RISK RATIOS

Short-Term Liquidity Risk

$$\text{Current Ratio} = \frac{\text{Current Assets}}{\text{Current Liabilities}}$$
(Page 355)

$$\text{Quick Ratio} = \frac{\text{Cash and Cash Equivalents} + \text{Short-Term Investments} + \text{Accounts Receivable}}{\text{Current Liabilities}}$$
(Page 357)

$$\text{Operating Cash Flow to Current Liabilities Ratio} = \frac{\text{Cash Flow from Operations}}{\text{Average Current Liabilities}}$$
(Page 357)

$$\text{Accounts Receivable Turnover} = \frac{\text{Sales}}{\text{Average Accounts Receivable}}$$
(Page 358)

$$\text{Inventory Turnover} = \frac{\text{Cost of Goods Sold}}{\text{Average Inventories}}$$
(Page 358)

$$\text{Accounts Payable Turnover} = \frac{\text{Purchases}}{\text{Average Accounts Payable}}$$
(Page 358)

Long-Term Solvency Risk

$$\text{Liabilities to Assets Ratio} = \frac{\text{Total Liabilities}}{\text{Total Assets}}$$
(Page 362)

$$\text{Liabilities to Shareholders' Equity Ratio} = \frac{\text{Total Liabilities}}{\text{Total Shareholders' Equity}}$$
(Page 362)

$$\text{Long-Term Debt to Long-Term Capital Ratio} = \frac{\text{Long-Term Debt}}{\text{Long-Term Debt} + \text{Total Shareholders' Equity}}$$
(Page 362)

$$\text{Long-Term Debt to Shareholders' Equity Ratio} = \frac{\text{Long-Term Debt}}{\text{Total Shareholders' Equity}}$$
(Page 362)

Interest Coverage Ratio

$$= \frac{\text{Net Income} + \text{Interest Expense} + \text{Income Tax Expense} + \text{Net Income Attributable to Noncontrolling Interests}}{\text{Interest Expense}}$$
(Page 363)

$$\text{Operating Cash Flow to Total Liabilities Ratio} = \frac{\text{Cash Flow from Operations}}{\text{Average Total Liabilities}}$$
(Page 364)

8E

Financial Reporting,
Financial Statement Analysis,
and Valuation

A STRATEGIC PERSPECTIVE

James M. Wahlen

Professor of Accounting

James R. Hodge Chair of Excellence
and Accounting Department Chair

Kelley School of Business, Indiana
University

Stephen P. Baginski

Professor of Accounting

Herbert E. Miller Chair in Financial
Accounting

J.M. Tull School of Accounting
Terry College of Business,
The University of Georgia

Mark T. Bradshaw

Associate Professor of Accounting

Department of Accounting

Carroll School of Management,
Boston College

CENGAGE
Learning®

Australia • Brazil • Japan • Korea • Mexico • Singapore • Spain • United Kingdom • United States

CENGAGE
Learning

Financial Reporting, Financial Statement Analysis and Valuation, 8e

James Wahlen, Stephen Baginski, Mark Bradshaw

Vice President, General Manager, Science, Math & Quantitative Business: Balraj Kalsi

Product Director: Rob Dewey

Product Manager: Matt Filimonov

Associate Content Developer: Conor Allen

Marketing Manager: Robin LeFevre

Content Project Managers: Darrell E. Frye and Nadia Saloom

Manufacturing Planner: Doug Wilke

Marketing Communications Manager: Eileen Corcoran

Production Service: Cenveo Publisher Services

Sr. Art Director: Stacy Jenkins Shirley

Internal and Cover Designer: Lou Ann Thesing

Cover Image: ©ALEAIMAGE/Getty Images

Intellectual Property

    Analyst: Christina Ciaramela

    Project Manager: Anne Sheroff

For product information and technology assistance, contact us at **Cengage Learning Customer & Sales Support, 1-800-354-9706**

For permission to use material from this text or product, submit all requests online at **www.cengage.com/permissions**
Further permissions questions can be emailed to **permissionrequest@cengage.com**

Unless otherwise noted, all items © Cengage Learning

Library of Congress Control Number: 2014940949
ISBN: 978-1-285-19090-7

Cengage Learning
20 Channel Center Street
Boston, MA 02210
USA

Cengage Learning is a leading provider of customized learning solutions with office locations around the globe, including Singapore, the United Kingdom, Australia, Mexico, Brazil, and Japan. Locate your local office at: **www.cengage.com/global**

Cengage Learning products are represented in Canada by Nelson Education, Ltd.

To learn more about Cengage Learning Solutions, visit **www.cengage.com**

Purchase any of our products at your local college store or at our preferred online store **www.cengagebrain.com**

Printed in the United States of America
Print Number: 01   Print Year: 2014

For our students,
with thanks for permitting us to take the journey with you

For Clyde Stickney and Paul Brown,
with thanks for allowing us the privilege to carry on their legacy of teaching through this book

For our families, with love,
Debbie, Jessica, Jaymie, Lynn, Drew, Marie, Kim, Ben, and Lucy

The process of financial reporting, financial statement analysis, and valuation is intended to help investors and analysts to deeply understand a firm's profitability and risk and to use that information to forecast future profitability and risk, and ultimately value the firm, enabling intelligent investment decisions. This process is central to the role of accounting, financial reporting, capital markets, investments, portfolio management, and corporate management in the world economy. When conducted with care and integrity, thorough and thoughtful financial statement analysis and valuation are fascinating and rewarding activities that can create tremendous value for society. However, as the recent financial crises in our capital markets reveal, when financial statement analysis and valuation is conducted carelessly and without integrity, it can create enormous loss of value in the capital markets and trigger deep recession in even the most powerful economies in the world. The stakes are high.

In addition, the game is changing. The world is shifting toward a new approach to financial reporting, and expectations for high quality and high integrity financial analysis and valuation are increasing among investors and securities regulators. Many of the world's most powerful economies, including the European Union, Canada, and Japan, have shifted to International Financial Reporting Standards (IFRS). The U.S. Securities and Exchange Commission (SEC) accepts financial statement filings based on IFRS from non-U.S. registrants, and is considering whether to converge financial reporting from U.S. Generally Accepted Accounting Principles (GAAP) to IFRS for U.S. registrants. Given the pace and breadth of financial reform legislation, it is clear that it is no longer "business as usual" on Wall Street and around the world for financial statement analysis and valuation.

Given the profound importance of financial reporting, financial statement analysis, and valuation, and given our rapidly changing world in accounting and the capital markets, this textbook provides you with a principled and disciplined approach to analysis and valuation. This textbook demonstrates and explains a thoughtful and thorough six-step framework you should use for financial statement analysis and valuation. You should begin an effective analysis of a set of financial statements with an evaluation of (1) the economic characteristics and current conditions of the industries in which a firm competes and (2) the particular strategies the firm executes to compete in each of these industries. Your analysis process should then move to (3) assessing how well the firm's financial statements reflect the economic effects of the firm's strategic decisions and actions. Your assessment requires an understanding of the accounting principles and methods used to create the financial statements, the relevant and reliable information that the financial statements provide, and the appropriate adjustments that you should make to improve the quality of that information. In this text we help you embrace financial reporting and financial statement analysis based on U.S. GAAP and IFRS. Next, you should (4) assess the profitability and risk of the firm using financial statement ratios and other analytical tools, and then (5) forecast the firm's future profitability and risk, incorporating information about expected changes in the economics of the industry and the firm's strategies. Finally, you can (6) value the firm using various valuation methods, making an investment decision by comparing likely ranges of the value of the share to the share price observed in the capital market. This six-step process forms the conceptual and pedagogical framework for this book, and it is a principled and disciplined approach you can use for intelligent analysis and valuation decisions.

All textbooks on financial statement analysis include step (4), assessing the profitability and risk of a company. Textbooks differ, however, with respect to their emphases on the other five steps. Consider the following depiction of these steps.

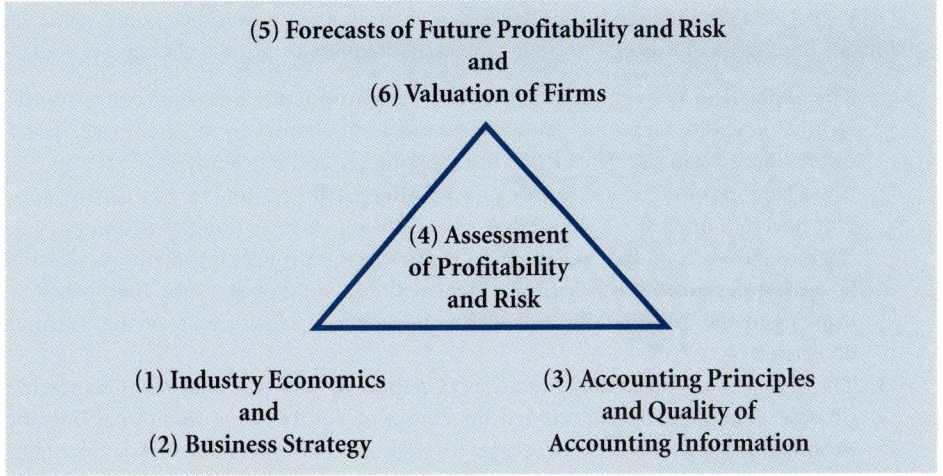

Our view is that these six steps must form an integrated approach for effective and complete financial statement analysis. We have therefore structured and developed this book to provide balanced, integrated coverage of all six elements. We sequence our study by beginning with industry economics and firm strategy, moving to a general consideration of GAAP and IFRS and the quality of accounting information, and providing a structure and tools for the analysis of profitability and risk. We then delve deeply into specific accounting issues and the determinants of accounting quality, and then conclude with forecasting and valuation. We anchor each step in the sequence on the firm's profitability and risk, which are the fundamental drivers of value. We continually relate each part to those preceding and following it to maintain this balanced, integrated perspective.

The premise of this book is that you will learn financial statement analysis most effectively by performing the analysis on actual companies. The book's narrative sets forth the important concepts and analytical tools and demonstrates their application using the financial statements of PepsiCo. Each chapter contains a set of questions, exercises, problems, and cases based primarily on financial statement data of actual companies. Each chapter also contains an integrative case involving Starbucks so you can apply the tools and methods throughout the text. A financial statement analysis package (FSAP) is available to aid you in your analytical tasks (discussed later).

Some of the Highlights of This Edition

The 8th edition continues to improve with two excellent coauthors, Stephen Baginski and Mark Bradshaw, who joined the authorship team for the 7th edition, replacing Clyde Stickney and Paul Brown. Clyde Stickney, the original author of the first three editions of this book and coauthor of the fourth, fifth, and sixth editions, is enjoying his well-earned retirement. Paul Brown, a coauthor of the fourth, fifth, and sixth editions, is now the president of Monmouth University. Mark and Steve are both internationally recognized research scholars and award-winning teachers in accounting, financial statement analysis, and valuation. They continue to bring many fresh new ideas and insights to produce a new edition with a strong focus on thoughtful and disciplined fundamental analysis, a broad and deep coverage of accounting issues including IFRS, and expanded analysis of companies within a global economic environment.

The next section highlights the content of each chapter. Listed below are some of the major highlights in this edition that impact all chapters or groups of chapters.

1. **The exposition of each chapter has been streamlined.** Known for being a well-written, accessible text, this edition presents each chapter in more concise, direct discussion, so you can get the key insights quickly and efficiently.

2. The chapters now include **quick checks after each section**, so you can be sure you have obtained the key insights from reading each section. In addition, each section and each of the end-of-chapter questions, exercises, problems, and cases is **cross-referenced to learning objectives**, so you can be sure that you can implement the critical skills and techniques associated with each of the learning objectives.

3. The chapters on profitability analysis (**Chapter 4**) and risk analysis (**Chapter 5**) provide **disaggregation of return on common equity** along traditional lines of profitability, efficiency, and leverage, as well as along operating versus financing lines.

4. The book's companion website, at www.cengagebrain.com, contains an **updated Appendix D** with descriptive statistics on 20 commonly used financial ratios computed over the past ten years for 48 industries. These ratios data enable you to benchmark your analyses and forecasts against industry averages.

5. The chapters on accounting quality have been **restructured to provide broader and deeper coverage of accounting for financing, investing, and operating activities**. The reorganization provides a logical flow, beginning in **Chapter 6** with a discussion of the determinants of accounting quality, how to evaluate accounting quality, and how to adjust reported earnings and financial statements to cleanse low-quality accounting items. Then the discussion proceeds across the primary business activities of firms in the natural sequence in which the activities occur—raising financial capital, investing that capital in productive assets, and operating the business. **Chapter 7** discusses accounting for financing activities. **Chapter 8** describes accounting for investing activities, and **Chapter 9** deals with accounting for operating activities.

6. The chapters on accounting quality have also been expanded to provide **more in-depth analysis of balance sheet quality, to augment income statement quality**.

7. Each chapter includes **relevant new discussion of current U.S. GAAP and IFRS, as well as how U.S. GAAP compares to IFRS**, and how you should deal with such differences in financial statement analysis. End-of-chapter materials contain many problems and cases involving non-U.S. companies, with **application of financial statement analysis techniques to IFRS-based financial statements**.

8. Each chapter provides references to specific standards in U.S. GAAP using the **new FASB Codification system**.

9. The chapters provide a number of **relevant insights from empirical accounting research**, pertinent to financial statement analysis and valuation.

10. The end-of-chapter material for each chapter contains portions of an **updated, integrative case applying the concepts and tools discussed in that chapter to**

Starbucks. This series of cases builds on the illustrations in the chapter in which the concepts and tools are applied to PepsiCo.

11. Each chapter contains **new or substantially revised and updated end-of-chapter material, including new problems and cases**. This material is relevant, real-world, and written for maximum learning value.

12. The Financial Statement Analysis Package (**FSAP**) available with this book has been **substantially revised and made more user-friendly**.

Overview of the Text

This section describes briefly the content and highlights of each chapter.

Chapter 1—Overview of Financial Reporting, Financial Statement Analysis, and Valuation. This chapter introduces you to the six interrelated sequential steps in financial statement analysis that serve as the organization structure for this book. It presents you with several frameworks for understanding the industry economics and business strategy of a firm and applies them to PepsiCo. It also reviews the purpose, underlying concepts, and content of each of the three principal financial statements, including those of non-U.S. companies reporting using IFRS. It also contains a section describing key provisions of the Sarbanes-Oxley Act of 2002. This chapter also provides the rationale for analyzing financial statements in capital market settings, including showing you some very compelling results from an empirical study of the association between unexpected earnings and market-adjusted stock returns as well as various empirical results showing that fundamental analysis can help investors generate above-market returns. The chapter's appendix, which can be found on this book's companion website at www.cengagebrain.com, presents an extensive discussion to help you do a term project involving the analysis of one or more companies. Our examination of the course syllabi of users of the previous edition indicated that most courses require students to engage in such a project. This appendix guides you in how to proceed, where to get information, and so on.

In addition to the updated integrative case involving Starbucks, the chapter includes an updated version of a case involving Nike.

Chapter 2—Asset and Liability Valuation and Income Recognition. This chapter covers three topics we believe you need to review from previous courses before delving into the more complex topics in this book.

- First, we discuss the link between the valuation of assets and liabilities on the balance sheet and the measurement of income. We believe that you will understand topics such as revenue recognition and accounting for marketable securities, derivatives, pensions, and other topics more easily when you examine them with an appreciation for the inherent trade-off of a balance sheet versus income statement perspective. This chapter also reviews the trade-offs faced by accounting standard setters, regulators, and corporate managers who attempt to simultaneously provide both reliable and relevant financial statement information. We also examine whether firms should recognize value changes immediately in net income or delay their recognition, sending them temporarily through other comprehensive income.

- Second, we present a framework for analyzing the dual effects of economic transactions and other events on the financial statements. This framework relies on the balance sheet equation to trace these effects through the financial statements. Even students who are well grounded in double-entry accounting find this framework helpful in visually identifying the effects of various complex business transactions, such as corporate acquisitions, derivatives, and leases. We use this framework in subsequent chapters to present and analyze transactions, as we discuss various GAAP and IFRS topics.

$A_{BEG} =$	L_{BEG}	+	CC_{BEG}	+	$AOCI_{BEG}$	+	RE_{BEG}
$+\Delta A$	$+\Delta L$		$+\Delta Stock$		$+OCI$		$+NI$ $- D$
$A_{END} =$	L_{END}	+	CC_{END}	+	$AOCI_{END}$	+	RE_{END}

[A=Assets, L=Liabilities, CC=Contributed Capital, AOCI=Accumulated Other Comprehensive Income, RE=Retained Earnings, Stock=Common and Preferred Capital Stock Accounts, OCI=Other Comprehensive Income, NI=Net Income, and D=Dividends.]

- Third, we discuss the measurement of income tax expense, particularly with regard to the treatment of temporary differences between book income and taxable income. Virtually every business transaction has income tax consequences, and it is crucial that you grasp the information conveyed in income tax disclosures. Discussing consideration of the income tax consequences early in the text enhances your learning in later chapters that cover complex topics such as restructuring charges, asset impairments, depreciation, and leases.

The end-of-chapter materials include various asset and liability valuation problems involving Walmart, Biosante Pharmaceuticals, Prepaid Legal Services, and Nike, as well as an integrative case involving Starbucks.

Chapter 3—Income Flows Versus Cash Flows: Understanding the Statement of Cash Flows. Chapter 3 reviews the statement of cash flows and presents a model for relating the cash flows from operating, investing, and financing activities to a firm's position in its product life cycle. The chapter demonstrates procedures you can use to prepare the statement of cash flows when a firm provides no cash flow information. The chapter also provides new insights that place particular emphasis on how you should use information in the statement of cash flows to assess earnings quality.

The end-of-chapter materials utilize cash flow and earnings data for a number of companies including eBay, Amazon, The Walt Disney Company, Fedex, Kroger, Coca-Cola, Texas Instruments, Sirius XM Radio, Sunbeam, AerLingus, and Fuso Pharmaceuticals. A case (Prime Contractors) illustrates the relation between earnings and cash flows as a firm experiences profitable and unprofitable operations and changes its business strategy. The classic W. T. Grant case illustrates the use of earnings and cash flow information to assess solvency risk and avoid bankruptcy.

Chapter 4—Profitability Analysis. This chapter discusses the concepts and tools for analyzing a firm's profitability, integrating industry economic and strategic factors that affect the interpretation of financial ratios. It then applies these concepts and tools to the analysis of the profitability of PepsiCo. The analysis of profitability centers on the rate of return on assets and its disaggregated components, the rate of return on common shareholders' equity and its disaggregated components, and earnings per share. The chapter contains a section on the well-publicized measurement of EVA (economic value added) and shows its relation to net income under GAAP. This chapter also considers analytical tools unique to certain industries, such as airlines, service firms, and financial institutions.

A number of problems and exercises at the end of the chapter cover profitability analyses for companies such as Nucor Steel, Boston Scientific, Valero Energy, Microsoft, Oracle, Dell, Sun Microsystems, Texas Instruments, Hewlett Packard, Georgia Pacific, General Mills, Abercrombie & Fitch, Hasbro, Coca-Cola, and many others. The integrative case on Starbucks involves analysis of Starbucks in both a time-series setting and in a cross-sectional setting in comparison to Panera Bread Company. Another case involves the time-series analysis of Walmart Stores and the cross-sectional analysis of its profitability versus Target and Carrefour.

Chapter 5—Risk Analysis. This chapter begins with a discussion of recently required disclosures on the extent to which firms are subject to various types of risk, including unexpected changes in commodity prices, exchange rates, and interest rates and how firms manage these risks. The chapter provides new insights and discussion about the benefits and dangers associated with financial flexibility and the use of leverage. This edition shows you how to decompose return on common equity into components that highlight the contribution of the inherent profitability of the firm's assets and the contribution from the strategic use of leverage to enhance the returns to common equity investors. The chapter provides you an approach to in-depth financial statement analysis of various risks associated with leverage, including short-term liquidity risk, long-term solvency risk, credit risk, bankruptcy risk, and systematic and firm-specific market risk. This chapter also describes and illustrates the calculation and interpretation of risk ratios and applies them to the financial statements of PepsiCo, focusing on both short-term liquidity risk and long-term solvency risk. We also explore credit risk and bankruptcy risk in greater depth.

A unique feature of the problems in Chapters 4 and 5 is the linking of the analysis of several companies across the two chapters, including problems involving Hasbro, Abercrombie & Fitch, Coca-Cola, Starbucks, and Walmart. Chapter-ending cases involve risk analysis for Starbucks and classic cases on credit risk analysis (Massachusetts Stove Company) and bankruptcy prediction (Fly-By-Night International Group).

Chapter 6—Accounting Quality. This chapter provides an expanded discussion of the quality of income statement and balance sheet information, emphasizing faithful representation of relevant and substantive economic content as the key characteristics and identifying conditions under which managers might likely engage in earnings management. The discussion provides a framework for accounting quality analysis, which is used in the discussions of various accounting issues in Chapters 7 to 9. We consider several financial reporting topics that primarily affect the persistence of earnings, including gains and losses from discontinued operations, changes in accounting principles, other comprehensive income items, impairment losses, restructuring charges, changes in estimates, and gains and losses from peripheral activities. The chapter concludes with an assessment of accounting quality by separating accruals and cash flows and an illustration of a model to assess the risk of financial reporting manipulation (Beneish's multivariate model for identifying potential financial statement manipulators).

Chapter-ending materials include problems involving Nestlé, Checkpoint Systems, Rock of Ages, Vulcan Materials, Northrop Grumman, Intel, Enron, and Sunbeam. End-of-chapter materials also include an integrative case involving the analysis of the earnings quality of Starbucks in light of the inclusion of several potentially nonrecurring items in earnings, as well as a case on the earnings quality of Citigroup.

Chapter 7—Financing Activities. This chapter has been structured along with Chapters 8 and 9 to discuss accounting issues in their natural sequence—raising financial capital, then investing the capital in productive assets, and then managing the operations of the business. Chapter 7 discusses the accounting principles and practices under U.S. GAAP and IFRS associated with firms' financing activities. The chapter begins by describing the financial statement reporting of capital investments by owners (equity issues) and distributions to owners (dividends and share repurchases), and the accounting for equity issued to compensate employees (stock options, stock appreciation rights, and restricted stock). The chapter demonstrates how shareholders' equity reflects the effects of transactions with non-owners which flow through the income statement (net income) and those which do not (other comprehensive income). The chapter then describes the financial reporting for long-term debt (bonds, notes payable, lease liabilities, and troubled debt), hybrid securities (convertible bonds, preferred stock), and derivatives used to hedge interest rate risk. The lease discussion demonstrates the adjustments required to convert operating leases to capital leases. Throughout the chapter we highlight the differences between U.S. GAAP and IFRS in the area of equity and debt financing, and we conclude the chapter with a discussion of likely forthcoming changes in the financial reporting for debt and leases.

In addition to various questions and exercises, the end-of-chapter material includes problems probing accounting for various financing alternatives, Ford Motor Credit's securitization of receivables, operating versus capital leases of The Gap and Limited Brands, and stock-based compensation at Coca-Cola and Eli Lilly. End-of-chapter cases include the integrative case involving Starbucks, a case on stock compensation at Oracle, and long-term financing and solvency risk at Southwest Airlines versus Lufthansa.

Chapter 8—Investing Activities. This chapter discusses various accounting principles and methods under U.S. GAAP and IFRS associated with a firm's investments in long-lived tangible assets, intangible assets, and financial instruments. The chapter demonstrates the accounting for a firm's investments in tangible productive assets including property, plant, and equipment, covering the initial decision to capitalize or expense and the use of choices and estimates to allocate costs through the depreciation process. The chapter demonstrates and explains alternative ways that firms account for intangible assets, highlighting research and development expenditures, software development expenditures, and goodwill, including the exercise of judgment in the allocation of costs through the amortization process. The chapter reviews and applies the rules for evaluating the impairment of different categories of long-lived assets, including goodwill. The chapter then describes accounting and financial reporting of intercorporate investments in securities (trading securities, available-for-sale securities, held-to-maturity securities, and noncontrolled affiliates) and corporate acquisitions (including the market value, equity, proportionate consolidation, and full consolidation methods). The chapter reviews accounting for variable-interest entities, including the requirement to consolidate them with the firm identified as the primary beneficiary. Finally, the chapter addresses foreign investments by preparing a set of translated financial statements using the all-current method and the monetary/nonmonetary method and describing the conditions under which each method best portrays the operating relationship between a U.S. parent firm and its foreign subsidiary.

The end-of-chapter questions, exercises, problems, and cases include a problem involving Molson Coors Brewing Company and its variable interest entities, an integrative application of the chapter topics to Starbucks, and a case involving Disney's acquisition of Marvel Entertainment.

Chapter 9—Operating Activities. Chapter 9 discusses how financial statements prepared under U.S. GAAP or IFRS capture and report the firm's operating activities. The chapter opens with discussion of how financial accounting measures and reports the revenues and expenses generated by a firm's operating activities, as well as the related assets, liabilities, and cash flows. This discussion reviews the criteria for recognizing revenue and expenses under the accrual basis of accounting and applies these criteria to various types of businesses. The chapter evaluates the financial statement effects of recognizing income prior to the point of sale, at the time of sale, and subsequent to sale. The chapter analyzes and interprets the effects of FIFO versus LIFO on financial statements and demonstrates how to convert the statements of a firm from a LIFO to a FIFO basis. The chapter identifies the working capital investments created by operating activities and the financial statement effects of credit policy and credit risk. The chapter also shows how to use the financial statement and note information for corporate income taxes to analyze the firm's tax strategies, pensions, and other post-employment benefits obligations. The chapter concludes with a discussion of how a firm uses derivative instruments to hedge the risk associated with commodities and with operating transactions denominated in foreign currency.

The end-of-chapter problems and exercises examine revenue and expense recognition for a wide variety of operating activities, including revenues for software, consulting, transportation, construction, manufacturing, and others. End-of-chapter problems also involve Coca-Cola's tax notes and include an integrative case involving Starbucks, a case on alternative revenue recognition timing for the Arizona Land Development Company, and a case involving Coca-Cola's pension disclosures.

Chapter 10—Forecasting Financial Statements. This chapter describes and illustrates the procedures you should use in preparing forecasted financial statements. This material plays a central role in the valuation of companies, discussed throughout Chapters 11 to 14. The chapter begins by giving you an overview of forecasting and the importance of creating integrated and articulated financial statement forecasts. It then illustrates the preparation of projected financial statements for PepsiCo. The chapter also demonstrates how to get forecasted balance sheets to balance and how to compute implied statements of cash flows from forecasts of balance sheets and income statements. The chapter also discusses forecast shortcuts analysts sometimes take, and when such forecasts are reliable and when they are not. The Forecast and Forecast Development spreadsheets within FSAP provide templates you can use to develop and build your own financial statement forecasts.

Short end-of-chapter problems illustrate techniques for projecting key accounts for firms like Home Depot, Intel, Hasbro, and Barnes and Noble, determining the cost structure of firms like Nucor Steel and Sony, and dealing with irregular changes in accounts. Longer problems and cases require the preparation of financial statements for cases discussed in earlier chapters involving Walmart and Starbucks. The end-of-chapter material also includes a classic case involving the projection of financial statements to assist the Massachusetts Stove Company in its strategic decision to add gas stoves to its wood stove line. The problems and cases specify the assumptions you should make to illustrate the preparation procedure. We link and use these longer problems and cases in later chapters that rely on these financial statement forecasts in determining share value estimates for these firms.

Chapter 11—Risk-Adjusted Expected Rates of Return and the Dividends Valuation Approach. Chapters 11 to 14 form a unit in which we demonstrate various approaches to valuing a firm. Chapter 11 focuses on fundamental issues of valuation that you will apply in all of the valuation chapters. This chapter provides you with an extensive discussion of the measurement of the cost of debt and equity capital and the weighted average cost of capital, as well as the dividends-based valuation approach. The chapter also discusses various issues of valuation, including forecasting horizons, projecting long-run continuing dividends, and computing continuing (sometimes called terminal) value. The chapter describes and illustrates the internal consistency in valuing firms using dividends, free cash flows, or earnings. Particular emphasis is placed on helping you understand that the different approaches to valuation are simply differences in perspective (dividends capture wealth distribution, free cash flows capture wealth realization in cash, and earning represent wealth creation), and that these approaches should produce internally consistent estimates of value. In this chapter we demonstrate the cost-of-capital measurements and the dividends-based valuation approach for PepsiCo, using the forecasted amounts from PepsiCo's financial statements discussed in Chapter 10. The chapter also presents techniques for assessing the sensitivity of value estimates, varying key assumptions such as the costs of capital and long-term growth rates. The chapter also discusses and illustrates the cost-of-capital computations and dividends valuation model computations within the Valuation spreadsheet in FSAP. This spreadsheet takes the forecast amounts from the Forecast spreadsheet and other relevant information and values the firm using the various valuation methods discussed in Chapters 11 to 14.

End-of-chapter material includes the computation of costs of capital across different industries and companies, including Whirlpool, IBM, and Target Stores, as well as short dividends valuation problems for companies like Royal Dutch Shell. Longer problems and cases involve computing costs of capital and dividends-based valuation of Walmart, Starbucks, and Massachusetts Stove Company from financial statement forecasts developed in Chapter 10's problems and cases.

Chapter 12—Valuation: Cash-Flow Based Approaches. Chapter 12 focuses on valuation using the present value of free cash flows. This chapter distinguishes free cash flows to all debt and equity stakeholders and free cash flows to common equity shareholders and the settings where one or the other measure of free cash flows is appropriate for valuation. The chapter develops and demonstrates valuation using free cash flows for common equity shareholders, and valuation using free cash flows to all debt and equity stakeholders. The chapter also considers and applies techniques for projecting free cash flows and measuring the continuing value after the forecast horizon. The chapter applies both of the discounted free cash flows valuation methods to PepsiCo, demonstrating how to measure the free cash flows to all debt and equity stakeholders, as well as the free cash flows to common equity. The valuations for PepsiCo use the forecasted amounts from PepsiCo's projected financial statements discussed in Chapter 10. The chapter also presents techniques for assessing the sensitivity of value estimates, varying key assumptions such as the costs of capital and long-term growth rates. The chapter also explains and demonstrates the consistency of valuation estimates across different approaches and shows that the dividends approach in Chapter 11 and the free cash flows approaches in Chapter 12 should and do lead to identical value estimates for PepsiCo. The Valuation spreadsheet in FSAP uses projected amounts from the Forecast spreadsheet and other relevant information and values the firm using both of the free cash flows valuation approaches.

Updated shorter problem material asks you to compute free cash flows from financial statement data for companies like 3M and Dick's Sporting Goods. Problem material also includes using free cash flows to value firms in leveraged buyout transactions, such as May Department Stores, Experian Information Solutions, and Wedgewood Products. Longer problem material includes the valuation of Walmart, Coca-Cola, Starbucks, and Massachusetts Stove Company. The chapter also introduces the Holmes Corporation case, which is an integrated case relevant for Chapters 10 to 13 in which you select forecast assumptions, prepare projected financial statements, and value the firm using the various methods discussed in Chapters 10 to 13. This case can be analyzed in stages with each chapter or as an integrated case after Chapter 13.

Chapter 13—Valuation: Earnings-Based Approaches. Chapter 13 emphasizes the role of accounting earnings in valuation, focusing on valuation methods using the residual income approach. The residual income approach uses the ability of a firm to generate income in excess of the cost of capital as the principal driver of a firm's value in excess of its book value. We apply the residual income valuation method to the forecasted amounts for PepsiCo from Chapter 10. The chapter also demonstrates that the dividends valuation methods, the free cash flows valuation methods, and the residual income valuation methods are consistent with a fundamental valuation approach. In the chapter we explain and demonstrate that these approaches yield identical estimates of value for PepsiCo. The Valuation spreadsheet in FSAP includes valuation models that use the residual income valuation method.

End-of-chapter materials include various problems involving computing residual income across different firms, including Abbott Labs, IBM, Target Stores, Microsoft, Intel, Dell, Southwest Airlines, Kroger, and Yum! Brands. Longer problems also involve the valuation of other firms such as Steak 'n Shake in which you are given the needed financial statement information. Longer problems and cases enable you to apply the residual income approach to Coca-Cola as well as to Walmart, Starbucks, and Massachusetts Stove Company, considered in Chapters 10, 11, and 12.

Chapter 14—Valuation: Market-Based Approaches. Chapter 14 demonstrates how to analyze and use the information in market value. In particular, the chapter describes and applies market-based valuation multiples, including the market-to-book ratio, the price-to-earnings ratio, and the price-earnings-growth ratio. The chapter describes and illustrates the theoretical and conceptual approaches to market multiples and contrasts them with the practical approaches to market multiples. The chapter demonstrates how the market-to-book ratio is consistent with residual ROCE valuation and the residual income model discussed in Chapter 13. The chapter also describes the factors that drive market multiples, so you can adjust multiples appropriately to reflect differences in profitability, growth, and risk across comparable firms. An applied analysis demonstrates how you can reverse engineer a firm's stock price to infer the valuation assumptions that the stock market appears to be making. We apply all of these valuation methods to PepsiCo. The chapter concludes with a new discussion of the role of market efficiency, as well as striking evidence on using earnings surprises to pick stocks and form portfolios (the Bernard-Thomas post-earnings announcement drift anomaly) as well as using value-to-price ratios to form portfolios (the Frankel-Lee strategy), both of which appear to help investors generate significant above-market returns.

End-of-chapter materials include problems involving computing and interpreting market-to-book ratios for pharmaceutical companies, Enron, Coca-Cola, Walmart, and Steak 'n Shake and the integrative case involving Starbucks.

Appendices. Appendix A includes the financial statements and notes for PepsiCo used in the illustrations throughout the book. Appendix B, available at www.cengagebrain.com, is PepsiCo's letter to the shareholders and management's discussion and analysis of operations, which we use when interpreting PepsiCo's financial ratios and in our financial statement projections. Appendix C presents the output from FSAP for PepsiCo, including the Data spreadsheet, the Analysis spreadsheet (profitability and risk ratio analyses), the Forecasts and Forecast Development spreadsheets, and the Valuations spreadsheet. Appendix D, also available online, provides descriptive statistics on 20 financial statement ratios across 48 industries over the years 2003 to 2013.

Chapter Sequence and Structure

Our own experience and our discussions with other professors suggest that there are various approaches to teaching the financial statement analysis course, each of which works well in particular settings. We have therefore designed this book for flexibility with respect to the sequence of chapter assignments. The following diagram sets forth the overall structure of the book.

Chapter 1: Overview of Financial Reporting, Financial Statement Analysis, and Valuation		
Chapter 2: Asset and Liability Valuation and Income Recognition	Chapter 3: Income Flows Versus Cash Flows	
Chapter 4: Profitability Analysis	Chapter 5: Risk Analysis	
Chapter 6: Accounting Quality		
Chapter 7: Financing Activities	Chapter 8: Investing Activities	Chapter 9: Operating Activities
Chapter 10: Forecasting Financial Statements		
Chapter 11: Risk-Adjusted Expected Rates of Return and the Dividends Valuation Approach		
Chapter 12: Valuation: Cash-Flow-Based Approaches	Chapter 13: Valuation: Earnings-Based Approaches	
Chapter 14: Valuation: Market-Based Approaches		

The chapter sequence follows the six steps in financial statement analysis discussed in Chapter 1. Chapters 2 and 3 provide the conceptual foundation for the three financial statements. Chapters 4 and 5 present tools for analyzing the financial statements. Chapters 6 to 9 describe how to assess the quality of accounting information under U.S. GAAP and IFRS and then examine the accounting for financing, investing, and operating activities. Chapters 10 to 14 focus primarily on forecasting financial statements and valuation.

Some schools teach U.S. GAAP and IFRS topics and financial statement analysis in separate courses. Chapters 6 to 9 are an integrated unit and sufficiently rich for the U.S. GAAP and IFRS course. The remaining chapters will then work well in the financial statement analysis course. Some schools leave the topic of valuation to finance courses. Chapters 1 to 10 will then work well for the accounting prelude to the finance course. Some instructors may wish to begin with forecasting and valuation (Chapters 10 to 14) and then examine data issues that might affect the numbers used in the valuations (Chapters 6 to 9). This textbook is adaptable to other sequences of the various topics.

Overview of the Ancillary Package

The Financial Statement Analysis Package (FSAP) is available on the companion website for this book (www.cengagebrain.com) to all purchasers of the text. The package performs various analytical tasks (common-size and rate of change financial statements, ratio computations, risk indicators such as the Altman-Z score and the Beneish manipulation index), provides a worksheet template for preparing financial statements forecasts, and applies amounts from the financial statement forecasts to valuing a firm using various valuation methods. A user manual for FSAP is embedded within FSAP.

Acknowledgments

Many individuals provided invaluable assistance in the preparation of this book and we wish to acknowledge their help in a formal manner here.

We wish to especially acknowledge many helpful comments and suggestions on the prior edition (many of which helped improve this edition) from Susan Eldridge at the University of Nebraska—Omaha and Christopher Jones at George Washington University. We are also very grateful for help with data collection from Matt Wieland of Indiana University Purdue University—Indianapolis.

The following colleagues have assisted in the development of this edition by reviewing or providing helpful comments on or materials for previous editions:

Kristian Allee, Michigan State University

Murad Antia, University of South Florida

Drew Baginski, University of Georgia

Michael Clement, University of Texas, Austin

Messod Daniel Beneish, Indiana University

Matthew Diamond, PepsiCo

Ellen Engel, University of Chicago

Aaron Hipscher, New York University

Robert Howell, Dartmouth College

Amy Hutton, Boston College

Prem Jain, Georgetown University

Ross Jennings, University of Texas at Austin

J. William Kamas, University of Texas at Austin

Michael Keane, University of Southern California

April Klein, New York University

Betsy Laydon, Indiana University

Yuri Loktionov, New York University

D. Craig Nichols, Syracuse University

Chris Noe, Massachusetts Institute of Technology

Virginia Soybel, Babson College

Christine Wiedman, University of Waterloo

Matthew Wieland, Indiana University Purdue University—Indianapolis

Michael Williamson, University of Texas at Austin

Julia Yu, University of Georgia

We wish to thank the following individuals at Cengage/South-Western, who provided guidance, encouragement, or assistance in various phases of the revision: Matt Filimonov, Krista Kellman, Conor Allen, Darrell Frye, and Nadia Saloom. Katherine Rybowiak did an outstanding job assisting with preparation of the solutions/instructor's manual. Thanks also to the review team at PepsiCo Inc., who reviewed the manuscript for this book to ensure that the company's financial information throughout its pages is correct: Matthew Diamond, Michael Mihok, Dawn Southerton, and Jeffrey Tjon.

Finally, we wish to acknowledge the role played by former students in our financial statement analysis classes for being challenging partners in our learning endeavors. We also acknowledge and thank Clyde Stickney and Paul Brown for allowing us to carry on their legacy by teaching financial statement analysis and valuation through this book. Lastly, and most importantly, we are deeply grateful for our families for being encouraging and patient partners in this work. We dedicate this book to each of you.

James M. Wahlen
Stephen P. Baginski
Mark T. Bradshaw

ABOUT THE AUTHORS

James M. Wahlen is the James R. Hodge Chair, Professor of Accounting, Chair of the Accounting Department, and the former Chairman of the MBA Program at the Kelley School of Business at Indiana University. He received his Ph.D. from the University of Michigan and has served on the faculties of the University of Chicago, University of North Carolina at Chapel Hill, INSEAD, the University of Washington, and Pacific Lutheran University. Professor Wahlen's teaching and research interests focus on financial accounting, financial statement analysis, and the capital markets. His research investigates earnings quality and earnings management, earnings volatility as an indicator of risk, fair value accounting for financial instruments, accounting for loss reserve estimates by banks and insurers, stock market efficiency with respect to accounting information, and testing the extent to which future stock returns can be predicted with earnings and other financial statement information. His research has been published in a wide array of academic and practitioner journals in accounting and finance. He has had public accounting experience in both Milwaukee and Seattle and is a member of the American Accounting Association. He has received numerous teaching awards during his career. In his free time Jim loves spending time with his wife and daughters, spoiling his incredibly adorable granddaughter Ailsa, outdoor sports (biking, hiking, skiing, golf), cooking (and, of course, eating), and listening to rock music (especially if it is loud and live).

Stephen P. Baginski is the Herbert E. Miller Chair in Financial Accounting at the University of Georgia's J.M. Tull School of Accounting. He received his Ph.D. from the University of Illinois in 1986, and he has taught a variety of financial and managerial undergraduate, MBA, and executive education courses at Indiana University, Illinois State University, the University of Illinois, Northeastern University, Florida State University, Washington University in St. Louis, the University of St. Galen, the Swiss Banking Institute at the University of Zurich, Bocconi, and INSEAD. Professor Baginski has published articles in a variety of journals including *The Accounting Review, Journal of Accounting Research, Contemporary Accounting Research, Review of Accounting Studies, The Journal of Risk and Insurance, Quarterly Review of Finance and Economics,* and *Review of Quantitative Finance and Accounting.* His research primarily deals with the causes and consequences of voluntary management disclosures of earnings forecasts, and he also investigates the usefulness of financial accounting information in security pricing and risk assessment. Professor Baginski has served on several editorial boards and as an associate editor at *Accounting Horizons* and *The Review of Quantitative Finance and Accounting.* He has won numerous undergraduate and graduate teaching awards at the department, college, and university level during his career, including receipt of the Doctoral Student Inspiration Award from students at Indiana University. Professor Baginski loves to watch college football, play golf, and run (very slowly) in his spare time.

Mark T. Bradshaw is an Associate Professor of Accounting at the Carroll School of Management of Boston College. Bradshaw received a Ph.D. from the University of Michigan Business School, and earned a BBA summa cum laude with highest honors in accounting and master's degree in financial accounting from the University of Georgia. He previously taught at University of Chicago, Harvard Business School, and University of Georgia. He has been a Certified Public Accountant since 1991 and was an auditor for Arthur Andersen & Co. in Atlanta. Bradshaw conducts research on capital markets, specializing in the examination of securities analysts and financial reporting issues. His research has been published in a variety of academic and practitioner journals, and he serves as Associate Editor for *Journal of Accounting and Economics*, *The Accounting Review*, and *Management Science*. He is also on the Editorial Board of *Review of Accounting Studies* and the *Journal of International Accounting Research*, and is a reviewer for numerous other accounting and finance journals. He has also authored a book with Brian Bruce, *Analysts, Lies, and Statistics—Cutting through the Hype in Corporate Earnings Announcements*. Approximately twenty-five pounds ago, Bradshaw was an accomplished cyclist. Currently focused on additional leisurely pursuits, he nevertheless routinely passes younger and thinner cyclists.

BRIEF CONTENTS

CONTENTS

Overview of Financial Reporting, Financial Statement Analysis, and Valuation

LEARNING OBJECTIVES

LO 1-1 Describe the six-step analytical framework that is the logical structure for financial statement analysis and valuation and the foundation for this book.

LO 1-2 Apply tools for assessing the economic characteristics and dynamics that drive competition in an industry, including (a) value chain analysis, (b) Porter's five forces framework, and (c) an economic attributes framework.

LO 1-3 Identify firm-specific strategies for achieving competitive advantage within an industry.

LO 1-4 Show familiarity with the purpose, underlying concepts, and format of the balance sheet, income statement, and statement of cash flows.

LO 1-5 Use tools to analyze a firm's profitability and risk, including financial ratios, common-size financial statements, and percentage change financial statements.

LO 1-6 Obtain an overview of how to use financial statement information to forecast the future business activities of a firm and to value a firm.

LO 1-7 Consider the role of financial statement analysis in an efficient capital market, and review empirical evidence on the association between changes in earnings and changes in stock prices.

LO 1-8 Review sources of financial information available for publicly held firms.

Chapter Overview

This book has three principal objectives, each designed to help you gain important knowledge and skills necessary for financial statement analysis and valuation:

1. To demonstrate how you can link the economics of an industry, a firm's strategy, and its financial statements, gaining important insights about the firm's profitability and its risk. Chapters 1–5 discuss the principal financial statements and tools for analyzing profitability and risk.

2. To enhance your understanding of the accounting principles and methods under U.S. Generally Accepted Accounting Principles (GAAP) and International Financial Reporting Standards (IFRS) that firms use to measure and report their financing, investing, and operating activities in a set of financial statements and, if necessary, the adjustments you may make to reported amounts to increase their relevance and reliability. Chapters 6–9 explore accounting principles in depth.

3. To demonstrate how you can use financial statement information to build forecasts of future financial statements and then use the expected future amounts of earnings, cash flows, and dividends in the valuation of firms. Chapters 10–14 focus on forecasting and valuation.

Financial statements play a central role in the analysis and valuation of a firm. Financial statement analysis is an exciting and rewarding activity, particularly when the objective is to assess whether the market is pricing a firm's shares fairly. Studying the intrinsic characteristics of a firm—such as its business model, product markets, and operating, investing, and financing decisions—and using this information to make informed judgments about the value of the firm can be done by anyone with an interest in learning and applying the many tools and techniques of analysis and valuation demonstrated in this text.

Security analysts are professionals whose primary objective is to value firms. Security analysts collect and analyze a wide array of information from financial statements and other sources to evaluate a firm's current and past performance and to predict its future performance. Then they use the expected future performance to measure the value of the firm's shares. Comparisons of thoughtful and intelligent estimates of the firm's share value with the market price for the shares provide the bases for making good investment decisions.

Besides being used to measure firm value, the tools of effective financial statement analysis can be applied in many other decision-making settings, including the following:

- Managing a firm and communicating results to investors, creditors, employees, and other stakeholders
- Assigning credit ratings or extending credit for a short-term period (for example, a bank loan used to finance accounts receivable or inventories) or a long-term period (for example, a bank loan or public bond issue used to finance the acquisition of property, plant, or equipment)
- Assessing the operating performance and financial health of a supplier, customer, competitor, or potential employer
- Evaluating firms for potential acquisitions, mergers, or divestitures
- Valuing the initial public offering of a firm's shares
- Consulting with a firm and offering helpful strategic advice
- Forming a judgment about damages sustained in a lawsuit
- Assessing the extent of auditing needed to form an opinion about a client's financial statements

Overview of Financial Statement Analysis

We view effective financial statement analysis as a three-legged stool, as Exhibit 1.1 depicts. The three legs of the stool in the figure represent effective analysis based on the following:

1. Identifying the *economic characteristics* of the *industries* in which a firm competes and mapping those characteristics into determinants of profitability and risk
2. Describing the *strategies* that a *firm* pursues to differentiate itself from competitors as a basis for evaluating a firm's competitive advantages, the sustainability and potential growth of a firm's earnings, and its risks

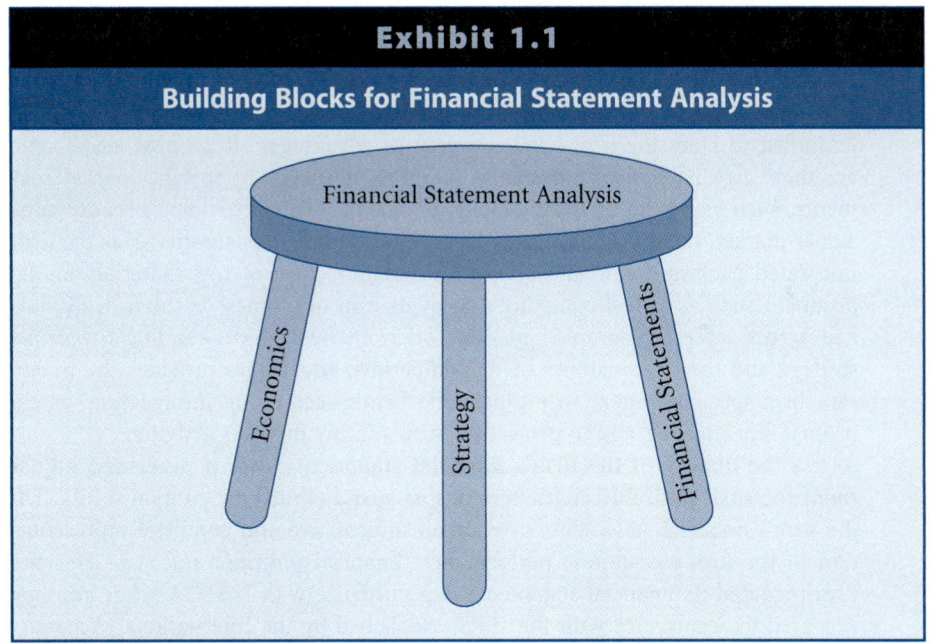

Exhibit 1.1

Building Blocks for Financial Statement Analysis

Financial Statement Analysis

Economics

Strategy

Financial Statements

3. Evaluating the firm's *financial statements*, including the accounting concepts and methods that underlie them and the quality of the information they provide

   Our approach to effective analysis of financial statements for valuation and many other decisions involves six interrelated sequential steps, depicted in Exhibit 1.2.

1. **Identify the economic characteristics and competitive dynamics of the industry in which a particular firm participates.** What dynamic forces drive competition in the industry? For example, does the industry include a large number of firms selling similar products, such as grocery stores, or only a small number of competitors selling unique products, such as pharmaceutical companies? Does technological change play an important role in maintaining a competitive advantage, as in computer software? Understanding the competitive forces in the firm's

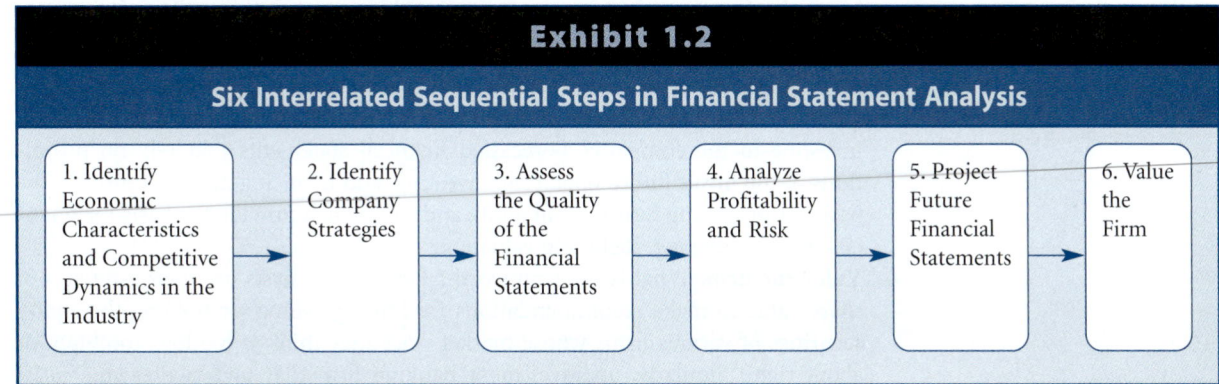

Exhibit 1.2

Six Interrelated Sequential Steps in Financial Statement Analysis

| 1. Identify Economic Characteristics and Competitive Dynamics in the Industry | 2. Identify Company Strategies | 3. Assess the Quality of the Financial Statements | 4. Analyze Profitability and Risk | 5. Project Future Financial Statements | 6. Value the Firm |

industry in the first step establishes the economic foundation and context for the remaining steps in the process.

2. **Identify strategies the firm pursues to gain and sustain a competitive advantage.** What business model is the firm executing to be different and successful in its industry? Does the firm have competitive advantages? If so, how sustainable are they? Are its products designed to meet the needs of specific market segments, such as ethnic or health foods, or are they intended for a broader consumer market, such as typical grocery stores and family restaurants? Has the firm integrated backward into the growing or manufacture of raw materials for its products, such as a steel company that owns iron ore mines? Is the firm diversified across several geographic markets or industries? Understanding the firm's strategy and the sustainability of its competitive advantages provides the necessary firm-specific context to evaluate the firm's accounting information, assess profitability and risk, and to project the firm's future business activities.

3. **Assess the quality of the firm's financial statements and, if necessary, adjust them for such desirable characteristics as sustainability or comparability.** Do the firm's financial statements provide an informative and complete representation of the firm's economic performance, financial position, and risk? Has the firm prepared its financial statements in accordance with U.S. GAAP or are they prepared in accordance with the IFRS established by the International Accounting Standards Board (IASB)? Do earnings include nonrecurring gains or losses, such as a write-down of goodwill, which you should evaluate differently from recurring components of earnings? Has the firm structured transactions or commercial arrangements or selected accounting methods so as to make the firm appear more profitable or less risky than economic conditions otherwise suggest? It is essential to understand the quality of the firm's accounting information in order to effectively analyze the firm's profitability and risk and to project its future balance sheets, income statements, and cash flows.

4. **Analyze the current profitability and risk of the firm using information in the financial statements.** Most financial analysts assess the profitability of a firm relative to the risks involved. What rate of return is the firm generating from the use of its assets? What rate of return is the firm generating for its common equity shareholders? Is the firm's profit margin increasing or decreasing over time? Are returns and profit margins higher or lower than those of its key competitors? How much leverage does the firm have in its capital structure? Ratios that reflect relations among particular items in the financial statements are the tools you can use to analyze profitability and risk. By understanding the firm's current and past profitability and risk, you will establish important information you will use in projecting the firm's future profitability and risk and in valuing its shares.

5. **Prepare forecasted financial statements.** What will be the firm's future resources, obligations, investments, cash flows, revenues, and expenses? What will be the likely future profitability and risk and, in turn, the likely future returns from investing in the company? Forecasted financial statements that rely on projections of the firm's future operating, investing, and financing activities provide the basis for projecting future profitability and risk, which provide the basis for financial decision making, including valuation.

6. **Value the firm.** What is the firm worth? Financial analysts use their estimates of share value to make recommendations for buying, selling, or holding the equity securities of various firms whose market price they think is too low, too high, or about right. Similarly, an investment banking firm that underwrites the initial

public offering of a firm's common stock must set the initial offering price, and an analyst in a corporation considering whether to acquire a company (or to divest a subsidiary or division) must assess a reasonable range of values to bid in order to acquire the target (or to expect to receive from the divestiture).

These six steps provide a logical, powerful sequence that will enable you to address very important and difficult questions, such as how to analyze and value a firm. These six interrelated steps represent the subject matter of this book. We use these six steps as the analytical framework for you to follow as you develop your skills in analyzing and valuing companies. This chapter introduces each step. Subsequent chapters develop the important concepts and tools for each step in considerably more depth.

Throughout this book, we use financial statements, notes, and other information provided by **PepsiCo, Inc.** (PepsiCo) and its subsidiaries to illustrate the various topics discussed. Appendix A at the end of the book includes the fiscal year 2012 financial statements and notes for PepsiCo, as well as statements by management and the opinion of the independent accountant regarding these financial statements. Appendix B (which can be found online at the book's companion website at www.cengagebrain. com) includes excerpts from a financial review provided by management that discusses the business strategy of PepsiCo; it also offers explanations for changes in PepsiCo's profitability and risk over time. Appendix C at the end of the book presents the output of the FSAP (Financial Statements Analysis Package), which is the financial statement analysis software that accompanies this book. The FSAP model is an Excel add-in that enables you to enter financial statement data, after which the model computes a wide array of profitability and risk ratios and creates templates for forecasting future financial statements and estimating a variety of valuation models. Appendix C presents the use of FSAP for PepsiCo, including PepsiCo's profitability and risk ratios, projected future financial statements, and valuation. FSAP is available at www.cengagebrain.com. You can use FSAP for many of the problems and cases in this book to aid in your analysis (FSAP applications are highlighted with the FSAP icon in the margin of the text). FSAP contains a user manual with guides to assist you. Appendix D (found online at the book's companion website at www.cengagebrain.com) presents tables of descriptive statistics on a wide array of financial ratios across 48 industries.

Step 1: Identify the Industry Economic Characteristics

The economic characteristics and competitive dynamics of an industry play a key role in influencing the strategies firms in the industry employ, their profitability and risk factors, and therefore the types of financial statement relations you should expect to observe. Consider, for example, the financial statement data for firms in four different industries shown in Exhibit 1.3. This exhibit expresses all items on the balance sheets and income statements as percentages of revenue. Consider how the economic characteristics of these industries affect their financial statements.

Grocery Store Chain

The products of a particular grocery store chain are difficult to differentiate from similar products of other grocery store chains, a trait that characterizes such products as *commodities*. In addition, low barriers to entry exist in the grocery store industry; an

Exhibit 1.3

Common-Size Financial Statement Data for Four Firms
(all figures as a percentage of revenue)

	Grocery Store Chain	Pharmaceutical Company	Electric Utility	Commercial Bank
BALANCE SHEET				
Cash and marketable securities	0.7%	11.0%	1.5%	261.9%
Accounts and notes receivable	0.7	18.0	7.8	733.5
Inventories	8.7	17.0	4.5	—
Property, plant, and equipment, net	22.2	28.7	159.0	18.1
Other assets	1.9	72.8	29.2	122.6
Total Assets	34.2%	147.5%	202.0%	1,136.1%
Current liabilities	7.7%	30.8%	14.9%	936.9%
Long-term debt	7.6	12.7	130.8	71.5
Other noncurrent liabilities	2.6	24.6	1.8	27.2
Shareholders' equity	16.3	79.4	54.5	100.5
Total Liabilities and Shareholders' Equity	34.2%	147.5%	202.0%	1,136.1%
INCOME STATEMENT				
Revenue	100.0%	100.0%	100.0%	100.0%
Cost of goods sold	(74.1)	(31.6)	(79.7)	—
Operating expenses	(19.7)	(37.1)	—	(41.8)
Research and development	—	(10.1)	—	—
Interest expense	(0.5)	(3.1)	(4.6)	(36.6)
Income taxes	(2.2)	(6.0)	(5.2)	(8.6)
Net Income	3.5%	12.1%	10.5%	13.0%

entrant needs primarily retail space and access to food products distributors. Thus, extensive competition and nondifferentiated products result in a relatively low net income to sales, or profit margin, percentage (3.5% in this case). Grocery stores, however, need relatively few assets to generate sales (34.2 cents in assets for each dollar of sales). The assets are described as turning over 2.9 times (100.0%/34.2%) per year. (Each dollar invested in assets generated, on average, $2.90 of revenues.) Each time the assets of this grocery store chain generate one dollar of revenue, it generates a profit of 3.5 cents. Thus, during a one-year period, the grocery store earns 10.15 cents (3.5% × 2.9) for each dollar invested in assets.

Pharmaceutical Company

The barriers to entry in the pharmaceutical industry are much higher than for grocery stores. Pharmaceutical firms must invest considerable amounts in research and development to create new drugs. The research and development process is lengthy with highly uncertain outcomes. Very few projects result in successful development of new drugs. Once new drugs have been developed, they must then undergo a lengthy government testing and approval process. If the drugs are approved, firms receive patents that give them exclusive rights to manufacture and sell the drugs for an extended period. These high entry barriers permit pharmaceutical firms to realize much higher profit margins on approved patent-protected products compared to the profit margins of grocery stores. Exhibit 1.3 indicates that the pharmaceutical firm generated a profit margin of 12.1%, more than three times that reported by the grocery store chain. Pharmaceutical firms, however, face product liability risks as well as the risk that competitors will develop superior drugs that make a particular firm's drug offerings obsolete. Because of these business risks, pharmaceutical firms tend to take on relatively small amounts of debt financing as compared to firms in industries such as electric utilities and commercial banks.

Electric Utility

The principal assets of an electric utility are its capital-intensive generating plants. Thus, property, plant, and equipment dominate the balance sheet. Because of the large investments required by such assets, electric utility firms generally demanded a monopoly position in a particular locale, and until recent years, usually obtained it. Government regulators permitted this monopoly position but set the rates that utilities charged customers for electric services. Thus, electric utilities have traditionally realized relatively high profit margins (10.5% in this case) to offset their relatively low total asset turnovers (0.495 = 100.0%/202.0% in this case). The monopoly position and regulatory protection reduced the risk of financial failure and permitted electric utilities to invest large amounts of capital in long-lived assets and take on relatively high proportions of debt in their capital structures. The economic characteristics of electric utilities have changed dramatically in recent years with gradual elimination of monopoly positions and the introduction of competition that affects rates, reducing profit margins considerably.

Commercial Bank

Through their borrowing and lending activities, commercial banks serve as intermediaries in the supply and demand for financial capital. The principal assets of commercial banks are investments in financial securities and loans to businesses and consumers. The principal financing for commercial banks comes from customers' deposits and short-term borrowings. Because customers can generally withdraw deposits at any time, commercial banks invest in securities that they can quickly convert into cash if necessary. Because money is a commodity, one would expect a commercial bank to realize a small profit margin on the revenue it earns from lending (interest revenue) over the price it pays for its borrowed funds (interest expense). The profit margins on lending are indeed relatively small. In contrast, the 13.0% margin for the commercial bank shown in Exhibit 1.3 reflects the much higher profit margins it generates from offering fee-based financial services such as structuring financing packages for businesses, guaranteeing financial commitments of business customers, and arranging mergers and acquisitions. Note that the assets of this commercial bank turn over just 0.09 (100.0%/ 1,136.1%) times per year, reflecting the net effect of interest revenues and fees from investments and loans of 6–8% per year, which requires a large investment in financial assets.

Tools for Studying Industry Economics

Three tools for studying the economic characteristics of an industry are (1) value chain analysis, (2) Porter's five forces classification framework, and (3) an economic attributes framework. The microeconomics literature suggests other analytical frameworks as well.

Value Chain Analysis

The value chain for an industry sets forth the sequence or chain of activities involved in the creation, manufacture, and distribution of its products and services. As an example, Exhibit 1.4 portrays an example of a value chain for the pharmaceutical industry. Pharmaceutical companies invest in research and development to discover and develop new drugs. When promising drugs emerge, a lengthy drug approval process begins. Estimates suggest that it takes seven to ten years and almost $1 billion to discover and obtain approval of new drugs. To expedite the approval process, reduce costs, and permit their scientists to concentrate on the more creative drug discovery phase, pharmaceutical companies often contract with clinical research firms to conduct the testing and shepherding of new drugs through the approval process.

To the extent prices are available for products or services at each stage in the value chain, you can study where value is added within an industry. For example, you can look at the prices paid to acquire firms with promising or newly discovered drugs to ascertain the value of the drug discovery phase. The prices that clinical research firms charge to test and obtain approval of new drugs signal the value added by this activity. The higher the value added from any activity, the higher the profitability should be from engaging in that phase.

You also can use the value chain to identify the strategic positioning of a particular firm within the industry. Traditionally, pharmaceutical firms have maintained a presence in the discovery through demand creation phases, leaving distribution to pharmacies and increasingly contracting out the drug testing and approval phase.

The manufacture of drugs involves combining various chemicals and other elements. For quality control and product purity reasons, pharmaceutical companies use highly automated manufacturing processes. Pharmaceutical companies employ sales forces to market drugs to doctors, hospitals, and health maintenance organizations. In an effort to create demand, these companies have increasingly advertised new products through multiple advertising media, suggesting that consumers ask their doctors about the drug. Drug distribution typically channels through pharmacies, although bulk mail-order and Internet purchases are increasingly common (and encouraged by health insurers).

Refer to Note 1, "Basis of Presentation and Our Divisions," to the financial statements of **PepsiCo** (Appendix A) for a description of PepsiCo's divisions and segments. PepsiCo operates four business units: PepsiCo Americas Foods (PAF), PepsiCo Americas Beverages

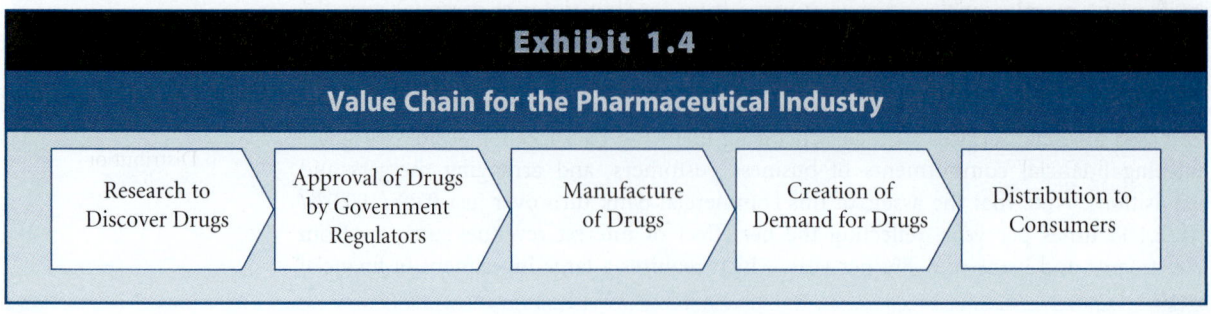

Exhibit 1.4

Value Chain for the Pharmaceutical Industry

Research to Discover Drugs → Approval of Drugs by Government Regulators → Manufacture of Drugs → Creation of Demand for Drugs → Distribution to Consumers

Exhibit 1.5

Division Revenues and Operating Profits for PepsiCo for 2012 (dollar amounts in millions)

	Revenues		Operating Profits		Operating Profit Margin
Frito-Lay North America	$13,574	20.7%	$ 3,646	40.0%	26.9%
Quaker Foods North America	2,636	4.0	695	7.6	26.4%
Latin America Foods	7,780	11.9	1,059	11.6	13.6%
PepsiCo Americas Beverages	21,408	32.7	2,937	32.2	13.7%
PepsiCo Europe	13,441	20.5	1,330	14.6	9.9%
Asia, Middle East & Africa	6,653	10.2	747	8.2	11.2%
Corporate unallocated	—	—	(1,302)	(14.3)	
Total	$65,492	100.0%	$ 9,112	100.0%	13.9%

(PAB), PepsiCo Europe, and PepsiCo Asia, Middle East and Africa (AMEA). The four business units include six reportable segments. PAF is organized into three divisions: Frito-Lay North America (FLNA; branded snacks, chips, and other food products), Quaker Foods North America (QFNA; cereal and related products), and Latin America Foods (LAF; branded snacks, chips, and other food products). PAB operates as a single-segment division, and it manufactures and distributes soft drinks and other beverages throughout North America. PepsiCo Europe and AMEA operate in markets outside North America and manufacture and sell branded snack foods, breakfast foods, soft drinks, and other beverages. Exhibit 1.5 shows the amounts taken from PepsiCo's Note 1, the proportions of revenues and operating profit that PepsiCo derived from each division, and the operating profit margin (operating profit divided by revenues) of each division for 2012.

Exhibit 1.6 illustrates a value chain for one of PepsiCo's principal businesses, the soft drink/beverage industry. Note that this is PepsiCo's legacy business, so for completeness you should also evaluate PepsiCo's other principal businesses, particularly in the snack food and breakfast food industries.

Although the classic PepsiCo soft drinks (for example, Pepsi, Diet Pepsi, and Mountain Dew) have not changed for many years, the company continually engages in new product development. Once a product appears to have commercial feasibility,

Exhibit 1.6

Value Chain for the Soft Drink/Beverage Industry

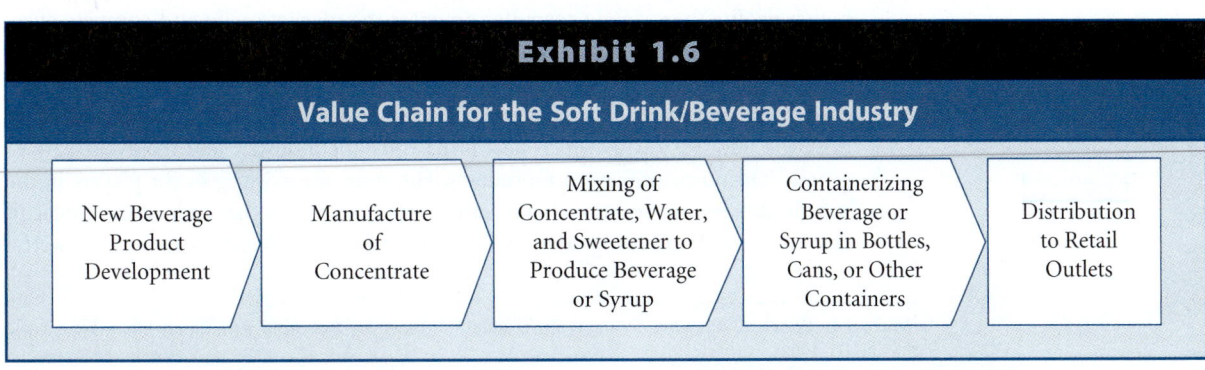

New Beverage Product Development → Manufacture of Concentrate → Mixing of Concentrate, Water, and Sweetener to Produce Beverage or Syrup → Containerizing Beverage or Syrup in Bottles, Cans, or Other Containers → Distribution to Retail Outlets

PepsiCo combines raw materials into a concentrate or syrup base. The ingredients and their mixes are highly confidential. PepsiCo transfers the concentrate to its bottlers (or, in the case of syrup, to its national fountain accounts), which combine it with water and sweeteners and then bottle it to produce the finished soft drink.

Porter's Five Forces Classification Framework

Porter suggests that five forces influence the level of competition and the profitability of firms in an industry.[1] Three of the forces—rivalry among existing firms, potential entry, and substitutes—represent horizontal competition among current or potential future firms in the industry and closely related products and services. The other two forces—buyer power and supplier power—depict vertical competition in the value chain, from the suppliers through the existing rivals to the buyers. We discuss each of these forces next and illustrate them within the soft drink/beverage industry. Exhibit 1.7 depicts Porter's five forces in the soft drink/beverage industry.

1. **Rivalry among Existing Firms.** Direct rivalry among existing firms is often the first order of competition in an industry. Some industries can be characterized by concentrated rivalry (such as a monopoly, a duopoly, or an oligopoly), whereas others have diffuse rivalry across many firms. Economists often assess the level of competition with industry concentration ratios, such as a four-firm concentration index that measures the proportion of industry sales controlled by the four largest competitors. Economics teaches that in general, the greater the industry concentration, the lower the competition between existing rivals and thus the more profitable the firms will be.

    PepsiCo and **Coca-Cola** dominate the soft drink/beverage industry in the United States. Because some consumers view the two companies' products as being similar, intense competition based on price could develop. Also, the soft drink market in the United States is mature (that is, not growing rapidly), so price cutting could become a strategy to gain market share. Although intense rivalries have a tendency to reduce profitability, in this case, PepsiCo and Coca-Cola appear to tacitly avoid competing based on price and compete instead on brand image, access to key distribution channels (for example, fast-food chains and grocery store shelf space), and other attributes. Growth opportunities do exist in other countries, which both companies pursue aggressively. Thus, we characterize industry rivalry as moderate.

2. **Threat of New Entrants.** How easily can new firms enter a market? Are there entry barriers such as large capital investment, technological expertise, patents, or regulations that inhibit new entrants? Do the existing rivals have distinct competitive advantages (such as brand names) that will make it difficult for other firms to enter and compete successfully? If so, firms in the industry will likely generate higher profits than if new entrants can enter the market easily and compete away any potential excess profits.

    The soft drink/beverage industry has no significant barriers to entry. This is evident by the numerous small juice, sports drink, water, and soft drink companies that exist; the frequency with which new firms enter the industry; and the availability of generic and no-name beverage products. However, the existing major players in the soft drink/beverage industry have competitive advantages that reduce the threat of new entrants. Brand recognition by PepsiCo and Coca-Cola serves as a very powerful

---

[1]Michael E. Porter, *Competitive Strategy: Techniques for Analyzing Industries and Competitors* (New York: Free Press), 1998.

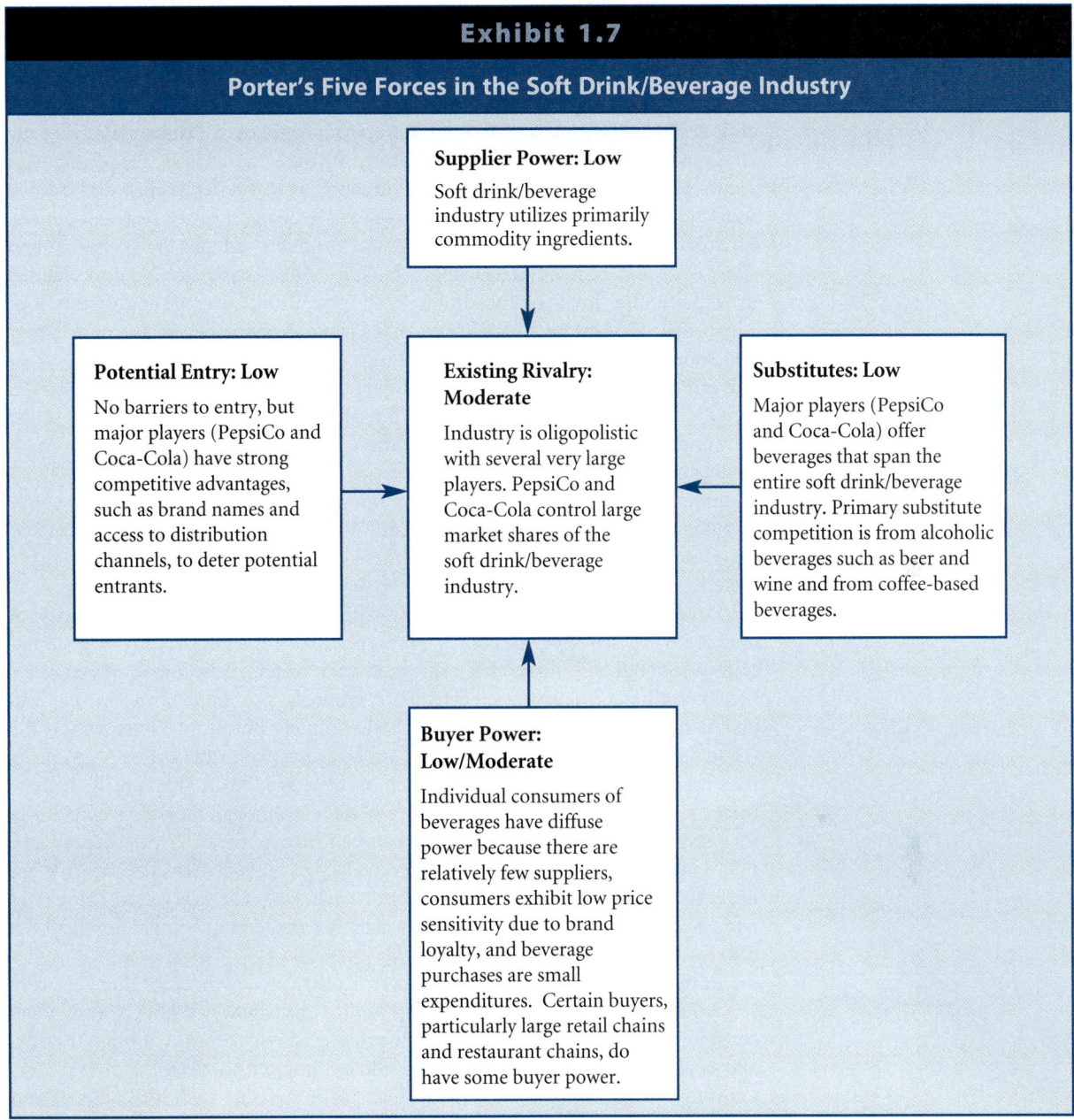

Exhibit 1.7

Porter's Five Forces in the Soft Drink/Beverage Industry

Supplier Power: Low

Soft drink/beverage industry utilizes primarily commodity ingredients.

Potential Entry: Low

No barriers to entry, but major players (PepsiCo and Coca-Cola) have strong competitive advantages, such as brand names and access to distribution channels, to deter potential entrants.

Existing Rivalry: Moderate

Industry is oligopolistic with several very large players. PepsiCo and Coca-Cola control large market shares of the soft drink/beverage industry.

Substitutes: Low

Major players (PepsiCo and Coca-Cola) offer beverages that span the entire soft drink/beverage industry. Primary substitute competition is from alcoholic beverages such as beer and wine and from coffee-based beverages.

Buyer Power: Low/Moderate

Individual consumers of beverages have diffuse power because there are relatively few suppliers, consumers exhibit low price sensitivity due to brand loyalty, and beverage purchases are small expenditures. Certain buyers, particularly large retail chains and restaurant chains, do have some buyer power.

deterrent to potential new competitors. Another deterrent is these two firms' domination of distribution channels. Most restaurant chains sign exclusive contracts to serve the beverages of one or the other of these two firms. Also, PepsiCo and Coca-Cola often dominate shelf space in grocery stores.

3. **Threat of Substitutes.** How easily can customers switch to substitute products or services? How likely are they to switch? When there are close substitutes in a market, competition increases and profitability diminishes (for example, between restaurants and grocery stores for certain types of prepared foods). Unique products with few substitutes, such as certain prescription medications, enhance profitability.

The carbonated soft drink industry faces substitute competition from an array of other beverages that consumers can substitute to quench their thirst. Fruit juices, bottled water, sports drinks, teas, coffees, milk, beers, and wines serve a similar thirst-quenching function to that of soft drinks. Over the years, Coca-Cola and PepsiCo have expanded their beverage portfolios to encompass virtually all nonalcoholic beverages. For example, PepsiCo purchased **Tropicana** and **Gatorade** to enhance its product offerings in juices, sports drinks, and bottled water, and has joint ventures with **Lipton** and **Starbucks** to sell teas and coffees. Because of the wide range of beverage products offered by PepsiCo and Coca-Cola and because of consumer buying habits, brand loyalty, and channel availability, the threat of substitutes in the soft drink/beverage industry is low. The primary substitute competition comes from alcoholic beverages such as beer and wine and from coffee-based beverages.

4. **Buyer Power.** Buyer power relates to the relative number of buyers and sellers in a particular industry and the leverage buyers have with respect to price. Are the buyers price takers or price setters? If there are many sellers of a product and a small number of buyers making very large purchase decisions, such as military equipment bought by governments or automobile parts purchased by automobile manufacturers, the buyer can exert significant downward pressure on prices and therefore on the profitability of suppliers. If there are few sellers and many buyers, as with beverages, the sellers have more bargaining power.

Buyer power also relates to buyers' price sensitivity and the elasticity of demand. How sensitive are consumers to product prices? If products are similar to those offered by competitors, consumers may switch to the lowest-priced offering. If consumers view a particular firm's products as unique, however, they will be less sensitive to price differences. Another dimension of price sensitivity is the relative cost of a product. Consumers are less sensitive to the prices of products that represent small expenditures, such as beverages, than they are to higher-priced products, such as automobiles. However, even though individual consumers may switch easily between brands or between higher- or lower-priced products, they make individual rather than large collective buying decisions; so they are likely to continue to be price takers (not price setters). The ease of switching does not make the buyer powerful; instead it increases the level of competition between the rivals.

In the beverage industry, buyer power is relatively low because there are very few suppliers and they have access to essential distribution channels. Individual consumers tend to exhibit relatively low price sensitivity because of brand loyalty, and beverages comprise relatively small dollar amount purchases. However, certain buyers (for example, large retail and grocery chains such as **Walmart** and large fast-food chains such as **McDonald's**) make such large beverage purchases on a national level that they can exert significant buyer power.

5. **Supplier Power.** A similar set of factors with respect to leverage in negotiating prices applies on the input side as well. If an industry is comprised of a large number of potential buyers of inputs that are produced by relatively few suppliers, the suppliers will have greater power in setting prices and generating profits. For example, many firms assemble and sell personal computers and laptops, but these firms face significant supplier power because **Microsoft** is a dominant supplier of operating systems and application software and **Intel** is a dominant supplier of microprocessors.

Beverage companies produce their concentrates and syrups with raw materials that are commodities. Although PepsiCo does not disclose every ingredient, PepsiCo is not likely to be dependent on one supplier (or even a few suppliers) for its raw materials. It also is unlikely that any of these ingredients are sufficiently unique that the suppliers could exert much power over PepsiCo. Given PepsiCo's size, the power more likely resides with PepsiCo than with its suppliers.

In summary:

- Competition in the soft drink/beverage industry rates low on supplier power, threat of new entrants, and threat of substitutes.
- The industry rates low on buyer power of consumers but moderate on buyer power of fast-food chains and large retail and grocery chains.
- The industry rates moderate on rivalry within the industry. Unless PepsiCo or Coca-Cola decides to compete on the basis of low price, you might expect these firms to continue to generate relatively high profitability.

Economic Attributes Framework

We find the following framework useful in studying the economic attributes of a business, in part because it ties in with items reported in the financial statements.

1. **Demand**
   - Are customers highly price-sensitive, as in the case of automobiles, or are they relatively insensitive, as in the case of soft drinks?
   - Is demand growing rapidly, as in the case of long-term health care, or is the industry relatively mature, as in the case of grocery stores?
   - Does demand move with the economic cycle, as in the case of construction of new homes and offices, or is demand insensitive to business cycles, as in the case of food products and medical care?
   - Does demand vary with the seasons, as in the case of summer clothing and ski equipment, or is demand relatively stable throughout the year, as in the case of most grocery store products?

2. **Supply**
   - Are many suppliers offering similar products, or are a few suppliers offering unique products?
   - Are there high barriers to entry, or can new entrants gain easy access?
   - Are there high barriers to exit, as in the case of firms that face substantial environment cleanup costs?

3. **Manufacturing**
   - Is the manufacturing process capital-intensive, as in the case of electric power generation; labor-intensive, as in the case of advertising, investment banking, auditing, and other professional services; or a combination of the two, as in the case of automobile manufacturing and airline transportation?
   - Is the manufacturing process complex with low tolerance for error, as in the case of heart pacemakers and microchips, or relatively simple with ranges of products that are of acceptable quality, as in the case of apparel and nonmechanized toys?

4. **Marketing**
   - Is the product promoted to other businesses, in which case a sales staff plays a key role, or is it marketed to consumers, so that advertising, location, and coupons serve as principal promotion mechanisms?

- Does steady demand pull products through distribution channels, or must firms continually create demand?

5. **Investing and Financing**
   - Are the assets of firms in the industry relatively short-term, as in the case of commercial banks, which require short-term sources of funds to finance them? Or are assets relatively long-term, as in the case of electric utilities, which require primarily long-term financing?
   - Is there relatively little risk in the assets of firms in the industry, such as from technological obsolescence, so that firms can carry high proportions of debt financing? Alternatively, are there high risks resulting from short product life cycles or product liability concerns that dictate low debt and high shareholders' equity financing?
   - Is the industry relatively profitable and mature, generating more cash flow from operations than is needed for acquisitions of property, plant, and equipment? Alternatively, is the industry growing rapidly and in need of external financing?

Exhibit 1.8 summarizes the economic attributes of the soft drink/beverage industry.

Exhibit 1.8

Economic Attributes of the Soft Drink/Beverage Industry

Demand

- Demand is relatively insensitive to price.
- There is low growth in the United States, but more rapid growth opportunities are available in other countries.
- Demand is not cyclical.

Supply

- Two principal suppliers (PepsiCo and Coca-Cola) sell branded products.
- Branded products and domination of distribution channels by two principal suppliers create significant competitive advantages.

Manufacturing

- Manufacturing process for concentrate/syrup is not capital-intensive.
- Bottling and distribution of final product are capital-intensive.
- Manufacturing process is simple (essentially a mixing operation) with some tolerance for quality variation.

Marketing

- Brand recognition and established demand pull products through distribution channels, but advertising can stimulate demand to some extent.

Investing and Financing

- Bottling operations and transportation of products to retailers require long-term financing.
- Profitability is relatively high and growth is slow in the United States, leading to excess cash flow generation. Growth markets in other countries require financing from internal domestic cash flow or from external sources.

Step 2: Identify the Company Strategies

LO 1-3

Identify firm-specific strategies for achieving competitive advantage within an industry.

Firms establish business strategies to differentiate themselves from competitors, but an industry's economic characteristics affect the flexibility that firms have in designing those strategies. In some cases, firms can create sustainable competitive advantages. **PepsiCo**'s size, brand name, and access to distribution channels give it sustainable competitive advantages over smaller, less-known beverage companies. Similarly, the reputation for quality family entertainment provides **Disney** with a sustainable advantage, whereas a reputation for low prices generates advantages for **Walmart**.

In many industries, however, products and ideas quickly get copied. Consider the following examples: cell phones, tablets, and computer hardware; chicken, pizza, and hamburger restaurant chains; and financial services. In these cases, firms may achieve competitive advantage by being the first with a new concept or idea (referred to as *first mover advantage*) or by continually investing in product development to remain on the leading edge of change in an industry. Such competitive advantages are difficult (but not impossible) to sustain for long periods of time.

Framework for Strategy Analysis

The set of strategic choices confronting a particular firm varies across industries. The following framework dealing with product and firm characteristics helps you identify and structure the set of trade-offs and choices a firm must face.

1. **Nature of Product or Service.** Is a firm attempting to create unique products or services for particular market niches, thereby achieving relatively high profit margins (referred to as a *product differentiation strategy*)? Or is it offering nondifferentiated products at low prices, accepting a lower profit margin in return for a higher sales volume and market share (referred to as a *low-cost leadership strategy*)? Is a firm attempting to achieve both objectives by differentiating (perhaps by creating brand loyalty or technological innovation) and being price competitive by maintaining tight control over costs?

2. **Degree of Integration in Value Chain.** Is the firm pursuing a vertical integration strategy, participating in all phases of the value chain, or selecting just certain phases in the chain? With respect to manufacturing, is the firm conducting all manufacturing operations itself (as usually occurs in steel manufacturing), outsourcing all manufacturing (common in athletic shoes), or outsourcing the manufacturing of components but conducting the assembly operation in-house (common in automobile and computer hardware manufacturing)?

   With respect to distribution, is the firm maintaining control over the distribution function or outsourcing it? Some restaurant chains, for example, own all of their restaurants, while other chains operate through independently owned franchises. Computer hardware firms have recently shifted from selling through their own sales staffs to using various indirect sellers, such as value-added resellers and systems integrators—in effect shifting from in-house sourcing to outsourcing the distribution function.

3. **Degree of Geographical Diversification.** Is the firm targeting its products to its domestic market or integrating horizontally across many countries? Operating in other countries creates opportunities for growth but exposes firms to risks from changes in exchange rates, political uncertainties, and additional competitors.

4. **Degree of Industry Diversification.** Is the firm operating in a single industry or diversifying across multiple industries? Operating in multiple industries permits firms to diversify product, cyclical, regulatory, and other risks encountered when operating in a single industry but raises questions about management's ability to understand and manage multiple and different businesses effectively.

Application of Strategy Framework to PepsiCo's Beverage Division

To apply this strategy framework to **PepsiCo**'s beverage division, we rely on the description provided by PepsiCo's management (Appendix B). Most U.S. firms include this type of management discussion and analysis in their Form 10-K filing with the Securities and Exchange Commission (SEC).

1. **Nature of Product or Service.** PepsiCo's beverage division competes broadly in the beverage industry, with offerings in soft drinks, fruit juices, bottled waters, sports drinks, teas, and coffees. However, its principal beverage products are soft drinks. Although one might debate whether its products differ from similar products offered by **Coca-Cola** and other competitors (a debate that invariably involves taste), PepsiCo relies on brand recognition and distribution channels to differentiate its products.

2. **Degree of Integration in Value Chain.** PepsiCo engages in new product development, manufactures concentrates and syrups, and bottles, distributes, and promotes its products. Maintaining product quality and efficient and effective distribution channels are critical to PepsiCo's success, so PepsiCo emphasizes the important role of much of the value chain. However, bottling operations are relatively simple, yet capital-intensive, and require long-term financing, typically debt. After many years of these operations being delegated to affiliated bottlers, PepsiCo recently began repurchasing financial interests in such operations, which has resulted in an increase in debt financing.

3. **Degree of Geographical Diversification.** Note 1 to PepsiCo's financial statements and Exhibit 1.5 indicate that the PepsiCo Americas Beverages division generated 33% of the firm's revenues during 2012. PepsiCo Europe and PepsiCo Asia, Middle East and Africa (AMEA) represented 21% and 10% of revenues, respectively. The remainder of revenues came from the three distinct foods divisions (Frito-Lay North America, Quaker Foods North America, and Latin America Foods). Note that the Europe and AMEA divisions include both beverage and food sales, so it is not possible from these disclosures to identify the exact amount of food versus beverage revenues for PepsiCo overall. Nevertheless, it is clear that PepsiCo is not strictly a beverage company.

4. **Degree of Industry Diversification.** To focus and streamline the presentation of industry analysis and strategic analysis techniques, our discussion thus far has focused on PepsiCo's beverages business. However, PepsiCo generates greater revenues and higher operating profit margins from the snack food and breakfast foods divisions than from the beverage division. As seen in Exhibit 1.5, PepsiCo's three foods divisions generated nearly 37% of the company's total revenues. Although PepsiCo is more industry-diverse than Coca-Cola, many economic characteristics of the beverage, snack food, and cereal industries are similar in nature, involving the selling of branded consumer products. These industries can be characterized as having low barriers to entry but a small number of powerful rivals with brand recognition and access to key distribution channels. These industries rely on commodity

raw materials for inputs, facing low supplier power, and relatively price-insensitive buyers because of brand loyalty and distribution channels. As a result, PepsiCo's strategies are relatively similar between the beverage and foods divisions, focusing on product development and promotion to leverage the brand recognition and maintaining access to important distribution channels.

■ The value chain for an industry sets forth the sequence or chain of activities involved in the creation, manufacture, and distribution of its products and services.

■ The Porter five forces framework is useful for identifying the level of competition and the profitability of firms in an industry.

■ Applying an economics attributes framework describes elements of supply, demand, and

other structural features of an industry, which are typically reflected in the financial statements.

■ The set of strategic choices confronting a particular firm varies across industries. Firms adopt different strategies to differentiate themselves from competitors, but available strategies are determined by an industry's economic characteristics.

Quick Check

Step 3: Assess the Quality of the Financial Statements

LO 1-4

Show familiarity with the purpose, underlying concepts, and format of the balance sheet, income statement, and statement of cash flows.

Firms prepare four principal financial statements to report the results of their activities: (1) balance sheet, (2) income statement, (3) statement of comprehensive income, and (4) statement of cash flows. Firms also prepare a fifth statement, the statement of shareholders' equity, which provides further detail of the shareholders' equity section of the balance sheet. A set of notes that elaborate on items included in these statements is also required. Together, the financial statements and notes provide an extensive set of information about the firm's financial position, performance, and cash flows, and permit users to develop insights about the firm's profitability, risk, and growth.

Using the financial statements and notes for **PepsiCo** in Appendix A as examples, this section presents a brief overview of the purpose and content of each of these three financial statements. Understanding accounting concepts and methods and evaluating the quality of a firm's financial statements is a central element of effective financial statement analysis and therefore one of the three central objectives of this book. Chapters 2 and 3 describe the fundamental accounting concepts and methods for measuring and reporting:

■ assets, liabilities, and shareholders' equity.
■ revenues, expenses, and income.
■ cash flows associated with operating, investing, and financing activities.

Chapters 6–9 describe specific accounting principles and methods in depth, opening with a discussion of accounting quality. In this chapter, we introduce the overall concept of accounting quality by highlighting the key elements of PepsiCo's financial statements and notes.

Accounting Principles

Firms produce financial statements and notes based on accounting standards and principles established by the accounting profession. For American firms, U.S. GAAP determines the valuation and measurement methods used in preparing financial statements. The SEC (Securities and Exchange Commission), an agency of the federal government, has the legal authority to specify acceptable accounting principles in the United States (www.sec.gov), but has, for the most part, delegated the responsibility for setting U.S. GAAP to the Financial Accounting Standards Board (FASB), a private-sector body within the accounting profession (www.fasb.org). The FASB is an independent board comprising seven members and a full-time professional staff. The FASB specifies acceptable accounting principles only after receiving extensive comments on proposed accounting standards from various preparers, auditors, and users of financial statements.

The IASB is an independent entity comprising 16 members and a full-time professional staff, which is responsible for developing international financial reporting standards (IFRS) (www.ifrs.org). Many countries have dropped their own country-specific accounting rules, formally accepting IFRS as the applicable accounting standards. Beginning in 2005, the financial statements of listed firms in the European Community were required to conform to the pronouncements of the IASB.

The SEC accepts financial statement filings prepared under IFRS from non-U.S. registrants, although it has not yet accepted IFRS-based financial statement filings from U.S. firms, a matter that remains under discussion. The FASB and IASB are working together closely to harmonize accounting standards and principles worldwide. Although substantial differences must be resolved between the two sets of standards (we will highlight existing differences throughout this book), the two boards have managed to find common ground on many major principles. Now when the two boards propose a new principle or a revision of an existing principle, they typically work jointly to develop the proposed principle and to collect and evaluate comments from various constituencies. They then agree on the final principle, which becomes part of both U.S. GAAP and IFRS. Global harmonization in accounting standards should facilitate better financial statement analysis, enabling analysts to evaluate and compare financial statements from firms across many countries, prepared under similar accounting principles. Accordingly, increasing comparability should make allocation of capital more efficient worldwide.

Balance Sheet—Measuring Financial Position

The balance sheet, or statement of financial position, presents a snapshot of the resources of a firm (assets) and the claims on those resources (liabilities and shareholders' equity) as of a specific date. The balance sheet derives its name from the fact that it reports the following balance, or equality:

$$\text{Assets} = \text{Liabilities} + \text{Shareholders' Equity}$$

That is, a firm's assets are in balance with, or equal to, the claims on those assets by creditors (liabilities) and owners (shareholders' equity). The balance sheet views resources from two perspectives: a list of the specific resources the firm controls (for example, cash, inventory, and equipment) and the obligations of the entity and ownership claims on the assets (for example, suppliers, employees, governments, financial institutions, and shareholders).

The assets portion of the balance sheet reports the effects of a firm's operating decisions (principally those involving assets used in day-to-day activities to produce and deliver products and services to customers) and investing decisions (principally those involving financial assets to generate interest income, dividends, and other returns on investment). Refer to the balance sheets for **PepsiCo** as of fiscal year-end 2008 through 2012 in Exhibit 1.9. PepsiCo's principal operating assets are cash and cash equivalents; accounts and notes receivable; inventories; prepaid expenses; property, plant, and equipment; and goodwill and other

Exhibit 1.9

PepsiCo, Inc., and Subsidiaries
Consolidated Balance Sheets
(in millions)

	2012	2011	2010	2009	2008
ASSETS					
Current Assets					
Cash and cash equivalents	$ 6,297	$ 4,067	$ 5,943	$ 3,943	$ 2,064
Short-term investments	322	358	426	192	213
Accounts and notes receivable, net	7,041	6,912	6,323	4,624	4,683
Inventories	3,581	3,827	3,372	2,618	2,522
Prepaid expenses and other current assets	1,479	2,277	1,505	1,194	1,324
Total Current Assets	$ 18,720	$ 17,441	$ 17,569	$ 12,571	$ 10,806
Property, plant and equipment, net	19,136	19,698	19,058	12,671	11,663
Amortizable intangible assets, net	1,781	1,888	2,025	841	732
Goodwill	16,971	16,800	14,661	6,534	5,124
Other nonamortizable intangible assets	14,744	14,557	11,783	1,782	1,128
Investments in noncontrolled affiliates	1,633	1,477	1,368	4,484	3,883
Other assets	1,653	1,021	1,689	965	2,658
Total Assets	$ 74,638	$ 72,882	$ 68,153	$ 39,848	$ 35,994
LIABILITES AND EQUITY					
Current Liabilities					
Short-term obligations	$ 4,815	$ 6,205	$ 4,898	$ 464	$ 369
Accounts payable and other current liabilities	11,903	11,757	10,923	8,127	8,273
Income taxes payable	371	192	71	165	145
Total Current Liabilities	$ 17,089	$ 18,154	$ 15,892	$ 8,756	$ 8,787
Long-term debt obligations	23,544	20,568	19,999	7,400	7,858
Other liabilities	6,543	8,266	6,729	5,591	6,541
Deferred income taxes	5,063	4,995	4,057	659	226
Total Liabilities	$ 52,239	$ 51,983	$ 46,677	$ 22,406	$ 23,412
Commitments and Contingencies	—	—	—	—	—
Preferred stock, no par value	$ 41	$ 41	$ 41	$ 41	$ 41
Repurchased preferred stock	(164)	(157)	(150)	(145)	(138)
Common Shareholders' Equity					
Common stock	26	26	31	30	30
Capital in excess of par value	4,178	4,461	4,527	250	351
Retained earnings	43,158	40,316	37,090	33,805	30,638
Accumulated other comprehensive loss	(5,487)	(6,229)	(3,630)	(3,794)	(4,694)
Repurchased common stock, in excess of par value	(19,458)	(17,870)	(16,745)	(13,383)	(14,122)
Total Common Shareholders' Equity	$ 22,417	$ 20,704	$ 21,273	$ 16,908	$ 12,203
Noncontrolling interests	105	311	312	638	476
Total Equity	$ 22,399	$ 20,899	$ 21,476	$ 17,442	$ 12,582
Total Liabilities and Equity	$ 74,638	$ 72,882	$ 68,153	$ 39,848	$ 35,994

Source: PepsiCo, Inc., Forms 10-K for the Fiscal Years Ended 2010–2012.

intangible assets. PepsiCo's principal financial assets from investing activities include short-term investment securities and investments in the equity securities of noncontrolled affiliates.

The liabilities and shareholders' equity portion of the balance sheet reports obligations that arise from a firm's operating decisions (involving obligations to pay employees and suppliers of goods and services) and financing decisions, involving raising debt capital from banks and other lenders as well as raising equity capital from investors in common stock. PepsiCo obtains financing from suppliers of goods and services (reported as accounts payable, other current liabilities, and other long-term liabilities), banks and other lenders (reported as both short- and long-term obligations), preferred equity investors (reported as preferred stock, offset by repurchased preferred stock), and common equity investors (reported as common shareholders' equity).

For sake of comparison, also refer to the balance sheets for **The Coca-Cola Company** as of fiscal year-end 2008 through 2012 in Exhibit 1.10. Notice that Coca-Cola's principal assets, liabilities, and financing from banks, lenders, and common equity investors are similar to those of PepsiCo.

Exhibit 1.10

The Coca-Cola Company
Consolidated Balance Sheets
(in millions)

	2012	2011	2010	2009	2008
ASSETS					
Current Assets					
Cash and cash equivalents	$ 8,442	$ 12,803	$ 8,517	$ 7,021	$ 4,701
Short-term investments	5,017	1,088	2,682	2,130	—
Total cash, cash equivalents, and short-term investments	$ 13,459	$ 13,891	$ 11,199	$ 9,151	$ 4,701
Marketable securities	3,092	144	138	62	278
Trade accounts receivable, less allowances of $53 and $83, respectively	4,759	4,920	4,430	3,758	3,090
Inventories	3,264	3,092	2,650	2,354	2,187
Prepaid expenses and other assets	2,781	3,450	3,162	2,226	1,920
Assets held for sale	2,973	—	—	—	—
Total Current Assets	$ 30,328	$ 25,497	$ 21,579	$ 17,551	$ 12,176
Equity method investments	9,216	7,233	6,954	6,217	5,316
Other investments, principally bottling companies	1,232	1,141	631	538	463
Other assets	3,585	3,495	2,121	1,976	1,733
Property, plant and equipment, net	$ 14,476	$ 14,939	$ 14,727	$ 9,561	$ 8,326
Trademarks with indefinite lives	6,527	6,430	6,356	6,183	6,059
Bottlers' franchise rights with indefinite lives	7,405	7,770	7,511	1,953	—
Goodwill	12,255	12,219	11,665	4,224	4,029
Other intangible assets	1,150	1,250	1,377	468	2,417
Total Assets	$ 86,174	$ 79,974	$ 72,921	$ 48,671	$ 40,519

(Continued)

Exhibit 1.10 (Continued)

	2012	2011	2010	2009	2008
LIABILITIES AND EQUITY					
Current Liabilities					
Accounts payable and accrued expenses	$ 8,680	$ 9,009	$ 8,859	$ 6,657	$ 6,205
Loans and notes payable	16,297	12,871	8,100	6,749	6,066
Current maturities of long-term debt	1,577	2,041	1,276	51	465
Accrued income taxes	471	362	273	264	252
Liabilities held for sale	796	—	—	—	—
Total Current Liabilities	$ 27,821	$ 24,283	$ 18,508	$ 13,721	$ 12,988
Long-term debt	14,736	13,656	14,041	5,059	2,781
Other liabilities	5,468	5,420	4,794	2,965	3,011
Deferred income taxes	4,981	4,694	4,261	1,580	877
Total Liabilities	$ 53,006	$ 48,053	$ 41,604	$ 23,325	$ 19,657
Shareowners' Equity					
Common stock	$ 1,760	$ 1,760	$ 880	$ 880	$ 880
Capital surplus	11,379	10,332	10,057	8,537	7,966
Reinvested earnings	58,045	53,621	49,278	41,537	38,513
Accumulated other comprehensive income (loss)	(3,385)	(2,774)	(1,450)	(757)	(2,674)
Treasury stock, at cost—2,571 and 2,514 shares, respectively	(35,009)	(31,304)	(27,762)	(25,398)	(24,213)
Equity Attributable to Shareowners	$ 32,790	$ 31,635	$ 31,003	$ 24,799	$ 20,472
Equity Attributable to Noncontrolling Interests	378	286	314	547	390
Total Equity	$ 33,168	$ 31,921	$ 31,317	$ 25,346	$ 20,862
Total Liabilities and Equity	$ 86,174	$ 79,974	$ 72,921	$ 48,671	$ 40,519

Source: The Coca-Cola Company, Forms 10-K for the Fiscal Years Ended 2010–2012.

Under U.S. GAAP, firms are required to report assets and liabilities in descending order of liquidity, so the assets that are closest to cash are listed first while the assets that are hardest to convert to cash are reported last. Similarly, the liabilities that are likely to be settled soonest are listed first while the liabilities likely to be settled furthest in the future are shown last.

Formats of balance sheets in some countries can differ from the format used in the United States. Under IFRS, for example, firms can choose to report the balance sheet with assets and liabilities listed in *descending* order of liquidity or they can report the balance sheet with long-term assets such as property, plant, and equipment and other noncurrent assets appearing first, followed by current assets. On the financing side, balance sheets prepared under IFRS may list shareholders' equity first, followed by noncurrent liabilities and current liabilities. Both formats under IFRS maintain the balance sheet equality but present accounts in a different sequence.

In the United Kingdom, for example, the balance sheet equation commonly takes the following form:

$$\text{Noncurrent Assets} + (\text{Current Assets} - \text{Current Liabilities}) - \text{Noncurrent Liabilities} = \text{Shareholders' Equity}$$

This format takes the perspective of shareholders by reporting the net assets available for shareholders after subtracting claims by creditors. You can always rearrange the components of published balance sheets to the format you consider most informative or comparable with others.

Assets—Recognition, Measurement, and Classification

Which of its resources should a firm recognize as assets? At what amount should the firm measure these assets? How should it classify them in the assets portion of the balance sheet? U.S. GAAP and IFRS establish the principles that firms must use to determine responses to those questions.

Defining what resources firms should recognize as assets is one of the most important definitions among all of the principles established by U.S. GAAP and IFRS:

> Assets are probable future economic benefits obtained or controlled by a particular entity as a result of past transactions or events.[2]

Assets are resources that have the potential to provide a firm with future economic benefits: the ability to generate future cash inflows (as with accounts receivable, inventories, and investment securities) or to reduce future cash outflows (as with prepayments) or to provide future service potential for operating activities (as with property, equipment, and intangibles). Therefore, asset recognition depends on managers' expectations for future economic benefits. A firm can recognize as assets only those resources for which it:

- controls the rights to future economic benefits as a result of a past transaction or event.
- can predict and measure, or quantify, the future benefits with a reasonable degree of precision and reliability.

If an expenditure does not meet *both* criteria, it cannot be capitalized as an asset and must be expensed. A firm should *derecognize* assets (that is, write off assets from the balance sheet) that it determines no longer represent future economic benefits (such as writing off uncollectible receivables or unsalable inventory). Resources that firms do not normally recognize as assets because they fail to meet one or both of the criteria include purchase orders received from customers; employment contracts with corporate officers and employees; and a quality reputation with employees, customers, or citizens of the community.

Most assets on the balance sheet are either *monetary* or *nonmonetary*. (We will define these categories more specifically in the discussion of foreign currency translation in Chapter 8.) Monetary assets include cash and claims to future payments of cash (such as receivables). **PepsiCo**'s monetary assets include cash, accounts and notes receivable, and investments in debt and equity securities of other firms. Under U.S. GAAP and IFRS, balance sheets report monetary assets using a variety of measurement attributes intended to enhance the relevance and reliability of reported asset values. Some monetary assets such as cash are reported at current value. Others, such as accounts receivable, are reported at net realizable value (the amounts the firm expects to collect).

---

[2]Financial Accounting Standards Board, *Statement of Financial Accounting Concepts No. 6*, "Elements of Financial Statements" (1985), par. 25.

For other assets, such as notes receivable and loans with cash receipts that extend beyond one year, the firm reports the monetary asset at the present value of the future cash flows using a discount rate that reflects the underlying uncertainty of collecting the cash as assessed at the time the claim initially arose. Still other assets, such as debt and equity investment securities, are typically reported at fair value, which represents those cash amounts the firm could expect to realize if it sold the securities. Chapter 2 provides more discussion of how accounting is a "mixed attribute" measurement system.

Nonmonetary assets are *tangible,* such as inventories, buildings, and equipment, and *intangible,* including brand names, patents, trademarks, licenses, and goodwill. In contrast to monetary assets, nonmonetary assets do not represent claims to future cash flows. The amount of cash firms receive from using or selling nonmonetary assets depends on market conditions at the time of their use or sale. Under U.S. GAAP and IFRS, firms might report nonmonetary assets at the:

- amounts initially paid to acquire them (acquisition, or historical, cost) adjusted for the use of the asset over time (accumulated depreciation or amortization).
- amounts currently required to replace them (replacement cost).
- amounts for which firms could currently sell them (net realizable value).
- present values of the amounts firms expect to receive in the future from selling or using the assets (present value of future cash flows).

Chapter 2 discusses alternative valuation methods and their implications for measuring earnings.

Perhaps PepsiCo's most valuable assets are its brand names (for example, Pepsi, Frito-Lay, and Quaker Oats), and brand names associated with specific products, like Mountain Dew and Doritos. PepsiCo and its subsidiaries created and developed these brand names through past expenditures on advertising, event sponsorships, product development, and quality control. Ascertaining the portion of these expenditures that creates reliably predictable future economic benefits and the portion that simply stimulates sales during the current period is too uncertain to justify recognizing an asset. The amounts that PepsiCo does report for amortizable intangible assets, goodwill, and other nonamortizable intangible assets result from PepsiCo's purchases of other companies, where the transaction provides market evidence of the value of acquired intangibles. PepsiCo's balance sheet reports $1,781 million of amortizable intangible assets and $14,744 million of nonamortizable intangibles, principally brand names. The remaining $16,971 million of intangible assets is goodwill, which represents the portion of the purchase price of other businesses that PepsiCo could not allocate to identifiable assets and liabilities. Every year, PepsiCo tests the value of all of its intangible assets for impairment, and if the evaluation indicates impairment, the intangible asset is written down to its estimated fair value. Chapter 8 discusses the accounting for goodwill and intangibles.

The classification of assets in the balance sheet varies widely in published annual reports. The principal asset categories are as follows:

Current Assets. Current assets include cash and other assets that a firm expects to collect, sell, or consume during the normal operating cycle of a business, usually one year. Cash; short-term investments; accounts and notes receivable; inventories; and prepayments for expenses such as rent, insurance, and advertising appear as current assets for PepsiCo.

Investments. This category includes short-term and long-term investments in the debt and equity securities of other entities. If a firm makes such investments for short-term purposes, it classifies them under current assets. Noncurrent assets include investments in noncontrolled affiliates. PepsiCo has recently acquired controlling interests in its affiliates (particularly its major bottlers), but still maintains investments in other noncontrolled affiliates. For these investments in noncontrolling interests, the company does not prepare consolidated financial statements; instead, it reports the investments on the balance sheet using the equity method (discussed in Chapter 8).

Property, Plant, and Equipment. This category includes the tangible, long-lived assets that a firm uses in operations over a period of years. Note 4, "Property, Plant and Equipment and Intangible Assets," to PepsiCo's financial statements (Appendix A) indicates that property, plant, and equipment includes land and improvements, buildings and improvements, machinery and equipment, and construction in progress. It reports property, plant, and equipment at acquisition cost and then subtracts the accumulated depreciation recognized on these assets since acquisition.

Intangibles. Intangibles include the rights established by law or contract to the future use of property. Patents, trademarks, licenses, and franchises are intangible assets. The most troublesome asset recognition questions revolve around which rights satisfy the criteria for an asset. As Chapter 8 discusses in more depth, firms generally recognize the intangibles acquired in external market transactions as assets. For example, brand names and goodwill are included in PepsiCo's balance sheet under the categories of amortizable and nonamortizable intangible assets, which are detailed in Note 4. However, firms do not recognize as assets intangibles developed internally by the firm (the Pepsi and Frito-Lay brand names, for example). The rationale for the different accounting treatment is that the value of intangibles acquired in external market transactions is more reliable than the value of internally developed intangibles.

Liabilities—Recognition, Valuation, and Classification

Under U.S. GAAP and IFRS, firms must report obligations as liabilities if they meet the **definition** of a liability:

> Liabilities are probable future sacrifices of economic benefits arising from present obligations of a particular entity to transfer assets or provide services to other entities in the future as a result of past transactions or events.[3]

Therefore, liabilities represent a firm's existing obligations to make payments of cash, goods, or services in a reasonably predictable amount at a reasonably predictable future time as a result of a past transaction or event. Liabilities reflect managers' expectations of future sacrifices of resources to satisfy existing obligations. Liabilities for **PepsiCo** include obligations to suppliers of goods and services (accounts payable and other current liabilities), governments (income taxes payable), and banks and other lenders (short-term and long-term debt obligations).

The most troublesome questions regarding liability recognition relate to *executory contracts* and *contingent obligations*. Under U.S. GAAP and IFRS, firms do not recognize executory contracts for labor, purchase order commitments, and some lease agreements as liabilities, because the firm has not yet received the benefits from these items and is not yet obligated to pay for them. For example, a firm should not recognize a liability when it places an order to purchase inventory, which is a contingent obligation; the obligation arises only when the firm receives the inventory. Likewise, the firms should not recognize a liability for future wages to employees; instead, it should

---

[3]*Ibid.,* par. 35.

recognize the liability once the employees have provided services. Notes to the financial statements disclose material executory contracts and other contingent claims. For example, refer to PepsiCo's long-term contractual commitments in Note 9, "Debt Obligations and Commitments" (Appendix A). PepsiCo lists noncancelable operating leases, purchasing commitments, and marketing commitments among its executory contracts.

Most liabilities are monetary, requiring future payments of cash. U.S. GAAP and IFRS report those due within one year at the amount of cash the firm expects to pay to discharge the obligation. If the payment dates extend beyond one year, U.S. GAAP and IFRS state the liability at the present value of the required future cash flows (discounted at an interest rate that reflects the underlying uncertainty of paying the cash as assessed at the time the obligation initially arose). Some liabilities, such as warranties, require delivery of goods or services instead of payment of cash, and the balance sheet states those liabilities at the expected future cost of providing these goods and services. Other liabilities also involve obligations to deliver goods or services when customers prepay, giving rise to deferred revenue liabilities. For example, such obligations can arise from the sale of gift cards redeemable for products or services and from advance purchases of insurance coverage, airfares, subscriptions, and membership fees. The balance sheet reports these liabilities at the amount of revenues that have been received from customers and not yet earned.

Balance sheets classify liabilities in various ways. Virtually all firms (except banks) use a current liabilities category, which includes obligations a firm expects to settle within one year. Balance sheets report the remaining liabilities in a section labeled "noncurrent liabilities" or "long-term debt." PepsiCo uses three noncurrent liability categories: long-term debt obligations, other liabilities, and deferred income taxes. Chapters 2 and 9 discuss deferred income taxes.

Shareholders' Equity Valuation and Disclosure

The shareholders' equity in a firm is a residual interest or claim. That is, the owners have a claim on all assets not required to meet the claims of creditors. Therefore, the valuation of assets and liabilities on the balance sheet determines the valuation of total shareholders' equity.[4]

Balance sheets show shareholders' equity separated into:

- amounts invested by shareholders for an ownership interest in a firm (**PepsiCo** uses the accounts *Common Stock* and *Capital in Excess of Par Value*).
- cumulative net income in excess of dividends declared (PepsiCo's account is *Retained Earnings*).
- shareholders' equity effects of the recognition or valuation of certain assets or liabilities (PepsiCo includes items related to available-for-sale investment securities, foreign currency translation, derivatives, and pensions in *Accumulated Other Comprehensive Loss*).
- treasury stock (PepsiCo purchases of its own shares, which it labels *Repurchased Common Stock, in Excess of Par Value*).

---

[4]The issuance of bonds with equity characteristics (such as convertible bonds), the issuance of equity claims with debt characteristics (such as redeemable preferred or common stock), and the issuance of obligations to be settled with the issuance of equity shares (such as stock options) cloud the distinction between liabilities and shareholders' equity.

PepsiCo also reports a small amount of contributed capital as preferred stock (which had been issued by Quaker prior to PepsiCo's acquisition of Quaker) minus the amount of repurchased preferred stock.

Assessing the Quality of the Balance Sheet as a Complete Representation of Economic Position

Analysts frequently examine the relation among items on the balance sheet when assessing a firm's financial position and credit risk. For example, an excess of current assets over current liabilities suggests that a firm has sufficient liquid resources to pay short-term creditors. Alternatively, a firm with strong cash flows and sufficient bargaining power (like **Walmart** or **Amazon**) can operate with current liabilities in excess of current assets. A relatively low percentage of long-term debt to shareholders' equity suggests that a firm likely has sufficient long-term assets to repay the long-term debt at maturity, or at least an ability to take on new debt financing using the long-term assets as collateral to repay debt coming due.

However, when using the balance sheet for these purposes, you must recognize the following:

- Certain valuable resources of a firm that generate future cash flows, such as a patent for a pharmaceutical firm or a brand name for a consumer products firm, appear as assets only if they were acquired from another firm and therefore have a measurable acquisition cost.
- Nonmonetary assets are reported at acquisition cost, net of accumulated depreciation or amortization, even though some of these assets may have current market values that exceed their recorded amounts. An example is the market value versus recorded value of land on the balance sheets of railroads and many urban department stores.
- Certain rights to use resources and commitments to make future payments may not appear as assets and liabilities. On the balance sheet of airlines, you generally do not see, for example, leased aircraft or commitments to make future lease payments on those aircraft. Also, on the balance sheets of steel, tire, and automobile companies, you do not see the rights to receive labor services or the commitments to make future payments for labor services under labor union contracts.
- Noncurrent liabilities appear at the present value of expected cash flows discounted at an interest rate determined at the time the liability initially arose instead of at a current market interest rate.

For certain firms under these circumstances, the balance sheet reporting may provide incomplete measures of the economic position of the firms. When using the balance sheet, you should consider making adjustments for items that impact balance sheet quality. Chapters 6–9 discuss these issues more fully.

Income Statement—Measuring Operating Performance

The second principal financial statement, the income statement, provides information about the profitability of a firm for a period of time. As is common among analysts and investors, we use the terms *net income, earnings,* and *profit* interchangeably when referring to the bottom-line amount on the income statement. Exhibit 1.11 presents the income statements for **PepsiCo** for the five years 2008 through 2012.

Net income equals revenues and gains minus expenses and losses. Revenues measure the inflows of assets and the settlements of obligations from selling goods and providing services to customers. Expenses measure the outflows of assets that a firm consumes and the obligations it incurs in the process of operating the business to generate revenues. As a measure of performance for a period, revenues represent the resources generated by a firm and expenses represent the resources consumed during that period. Gains and losses result from selling assets or settling liabilities for more or less than their book values in transactions that are only peripherally related to a firm's central operations. For example, the sale of a building by PepsiCo for more than its book value would appear as a gain on the income statement. Chapter 2 describes income measurement in detail, and Chapter 3 contrasts income measurement with cash flows. Chapter 9 describes accounting for operating activities, particularly recognizing revenues and expenses.

PepsiCo generates revenues from selling goods in three principal product categories: snack foods; various soft drink concentrates, syrups, and bottled beverages; and cereals and related items. PepsiCo also generates interest income from investments in debt instruments and equity method income from investments in noncontrolled affiliates (such as bottlers, until 2011).

Exhibit 1.11

PepsiCo, Inc., and Subsidiaries
Consolidated Statements of Income
(in millions, except per-share amounts)

	2012	2011	2010	2009	2008
Net Revenue	$65,492	$66,504	$57,838	$43,232	$43,251
Cost of sales	31,291	31,593	26,575	20,099	20,351
Gross profit*	$34,201	$34,911	$31,263	$23,133	$22,900
Selling, general and administrative expenses	24,970	25,145	22,814	15,026	15,877
Amortization of intangible assets	119	133	117	63	64
Operating Profit	$ 9,112	$ 9,633	$ 8,332	$ 8,044	$ 6,959
Bottling equity income	—	—	735	365	374
Interest expense	(899)	(856)	(903)	(397)	(329)
Interest income	91	57	68	67	41
Income before Income Taxes	$ 8,304	$ 8,834	$ 8,232	$ 8,079	$ 7,045
Provision for income taxes	2,090	2,372	1,894	2,100	1,879
Net Income	$ 6,214	$ 6,462	$ 6,338	$ 5,979	$ 5,166
Less: Net income attributable to noncontrolling interests	36	19	18	33	24
Net Income Attributable to PepsiCo	$ 6,178	$ 6,443	$ 6,320	$ 5,946	$ 5,142
Net income attributable to PepsiCo per common share:					
Basic	$ 3.96	$ 4.08	$ 3.97	$ 3.81	$ 3.26
Diluted	$ 3.92	$ 4.03	$ 3.91	$ 3.77	$ 3.21

*Gross profit line does not appear in PepsiCo's Consolidated Statement of Income but is included here for comparison to Coca-Cola.

Source: PepsiCo, Inc., Forms 10-K for the Fiscal Years Ended 2010–2012.

Costs of sales include the cost of manufacturing snack foods; the cost of producing concentrates, syrups, and bottled beverages; and the cost of manufacturing cereals and related items. Expenses also include selling, general, and administrative expenses (including advertising and other promotion costs) and interest expense on short- and long-term borrowing. PepsiCo reports amortization of intangible assets as a separate expense.

Compare PepsiCo's income statements to those of its closest rival, **Coca-Cola**. Exhibit 1.12 presents the income statements for Coca-Cola for the five years 2008 through 2012. Although PepsiCo is larger than Coca-Cola in terms of annual revenues, Coca-Cola is generally more profitable in terms of annual net income. For example, in 2012, PepsiCo generated total revenues of $65,492 million and net income of $6,178 million; during the same year, Coca-Cola generated total revenues of $48,017 and net income of $9,019.

When using the income statement to assess a firm's profitability, you are interested not only in its current and past profitability, but also in the likely level of sustainable earnings in the future (Step 5 in our six-step framework). When forecasting future earnings, you must project whether past levels of revenues and expenses will likely continue and grow. Chapters 4 and 6 discuss some of the accounting quality factors you should consider before making these judgments. Chapter 10 provides an extensive discussion of building forecasts of future financial statements.

Exhibit 1.12

The Coca-Cola Company
Consolidated Statements of Income
(in millions, except per-share amounts)

	2012	2011	2010	2009	2008
Net Operating Revenues	$48,017	$46,542	$35,119	$30,990	$31,944
Cost of goods sold	19,053	18,215	12,693	11,088	11,374
Gross Profit	28,964	28,327	22,426	19,902	20,570
Selling, general and administrative expenses	17,738	17,422	13,194	11,358	11,774
Other operating charges	447	732	819	313	350
Operating Income	$10,779	$10,173	$ 8,413	$ 8,231	$ 8,446
Interest income	471	483	317	249	333
Interest expense	397	417	733	355	438
Equity income (loss)—net	819	690	1,025	781	(874)
Other income (loss)—net	137	529	5,185	40	39
Income before Income Taxes	$11,809	$11,458	$14,207	$ 8,946	$ 7,506
Income taxes	2,723	2,812	2,370	2,040	1,632
Consolidated Net Income	$ 9,086	$ 8,646	$11,837	$ 6,906	$ 5,874
Less: Net income attributable to noncontrolling interests	67	62	50	82	67
Net Income Attributable to Shareowners	$ 9,019	$ 8,584	$11,787	$ 6,824	$ 5,807
Basic net income per share	$ 2.00	$ 1.88	$ 2.55	$ 2.95	$ 2.51
Diluted net income per share	$ 1.97	$ 1.85	$ 2.53	$ 2.93	$ 2.49

Source: The Coca-Cola Company, Forms 10-K for the Fiscal Years Ended 2010–2012.

Accrual Basis of Accounting

Exhibit 1.13 depicts the operating, or earnings, cycle for a typical manufacturing firm. Net income from this series of activities equals the amount of cash received from customers minus the amount of cash paid for raw materials, labor, and the services of production facilities. If the entire operating cycle occurred in one accounting period, few difficulties would arise in measuring operating performance. Net income would equal cash inflows minus cash outflows related to these operating activities. However, firms acquire raw materials in one accounting period and use them in several future accounting periods. They acquire buildings and equipment in one accounting period and use them during many future accounting periods. Firms commonly sell goods or services in an earlier period than the one in which customers pay. Firms often consume resources or incur obligations in one accounting period and pay for those resources or settle those obligations in subsequent periods.

Under a cash basis of accounting, a firm recognizes revenue when it receives cash from customers and recognizes expenses when it pays cash to suppliers, employees, and other providers of goods and services. Because a firm's operating cycle usually extends over several accounting periods, the cash basis of accounting provides a poor measure of economic performance for specific periods of time because it focuses on the timing of cash receipt and payment rather than on the period in which the firm successfully earned resources (revenues) and used resources in an effort to achieve that success (expenses). To overcome this deficiency of the cash basis, both U.S. GAAP and IFRS require that firms use the accrual basis of accounting in measuring performance on the income statement and in measuring assets, liabilities, and equity on the balance sheet.

Under the accrual basis of accounting, a firm recognizes revenue when it meets the following two criteria:

- **It has completed all (or substantially all) of the revenue-generating process by delivering products or services to customers.**
- **It is reasonably certain it has satisfied a liability or generated an asset that it can measure reliably.**

Most firms recognize revenue during the period in which they sell goods or render services. Consider the accrual basis of accounting applied to a manufacturing firm. The cost of manufacturing a product remains on the balance sheet as an asset (inventory) until the time of sale. At the time of sale, the firm recognizes revenue in the amount of cash it expects to collect. It recognizes the cost of manufacturing the product as a cost of the goods sold.

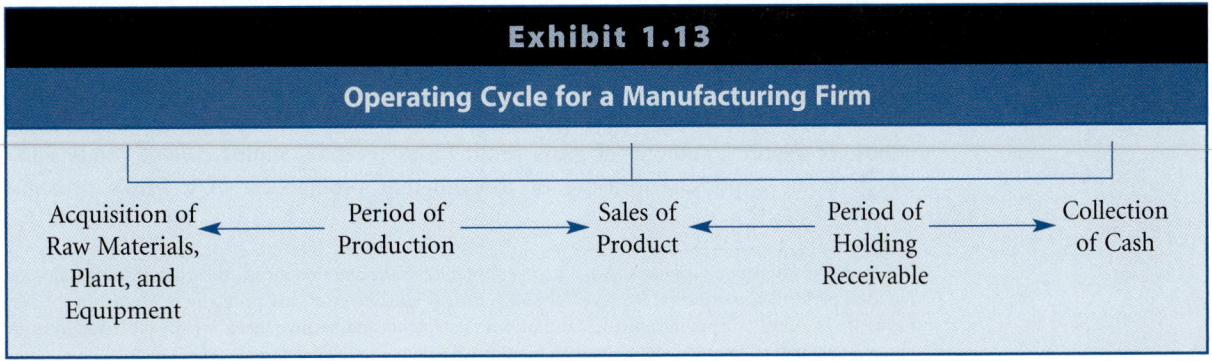

Exhibit 1.13

Operating Cycle for a Manufacturing Firm

Acquisition of Raw Materials, Plant, and Equipment → Period of Production → Sales of Product → Period of Holding Receivable → Collection of Cash

Other costs cannot be associated with particular revenues because they are costs of operating the business for a particular period of time (for example, the salary of the chief executive officer and rent on corporate offices.). Therefore, the firm recognizes such costs as expenses on the income statement in the period in which it consumes those resources.

Note that under accrual accounting a firm should not delay revenue recognition until it receives cash from customers as long as the firm can estimate with reasonable precision the amount of cash it will ultimately receive. The amount will appear in accounts receivable prior to the receipt of cash. The accrual basis provides a better measure of operating performance than the cash basis because it better captures the economics of a firm's periodic activities and performance than does simply reporting cash flows.[5]

Classification and Format in the Income Statement

Investors commonly assess a firm's value based on the firm's expected future sustainable earnings stream. As Chapter 10 discusses more fully, analysts predict future earnings, or net income, of a firm by projecting future business activities that will drive future revenues, expenses, profits, and cash flows. To inform analysts and other financial statement users about sustainable earnings, firms often report income from recurring business activities separately from income effects from unusual or nonrecurring activities (such as asset impairments, restructuring, discontinued business segments, and extraordinary events). To provide more useful information for prediction, U.S. GAAP requires that the income statement include some or all of the following sections or categories depending on the nature of the firm's income for a period:

- Income from continuing operations
- Income, gains, and losses from discontinued operations

Income from Continuing Operations

This first section reports the revenues and expenses of activities in which a firm anticipates an ongoing involvement. When a firm does not have discontinued segments in a particular year, all of its income items are related to continuing operations; so it does not need to use the continuing operations label.

Firms report their expenses in various ways. Most firms in the United States report expenses by their function: cost of goods sold for manufacturing, selling expenses for marketing, administrative expenses for administrative management, and interest expense for financing. Other firms, particularly those in the European community, tend to report expenses by their nature: raw materials, compensation, advertising, and research and development.

Many variations in income statement format appear in corporate annual reports. Most commonly, firms list various sources of revenues from selling their goods and services and then list the cost of goods sold. Some firms (**Coca-Cola** but not **PepsiCo**) choose to report a subtotal of gross profit (sales revenues minus cost of goods sold), which is an important measure of the inherent profitability of a firm's principal

---

[5]Of course, if you define *periodic activities and performance* as the amount of cash collected, then cash flows is the ideal performance measure. However, although cash is king, investors are primarily interested in the performance of a firm's operating activities, and income statements and balance sheets are the preferred measure based on decades of research, some of which is summarized later in the chapter.

products and services. Firms then list subtractions for the various operating expenses (for example, selling, general, and administrative expenses). This format reports a subtotal for operating income. The income statement then reports income amounts from investments (interest income and equity income), expenses associated with financing (interest expense), and nonoperating gains and losses. Firms commonly aggregate operating income with the nonoperating income items to report income before income taxes. Firms then subtract the provision for income taxes to compute and report the bottom-line net income.

Many firms, including **PepsiCo**, report restructuring charges and impairment losses in their income statements. Such items often reflect the write-down of assets or the recognition of liabilities arising from changes in economic conditions and corporate strategies. Because restructuring charges and impairment losses do not satisfy the criteria for discontinued operations, firms often report them in the continuing operations section of the income statement. If the amounts are material, they appear on a separate line to distinguish them from recurring income items. Chapters 4 and 6 discuss the benefits and possible pitfalls of segregating such amounts when analyzing profitability.

Income from Discontinued Operations

A firm that intends to remain in a line of business but decides to sell or close down some portion of that line (such as closing a single plant or dropping a line of products) generally will report any income, gain, or loss from such an action under continuing operations. On the other hand, if a firm decides to terminate its involvement in a line of business (such as selling or shutting down an entire division or subsidiary), it will report the income, gain, or loss from operating that line of business in the second section of the income statement, labeled "Income, Gains, and Losses from Discontinued Operations." Income, gains, and losses from discontinued operations appear on the income statement net of any income tax effects. Firms must report the results of discontinued operations separately from continuing operations so financials statement users can assess the portion of earnings that are likely to persist in the future.

Comprehensive Income

The FASB and IASB have determined that the balance sheet is the cornerstone of accounting and that income should be measured by changes in the values of assets and liabilities. To provide relevant and reliable measures of assets and liabilities, U.S. GAAP and IFRS use a variety of measurement attributes, some of which require firms to adjust asset or liability values to reflect changes in net realizable values, fair values, or present values. Valuation adjustments to assets and liabilities usually give rise to revenues (or gains) or to expenses (or losses). For example, if a firm determines that it will not collect some of its accounts receivable or will not be able to sell some items of inventory, it should adjust receivables and inventory to their net realizable values and recognize those adjustments as expenses or losses in net income.

The FASB and IASB have determined that four particular types of valuation adjustments represent unrealized gains or losses that should be reported in a statement of comprehensive income for reporting periods beginning after December 15, 2012.[6] Other comprehensive income items are accumulated over time in a special equity account

---

[6]Accounting Standards Codification 220, *Comprehensive Income*.

titled Accumulated Other Comprehensive Income or Loss (AOCI). These other comprehensive income items are not recognized in net income until they are realized in an economic transaction, such as when the related assets are sold or the liabilities are settled. The segregation of AOCI acts as a temporary "holding area" for such gains or losses until their ultimate settlement.

Review the consolidated statement of equity for **PepsiCo** in Appendix A. It details the four types of unrealized gain/loss items that are triggered by the revaluation of assets and liabilities. The accumulated effects of these items over several periods are reported as the components of accumulated other comprehensive loss: (1) currency translation adjustments; (2) cash flow hedges, net of tax; (3) certain changes in pension and retiree medical plan obligations, net of tax; and (4) unrealized losses/gains on securities, net of tax. Because PepsiCo uses U.S. GAAP instead of IFRS, it does not report the fifth possible item related to revaluations of property, plant, and equipment. Later chapters discuss the accounting for each of these items.

The FASB and IASB are aware that unrealized gains and losses of this nature affect the market value of firms, but users of financial statements might overlook them because they do not yet appear in net income. Therefore, firms must report *comprehensive income*.[7] Comprehensive income equals *all* revenues, expenses, gains, and losses for a period, both realized and unrealized. Comprehensive income includes net income plus or minus the other comprehensive income items. Refer to PepsiCo's consolidated statement of comprehensive income in Appendix A. Comprehensive income for PepsiCo for 2012 is as follows (in millions):

Net income	$6,214
Currency translation adjustment	737
Cash flow hedges, net of tax	18
Pension and retiree medical plan liability adjustments, net of tax	(72)
Unrealized losses on securities, net of tax	18
Other	36
Comprehensive income	$6,951
Comprehensive income attributable to noncontrolling interests	(31)
Comprehensive income attributable to PepsiCo	$6,920

Thus, PepsiCo's comprehensive income exceeded net income, primarily due to a large favorable effect of currency translation. Firms may present a single statement of comprehensive income, which includes the standard statement of net income, but continues with other comprehensive income to arrive at comprehensive income. Alternatively, firms may present other comprehensive income as part of a separate statement of comprehensive income, which begins with net income and adds or subtracts various elements of other comprehensive income to compute comprehensive income. PepsiCo uses the second method of disclosure. Appendix A indicates that PepsiCo uses the term *accumulated other comprehensive loss* on its consolidated balance sheet. In addition, PepsiCo reports the accumulated balances for each component of its other comprehensive income in Note 13, "Accumulated Other Comprehensive Loss Attributable to PepsiCo," to the financial statements.

---

[7]*Ibid.*

Assessing the Quality of Earnings as a Complete Representation of Economic Performance

Common stock prices in the capital markets usually react quickly when firms announce new earnings information, indicating that earnings play an important role in the valuation of firms. We provide some striking empirical evidence of the association between earnings and stock returns later in this chapter. In using earnings information for valuation, however, you must be alert to the possibility that reported earnings for a particular period represent an incomplete measure of current period profitability or are a poor predictor of ongoing sustainable profitability. For example, reported net income may include amounts that are not likely to recur in the future, such as restructuring charges, impairment charges, or gains and losses from discontinued operations. You may want to eliminate the effects of nonrecurring items when assessing operating performance for purposes of forecasting future earnings. (Chapters 6 and 10 discuss these ideas more fully.)

In some circumstances, managers use subtle means to manage earnings. For example, a firm might accelerate recognition of revenues, understate its estimate of bad debt expense or warranty expense, cut back on advertising or research and development expenditures, or delay maintenance expenditures as a means of increasing earnings in a particular period. Chapters 6–9 discuss the quality of accounting information and illustrate adjustments you might make to improve the quality of earnings.

Statement of Cash Flows

The third principal financial statement is the statement of cash flows. The purpose of the statement of cash flows is important but simple: to inform financial statement users about the sources and uses of cash, partitioned into its three business activities: operating, investing, and financing. This is an extremely useful statement, but because of the way it is reported by most companies, it can be confusing and either misinterpreted or ignored. The statement provides useful information to complement the income statement, demonstrating how cash flows differ from accrual-based income. As typically prepared, the statement begins with net income, and effectively "undoes" the accrual accounting procedures to recapture the underlying cash flows.

Rationale for the Statement of Cash Flows

The statement of cash flows provides information on the sources and uses of cash. Even profitable firms—especially those growing rapidly—sometimes find themselves strapped for cash and unable to pay suppliers, employees, and other creditors in a timely manner. This can occur for two principal reasons:

- The timing of cash receipts from customers does not necessarily coincide with the recognition of revenue, and the timing of cash expenditures does not necessarily coincide with the recognition of expenses under the accrual basis of accounting. In the usual case, cash expenditures precede the recognition of expenses, and cash receipts follow the recognition of revenue. Thus, a firm might have positive net income for a period but a negative net cash flow from operations.
- The firm may need to acquire new property, plant, and equipment; retire outstanding debt; or reacquire shares of its common stock when sufficient cash is not available.

In many cases, a profitable firm finding itself short of cash can obtain the needed funds from short- or long-term creditors or from equity investors. The firm must repay with interest the funds borrowed from creditors. Owners may require that the firm pay periodic dividends as an inducement to invest in the firm. Eventually, the firm must generate sufficient cash from operations if it is to survive.

Sometimes firms have excess cash, which can occur for two principal reasons:

- Firm operations may be profitable, with cash flows from operations equal to or greater than profits. This can occur, for example, when the firm is mature, stable, and profitable and does not need to invest excess cash flows in capital or growth opportunities (sometimes referred to as cash-cow firms).
- The firm may have engaged in cash-raising transactions by selling assets or divesting subsidiaries, issuing short- or long-term debt, or issuing equity shares.

You will find it useful to know which of the two reasons explain the firm's excess cash because they have different implications for the firm's strategy and are likely to influence how you value the firm.

Classification of Cash Flows

Cash flows are the connecting link between operating, investing, and financing activities. They permit each of these three principal business activities to continue functioning smoothly and effectively. The statement of cash flows also can be helpful in assessing a firm's past ability to generate free cash flows and for predicting future free cash flows. The concept of free cash flows is first introduced in Chapter 3. As discussed in Chapter 12, free cash flows are central to cash-flow-based valuation models.

The statement of cash flows classifies cash flows as relating to operating, investing, or financing activities.

Operating. Selling goods and providing services are among the most important ways a financially healthy company generates cash. Assessing cash flow from operations over several years indicates the extent to which operating activities have provided the necessary cash to maintain operating capabilities (and the extent to which firms have had to rely on other sources of cash).

Investing. The acquisition of long-lived productive assets, particularly property, plant, and equipment, usually represents major ongoing uses of cash. Firms must replace such assets as they wear out. If firms are to grow, they must acquire additional long-lived productive assets. Firms obtain a portion of the cash needed to acquire long-lived productive assets from sales of existing assets. However, such cash inflows are seldom sufficient to cover the cost of new acquisitions.

Financing. A firm obtains cash from short- and long-term borrowing and from issuing preferred and common stock. It uses cash to repay short- and long-term borrowing, to pay dividends, and to reacquire shares of outstanding preferred and common stock.

Exhibit 1.14 presents the consolidated statements of cash flows for **PepsiCo** for 2008 through 2012. The statement reveals that cash flow from operating activities exceeded the net cash outflow for investing activities in each year. Also, in every year PepsiCo used a significant amount of cash for investing activities, and in every year except 2010 used significant cash for financing activities. These patterns of cash inflows and outflows are typical of a mature, profitable firm. For comparative purposes, Exhibit 1.15 (pages 37–38) presents the consolidated statements of cash flows for Coca-Cola for 2008 through 2012, where the patterns of cash inflows and outflows are similar.

Firms sometimes engage in investing and financing transactions that do not directly involve cash. For example, a firm might acquire a building by assuming a mortgage obligation. It might issue common stock upon conversion of long-term debt, or it might acquire a firm with stock rather than cash. Firms disclose these transactions in a

Exhibit 1.14

PepsiCo, Inc. and Subsidiaries
Consolidated Statements of Cash Flows
(in millions)

	2012	2011	2010	2009	2008
OPERATING ACTIVITIES					
Net income	$ 6,214	$ 6,462	$ 6,338	$ 5,979	$ 5,166
Adjustments to reconcile net income to net cash provided by operating activities:					
Depreciation and amortization	2,689	2,737	2,327	1,635	1,543
Stock-based compensation expense	278	326	299	227	238
Merger and integration costs	16	329	808	—	—
Cash payments for merger and integration costs	(83)	(377)	(385)	—	—
Restructuring and impairment charges	279	383	—	36	543
Cash payments for restructuring charges	(343)	(31)	(31)	(196)	(180)
PBG/PAS merger costs	—	—	—	50	—
Cash payments for PBG/PAS merger costs	—	—	—	(49)	—
Restructuring and other charges related to the transaction with Tingyi	176	—	—	—	—
Cash payments for restructuring and other charges related to Tingyi	(109)	—	—	—	—
Gain on previously held equity interests in PBG and PAS	—	—	(958)	—	—
Assets write-off	—	—	145	—	—
Non-cash foreign exchange loss related to Venezuela devaluation	—	—	120	—	—
Excess tax benefits from share-based payment arrangements	(124)	(70)	(107)	(42)	(107)
Pension and retiree medical plan contributions	(1,865)	(349)	(1,734)	(1,299)	(219)
Pension and retiree medical plan expenses	796	571	453	423	459
Bottling equity income, net of dividends	—	—	42	(235)	(202)
Deferred income taxes and other tax charges and credits	321	495	500	284	573
Change in accounts receivable and notes receivable	(250)	(666)	(268)	188	(549)
Change in inventories	144	(331)	276	17	(345)
Change in prepaid expenses and other current assets	89	(27)	144	(127)	(68)
Change in accounts payable and other current liabilities	548	520	488	(133)	718
Change in income taxes payable	(97)	(340)	123	319	(180)
Other, net	(200)	(688)	(132)	(281)	(391)
Net Cash Provided by Operating Activities	$ 8,479	$ 8,944	$ 8,448	$ 6,796	$ 6,999
INVESTING ACTIVITIES					
Capital spending	$(2,714)	$(3,339)	$(3,253)	$(2,128)	$(2,446)
Sales of property, plant and equipment	95	84	81	58	98

(Continued)

Exhibit 1.14 (Continued)

	2012	2011	2010	2009	2008
Acquisitions and investments in noncontrolled affiliates	—	—	—	(500)	(1,925)
Acquisitions of PBG and PAS, net of cash and cash equivalents acquired	—	—	(2,833)	—	—
Acquisition of manufacturing and distribution rights from DPSG	—	—	(900)	—	—
Acquisition of WBD, net of cash and cash equivalents acquired	—	(2,428)	—	—	—
Investment in WBD	—	(164)	(463)	—	—
Cash payments related to the transaction with Tinyi	(306)	—	—	—	—
Other acquisitions and investments in noncontrolled affiliates	(121)	(601)	(83)	—	—
Divestitures	(32)	780	12	99	6
Cash restricted for pending acquisitions	—	—	—	15	(40)
Cash proceeds for sale of PBG and PAS stock	—	—	—	—	358
Short-term investments, by original maturity:					
More than three months—purchases	—	—	(12)	(29)	(156)
More than three months—maturities	—	21	29	71	62
Three months or less, net	61	45	(229)	13	1,376
Other investing, net	12	(16)	(17)	—	—
Net Cash Used for Investing Activities	$(3,005)	$(5,618)	$(7,668)	$(2,401)	$(2,667)
FINANCING ACTIVITIES					
Proceeds from issuances of long-term debt	$ 5,999	$ 3,000	$ 6,451	$ 1,057	$ 3,719
Payments of long-term debt	(2,449)	(1,596)	(59)	(226)	(649)
Debt repurchase	—	(771)	(500)	—	—
Short-term borrowings, by original maturity					
More than three months—proceeds	549	523	227	26	89
More than three months—payments	(248)	(559)	(96)	(81)	(269)
Three months or less, net	(1,762)	339	2,351	(963)	625
Cash dividends paid	(3,305)	(3,157)	(2,978)	(2,732)	(2,541)
Share repurchases—common	(3,219)	(2,489)	(4,978)	—	(4,720)
Share repurchases—preferred	(7)	(7)	(5)	(7)	(6)
Proceeds from exercises of stock options	1,122	945	1,038	413	620
Excess tax benefits from share-based payment arrangements	124	70	107	42	107
Acquisition of noncontrolling interests	(68)	(1,406)	(159)	—	—
Other financing	(42)	(27)	(13)	(26)	—
Net Cash (Used for)/Provided by Financing Activities	$(3,306)	$(5,135)	$ 1,386	$(2,497)	$(3,025)
Effect of exchange rate changes on cash and cash equivalents	$ 62	$ (67)	$ (166)	$ (19)	$ (153)

(Continued)

Exhibit 1.14 (Continued)

	2012	2011	2010	2009	2008
Net increase/(decrease) in Cash and Cash Equivalents	$ 2,230	$(1,876)	$ 2,000	$ 1,879	$ 1,154
Cash and Cash Equivalents, Beginning of Year	4,067	5,943	3,943	2,064	910
Cash and Cash Equivalents, End of Year	$ 6,297	$ 4,067	$ 5,943	$ 3,943	$ 2,064

Source: PepsiCo, Inc., Forms 10-K for the Fiscal Years Ended 2010–2012.

Exhibit 1.15

The Coca-Cola Company
Consolidated Statements of Cash Flows
(in millions)

	2012	2011	2010	2009	2008
OPERATING ACTIVITIES					
Consolidated net income	$ 9,086	$ 8,646	$ 11,837	$ 6,906	$ 5,874
Adjustments to reconcile net income to net cash provided by operating activities:					
Depreciation and amortization	1,982	1,954	1,443	1,236	1,228
Stock-based compensation expense	259	354	380	241	266
Deferred income taxes	632	1,035	604	353	(360)
Equity income or loss, net of dividends	(426)	(269)	(671)	(359)	1,128
Foreign currency adjustments	(130)	7	151	61	(42)
Gains on sales of assets	(98)	(220)	(645)	(43)	(130)
Other significant (gains) losses—net	—	—	(4,713)	—	—
Other operating charges	166	214	264	134	209
Other items	254	(354)	512	221	153
Net change in operating assets and liabilities	(1,080)	(1,893)	370	(564)	(755)
Net Cash Provided by Operating Activities	$ 10,645	$ 9,474	$ 9,532	$ 8,186	$ 7,571
INVESTING ACTIVITIES					
Purchases of short-term investments	$ (9,590)	$ (4,057)	$ (4,579)	—	—
Proceeds from disposals of short-term investments	5,622	5,647	4,032	—	—
Acquisitions and investments	(1,535)	(977)	(2,511)	$ (300)	$ (759)
Purchases of other investments	(5,266)	(787)	(132)	(2,152)	(240)
Proceeds from disposals of bottling companies and other investments	2,189	562	972	240	479
Purchases of property, plant and equipment	(2,780)	(2,920)	(2,215)	(1,993)	(1,968)
Proceeds from disposals of property, plant and equipment	143	101	134	104	129
Other investing activities	(187)	(93)	(106)	(48)	(4)
Net Cash Provided by (Used in) Investing Activities	$(11,404)	$ (2,524)	$ (4,405)	$ (4,149)	$(2,363)

(Continued)

Exhibit 1.15 (Continued)

	2012	2011	2010	2009	2008
FINANCING ACTIVITIES					
Issuances of debt	$ 42,791	$ 27,495	$ 15,251	$ 14,689	$ 4,337
Payments of debt	(38,573)	(22,530)	(13,403)	(12,326)	(4,308)
Issuances of stock	1,489	1,569	1,666	664	586
Purchases of stock for treasury	(4,559)	(4,513)	(2,961)	(1,518)	(1,079)
Dividends	(4,595)	(4,300)	(4,068)	(3,800)	(3,521)
Other financing activities	100	45	50	(2)	—
Net Cash Provided by (Used in) Financing Activities	$ (3,347)	$ (2,234)	$ (3,465)	$ (2,293)	$(3,985)
Effect of Exchange Rate Changes on Cash and Cash Equivalents	$ (255)	$ (430)	$ (166)	$ 576	$ (615)
Cash and Cash Equivalents					
Net increase (decrease) during the year	(4,361)	4,286	1,496	2,320	608
Balance at Beginning of Year	12,803	8,517	7,021	4,701	4,093
Balance at End of Year	$ 8,442	$ 12,803	$ 8,517	$ 7,021	$ 4,701

Source: The Coca-Cola Company, Forms 10-K for the Fiscal Years Ended 2010–2012.

supplementary schedule or note to the statement of cash flows in a way that clearly indicates that the transactions are investing and financing activities that do not affect cash.

The statement of cash flows is required under both U.S. GAAP and IFRS, but it is not a required financial statement in some countries. Increasingly, however, most large international firms are providing the statement on a voluntary basis. To help illustrate how the statement of cash flows links to the other financial statements, Chapter 3 describes procedures for preparing a statement of cash flows based only on information on the balance sheet and income statement. Chapter 10 demonstrates techniques for projecting future statements of cash flows from projected balance sheets and income statements.

Important Information with the Financial Statements

A firm's accounting system records the results of transactions, events, and commercial arrangements and generates the financial statements, but the financial statements do not stand alone. To provide more complete information for financial statement users, firms typically provide a substantial amount of important additional information with the financial statements. This section briefly introduces three important additional elements of information: (a) Notes, (b) Management's Discussion and Analysis, and (c) Managers' and Independent Auditors' Attestations.

Notes

The financial statements report the accounts and amounts that comprise the balance sheet, income statement, and statement of cash flows, but they do not explain how those accounts and amounts have been determined. The notes to financial statements are audited by the firm's independent auditors and are crucial for you to understand the accounting methods the firm has used to measure assets, liabilities, revenues, expenses, gains, and losses. The first note typically provides a summary of the key accounting principles the firm has used. Because each account balance reported on the financial statements was determined with the application of judgments, estimates, and accounting method choices, the notes typically describe and explain how each amount has been determined (with the exception of those deemed immaterial). For example, the notes explain how the firm is accounting for inventory and what cost methods the firm used to value inventory on hand as well as cost of goods sold. The notes explain how property, plant, and equipment are valued; how they are being depreciated; how much depreciation has been accumulated to date; and what the expected useful lives of the underlying assets are. Notes also provide important details about key financial statement estimates, such as fair values of investment securities, pension and postemployment benefit liabilities, income taxes, and intangible assets.

In its 2012 annual report, **PepsiCo** provides a total of 15 notes to explain the accounting principles, methods, and estimates used to prepare the financial statements. Immediately following the financial statements, the notes comprise an additional 36 pages of the annual report. You should read the notes carefully because they provide important information that is useful for understanding the firm's accounting and assessing its accounting quality.

Management Discussion and Analysis

Many firms accompany the financial statements and notes with extensive narrative and quantitative discussion and analysis from the managers. The Management Discussion and Analysis (MD&A) section of the financial statements provides insights into managers' strategies and their assessments and evaluation of the firm's performance. In some cases, MD&A disclosures provide glimpses into managers' expectations about the future of the company.

In its MD&A (Appendix B), PepsiCo describes the business as a whole, as well as the operations of the business in each of its divisions. In addition to qualitative descriptions, the MD&A section provides valuable details about the financial performance of each division, with managers' analysis comparing results of 2012 to 2011 and 2011 to 2010. In addition, PepsiCo's MD&A section provides important insights into the firm's business risks and the way PepsiCo is managing them, critical accounting policies PepsiCo has applied, and PepsiCo's liquidity and capital resource situation. It also provides valuable glimpses into a few of PepsiCo's plans for the future, such as its intention to continue to aggressively invest in emerging and developing markets and to make a pension contribution of approximately $240 million in 2013. Because the MD&A section provides insights from the managers' point of view, you should read it carefully but with a bit of skepticism, because it is not audited and managers tend to be optimistic when evaluating the strategies and performance of their own firms.

Management and Independent Auditor Attestation

The design and operation of the accounting system are the responsibility of a firm's managers. However, the SEC and most stock exchanges require firms with publicly traded common stock to have their accounting records and financial statements audited by independent auditors. The independent auditor's attestation as to the fairness and reliability of a firm's financial statements relative to U.S. GAAP or IFRS is an essential element in the integrity of the financial reporting process and the efficiency of the capital markets. Investors and other users of the financial statements can rely on financial statements for essential information about a firm only if they are confident that the independent auditor has examined the accounting records and has concluded that the financial statements are fair and reliable according to U.S. GAAP or IFRS.

In response to some managers' misrepresenting their financial statements and audit breakdowns in now infamous cases involving **Enron, Worldcom, Global Crossing, Qwest Communications,** and other firms, Congress passed the Sarbanes-Oxley Act of 2002. This act more clearly defines the explicit responsibility of managers for financial statements, the relation between the independent auditor and the firm audited, and the kinds of services permitted and not permitted. Exhibit 1.16 summarizes some of the more important provisions of the Sarbanes-Oxley Act as they relate to financial statements.

For many years, firms have included with their financial statements a report by management that states its responsibility for the financial statements. The Sarbanes-Oxley Act of 2002 now requires that the management report include an attestation that managers assume responsibility for establishing and maintaining adequate internal control structure and procedures (referred to as the *Management Assessment*). This new requirement now makes explicit management's responsibility not only for the financial statements, but also for the underlying accounting and control system that generates the financial statements.

The chief executive officer and the chief financial officer must sign this management report. PepsiCo's management report appears in Appendix A.

Exhibit 1.16

Summary of the Principal Provisions of the Sarbanes-Oxley Act of 2002

1. Violation of the provisions of the Sarbanes-Oxley Act of 2002 is a violation of the Securities Exchange Act of 1934, which governs the public trading of securities.

2. The Sarbanes-Oxley Act of 2002 created the Public Company Accounting Oversight Board (PCAOB), which has responsibility for setting generally accepted auditing standards, ethics standards, and quality-control standards for audits, overseen by the SEC.

3. The act precludes a registered public accounting firm from performing non-audit services contemporaneously with the audit. Certain services, such as tax work, are allowed if they are preapproved by the firm's audit committee or constitute less than 5% of the billing price for audit and other services.

4. The lead auditor or coordinating partner and the reviewing partner of the public accounting firm must rotate, or change, every five years.

5. Members of the audit committee of a firm's board of directors will have primary responsibility for appointment, oversight, and compensation of the registered public accounting firm.

6. At least one member of the audit committee of the board of directors must be a "financial expert."

7. The firm's chief executive officer and the chief financial officer must issue a statement along with the audit report stating that the financial statements and notes fairly present the operations and financial position of the firm.

8. Each annual report must contain an "internal control report" that states management's responsibility for establishing and maintaining an adequate internal control structure and procedures (Management Assessment Report). The annual report must also contain an assessment of the effectiveness of the internal control structure and procedures by the firm's auditor (Assurance Opinion). The assurance opinion can be unqualified, qualified, adverse, or a disclaimer. The chief executive officer and the chief financial officer must sign this management report.

The independent auditor also assesses a firm's internal control system, designs its audit tests in light of the quality of these internal controls, and then forms an opinion about the fairness of the amounts reported on the financial statements based on its audit tests. The independent auditor must now include opinions on the effectiveness of the internal control system (referred to as the *Assurance Opinion*) and the fairness of the amounts reported in the financial statements. This dual opinion makes explicit the independent auditor's responsibility for testing the effectiveness of the internal control system and judging the fairness of the amounts reported. PepsiCo's management assessment report and independent auditor's assurance opinion (KPMG, LLP) appear in Appendix A after Note 15, "Acquisitions and Divestitures." The last paragraph of the management assessment report reads as follows:

> PepsiCo has a strong history of doing what's right. We realize that great companies are built on trust, strong ethical standards and principles. Our financial results are delivered from that culture of accountability, and we take responsibility for the quality and accuracy of our financial reporting.

The last paragraph of the auditor's report includes opinions on both the internal control system and the financial statements:

> In our opinion, the consolidated financial statements referred to above present fairly, in all material respects, the financial position of PepsiCo, Inc. as of December 29, 2012 and December 31, 2011, and the results of its operations and its cash flows for each of the fiscal years in the three-year period ended December 29, 2012, in conformity with U.S. generally accepted accounting principles. Also in our opinion, PepsiCo, Inc. maintained, in all material respects, effective internal control over financial reporting as of December 29, 2012, based on criteria established in Internal Control—Integrated Framework issued by COSO.

Quick Check

- The financial statements, notes, MD&A section, and managers' and auditors' attestations provide analysts with an immense amount of useful information for understanding various aspects of a firm's operating, investing, and financing activities.
- The balance sheet reports the results of firms' decisions to acquire assets and the financing of those assets.
- The income statement primarily reflects the results of operating decisions (for example, product mix and pricing, sourcing of production and marketing, and use of plant and equipment). The income statement also reports amounts related to investing decisions (for example, interest and dividend income) and financing decisions (for example, interest expense).
- The statement of comprehensive income items reflect gains and losses from changes in values of certain assets and liabilities that are not reported in net income until such gains and losses are realized.
- The statement of cash flows reflects the sources of uses of cash during a period. The statement of cash flows classifies cash flows during a period into operating, investing, and financing categories. The operating section, as typically prepared, begins with net income and "undoes" the accrual-based accounting entries to reveal the underlying cash flows.
- The notes to the financial statements explain and describe the accounting methods, assumptions, estimates, and judgments used in recording the items appearing on the statements.
- The MD&A section provides managers' insights and evaluation of the firm's performance and risks.
- Management's attestation and the independent auditor's attestation provide statements about (and take responsibility for) the quality and effectiveness of the firm's internal control system and the fairness of its financial statements and notes in reporting a firm's financial position, performance, and cash flows. The independent audit adds credibility and reliability to the financial statements and notes prepared by management.

LO 1-5

Use tools to analyze a firm's profitability and risk, including financial ratios, common-size financial statements, and percentage change financial statements.

Step 4: Analyze Profitability and Risk

The first three steps of the six-step analytical framework establish three key building blocks:

- An understanding of the economics of the *industry* in which a firm competes
- An understanding of the particular strategies that the *firm* has chosen to compete in its industry
- An understanding of the information contained in the *financial statements* and *notes* that report the results of a firm's operating, investing, and financing activities and an assessment of the quality of the financial statements

You are now ready to conduct a financial statement analysis.

Most financial statement analysis aims to evaluate a firm's profitability and risk. This twofold focus stems from the emphasis of investment decisions on returns and risk. Investors acquire shares of common stock in a company because of the return they expect from such investments. This return includes any dividends received plus the change in the market price of the shares of stock while the investor holds them. A rational investor will not be indifferent between two investments that are expected to yield, for example, a 20% return if there are differences in the uncertainty, or risk, of earning that 20% return. The investor will demand a higher expected return from higher-risk investments to compensate for the additional risk assumed.

The income statement reports a firm's net income during the current year and prior years. Assessing the profitability of the firm during these periods, after adjusting as appropriate for nonrecurring or unsustainable items, permits you to evaluate the firm's current and past profitability and to begin forecasting its likely future profitability. Empirical research has shown an association between earnings and market rates of return on common stock, a point discussed in the next section of this chapter and in greater depth in Chapters 13 and 14.

Financial statements also are useful for assessing the risk of a firm. Empirical research has shown that volatility in reported earnings over time is correlated with stock market-based measures of firm risk, such as market equity beta. In addition, firms that cannot generate sufficient cash flow from operations will likely encounter financial difficulties and perhaps even bankruptcy. Firms that have high proportions of debt in their capital structures will experience financial difficulties if they are unable to repay the debt at maturity or replace maturing debt with new debt. Assessing the financial risk of a firm assists the investor in identifying the level of risk incurred when investing in the firm's common stock.

Tools of Profitability and Risk Analysis

Most of this book describes and illustrates tools for analyzing financial statements. In the next several pages, we simply introduce several of these tools as a broad overview.

Common-Size Financial Statements

One simple but powerful analytical tool is *common-size* financial statements, a tool that is helpful in highlighting relations in a financial statement. Common-size income statements and balance sheets express all items in the statement as a percentage of a common base. Common-size balance sheets often use total assets as the base. Sales revenue is a common base in a common-size income statement.

The first five columns of Exhibit 1.17 present common-size balance sheets for **PepsiCo** for 2008 through 2012. Note that various common-size percentages for PepsiCo remain quite stable while others change over this period. For example, PepsiCo experienced a decrease in the proportion of assets comprising most tangible and financial assets (including receivables, inventory, and property, plant, and equipment), but a sharp increase in the proportion of assets reflected by intangible assets. To better understand the reasons for the increased proportion of intangible assets, refer to the investing section of PepsiCo's statement of cash flows in Exhibit 1.14. It shows significant cash outflows for several acquisitions during 2008–2012. Acquisitions often result in significant intangibles being recognized. In addition, Note 4, "Property, Plant and Equipment and Intangible Assets" includes a breakdown of intangible assets by type and by segment.

The common-size balance sheets also show that the proportion of financing from liabilities rose from 65.0% in 2008 to 70.0% in 2012. Current liabilities remained relatively level, but both long-term debt and noncurrent deferred tax liabilities increased. This is consistent with the prior observation from the statement of cash flows that PepsiCo increased its long-term borrowing. The common-size balance sheet also reveals that retained earnings decreased as a proportion of total assets, falling from 85.1% in 2008 to 57.8% in 2012. This is due to the combined effects discussed already for the increases in intangible assets from acquisitions and the increase in long-term debt financing. The common-size balance sheets for **Coca-Cola** for 2008 through 2012, presented in the first five columns of Exhibit 1.19 (pages 47–48), reveal similar trends.

The first five columns of Exhibit 1.18 (page 46) present common-size income statements for PepsiCo for 2008 through 2012. Note that net income as a percentage of sales (also known as the *profit margin*) rose from 16.2% in 2008 to a high of 18.7% in 2009, but then declined to 12.7% in 2012. The common-size income statements show that most expenses as a percentage of sales revenue increased during this period. Management's discussion and analysis of operations presented in Appendix B explains some of these changes. The task of the financial analyst is to probe into the reasons for such changes, taking into consideration industry economics, company strategies, management's explanations, and the operating results of competitors. Chapter 4 explores the reasons for PepsiCo's decreased profit margin.

The common-size income statements for Coca-Cola for 2008 through 2012, presented in the first five columns of Exhibit 1.20 (page 49), reveal a similar decline in profit margin over the same period of time, which is again not surprising given the similar commodities inputs for both firms.

You must interpret common-size financial statements carefully. The amount for any one item in these statements is not independent of all other items. For example, the dollar amount for an item might increase between two periods, but its relative percentage in the common-size statement might decrease if the dollar amount increased at a slower rate than total assets. For example, PepsiCo's dollar amounts for property, plant, and equipment increased significantly between 2008 and 2012 (from $11.7 million to $19.1 million), but the common-size percentages decreased (from 32.4% to 25.6%). Common-size percentages provide a general overview of financial position and operating performance, but you must supplement them with other analytical tools.

Percentage Change Financial Statements

Another powerful analytical tool is *percentage change* financial statements, a tool that is helpful in highlighting the relative rates of growth in financial statement amounts from year to year and over longer periods of time. These statements present the percentage

Exhibit 1.17
Common-Size and Percentage Change Balance Sheets for PepsiCo (allow for rounding)

	Common-Size Balance Sheets					Percentage Change Balance Sheets			
	2012	2011	2010	2009	2008	2012	2011	2010	2009
ASSETS									
Cash and cash equivalents	8.4%	5.6%	8.7%	9.9%	5.7%	54.8%	(31.6)%	50.7%	91.0%
Short-term investments	0.4	0.5	0.6	0.5	0.6	(10.1)	(16.0)	121.9	(9.9)
Accounts and notes receivable, net	9.4	9.5	9.3	11.6	13.0	1.9	9.3	36.7	(1.3)
Inventories	4.8	5.3	4.9	6.6	7.0	(6.4)	13.5	28.8	3.8
Prepaid expenses and other current assets	2.0	3.1	2.2	3.0	3.7	(35.0)	51.3	26.0	(9.8)
Total Current Assets	25.1%	23.9%	25.8%	31.5%	30.0%	7.3%	(0.7)%	39.8%	16.3%
Property, plant and equipment, net	25.6	27.0	28.0	31.8	32.4	(2.9)	3.4	50.4	8.6
Amortizable intangible assets, net	2.4	2.6	3.0	2.1	2.0	(5.7)	(6.8)	140.8	14.9
Goodwill	22.7	23.1	21.5	16.4	14.2	1.0	14.6	124.4	27.5
Other nonamortizable intangible assets	19.8	20.0	17.3	4.5	3.1	1.3	23.5	561.2	58.0
Investments in noncontrolled affiliates	2.2	2.0	2.0	11.3	10.8	10.6	8.0	(69.5)	15.5
Other assets	2.2	1.4	2.5	2.4	7.4	61.9	(39.6)	75.0	(63.7)
Total Assets	100.0%	100.0%	100.0%	100.0%	100.0%	2.4%	6.9%	71.0%	10.7%
LIABILITIES AND SHAREHOLDERS' EQUITY									
Short-term obligations	6.5%	8.5%	7.2%	1.2%	1.0%	(22.4)%	26.7%	955.6%	25.7%
Accounts payable and other current liabilities	15.9	16.1	16.0	20.4	23.0	1.2	7.6	34.4	(1.8)
Income taxes payable	0.5	0.3	0.1	0.4	0.4	93.2	170.4	(57.0)	13.8
Total Current Liabilities	22.9%	24.9%	23.3%	22.0%	24.4%	(5.9)%	14.2%	81.5%	(0.4)%

(Continued)

Long-term debt obligations	31.5	28.2	29.3	18.6	21.8	14.5	2.8	170.3	(5.8)
Other liabilities	8.8	11.3	9.9	14.0	18.2	(20.8)	22.8	20.4	(14.5)
Deferred income taxes	6.8	6.9	6.0	1.7	0.6	1.4	23.1	515.6	191.6
Total Liabilities	70.0%	71.3%	68.5%	56.2%	65.0%	0.5%	11.4%	108.3%	(4.3)%
Preferred stock, no par value	0.1%	0.1%	0.1%	0.1%	0.1%	0.0%	0.0%	0.0%	0.0%
Repurchased preferred stock	(0.2)	(0.2)	(0.2)	(0.4)	(0.4)	4.5	4.7	3.4	5.1
Common stock, par value	0.0	0.0	0.0	0.1	0.1	(16.1)	0.0	3.3	0.0
Capital in excess of par value	5.6	6.1	6.6	0.6	1.0	(6.3)	(1.5)	1710.8	(28.8)
Retained earnings	57.8	55.3	54.4	84.8	85.1	7.0	8.7	9.7	10.3
Accumulated other comprehensive loss	(7.4)	(8.5)	(5.3)	(9.5)	(13.0)	(11.9)	71.6	(4.3)	(19.2)
Treasury stock	(26.1)	(24.5)	(24.6)	(33.6)	(39.2)	8.9	6.7	25.1	(5.2)
Noncontrolling interests	—	0.4%	0.5%	—	1.3%	(66.2)%	(0.3)%	(51.1)%	34.0%
Total Shareholders' Equity	30.0%	28.7	31.5	43.8%	35.0	7.2	(2.7)	23.1	38.6
Total Liabilities and Shareholders' Equity	100.0%	100.0%	100.0%	100.0%	100.0%	2.4%	6.9%	71.0%	10.7%

Exhibit 1.18

Common-Size and Percentage Change Income Statements for PepsiCo
(allow for rounding)

	Common-Size Income Statements					Percentage Change Income Statements			
	2012	2011	2010	2009	2008	2012	2011	2010	2009
Net Revenue	100.0%	100.0%	100.0%	100.0%	100.0%	(1.5%)	15.0%	33.8%	0.0%
Cost of sales	47.8	47.5	45.9	46.5	47.1	(1.0)	18.9	32.2	(1.2)
Gross Profit	52.2%	52.5%	54.1%	53.5%	52.9%	(2.0%)	11.7%	35.1%	1.0%
Selling, general, and administrative expenses	38.1	37.8	39.4	34.8	36.8	(0.7)	10.2	51.8	(5.5)
Other operating charges	0.2	0.2	0.2	0.1	0.1	(10.5)	13.7	85.7	(1.6)
Operating Profit	13.9%	14.5%	14.4%	18.6%	16.0%	(5.4%)	15.6%	3.6%	16.0%
Bottling equity income	0.0	0.0	1.3	0.8	0.9	0.0	(100.0)	101.4	(2.4)
Interest expense	(1.4)	(1.3)	(1.6)	(0.9)	(0.8)	5.0	(5.2)	127.5	20.7
Interest income	0.1	0.1	0.1	0.2	0.1	59.6	(16.2)	1.5	63.4
Other income (loss), net	0.0	0.0	0.0	0.0	0.0	0.0	0.0	0.0	0.0
Income before Income Taxes	12.7%	13.3%	14.2%	18.7%	16.2%	(6.0%)	7.3%	1.9%	15.1%
Provision for income taxes	3.2	3.6	3.3	4.9	4.3	(11.9)	25.2	(9.8)	11.8
Net Income	9.5%	9.7%	11.0%	13.8%	11.9%	(3.8%)	2.0%	6.0%	16.3%

Exhibit 1.19

Common-Size and Percentage Change Balance Sheets for Coca-Cola (allow for rounding)

	Common-Size Balance Sheets					Percentage Change Balance Sheets			
	2012	2011	2010	2009	2008	2012	2011	2010	2009
ASSETS									
Cash and cash equivalents	9.8%	16.0%	11.7%	14.4%	11.6%	(34.1)%	50.3%	21.3%	49.4%
Short-term investments	9.4	1.5	3.9	4.5	0.7	558.2	(56.3)	28.6	688.5
Accounts and notes receivable, net	5.5	6.2	6.1	7.7	7.6	(3.3)	11.1	17.9	21.6
Inventories	3.8	3.9	3.6	4.8	5.4	5.6	16.7	12.6	7.6
Prepaid expenses and other current assets	6.7	4.3	4.3	4.6	4.7	66.8	9.1	42.0	15.9
Total Current Assets	35.2%	31.9%	29.6%	36.1%	30.1%	18.9%	18.2%	23.0%	44.1%
Property, plant and equipment, net	16.8	18.7	20.2	19.6	20.5	(3.1)	1.4	54.0	14.8%
Amortizable intangible assets, net	1.3	1.6	1.9	1.0	6.0	(8.0)	(9.2)	194.2	(80.6)
Goodwill	14.2	15.3	16.0	8.7	9.9	0.3	4.7	176.2%	4.8
Other nonamortizable intangible assets	16.2	17.8	19.0	16.7	15.0	(1.9)	2.4	70.4	34.3
Investments in noncontrolled affiliates	12.1	10.5	10.4	13.9	14.3	24.8	10.4	12.3	16.9
Other assets	4.2	4.4	2.9	4.1	4.3	2.6	64.8	7.3	14.0
Total Assets	100.0%	100.0%	100.0%	100.0%	100.0%	7.8%	9.7%	49.8%	20.1%
LIABILITIES AND SHAREHOLDERS' EQUITY									
Short-term obligations	20.7%	18.6%	12.9%	14.0%	16.1%	19.9%	59.0%	37.9%	4.1%
Accounts payable and other current liabilities	11.0	11.3	12.1	13.7	15.3	5.2	1.7	33.1	7.3
Income taxes payable	0.5	0.5	0.4	0.5	0.6	30.1	32.6	3.4	4.8
Total Current Liabilities	32.3%	30.4%	25.4%	28.2%	32.1%	14.6%	31.2%	34.9%	5.6%

(Continued)

Exhibit 1.19 (Continued)

| | Common-Size Balance Sheets | | | | | Percentage Change Balance Sheets | | | |
	2012	2011	2010	2009	2008	2012	2011	2010	2009
Long-term debt obligations	17.1	17.1	19.3	10.4	6.9	7.9	(2.7)	177.5	81.9
Other liabilities	6.3	6.8	6.6	6.1	7.4	0.9	13.1	61.7	(1.5)
Deferred income taxes	5.8	5.9	5.8	3.2	2.2	6.1	10.2	169.7	80.2
Total Liabilities	61.5%	60.1%	57.1%	47.9%	48.5%	10.3%	15.5%	78.4%	18.7%
Preferred stock, no par value	0.0%	0.0%	0.0%	0.0%	0.0%	0.0%	0.0%	0.0%	0.0%
Repurchased preferred stock	0.0	0.0	0.0	0.0	0.0	0.0	0.0	0.0	0.0
Common stock, par value	2.0	2.2	1.2	1.8	2.2	0.0	100.0	0.0	0.0
Capital in excess of par value	13.2	12.9	13.8	17.5	19.7	10.1	2.7	17.8	7.2
Retained earnings	67.4	67.0	67.6	85.3	95.0	8.3	8.8	18.6	7.9
Accumulated other comprehensive loss	(3.9)	(3.5)	(2.0)	(1.6)	(6.6)	22.0	91.3	91.5	(71.7)
Treasury stock	(40.6)	(39.1)	(38.1)	(52.2)	(59.8)	11.8	12.8	9.3	4.9
	0.4	0.4	0.4	1.1	1.0	32.2	(8.9)	(42.6)	40.3
Total Shareholders' Equity	38.5%	39.9%	42.9%	52.1%	51.5%	3.9%	1.9%	23.6%	21.5%
Total Liabilities and Shareholders' Equity	100.0%	100.0%	100.0%	100.0%	100.0%	7.8%	9.7%	49.8%	20.1%

Exhibit 1.20

Common-Size and Percentage Change Income Statements for Coca-Cola (allow for rounding)

	Common-Size Income Statements					Percentage Change Income Statements			
	2012	2011	2010	2009	2008	2012	2011	2010	2009
Net Revenue	100.0%	100.0%	100.0%	100.0%	100.0%	3.2%	32.5%	13.3%	(3.0)%
Cost of sales	39.7	39.1	36.1	35.8	35.6	4.6	43.5	14.5	(2.5)
Gross Profit	60.3%	60.9%	63.9%	64.2%	64.4%	2.2%	26.3%	12.7%	(3.2)%
Selling, general, and administrative expenses	36.9	37.4	37.6	36.7	36.9	1.8	32.0	16.2	(3.5)%
Other operating charges	0.9	1.6	2.3	1.0	1.1	(38.9)	(10.6)	161.7	(10.6)
Operating Profit	22.4%	21.9%	24.0%	26.6%	26.4%	6.0%	20.9%	2.2%	(2.5)%
Bottling equity income	1.7	1.5	2.9	2.5	(2.7)	18.7	(32.7)	31.2	(189.4)
Interest expense	(0.8)	(0.9)	(2.1)	(1.1)	(1.4)	(4.8)	(43.1)	106.5	(18.9)
Interest income	1.0	1.0	0.9	0.8	1.0	(2.5)	52.4	27.3	(25.2)
Other income (loss) net	0.1	1.0	14.6	(0.1)	(0.1)	(85.0)%	(90.9)	(12326.2)	50.0
Income before Income Taxes	24.5%	24.5%	40.3%	28.6%	23.3%	3.0%	(19.5)%	59.7%	19.2%
Provision for income taxes	5.7	6.0	6.7	6.6	5.1	(3.2)	18.6	16.2	25.0
Income from Continuing Operations	18.8%	18.4%	33.6%	22.0%	18.2%	5.1%	(27.2)%	72.7%	17.5%

change in the amount of an item relative to its amount in the previous period or the compounded average percentage change over several prior periods.

The four rightmost columns of Exhibit 1.17 present percentage changes in balance sheet items during 2009 through 2012 for PepsiCo. Note the largest percentage changes in assets occur during 2010 for all intangible assets, consistent with the preceding observations with respect to acquisitions indicated on the statement of cash flows. Other large percentage changes between 2009 and 2010 occurred for long-term obligations and deferred income taxes, already discussed in the common-size analysis above. Note that the percentage change amounts for individual line items are highly variable. As noted above, these changes are often interdependent. For example, the increase in intangibles is tied to the increase in long-term debt. For comparison, the four rightmost columns of Exhibit 1.19 present the percentage changes in balance sheet items for Coca-Cola during 2009 through 2012, where we see similar volatility in changes.

You must exert particular caution when interpreting percentage change balance sheets for a particular year. If the amount for the preceding year that serves as the base is relatively small, even a small change in dollar amount can result in a large percentage change. This is the case, for example, with PepsiCo's deferred tax liability. The liability increased by 191.6% in 2009, but it amounted to a relatively small increase from $226 million to $659 million, which is small relative to the ending balance of $5,063 million in 2012. A large percentage change in an account that makes up a smaller portion of total financing is not as meaningful as a smaller percentage change in an account that makes up a larger portion of total assets or total financing.

The four rightmost columns of Exhibit 1.18 present percentage change income statement amounts for PepsiCo. Note that percentage changes in cost of sales generally tracks that of sales, consistent with cost of sales being a variable cost. In contrast, the percentage changes in net income show less of a relation, consistent with fixed or one-time expenses. For example, the percentage change in sales during 2009 was 0.0%, but net income rose 16.3%. You might direct particular concern to the growth rate in cost of sales during 2011, which significantly outpaced the growth in sales (18.9% versus 13.9%). This implies a lower degree of variable cost control, a loss of pricing power, or a shift in product mix to lower margin products, leading to shrinking gross profit margins. You should carefully investigate the reasons for this deterioration in PepsiCo's profitability. By comparison, the four rightmost columns of Exhibit 1.20 present the percentage change income statement amounts for **Coca-Cola** during the same span of years, and they reveal that Coca-Cola also exhibited percentage changes in the cost of sales that often outpaced those for sales.

Financial Statement Ratios

Perhaps the most useful analytical tools for assessing profitability and risk are *financial statement ratios*. Financial statement ratios express relations among various items from the three financial statements. Researchers and analysts have found that such ratios are effective indicators of various dimensions of profitability and risk and serve as useful signals of future profitability and risk. Chapters 4 and 5 discuss these financial ratios in depth. The discussion here merely introduces several of them. Appendix D presents descriptive statistics for many of the most commonly used financial ratios across 48 industries over the past eleven years.

Profitability Ratios. Perhaps the most commonly encountered financial ratio is EPS (earnings per share). Basic EPS equals net income available to the common shareholders (that is, net income minus dividends on preferred stock) divided by the weighted-average number of common shares outstanding. For 2012, basic EPS for PepsiCo (see Exhibit 1.11 and Note 11, "Net Income Attributable to PepsiCo per Common Share," in Appendix A) is $3.96 [($6,178 − $7)/1,557 shares]. Firms typically report both basic and diluted EPS on their income statements. As Chapter 14 makes clear, financial analysts often use a multiple of EPS (a price-earnings ratio) to derive what they consider an appropriate price for a firm's common stock.

Another profitability ratio, which plays a central role in this text, is the *return on common equity* (ROCE). ROCE equals net income available to the common shareholders divided by average common shareholders' equity for the year. ROCE for PepsiCo for 2012 is 28.5% {($6,178 − $7)/[0.5($22,399 + $20,899)]}. This ROCE is large relative to most firms. However, we should expect PepsiCo to generate a high rate of return for its shareholders because it has developed an effective and sustainable strategy as a major competitor in the beverage industry and one of the global leaders in the snack food industry, which we assessed to have relatively favorable competitive conditions. This example illustrates that it is difficult to interpret ROCE and other financial ratios without a frame of reference, which you build by conducting the industry analysis, the strategic analysis, and the accounting quality analysis. For PepsiCo, their valuable brands lead to higher revenues and earnings, but the value of internally generated brand value does not appear on the balance sheet.[8] Analysts compare ratios to corresponding ratios of earlier periods (*time-series analysis*), to corresponding ratios of other firms in the same industry (*cross-sectional analysis*), and to industry averages in order to interpret the ratios. Chapter 4 provides an in-depth analysis of PepsiCo's ROCE and other profitability ratios, including how to adjust reported profitability for unusual or nonrecurring items.

Risk Ratios. A simple method to assess the volatility of a firm's earnings over time and gauge uncertainty inherent in future earnings is to simply calculate the standard deviation in ROCE. Alternatively, to assess the ability of firms to repay short-term obligations, analysts frequently calculate various short-term liquidity ratios such as the current ratio, which equals current assets divided by current liabilities. The current ratio for PepsiCo at the end of 2012 is 1.10 ($18,720/$17,089). As with profitability ratios, this ratio is meaningful only when you perform a time-series and cross-sectional analysis. Like most firms, PepsiCo's current ratio has exceeded 1.0 in each of the past five years, so PepsiCo appears to have minimal short-term liquidity risk.

To assess the ability of firms to continue operating for a longer term (that is, to avoid bankruptcy), you look at various long-term solvency ratios, such the relative amount of long-term debt in the capital structure. The ratio of long-term debt to common shareholders' equity for PepsiCo at the end of 2012 is 1.05 ($23,544/$22,399). PepsiCo has been increasing its leverage, but given PepsiCo's level of profitability, strong cash flows, and solid short-term liquidity position, bankruptcy risk is low. Chapter 5 provides an in-depth analysis of PepsiCo's debt-to-equity and other risk ratios.

Step 5: Prepare Forecasted Financial Statements and Step 6: Value the Firm

LO 1-6

Obtain an overview of how to use financial statement information to forecast the future business activities of a firm and to value a firm.

Each of the steps in our six-step analysis and valuation framework is important, but the crucial (and most difficult) step is *forecasting* future financial statements. Such forecasts

---

[8]Thus, because assets are understated, then equity which equals assets minus liabilities is also understated, biasing ROCE upwards.

are the inputs into valuation models or other financial decisions, and the quality of the decisions rests on the reliability of the forecasts. The primary reason for the analysis of a firm's industry, strategy, accounting quality, and financial statement ratios is to use them as the starting point for deriving forecasts of future performance. Forecasted financial statements rely on assumptions you make about the future: Will the firm's strategy remain the same or change? At what rate will the firm generate revenue growth? Will the firm likely gain or lose market share relative to competitors? Will revenues grow because of increases in sales volume, prices, or both? How will its costs change? How much will the firm need to increase operating assets (inventory, plant, and equipment) to achieve its growth strategies? How much capital will the firm need to raise to finance growth in assets? Will it change the mix of debt versus equity financing? How will a change in the debt-equity mix change the risk of the firm? Responses to these and other questions provide the basis for preparing forecasted income statements, balance sheets, and statements of cash flows. You can compare financial ratios of forecasted financial statement items with the corresponding ratios from the reported financial statements to judge the reasonableness of the assumptions made. Chapter 10 describes and illustrates the techniques to project future financial statements and applies the techniques to build financial statement projections. Amounts from the forecasted financial statements serve as the basis for the valuation models in Step 6.

Capital market participants most commonly use financial statement analysis to *value* firms, which is the culmination of the previous five steps of the framework incorporated into a valuation model. Financial statements—specifically, key metrics from the statements such as earnings, dividends, and cash flows—play a central role in firm valuation. Thus, the emphasis of this book is to arm you with the knowledge necessary to apply sophisticated and comprehensive valuation models.

To develop reliable estimates of firm value, and therefore to make intelligent investment decisions, you must rely on well-reasoned and objective forecasts of the firm's future profitability and risk. Forecasts of future dividends, earnings, and cash flows form the basis for the most frequently used valuation models.

In some cases, analysts prefer to assess firm value using the classical dividends-based approach, which takes the perspective of valuing the firm from the standpoint of the cash that investors can expect to receive through dividends (or the sale of their shares). It also is common for analysts to assess firm value using measures of the firm's expected future free cash flows—cash flows that are available to be paid as dividends after necessary payments are made to reinvest in productive assets and meet required debt payments. An equivalent approach to valuation involves computing firm value based on the book value of equity and the earnings of the firm you expect to exceed the firm's cost of capital (similar in logic to "economic value-added" computations). In many circumstances, analysts find it necessary or desirable to estimate firm value using valuation heuristics such as price-earnings ratios and market-to-book value ratios. Chapters 11–14 describe the theory and demonstrate the practical applications of each of these approaches to valuation.

LO 1-7
Consider the role of financial statement analysis in an efficient capital market, and review empirical evidence on the association between changes in earnings and changes in stock prices.

Role of Financial Statement Analysis in an Efficient Capital Market

Security prices represent the aggregate information known by the capital markets about a firm. Market efficiency describes the degree to which the capital market impounds information into security prices. The larger the set of information that is priced and the greater the speed with which security prices reflect new information, the higher the degree of market efficiency. A highly efficient capital market would impound all publicly available value-relevant information (such as an announcement of surprisingly good or poor earnings in a particular period) quickly, completely, and without bias into share prices. In a less efficient market, share prices would react more slowly to value-relevant information. In the U.S. capital markets, the performance of large firms tends to have a wide following of buy-side and sell-side analysts, many institutional investors, and the financial press. The market is more efficient in adjusting the share prices of these large firms than those of smaller market firms, which have no analyst following, no institutional investors, and rare press coverage.

There are differing views as to the benefits of analyzing a set of financial statements in the context of market efficiency. One view is that stock market prices react with such a high degree of efficiency to published information about a firm that analysts and investors have more difficulty finding "undervalued" or "overvalued" securities by analyzing financial statements because the capital market quickly impounds new financial statement information into security prices.

However, consider the following:

- For markets to be efficient, analysts and investors must actually perform the analysis to bring about the appropriate prices. With their expertise and access to information about firms, financial analysts do the analysis quickly and engage in the trading necessary to achieve efficient pricing. They are agents of market efficiency.
- Research on capital market efficiency aggregates financial data for individual firms and studies the average reaction of the market to earnings and other financial statement information. A finding that the market is efficient *on average* does not preclude temporary mispricing of individual firms' shares.
- Research has shown that equity markets are not perfectly efficient. Anomalies include the tendency for market prices to adjust with a lag to new earnings information, systematic underreaction to the information contained in earnings announcements, and the ability to use a combination of financial ratios to detect under- and overpriced securities.[9]
- Management has incentives related to job security and compensation to report as favorable a picture as possible in the financial statements within the constraints of U.S. GAAP. Therefore, these reports may represent biased indicators of the economic performance and financial position of firms. Analysts must analyze and adjust these financial statements to remove such biases if market prices are to reflect underlying economic values.

Financial statement analysis is valuable in numerous settings outside equity capital markets, including credit analysis by a bank to support corporate lending, competitor analysis to identify competitive advantages, and merger and acquisition analysis to identify buyout candidates.

The Association between Earnings and Share Prices

To illustrate the striking relation between accounting earnings and stock returns and to foreshadow the potential to generate positive excess returns through analysis and

---

[9]For a summary of the issues and related research, see Ray Ball, "The Theory of Stock Market Efficiency: Accomplishments and Limitations," *Journal of Applied Corporate Finance* (Spring 1995), pp. 4–17.

forecasting, consider the results from empirical research by D. Craig Nichols and James Wahlen.[10] They studied the average cumulative market-adjusted returns generated by firms during the 12 months leading up to and including the month in which each firm announced annual earnings numbers. For a sample of 31,923 firm-years between 1988 and 2001, they found that the average firm that announced an increase in earnings (over the prior year's earnings) experienced stock returns that exceeded market average returns by 19.2%. On the other hand, the average firm that announced a decrease in earnings experienced stock returns that were 16.4% lower than the market average. Their results suggest that merely *the sign* of the change in earnings was associated with a 35.6% stock return differential in one year, on average, over their sample period. Exhibit 1.21 presents a graph of their results.

The results of the Nichols and Wahlen study indicate how informative accounting earnings are to the capital markets and emphasize the importance of forecasting the changes in earnings one year ahead. Analysts should view these results as encouraging because they imply that being able to simply forecast whether future earnings will be higher or lower than current earnings can yield investment profits. To be sure, Nichols and Wahlen knew with certainty which firms would announce earnings increases or decreases one year ahead. Analysts must forecast earnings changes and take positions in stocks on the basis of their earnings forecasts.

Note in the graph that the study also examined the relation between changes in cash flows from operations and cumulative market-adjusted stock returns. Using the same firm-years and study period, Nichols and Wahlen documented that firms experiencing positive changes in cash from operations experienced stock returns that beat the market by an average of 11.3%, whereas firms experiencing decreases in cash from operations experienced stock returns that were lower than the market by an average of 3.7%. These results suggest that the sign of the change in cash from operations was associated with a 15.0% stock return differential in one year, on average, during the study period. This implies that changes in cash flows also are strongly related to stock returns, but they are not as informative for the capital markets as are changes in earnings. This should not be surprising, because changes in cash flow are less indicative of a firm's performance in one period than are changes in earnings. For example, a firm experiencing a negative change in cash from operations could be attributable to cash flow distress (bad news) or a large investment of cash in growth opportunities (good news). A negative change in earnings, on the other hand, is almost always bad news. This explains, in part, why analysts, firm managers, the financial press, boards of directors, auditors, and therefore financial statement analysis textbook writers focus so much attention on analyzing and forecasting earnings numbers.

LO 1-8

Review sources of financial information available for publicly held firms.

Sources of Financial Statement Information

Firms whose bonds or common shares trade in public capital markets in the United States typically make the following information available:

---

[10]D. Craig Nichols and James Wahlen, "How Do Earnings Numbers Relate to Stock Returns? A Review of Classic Accounting Research with Updated Evidence," *Accounting Horizons* (December 2004), pp. 263–286. The portion of the Nichols and Wahlen study described here is a replication of path-breaking research in accounting by Ray Ball and Philip Brown, "An Evaluation of Accounting Income Numbers," *Journal of Accounting Research* (Autumn 1968), pp. 159–178.

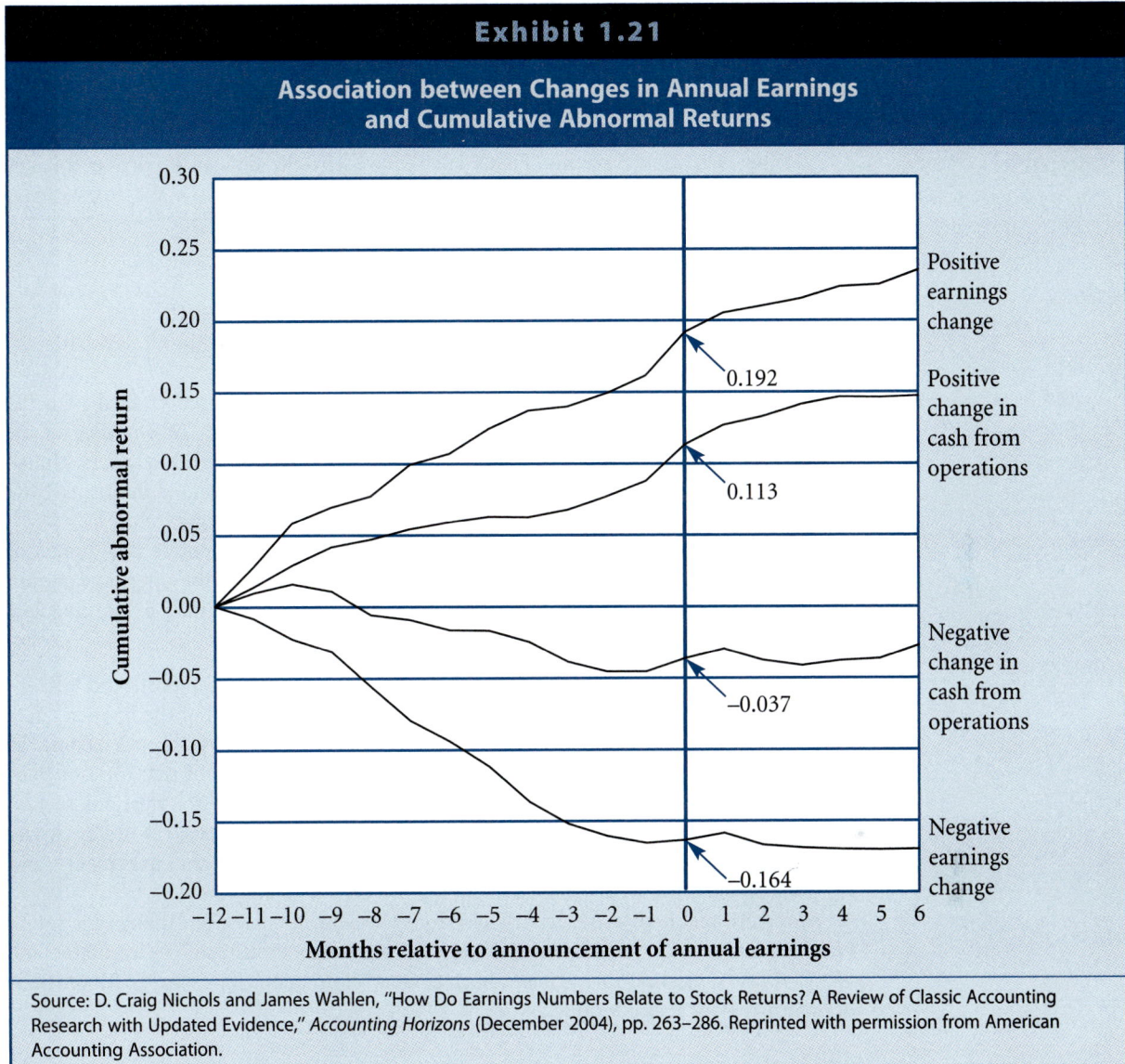

Exhibit 1.21

Association between Changes in Annual Earnings and Cumulative Abnormal Returns

Positive earnings change

0.192

Positive change in cash from operations

0.113

Negative change in cash from operations

−0.037

Negative earnings change

−0.164

Cumulative abnormal return

Months relative to announcement of annual earnings

Source: D. Craig Nichols and James Wahlen, "How Do Earnings Numbers Relate to Stock Returns? A Review of Classic Accounting Research with Updated Evidence," *Accounting Horizons* (December 2004), pp. 263–286. Reprinted with permission from American Accounting Association.

■ **Annual Report to Shareholders.** The glossy annual report includes balance sheets for the most recent two years and income statements and statements of cash flows for the most recent three years, along with various notes and supporting schedules. The annual report also includes a letter from the chairperson of the board of directors and from the chief executive officer summarizing the activities of the most recent year. The report typically includes management's discussion and analysis (MD&A) of the firm's operating performance, financial position, and liquidity. Firms vary with respect to the quality of information provided here. Some firms, such as **PepsiCo**, give helpful information about the firm's strategy and reasons for the changes in profitability, financial position, and risk. (See Appendix B.) Other firms merely repeat amounts presented in the financial statements without providing helpful explanations for operating results.

- **Form 10-K Annual Report.** The Form 10-K annual report filed with the SEC includes the same financial statements and notes as the corporate annual report with the addition of supporting schedules required by the SEC. For example, compared to the corporate annual report, Form 10-K often includes more detailed information on changes in the allowance for uncollectible accounts and other valuation accounts. Firms are required by the SEC to report several key items in the Form 10-K, including:
  - a description of the business (Item 1), including its risk factors (Item 1A).
  - a description of company properties (Item 2).
  - the management discussion and analysis (Item 7).
  - the financial statements, notes, and supplemental schedules (Item 8).

  Large firms must file their annual reports with the SEC within 60 days after the end of their annual accounting period.
- **Form 10-Q Quarterly Report.** The Form 10-Q quarterly report filed with the SEC includes condensed balance sheet and income statement information for the most recent three months, as well as comparative data for earlier quarters. Unlike the annual filing of Form 10-K, the financial statements included in Forms 10-Q are not audited.
- **Prospectus or Registration Statement.** Firms intending to issue new bonds or capital stock file a prospectus with the SEC that describes the offering (amount and intended uses of proceeds). The prospectus includes much of the financial information found in the Form 10-K annual report.

A large number of firms include all or a portion of their annual reports and SEC filings on their corporate websites. For example, PepsiCo provides all of the financial data and analysis provided in Appendices A and B on its website (www.pepsico.com). In addition, many firms provide additional financial data on their sites that are not published in the annual reports. Other useful information in the investor relations section of corporate websites may include (1) presentations made to analysts; (2) press releases pertaining to new products, customer acquisitions, and earnings announcements; and (3) transcripts or archived webcasts of conference calls with analysts.

Firms are required to file reports electronically with the SEC, and filings for recent years are available at the SEC website (www.sec.gov). Numerous commercial online and CD-ROM services also provide financial statement information (for example, **Bloomberg**, **Standard & Poor's**, and **Moody's**).

Summary

The purpose of this chapter is to provide a broad overview of the six-step analysis and valuation framework that is the focus of this book and a logical process for analyzing and valuing companies:

1. Identify the economic characteristics and competitive dynamics of the *industry* in which the firm participates.
2. Identify the strategies that the *firm* pursues to compete in its industry.
3. Assess the quality of the firm's *financial statements*, adjusting them, if necessary, for items lacking sustainability or comparability.
4. Analyze and interpret the *profitability* and *risk* of a firm, assessing the firm's performance and the strength of its financial position.
5. Prepare *forecasted financial statements*.
6. *Value* the firm.

You should not expect to fully understand these six steps at this stage of your studies. The remaining chapters discuss each step in greater depth. Chapter 2 discusses the important links between the valuation of assets and liabilities on the balance sheet and revenues and expenses on the income statement. Chapter 3 details the preparation and interpretation of the statement of cash flows for firms in different industries at various stages of growth. Chapter 4 describes common financial statement ratios used to assess profitability and illustrates their calculation and interpretation for **PepsiCo**. Chapter 5 parallels the preceding chapter by describing common financial statement ratios used to assess risk. Chapters 6–9 examine U.S. GAAP and IFRS for financing, investing, and operating activities and address concerns that affect the quality of earnings and financial position. Chapters 10–14 shift the focus to valuation. Chapter 10 demonstrates the preparation of forecasted financial statements. Chapters 11–14 examine various valuation models based on dividends, cash flows, earnings, and amounts for comparable firms. With firm valuation being the most frequent objective of financial statement analysis, these chapters represent a fitting culmination to the book.

Questions, Exercises, Problems, and Cases

Questions and Exercises

1.1 Porter's Five Forces Applied to the Air Courier Industry. Apply Porter's five forces to the air courier industry. Industry participants include such firms as **FedEx**, **UPS**, and **DHL**. (Hint: Access Gale's Business & Company Resource Center, Global Business Browser, or Standard & Poor's Industry Surveys to obtain the needed information.)   `LO 1-2`

1.2 Economic Attributes Framework Applied to the Specialty Retailing Apparel Industry. Apply the economic attributes framework discussed in the chapter to the specialty retailing apparel industry, which includes such firms as **Gap**, **Limited Brands**, and **Abercrombie & Fitch**. (Hint: Access Gale's Business & Company Resource Center, Global Business Browser, or Standard & Poor's Industry Surveys to obtain the needed information.)   `LO 1-2`

1.3 Identification of Commodity Businesses. A recent article in *Fortune* magazine listed the following firms among the top ten most admired companies in the United States: **Dell**, **Southwest Airlines**, **Microsoft**, and **Johnson & Johnson**. Access the websites of these four companies or read the Business section of their Form 10-K reports (www.sec.gov). Describe whether you would view their products or services as commodities. Explain your reasoning.   `LO 1-2`

1.4 Identification of Company Strategies. Refer to the websites and the Form 10-K reports of **Home Depot** (www.homedepot.com) and **Lowe's** (www.lowes.com). Compare and contrast their business strategies.   `LO 1-3`

1.5 Researching the FASB Website. Go to the website of the Financial Accounting Standards Board (www.fasb.org). Identify the most recently issued financial reporting standard and summarize briefly (in one paragraph) its principal provisions. Also search under Project Activities to identify the reporting issue with the most recent update. Describe the issue briefly and the nature of the action taken by the FASB.   `LO 1-4`

LO 1-4

1.6 Researching the IASB Website. Go to the website of the International Accounting Standards Board (www.ifrs.org). Search for the International Financial Reporting Standards (IFRS) summaries. Identify the most recently issued international financial reporting standard and summarize briefly (in one paragraph) its principal provisions.

LO 1-2

1.7 Effect of Industry Economics on Balance Sheets. Access the investor relations or corporate information section of the websites of **American Airlines** (www.aa.com), **Intel** (www.intel.com), and **Disney** (http://disney.com). Study the business strategies of each firm. Examine the financial ratios below and indicate which firm is likely to be American Airlines, Intel, and Disney. Explain your reasoning.

	Firm A	Firm B	Firm C
Property, plant, and equipment/assets	27.9%	34.6%	62.5%
Long-term debt/assets	18.2%	3.7%	35.7%

LO 1-3

1.8 Effect of Business Strategy on Common-Size Income Statements. Access the investor relations or corporate information section of the websites of **Apple Computer** (www.apple.com) and **Dell** (www.dell.com). Study the strategies of each firm. Examine the following common-size income statements and indicate which firm is likely to be Apple Computer and which is likely to be Dell. Explain your reasoning. Indicate any percentages that seem inconsistent with their strategies.

	Firm A	Firm B
Sales	100.0%	100.0%
Cost of goods sold	(82.1)	(59.9)
Selling and administrative expenses	(11.6)	(9.7)
Research and development	(1.1)	(3.1)
Income taxes	(1.4)	(8.9)
All other items	0.2	0.8
Net income	4.1%	19.2%

LO 1-3

1.9 Effect of Business Strategy on Common-Size Income Statements. Access the investor relations or corporate information section of the websites of **Dollar General** (www.dollargeneral.com) and **Macy's Inc.** (www.macysinc.com). Study the strategies of each firm. Examine the following common-size income statements and indicate which firm is likely to be Dollar General and which is likely to be Macy's. Explain your reasoning. Indicate any percentages that seem inconsistent with their strategies.

	Firm A	Firm B
Sales	100.0%	100.0%
Cost of goods sold	(70.7)	(60.3)
Selling and administrative expenses	(23.4)	(34.1)
Income taxes	(0.8)	(0.5)
All other items	(4.0)	(0.1)
Net income	1.0%	5.2%

Problems and Cases

1.10 Effect of Industry Characteristics on Financial Statement Relations.

LO 1-2, LO 1-5

Effective financial statement analysis requires an understanding of a firm's economic characteristics. The relations between various financial statement items provide evidence of many of these economic characteristics. Exhibit 1.22 (pages 60–61) presents common-size condensed balance sheets and income statements for 12 firms in different industries. These common-size balance sheets and income statements express various items as a percentage of operating revenues. (That is, the statement divides all amounts by operating revenues for the year.) Exhibit 1.22 also shows the ratio of cash flow from operations to capital expenditures. A dash for a particular financial statement item does not necessarily mean the amount is zero. It merely indicates that the amount is not sufficiently large enough for the firm to disclose it. Amounts that are not meaningful are shown as *n.m.* A list of the 12 companies and a brief description of their activities follow.

A. **Amazon.com**: Operates websites to sell a wide variety of products online. The firm operated at a net loss in all years prior to that reported in Exhibit 1.22.

B. **Carnival Corporation**: Owns and operates cruise ships.

C. **Cisco Systems**: Manufactures and sells computer networking and communications products.

D. **Citigroup**: Offers a wide range of financial services in the commercial banking, insurance, and securities business. Operating expenses represent the compensation of employees.

E. **eBay**: Operates an online trading platform for buyers to purchase and sellers to sell a variety of goods. The firm has grown in part by acquiring other companies to enhance or support its online trading platform.

F. **Goldman Sachs**: Offers brokerage and investment banking services. Operating expenses represent the compensation of employees.

G. **Johnson & Johnson**: Develops, manufactures, and sells pharmaceutical products, medical equipment, and branded over-the-counter consumer personal care products.

H. **Kellogg's**: Manufactures and distributes cereal and other food products. The firm acquired other branded food companies in recent years.

I. **MGM Mirage**: Owns and operates hotels, casinos, and golf courses.

J. **Molson Coors**: Manufactures and distributes beer. Molson Coors has made minority ownership investments in other beer manufacturers in recent years.

K. **Verizon**: Maintains a telecommunications network and offers telecommunications services. Operating expenses represent the compensation of employees. Verizon has made minority investments in other cellular and wireless providers.

L. **Yum! Brands**: Operates chains of name-brand restaurants, including **Taco Bell**, **KFC**, and **Pizza Hut**.

REQUIRED

Use the ratios to match the companies in Exhibit 1.22 with the firms listed above.

Exhibit 1.22

Common-Size Financial Statement Data for Firms in 12 Industries (Problem 1.10)

	1	2	3
BALANCE SHEET			
Cash and marketable securities	2,256.1%	4.1%	20.1%
Receivables	352.8	2.8	15.2
Inventories	—	2.4	7.9
Property, plant, and equipment, at cost	—	286.8	43.0
Accumulated depreciation	—	(59.8)	(20.4)
Property, plant, and equipment, net	—	227.0%	22.5%
Intangibles	—	36.5	43.4
Other assets	57.3%	7.2	24.0
Total Assets	2,666.2%	280.0%	133.2%
Current liabilities	2,080.8%	37.8%	32.7%
Long-term debt	390.9	69.1	12.7
Other long-term liabilities	92.6	5.6	21.1
Shareholders' equity	101.9	167.5	66.7
Total Liabilities and Shareholders' Equity	2,666.2%	280.0%	133.2%
INCOME STATEMENT			
Operating revenues	100.0%	100.0%	100.0%
Cost of sales (excluding depreciation) or operating expenses[a]	(54.6)	(61.6)	(29.0)
Depreciation and amortization	(2.0)	(9.9)	(4.4)
Selling and administrative	(1.4)	(12.1)	(29.3)
Research and development	(1.6)	—	(12.2)
Interest (expense)/income	9.5	(2.8)	(0.1)
Income taxes	(14.3)	(0.1)	(6.2)
All other items, net	(8.0)	0.1	1.6
Net Income	27.6%	13.6%	20.3%
Cash flow from operations/capital expenditures	n.m.	1.0	4.9

[a]See the problem narrative for items included in operating expenses.

LO 1-2, LO 1-5

1.11 Effect of Industry Characteristics on Financial Statement Relations.
Effective financial statement analysis requires an understanding of a firm's economic characteristics. The relations between various financial statement items provide evidence of many of these economic characteristics. Exhibit 1.23 (pages 62–63) presents common-size condensed balance sheets and income statements for 12 firms in different industries. These common-size balance sheets and income statements express various items as a percentage of operating revenues. (That is, the statement divides all amounts by operating revenues for

Exhibit 1.22 (Continued)

4	5	6	7	8	9	10	11	12
2.0%	10.6%	96.9%	4.1%	2,198.0%	26.0%	4.5%	1.9%	39.3%
8.9	12.0	8.8	4.2	1,384.8	4.0	13.3	2.0	5.1
7.0	2.1	3.0	1.5	—	8.9	4.0	1.3	—
55.4	221.5	33.8	278.8	—	7.8	41.4	61.1	32.9
(32.5)	(132.6)	(22.6)	(52.8)	—	(2.6)	(14.1)	(28.3)	(18.9)
22.9%	88.9%	11.2%	226.0%	—	5.3%	27.3%	32.9%	14.0%
39.8	75.2	40.5	6.0	101.9%	5.0	109.4	8.3	90.9
4.8	19.0	28.3	81.0	208.5	7.2	59.7	11.4	33.3
85.4%	207.9%	188.6%	322.9%	3,893.3%	56.4%	218.2%	57.9%	182.6%
27.7%	26.6%	37.8%	41.7%	2,878.4%	30.0%	20.7%	15.3%	43.4%
31.7	48.2	28.5	172.2	596.1	0.4	38.4	31.6	—
14.6	90.2	15.3	53.8	171.3	4.4	33.9	12.0	9.4
11.3	42.8	107.0	55.1	247.5	21.4	125.3	(1.0)	129.8
85.4%	207.9%	188.6%	322.9%	3,893.3%	56.4%	218.2%	57.9%	182.6%
100.0%	100.0%	100.0%	100.0%	100.0%	100.0%	100.0%	100.0%	100.0%
(58.1)	(40.1)	(36.1)	(56.0)	(73.4)	(85.8)	(59.5)	(75.1)	(26.1)
(2.9)	(15.0)	(1.5)	(10.8)	(5.0)	(1.5)	(5.7)	(4.9)	(2.8)
(23.7)	(27.6)	(27.6)	(19.3)	(5.1)	(2.6)	(27.9)	(7.6)	(33.7)
—	—	(14.6)	—	(7.7)	(5.1)	—	—	(8.5)
(2.5)	(1.9)	1.0	(8.5)	78.4	—	(1.8)	(2.0)	1.3
(3.8)	(3.4)	(4.3)	(2.6)	(16.0)	(1.0)	(2.2)	(2.8)	(4.7)
—	(5.5)	—	2.3	(28.8)	(0.3)	5.2	0.4	—
9.0%	6.6%	17.0%	5.3%	42.3%	3.7%	8.0%	8.0%	25.5%
2.7	1.5	9.8	1.0	n.m.	8.8	1.8	1.6	5.1

the year.) Exhibit 1.23 also shows the ratio of cash flow from operations to capital expenditures. A dash for a particular financial statement item does not necessarily mean the amount is zero. It merely indicates that the amount is not sufficiently large for the firm to disclose it. A list of the 12 companies and a brief description of their activities follow.

A. **Abercrombie & Fitch**: Sells retail apparel primarily through stores to the fashion-conscious young adult and has established itself as a trendy, popular player in the specialty retailing apparel industry.

Exhibit 1.23

Common-Size Financial Statement Data for Firms in 12 Industries (Problem 1.11)

	1	2	3
BALANCE SHEET			
Cash and marketable securities	11.6%	23.0%	9.2%
Receivables	18.2	48.4	25.0
Inventories	17.8	9.6	2.9
Property, plant, and equipment, at cost	87.8	101.2	272.3
Accumulated depreciation	(52.8)	(50.9)	(92.8)
Property, plant, and equipment, net	35.0%	50.3%	179.5%
Intangibles	15.2	8.2	—
Other assets	15.8	58.4	60.5
Total Assets	113.7%	197.9%	277.1%
Current liabilities	30.5%	60.0%	51.2%
Long-term debt	24.0	16.5	70.1
Other long-term liabilities	36.9	42.7	88.9
Shareholders' equity	22.4	78.7	66.9
Total Liabilities and Shareholders' Equity	113.7%	197.9%	277.1%
INCOME STATEMENT			
Operating revenues	100.0%	100.0%	100.0%
Cost of sales (excluding depreciation) or operating expenses[a]	(75.6)	(23.4)	(60.7)
Depreciation and amortization	(4.5)	(6.8)	(12.6)
Selling and administrative	(6.8)	(24.1)	—
Research and development	(4.4)	(20.1)	—
Interest (expense)/income	(1.2)	(1.1)	(4.8)
Income taxes	(1.2)	(8.4)	(3.3)
All other items, net	—	16.7	(10.6)
Net Income	6.3%	32.7%	8.1%
Cash flow from operations/capital expenditures	1.6	5.1	0.8

[a]See the problem narrative for items included in operating expenses.

B. **Allstate Insurance**: Sells property and casualty insurance, primarily on buildings and automobiles. Operating revenues include insurance premiums from customers and revenues earned from investments made with cash received from customers before Allstate pays customers' claims. Operating expenses include amounts actually paid or expected to be paid in the future on insurance coverage outstanding during the year.

C. **Best Buy**: Operates a chain of retail stores selling consumer electronic and entertainment equipment at competitively low prices.

D. **E. I. du Pont de Nemours**: Manufactures chemical and electronics products.

Exhibit 1.23 (Continued)

4	5	6	7	8	9	10	11	12
362.6%	6.0%	1.1%	1.6%	14.7%	8.3%	27.3%	8.8%	11.6%
47.7	8.9	4.1	15.7	2.7	43.2	697.5	4.0	16.8
—	8.7	10.6	—	10.5	5.0	—	0.5	5.3
10.3	46.4	15.4	6.9	66.1	13.1	3.2	132.4	18.3
(6.7)	(21.8)	(6.1)	(3.7)	(26.6)	(7.7)	(1.3)	(46.3)	(8.5)
3.6%	24.6%	9.3%	3.1%	39.5%	5.4%	1.9%	86.1%	9.8%
2.8	112.8	6.0	2.6	—	55.7	40.9	9.5	34.7
120.7	9.5	4.1	4.7	12.9	12.0	26.7	12.2	22.0
537.5%	170.6%	35.2%	27.8%	80.5%	129.6%	794.3%	121.0%	100.2%
391.7%	39.1%	18.7%	10.3%	12.7%	73.0%	122.1%	10.8%	37.5%
19.4	26.1	2.5	0.9	2.8	22.9	565.5	43.3	12.2
51.3	25.5	3.6	2.7	12.8	7.4	20.2	10.0	15.1
75.1	79.8	10.3	13.9	52.1	26.4	86.5	56.9	35.4
537.5%	170.6%	35.2%	27.8%	80.5%	129.6%	794.3%	121.0%	100.2%
100.0%	100.0%	100.0%	100.0%	100.0%	100.0%	100.0%	100.0%	100.0%
(91.6)	(49.2)	(75.6)	(82.5)	(33.3)	(87.4)	(29.1)	(63.3)	(76.4)
(0.9)	(3.9)	(1.8)	(0.8)	(5.1)	(1.8)	(1.7)	(5.1)	(4.2)
(10.7)	(23.9)	(18.2)	(15.3)	(49.4)	—	(25.0)	(4.9)	(6.0)
—	(2.6)	—	—	—	—	—	—	(2.5)
21.0	(1.7)	(0.2)	—	0.3	(0.6)	(32.7)	(2.2)	(0.6)
(6.9)	(5.1)	(1.5)	(0.5)	(5.0)	(4.1)	(3.7)	(7.8)	(1.5)
4.2	0.7	(0.5)	(0.1)	—	1.2	(3.3)	1.7	(2.1)
15.2%	14.3%	2.2%	0.8%	7.4%	7.5%	4.5%	18.3%	6.7%
18.7	4.6	1.4	1.6	1.3	6.6	100.9	2.8	3.6

E. **Hewlett-Packard**: Develops, manufactures, and sells computer hardware. The firm outsources manufacturing of many of its computer components.

F. **HSBC Finance**: Lends money to consumers for periods ranging from several months to several years. Operating expenses include provisions for estimated uncollectible loans (bad debts expense).

G. **Kelly Services**: Provides temporary office services to businesses and other firms. Operating revenues represent amounts billed to customers for temporary help services, and operating expenses include amounts paid to the temporary help employees of Kelly.

H. **McDonald's**: Operates fast-food restaurants worldwide. A large percentage of McDonald's restaurants are owned and operated by franchisees. McDonald's frequently owns the restaurant buildings of franchisees and leases them to franchisees under long-term leases.

I. **Merck**: A leading research-driven pharmaceutical products and services company. Merck discovers, develops, manufactures, and markets a broad range of products to improve human and animal health directly and through its joint ventures.

J. **Omnicom Group**: Creates advertising copy for clients and is the largest marketing services firm in the world. Omnicom purchases advertising time and space from various media and sells it to clients. Operating revenues represent commissions and fees earned by creating advertising copy and selling media time and space. Operating expenses includes employee compensation.

K. **Pacific Gas & Electric**: Generates and sells power to customers in the western United States.

L. **Procter & Gamble**: Manufactures and markets a broad line of branded consumer products.

REQUIRED

Use the ratios to match the companies in Exhibit 1.23 with the firms listed above.

LO 1-2, LO 1-5

1.12 Effect of Industry Characteristics on Financial Statement Relations: A Global Perspective. Effective financial statement analysis requires an understanding of a firm's economic characteristics. The relations between various financial statement items provide evidence of many of these economic characteristics. Exhibit 1.24 (pages 66–67) presents common-size condensed balance sheets and income statements for 12 firms in different industries. These common-size balance sheets and income statements express various items as a percentage of operating revenues. (That is, the statement divides all amounts by operating revenues for the year.) A dash for a particular financial statement item does not necessarily mean the amount is zero. It merely indicates that the amount is not sufficiently large for the firm to disclose it. A list of the 12 companies, the country of their headquarters, and a brief description of their activities follow.

A. **Accor** (France): World's largest hotel group, operating hotels under the names of Sofitel, Novotel, Motel 6, and others. Accor has grown in recent years by acquiring established hotel chains.

B. **Carrefour** (France): Operates grocery supermarkets and hypermarkets in Europe, Latin America, and Asia.

C. **Deutsche Telekom** (Germany): Europe's largest provider of wired and wireless telecommunication services. The telecommunications industry has experienced increased deregulation in recent years.

D. **E.ON AG** (Germany): One of the major public utility companies in Europe and the world's largest privately owned energy service provider.

E. **Fortis** (Netherlands): Offers insurance and banking services. Operating revenues include insurance premiums received, investment income, and interest revenue on loans. Operating expenses include amounts actually paid or amounts it expects to pay in the future on insurance coverage outstanding during the year.

F. **Interpublic Group** (U.S.): Creates advertising copy for clients. Interpublic purchases advertising time and space from various media and sells it to clients. Operating revenues represent the commissions or fees earned for creating advertising copy and selling media time and space. Operating expenses include employee compensation.

G. **Marks & Spencer** (U.K.): Operates department stores in England and other retail stores in Europe and the United States. Offers its own credit card for customers' purchases.

H. **Nestlé** (Switzerland): World's largest food processor, offering prepared foods, coffees, milk-based products, and mineral waters.

I. **Roche Holding** (Switzerland): Creates, manufactures, and distributes a wide variety of prescription drugs.

J. **Sumitomo Metal** (Japan): Manufacturer and seller of steel sheets and plates and other construction materials.

K. **Sun Microsystems** (U.S.): Designs, manufactures, and sells workstations and servers used to maintain integrated computer networks. Sun outsources the manufacture of many of its computer components.

L. **Toyota Motor** (Japan): Manufactures automobiles and offers financing services to its customers.

REQUIRED

Use the ratios to match the companies in Exhibit 1.24 with the firms listed above.

1.13 Value Chain Analysis and Financial Statement Relations.   LO 1-2, LO 1-5

Exhibit 1.25 (page 68) presents common-size income statements and balance sheets for seven firms that operate at various stages in the value chain for the pharmaceutical industry. These common-size statements express all amounts as a percentage of sales revenue. Exhibit 1.25 also shows the cash flow from operations to capital expenditures ratios for each firm. A dash for a particular financial statement item does not necessarily mean the amount is zero. It merely indicates that the amount is not sufficiently large for the firm to disclose it. A list of the seven companies and a brief description of their activities follow.

A. **Wyeth**: Engages in the development, manufacture, and sale of ethical drugs (that is, drugs requiring a prescription). Wyeth's drugs represent primarily mixtures of chemical compounds. Ethical-drug companies must obtain approval of new drugs from the U.S. Food and Drug Administration (FDA). Patents protect such drugs from competition until other drug companies develop more effective substitutes or the patent expires.

B. **Amgen**: Engages in the development, manufacture, and sale of drugs based on biotechnology research. Biotechnology drugs must obtain approval from the FDA and enjoy patent protection similar to that for chemical-based drugs. The biotechnology segment is less mature than the ethical-drug industry, with relatively few products having received FDA approval.

C. **Mylan Laboratories**: Engages in the development, manufacture, and sale of generic drugs. Generic drugs have the same chemical compositions as drugs that had previously benefited from patent protection but for which the patent has expired. Generic-drug companies have benefited in recent years from the patent expiration of several major ethical drugs. However, the major ethical-drug companies have increasingly offered generic versions of their ethical drugs to compete against the generic-drug companies.

D. **Johnson & Johnson**: Engages in the development, manufacture, and sale of over-the-counter health care products. Such products do not require a prescription and often benefit from brand recognition.

E. **Covance**: Offers product development and laboratory testing services for biotechnology and pharmaceutical drugs. It also offers commercialization services and market access services. Cost of goods sold for this company represents the salaries of personnel conducting the laboratory testing and drug approval services.

Exhibit 1.24

Common-Size Financial Statement Data for Firms in 12 Industries
(Problem 1.12)

	1	2	3
BALANCE SHEET			
Cash and marketable securities	313.7%	2.2%	21.8%
Receivables	412.9	8.4	48.8
Inventories	—	27.7	6.9
Property, plant, and equipment, at cost	6.6	186.9	66.2
Accumulated depreciation	(2.8)	(125.4)	(36.5)
Property, plant, and equipment, net	3.8%	61.4%	29.7%
Intangibles	2.4	—	—
Other assets	66.2	33.2	16.2
Total Assets	829.8%	133.0%	123.5%
Current liabilities	120.3%	18.3%	45.4%
Long-term debt	630.8	40.9	22.8
Other long-term liabilities	55.6	24.7	10.1
Shareholders' equity	23.1	49.0	45.1
Total Liabilities and Shareholders' Equity	829.8%	133.0%	123.5%
INCOME STATEMENT			
Operating revenues	100.0%	100.0%	100.0%
Cost of sales (excluding depreciation) or operating expenses[a]	(18.7)	(80.3)	(76.2)
Depreciation and amortization	(0.6)	(6.0)	(5.7)
Selling and administrative	(4.8)	(1.4)	(5.9)
Research and development	—	—	(3.6)
Interest (expense)/income	(69.7)	(0.3)	0.5
Income taxes	(1.1)	(5.1)	(3.5)
All other items, net	(0.4)	—	0.9
Net Income	4.7%	6.8%	6.5%
Cash flow from operations/capital expenditures	(5.5)	1.1	2.1

[a]See the problem narrative for items included in operating expenses.

F. **Cardinal Health**: Distributes drugs as a wholesaler to drugstores, hospitals, and mass merchandisers. Also offers pharmaceutical benefit management services in which it provides customized databases designed to help customers order more efficiently, contain costs, and monitor their purchases. Cost of goods sold for Cardinal Health includes the cost of drugs sold plus the salaries of personnel providing pharmaceutical benefit management services.

Exhibit 1.24 (Continued)								
4	5	6	7	8	9	10	11	12
4.9%	16.2%	32.7%	19.5%	17.9%	43.4%	4.7%	6.0%	6.5%
12.0	17.0	69.6	21.8	38.8	20.4	6.9	6.6	12.2
2.1	1.3	—	4.9	5.8	12.2	5.9	7.8	8.5
195.3	92.8	23.2	35.2	134.7	62.9	82.6	34.5	42.0
(127.9)	(36.9)	(15.2)	(23.6)	(76.0)	(24.9)	(29.3)	(17.7)	(22.8)
67.4%	55.9%	8.1%	11.6%	58.7%	38.0%	53.3%	16.8%	19.2%
87.5	31.6	46.3	27.2	26.5	32.3	4.4	14.1	34.1
25.9	25.5	17.5	18.4	28.5	12.7	4.9	7.7	16.1
199.7%	147.5%	174.1%	103.3%	176.2%	158.8%	80.1%	59.0%	96.6%
40.3%	70.2%	98.8%	40.8%	40.6%	25.3%	25.5%	32.2%	30.2%
8.8	24.9	25.7	9.1	21.3	6.2	23.4	10.8	5.8
80.7	6.3	14.2	13.1	43.5	15.0	8.1	3.6	10.7
69.9	46.0	35.6	40.3	70.8	112.4	23.2	12.4	50.0
199.7%	147.5%	174.1%	103.3%	176.2%	158.8%	80.1%	59.0%	96.6%
100.0%	100.0%	100.0%	100.0%	100.0%	100.0%	100.0%	100.0%	100.0%
(56.1)	(70.4)	(62.4)	(53.5)	(64.5)	(28.5)	(62.8)	(77.9)	(51.3)
(17.8)	(5.8)	(2.5)	(3.4)	(5.1)	(3.5)	(4.5)	(2.1)	(2.4)
(15.9)	—	(26.4)	(25.1)	(22.7)	(20.5)	(24.7)	(16.3)	(30.2)
—	—	—	(13.4)	—	(18.5)	—	—	(1.8)
(4.0)	(1.1)	(1.7)	1.2	(1.4)	0.5	(1.8)	(0.6)	(1.0)
(2.3)	(3.5)	(2.2)	(1.5)	(0.1)	(6.9)	(2.2)	(0.8)	(3.4)
(0.1)	(11.3)	(0.5)	0.2	1.1	0.1	1.6	0.1	7.6
3.8%	7.9%	4.2%	4.5%	7.3%	22.6%	5.6%	2.3%	17.3%
2.3	2.0	6.3	3.0	1.7	4.0	2.7	1.8	2.2

G. Walgreens: Operates a chain of drugstores nationwide. The data in Exhibit 1.25 for
   Walgreens include the recognition of operating lease commitments for retail space.

REQUIRED

Use the ratios to match the companies in Exhibit 1.25 with the firms listed above.

Exhibit 1.25

Common-Size Financial Statement Data for Seven Firms in the Pharmaceutical Industry (Problem 1.13)

	1	2	3	4	5	6	7
BALANCE SHEET							
Cash and marketable securities	12.5%	1.9%	63.7%	63.7%	12.1%	4.1%	20.1%
Receivables	22.7	5.7	13.8	16.0	18.7	3.9	15.2
Inventories	20.7	7.2	13.8	13.1	3.7	10.7	7.9
Property, plant, and equipment, at cost	34.2	3.9	66.6	73.9	74.2	22.6	43.0
Accumulated depreciation	(13.5)	(2.0)	(27.4)	(24.9)	(27.1)	(5.5)	(20.4)
Property, plant, and equipment, net	20.7%	1.9%	39.2%	49.0%	47.1%	17.1%	22.5%
Intangibles	109.3	6.1	95.5	20.5	5.8	2.3	43.4
Other assets	16.8	2.5	16.9	30.5	8.5	1.6	24.0
Total Assets	202.6%	25.2%	242.9%	192.8%	96.0%	39.7%	133.2%
Current liabilities	30.1%	11.5%	32.6%	30.0%	25.2%	10.7%	32.7%
Long-term debt	100.5	3.3	61.2	47.4	0.0	3.7	12.7
Other long-term liabilities	19.4	1.7	13.3	31.5	5.4	2.6	21.1
Shareholders' equity	52.6	8.8	135.9	84.0	65.4	22.7	66.7
Total Liabilities and Shareholders' Equity	202.6%	25.2%	242.9%	192.8%	96.0%	39.7%	133.2%
INCOME STATEMENT							
Operating revenues	100.0%	100.0%	100.0%	100.0%	100.0%	100.0%	100.0%
Cost of sales (excluding depreciation) or operating expenses	(59.7)	(94.4)	(15.3)	(27.4)	(62.5)	(72.2)	(29.0)
Depreciation and amortization	(8.3)	(0.4)	(7.2)	(4.1)	(3.9)	(1.5)	(4.4)
Selling and administrative	(12.2)	(3.1)	(20.1)	(25.9)	(13.7)	(21.1)	(29.3)
Research and development	(6.2)	0.0	(20.2)	(14.8)	0.0	0.0	(12.2)
Interest (expense)/income	(6.9)	(0.2)	0.2	(0.1)	0.4	(0.1)	(0.1)
Income taxes	(2.7)	(0.5)	(7.0)	(8.4)	(4.3)	(1.8)	(6.2)
All other items, net	0.1	0.0	(2.5)	(0.1)	(5.3)	0.0	1.6
Net Income	4.1%	1.3%	28.0%	19.3%	10.5%	3.2%	20.3%
Cash flow from operations/capital expenditures	2.3	3.0	8.9	4.4	4.0	2.2	4.9

INTEGRATIVE CASE 1.1

Starbucks

The first case at the end of this chapter and numerous subsequent chapters is a series of integrative cases involving **Starbucks**. The series of cases applies the concepts and analytical tools discussed in each chapter to Starbucks' financial statements and notes. The preparation of responses to the questions in these cases results in an integrated illustration of the six sequential steps in financial statement analysis discussed in this chapter and throughout the book.

Introduction

"They don't just sell coffee; they sell the *Starbucks Experience*," remarked Deb Mills while sitting down to enjoy a cup of Starbucks cappuccino with her friend Kim Shannon. Kim, an investment fund manager for a large insurance firm, reflected on that observation and what it might mean for Starbucks as a potential investment opportunity. Glancing around the store, Kim saw a number of people sitting alone or in groups, lingering over their drinks while chatting, reading, or checking e-mail and surfing the Internet through the store's wi-fi network. Kim noted that in addition to the wide selection of hot coffees, French and Italian style espressos, teas, and cold coffee-blended drinks, Starbucks also offered food items and baked goods, packages of roasted coffee beans, coffee-related accessories and equipment, and even its own line of CDs. Intrigued, Kim made a mental note to do a full financial statement and valuation analysis of Starbucks to evaluate whether its business model and common equity shares were as good as their coffee.

Growth Strategy

Kim's research quickly confirmed her friend's observation that Starbucks is about the *experience* of enjoying a good cup of coffee. The Starbucks 2012 Form 10-K (page 3) asserts the following:

> Our retail objective is to be the leading retailer and brand of coffee in each of our target markets by selling the finest quality coffee and related products, and by providing each customer a unique Starbucks Experience. The Starbucks Experience is built upon superior customer service as well as clean and well-maintained company operated stores that reflect the personalities of the communities in which they operate, thereby building a high degree of customer loyalty.

The *Starbucks experience* strives to create a "third place"—somewhere besides home and work where a customer can feel comfortable and welcome—through friendly and skilled customer service in clean and personable retail store environments. This approach enabled Starbucks to grow rapidly from just a single store near Pike's Place Market in Seattle to a global company with 18,066 locations worldwide at the end of fiscal 2012. Of that total, Starbucks owned and operated 9,405 stores (7,857 stores in the Americas; 882 stores in the Europe, Middle East & Africa (EMEA) region; and 666 stores in the China and Asia Pacific (CAP) region). In addition, licensees owned and operated a total of 8,661 stores (5,046 stores in the Americas; 987 stores in the EMEA region; and 2,628 stores in the CAP region).

Most of Starbucks' stores at the end of fiscal 2012 were located in the United States, amounting to one Starbucks retail location for every 28,000 U.S. residents. However, Starbucks was clearly not a company content to focus simply on the U.S. market, as it was extending the reach of its stores globally, with thousands of stores outside the United States. At the end of fiscal 2012, Starbucks owned and operated stores in a number of countries around the world, including 878 stores in Canada, 593 stores in the United Kingdom, and 408 stores in China.

Starbucks' success can be attributed in part to its successful development and expansion of a European idea—enjoying a fine coffee-based beverage and sharing that experience with others in a comfortable, friendly environment with pleasant, competent service. Starbucks imported the idea of the French and Italian café into the busy North American lifestyle. Ironically, Starbucks successfully extended its brand and style of a café into the European continent. On January 16, 2004, Starbucks opened its first coffeehouse in France—in the heart of Paris at 26 Avenue de l'Opera—and had a total of 67 stores in France by the end of 2012. The success of Starbucks' retail coffeehouse concept is illustrated by the fact that by the end of 2012, Starbucks had opened over 1,100 company-operated and licensed locations in Europe, with the majority of them in the United Kingdom.

Not long ago, Starbucks' CEO Howard Schultz stated that his vision and ultimate goal for Starbucks was to have 20,000 Starbucks retail locations in the United States, to have another 20,000 retail locations in international markets worldwide, and to have Starbucks recognized among the world's leading brands. Kim Shannon wondered whether Starbucks could ultimately achieve that level of global penetration because she could name only a few such worldwide companies. Among those that came to mind were **McDonald's**, with more than 34,000 retail locations in 118 countries; **Subway**, with more than 34,000 locations in 90 countries; and **Yum! Brands**, with more than 40,000 restaurants in 130 countries under brand names such as **KFC**, **Pizza Hut**, and **Taco Bell**.

Growth in the number of retail stores had been one of the primary drivers of Starbucks' growth in revenues. The most significant area of expansion of the Starbucks model in recent years has been the rapid growth in the number of licensed retail stores. At the end of fiscal 1999, Starbucks had only 363 licensed stores, but by the end of fiscal 2012, the number of licensed stores had mushroomed to 8,661.

Recent Performance

Performance in recent years caused Kim to question whether Starbucks had already reached (or perhaps exceeded) its full potential. She wondered whether it could generate the impressive growth in new stores and revenues that it had created in the past.

In fiscal year 2008, Starbucks opened 1,669 net new retail locations (698 net new company-owned stores and 971 new licensed stores), but this number was well below the initial target of 2,500 new stores and well below the 2,571 new stores opened in 2007. Late in 2008, Starbucks announced a plan to close approximately 600 underperforming stores in the United States as well as 64 underperforming stores in Australia. The store closings triggered restructuring charges that reduced Starbucks' operating income by $266.9 million in 2008.

During fiscal 2009, they increased the restructuring plan to close a total of approximately 800 U.S. stores (an increase of 200), and managed to close 566 U.S. stores during the year. They also announced a plan to close 100 stores in various international markets. The 2009 store closings triggered additional restructuring charges that reduced Starbucks' operating income by $332.4 million in 2009. In 2009, for the first time in company history, Starbucks' net store growth was negative, with a net of 474 stores closed in the United States (92 stores opened net of 566 closed) and only 89 net new international stores opened (130 stores opened net of 41 closed), for a net total closure of 385 company operated stores.

In fiscal 2009, total revenues fell to $9.775 billion from $10.383 billion in fiscal 2008. Fiscal 2009 marked the first year of revenue decline (5.9%) in company history. Prior to 2009, Starbucks had generated impressive revenue growth rates of 10.3% in fiscal 2008; 20.9% growth in fiscal 2007; and 22.2% in fiscal 2006.

Starbucks' revenue growth is not just driven by opening new stores; it is also driven by sales growth among existing stores. Through 2007, Starbucks could boast of a streak of

16 consecutive years in which it achieved comparable store sales growth rates equal to or greater than 5%, but that string was broken with negative 3% comparable store sales growth in 2008. Unfortunately, things got worse in 2009, because Starbucks' company-operated stores generated a negative 6% growth in comparable U.S. store sales, a negative 2% growth in comparable international store sales, and a negative 6% growth in comparable store sales overall.

In response to the downturn in Starbucks' business, in January, 2009, Howard Schultz returned from retirement and reassumed his role as president and CEO of Starbucks in order to restructure the business and its potential for growth. Focal points of his transformation plan included taking a more disciplined approach to new store openings, reinvigorating the Starbucks Experience, developing and implementing even better service and quality, while cutting operating and overhead costs. In addition, the transformation plans included introducing more new beverage and food offerings, such as baked goods, breakfast items and chilled and other foods. A key to Starbucks profit growth lies in increasing same store sales growth via new products. Starbucks regularly introduces new specialty coffee-based drinks and coffee flavors, as well as iced coffee-based drinks, such as the very successful line of Frappuccino drinks and Shaken Iced Refreshment drinks.

Under Schultz's renewed leadership, comparable store sales growth rebounded impressively, to 7% growth among U.S. stores and 6% among international stores. Starbucks' store openings were very conservative in 2010, owing in part to the difficult economic conditions in the primary markets. In the United States, Starbucks only opened a net 3 new stores in 2010—opening 60 licensed stores while closing 57 company-owned stores. Internationally, Starbucks opened 220 new stores in 2010—opening 235 licensed stores while closing 15 company-owned stores. Overall revenue growth also rebounded, reaching $10.7 billion (up 9.5% from 2009).

Starbucks continued this modest new store growth trajectory into 2011. Among company-owned stores, Starbucks opened 49 but closed 51 in the United States and opened 180 but closed 36 international stores. Starbucks' licensees opened 345 new stores internationally and 133 new stores in the United States. Unfortunately, because **Borders' Bookstores** went bankrupt in 2011, it closed the 475 Starbucks' stores that it had licensed. This caused a net negative growth of 342 licensee closings in 2011 in the United States. Overall revenue again sustained healthy growth, with total revenues reaching $11.7 billion (up 9.3% from 2010).

Kim was even more encouraged with Starbucks' growth in fiscal 2012. During that period, Starbucks opened a total of 1,063 new stores. Of those, Starbucks opened 234 company-owned and 270 licensed stores in the Americas. In the EMEA region, Starbucks opened 10 company-owned and 101 licensed stores, as well as 154 company-owned and 294 licensed stores in the CAP region. Overall revenue reached $13.3 billion (up 14% from 2011).

Starbucks also continues to expand the scope of its business model through new channel development in order to "reach customers where they work, travel, shop, and dine." To further expand the business model, Starbucks terminated its licensing and distribution agreement with **Kraft Foods** and now manages its own marketing and distribution of Starbucks whole bean and ground coffee to grocery stores and warehouse club stores. By the end of fiscal 2012, Starbucks whole bean and ground coffees were available throughout the United States in approximately 39,000 grocery and warehouse club stores. Further, Starbucks sells whole bean and ground coffee through institutional foodservice companies that service business, education, office, hotel, restaurant, airline, and other foodservice accounts. For example, in 2012 Starbucks (and their subsidiary, Seattle's Best Coffee) were the only superpremium national brand coffees promoted by **Sysco Corporation** to such foodservice accounts. Finally, Starbucks had formed partnerships to produce and distribute bottled Frappuccino and DoubleShot drinks with **PepsiCo** and premium ice creams with **Unilever**.

Despite Starbucks' past difficulties with store closings, restructuring charges, and negative comparable store sales growth rates, Kim could see some very positive aspects of Starbucks' financial performance and condition. She noted that Starbucks had been profitable in 2008 and 2009, despite the difficulties. She also noted that Starbucks generated record high profits in 2010, 2011, and 2012, suggesting the restructuring and turnaround efforts were proving successful. The restructuring plan was seemingly complete and had helped Starbucks to reduce costs. Further, she noted that Starbucks' operating cash flows had remained fairly strong throughout this period. With its positive operating cash flows, Starbucks had retired all of the $713 million in commercial paper and short-term borrowings during 2009, initiated the first dividend in company history in 2010, resumed repurchasing common shares in 2010, and had grown the combined balances in cash and short-term investments over $2.0 billion by fiscal year-end 2012.

Product Supply

Starbucks purchases green coffee beans from coffee-producing regions around the world and custom roasts and blends them to its exacting standards. Although coffee beans trade in commodity markets and experience volatile prices, Starbucks purchases higher-quality coffee beans that sell at a premium to commodity coffees. Starbucks purchases its coffee beans under fixed-price purchase contracts with various suppliers, with purchase prices reset annually. Starbucks also purchases significant amounts of dairy products from suppliers located near its retail stores. Starbucks purchases paper and plastic products from several suppliers, the prices of which vary with changes in the prices of commodity paper and plastic resin.

Competition in the Specialty Coffee Industry

After some reflection, Kim realized that Starbucks faced intense direct competition. Kim could think of a wide array of convenient retail locations where a person can purchase a cup of coffee. Kim reasoned that Starbucks competes with a broad scope of coffee beverage retailers, including fast-food chains (for example, **McDonald's**), doughnut chains (for example, **Krispy Kreme**, **Dunkin' Donuts**, and **Tim Hortons**), and convenience stores associated with many gas stations, but that these types of outlets offer an experience that is very different from what Starbucks offers. In particular, Kim was aware that McDonald's had started to expand development of its McCafé shops, which sold premium coffee drinks (lattes, cappuccinos, and mochas) in McDonald's restaurants. It appeared to Kim that the McCafé initiative was intended to be a direct competitive challenge to Starbucks' business.

Kim also identified a number of companies that were growing chains of retail coffee shops that could be compared to Starbucks, including firms such as **Panera Bread Company**; **Diedrich Coffee**; **New World Restaurant Group, Inc.**; and **Caribou Coffee Company, Inc.** (a privately held firm). However, these firms were much smaller than Starbucks, with the largest among them being the Panera Bread Company, with approximately 1,700 bakery-cafés systemwide at the end of 2012. On the other end of the spectrum, Kim was aware that Starbucks faced competition from local independent coffee shops and cafés.

Kim recognized that despite facing extensive competition, Starbucks had some distinct competitive advantages. Very few companies were implementing a business strategy comparable to that of Starbucks, with emphasis on the quality of the experience, the products, and the service. In addition, only the fast-food chains and the doughnut chains operated on the same scale as Starbucks. Finally, Starbucks had developed a global brand that was synonymous with the quality of the *Starbucks experience*. Recently, Interbrand ranked the Starbucks brand as one of the world's top 100 most valuable brand names, estimating it to be worth in excess of $4 billion.

The Valuation Controversy

In beginning to research Starbucks' share price (ticker: SBUX), Kim realized that it had experienced a wild ride over the past five years, following a very similar pattern to Starbucks' earnings performance during that time. Starbucks had been one of the hottest companies in the capital market, in large part due to its impressive growth in sales and earnings, up until December of 2006. SBUX's share price had appreciated dramatically, generating cumulative returns that far exceeded those of the S&P 500 over that period. The market for Starbucks' shares cooled beginning in early 2007, with share prices falling from a high of nearly $40 to a low of under $8 in November of 2008. Since that low point, Starbucks' share price began a dramatic recovery. Over the calendar year 2012, SBUX stock price ranged between $42 and $62 per share, and was currently trading at $50 per share, implying a PE ratio of over 28 (based on trailing 12 months earnings per share of $1.79), an earnings multiple that is well above the industry average.

Kim further discovered that the capital markets and analysts have mixed opinions on the SBUX stock value. Kim found one-year-ahead price targets from 24 analysts, ranging from a low of $49 to a high of $65, with a mean (median) price target of $59 ($60). She found that 30 analysts issued investment recommendations for SBUX: eleven recommend strong buy, ten recommend buy, nine recommend hold, and no analysts recommend sell. The consensus analysts' earnings per share forecasts are $2.15 for fiscal 2013 and $2.62 for fiscal 2014.

Financial Statements

Exhibit 1.26 presents comparative balance sheets, Exhibit 1.27 presents comparative income statements, and Exhibit 1.28 (pages 76–77) presents comparative statements of cash flows for Starbucks for the four fiscal years ending September 30, 2012.

REQUIRED

Respond to the following questions relating to Starbucks.

Industry and Strategy Analysis

  a. Apply Porter's five forces framework to the specialty coffee retail industry.
  b. How would you characterize the strategy of Starbucks? How does Starbucks create value for its customers? What critical risk and success factors must Starbucks manage?

Balance Sheet

  c. Describe how "cash" differs from "cash equivalents."
  d. Why do investments appear on the balance sheet under both current and noncurrent assets?
  e. Accounts receivable are reported net of allowance for uncollectible accounts. Why? Identify the events or transactions that cause accounts receivable to increases and decrease. Also identify the events or transactions that cause the allowance account to increase and decrease.
  f. How does accumulated depreciation on the balance sheet differ from depreciation expense on the income statement?
  g. Deferred income taxes appear as a current asset on the balance sheet. Under what circumstances will deferred income taxes give rise to an asset?
  h. Accumulated other comprehensive income includes unrealized gains and losses from marketable securities and investments in securities as well as unrealized gains and losses from translating the financial statements of foreign subsidiaries into U.S. dollars. Why are these gains and losses not included in net income on the income statement? When, if ever, will these gains and losses appear in net income?

Exhibit 1.26

Starbucks Corporation Comparative Balance Sheets
(amounts in millions)
(Integrative Case 1.1)

Fiscal Year Ended	2012	2011	2010	2009
ASSETS				
Current assets:				
Cash and cash equivalents	$1,189	$1,148	$1,164	$ 600
Short-term investments available-for-sale securities	848	903	286	67
Accounts receivable, net	486	387	303	271
Inventories	1,242	966	543	665
Prepaid expenses and other current assets	197	162	157	147
Deferred income taxes, net	239	230	304	287
Total current assets	$4,200	$3,795	$2,756	$2,036
Long-term investments available-for-sale securities	$ 116	$ 107	$ 192	$ 71
Equity and cost investments	460	372	342	352
Property, plant and equipment, net	2,659	2,355	2,417	2,536
Other assets	385	409	418	322
Goodwill	399	322	262	259
Total Assets	$8,219	$7,360	$6,386	$5,577
LIABILITIES AND SHAREHOLDERS' EQUITY				
Current liabilities:				
Accounts payable	$ 398	$ 540	$ 283	$ 267
Accrued compensation and other accrued expenses	1,134	941	936	772
Insurance reserves	168	146	146	154
Deferred revenue	510	449	414	389
Total Current Liabilities	$2,210	$2,076	$1,779	$1,581
Long-term debt	550	550	549	549
Other long-term liabilities	345	348	375	390
Total Liabilities	$3,105	$2,973	$2,704	$2,520
Shareholders' equity:				
Common stock ($0.001 par value)	$ 1	$ 1	$ 1	$ 1
Additional paid-in capital	39	41	106	147
Other additional paid-in-capital	—	—	39	39
Retained earnings	5,046	4,297	3,471	2,793
Accumulated other comprehensive income	23	46	57	65
Total Shareholders' Equity	$5,109	$4,385	$3,675	$3,046
Non-controlling Interests	6	2	8	11
Total Equity	$5,115	$4,387	$3,682	$3,057

Source: Starbucks Corporation, Forms 10-K for the Fiscal Years ended September 30, 2012, and October 2, 2011.

Exhibit 1.27

Starbucks Corporation Comparative Income Statements
(amounts in millions, except per-share data)
(Integrative Case 1.1)

Fiscal Year Ended	30-Sep 2012	2-Oct 2011	3-Oct 2010	27-Sep 2009
Net revenues:				
Company-operated retail	$10,535	$ 9,632	$ 8,964	$8,180
Specialty:				
Licensing	1,210	1,008	875	1,222
Foodservice and other	1,555	1,061	869	373
Total Net Revenues	$13,300	$11,700	$10,707	$9,775
Cost of sales including occupancy costs	$ 5,813	$ 4,916	$ 4,417	$4,325
Store operating expenses	3,918	3,595	3,472	3,425
Other operating expenses	430	393	280	264
Depreciation and amortization expenses	550	523	510	535
General and administrative expenses	801	749	705	453
Restructuring charges	—	—	53	332
Total Operating Expenses	$11,513	$10,176	$ 9,436	$9,993
Gain on sale of properties	—	$ 30	—	$ 0
Income from equity investees	$ 211	174	$ 148	114
Operating Income	$ 1,997	$ 1,729	$ 1,419	$ 504
Interest income and other, net	94	116	50	5
Interest expense	(33)	(33)	(33)	(53)
Earnings before Income Taxes	$ 2,059	$ 1,811	$ 1,437	$ 456
Income taxes	674	563	489	144
Net earnings including noncontrolling interests	$ 1,385	$ 1,248	$ 948	$ 312
Net earnings (loss) attributable to noncontrolling interests	1	2	3	(4)
Net Earnings Attributable to Starbucks	$ 1,384	$ 1,246	$ 946	$ 316
Earnings per share—basic	$ 1.83	$ 1.66	$ 1.27	$ 0.43
Earnings per share—diluted	$ 1.79	$ 1.62	$ 1.24	$ 0.43

Source: Starbucks Corporation, Forms 10-K for the Fiscal Years ended September 30, 2012, and October 2, 2011.

Income Statement

i. Starbucks reports three principal sources of revenues: (1) company-operated stores, (2) licensing, and (3) foodservice and other consumer products. Using the narrative information provided in this case, describe the nature of each of these three sources of revenue.

j. What types of expenses does Starbucks likely include in (1) cost of sales, (2) occupancy costs, and (3) store operating expenses?

k. Starbucks reports income from equity investees on its income statement. Using the narrative information provided in this case, describe the nature of this type of income.

Exhibit 1.28

Starbucks Corporation Comparative Statements of Cash Flows
(amounts in millions)
(Integrative Case 1.1)

Fiscal Year Ended	30-Sep 2012	2-Oct 2011	3-Oct 2010	27-Sep 2009
OPERATING ACTIVITIES:				
Net earnings	$ 1,385	$ 1,248	$ 948	$ 392
Adjustments to reconcile net earnings to net cash provided by operating activities:				
Depreciation and amortization	581	550	541	563
Gain on sale of properties	—	(30)	—	—
Provision for impairments and asset disposals	—	—	—	224
Deferred income taxes, net	61	106	(42)	(70)
Equity in income of investees	(61)	(66)	(61)	(78)
Distributions of income from equity investees	—	—	—	53
Stock-based compensation	154	145	114	2
Tax benefit from exercise of stock options	—	—	—	2
Excess tax benefit from exercise of stock options	—	—	—	(16)
Other	24	33	76	5
Cash provided/(used) by changes in operating assets and liabilities:				
Accounts receivable	(90)	(89)	(33)	—
Inventories	(273)	(422)	123	29
Accounts payable	105	228	(4)	(53)
Accrued liabilities and insurance services	24	(82)	(19)	—
Accrued taxes	—	—	—	57
Deferred revenue	61	36	24	16
Other operating assets	—	—	—	121
Other operating liabilities	—	—	—	61
Prepaid expenses, other current assets and other assets	(20)	(23)	17	—
Net cash provided by operating activities	$ 1,750	$ 1,612	$1,705	$ 1,389
INVESTING ACTIVITIES:				
Purchase of investments	(1,749)	(966)	(549)	—
Purchase of available-for-sale securities	—	—	—	(129)
Maturities and calls of investments	1,796	430	210	—
Maturity of available-for-sale securities	—	—	—	111
Sale of available-for-sale securities	—	—	—	5
Acquisitions, net of cash acquired	(129)	(56)	(12)	—
Net purchases of equity, other investments and other assets	—	—	—	(5)
Additions to property, plant and equipment	(856)	(532)	(446)	(446)
Cash proceeds from sale of property, plant and equipment	5	117	5	—
Proceeds from sale of property, plant and equipment	—	—	—	43

(Continued)

Exhibit 1.28 (Continued)

Fiscal Year Ended	30-Sep 2012	2-Oct 2011	3-Oct 2010	27-Sep 2009
Other	(42)	(13)	2	—
Net cash used by investing activities	$ (974)	$(1,020)	$ (790)	$ (421)
FINANCING ACTIVITIES:				
Proceeds from issuance of commercial paper	—	—	—	20,965
Repayments of commercial paper	—	—	—	(21,379)
(Payments)/Proceeds from short-term borrowings	(31)	31	—	1,338
Repayments of short-term borrowings	—	—	—	(1,638)
Purchase of non-controlling interest	—	(28)	(46)	—
Proceeds from issuance of common stock	237	250	133	57
Excess tax benefit from exercise of stock options	170	104	37	16
Principal payments on long-term debt	—	—	—	(1)
Cash dividends paid	(513)	(390)	(171)	—
Repurchase of common stock	(549)	(556)	(286)	—
Other	(1)	(5)	(8)	(2)
Net cash used by financing activities	$ (746)	$ (608)	$ (346)	$ (642)
Effect of exchange rate changes on cash and cash equivalents	10	(1)	(5)	4
Net increase/(decrease) in cash and cash equivalents	$ 41	$ (16)	$ 564	$ 330
CASH AND CASH EQUIVALENTS:				
Beginning of period	1,148	1,164	600	270
End of the period	$ 1,189	$ 1,148	$1,164	$ 600
SUPPLEMENTAL DISCLOSURE OF CASH FLOW INFORMATION:				
Cash paid during the period for:				
Interest, net of capitalized interest	34	34	32	40
Income taxes	417	350	527	162

Source: Starbucks Corporation, Forms 10-K for the Fiscal Years ended September 30, 2012, and October 2, 2011.

Statement of Cash Flows

l. Why does net income differ from the amount of cash flow from operating activities?

m. Why does Starbucks add the amount of depreciation and amortization expense to net income when computing cash flow from operating activities?

n. Why does Starbucks show an increase in inventory as a subtraction when computing cash flow from operations?

o. Why does Starbucks show a decrease in accounts payable as a subtraction when computing cash flow from operations?

p. Starbucks includes short-term investments in current assets on the balance sheet, yet it reports purchases and sales of investment securities as investing activities on the statement of cash flows. Explain why changes in investment securities are investing activities while changes in most other current assets (such as accounts receivable and inventories) are operating activities.

q. Starbucks includes changes in short-term borrowings as a financing activity on the statement of cash flows. Explain why changes in short-term borrowings are a financing activity when most other changes in current liabilities (such as accounts payable and other current liabilities) are operating activities.

Relations between Financial Statements

r. Prepare an analysis that explains the change in retained earnings from $4,297 at the end of fiscal 2011 to $5,046 at the end of fiscal 2012.

s. Prepare an analysis that explains the changes in property, plant, and equipment from $6,163 at the end of fiscal 2011 to $6,903 at the end of fiscal 2012 and accumulated depreciation from $3,808 at the end of fiscal 2011 to $4,244 at the end of fiscal 2012. You may need to deduce certain amounts that Starbucks does not disclose. For simplicity, assume that all of the depreciation and amortization expense is depreciation.

Interpreting Financial Statement Relations

Exhibit 1.29 presents common-size and percentage change balance sheets and Exhibit 1.30 (page 81) presents common-size and percentage change income statements for Starbucks for 2009–2012. The percentage change statements report the annual percentage change in each account from 2010 through 2012. Respond to the following questions.

t. The dollar amount shown for cash and cash equivalents (see Exhibit 1.26) increased between the end of fiscal 2011 and the end of fiscal 2012, yet the percentage of total assets comprising these assets declined (see Exhibit 1.29). Explain.

u. From 2009 through 2012, the proportion of total liabilities declined while the proportion of shareholders' equity increased. What are the likely explanations for these changes?

v. How has the revenue mix of Starbucks changed from 2009 to 2012? Relate these changes to Starbucks' business strategy.

w. Net earnings as a percentage of total revenues increased from 3.2% in fiscal 2009 to 10.4% in fiscal 2012. Identify the most important reasons for this change.

LO 1-4, LO 1-5

CASE 1.2

Nike: Somewhere between a Swoosh and a Slam Dunk

Nike, Inc.'s principal business activity involves the design, development, and worldwide marketing of high-quality footwear, apparel, equipment, and accessory products for serious and recreational athletes. Almost 25,000 employees work for the firm as of 2009. Nike boasts the largest worldwide market share in the athletic footwear industry and a leading market share in sports and athletic apparel.

This case uses Nike's financial statements and excerpts from its notes to review important concepts underlying the three principal financial statements (balance sheet, income statement, and statement of cash flows) and relations among them. The case also introduces tools for analyzing financial statements.

Industry Economics

Product Lines

Industry analysts debate whether the athletic footwear and apparel industry is a performance-driven industry or a fashion-driven industry. Proponents of the performance view point to Nike's

Exhibit 1.29

Starbucks Corporation Common-Size and Percentage Change Balance Sheets (allow for rounding) (Integrative Case 1.1)

Fiscal Year Ended	Common-Size Balance Sheets				Percentage Change Balance Sheets		
	2012	2011	2010	2009	2012	2011	2010
ASSETS							
Current assets:							
Cash and cash equivalents	14.5%	15.6%	18.2%	10.8%	3.5%	(1.4)%	94.1%
Short-term investments available-for-sale securities	10.3	12.3	4.5	1.2	(6.0)	216.1	329.3
Accounts receivable, net	5.9	5.3	4.7	4.9	25.7	27.7	11.7
Inventories	15.1	13.1	8.5	11.9	28.5	77.8	(18.3)
Prepaid expenses and other current assets	2.4	2.2	2.5	2.6	21.7	3.2	6.3
Deferred income taxes, net	2.9	3.1	4.8	5.1	3.6	(24.3)	6.1
Total Current Assets	51.1%	51.6%	43.2%	36.5%	10.7%	37.7%	35.4%
Long-term investments available-for-sale securities	1.4%	1.5%	3.0%	1.3%	8.4%	(44.2)%	169.4%
Equity and cost investments	5.6	5.1	5.3	6.3	23.5	9.0	(3.1)
Property, plant and equipment, net	32.3	32.0	37.8	45.5	12.9	(2.5)	(4.7)
Other assets	4.7	5.6	6.5	5.8	(5.9)	(2.0)	29.7
Goodwill	4.9	4.4	4.1	4.6	24.1	22.6	1.3
Total Assets	100.0%	100.0%	100.0%	100.0%	11.7%	15.3%	14.5%
LIABILITIES AND SHAREHOLDERS' EQUITY							
Current liabilities:							
Accounts payable	4.8	7.3	4.4	4.8	(26.3)	91.1	5.8
Accrued compensation and other accrued expenses	13.8	12.8	14.7	13.8	20.5	0.5	21.3
Insurance reserves	2.0	2.0	2.3	2.8	15.2	(0.4)	(5.2)

(Continued)

Exhibit 1.29 (Continued)

Fiscal Year Ended	Common-Size Balance Sheets				Percentage Change Balance Sheets		
	2012	2011	2010	2009	2012	2011	2010
Deferred revenue	6.2	6.1	6.5	7.0	13.6	8.5	6.5
Total Current Liabilities	26.9%	28.2%	27.9%	28.3%	6.5%	16.7%	12.5%
Long-term debt	6.7%	7.5%	8.6%	9.8%	0.0%	0.0%	0.0%
Other long-term liabilities	4.2	4.7	5.9	7.0	(0.7)	(7.3)	(3.7)
Total Liabilities	37.8%	40.4%	42.3%	45.2%	4.4%	10.0%	7.3%
Shareholders' equity:							
Common stock ($0.001 par value)	0.0%	0.0%	0.0%	0.0%	0.0%	0.0%	0.0%
Additional paid-in capital	0.5	0.5	1.3	1.8	(2.7)	(61.9)	(27.8)
Other additional paid-in-capital	0.0	0.0	0.5	0.5	n.a.	(100.0)	0.0
Retained earnings	61.4	52.3	42.2	34.0	17.4	23.8	24.3
Accumulated other comprehensive income	0.3	0.6	0.7	0.8	(51.0)	(19.1)	(12.5)
Total Shareholders' Equity	62.2%	59.6%	57.5%	54.6%	16.5%	19.3%	20.7%
Non-controlling Interests	0.1	0.0	0.1	0.2	129.2	(68.4)	(32.1)
Total Equity	62.2%	59.6%	57.7%	54.8%	16.6%	19.1%	20.5%
TOTAL LIABILITIES AND SHAREHOLDERS' EQUITY	100.0%	100.0%	100.0%	100.0%	11.7%	15.3%	14.5%

Exhibit 1.30

Starbucks Corporation Common-Size and Percentage Change Income Statements (allow for rounding) (Integrative Case 1.1)

Fiscal Year Ended	Common-Size				Percentage Change		
	2012	2011	2010	2009	2012	2011	2010
Net revenues:							
Company-operated retail	79.2%	82.3%	83.7%	83.7%	9.4%	7.5%	9.6%
Specialty:							
Licensing	9.1	8.6	8.2	12.5	20.1	15.1	(28.4)
Foodservice and other	11.7	9.1	8.1	3.8	46.6	22.1	132.9
Total net revenues	100.0%	100.0%	100.0%	100.0%	13.7	9.3	9.5
Cost of sales including occupancy costs	43.7	42.0	41.2	44.2	18.3	11.3	2.1
Store operating expenses	29.5%	30.7%	32.4%	35.0%	9.0	3.5	1.4
Other operating expenses	3.2	3.4	2.6	2.7	9.4	40.4	5.8
Depreciation and amortization expenses	4.1	4.5	4.8	5.5	5.2	2.5	(4.6)
General and administrative expenses	6.0	6.4	6.6	4.6	6.9	6.3	55.5
Restructuring charges	0.0	0.0	0.5	3.4	n.a.	(100.0)	(84.0)
Total operating expenses	86.6	87.0	88.1	102.2	13.1	7.8	(5.6)
Gain on sale of properties	0.0	0.3	0.0	0.0			
Income from equity investees	1.6	1.5	1.4	1.2	21.3	17.3	29.9
Operating income	15.0%	14.8%	13.3%	5.2%	15.6	21.8	181.6
Interest income and other, net	0.7%	1.0%	0.5%	0.1%	(18.6)	130.4	867.3
Interest expense	(0.2)	(0.3)	(0.3)	(0.5)	(1.8)	1.8	(38.8)
Earnings before income taxes	15.5%	15.5%	13.4%	4.7%	13.7	26.0	215.1
Income taxes	5.1	4.8	4.6	1.5	19.8	15.2	239.4
Net earnings including noncontrolling interests	10.4	10.7	8.9	3.2	11.0	31.6	203.9
Net earnings (loss) attributable to noncontrolling interests	0.0	0.0	0.0	0.0	(60.9)	(14.8)	(171.1)
Net earnings attributable to Starbucks	10.4%	10.6%	8.8%	3.2%	11.1	31.7	199.7

dominant market position, which results in part from continual innovation in product development. Proponents of the fashion view point to the difficulty of protecting technological improvements from competitor imitation, the large portion of total expenses comprising advertising, the role of sports and other personalities in promoting athletic shoes, and the fact that a high percentage of athletic footwear and apparel consumers use the products for casual wear rather than the intended athletic purposes (such as playing basketball or running).

Growth

There are only modest growth opportunities for footwear and apparel in the United States. Concern exists with respect to volume increases (how many pairs of athletic shoes will consumers tolerate in their closets) and price increases (will consumers continue to pay prices for innovative athletic footwear that is often twice as costly as other footwear).

Athletic footwear companies have diversified their revenue sources in two directions in recent years. One direction involves increased emphasis on international sales. With dress codes becoming more casual in Europe and East Asia and interest in American sports such as basketball becoming more widespread, industry analysts view international markets as the major growth markets during the next several years. Increased emphasis on soccer (European football) in the United States aids companies such as Adidas that have reputations for quality soccer footwear.

The second direction for diversification is sports and athletic apparel. The three leading athletic footwear companies capitalize on their brand name recognition and distribution channels to create a line of sportswear that coordinates with their footwear. Team uniforms and matching apparel for coaching staffs and fans have become a major growth avenue. For example, to complement Nike's footwear sales, Nike acquired **Umbro**, a major brand-name line of jerseys, shorts, jackets, and other apparel in the soccer market.

Production

Essentially all athletic footwear and most apparel are produced in factories in Asia, primarily China (40%), Indonesia (31%), Vietnam, South Korea, Taiwan, and Thailand. The footwear companies do not own any of these manufacturing facilities. They typically hire manufacturing representatives to source and oversee the manufacturing process, helping to ensure quality control and serving as a link between the design and the manufacture of products. The manufacturing process is labor-intensive, with sewing machines used as the primary equipment. Footwear companies typically price their purchases from these factories in U.S. dollars.

Marketing

Athletic footwear and sportswear companies sell their products to consumers through various independent department, specialty, and discount stores. Their sales forces educate retailers on new product innovations, store display design, and similar activities. The market shares of Nike and the other major brand-name producers dominate retailers' shelf space, and slower growth in sales makes it increasingly difficult for the remaining athletic footwear companies to gain market share. The slower growth also has led the major companies to increase significantly their advertising and payments for celebrity endorsements. Many footwear companies, including Nike, have opened their own retail stores, as well as factory outlet stores for discounted sales of excess inventory.

Athletic footwear and sportswear companies have typically used independent distributors to market their products in other countries. With increasing brand recognition and anticipated growth in international sales, these companies have recently acquired an increasing number of their distributors to capture more of the profits generated in other countries and maintain better control of international marketing.

Financing

Compared to other apparel firms, the athletic footwear firms generate higher profit margins and rates of return. These firms use cash flow generated from this superior profitability to finance needed working capital investments (receivables and inventories). Long-term debt tends to be relatively low, reflecting the absence of significant investments in manufacturing facilities.

Nike Strategy

Nike targets the serious athlete with performance-driven footwear and athletic wear, as well as the recreational athlete. The firm has steadily expanded the scope of its product portfolio from its primary products of high-quality athletic footwear for running, training, basketball, soccer, and casual wear to encompass related product lines such as sports apparel, bags, equipment, balls, eyewear, timepieces, and other athletic accessories. In addition, Nike has expanded its scope of sports, now offering products for swimming, baseball, cheerleading, football, golf, lacrosse, tennis, volleyball, skateboarding, and other leisure activities. In recent years, the firm has emphasized growth outside the United States. Nike also has grown by acquiring other apparel companies, including **Cole Haan** (dress and casual footwear), **Converse** (athletic and casual footwear and apparel), **Hurley** (apparel for action sports such as surfing, skateboarding, and snowboarding), and Umbro (footwear, apparel, and equipment for soccer). The firm sums up the company's philosophy and driving force behind its success as follows:

> Nike designs, develops, and markets high quality footwear, apparel, equipment and accessory products worldwide. We are the largest seller of athletic footwear and apparel in the world. Our strategy is to achieve long-term revenue growth by creating innovative, "must-have" products; building deep, personal consumer connections with our brands; and delivering compelling retail presentation and experiences.

To maintain its technological edge, Nike engages in extensive research at its research facilities in Beaverton, Oregon. It continually alters its product line to introduce new footwear, apparel, equipment, and evolutionary improvements in existing products.

Nike maintains a reputation for timely delivery of footwear products to its customers, primarily as a result of its "Futures" ordering program. Under this program, retailers book orders five to six months in advance. Nike guarantees delivery of the order within a set time period at the agreed price at the time of ordering. Approximately 89% of the U.S. footwear orders received by Nike during 2009 came through its Futures program. This program allows the company to improve production scheduling, thereby reducing inventory risk. However, the program locks in selling prices and increases Nike's risk of increased raw materials and labor costs. Independent contractors manufacture virtually all of Nike's products. Nike sources all of its footwear and approximately 95% of its apparel from other countries.

The following exhibits present information for Nike:

Exhibit 1.31: Consolidated balance sheets for 2007, 2008, and 2009
Exhibit 1.32: Consolidated income statements for 2007, 2008, and 2009
Exhibit 1.33: Consolidated statements of cash flows 2007, 2008, and 2009
Exhibit 1.34: Excerpts from the notes to Nike's financial statements
Exhibit 1.35: Common-size and percentage change income statements
Exhibit 1.36: Common-size and percentage change balance sheets

Exhibit 1.31

Consolidated Balance Sheet for Nike, Inc.
(amounts in millions)
(Case 1.2)

As of Fiscal Year-End May 31	2007	2008	2009
ASSETS			
Current Assets			
Cash and equivalents	$ 1,856.7	$ 2,133.9	$ 2,291.1
Short-term investments	990.3	642.2	1,164.0
Accounts receivable	2,494.7	2,795.3	2,883.9
Inventories	2,121.9	2,438.4	2,357.0
Prepaid expenses and other assets	393.2	602.3	765.6
Deferred income taxes, net	219.7	227.2	272.4
Total Current Assets	$ 8,076.5	$ 8,839.3	$ 9,734.0
Property and equipment, gross	$ 3,619.1	$ 4,103.0	$ 4,255.7
Accumulated depreciation	(1,940.8)	(2,211.9)	(2,298.0)
Property and equipment, net	$ 1,678.3	$ 1,891.1	$ 1,957.7
Identifiable intangible assets	409.9	743.1	467.4
Goodwill	130.8	448.8	193.5
Deferred income taxes and other assets	392.8	520.4	897.0
Total Assets	$10,688.3	$12,442.7	$13,249.6
LIABILITIES AND SHAREHOLDERS' EQUITY			
Current Liabilities			
Current portion of long-term debt	$ 30.5	$ 6.3	$ 32.0
Notes payable	100.8	177.7	342.9
Accounts payable	1,040.3	1,287.6	1,031.9
Accrued liabilities	1,303.4	1,761.9	1,783.9
Income taxes payable	109.0	88.0	86.3
Total Current Liabilities	$ 2,584.0	$ 3,321.5	$ 3,277.0
Long-term debt	409.9	441.1	437.2
Deferred taxes and other long-term liabilities	668.7	854.5	842.0
Total Liabilities	$ 3,662.6	$ 4,617.1	$ 4,556.2
Redeemable preferred stock	$ 0.3	$ 0.3	$ 0.3
Common Shareholders' Equity			
Common stock	2.8	2.8	2.8
Capital in excess of stated value	1,960.0	2,497.8	2,871.4
Retained earnings	4,885.2	5,073.3	5,451.4
Accumulated other comprehensive income	177.4	251.4	367.5
Total Common Shareholders' Equity	$ 7,025.4	$ 7,825.3	$ 8,693.1
Total Liabilities and Shareholders' Equity	$10,688.3	$12,442.7	$13,249.6

Source: Nike, Inc., Form 10-K for the Fiscal Year ended May 31, 2009.

Exhibit 1.32

Consolidated Income Statement for Nike, Inc. (amounts in millions except per share figures) (Case 1.2)

Fiscal Years Ended May 31	2007	2008	2009
Revenues	$16,325.9	$ 18,627.0	$ 19,176.1
Cost of sales	(9,165.4)	(10,239.6)	(10,571.7)
Gross Profit	$ 7,160.5	$ 8,387.4	$ 8,604.4
Selling and administrative expenses	(5,028.7)	(5,953.7)	(6,149.6)
Restructuring charges	—	—	(195.0)
Goodwill impairment	—	—	(199.3)
Intangible and other asset impairment	—	—	(202.0)
Other income (expenses)	0.9	(7.9)	88.5
Operating Income	$ 2,132.7	$ 2,425.8	$ 1,947.0
Interest and other income	116.9	115.8	49.7
Interest expense	(49.7)	(38.7)	(40.2)
Income before income taxes	$ 2,199.9	$ 2,502.9	$ 1,956.5
Provision for income taxes	(708.4)	(619.5)	(469.8)
Net Income	$ 1,491.5	$ 1,883.4	$ 1,486.7
Net income per share			
Basic	$ 2.96	$ 3.80	$ 3.07
Diluted	$ 2.93	$ 3.74	$ 3.03

Source: Nike, Inc., Form 10-K for the Fiscal Year ended May 31, 2009.

REQUIRED

Study the financial statements and notes for Nike and respond to the following questions.

Income Statement

a. Identify the time at which Nike recognizes revenues. Does this timing of revenue recognition seem appropriate? Explain.

b. Identify the cost-flow assumption(s) that Nike uses to measure cost of goods sold. Does Nike's choice of cost-flow assumption(s) seem appropriate? Explain.

c. Nike reports property, plant, and equipment on its balance sheet and discloses the amount of depreciation for each year in its statement of cash flows. Why doesn't depreciation expense appear among its expenses on the income statement?

d. Identify the portion of Nike's income tax expense of $469.8 million for 2009 that is currently payable to governmental entities and the portion that is deferred to future years. Why is the amount currently payable to governmental entities in 2009 greater than the income tax expense?

Exhibit 1.33

Consolidated Statement of Cash Flows for Nike
(amounts in millions)
(Case 1.2)

Fiscal Years Ended May 31	2007	2008	2009
OPERATING ACTIVITIES:			
Net income	$ 1,491.5	$ 1,883.4	$1,486.7
Depreciation	269.7	303.6	335.0
Deferred income taxes, net	34.1	(300.6)	(294.1)
Stock-based compensation	147.7	141.0	170.6
Impairments of goodwill, intangibles and other assets	—	—	401.3
Gain on divestiture	—	(60.6)	—
Amortization and other	0.5	17.9	48.3
Changes in operating assets and liabilities:			
Increase in accounts receivable	(39.6)	(118.3)	(238.0)
Decrease (Increase) in inventories	(49.5)	(249.8)	32.2
Decrease (Increase) in prepaid expenses	(60.8)	(11.2)	14.1
(Decrease) Increase in payables and accrued liabilities	85.1	330.9	(220.0)
Cash Provided by Operations	$ 1,878.7	$ 1,936.3	$1,736.1
INVESTING ACTIVITIES:			
Purchases, sales, maturities of investment securities	$ 382.4	$ 380.4	$ (518.7)
Net additions to property, plant and equipment	(285.2)	(447.3)	(423.7)
Acquisition of subsidiary, net of cash acquired	—	(571.1)	—
Proceeds from divestiture	—	246.0	—
Other investing activities	(4.3)	(97.8)	144.3
Cash Used in (provided by) Investing Activities	$ 92.9	$ (489.8)	$ (798.1)
FINANCING ACTIVITIES:			
Proceeds from notes payable	$ 52.6	$ 63.7	$ 177.1
Net (payments on) proceeds from long-term debt	(213.9)	(35.2)	(6.8)
Proceeds from exercise of stock options	322.9	343.3	186.6
Excess tax benefit from exercise of stock options	55.8	63.0	25.1
Repurchases of common equity shares	(985.2)	(1,248.0)	(649.2)
Dividends—common and preferred	(343.7)	(412.9)	(466.7)
Cash Used by Financing Activities	$(1,111.5)	$(1,226.1)	$ (733.9)
Effects of exchange rate changes on cash	$ 42.4	$ 56.8	$ (46.9)
Net Change in Cash and Cash Equivalents	$ 902.5	$ 277.2	$ 157.2
Beginning Cash and Cash Equivalents	954.2	1,856.7	2,133.9
Ending Cash and Cash Equivalents	$ 1,856.7	$ 2,133.9	$2,291.1

Source: Nike, Inc., Form 10-K for the Fiscal Year ended May 31, 2009.

Exhibit 1.34

Excerpts from Notes to Consolidated Financial Statements for Nike
(amounts in millions)
(Case 1.2)

Summary of Significant Accounting Policies

Recognition of Revenues: Nike recognizes wholesale revenues when the risks and rewards of ownership have passed to the customer, based on the terms of sale. This occurs upon shipment or upon receipt by the customer depending on the country of the sale and the agreement with the customer. Nike recognizes revenue at time of retail sales to its customers. Provisions for sales discounts and returns are made at the time of sale.

Allowance for Uncollectible Accounts Receivable: Accounts receivable consists principally of amounts receivable from customers. Nike makes ongoing estimates relating to the collectability of our accounts receivable and maintains an allowance for estimated losses resulting from the inability of our customers to make required payments. The allowance for uncollectible accounts receivable was $110.8 million and $78.4 million at May 31, 2009 and 2008, respectively.

Inventory Valuation: Inventories appear at lower of cost or market. Nike determines cost using the first-in, first-out (FIFO) method.

Property, Plant and Equipment and Depreciation: Property, plant and equipment are recorded at acquisition cost. Nike computes depreciation using the straight-line method. Estimated useful lives are over 2 to 40 years for buildings and leasehold improvements; over 2 to 15 years for machinery and equipment; and over 3 to 10 years for computer software.

Identifiable Intangible Assets and Goodwill: This account represents the excess of the purchase price of acquired businesses over the market values of identifiable net assets, net of amortization to date on assets with limited lives.

Foreign Currency Translation: Adjustments resulting from translating foreign functional currency financial statements into U.S. dollars and gains and losses from derivatives that Nike uses to hedge changes in exchange rate are included in accumulated other comprehensive income.

Income Taxes: Nike provides deferred income taxes for temporary differences between income before taxes for financial reporting and tax reporting. Income tax expense includes the following:

	2007	2008	2009
Currently Payable	$674.1	$ 920.1	$ 763.9
Deferred	34.3	(300.6)	(294.1)
Income Tax Expense	$708.4	$ 619.5	$ 469.8

Stock Repurchases: Nike repurchases outstanding shares of its common stock each year and retires them. Any difference between the price paid and the book value of the shares appears as an adjustment of retained earnings.

Source: Nike, Inc., Form 10-K for the Fiscal Year ended May 31, 2009.

Exhibit 1.35

Common-Size and Percentage Change Income Statements for Nike
(Case 1.2)

Fiscal Years Ended May 31	Common-Size Income Statements			Percentage Change Income Statements			Compound Growth
	2007	2008	2009	2008	2009		
Revenues	100.0%	100.0%	100.0%	14.1%	2.9%		8.4%
Cost of sales	(56.1)	(55.0)	(55.1)	11.7	3.2		7.4
Gross Profit	43.9%	45.0%	44.9%	17.1	2.6		9.6
Selling and administrative expenses	(30.8)	(32.0)	(32.1)	18.4	3.3		10.6
Restructuring charges	0.0	0.0	(1.0)	n.m.	n.m.		n.m.
Goodwill impairment	0.0	0.0	(1.0)	n.m.	n.m.		n.m.
Intangible and other asset impairment	0.0	0.0	(1.1)	n.m.	n.m.		n.m.
Other income (expenses)	0.0	0.0	0.5	n.m.	n.m.		n.m.
Operating Income	13.1%	13.0%	10.2%	13.7	(19.7)		(4.5)
Interest and other income	0.7	0.6	0.3	(0.9)	(57.1)		(34.8)
Interest expense	(0.3)	(0.2)	(0.2)	(22.1)	3.9		(10.1)
Income before income taxes	13.5%	13.4%	10.3%	13.8	(21.8)		(5.7)
Provision for income taxes	(4.4)	(3.3)	(2.5)	(12.5)	(24.2)		(18.6)
Net Income	9.1%	10.1%	7.8%	26.3	(21.1)		(0.2)

Exhibit 1.36

Common-Size and Percentage Change Balance Sheets for Nike
(Case 1.2)

As of Fiscal Year End May 31	Common-Size Balance Sheets			Percentage Change Balance Sheets		Compound Growth
	2007	2008	2009	2008	2009	
ASSETS						
Current Assets						
Cash and equivalents	17.4%	17.1%	17.3%	14.9%	7.4%	11.1%
Short-term investments	9.3	5.2	8.8	(35.2)	81.3	8.4
Accounts receivable	23.3	22.5	21.8	12.0	3.2	7.5
Inventories	19.9	19.6	17.8	14.9	(3.3)	5.4
Prepaid expenses and other assets	3.7	4.8	5.8	53.2	27.1	39.5
Deferred income taxes, net	2.0	1.8	2.0	3.4	19.9	11.3
Total Current Assets	75.6%	71.0%	73.5%	9.4	10.1	9.8
Property and equipment, gross	33.9%	33.0%	32.1%	13.4	3.7	8.4
Accumulated depreciation	(18.2)	(17.8)	(17.3)	14.0	3.9	8.8
Property and equipment, net	15.7%	15.2%	14.8%	12.7	3.5	8.0
Identifiable intangible assets	3.8	6.0	3.5	81.3	(37.1)	6.8
Goodwill	1.2	3.6	1.4	243.1	(56.9)	21.6
Deferred income taxes and other assets	3.7	4.2	6.8	32.5	72.4	51.1
Total Assets	100.0%	100.0%	100.0%	16.4	6.5	11.3

(Continued)

Exhibit 1.36 (Continued)

As of Fiscal Year End May 31	Common-Size Balance Sheets			Percentage Change Balance Sheets		
	2007	2008	2009	2008	2009	Compound Growth
LIABILITIES AND STOCKHOLDERS' EQUITY						
Current Liabilities						
Current portion of long-term debt	0.3%	0.1%	0.2%	(79.3)	407.9	2.4
Notes payable	1.0	1.4	2.6	76.3	93.0	84.4
Accounts payable	9.7	10.3	7.8	23.8	(19.9)	(0.4)
Accrued liabilities	12.2	14.2	13.4	35.2	1.2	17.0
Income taxes payable	1.0	0.7	0.7	(19.3)	(1.9)	(11.0)
Total Current Liabilities	24.2%	26.7%	24.7%	28.5	(1.3)	12.6
Long-term debt	3.8	3.5	3.3	7.6	(0.9)	3.3
Deferred taxes and other long-term liabilities	6.3	6.9	6.4	27.8	(1.5)	12.2
Total Liabilities	34.3%	37.1%	34.4%	26.1	(1.3)	11.5
Redeemable preferred stock	0.0	0.0	0.0	0.0	0.0	0.0
Common Shareholders' Equity						
Common stock	0.0	0.0	0.0	0.0	0.0	0.0
Capital in excess of stated value	18.3	20.1	21.7	27.4	15.0	21.0
Retained earnings	45.7	40.8	41.1	3.9	7.5	5.6
Accumulated other comprehensive income	1.7	2.0	2.8	41.7	46.2	43.9
Total Common Shareholders' Equity	65.7%	62.9%	65.6%	11.4	11.1	11.2
Total Liabilities and Shareholders' Equity	100.0%	100.0%	100.0%	16.4%	6.5%	11.3%

Balance Sheet

e. Why do accounts receivable appear net of allowance for doubtful accounts? Identify the events or transactions that cause the allowance account to increase or decrease.

f. Identify the depreciation method(s) that Nike uses for its buildings and equipment. Does Nike's choice of depreciation method(s) seem appropriate?

g. Nike includes identifiable intangible assets on its balance sheet as an asset. Does this account include the value of the Nike name and Nike's "swoosh" trademark? Explain.

h. Nike includes deferred income taxes among current assets, noncurrent assets, and noncurrent liabilities. Under what circumstances will deferred income taxes give rise to an asset? To a liability?

i. Nike reports accumulated other comprehensive income of $367.5 million at the end of 2009 and $251.4 million at the end of 2008, implying that other comprehensive income items amounted to $116.1 million during 2009. Why is this "income" reported as part of shareholders' equity and not part of net income in the income statement?

Statement of Cash Flows

j. Why does the amount of net income differ from the amount of cash flow from operations?

k. Why does Nike add depreciation expense back to net income when calculating cash flow from operations?

l. Why does Nike subtract deferred income taxes from net income when calculating cash flow from operations for 2009?

m. Why does Nike subtract increases in accounts receivable to net income when calculating cash flow from operations for 2009?

n. Why does Nike adjust net income by subtracting increases in inventory and adding decreases in inventory when calculating cash flow from operations?

o. When calculating cash flow from operations, why does Nike adjust net income by adding increases and subtracting decreases in accounts payable and other current liabilities?

p. Nike recognized a gain from the divestiture of the subsidiary for the Bauer line of hockey apparel and equipment in 2008. Why does Nike subtract the gain on the divestiture from the operating activities? Why does Nike include the proceeds from the divestiture as an investing activity?

q. Given that notes payable appear on the balance sheet as a current liability, why does Nike include increases in this liability as a financing activity rather than as an operating activity?

Relations between Financial Statement Items

r. Compute the amount of cash collected from customers during 2009.

s. Compute the amount of cash payments made to suppliers of merchandise during 2009.

t. Prepare an analysis that accounts for the change in property, plant, and equipment and accumulated depreciation during 2009. You will have to plug certain amounts if Nike does not disclose them.

u. Identify the reasons for the change in retained earnings during 2009.

Interpreting Financial Statement Relations

v. Exhibit 1.35 presents common-size and percentage change income statements for Nike for 2007, 2008, and 2009. What are the likely reasons for the higher net income/sales revenue percentages for Nike between 2007 and 2008? What are the likely reasons for the lower net income/sales revenue percentages for Nike between 2008 and 2009?

w. What are the likely reasons for the decrease in the cost of goods sold to sales percentages between 2007 and 2009?

x. What are the likely reasons for the increase in the selling and administrative expenses to sales percentages between 2007 and 2009?

y. Exhibit 1.36 presents common-size and percentage change balance sheets for Nike at the end of 2007, 2008, and 2009. What is the likely explanation for the relatively small percentages for property, plant, and equipment?

z. What is the likely explanation for the relatively small percentages for notes payable and long-term debt?

a.a. What is the likely explanation for the small decreases in property, plant, and equipment for Nike for 2008 and 2009?

b.b. Refer to the statement of cash flows for Nike in Exhibit 1.33. Cash flow from operations exceeded net income during all three years. Why?

c.c. How has Nike primarily financed its acquisitions of property, plant, and equipment during the three years?

d.d. What are the likely reasons for the repurchases of common stock during the three years?

e.e. The dividends paid by Nike increased each year ($343.7 million in 2007, $412.9 million in 2008, and $466.7 million in 2009). Given that Nike repurchased its stock each year, what is the likely explanation for the increasing amount of dividends?

Asset and Liability Valuation and Income Recognition

LO 2-1 Define the mixed attribute accounting model used to measure assets and liabilities.

LO 2-2 Describe how the mixed attribute accounting model provides for more relevant and representationally faithful information to financial statement users.

LO 2-3 Explain how changes in valuations of assets and liabilities on the balance sheet are recognized on the income statement or statement of comprehensive income.

LO 2-4 Provide an overview of the pervasive importance of income tax effects on reported financial statements.

LO 2-5 Reconcile financial reporting with tax reporting by adjusting for permanent differences and deferred tax assets and liabilities.

LO 2-6 Work with an analytical framework that maps the effects of business transactions and events to the balance sheet and income statement.

Chapter Overview

In this chapter, we review basic financial accounting concepts at a high level, focusing primarily on the features of accounting that lead to what is called the mixed attribute accounting model. To effectively analyze financial statements, you must clearly understand how they are prepared and what economic events and transactions they represent. You might legitimately question whether it is necessary to understand individual transactions—like purchasing inventory or incurring a specific current liability—if the primary concern is to learn how to analyze financial statements at a higher level. After all, firms engage in thousands or even millions of transactions during the year. The reasons for the need to understand how specific events and transactions affect the financial statements are twofold:

■ First, to be able to make appropriate interpretations about a firm's profitability and risk, you must understand the effects of numerous transactions that balance sheet and income statement amounts represent.

■ Second, given the increased complexity of many transactions, effective financial statement analysis requires an ability to deduce how discrete events impact each of the financial statements, especially if your analysis leads you to restate financial statements excluding the effects of some event or under alternative accounting treatment.

This chapter will discuss the building blocks underlying the balance sheet and income statement.[1] Because it is difficult to discuss a line item on one financial statement without referencing another line item or another financial statement, the approach in this chapter is to briefly discuss elements of both the balance sheet and income statement.

Introduction to the Mixed Attribute Accounting Model

Consider the fundamental accounting identity:

$$\text{Assets} = \text{Liabilities} + \text{Shareholders' Equity}$$

LO 2-1

Define the mixed attribute accounting model used to measure assets and liabilities.

At the instant a firm is formed and receives financing (through equity investments of shareholders and/or debt financing from banks), the balance sheet of a company is simple and the valuation of the assets and liabilities is straightforward. For example, suppose an entrepreneur starts a consulting company by borrowing $1,000,000 from a bank. Initially, the value of the assets—all cash at this point—would be $1,000,000, equal to the entrepreneur's liability to the bank. However, valuing the company's assets and the liability becomes less clear (but more interesting) as the company begins deploying that cash, as time progresses, and as operating activities commence. The following are a number of simple but challenging examples that might arise, which you will learn to account for and analyze throughout this chapter and the remainder of this text:

1. The entrepreneur purchases an automobile for use in the business. Is the value of the automobile what the entrepreneur paid for it or what the entrepreneur could sell it for in the used market? If the company also had to pay registration and certain legal fees as part of the acquisition of the automobile, are those fees a part of the value of the automobile?

2. Should the company have to periodically reduce the value of the automobile to reflect the wear and tear and associated decline in its value? If so, how should the company compute the amount of the decline in value each period?

3. If the company acquires a building in which the entrepreneur will work, should the company periodically adjust the value of the building, as it does with the automobile? Unlike an automobile that clearly declines in value over time, the value of a building might increase. If so, should the amount at which the company values the building on the balance sheet be increased? Absent a sale of the building, how would someone estimate the value of the building?

4. The entrepreneur performs consulting services for ten clients and bills each client $5,000. The company now has an asset (accounts receivable) reflecting the amount due from each client, totaling $50,000. However, it is statistically likely that one of the clients will end up not paying the entire bill. Should the company adjust the value of the $50,000 asset to reflect this fact? If so, how much should the value of the asset be reduced? Is the reason for reflecting this

---

[1]As noted in Chapter 1, the primary financial statements include the balance sheet and income statement, with the statement of cash flows providing a link between the information in these two statements. Chapter 3 will take up a joint analysis of the income statement and statement of cash flows.

amount in the financial statements to value the accounts receivable on the balance sheet appropriately, or is it to ensure that a cost of doing business (that is, selling to people who do not pay) is properly reflected on the income statement, or is it both?

5. The entrepreneur invests some of the remaining cash from the bank loan into a mutual fund. After several months, the value of the mutual fund investment has increased. Should the company adjust the value of this investment on its balance sheet? What should the company do if the investment falls back to the initial amount invested? What if the value falls below the initial amount invested? Should the company report each of these adjustments to the balance sheet as a gain or a loss on the income statement?

If these hypothetical questions are prompted by an example of a company with limited assets and liabilities, imagine how the valuation of assets and liabilities becomes increasingly complex when real companies engage in numerous and diverse activities. There are the many different approaches companies must use to value assets and liabilities in their financial statements under U.S. GAAP and IFRS, depending on the nature of the asset or liability. This variety provides insight into what is meant by the term *mixed attribute accounting model.*[2]

Double-Entry Bookkeeping

An important feature of accounting is that the valuation of assets and liabilities on the balance sheet and the recognition and measurement of income on the income statement are not separable. Double-entry bookkeeping views transactions as having two equal sides, which requires that at least two accounts be affected when transactions and events are recorded. That is, the "double" in double-entry bookkeeping refers to the fact that there must be *at least* one debit to some account and *at least* one credit to another. For example, the incorporation of the hypothetical business above led to an increase in an asset (cash) and an increase in a liability (the bank loan and promise to repay). Exhibit 2.1 provides additional examples of transactions effecting combined financial statement impacts on the accounting equation.[3]

Relative Usefulness

The intent of the accounting system is to provide relevant and representationally faithful information about both the balance sheet and the income statement, but emphasizing the usefulness of one often affects the usefulness of the other. The two statements are obviously complementary as the balance sheet presents information *as of* a point in time, whereas the income statement presents information about flows *between* two points in time. The *mixed attribute accounting model* that

---

[2]One way to approach the complexity described in this chapter is to apply a standardized framework to analyze the impact of events and transactions on the financial statements; we present this framework later on in this chapter.

[3]After a discussion of asset and liability valuation, the chapter will turn to income recognition. Keep in mind the discussion from Chapter 1 regarding the important difference between *net* income and *comprehensive* income; comprehensive income exists to accommodate various fair value adjustments to balance sheet items.

Exhibit 2.1

Examples of Combined Financial Statement Impacts of Various Events and Transactions

Combined Financial Statement Impacts[a]	Examples
Asset and Revenue	Services are provided. *(1) Accounts Receivable increases and (2) Revenue increases*
Asset and Expense	Current month wages are incurred and paid. *(1) Cash decreases and (2) Wages Expense increases*
Asset and Asset	A customer pays for services provided previously. *(1) Cash increases and (2) Accounts Receivable decreases*
Asset and Liability	A customer prepays for services. *(1) Cash increases and (2) Unearned Revenue increases*
Asset and Equity	A company raises capital by issuing shares for cash. *(1) Cash increases and (2) Common Stock and Paid-in Capital increase*
Liability and Liability	A company refinances a short-term loan. *(1) Short-Term Debt decreases and (2) Long-Term Debt increases*
Liability and Equity	A company declares a cash dividend. *(1) Dividends Payable increases and (2) Retained Earnings decreases*
Liability and Revenue	Service is provided to a customer who had prepaid. *(1) Unearned Revenue decreases and (2) Revenue increases*
Liability and Expense	Salaries accrued but not paid at month end are recorded. *(1) Salaries Payable increases and (2) Salaries Expense increases*

[a]It is helpful to recall the definitions of revenues and expenses to better understand the links among income statement and balance sheet items in this exhibit. Revenues are defined as "inflows or other enhancements of assets of an entity or settlements of its liabilities (or a combination of both) from delivering or producing goods, rendering services, or other activities that constitute the entity's ongoing major or central operations." Similarly, expenses are defined as "outflows or other using up of assets or incurrences of liabilities (or a combination of both) from delivering or producing goods, rendering services, or carrying out other activities that constitute the entity's ongoing major or central operations." *Statement of Financial Accounting Concepts No. 6,* "Elements of Financial Statements."

characterizes most accounting standards implies that there is a mix of emphases on balance sheet versus income statement accounts. The varying emphases on different accounts are a direct result of the attempt by standard setters to optimize relevant information given various constraints on the representational faithfulness of measurement.

Academic research has examined the overall relative usefulness of the balance sheet and income statement to explain common stock prices. The evidence supports the notion that over the past several decades, financial statements appear to have become more in line with a balance sheet emphasis relative to an income statement emphasis. Based on data from a study by Collins, Maydew, and Weiss (1997), Exhibit 2.2 shows the incremental power of earnings (income statement emphasis) and book value of equity (balance sheet emphasis) to explain common stock prices over four decades. A decreasing trend line suggests a decline in the ability of a measure to explain security prices relative to the other. Consistent with the claims of many observers, the incremental explanatory power of book values increased relative to earnings over the period.

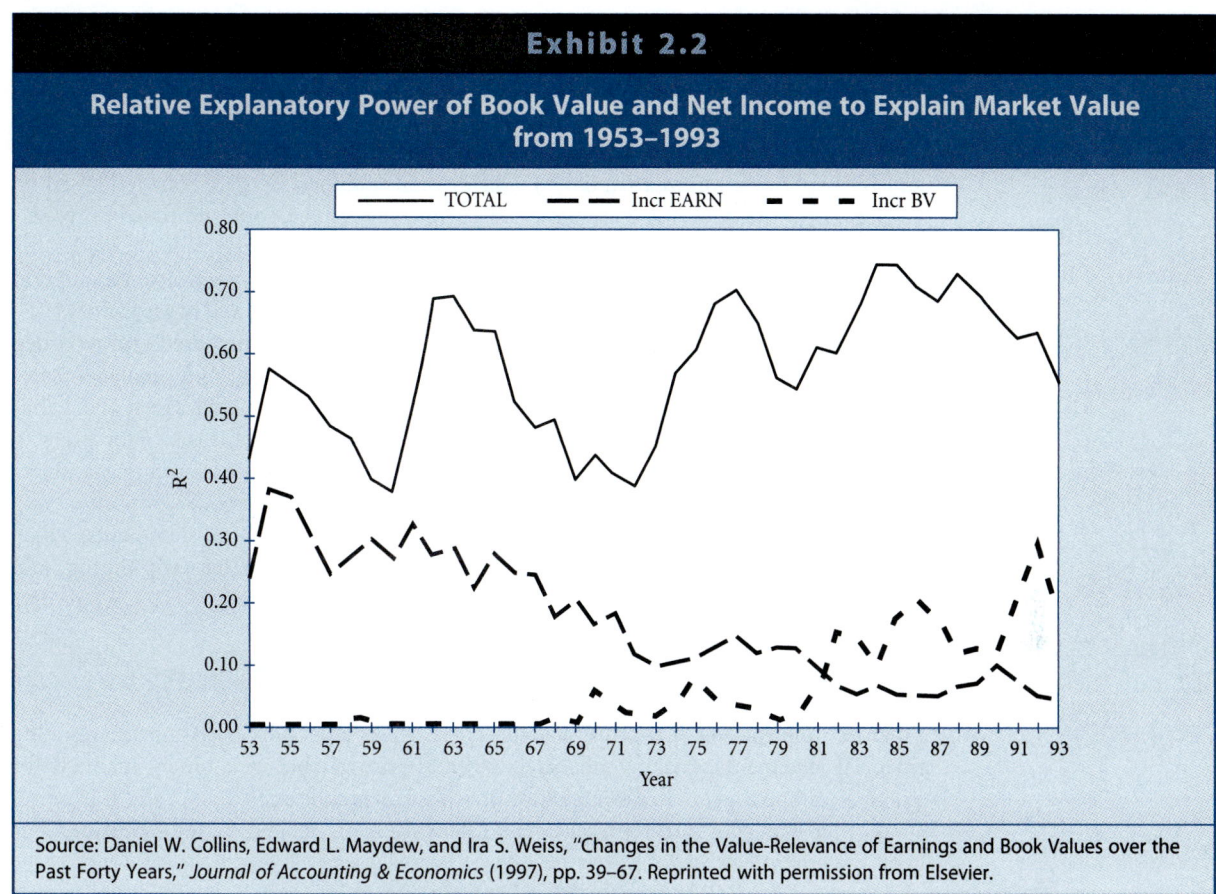

Exhibit 2.2

Relative Explanatory Power of Book Value and Net Income to Explain Market Value from 1953–1993

Source: Daniel W. Collins, Edward L. Maydew, and Ira S. Weiss, "Changes in the Value-Relevance of Earnings and Book Values over the Past Forty Years," *Journal of Accounting & Economics* (1997), pp. 39–67. Reprinted with permission from Elsevier.

Moreover, the study documented that the overall ability of both book value and earnings has increased over this four-decade period, consistent with increasing usefulness of financial statements.[4]

Asset and Liability Valuation and the Trade-Off between Relevance and Representational Faithfulness

LO 2-2

Describe how the mixed attribute accounting model provides for more relevant and representationally faithful information to financial statement users.

As described in Chapter 1, the balance sheet reports the assets of a firm and the claims on those assets by creditors (liabilities) and owners (shareholders' equity) at a moment in time. A useful way to think about assets, liabilities, and shareholders' equity is that liabilities and shareholders' equity represent the capital contributed by suppliers, lending institutions, and shareholders so that the company can acquire operating assets to use in profit-generating activities. Our focus in this section is on a conceptual

---

[4]Some observers of accounting regulators like the FASB and IASB have argued that the recent trend in new accounting rules reflects gravitation away from an income statement emphasis to a balance sheet emphasis.

understanding of how assets and liabilities should be valued and reported in the financial statements.[5]

Assets provide economic benefits to a firm in the future, and liabilities require firms to sacrifice economic resources in the future. Although assets and liabilities clearly have a future orientation, balance sheet accounting for assets and liabilities under U.S. GAAP and IFRS follows a *mixed attribute accounting model*. Some assets are reported based on original (historic) cost, some are based on current fair values, some are based on realizable values, and others are based on a hybrid approach. Similarly, some liabilities are measured at the initial amount of the incurred liability, whereas others are measured at the current value of the liability based on prevailing interest rates and other factors.

An obvious question is, why aren't all assets and liabilities measured and recorded using the same measurement attribute? Wouldn't that greatly simplify financial statement analysis? For example, it might seem obvious that reporting all assets and liabilities at historical values or all at current fair values would make it easier for users to understand financial statements. The reason most high-quality accounting standards follow a mixed attribute model is because regulators attempt to provide an optimal mix of *relevant* and *representationally faithful* information in the financial statements, which helps users better translate the information into assessments of the risk, timing, and amounts of future cash flows.

Relevance and Representational Faithfulness

Financial information is *relevant* if it can affect a user's decision based on the reported financial statements. Making financial information available in a timely manner, for example, is one aspect of relevance. Information is *representationally faithful* if it represents what it purports to represent. The following is articulated by the FASB in Concepts Statement No. 9:

> Relevant financial information is capable of making a difference in the decisions made by users. Information may be capable of making a difference in a decision even if some users choose not to take advantage of it or already are aware of it from other sources.

> Financial reports represent economic phenomena in words and numbers. To be useful, financial information not only must represent relevant phenomena, but it also must faithfully represent the phenomena that it purports to represent. To be a perfectly faithful representation, a depiction would have three characteristics. It would be complete, neutral, and free from error. Of course, perfection is seldom, if ever, achievable. The Board's objective is to maximize those qualities to the extent possible.[6]

As a consequence of this balancing act to make the overall financial statements as useful as possible to external users, accounting standards require that some assets and liabilities be valued based on more representationally faithful information and others must be based on more representaionally faithful information.

---

[5]For purposes here, do not become anxious about mastering procedures for analyzing specific assets or liabilities. Such analyses are addressed in subsequent chapters.

[6]Financial Accounting Standards Board, *Statement of Financial Accounting Concepts No. 8*, "Chapter 1, The Objective of General Purpose Financial Reporting, and Chapter 3, Qualitative Characteristics of Useful Financial Information" (September 2010).

Accounting Quality

One way to view financial accounting amounts is that they reflect the following symbolic equation,

$$\text{Financial Accounting Amounts} = f(\text{Economics, Measurement Error, Bias})$$

In words, this means that users can view financial accounting numbers as a function of several features of the financial reporting process. First, and most importantly, the aim of financial statements is to provide useful information regarding the 'true economics' of a firm's financial position or operations. This means that the financial statements capture and report, in an unbiased manner, the underlying economics. Managers are responsible for preparing financial statements because they should be in the best position to do so, given their intimate involvement in and knowledge of the firms' operations. Such information is clearly relevant to users who analyze financial information.

The other two features offset the quality of financial statements. Measurement error in reported financial numbers exists because many events and circumstances require estimates. For example, managers must estimate the collectability of accounts receivable, the depreciation parameters for fixed assets, the ultimate liability for postretirement benefits, and so on. Good faith estimates sometimes turn out to be too high, and sometimes too low. The hope is that, on average, such measurement errors cancel each other out. The accounting discretion available to managers in making and reporting accounting estimates, which can lead to measurement error, is granted because this discretion can increase the relevance of the financial statements.

However, managers can also misuse their accounting discretion to inject bias into the reported financial amounts. Managers might bias their estimates in order to help the company appear more profitable or less risky to stakeholders, or for their own personal gain. Managers commonly receive bonus compensation based on realized earnings. The incentive to produce higher earnings, and thus realize higher compensation, can induce a manager to bias necessary estimates. For example, a manager might underestimate the amount of receivables that will ultimately be uncollectible. As a consequence, bad debt expense would be understated, and earnings would be overstated.

Trade-Off

Both measurement error and bias decrease the relevance and representational faithfulness of reported financial information. As noted, these features of reported financial numbers are due to discretion available to managers. Thus, why not remove discretion from managers? The answer pertains to the trade-off of relevance and representational faithfulness already discussed. Without discretion, all firms would have to apply the same accounting principles. For example, accounting rules might stipulate that all firms must recognize a 5% allowance for uncollectible accounts receivable. This would certainly be representationally faithful to the extent that it can be mathematically verified, and it would prevent managers from introducing any subjective bias into the valuation of the allowance for bad debts. However, it would probably not be relevant for many firms where the experienced actual default rate is other than 5%.

As accounting standards are developed, standard setters are mindful of this trade-off between relevance and representational faithfulness and whether capturing the economics outweighs the incidence of measurement error or bias. What results is the mixed attribute accounting model, whereby valuations of assets and liabilities reflect various combinations of historical data, current up-to-date information, and expectations of future outcomes. The astute analyst draws advantage from the information available in the mixed attributes of asset and liability valuation.

The remainder of this section provides brief descriptions and examples of the primary valuation alternatives that are most common for balance sheet accounts. This discussion sets the stage for a more detailed understanding of financial statement information in later chapters.

Primary Valuation Alternatives: Historical Cost versus Fair Value

Historical cost is simply the cost the firm originally incurred to acquire an asset or the original (principal) amount of an incurred liability. *Fair value*, on the other hand, reflects the value of the asset or liability based on current market conditions. At the time of an arm's-length transaction, the historical cost of assets and the original amount of liabilities are equal to their fair values. Over time, their fair values may change. In some instances, adjustments are made to reflect fair values on the balance sheet.[7]

Historical Cost

The historical, or acquisition, cost of an asset is the amount paid initially to acquire the asset. Such historical costs include all costs required to prepare the asset for its intended use, but does not include costs to operate the asset. At the time assets are obtained, acquisition cost valuations are ideal because they are *relevant* insofar as they measure the amounts that firms actually paid to acquire resources, and they are *representationally faithful* because they are unbiased, objective, and verifiable through invoices, canceled checks, and other documents that provide clear support for the valuation.

For example, assume **Mollydooker Wines** paid employees $700,000 to oversee the growing of grapes in its vineyards, to harvest the grapes, and to process the grapes into wine. Depreciation on buildings and equipment pertaining to wine production totaled $250,000. Mollydooker also incurred other operating costs of $150,000 related to wine production. The historical cost of the wine in inventory prior to commencement of aging totaled $1,100,000 ($700,000 + $250,000 + $150,000). Mollydooker Wines will subsequently increase the inventory account in later periods by capitalizing additional costs incurred during the aging process, eventually recording all costs of producing the wine as inventory prior to eventual sale.

One question that often arises concerns the costs to include in the asset amount. Should the acquisition cost of the wine include interest on funds that Mollydooker borrowed to finance production of the wine? Variation in practice exists, and accounting procedures for material amounts should be disclosed in the financial statement footnotes.

A second question concerns the relevance of historical cost valuations to financial statement users. At the time a firm acquires an asset, historical cost valuations are timely and objectively measured, so are both *relevant* and *representationally faithful* to financial statement users. As time passes, however, the historical cost valuation retains

---

[7]Many market observers have concluded that the FASB and IASB have embarked in an increasing effort to measure assets and liabilities at fair values rather than historic cost, although members of both boards dispute this. Indeed, one interpretation of Exhibit 2.2 is that the increasing ability of book values relative to earnings to explain firm market values is a result of this effort.

representational faithfulness but can lose relevance if the valuation becomes dated and does not reflect current values.

Adjusted Historical Cost. Often, firms adjust historical costs downwards. For some assets, the service potential is consumed gradually (like machinery that has a limited life) or immediately (like inventory, which provides all of its benefits when it is sold). As the service potential of an asset is consumed, the consumed portion is expensed (that is, the asset is reduced and an expense is increased). For machinery, the expense is depreciation; for inventory, the expense is cost of goods sold. Over the life during which a firm enjoys the benefits of an asset, the firm should either derecognize—that is, remove the asset from the balance sheet—the asset when its value has been consumed (for example, inventory) or ratably adjust the acquisition cost downward through systematic depreciation or amortization (for example, machinery).

Like historical costs, adjusted historical costs involve a trade-off between *relevance* and *representational faithfulness*. For example, consider a firm that acquires computer equipment for $5 million and depreciates it over four years to an estimated salvage value of $1 million. The valuation of the computer equipment at the end of the four years is based on a combination of a representationally faithful acquisition cost ($5 million) and a good faith estimate of the portion eventually realized through sale or trade-in of the used equipment ($1 million). These estimates attempt to provide valuations that are relevant. Even though the estimates are made in good faith, they are of uncertain amounts and may turn out to be incorrect.

Firms use historical cost valuations and adjusted historical cost valuations for *nonmonetary* assets—those that are not characterized by fixed and determinable amounts of future cash flows. For example, inventories, land, buildings, equipment, and goodwill are examples of nonmonetary assets. When the future economic benefits of an asset are sufficiently uncertain, firms use historical cost and adjusted historical cost as a representationally faithful measure of the asset's value.

Monetary assets and liabilities, on the other hand, represent amounts of cash the firm can expect to receive or pay in the future. Cash, accounts receivable, and notes receivable are monetary assets; accounts, notes, and bonds payable are monetary liabilities. Firms typically value monetary assets and liabilities using present values, although U.S. GAAP and IFRS permit firms to ignore the discounting process for monetary assets and liabilities due within one year.

Present Value. Another type of historical cost is initial present value. If markets are not sufficiently active to provide reliable evidence of fair value, firms can use the present value of expected cash flows to approximate the fair value assets and liabilities.[8] Present value methods are often used with receivables and payables.

Selling goods or services on account to customers or lending funds to others creates either an account receivable or a note receivable for the selling or lending firm. Purchasing goods or services on account from a supplier or borrowing funds from others creates a liability (for example, accounts payable, notes payable, and bonds payable). Discounting the expected future cash flows under such arrangements to a present value expresses those cash flows in terms of a current cash-equivalent value. When the

---

[8]For a conceptual discussion of present value approaches, see Financial Accounting Standards Board, *Statement of Financial Accounting Concepts No. 7,* "Using Cash Flow Information and Present Value Accounting Measurement" (February 2000). For the authoritative literature on fair value measurement approaches, see *FASB Codification Topic 820,* "Fair Value Measurements and Disclosures."

monetary asset or liability is first entered in the financial statements, the present value computation (if the cash flows span more than one year) uses interest rates appropriate for the particular financing arrangement at that time.

For example, assume **Jordan's Furniture** sells a sofa to a customer on January 1, permitting the customer to delay payment of the $500 selling price for five years. An assessment of the customer's credit standing suggests that 6% per year is an appropriate interest rate for this extension of credit (even though there is no explicitly stated interest rate to the customer). The present value of $500 to be received in five years, when discounted back at 6%, is $373.63. A strict application of the initial present value of cash flows valuation method results in reporting sales revenue and a receivable of $373.63 on January 1 and interest revenue and an increase in the receivable of $22.42 (0.06 × $373.63) at December 31. The following year, interest revenue and an increase in the receivable of $23.76 [0.06 × (373.63 + 22.42)] would be recognized, and so on for the next three years, at the end of which the receivable would equal the $500 then due from the customer.

Because financing arrangements between sellers and buyers usually specify the timing and amounts of future cash flows, valuing monetary assets and liabilities at the initial present value of cash flows using historical interest rates is relevant and representationally faithful.[9] Moreover, for multi-year collection periods, the relevance of the present values (versus nominal values) justifies the extra efforts to discount assets or liabilities to the present value of future cash flows. Some subjectivity may exist in establishing an appropriate interest rate at the time of the transaction. The borrower, for example, might choose to use the interest rate at which it could borrow on similar terms from a bank, whereas the seller might use the interest rate that would discount the cash flows to a present value equal to the cash selling price of the good or service sold. These small differences in interest rates usually do not result in material differences in valuation between the entities involved in the transaction.

Fair Value

Because historical cost approaches to valuing assets and liabilities can lose relevance as valuations become old and outdated and do not reflect current economic conditions, the FASB and IASB have increasingly developed accounting standards that value assets and liabilities using *current* or *fair value approaches*, which emphasize relevance while retaining representational faithfulness. The FASB defines fair value as "the price that would be received to sell an asset or paid to transfer a liability in an orderly transaction between market participants at the measurement date."[10] This definition explicitly characterizes fair value as a measure of "exit price," which is the amount for which a firm could sell an asset or pay to settle or transfer a liability. The IASB defines fair value slightly differently, as "the amount for which an asset could be exchanged, or a liability settled, between knowledgeable, willing parties in an arm's-length transaction."[11] This definition allows for the use of an exit price or an entry price (the amount for which a

---

[9]The previous discussion about historical cost presumed that such values are driven by some measure of cash exchange. However, initial present values could also form the basis of historical cost, such as when an asset is acquired by issuing a note payable.

[10]Financial Accounting Standards Board, *Statement of Financial Accounting Standards No. 157,* "Fair Value Measurements" (September 2006). *FASB Codification Topic 820.*

[11]International Accounting Standards Board, *International Accounting Standards No. 39,* "Financial Instruments: Recognition and Measurement" (December 1998). At the time of publication of this text, the IASB was considering a change to the definition of fair value, which matched the exit price notion explicit in the FASB definition.

firm could buy or sell an asset or incur or settle a liability). Differences could arise between entry and exit price approaches, for example, when the market in which a purchase takes place is different from the one in which a sale takes place (such as a securities firm that transacts with retail customers, institutional investors, or other securities firms). In addition to the use of quoted market prices as inputs into current values, accountants sometimes use present value techniques to estimate certain current values (for example, Level 3 assets, discussed below).

Clearly, fair values are of interest to financial statement users, particularly in settings where fair values have diverged greatly from acquisition costs of assets or initial present values of liabilities. An obvious example is found in financial institutions, where the values of financial assets and liabilities change immediately with interest rates. Obtaining "the price" at which assets and liabilities can be exchanged can provide extremely relevant and representationally faithful measurements when they are based on observable prices in orderly markets for stocks, bonds, securities, commodities, derivatives, and other items. However, obtaining "the price" can require management estimates when there is no quoted price in an active market for an asset or a liability. Generally, prices are more readily available for financial assets (and commodities) and liabilities than for nonmonetary assets or liabilities, which is why the trend in financial reporting is to employ fair values for most financial assets and liabilities.

Even among financial assets and liabilities, however, there is wide variation in the availability of quoted market prices. Accordingly, there is a three-tiered hierarchy within U.S. GAAP and IFRS that distinguishes among different sources of fair value estimates.[12]

Source of Fair Value Estimate	Representational Faithfulness
• "Level 1" inputs for estimating fair values are based on inputs that are readily available via prices for identical assets or liabilities in actively traded markets such as securities exchanges.	High
• "Level 2" inputs for estimating fair values include quoted prices for similar assets or liabilities in active or inactive markets, other *observable* information such as yield curves and price indexes, and other *observable* data such as market-based correlation estimates.	Medium to High
• "Level 3" inputs for estimating fair values include a firm's own assumptions about the fair value of an asset or a liability, such as using various data about future cash flows and discount rates to estimate present values.	Possibly Low

As of 2009, it is estimated that the S&P 500 companies report over $6 trillion of assets under fair value (the vast majority of which are financial assets); of those, approximately 10% incorporate Level 3 inputs for fair value estimation.

Fair value approaches to valuation for financial assets and liabilities is becoming commonplace within U.S. GAAP and IFRS. Reporting financial assets and liabilities at fair values also is referred to as "mark-to-market" accounting. Although the relevance of fair values is obvious, given the subjective nature of current value estimation along

---

[12]These are specified in SFAS No. 157, *FASB Codification Topic 820*, and IFRS No. 7. The International Accounting Standards Board amended IFRS No. 7 to incorporate the Level 1, Level 2, and Level 3 disclosures as well.

the continuum of representational faithfulness from Level 1 to Level 3 inputs for assets and liabilities, the representational faithfulness of such valuations is sometimes questioned. For example, Level 1 inputs are applicable for most assets traded on active exchanges with published market quotes, whereas Level 3 inputs relate primarily to illiquid investments such as mortgaged-backed securities. Recent rules released by the FASB and IASB allow firms the option to measure and report certain financial instruments at fair value (with subsequent changes to flow through earnings). The decision to use fair value or historical cost must be made at the inception of the financial asset or liability and retained over the life of that financial instrument; however, firms can make different choices for different instruments. The "fair value option" will be most applicable for financial institutions.[13] Nevertheless, valuations of numerous nonmonetary assets also rely on fair value estimates, either of the asset itself or of the current present value of cash flows expected to be generated by an asset.

Current Replacement Cost. Another form of fair value usage is *current replacement cost*, which is the amount a firm would have to pay currently to acquire or produce an asset it now holds. By virtue of the term's reference to an external market, this is a special case of applying the fair value approach. However, whereas straightforward fair values generally pertain to financial assets and commodities, current replacement cost generally applies to nonmonetary assets. The most common use of current replacement cost is through the application of lower-of-cost-or-market valuation of inventories. Current replacement cost valuations generally reflect greater subjectivity than acquisition cost valuations, but they are the least subjective and most representationally faithful when based on observable market prices from recent transactions in which similar assets or liabilities have been exchanged in active markets. For example, you could obtain reliable measures of current replacement costs of raw commodities by referencing spot prices in commodities markets. When active markets do not exist, as is often the case for inventory or equipment designed specifically for a particular firm's needs, the degree of subjectivity increases. Thus, although replacement cost values are more relevant, subjectivity in estimating them in most markets reduces the representational faithfulness of such values. Nevertheless, users of financial statements may find current replacement cost valuations used occasionally and more relevant than out-of-date acquisition cost valuations.

Net Realizable Value. A hybrid form of historical cost and fair value measurement is the use of *net realizable value*, which is the net amount a firm would receive if it sold an asset (for example, inventory for which current value has declined below cost). Net realizable value is another special case of a fair value approach, but it also shares features of adjusted historical cost valuation, because historical cost provides a reference point to determine whether net realizable valuation is applicable. Thus, this is a hybrid approach and the examples that will be discussed exhibit similarities with other valuation approaches (both historical cost and current value). We include net realizable value within our discussion of current value approaches because of the reference to exit prices. The difference is that rather than estimating the cost of acquiring a similar asset in a hypothetical transaction, the net realizable value approach focuses on

---

[13]Financial Accounting Standards Board, *Statement of Financial Accounting Standards No. 159,* "The Fair Value Option for Financial Assets and Financial Liabilities" (February 2007). *FASB Codification Topic 825;* International Accounting Standards Committee, *International Accounting Standards No. 39,* "Financial Instruments: Recognition and Measurement" (revised June 2005); International Accounting Standards Committee, *International Accounting Standards No. 40,* "Investment Properties" (revised December 2003).

the amount a firm is likely to realize given prevailing market conditions, offset by any pertinent selling costs.

Contrasting Illustrations of Asset and Liability Valuations, and Nonrecognition of Certain Assets

The previous discussion focused on different approaches to asset and liability valuation. As noted, the differing ability to reliably measure many assets and liabilities results in a mixed approach to asset and liability valuation. Some assets and liabilities are measured at historical cost, whereas others can reliably be measured using relevant fair values. Sometimes measurement is so imprecise that accounting standards preclude recognition of various assets (and sometimes liabilities) altogether. For example, uncertainty is extremely high for the ability to value profitable growth opportunities, internally developed intangibles like brand names and supply chain networks, and other intellectual property such as the value of research and development assets. If every asset and liability were able to be reliably valued at fair values, the fair value of assets minus the fair value of liabilities would explain well the fair value—or market value—of the firm. Obviously, this is hypothetical because a significant component of the value of many firms is the opportunity to capitalize on future growth options and profitability, for which reliable measurement is nearly impossible.

In this section, we provide balance sheets for two firms with similar market values to highlight the varying ability of measured assets and liabilities to map into book values and market values. Exhibit 2.3 shows the balance sheet for **BlackRock Kelso Capital**

Exhibit 2.3

BlackRock Kelso Capital Corporation Balance Sheets

	December 31, 2012	December 31, 2011
Assets		
Investments at fair value:		
Non-controlled, non-affiliated investments		
(cost of $849,028,227 and $959,635,127)	$ 850,511,125	$ 890,691,404
Non-controlled, affiliated investments		
(cost of $50,983,674 and $59,633,913)	67,750,172	71,035,799
Controlled investments (cost of $137,337,392 and $78,601,629)	143,336,244	87,225,239
Total investments at fair value (cost of $1,037,349,293 and $1,097,870,669)	1,061,597,541	1,048,952,442
Cash and cash equivalents	9,122,141	7,478,904
Cash denominated in foreign currencies (cost of $0 and $300,380)	—	300,089
Unrealized appreciation on forward foreign currency contracts	369,417	—
Receivable for investments sold	504,996	2,734,705
Interest receivable	14,048,248	16,474,871
Dividends receivable	—	8,493,799
Prepaid expenses and other assets	4,375,527	6,740,517
Total Assets	$ 1,090,017,870	$ 1,091,175,327

(Continued)

Exhibit 2.3 (Continued)

Liabilities

Payable for investments purchased	$ 440,243	$ 421,597
Unrealized depreciation on forward foreign currency contracts	—	1,106,241
Debt	346,850,000	343,000,000
Interest payable	5,277,132	5,592,184
Dividend distributions payable	19,196,418	19,040,586
Base management fees payable	5,626,893	5,293,755
Incentive management fees payable	20,277,930	11,878,159
Accrued administrative services	277,000	144,625
Other accrued expenses and payables	4,692,562	3,689,331
Total Liabilities	402,638,178	390,166,478

Net Assets

Common stock, par value $.001 per share, 200,000,000 common shares authorized, 75,257,888 and 74,636,091 issued and 73,832,381 and 73,210,584 outstanding	75,258	74,636
Paid-in capital in excess of par	917,534,577	983,082,373
Distributions in excess of taxable net investment income	(22,291,022)	(26,165,703)
Accumulated net realized loss	(219,270,607)	(194,505,823)
Net unrealized appreciation (depreciation)	20,808,162	(51,999,958)
Treasury stock at cost, 1,425,507 and 1,425,507 shares held	(9,476,676)	(9,476,676)
Total Net Assets	687,379,692	701,008,849
Total Liabilities and Net Assets	$ 1,090,017,870	$ 1,091,175,327
Net Asset Value Per Share	$ 9.31	$ 9.58

Source: BlackRock Kelso Capital Corporation, Form 10-K, for the fiscal year ended December 31, 2012.

Corporation (Nasdaq GS: BKCC), a publicly traded private equity firm that makes investments in middle market firms, those with market valuations between $10 and $50 million. Accordingly, most of the assets on BlackRock Kelso Capital's balance sheet reflect investments explicitly valued at fair value ($1.061 billion out of $1.090 billion in total assets). The remaining recognized assets reflect cash, various short-term receivables, and a small amount of prepaid expenses and other assets, and the reported values of these assets likely also approximate fair value. On the liabilities side of the balance sheet, the largest liability reflects debt ($347 million out of $403 million in liabilities), which likely approximates fair value. Finally, the remaining liabilities are short-term and their values are also likely at or near fair value. Thus, given that this firm's assets and liabilities all approximate fair values, the book value of the firm is likely to correspond well to market value (again, ignoring the value of unrecognized growth options). Indeed, the resulting book value of $687 million is quite close to the market of just over $700 million in the months after the announcement of 2012 results.

In contrast to the previous example, where most assets and liabilities are recognized at fair value on the balance sheet, consider Exhibit 2.4, which shows the balance sheet for Halozyme Therapeutics (Nasdaq GS: HALO). Halozyme is a biopharmaceutical company that conducts research and development to commercialize products that

Exhibit 2.4

Halozyme Therapeutics, Inc.
Consolidated Balance Sheets

	December 31, 2012	December 31, 2011
Assets		
Current assets:		
Cash and cash equivalents	$ 99,901,264	$ 52,825,527
Accounts receivable, net	15,703,087	2,262,465
Inventories	2,670,696	567,263
Prepaid expenses and other assets	12,752,888	8,332,242
Total current assets	131,027,935	63,987,497
Property and equipment, net	3,700,462	1,771,048
Total Assets	$ 134,728,397	$ 65,758,545
Liabilities and Stockholders' Equity		
Current liabilities:		
Accounts payable	$ 2,271,689	$ 7,556,859
Accrued expenses	7,783,447	5,615,574
Deferred revenue, current portion	8,891,017	4,129,407
Total current liabilities	18,946,153	17,301,840
Deferred revenue, net of current portion	34,954,966	36,754,583
Long-term debt, net	29,661,680	—
Lease financing obligation	1,450,000	—
Deferred rent, net of current portion	861,879	802,006
Total Liabilities	85,874,678	54,858,429
Stockholders' equity:		
Preferred stock—$0.001 par value; 20,000,000 shares authorized; no shares issued and outstanding	—	—
Common stock—$0.001 par value; 150,000,000 shares authorized; 112,709,174 and 103,989,272 shares issued and outstanding at December 31, 2012 and 2011, respectively	112,709	103,990
Additional paid-in capital	347,314,658	255,817,772
Accumulated deficit	(298,573,648)	(245,021,646)
Total stockholders' equity	48,853,719	10,900,116
Total Liabilities and Stockholders' Equity	$ 134,728,397	$ 65,758,545

Source: Halozyme Therapeutics, Inc., Form 10-K, for the fiscal year ended December 31, 2012.

advance patient care. Like BlackRock Kelso Capital Corporation discussed above, Halozyme also had a market value of approximately $700 million in 2012. However, reported values of assets and liabilities on the balance sheet of Halozyme diverge substantially from market value. The company has $135 million of assets and $86 million of liabilities, for a net book value of $49 million. What explains the $651 million difference between the net book value and market value?

Most of Halozyme's *recognized* assets likely approximate fair value. For example, $100 million of the total assets of $135 million are cash and cash equivalents. The rest reflect receivables, inventories, prepaid expenses, and property and equipment. It is possible that the depreciated property and equipment have market values above the adjusted historical cost of $3.7 million, but any such difference is unlikely to explain the $651 million difference noted above. The explanation for the divergence between the reported book value and the market value is that Halozyme has assets that the mixed attribute accounting system has not recognized in the financial statements. Indeed, the company's website indicates that "The company's product portfolio is primarily based on intellectual property covering the family of human enzymes known as hyaluronidases and additional enzymes that affect the extracellular matrix." This intellectual property represents the knowledge acquired from research and clinical trials, patents, and positioning, which will translate into marketable products in the future. In addition, Halozyme likely has the ability to strategically deploy these assets into various opportunities yet to arise. It would be quite difficult to reliably incorporate Halozyme's positioning for future growth into the balance sheet, but the market has attempted to price it at $651 million ($700 market price – $49 million book value).

Unfortunately, important assets like these are not easily recognized under most accounting standards. When companies like Halozyme invest capital and other resources into research and development, those companies are generally required to expense such expenditures rather than recognize "knowledge" assets. Clearly, the value of such assets is relevant to financial statement users, but the representational faithfulness of such estimates is so tenuous that standard setters have defaulted towards expensing these amounts rather than potentially contaminating the balance sheet with immense measurement error and/or managerial bias. Thus, investors are left to come up with their own fair values of such assets, with the measurement error in such estimates explaining the higher-than-average stock price volatility of such firms.[14]

Summary of U.S. GAAP and IFRS Valuations

U.S. GAAP and IFRS do not utilize a single valuation method for all assets and liabilities. Instead, they use numerous valuation approaches for different assets and liabilities. U.S. GAAP and IFRS, for example, stipulate that firms use historical values for some assets and liabilities and current, or fair, values for other assets and liabilities. For this reason, U.S. GAAP and IFRS are mixed attribute accounting models. Revisions to U.S. GAAP and IFRS increasingly require use of fair values in the valuation of certain assets and liabilities. When accounting rules require firms to use fair value for an asset, firms might measure fair value using quoted market prices, current replacement cost, or net realizable value. If markets are not sufficiently active to provide reliable evidence of fair value, firms can use the present value of expected cash flows to approximate fair value. The fair value approach is generally more representationally faithful for financial assets and liabilities that either have observable market prices or contractual future cash flows. Exhibit 2.5 summarizes the use of these valuation methods for various assets and liabilities, which later chapters discuss more fully.

---

[14]The fair values of these unrecorded assets are estimated by analysts and investors when they forecast the future cash flows that these assets produce. Clearly, in the case of Halozyme, the investors and analysts are relying heavily on their knowledge and expertise in the company and the industry in forecasting the rate at which Halozyme will transform its intellectual property into future profitable growth. Using company-specific financial statement information combined with industry knowledge to forecast future cash flows, dividends, and earnings and transforming these forecasts into fair value estimates is the dominant theme in Chapters 10–14.

Exhibit 2.5

Examples of Valuation Methods for Various Assets and Liabilities

Historical Cost

- *Acquisition cost:* Land, intangibles with indefinite lives, goodwill, prepayments
- *Adjusted historical cost:* Buildings, equipment and other depreciable assets, intangibles with limited lives, natural resources subject to depletion
- *Initial present value:* Investments in bonds held to maturity, long-term receivables and payables, noncurrent unearned revenue, current receivables and payables (but U.S. GAAP and IFRS ignore the discounting process on the grounds that discounted and undiscounted cash flows do not result in materially different valuations)

Fair Value

- Investments in marketable equity securities, investments in debt securities classified as either trading securities or securities available for sale, financial instruments and derivative instruments subject to hedging activities, assets and liabilities of a business acquired using the acquisition method, assets and liabilities of a business to be discontinued

Hybrid of Historical and Fair Values

- Current replacement cost of long-lived assets relative to acquisition cost
- Lower of cost or fair value for inventory, net realizable value of inventory, accounts receivable net of an allowance for uncollectible accounts

Income Recognition

We now turn from the balance sheet to the income statement. The two are integrated. The revenues, expenses, gains, and losses reported on the income statement describe changes in assets and liabilities, and net income from the income statement is transferred into retained earnings on the balance sheet at year end.[15] The terms *earnings*, *income*, and *profits* are generally used interchangeably in this text and among analysts, managers, and investors. Historically, earnings, income, and profits refer to *net income*, which is different from *comprehensive income*. As discussed in the previous chapter, comprehensive income equals net income plus other comprehensive income.

In an ideal world, net income for a period would equal all changes in the economic (or fair) value of the assets and liabilities of a firm during that period. However, as discussed in the previous section, it is sometimes very difficult or impossible to measure the economic values of certain types of assets and liabilities with perfect representational faithfulness. Therefore, financial statement users must wrestle with the mixed attribute accounting model, whereby assets and liabilities appear on the balance sheet under different valuation approaches. This is one reason why income recognition sometimes does not reflect all changes in the economic value of a firm. In addition, it is very difficult for

LO 2-3

Explain how changes in valuations of assets and liabilities on the balance sheet are recognized on the income statement or statement of comprehensive income.

---

[15]The income statement reports earnings from a firm's operating activities for a period of time (as the difference between revenues and expenses), but also reports gains or losses realized from investing activities (for example, sale of marketable securities at a gain or loss) and financing activities (for example, retirement of debt before maturity at a gain or loss).

a firm to reliably estimate and report the future value it hopes to generate by introducing new products, entering new markets, creating operating efficiencies, and taking other strategic actions to create future value for shareholders. Therefore, the accounting and financial reporting standards discipline the accounting system and only permit firms to recognize revenues, expenses, and gains and losses that can be reliably measured in terms of changes in assets and liabilities during each period. The relevance versus representational faithfulness trade-off impacts the income statement as well.

Recall that valuation of assets and liabilities falls within a continuum from historical value to current (fair) value approaches. Similarly, we can relate approaches to reporting changes in value on the income statement by appealing to the same continuum, as shown in Exhibit 2.6.

The defining characteristic of Approach 3 is the dynamic between recognition of changes in economic value on the balance sheet and income statement. Sometimes changes in economic value are not recognized on the balance sheet and net income until they are actually realized (Approach 1), sometimes they are recognized immediately when the changes occur (Approach 3), and sometimes the balance sheet recognition precedes income statement recognition (Approach 2). Note that in Approach 2, the change is not recognized in net income, but is included in the broader other comprehensive income.

Accrual Accounting

Before expanding on the three approaches, a review of accrual accounting is in order. The following point highlights the fundamental reason for the existence of accrual accounting:

> Over sufficiently long time periods, net income equals cash inflows minus cash outflows, other than cash flows with owners (for example, issuing or repurchasing common stock, and paying dividends). Asset and liability valuation and income measurement determine when and how the financial statements report these value changes. All value changes eventually affect net income and retained earnings.

Exhibit 2.6			
How Changes in Economic Value Can Be Recognized on the Balance Sheet and Income Statement			
	Approach 1	*Approach 2*	*Approach 3*
Recognize Changes in Economic Value on the Balance Sheet and the Income Statement:	when they are *realized* in a market transaction (such as when a firm sells an asset or pays a liability).	when the value changes *occur* over time, in which case the balance sheet is adjusted, but recognition in net income is delayed until the value changes are *realized* in a market transaction (such as with fair value gains or losses on certain types of investment securities).*	when they *occur*, even though they are not yet realized in a market transaction (such as with an impairment charge).
*In the interim, the value change will be reflected in other comprehensive income.			

The ultimate goal of a firm is to create wealth for stakeholders by generating more cash inflows than it incurs cash outflows. Thus, a very simplistic option for reporting financial performance would be simply to report cash inflows and outflows. However, simply reporting cash inflows and outflows would suffer from timing issues as a measure of firm performance and financial condition. To review this basic premise, consider a stylized example of three transactions under accrual accounting versus cash flow reporting approaches, as presented in Exhibit 2.7.

In this stylized example, a firm purchases supplies (December 31, 2013), uses the supplies to provide services to a customer the next year, and collects cash for the billed services the following year. Under cash flow reporting, income from this transaction appears in three reporting periods in the following pattern: –$100, $0, and $1,000, whereas under accrual accounting, the net of $900 appears in a single period in which the activity occurs. In this example, we see that reporting cash inflows and outflows yields a series of performance measures that vary from negative to zero to positive, whereas accrual accounting measures and reports when and how the value changes are generated. The accrual accounting approach moves the timing of income and expenses to the period in which the real activity occurs (2014). The investment in supplies in 2013 and the collection of the account receivable in 2015 are handled by accruals, which can be thought of as "placeholders" on the balance sheet (assets in this example). Under accrual accounting, the supplies are classified as inventory, which, like many nonmonetary assets, is "an expense waiting to happen." The amounts billed for services is classified as a receivable (with the offset being the revenue recorded), which, like many monetary assets, is a "cash inflow waiting to happen."

Exhibit 2.7			
Stylized Example to Demonstrate the Advantages of Accrual Accounting Relative to Cash Flow Reporting			
Date	**Transaction**		
December 31, 2013	Firm purchases supplies for $100		
August 17, 2014	Firm uses supplies to provide services, billed at $1,000		
January 1, 2015	Customer pays $1,000 for services billed		
	2013	**2014**	**2015**
Net cash flow reporting	–$100	$0	$1,000
Accrual accounting	$0	$900	$0
		($1,000 billed − $100 supplies)	

Although stylized, this example is symbolic of real-world evidence. Noted accounting author Patricia Dechow examined the relative ability of cash flows and accounting earnings to capture firm performance. She predicts and finds that

> "... for firms in steady state (that is, firms with cash requirements for working capital, investments, and financing that are relatively stable), cash flows have few timing and matching problems and are a relatively useful measure of firm performance. However, for firms operating in volatile environments with large

changes in their working capital and investment and financing activities, cash flows … have more severe timing and matching problems. Thus, cash flows' ability to reflect firm performance will decline as the firms' working capital requirements and investment and financing activities increase. Accruals … mitigate timing and matching problems in cash flows. As a consequence, earnings … better reflect firm performance than cash flows, in firms with more volatile operating, investment and financing activities …. [Finally], cash flows and earnings … [are] equally useful in industries with short operating cycles. However, in industries with long operating cycles, cash flows are … relatively poor measures of firm performance."[16]

Quick Check

■ Reporting cash inflows and outflows is representationally faithful but is often not relevant for predicting future cash flows.
■ Reporting income under accrual accounting procedures provides a measure of financial performance that is more relevant for users

interested in predicting the ultimate payoff of cash flows, albeit with a potential for information to be less representationally faithful.[17]

Next, we discuss the three alternative approaches to income measurement. Please note that because Approach 2 is a hybrid of Approach 1 and Approach 3, the discussion of Approach 2 follows the discussion of Approach 3.

Approach 1: Economic Value Changes Recognized on the Balance Sheet and Income Statement *When Realized*

Just as the conventional method of asset and liability valuation leans on historical value approaches (but with a decreasing emphasis), the conventional approach to income measurement relies on *realization* as the trigger for recognizing components of income. "Realization" for revenues occurs when firms receive cash, a receivable, or some other asset subject to representationally faithful measurement from a customer for goods sold or services performed (or when the firm satisfies a liability to a customer by delivering goods or services owed). The receipt of this asset validates the amount of the value change, and accountants characterize the firm as having *realized* the value change. This ensures that the amounts recorded as revenue are both relevant and representationally faithful.

For expenses, the concept of "realization" is somewhat different because expenses frequently reflect the consumption of assets or incurrence of liabilities, which often is

---

[16]Patricia M. Dechow, "Accounting Earnings and Cash Flows as Measures of Firm Performance: The Role of Accounting Accruals," *Journal of Accounting & Economics* (July 1994), pp. 3–42.

[17]The FASB's Conceptual Framework, which is the foundation for U.S. GAAP, is based on observations similar to those documented by Dechow. In *Statement of Financial Accounting Concepts No. 1*, the FASB states "Information about enterprise earnings and its components measured by accrual accounting generally provides a better indication of enterprise performance than does information about current cash receipts and payments." This will be discussed in more detail in Chapter 3.

not as directly observable as an event like a sale to a customer. The conventional way of thinking about recognizing expenses is that they are *matched* to the revenues they help generate, but this convention applies only to certain expenses that can be clearly linked to realization of revenues, such as costs of goods sold or selling commissions.[18] For example, a sale of lumber by **The Home Depot** indicates that revenues have been realized, which then triggers derecognition of the inventory and the accompanying recognition of an expense for cost of goods sold. More commonly, expenses are recognized in the particular period in which they are realized by the consumption of resources (such as paying salaries to employees) or the passage of time (such as rent or interest).

As presented in the discussion of asset and liability valuation, delaying the recognition of value changes for assets and liabilities until triggered by some realization (such as a sale or consumption) means that the balance sheet reports assets and liabilities at historical values. When historical values are used, valuation changes in assets and liabilities are not recognized until they are realized, meaning that some event (such as a sale) establishes a reliable basis for measuring and reporting the changes in the assets and liabilities on the financial statements. In this case, realization affects the balance sheet and the income statement simultaneously, which characterizes Approach 1. For example, a firm that holds land it acquired at $300,000 but is now clearly worth $900,000 does not recognize the $600,000 gain until the land is actually sold. An intuitive way to think about Approach 1 is that the accountant takes a "wait-and-see" approach.

Note that the receipt or disbursement of cash is *not* a requirement for realization. Because cash flows may precede, coincide with, or follow the value change, the balance sheet utilizes various *accruals* and *deferrals* as placeholders for cash flows (such as accounts receivable, accounts payable, or prepayments).

Approach 3: Economic Value Changes Recognized on the Balance Sheet and the Income Statement *When They Occur*

Approach 3 compels firms to revalue assets and liabilities to fair value each period and recognize the *unrealized* gains and losses in net income in that same period. This approach to income recognition aligns well with the current value approach for assets and liabilities because the changes in economic value are reflected on the income statement *even if they are not yet realized*. With exceptions discussed next for Approach 2, U.S. GAAP generally does not permit firms to revalue assets upward for value increases, which would recognize the unrealized gain as part of net income. The reason for this is that the combination of representational faithfulness concerns for the estimated increases in economic value and managers' self-interested incentives to report higher book values and income might lead to poor quality financial statements (despite the potential for greater relevance). Instead, firms must await the validation of such increases in value through a market transaction (that is, realization) to provide a sound, reliable basis for recognizing the gain.

U.S. GAAP is not symmetric regarding recognition of value increases and decreases. Firms must generally write down assets when fair values decrease below book values and recognize the decline in economic value immediately in income, but this is generally not permissible for increases in fair values. For example, suppose **Smithfield Foods**

---

[18]As regulators gravitate away from the historical value approaches to assets and liabilities (toward current value approaches), the emphasis and popularity of the matching objective is becoming diminished. However, it remains useful when considering when and how to recognize certain expenses (for example, depreciation).

has live hog inventory valued at $882 million. Despite the fact that swine flu is not spread by eating properly cooked pork, a swine flu epidemic sends the market price of live hogs down approximately 5% on the Chicago Mercantile Exchange. As a consequence, Smithfield Foods' inventory is overstated by $44 million. This decline in inventory fair value is recognized on both the balance sheet and income statement based on the new market prices. The new value of live hog inventory is $838 million, and this decline in economic value is recognized in income as a lower-of-cost-or-market adjustment for inventory of $44 million.

In contrast, IFRS allows for a number of situations where firms are permitted to increase asset valuations. For example, upon initial adoption of IFRS, firms may elect to value property and equipment at fair value. In addition, firms can record investment property (such as rental property), intangible assets, and some financial assets at fair values even when those fair values rise above carrying values. Note, however, that when firms report unrealized changes in economic value in current earnings under IFRS, additional disclosures must accompany the use of fair values, including the methodology of determining fair value. These additional disclosures are an attempt to increase the transparency of the fair values and therefore the representational faithfulness of these amounts. Also note that under IFRS, if a firm elects to recognize increased fair values of assets, it must do so for entire classes of similar assets (for example, all real estate, not just single properties) and it must continue to revalue such classes of assets thereafter (even if fair values decline). These requirements are meant to discourage firms from cherry-picking which assets to revalue upward and when.

Approach 2: Economic Value Changes Recognized on the Balance Sheet *When They Occur* but Recognized on the Income Statement *When Realized*

The value changes of certain types of assets and liabilities are of particular interest to financial statement users and are measurable with a sufficiently high degree of reliability that U.S. GAAP and IFRS require firms to revalue them to fair value each period. U.S. GAAP and IFRS recognize, however, that the value change is *unrealized* until the firm sells the asset or settles the liability. The ultimate *realized* gain or loss will likely differ from the unrealized gain or loss each period, particularly if the market values of the underlying assets or liabilities are volatile. Therefore, U.S. GAAP and IFRS require firms to delay including the gain or loss in *net income* until realization of the gain or loss occurs. However, such gains or losses do appear as part of *comprehensive income* (as discussed in Chapter 1). The most common types of unrealized gains and losses that receive treatment under Approach 2 include:

- foreign currency translation effects.
- fair value gains and losses on financial assets classified as available-for-sale investments and derivatives designated as hedges of future cash flows.
- certain adjustments to pension and post-retirement benefit obligations.[19]

---

[19]These items are discussed in more detail in Chapters 6, 8, and 9. In addition, other amounts bypass the income statement and statement of comprehensive income and are recorded directly to equity. Examples include corrections of errors and retroactive adjustments required under certain changes in accounting principles. Accounting Principles Board Opinion No. 9, "Reporting the Results of Operations" (December 1966). *FASB Codification Topic 250;* International Accounting Standards Board, *International Accounting Standards No. 8,* "Accounting Policies, Changes in Accounting Estimates and Errors" (revised January 2008).

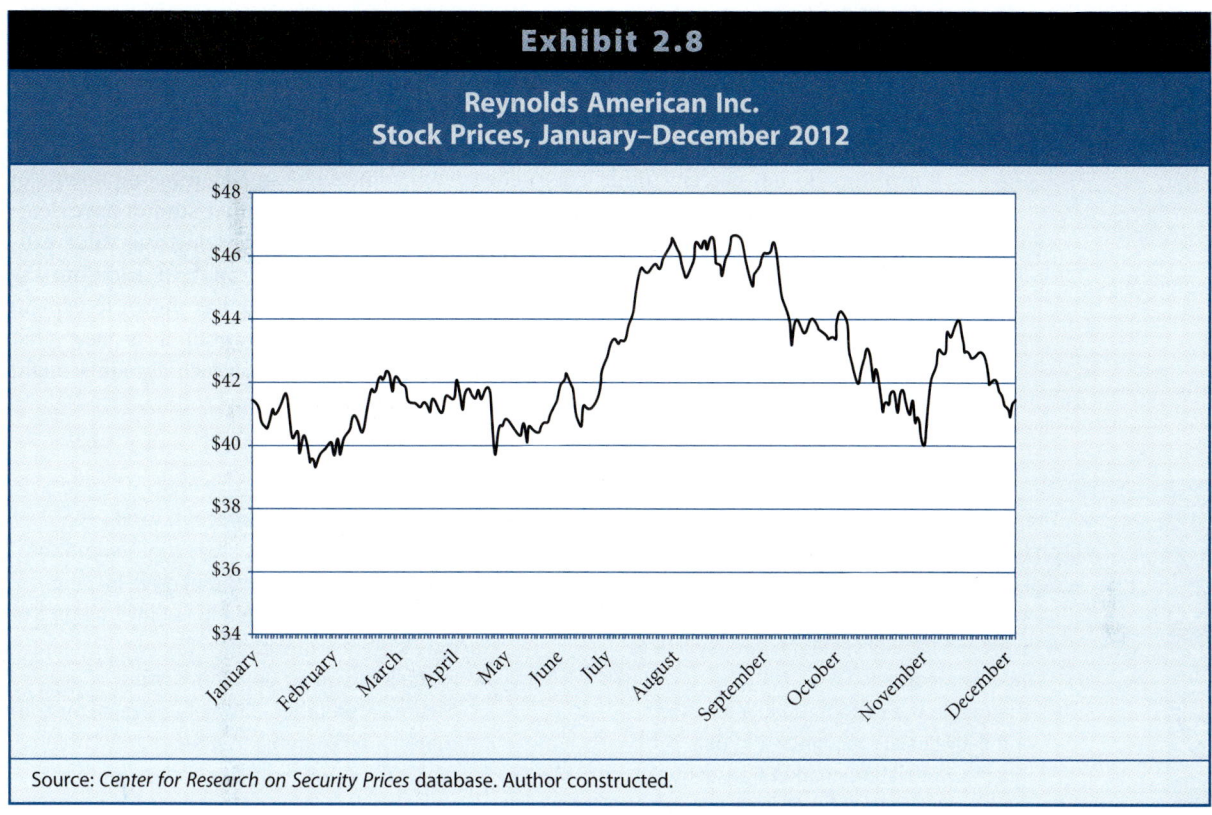

Exhibit 2.8

**Reynolds American Inc.
Stock Prices, January–December 2012**

Source: *Center for Research on Security Prices* database. Author constructed.

To put this in context, consider the actual monthly share prices of **Reynolds American Inc.** (NYSE: RAI) during calendar year 2012, shown graphically in Exhibit 2.8. Reynolds American is one of the largest tobacco companies in the world, and its stock is held in many investment portfolios. Consider how the price fluctuations in RAI's stock would have affected the financial statements of firms holding this investment during 2012. The stock price ended the year at $41.43, virtually unchanged from its price at the beginning of the year, $41.42. However, firms report results quarterly, so a firm with a December fiscal year-end would have seen the value of an investment in Reynolds American virtually unchanged at $41.44 at the end of first quarter; increase 8.3% from the first-quarter close to $44.87 at the end of the second quarter; decrease 3.4% to $43.34 during the third quarter; and finally fall another 4.4% back to $41.43. If applied to each quarter's financial statements, Approach 3 would have resulted in a volatile seesaw of net income recognition across the four quarters, although the year-over-year valuation of the investment was essentially flat. The intent here is not to argue that either approach is superior to the other, but just to highlight their differences.

As a hybrid of Approaches 1 and 3, Approach 2 attempts to capture the relevant economic value changes recognized for assets and liabilities under Approach 3, using the current value approach for asset and liability valuation. At the same time, Approach 2 incorporates the representational faithfulness feature of Approach 1 by delaying recognition of the economic value change in net income until the change is realized in a market transaction. Instead, such changes appear as part of other comprehensive income on the statement of comprehensive income.

The practice of delaying the recognition of fair value changes in net income under Approach 2 presumes that the investors assign greater relevance to *net income* as the summary measure of performance for a firm, but view amounts recognized as *other comprehensive income* as being of secondary relevance. Indeed, in a study of comprehensive income disclosures shortly after they were first required, it was concluded that investors do not perceive other comprehensive income to be important components of a firm's performance, given net income.[20] However, numerous other studies have demonstrated a strong association between security prices and underlying fair value estimates and between the changes in fair values and stock returns.[21] In addition, the volatility of fair value changes reflected in comprehensive income has shown to explain numerous measures of risk for commercial banks.[22] Thus, overall it is clear that investors view fair value amounts as relevant despite the risk that such amounts might be less representationally faithful than historical valuations.

Quick Check

- The traditional accounting model relies mostly on historical values for assets and liabilities and delays income recognition until realization (Approach 1). Under this approach:
  - asset and liability valuation directly link to income recognition.
  - changes in the economic value of assets and liabilities are recognized in net income when some market transaction triggers realization of the economic value changes.
- However, the FASB and IASB are more often requiring the use of fair values for certain assets and liabilities. Using the fair value approach for assets and liabilities generally translates into Approach 3, which recognizes such economic value changes in income immediately.

- As a hybrid of these approaches, some economic value changes are recognized on the balance sheet and in comprehensive income before they are recognized in net income on the income statement (Approach 2).
  - In the intervening time, firms use accumulated other comprehensive income (in shareholders' equity) as a temporary "holding tank" for unrealized gains and losses for which the assets and liabilities have been marked to fair value but the gains and losses are yet to be realized in a market transaction.
  - When the change in economic value is realized, the firm formally recognizes the gains and losses by removing them from accumulated other comprehensive income and reporting them within net income.

Evolution of the Mixed Attribute Accounting Model

The mixed attribute accounting model does a fairly good job of capturing economic events and transactions in a way that maintains the overall representational faithfulness of the financial statements. (Recall the increasing usefulness of financial statements indicated in Exhibit 2.2.) The FASB, and now the IASB, is constantly monitoring the needs of financial statement users and adapting the financial reporting rules to those needs.

[20]Dan Dhaliwal, K. R. Subramanyam, and Robert Trezevant, "Is Comprehensive Income Superior to Net Income as a Measure of Firm Performance?" *Journal of Accounting & Economics* (1999), pp. 1–3, 43–67.

[21]Thomas J. Carroll, Thomas J. Linsmeier, and Kathy R. Petroni, "The Reliability of Fair Value versus Historical Cost Information: Evidence from Closed-End Mutual Funds," *Journal of Accounting, Auditing and Finance* (2003), pp. 1–23.

[22]Leslie D. Hodder, Patrick E. Hopkins, and James M. Wahlen, "Risk-Relevance of Fair Value Income Measures for Commercial Banks," *The Accounting Review* (April 2006).

The FASB and IASB are actively overhauling the conceptual frameworks upon which the accounting model is based, with the goal of making the accounting for similar events and transactions consistent across firms and across time. However, because of the trade-off between relevance and representational faithfulness it is unlikely that financial reporting will move toward any extreme, such as full historical values or full fair values. Instead, the evolution of the mixed attribute accounting model reflects a continuous improvement in financial reporting that adapts to the evolving needs of financial statement users. Also, an important fact to keep in mind is that the quality of financial reporting can be enhanced (or offset) by other features of the economic environment, such as managers' voluntary disclosures, corporate governance practices, and shareholder protection, regulation, and enforcement. For example, it has been demonstrated that the usefulness of accrual accounting is higher in countries that have institutional features that protect shareholders (such as common law legal systems and shareholders' rights provisions).[23]

Income Taxes

LO 2-4

Provide an overview of the pervasive importance of income tax effects on reported financial statements.

The discussion thus far has considered the measurement of assets, liabilities, revenues, gains, expenses, and losses before considering any income tax effects. Everyone is aware that taxes are a significant aspect of doing business, but few understand how taxes impact financial statements. The objective of this brief discussion is to familiarize you with the basic concepts underlying the treatment of income taxes in the financial statements. To fully understand business transactions and the impact they have on firms, you need to understand their income tax effects. Further, analyzing profitability (in Chapter 4) requires that you understand tax effects on profitability. Thus, an overview of the required accounting for income taxes under U.S. GAAP and IFRS is necessary.

The fundamental reason for the difficulty in understanding the financial reporting of income taxes is that financial reporting of income uses one set of rules (U.S. GAAP, for example), while taxable income uses another set of rules (the Internal Revenue Code, for example). The differences between these sets of rules triggers differences in the timing and amount of tax expense on the income statement and the actual taxes payable to the government, which necessitates recognizing deferred income tax assets and liabilities. These differences are analogous to differences between financial reporting rules and cash basis accounting, which necessitate the use of various accruals such as accounts receivable and accounts payable. Thus, an understanding of financial statement analysis requires the appreciation that there are (at least) three primary methods by which financial performance can be measured, as shown in Exhibit 2.9.

Overview of Financial Reporting of Income Taxes[24]

LO 2-5

Reconcile financial reporting with tax reporting by adjusting for permanent differences and deferred tax assets and liabilities.

Income taxes significantly affect all of the financial statements and the analysis of a firm's reported profitability (income tax expense is a subtraction in computing net

---

[23]Mingyi Hung, "Accounting Standards and Value Relevance of Financial Statements: An International Analysis," *Journal of Accounting & Economics* (December 2000).

[24]Our discussion proceeds as if accounting for income taxes follows an income statement perspective. However, this is not technically correct, as accounting standards require a balance sheet perspective. We have found that exposition using the income statement perspective is more intuitive for students than the technically correct balance sheet perspective.

Exhibit 2.9

Alternative Perspectives for Determining Financial Performance

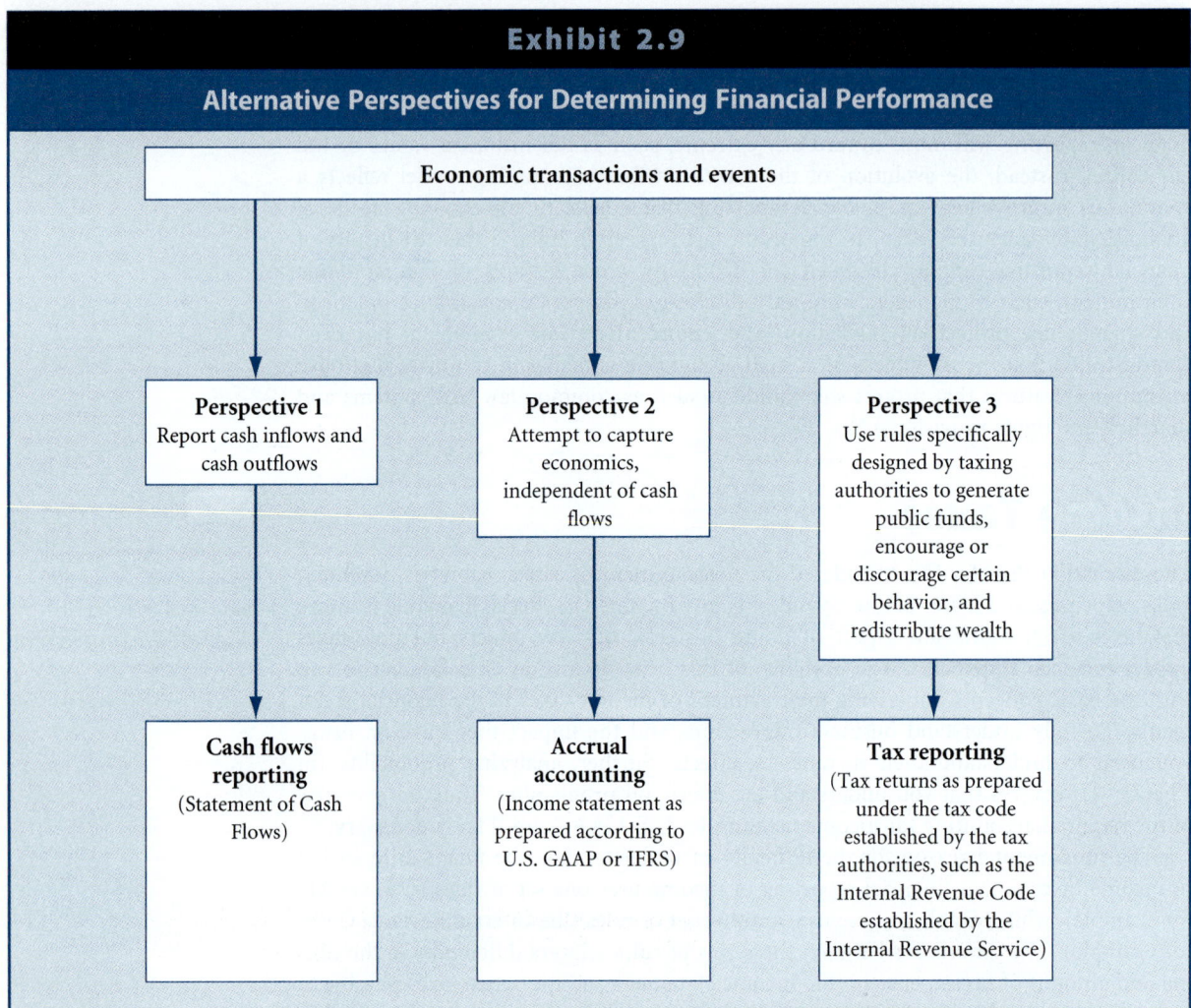

income), cash flows (income taxes paid are an operating use of cash), and assets and liabilities (for accrued taxes payable and deferred tax assets or liabilities). Income tax expense under accrual accounting for a period does not necessarily equal income taxes owed under the tax laws for that period (for which the firm must pay cash). The discussion first helps you clarify nomenclature that differs between financial reporting of income taxes (in financial statements) and elements of income taxes for tax reporting (on tax returns). Exhibit 2.10 demonstrates the primary differences.

Both financial reporting and tax reporting begin with revenues, but revenue recognition rules for financial reporting do not necessarily lead to the same figure for revenues as reported for tax reporting. Under tax reporting, firms report "deductions" rather than "expenses." Revenues minus deductions equal "taxable income" (rather than "income before taxes," or "pretax income"). Finally, taxable income determines "taxes owed," which can be substantially different from "tax expense" on the income statement, as highlighted later in this section. The balance sheet recognizes the difference between the two amounts as deferred tax assets or deferred tax liabilities. The balance sheet also recognizes any taxes owed at year-end (beyond the estimated tax payments firms may have made throughout the year) as a current liability for income taxes payable.

Exhibit 2.10

Differences in Nomenclature for Financial Reporting and Tax Reporting

Financial Reporting	Tax Reporting
Revenues (U.S. GAAP)	Revenues (tax rules)
− Expenses	− Deductions
= Income before taxes (or Pretax income)	= Taxable income
− Income tax expense	⇒ Taxes owed
= Net income	[no counterpart]

A simple example illustrates the issues in accounting for income taxes. Exhibit 2.11 sets forth information for the first two years of a firm's operations. The first column for each year shows the financial reporting amounts (referred to as "book amounts"). The second column shows the amounts reported to income tax authorities (referred to as "tax amounts" or "tax reporting"). To clarify some of the differences between book and tax effects in the first two columns, the third column indicates the effect of each item on cash flows. Assume for this example and those throughout this chapter that the income tax rate is 40%. Additional information on each item is as follows:

- *Sales Revenue:* The firm reports sales of $500 each year for both book and tax reporting. Assume that it collects the full amount each year in cash (that is, the firm has no accounts receivable).
- *Interest Income on Municipal Bonds:* The firm earns $25 of interest on municipal bonds. The firm includes this amount in its book income. The federal government

---

Exhibit 2.11

Illustration of the Effects of Income Taxes on Net Income, Taxable Income, and Cash Flows

	First Year			Second Year		
	Book Amounts	Tax Amounts	Cash Flow Amounts	Book Amounts	Tax Amounts	Cash Flow Amounts
Sales revenue	$ 500	$ 500	$ 500	$ 500	$ 500	$ 500
Interest on municipal bonds	25	—	25	25	—	25
Purchase of equipment	—	—	(120)	—	—	—
Depreciation expense	(60)	(80)	—	(60)	(40)	—
Warranty expense	(10)	(4)	(4)	(10)	(12)	(12)
Other expenses	(300)	(300)	(300)	(300)	(300)	(300)
Net Income before Taxes or Taxable Income	$ 155	$ 116		$ 155	$ 148	
Income tax expense or payable	(52)	(46.4)	(46.4)	(52)	(59.2)	(59.2)
Net Income or Net Cash Flows	$ 103		$ 54.6	$ 103		$153.8

does not tax interest on state and municipal bonds, so this amount is excluded from taxable income.

- *Depreciation Expense:* The firm purchases equipment for $120 cash, and the equipment has a two-year life. It depreciates the equipment using the straight-line method for financial reporting, recognizing $60 of depreciation expense on its books each year. Income taxing authorities permit the firm to deduct $80 of depreciation of the asset in the first year, and only $40 of depreciation for tax reporting in the second year.
- *Warranty Expense:* The firm estimates that the cost of providing warranty services on products sold equals 2% of sales. It recognizes warranty expense of $10 (0.02 × $500) each year for financial reporting, which links the estimated cost of warranties against the revenue from the sale of products subject to warranty. Income tax laws do not permit firms to claim a deduction for warranties in computing taxable income until they make cash expenditures to provide warranty services. Assume that the firm incurs cash costs of $4 in the first year and $12 in the second year.
- *Other Expenses:* The firm incurs and pays other expenses of $300 each year.
- *Income before Taxes and Taxable Income:* Based on the preceding assumptions, income before taxes for financial reporting is $155 each year. Taxable income is $116 in the first year and $148 in the second year.
- *Taxes Payable:* Assume for purposes here that the firm pays all income taxes at each year-end.

Income before taxes for financial reporting differs from taxable income for the following principal reasons:

1. **Permanent Differences:** There are revenues and expenses that firms include in net income for financial reporting but that never appear on the income tax return. The amount of interest earned on the municipal bond is a permanent revenue difference. Examples of expenses that would be disallowed as deductions include executive compensation above a specified cap, certain entertainment expenses, political and lobbying expenses, and some fines and penalties.
2. **Temporary Differences:** There are revenues and expenses that firms include in both net income and taxable income but in different periods. These timing differences are "temporary" until they "reverse." Straight-line versus accelerated depreciation expense is a temporary difference. The firm recognizes total depreciation of $120 over the life of the equipment for both financial and tax reporting but in a different pattern over time. Similarly, warranty expense is a temporary difference. The firm recognizes a total of $20 of warranty expense over the two-year period for financial reporting. It deducts only $16 over the two-year period for tax reporting. If the firm's estimate of total warranty costs turns out to be correct, the firm will deduct the remaining $4 of warranty expense for tax reporting in future years when it provides warranty services.

A central conceptual question in accounting for income taxes concerns the measurement of income tax expense on the income statement for financial reporting.

1. Should the firm compute income tax expense based on book income before taxes ($155 for each year in Exhibit 2.11)?
2. Should the firm compute income tax expense based on book income before taxes but excluding permanent differences [$130 ($155 – $25) for each year in Exhibit 2.11]?
3. Should the firm compute income tax expense based on taxable income ($116 in the first year and $148 in the second year in Exhibit 2.11)?

U.S. GAAP and IFRS require firms to follow the second approach, which complicates an understanding of income tax accounting because the amount upon which tax expense is based does not necessarily appear on the income statement (that is, income before taxes minus permanent differences). For this reason, U.S. GAAP and IFRS require disclosure within the income tax footnote to the financial statements that shows how the firm calculates income tax expense. This should clear up a misconception that income tax expense is the amount of income taxes currently owed (the third approach). If a firm does not have any permanent differences, there is no difference between the first and second approaches.

The rationale behind basing income tax expense on income before taxes minus permanent differences is that it aligns the recognition of *all* tax consequences of items and events already recognized in the financial statements or on tax returns in the period they occur. Thus, tax expense is based on book income, which often diverges from what is shown on the tax returns. Permanent differences do not affect taxable income or income taxes paid in any year, and firms do not recognize income tax expense or income tax savings on permanent differences.

Continuing the example above, under the second approach, income tax expense is $52 (0.4 × $130) in each year. The impact on the financial statements of recognizing the tax expense, taxes paid, and associated deferred tax accounts is as follows:[25]

Assets		=	Liabilities		+	Shareholders' Equity		
						Contributed Capital (CC)	Accumulated Other Comprehensive Income (AOCI)	Retained Earnings (RE)
Cash	−46.4		Deferred Tax Liability – Depreciation	8.0				Income Tax Expense 52.0
Deferred Tax Asset – Warranty	2.4							

Income tax expense of 52.0 is recognized, which reduces net income, whereas the firm only pays cash taxes of 46.4. The deferred tax asset measures the future tax saving that the firm will realize when it provides warranty services in future years and claims a tax deduction for the realization of expenses that are estimated in the first year. The firm expects to incur $6 ($10 – $4) of warranty costs in the second year and later years. When it incurs these costs, it will reduce its taxable income, which will result in lower taxes owed for the year, all else equal. Hence, the deferred tax asset of $2.4 (0.4 × $6) reflects the expected future tax savings from the future deductibility of amounts already expensed for financial reporting but not yet deducted for tax reporting. The $8 (0.4 × $20) deferred tax liability measures taxes that the firm must pay in the second year when it recognizes $20 less depreciation for tax reporting than for financial reporting.

The following summarizes the differences between book and tax amounts and the underlying cash flows. The $25 of interest on municipal bonds is a cash flow, but it is not reported on the tax return (it is a permanent difference). Depreciation is an expense that is a temporary difference between tax reporting and financial reporting but does not use cash. The firm recognized warranty expense of $10 in measuring net income but used only $4 of cash in satisfying warranty claims, which is the amount allowed to be deducted on the tax return. Finally, the firm recognized $52 of income tax expense in measuring net income but used only $46.4 cash for income taxes due to permanent and temporary differences. Overall, net income is $103, taxable income is $116, and net cash flows are

[25]See the section at the end of this chapter for a formal description of the above framework for analyzing the financial statement impacts of transactions and events.

$54.6. The discrepancy between net income and net cash flows is in large part due to the difference between cash invested in long-term assets relative to periodic depreciation.

In the second year, the impact on the financial statements of the income tax effects is as follows:

Assets		=	Liabilities		+	Shareholders' Equity		
						CC	AOCI	RE
Cash	−59.2		Deferred Tax Liability –					Income Tax Expense −59.2
Deferred Tax Asset –			Depreciation	−8.0				
Warranty	−0.8							

As in the first year, income tax is recognized as the effective tax rate times the pretax income, and cash paid for taxes equals the tax rate times taxable income. The temporary difference related to depreciation completely reverses in the second year, so the firm reduces the deferred tax liability to zero, which increases income taxes currently payable by $8. The temporary difference related to the warranty partially reversed during the second year, but the firm created additional temporary differences in that year by making another estimate of future warranty expense. For the two years as a whole, warranty expense for financial reporting of $20 ($10 + $10) exceeds the amount recognized for tax reporting of $16 ($4 + $12). Thus, the firm will recognize a deferred tax asset representing future tax savings of $1.6 (0.4 × $4). The deferred tax asset had a balance of $2.4 at the end of the first year, so the adjustment in the second year reduces the balance of the deferred tax asset by $0.8 ($2.4 – $1.6).

Now consider the cash flow effects for the second year. Cash flow from operations is $153.8. Again, depreciation expense is a noncash expense of $60. The firm recognized warranty expense of $10 for financial reporting but used $12 of cash to satisfy warranty claims. The $2 subtraction also equals the net reduction in the warranty liability during the second year, as the following analysis shows:

Warranty liability, beginning of second year	$ 6
Warranty expense, second year	10
Warranty claims, second year	(12)
Warranty liability, end of second year	$ 4

The firm recognized $52 of income tax expense but used $59.2 of cash for income taxes. The additional $7.2 of cash used to pay taxes in excess of the tax expense reduces the net deferred tax liability position. The $7.2 subtraction also equals the net change in the deferred tax asset ($0.8 decrease) and deferred tax liability ($8 decrease) during the second year, summarized as:[26]

Net deferred tax liability, beginning of second year ($2.4 asset − $8 liability)	$ 5.6
Income tax expense, second year	52.0
Income taxes paid, second year	(59.2)
Negative net deferred tax liability, or net deferred tax *asset,* end of second year ($1.6 asset − $0 liability)	$ (1.6)

---

[26]We are presenting the *net* change in deferred tax balances for ease of presentation. However, note that the deferred tax liability for the equipment would be classified as noncurrent and the deferred tax asset for the warranties is (usually) classified as current, so in practice, deferred taxes do not appear net.

At the end of the second year, the following totals for net income, cash flows, and tax amounts are as follows:

	First Year	Second Year	Totals
Net income	$ 103.0	$ 103.0	$ 206.0
Net cash flows	54.6	153.8	208.4
Taxable income	$ 116.0	$ 148.0	$ 264.0
Taxes paid	−46.4	−59.2	−105.6
	$ 69.6	$ 88.8	$ 158.4

The total amounts for net income and net cash flows differ by 2.4, which reflects the following:

Warranty liability for payments not yet made	$ 4.0
Offset by related deferred tax asset	−1.6
	$ 2.4

The remaining net cash flows associated with the warranty will be the $4.0 cash outflow, offset by the $1.6 tax expense savings when those warranty payments are deductible. When the warranty liability is finally settled, net income will equal net cash flows. In addition, total net cash flows of $208.4 exceed the net of taxable income and taxes paid of $158.4, a difference of $50.0. This difference reflects the total of permanent differences across the two years ($25.0 + $25.0). We reconciled net cash flows to net income above, so this additional $50.0 difference reflects a *permanent difference* between what is reported on the tax returns and what appears in the financial statements (both the income statement and statement of cash flows).

Measuring Income Tax Expense: A Bit More to the Story (to Be Technically Correct)

The preceding illustration followed what might be termed an *income statement approach* to measuring income tax expense. It compared revenues and expenses recognized for book and tax purposes, eliminated permanent differences, and computed income tax expense based on book income before taxes excluding permanent differences. However, FASB Statement No. 109 and IAS 12[27] require firms to follow a *balance sheet approach* when computing income tax expense. For example, Statement No. 109 (para. 11) states the following:

> … a difference between the tax basis of an asset or a liability and its reported amount in the [balance sheet] will result in taxable or deductible amounts in some future year(s) when the reported amounts of assets are recovered and the reported amounts of liabilities are settled.

---

[27]Financial Accounting Standards Board, *Statement of Financial Accounting Standards No. 109,* "Accounting for Income Taxes" (1992). *FASB Codification Topic 740;* International Accounting Standards Committee, *International Accounting Standards No. 12,* "Income Taxes" (October 1996).

Similarly, IAS 12 states:

> It is inherent in the recognition of an asset or liability that the reporting entity expects to recover or settle the carrying amount of that asset or liability. If it is probable that recovery or settlement of that carrying amount will make future tax payments larger (smaller) than they would be if such recovery or settlement were to have no tax consequences, this Standard requires an entity to recognize a deferred tax liability (deferred tax asset), with certain limited exceptions.

Thus, in the context of the preceding example, the perspective under the balance sheet approach is as follows:

Step 1. In the illustration, the book basis (that is, the amount on the balance sheet) of the equipment at the end of the first year is $60 ($120 cost − $60 accumulated depreciation) and the tax basis (that is, what would appear if the firm prepared a tax reporting balance sheet) is $40 ($120 − $80). Both the book and tax basis are zero at the end of the second year. The book basis of the warranty liability at the end of the first year is $6 ($10 − $4), and the tax basis is zero. (That is, the firm recognizes a deduction for tax purposes when it pays warranty claims and would therefore show no liability if it were to prepare a tax balance sheet.) The book basis of the warranty liability at the end of the second year is $4 ($6 + $10 − $12), and the tax basis remains zero.

Step 2. After identifying book and tax differences, eliminate those that will not have a future tax consequence (that is, permanent differences). There are no permanent differences in the book and tax bases of assets and liabilities in the example. However, suppose the firm had not yet received the $25 of interest on the municipal bond investment by the end of the first year. It would show an interest receivable on its financial reporting balance sheet of $25, but no receivable would appear on its tax balance sheet, because the tax law does not tax such interest; the difference between the book and tax basis is a permanent difference. The firm would eliminate this book-tax difference before moving to the next step.

Step 3. Next, separate the remaining differences into those that give rise to future tax *deductions* and those that give rise to future taxable *income*. Exhibit 2.12 summarizes the possibilities and gives several examples of these temporary differences, as later chapters discuss. The difference between the book basis ($6) and the tax basis ($0) of the warranty liability at the end of the first year means that the firm will have future tax deductions (assuming that the book basis of the estimate is accurate). The difference between the book basis ($60) and the tax basis ($40) of the equipment at the end of the first year gives rise to future taxable income (meaning that depreciation deductions will be lower, which will increase taxable income, all else equal). We multiply these differences by the marginal tax rate expected to apply *in those future periods*. In the example, the future tax deduction for the warranties results in a deferred tax asset at the end of the first year of $2.4 [0.4 × ($6 book basis − $0 tax basis)]. The future taxable income (due to the lower future depreciation of the equipment) results in a deferred tax liability at the end of the first year of $8 [0.4 × ($60 book basis − $40 tax basis)].

Step 4. Finally, the rules for income tax accounting require managers to assess the likelihood that the firm will realize the future benefits of any recognized deferred tax assets. This assessment should consider the nature (whether cyclical or non-cyclical, for example) and characteristics (growing, mature, or declining, for

Exhibit 2.12		
Examples of Temporary Differences		
	Assets	**Liabilities**
Future Tax Deduction *(results in deferred tax assets)*	Tax basis of assets exceeds financial reporting basis. *Example:* Accounts receivable using the direct charge-off method for uncollectible accounts for tax purposes exceeds accounts receivable (net) using the allowance method for financial reporting.	Tax basis of liabilities is less than financial reporting basis. *Example:* Tax reporting does not recognize an estimated liability for warranty claims (firms can deduct only actual expenditures on warranty claims), whereas firms must recognize such a liability for financial reporting to match warranty expense with sales revenue in the period of sale.
Future Taxable Income *(results in deferred tax liabilities)*	Tax basis of assets is less than financial reporting basis. *Example:* Depreciation is computed using accelerated depreciation for tax purposes and the straight-line method for financial reporting.	Tax basis of liabilities exceeds financial reporting basis. *Example:* Leases are recognized by a lessee, the user of the leased assets, as a capital lease for tax reporting and an operating lease for financial reporting.

example) of a firm's business and its tax planning strategies for the future. If realization of the benefits of deferred tax assets is "more likely than not" (that is, the likelihood exceeds 50%), then deferred tax assets equal the amounts computed in Step 3. However, if it is "more likely than not" that the firm will *not* realize some or all of the deferred tax assets, then the firm must reduce the deferred tax asset using a valuation allowance (similar in concept to the allowance for uncollectible accounts receivable). The valuation allowance reduces the deferred tax assets to the amounts the firm expects to realize in the form of lower tax payments in the future (similar to a net realizable value approach). For purposes here, assume that the firm in the preceding illustration considers it more likely than not that it will realize the tax benefits of the deferred tax assets related to warranties and therefore recognizes no valuation allowance.

The result of this four-step procedure for the example is a deferred tax asset and a deferred tax liability at each balance sheet date. The amounts in the preceding illustration are as follows:

	January 1, First Year	December 31, First Year	December 31, Second Year
Deferred tax asset – warranties	$0.0	$2.4	$1.6
Deferred tax liability – equipment	0.0	8.0	0.0

Income tax expense for each period equals:

1. Income taxes currently payable on taxable income
2. Plus (minus) any increases (decreases) in deferred tax liabilities
3. Plus (minus) any decreases (increases) in deferred tax assets.

Thus, income tax expense in the preceding illustration is as follows:

	First Year	Second Year
Income taxes currently payable on taxable income	$46.4	$59.2
Plus (minus) increase (decrease) in deferred liability	8.0	(8.0)
Minus (plus) increase (decrease) in deferred tax asset	(2.4)	0.8
Income tax expense	$52.0	$52.0

The income statement approach illustrated in the first section and the balance sheet approach illustrated in this section yield identical results whenever (1) enacted tax rates applicable to future periods do not change and (2) the firm recognizes no valuation allowance on deferred tax assets. Legislated changes in tax rates applicable to future periods will cause the tax effects of previously recognized temporary differences to differ from the amounts in the deferred tax asset and deferred tax liability accounts. The firm revalues the deferred tax assets and liabilities for the change in tax rates and flows through the effect of the change to income tax expense in the year of the legislated change. A change in the valuation allowance for deferred tax assets likewise flows through immediately to income tax expense.

Reporting Income Taxes in the Financial Statements

Understanding income tax accounting becomes difficult because firms may not include all income taxes for a period on the line for income tax expense in the income statement. Some amounts may appear elsewhere:

- *Discontinued Operations:* Under U.S. GAAP, firms report the results of discontinued operations in a separate section of the income statement, net of the income tax effects. Thus, income tax expense reflects income taxes on income from continuing operations only. IFRS does not permit extraordinary item categorizations, but exceptional or material items may be disclosed separately, including income tax effects.
- *Other Comprehensive Income:* Unrealized changes in the market value of marketable securities classified as "available for sale," unrealized changes in the market value of hedged financial instruments and derivatives classified as cash flow hedges, unrealized foreign currency translation adjustments, and certain changes in pension and other post-employment benefit assets and liabilities appear in other comprehensive income, net of their tax effects. These items usually give rise to deferred tax assets or deferred tax liabilities because the income tax law includes such gains and losses in taxable income when realized. Thus, a portion of the change in deferred tax assets and liabilities on the balance sheet does not flow through income tax expense on the income statement.

PepsiCo's Reporting of Income Taxes

PepsiCo reports information on income taxes in Note 5, "Income Taxes," to its financial statements (Appendix A), excerpts of which appear in Exhibit 2.13. Income tax expense for 2012 of $2,090 million includes $2,004 million currently owed and $86 million deferred. Thus, excluding permanent differences, PepsiCo's income for financial reporting exceeded its taxable income for 2012 (as evidenced by the $86 of deferred tax expense, reflecting income tax liabilities that will be due in the future).

At the end of 2012, PepsiCo's deferred tax liabilities exceeded its deferred tax assets, for a net deferred tax liability of $4,323 million. In the previous year, PepsiCo also ended with a net deferred tax liability of $4,150 million. The $173 million increase in the net deferred tax liability reflects a modest increase in deferred tax liabilities of $132 million and a $41 million decrease in net deferred tax assets.

Exhibit 2.13			
PepsiCo Excerpts from Note 5 on Income Taxes (amounts in millions)			
Income Statement for Year	**2012**	**2011**	**2010**
Provision for income taxes—continuing operations:			
Current	$ 2,004	$ 1,617	$1,797
Deferred	86	755	97
Total	$ 2,090	$ 2,372	$1,894
Balance Sheet at End of Year	**2012**	**2011**	
Gross deferred tax liabilities (details omitted)	$ 7,948	$ 7,816	
Gross deferred tax assets (details omitted)	$ 4,858	$ 4,930	
Valuation allowances	(1,233)	(1,264)	
Deferred tax assets, net	$ 3,625	$ 3,666	
Net Deferred Tax (Assets) Liabilities	$ 4,323	$ 4,150	
	2012	**2011**	
Deferred taxes included within:			
ASSETS:			
Prepaid expenses and other current assets	$ 740	$ 845	
LIABILITIES:			
Deferred income taxes	5,063	4,995	
Analysis of valuation allowances:			
Balance, beginning of year	$ 1,264	$ 875	
Provision	68	464	
Other deductions	(99)	(75)	
Balance, end of year	$ 1,233	$ 1,264	

Source: PepsiCo, Inc., Form 10-K, for the fiscal year ended December 29, 2012.

Note that Exhibit 2.13 also indicates that PepsiCo's gross deferred tax assets in both 2011 and 2012 were accompanied by valuation allowances. For 2012, the valuation allowance was $1,233 million on the gross deferred tax assets of $4,858 million. The valuation allowance likely relates to $10.4 billion of operating loss carryforwards (which create large deferred tax assets) that have various expiration dates. (See Note 5 to PepsiCo's consolidated financial statements in Appendix A.) If PepsiCo's management determines that it is more likely than not that some portion of these carryforwards will not be used, a valuation allowance must be established.

Finally, the last table in Exhibit 2.13 indicates that PepsiCo's deferred tax assets and liabilities appear in two locations on the balance sheet—current assets ("Prepaid expenses and other current assets"), and noncurrent liabilities ("Deferred income taxes").

You will return to the study of income taxes in Chapter 9 to explore in greater depth the concepts and procedures of accounting for income taxes.

LO 2-6

Work with an analytical framework that maps the effects of business transactions and events to the balance sheet and income statement.

Framework for Analyzing the Effects of Transactions on the Financial Statements

In each period, firms prepare financial statements that aggregate and summarize the results of numerous transactions. This section presents and illustrates an analytical framework for understanding the effects of various transactions on the financial statements, which is built on basic financial accounting. Understanding the impact of individual transactions is important, because financial statement analysis requires an understanding of the composition of current financial statements. Understanding the composition of the current financial statements is necessary for analyzing cash flows (Chapter 3), profitability (Chapter 4), risk (Chapter 5), and especially accounting quality (Chapter 6), all of which help the analyst project future results (Chapter 10) so that the analyst can estimate the value of a firm (Chapters 11–14).

Overview of the Analytical Framework

The analytical framework relies on the balance sheet equation:

$$\text{Assets (A)} = \text{Liabilities (L)} + \text{Total Shareholders' Equity (TSE)}$$

We can expand total shareholders' equity (TSE) into its component parts, which will help identify the sources of changes in shareholders' net investment in a firm:

$$\begin{array}{c}\text{Total Shareholders'}\\\text{Equity}\end{array} = \begin{array}{c}\text{Contributed}\\\text{Capital (CC)}\end{array} + \begin{array}{c}\text{Accumulated Other}\\\text{Comprehensive Income (AOCI)}\end{array} + \begin{array}{c}\text{Retained}\\\text{Earnings (RE)}\end{array}$$

Contributed Capital (CC) accumulates net stock transactions with shareholders and includes accounts such as Common Stock, Additional Paid-in Capital, Treasury Stock, and other paid-in capital accounts. Accumulated Other Comprehensive Income (AOCI) is the "holding tank" discussed in Chapters 1 and 2, where unrealized gains or losses on certain assets and liabilities are held until realization occurs. Finally, Retained Earnings (RE) is simply the accumulation of all net income minus dividends (and occasionally other transactions).

Firms prepare balance sheets at the beginning and end of a period. Thus, for each component of the balance sheet equation, the following equations hold:

$$A_{BEG} + \Delta A = A_{END}$$
$$L_{BEG} + \Delta L = L_{END}$$
$$TSE_{BEG} + \Delta TSE = TSE_{END}$$

where *BEG* and *END* subscripts refer to beginning-of-period and end-of-period balances, respectively, and Δ indicates changes in balances. Changes in assets, liabilities, and total shareholders' equity over a period reflect the net effect of all individual transactions during the period, which is why it is important to understand how individual transactions affect the financial statements. Changes in total shareholders' equity have multiple components, so it reflects the net of stock transactions with owners, the "holding tank" of unrealized gains and losses on certain assets and liabilities, and the accumulation of net income minus dividends. Because of this mix of elements in TSE, it is helpful to partition the change in total shareholders' equity into these components:

$$\Delta TSE = \begin{array}{c} \text{Stock Transactions} \\ (\Delta \text{ Stock}) \end{array} + \begin{array}{c} \text{Other Comprehensive} \\ \text{Income (OCI)} \end{array} + \text{Net Income (NI)} - \text{Dividends (D)}$$

Thus, as a working framework for capturing beginning-of-period and end-of-period balance sheets as well as changes during the period (which include changes due to net income recognized on the income statement), we use the following framework to summarize transactions and events throughout this book:

$A_{BEG} =$	L_{BEG}	+	CC_{BEG}	+	$AOCI_{BEG}$	+	RE_{BEG}
$+\Delta A$	$+\Delta L$		$+\Delta Stock$		$+OCI$		$+NI$ $- D$
$A_{END} =$	L_{END}	+	CC_{END}	+	$AOCI_{END}$	+	RE_{END}

To demonstrate this analytical framework, the following examples illustrate how to apply this framework to several of the transactions described earlier in this chapter. For the transactions we analyze, we present the analytical framework showing how the transaction affects (increases or decreases shown by +/− signs and amounts) the categories of the balance sheet. We also present the journal entries to show how each transaction will affect specific financial statement accounts.

Example 1—Capital Expenditures

In-N-Out Burger sells land with an acquisition cost of $210,000 for $300,000 in cash. For simplicity, assume that In-N-Out Burger pays taxes immediately at a 40% rate.

	Assets		=	Liabilities	+	Shareholders' Equity		
						CC	AOCI	RE
1.	Cash Land	+300,000 −210,000						Gain on Sale of Land +90,000

Cash	300,000	
Land		210,000
Gain on Sale of Land		90,000

	Assets		=	Liabilities	+	Shareholders' Equity		
						CC	AOCI	RE
2.	Cash	−36,000						Income Tax Expense 36,000

Income Tax Expense	36,000		(0.40 × [300,000 − 210,000])
Cash		36,000	

Note that if you wanted to compute overall changes in balance sheet accounts across a set of transactions, you need only sum the amounts within any partition. For example, the overall impact on assets of the above transactions is a net increase of $54,000, equal to the aggregation of +$300,000, −$210,000, and −$36,000. Similarly, to compute the net impact on income, sum the amounts in the Retained Earnings column. In the above transactions, the impact on *net income* is +$90,000 and −$36,000, or net income of $54,000. Not surprisingly, the change in assets in this example exactly equals the change in retained earnings (because there were no effects on liabilities, contributed capital, or accumulated other comprehensive income).

Example 2—Sale of Inventory

Consider the following three events for **Mollydooker Wines**:

1. The sale of wine for $2,000,000 on account (Accounts Receivable)
2. The derecognition of the wine inventory with an accumulated cost of $1,600,000
3. The immediate payment of income taxes at a 40% rate

	Assets		=	Liabilities		+	Shareholders' Equity		
							CC	AOCI	RE
1.	Accounts Receivable	+2,000,000							Sales +2,000,000
	Accounts Receivable			2,000,000					
	Sales						2,000,000		

	Assets		=	Liabilities		+	Shareholders' Equity		
							CC	AOCI	RE
2.	Inventory	−1,600,000							Cost of Goods Sold −1,600,000
	Cost of Goods Sold			1,600,000					
	Inventory						1,600,000		

	Assets		=	Liabilities		+	Shareholders' Equity		
							CC	AOCI	RE
3.	Cash	−160,000							Income Tax Expense −160,000
	Income Tax Expense			160,000			(0.40 × [2,000,000 − 1,600,000])		
	Cash						160,000		

Summing the increases and decreases in any column indicates the net effect of the wine sale (after taxes). For example, the change in assets as a result of this transaction is $2,000,000 −$1,600,000 −$160,000 = $240,000. Similarly, shareholders' equity increased by the same amount. This transaction has no other effect on Mollydooker's balance sheet. The income effects of this transaction are the sum of any effects reflected under RE that would appear on the income statement, which for this transaction would be +$2,000,000 (Sales), −$1,600,000 (Cost of Goods Sold), and −$160,000 (Tax Expense), for a net impact on income of +$240,000.

Example 3—Inventory Valuation

Smithfield Foods records an inventory write-down for live hog inventory, driven by the drop in market prices of live hogs. Live hog inventory with a book value of $882 million is written down by approximately 5%, or $44 million. Income tax law does not permit Smithfield Foods to deduct the write-down on the live hog inventory until the loss is realized. Thus, the 40% tax effect of the write-down becomes a deferred tax asset until that time. This leads to the recording of the following two effects:

Assets	=	Liabilities	+	Shareholders' Equity		
				CC	AOCI	RE
1. Inventory −44,000,000						Inventory Write-Down Loss −44,000,000

Inventory Write-Down Loss	44,000,000	
Inventory		44,000,000

Assets	=	Liabilities	+	Shareholders' Equity		
				CC	AOCI	RE
2 Deferred Tax Asset +17,600,000						Income Tax Expense +17,600,000

Deferred Tax Asset	17,600,000	(0.40 × 44,000,000)
Income Tax Expense		17,600,000

The overall impact of the $44 million write-down is to decrease assets by $26.4 million ($44 million write-down offset by $17.6 million deferred tax effect). The same amount flows through to net income as well, reducing retained earnings.

Example 4—External Financing

Petroleo Brasileiro purchases computer equipment from **Sun Microsystems** and signs a five-year note payable in the amount of $998,178 (present value of $250,000 a year for five years at 8%). The purchase, use of the equipment, and first-year principal and interest payment trigger the following events to be recognized (ignore income taxes for this example):

1. Purchase of the computer equipment and signing of the note payable
2. Depreciation of $199,636 ($998,178 ÷ 5) on the computer for the first year based on a five-year useful life
3. Interest expense for the first year of $79,854 (0.08 × $998,178), the cash payment of $250,000, and the reduction in principal of $170,146 ($250,000 − $79,854)

Assets	=	Liabilities	+	Shareholders' Equity		
				CC	AOCI	RE
1. Computer Equipment +998,178		Note Payable +998,178				

Computer Equipment	998,178	
Note Payable		998,178

Assets	=	Liabilities	+	Shareholders' Equity		
				CC	AOCI	RE
2. Accumulated Depreciation −199,636						Depreciation Expense −199,636

Depreciation Expense	199,636	
Accumulated Depreciation		199,636

Assets	=	Liabilities	+	Shareholders' Equity		
				CC	AOCI	RE
3. Cash −250,000		Note Payable −170,146				Interest Expense −79,854

Interest Expense	79,854	
Note Payable	170,146	
Cash		250,000

Example 5—Other Comprehensive Income

Microsoft invests in marketable equity securities. The following events occur:

1. Initial $4,500,000 investment in marketable equity securities
2. Increase in fair value as of December 31 to $4,900,000
3. Deferred tax effect of the unrealized gain (assume 40%)
4. Sale of marketable equity securities in June for $5,000,000
5. Settlement of the tax liability (assume taxes paid immediately after the sale)

	Assets	=	Liabilities	+	Shareholders' Equity		
					CC	AOCI	RE
1.	Marketable Equity Securities +4,500,000 Cash −4,500,000						

Marketable Equity Securities	4,500,000	
Cash		4,500,000

	Assets	=	Liabilities	+	Shareholders' Equity		
					CC	AOCI	RE
2.	Marketable Equity Securities +400,000					Unrealized Holding Gain +400,000	

Marketable Equity Securities	400,000	
Unrealized Holding Gain		400,000

	Assets	=	Liabilities	+	Shareholders' Equity		
					CC	AOCI	RE
3.			Deferred Tax Liability +160,000			Unrealized Holding Gain −160,000	

Unrealized Holding Gain	160,000	
Deferred Tax Liability		160,000

	Assets	=	Liabilities	+	Shareholders' Equity		
					CC	AOCI	RE
4.	Cash +5,000,000 Marketable Equity Securities −4,900,000					Unrealized Holding Gain −400,000	Gain on Sale of Marketable Equity Securities +500,000

Cash	5,000,000	
Unrealized Holding Gain	400,000	
Marketable Equity Securities		4,900,000
Gain on Sale of Marketable Equity Securities		500,000

	Assets	=	Liabilities	+	Shareholders' Equity		
					CC	AOCI	RE
5.	Cash −200,000		Deferred Tax Liability −160,000			Unrealized Holding Gain +160,000	Income Tax Expense −200,000

Income Tax Expense	200,000		(0.40 × 500,000)
Deferred Tax Liability	160,000		
Unrealized Holding Gain		160,000	
Cash		200,000	

This example demonstrates the mechanics of how other comprehensive income affects the financial statements. At the end of the year, when Microsoft has an unrealized gain of $400,000, the value of the marketable equity securities is written up to its fair value of $4,900,000. Because this increase has not been realized in a market transaction (such as a sale), Microsoft puts this gain in the accumulated other comprehensive income "holding tank" rather than recognize it as part of net income. However, note that Microsoft will be required to present this amount as part of other comprehensive income on the statement of comprehensive income. The amount recognized as other comprehensive income is then closed out to the accumulated other comprehensive income account and labeled as unrealized holding gain or loss. When Microsoft sells the marketable equity securities in June, the $400,000 is removed from the "holding tank" of accumulated other comprehensive income and recognized in income as gain on sale, along with an additional $100,000 that occurred subsequent to December. Of course, the associated tax effects are accumulated and reversed from accumulated other comprehensive income as well. The overall net effect is that Microsoft realizes a $500,000 gain, offset by $200,000 of income tax expense, for an increase in net assets of $300,000.

Summary

This chapter provides a conceptual foundation for understanding the balance sheet and the income statement.

- ■ U.S. GAAP, IFRS, and other major sets of accounting standards are best characterized as mixed attribute accounting models. Assets and liabilities on the balance sheet are valued using various methods based on historical and current values, depending on the nature of the asset or liability.
  - ● The conventional accounting model uses historical, or acquisition, costs to value assets and liabilities and delays the recognition of value changes until external market transactions validate their amounts. Use of acquisition costs generally results in more representationally faithful asset and liability valuations than do current values, but such valuation can lose relevance, especially as the time from the initial transaction passes and historical values diverge from current values.
- ■ Recognizing value changes for assets and liabilities still leaves open the question of when the value change should affect net income. Such value changes may affect net income immediately or may affect it later, initially being temporarily held as accumulated other comprehensive income (in shareholders' equity) until validated through an external market transaction.
  - ● Over sufficiently long time periods, net income equals cash inflows minus cash outflows (excluding cash transactions with owners). Different approaches to asset and liability valuation and to income measurement affect the pattern of net income over time, but not its ultimate amount.
- ■ Almost every transaction affecting net income has an income tax effect. The financial reporting issue is whether firms should recognize the income tax effect when the related revenue or expense affects net income or when it affects taxable income.
  - ● U.S. GAAP requires firms to measure income tax expense each period based on the pretax income for financial reporting, excluding permanent differences.
- ■ When income tax expense differs from income taxes currently owed on taxable income, firms recognize deferred tax assets and deferred tax liabilities.
  - ● Deferred tax assets arise when taxable income exceeds book income. Firms prepay taxes now but reduce taxes paid later when the temporary difference reverses and book income exceeds taxable income.
  - ● Deferred tax liabilities are the opposite, arising when book income exceeds taxable income. Firms delay paying taxes now, but will pay the taxes later when the temporary differences reverse and taxable income exceeds book income.

Questions, Exercises, Problems, and Cases

Questions and Exercises

LO 2-2

2.1 Relevance versus Representational Faithfulness. "Some asset valuations using historical costs are highly relevant and very representationally faithful, whereas others may be representationally faithful but lack relevance. Some asset valuations based on fair values are highly relevant and very representational faithful, whereas others may be relevant but lack representational faithfulness." Explain and provide examples of each.

LO 2-3

2.2 Asset Valuation and Income Recognition. "Asset valuation and recognition of net income closely relate." Explain, including conditions when they do not.

LO 2-2

2.3 Trade-Offs among Acceptable Accounting Alternatives. Firms value inventory under a variety of assumptions, including two common methods: last-in first-out (LIFO) and first-in first-out (FIFO). Ignore taxes, assume that prices increase over time, and assume that a firm's inventory balance is stable or grows over time. Which inventory method provides a balance sheet that better reflects the underlying economics, and why? Which method provides an income statement that better reflects the underlying economics, and why?

LO 2-2, LO 2-3

2.4 Income Flows versus Cash Flows. The text states, "Over sufficiently long time periods, net income equals cash inflows minus cash outflows, other than cash flows with owners." Demonstrate the accuracy of this statement in the following scenario: Two friends contributed $50,000 each to form a new business. The owners used the amounts contributed to purchase a machine for $100,000 cash. They estimated that the useful life of the machine was five years and the salvage value was $20,000. They rented out the machine to a customer for an annual rental of $25,000 a year for five years. Annual cash operating costs for insurance, taxes, and other items totaled $6,000 annually. At the end of the fifth year, the owners sold the equipment for $22,000, instead of the $20,000 salvage value initially estimated. (*Hint: Compute the total net income and the total cash flows other than cash flows with owners for the five-year period as a whole.*)

LO 2-1

2.5 Measurement of Acquisition Cost. **United Van Lines** purchased a truck with a list price of $250,000 subject to a 6% discount if paid within 30 days. United Van Lines paid within the discount period. It paid $4,000 to obtain title to the truck with the state and an $800 license fee for the first year of operation. It paid $1,500 to paint the firm's name on the truck and $2,500 for property and liability insurance for the first year of operation. What acquisition cost of this truck should United Van Lines record in its accounting records? Indicate the appropriate accounting treatment of any amount not included in acquisition cost.

LO 2-1

2.6 Measurement of a Monetary Asset. Assume **Boeing** sold a 767 aircraft to **American Airlines** on January 1, 2009. The sales agreement required American Airlines to pay $10 million immediately and $10 million on December 31 of each year for 20 years, beginning on December 31, 2009. Boeing and American Airlines judge that 8% is an appropriate interest rate for this arrangement.

    a. Compute the present value of the receivable on Boeing's books on January 1, 2009, immediately after receiving the $10 million down payment.

    b. Compute the present value of the receivable on Boeing's books on December 31, 2009.

    c. Compute the present value of the receivable on Boeing's books on December 31, 2010.

LO 2-1

2.7 Measurement of a Nonmonetary Asset. Assume **American Airlines** acquires a regional airline in the midwestern United States for $450 million. American Airlines allocates $150 million of the purchase price to landing rights at various airports. The landing rights expire in five years. What type of measurement is applicable to the valuation of the landing rights at acquisition and at the end of each of the five years?

2.8 Fair Value Measurements. The text discusses inputs managers might use to determine fair values of assets and liabilities and identifies different classifications of assets identified in SFAS No. 157. Suppose a major university endowment has investments in a wide array of assets, including (a) common stocks; (b) bonds; (c) real estate; (d) timber investments, which receive cash flows from sales of timber; (e) private equity funds; and (f) illiquid asset-backed securities. Consider how the portfolio manager would estimate the fair values of each of those classes of assets, and characterize the inputs you identify as Level 1, Level 2, or Level 3.

`LO 2-2`

2.9 Computation of Income Tax Expense. A firm's income tax return shows $50,000 of income taxes owed for 2009. For financial reporting, the firm reports deferred tax assets of $42,900 at the beginning of 2009 and $38,700 at the end of 2009. It reports deferred tax liabilities of $28,600 at the beginning of 2009 and $34,200 at the end of 2009.

`LO 2-5`

  a. Compute the amount of income tax expense for 2009.
  b. Assume for this part that the firm's deferred tax assets are as stated above for 2009 but that its deferred tax liabilities were $58,600 at the beginning of 2009 and $47,100 at the end of 2009. Compute the amount of income tax expense for 2009.
  c. Explain contextually why income tax expense is higher than taxes owed in Part a and lower than taxes owed in Part b.

2.10 Computation of Income Tax Expense. A firm's income tax return shows income taxes for 2009 of $35,000. The firm reports deferred tax assets before any valuation allowance of $24,600 at the beginning of 2009 and $27,200 at the end of 2009. It reports deferred tax liabilities of $18,900 at the beginning of 2009 and $16,300 at the end of 2009.

`LO 2-5`

  a. Assume for this part that the valuation allowance on the deferred tax assets totaled $6,400 at the beginning of 2009 and $7,200 at the end of 2009. Compute the amount of income tax expense for 2009.
  b. Assume for this part that the valuation allowance on the deferred tax assets totaled $6,400 at the beginning of 2009 and $4,800 at the end of 2009. Compute the amount of income tax expense for 2009.

Problems and Cases

2.11 Costs to Be Included in Historical Cost Valuation. At a cost of $200,000, Assume **In-N-Out Burger** acquired a tract of land for a restaurant site. It paid attorneys $7,500 to conduct a title search and to prepare the required legal documents for the purchase. State real estate transfer taxes totaled $2,500. Building permits totaled $1,200. Compute the acquisition cost of the land.

`LO 2-1`

2.12 Effect of Valuation Method for Nonmonetary Asset on Balance Sheet and Income Statement. Assume **Walmart** acquires a tract of land on January 1, 2009, for $100,000 cash. On December 31, 2009, the current market value of the land is $150,000. On December 31, 2010, the current market value of the land is $120,000. The firm sells the land on December 31, 2011, for $180,000 cash.

`LO 2-2, LO 2-3`

REQUIRED

Ignore income taxes. Indicate the effect on the balance sheet and income statement of the preceding information for 2009, 2010, and 2011 under each of the following valuation methods (Parts a–c).

a. Valuation of the land at acquisition cost until sale of the land (Approach 1)

b. Valuation of the land at current market value but including unrealized gains and losses in accumulated other comprehensive income until sale of the land (Approach 2)

c. Valuation of the land at current market value and including market value changes each year in net income (Approach 3)

d. Why is retained earnings on December 31, 2011, equal to $80,000 in all three cases despite the reporting of different amounts of net income each year?

LO 2-2, LO 2-3 **2.13 Effect of Valuation Method for Monetary Asset on Balance Sheet and Income Statement.** Refer to Problem 2.12. Assume that **Walmart** has accounted for the value of the land at acquisition cost and sells the land on December 31, 2011, for a two-year note receivable with a present value of $180,000 instead of for cash. The note bears interest at 8% and requires cash payments of $100,939 on December 31, 2012 and 2013. Interest rates for notes of this risk level increase to 10% on December 31, 2012, resulting in a market value for the note on this date of $91,762.

REQUIRED

Ignore income taxes. Indicate the effect on the balance sheet and income statement of the preceding information for 2011, 2012, and 2013 under each of the following valuation methods.

a. Valuation of the note at the present value of future cash flows using the historical market interest rate of 8% (Approach 1)

b. Valuation of the note at the present value of future cash flows, adjusting the note to fair value upon changes in market interest rates and including unrealized gains and losses in net income (Approach 3)

c. Why is retained earnings on December 31, 2013, equal to $101,878 in both cases despite the reporting of different amounts of net income each year?

LO 2-2, LO 2-3 **2.14 Effect of Valuation Method for Nonmonetary Asset on Balance Sheet and Income Statement.** Assume **Southern Copper Corporation (PCU)** acquired mining equipment for $100,000 cash on January 1, 2009. The equipment had an expected useful life of four years and zero salvage value. PCU calculates depreciation using the straight-line method over the remaining expected useful life in all cases. On December 31, 2009, after recognizing depreciation for the year, PCU learns that new equipment now offered on the market makes the purchased equipment partially obsolete. The market value of the equipment on December 31, 2009, reflecting this obsolescence, is $60,000. The expected useful life does not change. On December 31, 2010, the market value of the equipment is $48,000. PCU sells the equipment on January 1, 2012, for $26,000.

REQUIRED

Ignore income taxes.

a. Assume for this part that PCU accounts for the equipment using historical cost adjusted for depreciation and impairment losses. Indicate the effects of the following events on the balance sheet and income statement.

(1) Acquisition of the equipment for cash on January 1, 2009

(2) Depreciation for 2009

(3) Impairment loss for 2009

(4) Depreciation for 2010

(5) Depreciation for 2011

(6) Sale of the equipment on January 1, 2012

b. Assume that PCU accounts for the equipment using current fair market values adjusted for depreciation and impairment losses (with changes in fair market values recognized in net income). Using the analytical framework discussed in the chapter, indicate the effect of the following events on the balance sheet and income statement.

(1) Acquisition of the equipment for cash on January 1, 2009

(2) Depreciation for 2009

(3) Impairment loss for 2009

(4) Depreciation for 2010

(5) Recognition of unrealized holding gain or loss for 2010

(6) Depreciation for 2011

(7) Recognition of unrealized holding gain or loss for 2011

(8) Sale of the equipment on January 1, 2012

c. After the equipment is sold, why is retained earnings on January 1, 2012, equal to a negative $74,000 in both cases despite having shown a different pattern of expenses, gains, and losses over time?

2.15 Effect of Valuation Method for Monetary Asset on Balance Sheet and Income Statement.

LO 2-2, LO 2-3

Alfa Romeo incurs direct cash costs of $30,000 in manufacturing a red convertible automobile during 2009. Assume that it incurs all of these costs in cash. Alfa Romeo sells this automobile to you on January 1, 2010, for $45,000. You pay $5,000 immediately and agree to make annual payments of $14,414 on December 31, 2010, 2011, and 2012. Based on the interest rate appropriate for this note of 4% on January 1, 2012, the present value of the note is $40,000. The interest rate appropriate for this note is 5% on December 31, 2010, resulting in a present value of the remaining cash flows of $26,802. The interest rate appropriate for this note is 8% on December 31, 2011, resulting in a present value of the remaining cash flows of $13,346.

REQUIRED

Ignore income taxes.

a. Assume that Alfa Romeo accounts for this note throughout the three years using its initial present value and the historical interest rate (Approach 1). Indicate the effects of the following events on the balance sheet and income statement.

(1) Manufacture of the automobile during 2009

(2) Sale of the automobile on January 1, 2010

(3) Cash received and interest revenue recognized on December 31, 2010

(4) Cash received and interest revenue recognized on December 31, 2011

(5) Cash received and interest revenue recognized on December 31, 2012

b. Assume that Alfa Romeo values this note receivable at fair value each year with fair value changes recognized in net income (Approach 3). Changes in market interest rates affect the valuation of the note on the balance sheet immediately and the computation of interest revenue for the next year. Indicate the effects of the following events on the balance sheet and income statement.

(1) Manufacture of the automobile during 2009

(2) Sale of the automobile on January 1, 2010

(3) Cash received and interest revenue recognized on December 31, 2010

(4) Note receivable revalued and an unrealized holding gain or loss recognized on December 31, 2010

(5) Cash received and interest revenue recognized on December 31, 2011

(6) Note receivable revalued and an unrealized holding gain or loss recognized on December 31, 2011

(7) Cash received and interest revenue recognized on December 31, 2012

c. Why is retained earnings on December 31, 2012, equal to $18,242 in both cases, despite having shown a different pattern of income over time?

d. Discuss the trade-off in financial reporting when moving from Approach 1 in Part a to Approach 3 in Part b.

 2.16 Deferred Tax Assets. Components of the deferred tax asset of **Biosante Pharmaceuticals, Inc.,** are shown in Exhibit 2.14. The company had no deferred tax liabilities.

Exhibit 2.14

Biosante Pharmaceuticals, Inc.
Income Tax Disclosures (Problem 2.16)

	2008	2007
Net operating loss carryforwards	$ 23,609,594	$ 17,588,392
Tax basis in intangible assets	403,498	538,819
Research and development credits	3,415,143	2,569,848
Stock option expense	1,462,065	1,017,790
Other	56,063	103,235
Gross Deferred Tax Asset	$ 28,946,363	$ 21,818,084
Valuation allowance	(28,946,363)	(21,818,084)
Net Deferred Tax Asset	$ 0	$ 0

At December 31, 2008, the company had approximately $62,542,000 of net operating loss carryforwards available to reduce future taxable income for a period of up to 20 years. The net operating loss carryforwards expire in 2018–2028. The net operating loss carryforwards as well as amortization of various intangibles, principally acquired in-process research and development, generate deferred tax benefits that have been recorded as deferred tax assets and are entirely offset by a tax valuation allowance. The valuation allowance has been provided at 100% to reduce the deferred tax assets to zero, the amount management believes is more likely than not to be realized. In addition, the company has provided a full valuation allowance against $3,415,143 of research and development credits, which are available to reduce future income taxes, if any, through 2028.

Source: Biosante Pharmaceuticals, Inc., Form 10-K, for the fiscal year ended December 31, 2008.

REQUIRED

a. At the end of 2008, the largest deferred tax asset is for net operating loss carryforwards. (Net operating loss carryforwards [also referred to as tax loss carryforwards] are amounts reported as taxable losses on tax filings. Because the tax authorities generally do not "pay" corporations for incurring losses, companies are allowed to "carry forward" taxable losses to future years to offset taxable income. These future tax benefits give rise to deferred tax assets.) As of the end of 2008, what is the dollar amount of the company's net operating loss carryforwards? What is the dollar amount of the deferred tax asset for the net operating loss carryforwards? Describe how these two amounts are related.

b. Biosante has gross deferred tax assets of $28,946,363. However, the net deferred tax assets balance is zero. Explain.

c. The valuation allowance for the deferred tax asset increased from $21,818,084 to $28,946,363 between 2007 and 2008. How did this change affect the company's net income?

2.17 Interpreting Income Tax Disclosures. The financial statements of ABC Corporation, a retail chain, reveal the information for income taxes shown in Exhibit 2.15.

Exhibit 2.15

ABC Corporation Income Tax Disclosures
(amounts in millions) (Problem 2.17)

For the Year Ended January 31:	2014	2013	
Income before income taxes			
United States	$ 3,031	$ 2,603	
Income tax expense			
Current:			
Federal	$ 908	$ 669	
State and local	144	107	
Total Current	$ 1,052	$ 776	
Deferred:			
Federal	$ 83	$ 184	
State and local	11	24	
Total Deferred	$ 94	$ 208	
Total	$ 1,146	$ 984	

January 31:	2014	2013	2012
Components of deferred tax assets and liabilities			
Deferred tax assets:			
Self-insured benefits	$ 179	$ 143	$ 188
Deferred compensation	332	297	184
Inventory	47	44	56
Postretirement health care obligation	38	42	41
Uncollectible accounts	147	133	113
Other	128	53	166
Total Deferred Tax Assets	$ 871	$ 712	$ 748
Deferred tax liabilities:			
Depreciation	$ (1,136)	$ (945)	$ (826)
Pensions	(268)	(218)	(190)
Other	(96)	(84)	(59)
Total Deferred Tax Liabilities	$ (1,500)	$ (1,247)	$ (1,075)
Net Deferred Tax Liability	$ (629)	$ (535)	$ (327)

REQUIRED

a. Assuming that ABC had no significant permanent differences between book income and taxable income, did income before taxes for financial reporting exceed or fall short of taxable income for 2013? Explain.

b. Did income before taxes for financial reporting exceed or fall short of taxable income for 2014? Explain.

c. Will the adjustment to net income for deferred taxes to compute cash flow from operations in the statement of cash flows result in an addition or a subtraction for 2013? For 2014?

d. ABC does not contract with an insurance agency for property and liability insurance; instead, it self-insures. ABC recognizes an expense and a liability each year for financial reporting to reflect its average expected long-term property and liability losses. When it experiences an actual loss, it charges that loss against the liability. The income tax law permits self-insured firms to deduct such losses only in the year sustained. Why are deferred taxes related to self-insurance disclosed as a deferred tax asset instead of a deferred tax liability? Suggest reasons for the direction of the change in amounts for this deferred tax asset between 2012 and 2014.

e. ABC treats certain storage and other inventory costs as expenses in the year incurred for financial reporting but must include these in inventory for tax reporting. Why are deferred taxes related to inventory disclosed as a deferred tax asset? Suggest reasons for the direction of the change in amounts for this deferred tax asset between 2012 and 2014.

f. Firms must recognize expenses related to postretirement health care and pension obligations as employees provide services, but claim an income tax deduction only when they make cash payments under the benefit plan. Why are deferred taxes related to health care obligation disclosed as a deferred tax asset? Why are deferred taxes related to pensions disclosed as a deferred tax liability? Suggest reasons for the direction of the change in amounts for these deferred tax items between 2012 and 2014.

g. Firms must recognize expenses related to uncollectible accounts when they recognize sales revenues, but claim an income tax deduction when they deem a particular customer's accounts uncollectible. Why are deferred taxes related to this item disclosed as a deferred tax asset? Suggest reasons for the direction of the change in amounts for this deferred tax asset between 2012 and 2014.

h. ABC uses the straight-line depreciation method for financial reporting and accelerated depreciation methods for income tax purposes. Why are deferred taxes related to depreciation disclosed as a deferred tax liability? Suggest reasons for the direction of the change in amounts for this deferred tax liability between 2012 and 2014.

LO 2-4, LO 2-5 **2.18 Interpreting Income Tax Disclosures.** Prepaid Legal Services (PPD) is a company that sells insurance for legal expenses. Customers pay premiums in advance for coverage over some specified period. Thus, PPD obtains cash but has unearned revenue until the passage of time over the specified period of coverage. Also, the company pays various costs to acquire customers (such as sales materials, commissions, and prepayments to legal firms who provide services to customers). These upfront payments are expensed over the specified period that customers' contracts span. Exhibit 2.16 provides information from PPD's income tax note.

REQUIRED

a. Assuming that PPD had no significant permanent differences between book income and taxable income, did income before taxes for financial reporting exceed or fall short of taxable income for 2007? For 2008? Explain.

b. Will the adjustment to net income for deferred taxes to compute cash flow from operations in the statement of cash flows result in an addition or a subtraction for 2007? For 2008?

c. PPD must report as taxable income premiums collected from customers, although the company defers recognizing them as income for financial reporting purposes until they are earned over the contract period. Why are deferred taxes related to deferred revenue disclosed as a deferred tax asset instead of a deferred tax liability? Suggest reasons for the direction of the change in amounts for this deferred tax asset between 2007 and 2008.

Exhibit 2.16

Prepaid Legal Services Income Tax Disclosures
(Problem 2.18)

The provision for income taxes consists of the following:

	2008	2007	2006
Current	$ 36,840	$ 33,864	$27,116
Deferred	385	(552)	774
Total Provision for Income Taxes	$ 37,225	$ 33,312	$27,890

Deferred tax liabilities and assets at December 31, 2008 and 2007, are comprised of the following:

	2008	2007
Deferred tax liabilities relating to:		
Deferred member and associate service costs	$ 6,919	$ 7,367
Property and equipment	8,693	7,829
Unrealized investment gains	159	131
Total Deferred Tax Liabilities	$ 15,771	$ 15,327
Deferred tax assets relating to:		
Expenses not yet deducted for tax purposes	$ 4,028	$ 3,552
Deferred revenue and fees	11,138	11,564
Other	110	101
Total Deferred Tax Assets	$ 15,276	$ 15,217
Net Deferred Tax Liability	$ (495)	$ (110)

Source: Prepaid Legal Services, Inc., Form 10-K, for the fiscal year ended December 31, 2012.

d. Firms are generally allowed to deduct cash costs on their tax returns, although they might defer some of these costs for financial reporting purposes. As noted above, PPD defers various costs associated with obtaining customers. Why are deferred taxes related to this item disclosed as a deferred tax liability? Suggest reasons for the direction of the change in amounts for this deferred tax asset between 2007 and 2008.

e. Like most companies, PPD uses the straight-line depreciation method for financial reporting and accelerated depreciation methods for income tax purposes. Why are deferred taxes related to depreciation disclosed as a deferred tax liability? Suggest reasons for the direction of the change in amounts for this deferred tax liability between 2007 and 2008.

f. Based only on the selected disclosures from the income tax footnote provided in Exhibit 2.16 and your responses to Parts d and e above, do you believe that PPD reported growing or declining revenue and profitability in 2008 relative to 2007? Explain.

2.19 Interpreting Income Tax Disclosures. The financial statements of **Nike, Inc.**, reveal the information regarding income taxes shown in Exhibit 2.17.

LO 2-4, LO 2-5

REQUIRED

a. Assuming that Nike had no significant permanent differences between book income and taxable income, did income before taxes for financial reporting exceed or fall short of taxable income for 2007? Explain.

Exhibit 2.17

Nike, Inc., Income Tax Disclosures (amounts in millions) (Problem 2.19)

Income before income taxes is as follows:	2008	2007	2006
Income before income taxes:			
United States	$ 713.0	$ 805.1	$ 838.6
Foreign	1,789.9	1,394.8	1,303.0
	$ 2,502.9	$ 2,199.9	$ 2,414.6

The provision for income taxes consists of the following:	2008	2007	2006
Current:			
United States			
Federal	$ 469.9	$ 352.6	$ 359.0
State	58.4	59.6	60.6
Foreign	391.8	261.9	356.0
	$ 920.1	$ 674.1	$ 775.6
Deferred:			
United States			
Federal	$ (273.0)	$ 38.7	$ (4.2)
State	(5.0)	(4.8)	(6.8)
Foreign	(22.6)	0.4	(15.0)
	$ (300.6)	$ 34.3	$ (26.0)
Total Provision for Income Taxes	$ 619.5	$ 708.4	$ 749.6

Deferred tax assets and (liabilities) are comprised of the following:	2008	2007
Deferred tax assets:		
Allowance for doubtful accounts	$ 13.1	$ 12.4
Inventories	49.2	45.8
Sales returns reserves	49.2	42.1
Deferred compensation	158.4	132.5
Stock-based compensation	55.2	30.3
Reserves and accrued liabilities	57.0	46.2
Property, plant, and equipment	7.9	16.3
Foreign loss carry-forwards	40.1	37.5
Foreign tax credit carry-forwards	91.9	3.4
Hedges	42.9	26.2
Other	40.5	33.0
Total Deferred Tax Assets	$ 605.4	$ 425.7
Valuation allowance	(40.7)	(42.3)
Total Deferred Tax Assets after Valuation Allowance	$ 564.7	$ 383.4

(Continued)

Exhibit 2.17 (Continued)		
Deferred tax liabilities:		
Undistributed earnings of foreign subsidiaries	$ (113.2)	$ (232.6)
Property, plant, and equipment	(67.4)	(66.1)
Intangibles	(214.2)	(97.2)
Hedges	(1.3)	(2.5)
Other	(0.7)	(17.8)
Total Deferred Tax Liability	$ (396.8)	$ (416.2)
Net Deferred Tax Asset (Liability)	$ 167.9	$ (32.8)

Source: Nike, Inc., Form 10-K, for the fiscal year ended May 31, 2012.

b. Did book income before taxes for financial reporting exceed or fall short of taxable income for 2008? Explain.

c. Will the adjustment to net income for deferred taxes to compute cash flow from operations in the statement of cash flows result in an addition or a subtraction for 2008?

d. Nike recognizes provisions for sales returns and doubtful accounts each year in computing income for financial reporting. Nike cannot claim an income tax deduction for these returns and doubtful accounts until customers return goods or accounts receivable become uncollectible. Why do the deferred taxes for returns and doubtful accounts appear as deferred tax assets instead of deferred tax liabilities? Suggest possible reasons why the deferred tax asset for sales returns and doubtful accounts increased between 2007 and 2008.

e. Nike recognizes an expense related to deferred compensation as employees render services but cannot claim an income tax deduction until it pays cash to a retirement fund. Why do the deferred taxes for deferred compensation appear as a deferred tax asset? Suggest possible reasons why the deferred tax asset increased between 2007 and 2008.

f. Nike states that it recognizes a valuation allowance on deferred tax assets related to foreign loss carryforwards because the benefits of some of these losses will expire before the firm realizes the benefits. Why might the valuation allowance have decreased slightly between 2007 and 2008?

g. Nike reports a large deferred tax liability for Intangibles. In another footnote, Nike states, "During the fourth quarter ended May 31, 2008 the Company completed the acquisition of Umbro Plc ("Umbro"). As a result, $378.4 million was allocated to unamortized trademarks, $319.2 million was allocated to goodwill and $41.1 million was allocated to other amortized intangible assets consisting of Umbro's sourcing network, established customer relationships and the United Soccer League Franchise." Why would Nike report a deferred tax liability associated with this increase in intangible assets on the balance sheet?

h. Nike recognizes its share of the earnings of foreign subsidiaries each year for financial reporting but recognizes income from these investments for income tax reporting only when it receives a dividend. Why do the deferred taxes related to these investments appear as a deferred tax liability?

i. Why does Nike recognize both deferred tax assets and deferred tax liabilities related to investments in foreign operations?

LO 2-6

2.20 Analyzing Transactions. Using the analytical framework, indicate the effect of the following related transactions of a firm.

a. January 1: Issued 10,000 shares of common stock for $50,000.

b. January 1: Acquired a building costing $35,000, paying $5,000 in cash and borrowing the remainder from a bank.

c. During the year: Acquired inventory costing $40,000 on account from various suppliers.

d. During the year: Sold inventory costing $30,000 for $65,000 on account.

e. During the year: Paid employees $15,000 as compensation for services rendered during the year.

f. During the year: Collected $45,000 from customers related to sales on account.

g. During the year: Paid merchandise suppliers $28,000 related to purchases on account.

h. December 31: Recognized depreciation on the building of $7,000 for financial reporting. Depreciation expense for income tax purposes was $10,000.

i. December 31: Recognized compensation for services rendered during the last week in December but not paid by year-end of $4,000.

j. December 31: Recognized and paid interest on the bank loan in Part b of $2,400 for the year.

k. Recognized income taxes on the net effect of the preceding transactions at an income tax rate of 40%. Assume that the firm pays cash immediately for any taxes currently due to the government.

LO 2-6

2.21 Analyzing Transactions. Using the analytical framework, indicate the effect of each of the three independent sets of transactions described next.

(1) a. January 15, 2014: Purchased marketable equity securities for $100,000.

b. December 31, 2014: Revalued the marketable securities to their market value of $90,000. Unrealized changes in the market value of marketable equity securities appear in accumulated other comprehensive income.

c. December 31, 2014: Recognized income tax effects of the revaluation in Part b at an income tax rate of 40%. The income tax law includes changes in the market value of equity securities in taxable income only when the investor sells the securities.

d. January 5, 2015: Sold the marketable equity securities for $94,000.

e. January 5, 2015: Recognized the tax effect of the sale of the securities in Part d. Assume that the tax is paid in cash immediately.

(2) a. During 2015: Sold inventory on account for $500,000.

b. During 2015: The cost of the goods sold in Part b is $400,000.

c. During 2015: Estimated that uncollectible accounts on the goods sold in Part a will equal 2% of the selling price.

d. During 2015: Estimated that warranty claims on the goods sold in Part a will equal 4% of the selling price.

e. During 2015: Actual accounts written off as uncollectible totaled $3,000.

f. During 2015: Actual cash expenditures on warranty claims totaled $8,000.

g. December 31, 2015: Recognized income tax effects of the preceding six transactions. The income tax rate is 40%. The income tax law permits a deduction for uncollectible accounts when a firm writes off accounts as uncollectible and for warranty claims when a firm makes warranty expenditures. Assume that any tax is paid in cash immediately.

(3) a. January 1, 2015: Purchased $100,000 face value of zero-coupon bonds for $68,058. These bonds mature on December 31, 2019, and are priced on the market at the time of issuance to yield 8% compounded annually. Zero-coupon bonds earn interest as time passes for financial and tax reporting, but the issuer does not pay

interest until maturity. Assume that any tax owed on taxable income is paid in cash immediately.

b. December 31, 2015: Recognized interest revenue on the bonds for 2015.

c. December 31, 2015: Recognized income tax effect of the interest revenue for 2015. The income tax law taxes interest on zero-coupon bonds as it accrues each year.

d. December 31, 2016: Recognized interest revenue on the bonds for 2016.

e. December 31, 2016: Recognized income tax effect of the interest revenue for 2016.

f. January 2, 2017: Sold the zero-coupon bonds for $83,683.

g. January 2, 2017: Recognized the income tax effect of the gain or loss on the sale. The applicable income tax rate is 40%, which affects cash immediately.

INTEGRATIVE CASE 2.1

LO 2-1, LO 2-2, LO 2-3, LO 2-4

Starbucks

The financial statements of **Starbucks Corporation** are presented in Exhibits 1.26–1.28 (see pages 74–77). The income tax note to those financial statements reveals the information regarding income taxes shown in Exhibit 2.18.

REQUIRED

a. Assuming that Starbucks had no significant permanent differences between book income and taxable income, did income before taxes for financial reporting exceed or fall short of taxable income for 2012? Explain.

b. Will the adjustment to net income for deferred taxes to compute cash flow from operations in the statement of cash flows result in an addition or subtraction for 2012?

c. Starbucks rents retail space for its coffee shops. It must recognize rent expense as it uses rental facilities but cannot claim an income tax deduction until it pays cash to the landlord. Suggest the scenario that would give rise to a deferred tax asset instead of a deferred tax liability related to occupancy cost ("Accrued occupancy costs").

d. Starbucks recognizes an expense related to retirement benefits as employees rendered services but cannot claim an income tax deduction until it pays cash to a retirement fund. Why do the deferred taxes for deferred compensation appear as a deferred tax asset ("Accrued compensation and related costs")? Suggest possible reasons why the deferred tax asset decreased slightly between the end of 2011 and the end of 2012.

e. Starbucks reports deferred revenue for sales of store value cards, such as the Starbucks Card and gift certificates. These amounts are taxed when collected, but not recognized in financial reporting income until tendered at a store. Why does the tax effect of deferred revenue appear as a deferred tax asset?

f. Starbucks recognizes a valuation allowance on its deferred tax assets to reflect net operating losses of consolidated foreign subsidiaries. Why might the valuation allowance have increased between 2011 and 2012?

g. Starbucks uses the straight-line depreciation method for financial reporting and accelerated depreciation for income tax reporting. Like most firms, the largest deferred tax liability is for property, plant, and equipment (depreciation). Explain how depreciation leads to a deferred tax liability. Suggest possible reasons why the amount of the deferred tax liability related to depreciation increased between 2011 and 2012.

Exhibit 2.18

Starbucks Income Tax Disclosures
(amounts in millions) (Integrative Case 2.1)

For the Year Ended September 30 and October 2, respectively:	2012	2011
Income Tax Expense		
Current:		
Federal	$466.0	$344.7
State	79.9	61.2
Foreign	76.8	37.3
Deferred	51.7	119.9
Total	$674.4	$563.1

As of the Year Ended September 30 and October 2, respectively:	2012	2011
Components of Deferred Tax Assets and Liabilities		
Deferred tax assets:		
Property, plant, and equipment	$ 62.7	$ 46.4
Accrued occupancy costs	72.0	55.9
Accrued compensation and related costs	66.9	69.6
Other accrued liabilities	15.7	27.8
Asset retirement obligation asset	20.1	19.0
Deferred revenue	43.7	47.8
Asset impairments	38.5	60.0
Tax credits	14.6	23.0
Stock based compensation	131.8	128.8
Net operating losses	99.2	85.5
Other	80.9	58.6
Total Deferred Tax Assets	$ 646.1	$ 622.4
Valuation allowance	(154.2)	(137.4)
Net Deferred Tax Assets	$ 491.9	$ 485.0
Deferred tax liabilities:		
Property, plant, and equipment	$ (89.0)	$ (66.4)
Intangible assets and goodwill	(34.0)	(25.2)
Other	(44.8)	(18.1)
Total Deferred Tax Liabilities	$ (167.8)	$ (109.7)
Net Deferred Tax Asset	$ 324.1	$ 375.3

Source: Starbucks Corporation, Form 10-K, for the fiscal year ended September 30, 2012.

Income Flows versus Cash Flows: Understanding the Statement of Cash Flows

LEARNING OBJECTIVES

LO 3-1   Identify the purpose of the statement of cash flows.

LO 3-2   Describe the structure and interpretation of operating, investing, and financing cash flow activities on the statement of cash flows.

LO 3-3   Evaluate how the statement of cash flows captures the various stages of firms' life cycles.

LO 3-4   Explain how net income and cash flows from operations are related and how the cash flow statement articulates information in the income statement and balance sheet.

LO 3-5   Prepare a statement of cash flows from balance sheet and income statement data.

LO 3-6   Recognize additional uses of the statement of cash flows, such as for accounting and risk analysis.

Chapter Overview

The previous chapter discussed general principles for the valuation of assets and liabilities on the *balance sheet* and the recognition of components of income on the *income statement*. This chapter's focus is on the *statement of cash flows*.[1] In addition to a balance sheet and an income statement, U.S. GAAP and IFRS require firms to include a statement of cash flows in their published financial statements each period.[2]

This chapter examines the statement of cash flows in greater depth than the overview presented in Chapter 1. First, we explore the partitioning of cash flows into operating, investing, and financing activities; we then examine how various patterns of cash flows map into various stages of firm life cycles. Second, the chapter illustrates how the balance sheet, income statement, and statement of cash flows are linked. Third, the

---

[1]Prior to 1988, firms reported a statement of changes in financial position, which provided some similar information but focused on "funds" and did not require firms to report cash flows during a period.

[2]There are two substantive differences in statements of cash flows between U.S. GAAP and IFRS. First, IFRS defines cash and cash equivalents to include an offset for bank overdrafts, whereas these are treated as working capital under U.S. GAAP. Second, there are differences in the classification of dividends and interest, discussed later in the chapter.

chapter walks you through the nuts and bolts of preparing the statement of cash flows using information from the balance sheet and income statement. If you understand how to prepare a cash flow statement, you will have a much greater ability to interpret the information in the statement of cash flows. Finally, the last part of the chapter provides a prelude to how analysts can integrate an understanding of the relation between net income and cash flows to draw inferences about earnings quality, liquidity and credit risk, or calculate free cash flows, which are discussed in more detail in later chapters.

LO 3-1

Identify the purpose of the statement of cash flows.

Purpose of the Statement of Cash Flows

The objective of providing a statement of cash flows is to assist users in understanding the cash inflows and outflows that support a firm's primary activities. This information is sometimes difficult to extract from the accrual accounting information on the balance sheet and income statement. Just as the income statement gives you an understanding of how the business changed during the period through the perspective of profits or losses, the statement of cash flows gives you an understanding of how the business changed during the period through the lens of the Cash account.

Under the frequently used indirect method for both U.S. GAAP and IFRS, the first line of the statement of cash flows is net income, which is reconciled to the net change in cash during the period. An oversimplification of the statement of cash flows is that it reports all of the sources and uses of cash during a period. However, the statement of cash flows provides numerous insights not available from either the balance sheet or the income statement. The statement of cash flows:

- reconciles the change in cash on the balance sheet and net income reported in the income statement.
- is logically organized in three sections (*operating* activities, *investing* activities, and *financing* activities), which correspond to the primary pursuits necessary to generate profits. Provides information about cash flows to and from entities, such as customers, suppliers, creditors, and investors, with whom the firm conducts business.
- assists analysts with numerous other tasks, such as uncovering accounting discretion, calculating free cash flows and identifying other information unavailable elsewhere in the financial reports.

It is cash flows that precede the recognition of most balance sheet and income statement line items. The accountant's job is to take observed cash flows, along with other events, employ accrual accounting procedures, and prepare the income statement and balance sheet under accrual accounting principles. As noted in the previous chapter, accrual accounting exists to help investors better predict the nature, amount, and timing of future cash flows. Thus, we emphasize that the statement of cash flows is essentially an "unraveling" of the accrual accounting procedures employed in the preparation of the balance sheet and income statement, in order to reveal the underlying cash flows.

Cash Flows versus Net Income

A firm's cash flows will differ from net income each period because:

- cash receipts from customers do not necessarily occur in the same period revenue is recognized.

- cash expenditures do not necessarily occur in the same period expenses are recognized.
- cash inflows and outflows from investing and financing activities do not immediately flow through the income statement.

Recall that a primary objective in preparing an income statement is the matching of economic resources used or consumed (expenses) during the period with economic resources earned (revenues) during the period. Under accrual accounting, the timing of the inflow and outflow of cash is ignored. However, cash is essential for operating, investing, and financing activities. Thus, firms must provide the statement of cash flows, a financial statement that reports the flows of cash in and out of the firm each period.

Cash Flows and Financial Analysis

An understanding of a firm's cash flows is an integral part of each of the six steps in financial statement analysis discussed in Chapter 1:

- **Identify the Economic Characteristics of a Business:** You will see dramatic differences in the pattern of cash flows from operating, investing, and financing activities among various types of businesses as well as within a firm throughout various stages of the firm's life cycle. For example, high-growth, capital-intensive firms generally experience insufficient cash flow from operations to finance capital expenditures (investing activities); thus, they require external sources of capital (financing activities). In contrast, mature companies usually can use cash flows from operations to finance capital expenditures and to repay debt, pay dividends, or repurchase common stock (financing activities).
- **Identify the Strategy of the Firm:** The statement of cash flows will reveal to you the overall strategy of a firm, especially how the firm is generating and using cash to execute its operating, investing and financing strategies, as well as its trajectory of growth. For example, a firm opting for organic growth will exhibit large positive cash flows from operations, which are funneled into investing activities. On the other hand, a firm pursuing a strategy of growth by acquiring other firms will report significant cash outflows for corporate acquisitions (investing activities) and, perhaps, large cash inflows from financing activities. The statement of cash flows provides a "reality check" on the firm's stated strategies, by showing you how the firm is actually generating and using cash.
- **Identify Nonrecurring, Unusual Items and Provide Insight into the Use of Accounting Discretion by Managers:** The cash flow statement provides you with information into the cash versus non-cash components of unusual items, such as one-time gains or losses and discontinued operations. In addition, an analyst who chooses to eliminate nonrecurring or unusual items from net income to more clearly assess operating profitability also should adjust the relevant parts of the cash flow statement. You will also find that the reconciling adjustments in the operating section can sometimes reveal the extent to which managers use accounting discretion to affect reported earnings.
- **Analyze Profitability and Risk:** You learned in Chapter 2 that over sufficiently long periods, net income equals the net cash flows from operating, investing, and non-owner financing activities. Thus, a reality check on reported net income is that it should converge to operating cash flows as a firm matures and transitions into more of a "steady state," although they both will fluctuate from one period to the next. Also, the ability of a firm to generate sufficient cash flow from

operations to finance capital expenditures and adequately service debt obligations is a key signal of the financial health of the firm.

- **Prepare Forecasted Financial Statements:** As Chapter 10 will show you, forecasting is the most important part of firm valuation. Forecasting profitability is incomplete without forecasts of all balance sheet items. Together, the forecasted income statement and balance sheet imply a series of cash flows. For example, you may forecast continued growth in net income when you see continued investments in productive assets. However, a key determinant of such forecasts is how the firm will generate the cash necessary to finance future growth. Will operations generate sufficient cash flow, or will external financing be required?

- **Value the Firm:** Chapter 12 discusses firm valuation based on "free cash flows" to equity shareholders, which is cash flow available for distribution to investors after necessary reinvestments in operating assets or required payments to debtholders are made. The statement of cash flows provides the information needed to calculate free cash flows.

- The statement of cash flows reveals the cash flows relative to reported profitability.

- Incorporating analysis of the statement of cash flows is an integral part of the six-step process of financial statement analysis.

Describe the structure and interpretation of operating, investing, and financing cash flow activities on the statement of cash flows.

The Relations among the Cash Flow Activities

The organization of the statement of cash flows partitions a firm's activities into three logical sections: operating activities, investing activities, and financing activities. One intuitive way to think about a firm is that it generates cash inflows and outflows every day from its operating activities, and continually reinvests cash by investing it in long term productive assets; cash shortfalls trigger the need for new financing, whereas excess cash flows allow firms to distribute cash by paying off debt or paying dividends to shareholders. The three sections of the statement of cash flows follow this logical progression.

Operating activities include all activities directly involving the production and delivery of goods or services; examples include cash received from customers and cash used to purchase raw materials and to compensate employees. As we will discuss later, most firms report this section under what is referred to as the "indirect method," which undoes the accrual accounting entries that determine net income in order to reveal the underlying cash flows. The *investing activities* section chronicles expenditures for (and proceeds from dispositions of) assets, such as equipment and joint ventures, that are intended to be used to generate cash flows. Also included in the investing section are cash flows related to acquisitions and divestitures. The section summarizing *financing activities* of the firm includes cash received from (or returned to) capital providers such as banks, other lending institutions, and shareholders. The subtotals for net operating, investing, and financing cash flows provide the net increase or decrease in cash and cash equivalents.

As an example, refer to **PepsiCo**'s Consolidated Statement of Cash Flows in Appendix A. Note the three activity sections presented in the statement of cash flows. For all years presented, PepsiCo generates very large positive cash flows from operating activities and negative cash flows for both investing and financing activities. For example, in 2012, PepsiCo generated $8,479 million from operating activities and used $3,005 million and $3,306 million for investing and financing activities, respectively. Thus, PepsiCo generates a great deal of cash from its core operations (as shown in the operating section) and uses much of it to invest in productive assets (shown in the investing section) and to return cash to capital providers (shown in the financing section). For PepsiCo, the net of operating, investing, and financing activities is an increase in cash and cash equivalents of $2,230 million (which includes an adjustment for the effects of exchange rate changes on cash balances).

Note several important line items in PepsiCo's statement of cash flows for 2012. First, the largest adjustment in the operating section is for the addback of depreciation and amortization, which adds $2,689 million to PepsiCo's $6,214 million of net income. The sum of other non-working capital adjustments (from "Stock-based compensation expense" through "Deferred income taxes and other tax charges and credits") is negative $658 million, indicating a net negative adjustment to net income due to these items. The large depreciation and amortization adjustment is offset partly by the net negative adjustment for the other non-working capital items, which is typical of a large, mature company such as PepsiCo. Second, the net cash flows from changes in working capital accounts (from "Change in accounts and notes receivable" through "Other, net") is $234 million, indicating a net decrease of investments in working capital during 2012. Third, investing cash flows primarily reflects capital spending ($2,714 million). The financing section shows that PepsiCo raised $3,550 million in net long-term debt. PepsiCo also used $3,305 million to pay dividends and $3,226 million to repurchase common and preferred shares. The net increase in long-term debt coupled with the dividends and share repurchases contributes to an increase in PepsiCo's leverage.

- Operating activities are those involving the production or delivery of the firm's primary products or services.
- Investing activities include the acquisition or disposal of long-lived productive operating assets, as well as the investment or sale of other assets that generate cash flows.

- Financing activities summarize the cash received from or returned to providers of capital.

Quick Check

Cash Flow Activities and a Firm's Life Cycle

LO 3-3

Evaluate how the statement of cash flows captures the various stages of firms' life cycles.

A helpful framework for intuitively grasping the information conveyed through the organization of cash flows involves the product life cycle concept from economics and marketing. Individual products (like goods or services) move through four phases: (1) introduction, (2) growth, (3) maturity, and (4) decline. Firms also evolve through these phases, as graphically depicted in Exhibit 3.1, which shows stylized patterns for revenues, net income, and cash flows over the life cycle.

Exhibit 3.1

Stylized Patterns of Revenues, Net Income, and Cash Flows from Operations, Investing, and Financing at Various Stages of a Product or Business Life Cycle

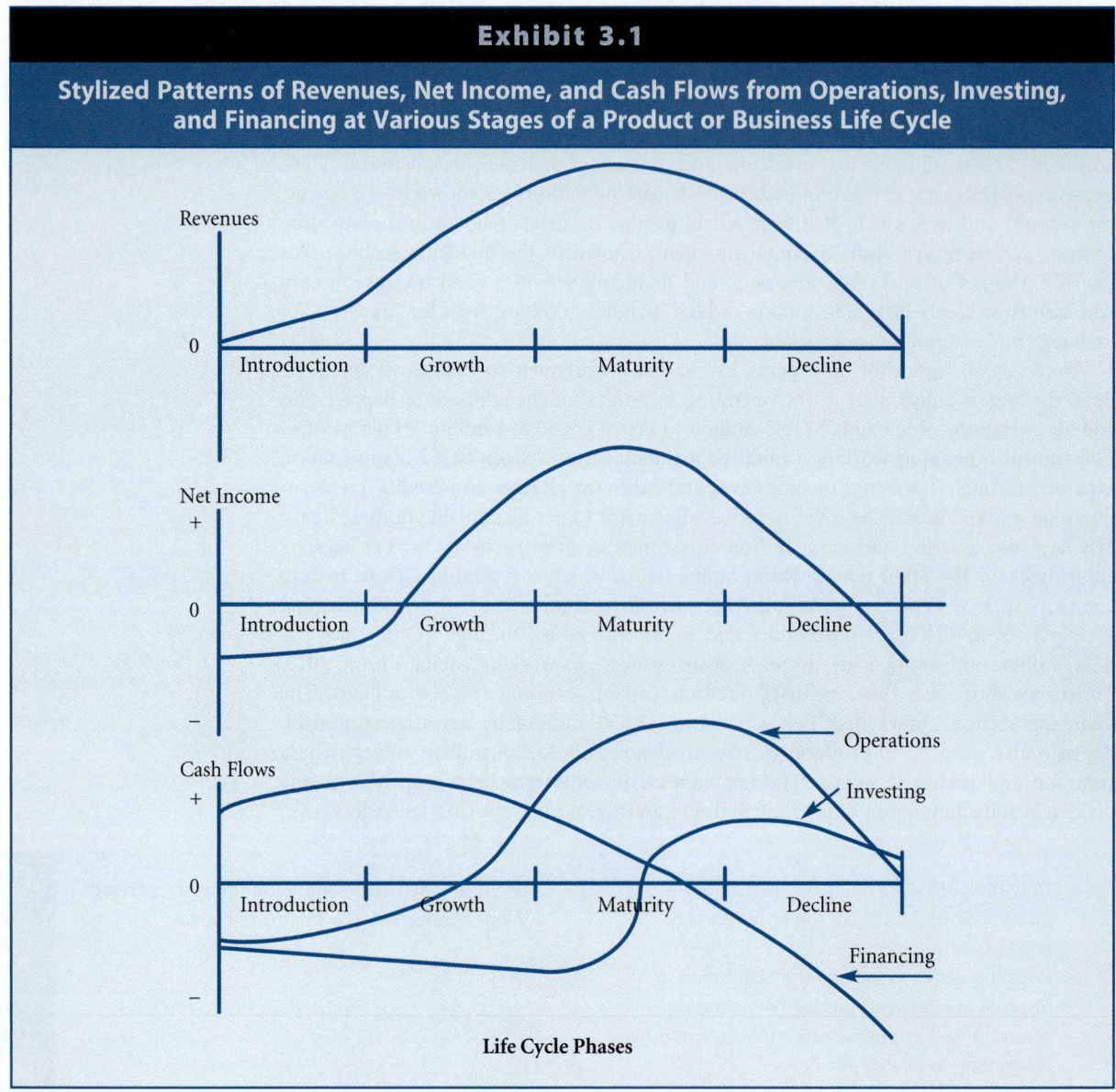

A Firm's Life Cycle: Revenues

The top graph shows the pattern of revenues throughout the four phases, which typically follows a period of growth, peaking during maturity, and a subsequent decline as customers switch to alternatives. Obviously, the length of these phases and the steepness of the revenue curve vary by type and success of a product. Products subject to rapid technological change, such as semiconductors and computer software, or driven by fads, such as clothing fashions, move through these four phases in just a few years. Other products, such as venerable staple products like **Campbell's** soup, **Disney** movies, **Marlboro** cigarettes, **Gillette** razors, **Kellogg's** cereal, and **Michelin** tires can remain in the maturity phase for many years. Although it is difficult to pinpoint the precise location of a product on its life cycle curve, one can generally identify the phase and whether the product is in the early or later portion of a phase.

A typical firm provides numerous products or services, so the applicability of the theory and evidence for single products is more difficult when firms are diversified across numerous products at different stages of their life cycle. Nevertheless, these patterns are descriptive of firm performance over time as they introduce new products and discontinue older ones.

A Firm's Life Cycle: Net Income

The middle panel of Exhibit 3.1 shows the trend of net income over the life cycle of a product or firm. Net losses usually occur in the introduction and early growth phases because revenues are less than the cost of designing and launching new products. Then, net income peaks during the maturity phase, followed by a decline.

A Firm's Life Cycle: Cash Flows

The lower panel of Exhibit 3.1 shows the cash flows from operating, investing, and financing activities during the four life cycle phases. As with revenues, the length of phases and steepness of the net income and cash flow curves vary depending on the success and sustainability of a product or a firm's operations and strategy. For example, **PepsiCo**'s systematically large positive net income and cash flows from operations are consistent with PepsiCo's products (in aggregate) being both mature and profitable.

During the initial introduction of a product or business, revenues are minimal; therefore, net income and net cash flows from operating and investing activities are typically low or negative, and the firm relies heavily on cash flows from financing activities. As the growth phase accelerates, operations become profitable and begin to generate cash. However, firms must use the cash generated to fund activities such as selling products on credit (that is, accounts receivable) and building up inventory in anticipation of higher sales volume in the future. Thus, because these expenditures are accounted for as assets on the balance sheet rather than being expensed immediately, compared to cash flows from operations, net income usually turns positive earlier than do cash flows. The extent of the negative cash flows from investing activities depends on the rate of growth and the degree of capital expenditure needs and asset intensity. Continuing from the introduction phase, firms obtain most of the cash they need during the introduction and growth phase by borrowing or issuing stock to external investors.

As products and businesses move through the maturity phase, the cash flow pattern changes dramatically. Operations become profitable and generate substantial positive cash flows because of market acceptance of the product and a leveling off of working capital needs and asset acquisitions. Also, with revenues leveling off, firms invest to *maintain* rather than *increase* productive capacity. During the later stages of the maturity phase, net cash flows from sales of unneeded plant assets sometimes result in a net positive cash flow from investing activities. Firms can use the excess cash flow from operations and, to a lesser extent, from the sale of investments to repay debt incurred during the introduction and growth phases, to pay dividends, and to repurchase outstanding common stock. During the decline phase, cash flows from operations and investing activities taper off as customers become satiated or switch to alternative products, thus decreasing sales. At this point, firms use cash flows to repay outstanding debt from the introduction and growth phases and can pay dividends or repurchase common stock from equity investors.

Few business firms rely on a single product; most have a range of products at different stages of the life cycle. A multiproduct firm such as PepsiCo can use cash generated from products in the maturity phase of their life cycle to finance products in the introduction and growth phases and therefore not need as much external financing. Furthermore, the statement of cash flows discussed in this chapter reports amounts for a firm as a whole and not for each product. If the life cycle concept is to assist in interpreting statements of cash flows, you should appreciate how individual products aggregate at the firm level.

Knowledge of competitive industry dynamics and trends can help guide you through an assessment of firm-level cash flows. For example, investor excitement in technology-driven industries such as biotechnology most often peaks during the growth phase. Although such firms may have some products at various stages of the product life cycle, the interest is in forecasting the emergence of new technologies that translate into new products that might generate large profits and cash flows. A good example is Apple, because their iPads represent growth potential in the face of declining desktop sales. In contrast, many consumer food companies are characterized as being well into the maturity phase of overall product life cycles. Branded consumer food products can remain in their maturity phase for many years with proper product quality control and promotion, such as General Mills' Cheerios.

Companies continually bring new products to the market that replace similar products that are out of favor, but the life cycle of these products tends to be more like products in the maturity phase than introductory products in the growth phase. Certain industries in well-developed economies like the United States, including textiles, appliance repair, and automotive, are probably in the early decline phase because of foreign competition, price declines, and/or outdated technology. Some companies in these industries have built technologically advanced production facilities to compete more effectively on a worldwide basis and have, therefore, reentered the maturity phase. Other firms have diversified geographically to realize the benefits of shifts to foreign production, which also prolongs their ability to enjoy the maturity phase of their portfolio of products.

Four Companies: Four Different Stages of the Life Cycle

We conclude this section by surveying statements of cash flows for several firms to contrast how these statements capture various stages of the product life cycle (that is, introduction, growth, maturity, and decline).

Advanced Cell Technology, Inc. (Introduction Phase)

Advanced Cell Technology (OTC BB: ACTC), a company that intends to develop stem cell technologies for medical therapies, has not yet developed any commercial products but has a pipeline of clinical trials and several products in preclinical development. Advanced Cell Technology is a small company in a nascent industry. They went public in 2005, but their stock price has languished below twenty cents for years. The company's statements of cash flows for 2010–2012 (Exhibit 3.2) show the typical pattern of a firm in the introduction phase. Note:

- the negative cash flows from both operating and investing activities, funded by large positive cash flows from financing activities.
- the large net losses ($72.8 million in 2011 and $28.5 million in 2012).

Exhibit 3.2

Advanced Cell Technology Inc.
Statement of Cash Flows

	2012	2011	2010
CASH FLOWS FROM OPERATING ACTIVITIES:			
Net loss	$(28,526,261)	$(72,795,119)	$(54,373,332)
Adjustments to reconcile net loss to net cash used in operating activities:			
Depreciation	58,637	67,161	138,050
Amortization of deferred charges	117,436	91,600	91,600
Amortization of deferred revenue	(466,487)	(506,419)	(725,044)
Redeemable preferred stock dividend accrual	135,235	122,605	95,883
Stock based compensation	3,691,149	3,856,501	967,721
Amortization of deferred issuance costs	807,989	1,201,741	617,568
Amortization of discounts	161,379	180,172	12,443,112
Adjustments to fair value of derivatives	(889,883)	(11,444,988)	6,209,898
Shares of common stock issued for services	—	475,900	11,194,866
Shares of common stock issued for compensation	1,816,630	2,673,960	55,168
Non-cash financing costs	3,671,970	60,834,170	3,375,745
Loss on settlement of litigation	—	294,144	11,132,467
Gain on forgiveness of debt	—	—	(197,370)
(Gain) Loss on disposal of fixed assets	17,138	—	(9,500)
Amortization of deferred joint venture obligations	—	(6,870)	(56,602)
Warrant and options issued for consulting services	60,388	834,443	—
Changes in operating assets and liabilities			
Grants receivable	(96,425)	—	—
Prepaid expenses and other current assets	34,204	(241,248)	9,054
Deferred revenue	300,000	—	150,000
Accounts payable and other current liabilities	4,500,544	734,960	97,784
Net cash used in operating activities	(14,606,357)	(13,627,287)	(8,782,932)
CASH FLOWS FROM INVESTING ACTIVITIES:			
Purchases of property and equipment	(96,260)	(36,830)	(207,402)
Payment of lease deposits	(15,090)	—	(12,596)
Net cash used in investing activities	(111,350)	(36,830)	(219,998)
CASH FLOWS FROM FINANCING ACTIVITIES:			
Proceeds from exercise of warrants and options	—	3,377,715	719,636
Proceeds from issuance of convertible debentures	—	—	1,685,000
Proceeds from convertible promissory notes	—	—	5,880,000
Proceeds from issuance of preferred stock	6,000,000	7,500,000	14,068,865
Proceeds from issuance of common stock	2,941,102	—	—
Costs associated with issuance of common stock	(84,550)	—	—
Net cash provided by financing activities	8,856,552	10,877,715	22,353,501
NET DECREASE IN CASH AND CASH EQUIVALENTS	(5,861,155)	(2,786,402)	13,350,571
CASH AND CASH EQUIVALENTS, BEGINNING BALANCE	13,103,007	15,889,409	2,538,838
CASH AND CASH EQUIVALENTS, ENDING BALANCE	$ 7,241,852	$ 13,103,007	$ 15,889,409

- the large and negative cash flows from operating activities (negative $14.6 million for 2012).
- the source of the cash flows—primarily financing activities.

In addition, note that the cash balance has fallen steadily from a peak of $15.9 million in 2010 to the 2012 balance of $7.2 million. Advanced Cell Technology obtained substantial capital from financing activities in each of the prior three years, but the amounts are declining, presumably as investors grow weary of supplying additional capital without any tangible returns, or that the company is nearing a time where they have a marketable product. In addition to plowing cash into operations, Advanced Cell Technology also used some cash in investing activities, but these amounts are minor relative to the cash flows used in operations. This should not be surprising given the business model of engaging in research and development.[3] Overall, the statement of cash flows clearly paints a picture of a company in the introductory phase of its life cycle.

Black Diamond Group (Growth Phase)

Black Diamond is a Canadian company that incorporated in 2009 and rents modular structures used as workforce accommodation and temporary workspaces, and also provides logistics and maintenance services. Customers typically include very large structural projects, such as construction, paving, or oil drilling, that require temporary structures for workers or those who are temporarily displaced. Numerous analysts have strong buy ratings on the company's common stock.

The statement of cash flows in Exhibit 3.3 shows typical characteristics of a growth firm. First, profits are increasing, as net income grew approximately 16% from $41.0 million to $47.4 million in 2012. Even more impressive, cash flows from operations increased 50%, from $68.8 million to $103.5 million. At the same time, capital expenditures increased substantially, which increased the cash used for investing activities from $85.2 million to $164.0 million. Such large increases in capital expenditures are seen as a signal of management bullishness about future growth. Finally, as is typical of rapidly growing companies, growth in cash flows frequently is not enough to fuel the investments required to sustain growth, so Black Diamond realizes substantial inflows of capital through financing activities, which are approximately $40 million in both 2011 and 2012. Looking at the details in the financing section of the statement of cash flows, the majority of the capital inflow is from the issuance of equity shares, although some long-term debt was issued and repaid during the two years presented. What is somewhat unusual, however, is that Black Diamond pays substantial dividend payments, which is typically associated only with mature firms or those returning capital to shareholders in the decline phase.

Cedar Fair L.P. (Maturity Phase)

Founded in 1983 in Sandusky, Ohio, **Cedar Fair L.P.** is among the largest amusement park companies in the world. The company's statement of cash flows (Exhibit 3.4) exhibits the typically large positive cash flows from operating activities and negative cash flows for both investing and financing activities. The company generates large and

---

[3]As you are aware, although cash spent on research and development (R&D) is generally viewed as an investment (and hence an investment activity), measurement problems (like those discussed in the last chapter) prevent the recognition of internally developed intangible assets like "R&D knowledge."

Exhibit 3.3

Black Diamond Group
Statement of Cash Flows
for the years ended December 31,
(expressed in thousands)

	2012	2011
	CDN$	CDN$
Operating activities		
Net Income attributable to Black Diamond Group Limited	47,394	40,979
Add (deduct) non-cash items:		
Depreciation of property and equipment	34,665	27,285
Amortization of intangible assets	879	1,415
Net income attributable to non-controlling interest	3,761	3,602
Unrealized foreign exchange loss	36	7
Finance costs	5,747	4,884
Deferred income taxes	7,061	13,996
Share-based compensation expense	3,321	1,843
	102,864	94,011
Book value of used fleet sales in operating activities	6,817	14,171
Change in long-term receivables	(2,708)	—
Change in non-cash working capital related to operating activities	(3,458)	(39,378)
Net cash from operating activities	**103,515**	**68,804**
Investing activities		
Purchase of property and equipment	(163,628)	(94,656)
Change in non-cash working capital related to investing activities	(404)	9,506
Net cash used in investing activities	**(164,032)**	**(85,150)**
Financing activities		
Proceeds from long-term debt	10,000	62,000
Repayment of long-term debt	—	(41,000)
Costs of long-term debt issuance and refinancing	(97)	(949)
Repayment of finance lease	—	(561)
Interest in the year	(5,470)	(4,765)
Net proceeds from issuance of shares	57,465	48,772
Dividend payments	(26,983)	(20,138)
Distribution to non-controlling interest	(1,218)	(1,451)
Purchase of shares in trust	(993)	(220)
Sale of shares in trust	206	206
Bank indebtedness	—	(6,776)
Share options exercised	7,587	1,655
Change in non-cash working capital related to financing activities	(241)	2,573
Net cash from financing activities	**40,256**	**39,346**

(Continued)

Exhibit 3.3 (Continued)

Increase (decrease) in cash and cash equivalents	(20,261)	23,000
Cash and cash equivalents, beginning of year	22,990	—
Effect of foreign currency rate changes on cash and cash equivalents	(32)	(10)
Cash and cash equivalents, end of year	**2,697**	**22,990**

Exhibit 3.4

Cedar Fair, L.P.
Statement of Cash Flows
(amounts in thousands)

For the years ended December 31,	2012	2011	2010
CASH FLOWS FROM OPERATING ACTIVITIES			
Net income (loss)	$ 101,857	$ 65,296	$ (33,052)
Adjustments to reconcile net income (loss) to net cash from operating activities:			
Depreciation and amortization	126,306	125,837	128,856
Non-cash equity based compensation expense	4,476	(239)	(89)
Loss on early debt extinguishment	—	—	35,289
Loss on impairment of goodwill and other intangibles	—	—	2,293
Loss on impairment / retirement of fixed assets, net	30,336	11,355	62,752
Gain on sale of other assets	(6,625)	—	—
Net effect of swaps	(1,492)	(13,119)	18,194
Amortization of debt issuance costs	10,417	10,000	5,671
Unrealized foreign currency (gain) loss on notes	(8,758)	8,753	(17,464)
Other non-cash income	—	—	(1,893)
Deferred income taxes	27,502	677	(14,664)
Excess tax benefit from unit-based compensation expense	(1,208)	—	—
Change in operating assets and liabilities:			
(Increase) decrease in current assets	(1,420)	1,686	(11,855)
(Increase) decrease in other assets	(2,739)	173	6
Increase (decrease) in accounts payable	170	(1,144)	652
Increase (decrease) in accrued taxes	1,883	835	(2,242)
Increase (decrease) in self-insurance reserves	2,676	(206)	(383)
(Decrease) increase in deferred revenue and other current liabilities	(1,345)	14,170	7,653
Increase (decrease) in other liabilities	3,897	(5,897)	2,391
Net cash from operating activities	285,933	218,177	182,115
CASH FLOWS FOR INVESTING ACTIVITIES			
Sale of other assets	16,058	—	—
Capital expenditures	(96,232)	(90,190)	(71,706)
Net cash for investing activities	(80,174)	(90,190)	(71,706)

(Continued)

Exhibit 3.4 (Continued)

CASH FLOWS FOR FINANCING ACTIVITIES			
Net (payments) borrowings on revolving credit loans - previous credit agreement	—	—	(86,300)
Net (payments) borrowings on revolving credit loans - existing credit agreement	—	(23,200)	23,200
Term debt borrowings	—	22,938	1,175,000
Note borrowings	—	—	399,383
Derivative settlement	(50,450)	—	—
Term debt payments, including early termination penalties	(25,000)	(23,900)	(1,566,890)
Distributions paid to partners	(88,813)	(55,347)	(13,834)
Payment of debt issuance costs	—	(21,214)	(43,264)
Exercise of limited partnership unit options	76	5	7
Excess tax benefit from unit-based compensation expense	1,208	—	—
Net cash for financing activities	(162,979)	(100,718)	(112,698)
EFFECT OF EXCHANGE RATE CHANGES ON CASH AND CASH EQUIVALENTS	526	(1,510)	126
CASH AND CASH EQUIVALENTS			
Net increase (decrease) for the year	43,306	25,759	(2,163)
Balance, beginning of year	35,524	9,765	11,928
Balance, end of year	$ 78,830	$ 35,524	$ 9,765

---

persistent net income ($101.9 million in 2012, up from $65.3 million in 2011) and enormous cash flows from operating activities ($285.9 million in 2012). With such large amounts generated by cash flows from operating activities, the company relied very little on external financing; instead, it tended to pay large distributions to partners (the company is a partnership) and paying down lines of credit and term debt. Also, Cedar Fair continued to use significant cash for investing activities (a net total of $80.2 million in 2012). Indeed, the company believes that annual park attendance is strongly affected by the introduction of new rides and attractions each year, explaining the continuing investment activities. In contrast to Advanced Cell Technology above, where the balance of cash has been steadily depleted, Cedar Fair has seen an increase in cash on hand from $9.8 million in 2010 to $78.8 million at the end of 2012. Overall, Cedar Fair exhibits patterns of cash flows typical of a mature firm.

Warner Music Group (Decline Phase)

Exhibit 3.5 shows the statement of cash flows for Warner Music Group during its final years before being acquired by a private company. The company traces its origins back to 1929, and became one of the world's largest and most influential music content companies. It generated revenues from the marketing, licensing and sale of music through various formats, historically physical formats such as vinyl, cassette, and compact disk. Like other music content companies, Warner Music Group suffered as the music

Exhibit 3.5

Warner Music Group
Statement of Cash Flows
(amounts in millions)

	Fiscal Year Ended September 30		
	2010	**2009**	**2008**
Cash flows from operating activities			
Net loss	$ (145)	$ (104)	$ (51)
Loss from discontinued operations	—	—	21
Loss from continuing operations	(145)	(104)	(30)
Adjustments to reconcile net loss to net cash provided by operating activities:			
Gain on sale of equity-method investment	—	(36)	—
Gain on foreign exchange transaction	—	(9)	—
Gain on sale of building	—	(3)	—
Impairment of equity-method investments	—	11	—
Impairment of cost-method investments	1	29	—
Depreciation and amortization	258	262	268
Deferred taxes	—	—	(3)
Non-cash interest expense	20	62	46
Non-cash, stock-based compensation expense	10	11	11
Other non-cash adjustments	—	—	(3)
Changes in operating assets and liabilities:			
Accounts receivable	118	(8)	28
Inventories	8	10	2
Royalty advances	16	(20)	(6)
Accounts payable and accrued liabilities	(147)	15	(13)
Accrued interest	2	25	(3)
Other balance sheet changes	9	(8)	7
Net cash provided by operating activities	150	237	304
Cash flows from investing activities			
Capital expenditures	(51)	(27)	(32)
Acquisition of publishing rights	(36)	(11)	(25)
Investments and acquisitions of businesses, net of cash acquired	(7)	(16)	(132)
Proceeds from the sale of investments	9	125	25
Repayments of loans by (loans to) third parties	—	3	(3)
Proceeds from the sale of building	—	8	—
Net cash (used in) provided by investing activities	(85)	82	(167)

(Continued)

Exhibit 3.5 (Continued)

Cash flows from financing activities			
Debt repayments	—	(1,379)	(17)
Proceeds from issuance of Acquisition Corp. Senior Secured Notes	—	1,059	—
Deferred financing costs paid	—	(23)	—
Dividends paid	—	—	(42)
Distributions to noncontrolling interest holders	(3)	(3)	—
Net cash used in financing activities	(3)	(346)	(59)
Effect of foreign currency exchange rate changes on cash	(7)	—	—
Net increase (decrease) in cash and equivalents	55	(27)	78
Cash and equivalents at beginning of period	384	411	333
Cash and equivalents at end of period	$ 439	$ 384	$ 411

industry experienced a distribution transformation with the development of digital music and other delivery platforms like Internet streaming. As is typical of a firm in decline, Warner Music Group:

- reported a string of net losses (increased from $51 million to $145 million between 2008 and 2010).
- generated positive cash flows from operations, but at a substantially decreasing rate (declined from $304 million to $150 million).
- investing activities appeared volatile (negative in 2008 and 2010, but positive in 2009 as the company disposed of certain investments).
- raised very little capital from external financing sources, (other than a simultaneous issuance and higher retirement of debt in 2009).

Subsequently, the company was acquired by a private conglomerate, **Access Industries**.

Quick Check

- The organization of the statement of cash flows into operating, investing, and financing activities helps identify a firm's stage in its life cycle.
- Start-up firms typically have negative profits, negative cash flows from operations, negative cash flows for investing activities, and positive cash flows from financing activities.
- Growth firms typically have increasing profits or decreasing losses, positive cash flows from operations, negative cash flows for investing

activities, and positive cash flows from financing activities.
- Mature firms typically have large positive profits, large positive cash flows from operations, stable cash flows from investing activities, and negative cash flows from financing activities.
- Decline firms typically have decreasing profits or increasing losses, declining cash flows from operations, low or positive cash flows for investing activities, and negative cash flows from financing activities.

Understanding the Relations among Net Income, Balance Sheets, and Cash Flows

As noted in Chapter 2, one alternative to measuring financial performance under accrual accounting is simply to measure cash inflows and outflows. If an analyst takes a primitive "cash is king" perspective, the statement of cash flows provides fundamental information on the flows of cash in and out of a firm. However, over short horizons such as a fiscal quarter or year, cash inflows and outflows are not very informative with regard to a firm's profitability now or in the future. For example, recall the **Warner Music Group** example highlighted in the prior section, where increasing losses were associated with positive, but declining, cash flows from operations.

One criticism sometimes lobbied at accrual accounting is that it is unreliable because managers can so easily manipulate it. However, checks and balances such as auditors, regulators, boards of directors, the press, and activist investors scrutinize reported profits, restricting such nefarious behavior. Cash flows, on the other hand, are not subject to reporting standards, so managers can much more easily manipulate cash flows relative to their ability to manipulate earnings. As a simple example, consider the decision to pay a supplier on December 31 versus January 1 of the following year. This decision affects cash flows, but not earnings. Further, the timing of that cash flow would not likely alter any expectations of future performance or cash flows. Thus, whereas accrual accounting has the objective of helping users assess the current financial position and the nature, amount, and timing of future cash flows, the objective of cash flow reporting is to simply track the flows of cash. Accrual accounting goes beyond measurement of cash flows to measure *economic* inflows and outflows. Economic resources and obligations generate assets and liabilities (the balance sheet), which in turn allow for an improved measure of performance based on economic resources generated and consumed (the income statement). As emphasized above, the statement of cash flows, although quite useful, merely undoes the accrual accounting that transformed cash flows into balance sheets and income statements. Recall Exhibit 1.21, which shows that the difference in stock returns between firms with positive and negative changes in earnings is 35.6%, whereas the change in stock returns between firms with positive and negative operating cash flows is only 15.0%, which indicates periodic earnings are much more associated with stock prices than are cash flows.

The statement of cash flows is closely tied to net income, but serves several additional roles. You need an understanding of the following three relations to be able to interpret the statement of cash flows:

1. The overall relations among the net cash flows from operating, investing, and financing activities
2. The relation between the change in the cash balance on the balance sheet and the net changes reflected on the statement of cash flows
3. The specific relation between net income and cash flows from operations

The first topic was discussed in the previous section that covered four examples of firms in various stages of their life cycle. The second and third topics are discussed next. Because the third relation is most important, it is addressed in two parts. First, the discussion focuses specifically on the operating section of the statement of cash flows, highlighting the types of adjustments necessary to reconcile net income to cash flows from operations; then a more general discussion covers the overall relation between net income and cash flows from operations.

The Relation between Cash Balances and Net Cash Flows

The primary purpose of the statement of cash flows is to provide financial statement users with information about a firm's cash receipts and payments that cause the change in the cash balance on the balance sheet. This is accounting in its simplest form:

Beginning Cash + Cash Receipts – Cash Expenditures = Ending Cash Balance

Net cash flows for a period should equal the change in cash for the period. FASB's *Codification Topic 230* and IASB's *International Accounting Standard 7* define cash flows in terms of their effect on the balance of *cash and cash equivalents*. Cash equivalents include highly liquid short-term investments that are readily convertible into cash, including very short-term Treasury bills, commercial paper, and money market funds. Both U.S. GAAP and IFRS indicate that a maturity date of three months or less would generally qualify short-term investments as cash equivalents. Throughout this book, the term *cash* is used to mean cash and cash equivalents as defined under both U.S. GAAP and IFRS.

On the statement of cash flows, the net cash flows equal the (net) sum of cash flows provided by or used for operating, investing, and financing activities. Refer again to **PepsiCo**'s statement of cash flows in Appendix A. The net cash flow for PepsiCo during 2012 is the sum of $8,479 million (operations), –$3,005 million (investing), and –$3,306 million (financing), a net positive change in cash of $2,168 million. The balance sheet indicates that cash and cash equivalents rose from $4,067 million to $6,297 million during 2012, an increase of $2,230 million. The difference between net cash flows of $2,168 million and the actual increase in cash and cash equivalents of $2,230 million is $62 million. This reconciling amount is highlighted at the bottom of the statement of cash flows as the effect of exchange rate changes on the measurement of cash and cash equivalents (which is done using the fair value approach described in Chapter 2). This difference shows that PepsiCo's cash and cash equivalents experienced positive effects from exchange rate changes, which further increased the U.S. dollar value of PepsiCo's cash balance at the end of 2012.

The Operating Section of the Statement of Cash Flows

Many would argue that the first section of the statement of cash flows—cash flows from operating activities—is the most important, because it provides information on the firm's core activities. These activities include cash received from selling goods and services to customers offset by cash paid to suppliers, employees, governments, and other providers of goods and services. This section also is where an analyst can gather information about the *quality of earnings*. An analysis of the timing of cash flows in the operating section exposes the drivers of reported profitability on the income statement, which can sometimes raise red flags for earnings manipulation.[4]

---

[4]Analysis of earnings quality will be previewed at the end of this chapter and discussed fully in Chapter 6.

First, we briefly mention the two formats of the operating section that are permissible under U.S. GAAP and IFRS. Regardless of the format used, a reconciliation of net income to cash flows from operations must be shown, and we will emphasize the information available to the analyst from understanding this reconciliation. Second, we examine the different types of adjustments to net income that appear in the operating section. Finally, we provide several illustrative examples.

The Operating Section: Format Alternatives

Under U.S. GAAP and IFRS, firms may present cash flows from operations in one of two formats: the direct method or the indirect method. The *direct method*, which is preferred by both the FASB and IASB, lists individual classes of cash receipts and cash payments, such as cash collected from customers, cash paid to suppliers, and cash paid to employees. In contrast, the *indirect method* reconciles reported net income to cash flows from operations by "undoing" non-cash (accrual) components of earnings. Despite a preference for the direct method by standard setters, almost all companies report cash flows using the indirect method. In 2011, the AICPA surveyed 500 firms and identified only 5 that used the direct method.[5] The reluctance to report under the direct method seems to be based on practicality, because the FASB and IASB require that firms using the direct method also provide a separate schedule for the reconciliation between net income and operating cash flows (in other words, an indirect method operating section).

Exhibit 3.6 provides a rare example of the direct method for the operating cash flows in the statement for the drugstore chain **CVS Caremark**. Notice that the net operating cash flows are $6,671 million for 2012, which is shown in the top section of the statement. Notice also that this same amount is shown at the bottom of the statement in an addendum for the reconciliation of net income to net cash provided by operating activities. Regardless of the method of presentation, net operating cash flows are the same, $6,671 million. The line item descriptions in the direct method are more intuitive than those in the indirect method, because the line items all represent cash flows. Under the indirect method, not a single line item is an actual cash flow (being adjustments for non-cash components of net income instead). For example, "Cash paid for inventory" is more straightforward than the change in inventories (net of effects from acquisitions) shown as a reconciling item in the indirect method (at the bottom of Exhibit 3.6). This chapter later describes how you can compute the more intuitive figures such as cash paid for inventory from information in the balance sheet and income statement.

Under the *indirect method*, firms begin with net income to calculate cash flows from operations. The assumption implicit in starting with net income is that revenues increased cash and expenses decreased cash, but remember that with accrual accounting, revenues and expenses are not necessarily simultaneous with cash receipts or payments. Because of differences in the timing of cash flows and income statement recognition, net income must be reconciled to cash flows by adjusting for non-cash effects. Again, even though CVS Caremark reports a direct method operating section, it must also report an indirect method reconciliation, as shown at the bottom of Exhibit 3.6.

Most firms use the indirect method because it reconciles net income with the net amount of cash received from or used for operations, which provides a direct link to the income statement. Critics of the indirect method suggest that the rationale for some of the reconciling items is difficult for less sophisticated users to understand. For example, a decrease in receivables is an increase in cash flows (because cash is collected from customers); however, this adjustment is typically labeled as "Decrease in accounts receivable."

---

[5] AICPA, *Accounting Trends & Techniques* (2012).

Exhibit 3.6

CVS Caremark
Statement of Cash Flows: Operating Section under
Direct and Indirect Methods (amounts in millions)

	Year Ended December 31,		
	2012	**2011**	**2010**
Cash flows from operating activities:			
Cash receipts from customers	$113,205	$ 97,688	$ 94,503
Cash paid for inventory and prescriptions dispensed by retail network pharmacies	(90,032)	(75,148)	(73,143)
Cash paid to other suppliers and employees	(13,643)	(13,635)	(13,778)
Interest received	4	4	4
Interest paid	(581)	(647)	(583)
Income taxes paid	(2,282)	(2,406)	(2,224)
Net cash provided by operating activities	6,671	5,856	4,779
Cash flows from investing activities:			
Purchases of property and equipment	(2,030)	(1,872)	(2,005)
Proceeds from sale-leaseback transactions	529	592	507
Proceeds from sale of property and equipment	23	4	34
Acquisitions (net of cash acquired) and other investments	(378)	(1,441)	(177)
Purchase of available-for-sale investments	—	(3)	—
Maturity of available-for-sale investments	—	60	1
Proceeds from sale of subsidiary	7	250	—
Net cash used in investing activities	(1,849)	(2,410)	(1,640)
Cash flows from financing activities:			
Increase (decrease) in short-term debt	(60)	450	(15)
Proceeds from issuance of long-term debt	1,239	1,463	991
Repayments of long-term debt	(1,718)	(2,122)	(2,103)
Purchase of noncontrolling interest in subsidiary	(26)	—	—
Dividends paid	(829)	(674)	(479)
Derivative settlements	—	(19)	(5)
Proceeds from exercise of stock options	836	431	285
Excess tax benefits from stock-based compensation	28	21	28
Repurchase of common stock	(4,330)	(3,001)	(1,500)
Other	—	(9)	—
Net cash used in financing activities	(4,860)	(3,460)	(2,798)
Net increase (decrease) in cash and cash equivalents	(38)	(14)	341
Cash and cash equivalents at the beginning of the year	1,413	1,427	1,086
Cash and cash equivalents at the end of the year	$ 1,375	$ 1,413	$ 1,427
Reconciliation of net income to net cash provided by operating activities:			
Net income	$ 3,875	$ 3,457	$ 3,424

(Continued)

Exhibit 3.6 (Continued)

Adjustments required to reconcile net income to net cash provided by operating activities:			
Depreciation and amortization	1,753	1,568	1,469
Stock-based compensation	132	135	150
Loss on early extinguishment of debt	348	—	—
Gain on sale of subsidiary	—	(53)	—
Deferred income taxes and other noncash items	(106)	144	30
Change in operating assets and liabilities, net of effects from acquisitions:			
Accounts receivable, net	(387)	(748)	532
Inventories	(858)	607	(352)
Other current assets	3	(420)	(4)
Other assets	(99)	(49)	(210)
Accounts payable and claims and discounts payable	1,147	1,128	(40)
Accrued expenses	753	85	(176)
Other long-term liabilities	110	2	(44)
Net cash provided by operating activities	$ 6,671	$ 5,856	$ 4,779

The equivalent line item with the direct method is the more intuitive "Cash receipts from customers." Although only a moderate amount of effort is required to understand the reconciliation adjustments, certain peculiarities challenge even the most seasoned analysts.

The Operating Section: Adjustments for the Indirect Method

The calculation of cash flows from operations under the indirect method involves two types of adjustments to net income—working capital and non-working capital adjustments. Both of these adjustments, explained below, are necessary because of timing differences between income recognition and cash flow realization. Common non-working capital adjustments include depreciation, amortization, deferred taxes, and gains/losses on asset dispositions. These adjustments affect current period net income, but do not affect current period cash flows, so must be 'adjusted out' of the starting point of the statement of cash flows—net income. As an example, consider depreciation expense. Depreciation expense reduces net income, but it is a non-cash expense. Thus, in reconciling net income to cash flows from operations, non-cash expenses such as depreciation must be added back to net income. Working capital adjustments, on the other hand, are adjustments for changes in operating working capital accounts during the period.[6] Common adjustments include increases and decreases in accounts receivable, inventories, and accounts payable.

We now discuss adjustments under the indirect method of preparing the operating section of the statement of cash flows. Following the typical format of the operating section, we first highlight the most common non-working capital adjustments and then discuss the working capital adjustments.

---

[6]Working capital means current assets minus current liabilities. Operating working capital accounts generally include all current assets except marketable securities and all current liabilities except short-term loans and the current portion of long-term debt. A later section of this chapter explains the rationale for excluding these items from operating working capital.

Non-Working Capital Adjustments

Depreciation and amortization expense. [7] Depreciation expense reduces net property, plant, and equipment and net income. However, depreciation expense does not require an *operating* cash outflow in the period of the expense. Cash flows paid out for depreciable assets are classified as *investing* activities in the year of acquisition. **PepsiCo**, for example, lists such acquisitions as "Capital spending" in the investing section of its statement of cash flows (in Appendix A). The addback of depreciation expense to net income when computing cash flows from operations reverses the effect of the subtraction of depreciation expense when computing net income. Similarly, amortization expense reflects the consumption of intangible assets, and it must be added back to net income in computing operating cash flows. PepsiCo includes depreciation on buildings and equipment and amortization of intangibles on a single line as an addback to net income in computing cash flows from operations, which is a common practice. PepsiCo's "Depreciation and amortization" adjustment, which is $2,689 million, is the single largest non-working capital adjustment to net income. Thus, the net income of $6,214 million is adjusted upward by $2,689 million to add back the non-cash expenses of depreciation and amortization.

Bad debt expense. Like depreciation and amortization expense for fixed and intangible assets, bad debt expense reduces net accounts receivable and net income. However, bad debt expense is a non-cash expense, so must be added back to net income, similar to depreciation and amortization. You will not always see a specific addback for bad debt expense because the amount may be relatively immaterial and/or may be netted with the working capital accounts receivable adjustment. For example, PepsiCo does not show an adjustment for bad debt expense (so it is either immaterial or included within "Change in accounts and notes receivable). Bad debts are relatively more material for companies like **Target**, which deal with a wide variety of retail customers. See Exhibit 3.7, where Target shows a $154 million addback for bad debt expense in its computation of cash flow provided by operations.

Deferred tax expense. Firms recognize deferred tax assets and/or deferred tax liabilities on the balance sheet when they use different methods of accounting for financial reporting and income tax reporting. The total amount of income tax expense, including both current and deferred components, will differ from the amount of income taxes owed or payable for the fiscal year (from the tax return). Thus, firms must add back the excess of income tax expense over income taxes owed for the year (approximated by current tax expense). PepsiCo shows an addback for deferred income taxes of $321 million in 2012, suggesting that income tax expense exceeds income taxes actually paid for the year.

---

[7] Adjustments for depreciation and amortization on the statement of cash flows are more complex than implied in this discussion because depreciation is often allocated to the cost of inventory. If the balance of inventory changes during a period, the change may include allocated depreciation to the cost basis of inventory. Thus, the allocation of depreciation (and amortization) to inventory creates a discrepancy between amounts expensed and the addback on the statement of cash flows. Firms handle this discrepancy a variety of ways, which makes it rare that depreciation expense on the income statement equals the depreciation adjustment on the statement of cash flows. (Similarly, the change in inventory balances on the balance sheet rarely equals the working capital adjustment for increases or decreases in inventory on the statement of cash flows.) This is one of the compelling motivations for requiring a statement of cash flows to be provided by management, which has the information to prepare cash flow statements more precisely than external users can by using approximations from the other financial statements. We will discuss the technical aspects of preparing a cash flow statement towards the end of the chapter.

Exhibit 3.7

Target Corporation
Statement of Cash Flows: Operating Section
(amounts in millions)

	2011	2010	2009
Operating activities			
Net earnings	$2,929	$2,920	$2,488
Reconciliation to cash flow			
Depreciation and amortization	2,131	2,084	2,023
Share-based compensation expense	90	109	103
Deferred income taxes	371	445	364
Bad debt expense	154	528	1,185
Non-cash (gains)/losses and other, net	22	(145)	143
Changes in operating accounts:			
Accounts receivable originated at Target	(187)	(78)	(57)
Inventory	(322)	(417)	(474)
Other current assets	(150)	(124)	(129)
Other noncurrent assets	43	(212)	(114)
Accounts payable	232	115	174
Accrued and other current liabilities	218	149	257
Other noncurrent liabilities	(97)	(103)	(82)
Cash flow provided by operations	5,434	5,271	5,881

Employee stock option compensation. Stock-based compensation, such as employee stock options that permit employees to purchase shares of the firm's common stock for less than their market value, is recognized as an expense on the income statement.[8] This expense reduces net income and increases a shareholders' equity account, but it does not affect cash flows. Because the expense does not use cash, firms add back stock-based compensation expense to net income when computing cash flows from operations. In 2012, PepsiCo lists an addback of $278 million for "Stock-based compensation expense" in the operating section of its statement of cash flows. Incidentally, when employees exercise stock options, it is common that they pay the strike price to the firm, and this resulting cash inflow to the company appears in the financing section of the statement of cash flows. In 2012, PepsiCo lists $1,122 million from such stock issuances as "Proceeds from exercises of stock options" in the financing section of its statement of cash flows.

Gains and losses. Companies that sell an item of property, plant, or equipment report the full cash proceeds with the investing activities on the statement of cash flows. For example, refer to the line for $95 million of "Sales of property, plant and equipment" for PepsiCo in 2012. When assets are sold for amounts that differ from their book value, net income includes gains and losses on these sales (that is, sale proceeds minus book value of the item sold). Therefore, the operating section of the statement of

---

[8]Stock-based compensation expenses are discussed more fully in Chapter 7.

cash flows shows an addback for a loss and a subtraction for a gain to offset their effects on net income and to avoid double counting the gain or loss, given that the investing section includes the full cash proceeds from the asset sale. The absence of a line item for gains or losses on PepsiCo's statement of cash flows suggests that these amounts are sufficiently small and likely included in the line "Other, net."

For an example of how gains and losses on the disposal of fixed assets affect the operating section, refer back to the example for Cedar Fair in Exhibit 3.4. For 2012, the company shows an adjustment for "Gain on sale of other assets" of −$6.625 million. It appears as a subtraction because the gain is included in the firm's overall net income (that is, the starting point of the statement of cash flows), but the total cash proceeds from the sale are included in the investing section as "Sale of other assets," totaling $16,058 million. Without this adjustment, the gain would be double counted on the statement of cash flows (once in net income and a second time in the investing section).

Equity method income. Firms holding investments of 20–50% of the common shares in another entity generally use the equity method to account for the investment.[9] As an investor, the firm recognizes in net income its share of the investee's earnings each period and increases the balance of the investment account accordingly. It reduces the investment account for any cash dividends received. Therefore, net income reflects the investor's share of the investee's earnings, not the cash received. The statement of cash flows usually shows a subtraction from net income for the investor's share of the investee's earnings and an addition for the dividends received. Often, firms will simply report the net of these two amounts. For example, in 2010 PepsiCo reports "Bottling equity income, net of dividends" as a $42 million addition when converting net income to cash flows from operations. Subsequently, PepsiCo consolidated with the bottlers, so adjustments for this line item do not appear in the columns for 2011 and 2012.

Noncontrolling interests. Firms with subsidiaries sometimes do not own 100% of those subsidiaries. Although the parent controls the operations of the subsidiaries, other investors have a noncontrolling or minority interest. The parent consolidates 100% of the subsidiaries assets, liabilities, and income, but shows deductions for the noncontrolling interest. For example, PepsiCo reports net income of $6,214 million in 2012, but shows a deduction at the bottom of the income statement of $36 million for "Net income attributable to noncontrolling interests," leading to "Net income attributable to PepsiCo" of $6,178 million. This noncontrolling interest is a non-cash deduction, so must be added back, which PepsiCo effectively accomplishes by beginning the statement of cash flows with net income of $6,214.

Other comprehensive income. As discussed in prior chapters, other comprehensive income represents non-cash adjustments to certain financial securities, foreign currency gains/losses, and various postretirement benefit items. Thus, such amounts would also be added back to net income. However, most companies accomplish this by starting with net income in the statement of cash flows, rather than comprehensive income.

Employee-related costs such as pensions. There are two types of pension plans— defined contribution and defined benefit.[10] Defined benefit plans may give rise to large differences between pension expense and actual cash flows, but this is not true for defined contribution plans (for example, numerous estimates are required for the length

---

[9]Accounting for investments is more fully covered in Chapter 8.

[10]Pension plans are fully covered in Chapter 9.

of time an employee will work, the length of time an employee will realize postretirement benefits, the growth in the cost of those benefits, and the return on investments set aside to cover those future costs). As a result, companies with defined benefit plans adjust net income for the net difference between the expense and cash transactions. Alternatively, companies such as PepsiCo separately add back the pension expense and deduct the actual cash contributed to fund pension assets and postretirement benefits. For example, in 2012, PepsiCo reports an addback of "Pension and retiree medical plan expenses" of $796 million and a deduction for "Pension and retiree medical plan contributions" of $1,865 million. This indicates that PepsiCo funded almost twice the amount recognized as expense, which means cash flows will be lower than net income, all else equal.

Excess tax benefits from share-based compensation plans. *[This topic is considered difficult.]* Companies are required to expense an estimate of the fair value of stock options granted to employees over the vesting period. This expense lowers income, resulting in lower tax expense. When an employee exercises stock options, she will owe taxes on the difference between the stock price at the time of exercise and the amount she has to pay to exercise the option (the strike price). At this time, the company is entitled to an actual tax deduction equal to the amount the employee realizes as taxable income [that is, total number of shares × (share price – strike price)]. Often, the amount of the tax deduction for compensation is in *excess* of the cumulative compensation expense that has already been recognized. The excess lowers taxes actually paid (reducing a deferred tax asset), but does not reduce tax expense recognized on the income statement. Instead, the tax benefit is recognized as a direct "credit" to paid-in-capital in the statement of shareholders' equity. There is wide variation in practice, but the proper way to report these amounts is as an "excess benefit from share-based compensation," which affects the statement of cash flows as follows:

1. The adjustment is shown as an addback to net income in the operating section (to reflect the amount of tax savings that had bypassed the income statement by being recorded directly to equity). After this adjustment, all tax benefits related to the applicable options are properly classified as an operating activity, as required.[11]
2. This amount is then deducted from operating activities, because the underlying transaction is an equity transaction with shareholders (who are also employees), and hence should be classified as a financing activity.
3. A positive cash flow for the amount of tax savings that increased equity is shown in the financing activities section (that is, the reclassification of the amount adjusted out of operating activities in Step 2 above).

Note that the ultimate classification of these tax benefits as a financing activity pairs with the classification of the cash flows pertaining to stock option exercises as a financing activity. The **Facebook** example discussed later in the chapter (Exhibit 3.8) shows this treatment. Facebook is an extreme example because (a) the use of options for compensation is large and (b) the stock price has performed very well, leading to a large amount of employee exercises that produce tax deductions for the company. For most other companies, the first adjustment is netted among other adjustments, although the reclassification from operating to financing activities is frequently shown. For example, PepsiCo's statement of cash flows shows a deduction in the operating section of

---

[11]Both SFAS No. 95 "Statement of cash flows" and EITF 00-15 require that all tax benefits from share-based compensation plans should be classified as operating cash flows. SFAS No. 123(R), however, required the excess tax benefits to be shown as financing cash flows, not operating. See *FASB Codification Topic 718* for current guidance.

$124 million for "Excess tax benefits from share-based payment arrangements," and this same $124 million adjustment appears in the financing section as a *positive* cash flow.

Impairment- and restructuring-related charges. Write-offs and write-downs of assets reduce net income through impairment charges, but there are usually no associated cash transactions. Thus, impairment charges must be added back to net income in the computation of operating cash flows. Similarly, restructuring charges are estimated and the associated cash flows generally follow later. Thus, restructuring charges appear as add-backs to income, and the actual cash payments for restructuring appear as subtractions from income in the operating section. For 2012, PepsiCo shows an addback for "Restructuring and impairment charges" of $279 million and a deduction for "Cash payments for restructuring charges" of $343 million. Thus, PepsiCo paid more for restructurings than was expensed, resulting in a net negative adjustment to net income of $64 million ($343 million − $279 million). PepsiCo also shows similar adjustments for restructuring charges related to Tingyi and merger and integration costs.

Operating Working Capital Adjustments

The second type of adjustment used to reconcile net income to cash flows from operations involves changes in the working capital (current asset and current liability) accounts. Net income must be adjusted for the cash flows associated with these changes. Again, we discuss each of the most common working capital adjustments reported in the operating section of the statement of cash flows.

Accounts receivable. Revenue recognition is based on the economics of a sale rather than the realization of cash. Unless a customer pays in cash, recognition of revenue increases accounts receivable. An increase in accounts receivable indicates that a firm did not collect as much cash as the amount of revenues included in net income, and a decrease indicates that a firm collected more cash than it recognized as revenues. Thus, to account for the amount of revenue that is in net income but does not reflect cash collected, increases in accounts receivable are subtracted from net income; decreases in accounts receivable are added to net income.

Inventories. Two features of inventory accounting lead to adjustments to net income in computing operating cash flows. When inventory balances increase, the cash flow statement subtracts this amount because it does imply a cash outlay. Similarly, when inventory balances decrease, the cash flow statement includes a positive adjustment because the decrease is expensed as cost of goods sold, but some of this amount relates to inventory that was paid for in a prior reporting period. Second, it also is important to understand how non-cash allocations of depreciation and amortization are idiosyncratically adjusted on the cash flow statement, as highlighted previously in footnote 7 of this chapter.

Prepaid expenses. Prepaid expenses are simply cash payments that have yet to be expensed. Increases in prepaid expenses indicate cash payments in excess of amounts recognized as expenses in computing net income; decreases in prepaid expenses represent amounts that were expensed but for which there was no equivalent simultaneous cash flow. Thus, the cash flow statement must subtract increases in prepaid expenses or add decreases in prepaid expenses.

Accounts payable and accrued expenses. An increase in current liabilities for accounts payable and accrued operating expenses means that a firm did not use as much cash for inventory purchases and operating expenses as the amounts appearing on the income statement. For example, suppose a firm was invoiced for services received at the end of the fiscal year but did not pay the invoices until the following fiscal year. The firm would recognize the services as expense and the increase in liabilities. The expense reduces net income, but no cash has been paid, so the amount needs to be added back to net income in computing operating cash flows. On the other hand, decreases in accounts payable and accrued expenses would indicate cash payments of such liabilities exceeded expenses that increased those liabilities, implying net cash outflows.

Income taxes payable. Firms typically do not pay all taxes due for a particular year during that year. Some taxes paid within a year relate to taxes due for the preceding year; some taxes due for the current year are paid the following year. Recall from the earlier discussion about non-working capital adjustments that the addition to (or subtraction from) net income for deferred income tax expense (or benefit) converts income tax expense to income taxes currently payable. The adjustment for changes in income taxes payable similarly converts income taxes currently payable to the income taxes actually paid.

Other current assets and liabilities. In addition to the working capital accounts discussed previously, there are other current accounts such as marketable securities, short-term investments, commercial paper, and other short-term borrowings. The cash flows pertaining to these items are shown in investing (marketable securities, short-term investments) or financing activities (commercial paper, short-term borrowings).

Why Do Adjustments Rarely Equal the Changes in Assets and Liabilities on the Balance Sheet?

The reconciling adjustments throughout the statement of cash flows relate to non-cash accounts on the balance sheet, but it is rare that changes in the actual balance sheet accounts equal the reconciling adjustments on the statement of cash flows. For example, in 2012, **PepsiCo**'s balance for accounts and notes receivable increased from $6,912 million in 2011 to $7,041 million, an increase of $129 million. However, the adjustment on the statement of cash flows—"Change in accounts and notes receivable"—is −$250 million. Similarly, PepsiCo's balance sheet shows "Accounts payable and other current liabilities" increased from $11,757 million to $11,903 million, an increase of $146 million. However, the adjustment on the statement of cash flows shows a positive adjustment of $548 million. Why do adjustments on the statement of cash flows rarely match the actual changes in the corresponding line items on the balance sheet?

There are four primary reasons that changes we see on the balance sheet do not match the adjustment on the statement of cash flows:

1. **Acquisitions and divestitures.** If a company acquires another firm for cash, that cash flow appropriately shows up in the investing section of the statement of cash flows. Acquisitions often result in the acquiring company taking over various current assets and liabilities of the acquiree, like receivables, inventory, and payables. These current assets and liabilities will be included in the consolidated balance sheet at the end of the year. However, it would be inappropriate to let the change in the balance sheet totals show up as an adjustment in the operating section of the statement of cash flows, as this would result in double counting. To clarify, assume Company X acquired Company Y for $1,000,000 cash, receiving $300,000 of Company Y's accounts receivable in the process. Company X will include the additional $300,000 of accounts receivable on its balance sheet. In Company X's statement of cash flows, the acquisition would appear as a $1,000,000 subtraction

in the investing section. In the operating section, the $300,000 would not be included in the "Change in accounts receivable" adjustment. Divestitures would have similar effects, but the direction would be the opposite.

2. **Non-cash transactions.** Non-cash transactions include non-cash acquisitions using common stock, the acquisition of assets under lease agreements, asset exchanges, financed asset acquisitions or settlement of liabilities, debt-for-equity swaps, and other transactions which increase or decrease assets, liabilities, or equities, but do not involve the exchange of cash. Similar to the discussion above, for any such line items on the balance sheet, the changes in balances from beginning to end of year would need to be adjusted when preparing the statement of cash flows. For example, reconsider the Company X example, but assume the acquisition of Company Y was accomplished by issuing common shares to Company Y's shareholders rather than paying them cash. Significant non-cash transactions are supposed to be highlighted separately, along with cash paid for interest and taxes, either as an addendum to the statement of cash flows or in a footnote.

3. **Changes in contra accounts.** Some assets, like accounts receivable and fixed assets, include contra accounts. If those assets are shown net on the balance sheet, then changes in the contra accounts can also cause the change on the balance sheet to not match the adjustments in the operating section of the statement of cash flows. For example, assume that Company Z has the following balances for net accounts receivable:

	2012	2013
Accounts receivable	$500,000	$500,000
Allowance for bad debts	(25,000)	(40,000)
Net accounts receivable	$475,000	$460,000

Assume that during 2012 Company Z worried that changes in the economy will adversely affect the customers who owe the $500,000, so it increased its allowance for bad debts from $25,000 to $40,000. The change in net accounts receivable is −$15,000, which was the result of recognizing non-cash bad debt expense of $15,000. The bad debt expense would decrease net income and would typically appear in the operating section of the statement of cash flows separately as an addback to net income. Refer back to the Target example in Exhibit 3.7. Notice that an adjustment for changes in bad debt expense appears separately from the adjustment for changes in accounts receivable.

4. **Foreign currency translation.** Globally diversified companies have assets and liabilities located in many countries and frequently denominated in various currencies. When consolidated balance sheets are prepared, the translation of current assets and liabilities from the local currency into the currency of the consolidated parent can change the balances of assets and liabilities, which is a non-cash change. For reasons similar to those discussed for the examples above, the inclusion of foreign currency translation gains or losses within the balances of assets or liabilities would lead to adjustments in the operating section not matching the changes in line item balances on from the balance sheet.

On occasion, some firms alert readers of the financial statements that changes in working capital in the operating section of the statement of cash flows do not equal changes in the corresponding accounts on the comparative balance sheet by phrasings in the operating section such as "changes in operating working capital, *excluding effects of acquisitions and dispositions."* Some of the examples in the next section will show such wording. Note also that this inability to reconcile balance sheet changes perfectly also applies to non-working capital accounts such as property, plant, and equipment; long-term investments; long-term debt; and other liabilities.

The Operating Section: Illustrations of Adjustments for the Indirect Method

The organization and line item descriptions of the operating section vary across firms. This variability is partly due to the fact that firms vary significantly in their operations (along dimensions such as technology, product markets, and customers). Thus, this section focuses on several examples of the operating section to illustrate the variety of presentations that firms use. We will discuss select line items from each example and will not dwell on unusual or idiosyncratic adjustments.

Facebook Inc. Facebook is the most popular social media website in the world. The operating section of Facebook's statement of cash flows is shown in Exhibit 3.8. The

Exhibit 3.8

Facebook Inc.
Statement of Cash Flows: Operating Section
(amounts in millions)

	Year Ended December 31,		
	2012	**2011**	**2010**
Cash flows from operating activities			
Net income	$ 53	$1,000	$ 606
Adjustments to reconcile net income to net cash provided by operating activities:			
Depreciation and amortization	649	323	139
Loss on write-off of equipment	15	4	3
Share-based compensation	1,572	217	20
Deferred income taxes	(186)	(30)	23
Tax benefit from share-based award activity	1,033	433	115
Excess tax benefit from share-based award activity	(1,033)	(433)	(115)
Changes in assets and liabilities:			
Accounts receivable	(170)	(174)	(209)
Income tax refundable	(451)	—	—
Prepaid expenses and other current assets	(14)	(24)	(38)
Other assets	2	(5)	(6)
Accounts payable	1	6	12
Platform partners payable	(2)	96	75
Accrued expenses and other current liabilities	160	37	20
Deferred revenue and deposits	(60)	49	37
Other liabilities	43	50	16
Net cash provided by operating activities	1,612	1,549	698

most striking aspect of Facebook's operating activities is that the company has reported net income of only $53 million, but net cash flows from operating activities of $1.612 *billion*. The largest non-cash adjustment is for share-based compensation, which totals $1,572 million, followed by the adjustment for depreciation and amortization, totaling $649 million. Offsetting these addbacks somewhat is a $451 million deduction for an income tax refund. In footnotes to the financial statements, Facebook explains that they recognized an income tax credit of $451 million, which was a non-cash increase in net income. Most of the other adjustments are small, with the exception of adjustments for tax benefits from share-based award activity. As described earlier in the chapter, Facebook receives a tax benefit when employees exercise options, and the excess of this tax benefit relative to the reduction in tax expense previously recognized when options were expensed is credited directly to paid-in-capital. The excess deductions give rise to tax savings that are a source of cash flows, so Facebook adds these back to net income. However, this tax benefit needs to be classified as a financing activity, so it is deducted in the operating section, and added back to the financing section. The overall effect of these adjustments is a dramatic swing from a small net income to a very large cash flow from operations.

Blackboard Inc. Blackboard Inc., a company based in Washington, D.C., provides software applications used in education, such as course website management and mobile applications. The operating section of the 2008 statement of cash flows is provided in Exhibit 3.9.

Blackboard shows an enormous difference between net income and operating cash flows for 2008 ($2.8 million net income versus $79.8 million operating cash flows). The largest non-working capital adjustments are typical and include depreciation and amortization ($15.7 million), amortization of acquired intangibles ($37.9 million), and stock-based compensation ($15.1 million).

For working capital adjustments, note that Blackboard provides the useful description "net of effect of acquisitions," which, as discussed, notifies the reader that simple changes in balance sheet amounts are unlikely to correspond to the reconciling amounts on the statement of cash flows because acquisitions are reported under investing activities and include working capital accounts acquired. For example, Blackboard shows a $31.7 million negative adjustment for accounts receivable, indicating that accounts receivable increased. Because these amounts have not been collected, they are deducted from net income to compute operating cash flows. Also, the large positive adjustment for deferred revenues of $45.2 million indicates that cash was received in advance from customers, and these amounts have yet to be recognized in income; so net income must be increased for these cash flows. These adjustments, however, contrast with information on the balance sheet (amounts in millions), as follows:

	2008	2007	Change
Accounts receivable	$ 93.4	$ 53.6	↑ $39.8
Deferred revenue	$184.7	$129.5	↑ $55.2

The discrepancy between the actual change in accounts receivable of $39.8 million and the $31.7 million reconciling adjustment on the statement of cash flows ($8.1 million) reflects accounts receivable assumed through acquisitions during 2008. Similarly, deferred revenue increased $55.2 million on the balance sheet, but the statement of cash flows shows an adjustment of only $45.2 million, indicating that the difference ($10.0 million) reflects deferred revenues assumed as part of acquisitions.

Exhibit 3.9

Blackboard Inc.
Statement of Cash Flows: Operating Section
(amounts in thousands)

	Year Ended December 31,		
	2008	2007	2006
CASH FLOWS FROM OPERATING ACTIVITIES			
Net (loss) income	$ 2,820	$12,865	$(10,737)
Adjustments to reconcile net (loss) income to net cash provided by operating activities:			
Deferred tax benefit	(8,113)	(2,830)	(5,075)
Excess tax benefits from exercise of stock options	(2,107)	(6,845)	(3,317)
Amortization of debt discount	1,653	1,840	1,701
Depreciation and amortization	15,703	10,681	8,980
Amortization of intangibles resulting from acquisitions	37,866	22,122	17,969
Change in allowance for doubtful accounts	161	(2)	(109)
Stock-based compensation	15,127	12,043	8,056
Gain on investment in common stock warrants	(3,980)	—	—
Changes in operating assets and liabilities, net of effect of acquisitions:			
Accounts receivable	(31,721)	(225)	(21,780)
Inventories	306	288	(571)
Prepaid expenses and other current assets	(2,594)	(1,233)	(42)
Deferred cost of revenues	(394)	372	(5,129)
Accounts payable	(4,018)	952	133
Accrued expenses	4,227	9,394	(5,588)
Deferred rent	9,675	1,101	(245)
Deferred revenues	45,224	8,834	38,640
Net Cash Provided by Operating Activities	$ 79,835	$69,357	$ 22,886

Cengage Learning Holdings II, L.P. Cengage Learning is a major provider of print and digital educational materials for students in higher education, professional, and international markets, and is the publisher of this text. The operating section of Cengage's statement of cash flows is shown in Exhibit 3.10. Like Blackboard, Cengage also reports cash flows well in excess of reported net income (or loss) each year. Several items are noteworthy. First, there are several large non-cash adjustments for amortization expense. For example, the first one listed is for "Amortization of pre-publication costs." Cengage aggregates costs necessary to prepare books and other materials for publication in an asset called "pre-publication costs." When the book or product is available for distribution and sale, the pre-publication costs are expensed as sales are recognized. Being a non-cash expense that reduces net income, such amortization is added back in the statement of cash flows. Second, Cengage reports a negative

Exhibit 3.10

Cengage Learning Holdings II, L.P.
Statement of Cash Flows: Operation Section
(amounts in millions)

	Years Ended June 30,		
	2012	**2011**	**2010**
Cash Flows from Operating Activities			
Net income (loss)	$ 18.2	$ (26.9)	$ 7.4
Loss from discontinued operations, net of tax	—	3.8	0.7
Income (loss) from continuing operations	18.2	(23.1)	8.1
Adjustments to reconcile income (loss) from continuing operations to net cash provided by operating activities of continuing operations:			
Amortization of pre-publication costs	161.2	142.2	140.7
Depreciation	54.9	47.3	47.0
Amortization of identifiable intangible assets	164.3	167.5	164.8
Amortization of debt discounts and deferred financing costs	16.6	16.5	18.7
Interest capitalized on long-term debt	0.7	17.5	19.0
Non-cash interest on derivative instruments	31.7	57.0	57.1
Repayments of long term debt, in lieu of interest	(35.0)	(4.4)	(7.3)
Non-cash equity-based compensation expense	4.4	8.1	5.4
Restructuring charges	—	0.6	10.5
Cash payments for restructurings	(1.3)	(8.6)	(5.4)
Mark-to-market of derivative instruments	(27.8)	(63.5)	(66.9)
Gain on early extinguishment of debt	(39.1)	(1.9)	(9.2)
(Benefit from) provision for deferred taxes	(7.8)	(4.4)	3.6
Equity losses of affiliates, net of taxes	3.1	2.9	2.4
Changes in operating assets and liabilities, net of acquisitions	68.5	(6.9)	11.8
Other, net	13.6	16.9	(3.3)
Net cash provided by operating activities of continuing operations	426.2	363.7	397.0
Net cash used in operating activities of discontinued operations	—	(0.6)	(0.3)
Net cash provided by operating activities	426.2	363.1	396.7

18. SUPPLEMENTAL CASH FLOW INFORMATION

Details of "Changes in operating assets and liabilities, net of acquisitions" are:

	Years Ended June 30,		
(in millions)	**2012**	**2011**	**2010**
Accounts receivable, net	$(15.2)	$ 68.0	$(65.2)
Inventories	14.1	(12.5)	14.8
Prepaid expenses and other current assets	(2.8)	14.7	(9.9)
Accounts payable and accrued expenses	59.8	(69.9)	23.9

(Continued)

Exhibit 3.10 (Continued)			
Accrued interest payable	16.2	(0.7)	25.1
Deferred revenue	9.3	4.3	10.7
Current taxes payable	5.1	(12.7)	6.8
Author advances	(4.0)	4.8	(2.7)
Other, net	(14.0)	(2.9)	8.3
	$ 68.5	$ (6.9)	$ 11.8

adjustment for "Gain on early extinguishment of debt." Sometimes, companies can retire debt early at amounts less than the book value, which results in a gain when the debt is retired. The gain increases net income but is non-cash, because it is the amount of the debt's book value above the cash used to retire the debt. The adjustment is necessary to remove this component of income that is not associated with cash flows. Third, Cengage lumps all reconciling adjustments together and, like Blackboard, also labels those adjustments as "Changes in operating assets and liabilities, net of acquisitions." The net of all working capital adjustments is $68.5 million, and from the note excerpt shown below the operating section, these adjustments are all typical and fluctuate from year to year. For example, the largest working capital adjustment is the $59.8 million positive adjustment for accounts payable and accrued expenses, indicating that Cengage let these liabilities rise during 2012, providing a source of cash. Receivables also rose during 2012, resulting in a use of cash of $15.2 million. The overall picture that emerges from the operating section is of a company with relatively low profits, but very high cash flows from operations.

Givaudan SA. All of the examples discussed thus far report under U.S. GAAP. Exhibit 3.11 shows the operating section of the statement of cash flows for **Givaudan SA**, a Swiss company that is one of the world's leading manufacturers of fragrances and flavorings. Under U.S. GAAP, interest paid and received and dividends received must be included as operating cash flows. In contrast, IFRS permits discretion over where companies classify interest paid and received and dividends received; both standards require dividends *paid* to be classified as a financing activity. First, note that Givaudan adjusts net income to operating income prior to beginning the operating section, and one of these adjustments is to add back interest expense. Second, interest paid is then deducted within the financing section. Third, interest received is shown within the financing section. Finally, as an aside, note that IFRS companies often show the amount of income taxes actually paid directly within the operating section.

This and previous illustrations indicate that while certain information must be presented to enable financial statement users to reconcile net income to operating cash flows, the formats and included adjustments can vary significantly. Thus, it is important to understand the substance of how accountants reconcile reported income to cash flows, not necessarily to memorize the format or sign of adjusting items.

The Relation between Net Income and Cash Flows from Operations

What is the general relation between net income and cash flows from operations? When should one exceed the other? Should they be approximately the same over a

Exhibit 3.11

Givaudan SA
Statement of Cash Flows
(in millions of Swiss francs)

	Note	2012	2011
Income for the period		411	252
Income tax expense	14	103	66
Interest expense	12	72	75
Non-operating income and expense		21	50
Operating income		**607**	**443**
Depreciation of property, plant and equipment	21	108	105
Amortisation of intangible assets	22	155	205
Impairment of long-lived assets	20, 21		5
Other non-cash items			
– share-based payments		13	13
– pension expenses		63	37
– additional and unused provisions, net		18	13
– other non-cash items		(24)	43
Adjustments for non-cash items		**333**	**421**
(Increase) decrease in inventories		90	(117)
(Increase) decrease in accounts receivable		(64)	(92)
(Increase) decrease in other current assets		(20)	(7)
Increase (decrease) in accounts payable		13	14
Increase (decrease) in other current liabilities		(2)	(11)
(Increase) decrease in working capital		**17**	**(213)**
Income taxes paid		(84)	(73)
Pension contributions paid		(70)	(75)
Provisions used		(27)	(47)
Purchase and sale of own equity instruments, net		14	—
Impact of financial transactions on operating, net		(9)	
Cash flows from (for) operating activities		**781**	**456**
Increase in long-term debt		1	839
(Decrease) in long-term debt		(50)	
Increase in short-term debt		309	131
(Decrease) in short-term debt		(732)	(1,132)
Interest paid		(76)	(77)
Distribution to the shareholders paid	26	(200)	(196)
Purchase and sale of derivative financial instruments financing, net		(17)	
Others, net		(5)	(6)
Cash flows from (for) financing activities		**(770)**	**(441)**
Acquisition of property, plant and equipment	21	(156)	(187)
Acquisition of intangible assets	22	(72)	(86)

(Continued)

Exhibit 3.11 (Continued)

Increase in share capital of jointly controlled entities			(1)
Proceeds from the disposal of property, plant and equipment	21	8	11
Sale of jointly controlled entity	8	10	
Sale of intangible assets	9	27	
Interest received		3	2
Purchase and sale of available-for-sale financial assets, net		5	1
Purchase and sale of derivative financial instruments, net			29
Others, net		(8)	(35)
Cash flows from (for) investing activities		**(183)**	**(266)**
Net increase (decrease) in cash and cash equivalents		**(172)**	**(251)**
Net effect of currency translation on cash and cash equivalents		(5)	(9)
Cash and cash equivalents at the beginning of the period		545	805
Cash and cash equivalents at the end of the period		**368**	**545**

long time period, and, if so, how long? As you saw in the previous examples, net income tends to be primarily below cash flows from operations, but you will also see exceptions. Not surprisingly, the relation between net income and cash flows depends on numerous factors, including economic characteristics of the industry, the firm, its rate of growth, and even discretionary reporting choices made by managers. However, in recent years, operating cash flows exceeds net income in approximately 80% of reporting firms.

The tendency for operating cash flows to exceed net income is not surprising for several reasons. First, the largest adjustments to net income in the operating section are generally non-working capital adjustments for changes in noncurrent assets, noncurrent liabilities, and shareholders' equity accounts, and these are primarily addbacks to net income rather than subtractions. These addbacks include depreciation expense (noncurrent assets), deferred tax expense (noncurrent liability), and share-based compensation (shareholders' equity). Almost all firms report depreciation, but primary cash flows pertaining to capital expenditures for the underlying assets are negative and appear in the investing section (as opposed to the operating section). Similarly (and related to property, plant, and equipment), a majority of firms report deferred tax liabilities, which reflect negative cash flows that are deferred to future years, although an expense is recognized currently. This contributes to current cash flows exceeding net income for many firms. Also, stock-based compensation remains a popular form of paying employees. The amount of non-cash expense is often significant, whereas small cash flows associated with these arrangements appear in the financing section (primarily cash inflows from employees who pay the exercise price on options and the contemporaneous tax savings). Finally, recent years are characterized by a large number of asset write-downs and restructuring charges, which reduce net income but not operating cash flows.

Firms that are growing rapidly can reflect various relations between operating cash flows and net income. Growth firms often report substantial adjustments for changes in accounts receivable, inventories, and current operating liabilities. When a firm increases its sales, its working capital accounts tend to increase as well. Suppose a firm doubles its sales over several years. It is likely that the company also would increase its sales made on credit (accounts receivable), increase products available for sale (inventory), and increase its own credit with vendors (payables). Most growing firms expand their accounts receivable and inventories (that is, uses of cash) more rapidly than their current operating liabilities (that is, sources of cash) and find that the net effect of changes in operating working capital is a subtraction from net income when computing cash flows from operations, which can make cash flows from operations less than net income. Alternatively, if expansions of working capital assets are accompanied by approximately equal increases in working capital liabilities, cash used in the expansion of receivables and inventory can be offset by cash provided by increasing payables. As a result, the primarily positive non-working capital adjustments discussed previously will dominate, leading to operating cash flows greater than net income.

Another factor that may cause cash flow from operations to differ from net income is the length of the operating cycle, which encompasses the period of time from when a firm commences production until it receives cash from customers for the sale of the products. Firms such as construction companies and aerospace manufacturers with relatively long operating cycles often experience a long lag between the expenditures of cash for design, development, raw materials, and labor and the receipt of cash from customers. Unless such firms receive cash advances from their customers prior to completion and delivery of the products or delay payments to their suppliers, the net effect of changes in operating working capital accounts is a subtraction from net income when computing cash flows from operations. The longer the operating cycle and the more rapid the growth of a firm, the larger the difference between net income and cash flows from operations. Consider a winery, which must plant vines, cultivate them for years, harvest grapes, ferment the juice, age wine in barrels for months or years, then bottle it, sell it, and ship it; significant cash outflows are required years before the winery will realize any cash inflows. Firms with short operating cycles, such as restaurants and service firms, experience less of a lag between the creation and delivery of their products and the collection of cash from customers. Thus, for these firms, changes in operating working capital accounts play a relatively minor role in creating a wedge between net income and cash flows from operations.

Exhibit 3.12 shows graphically the relation between net income and cash flows for **PepsiCo** from 2008–2012. First, note that cash flows from operations are positive every year but cash flows from both investing and financing activities are negative each year, with the exception of 2010, when financing cash flows are positive due to the acquisition of PepsiCo's bottlers (and investing cash flows are more negative than normal). This is consistent with the typical pattern for a mature, profitable firm. Second, cash flows from operations exceeds net income every year. Why are cash flows from operations in excess of net income for PepsiCo every year? Is it due to non-working capital or working capital adjustments? The plots for non-working capital and working capital adjustments indicate that the non-working capital adjustments are always (net) positive, but the working capital adjustments are both positive and negative and tend to vary around zero. Thus, the excess of cash flows from operations over net income is clearly due to the large positive non-working capital adjustments. Third, the most volatile pattern for the components of cash flows from operations is for the non-working and working capital adjustments. Therefore, the significant variation in these adjustments contributes directly to the variation in net income and the computation of cash flows from operations.

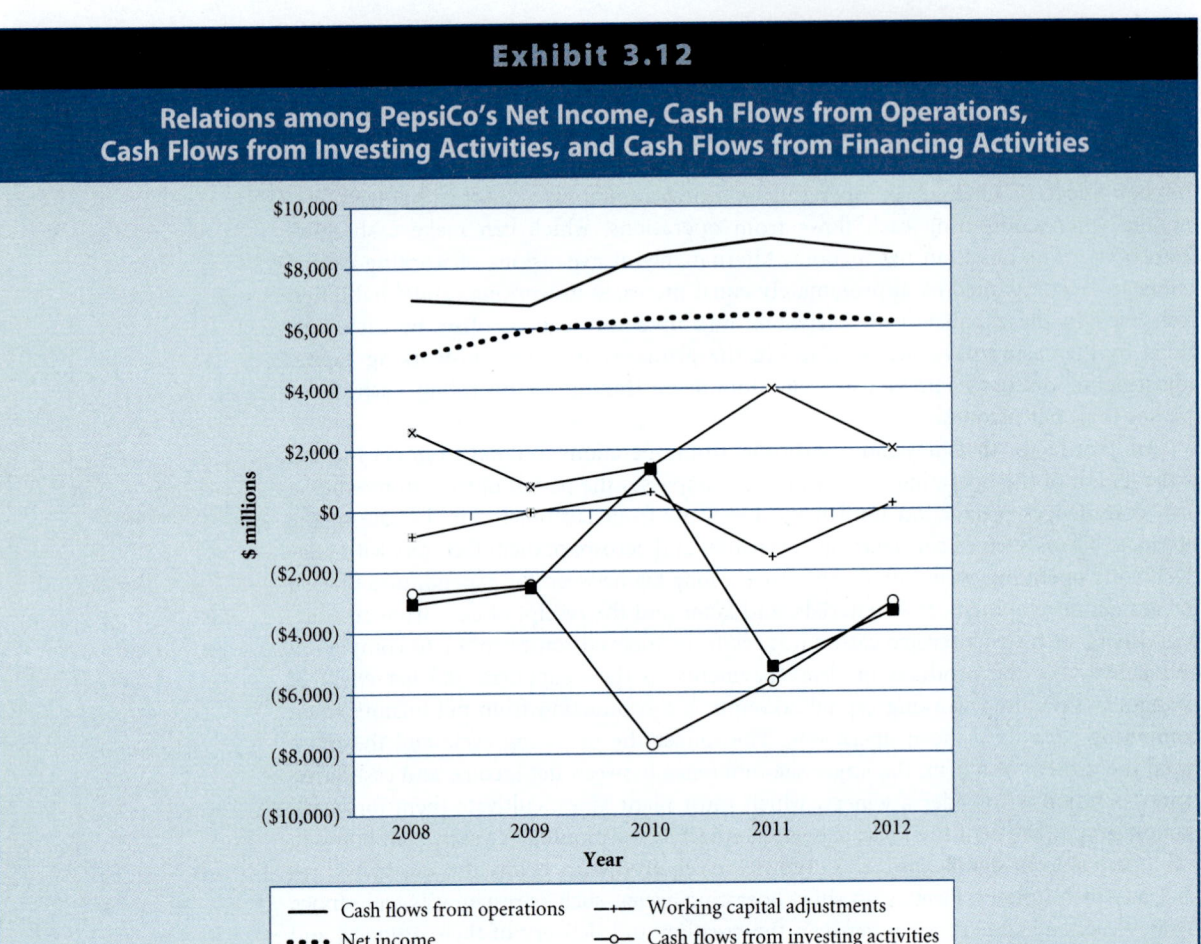

Exhibit 3.12

Relations among PepsiCo's Net Income, Cash Flows from Operations, Cash Flows from Investing Activities, and Cash Flows from Financing Activities

Quick Check

- The operating section reconciles net income to cash flows from operations.
- Two options exist for reconciling net income—the indirect or direct method—and most firms use the indirect method.

- Adjustments for working capital and non-working capital reflect the reversal of accounting entries recorded to compute balance sheet and income statement line items.

LO 3-5

Prepare a statement of cash flows from balance sheet and income statement data.

Preparing the Statement of Cash Flows

This section illustrates a procedure for preparing an *implied* statement of cash flows using information from the balance sheet and income statement. The implied statement of cash flows assumes that all of the changes in non-cash assets, liabilities, and shareholders' equity accounts imply cash flows. For example, an increase in a liability implies borrowing, while a decrease implies payment. Due to the four factors discussed earlier in the chapter for why changes rarely match the actual cash flow adjustments, the implied statement of cash flows that you prepare merely approximates the amounts the statement of cash flows would report if the analyst had full access to a firm's accounting records. For example, you can assume that all changes in operating working capital accounts are operating transactions even though some of these changes might arise from a corporate acquisition or divestiture, which are investing activities. As a second example, consider a firm that acquires another firm by paying cash and assuming its liabilities (like the **Blackboard** illustration earlier in the chapter). Only the cash outflow appears in the investing section of the statement of cash flows. Acquiring assets by assuming liabilities is a non-cash acquisition of assets, and these do not appear in the statement of cash flows (because they do not affect cash). However, firms must report them either below the statement of cash flows or in a supplemental note to the financial statements. Absent information about non-cash exchanges, the preparation procedure described in this section assumes that all of the change in each account involves a cash flow that relates to one of the three activities reported in the statement of cash flows. Despite these concerns, the estimated amounts should approximate the actual amounts closely enough for the analyst to make meaningful interpretations.

We further emphasize the above caveat by noting that cash flow statements provided by managers are not a calculation of cash flows, per se. For example, because the statement of cash flows frequently shows an addback for depreciation expense, students sometimes mistakenly infer that if a firm changes depreciation assumptions that, say, increase depreciation expense, then cash flows from operations would increase. To the contrary, cash flows from operations are what they are regardless of a firm's depreciation policies. A change in depreciation policy for financial reporting is always cash flow neutral.

To illustrate, suppose that after preparing financial statements, a firm receives new information that requires it to shorten the depreciable life of its assets, beginning with the most recently completed year. Consequently, it will need to redo those financial statements. The shortened depreciable life would trigger an increase in depreciation expense. The higher depreciation expense would trigger lower net income. This lower net income would be the revised starting point of the statement of cash flows. The depreciation addback in the operating section would be the new, higher depreciation expense. These changes would cancel each other out, and the resulting cash flows from operations would be identical to those initially reported in the financial statements.

Algebraic Formulation

You know from the accounting equation that

$$\text{Assets} = \text{Liabilities} + \text{Shareholders' Equity}$$

This equality holds for balance sheets at the beginning and end of each period. If you subtract the amounts on the balance sheet at the beginning of the period from the corresponding amounts on the balance sheet at the end of the period, you obtain the following equality for changes (Δ) in balance sheet amounts:

$$\Delta \text{ Assets} = \Delta \text{ Liabilities} + \Delta \text{ Shareholders' Equity}$$

You can now expand the change in assets as follows:

$$\Delta \text{ Cash} + \Delta \text{ Non-Cash Assets} = \Delta \text{ Liabilities} + \Delta \text{ Shareholders' Equity}$$

Rearranging terms,

$$\Delta \text{ Cash} = \Delta \text{ Liabilities} + \Delta \text{ Shareholders' Equity} - \Delta \text{ Non-Cash Assets}$$

The statement of cash flows explains the reasons for the change in cash during a period. You can see that the change in cash equals the change in all other (non-cash) balance sheet amounts. The negative sign on Δ Non-Cash Assets also explains why signs on adjustments of non-cash assets in the operating section are signed opposite to their actual change.

Refer to Exhibit 3.13, which shows the comparative balance sheet of Footloose Shoe Store for the years ending December 31, Year 4, Year 3, and Year 2. The balance sheets at the end of Year 2 and Year 3 report the following equalities:

	Cash	+	Non-Cash Assets	=	Liabilities	+	Shareholders' Equity
Year 2	$13,698	+	$132,136	=	$105,394	+	$40,440
Year 3	12,595	+	129,511	=	85,032	+	57,074
Changes	$(1,103)	+	$ (2,625)	=	$(20,362)	+	$16,634

Subtracting the amounts at the end of Year 2 from the amounts at the end of Year 3, you obtain the following:

$$\Delta \text{ Cash} + \Delta \text{ Non-Cash Assets} = \Delta \text{ Liabilities} + \Delta \text{ Shareholders' Equity}$$
$$\$(1,103) + \$(2,625) = \$(20,362) + \$16,634$$

Rearranging terms,

$$\Delta \text{ Cash} = \Delta \text{ Liabilities} + \Delta \text{ Shareholders' Equity} - \Delta \text{ Non-Cash Assets}$$
$$\$(1,103) = \$(20,362) + \$16,634 - \$(2,625)$$

The decrease in cash of $1,103 equals the decrease in liabilities plus the increase in shareholders' equity minus the decrease in non-cash assets.

To link the above decomposition of the balance sheet equation into the format of the statement of cash flows, partition non-cash assets and liabilities into working capital and non-working capital components. Also assume that all non-working capital liabilities reflect debt financing. Indicating the components with "WC" and "NWC" subscripts, the equation becomes:

$$\Delta \text{ Cash} = \Delta \text{ Liabilities}_{WC} + \Delta \text{ Liabilities}_{NWC} + \Delta \text{ Shareholders' Equity} - \Delta \text{ Non-Cash Assets}_{WC} - \Delta \text{ Non-Cash Assets}_{NWC}$$

Rearranging terms,

$$\Delta \text{ Cash} = \Delta \text{ Liabilities}_{WC} - \Delta \text{ Non-Cash Assets}_{WC} - \Delta \text{ Non Cash Assets}_{NWC} + \Delta \text{ Liabilities}_{NWC} + \Delta \text{ Shareholder's Equity}$$

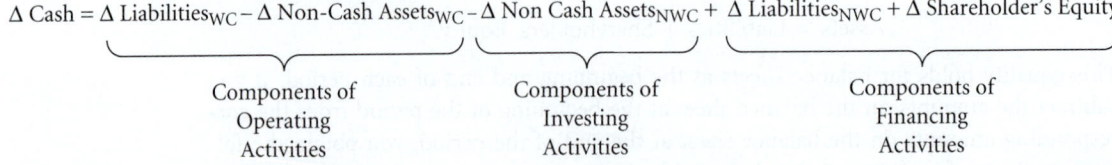

| Components of Operating Activities | Components of Investing Activities | Components of Financing Activities |

The rearrangement of the familiar balance sheet equation (and use of simplifying assumptions) yields the intuitive equation above, which *figuratively* maps into the information on the statement of cash flows. The mapping is figurative and is not technically representative, however, because net income is included in ΔShareholders' Equity above and is an operating activity.

Exhibit 3.13

Footloose Shoe Store
Balance Sheet

	December 31, Year 2	December 31, Year 1
ASSETS		
Cash	$ 12,595	$ 13,698
Accounts receivable	1,978	1,876
Inventories	106,022	98,824
Other current assets	—	3,591
Total Current Assets	$120,595	$117,989
Property, plant, and equipment, at cost	$ 65,285	$ 63,634
Less accumulated depreciation	(45,958)	(37,973)
Net property, plant, and equipment	$ 19,327	$ 25,661
Intangible assets	2,184	2,184
Total Assets	$142,106	$145,834
LIABILITIES AND SHAREHOLDERS' EQUITY		
Accounts payable	$ 15,642	$ 21,768
Notes payable	—	—
Current portion of long-term debt	10,997	18,256
Other current liabilities	6,912	4,353
Total Current Liabilities	$ 33,551	$ 44,377
Long-term debt	51,481	61,017
Total Liabilities	$ 85,032	$105,394
Common stock	$ 1,000	$ 1,000
Additional paid-in capital	124,000	124,000
Retained earnings	(67,926)	(84,560)
Total Shareholders' Equity	$ 57,074	$ 40,440
Total Liabilities and Shareholders' Equity	$142,106	$145,834

Classifying Changes in Balance Sheet Accounts

Converting the balance sheet and income statement into a statement of cash flows requires the analyst to classify the change in each non-cash balance sheet account (right side of the preceding equation) into an operating, investing, or financing activity. Some of the changes in balance sheet accounts clearly fit into one of the three categories. (For example, the change in long-term debt is usually a financing transaction.) However, some balance sheet changes (for example, retained earnings) result from the netting of several changes, some of which relate to operations (net income) and some of which relate to financing activities (dividends). The analyst should use whatever information the financial statements and notes provide about changes in balance sheet accounts to classify the net change properly in each account each period.

Exhibit 3.14 classifies the changes in the non-cash balance sheet accounts and provides a schematic worksheet for the preparation of the statement of cash flows. The text

---

Exhibit 3.14

Worksheet for Preparation of Statement of Cash Flows

Balance Sheet Accounts	Amount of Balance Sheet Changes	Operating	Investing	Financing
(INCREASE) DECREASE IN ASSETS				
(1) Accounts receivable	X	X		
(2) Marketable securities	X		X	
(3) Inventories	X	X		
(4) Other current assets	X	X		
(5) Investments in securities	X		X	
(6) Property, plant, and equipment cost	X		X	
(7) Accumulated depreciation	X	X		
(8) Intangible assets	X	X	X	
INCREASE (DECREASE) IN LIABILITIES AND SHAREHOLDERS' EQUITIES				
(9) Accounts payable	X	X		
(10) Notes payable	X			X
(11) Current portion of long-term debt	X			X
(12) Other current liabilities	X	X		
(13) Long-term debt	X			X
(14) Deferred income taxes	X	X		
(15) Other noncurrent liabilities	X	X		
(16) Common stock	X			X
(17) Additional paid-in capital	X			X
(18) Retained earnings	X	X (net income)		X (dividends)
(19) Treasury stock	X			X
(20) Other accumulated comprehensive income				
(21) Cash	X	X	X	X

will refer to this exhibit in walking through the preparation of a statement of cash flows for Footloose Shoe Store and in several exercises at the end of the chapter. The classification of each of these changes is discussed next.

1. Accounts Receivable

Cash collections from customers during a period equal sales for the period plus accounts receivable at the beginning of the period minus accounts receivable at the end of the period, or alternatively, sales minus the change in accounts receivable.

$$\text{Cash Collected from Customers} = \text{Sales} - \Delta \text{ Accounts Receivable}$$

An increase in accounts receivable indicates that less cash was collected than was recognized in revenues, so the adjustment is a subtraction, and vice versa for decreases in accounts receivable. Thus, the change in accounts receivable clearly relates to operations. Line (18) of Exhibit 3.14 shows net income as a source of cash from operations, which includes sales revenues. Thus, the amount for sales revenue included in the amount on line (18) adjusted for the change in accounts receivable on line (1) results in the amount of cash received from customers.

2. Marketable Securities

Firms typically acquire marketable securities when they temporarily have excess cash and sell these securities when they need cash. U.S. GAAP and IFRS ignore the reason for the source or use of this cash and classify the cash flows associated with purchases and sales of marketable securities as investing activities. Because net income includes gains or losses on sales of marketable securities, you must subtract gains and add back losses to net income in deriving cash flow from operations. Failure to offset the gain or loss included in earnings results in reporting too much (sales of marketable securities at a gain) or too little (sales of marketable securities at a loss) cash flow from operations.

3. Inventories

Purchases of inventory during a period equal cost of goods sold plus the change in inventory.

$$\text{Purchases of Inventory} = \text{Cost of Goods Sold} + \Delta \text{ Inventory}$$

Line (18) includes cost of goods sold as an expense in measuring net income. The change in inventories on line (3) coupled with cost of goods sold included in net income on line (18) results in the cash flow for purchases for the period. The presumption is that the firm made a cash outflow equal to the amount of purchases. If the firm does not pay cash for all of these purchases, accounts payable will change. You adjust for the change in accounts payable on line (9), discussed later.

4. Other Current Assets

Other current assets typically include prepayments for various operating costs, such as insurance and rent. Unless the financial statements and notes present information to the contrary, the presumption is that the change in other current assets relates to operations. Under this presumption, the related expenses are included in net income, so we must adjust these amounts for any changes in other current assets to convert those expenses into the cash amounts. The logic is the same as that for inventory.

5. Investments in Securities

The Investments in Securities account can change for the following reasons:

Source of Change	Classification in Statement of Cash Flows
Recognition of income or loss using equity method	Operating (subtraction or addition)
Acquisition or sale of investments	Investing (outflow or inflow)
Receipt of dividend from investee	Operating (inflow)
Purchases or sales of securities classified as "trading" securities	Operating (outflow or inflow)

We discussed the adjustment for equity method income for **PepsiCo** earlier in the chapter. These types of investments are generally separately disclosed. If a firm's balance sheet, income statement, or notes provide information that permits the disaggregation of the net change in investments in securities into these separate components, you can make appropriate classifications of the components. Absent such information, however, it is natural to classify the change in investment securities other than trading securities as an investing activity.

6. Property, Plant, and Equipment

Cash flows related to purchases and sales of fixed assets are classified as investing activities. Because net income includes any gains or losses from sales of fixed assets, you offset their effect on earnings by adding back losses and subtracting gains from net income when computing cash flows from operations. You then include the full amount of the proceeds from sales of fixed assets as an investing activity. Impairment charges, if applicable, would be a non-cash charge that must be added back to net income in the operating section to appropriately report operating cash flows.

7. Accumulated Depreciation

The amount of depreciation expense recognized each period reduces net income but does not use cash. Thus, add back depreciation expense on line (7). This treatment is appropriate because depreciation expense is not a cash flow (ignoring income tax consequences). If a firm sells depreciable assets during a period, the net change in accumulated depreciation includes both the accumulated depreciation removed from the account for assets sold and depreciation expense for the period. Thus, you cannot assume that the change in the Accumulated Depreciation account relates only to depreciation expense unless disclosures indicate that the firm did not sell depreciable assets during the year.

8. Intangible Assets

Intangible assets on the balance sheet include patents, copyrights, goodwill, and similar assets. A portion of the change in these accounts represents amortization, which requires an addback to net income when computing cash flows from operations. Unless the financial statements and notes provide contrary information, the presumption is that the remaining change in these accounts is an investing activity. Many firms include another line item on their balance sheets labeled "Other Noncurrent Assets." You should use whatever information firms disclose to determine the appropriate classification of the change in this account.

9. Accounts Payable

Under the assumption that all accounts payable are due to suppliers from which the firm makes purchases, the cash outflow for accounts payable equals inventory purchases during the period minus the change in accounts payable.

$$\text{Cash Paid to Suppliers} = \text{Purchases of Inventory} - \Delta \text{ Accounts Payable}$$

The amount for inventory purchases of the period was derived as part of the calculations in line (3) for inventories. The adjustment on line (9) for the change in accounts payable converts cost of goods sold that is included within net income to cash payments for purchases and, like inventories, is an operating activity.

10. Notes Payable

Notes Payable is the account generally used when a firm engages in short-term borrowing from a bank or another financial institution. The typical classification of such borrowings is as a financing activity on the statement of cash flows even though the firm might use the proceeds to finance accounts receivable, inventories, or other working capital needs. The presumption underlying the classification of bank borrowing as a financing activity is that firms derive operating cash inflows from their customers, not by borrowing from banks.

11. Current Portion of Long-Term Debt

The change in the current portion of long-term debt during a period equals (a) the reclassification of long-term debt from a noncurrent liability to a current liability (that is, debt that the firm expects to repay within one year of the balance sheet date) minus (b) the current portion of long-term debt actually repaid during the period. The latter amount represents the cash outflow from this financing transaction. The amount arising from the reclassification in connection with line (13) will be considered shortly.

12. Other Current Liabilities

Firms generally use this account for obligations related to goods and services used in operations other than purchases of inventories. Thus, changes in other current liabilities appear as operating activities.

13. Long-Term Debt

This account changes for the following reasons:

- Issuance of new long-term debt
- Reclassification of long-term debt from a noncurrent to a current liability (current portion of long-term debt)
- Retirement of long-term debt
- Conversion of long-term debt to preferred or common stock

These items are clearly financing transactions, but they do not all affect cash. The issuance of new debt and the retirement of old debt do affect cash flows. When long-term debt approaches maturity, the reclassification of long-term debt offsets the corresponding increase in the current portion of long-term debt, and they effectively cancel each other. This is appropriate because the reclassification does not affect cash flow. Likewise, any portion of the change in long-term debt on line (13) due to a conversion of debt into common stock offsets a similar change on lines (16) and (17). You enter reclassifications and conversions of debt, such as those described previously, on the worksheet for the preparation of a statement of cash flows because such transactions help explain changes in balance sheet accounts. However, these transactions do not appear on the formal statement of cash flows because they do not involve actual cash flows.

14. Deferred Income Taxes

Income taxes currently payable equal income tax expense [included on line (18) as a negative element of net income] plus or minus the change in deferred taxes during the period. Thus, changes in deferred income taxes appear as an operating activity.

15. Other Noncurrent Liabilities

This account includes unfunded pension and retirement benefit obligations, long-term deposits received, and other miscellaneous long-term liabilities. Changes in these types of obligations are operating activities, absent information to the contrary.

16, 17, and 19. Common Stock, Additional Paid-in Capital, and Treasury Stock

These accounts change when a firm issues new common stock or repurchases and retires outstanding common stock, and they appear as financing activities. The Additional Paid-in Capital account also changes when firms recognize compensation expense related to stock options. This is a non-cash expense that, like depreciation, requires an addback to net income to compute cash flows from operations.

18. Retained Earnings

Retained earnings increase by the amount of net income and decrease with the declaration of dividends each period.

$$\text{Ending Retained Earnings} = \text{Beginning Retained Earnings} + \text{Net Income} - \text{Dividends}$$
$$\Rightarrow \Delta\,\text{Retained Earnings} = \text{Net Income} - \text{Dividends}$$

Net income is an operating activity, and dividends are a financing activity.

20. Accumulated Other Comprehensive Income

Recall that accumulated other comprehensive income is a component of shareholders' equity and includes various fair value gains and losses that have not been realized. Examples include gains and losses from foreign currency translation, certain investment securities, derivative instruments, and certain pension items. The change in accumulated other comprehensive income on the balance sheet represents the amount of other comprehensive income for the period, net of any accumulated other comprehensive income items that were realized in cash and therefore recognized in net income during the period. Also recall that

$$\text{Net Income} + \text{Other Comprehensive Income} = \text{Comprehensive Income}$$

Other comprehensive income represents only non-cash adjustments (that is, gains and losses that have not been realized). Accumulated other comprehensive income items that are realized in cash are already recognized in net income for the period. Therefore, the change in accumulated other comprehensive income on the balance sheet needs no further recognition on the statement of cash flows, because the statement of cash flows starts with net income, not comprehensive income.

Illustration of the Preparation Procedure

Based on the data for Footloose Shoe Store, the procedure for preparing the statement of cash flows is illustrated in Exhibit 3.15. In addition to the balance sheet data shown there, net income was $16,634 for Year 2. The first column of Exhibit 3.15 shows the change in each non-cash balance sheet account that nets to the $1,103 decrease in cash for the period. You should observe with particular care the direction of the change. Recall the earlier decomposition of the balance sheet equation. Possible combinations of net changes in cash, liabilities, shareholders' equity, and non-cash assets can be described as follows:

Δ Cash	=	Δ Liabilities	+	Δ Shareholders' Equity	−	Δ Non-Cash Assets
Increase	=	Increase				
Decrease	=	Decrease				
Increase	=			Increase		
Decrease	=			Decrease		
Decrease	=					Increase
Increase	=					Decrease

Exhibit 3.15

Footloose Shoe Store
Worksheet for Statement of Cash Flows
Year 3

Balance Sheet Accounts	Amount of Balance Sheet Changes	Operating	Investing	Financing	Cross-Reference to Statement of Cash Flows in Exhibit 3.16
(INCREASE) DECREASE IN ASSETS					
Accounts receivable	$ (102)	$ (102)	—	—	❶
Inventories	(7,198)	(7,198)	—	—	❷
Other current assets	3,591	3,591	—	—	❸
Property, plant, and equipment	(1,651)	—	$(1,651)	—	❹
Accumulated depreciation	7,985	7,985	—	—	❺
Intangible assets	—	—	—	—	
INCREASE (DECREASE) IN LIABILITIES AND SHAREHOLDERS' EQUITIES					
Accounts payable	$ (6,126)	$ (6,126)	—	—	❻
Notes payable	—	—	—	—	❼
Current portion of long-term debt	(7,259)	—	—	$ (7,259)	❽
Other current liabilities	2,559	2,559	—	—	❾
Long-term debt	(9,536)	—	—	(9,536)	❽
Common stock	—	—	—	—	
Additional paid-in capital	—	—	—	—	
Retained paid-in capital	16,634	16,634	—	—	
Cash	$ (1,103)	$17,343	$(1,651)	$(16,795)	❿

Thus, changes in liabilities and shareholders' equity have the same directional effect on cash, whereas changes in non-cash assets have the opposite directional effect. Bank borrowings increase liabilities and cash; debt repayments decrease liabilities and cash. Issuing common stock increases shareholders' equity and cash; paying dividends or repurchasing outstanding common stock reduces shareholders' equity and cash. Purchasing equipment increases non-cash assets and reduces cash; selling equipment reduces non-cash assets and increases cash.

You classify the change in each account as an operating, investing, or financing activity because you have no information that more than one activity caused the change in the account. Observe the following inferences for Year 2:

1. Operating activities were a net source of cash for the period. Cash flows from operations approximately equaled net income. Footloose Shoe Store increased its inventories but reduced accounts payable. Most firms attempt to increase accounts payable to finance increases in inventories. The reduced accounts payable suggests a desire to pay suppliers more quickly, perhaps to take advantage of cash discounts, or pressure from suppliers to pay more quickly.

2. Cash flows from operations was more than sufficient to finance the increase in property, plant, and equipment. Note that capital expenditures were small relative to the amount of depreciation for the year, suggesting that the firm is not increasing its capacity.

3. Footloose Shoe Store used the cash derived from operations in excess of capital expenditures to repay long-term debt.

Exhibit 3.16 presents the statement of cash flows for Footloose Shoe Store for Year 2 using the amounts taken from the worksheet in Exhibit 3.15. The far right columns of Exhibits 3.15 and 3.16 provide cross-references for clarifying how the worksheet is used to prepare the statement of cash flows.

Exhibit 3.16

Footloose Shoe Store
Statement of Cash Flows

	Year 2	Cross-Reference of Year 2 Amounts to Exhibit 3.15
OPERATING		
Net Income	$ 16,634	
Depreciation	7,985	❺
(Increase) Decrease in accounts receivable	(102)	❶
(Increase) Decrease in inventories	(7,198)	❷
(Increase) Decrease in other current assets	3,591	❸
Increase (Decrease) in accounts payable	(6,126)	❻
Increase (Decrease) in other current liabilities	2,559	❾
Cash Flows from Operating Activities	$ 17,343	❿
INVESTING		
Sale (acquisition) of property, plant, and equipment	$ (1,651)	❹
Cash Flows from Investing Activities	$ (1,651)	❿
FINANCING		
Increase in notes payable	—	❼
Repayment of long-term debt	(16,795)	❽
Cash Flows from Financing Activities	$(16,795)	❿
Net Change in Cash	$ (1,103)	❿
Cash at beginning of year	13,698	
Cash at End of Year	$ 12,595	

Quick Check

■ Changes in cash mechanically equal changes in liabilities and equity minus changes in non-cash assets.

■ If you understand how a statement of cash flows is prepared, you will better be able to effectively use the statement of cash flows.

Usefulness of the Statement of Cash Flows for Accounting and Risk Analysis

LO 3-6

Recognize additional uses of the statement of cash flows, such as for accounting and risk analysis.

Chapter 6 explores the analysis of accruals as part of assessing earnings and overall accounting quality. Accruals represent the non-cash accounting adjustments that are employed to prepare income statements and balance sheets, such as recognizing sales on account, accruing expenses incurred but not paid, and so on. As discussed in the previous chapter, these accounting adjustments involve managerial discretion. One nice feature of the statement of cash flows is that accruals are captured in its operating section.

As a prelude to the analysis of accruals to assess earnings quality, Exhibit 3.17 shows two versions of the 1998 statement of cash flows for **MicroStrategy, Inc.**—one as originally reported and the other as subsequently restated for changes in the accounting for revenues. MicroStrategy is a provider of software that enables businesses to conduct transaction data through various channels and to examine information about customers, partners, and supply chains. The company was aggressive at recognizing revenue upon signing a contract with customers (and often before that), and the restatement announced in March 2000 included revised procedures for recognizing revenues only after sales contracts were completed and over the contract period rather than immediately. The most important point made in Exhibit 3.17 is that regardless of the accounting practices (before or after restatement), *the cash flows do not change.* How could different accounting treatment create or destroy cash flows?

For 1998, software license revenues of $72.721 million were restated downward to $61.635 million and net income was restated downward from a *profit* of $6.178 million to a *loss* of $2.255 million. The restatement affected the balance sheet through decreases in accounts receivable (for revenues recognized premature to the finalization of the contract), increases in deferred revenue (for revenue recognized immediately rather than spread over the contract period), and other miscellaneous adjustments. As Exhibit 3.17 shows, MicroStrategy used $2.548 million of cash for operations, which is unaffected by the restatement of revenues (and associated balance sheet data). As originally reported, non-working capital adjustments totaled $4.183 million, which totaled $5.185 million after the restatement; more importantly, working capital adjustments fell from −$12.909 million to −$5.478 million.

Several features of MicroStrategy's original operating section of the statement of cash flows stand out. First, as you have seen in other examples discussed earlier in the chapter, the typical relation of net income being less than operating cash flows is reversed for MicroStrategy. Although net income can legitimately exceed cash flows from operations, especially for growth firms, it is a red flag for accounting quality issues because of managerial discretion necessary in the reporting of non-working capital and working capital adjustments. Second, the existence of negative cash flows from operations but positive net income represents a situation in which managers may be keenly interested in reporting profits rather than losses, increasing incentives to adopt aggressive accounting practices. Third, the magnitude of the working capital adjustments exceeds that of non-working capital adjustments, which indicates that the accounting for working capital accounts has an elevated importance for the level of reported earnings. For example, accounts receivable and deferred revenues are directly associated with the recognition of revenues.

As originally reported, MicroStrategy showed a negative adjustment for accounts receivable of $17.525 million, indicating that accounts receivable increased (and revenue was recognized); on the other hand, the originally reported change in deferred revenue was relatively smaller, increasing cash flows by $2.267 million (as customers prepaid and MicroStrategy actually deferred revenue). After the restatement, however, the

Exhibit 3.17

MicroStrategy, Inc.
Statement of Cash Flows for 1998
(amounts in thousands)

	As Originally Reported	Restated
OPERATING ACTIVITIES		
Net income (loss)	$ 6,178	$ (2,255)
Adjustments to reconcile net income (loss) to net cash from operating activities:		
Depreciation and amortization	3,250	3,250
Provision for doubtful accounts, net of write-offs and recoveries	815	815
Net change in deferred taxes	(45)	0
Other	163	1,120
Changes in operating assets and liabilities, net of effect of foreign exchange rate changes:		
Accounts receivable	(17,525)	(10,835)
Prepaid expenses and other current assets	(711)	(3,758)
Accounts payable and accrued expenses, compensation, and benefits	5,948	5,508
Deferred revenue	2,267	3,795
Deposits and other assets	(188)	(188)
Long-term accounts receivable	(2,700)	0
Net Cash Used in Operating Activities	$ (2,548)	$ (2,548)
INVESTING ACTIVITIES		
Acquisition of property and equipment	$ (9,295)	$ (9,295)
Net Cash Used in Investing Activities	$ (9,295)	$ (9,295)
FINANCING ACTIVITIES		
Proceeds from sale of Class A common stock and exercise of stock options, net of offering costs	$ 48,539	$ 48,539
Repayments on short-term line of credit, net	(4,508)	(4,508)
Repayments of dividend notes payable	(5,000)	(5,000)
Proceeds from issuance of note payable	862	862
Principal payments on notes payable	(4,190)	(4,190)
Net Cash Provided by Financing Activities	$ 35,703	$ 35,703
Effect of foreign exchange rate changes on cash	$ 125	$ 125
Net Increase in Cash and Cash Equivalents	$ 23,985	$ 23,985
Cash and cash equivalents, beginning of year	3,506	3,506
Cash and Cash Equivalents, End of Period	$ 27,491	$ 27,491

increase in receivables declined to $10.835 million (pushing revenue recognition to future years) and the increase in deferred revenue increased to $3.795 million (deferring even more of the revenues for which customers had prepaid). Both of these changes reflect less aggressive accounting practice in terms of revenue recognition. Finally, the average total assets of MicroStrategy for 1998 was $56.377 million (not shown in Exhibit 3.17), so total accruals is approximately 15.5% of average total assets [{6,178 − (−2,548)} / 56,377]. The median value of asset-scaled total accruals for all firms is approximately − 0.04. Thus, a value of +0.155 is remarkably high, and as will be discussed in more depth in Chapter 6. Higher values of this metric are suggestive of lower earnings quality, which certainly characterized MicroStrategy's originally reported 1998 financial statements.

The restatement was costly to the company's shareholders as the price of MicroStrategy common shares fell from $227 to $113 within five days of the announcement of the restatement. Clearly, the financial statements as originally reported contained clues investors could have used to raise concerns about the quality of earnings possibly being low.

In addition to the analysis of accounting quality, the statement of cash flows is useful for liquidity and credit risk analysis. Chapter 5 discusses how you can use information on cash flows to assess a firm's ability to fund its operations and investments and to meet its debt obligations. Also, Chapter 12 discusses how the statement of cash flows can be used to compute free cash flows, which are widely used to estimate firm value.

■ The statement of cash flows is useful in assessing the quality of earnings and elements of the balance sheet.

■ Subsequent chapters will illustrate the use of cash flows information to assess financial risk.

Quick Check

Summary

As a complement to the balance sheet and the income statement, the statement of cash flows is an informative statement for analysts for the following reasons:

■ Analysts who understand the types of information this statement presents and the kinds of interpretations that are appropriate find that the statement of cash flows reveals information about the economic characteristics of a firm's industry, its strategy, and the stage in its life cycle.

■ An understanding of the mechanics of statement of cash flows preparation enables an analyst to better understand the linkages between the income statement and balance sheet.

■ The statement of cash flows provides information to assess the financial health of a firm. Analysts increasingly recognize that cash flows do not necessarily track income flows. A firm with a healthy income statement is not necessarily financially healthy. Likewise, a firm with healthy cash flows is not necessarily financially healthy. Cash requirements to service debt, for example, may outstrip the ability of operations to generate cash. Or, cash flows might be high because the firm is liquidating assets.

■ The statement of cash flows highlights accounting accruals and can be an important tool in performing risk analysis and analysis of earnings quality, which are necessary for forecasting future results and valuing the firm.

Questions, Exercises, Problems, and Cases

Questions and Exercises

LO 3-1

3.1 Need for a Statement of Cash Flows. "The accrual basis of accounting creates the need for a statement of cash flows." Explain.

LO 3-3

3.2 Articulation of the Statement of Cash Flows with Other Financial Statements. Describe how the statement of cash flows is linked to each of the other financial statements (income statement and balance sheet). Also review how the other financial statements are linked with each other.

LO 3-3

3.3 Classification of Interest Expense. Under U.S. GAAP, the statement of cash flows classifies cash expenditures for interest expense as an operating activity but classifies cash expenditures to redeem debt as a financing activity. Explain this apparent paradox.

LO 3-3

3.4 Classification of Cash Flows Related to the Cost of Financing. Under U.S. GAAP, the statement of cash flows classifies cash expenditures for interest expense on debt as an operating activity but classifies cash expenditures for dividends to shareholders as a financing activity. Explain this apparent paradox.

LO 3-3

3.5 Classification of Changes in Short-Term Financing. The statement of cash flows classifies changes in accounts payable as an operating activity but classifies changes in short-term borrowing as a financing activity. Explain this apparent paradox.

LO 3-3

3.6 Classification of Cash Flows Related to Share-Based Compensation. One reason companies use stock options to compensate employees is to conserve cash. Under current tax law, companies get to deduct compensation when the employees actually exercise options. Explain how the cash flow savings from stock option exercises affect the statement of cash flows.

LO 3-3

3.7 Treatment of Non-Cash Exchanges. The acquisition of equipment by assuming a mortgage is a transaction that firms cannot report in their statement of cash flows but must report in a supplemental schedule or note. Of what value is information about this type of transaction? What is the reason for its exclusion from the statement of cash flows?

LO 3-4

3.8 Computing Cash Collections from Customers. Caterpillar manufactures heavy machinery and equipment and provides financing for purchases by its customers. Caterpillar reported sales and interest revenues of $51,324 million for Year 1. The balance sheet showed current and noncurrent receivables of $15,752 million at the beginning of Year 1 and $18,448 million at the end of Year 1. Compute the amount of cash collected from customers during Year 1.

LO 3-4

3.9 Computing Cash Payments to Suppliers. Lowe's Companies, a retailer of home improvement products, reported cost of goods sold of $31,729 million for Year 1. It reported merchandise inventories of $7,611 million at the beginning of Year 1 and $8,209 million at the end of Year 1. It reported accounts payable to suppliers of $3,713 million at the beginning of fiscal Year 1 and $4,109 million at the end of fiscal Year 1. Compute the amount of cash paid to merchandise suppliers during Year 1.

3.10 Computing Cash Payments for Income Taxes. Visa Inc., a credit card company, reported income tax expense of $1,648 million for Year 1, comprising $1,346 million of current taxes and $302 million of deferred taxes. The balance sheet showed income taxes payable of $122 million at the beginning of Year 1 and $327 million at the end of Year 1. Compute the amount of income taxes paid in cash during Year 1.

LO 3-4

3.11 Interpreting the Relation between Net Income and Cash Flow from Operations. Combined data for three years for two firms follows (in millions).

LO 3-2

	Firm A	Firm B
Net income	$2,381	$2,825
Cash flow from operations	1,133	7,728

One of these firms is **Amazon.com**, a rapidly growing Internet retailer, and the other is **Kroger**, a retail grocery store chain growing at approximately the same rate as the population. Identify each firm and explain your reasoning.

3.12 Interpreting the Relation between Net Income and Cash Flow from Operations. Three years of combined data for two firms follows (in millions).

LO 3-2

	Firm A	Firm B
Net income	$ 996	$2,846
Cash flow from operations	3,013	3,401

The two firms experienced similar growth rates in revenues during the three-year period. One of these firms is **Accenture Ltd.**, a management consulting firm, and the other is **Southwest Airlines**, a provider of airline transportation services. Identify each firm and explain your reasoning.

3.13 Interpreting Relations among Cash Flows from Operating, Investing, and Financing Activities. Three years of combined data for two firms follows (in millions).

LO 3-2

	Firm A	Firm B
Net income	$ 2,378	$ 2,399
Cash flow from operations	7,199	3,400
Cash flow from investing	(6,764)	(678)
Cash flow from financing	570	(2,600)

One of these firms is **FedEx**, a relatively high-growth firm that provides courier services, and the other is **Kellogg Company**, a more mature consumer foods processor. Identify each firm and explain your reasoning.

3.14 Interpreting Relations among Cash Flows from Operating, Investing, and Financing Activities. Three years of combined data for two firms follows (in millions).

	Firm A	Firm B
Cash flow from operations	$ 2,639	$ 2,759
Cash flow from investing	(3,491)	(1,281)
Cash flow from financing	1,657	(1,654)

One of these firms is **eBay**, an online retailer with a three-year growth in sales of 337.3%, and the other is **TJX Companies, Inc.,** a specialty retail store with a three-year growth in sales of 39.3%. Identify each firm and explain your reasoning.

Problems and Cases

3.15 Interpreting the Statement of Cash Flows. The **Coca-Cola Company** (Coca-Cola), like **PepsiCo**, manufactures and markets a variety of beverages. Exhibit 3.18 presents a statement of cash flows for Coca-Cola for three years.

Exhibit 3.18

**The Coca-Cola Company
Statement of Cash Flows
(amounts in millions)
(Problem 3.15)**

Year Ended December 31,	Year 3	Year 2	Year 1
OPERATING ACTIVITIES			
Net income	$ 5,807	$ 5,981	$ 5,080
Depreciation and amortization	1,228	1,163	938
Stock-based compensation expense	266	313	324
Deferred income taxes	(360)	109	(35)
Equity income or loss, net of dividends	1,128	(452)	124
Foreign currency adjustments	(42)	9	52
Gains on sales of assets, including bottling interests	(130)	(244)	(303)
Other operating charges	209	166	159
Other items	153	99	233
Net change in operating assets and liabilities	(688)	6	(615)
Net Cash Provided by Operating Activities	$ 7,571	$ 7,150	$ 5,957
INVESTING ACTIVITIES			
Acquisitions and investments, principally beverage and bottling companies and trademarks	$ (759)	$(5,653)	$ (901)
Purchases of other investments	(240)	(99)	(82)
Proceeds from disposals of bottling companies and other investments	479	448	640

(Continued)

Exhibit 3.18 (Continued)			
Purchases of property, plant, and equipment	(1,968)	(1,648)	(1,407)
Proceeds from disposals of property, plant, and equipment	129	239	112
Other investing activities	(4)	(6)	(62)
Net Cash Used in Investing Activities	$(2,363)	$(6,719)	$(1,700)
FINANCING ACTIVITIES			
Issuances of debt	$ 4,337	$ 9,979	$ 617
Payments of debt	(4,308)	(5,638)	(2,021)
Issuances of stock	586	1,619	148
Purchases of stock for treasury	(1,079)	(1,838)	(2,416)
Dividends	(3,521)	(3,149)	(2,911)
Net Cash Provided by (Used in) Financing Activities	$(3,985)	$ 973	$(6,583)
Effect of exchange rate changes on cash and cash equivalents	$ (615)	$ 249	$ 65
CASH AND CASH EQUIVALENTS			
Net Increase (Decrease) During the Year	$ 608	$ 1,653	$(2,261)
Balance at beginning of year	4,093	2,440	4,701
Balance at End of Year	$ 4,701	$ 4,093	$ 2,440

Source: The Coca-Cola Company, Form 10-K for the Fiscal Year Ended 2008.

REQUIRED

Discuss the relations between net income and cash flow from operations and among cash flows from operating, investing, and financing activities for the firm over the three-year period. Identify characteristics of Coca-Cola's cash flows that you would expect for a mature company.

3.16 Interpreting the Statement of Cash Flows. Texas Instruments pri-
marily develops and manufactures semiconductors for use in technology-based products for various industries. The manufacturing process is capital-intensive and subject to cyclical swings in the economy. Because of overcapacity in the industry and a cutback on spending for technology products due to a recession, semiconductor prices collapsed in Year 1 and commenced a steady comeback during Years 2 through 4.

`LO 3-3`

  Exhibit 3.19 presents a statement of cash flows for Texas Instruments for Year 0 to Year 4.

REQUIRED

Discuss the relations between net income and cash flows from operations and among cash flows from operating, investing, and financing activities for the firm over the five-year period.

3.17 Interpreting the Statement of Cash Flows. Tesla Motors manufac-
tures high-performance electric vehicles that are extremely slick looking. Exhibit 3.20 presents the statement of cash flows for Tesla Motors for 2010–2012.

`LO 3-2, LO 3-3`

REQUIRED

Discuss the relations among net income, cash flows from operations, cash flows from investing activities, and cash flows from financing activities for the firm over the three-year period.

Exhibit 3.19

Texas Instruments
Statement of Cash Flows
(amounts in millions)
(Problem 3.16)

	Year 4	Year 3	Year 2	Year 1	Year 0
OPERATIONS					
Net income (loss)	$ 1,861	$ 1,198	$ (344)	$ (201)	$ 3,087
Depreciation and amortization	1,549	1,528	1,689	1,828	1,376
Deferred income taxes	68	75	13	19	1
Other additions (Subtractions)	(179)	(469)	709	(68)	(2,141)
(Increase) Decrease in accounts receivable					
(Increase) Decrease in accounts inventories	(238)	(197)	(114)	958	(372)
(Increase) Decrease in inventories	(272)	(194)	(39)	482	(372)
(Increase) Decrease in prepayments	134	(183)	191	(235)	56
Increase (Decrease) in accounts payable	(71)	264	(81)	(687)	246
Increase (Decrease) in other current liabilities	294	129	(32)	(277)	309
Cash Flow from Operations	$ 3,146	$ 2,151	$ 1,992	$ 1,819	$ 2,185
INVESTING					
Fixed assets acquired	$ (1,298)	$ (800)	$ (802)	$ (1,790)	$(2,762)
Change in marketable securities	145	86	(238)	164	834
Acquisition of businesses	(8)	(128)	(69)	—	(3)
Other investing transactions	—	—	—	—	107
Cash Flow from Investing	$ (1,161)	$ (842)	$ (1,109)	$ (1,626)	$(1,824)
FINANCING					
Increase in short-term borrowing	$ —	$ —	$ 9	$ —	$ 23
Increase in long-term borrowing	—	—	—	3	250
Issue of common stock	192	157	167	183	242
Decrease in short-term borrowing	(6)	(8)	(16)	(3)	(19)
Decrease in long-term borrowing	(429)	(418)	(22)	(132)	(307)
Acquisition of common stock	(753)	(284)	(370)	(395)	(155)
Dividends	(154)	(147)	(147)	(147)	(141)
Other financing transactions	15	260	14	(16)	(290)
Cash Flow from Financing	$ (1,135)	$ (440)	$ (365)	$ (507)	$ (397)
Change in Cash	$ 850	$ 869	$ 518	$ (314)	$ (36)
Cash—Beginning of year	1,818	949	431	745	781
Cash—End of Year	$ 2,668	$ 1,818	$ 949	$ 431	$ 745
Change in sales from previous year	+27.9%	+17.3%	+2.2%	−30.9%	−1.9%

Source: Texas Instruments Inc., Form 10-K for the Fiscal Years Ended 2004 and 2002.

Exhibit 3.20

Tesla Motors
Statement of Cash Flows
(amounts in thousands)
(Problem 3.17)

	Year Ended December 31,		
	2012	2011	2010
Cash Flows From Operating Activities			
Net loss	$(396,213)	$(254,411)	$(154,328)
Adjustments to reconcile net loss to net cash used in operating activities:			
Depreciation and amortization	28,825	16,919	10,623
Change in fair value of warrant liabilities	1,854	2,750	5,022
Discounts and premiums on short-term marketable securities	56	(112)	—
Stock-based compensation	50,145	29,419	21,156
Excess tax benefits from stock-based compensation	—	—	(74)
Loss on abandonment of fixed assets	1,504	345	8
Inventory write-downs	4,929	1,828	951
Changes in operating assets and liabilities			
Accounts receivable	(17,303)	(2,829)	(3,222)
Inventories and operating lease vehicles	(194,726)	(13,638)	(28,513)
Prepaid expenses and other current assets	1,121	(248)	(4,977)
Other assets	(482)	(288)	(463)
Accounts payable	187,821	19,891	(212)
Accrued liabilities	9,603	10,620	13,345
Deferred development compensation	—	—	(156)
Deferred revenue	(526)	(1,927)	4,801
Reservation payments	47,056	61,006	4,707
Other long-term liabilities	10,255	2,641	3,515
Net cash used in operating activities	(266,081)	(128,034)	(127,817)
Cash Flows From Investing Activities			
Purchases of marketable securities	(14,992)	(64,952)	—
Maturities of short-term marketable securities	40,000	40,000	—
Payments related to acquisition of Fremont manufacturing facility and related assets	—	—	(65,210)
Purchases of property and equipment excluding capital leases	(239,228)	(184,226)	(40,203)
Withdrawals out of (transfers into) our dedicated Department of Energy account, net	8,620	50,121	(73,597)
Increase in other restricted cash	(1,330)	(3,201)	(1,287)
Net cash used in investing activities	(206,930)	(162,258)	(180,297)
Cash Flows From Financing Activities			
Proceeds from issuance of common stock in public offerings, net	221,496	172,410	188,842
Proceeds from issuance of common stock in private placements	—	59,058	80,000

(Continued)

Exhibit 3.20 (Continued)

Principal payments on capital leases and other debt	(2,832)	(416)	(315)
Proceeds from long-term debt and other long-term liabilities	188,796	204,423	71,828
Principal payments on long-term debt	(12,710)	—	—
Proceeds from exercise of stock options and other stock issuances	24,885	10,525	1,350
Excess tax benefits from stock-based compensation	—	—	74
Deferred common stock and loan facility issuance costs	—	—	(3,734)
Net cash provided by financing activities	419,635	446,000	338,045
Net increase (decrease) in cash and cash equivalents	(53,376)	155,708	29,931
Cash and cash equivalents at beginning of period	255,266	99,558	69,627
Cash and cash equivalents at end of period	$ 201,890	$ 255,266	$ 99,558

Source: Tesla Motors, Inc., Form 10-K for the Fiscal Year Ended December 31, 2012.

Describe what stage of life cycle these relations suggest for Tesla Motors. Why are negative operating cash flows less than the net losses? Where is Tesla obtaining cash, and what are they doing with it? What do you think will happen with cash flows in 2013?

LO 3-3

3.18 Interpreting the Statement of Cash Flows. Gap Inc. operates chains of retail clothing stores under the names of **Gap**, **Banana Republic**, and **Old Navy**. Exhibit 3.21 presents the statement of cash flows for Gap for Year 0 to Year 4.

Exhibit 3.21

Gap Inc. Statement of Cash Flows
(amounts in millions)
(Problem 3.18)

	Year 4	Year 3	Year 2	Year 1	Year 0
OPERATIONS					
Net income (loss)	$ 1,150	$ 1,031	$ 478	$ (8)	$ 877
Depreciation	620	675	706	811	590
Other additions and subtractions	(28)	180	166	30	92
(Increase) Decrease in inventories	(90)	385	(258)	213	(455)
(Increase) Decrease in prepayments	(18)	5	33	(13)	(61)
Increase (Decrease) in accounts payable	42	(10)	(47)	42	250
Increase (Decrease) in other current liabilities	(56)	(106)	165	243	(3)
Cash Flow from Operations	$ 1,620	$ 2,160	$ 1,243	$ 1,318	$ 1,290
INVESTING					
Fixed assets acquired	$ (442)	$ (261)	$ (308)	$ (940)	$ (1,859)
Changes in marketable securities	259	(2,063)	(313)	—	—
Other investing transactions	343	6	(8)	(11)	(16)
Cash Flow from Investing	$ 160	$ (2,318)	$ (629)	$ (951)	$ (1,875)

(Continued)

Exhibit 3.21 (Continued)					
FINANCING					
Increase in short-term borrowing	$ —	$ —	$ —	$ —	$ 621
Increase in long-term borrowing	—	85	1,346	1,194	250
Issue of capital stock	130	26	153	139	152
Decrease in short-term borrowing	—	0	(42)	(735)	—
Decrease in long-term borrowing	(871)	(668)	—	(250)	—
Acquisition of capital stock	(976)	—	—	(1)	(393)
Dividends	(79)	(79)	(78)	(76)	(75)
Other financing transactions	—	28	27	(11)	(11)
Cash Flow from Financing	$ (1,796)	$ (608)	$ 1,406	$ 260	$ 544
Change in Cash	$ (16)	$ (766)	$ 2,020	$ 627	$ (41)
Cash—Beginning of year	2,261	3,027	1,007	380	421
Cash—End of Year	$ 2,245	$ 2,261	$ 3,0.27	$ 1,007	$ 380
Change in sales from previous year	+2.6%	+9.7%	+4.4%	+1.3%	+17.5%

Source: Gap Inc., Form 10-K for the Fiscal Years Ended 2005 and 2003.

REQUIRED

Discuss the relations between net income and cash flow from operations and among cash flows from operating, investing, and financing activities for the firm over the five-year period.

3.19 Interpreting the Statement of Cash Flows. Sirius XM Radio Inc. is a LO 3-3 satellite radio company, formed from the merger of Sirius and XM in 2008. Exhibit 3.22 presents a statement of cash flows for Sirius XM Radio for 2006, 2007, and 2008. Sirius XM and its predecessor, Sirius, realized revenue growth of 49% in 2007 and 81% in 2008. The merger was a stock-for-stock merger.

Exhibit 3.22			
Sirius XM Radio Inc. **Statement of Cash Flows** **(amounts in thousands)** **(Problem 3.19)**			
	2008	**2007**	**2006**
CASE FLOWS FROM OPERATING ACTIVITIES			
Net loss	$(5,313,288)	$(565,252)	$(1,104,867)
Adjustments to reconcile net loss to net cash used in operating activities:			
Depreciation and amortization	203,752	106,780	105,749
Impairment loss	4,766,190	—	10,917
Non-cash interest expense, net of amortization of premium	(6,311)	4,269	3,107
Provision for doubtful accounts	21,589	9,002	9,370

(Continued)

Exhibit 3.22 (Continued)

Non-cash loss from redemption of debt	98,203	—	—
Loss on disposal of assets	4,879	(428)	1,661
Loss on investments, net	28,999	—	4,445
Share-based payment expense	87,405	78,900	437,918
Deferred income taxes	2,476	2,435	2,065
Other non-cash purchase price adjustments	(67,843)	—	—
Changes in operating assets and liabilities, net of assets and liabilities acquired:			
Accounts receivable	(32,121)	(28,881)	(1,871)
Inventory	8,291	4,965	(20,246)
Prepaid expenses and other current assets	(19,953)	11,118	(42,132)
Other long-term assets	(13,338)	(729)	(39,878)
Accounts payable and accrued expenses	(65,481)	66,169	26,366
Accrued interest	23,081	(8,920)	1,239
Deferred revenue	55,778	169,905	181,003
Other long-term liabilities	64,895	1,901	3,452
Net Cash Used in Operating Activities	$ (152,797)	$(148,766)	$ (421,702)
CASH FLOWS FROM INVESTING ACTIVITIES			
Additions to property and equipment	$ (130,551)	$ (65,264)	$ (92,674)
Sales of property and equipment	105	641	127
Purchases of restricted and other investments	(3,000)	(310)	(12,339)
Acquisition of acquired entity cash	819,521	—	—
Merger-related costs	(23,519)	(29,444)	—
Purchase of available-for-sale securities	—	—	(123,500)
Sale of restricted and other investments	65,869	40,191	255,715
Net Cash Provided by (Used in) Investing Activities	$ 728,425	$ (54,186)	$ 27,329
CASH FLOWS FROM FINANCING ACTIVITIES			
Proceeds from exercise of warrants and stock options and from share/borrow arrangement	$ 471	$ 4,097	$ 25,787
Long-term borrowings, net of related costs	531,743	244,879	—
Payment of premiums on redemption of debt and payments to minority interest holder	(20,172)	—	—
Repayment of long-term borrowings	(1,146,044)	(625)	—
Net Cash (Used in) Provided by Financing Activities	$ (634,002)	$ 248,351	$ 25,787
Net (Decrease) Increase in Cash and Cash Equivalents	$ (58,374)	$ 45,399	$ (368,586)
Cash and cash equivalents at beginning of period	438,820	393,421	762,007
Cash and Cash Equivalents at End of Period	$ 380,446	$ 438,820	$ 393,421

Source: Sirius XM Radio Inc., Form 10-K for the Fiscal Year Ended December 31, 2008.

REQUIRED

Discuss the relations among net loss and cash flow from operations and the pattern of cash flows from operating, investing, and financing activities during the three years.

3.20 Interpreting the Statement of Cash Flows. Sunbeam Corporation `LO 3-5`
manufactures and sells a variety of small household appliances, including toasters, food processors, and waffle grills. Exhibit 3.23 presents a statement of cash flows for Sunbeam for Year 5,
Year 6, and Year 7. After experiencing decreased sales in Year 5, Sunbeam hired Albert Dunlap
in Year 6 to turn the company around. Albert Dunlap, known in the industry as "Chainsaw Al,"

Exhibit 3.23

Sunbeam Corporation
Statement of Cash Flows
(amounts in millions)
(Problem 3.20)

	Year 7	Year 6	Year 5
OPERATIONS			
Net income (loss)	$ 109.4	$(228.3)	$ 50.5
Depreciation and amortization	38.6	47.4	44.2
Restructuring and asset impairment charges	—	283.7	—
Deferred income taxes	57.8	(77.8)	25.1
Other additions	13.7	46.2	10.8
Other subtractions	(84.6)	(27.1)	(21.7)
(Increase) Decrease in accounts receivable	(84.6)	(13.8)	(4.5)
(Increase) Decrease in inventories	(100.8)	(11.6)	(4.9)
(Increase) Decrease in prepayments	(9.0)	2.7	(8.8)
Increase (Decrease) in accounts payable	(1.6)	14.7	9.2
Increase (Decrease) in other current liabilities	52.8	(21.9)	(18.4)
Cash Flow from Operations	$ (8.3)	$ 14.2	$ 81.5
INVESTING			
Fixed assets acquired	$ (58.3)	$ (75.3)	$(140.1)
Sale of businesses	91.0	—	65.3
Acquisitions of businesses	—	(.9)	(33.0)
Cash Flow from Investing	$ 32.7	$ (76.2)	$(107.4)
FINANCING			
Increase (Decrease) in short-term borrowing	$ 5.0	$ 30.0	$ 40.0
Increase in long-term debt	—	11.5	—
Issue of common stock	26.6	9.2	9.8
Decrease in long-term debt	(12.2)	(1.8)	(5.4)
Acquisition of common stock	—	—	(13.0)
Dividends	(3.4)	(3.3)	(3.3)
Other financing transactions	.5	(.4)	(.2)
Cash Flow from Financing	$ 16.5	$ 45.2	$ 27.9
Change in Cash	$ 40.9	$ (16.8)	$ 2.0
Cash—Beginning of year	11.5	28.3	26.3
Cash—End of Year	$ 52.4	$ 11.5	$ 28.3

Source: Sunbeam Corporation, Form 10-K for the Fiscal Year Ended 1997.

had previously directed restructuring efforts at Scott Paper Company. The restructuring effort at Sunbeam generally involved firing employees and cutting costs aggressively. Most of these restructuring efforts took place during Year 6. The market expected significantly improved results in Year 7. Reported sales increased 18.7% between Year 6 and Year 7, and net income improved. However, subsequent revelations showed that almost half of the sales increase resulted from fraudulent early recognition of revenues in the fourth quarter of Year 7 that the firm should have recognized in the first quarter of Year 8. Growth in revenues for Years 5, 6, and 7 was −2.6%, −3.2%, and 18.7%, respectively.

REQUIRED

a. Using the information provided and the statement of cash flows for Year 5 in Exhibit 3.23, identify any signals that Sunbeam was experiencing operating difficulties and was in need of restructuring.

b. Using information in the statement of cash flows for Year 6, identify indicators of the turnaround efforts and any relations among cash flows that trouble you.

c. Using information in the statement of cash flows for Year 7, indicate any signals that the firm might have engaged in aggressive revenue recognition and had not yet fixed its general operating problems.

LO 3-5

3.21 Interpreting the Statement of Cash Flows. Montgomery Ward operates a retail department store chain. It filed for bankruptcy during the first quarter of Year 12. Exhibit 3.24 presents a statement of cash flows for Montgomery Ward for Year 7 to Year 11.

Exhibit 3.24

Montgomery Ward
Statement of Cash Flows
(amounts in millions)
(Problem 3.21)

	Year 11	Year 10	Year 9	Year 8	Year 7
OPERATIONS					
Net income	$ (237)	$ (9)	$ 109	$ 101	$ 100
Depreciation	122	115	109	98	97
Other addbacks	13	8	24	25	32
Other subtractions	(197)	(119)	(29)	—	—
(Increase) Decrease in accounts receivable	(32)	(54)	(38)	(9)	9
(Increase) Decrease in inventories	225	(112)	(229)	(204)	(38)
(Increase) Decrease in prepayments	27	(32)	(39)	(58)	36
Increase (Decrease) in accounts payable	(222)	85	291	148	(17)
Increase (Decrease) in other current liabilities	(55)	(64)	(45)	28	(64)
Cash Flow from Operations	$ (356)	$ (182)	$ 153	$ 129	$ 155
INVESTING					
Fixed assets acquired	$ (75)	$ (122)	$ (184)	$ (142)	$ (146)
Change in marketable securities	20	(14)	(4)	(27)	137
Other investing transactions	(93)	27	(113)	6	9
Cash Flow from Investing	$ (148)	$ (109)	$ (301)	$ (163)	$ —

(Continued)

Exhibit 3.24 (Continued)					
FINANCING					
Increase in short-term borrowing	$ 588	$ 16	$ 144	$ —	$ —
Increase in long-term borrowing	—	205	168	100	—
Issue of capital stock	3	193	78	1	1
Decrease in short-term borrowing	—	—	—	—	—
Decrease in long-term borrowing	(63)	(17)	(275)	(18)	(403)
Acquisition of capital stock	(20)	(98)	(9)	(11)	(97)
Dividends	(9)	(4)	(24)	(23)	(19)
Other	—	—	1	2	2
Cash Flow from Financing	$ 499	$ 295	$ 83	$ 51	$ (516)
Change in Cash	$ (5)	$ 4	$ (65)	$ 17	$ (361)
Cash—Beginning of year	37	33	98	81	442
Cash—End of Year	$ 32	$ 37	$ 33	$ 98	$ 81
Change in sales from previous year	−10.0%	−.5%	+17.2%	+3.7%	+2.0%

Source: Montgomery Ward, Form 10-K for the Fiscal Years Ended 1996 and 1994.

The firm acquired **Lechmere**, a discount retailer of sporting goods and electronic products, during Year 9. It acquired **Amoco Enterprises**, an automobile club, during Year 11. During Year 10, it issued a new series of preferred stock and used part of the cash proceeds to repurchase a series of outstanding preferred stock. The "other subtractions" in the operating section for Year 10 and Year 11 represent reversals of deferred tax liabilities.

REQUIRED

Discuss the relations between net income and cash flow from operations and among cash flows from operating, investing, and financing activities for the firm over the five-year period. Identify signals of Montgomery Ward's difficulties that might have led to its filing for bankruptcy.

3.22 Extracting Performance Trends from the Statement of Cash Flows. `LO 3-3, LO 3-5`

The **Apollo Group** is one of the largest providers of private education, and runs numerous programs and services, including the **University of Phoenix**. Exhibit 3.25 provides the statement of cash flows for 2012.

REQUIRED

Discuss the relations between net income and cash flow from operations and among cash flows from operating, investing, and financing activities for the firm, especially for 2012. Identify signals that might raise concerns for an analyst.

3.23 Interpreting a Direct Method Statement of Cash Flows. Aer `LO 3-1`

Lingus is an international airline based in Ireland. Exhibit 3.26 provides the statement of cash flows for Year 1 and Year 2, which includes a footnote from the financial statements. Year 2 was characterized by weakening consumer demand for air travel due to a recession and record high fuel prices. In addition, Year 2 includes exceptional items totaling €141 million, which reflect a staff restructuring program for early retirement (€118 million), takeover defense costs due to a bid by **Ryanair** (€18 million), and other costs (€5 million).

Exhibit 3.25

The Apollo Group
Statement of Cash Flows
(amounts in thousands)
(Problem 3.22)

	Year Ended August 31,		
	2012	2011	2010
Cash flows provided by (used in) operating activities:			
Net income	$ 417,006	$ 535,796	$ 521,581
Adjustments to reconcile net income to net cash provided by operating activities:			
Share-based compensation	78,705	70,040	64,305
Excess tax benefits from share-based compensation	(1,150)	(4,014)	(6,648)
Depreciation and amortization	178,234	159,006	147,035
Amortization of lease incentives	(15,510)	(18,822)	(13,358)
Amortization of deferred gains on sale-leasebacks	(2,798)	(2,221)	(1,705)
Impairment on discontinued operations	—	—	9,400
Goodwill and other intangibles impairment	16,788	219,927	184,570
Non-cash foreign currency (gain) loss, net	(497)	1,662	643
Gain on sale of discontinued operations	(26,678)	—	—
Provision for uncollectible accounts receivable	146,742	181,297	282,628
Litigation charge (credit), net	4,725	(11,951)	177,982
Deferred income taxes	21,850	55,823	(125,399)
Changes in assets and liabilities, excluding the impact of acquisitions and business dispositions:			
Restricted cash and cash equivalents	61,073	64,725	(11,828)
Accounts receivable	(129,773)	(121,120)	(265,996)
Prepaid taxes	9,303	(25,241)	10,421
Other assets	(11,568)	(9,900)	2,183
Accounts payable	12,525	(3,913)	21,624
Student deposits	(58,740)	(70,120)	3,445
Deferred revenue	(39,154)	(79,488)	32,887
Accrued and other liabilities	(109,783)	(44,364)	(528)
Net cash provided by operating activities	551,300	897,122	1,033,242
Cash flows provided by (used in) investing activities:			
Additions to property and equipment	(115,187)	(162,573)	(168,177)
Acquisitions, net of cash acquired	(73,736)	—	(5,497)
Maturities of marketable securities	—	10,000	5,000
Proceeds from sale-leaseback, net	—	169,018	—
Proceeds from dispositions, net	76,434	21,251	—
Collateralization of letter of credit	—	126,615	(126,615)
Other investing activities	(1,694)	—	—
Net cash (used in) provided by investing activities	(114,183)	164,311	(295,289)

(Continued)

Exhibit 3.25 (Continued)

Cash flows provided by (used in) financing activities:			
Payments on borrowings	(562,269)	(437,925)	(477,568)
Proceeds from borrowings	629,145	410,051	475,454
Apollo Group Class A common stock purchased for treasury	(811,913)	(783,168)	(446,398)
Issuance of Apollo Group Class A common stock	11,949	24,903	19,671
Noncontrolling interest contributions	—	6,875	2,460
Excess tax benefits from share-based compensation	1,150	4,014	6,648
Net cash used in financing activities	(731,938)	(775,250)	(419,733)
Exchange rate effect on cash and cash equivalents	(468)	712	(1,697)
Net (decrease) increase in cash and cash equivalents	(295,289)	286,895	316,523
Cash and cash equivalents, beginning of year	1,571,664	1,284,769	968,246
Cash and cash equivalents, end of year	$1,276,375	$1,571,664	$1,284,769

Source: The Apollo Group, Form 10-K for the Fiscal Year Ended 2012.

Exhibit 3.26

**Aer Lingus
Statement of Cash Flows
(amounts in millions)
(Problem 3.23)**

	Year 2	Year 1
CASH FLOWS FROM OPERATING ACTIVITIES		
Cash (used in) generated from operations (see Note 27)	€ (8,627)	€ 59,122
Interest paid	(17,684)	(22,437)
Income tax received (paid)	5,046	(4,002)
Net Cash (Used in) Generated from Operating Activities	€ (21,265)	€ 32,683
CASH FLOWS FROM INVESTING ACTIVITIES		
Purchases of property, plant, and equipment	€(114,490)	€(200,604)
Purchases of intangible assets	(5,619)	(4,294)
Proceeds from sale of investment	—	11,374
Disposal of available-for-sale financial assets	—	9,031
(Increase) Decrease in deposits and restricted cash with maturity greater than 3 months	(44,099)	138,066
Dividends received	—	2,998
Interest received	46,766	60,008
Net Cash (Used in) Generated from Investing Activities	€(117,442)	€ 16,579
CASH FLOWS FROM FINANCING ACTIVITIES		
Costs arising from issuance of ordinary shares	€ —	€ (3,720)
Proceeds from borrowings	186,135	2,090
Repayments of borrowings	(38,695)	(61,104)
Net Cash Generated from (Used in) Financing Activities	€ 147,440	€ (62,734)

(Continued)

Exhibit 3.26 (Continued)

Net Increase (Decrease) in Cash, Cash Equivalents and Bank Overdrafts	€ 8,733	€ (13,472)
Cash, cash equivalents, and bank overdrafts at beginning of year	€ (12,185)	€ (1,226)
Exchange gains on cash, cash equivalents, and bank overdrafts	9,533	2,513
Cash, Cash Equivalents, and Bank Overdrafts at End of Year	€ 6,081	€ (12,185)
NOTE 27 CASH GENERATED FROM OPERATIONS		
(Loss) Profit before tax	€(119,696)	€ 124,726
Adjustments for:		
Depreciation	69,558	63,664
Amortisation	2,307	5,635
Net movements in provisions for liabilities and charges	(13,084)	(14,690)
Net fair value losses on derivative financial instruments	945	40
Finance income	(60,860)	(65,143)
Finance cost	22,018	22,572
Net exceptional items	140,888	(3,517)
Other (gains) losses	(8,796)	8,880
Changes in working capital		
Inventories	360	(140)
Trade and other receivables	(16,329)	181
Trade and other payables	(25,938)	20,914
Payment to supplemental pension arrangements	—	(104,000)
Cash Generated from Operations	€ (8,627)	€ 59,122

Source: Aer Lingus Group Plc, Annual Report for the Fiscal Year Ended December 31, 2008.

REQUIRED

a. Based on information in the statement of cash flows, compare and contrast the cash flows for Years 1 and 2. Explain significant differences in individual reconciling items and direct cash flows.

b. The format of Aer Lingus' statement of cash flows is the direct method, as evidenced by the straightforward titles used in the operating section. How is this statement different from the presentation that Aer Lingus would report using the indirect method?

 3.24 Identifying Industry Differences in Statement of Cash Flows.
Exhibit 3.27 presents common-size statements of cash flows for eight firms in various industries. All amounts in the common-size statements of cash flows are expressed as a percentage of cash flow from operations. In constructing the common-size percentages for each firm, reported amounts for each firm for three consecutive years were summed and the common-size percentages are based on the summed amounts. This procedure reduces the effects of a nonrecurring item in a particular year, such as a major debt or a common stock issue. Exhibit 3.27 also shows the compound annual rate of growth in revenues over the three-year period.
The eight companies are as follows:

■ **Biogen** creates and manufactures biotechnology drugs. Many drugs are still in the development phase in this high-growth, relatively young industry. Research and manufacturing facilities are capital-intensive, although the research process requires skilled scientists.

Exhibit 3.27

Common-Size
Statements of Cash Flows for Selected Companies
(Problem 3.24)

	1	2	3	4	5	6	7	8
OPERATIONS								
Net income	34.9%	38.6%	40.9%	45.4%	61.2%	62.4%	76.5%	97.6%
Depreciation	47.9	55.2	62.9	37.7	46.0	22.3	38.0	23.3
Other	3.1	24.3	5.1	(5.0)	9.4	11.6	2.3	3.9
(Increase) Decrease in accounts receivable	6.5	(4.8)	(.6)	(12.4)	(34.2)	(7.8)	(6.8)	(8.5)
(Increase) Decrease in Inventories	1.5	(15.1)	(1.2)	(14.4)	(11.9)	(3.1)	(7.4)	(58.4)
Increase (Decrease) in accounts payable	1.5	3.1	(5.6)	12.4	3.0	2.9	12.6	39.9
Increase (Decrease) in other current liabilities	4.6	(1.3)	(1.5)	36.3	26.5	11.7	(15.2)	2.2
Cash Flow from Operations	100.0%	100.0%	100.0%	100.0%	100.0%	100.0%	100.0%	100.0%
INVESTING								
Fixed assets acquired	(37.1%)	(64.0%)	(81.1%)	(165.7%)	(44.7%)	(13.4%)	(39.3%)	(153.4%)
Change in marketable securities	—	—	(2.8)	(75.1)	(14.8)	(3.5)	5.9	(17.5)
Other investing transactions	(7.7)	8.5	16.4	(28.4)	(15.9)	(17.3)	(40.6)	23.2
Cash Flow from Investing	(44.8%)	(55.5%)	(67.5%)	(269.2%)	(75.4%)	(34.2%)	(74.0%)	(147.7%)
FINANCING								
Change in short-term debt	(0.6%)	—	(7.4%)	—	(2.4%)	—	7.9%	—
Increase in long-term debt	19.5	41.4%	8.4	75.7%	—	33.1%	24.0	46.9%
Issue of capital stock	11.2	9.9	—	82.5	17.7	1.7	6.7	13.5
Decrease in long-term debt	(36.0)	(85.0)	(9.1)	(2.7)	(7.0)	(27.6)	(3.1)	(1.2)
Repurchase of capital stock	(18.9)	(1.5)	(0.1)	—	(50.7)	(21.4)	(26.9)	—
Dividends	(29.5)	(10.9)	(29.9)	—	—	(46.1)	(43.5)	(11.5)
Other financing transactions	—	—	(0.2)	—	—	0.6	9.8	1.9
Cash Flow from Financing	(54.3%)	(46.1%)	(38.3%)	155.5%	(42.4%)	(59.7%)	(25.1%)	49.6%
Net Change in Cash	0.9%	(1.6%)	(5.8%)	13.7%	(17.8%)	6.1%	0.9%	1.9%
Growth in Revenues	(3.6%)	5.7%	5.7%	23.0%	18.2%	7.7%	8.6%	28.3%

- **Chevron Texaco** explores, extracts, refines, and markets petroleum products. Extraction and refining activities are capital-intensive. Petroleum products are in the mature phase of their product life cycle.
- **H. J. Heinz** manufactures and markets branded consumer food products. Heinz has acquired several other branded food products companies in recent years.
- **Home Depot** sells home improvement products. Home Depot competes in a new retail category known as "category killer" stores. Such stores offer a wide selection of products in a particular product category (for example, books, pet products, or office products). In recent years, these stores have taken away significant market share from more diversified department and discount stores.
- **Inland Steel** manufactures steel products. Although steel plants are capital-intensive, they also use unionized workers to process iron into steel products. Demand for steel products follows cyclical trends in the economy. Steel manufacturing in the United States is in the mature phase of its life cycle.
- **Pacific Gas & Electric** provides electric and gas utility services. The electric utility industry in the United States has excess capacity. Increased competition from less regulated, more open markets has forced down prices and led some utilities to reduce their capacity.
- **ServiceMaster** provides home cleaning and restoration services. ServiceMaster has recently acquired firms offering cleaning services for health care facilities and has broadened its home services to include termite protection, garden care, and other services. ServiceMaster operates as a partnership. Partnerships do not pay income taxes on their earnings each year. Instead, partners (owners) include their share of the earnings of ServiceMaster in their taxable income.
- **Sun Microsystems** creates, manufactures, and markets computers, primarily to the scientific and engineering markets and to network applications. Sun follows an assembly strategy in manufacturing computers, outsourcing the components from other firms worldwide. (Note: The figures in Exhibit 3.27 are prior to Sun's acquisition by Oracle Corporation.)

REQUIRED

Use the clues in the common-size statements of cash flows to match the companies in Exhibit 3.27 with the companies listed here. Discuss the reasoning for your selection in each case.

 3.25 Preparing a Statement of Cash Flows from Balance Sheets and Income Statements. Nojiri Pharmaceutical Industries develops, manufactures, and markets pharmaceutical products in Japan. The Japanese economy experienced recessionary conditions in recent years. In response to these conditions, the Japanese government increased the proportion of medical costs that is the patient's responsibility and lowered the prices for prescription drugs. Exhibits 3.28 and 3.29 present the firm's balance sheets and income statements for Years 1 through 4.

REQUIRED

a. Prepare a worksheet for the preparation of a statement of cash flows for Nojiri Pharmaceutical Industries for each of the years ending March 31, Year 2 to Year 4. Follow the format of Exhibit 3.14 in the text. Notes to the financial statements indicate the following:
   (1) The changes in Accumulated Other Comprehensive Income relate to revaluations of Investments in Securities to market value. The remaining changes in Investments in Securities result from purchases and sales. Assume that the sales occurred at no gain or loss.
   (2) No sales of property, plant, and equipment took place during the three-year period.
   (3) The changes in Other Noncurrent Assets are investing activities.
   (4) The changes in Employee Retirement Benefits relate to provisions made for retirement benefits net of payments made to retired employees, both of which the statement of cash flows classifies as operating activities.
   (5) The changes in Other Noncurrent Liabilities are financing activities.

Exhibit 3.28

Nojiri Pharmaceutical Industries
Balance Sheets
(amounts in millions)
(Problem 3.25)

March 31:	Year 4	Year 3	Year 2	Year 1
ASSETS				
Cash	¥ 6,233	¥ 4,569	¥ 4,513	¥ 5,008
Accounts and notes receivable—Trade	19,003	17,828	19,703	19,457
Inventories	7,693	7,948	8,706	8,607
Deferred income taxes	1,355	1,192	948	824
Prepayments	432	325	640	634
Total Current Assets	¥ 34,716	¥ 31,862	¥ 34,510	¥ 34,530
Investments	3,309	2,356	3,204	4,997
Property, plant, and equipment, at cost	71,792	71,510	71,326	71,018
Less accumulated depreciation	(40,689)	(38,912)	(36,854)	(35,797)
Deferred income taxes	236	1,608	1,481	494
Other assets	4,551	3,904	3,312	3,463
Total Assets	¥ 73,915	¥ 72,328	¥ 76,979	¥ 78,705
LIABILITIES AND SHAREHOLDERS' EQUITY				
Accounts and notes payable—Trade	¥ 10,087	¥ 9,629	¥ 10,851	¥ 10,804
Notes payable to banks	10,360	10,328	9,779	10,023
Current portion of long-term debt	100	200	—	—
Other current liabilities	7,200	6,170	9,779	7,565
Total Current Liabilities	¥ 27,747	¥ 26,327	¥ 30,409	¥ 28,392
Long-term debt	8,140	7,889	6,487	8,147
Deferred income taxes	3,361	—	—	—
Employee retirement benefits	809	905	1,087	1,166
Other noncurrent liabilities	175	174	200	216
Total Liabilities	¥ 40,232	¥ 35,295	¥ 38,183	¥ 37,921
Common stock	¥ 10,758	¥ 10,758	¥ 10,758	¥ 10,758
Additional paid-in capital	15,012	15,012	15,012	15,012
Retained earnings	9,179	11,838	13,697	15,014
Accumulated other comprehensive income	(342)	(490)	(659)	—
Treasury stock	(924)	(85)	(12)	—
Total Shareholders' Equity	¥ 33,683	¥ 37,033	¥ 38,796	¥ 40,784
Total Liabilities and Shareholders' Equity	¥ 73,915	¥ 72,328	¥ 76,979	¥ 78,705

b. Prepare a comparative statement of cash flows for Year 2, Year 3, and Year 4.

c. Discuss the relations among net income and cash flow from operations and the pattern of cash flows from operating, investing, and financing transactions for Year 2, Year 3, and Year 4.

Exhibit 3.29

Nojiri Pharmaceutical Industries
Income Statements
(amounts in millions)
(Problem 3.25)

Year Ended March 31:	Year 4	Year 3	Year 2
Sales	¥ 41,352	¥ 41,926	¥ 44,226
Cost of goods sold	(27,667)	(27,850)	(28,966)
Selling and administrative expenses	(13,396)	(15,243)	(15,283)
Interest expense	(338)	(364)	(368)
Income tax expense	(1,823)	443	34
Net Income	¥ (1,872)	¥ (1,088)	¥ (357)

LO 3-4 **3.26 Preparing a Statement of Cash Flows from Balance Sheets and Income Statements.** Flight Training Corporation is a privately held firm that provides fighter pilot training under contracts with the U.S. Air Force and the U.S. Navy. The firm owns approximately 100 Lear jets that it equips with radar jammers and other sophisticated electronic devices to mimic enemy aircraft. The company recently experienced cash shortages to pay its bills. The owner and manager of Flight Training Corporation stated, "I was just dumbfounded. I never had an inkling that there was a problem with cash." Exhibits 3.30 and 3.31 present comparative balance sheets and income statements for Years 2 through 4.

Exhibit 3.30

Flight Training Corporation
Balance Sheets
(amounts in thousands)
(Problem 3.26)

December 31:	Year 4	Year 3	Year 2	Year 1
CURRENT ASSETS				
Cash	$ 159	$ 583	$ 313	$ 142
Accounts receivable	6,545	4,874	2,675	2,490
Inventories	5,106	2,514	1,552	602
Prepayments	665	829	469	57
Total Current Assets	$ 12,475	$ 8,800	$ 5,009	$ 3,291
NONCURRENT ASSETS				
Property, plant, and equipment	$106,529	$76,975	$24,039	$17,809
Less accumulated depreciation	(17,231)	(8,843)	(5,713)	(4,288)

(Continued)

Exhibit 3.30 (Continued)

Net property, plant, and equipment	$ 89,298	$68,132	$18,326	$13,521
Other assets	$ 470	$ 665	$ 641	$ 1,112
Total Assets	$102,243	$77,597	$23,976	$17,924
CURRENT LIABILITIES				
Accounts payable	$ 12,428	$ 6,279	$ 993	$ 939
Notes payable	—	945	140	1,021
Current portion of long-term debt	60,590	7,018	1,789	1,104
Other current liabilities	12,903	12,124	2,423	1,310
Total Current Liabilities	$ 85,921	$26,366	$ 5,345	$ 4,374
NONCURRENT LIABILITIES				
Long-term debt	$ —	$41,021	$ 9,804	$ 6,738
Deferred income taxes	—	900	803	—
Other noncurrent liabilities	—	—	226	—
Total Liabilities	$ 85,921	$68,287	$16,178	$11,112
SHAREHOLDERS' EQUITY				
Common stock	$ 34	$ 22	$ 21	$ 20
Additional paid-in capital	16,516	5,685	4,569	4,323
Retained earnings	(29)	3,802	3,208	2,469
Treasury stock	(199)	(199)	—	—
Total Shareholders' Equity	$ 16,322	$ 9,310	$ 7,798	$ 6,812
Total Liabilities and Shareholders' Equity	$102,243	$77,597	$23,976	$17,924

Exhibit 3.31

Flight Training Corporation
Income Statements
(amounts in thousands)
(Problem 3.26)

Year Ended December 31:	Year 4	Year 3	Year 2
Sales	$54,988	$36,597	$20,758
Cost of services	$47,997	$29,594	$14,247
Selling and administrative	5,881	2,972	3,868
Interest	5,841	3,058	1,101
Income taxes	(900)	379	803
Total Expenses	$58,819	$36,003	$20,019
Net Income	$ (3,831)	$ 594	$ 739

REQUIRED

a. Prepare a worksheet for the preparation of a statement of cash flows for Flight Training Corporation for each of the years ending December 31, Year 2 through Year 4. Follow the format of Exhibit 3.14 in the text. Notes to the financial statements indicate the following:

(1) The firm did not sell any aircraft during the three-year period.

(2) Changes in other noncurrent assets are investing transactions.

(3) Changes in deferred income taxes are operating transactions.

(4) Changes in other noncurrent liabilities and treasury stock are financing transactions.

(5) The firm violated covenants in its borrowing agreements during Year 4. Therefore, the lenders can require Flight Training Corporation to repay its long-term debt immediately. Although the banks have not yet demanded payment, the firm reclassified its long-term debt as a current liability.

b. Prepare a comparative statement of cash flows for Flight Training Corporation for each of the years ending December 31, Year 2 through Year 4.

c. Comment on the relations among net income and cash flow from operations and the pattern of cash flows from operating, investing, and financing activities for each of the three years.

d. Describe the likely reasons for the cash flow difficulties of Flight Training Corporation.

LO 3-4

3.27 Preparing a Statement of Cash Flows from Balance Sheets and Income Statements. BTB Electronics Inc. manufactures parts, components, and processing equipment for electronics and semiconductor applications in the communications, computer, automotive, and appliance industries. Its sales tend to vary with changes in the business cycle because the sales of most of its customers are cyclical. Exhibit 3.32 presents balance sheets for BTB as of December 31, Year 7 through Year 9, and Exhibit 3.33 presents income statements for Year 8 and Year 9.

Exhibit 3.32

BTB Electronics Inc.
Balance Sheets
(amounts in thousands)
(Problem 3.27)

December 31:	Year 9	Year 8	Year 7
ASSETS			
Cash	$ 367	$ 475	$ 430
Accounts receivable	2,545	3,936	3,768
Inventories	2,094	2,966	2,334
Prepayments	122	270	116
Total Current Assets	$ 5,128	$ 7,647	$ 6,648
Property, plant, and equipment, net	4,027	4,598	3,806
Other assets	456	559	193
Total Assets	$ 9,611	$12,804	$10,647

(Continued)

Exhibit 3.32 (Continued)

LIABILITIES AND SHAREHOLDERS' EQUITY

Accounts payable	$ 796	$ 809	$ 1,578
Notes payable to banks	2,413	231	11
Other current liabilities	695	777	1,076
Total Current Liabilities	$ 3,904	$ 1,817	$ 2,665
Long-term debt	2,084	4,692	2,353
Deferred income taxes	113	89	126
Total Liabilities	$ 6,101	$ 6,598	$ 5,144
Preferred stock	$ 289	$ 289	$ —
Common stock	85	85	83
Additional paid-in capital	4,395	4,392	4,385
Retained earnings	(1,259)	1,440	1,035
Total Shareholders' Equity	$ 3,510	$ 6,206	$ 5,503
Total Liabilities and Shareholders' Equity	$ 9,611	$12,804	$10,647

Exhibit 3.33

BTB Electronics Inc.
Income Statements
(amounts in thousands)
(Problem 3.27)

Year Ended December 31:	Year 9	Year 8
Sales	$ 11,960	$ 22,833
Cost of goods sold	(11,031)	(16,518)
Selling and administrative expenses	(3,496)	(4,849)
Interest expense	(452)	(459)
Income tax expense	328	(590)
Net Income	$ (2,691)	$ 417
Dividends on preferred stock	(8)	(12)
Net Income Available to Common	$ (2,699)	$ 405

REQUIRED

a. Prepare a worksheet for the preparation of a statement of cash flows for BTB Electronics Inc. for Years 8 and 9. Follow the format of Exhibit 3.14 in the text. Notes to the firm's financial statements reveal the following (amounts in thousands):

(1) Depreciation expense was $641 in Year 8 and $625 in Year 9. No fixed assets were sold during these years.

(2) Other Assets represents patents. Patent amortization was $25 in Year 8 and $40 in Year 9. BTB sold a patent during Year 9 at no gain or loss.

(3) Changes in Deferred Income Taxes are operating activities.

b. Discuss the relations among net income and cash flow from operations and the pattern of cash flows from operating, investing, and financing activities.

INTEGRATIVE CASE 3.1

Starbucks

LO 3-3   Exhibit 3.34 presents a statement of cash flows for **Starbucks** for 2010, 2011, and 2012. This statement is an expanded version of the statement of cash flows for Starbucks shown in Exhibit 1.28.

Exhibit 3.34

Starbucks Corporation
Comparative Statements of Cash Flows
(amounts in millions)
(Case 3.1)

Fiscal Year Ended	Sep 30, 2012	Oct 2, 2011	Oct 3, 2010
OPERATING ACTIVITIES:			
Net earnings including noncontrolling interests	$ 1,384.7	$ 1,248.0	$ 948.3
Adjustments to reconcile net earnings to net cash provided by operating activities:			
Depreciation and amortization	580.6	550.0	540.8
Gain on sale of properties	—	(30.2)	—
Deferred income taxes, net	61.1	106.2	(42.0)
Income earned from equity method investees, net of distributions	(49.3)	(32.9)	(17.2)
Gain resulting from acquisition of joint ventures	—	(55.2)	(23.1)
Stock-based compensation	153.6	145.2	113.6
Other	23.6	33.3	75.5
Cash provided/(used) by changes in operating assets and liabilities:			
Accounts receivable	(90.3)	(88.7)	(33.4)
Inventories	(273.3)	(422.3)	123.2
Accounts payable	(105.2)	227.5	(3.6)
Accrued liabilities and insurance reserves	23.7	(81.8)	(18.7)
Deferred revenue	60.8	35.8	24.2
Prepaid expenses, other current assets and other assets	(19.7)	(22.5)	17.3
Net cash provided by operating activities	1,750.3	1,612.4	1,704.9
INVESTING ACTIVITIES:			
Purchase of investments	(1,748.6)	(966.0)	(549.0)
Maturities and calls of investments	1,796.4	430.0	209.9
Acquisitions, net of cash acquired	(129.1)	(55.8)	(12.0)
Additions to property, plant and equipment	(856.2)	(531.9)	(445.8)
Cash proceeds from sale of property, plant, and equipment	5.3	117.4	5.1
Other	(41.8)	(13.2)	2.3
Net cash used by investing activities	(974.0)	(1,019.5)	(789.5)

(Continued)

Exhibit 3.34 (Continued)

FINANCING ACTIVITIES:

(Payments)/proceeds from short-term borrowings	(30.8)	30.8	—
Purchase of noncontrolling interest	—	(27.5)	(45.8)
Proceeds from issuance of common stock	236.6	250.4	132.8
Excess tax benefit from exercise of stock options	169.8	103.9	36.9
Cash dividends paid	(513.0)	(389.5)	(171.0)
Repurchase of common stock	(549.1)	(555.9)	(285.6)
Minimum tax withholdings on share-based awards	(58.5)	(15.0)	(4.9)
Other	(0.5)	(5.2)	(8.4)
Net cash used by financing activities	(745.5)	(608.0)	(346.0)
Effect of exchange rate changes on cash and cash equivalents	9.7	(0.8)	(5.2)
Net increase (decrease) in cash and cash equivalents	40.5	(15.9)	564.2

CASH AND CASH EQUIVALENTS:

Beginning of period	1,148.1	1,164.0	599.8
End of period	$ 1,188.6	$ 1,148.1	$1,164.0

Source: Starbucks Corporation, Form 10-K for the Fiscal Year ended September 30, 2012.

REQUIRED

a. Explain why equity in income of investees appears as a subtraction when net income is converted to cash flow from operations.

b. Compute the amount of cash received from investees as dividends each year. To answer this question, you need to refer to the income statement of Starbucks in Exhibit 1.27 in Chapter 1 (Integrative Case 1.1).

c. Explain why stock-based compensation appears as an addition to net income to compute cash flow from operations.

d. Discuss the relation between net income and cash flow from operations for each of the three years.

e. Discuss the relations among cash flows from operating, investing, and financing activities for each of the three years.

f. Refer to the income statement for Starbucks in Exhibit 1.27). Compute the amount of EBITDA for 2010, 2011, and 2012.

g. Discuss the relations among net income, non-working capital adjustments, working capital adjustments, operating cash flows, and EBITDA for the three years. Are the patterns similar or different? What are the primary determinants of the differences between the summary measures net income, operating cash flows, and EBITDA?

h. The income statement in Exhibit 1.27 shows depreciation and amortization expense as follows:

2012	2011	2010
$550.3	$523.3	$510.4

However, the statement of cash flows shows addbacks for depreciation and amortization as follows:

2012	2011	2010
$580.6	$550.0	$540.8

Explain why the amount on the income statement differs from the amount on the statement of cash flows each year.

CASE 3.2

Prime Contractors

LO 3-2, LO 3-3, LO 3-5

Prime Contractors (Prime) is a privately owned company that contracts with the U.S. government to provide various services under multiyear (usually five-year) contracts. Its principal services are as follows:

Refuse: Picks up and disposes of refuse from military bases.

Shuttle: Provides parking and shuttle services on government-sponsored research campuses.

Animal Care: Provides feeding and veterinary care for animals used in research at government-sponsored facilities.

Prime's sales mix for the years ending September 30, Year 6 to Year 10, is as follows:

	Refuse Services	Shuttle Services	Animal Care Services
Year 6	59.9%	40.1%	—
Year 7	48.5%	31.2%	20.3%
Year 8	20.7%	22.0%	57.3%
Year 9	11.4%	26.9%	61.7%
Year 10	7.1%	22.5%	70.4%

As the sales mix data indicate, Prime engaged in a strategic shift beginning in Year 7. It began to exit the refuse services business and geared up its animal care services business. Exhibit 3.35 presents a statement of cash flows for Prime for Years 6 through 10.

REQUIRED

a. What evidence do you see in Exhibit 3.35 of Prime's strategic shift from refuse services to animal care services?

b. Discuss how Prime's net income could decline between Year 6 and Year 8 while its cash flow from operations increased.

c. Discuss how Prime's net income could increase between Year 8 and Year 10 while its cash flow from operations decreased.

d. What is the likely reason that the adjustment for deferred income taxes when converting net income to cash flow from operations was an addition in Year 6 to Year 8 but a subtraction in Year 9 and Year 10?

e. Explain why gains on the disposition of fixed assets appear as a subtraction from net income when cash flow from operations is computed.

f. Prime increased its long-term debt net in Year 6 and Year 7 but decreased it net in Year 8 to Year 10. What is the likely reason for this shift in financing?

Exhibit 3.35

Prime Contractors
Statement of Cash Flows
(amounts in thousands)
(Case 3.2)

	Year 10	Year 9	Year 8	Year 7	Year 6
OPERATIONS					
Net income	$ 568	$ 474	$ 47	$ 249	$ 261
Depreciation	595	665	827	616	306
Deferred income taxes	(139)	(110)	55	180	159
Loss (Gain) on disposition of fixed assets	(82)	(178)	—	—	20
Other additions and subtractions	(4)	(19)	(52)	(7)	2
(Increase) Decrease in accounts receivable	62	(865)	(263)	(647)	(1,421)
(Increase) Decrease in other current assets	19	(9)	(40)	(26)	(38)
Increase (Decrease) in accounts payable	(174)	(272)	(33)	(177)	507
Increase (Decrease) in other current liabilities	(310)	926	423	100	268
Cash Flow from Operations	$ 535	$ 612	$ 964	$ 288	$ 64
INVESTING					
Fixed assets sold	$ 146	$ 118	$ —	$ —	$ 80
Fixed assets acquired	(15)	(19)	(56)	(911)	(2,003)
Other investing transactions	37	—	—	62	(17)
Cash Flow from Investing	$ 168	$ 99	$ (56)	$ (849)	$ (1,940)
FINANCING					
Increase (Decrease) in short-term borrowing	$ 324	$ 12	$ (127)	$ 276	$ 204
Increase in long-term borrowing	—	—	208	911	1,987
Decrease in long-term borrowing	(960)	(742)	(1,011)	(658)	(423)
Cash Flow from Financing	$ (634)	$ (730)	$ (930)	$ 529	$ 1,768
Change in Cash	$ 69	$ (19)	$ (22)	$ (32)	$ (108)
Cash—Beginning of year	6	25	47	79	187
Cash—End of Year	$ 75	$ 6	$ 25	$ 47	$ 79
Change in sales from previous year	+15.5%	+18.0%	+38.5%	+47.1%	+53.5%

CASE 3.3

W. T. Grant Company[12]

LO 3-5

When it filed for bankruptcy in October 1975, **W. T. Grant** (Grant) was the seventeenth largest retailer in the United States, with almost 1,200 stores, more than 82,000 employees, and sales of $1.7 billion. It had paid dividends consistently since 1906. The collapse of Grant came largely as a surprise to the capital markets, particularly to the banks that provided short-term working capital loans. Grant had altered its business strategy in the mid-1960s to transform itself from an urban discount store chain to a suburban house goods store chain. Its failure serves as a classic study of poor implementation of what seemed like a sound business strategy. What happened to Grant and why did it happen are questions that, with some analysis, can be answered. On the other hand, why the symptoms of Grant's prolonged illness were not diagnosed and treated earlier is difficult to understand.

The Strategic Shift

Prior to the mid-1960s, Grant built its reputation on sales of low-priced soft goods (clothing, linens, and sewing fabrics). It placed its stores in large urban locations and appealed primarily to lower-income consumers.

However, the mid-1960s marked the beginning of urban unrest and movement to the suburbs. To service the needs of these new homeowners, suburban shopping centers experienced rapid growth. **Sears** led the way in this movement, establishing itself as the anchor store in many of the more upscale locations. **Montgomery Ward** and **JCPenney** followed suit. At this time, Sears held a dominant market share in the middle-income consumer market. However, it saw an opportunity to change its product line, becoming more upscale, to compete with the established department stores (for example, **Macy's** and **Marshall Field's**), which had not yet begun their move to the suburbs. To implement this new strategy, Sears introduced its Sears Best line of products.

The outward population move to the suburbs and increased competition from growing discount chains such as **Kmart** caused Grant to alter its strategy as well. One aspect of this strategic shift was rapid expansion of new stores into suburban shopping centers. Between 1963 and 1973, Grant opened 612 new stores and expanded 91 others. It concentrated most of that expansion in the 1969–1973 period when it opened 369 new stores, 15 on one particularly busy day. Because Grant's reputation had been built on sales to lower-income consumers, it was often unable to locate its new stores in the choicest shopping centers. Louis C. Lustenberger, president of Grant from 1959 to 1968, started the expansion program, although later, as a director, he became concerned over dimensions of the growth and the problems it generated. After Lustenberger stepped down, the pace of expansion accelerated under the leadership of Chairman Edward Staley and President Richard W. Mayer.

A second aspect of Grant's strategy involved a change in its product line. Grant perceived a vacuum in the middle-income consumer market when Sears moved more upscale. Grant introduced a higher-quality, medium-priced line of products into its new shopping center stores to fill this vacuum. In addition, it added furniture and private-brand appliances to its product line and implemented a credit card system. With much of the move to the suburbs representing

---

[12]This case was coauthored with Professor James A. Largay.

middle-income consumers, Grant attempted to position itself as a primary supplier to outfit the new homes being constructed.

To implement this new strategy, Grant chose a decentralized organizational structure. Each store manager controlled credit extension and credit terms. At most stores, Grant permitted customers 36 months to pay for their purchases; the minimum monthly payment was $1 regardless of total purchases. Bad debt expenses averaged 1.2% of sales each year until fiscal 1975, when a provision of $155.7 million was made. Local store managers also made inventory and pricing decisions. Merchandise was acquired from regional Grant warehouses or ordered directly from the manufacturer. At this time, Grant did not have an information system in place that permitted one store to check the availability of a needed product from another store. Compensation of employees was considered among the most generous in the industry, with most employees owning shares of Grant's common stock acquired under employee stock option plans. Compensation of store managers included salary plus stated percentages of the store's sales and profits.

To finance the expansion of receivables and inventory, Grant used commercial paper, bank loans, and trade credit. To finance the expansion of store space, Grant entered into leasing arrangements. Because Grant was liquidated before the FASB issued *Statement of Financial Accounting Standards No. 13,* requiring the capitalization of capital leases on the balance sheet and the disclosure of information on operating leases in the notes to the financial statements, it did not disclose its long-term leasing arrangements. Property, plant, and equipment reported on its balance sheet consisted mostly of store fixtures. Grant's long-term debt included debentures totaling $200 million issued in 1971 and 1973. Based on per-square-foot rental rates at the time, Grant's disclosures of total square footage of space, and an 8% discount rate, the estimated present values of Grant's leases are as follows (in thousands):

January 31	Present Value of Lease Commitments	January 31	Present Value of Lease Commitments
1966	$394,291	1971	$496,041
1967	$400,090	1972	$626,052
1968	$393,566	1973	$708,666
1969	$457,111	1974	$805,785
1970	$486,837	1975	$821,565

Advance and Retreat—The Attempt to Save Grant

By 1974, it became clear that Grant's problems were not of a short-term operating nature. In the spring of 1974, both Moody's and Standard & Poor's eliminated their credit rating for Grant's commercial paper. Banks entered the picture in a big way in the summer of 1974. To provide financing, a group of 143 banks agreed to offer lines of credit totaling $525 million. Grant obtained a short-term loan of $600 million in September 1974, with three New York money center banks absorbing approximately $230 million of the total. These three banks also loaned $50 million out of a total of $100 million provided to Grant's finance subsidiary.

Support of the banks during the summer of 1974 was accompanied by a top management change. Staley and Mayer stepped down in the spring and were replaced in August 1974 by

James G. Kendrick, brought in from Zeller's Ltd., Grant's Canadian subsidiary. As chief executive officer, Kendrick moved to cut Grant's losses. He slashed payroll significantly, closed 126 unprofitable stores, and phased out the big-ticket furniture and appliance lines. New store space opened in 1975 was 75% less than in 1974.

The positive effects of these moves could not overcome the disastrous events of early 1975. In January, Grant defaulted on about $75 million in interest payments, and in February, results of operations for the year ended January 31, 1975, were released. Grant reported a loss of $177 million, with substantial losses from credit operations accounting for 60% of the total.

The banks now assumed a more active role in what was becoming a struggle to save Grant. Robert H. Anderson, a vice president of Sears, was offered a lucrative $2.5 million contract. He decided to accept the challenge to turn the company around, joining Grant as its new president in April 1975. Kendrick remained as chairman of the board. The banks holding 90% of Grant's debt extended their loans from June 2, 1975, to March 31, 1976. The balance of about $56 million was repaid on June 2. A major problem confronting Anderson was how to maintain the continued flow of merchandise to Grant stores. Suppliers became skeptical of Grant's ability to pay for merchandise, and in August 1975, the banks agreed to subordinate $300 million of debt to the suppliers' claims for merchandise shipped. With the approach of the Christmas shopping season, the need for merchandise became critical. Despite the banks' subordination of their claims to those of suppliers and the intensive cultivation of suppliers by Anderson, Grant did not receive sufficient quantities of merchandise in the stores.

During this period, Grant reported a $111.3 million net loss for the six months ended on July 31, 1975. Sales had declined 15% from the comparable period in 1974. Kendrick observed that a return to profitability before the fourth quarter was unlikely.

On October 2, 1975, Grant filed a Chapter 11 bankruptcy petition. The rehabilitation effort was formally underway, and the protection provided by Chapter 11 permitted a continuation of the reorganization and rehabilitation activities for the next four months. On February 6, 1976, after store closings and liquidations of inventories had generated $320 million in cash, the creditors committee overseeing the bankruptcy voted for liquidation and W. T. Grant ceased to exist.

Financial Statements for Grant

Two changes in accounting principles affect Grant's financial statements. Prior to fiscal 1970, Grant accounted for the investment in its wholly owned finance subsidiary using the equity method. Beginning with the year ending January 31, 1970, Grant consolidated the finance subsidiary. Prior to fiscal 1975, Grant recorded the total finance charge on credit sales as income in the year of the sale. Therefore, accounts receivable included the full amount to be received from customers, not the present value of such amount. Beginning with the fiscal year ending January 31, 1975, Grant recognized finance changes on credit sales over the life of the installment contract.

Exhibit 3.36 presents comparative balance sheets and Exhibit 3.37 presents statements of income and retained earnings for Grant based on the amounts originally reported for each year. Exhibits 3.38, 3.39, and 3.40 present balance sheets, income statements, and statements of cash flow, respectively, based on revised amounts reflecting retroactive restatement for the two changes in accounting principles described earlier. These three statements consolidate the finance subsidiary for all years. Grant provided the necessary data to restate for the change in income recognition of finance charges for the 1971 to 1975 fiscal years only. Exhibit 3.41

presents selected other data for Grant, the variety chain store industry, and the aggregate economy.

REQUIRED

Using the narrative information and the financial data provided in Exhibits 3.36–3.41, your mission is to apply tools of financial analysis to determine the major causes of Grant's financial problems. If you had been performing this analysis contemporaneously with the release of publicly reported information, when would you have become skeptical of the ability of Grant to continue as a viable going concern? To assist in this analysis, Exhibits 3.42–3.44 present selected ratio and growth rate information based on the following assumptions:

- Exhibit 3.42: Based on the amounts as originally reported for each year (Exhibits 3.36 and 3.37)
- Exhibit 3.43: Based on the amounts as retroactively restated for changes in accounting principles (Exhibits 3.38–3.40)
- Exhibit 3.44: Same as Exhibit 3.42 except that assets and liabilities reflect the capitalization of leases using the amounts presented in the case

Exhibit 3.36

W. T. Grant Company
Comparative Balance Sheets
(as originally reported in thousands)
(Case 3.3)

January 31:	1966	1967	1968	1969
ASSETS				
Cash and marketable securities	$ 22,559	$ 37,507	$ 25,047	$ 28,460
Accounts receivable[c]	110,943	110,305	133,406	154,829
Inventories	151,365	174,631	183,722	208,623
Other current assets	—	—	—	—
Total Current Assets	$284,867	$322,443	$342,175	$391,912
Investments	38,419	40,800	56,609	62,854
Property, plant, and equipment, net	40,367	48,071	47,572	49,213
Other assets	1,222	1,664	1,980	2,157
Total Assets	$364,875	$412,978	$448,336	$506,136
LIABILITIES AND SHAREHOLDERS' EQUITY				
Short-term debt	$ —	$ —	$ 300	$ 180
Accounts payable—Trade	58,252	75,885	79,673	102,080
Current deferred taxes	37,590	47,248	57,518	64,113
Total Current Liabilities	$ 95,842	$123,133	$137,491	$166,373
Long-term debt	70,000	70,000	62,622	43,251
Noncurrent deferred taxes	6,269	7,034	7,551	7,941
Other long-term liabilities	4,784	4,949	4,858	5,519
Total Liabilities	$176,895	$205,116	$212,522	$223,084
Preferred stock	$ 15,000	$ 15,000	$ 14,750	$ 13,250
Common stock	15,375	15,636	16,191	17,318
Additional paid-in capital	25,543	27,977	37,428	59,945
Retained earnings	132,062	149,249	167,445	192,539
Total	$187,980	$207,862	$235,814	$283,052
Less cost of treasury stock	—	—	—	—
Total Stockholders' Equity	$187,980	$207,862	$235,814	$283,052
Total Liabilities and Shareholders' Equity	$364,875	$412,978	$448,336	$506,136

[a] In the year ending January 31, 1970, W. T. Grant changed its consolidation policy and commenced consolidating its wholly owned finance subsidiary.

[b] In the year ending January 31, 1975, W. T. Grant changed its method of recognizing finance income on installment sales. In prior years, Grant recognized all finance income in the year of the sale. Beginning in the 1975 fiscal period, it recognized finance income over the time the installment receivable was outstanding.

[c] Accounts receivable comprises the following:

January 31:	1966	1967	1968	1969
Customer installment receivables	$114,470	$114,928	$140,507	$162,219
Less allowances for uncollectible accounts	(7,065)	(9,383)	(11,307)	(13,074)
Unearned credit insurance	—	—	—	—
Unearned finance income	—	—	—	—
Net	$107,405	$105,545	$129,200	$149,145
Other receivables	3,538	4,760	4,206	5,684
Total receivables	$110,943	$110,305	$133,406	$154,829

Source: W. T. Grant Company, Form 10-K for the Fiscal Years Ended 1966, 1967, 1968, 1969, 1970, 1971, 1972, 1973, 1974, and 1975.

Exhibit 3.36 (Continued)

1970[a]	1971	1972	1973	1974	1975[b]
$ 32,977	$ 34,009	$ 49,851	$ 30,943	$ 45,951	$ 79,642
368,267	419,731	477,324	542,751	598,799	431,201
222,128	260,492	298,676	399,533	450,637	407,357
5,037	5,246	5,378	6,649	7,299	6,581
$628,409	$719,478	$831,229	$ 979,876	$1,102,686	$ 924,781
20,694	23,936	32,367	35,581	44,251	49,764
55,311	61,832	77,173	91,420	100,984	101,932
2,381	2,678	3,901	3,821	5,063	5,790
$706,795	$807,924	$944,670	$1,110,698	$1,252,984	$1,082,267
$182,132	$246,420	$237,741	$ 390,034	$ 453,097	$ 600,695
104,144	118,091	124,990	112,896	104,883	147,211
80,443	94,785	112,846	130,137	132,085	2,000
$366,719	$459,296	$475,577	$ 633,067	$ 690,065	$ 749,906
35,402	32,301	128,432	126,672	220,336	216,341
8,286	8,518	9,664	11,926	14,649	—
5,700	5,773	5,252	4,694	4,196	2,183
$416,107	$505,888	$618,925	$ 776,359	$ 929,246	$ 968,430
$ 11,450	$ 9,600	$ 9,053	$ 8,600	$ 7,465	$ 7,465
17,883	18,180	18,529	18,588	18,599	18,599
71,555	78,116	85,195	86,146	85,909	83,914
211,679	230,435	244,508	261,154	248,461	37,674
$312,567	$336,331	$357,285	$ 374,488	$ 360,434	$ 147,652
(21,879)	(34,295)	(31,540)	(40,149)	(36,696)	(33,815)
$290,688	$302,036	$325,745	$ 334,339	$ 323,738	$ 113,837
$706,795	$807,924	$944,670	$1,110,698	$1,252,984	$1,082,267

1970[a]	1971	1972	1973	1974	1975[b]
$381,757	$433,730	$493,859	$556,091	$602,305	$518,387
(15,270)	(15,527)	(15,750)	(15,770)	(18,067)	(79,510)
(5,774)	(9,553)	(12,413)	(8,768)	(4,923)	(1,386)
—	—	—	—	—	(37,523)
$360,713	$408,650	$465,696	$531,553	$579,315	$399,968
7,554	11,081	11,628	11,198	19,484	31,233
$368,267	$419,731	$477,324	$542,751	$598,799	$431,201

Exhibit 3.37

W. T. Grant Company
Statements of Income and Retained Earnings
(as originally reported in thousands)
(Case 3.3)

Year Ended January 31:	1967	1968	1969	1970	1971	1972	1973	1974	1975
Sales	$920,797	$979,458	$1,096,152	$1,210,918	$1,254,131	$1,374,811	$1,644,747	$1,849,802	$1,761,952
Concessions	2,249	2,786	3,425	3,748	4,986	3,439	3,753	3,971	4,238
Equity in earnings	2,072	2,987	3,537	2,084	2,777	2,383	5,116	4,651	3,086
Finance charges	—	—	—	—	—	—	—	—	91,141
Other income	1,049	2,010	2,205	2,864	2,874	3,102	1,188	3,063	3,376
Total Revenues	$926,167	$987,241	$1,105,319	$1,219,614	$1,264,768	$1,383,735	$1,654,804	$1,861,487	$1,863,793
Cost of goods sold	$631,585	$669,560	$741,181	$817,671	$843,192	$931,237	$1,125,261	$1,282,945	$1,303,267
Selling, general, and administration	233,134	253,561	287,883	307,215	330,325	374,334	444,879	491,287	769,253
Interest	4,970	4,907	4,360	14,919	18,874	16,452	21,127	78,040	86,079
Taxes:									
Current	13,541	17,530	25,600	24,900	21,140	13,487	9,588	(6,021)	(19,439)
Deferred	11,659	9,120	8,400	13,100	11,660	13,013	16,162	6,807	(98,027)
Total Expenses	$894,889	$954,678	$1,067,424	$1,177,805	$1,225,191	$1,348,523	$1,617,017	$1,853,058	$2,041,133
Net income	$ 31,278	$ 32,563	$ 37,895	$ 41,809	$ 39,577	$ 35,212	$ 37,787	$ 8,429	$ (177,340)
Dividends	(14,091)	(14,367)	(17,686)	(19,737)	(20,821)	(21,139)	(21,141)	(21,122)	(4,457)
Change in accounting principles:									
Consolidation of finance subsidiary	—	—	4,885	(2,932)	—	—	—	—	—
Recognition of financing charges	—	—	—	—	—	—	—	—	(28,990)
Change in retained earnings	$ 17,187	$ 18,196	$ 25,094	$ 19,140	$ 18,756	$ 14,073	$ 16,646	$ (12,693)	$ (210,787)
Retained earnings—Beginning of period	132,062	149,249	167,445	192,539	211,679	230,435	244,508	261,154	248,461
Retained Earnings—End of Period	$149,249	$167,445	$ 192,539	$ 211,679	$ 230,435	$ 244,508	$ 261,154	$ 248,461	$ 37,674

Source: W. T. Grant Company, Form 10-K for the Fiscal Years Ended 1967, 1968, 1969, 1970, 1971, 1972, 1973, 1974, and 1975.

Exhibit 3.38

W. T. Grant Company
Comparative Balance Sheets
(as retroactively reported for changes in accounting principles in thousands)
(Case 3.3)

January 31:	1966	1967	1968	1969	1970[a]	1971	1972	1973	1974	1975[b]
ASSETS										
Cash and marketable securities	$ 22,638	$ 39,040	$ 25,141	$ 25,639	$ 32,977	$ 34,009	$ 49,851	$ 30,943	$ 45,951	$ 79,642
Accounts receivable[c]	172,706	230,427	272,450	312,776	368,267	358,428	408,301	468,582	540,802	431,201
Inventories	151,365	174,631	183,722	208,623	222,128	260,492	298,676	399,533	450,637	407,357
Other current assets	3,630	4,079	3,982	4,402	5,037	5,246	5,378	6,649	7,299	6,581
Total Current Assets	$350,339	$448,177	$485,295	$551,440	$628,409	$658,175	$762,206	$905,707	$1,044,689	$ 924,781
Investments	13,405	14,791	16,754	18,581	20,694	23,936	32,367	35,581	44,251	49,764
Property, plant, and equipment, net	40,372	48,076	47,578	49,931	55,311	61,832	77,173	91,420	100,984	101,932
Other assets	1,222	1,664	1,980	2,157	2,381	2,678	3,901	3,821	5,063	5,790
Total Assets	$405,338	$512,708	$551,607	$622,109	$706,795	$746,621	$875,647	$1,036,529	$1,194,987	$1,082,267
LIABILITIES AND SHAREHOLDERS' EQUITY										
Short-term debt	$ 37,314	$ 97,647	$ 99,230	$118,125	$182,132	$246,420	$237,741	$ 390,034	$ 453,097	$ 600,695
Accounts payable	58,252	75,885	79,673	102,080	104,144	118,091	124,990	112,896	104,883	147,211
Current deferred taxes	36,574	44,667	56,545	65,073	80,443	58,536	72,464	87,431	103,078	2,000
Total Current Liabilities	$132,140	$218,199	$235,448	$285,278	$366,719	$423,047	$435,195	$ 590,361	$ 661,058	$ 749,906
Long-term debt	70,000	70,000	62,622	43,251	35,402	32,301	128,432	126,672	220,336	216,341
Noncurrent deferred taxes	6,269	7,034	7,551	7,941	8,286	8,518	9,664	11,926	14,649	—
Other long-term liabilities	4,785	5,159	5,288	5,519	5,700	5,773	5,252	4,694	4,196	2,183
Total Liabilities	$213,194	$300,392	$310,909	$341,989	$416,107	$469,639	$578,543	$ 733,653	$ 900,239	$ 968,430

(Continued)

Exhibit 3.38 (Continued)

W. T. Grant Company
Comparative Balance Sheets
(as retroactively reported for changes in accounting principles in thousands)
(Case 3.3)

January 31:	1966	1967	1968	1969	1970[a]	1971	1972	1973	1974	1975[b]
Preferred stock	$ 15,000	$ 15,000	$ 14,750	$ 13,250	$ 11,450	$ 9,600	$ 9,053	$ 8,600	$ 7,465	$ 7,465
Common stock	15,375	15,636	16,191	17,318	17,883	18,180	18,529	18,588	18,599	18,599
Additional paid-in capital	25,543	27,977	37,428	59,945	71,555	78,116	85,195	86,146	85,909	83,914
Retained earnings	136,226	153,703	172,329	189,607	211,679	205,381	215,867	229,691	219,471	37,674
Total	$192,144	$212,316	$240,698	$280,120	$312,567	$311,277	$328,644	$343,025	$331,444	$147,652
Less cost of treasury stock	—	—	—	—	(21,879)	(34,295)	(31,540)	(40,149)	(36,696)	(33,815)
Total Stockholders' Equity	$192,144	$212,316	$240,698	$280,120	$290,688	$276,982	$297,104	$302,876	$294,748	$113,837
Total Liabilities and Shareholders' Equity	$405,338	$512,708	$551,607	$622,109	$706,795	$746,621	$875,647	$1,036,529	$1,194,987	$1,082,267

Note: [a] See note (a) to Exhibit 3.36.
[b] See note (b) to Exhibit 3.36.
[c] Accounts receivable comprises the following:

	1966	1967	1968	1969	1970[a]	1971	1972	1973	1974	1975[b]
Customer installment receivables				$381,757	$433,730	$493,859	$556,091	$602,305	$518,387	
Less allowances for uncollectible Accounts		*NOT DISCLOSED ON A FULLY*		(15,270)	(15,527)	(15,750)	(15,770)	(18,067)	(79,510)	
Unearned credit insurance		*CONSOLIDATED BASIS WITH FINANCE*		(5,774)	(9,553)	(12,413)	(8,768)	(4,923)	(1,386)	
Unearned finance income		*SUBSIDIARY*		—	(61,303)	(69,023)	(74,169)	(57,997)	(37,523)	
				$360,713	$347,347	$396,073	$457,384	$521,318	$399,968	
Net other Receivables				7,554	11,081	11,628	11,198	19,484	31,233	
Total Receivables	$172,706	$230,427	$272,450	$312,776	$368,267	$358,428	$408,301	$468,582	$540,802	$431,201

Source: W. T. Grant Company, Form 10-K for the Fiscal Years Ended 1966, 1967, 1968, 1969, 1970, 1971, 1972, 1973, 1974, and 1975.

Exhibit 3.39

W. T. Grant Company
Statements of Income and Retained Earnings
(as retroactively revised for changes in accounting principles in thousands)
(Case 3.3)

Year Ended January 31:	1967	1968	1969	1970	1971	1972	1973	1974	1975
Sales	$920,797	$979,458	$1,096,152	$1,210,918	$1,254,131	$1,374,812	$1,644,747	$1,849,802	$1,761,952
Concessions	2,249	2,786	3,425	3,748	4,986	3,439	3,753	3,971	4,238
Equity in earnings	1,073	1,503	1,761	2,084	2,777	2,383	5,116	4,651	3,086
Finance charges	—	—	—	—	63,194	66,567	84,817	114,920	91,141
Other income	1,315	2,038	2,525	2,864	2,874	3,102	1,188	3,063	3,376
Total Revenues	$925,434	$985,785	$1,103,311	$1,219,614	$1,327,962	$1,450,303	$1,739,621	$1,976,407	$1,863,793
Cost of goods sold	$631,585	$669,560	$741,181	$817,671	$843,192	$931,237	$1,125,261	$1,282,945	$1,303,267
Selling, general, and administration	229,130	247,093	278,031	307,215	396,877	445,244	532,604	601,231	769,253
Interest	7,319	8,549	9,636	14,919	18,874	16,452	21,127	78,040	86,079
Taxes:									
Current	14,463	18,470	27,880	24,900	22,866	13,579	11,256	(6,021)	(19,439)
Deferred	11,369	9,120	8,400	13,100	9,738	12,166	14,408	9,310	(98,027)
Total Expenses	$893,866	$952,792	$1,065,128	$1,177,805	$1,291,547	$1,418,678	$1,704,656	$1,965,505	$2,041,133
Net income	$ 31,568	$ 32,993	$ 38,183	$ 41,809	$ 36,415	$ 31,625	$ 34,965	$ 10,902	$ (177,340)
Dividends	(14,091)	(14,367)	(17,686)	(19,737)	(20,821)	(21,139)	(21,141)	(21,122)	(4,457)
Change in accounting principles:									
Consolidation of finance subsidiary	—	—	(3,219)	—	—	—	—	—	—
Recognition of financing charges	—	—	—	—	(21,892)	—	—	—	—
Change in retained earnings	$ 17,477	$ 18,626	$ 17,278	$ 22,072	$ (6,298)	$ 10,486	$ 13,824	$ (10,220)	$ (181,797)
Retained earnings— Beginning of period	136,226	153,703	172,329	189,607	211,679	205,381	215,867	229,691	219,471
Retained Earnings—End of Period	$153,703	$172,329	$ 189,607	$ 211,679	$ 205,381	$ 215,867	$ 229,691	$ 219,471	$ 37,674

Source: W. T. Grant Company, Form 10-K for the Fiscal Years Ended 1967, 1968, 1969, 1970, 1971, 1972, 1973, 1974, and 1975.

Exhibit 3.40

W. T. Grant Company
Statement of Cash Flows
(as retroactively revised for changes in accounting principles in thousands)
(Case 3.3)

Year Ended January 31:	1967	1968	1969	1970	1971	1972	1973	1974	1975
OPERATIONS									
Net income	$ 31,568	$ 32,993	$ 38,183	$ 41,809	$ 36,415	$ 31,625	$ 34,965	$ 10,902	$(177,340)
Depreciation	7,524	8,203	8,388	8,972	9,619	10,577	12,004	13,579	14,587
Other	66	(856)	(1,140)	(1,559)	(2,470)	(1,758)	(1,699)	(1,345)	(16,993)
(Increase) Decrease in receivables	(57,721)	(42,023)	(40,326)	(55,491)	(11,981)	(49,873)	(60,281)	(72,220)	109,601
(Increase) Decrease in inventories	(23,266)	(9,091)	(24,901)	(13,505)	(38,364)	(38,184)	(100,857)	(51,104)	43,280
(Increase) Decrease in prepayments	(449)	97	(420)	(635)	(209)	(132)	(1,271)	(650)	718
Increase (Decrease) in accounts payable	17,633	3,788	22,407	2,064	13,947	6,899	(12,094)	(8,013)	42,328
Increase (Decrease) in other current liabilities	8,093	11,878	8,528	15,370	(21,907)	13,928	14,967	15,647	(101,078)
Cash Flow from Operations	$(16,552)	$ 4,989	$ 10,719	$ (2,975)	$(14,950)	$(26,918)	$(114,266)	$ (93,204)	$ (84,897)
INVESTING									
Acquisition of property, plant, and equipment	$(15,257)	$ (7,763)	$(10,626)	$(14,352)	$(16,141)	$(25,918)	$ (26,251)	$ (23,143)	$ (15,535)
Acquisition of investments	(269)	(418)	(35)	—	(436)	(5,951)	(2,216)	(5,700)	(5,282)
Cash Flow from Investing	$(15,526)	$ (8,181)	$(10,661)	$(14,352)	$(16,577)	$(31,869)	$ (28,467)	$ (28,843)	$ (20,817)

(Continued)

FINANCING	1967	1968	1969	1970	1971	1972	1973	1974	1975
Increase (Decrease) in short-term borrowing	$ 60,333	$ 1,583	$ 18,895	$ 64,007	$ 64,288	$ (8,679)	$ 152,293	$ 63,063	$ 147,598
Increase (Decrease) in long-term borrowing	—	(1,500)	(1,500)	(1,687)	(1,538)	98,385	(1,584)	93,926	(3,995)
Increase (Decrease) in capital stock	2,695	3,958	844	(17,860)	(8,954)	7,407	(8,227)	1,833	886
Dividends	(14,091)	(14,367)	(17,686)	(19,737)	(20,821)	(21,139)	(21,141)	(21,122)	(4,457)
Cash Flow from Financing	$ 48,937	$(10,326)	$ 553	$ 24,723	$ 32,975	$ 75,974	$ 121,341	$137,700	$ 140,032
Other	$ (457)	$ (381)	$ (113)	$ (58)	$ (416)	$ (1,345)	$ 2,484	$ (645)	$ (627)
Change in Cash	$ 16,402	$(13,899)	$ 498	$ 7,338	$ 1,032	$ 15,842	$ (18,908)	$ 15,008	$ 33,691

Source: W. T. Grant Company, Form 10-K for the Fiscal Years Ended 1967, 1968, 1969, 1970, 1971, 1972, 1973, 1974, and 1975.

Exhibit 3.41

W. T. Grant
Company Other Data
(Case 3.3)

December 31:	1965	1966	1967	1968	1969	1970	1971	1972	1973	1974
W. T. Grant Co.										
Sales (millions)[a]	$ 839.7	$ 920.8	$ 979.5	$1,096.1	$1,210.9	$1,254.1	$1,374.8	$1,644.7	$1,849.8	$1,762.0
Number of stores	1,088	1,104	1,086	1,092	1,095	1,116	1,168	1,208	1,189	1,152
Store area (thousands of square feet)		[a]Data Not Available			—	38,157	44,718	50,619	53,719	54,770
Dividends per share[a]	$ 0.80	$ 1.10	$ 1.10	$ 1.30	$ 1.40	$ 1.40	$ 1.50	$ 1.50	$ 1.50	$ 0.30
Stock Price										
—High	31 1/8	35 1/8	37 3/8	45 1/8	59	52	70 5/8	48 3/4	44 3/8	12
—Low	18	20 1/2	20 3/4	30	39 1/4	26 7/8	41 7/8	38 3/4	9 7/8	1 1/2
—Close (12/31)	31 1/8	20 3/4	34 3/8	42 5/8	47	47 1/8	47 3/4	43 7/8	10 7/8	1 7/8
Variety Chain Store Industry										
Sales (millions)	$5,320.0	$5,727.0	$6,078.0	$6,152.0	$6,426.0	$6,959.0	$6,972.0	$7,498.0	$8,212.0	$8,714.0
Standard & Poor's Variety Chain Stock Price Index										
—High	31.0	31.2	38.4	53.6	66.1	61.4	92.2	107.4	107.3	73.7
—Low	24.3	22.4	22.3	34.7	48.8	40.9	60.2	82.1	60.0	39.0
—Close (12/31)	31.0	22.4	37.8	50.5	59.6	60.4	88.0	106.8	66.2	41.9
AGGREGATE ECONOMY										
Gross national product (billions)	$ 684.9	$ 747.6	$ 789.7	$ 865.7	$ 932.1	$1,075.3	$1,107.5	$1,171.1	$1,233.4	$1,210.0
Average bank short-term lending rate	4.99%	5.69%	5.99%	6.68%	8.21%	8.48%	6.32%	5.82%	8.30%	11.28%
Standard & Poor's 500 Stock Price Index										
—High	92.6	94.1	97.6	108.4	106.2	93.5	104.8	119.1	120.2	99.8
—Low	81.6	73.2	80.4	87.7	89.2	69.3	90.2	101.7	92.2	62.3
—Close (12/31)	92.4	80.3	96.5	103.9	92.1	92.2	102.1	118.1	97.6	68.6

[a] These amounts are for the fiscal year ending January 31 of the year after the year indicated in the column. For example, sales for W. T. Grant of $839.7 in the 1965 column are for the fiscal year ending January 31, 1966.

Source: W. T. Grant Company, Form 10-K for the Fiscal Years Ended 1965, 1966, 1967, 1968, 1969, 1970, 1971, 1972, 1973, and 1974.

Exhibit 3.42

W. T. Grant Company
Financial Ratios and Growth Rates Based on Amounts as Originally Reported
(Case 3.3)

Financial Ratios	1967	1968	1969	1970	1971	1972	1973	1974	1975
PROFITABILITY ANALYSIS									
Profit margin for ROA	3.7%	3.6%	3.7%	4.1%	3.9%	3.2%	3.0%	2.6%	(7.5%)
Assets turnover	2.4	2.3	2.3	2.0	1.7	1.6	1.6	1.6	1.5
Return on assets (ROA)	8.7%	8.2%	8.4%	8.2%	6.5%	5.0%	4.7%	4.1%	(11.4%)
Return on common shareholders' equity (ROCE)	16.8%	15.5%	15.2%	15.1%	13.7%	11.4%	11.7%	2.5%	(84.1%)
OPERATING PERFORMANCE									
Cost of goods sold/sales	68.6%	68.4%	67.6%	67.5%	67.2%	67.7%	68.4%	69.4%	74.0%
Selling and administrative expenses/sales	25.3%	25.9%	26.3%	25.4%	26.3%	27.2%	27.0%	26.6%	43.7%
ASSET TURNOVERS									
Accounts receivable	8.3	8.0	7.6	4.6	3.2	3.1	3.2	3.2	3.4
Inventory	3.9	3.7	3.8	3.8	3.5	3.3	3.2	3.0	3.0
Fixed asset	20.8	20.5	22.7	23.2	21.4	19.8	19.5	19.2	17.4
SHORT-TERM LIQUIDITY RISK									
Current ratio	2.62	2.49	2.36	1.71	1.57	1.75	1.55	1.60	1.23
Quick ratio	1.20	1.15	1.10	1.09	0.99	1.11	0.91	0.93	0.68
Days receivables	44	45	48	79	115	119	113	113	107
Days inventory	94	98	97	96	104	110	113	121	120
Days payables	37	42	43	45	46	46	35	30	37
Operating cash flow/current liabilities	(15.1%)	3.8%	7.1%	(1.1%)	(3.6%)	(5.8%)	(20.6%)	(14.1%)	(11.8%)

(Continued)

Exhibit 3.42 (Continued)

W. T. Grant Company
Financial Ratios and Growth Rates Based on Amounts as Originally Reported
(Case 3.3)

Financial Ratios	1967	1968	1969	1970	1971	1972	1973	1974	1975
LONG-TERM LIQUIDITY RISK									
Liabilities/Assets	49.7%	47.4%	44.1%	58.9%	62.6%	65.5%	69.9%	74.2%	85.9%
Long-term debt/assets	17.0%	14.0%	8.5%	5.0%	4.0%	13.6%	11.4%	17.6%	20.0%
Operating cash flow/total liabilities	(8.7%)	2.4%	4.9%	(0.9%)	(3.2%)	(4.8%)	(16.4%)	(10.9%)	(9.0%)
Interest coverage ratio	12.4	13.1	17.5	6.4	4.8	4.8	4.0	1.1	(2.4)
Growth Rates		**1968**	**1969**	**1970**	**1971**	**1972**	**1973**	**1974**	**1975**
Accounts receivable		20.9%	16.1%	137.9%	14.0%	13.7%	13.7%	10.3%	(28.0%)
Inventories		5.2%	13.6%	6.5%	17.3%	14.7%	33.8%	12.8%	(9.6%)
Fixed assets		(1.0%)	3.4%	12.4%	11.8%	24.8%	18.5%	10.5%	0.9%
Total Assets		8.6%	12.9%	39.6%	14.3%	17.0%	17.6%	12.8%	(13.6%)
Accounts payable		5.0%	28.1%	2.0%	13.4%	5.8%	(9.7%)	(7.1%)	40.4%
Bank loans		—	(40.0%)	N/A	35.3%	(3.5%)	64.1%	16.2%	32.6%
Long-term debt		(10.5%)	(30.9%)	(18.1%)	(8.8%)	297.6%	(1.4%)	73.9%	(1.8%)
Shareholders' equity		13.4%	20.0%	2.7%	3.9%	7.8%	2.6%	(3.2%)	(64.8%)
Sales		6.4%	11.9%	10.5%	3.6%	9.6%	19.6%	12.5%	(4.7%)
Cost of goods sold		6.0%	10.7%	10.3%	3.1%	10.4%	20.8%	14.0%	1.6%
Selling and administrative expenses		8.8%	13.5%	6.7%	7.5%	13.3%	18.8%	10.4%	56.6%
Net Income		4.1%	16.4%	10.3%	(5.3%)	(11.0%)	7.3%	(77.7%)	(2,203.9%)

Exhibit 3.43

W. T. Grant Company
Financial Ratios and Growth Rates Based on Amounts Retroactively Restated for Changes in Accounting Principles (Leases Not Capitalized) (Case 3.3)

Financial Ratios	1967	1968	1969	1970	1971	1972	1973	1974	1975
PROFITABILITY ANALYSIS									
Profit margin for ROA	3.8%	3.8%	3.9%	4.1%	3.7%	2.9%	2.8%	2.8%	(7.5%)
Assets turnover	2.0	1.8	1.9	1.8	1.7	1.7	1.7	1.7	1.5
Return on assets (ROA)	7.7%	7.0%	7.4%	7.5%	6.4%	5.0%	4.8%	4.6%	(11.6%)
Return on common shareholders' equity (ROCE)	16.6%	15.3%	15.3%	15.1%	13.2%	11.3%	11.9%	3.6%	(90.2%)
OPERATING PERFORMANCE									
Cost of goods sold/sales	68.6%	68.4%	67.6%	67.5%	67.2%	67.7%	68.4%	69.4%	74.0%
Selling and administrative expenses/sales	24.9%	25.2%	25.4%	25.4%	31.6%	32.4%	32.4%	32.5%	43.7%
ASSETS TURNOVERS									
Accounts receivable	4.6	3.9	3.7	3.6	3.5	3.6	3.8	3.7	3.6
Inventory	3.9	3.7	3.8	3.8	3.5	3.3	3.2	3.0	3.0
Fixed asset	20.8	20.5	22.5	23.0	21.4	19.8	19.5	19.2	17.4
SHORT-TERM LIQUIDITY RISK									
Current ratio	2.05	2.06	1.93	1.71	1.56	1.75	1.53	1.58	1.23
Quick ratio	1.23	1.26	1.19	1.09	0.93	1.05	0.85	0.89	0.68
Days receivables	80	94	97	103	106	102	97	100	101
Days inventory	94	98	97	96	104	110	113	121	120
Days payables	37	42	43	45	46	46	35	30	37
Operating cash flow/ current liabilities	(9.4%)	2.2%	4.1%	(0.9%)	(3.8%)	(6.3%)	(22.3%)	(14.9%)	(12.0%)
LONG-TERM LIQUIDITY RISK									
Liabilities/Assets	58.6%	56.4%	55.0%	58.9%	62.9%	66.1%	70.8%	75.3%	89.5%
Long-term debt/assets	13.7%	11.4%	7.0%	5.0%	4.3%	14.7%	12.2%	18.4%	20.0%
Operating cash flow/liabilities	(6.4%)	1.6%	3.3%	(0.8%)	(3.4%)	(5.1%)	(17.4%)	(11.4%)	(9.1%)
Interest coverage ratio	8.8	8.1	8.7	6.4	4.7	4.5	3.9	1.2	(2.4)

(Continued)

Exhibit 3.43 (Continued)

W. T. Grant Company
Financial Ratios and Growth Rates Based on Amounts Retroactively Restated for Changes in Accounting Principles
(Leases Not Capitalized)
(Case 3.3)

Growth Rates	1968	1969	1970	1971	1972	1973	1974	1975
Accounts receivable	18.2%	14.8%	17.7%	(2.7%)	13.9%	14.8%	15.4%	(20.3%)
Inventories	5.2%	13.6%	6.5%	17.3%	14.7%	33.8%	12.8%	(9.6%)
Fixed assets	(1.0%)	4.9%	10.8%	11.8%	24.8%	18.5%	10.5%	0.9%
Total assets	7.6%	12.8%	13.6%	5.6%	17.3%	18.4%	15.3%	(9.4%)
Accounts payable	5.0%	28.1%	2.0%	13.4%	5.8%	(9.7%)	(7.1%)	40.4%
Bank loans	1.6%	19.0%	54.2%	35.3%	(3.5%)	64.1%	16.2%	32.6%
Long-term debt	(10.5%)	(30.9%)	(18.1%)	(8.8%)	297.6%	(1.4%)	73.9%	(1.8%)
Shareholders' equity	13.4%	16.4%	3.8%	(4.7%)	7.3%	1.9%	(2.7%)	(61.4%)
Sales	6.4%	11.9%	10.5%	3.6%	9.6%	19.6%	12.5%	(4.7%)
Cost of goods sold	6.0%	10.7%	10.3%	3.1%	10.4%	20.8%	14.0%	1.6%
Selling and administrative expenses	7.8%	12.5%	10.5%	29.2%	12.2%	19.6%	12.9%	27.9%
Net Income	4.5%	15.7%	9.5%	(12.9%)	(13.2%)	10.6%	(68.8%)	(1,726.7%)

Exhibit 3.44

W. T. Grant Company
Financial Ratios and Growth Rates Based on Amounts Retroactively Restated for Changes in Accounting Principles
(Leases Capitalized)
(Case 3.3)

Financial Ratios	1967	1968	1969	1970	1971	1972	1973	1974	1975
PROFITABILITY ANALYSIS									
Profit margin for ROA	3.8%	3.8%	3.9%	4.1%	3.7%	2.9%	2.8%	2.8%	(7.5%)
Assets turnover	1.1	1.1	1.1	1.1	1.0	1.0	1.0	1.0	0.9
Return on assets (ROA)	4.1%	4.0%	4.3%	4.4%	3.8%	2.9%	2.8%	2.7%	(6.8%)
Return on common									
Shareholders' equity (ROCE)	16.6%	15.3%	15.3%	15.1%	13.2%	11.3%	11.9%	3.6%	(90.2%)
OPERATING PERFORMANCE									
Cost of goods sold/sales	68.6%	68.4%	67.6%	67.5%	67.2%	67.7%	68.4%	69.4%	74.0%
Selling and administrative									
expenses/sales	24.9%	25.2%	25.4%	25.4%	31.6%	32.4%	32.4%	32.5%	43.7%
ASSET TURNOVERS									
Accounts receivable	4.6	3.9	3.7	3.6	3.5	3.6	3.8	3.7	3.6
Inventory	3.9	3.7	3.8	3.8	3.5	3.3	3.2	3.0	3.0
Fixed Asset	2.1	2.2	2.3	2.3	2.3	2.2	2.2	2.2	1.9
SHORT-TERM LIQUIDITY RISK									
Current ratio	2.05	2.06	1.93	1.71	1.56	1.75	1.53	1.58	1.23
Quick ratio	1.23	1.26	1.19	1.09	0.93	1.05	0.85	0.89	0.68
Days receivables	80	94	97	103	106	102	97	100	101
Days inventory	94	98	97	96	104	110	113	121	120
Days payables	37	42	43	45	46	46	35	30	37
Operating cash flow/									
current liabilities	(9.4%)	2.2%	4.1%	(0.9%)	(3.8%)	(6.3%)	(22.3%)	(14.9%)	(12.0%)
LONG-TERM LIQUIDITY RISK									
Liabilities/Assets	76.7%	74.5%	74.0%	75.6%	77.7%	80.2%	82.6%	85.3%	94.0%
Long-term debt/assets	51.5%	48.3%	46.4%	43.8%	42.5%	50.2%	47.9%	51.3%	54.5%
Operating cash flow/liabilities	(2.5%)	0.7%	1.4%	(0.3%)	(1.6%)	(2.5%)	(8.6%)	(5.9%)	(4.9%)
Interest coverage	8.8	8.1	8.7	6.4	4.7	4.5	3.9	1.2	(2.4)

(Continued)

Exhibit 3.44 (Continued)

W. T. Grant Company
Financial Ratios and Growth Rates Based on Amounts Retroactively Restated for Changes in Accounting Principles
(Leases Capitalized)
(Case 3.3)

Growth Rates	1968	1969	1970	1971	1972	1973	1974	1975
Accounts receivable	18.2%	14.8%	17.7%	(2.7%)	13.9%	14.8%	15.4%	(20.3%)
Inventories	5.2%	13.6%	6.5%	17.3%	14.7%	33.8%	12.8%	(9.6%)
Fixed assets	1.6%	14.9%	6.9%	2.9%	26.1%	13.8%	13.3%	1.8%
Total assets	3.5%	14.2%	10.6%	4.1%	20.8%	16.2%	14.6%	(4.8%)
Accounts payable	5.0%	28.1%	2.0%	13.4%	5.8%	(9.7%)	(7.1%)	40.4%
Bank loans	1.6%	19.0%	54.2%	35.3%	(3.5%)	64.1%	16.2%	32.6%
Long-term debt	(3.0%)	9.7%	4.4%	1.2%	42.8%	10.7%	22.8%	1.1%
Shareholders' equity	13.4%	16.4%	3.8%	(4.7%)	7.3%	1.9%	(2.7%)	(61.4%)
Sales	6.4%	11.9%	10.5%	3.6%	9.6%	19.6%	12.5%	(4.7%)
Cost of goods sold	6.0%	10.7%	10.3%	3.1%	10.4%	20.8%	14.0%	1.6%
Selling and administrative expenses	7.8%	12.5%	10.5%	29.2%	12.2%	19.6%	12.9%	27.9%
Net Income	4.5%	15.7%	9.5%	(12.9%)	(13.2%)	10.6%	(68.8%)	(1,726.7%)

Profitability Analysis

LEARNING OBJECTIVES

LO 4-1 Evaluate firm profitability using the primary measure of firm performance—net income—as well as techniques such as per-share analysis, common-size analysis, percentage change analysis, segment profitability analysis, and alternative measures of income.

LO 4-2 Explain the importance of rate of return analysis in succinctly summarizing firm performance, and demonstrate how to interpret the return on assets (ROA) and its components: profit margin and total assets turnover.

LO 4-3 Analyze and interpret the return on common shareholders' equity (ROCE), including the conditions when a firm successfully uses financial leverage to increase the return to common shareholders.

LO 4-4 Link the effects of economic and strategic factors to the interpretation of ROA and ROCE.

LO 4-5 Describe the benefits and limitations of using ratios like ROA and ROCE as part of understanding the historical performance of a company.

Chapter Overview

The ultimate objective in most financial statement analyses is to value a firm's equity securities. The value of an equity security depends critically on the future *profitability* you anticipate relative to the *risk* involved. However, even if the objective is not valuation but simply performance assessment, financial statement analysis examines a firm's *profitability* and its *risk*. Examining the recent profitability of a firm provides information that helps you project future profitability and the expected return from investing in the firm's equity securities. Evaluations of risk involve judgments about a firm's success in managing various dimensions of risk in the past and its ability to manage risks in the future.

This chapter describes several commonly used financial statement analysis techniques for analyzing profitability, and Chapter 5 presents various techniques for using financial statements in assessing risk. Both chapters apply these tools of analysis to the financial statements of **PepsiCo**, and we recommend that you trace the calculation of each financial ratio discussed in these chapters to these financial statements so that you understand exactly how to do these computations. The analytical tools discussed in Chapters 4 and 5 provide the framework for the discussion of accounting quality analysis issues in Chapters 6–9 and the forecasting and valuation of firms in Chapters 10–14.

As discussed in Chapter 1, we view financial statement analysis as a three-legged stool (see Exhibit 1.1), which requires understanding

1. the economics of a firm's industry and markets.
2. the firm's specific strategy within its industry.
3. the information captured in its financial statements.

The analysis of profitability includes, among other things, the analysis of various financial ratios based on numbers from the financial statements. We will discuss many ratios in this chapter. An important concept at this point is that ratios are not metrics that you have to memorize, but are useful tools that you may construct and use in different ways to capture information relevant to your particular task. Although we demonstrate the most common and theoretically sound approaches to computing and interpreting ratios, you can always use these ratios somewhat differently. For example, analysts may vary whether they include gross or net sales or beginning, average, or ending asset balances in a ratio. When assessing ratios prepared by others, you need to understand how those ratios were defined and computed. Although differences in ratio definitions do not always generate substantive differences in inferences, sometimes they do.

Chapter 1 introduced the economic characteristics of the beverage industry and the strategy of PepsiCo to compete in this industry. We incorporate this information and other information provided by PepsiCo in its management discussion and analysis (MD&A) into our interpretations of PepsiCo's financial ratios. Appendix C provides a printout for PepsiCo of FSAP (Financial Statement Analysis Package) available with this book, containing financial ratios computed for PepsiCo. Finally, Appendix D, available at www.cengagebrain.com, provides medians across 48 industries for ROA, ROCE, and other commonly used ratios, which provides useful benchmarks for many of the ratios we discuss in this chapter.

LO 4-1

Evaluate firm profitability using the primary measure of firm performance—net income—as well as techniques such as per-share analysis, common-size analysis, percentage change analysis, segment profitability analysis, and alternative measures of income.

Overview of Profitability Analysis Based on Various Measures of Income

Investors in a firm are keenly interested in profitability to assess how well the managers are using the capital they have invested in the firm to generate returns on that investment. Other stakeholders, such as creditors, employees, suppliers, and customers, are similarly interested in profitability as a measure of the continuing viability of the firm. Thus, profitability analysis is a way to evaluate whether managers are effectively executing a firm's strategy. With this in mind, we view financial statement analysis as a form of hypothesis testing. For example, knowing that **PepsiCo** is a leading manufacturer of beverages, snack foods, and breakfast foods with well-recognized brands and an international presence, we might hypothesize that PepsiCo is more profitable than the average firm. We can obtain data from the financial statements for PepsiCo and comparable firms to see if this hypothesis actually describes PepsiCo's performance. Because there are numerous ways to measure profitability, it is important to approach the many tools for analyzing profitability in an organized manner. In this chapter, using PepsiCo as an example, we discuss the analysis of profitability as a step-by-step examination of different layers of financial information.

Although firms must report comprehensive income, net income remains the key measure of profitability and is more strongly associated with stock returns.[1] This result is surely due to net income exhibiting fairly high persistence and other comprehensive income items exhibiting very low persistence. Thus, we focus on net income as our primary measure of profitability, with the caveat that components of other comprehensive income for certain firms should not be automatically dismissed.

---

[1]Dan Dhaliwal, K. R. Subramanyam, and Robert Trezevant, "Is Comprehensive Income Superior to Net Income as a Measure of Firm Performance?" *Journal of Accounting and Economics* Vol. 26, Issues 1–3 (January 1999), pp. 43–67.

Exhibit 4.1 provides a diagram of the approaches to analyzing net income. The diagram begins with net income from the income statement. From net income, two branches represent alternative approaches to obtaining further insight into a firms' profitability. On the left, the approach is to analyze different transformations of net income; on the right, the approach is to compute rate of return analyses. The transformations of net income include per-share analysis, common-size analysis, percentage change analysis, and alternative definitions of profits. These are straightforward approaches to understand profitability. The rate of return analyses include return on assets (ROA) and return on common equity (ROCE), which integrate information from the income statement and the balance sheet. Most of this chapter will focus on understanding how to interpret ROCE and ROA, as these are key metrics in the discussions of accounting quality in Chapters 6–9 and forecasting and valuation in Chapters 10–14.

As Exhibit 4.1 shows, ROA and ROCE can be broken down into measures of profit margin, turnover, and leverage, which facilitate a deeper understanding of how a firm is generating wealth for its shareholders. The dashed lines for the decomposition of ROCE into margin (and leverage) highlight that there are differences in the calculations for ROA and ROCE, as will be discussed later (under the section "Relating ROA to ROCE"). Finally, the measures of margin, turnover, and leverage can be even more deeply analyzed using various financial ratios prepared from different line items in the financial statements. Note that the two branches of analysis of net income displayed in Exhibit 4.1 are interrelated, especially the use of common-size analysis and alternative definitions of profits. Both of these can be incorporated into rate of return analysis, as we will do later in the chapter.

Exhibit 4.1

Diagram of Alternative Approaches to Analyzing Net Income

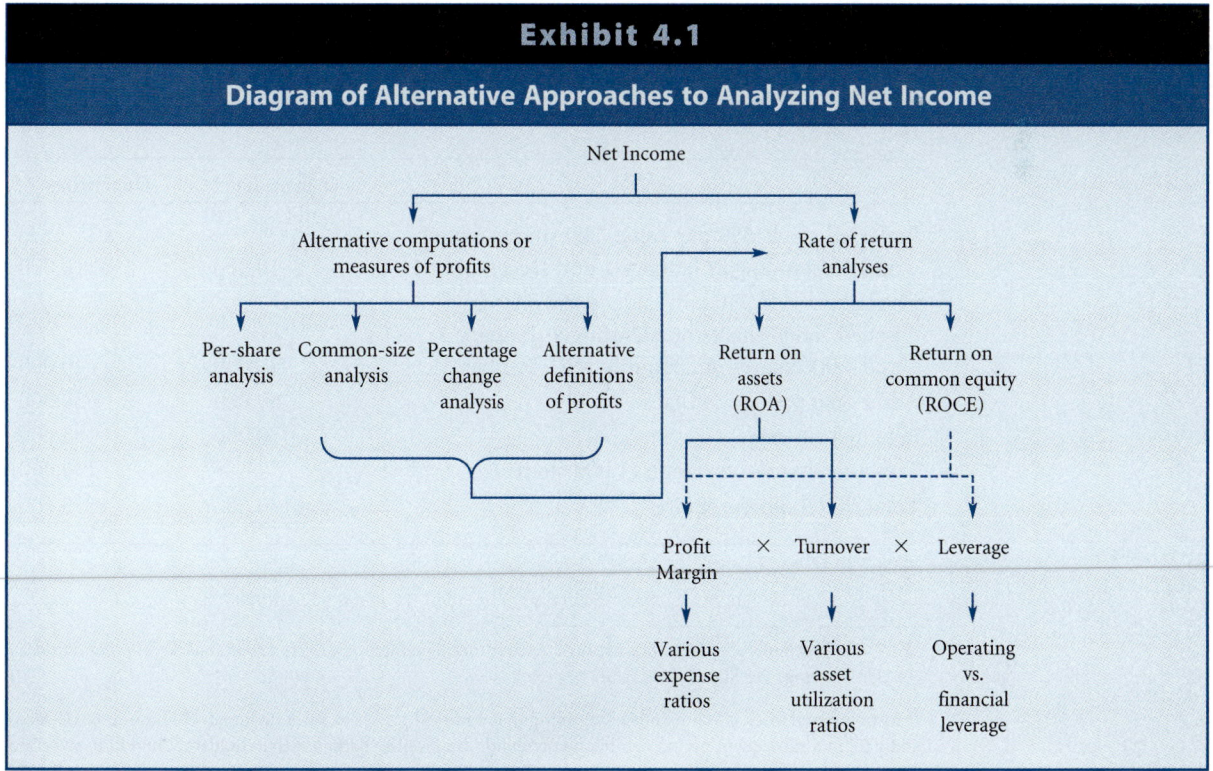

Earnings Per Share (EPS)

One of the most frequently used measures of profitability is earnings per share (EPS). Analysts and investors frequently use multiples of EPS, referred to as *price-earnings ratios*, to value firms. EPS is the only additional financial metric that U.S. GAAP requires firms to disclose on the face of the income statement and is covered explicitly by the opinion of the independent auditor.[2] This section briefly describes the calculation of EPS and discusses some of its uses and limitations.

Calculating Basic EPS

Firms have *simple* capital structures if they do not have

- outstanding convertible bonds or convertible preferred stock that holders can exchange for shares of common stock.
- options or warrants that holders can use to acquire common stock.

For such firms, the accountant calculates basic EPS as follows:

$$\frac{\text{Basic EPS}}{\text{(Simple Capital Structure)}} = \frac{\text{Net Income} - \text{Preferred Stock Dividends}}{\text{Weighted-Average Number of Common Shares Outstanding}}$$

The deduction of preferred stock dividends from net income yields net income available to common shareholders, the residual claimants on a firm's profits.[3] The numerator of basic EPS is adjusted for preferred stock dividends because the denominator includes only common shares outstanding. The denominator is a *weighted average* of common shares outstanding during the period, reflecting new stock issues, treasury stock acquisitions, and similar transactions that occur through the year.

Example 1. Cat Corporation had the following capital structure during its most recent year:

	January 1	December 31
Preferred stock, $20 par value, 500 shares issued and outstanding at January 1 and December 31	$ 10,000	$ 10,000
Common stock, $10 par value, 4,000 shares issued; 4,000 shares outstanding at January 1 and 3,000 shares outstanding at December 31	40,000	40,000
Additional paid-in capital	50,000	50,000
Retained earnings	80,000	85,600
Treasury shares—common (1,000 shares)	—	(30,000)
Total shareholders' equity	$180,000	$155,600

---

[2]*FASB Codification Topic 260.* International Accounting Standards Board, *International Accounting Standard No. 33,* "Earnings Per Share" (2003).

[3]Most preferred stock is "cumulative," meaning that a missed preferred stock dividend will have to be declared and paid in a subsequent period before any dividends are given to common shareholders. Therefore, preferred stock dividends are subtracted even if they have not been declared.

Retained earnings changed during the year as follows:

Retained earnings, January 1	$80,000
Net income	7,500
Preferred stock dividends	(500)
Common stock dividends	(1,400)
Retained earnings, December 31	$85,600

Assume the preferred stock is not convertible into common stock, the firm acquired 1,000 shares of treasury stock on July 1, and no stock options or warrants are outstanding. Then, the calculation of basic earnings per share for Cat Corporation follows:

$$\text{Basic EPS} = \frac{\$7,500 - \$500}{(0.5 \times 4,000) + (0.5 \times 3,000)} = \frac{\$7,000}{3,500} = \$2 \text{ per share}$$

Calculating Diluted EPS with Complex Capital Structure

Firms that have convertible securities and/or stock options or warrants outstanding have *complex* capital structures. Such firms must present two EPS amounts: *basic EPS* and *diluted EPS*. Diluted EPS reflects the dilution potential of convertible securities, options, and warrants. Dilution refers to the reduction in basic EPS that would result if holders of convertible securities exchanged them for shares of common stock or if holders of stock options or warrants exercised them. Firms include in diluted EPS calculations only those securities, options, and warrants that are exercisable and would reduce EPS; income and share dilution effects of equity instruments are excluded from both the numerator and denominator if they are not yet exercisable (for example, options that have not yet vested) or if their conversion would *increase* EPS (such securities would be referred to as "out of the money" and their effect on EPS as "antidilutive"). Accordingly, diluted EPS will always be less than (or equal to) basic EPS. This section describes the calculation of diluted EPS in general terms.

$$\frac{\text{Diluted EPS}}{\text{(Complex Capital Structure)}} = \frac{\text{Net Income} - \text{Preferred Stock Dividends} + \text{Adjustments for Dilutive Securities}}{\text{Weighted-Average Number of Common Shares Outstanding} + \text{Weighted-Average Number of Shares Issuable from Dilutive Securities}}$$

Adjustments for dilutive securities and the adjustment to weighted-average number of shares outstanding presume that the dilutive securities are converted to common shares *as of the beginning of the year*. To calculate diluted EPS, the accountant assumes the conversion of convertible bonds and convertible preferred stock and the exercise of stock options and warrants if their effect would be dilutive. The accountant adds back (1) interest expense (net of taxes) on convertible bonds and (2) dividends on convertible preferred stock the firm subtracted in computing net income attributable to common shareholders. Consistency would suggest that the accountant also add back to net income any compensation expense recognized on the employee stock options. However, U.S. GAAP and IFRS do not stipulate such an addback, but instead require firms to incorporate any unamortized compensation expense on those options into the calculation of the denominator of diluted EPS, as discussed next.

In the denominator of the diluted EPS computation, you increase common shares for the additional shares that are presumed to be issued at the beginning of the year (for conversion of bonds, conversion of preferred stock, and the exercise of stock options and warrants). The computation of additional shares due to the exercise of stock options assumes that the firm would repurchase common shares on the open market using an amount equal to the sum of (1) any cash proceeds from such exercise, (2) any unamortized compensation expense on those options, and (3) any tax benefits that would be credited to Additional Paid-in Capital.[4] Only the net incremental shares issued (shares issued under options minus assumed shares repurchased) enter the computation of diluted EPS.

Example 2. Assume that Dawg Corporation has the same capital structure as Cat Corporation, except the preferred stock of Dawg Corporation is convertible into 1,000 shares of common stock. Also assume that Dawg Corporation has stock options outstanding that holders can currently exchange for 300 incremental shares of common stock.[5] The calculation of diluted EPS is as follows:

$$\text{Diluted EPS} = \frac{\$7,500 - \$500 + \$500}{[0.5 \times (4,000 + 3,000)] + [1.0 \times (1,000 + 300)]} = \frac{\$7,500}{4,800}$$
$$= \$1.56$$

The calculation assumes the conversion of the convertible preferred stock into common stock as of January 1. If conversion had taken place, the firm would have had no preferred dividends during the year. Thus, the accountant adds back $500 of preferred dividends to the numerator. The weighted-average number of shares in the denominator increases for the 1,000 common shares the firm would issue on conversion of the preferred stock. The weighted-average number of shares in the denominator also increases for the incremental shares issuable under stock option plans.

Refer to the income statement of **PepsiCo** in Appendix A. PepsiCo reports basic EPS of $3.96 and diluted EPS of $3.92 for 2012. PepsiCo's Note 11, "Net Income Attributable to PepsiCo per Common Share," shows the calculation of its EPS amounts. Basic EPS shows a subtraction from net income for preferred dividends (related to ESOP convertible preferred stock). It also shows a subtraction for the redemption premium that PepsiCo paid when it redeemed some of the outstanding preferred stock.[6] For the calculation of diluted EPS, PepsiCo assumes the conversion of the preferred stock as of the beginning of the year, so the numerator adds back the dividends and redemption premium subtracted in the basic EPS calculation. Similarly, the denominator adds additional common shares assumed to be issued under stock option plans and from the convertible ESOP convertible preferred stock.

Criticisms of EPS

Critics of EPS as a measure of profitability point out that it does not consider the amount of assets or capital required to generate a particular level of earnings. Two firms

---

[4]Understanding the rationale for including unamortized compensation expense in the computation of the net incremental shares issuable requires an understanding of the accounting for stock options, which is discussed in Chapter 7. Basically, U.S. GAAP and IFRS view the value of stock options, which is expensed over the period of benefit, as a substitute for cash compensation. Assuming unamortized expense leads to repurchased shares presumes that a firm realizes a pseudo cash savings in this amount.

[5]We are simplifying this example with the assumption of 300 *incremental* shares. An actual calculation would require separate computation of the proceeds from exercise, unamortized compensation expense, and associated tax benefits.

[6]The treatment of redemption premia in calculating basic EPS is rare.

with the same earnings and EPS are not equally profitable if one firm requires twice the amount of assets or capital to generate those earnings compared to the other firm. Also, the number of shares of common stock outstanding serves as a poor measure of the amount of capital in use. The number of shares outstanding usually reflects a firm's attempts to achieve a desirable trading range for its common stock. For example, suppose a firm has an aggregate market value for its common shares of $10 million. If the firm has 500,000 shares outstanding, the shares would trade around $20 per share. If, instead, the firm has 1 million shares outstanding, the shares would trade around $10 per share. The amount of capital in place is the same in both instances, but the number of shares outstanding (and therefore EPS) is different. Also, EPS is an ambiguous measure of changes in profitability over time because changes in shares outstanding over time can have disproportionate effects on the numerator and denominator. For example, a firm could experience a decline in earnings during a year but report higher EPS than it did the previous year if it repurchased a sufficient number of shares early in the period. When assessing earnings performance, you must separate the impact of these two factors on EPS.

Despite these criticisms of EPS as a measure of profitability, it remains one of the focal points of the quarterly earnings announcement season, and analysts frequently use it in valuing firms. The reason for its ubiquity is the direct comparability of a firm's earnings per share to its stock price per share. Later, Chapter 14 discusses the use of EPS in valuation.

Common-Size Analysis

Common-size analysis converts financial statement line items into percentages of either sales (for the income statement) or total assets (for the balance sheet). Through the use of a common denominator, common-size analysis enables you to compare financial statements across firms and across time (for the same firm). For example, suppose a firm has ten times the sales of a competitor. The profitability of the two firms can be compared more meaningfully by scaling net income and the individual expense line items to a common denominator (each firm's total revenues) to remove the large discrepancy in the size of the two firms' operations. Common-size analysis is also a very helpful comparison tool when evaluating financial statements reported using different currencies (for example, PepsiCo with U.S. dollars and Nestle with Euros).

Chapter 1 introduced common-size financial statements and examined **PepsiCo** and **Coca-Cola** (both a cross-sectional and a time-series analysis, and based on reported amounts) for 2008–2012. Refer to Exhibits 1.18 and 1.20. The 2012 common-size figures scaled by revenues suggest that Coca-Cola shows a more favorable gross profit (revenues minus cost of goods sold) of 60.3% of revenues, relative to 52.2% for PepsiCo. Selling, general, and administrative expenses are lower for Coca-Cola at 36.9% of revenues relative to 38.1% for PepsiCo. Other line items contribute relatively minor differences, and the substantial difference in gross profits contributes to higher common-size net income for Coca-Cola relative to PepsiCo. Common-size analysis is a simple but powerful approach to understanding profitability. Common-size income statements provide quick and easy methods to compute firms' profit margins—including gross profit, operating profit, and net profit margins. For example, the analyses in Exhibits 1.18 and 1.20 suggest that Coca-Cola realizes substantially higher profitability per dollar of sales than PepsiCo. However, to more deeply understand this comparison, you must perform additional analysis to understand that a primary explanation for the higher gross profit at Coca-Cola is substantially greater presence and profitability in international beverage markets, despite PepsiCo's domestic operations being more profitable than those of Coca-Cola.

The common-size analysis of profitability across firms can be extended to time-series analysis as well. Examining the time series for each company may suggest the direction in which various expenses are trending. As noted previously, the primary difference between PepsiCo's and Coca-Cola's profitability in 2012 is due to the higher gross profit margins for Coca-Cola. Examining the trend in gross profit over the period 2008–2012 indicates that Coca-Cola's gross profit has trended downwards from 64.4% in 2008 to 60.3% in 2012. In contrast, PepsiCo's gross profit has ranged between 52.2 and 54.1%, with no clear trend. The different trends suggest that Coca-Cola's input costs are rising at a higher rate than increases in sales revenue and/or that it is shifting its revenue mix to lower margin products and markets. Indeed, Coca-Cola's MD&A indicates that commodity costs, temporary shifts in package mix, and unfavorable foreign currency changes all contributed to the declining margins.

When you perform common-size analysis, be aware that percentages can change because of

- changes in expenses in the numerator independent of changes in sales (for example, an increase in employee compensation levels).
- changes in sales independent of changes in expenses (for example, because the expense being examined is fixed for the period).
- interaction effects between the numerator and denominator (an increase in advertising expenses leads to an increase in sales, but possibly at different rates).
- coincident but independent changes in the numerator and denominator (that is, combinations of the other three possibilities).

Thus, although common-size analysis is useful, to fully understand the trends it reveals you must dig deeper into the economics of the firm's environment and the firm's strategy during the period being analyzed, as well as conduct further financial analysis using finer partitions of data. **That is why the six-step analytical framework of this book begins with an analysis of the firm's economic environment and strategy.** Note that FSAP performs the task of computing common-size financial statements automatically.

Percentage Change Analysis

Another way to analyze financial data is to compute percentage changes in individual line items, which also can be compared across firms and across time. However, the focus is not on the financial data themselves, but on the changes in individual line items through time. Percentage change analysis was introduced briefly in Chapter 1 along with common-size analysis. In addition to common-size figures, Exhibits 1.17 and 1.19 (balance sheets) and Exhibits 1.18 and 1.20 (income statements) also provide percentage change figures for **PepsiCo** and **Coca-Cola**, respectively, over 2009–2012. Note the loss of one year of data relative to common-size analysis, which simply reflects that the first year for which percentage changes can be computed for the 2008–2012 series is 2009 (that is, five years of data yield four changes).

In the common-size analysis discussed above, we noted a significant difference in the gross profit margins between PepsiCo and Coca-Cola. We can examine whether there are trends in gross profits as a percentage of sales for PepsiCo relative to Coca-Cola. Refer to Exhibits 1.18 and 1.20, which show four-year percentage change analyses for PepsiCo and Coca-Cola, respectively. PepsiCo's revenue growth rate exceeded that of Coca-Cola in 2010, but this reversed in 2011. More importantly, after 2009 the percentage change of Coca-Cola's cost of sales exceeded the percentage change in revenues for each year, which resulted in decreased gross profit margins. In addition, both companies show large increases in SG&A expenses, especially in 2010 for PepsiCo and in 2011 for Coca-Cola. When forecasting (a focus of Chapter 10), a helpful starting point is to examine prior percentage changes (and common-size data) to identify trends that may persist in the future. With knowledge of the company's strategic plans and recent trends, many changes can be anticipated. However, a limitation of percentage change analysis is that nonrecurring items or changes in "other" categories can be associated with extreme percentage changes.

Alternative Definitions of Profits

When you assess the profitability of a firm, the concern is with all revenues, expenses, gains, and losses that affected the economic value of the firm. However, when you use measures of past profitability to forecast the firm's future profitability, the emphasis is on those items that are expected to persist. If net income in the recent past includes nonrecurring gains from sales of assets or nonrecurring losses from unusual asset impairment or restructuring charges, you might decide to eliminate those items from past earnings when forecasting future earnings. For purposes of valuation, the goal is to forecast the sustainable earnings of a firm. The famous investment text by Benjamin Graham and David Dodd refers to this concept of earnings persistence as "earnings power."[7] Sustainable earnings, or earnings power, is the level of earnings and the growth in the level of earnings expected to persist in the future. Nonrecurring gains and losses may occur in future periods, but you cannot anticipate their occurrence, timing, or amount with sufficient precision to include them in sustainable earnings. Thus, a key to developing forecasts that are useful for valuation is to identify components of bottom-line earnings that are recurring.

Segment Profitability

Many firms consist of more than one operating segment. Both U.S. GAAP and IFRS require that companies provide measures of profitability and certain additional information for each segment. The definition of segments follows the "management approach," which leaves the identification of operating segments up to managers based on how they manage the operations of the company. For example, **PepsiCo** discloses four business units (Americas foods, Americas beverages, Europe, and Asia, Middle East and Africa) and PepsiCo further partitions these business units into six reportable segments (see discussion later in this chapter). Most often, disclosure of segment profitability data is presented in the footnotes to the financial statements. Given the open-ended management approach to these required disclosures, there is generally wide variation in the details provided by firms, which makes cross-sectional comparisons of segments challenging. However, firms are required to reconcile revenues and other disclosed items presented for segments to the corresponding totals for the firm. It is important to note that firms often do not allocate all general and administrative expenses to individual segments (allocating a portion to the "corporate" segment), so it also is challenging to compare performance of a segment within a multisegment firm to that of a pure-play firm, for which such expenses are included on the income statement.

---

[7]Benjamin Graham and David Dodd, *Security Analysis* (New York: McGraw-Hill), 1934.

Comprehensive Income

Financial statement users typically analyze net income as the summary bottom-line measure of performance. However, both U.S. GAAP and IFRS require presentation of comprehensive income, which is defined as:

> The change in equity (net assets) of a business entity during a period from transactions and other events and circumstances from nonowner sources. It includes all changes in equity during a period except those resulting from investments by owners and distributions to owners.[8]

Thus, items included as part of "other comprehensive income" are added to or deducted from net income. Such items include certain foreign currency translation items, defined benefit pension plan and other postretirement plan adjustments, certain unrealized gains and losses on investment securities and derivatives, and other adjustments.

The overriding objective of reporting items of other comprehensive income is to present an *all-inclusive* picture of a company's economic events during a period, where items included as other comprehensive income are generally more likely to be *temporary* in nature and may likely reverse prior to ultimate realization of the currently recognized gains and losses. Reliance on comprehensive income as a summary measure of performance is generally not emphasized as much as an understanding of the components. The primary interest of analysts in examining the components of other comprehensive income is to assess situations in which certain components are likely to persist. However, because of the volatility and uncertainty surrounding most of these items, they are generally not helpful for predicting future income.

Operating Income, EBIT, EBITDA, and Other Profit Measures

Another factor driving the analysis of different aggregations of income statement line items is that firms have different organizational and capital structures. As a consequence, it is sometimes helpful to examine profitability prior to considering a variety of expenses that vary depending on different organizational or capital structures. Thus, analysts are sometimes interested in analyzing different levels of profitability, such as gross profit, operating income, EBIT, EBITDA, EBITDAR, NOPAT, EBIAT, and earnings excluding any number of recognized expenses.[9] The most common of these is EBITDA, which many analysts and investors unfortunately confuse as a proxy for a firm's cash flows. As discussed later in our discussion of earnings quality (Chapter 6), it does not make sense to use EBITDA in lieu of operating cash flows, which are easily found on the statement of cash flows. Each metric identified above can be informative, but none (including net income) should be viewed as the single complete measure of financial performance.

As we saw in the common-size income statement analysis in Exhibits 1.18 and 1.20, gross profit is a key component of profitability when comparing **PepsiCo** and **Coca-Cola**, but the income statement that PepsiCo actually files with the SEC (in Appendix A) does *not* report a separate line item for gross profit. Similarly, measures of profitability at different levels of the income statement, such as EBITDA, are rarely disclosed on firms' income statements. Thus, you should be adept at reconfiguring income statements to suit different purposes, especially comparisons across companies where you inevitably must use judgment to normalize financial information into the same format.

---

[8]*FASB Codification 220-10-20.*

[9]The acronyms mentioned are as follows: EBIT = earnings before interest and taxes; EBITDA = earnings before interest, taxes, depreciation, and amortization; EBITDAR = earnings before interest, taxes, depreciation, amortization, and rent; NOPAT = net operating profits after tax; EBIAT = earnings before interest after tax.

Pro Forma, Adjusted, or Street Earnings

Managers frequently discuss specific computations of "earnings" that exclude certain line items and refer to such earnings as "pro forma" or "adjusted" earnings; collectively, such presentations of earnings, which are widely followed on Wall Street, are called "Street" earnings. As director of research at First Call, Chuck Hill commented, "What companies are trying to do is entice analysts into excluding certain charges and value them only on that basis."[10] Exhibit 4.2 shows a hypothetical approach to computing pro forma earnings by sequentially arguing that certain line items on the income statement are nonrecurring or are not relevant to the assessment of current profitability. The example shows revenues of $100, total expenses of $50, and net income of $50. Consider a manager who argues that Expense 5 is a one-time expense, such as severance payments to workers from a closed plant. The manager would report pro forma earnings of $60 after excluding this charge (Pro Forma 1 in Exhibit 4.2). Expense 4 might be for an expenditure such as advertising or R&D (research and development); so a manager might claim that these expenditures generate assets and are not relevant for assessing current performance. Excluding Expense 4 yields pro forma earnings of $70 (Pro Forma 2 in Exhibit 4.2). The manager also might claim that expenses such as depreciation and amortization should be ignored and not deducted in the measurement of "earnings" simply because such expenses do not involve cash outflows in the current period. If Expense 3 in Exhibit 4.2 represents depreciation and amortization, the manager might report and discuss Pro Forma 3, which reports earnings of $80. A scheming manager even might be inclined to argue against including *all* expenses, ending up reporting pro forma earnings equal to revenues (Pro Forma 5 in Exhibit 4.2). This may seem far-fetched, but it is what Internet firms did during the growth of this sector in the late 1990s. Managers of such firms argued that the key to assessing performance was the level of and growth in revenues, which reflected first-mover advantages to gain market share and growth in customers who would secure the firm's profitability in the future. Needless to say, most market observers agree that the valuation of such firms reached irrational levels and resulted in a subsequent stock market crash, partially attributable to the temporary disregard for profitability measured to include operating expenses.

Exhibit 4.2

Pro Forma Earnings Example

		U.S. GAAP	Pro Forma 1	Pro Forma 2	Pro Forma 3	Pro Forma 4	Pro Forma 5
Revenues		$100	$100	$100	$100	$100	$100
− Expenses:	*Expense 1*	(10)	(10)	(10)	(10)	(10)	—
	Expense 2	(10)	(10)	(10)	(10)	—	—
	Expense 3	(10)	(10)	(10)	—	—	—
	Expense 4	(10)	(10)	—	—	—	—
	Expense 5	(10)	—	—	—	—	—
= Earnings		$ 50	$ 60	$ 70	$ 80	$ 90	$100

---

[10]Elizabeth MacDonald, "Varied Profit Reports by Firms Create Confusion," *The Wall Street Journal* (August 24, 1999), p. C1.

An empirical research study revealed a significant increase in the trend of managers reporting pro forma earnings higher than bottom-line net income, primarily by excluding certain charges and expenses from reported "pro forma" earnings.[11] Exhibit 4.3 shows results from the study. The widening gap between plots in the graph makes it clear that firms increasingly excluded expenses from reported pro forma earnings beginning as far back as the late 1980s. A study of how managers highlight nonrecurring gains and losses revealed that managers tend to highlight unusual or one-time expenses or losses in the quarter in which they occur, but when that quarter is used as a benchmark for the announcement of the same quarter's earnings in the next year, managers tend not to remind investors that the previous year included an unusual or one-time expense or loss.[12] This makes the earnings announcement at that time appear more favorable in terms of year-to-year improvement in profitability.

In reaction to perceived abuses in the reporting of profits, the U.S. Securities and Exchange Commission (SEC) became concerned that the emphasis placed on pro forma earnings by managers risked misleading the average investor. The SEC issued Regulation G in 2003, which deals with what the SEC calls "non-GAAP" earnings, otherwise known in the investment community as pro forma earnings. Regulation G prohibits firms from placing more emphasis on pro forma earnings relative to bottom-line U.S. GAAP earnings or from identifying an amount as nonrecurring or unusual when such amounts have occurred in the past or are likely to recur in the future. Nevertheless, the reporting of non-GAAP (or pro forma) earnings is not prohibited outright, so investors must be diligent in understanding the composition of alternative measures of profits.

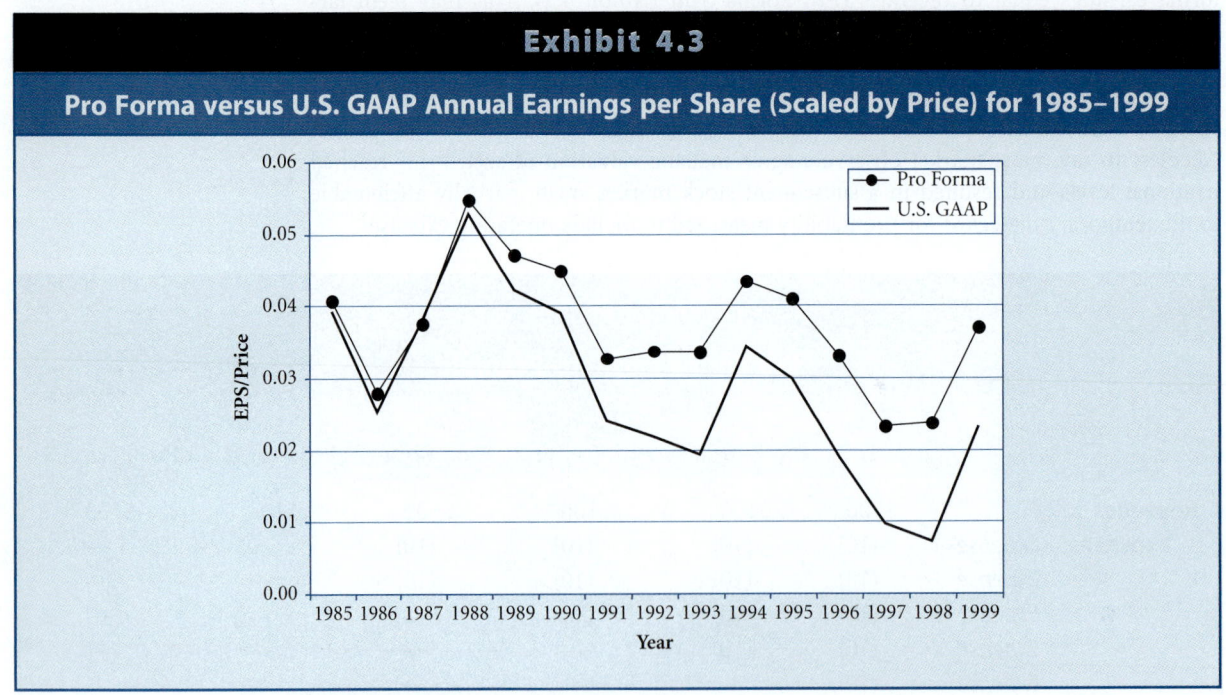

Exhibit 4.3

Pro Forma versus U.S. GAAP Annual Earnings per Share (Scaled by Price) for 1985–1999

---

[11]Mark T. Bradshaw and Richard G. Sloan, "GAAP versus the Street: An Empirical Assessment of Two Alternative Definitions of Earnings," *Journal of Accounting Research*, Vol. 40, No. 1 (March 2002), pp. 41–66.

[12]Catherine M. Schrand and Beverly R. Walther, "Strategic Benchmarks in Earnings Announcements: The Selective Disclosure of Prior-Period Earnings Components," *The Accounting Review*, Vol. 75, No. 2 (April 2000), pp. 151–177.

For example, firms often include financial highlights in their annual reports but use small fonts for footnotes indicating that certain charges have been excluded from the figures presented. However, most firms now make it easier for investors to understand how management views nonrecurring or unusual charges with separate disclosures. For example, in **PepsiCo**'s MD&A (Appendix B), the company includes a section titled "Items Affecting Comparability," which quantifies numerous items that are either nonrecurring or volatile. For example, PepsiCo's year-over-year comparisons are significantly impacted by merger and integration charges, restructuring and impairment charges, and a variable 52- to 53-week fiscal year convention.

Quick Check

- Earnings per share analysis is a basic measure of profitability, primarily because it shares the same denominator as price per share.
- Common-size analysis converts financial statement line items to percentages, enabling the comparison of financial results across firms or across time.
- Percentage change analysis is similarly useful for comparing trends across firms and across time.
- Numerous measures of profitability can supplement the analysis of net income, including segment-level profitability, operating income and similar metrics like EBIT and EBITDA, and earnings adjusted for the effects of unusual or nonrecurring items.

Return on Assets (ROA)

LO 4-2

Explain the importance of rate of return analysis in succinctly summarizing firm performance, and demonstrate how to interpret the return on assets (ROA) and its components: profit margin and total assets turnover.

The right branch of Exhibit 4.1 relates to analyses of profitability using rate of return measures, which presume that a certain amount of investment generates economic profits. A simple example is interest earned on a savings account. A straightforward computation of the rate of return on such an investment is the interest income earned divided by the amount deposited. Conceptually, the analysis of returns to creditors and equity shareholders is similar. In the analysis of financial statements, the two most common measures of rate of return are ROA and ROCE, or sometimes just ROE (return on equity). Our discussion of rate of return analysis begins with ROA. The next section transitions to an examination of ROCE.

The rate of ROA measures a firm's success in using assets to generate earnings independent of the financing of those assets. Thus, a properly calculated ROA will be unaffected by the proportion of debt versus equity financing and the costs of those types of capital. ROA is calculated as:

$$\text{ROA} = \frac{\text{Net Income} + \begin{array}{c}(1 - \text{Tax Rate}) \times \\ (\text{Interest Expense})\end{array} + \begin{array}{c}\text{Noncontrolling Interest} \\ \text{in Earnings}\end{array}}{\text{Average Total Assets}}$$

The numerator of ROA adjusts net income to exclude the effects of any financing costs. Thus, the measure of profits pertinent to ROA is net income *before* financing costs.[13] Because accountants subtract interest expense when computing net income, you must add it back when computing ROA. However, firms deduct interest expense in

---

[13]If a firm has income from discontinued operations or extraordinary gains or losses, you might exclude those items and start with net income from continuing operations instead of net income if the objective is to measure a firm's sustainable profitability.

measuring *taxable* income. Therefore, the *incremental* effect of interest expense on net income equals interest expense times one minus the marginal tax rate.[14] That is, you add back the full amount of interest expense to net income and then eliminate the tax savings from that interest expense.

The tax savings from interest expense depends on the statutory tax rate in the tax jurisdiction where the firm raises its debt, and these vary substantially. For example, as of the date this text was written, the statutory federal tax rate is 35% in the United States, 28% in Norway, 23% in the United Kingdom, 15% in Canada, and 0% in the Cayman Islands. In the United States, firms must disclose in a note to the financial statements why the average income tax rate (defined as income tax expense divided by net income before income taxes) differs from the federal statutory tax rate of 35%. The statutory federal rate will differ from a firm's average tax rate because of

1. state, local, and foreign tax rates that differ from 35% (Chapter 9 provides a discussion of these effects).
2. revenues and expenses that firms include in accounting income but that do not impact taxable income (that is, permanent differences, as described in Chapter 2).

You can approximate the combined statutory federal, state, local, and foreign tax rate applicable to tax savings from interest expense using 35% plus or minus the amounts disclosed related to Item 1 above. Permanent differences in Item 2 usually do not relate to interest expense and therefore should not affect the statutory tax rate applicable to interest expense deductions. To simplify the calculations, we will follow the common practice of using the *statutory* federal tax rate of 35% in the computations of the tax savings from interest in the numerator of ROA throughout this book. Because accountants do not subtract dividends on preferred and common stocks in measuring net income, calculating the numerator of ROA requires no adjustment for dividends.[15]

The rationale for adding back the noncontrolling interest in earnings relates to attaining consistency in the numerator and the denominator of ROA. The denominator of ROA includes all assets of the consolidated entity, not just the parent company's share. Net income in the numerator, however, represents the parent's earnings plus the parent's share of the earnings of consolidated subsidiaries. Consistency with the inclusion of all of the assets of the consolidated entity in the denominator of ROA requires that the numerator include all of the earnings of the consolidated entity, not just the parent's share. The add-back of the noncontrolling interest in earnings accomplishes this objective. Most publicly traded corporations do not disclose the noncontrolling interest in earnings because its amount, if any, is usually immaterial. Thus, you typically make this adjustment only for significant noncontrolling interests. **PepsiCo** reports a small but growing amount of noncontrolling interest, so we will make this adjustment in the PepsiCo computations that follow.

Calculating the numerator of ROA is accomplished most easily by starting with net income.[16] Because net income before financing costs in the numerator of ROA

---

[14]The marginal tax rate times interest expense is the *interest tax shield*. An interest tax shield is the reduction in taxes payable for firms that deduct interest expense in the computation of income tax liability.

[15]One could argue that you should exclude returns from short-term investments of excess cash (that is, interest revenue) from the numerator of ROA and the short-term investments from the denominator of ROA under the view that such investments are negative financings (that is, savings rather than borrowings). Such adjustments will be trivial for most firms, so for parsimony we do not make this adjustment when computing ROA.

[16]Equivalently, however, one could start with earnings before interest and taxes and deduct taxes applicable to pre-tax profits. Often analysts calculate EBIAT by deducting tax expense from the income statement, not including the adjustment for taxes on interest. For firms with limited amounts of interest-bearing debt, this is not a material omission. However, as with any ratio or financial computation, analysts should know whether trade-offs are being made for computational ease but at the expense of deviating from a theoretically correct construct.

reports the results for a period of time, a typical denominator uses a measure of average assets in use during that same period. This computation aligns the income measure in the numerator with the average assets in place during the period. Using average total assets is not mandatory, however, in the sense that using beginning total assets is not necessarily wrong. (In fact, if total assets have not changed significantly during the period, there will be little difference between the beginning amount and the average.) The use of average total assets is a simple way to account for the changing level of investments in total assets upon which profits are judged. Thus, for a nonseasonal business, an average of assets at the beginning and end of the year is usually satisfactory. For a seasonal business, you might use an average of assets at the end of each quarter.

Refer to the financial statements for PepsiCo in Appendix A. Also refer to the ROA and other ratio computations in the Analysis Spreadsheet of the FSAP presented in Appendix C. The calculation of ROA for 2012 is as follows:

$$ROA = \frac{\begin{array}{c}\text{Net Income from}\\\text{Continuing Operations}\end{array} + \begin{array}{c}(1 - \text{Tax Rate})\times\\(\text{Interest Expense})\end{array} + \begin{array}{c}\text{Noncontrolling}\\\text{Interest in Earnings}\end{array}}{\text{Average Total Assets}}$$

$$9.2\% = \frac{\$6,178 + (1 - 0.35)(\$899) + \$36}{0.5(\$74,638 + \$72,882)}$$

Adjustments for Nonrecurring or Special Items

As noted earlier in the chapter, you should consider whether reported net income includes any nonrecurring or special items that might affect assessments of a firm's ongoing profitability. The notes to the financial statements and the MD&A provide information for making these assessments. **PepsiCo** includes a section in its MD&A (Appendix B) labeled "Items Affecting Comparability." For 2012, PepsiCo lists several items affecting net income that you might consider unusual or nonrecurring (such as restructuring and impairment charges, a pension charge, and a court decision regarding tax benefits). If the objective is to measure the profitability performance of PepsiCo that particular year, this items should not be excluded, as they impacted PepsiCo's reported net income. However, if the objective is to measure the sustainable profitability of PepsiCo, you might decide to exclude the reported amounts for such items. Collectively, the six amounts listed by PepsiCo net to –$276 million, or approximately 5% of the numerator in our unadjusted ROA calculation above.

When deciding whether to eliminate any of these special items as part of assessing sustainable profitability, you should consider whether the event that triggered the charge or gain is likely to persist. Sometimes companies provide forward-looking information that helps you assess the persistence of such amounts, but more often they do not. If an amount is likely to persist, then you might leave it in the reported profitability in the numerator of ROA, but if it is likely to be nonrecurring, then you would remove its effect from the numerator. One could argue that "if it is not one thing, it will be another" and implicitly acknowledge that nonrecurring or unusual charges are more common than the nomenclature implies. A third approach is to leave the special items in earnings but de-emphasize them when contextually analyzing ongoing profitability, which is also a fairly common approach.

We follow the second approach and eliminate some items in 2010–2012 based on whether they are peripheral to PepsiCo's central operations. These are discussed below. Note that we view the decision whether to eliminate these items as very close to call and could easily have concluded to not eliminate them based on their recurring nature in the recent past. In Chapter 10, we project future financial statements for PepsiCo based on the assumption that these charges will not be recurring. Our decision to eliminate the charges also reflects the pedagogical benefits of describing the elimination procedure.

PepsiCo's MD&A highlights the following six items for 2012:[17]

Net income attributable to PepsiCo	2012	2011	2010
Mark-to-market net impact gains/(losses)	$ 41	$ (71)	$ 58
Merger and integration charges	$ (12)	$ (271)	$ (648)
Restructuring and impairment charges	$ (215)	$ (286)	—
Restructuring and other charges related to the transaction with Tingyi	$ (176)	—	—
Pension lump sum settlement charge	$ (131)	—	—
Tax benefit related to tax court decision	$ 217	—	—
53rd week	—	$ 64	—
Inventory fair value adjustments	—	$ (28)	$ (333)
Gain on previously held equity interests	—	—	$ 958
Venezuela currency devaluation	—	—	$ (120)
Asset write-off	—	—	$ (92)
Foundation contribution	—	—	$ (64)
Debt repurchase	—	—	$ (114)

The following paragraphs describe each of the items in more detail and state our reasoning for either excluding the amounts or leaving them in reported profits.

1. **Mark-to-market net impact gains/(losses).** These amounts result from fluctuations in commodity derivatives, which PepsiCo's corporate finance group manages on behalf of all divisions. Prices of commodity derivatives are volatile, so it is not surprising that PepsiCo realizes adjustments in all three years. The question is whether to cleanse reported earnings of such charges when analyzing profitability. The argument to exclude them is that price movements of commodities are unpredictable. However, because the commodity derivatives cover "agricultural products, metals and energy," it seems compelling that these are primary inputs into PepsiCo's core operations and hence not tangential. Thus, we will *not* exclude these charges from reported income during 2010–2012.

2. **Merger and integration charges.** In 2012, PepsiCo incurred $12 million for charges related to the acquisition of Wimm-Bill-Dann Foods, Russia's leading food and beverage company. The company frequently incurs such charges, which support the worldwide presence of PepsiCo brands. Given that this seems integral to PepsiCo's strategy, we will *not* exclude these charges.

3. **Restructuring and impairment charges.** In 2012, PepsiCo incurred charges related to a multi-year "Productivity Plan," which focuses on numerous improvements in global operations. The MD&A notes that "we expect to incur pretax charges of approximately $910 million, $279 million of which was reflected in

---

[17]There are additional amounts listed for 2011 and 2010 in the MD&A, some large like a $958 million gain on equity interests in 2010. Our primary focus is on 2012 and our intent in making adjustments is to demonstrate the process, so we will restrict our discussion to the six adjustments present for 2012, three of which also affect earlier years. Our adjustments for earlier years, however, will selectively adjust for other items.

our 2012 results, $383 million of which was reflected in our 2011 results, and the balance of which will be reflected in our 2013 through 2015 results." These charges will thus recur for the next two years, so we could justify not adjusting these amounts. However, because we often require forecasts for five or more years when performing valuation, an alternative is to adjust reported amounts for these charges, but then individually forecast such charges during 2014 and 2015. We *will* adjust ROA for these amounts in our historical analysis, and implicitly include them in forecasts of SG&A (discussed in Chapter 10).

4. **Restructuring and other charges related to the transaction with Tingyi.** In 2012, PepsiCo engaged in a transfer of certain bottling operations to a Tingyi, a franchise bottler in China. The charges related to this transaction primarily consist of employee-related charges. This amount is large and similar to the Productivity Plan restructuring charges noted above. Thus, we *will* also make adjustments to ROA for these charges.

5. **Pension lump sum settlement charge.** In the fourth quarter of 2012, PepsiCo offered some former employees receiving vested pension payments the option of receiving a one-time lump sum payment, which resulted in this settlement charge. Given the nonrecurring nature of this transaction, we *will* adjust ROA for this charge.

6. **Tax benefit related to tax court decision.** For 2012, this amount reflects a non-cash tax benefit related to a favorable tax court settlement related to how the company classified financial instruments. The nonrecurring nature of this charge supports adjusting reported profitability for this amount. Thus, we *will* adjust ROA for the tax benefit because the amounts are part of a negotiated settlement with taxing authorities, which is inherently unpredictable.

In summary, for 2010–2012, we adjust net income for the last three items listed above (that is, the restructuring charges and the tax benefit). In addition, selective adjustments are made for other items that affected 2010–2011 but did not affect 2012. These disclosures reflect adjustments to "Net income attributable to PepsiCo," which is after the deduction for noncontrolling interest, so our adjustments will need to start with the appropriate level of profitability. In other words, we start with net income attributable to PepsiCo when adding or subtracting the effects of the special items. All adjustments should be net of income tax effects. If firms disclose the income tax effect, we use the reported amounts. Otherwise, we assume that the current marginal federal tax rate applies. It is important to carefully consider the sign of the adjustments in Exhibit 4.4. Income-reducing charges such as impairments and restructuring charges are *added back* to income before income taxes, which is intuitive.

The adjusted ROA for PepsiCo for 2012 is as follows:

$$9.6\% = \frac{\$6,483 + (1 - 0.35)(\$899) + \$36}{0.5(\$74,638 + \$72,882)} = \frac{\$7,103}{\$73,760}$$

We make similar adjustments for impairment and restructuring charges in 2011 and 2010. As shown in Exhibit 4.4, adjusted net income is higher than reported net income for 2012 and 2011, but in 2010 adjusted income is lower than reported net income.

Calculations for both unadjusted and adjusted ROA are shown for all three years in Exhibit 4.5. ROA based on reported net income is 9.2%, 10.0%, and 12.8% in 2012, 2011, and 2010, respectively, while ROA based on adjusted net income is 9.6%, 10.3%, and 12.4%, respectively. Analyzing the time series of PepsiCo's ROA based on

Exhibit 4.4

Adjustments to Reported Net Income for Unusual and Nonrecurring Items for PepsiCo (amounts in millions)

	2012	2011	2010
Net income attributable to PepsiCo	$6,178	$6,443	$6,320
Restructuring and impairment charges ($215 + $176 for 2012)	391	286	—
Pension lump sum settlement charge	131	—	—
Tax benefit related to tax court decision	(217)	—	—
53rd week	—	(64)	—
Inventory fair value adjustments	—	—	333
Gain on previously held equity interests	—	—	(958)
Venezuela currency devaluation	—	—	120
Asset write-off	—	—	92
Foundation contribution	—	—	64
Debt repurchase	—	—	114
Adjusted net income attributable to PepsiCo	$6,483	$6,665	$6,085

reported or adjusted net income, performance in 2012 continues a downward trend from previous years. Refer to the Analysis Spreadsheet in the FSAP model for a five-year time series of these and other ratios computed based on as-reported and adjusted figures (also presented in Appendix C).

Exhibit 4.5

Calculations of Unadjusted and Adjusted ROA for PepsiCo (data for total assets from Appendix C and adjusted net income data from Exhibit 4.4)

	2012	2011	2010
Total assets—beginning of year	$72,882	$68,153	$39,848
Total assets—end of year	74,638	72,882	68,153
Average total assets	73,760	70,518	54,001
Net income attributable to PepsiCo	6,178	6,443	6,320
Adjusted net income attributable to PepsiCo	6,483	6,665	6,085
Interest expense	899	856	903
Net income + (1 − 0.35) × Interest expense	6,798	7,018	6,925
Adjusted net income + (1 − 0.35) × Interest expense	7,103	7,240	6,690
ROA (unadjusted)	9.2%	10.0%	12.8%
ROA (adjusted)	9.6%	10.3%	12.4%

Two Comments on the Calculation of ROA

First, some analysts subtract average non-interest-bearing liabilities (such as accounts payable and accrued liabilities) from average total assets in the denominator of ROA, the argument being that these items are sources of indirect financing. An alternative argument for reducing total assets by non-interest-bearing liabilities is that ROA is better characterized as a return on *invested* capital when items that are not directly invested capital (such as accounts payable) are purged from total assets.

Economics suggests that when liabilities do not provide for *explicit* interest charges, the creditor charges *implicit* interest by adjusting the terms of the contract, such as offering discounts for those who do pay immediately or setting higher prices for those who do not pay immediately. The numerator of the ROA calculation is a measure of income before deducting financing costs; therefore, an alternative approach would be to use total assets in the denominator (i.e., do not subtract non-interest-bearing liabilities) but adjust net income for both explicit and implicit financing costs. Unfortunately, it is quite difficult to reliably estimate the implicit interest charges associated with non-interest-bearing liabilities such as accounts payable and accrued liabilities and to reclassify the implicit increments for financing charges in cost of goods sold and selling, general, and administrative expenses to interest expense (which is added back to net income). Adjusting prefinancing income this way would increase the measure of operating income in the numerator, increasing calculated ROA. (The alternative of reducing the denominator by subtracting non-interest-bearing liabilities from total assets also would increase calculated ROA.) Despite the reasonable arguments for adjusting income in the ROA calculation to account for implicit interest or adjusting total assets for indirectly invested capital, in all but extreme cases such adjustments generally result in only minor changes in time-series or cross-sectional analyses of ROA. Combined with the low degree of precision in estimating such amounts, the examples and problems in this book follow the conventional practice of using average total assets in the denominator of ROA, making no adjustment for non-interest-bearing liabilities.

Second, it is important to note that although we adjusted the numerator of ROA for unusual or nonrecurring items, we did not adjust the denominator. This implicitly assumes the unusual or nonrecurring items are not persistent but that their effects on total assets *are* persistent. For example, consider the restructuring charges that were added back to net income. These impairment charges probably reduced the carrying value of some assets. Our adjustment added back to net income the effect of the charges on the income statement but did not add back the effects of the restructuring charges in the ending balance of total assets, which will be lower because of the write-down. Thus, our adjustment to the numerator (an increase) was coupled with the impact of the unadjusted balance sheet effects in the denominator (a decrease), leading to an upward bias in our calculation of adjusted ROA. The logic behind this seemingly inconsistent treatment is motivated by a desire to compute *sustainable* ROA. The current period restructuring charges should not persist in future periods, but the asset write-downs are permanent (some assets are now worth less or may have been written off entirely); thus, the adjusted ROA provides a better indicator of the ROA we might expect to observe next period even though it is a biased measured of the current period's ROA. Again, our approach reflects conventional practice, but the astute analyst should understand that blindly ignoring negative charges on the income statement but allowing them to affect the balance sheet can affect calculations of adjusted performance. This caveat echoes the cautionary discussion earlier in the chapter regarding the potentially misleading practice of managers emphasizing pro forma earnings.

Disaggregating ROA

You obtain further insight into the behavior of ROA by disaggregating it into profit margin for ROA and total assets turnover (also simply referred to as *assets turnover*) components as follows:

ROA	=	**Profit Margin for ROA**	×	**Assets Turnover**
$\dfrac{\text{Net Income} + \text{Interest Expense (net of taxes)} + \text{Noncontrolling Interest in Earnings}}{\text{Average Total Assets}}$	=	$\dfrac{\text{Net Income} + \text{Interest Expense (net of taxes)} + \text{Noncontrolling Interest in Earnings}}{\text{Sales}}$	×	$\dfrac{\text{Sales}}{\text{Average Total Assets}}$

The profit margin for ROA indicates the ability of a firm to utilize its assets to generate earnings for a particular level of sales.[18] Assets turnover indicates the ability to manage the level of investment in assets for a particular level of sales or, to put it another way, the ability to generate sales from a particular level of investment in assets. The *assets turnover ratio* indicates the firm's *ability to use assets to generate sales*, and the *profit margin for ROA* indicates the firm's *ability to use sales to generate profits*.

The disaggregation of ROA for **PepsiCo** for 2012, after adjusting for nonrecurring items, is as follows:

ROA	=	**Profit Margin for ROA**	×	**Assets Turnover**
$\dfrac{\$7,103}{\$73,760}$	=	$\dfrac{\$7,103}{\$65,492}$	×	$\dfrac{\$65,492}{\$73,760}$
9.6%	=	10.8%	×	0.89

Exhibit 4.6 summarizes ROA, profit margin for ROA, and assets turnover for PepsiCo for 2010–2012. PepsiCo's profit margin for ROA is declining. In addition, PepsiCo has decreased assets turnover. In the next section, we discuss another measure of profitability—return on common shareholders' equity (ROCE). After that discussion, we explore the economic and strategic factors underlying both measures of profitability.

Exhibit 4.6			
ROA, Profit Margin, and Assets Turnover for PepsiCo: 2010–2012 (adjusted data)			
	2012	**2011**	**2010**
ROA	9.6%	10.3%	12.4%
Profit Margin for ROA	10.8%	11.0%	11.6%
Assets Turnover	0.89	0.93	1.07

---

[18]One might argue that you should use total *revenues*, not just *sales*, in the denominator because assets generate returns in forms other than sales (for example, interest revenue and equity in earnings of affiliates). However, interpretations of various expense ratios (discussed later in this chapter) are usually easier when we use sales in the denominator, and it is generally easier to separately analyze the returns from other revenues.

■ Return on assets (ROA) is an overall measure of the profitability of a firm and is unaffected by the way in which a firm is financed.

■ The numerator of ROA is the level of profits before deducting financing costs but after deducting taxes (exclusive of the tax benefit of debt financing).

■ ROA can be computed based on the profits reported by a company, or it can be adjusted to

exclude the effects of unusual or nonrecurring items, so that the computation yields a better measure of the core operations of the company.

■ ROA can be disaggregated into profit margin for ROA and assets turnover, which provide insight into the sources of a company's overall profitability.

Quick Check

Return on Common Shareholders' Equity (ROCE)

LO 4-3

Analyze and interpret the return on common shareholders' equity (ROCE), including the conditions when a firm successfully uses financial leverage to increase the return to common shareholders.

ROA measures the profitability of operations *before* considering the effects of financing. That is, ROA ignores the proportion of debt versus equity financing that a firm uses to finance the assets. ROA is important for analysts interested in the profitability and efficiency of the firm's core operations.

Return on common equity (ROCE), on the other hand, measures the return to common shareholders after subtracting from revenues not only operating expenses (such as cost of goods sold, selling and administration expenses, and income taxes) but also the costs of financing debt and preferred stock.[19] The latter includes interest expense on debt and required dividends on preferred stock (if any). Thus, ROCE incorporates the results of a firm's operating, investing, *and financing* decisions. When we talk about valuation in later chapters, the perspective of ROA maps into the valuation of cash flows or earnings to all investors, whereas ROCE maps into the valuation of cash flows or earnings to equity investors. You calculate ROCE as follows:

$$\text{ROCE} = \frac{\text{Net Income} - \text{Noncontrolling Interest in Earnings} - \text{Preferred Stock Dividends}}{\text{Average Common Shareholders' Equity}}$$

The numerator measures the amount of net income for the period available to the common shareholders after subtracting all amounts allocable to noncontrolling interests and preferred shareholders. The accountant subtracts interest expense on debt in measuring net income, so the calculation of the numerator of ROCE requires no adjustment for creditors' claims on earnings. However, you must subtract dividends paid or payable on preferred stock from net income to obtain income attributable to the common shareholders.[20]

The denominator of ROCE measures the average amount of total common shareholders' equity in use during the period. An average of the total common shareholders'

---

[19]Some analysts use the acronym ROCE to refer to "return on capital employed." The numerator of return on capital employed is net income before interest expense (net of tax savings) on long-term debt. The denominator is the average amount of long-term debt and shareholders' equity during the year. The rate of return on capital employed generally falls between ROA and ROCE as we have defined these ratios. We do not use return on capital employed in this book, but it is important to realize the confusion that blind adherence to acronyms can cause. Indeed, use of ROE is probably more common than ROCE, but we use the latter to emphasize that the construct we want is return on *common* shareholders' equity.

[20]Chapter 14 indicates that for purposes of valuation, you might instead compute ROCE using comprehensive income available to common shareholders, not net income available to common shareholders.

equity at the beginning and end of the year is appropriate unless a firm made a significant new common stock issue or buyback during the year. If the latter occurred, you should use an average of the common shareholders' equity at the end of each quarter to better reflect the outstanding common shareholders' equity during the year.

Common shareholders' equity equals total shareholders' equity minus the noncontrolling interest in the net assets of consolidated subsidiaries minus the par value of preferred stock. Because net income to common shareholders in the numerator reflects a subtraction for the noncontrolling interest in earnings of consolidated subsidiaries, the denominator should exclude the noncontrolling interest in net assets (if any). Firms seldom issue preferred stock significantly above par value, so you can assume that the amount in the additional paid-in capital account relates to common stock.

PepsiCo reports preferred stock outstanding. Also, PepsiCo reports a small noncontrolling interest in its income statement and balance sheet. The calculation of the ROCE of PepsiCo for 2012, using the *reported* amounts of net income, which is shown on the "Analysis Spreadsheet" of FSAP, is as follows (in millions):

$$\text{ROCE} = \frac{\text{Net Income} - \text{Preferred Stock Dividends}}{\text{Average Common Shareholders' Equity}}$$

$$28.5\% = \frac{\$6,214 - \$36 - \$7}{0.5(\$22,399 + \$20,899)}$$

The calculation of the ROCE of PepsiCo for 2012, using the *adjusted* amounts of net income discussed previously and displayed in Exhibit 4.4, is as follows (in millions):

$$\text{ROCE} = \frac{\text{Adjusted Net Income Attributable to PepsiCo} - \text{Preferred Stock Dividends}}{\text{Average Common Shareholders' Equity}}$$

$$29.9\% = \frac{\$6,483 - \$7}{0.5(\$22,399 + \$20,899)}$$

The amount for preferred stock dividends appears in Note 11, "Net Income per Common Share from Continuing Operations" (Appendix A).[21] For purposes of our analysis of PepsiCo in this chapter, we demonstrate how to calculate net income available to common shareholders using the full preferred stock dividends, including a redemption premium.[22] Adjusting reported net income for the preferred stock dividends and redemption premium, the ROCE of PepsiCo was 30.4% in 2011 and 32.5% in 2010, consistent with the downward trend in ROA discussed earlier in the chapter.

---

[21]The $7 million amount for preferred dividends in the numerator is actually a preferred dividend of $1 million and a redemption premium on preferred stock of $6 million. The SEC requires firms that redeem preferred stock for more than its book, or carrying, value to subtract the excess from net income when computing net income available to common shareholders in the computation of earnings per share. See Securities and Exchange Commission, *EITF Abstracts*, Topic No. D 42, "The Effect on the Calculation of Earnings per Share for the Redemption or Induced Conversion of Preferred Stock" (1994); *FASB Codification Topic 260*. To maintain consistency in the calculation of ROCE and earnings per share, we subtract the redemption premium in the numerator of both ratios. Analysts will likely encounter such redemption premiums infrequently.

[22]However, users of FSAP should note that due to the rarity of this item and its relative immateriality, FSAP follows the standard approach of adjusting only for the preferred stock dividend and treats the redemption premium as other expense. The alternative exposition in the chapter is intended to highlight the judgment required when analyzing financial statements, particularly when firms engage in unusual or nonrecurring transactions.

Benchmarks for ROCE

Having computed ROCE for **PepsiCo** of 28.5% (as reported) or 29.9% (adjusted) for 2012, is this is "good" or "bad" performance? One benchmark is the average ROCE of other firms (recall Appendix D includes benchmarking data for many ratios across 48 industries). The average ROCE for the cross-section of publicly traded firms in the United States is approximately 10%–12%, so PepsiCo is well above the average ROCE; hence, its current ROCE is certainly "good" by this benchmark.[23] Also, the ROCE of a similar firm such as **Coca-Cola** can serve as a benchmark. For 2012, Coca-Cola had an ROCE of 27.7%, so PepsiCo generated a slightly higher ROCE than Coca-Cola.

A more direct benchmark against which to judge ROCE is the return demanded by common shareholders for a firm's use of their capital. Because common shareholders are the residual claimants of the firm, accountants do not treat the cost of common shareholders' equity capital as an expense when computing net income. On the other hand, a firm that generates ROCE less than the cost of common equity capital destroys value for shareholders, whereas a firm that generates ROCE in excess of the cost of capital creates value. ROCE measures the return to the common shareholders but does not indicate whether this rate of return exceeds or falls short of the cost of common equity capital.

To illustrate, PepsiCo's ROCE for 2012 as computed above is 29.9%. Chapter 11 provides a discussion of how to compute the cost of equity capital. In that chapter, the cost of equity capital for PepsiCo is estimated to be 7.5%. Based on this cost of common equity capital, PepsiCo generated an excess return of 22.4% (29.9% – 7.5%). If the cost of common equity capital would have been, for example, 40% (which is an unreasonable premise), PepsiCo would not have generated a return sufficient to cover the cost of common equity capital.

Conceptually, the cost of common equity capital is the rate of return the common shareholders demand as compensation for sacrificing consumption of their investment in other ways and for bearing the risk of investing in a particular firm. Measuring the cost of common equity capital is more difficult than measuring the cost of debt, because debt instruments typically specify an interest rate and effective interest rates can be easily determined. The dividend on common stock is not an accurate measure of the cost of common equity capital because managers and boards of directors determine dividend payout policies, whereas equity investors determine the cost of equity capital.

The importance of ROCE is highlighted by its central use in assessing profitability and estimating firm value. As will be shown later in Chapter 13, a measure known as *residual income* (also called *abnormal earnings*) quantifies the profits earned by a company after deducting a charge for the cost of equity capital, calculated as follows:

Residual Income = Net Income Available to Common Shareholders − (Cost of Equity Capital × Beginning Common Shareholders' Equity)

Residual income is a measure of the wealth a firm generates for its common shareholders in a period beyond the required return on their investment in the firm. In recent years, the financial press and some corporate managers have given considerable attention to similar measures of profits after deducting a charge for the use of capital.[24] The concept behind these refined measures of profits is that a firm does not create value

---

[23]Average ROCEs depend on many factors, including the period of measurement, samples of firms used, and definitions of accounting data used in the numerator and denominator of the ROCE calculation.

[24]For example, various consulting firms promote similar measures such as Stern Stewart's *economic value added* (EVA)®, HOLT Value Associates' *cash flow return on investment* (CFROI), L.E.K. Consulting's *shareholder value added* (SVA), Marakon's *discounted economic profits* (EP), and KPMG's *economic value management* (EVM).

Exhibit 4.7

Evolution of Future ROCE Conditional on Current ROCE

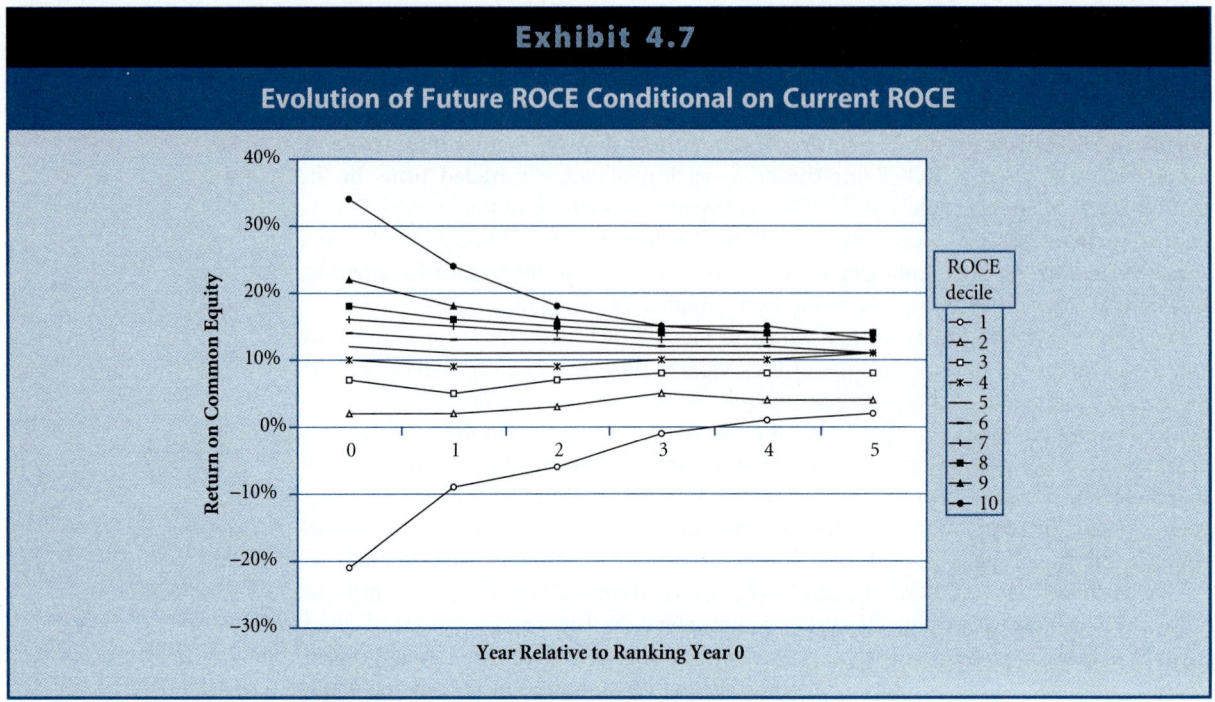

unless it earns more than the cost of all of its capital, including common shareholders' equity capital. The intuition under this approach is that valuations are higher as firms generate future ROCE higher than the cost of equity capital. Thus, the benchmark for ROCE that will be most useful in the remainder of this text is the cost of equity capital.

In addition, it is helpful to see how ROCE is subject to the same life cycle and competitive pressures discussed earlier in the chapter. For example, Exhibit 4.7 plots the results from a study of the behavior of ROCE across time.[25] It partitioned firms into deciles based on beginning ROCE and then tracked the average ROCE for each decile over subsequent years. The graph indicates that the initial spread in ROCE is very large, with the most profitable firms generating ROCEs in excess of 30% and the least profitable firms generating returns below negative 20%. However, competitive pressures erode the abnormally high ROCEs of the most profitable firms, and survival (or bankruptcy or an acquisition) results in the poorest performing firms increasing ROCE to positive levels. This does not imply that all firms with above-average ROCEs will realize lower ROCEs in the future, but it is the dominant pattern. A few companies with sustainable strategic advantages and/or substantial off-balance-sheet assets and equity (such as PepsiCo's valuable brand names) can generate ROCEs well above the average for an extended numbers of years.

Relating ROA to ROCE

ROA measures operating performance independent of financing, while ROCE explicitly considers the cost of debt and preferred stock financing. Exhibit 4.1 diagrams the relation between ROA and ROCE and shows that both can be broken down into margin,

---

[25]See Victor L. Bernard, "Accounting-Based Valuation Methods, Determinants of Market-to-Book Ratios, and Implications for Financial Statement Analysis." Unpublished manuscript, University of Michigan Business School, Kresge Library (January 1994).

turnover, and leverage (although differences are highlighted with dashed lines). An expanded diagram of the relation between ROA and ROCE is as follows:[26]

Return on Assets		**Return to Creditors**	**Return to Preferred Shareholders**	**Return to Common Shareholders**
Net Income + Interest Expense Net of Taxes	→	Interest Expense Net of Taxes	Preferred Dividends	Net Income to Common
——————		——————	——————	——————
Average Total Assets		Average Total Liabilities	Average Preferred Shareholders' Equity	Average Common Shareholders' Equity

This diagram allocates each dollar of pre-financing earnings to the various providers of capital. Creditors receive their return first in the form of interest payments. The cost of this capital to the firm is interest expense net of the income tax benefit derived from deducting interest in calculating taxable income. Many liabilities, such as accounts payable and salaries payable, carry no explicit interest cost.

Preferred stock carries a cost equal to the preferred dividend amount. Historically, firms could not deduct preferred dividends when calculating taxable income, but in recent years, some firms have been successful in structuring preferred stock issues so that they qualify for tax deductibility of dividends paid. In those cases, you should adjust preferred dividends for the related tax savings.

The portion of net income that is *not* allocated to creditors or preferred shareholders is available for the common shareholders, who are the residual claimants. Likewise, the portion of a firm's assets not financed with capital provided by creditors or preferred shareholders represents the capital provided by the common shareholders.[27]

Now consider the relation between ROA and ROCE.

- Under what circumstances will ROCE exceed ROA?
- Under what circumstances will ROCE be less than ROA?

The key to answering those questions lies in understanding how the use of financing from sources other than common shareholders can harm or benefit common shareholders.

ROCE will exceed ROA whenever ROA exceeds the cost of capital provided by creditors and preferred shareholders. Alternatively stated, if common equity holders can rely on lower-cost financing by creditors and preferred shareholders, and use that capital to generate higher rates of return, then they have leveraged such financing for assets that produce a return sufficiently high to pay interest and preferred stock dividends and yield an excess return, which then belongs to the common shareholders.

Common business terminology refers to the practice of using lower-cost creditor and preferred stock capital to increase the return to common shareholders as *financial leverage* or *capital structure leverage*. To clarify the concept, consider the two scenarios shown in Exhibit 4.8.

Under Scenario 1 in Exhibit 4.8, the firm has one common equity investor who invests $100 to fund a firm that generates an ROA of 10%. At the end of the year, income available to the common equity investor is $10, reflecting the ROA and ROCE of 10% ($10 income ÷ $100 investment). Alternatively, in Scenario 2 the single equity investor

---

[26]Note that the relation does not appear as an equation. We use an arrow instead of an equal sign to indicate that the return on assets gets allocated to the various suppliers of capital. To accurately express the relation as an equality, you would need to know the weights of each source of financing in the capital structure.

[27]If a firm does not own 100% of the common stock of a consolidated subsidiary, the accountant must allocate a portion of the ROA to the noncontrolling shareholders. For such firms (including PepsiCo) a fourth term would appear on the right side of the arrow: noncontrolling interest in earnings/average noncontrolling interest in net assets.

Exhibit 4.8

ROCE: Example of How Equity Investors Strategically Use Leverage to Their Returns on Investment

	Scenario 1	Scenario 2
Equity investment	$ 100	$ 10
Debt financing	0	90
Total assets	$ 100	$ 100
ROA	10%	10%
After-tax cost of financing		5%
Net income available to equity:		
Scenario 1 (10% × $100)	$10.00	
Scenario 2 [$10 – ($90 × 5%)]		$5.50
ROCE:		
Scenario 1 ($10 ÷ $100)	10%	
Scenario 2 ($5.50 ÷ $10)		55%

could have invested only $10 and borrowed $90 to have the same amount to invest ($100) and generate the same return (10%). Suppose creditors provide the $90 loan at an after-tax interest cost to the firm of 5%. At the end of the year, the firm would have generated the same income of $10, but the after-tax cost of financing would be $4.50 ($90 debt × 5%), leaving income available to the common shareholder of $5.50. *Although the net income is lower in Scenario 2, the ROCE is 55%, much higher, reflecting the strategic use of leverage by the equity investor.* A much smaller investment of $10 (rather than $100) combined with debt financing of $90 enables the common equity investor to realize a substantially higher rate of return. In this case, rather than a 10% return on equity, the equity investor would have realized a 55% return on equity ($5.50 income ÷ $10 investment). This example demonstrates the advantages of the strategic use of financial leverage to increase returns to equity investors; deploying assets that generate 10% but partially financing them with capital that costs only 5% generates "abnormal" returns. At the same time, increased leverage triggers greater risk, which we will discuss in Chapter 5.

Consider our analysis of **PepsiCo**, which generated an adjusted ROA of 9.6% during 2012. The after-tax cost of capital provided by creditors during 2012 was 1.1% [(1 − 0.35)($899)/0.5($52,239 + $51,983)].[28] The difference between the 1.1% cost of creditor capital and the 9.6% ROA generated on assets financed with debt capital belongs to the common shareholders. In other words, PepsiCo has approximately $52 billion in assets financed at a cost of 1.1% (or approximately $584 million), but these assets generate a return of 9.6% (or approximately $5 billion).

PepsiCo's financial leverage worked to the advantage of its common shareholders from 2010 through 2012 because its ROA exceeded the cost of all non-common equity financing. This resulted in ROCE exceeding ROA in every year: 2010: 31.2%>12.4%; 2011: 31.4%>10.3%; and 2012: 29.9%>9.6%. Next, we explore the possible reasons for the superior returns generated for equity investors when ROCE exceeds ROA.

---

[28]The amounts in the denominator for PepsiCo equal total assets minus total shareholders' equity, or equivalently, total liabilities. The after-tax cost of creditor capital seems low, but recall that many liabilities do not carry an explicit interest cost.

Disaggregating ROCE

We can disaggregate ROCE into several components to aid in its interpretation, just like we did with ROA. The disaggregated components of ROCE are profit margin for ROCE, assets turnover, and capital structure leverage.

ROCE	=	Profit Margin for ROCE	×	Assets Turnover	×	Capital Structure Leverage

$$\frac{\text{Net Income Available to Common Shareholders}}{\text{Average Common Shareholders' Equity}} = \frac{\text{Net Income Available to Common Shareholders}}{\text{Sales}} \times \frac{\text{Sales}}{\text{Average Total Assets}} \times \frac{\text{Average Total Assets}}{\text{Average Common Shareholders' Equity}}$$

Note that the first distinction between profit margin for ROA and profit margin for ROCE is the different numerator used. The numerator of profit margin for ROCE is net income available to common shareholders, and the numerator for profit margin for ROA is net income with after-tax interest expense and noncontrolling interest added back, which yields a measure of profits before deducting financing costs. The different numerators are aligned with the different denominators (common equity for ROCE and total assets for ROA).

Assets turnover is identical to that used to disaggregate ROA. The additional component in the disaggregation of ROCE is the capital structure leverage ratio, which measures the degree to which a firm strategically utilizes financial leverage to finance assets. The difference between the numerator and the denominator of the capital structure leverage ratio is the amount of liabilities (and preferred shareholders' equity, if any) in the capital structure. The larger the amount of capital obtained from these sources, the smaller the amount of capital obtained from common shareholders and therefore the larger the capital structure leverage ratio. Another way to interpret the capital structure leverage ratio is as follows:

$$\frac{\text{Total Assets}}{\text{Common Shareholders' Equity}} = \frac{\text{Debt} + \text{Preferred Equity} + \text{Common Shareholders' Equity}}{\text{Common Shareholders' Equity}} = 1 + \frac{\text{Debt} + \text{Preferred Equity}}{\text{Common Shareholders' Equity}}$$

Thus, capital structure leverage is simply one plus the debt-to-equity ratio for a firm with no preferred stock or one plus the ratio of debt plus preferred equity to common shareholder equity for a firm with preferred stock.

Before proceeding with a disaggregation of **PepsiCo**'s ROCE, we note that there are many more ways to disaggregate ROA or ROCE than are discussed in this chapter. We will explore one alternative method of decomposing ROCE in the next chapter, which highlights the importance of benchmarking returns generated by the firm's assets against the cost of borrowing from creditors. The disaggregation of ROCE for PepsiCo for 2012 under the basic decomposition discussed in this chapter is as follows:

ROCE	=	Profit Margin for ROCE	×	Assets Turnover	×	Capital Structure Leverage
$\dfrac{\$6,483 - 7}{0.5(\$22,399 + \$20,899)}$	=	$\dfrac{\$6,483 - 7}{\$65,492}$	×	$\dfrac{\$65,492}{0.5(\$74,638 + \$72,882)}$	×	$\dfrac{0.5(\$74,638 + \$72,882)}{0.5(\$22,399 + \$20,899)}$
29.9%	=	9.9%	×	0.89	×	3.41

Exhibit 4.9 presents the disaggregation of ROCE of PepsiCo for 2010–2012. The increasing ROCE of PepsiCo results from the net effect of (1) decreasing profit margins, (2) decreasing assets turnover, and (3) an increase in capital structure leverage. The decreasing profit margin for ROCE mirrors that discussed previously for ROA. The calculation of assets turnover is the same in the decomposition of ROA and ROCE, so it

Exhibit 4.9

Disaggregation of ROCE of PepsiCo: 2010–2012

	ROCE	=	Profit Margin for ROCE	=	Total Assets Turnover	=	Capital Structure Leverage
2012	29.9%	=	9.9%	×	0.888	×	3.407
2011*	31.4%	=	10.1%	×	0.934	×	3.328
2010	31.2%	=	10.5%	×	1.071	×	2.775

*For 2011, calculations use sales adjusted for the $623 million and net income adjusted for $64 million reflecting the impact of the 53rd week, in addition to the adjustments discussed previously (see "Items Affecting Comparability" in PepsiCo's MD&A).

also mirrors the previous discussion about the decomposition of ROA. The primary difference between the ROA and ROCE decompositions is the capital structure leverage component. We must examine changes in PepsiCo's capital structure by examining changes in each source of financing. The change in preferred equity on the balance sheet is minimal, so it cannot explain the increased leverage. (See Appendix A.) The balance sheet does indicate a small change in total liabilities (which increased from $51,983 million in 2011 to $52,239 million in 2012) and common shareholders' equity (which increased from $20,899 million to $22,399 million).

The profit margin for ROCE and total assets turnover have both been steadily declining each year, while capital structure leverage has been increasing. Companies rarely discuss profit margin for ROCE or total assets turnover directly, but you may glean insight by reading explanations for changes in profits and balance sheet items in the MD&A. PepsiCo describes the decline in operating profit margin in 2012 as reflecting "cost increases reflecting strategic investments, higher commodity costs, higher advertising and marketing expenses, and unfavorable foreign currency exchanges, partially offset by effective net pricing." Additionally, profit margin for ROCE is negatively affected by increased interest expense associated with the increased level of borrowings.

We can gain insight into the change in total assets turnover by examining relative changes in sales (the numerator) and total assets (the denominator). For 2012, sales declined 0.6% (adjusting sales for the 53rd week in 2011) while total assets increased 2.4%. The declining numerator and increasing denominator led to a decline in the overall total assets turnover.

Above we noted that interest expense negatively affected margin, driven by increasing debt levels. The statement of cash flows and Note 9, "Debt Obligations and Commitments" indicate that PepsiCo has been issuing more long-term debt than it is repaying for each year. For example, in 2012, PepsiCo issued $5.999 billion of long-term debt, but repaid only $2.449 billion. These increases in leverage are described as being used for "general corporate purposes."

Quick Check

- Return on common shareholders' equity (ROCE) is a measure of the profitability of common shareholder investment in a firm, after deducting all costs of financing from other sources (such as debt, preferred equity, and noncontrolling interests).

- Like ROA, ROCE can be disaggregated into components to reveal insight into the sources of profitability for common shareholders.
- ROCE can be disaggregated into profit margin for ROCE, assets turnover, and leverage.

Economic and Strategic Factors in the Interpretation of ROA and ROCE[29]

LO 4-4

Link the effects of economic and strategic factors to the interpretation of ROA and ROCE.

ROA and ROCE differ across industries depending on their economic characteristics and across firms within an industry depending on the design and implementation of their strategies. This section explores economic and strategic factors that impact the interpretation of the margin and turnover components of ROA and ROCE. *We defer additional discussion of the leverage component of ROCE to Chapter 5.* Exhibit 4.10 depicts graphically the 15-year average of the median annual ROAs, profit margins for ROA, and assets turnovers of 23 industries for 1990–2004. The two *isoquants* reflect ROAs of 3% and 6%. The isoquants show the various combinations of profit margin for ROA and assets turnover that yield an ROA of 3% and 6%. For instance, an ROA of 6% results from any of the following profit margins for ROA × assets turnover combinations: 6% × 1.0, 3% × 2.0, 2% × 3.0, 1% × 6.0.

Financial statement analysis focuses on the ROAs of specific firms (or even segments of specific firms) for particular years (or even quarters). The data for ROA, profit margin for ROA, and assets turnover underlying the plots in Exhibit 4.10 reflect aggregated amounts across firms within industries and across years. What factors

Exhibit 4.10

Median ROA, Profit Margin for ROA, and Assets Turnover for 23 Industries for 1990–2004

[Scatter plot: x-axis "Assets Turnover" ranging 0.0 to 3.0; y-axis "Profit Margin for ROA" ranging 0% to 14%. Two isoquant curves labeled ROA=3% and ROA=6%. Industries plotted: Utilities, Oil & Gas Extraction, Hotels, Petroleum, Paper, Printing & Publishing, Personal Services, Amusements, Agricultural Production, Health Services, Lumber, Food Products, Retailing–Apparel, Metals, Transportation Equipment, Retailing–General Merchandise, Airlines, Communications, Restaurants, Wholesalers–Durables, Industrial Equipment, Wholesalers–Nondurables, Grocery Stores.]

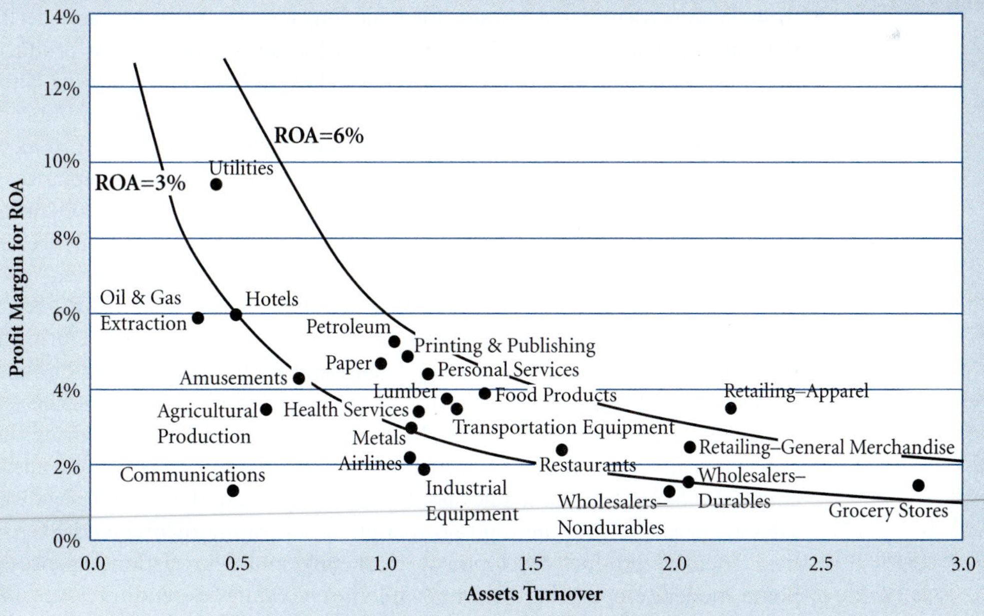

[29]The material in this section draws heavily from Thomas I. Selling and Clyde P. Stickney, "The Effects of Business Environments and Strategy on a Firm's Rate of Return on Assets," *Financial Analysts Journal* (January/February 1989), pp. 43–52.

explain the consistently high or consistently low ROAs of some industries relative to the average of all industries? Further, what explains the fact that certain industries have high profit margins and low assets turnovers while other industries experience low profit margins and high assets turnovers?

The microeconomics and business strategy literature provides useful background for interpreting the behavior of ROA, profit margin, and assets turnover. As a prelude to the discussion that follows, consider the two extreme industries in Exhibit 4.10. Utilities show the highest profit margins, which can be explained by significant barriers to entry (both regulatory and enormous fixed costs). Barriers to entry in this industry permit existing firms to realize higher profit margins due to limited competition, and turnover is lower because of the large asset base required, such as power generation plants and distribution networks. On the other hand, grocery stores show the highest assets turnover. Given lower barriers to entry and significant competition, the firms in this industry survive on the ability to run efficient operations and generate substantial assets turnover, consistent with the perpetual efforts by such companies to generate foot traffic through ever-changing sales and promotions.

Economic theory suggests that higher levels of perceived risk in any activity should lead to higher levels of expected return if that activity is to attract capital from investors. ROAs based on reported financial statement data provide useful information for tracking the past periodic performance of a firm and its segments (realized ROA) and for developing expectations about future earnings potential (expected ROA). Elements of risk can cause realized ROA to diverge from expected ROA. We briefly discuss three elements of risk that are useful in understanding differences in ROAs across firms and changes over time: (1) product life cycles, (2) operating leverage, and (3) cyclicality of sales.

Product Life Cycle. An element of risk that affects ROA relates to the stage and length of a firm's product life cycle, a concept discussed in Chapter 3. Products move through four identifiable phases: introduction, growth, maturity, and decline. During the introduction and growth phases, a firm focuses on developing products (product R&D spending) and building capacity (capital spending). The objective is to gain market acceptance, productive capacity, and market share. Considerable uncertainty may exist during these phases regarding the market viability of a firm's products. Products that have survived into the maturity phase have gained market acceptance. Also, firms have probably been able to cut back capital expenditures on new operating capacity. During the maturity phase, however, competition becomes more intense and the emphasis shifts to reducing costs through improved capacity utilization (economies of scale) and more efficient production (process R&D spending aimed at reducing manufacturing costs through better utilization of labor and materials). During the decline phase, firms exit the industry as sales decline and profit opportunities diminish.

Exhibit 4.11 depicts the behavior of revenues, operating income, investment, and ROA that corresponds to the four phases of the product life cycle. During the introduction and early growth phases, expenditures on product development and marketing, coupled with relatively low sales levels, lead to operating losses and negative ROAs. As sales accelerate during the high-growth phase, operating income and ROAs turn positive. Extensive product development, marketing, and depreciation expenses during this phase moderate operating income, while heavy capital expenditures to build capacity for expected higher future sales increase the denominator of ROA. Thus, ROA does not grow as rapidly as sales. ROA increases significantly during the maturity phase due to benefits of economies of scale and learning curve phenomena and to curtailments of capital expenditures. ROA deteriorates during the decline phase as operating income decreases, but ROA may remain positive or even increase for some time into this phase

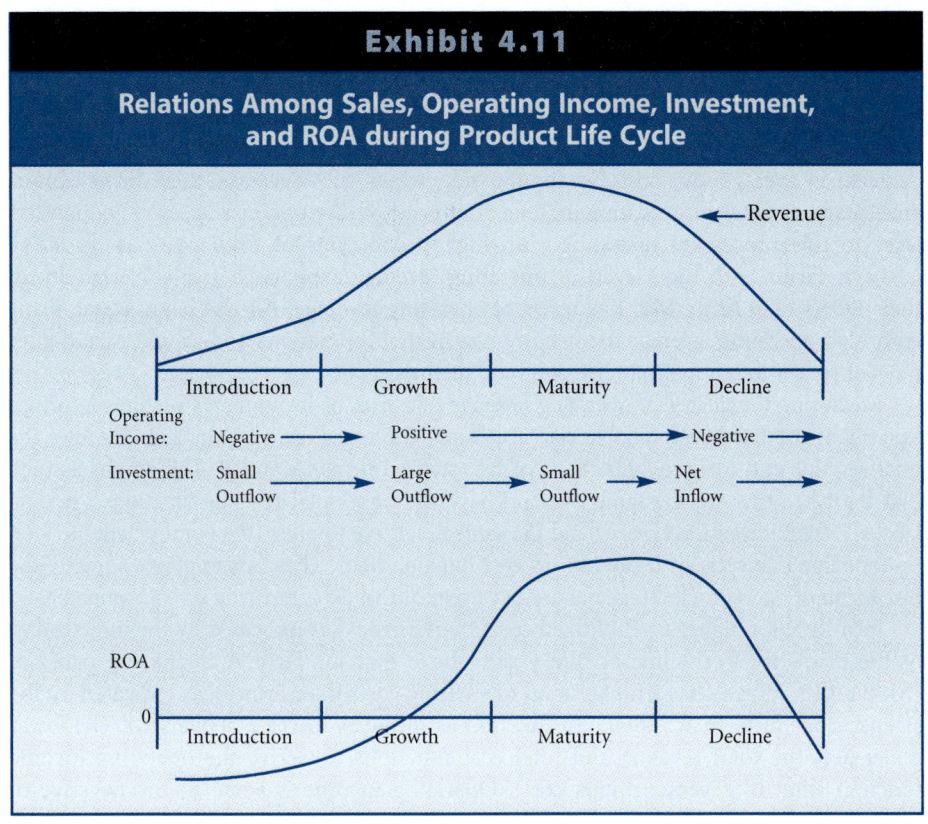

Exhibit 4.11

Relations Among Sales, Operating Income, Investment, and ROA during Product Life Cycle

(particularly if the depreciable assets have been largely depreciated). This movement in ROA appears negatively correlated with the level of risk. Risks are probably greatest in the introduction and growth stages, when ROA is low or negative, and least in the maturity phase, when ROA is high.

Note that the product life cycle theory focuses on individual products. We can extend the theory to an industry level by examining the average stage in the product life cycle of all products in that industry. For instance, products in the computer industry range from the introduction to the decline phases, but the overall industry is probably in the latter part of the high-growth phase. The beverage and food-processing industries, the primary markets of **PepsiCo**, are mature, although PepsiCo and its competitors continually introduce new products. We might view the steel industry, at least in the United States, as in the early decline phase, although some companies have modernized production sufficiently to stave off the decline.

In addition to the stage in the product life cycle, the length of the product life cycle also is an element of risk. Products with short product life cycles require more frequent expenditures to develop replacement or new products, thereby increasing risks. The product life cycles of most computer products run just a few years. Most pharmaceutical products experience product life cycles of approximately seven years. In contrast, the life cycles of PepsiCo's soft drinks, branded food products, and some toys (for example, Barbie® dolls and Matchbox® cars) are much longer.

Operating Leverage. Firms operate with different mixtures of fixed and variable costs in their cost structures. Firms in the utilities, communications, hotel, petroleum, and chemical industries are capital-intensive. Depreciation and many operating costs are more or less fixed for any given period. Most retailers and wholesalers, on the other hand, have high proportions of variable costs in their cost structures. Firms with high proportions of fixed costs experience significant increases in operating income as sales increase, a phenomenon known as *economies of scale.* The increased income occurs because the firms spread fixed costs over a larger number of units sold, resulting in a decrease in average unit cost. On the flip side, when sales decrease, these firms experience sharp declines in operating income, the result of *diseconomies of scale.* Economists refer to this process of operating with high proportions of fixed costs as *operating leverage.* Firms with high levels of operating leverage experience greater variability in their ROAs than firms with low levels of operating leverage. All else being equal, firms with high operating leverage incur more risk in their operations and should earn higher rates of return to compensate investors for such risk.

Measuring the degree of operating leverage of a firm or its segments requires information about the fixed and variable cost structure. The top panel of Exhibit 4.12 shows the total revenue and total cost functions of two stylized firms, A and B. The graphs assume that the two firms are the same size and have the same total revenue functions (the line labeled "Total Revenue: A or B") and the same break-even points (the point where the total revenue line intersects with each firm's cost function line). These assumptions simplify the discussion of operating leverage but are not necessary when comparing actual companies.

Firm B has a higher level of fixed costs than Firm A, as indicated by the intersection of the firm's total cost line on the y-axis above that for Firm A in the top panel of Exhibit 4.12. Firm A has a higher level of variable costs than Firm B, as indicated by the steeper slope of Firm A's total cost function as revenues increase above zero. The lower panel nets the total revenue and total cost functions to derive the operating income function (that is, revenue minus cost). Operating income is equal to the negative of fixed costs when revenues are zero and operating income is zero at when revenues equal the sum of fixed and variable costs (that is, at breakeven). We use the slope of the

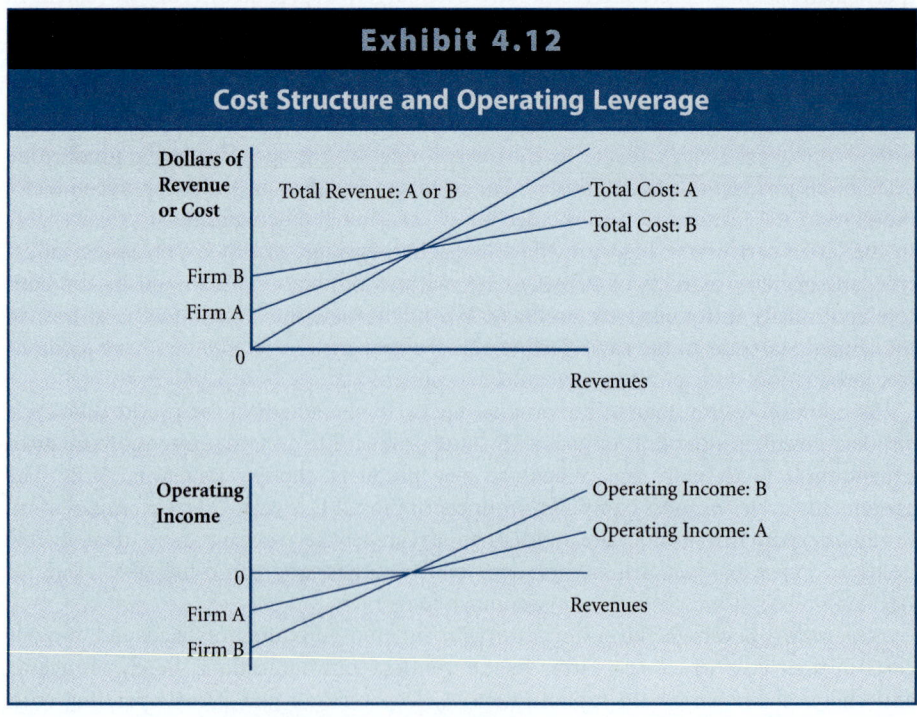

Exhibit 4.12

Cost Structure and Operating Leverage

operating income line as a measure of the extent of operating leverage. Firm B, with its higher fixed costs and lower variable-cost mix, has more operating leverage. As revenues increase, its operating income increases more rapidly than that of Firm A. On the downside, however, income decreases more rapidly for Firm B as revenues decrease.

Unfortunately, firms do not publicly disclose information about their fixed and variable cost structures. To examine the influence of operating leverage on the behavior of ROA for a particular firm or its segments, you must estimate the fixed versus variable cost structure. One approach to such estimation is to study the various cost items of a firm and attempt to identify those that are likely to behave as fixed costs. Firms incur some costs in particular amounts, referred to as *committed fixed costs,* regardless of the actual level of activity during the period. Examples include depreciation, amortization, and rent. Firms can alter the amount of other costs, referred to as *discretionary fixed costs,* in the short run in response to operating conditions, but in general, these costs do not vary directly with the level of activity. Examples include research and development, maintenance, advertising, and central corporate staff expenses. Whether you should classify these latter costs as fixed costs or as variable costs in measuring operating leverage depends on their behavior in a particular firm. Given sufficient time-series data, you could estimate the level of fixed costs by estimating a regression of an operating expense on a variable that drives the variable component of the operating expense. For example, to estimate the fixed component of cost of goods sold, you could estimate the following regression:

$$\text{Cost of Goods Sold}_t = \alpha + \beta * \text{Sales}_t + \varepsilon_t$$

The estimated intercept, α, would be your best estimate of the fixed component of cost of goods sold, and β would be the estimate of the variable component (as a percentage of sales). Although ideal in theory, you need to use data from past quarters or years, which likely become outdated as the firm changes its strategy and operating structure. As an example of a simpler approach for assessing the relative contribution of fixed versus variable costs—continuing with the cost of goods sold example—you can test for the existence of significant fixed costs by examining the *percent change in cost of goods sold relative to the percent change in sales.* Firms with substantial fixed costs will behave like Firm B in Exhibit 4.12 and show percentage changes in cost of goods sold that are less than the percentage changes in sales. (Chapter 10 provides more discussion of how to estimate fixed versus variable costs and use that information in forecasting future expenses and income.)

Cyclicality of Sales. The sales of certain goods and services are particularly sensitive to conditions in the economy. Examples include construction services, industrial equipment, computers, automobiles, and other durable goods. When the economy is in an upswing (healthy GNP growth, low unemployment, and low interest rates), customers purchase these relatively high-priced items, and sales of these firms grow accordingly. On the other hand, when the economy enters a recession, customers curtail their purchases, and the sales of these firms decrease significantly. Contrast these cyclical sales patterns with those of grocery stores, food processors, nonfashion clothing, and electric utilities. Those industries sell products that most consumers consider necessities. Also, their products tend to carry lower per-unit costs, reducing the benefits of delaying purchases to realize cost savings. Firms with cyclical sales patterns incur more risk than firms with noncyclical sales.

One means of reducing the risk inherent in cyclical sales is to strive for a high proportion of variable cost in the cost structure. Examples of variable-cost strategies include paying employees an hourly wage instead of a fixed salary and renting buildings and equipment under short-term cancelable leases instead of purchasing them. Cost levels should change proportionally with sales, thereby maintaining stable profit margin percentages and reducing risk. Of course, this depends on whether the firm can make timely adjustments to cost structures in response to changes in demand, such as the ability to furlough workers or return leased equipment to lessors.

The nature of the activities of some firms is such that they must carry high levels of fixed costs (that is, operating leverage). Examples include capital-intensive service firms such as airlines and railroads. Firms in these industries may attempt to transform the cost of their physical capacity from a fixed cost to a variable cost by engaging in short-term leases or outsourcing. However, lessors then bear the risk of cyclical sales and demand higher returns (referred to by economists as *rents*). Thus, some firms are especially risky because they bear a combination of operating leverage and cyclical sales risk. A noncyclical sales pattern can compensate for high operating leverage and effectively neutralize this element of risk. Electric utilities, for example, carry high levels of fixed costs. However, their dominant positions in most service areas reduce their operating risks and permit them to achieve stable profitability.

Trade-Offs between Profit Margin and Assets Turnover

Refer again to the average industry ROAs in Exhibit 4.10. The location of several industries is consistent with their incurring one or more of these elements of risk. The relatively high ROAs of the utilities and petroleum industries are consistent with high operating leverage. Paper, petroleum, and transportation equipment experience cyclical sales, and apparel retailers face the risk of their products becoming obsolete. Some of the industry locations in Exhibit 4.10 appear inconsistent with these elements of risk. Oil and gas extraction, agricultural production, and communications are capital-intensive, yet their ROAs are the lowest of the 23 industries. One might view these positions as disequilibrium situations. Generating such low ROAs will not likely attract capital over the longer term.

The ROA locations of several industries appear to be affected by U.S. GAAP. A principal resource of food products firms such as **General Mills** and **Campbell's Soup** is the value of their brand names. Yet U.S. GAAP requires these firms to immediately expense advertising and other costs incurred to develop these brand names. Thus, their asset bases are understated and their ROAs are overstated.[30] Likewise, the publishing industry does not recognize the value of copyrights or authors' contracts as assets, resulting in an overstatement of ROAs. A similar overstatement problem occurs for service firms, for which the value of their employees does not appear as an asset.

In addition to the differences in ROA depicted in Exhibit 4.10, we also must examine reasons for differences in the relative mix of profit margin and assets turnover. Explanations come from the microeconomics and business strategy literature.

Microeconomic Theory. Exhibit 4.13 sets out some important economic factors that constrain certain firms and industries to operate with particular combinations of profit margins and assets turnovers. Firms and industries characterized by heavy fixed capacity costs and lengthy periods required to add new capacity operate under a

---

[30]The immediate expensing of advertising costs understates net income as well, but the difference between the amount expensed and amortization of amounts from the current and prior periods that perhaps should have been capitalized results in less distortion of net income than of total assets.

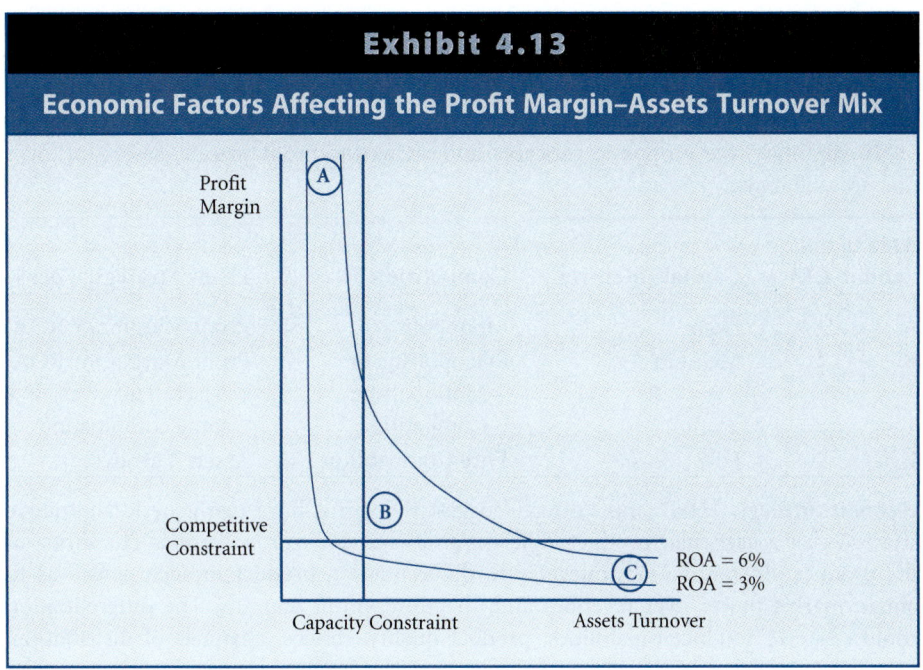

Exhibit 4.13

Economic Factors Affecting the Profit Margin–Assets Turnover Mix

capacity constraint. There is an upper limit on the size of assets turnover achievable. To attract sufficient capital, these firms must generate a relatively high profit margin. Therefore, such firms operate in the area of Exhibit 4.13 marked Ⓐ. The firms usually achieve high profit margins through some form of entry barrier. The entry barrier may take the form of large required capital outlays, high risks, or regulation. Such factors help explain the profit margin–assets turnover mix of utilities, oil and gas extraction, communications, hotels, and amusements in Exhibit 4.10.

Firms whose products are commodity-like where there are few entry barriers and where competition is intense operate under a competitive constraint. There is an upper limit on the achievable level of profit margin for ROA. To attract sufficient capital, these firms must strive for high assets turnover. Therefore, such firms will operate in the area of Exhibit 4.13 marked Ⓒ. Firms achieve the high assets turnovers by keeping costs as low as possible (for example, minimizing fixed overhead costs, purchasing in sufficient quantities to realize discounts, and integrating vertically or horizontally to obtain cost savings). These firms match such actions to control costs with aggressively low prices to gain market share and drive out marginal firms. Most retailers and wholesalers operate in the low profit margin–high assets turnover area of Exhibit 4.10.

Firms that operate in the area of Exhibit 4.13 marked Ⓑ are not as subject to capacity or competitive constraints as severe as those that operate in the tails of the ROA curves. Therefore, they have more flexibility to take actions that will increase profit margin for ROA, assets turnover, or both to achieve a higher ROA. As already suggested, firms operating in area Ⓐ might attempt to reposition the capacity constraint to the right by outsourcing some of their production. Such an action reduces the amount of fixed assets needed per dollar of sales (that is, increases the fixed assets turnover) but likely will reduce the profit margin for ROA (because of the need to share some of the margin with the outsourcing company). Firms operating in area Ⓒ might add products with a higher profit margin for ROA. Grocery stores, for example, have added fresh flowers, salad bars, fresh bakery products, and pharmaceutical prescription services to their product offerings in recent years in an effort to increase their profit margin for ROA and advance beyond the competitive constraint common for grocery products.

In summary, the economic concepts underlying the profit margin–assets turnover mix are as follows:

Area in Exhibit 4.13	Capital Intensity	Competition	Likely Strategic Focus
A	High	Monopoly	Profit Margin for ROA
B	Medium	Oligopolistic or Monopolistic Competition	Profit Margin for ROA, Assets Turnover, or some combination
C	Low	Pure Competition	Assets Turnover

Business Strategy. Hall[31] and Porter[32] suggest that firms have two generic alternative strategies for a particular product: *differentiation* and *low-cost leadership*. The thrust of the product differentiation strategy is to differentiate a product in such a way as to obtain market power over revenues and, therefore, profit margins. The differentiation could relate to product capabilities, product quality, service, channels of distribution, or some other factor. The thrust of the low-cost leadership strategy is to become the lowest-cost producer, thereby enabling the firm to charge the lowest prices and to achieve higher sales volumes. Such firms can achieve the low-cost position through economies of scale, production efficiencies, outsourcing, or similar factors or by asset parsimony (maintaining strict controls on investments in receivables, inventories, and capital expenditures).[33]

In terms of Exhibit 4.13, movements in the direction of area Ⓐ from any point along the ROA curves focus on product differentiation. Likewise, movements in the direction of area Ⓒ from any point along the ROA curves focus on low-cost leadership. For an example, look at the average profit margins for ROA and assets turnovers for three types of retailers.

	Profit Margin for ROA	Assets Turnover
Specialty Retailers	2.97%	2.21
General Merchandise Stores	2.38%	2.02
Grocery Stores	1.43%	2.82

In the retailing industry, specialty retailers have differentiated themselves by following a niche strategy and have achieved a higher profit margin for ROA than the other two segments. Competition severely constrains the profit margin for ROA of grocery stores, and they must pursue more low-cost leadership strategies. Thus, a firm does not have to be in

[31]W. K. Hall, "Survival Strategies in a Hostile Environment," *Harvard Business Review* (September–October 1980), pp. 78–85.

[32]M. E. Porter, *Competitive Strategy: Techniques for Analyzing Industries and Competitors* (New York: Free Press), 1998. Porter suggests that firms also might pursue a niche strategy. Because a niche strategy essentially represents differentiation within a market segment, we include it here under product differentiation strategy.

[33]Research in business strategy suggests that firms can simultaneously pursue product differentiation and low-cost leadership because product differentiation is revenue-oriented (output) and low-cost leadership is more expense-oriented (input).

the tails of the ROA curves to be described as a product differentiator or a low-cost leader. The appropriate basis of comparison is not other industries, but other firms in the same industry. Remember, however, that the relative location along the ROA curve affects a firm's flexibility to trade off profit margin (product differentiation) for assets turnover (low-cost leadership). More importantly, within an industry, firms are dispersed among the profit margin and asset turnover dimensions. For example, within grocery stores, **Kroger** has higher assets turnover and lower profit margin, whereas **Whole Foods** has higher profit margin but lower assets turnover. Summarizing, differences in the profit margin for ROA–assets turnover mix relate to economic factors external to a firm (such as degree of competition, extent of regulation, entry barriers, and similar factors) and to internal strategic choices (such as product differentiation and low-cost leadership). The external and internal factors are, of course, interdependent and dynamic.

PepsiCo's Positioning Relative to the Consumer Foods Industry

PepsiCo is part of the consumer foods industry. The median ROA, profit margin for ROA, and assets turnover for the consumer foods industry and the average amounts for PepsiCo for 2010–2012 are as follows:

	Consumer Foods Industry	PepsiCo
ROA	8.4%	9.6%
Profit Margin for ROA	6.8%	10.8%
Assets Turnover	1.4	0.9

Note that the average ROA of PepsiCo significantly exceeds that for the consumer foods industry because of higher profit margins for ROA earned by PepsiCo. Possible economic or strategic explanations for the higher profit margin for ROA include (1) more value to PepsiCo's brand names than obtained by other food products companies, (2) greater pricing power because of PepsiCo's and **Coca-Cola**'s domination of the beverage industry, (3) greater pricing power because of PepsiCo's influence over its bottlers, and (4) greater efficiencies due to PepsiCo's size or quality of management. The next section explores this higher profit margin for ROA more fully.

Analyzing the Profit Margin for ROA

Profit margin for ROA captures the overall profitability of a firm's operations and is measured as the amount of after-tax profit generated (before financing costs) as a percentage of sales. Thus, the analysis of profit margin focuses on all expenses (other than interest expense) that reduce sales to after-tax profit. ROA for **PepsiCo** declined steadily from 2010 through 2012, falling from 12.4% to 9.6%. The disaggregation of ROA into the profit margin for ROA and assets turnover components in Exhibit 4.6 (using adjusted ROA) reveals that the decline in ROA results from a steadily decline in both assets turnover and profit margin for ROA.

This disaggregation is like peeling an onion. ROA is the outer layer. Peeling away that layer reveals the profit margin for ROA and assets turnover. We can peel the onion an additional layer by separately examining the components of the profit margin for

ROA and the components of assets turnover. Using common-size analysis, we can express individual income statement amounts as percentages of sales to identify reasons for changes in the profit margin for ROA. Exhibit 4.14 presents these revenue and expense percentages for PepsiCo. We maintain consistency with our earlier decision to adjust reported amounts for various special items through an adjustment at the bottom of the exhibit.

Note from Exhibit 4.14 that PepsiCo's profit margin for ROA decreased sharply in 2011 because of the following factors:

- Decrease in bottling equity income relative to sales
- Increase in the cost of sales as a percentage of sales

This was partially offset by a decrease in selling, general, and administrative expenses relative to sales, a decrease in interest expense as a percentage of sales, and an increase in the provision for income taxes relative to sales.

It is important to understand that the above summary contains some degree of measurement error relating to the adjustments made earlier because the special items that we adjusted directly to reported income should actually be adjusted at the individual line item level in Exhibit 4.14, including cost of sales and selling, general, and administrative expenses. As discussed in Note 3, "Restructuring, Impairment and Integration Charges" (Appendix A), PepsiCo's $279 million of restructuring charges in 2012 reflects severance and other employee costs, asset impairments, and other costs, which would likely affect cost of sales and SG&A.

Your task as an analyst is to identify reasons for the changes in the revenue and expense percentages shown in Exhibit 4.14. The MD&A is supposed to provide information for interpreting such changes in these profitability percentages. However, firms vary with respect to the informativeness of these discussions. Some firms give specific reasons for changes in various financial ratios. Other firms simply indicate the amount or rate of increase or decrease without providing explanations for the changes. Even when firms provide explanations, you should assess their reasonableness in light of

Exhibit 4.14

Analysis of the Profit Margin for PepsiCo: 2010–2012

	2012	2011	2010
Net revenue	100.0%	100.0%	100.0%
Bottling equity income	0.0	0.0	1.3
Interest income and other	0.1	0.1	0.1
Cost of sales	(47.8)	(47.5)	(45.9)
Selling, general, and administrative expenses	(38.1)	(37.8)	(39.4)
Other operating charges	(0.2)	(0.2)	(0.2)
Interest expense	(1.4)	(1.3)	(1.6)
Provision for income taxes	(3.2)	(3.6)	(3.3)
Adjustments for special items	0.5	0.3	(0.4)
Numerator addbacks for after tax interest and noncontrolling interest	0.9	0.9	1.0
Profit margin for ROA	10.8%	10.9%	11.6%

conditions in the economy and the industry, as well as the firm's stated strategy and the results for the firms' competitors. You should also be vigilant when a firm does not provide discussion or an explanation for a significant shift in a financial ratio; it implies that the firm is not being forthcoming with useful information.

Below we focus only on the most noticeable changes in components of profit margin and use information provided by PepsiCo in its MD&A (Appendix B) to identify reasons for changes in the profit margin for ROA.

PepsiCo Bottling Equity Income

Note 8, "Related Party Transactions" (Appendix A), indicates that in February of 2010, **PepsiCo** completed acquisitions of **PepsiCo Bottling Group** (PBG) and **PepsiAmericas** (PAS), and began consolidating the results of these bottlers. Prior to that time, PepsiCo accounted for investments in these bottlers under the equity method, where PepsiCo's percentage ownership of the bottlers' net income was recognized as bottling equity income. Once these bottlers became fully consolidated, this line item was no longer necessary, explaining the decline to zero in 2011. PepsiCo's share of the bottlers' revenues and expenses is now mixed within its other operations (as are the bottlers' assets and liabilities).

PepsiCo Cost of Goods Sold

Interpreting changes in the cost of goods sold to sales percentage is often difficult because explanations might relate to sales revenue only, to cost of goods sold only, or to common factors affecting both. Consider, for example, the following possible explanations for a decrease in the cost of goods sold to sales percentage for a firm:

1. An increase in demand for products in excess of available capacity in an industry will likely result in an increase in selling prices. Even though the cost of manufacturing the product does not change, the cost of goods sold percentage will decrease.

2. As a result of product improvements or effective advertising, a firm's market share for its product increases. The firm allocates the fixed cost of manufacturing the product over a larger volume of production, thereby lowering its per-unit cost. Even though selling prices do not change, the cost of goods sold to sales percentage will decrease.

3. A firm lowers the price for its product to gain a larger market share. It lowers its manufacturing cost per unit by purchasing raw materials in larger quantities to take advantage of quantity discounts. Cost of goods sold per unit declines more than selling price per unit, causing the cost of goods sold to sales percentage to decline.

4. A firm sells multiple products with different cost of goods sold to sales percentages. The product mix shifts toward products with higher profit margins, thereby lowering the overall cost of goods sold to sales percentage.

Thus, you must consider changes in selling prices, manufacturing costs, and product mix when interpreting changes in the cost of goods sold percentage. Exhibit 4.14 indicates that **PepsiCo**'s cost of goods sold to sales percentage increased between 2010 and 2011, where it has remained in 2012. Management's discussion of the results of operations indicates in several places that PepsiCo encountered higher commodity costs. Because PepsiCo acquired its bottlers in 2010, they no longer provide disclosures regarding the bottlers' gross profit. However, if you examine older Forms 10-K, which include such disclosures, you find that the bottlers had a higher cost of sales to sales percentage than PepsiCo's other divisions. For example, in 2009 cost of sales as a percentage of sales was 55.8% for PBG and 60.0% for PAS. Consolidating these operations into PepsiCo's financial results surely contributed to the increase in cost of sales as a percentage of sales.

PepsiCo Selling, General, and Administrative Expenses (including adjustments for special items)

Most firms combine selling, general, and administrative expenses into one line item on the income statement. Combining these expense items is unfortunate from an analysis perspective because different factors tend to drive these expenses. Selling expenses include sales commissions, advertising, and promotion materials, which usually vary with the level of sales. General expenses include overhead expenses such as rent, utilities, communications, and insurance, whereas administrative expenses include top management's salaries and the cost of operating staff departments such as information systems, legal services, and R&D. These costs tend to be more static and do *not* vary with the level of sales.

PepsiCo's selling, general, and administrative expenses to sales percentages fell between 2010 and 2011 (from 39.4% to 37.8%), and increased slightly in 2012 (to 38.1%). Reported sales decreased slightly—approximately 1.5%—between 2011 and 2012, so the spreading of relatively fixed administrative costs over a slightly smaller sales base might explain the increase in SG&A as a percentage of sales from 37.8% to 38.1%; removing the effect of the 53rd week of sales in 2011 shrinks the year-over-year decline in sales to 0.6%. Between 2010 and 2011, sales increased 15% (again, slightly less if you remove the 53rd week from 2011 sales), which would have spread fixed costs over a much larger sales base, contributing to the decline in SG&A as a percentage of sales. Management's discussion of operations (Appendix B) does not give sufficient information to ensure an understanding of the detailed breakdown of selling, general, and administrative expenses. Additionally, as seen previously, the MD&A indicates a large amount of special charges recognized in 2010 as part of PepsiCo's Productivity Plan, and many of these were recorded as SG&A (frequently as corporate unallocated expenses).

PepsiCo Segment Data

The aggregate results in the common-size income statements for **PepsiCo** examined in Exhibit 4.14 mask potentially important differences in profitability in different product lines or geographic markets. Fortunately, as highlighted earlier in the chapter, both U.S. GAAP and IFRS require firms to provide financial data for their operating segments, products and services, and major customers.[34] Note 1, "Basis of Presentation and Our Divisions," to PepsiCo's financial statements (Appendix A) presents these segment data for 2010–2012. PepsiCo reports product segment data for six divisions: Frito-Lay North America; Quaker Foods North America; Latin American Foods; PepsiCo Americas Beverages; Europe; and Asia, Middle East and Africa.

The segment disclosures permit you to examine ROA, profit margin, and assets turnover at an additional level of depth, in effect peeling the onion one more layer. Firms such as PepsiCo report revenues, operating profits, and other aggregate information by segment. Unfortunately, to avoid disclosure of sensitive information, firms do

---

[34]*FASB Codification No. 280;* International Accounting Standards Board, *International Financial Reporting Standards No. 8,* "Operating Segments" (November 2006).

not generally report cost of goods sold and selling, general, and administrative expenses for each segment. That means we cannot reconcile changes in segment profit margins to changes in the overall levels of these two expense percentages. Firms also report segment data pretax, meaning that the segment 'ROAs' and profit margins exceed those for the overall company to a considerable extent.

Exhibit 4.15 presents sales mix data for PepsiCo. PepsiCo's sales mix has shifted slightly during the three years from its North America food and beverage divisions to international segments, with growth in representation of sales for Europe and Latin America Foods. An important insight that is conveyed by the common-size analysis in Exhibit 4.15 is that the two North American food segments account for approximately one-fourth of PepsiCo's total sales, but the growth seems to be in two segments that reflect approximately one-third of PepsiCo's sales—Europe and Latin America Foods. The largest segment is the Americas Beverages segment, which shows a noticeable decline from 35.3% of total sales in 2010 to 32.7% in 2012. PepsiCo may more accurately be deemed to be a food company than a beverage company (especially because the highest profit margins and asset turnovers reside in the foods segments, as we will see next).

Exhibit 4.16 presents ROAs, profit margins, and assets turnovers for each of PepsiCo's segments. Note that our methods of computation here differ from those we performed previously for PepsiCo consolidated. First, we compute segment ROAs and assets turnover using assets at the *end of the period* to simplify the calculations. The difficulty you often encounter with using average segment assets is that firms frequently change their definition of segments over time and firms report the three most recent years of segment asset data in their current annual report. You would need to access asset data for the fourth year back in order to compute average assets for the three years and hope that the firm maintained a consistent definition of segments. Firms that have changed their segment definitions within the last year will not consistently show assets with current segment definitions. For a stable, mature company such as PepsiCo, the use of assets at the end of the period instead of the average for the period will affect the level of the ROAs and the assets turnover ratios but will not likely have a material effect on the trend of these segment ratios over time unless the firm made a significant corporate acquisition or divestiture during one of the years. Second, note that the numerator of our profitability calculations is based on pretax operating profits rather than the usual

Exhibit 4.15			
Sales Mix Data for PepsiCo			
Reportable Segments	**2012**	**2011**	**2010**
Frito-Lay North America	20.7%	20.0%	21.7%
Quaker Foods North America	4.0	4.0	4.6
Latin America Foods	11.9	10.8	10.9
PepsiCo Americas Beverages	32.7	33.7	35.3
Europe	20.5	20.4	16.6
Asia, Middle East & Africa	10.2	11.1	10.9
Total	100.0%	100.0%	100.0%

Exhibit 4.16

Product Segment Pretax Profitability Analysis for PepsiCo

ROA

	2012	2011	2010
Frito-Lay North America	69.1%	67.3%	64.0%
Quaker Foods North America	72.9%	78.4%	69.8%
Latin America Foods	22.2%	23.9%	24.8%
PepsiCo Americas Beverages	9.8%	10.7%	9.9%
Europe	7.1%	7.1%	8.4%
Asia, Middle East & Africa	15.6%	14.8%	12.7%

	Profit Margin for ROA			**Assets Turnover**		
	2012	2011	2010	2012	2011	2010
Frito-Lay North America	27.1%	27.8%	26.9%	2.55	2.43	2.38
Quaker Foods North America	26.7%	30.7%	27.9%	2.73	2.55	2.50
Latin America Foods	14.3%	15.7%	15.9%	1.56	1.52	1.56
PepsiCo Americas Beverages	14.2%	15.1%	15.3%	0.69	0.71	0.65
Europe	10.2%	9.6%	11.4%	0.70	0.73	0.74
Asia, Middle East & Africa	13.5%	12.1%	11.3%	1.16	1.22	1.13

appropriate measure, net income adjusted for after-tax interest expense. This decision also is made because PepsiCo does not disclose this information at the segment level. Financing policies and activities frequently reside with the corporate division; thus, they are not allocated to operating segments. As with our use of end-of-period total assets, this procedure is not likely to prevent us from gaining objective insight into the relative profitability and efficiency of the segments being analyzed. The primary limitation of these assumptions is that we cannot precisely reconcile the segment calculations with those for the consolidated results of PepsiCo. *Data availability and practicality frequently drive financial analysis decisions and techniques*, which further emphasizes our earlier cautionary note that the astute analyst does not memorize ratios, but understands the rationale for how to interpret various measures.

The top portion of Exhibit 4.16 indicates that the segments with the highest ROAs by far are Frito-Lay North America and Quaker Foods North America. The lower portion of Exhibit 4.16 shows the breakdown of ROA into profit margin and assets turnover. The profit margins generally mirror the distribution of ROA in the upper portion of Exhibit 4.16, with both North America foods divisions showing the highest profit margins. Similarly, these divisions also have the highest assets turn-overs, followed by Latin America Foods. The overall higher level of profitability and asset utilization for the foods divisions is consistent with our discussions of life cycle theory in Chapter 3 (Exhibit 3.1) and earlier in this chapter (Exhibit 4.11). The North America segments are older and more mature than the other segments, so it is understandable that the Americas divisions are more profitable and efficient. PepsiCo Americas Beverages, in contrast, appears to be in a decline phase. ROA and profit margins seem to be in decline, consistent with efforts discussed previously about PepsiCo's Productivity Plan, which triggered many of the special charges we have discussed and is related to PepsiCo's 2010 decision to acquire the PBG and PAS bottlers to respond to changing consumer preferences for niche beverages in lieu of well-established brands.

Growth segments like PepsiCo's Europe division are not as profitable due to required investments in growing sales volume and refining production and distribution operations to levels comparable to more mature segments. If PepsiCo proves as success-ful internationally as it has been in the Americas, profit margins and assets turnovers for these segments should improve in the future. Because of this regularity, segment dis-closures are frequently most helpful in the forecasting part of financial statement analy-sis and valuation, which we will return to in Chapter 10.

A caveat of segment reporting analysis relates to the data used. The information in Note 1 of PepsiCo's footnotes is the basis of calculations for Exhibits 4.15 and 4.16. Exhibit 4.15 is based on sales that reconcile to the total for consolidated results for PepsiCo; that is, the total sales of all six segments add up to the total sales for PepsiCo consolidated. However, Exhibit 4.16 is based on operating profits that do *not* reconcile with consolidated total operating profit for PepsiCo. As indicated in Note 1 of PepsiCo's footnotes, the difference between total operating profit of $9,112 million in 2012 and the $10,414 million sum of the operating profits of the individual operating segments is caused by corporate unallocated expenses of $1,302 million. PepsiCo includes these expenses in selling, general, and administrative expenses on its income statement but does not allocate them to its operating segments when disclosing segment data. Follow-ing are the corporate unallocated expenses as a percentage of sales for the three years (in millions):

2010: $1,327/$57,838 = 2.3%
2011: $1,233/$66,504 = 1.9%
2012: $1,302/$65,492 = 2.0%

If a large amount of expenses is not allocated to segments in segment disclosures, you must exert caution when interpreting segment profit margins and ROAs. Changes in the amount of expenses allocated versus not allocated to segments, a choice made by management, clearly affect these ratios. PepsiCo reports a fairly steady amount of unal-located corporate expenses each year, around 2.0%. Thus, this probably does not affect our prior analysis of the segment disclosures, but it is a reporting choice that you should examine for reasonableness.

Summary of Profit Margin Analysis for PepsiCo

We noted at the beginning of this section that **PepsiCo**'s profit margin for ROA declined from 11.6% to 10.8% during 2010 through 2012. This reflected increasing cost of sales and SG&A as a percentage of sales. We used common-size analysis to identify the primary contributions to the observed profit margins and analyzed each item to better understand the factors contributing to the overall profit margin for PepsiCo. The summary of our findings for the analysis of profit margins is as follows:

- Bottling equity income disappeared as a separate line item on the income statement in 2011 because PepsiCo decided to acquire its bottlers as part of a restructuring of the company to be more efficient in responding to changes in the consumer beverages market.
- Cost of sales increased due to higher commodity costs, and probably due to the higher cost structure of the bottling operations now consolidated within PepsiCo's operations.
- Selling, general, and administrative expenses decreased in 2011, due primarily to a large number of restructuring and other special charges being recognized in 2010. Sales slightly decreased in 2012, leading to the spreading of costs over a smaller sales base, resulting in a slight increase in these expenses as a percentage of sales.
- Segment analysis suggested that the most profitable divisions are the North America foods divisions, but that the Americas Beverages division is decreasing as a percentage of total sales, and its margins are lower than the foods divisions.

Having examined the first component of ROA—profit margin—we examine next the other component—total assets turnover.

Analyzing Total Assets Turnover

Total assets turnover captures how efficiently assets are being utilized to generate revenues. Higher revenues generated with a given level of assets indicates more efficient use of those assets. Exhibit 4.6 showed that **PepsiCo**'s total assets turnover steadily decreased from 2010 to 2012, falling from 1.07 to 0.89. The first step you might take toward understanding changes in total assets turnover is to be aware of the relative changes in the numerator (sales) and denominator (average total assets) across the years. In 2011, sales increased 15%, but this was outpaced by a 31% increase in average total assets; similarly, in 2012, average total assets increased 4.5% relative to a 1.5% decrease in sales. Thus, in both years, total assets turnover declined. A significant change across these years is the acquisition of the bottlers, PBG and PAS, and the Russian food and beverage company, WBD, which increased assets, primarily through fair value recognition of various intangible assets like goodwill and brands. These additions to assets have yet to be matched by commensurate increases in sales, leading to the overall declines in total assets turnover.

Unlike the analysis of profit margin, where we decomposed the numerator by examining different expenses that determined operating profit, the analysis of total assets turnover can best be achieved by decomposing the denominator. We can gain greater insight into changes in total assets turnover by examining turnover ratios for particular classes of assets under the logic that turnover ratios for individual assets aggregate to total assets turnover. The following three turnover ratios are among the most popular, largely driven by the importance of each of these assets:

- Accounts receivable turnover
- Inventory turnover
- Fixed assets turnover

Management's discussion and analysis of operations usually provides detailed explanations for operating profits, but it does not include explanations for changes in assets turnovers; so you must search for possible clues. This is unfortunate because small changes in assets turnover can have enormous effects on the overall profitability of a firm (that is, ROA and ROCE).

Accounts Receivable Turnover

The rate at which accounts receivable turn over indicates the average time until firms collect them in cash. You calculate accounts receivable turnover by dividing net sales on account by average accounts receivable. Most sales transactions between businesses are on account, not for cash. Except for retailers and restaurants that deal directly with consumers, the assumption that all sales are on account is usually reasonable. The calculation of the accounts receivable turnover for 2012 for **PepsiCo** is as follows (in millions):

$$\text{Accounts Receivable Turnover} = \frac{\text{Net Sales on Account}}{\text{Average Accounts Receivable}}$$

$$9.4 = \frac{\$65,492}{0.5(\$7,041 + \$6,912)}$$

PepsiCo's accounts receivable turnover was 10.0 in 2011 and 10.6 in 2010.

Accounts receivable turnover is often framed in terms of the average number of days receivables are outstanding before firms collect them in cash. The calculation divides 365 days by the accounts receivable turnover.[35] The average number of days that accounts receivable were outstanding was 38.8 days (365/9.4) during 2012, 36.5 days (365/10.0) during 2011, and 34.4 days (365/10.6) during 2010. One also could calculate the days' sales included in the *ending* accounts receivable balance, in which case the calculation would be ending accounts receivable divided by average daily sales (sales/365). The slight increase in accounts receivable at the end of 2012 and the slight decline in sales from 2011, yields a slightly higher days' sales in the ending receivables [$7,041/ ($65,492/365) = 39.2]. These computations clearly indicate that PepsiCo is collecting accounts receivable more slowly. Many firms transact business with credit sales terms of 30 days. Although customers are paying more slowly, most of PepsiCo's customers pay within a reasonable period of just over one month.

The interpretation of changes in the accounts receivable turnover and average collection period also relates to a firm's credit extension policies. Firms often use credit terms as a means of stimulating sales. For example, in an effort to stimulate sales, firms might permit customers to delay making payments on purchases of lawn mowers until after the summer and on snowmobiles until after the winter. Such actions would lead to a decrease in the accounts receivable turnover and an increase in the number of days receivables are outstanding. The changes in these accounts receivable ratios would not necessarily signal negative news if the increase in net income from the additional sales exceeded the cost of carrying accounts receivable for the extra time. Firms also can use credit policy to provide implicit financing to support affiliated companies, such as credit extended by automobile manufacturers to dealerships, by producers to closely related distributors (such as PepsiCo and **Coca-Cola** to affiliated companies), and by restaurant chains to franchisees or licensees (such as **McDonald's** to franchisees and **Starbucks** to licensees).

---

[35]Sometimes you may see the use of 360 days in calculations like this. Although this choice introduces slight measurement error biasing toward faster turnover, as long as it is used consistently in all calculations, it is unlikely to have a significant effect on inferences.

Retailing firms, particularly department store chains such as **Sears** and **Macy's**, offer their own credit cards to customers. They use credit cards to stimulate sales. Interpreting an increase in the number of days accounts receivable are outstanding involves two conflicting signals. The increase might suggest greater risk of uncollectibility, but it also provides additional interest revenues. Some firms price their products to obtain a relatively low gross margin from the sale and depend on interest revenue as a principal source of earnings. Thus, you must consider a firm's credit strategy and policies when interpreting the accounts receivable turnover and days receivables outstanding ratios.

PepsiCo does not explain the slower accounts receivable turnover. A significant proportion of PepsiCo's accounts receivable likely relates to amounts owed PepsiCo by retailers. PepsiCo might have intentionally granted more favorable repayment terms to support its bottlers and grocery retailers during the recessionary economy of 2010–2012. Another possibility is that repayment terms in other countries may differ from those in the United States. An increased percentage of sales from countries with longer repayment times might account for the slower accounts receivable turnover. In any case, the increase in the number of days it takes to collect accounts receivable from 34.4 days in 2010 to 38.8 days in 2012 does not seem to be a major concern. Assuming that PepsiCo borrowed short-term debt at 4% interest to finance the greater number of days receivables were outstanding, it would have cost PepsiCo approximately $3.3 million $\{[(38.8 - 34.4)/365] \times 0.04 \times [0.5(\$7,041 + \$6,912)]\}$ during 2012. PepsiCo's interest expense for 2012 was $899 million. Under these assumptions, the increase in collection period would have increased interest expense by only 0.37% ($3.3/$899).

Inventory Turnover

The rate at which inventories turn over indicates the length of time needed to produce, hold, and sell inventories. You calculate inventory turnover by dividing cost of goods sold by the average inventory during the period. The calculation of inventory turnover for **PepsiCo** for 2012 is as follows (in millions):

$$\text{Inventory Turnover} = \frac{\text{Cost of Goods Sold}}{\text{Average Inventories}}$$

$$8.4 = \frac{\$31,291}{0.5(\$3,581 + \$3,827)}$$

Thus, PepsiCo's inventory was on hand for an average of 43.5 days (365/8.4) during 2012. PepsiCo's inventory turnover was 8.8 (41.5 days) in 2011 and 8.9 (41.0 days) in 2010. Thus, the inventory turnover slowed by 2.5 days during the three-year period.

PepsiCo does not explain the slower inventory turnover, but one possibility is that the recent consolidation of their bottlers would have added their inventory. Second, worldwide economic conditions led to reduced purchases of premium snacks or beverages, both of which could have led to reduced inventory turnover. Average inventory levels were up in 2012, although ending inventory is actually slightly down from the end of 2011. The MD&A (Appendix B) indicates a large decline in sales for the PepsiCo Americas Beverages division, reflecting slowdowns in sales of carbonated beverages, Tropicana, and Gatorade. Large sales declines coupled with steady inventory levels would decrease turnover. However, this is speculative, because sales increases in other divisions might offset such turnover declines. Another possibility is that PepsiCo experienced a shift in sales mix due to its expansion in international markets with different consumer preferences. Unfortunately, you cannot assess the latter possibility without a breakout of the various products by segment.

The interpretation of the inventory turnover figure involves two opposing considerations. A firm would like to sell as many goods as possible with a minimum of capital tied up in inventories. Moreover, inventory is subject to obsolescence or spoilage, especially in the case of food products. An increase in the rate of inventory turnover between periods would seem to indicate more profitable use of the investment in inventory and lowering costs for financing and carrying inventory. On the other hand, a firm does not want to have so little inventory on hand that shortages result and the firm misses sales opportunities. An increase in the rate of inventory turnover in this case may mean a loss of sales opportunities, thereby offsetting any cost savings achieved by a decreased investment in inventory. Firms must make trade-offs in deciding the optimum level of inventory and thus the desirable rate of inventory turnover. For example, in 2012, the high-end jeweler **Tiffany** had an inventory turnover of 509 days, whereas **Apple**'s turnover was only 3 days.

You may gain insight into changes in inventory turnover by examining the changes in relation to changes in the cost of goods sold to sales percentage. Consider the following scenarios and possible interpretations:

- **Increasing cost of goods sold to sales percentage, coupled with an increasing inventory turnover.**
  - The firm lowers prices to sell inventory more quickly.
  - The firm shifts its product mix toward lower-margin, faster-moving products.
  - The firm outsources the production of a higher proportion of its products, requiring it to share profit margin with the outsourcer but reducing the amount of raw materials and work-in-process inventories.
- **Decreasing cost of goods sold to sales percentage, coupled with a decreasing inventory turnover.**
  - The firm raises prices to increase its gross margin, but inventory sells more slowly.
  - The firm shifts its product mix toward higher-margin, slower-moving products.
  - The firm produces a higher proportion of its products instead of outsourcing, thereby capturing more of the gross margin but requiring the firm to carry raw materials and work-in-process inventories.
- **Increasing cost of goods sold to sales percentage, coupled with a decreasing inventory turnover.**
  - Weak economic conditions lead to reduced demand for the firm's products, necessitating price reductions to move goods. Despite price reductions, inventory builds up.
- **Decreasing cost of goods sold to sales percentage, coupled with an increasing inventory turnover.**
  - Strong economic conditions lead to increased demand for the firm's products, allowing price increases. An inability to replace inventory as fast as the firm sells it leads to an increased inventory turnover.
  - The firm implements a just-in-time inventory system, reducing storage costs, product obsolescence, and the amount of inventory held.

Some analysts calculate the inventory turnover ratio by dividing sales, rather than cost of goods sold, by the average inventory. As long as there is a reasonably constant relation between selling prices and cost of goods sold, you can identify changes in the trend of the inventory turnover using either measure. It is inappropriate to use sales in the numerator if you want to use the inventory turnover ratio to calculate the average number of days that inventory is on hand until sale or if you want to compare inventory turnover across firms with different markups and gross profit margins.

The cost-flow assumption (FIFO, LIFO, or weighted-average) for inventories and cost of goods sold can significantly affect both the inventory turnover ratio and the cost of goods sold to sales percentage. Chapter 9 discusses the impact of the cost-flow assumption and illustrates adjustments you might make to deal with these effects.

Fixed Assets Turnover

The fixed assets turnover ratio measures the relation between sales and the investment in property, plant, and equipment. Fixed assets turnover equals sales divided by average fixed assets (net of accumulated depreciation) during the year. The fixed assets turnover ratio for **PepsiCo** for 2012 is as follows:

$$\text{Fixed Assets Turnover} = \frac{\text{Sales}}{\text{Average Fixed Assets}}$$

$$3.4 = \frac{\$65{,}492}{0.5(\$19{,}136 + \$19{,}698)}$$

The fixed assets turnover for PepsiCo was 3.4 in 2011 and 3.6 in 2010. An increasing fixed assets turnover ratio generally indicates greater efficiency in the use of existing fixed assets, and lower turnover suggests the opposite. The analysis of fixed assets turnover is also affected by acquisitions and divestitures, particularly if such transactions relate to distinct lines of business with different fixed asset requirements. Like other ratios, you must carefully interpret changes in the fixed assets turnover ratio. Firms invest in fixed assets in anticipation of higher production and sales in future periods. Thus, a temporarily low or decreasing rate of fixed assets turnover may be a positive signal of an expanding firm preparing for future growth. On the other hand, a firm may reduce its capital expenditures if the near-term outlook for its products is poor, which might lead to an increase in the fixed assets turnover ratio.

In recent years, many firms have increased the proportion of production outsourced to other manufacturers. This action allows firms to achieve the same (or increasing) sales levels with less fixed assets, thereby increasing the fixed assets turnover. However, PepsiCo did the opposite by acquiring its bottlers in 2010, which increased its asset base and contributed towards the subsequent declines in fixed assets turnover. The acquired companies profitability in relation to its asset base also plays a significant role. In this case, PBG was not as profitable as we were yet. They had a very large fixed asset base. Due to its bottling operations. Therefore, their ratio was significantly lower than ours.

Other Asset Turnover Ratios

Although turnover ratios are most common for the receivables, inventory, and fixed assets, any asset can be examined as a turnover ratio as long as the appropriate numerator is used in the calculation. For example, firms maintain varying levels of cash, and analysts are often interested in the efficiency with which cash is managed. Thus, an investor can gauge the strategic maintenance of cash balances by a cash turnover ratio. The cash turnover ratio is computed by dividing sales by the average cash balance during the year. The cash turnover ratio for **PepsiCo** for 2012 is as follows:

$$\text{Cash Turnover} = \frac{\text{Sales}}{\text{Average Cash and Cash Equivalents}}$$

$$12.6 = \frac{\$65{,}492}{0.5(\$6{,}297 + \$4{,}067)}$$

Thus, PepsiCo maintains a cash balance of approximately 29.0 days' sales (365/12.6). Calculated with *sales* in the numerator, this implies that PepsiCo replenishes its cash balance approximately every month. Alternatively, you could view cash as a means of funding other working capital (inventory, for example). With this perspective, you might calculate the cash turnover ratio with cost of goods sold in the numerator. The computations are similar to those above, but the interpretation is different.

Similarly, you might want an overall metric for the efficiency with which all current assets are managed (rather than individually). Accordingly, you would compute a current assets turnover ratio by dividing sales by the average current assets during the year. The current assets turnover ratio for PepsiCo for 2012 is as follows:

$$\text{Current Assets Turnover} = \frac{\text{Sales}}{\text{Average Current Assets}}$$

$$3.6 = \frac{\$65{,}492}{0.5(\$18{,}720 + \$17{,}441)}$$

Thus, PepsiCo turns over its current assets approximately every fiscal quarter. The current assets turnover ratio conveys information similar to that for individual asset turnover ratios for cash, receivables, or inventory. However, the current assets turnover ratio is often more representative because the volatility of *total* current assets is less than the volatility of an *individual* current asset. For example, stronger-than-expected end-of-year sales might result in ending receivables being temporarily above normal levels and inventory being temporarily below current levels. This would cause the receivables turnover ratio to be deflated but the inventory turnover ratio to be inflated. All else equal, however, the current assets turnover ratio would be less likely to be affected because the volatilities in receivables balances and inventory levels tend to offset each other.

Summary of Assets Turnover Analysis

PepsiCo's total assets turnover has been declining between 2010 and 2012. We first noted that structural changes associated with PepsiCo's acquisitions of PBG, PAS, and WBD increased assets, especially the recognition of intangible assets. We also examined the three primary asset turnover ratios: accounts receivable, inventory, and fixed assets. All three turnover ratios decreased slightly across these years. Accounts receivable make up approximately 9% of total assets, and inventories make up approximately 5% of total assets. However, fixed assets make up 25% of total assets. Thus, one would expect that the pattern in fixed assets turnover would dominate among these three, especially given only small changes in accounts receivable and inventory turnovers. However, other assets beside receivables, inventories, and fixed assets affect the total assets turnover computation. The utilization of these other assets is sometimes important. For example, the percentage of total assets represented by intangible assets rose from 23.0% in 2009 (before acquiring the bottlers) to 44.9% in 2012.

Summary of ROA Analysis

Recalling the analogy of decomposing profitability to peeling back layers of an onion, our analysis of operating profitability involves four levels of depth:

Level 1: ROA for the firm as a whole
Level 2: Disaggregation of ROA into profit margin for ROA and assets turnover for the firm as a whole
Level 3a: Disaggregation of profit margin into expense ratios for various cost items
Level 3b: Disaggregation of assets turnover into turnovers for individual assets
Level 4: Analysis of profit margins and asset turnovers for the segments of a firm

Exhibit 4.17

Profitability Analysis for PepsiCo at Levels 1, 2, and 3

Level 1 Analysis

ROA

	2012	2011	2010
	9.6%	10.3%	12.4%

Level 2 Analysis

Profit Margin for ROA				Assets Turnover		
2012	2011	2010		2012	2011	2010
10.9%	10.9%	11.6%		0.89	0.94	1.07

Level 3 Analysis

	2012	2011	2010		2012	2011	2010
Net sales	100.0%	100.0%	100.0%	Receivable Turnover	9.4	10.0	10.6
Bottling equity income	0.0	0.0	1.3	Inventory Turnover	8.4	8.8	8.9
Interest income	0.1	0.1	0.1	Fixed Assets Turnover	3.4	3.4	3.6
Cost of sales	(47.8)	(48.0)	(45.9)				
Selling, general, and administrative expenses	(38.1)	(38.2)	(39.4)				
Other operating charges	(0.2)	(0.2)	(0.2)				
Interest expense	(1.4)	(1.3)	(1.6)				
Provision for income taxes (adjusted)	(2.9)	(3.6)	(3.3)				
Tax effect of interest addback in numerator	0.9	0.8	1.0				
Profit margin for ROA	10.8%	11.0%	11.6%				

Exhibit 4.17 summarizes this analysis in a format used throughout the remainder of this book and included in FSAP.

This layered approach to analyzing financial statements provides a disciplined approach that can be applied to any firm.

Supplementing ROA in Profitability Analysis

ROA uses average total assets as a base for assessing a firm's effectiveness in using resources to generate earnings. For some firms and industries, total assets may be less informative for this purpose because, as Chapter 2 discusses, accounting practices (1) do not assign asset values to certain valuable resources (brand names, technological knowledge, and human capital) and (2) report assets at acquisition costs instead of current market values (forests for forest products companies and land for railroads).

To supplement straightforward financial statement analysis, analysts often supplement ROA by relating sales, expenses, and earnings to *nonfinancial* attributes when evaluating profitability. This section discusses techniques for assessing profitability unique to several industries. The discussion is not intended to be exhaustive for all industries, but to provide a flavor for the types of supplemental measures used.

Analyzing Retailers

A key resource of retailers is their retail space. Some retailers own their stores, while others lease their space. You can constructively capitalize the present value of operating lease commitments to ensure that total assets include store buildings under operating leases. An alternative approach when analyzing retailers is to express sales, operating expenses, and operating income on a per-store basis or per square foot of retail selling space. This supplemental base for evaluating profitability circumvents the issue of whether firms own or lease their space. It also eliminates the effects on the denominator of ROA of using different depreciation methods and depreciable lives and having fixed assets with different ages. However, it does not eliminate the effect of different depreciation methods or depreciable lives on income in the numerator. An equally important metric for retail firms is growth in "same store" or "comparable store" sales. Analysts are interested in changes in revenues due to changes in the number of retail stores as well as in changes in revenues due to changes in the average sales per retail store. Thus, a key measure reported by firms in this industry is the change in sales on a comparable store basis (based on the number of stores open throughout the period).

Exhibit 4.18 presents per-square-foot and comparable store data for **Target Corporation** (Target) and **Walmart Stores** (Walmart), as well as profit margin for ROA, assets turnover, and ROA (for 2009). The superior ROA of Walmart results from much higher sales per square foot, which corresponds to its higher assets turnover. However, Target's profit margin is actually higher than that of Walmart. Overall, for this year, Walmart is more profitable in terms of ROA and Walmart actually grew comparable stores sales versus a decline in comparable store sales for Target over the same period.

Exhibit 4.18		
Profitability Ratios for Target and Walmart		
	Target	**Walmart**
Per Square Foot:		
Sales	$ 302	$ 454
Cost of goods sold	(205)	(342)
Selling and administrative	(76)	(86)
Operating income	$ 21	$ 26
Profit margin for ROA	4.30%	3.82%
Assets turnover	1.47	2.45
ROA	6.3%	9.4%
Comparable store sales change	(2.9)%	3.5%

Analyzing Airlines

Aircraft provide airlines with a fixed amount of capacity during a particular period. The total number of seats *available* to carry passengers times the number of miles flown equals the available capacity. The number of seats *occupied* times the number of miles flown equals the amount of capacity used (referred to as revenue passenger miles). Common practice in the airline industry is to compute the revenues and expenses per available seat mile and per revenue passenger mile flown to judge pricing, cost structure, and profitability.

Exhibit 4.19 presents selected profitability data for **American Airlines**, **JetBlue**, and **Airtran** (for 2008). American operates both domestic and international routes, while JetBlue and Airtran provide primarily domestic services. The employees of American and Airtran are unionized, while those of JetBlue are not. All three airlines are publicly owned. The first three columns present revenues, expenses, and operating income before income taxes per available seat mile, and the last three columns present the same income items per revenue passenger mile flown.

The costs of an airline (such as depreciation and compensation) are largely fixed for a particular year. Thus, the operating expenses per available seat mile indicate the costs of operating each airline. Fuel costs were significant for all airlines, but JetBlue had the lowest cost; American had the highest. Compensation costs also were highest at American, as were all other operating expenses. This resulted in a significant operating loss for American, despite also having the highest revenue per seat mile. Airtran had lower costs than American, but because operating revenues on a per-mile basis were lower, it also realized an operating loss. In contrast, JetBlue had the lowest operating revenue on a per-mile basis, but due to low fuel, compensation, and other costs, it was profitable. The profit margins were similar (and negative) for American and Airtran but were positive for JetBlue. The assets turnover for Airtran was highest, which combined with the negative profit margin to yield Airtran's negative ROA. Given similar profit margins, the difference in ROA between Airtran and American is driven by assets turnover differences. The explanation for the higher assets turnover for Airtran relative to American is that in the year shown, Airtran leases 100 of 136 aircraft, versus 220 out of 892 for American (not shown in Exhibit 4.19). JetBlue had the lowest assets turnover, but it had a positive profit margin, which produced a positive but low ROA.

Exhibit 4.19

Profitability Ratios for American, JetBlue, and Airtran

	Per Available Seat Mile			Per Revenue Passenger Mile		
	American	JetBlue	Airtran	American	JetBlue	Airtran
Operating revenues	14.53¢	10.44¢	10.72¢	18.04¢	13.00¢	13.47¢
Fuel	(5.51)	(4.17)	(5.02)	(6.84)	(5.19)	(6.30)
Compensation	(4.07)	(2.14)	(1.99)	(5.05)	(2.66)	(2.51)
Other operating expenses	(6.11)	(3.79)	(4.01)	(7.58)	(4.73)	(5.04)
Operating income	(1.16)¢	0.34¢	(0.30)¢	(1.43)¢	0.42¢	(0.38)¢
Profitability decomposition:						
Profit margin for ROA				(8.7)%	2.2%	(8.7)%
Assets turnover				0.68	0.58	1.24
ROA				(5.9)%	1.3%	(10.8)%

You can also apply similar metrics to other firms with fixed capacity. For example, the analysis of hospitals often focuses on income data per available bed or per patient day. The analysis of hotels uses income data per room. The analysis of cable and telecommunications companies examines income data per subscriber. For-profit education firms are judged based on income data per student. General nonfinancial metrics like customer satisfaction, market share, and sales growth. The takeaway is that specialization by industry is common among analysts, due to the importance of understanding the economics of the industry, which includes the usefulness of various industry-specific metrics.

Analyzing Service Firms

Using ROA to analyze the profitability of firms that provide services can result in misleading conclusions because their most important resources, employees who deliver the services, do not appear on the balance sheet as assets under U.S. GAAP. One approach to deal with this omission is to express income on a per-employee basis. However, you must use these data cautiously because of differences among firms in their use of full- versus part-time employees and their mix of direct service providers versus support personnel.

Exhibit 4.20 presents profitability data for three service firms (for 2008). **VisionChina Media** is one of China's largest mobile TV advertising networks, with extensive coverage in public transportation facilities (<500 employees). **Monster Worldwide** is an online recruitment firm that links employers with people seeking employment (approximately 7,000 employees). **Accenture** is a multinational management consulting firm (>175,000 employees). VisionChina has the highest operating revenues per employee, followed by Monster, then Accenture. This is due to the combined exclusivity of VisionChina's network throughout China and the fact that the service it provides—advertising via mobile video terminals—does not rely on people to provide the service. In sharp contrast, Accenture's services are provided almost exclusively by employees. Also, compensation expense is highest for Accenture, followed by Monster and VisionChina, with VisionChina having the lowest compensation costs per employee.[36] Administrative and other expenses are highest for VisionChina, which incurs substantial costs for media equipment (essentially

Exhibit 4.20			
Profitability Data for VisionChina Media, Monster Worldwide, and Accenture			
Per Employee:	**VisionChina Media**	**Monster Worldwide**	**Accenture**
Operating revenues	$ 220,044	$193,328	$130,909
Compensation	(5,619)	(78,168)	(92,259)
Administrative and other expenses	(126,293)	(90,706)	(23,713)
Operating income before income taxes	$ 88,132	$ 24,454	$ 14,937
Profitability decomposition:			
Profit margin for ROA	45.1%	9.4%	7.5%
Assets turnover	0.44	0.67	1.88
ROA	19.8%	6.3%	14.1%

---

[36]The individual line items require judgment, as neither company separately discloses an income statement line item for salaries and benefits. Thus, you must examine additional disclosures when available to best prepare cross-sectionally comparable expense classifications.

cost of sales) and other media under certain agreements, which Monster and Accenture do not report. This difference in business models can be seen with the significantly lower assets turnover for VisionChina, which actually maintains substantial investments in assets, as it is not purely a "service" firm. Assets turnover is highest for Accenture, which maintains limited fixed assets and possesses brand recognition and an extensive professional network. Operating revenues and operating income before taxes per employee are lowest at Accenture (with the largest workforce), but Accenture generates a very high ROA due to the high assets turnover. Monster's operating revenues and operating income before taxes per employee are between those of Accenture and VisionChina, but its ROA is lowest.

Per-employee data might usefully supplement traditional financial ratios for numerous other industries, including investment banking, temporary help firms, engineering firms, advertising firms, professional sports teams, information technology, and other service firms. The use of per-employee data also might supplement the analysis of firms that use fixed assets in the provision of services, such as airlines, health care providers, and hotels.

Analyzing Technology-Based Firms

ROA can be an even more misleading ratio for analyzing technology-based firms than for analyzing service firms if the two most important resources of technology firms do not appear in their assets: (1) their people and (2) their technologies. Employees contribute to the creation of technologies, but the most important resource not recognized is the value of the technologies (when those technologies have been internally generated rather than acquired). U.S. GAAP requires firms to expense R&D costs in the year incurred. Thus, both assets and net income are understated during periods in which firms invest heavily in R&D. Subsequently after R&D has led to the introduction of successful, profitable new products, assets are understated but income is overstated because the firms have already expensed investments in R&D. Comparisons across firms with different R&D strategies is affected by whether the firm expenses internally developed R&D or purchases it externally and capitalizes it.

Researchers Lev and Sougiannis proposed studying the relation between R&D expenditures in a particular year and the resulting revenues in subsequent years to determine a basis for recognizing a technology asset on the balance sheet and recomputing net income each year.[37] The technology "asset" would equal the present value of the future revenue stream net of the R&D expenditure during the year. You would then amortize this "asset" over the future periods of benefit based on the projected stream of revenues. Traditional financial ratio analysis works reasonably well for established technology firms that have products in all stages of their life cycles. Traditional financial ratio analysis does not work as well for start-up firms and firms with most of their products in the early high-growth stages of their life cycles. Thus, many analysts take as-reported income statement and balance sheets for such companies and recast them to allow for the capitalization of technology assets (and subsequent amortization), similar to the proposal by Lev and Sougiannis. This further emphasizes the need for analysts to understand financial statements and business operations rather than memorize ratio formulas or scripted analysis techniques.

---

[37]Baruch Lev and Theodore Sougiannis, "The Capitalization, Amortization, and Value-Relevance of R&D," *Journal of Accounting and Economics* (1996), pp. 107–138.

- Firms generally face a tradeoff between profit margin and assets turnover.
- High profit margins tend to reflect high barriers to competitive entry, and low assets turnovers tend to reflect requirements for large capital investments (which can be a barrier to entry).
- Low profit margins tend to reflect low barriers to competitive entry, and higher assets turnovers

due to relatively lower requirements for capital investments.
- Product life cycle theory can be adapted to the profitability of firms during different stages.
- Profit margin for ROA or ROCE can be disaggregated by examining various expense ratios, typically through common-size analysis.
- Assets turnover can be disaggregated into various asset turnover ratios.

Benefits and Limitations of Using Financial Statement Ratios

LO 4-5

Describe the benefits and limitations of using ratios like ROA and ROCE as part of understanding the historical performance of a company.

Financial ratios are easy to compute, and there are many sources of financial data that do the computing for investors, including free websites such as Yahoo! Finance and Smartmoney.com. The most important and valuable step, however, is *interpreting and gleaning key insights from a financial ratio.* To do this successfully, you must know how a ratio was computed. For example, was ROA computed correctly such that the numerator includes net profits after taxes but before interest, or is it based on someone else's calculation that simply uses EBIT in the numerator? Differences in computations do not always create significant differences in ratio calculations, but the astute analyst must be aware of the underlying data embedded in ratios. The second, and most crucial, aspect of interpreting ratios is doing so with an understanding of the firm's economic environment and business strategy. As noted earlier in the chapter, you *must* understand a firm's industry, organizational structure, and strategy to develop hypotheses about what to expect in terms of financial position, profitability, risk, and growth.

Analyzing financial statement ratios is the forensic part of the process of searching for insights and answers to questions about how the firm is performing. In this step, you must dig deep to understand why ratios are what they are. As we saw with **PepsiCo**, a company often provides only limited insight into questions raised by your ratio analysis. At a minimum, however, you should discern whether the ratios reflect the economics of the industry and the specific strategy of the firm. Further, using several benchmarks, you should understand whether a firm is performing better or worse than its peers or is performing better or worse through time. Underlying accounting choices can also affect the ratios you construct. In summary, the first three steps of the six-step process discussed in Chapter 1 (that is, (1) identify economic characteristics of the industry, (2) identify company strategies, and (3) assess the quality of the financial statements) link directly to the use of ratios to validate your understanding of the profitability and risk of a firm and to generate new insights not discovered in the first three steps.

You can compare financial ratios for a particular firm with similar ratios for the same firm for earlier periods (time-series analysis), as we did in this chapter for PepsiCo, or with those of other firms for the same period (cross-sectional analysis), as we did for PepsiCo and **Coca-Cola** and several other sets of firms in this chapter. The next section discusses some of the general issues involved in making such comparisons.

Comparisons with Earlier Periods

You can draw useful insights by comparing a firm with itself over time. We applied this analysis when examining PepsiCo's ROA decomposition earlier in the chapter. A firm's past financial ratios serve as a benchmark for interpreting its current period financial ratios. You can study the impact of economic conditions (recession and inflation), industry conditions (shift in regulatory status and new technology), and firm-specific conditions (shift in corporate strategy and new management) on the time-series pattern of these ratios.

Some questions you should raise before using ratios of past financial statement data as a basis for interpreting ratios for the current period are as follows:

- Has the firm made a significant change in its product, geographic, or customer mix that affects the comparability of financial statement ratios over time?
- Has the firm made a major acquisition or divestiture?
- Has the firm changed its methods of accounting over time? For example, does the firm now consolidate a previously unconsolidated entity?
- Are there any unusual or nonrecurring amounts that impair a comparable analysis of financial results across years?

Analysts should not use past performance as a basis for comparison without considering the level of past and current performance. For example, prior performance might have been at an unsatisfactory level. Improvement during the current year may still leave the firm at an undesirable level. An improved profitability ratio may mean little if the firm still ranks last in its industry in terms of profitability in all years. Similarly, if the firm's prior performance was exceptional but declined in the current period, the firm still may have performed well in the current period.

Another concern involves interpreting the relative rate of change in a ratio over time. Your interpretation of a 10% increase in profit margin for ROA differs depending on whether other firms in the industry experienced a 15% versus a 5% increase. Comparing a particular firm's ratios with those of similar firms lessens the concerns discussed here. Careful time-series analyses of a firm's financial ratios will not only yield key insights about how and why the firm's profitability has been changing over time, but also will provide valuable information about trends. Chapter 10 discusses techniques for building detailed and careful forecasts of financial statements, and we rely heavily on the information and trends gathered from time-series analysis of ratios. In that chapter, we project future financial statements for PepsiCo for the next five years, and the information in the current and past financial ratios provides valuable insights to help us make more reliable forecasts.

Comparisons with Other Firms

The major task in performing a cross-sectional analysis is identifying the other firms to use for comparison. The objective is to select firms with similar products and strategies and similar size and age. Few firms may meet these criteria, and no firms will meet these criteria perfectly. Coca-Cola, for example, is a logical comparison firm for PepsiCo. However, Coca-Cola derives virtually all of its revenues from beverages, whereas PepsiCo derives revenues from beverages and food products, which makes the comparison less than perfect. Comparable firms are rarely perfectly comparable. Even the comparison of similar firms such as Target and Walmart gets complicated, because Target's operations include a segment for its branded credit card and Walmart's operations include the Sam's Club warehouse store chain. You must accept the fact that cross-sectional comparisons of ratios between firms will require subjective judgment about how the differences across firms in business model, strategy, and accounting affect the ratios.

An alternative approach uses average industry ratios, such as those provided in Appendix D of this text; published by **Moody's**, **Dun & Bradstreet**, and **Robert Morris Associates**; or derived from computerized databases such as **Compustat**. These average industry ratios provide an overview of the performance of an industry, aiming to capture the commonalities across many firms. When using standardized ratios prepared by various databases, you should consider the following issues:

1. **Definition of the industry:** Publishers of industry average ratios generally classify diversified firms into the industry of their major product. PepsiCo, for example, appears as a "beverage" company even though it generates a large percentage of its revenues from consumer foods. The industry may also exclude privately held and foreign firms if data are not available for those firms. If these types of firms are significant for a particular industry, you should recognize the possible impact of their absence from the published data.
2. **Calculation of industry average:** Industry averages can be a simple (unweighted) average or a weighted average of the ratios of the included firms. Further, it is helpful to know whether summary industry averages are based on the mean or median.
3. **Distribution of ratios around the mean:** To interpret a deviation of a particular firm's ratio from the industry average requires information on the distribution around the mean. You interpret a ratio that is 10% larger than the industry mean differently depending on whether the standard deviation is 5% versus 15% greater or less than the mean. Useful sources of industry ratios give either the quartiles or the range of the distribution.
4. **Definition of financial statement ratios:** As already emphasized, you should examine the definition of each published ratio. For instance, is the rate of ROCE based on average or beginning-of-the-period common shareholders' equity? Are any adjustments made to reported net income, such as for nonrecurring or unusual charges?

Average industry ratios serve as a useful basis of comparison as long as you recognize their possible limitations. To assist the reader, Appendix D presents data on the distribution of the most common financial statement ratios across time for 48 industries.

Summary

This chapter introduced the fourth step of the six-step process of financial statement analysis, which is to analyze profitability and risk. We examined the two primary summary measures of profitability—ROA and ROCE. Additionally, we examined various financial statement ratios useful for understanding the drivers of ROA or ROCE. Enhanced understanding of these financial ratios results from using and interpreting the ratios, not from memorizing them. The FSAP software available with this book facilitates calculation of the ratios and permits you to devote more time to interpretations. As noted in the chapter, however, it cannot be overemphasized how important the interpretation of financial statement ratios is. This is a necessarily qualitative and intellectual process, which requires you to have understood the firm's specific strategy in the context of the industry and to be aware of any underlying accounting choices that affect the data used in the computation of the financial ratios being examined.

We highlighted alternative methods for examining profitability. The first part of the chapter focused on simple approaches, such as earnings per share, common-size, and percentage change analysis, as well as subjective redefinition of profits. However, the majority of the chapter focused on how to interpret different levels of profitability ratios. Exhibit 4.21 summarizes many of the key profitability ratios discussed in this chapter.

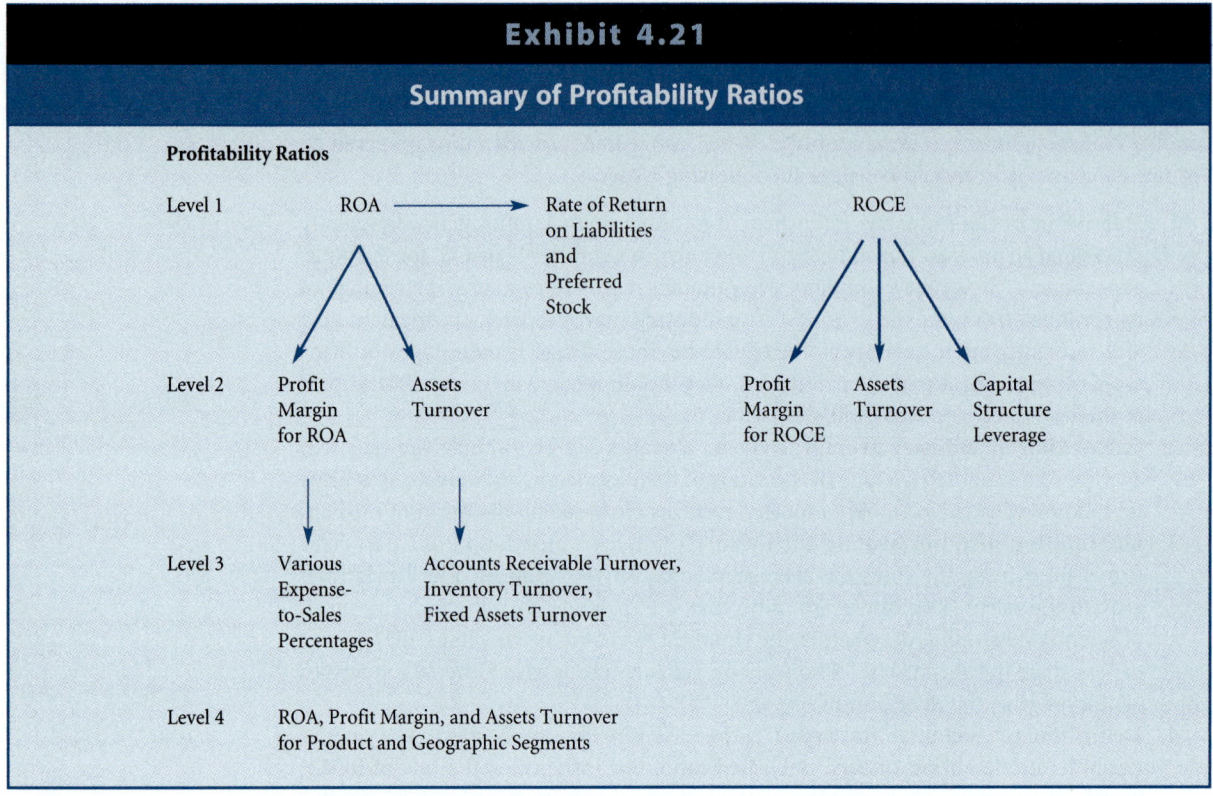

Exhibit 4.21

Summary of Profitability Ratios

Profitability analysis proceeds through four levels of depth. Level 1 involves measures of profitability for a firm as a whole: the rate of ROA and the rate of ROCE. Level 2 disaggregates ROA and ROCE into important components. ROA disaggregates into profit margin for ROA and assets turnover. ROCE disaggregates into profit margin for ROCE, assets turnover, and capital structure leverage components. Level 3 disaggregates the profit margin into various expense-to-sales percentages and disaggregates assets turnover into individual asset turnovers. Level 4 uses product and geographic segment data to study ROA, profit margin, and assets turnover more fully.

Questions, Exercises, Problems, and Cases

Questions and Exercises

LO 4-1   **4.1 Common-Size Analysis.** Common-size analysis is a simple way to make financial statements of different firms comparable. What are possible shortcomings of comparing two different firms using common-size analysis?

LO 4-1   **4.2 Earnings per Share.** Firm A reports an increase in earnings per share; Firm B reports a decrease in earnings per share. Is this unconditionally informative about each firm's performance? If not, why is earnings per share so commonly discussed in the financial press?

LO 4-1   **4.3 Pro Forma Earnings.** Firms often provide supplemental disclosures that report and discuss income figures that do not necessarily equal bottom-line net income from the income statement. Discuss the merits and shortcomings of this managerial practice.

4.4 Profit Margin for ROA versus ROCE. Describe the difference between the profit margin for ROA and the profit margin for ROCE. Explain why each profit margin is appropriate for measuring the rate of ROA and the rate of ROCE, respectively.

`LO 4-2`

4.5 Concept and Measurement of Financial Leverage. Define financial leverage. Explain how financial leverage works to the benefit of the common shareholders.

`LO 4-3`

4.6 Advantages of Financial Leverage. A company president remarked, "The operations of our company are such that we can take advantage of only a minor amount of financial leverage." Explain the likely reasoning the company president had in mind to support this statement.

`LO 4-3`

4.7 Disadvantages of Financial Leverage. The intuition behind the benefits of financial leverage is that a firm can borrow funds that bear a certain interest rate but invest those funds in assets that generate returns in excess of that rate. Why would firms with high ROAs not keep leveraging up their firm by borrowing and investing the funds in profitable assets?

`LO 4-3`

4.8 Concept of Residual Income. Explain the intuition of residual income. Distinguish between net income available to the common shareholders and residual income.

`LO 4-3`

4.9 Return on Common Shareholders' Equity versus Basic Earnings per Common Share. Analysts can compare ROCEs across companies but should not compare basic EPSs despite the fact that both ratios use net income to the common shareholders in the numerator. Explain.

`LO 4-3`

4.10 Calculating ROA and Its Components. Nucor, a steel manufacturer, reported net income for 2008 of $1,831 million on sales of $23,663 million. Interest expense for 2008 was $135 million, and noncontrolling interest was $314 million for 2008. The income tax rate is 35%. Total assets were $9,826 million at the beginning of 2008 and $13,874 million at the end of 2008. Compute the rate of ROA for 2008 and disaggregate ROA into profit margin for ROA and asset turnover components.

`LO 4-2`

4.11 Calculating ROCE and Its Components. Phillips-Van Heusen, an apparel manufacturer, reported net income (amounts in thousands) for Year 4 of $58,615 on sales of $1,460,235. It declared preferred dividends of $21,122. Preferred shareholders' equity totaled $264,746 at both the beginning and end of Year 4. Common shareholders' equity totaled $296,157 at the beginning of Year 4 and $364,026 at the end of Year 4. Phillips-Van Heusen had no noncontrolling interest in its equity. Total assets were $1,439,283 at the beginning of Year 4 and $1,549,582 at the end of Year 4. Compute the rate of ROCE for Year 4 and disaggregate it into profit margin for ROCE, assets turnover, and capital structure leverage ratio components.

`LO 4-3`

4.12 Calculating Basic and Diluted EPS. TJX, Inc., an apparel retailer, reported net income (amounts in thousands) of $609,699 for Year 4. The weighted average of common shares outstanding during Year 4 was 488,809 shares. TJX, Inc., subtracted interest expense net of tax saving on convertible debt of $4,482. If the convertible debt had been converted into common stock, it would have increased the weighted-average common shares outstanding by 16,905 shares. TJX, Inc., has outstanding stock options that, if exercised, would increase the weighted average of common shares outstanding by 6,935 shares. Compute basic and diluted earnings per share for Year 4, showing supporting computations.

`LO 4-1`

LO 4-3 **4.13 Relating ROA and ROCE.** Boston Scientific, a medical device manufacturer, reported net income (amounts in millions) of $1,062 on sales of $5,624 during Year 4. Interest expense totaled $64. The income tax rate was 35%. Average total assets were $6,934.5, and average common shareholders' equity was $3,443.5. The firm did not have preferred stock outstanding or noncontrolling interest in its equity.

a. Compute the rate of ROA. Disaggregate ROA into profit margin for ROA and assets turnover components.

b. Compute the rate of ROCE. Disaggregate ROCE into profit margin for ROCE, assets turnover, and capital structure leverage ratio components.

c. Calculate the amount of net income to common shareholders derived from the excess return on creditors' capital and the amount from the return on common shareholders' capital.

LO 4-3 **4.14 Relating ROA and ROCE.** Valero Energy, a petroleum company, reported net income of $1,803.8 on revenues of $54,618.6 for Year 4. Interest expense totaled $359.7, and preferred dividends totaled $12.5. Average total assets for Year 4 were $17,527.9. The income tax rate is 35%. Average preferred shareholders' equity totaled $204.3, and average common shareholders' equity totaled $6,562.3. All amounts are in millions.

a. Compute the rate of ROA. Disaggregate ROA into profit margin for ROA and assets turnover components.

b. Compute the rate of ROCE. Disaggregate ROCE into profit margin for ROCE, assets turnover, and capital leverage ratio components.

c. Calculate the amount of net income to common shareholders derived from the excess return on creditors' capital, the excess return on preferred shareholders' capital, and the return on common shareholders' capital.

Problems and Cases

LO 4-1 **4.15 Analyzing Operating Profitability.** Exhibit 4.22 presents selected operating data for three retailers for a recent year. Macy's operates several department store chains selling consumer products such as brand-name clothing, china, cosmetics, and bedding and has a large presence in the bridal and formalwear markets (under store names Macy's and Bloomingdale's). Home Depot sells a wide range of building materials and home improvement products, which includes lumber and tools, riding lawn mowers, lighting fixtures, and

Exhibit 4.22

Selected Data for Three Retailers
(amounts in millions)
(Problem 4.15)

	Macy's	Home Depot	Supervalu
Sales	$24,892	$71,288	$44,564
Cost of goods sold	15,009	47,298	34,451
Interest expense	588	624	633
Net income	(4,803)	2,260	(2,855)
Average inventory	4,915	11,202	2,743
Average fixed assets	10,717	26,855	7,531
Average total assets	24,967	42,744	19,333

kitchen cabinets and appliances. **Supervalu** operates grocery stores under numerous brands (including **Albertsons**, **Cub Foods**, **Jewel-Osco**, **Shaw's**, and **Star Market**).

REQUIRED

a. Compute the rate of ROA for each firm. Disaggregate the rate of ROA into profit margin for ROA and assets turnover components. Assume that the income tax rate is 35% for all companies.

b. Based on your knowledge of the three retail stores and their respective industry concentrations, describe the likely reasons for the differences in the profit margins for ROA and assets turnovers.

4.16 Calculating and Interpreting Accounts Receivable Turnover Ratios.

Microsoft Corporation (Microsoft) and **Oracle Corporation** (Oracle) engage in the design, manufacture, and sale of computer software. Microsoft sells and licenses a wide range of systems and application software to businesses, computer hardware manufacturers, and consumer retailers. Oracle sells software for information management almost exclusively to businesses. Exhibit 4.23 presents selected data for the two firms for three recent years.

Exhibit 4.23			
Selected Data for Microsoft and Oracle **(amounts in millions)** **(Problem 4.16)**			
	Year 3	**Year 2**	**Year 1**
Microsoft			
Sales	$58,437	$60,420	$51,122
Average accounts receivable	12,391	12,464	10,327
Change in sales from previous year	−3.3%	+18.2%	+15.5%
Oracle			
Sales	$23,252	$22,430	$17,996
Average accounts receivable	4,430	5,799	4,589
Change in sales from previous year	+3.7%	+24.6%	+25.2%

REQUIRED

a. Calculate the accounts receivable turnover ratio for Microsoft and Oracle for Year 1, Year 2, and Year 3.

b. Suggest possible reasons for the differences in the accounts receivable turnovers of Microsoft and Oracle during the three-year period.

c. Suggest possible reasons for the changes in the accounts receivable turnover for the two firms over the three-year period.

4.17 Calculating and Interpreting Inventory Turnover Ratios. Dell

produces computers and related equipment on a made-to-order basis for consumers and businesses. **Sun Microsystems** designs and manufactures higher-end computers that function as servers and for use in computer-aided design. Sun Microsystems sells primarily to businesses. It also provides services to business customers in addition to product sales of computers. Selected data for each firm for three recent years appear in Exhibit 4.24. (Dell's fiscal year-end is in January; Sun's fiscal year-end is in June. Subsequently in 2010, Oracle acquired Sun.)

Exhibit 4.24

Selected Data for Dell and Sun Microsystems
(amounts in millions)
(Problem 4.17)

	Year 3	Year 2	Year 1
Dell			
Cost of goods sold	$49,375	$48,855	$47,433
Average inventories	1,024	920	618
Change in sales from previous year	+1.1%	+3.0%	+4.1%
Sun Microsystems			
Cost of goods sold	$ 5,948	$ 6,639	$ 6,778
Average inventories	623	602	532
Change in sales from previous year	−10.4%	−2.1%	+3.7%

REQUIRED

a. Calculate the inventory turnover ratio for each firm for the three years.
b. Suggest reasons for the differences in the inventory turnover ratios of these two firms.
c. Suggest reasons for the changes in the inventory turnover ratios during the three-year period.

4.18 Calculating and Interpreting Accounts Receivable and Inventory Turnover Ratios. **Nucor** and **AK Steel** are steel manufacturers. Nucor produces steel in mini-mills. Mini-mills transform scrap ferrous metals into standard sizes of rolled steel, which Nucor then sells to steel service centers and distributors. Its steel falls on the lower end in terms of quality (strength and durability). AK Steel is an integrated steel producer, transforming ferrous metals into rolled steel and then into various steel products for the automobile, appliance, construction, and other industries. Its steel falls on the higher end in terms of quality. Exhibit 4.25 sets forth various data for these two companies for two recent years.

REQUIRED

a. Calculate the accounts receivable turnovers for Nucor and AK Steel for Year 1 and Year 2.
b. Describe the likely reasons for the differences in the accounts receivable turnovers for these two firms.
c. Describe the likely reasons for the trend in the accounts receivable turnovers of these two firms during the two-year period.
d. Calculate the inventory turnovers for Nucor and AK Steel for Year 1 and Year 2.
e. Describe the likely reasons for the differences in the inventory turnovers of these two firms.
f. Describe the likely reasons for the trend in the inventory turnovers of these two firms during the two-year period.

4.19 Calculating and Interpreting Fixed Assets Turnover Ratios.
Texas Instruments (TI) designs and manufactures semiconductor products for use in computers, telecommunications equipment, automobiles, and other electronics-based products. The manufacturing of semiconductors is highly capital-intensive. **Hewlett-Packard Corporation** (HP) manufactures computer hardware and various imaging products, such as printers and fax machines. Exhibit 4.26 presents selected data for TI and HP for three recent years.

Exhibit 4.25

Selected Data for Nucor and AK Steel
(amounts in millions)
(Problem 4.18)

	Year 3	Year 2
Nucor		
Sales	$23,663	$16,593
Cost of goods sold	19,612	13,035
Average accounts receivable	1,420	1,340
Average inventories	2,005	1,371
Change in sales from previous year	+42.6%	+12.5%
AK Steel		
Sales	$ 7,644	$ 7,003
Cost of goods sold	6,479	5,904
Average accounts receivable	572	686
Average inventories	607	752
Change in sales from previous year	+9.2%	+15.3%

Exhibit 4.26

Selected Data for Texas Instruments and Hewlett-Packard
(amounts in millions)
(Problem 4.19)

	Year 3	Year 2	Year 1
Texas Instruments			
Sales	$ 12,501	$ 13,835	$ 14,255
Cost of goods sold	6,256	5,432	5,775
Capital expenditures	763	686	1,272
Average fixed assets	3,457	3,780	3,925
Percentage fixed assets depreciated	54.9%	52.3%	49.0%
Percentage change in sales	−9.6%	−3.0%	+6.4%
Hewlett-Packard			
Sales	$114,552	$118,364	$104,286
Cost of goods sold	86,351	87,065	76,965
Capital expenditures	3,695	2,990	3,040
Average fixed assets	11,050	9,318	7,331
Percentage fixed assets depreciated	74.7%	72.4%	87.0%
Percentage change in sales	−3.2%	+13.5%	+13.8%

REQUIRED

    a. Compute the fixed assets turnover for each firm for Years 1, 2, and 3.

    b. Suggest reasons for the differences in the fixed assets turnovers of TI and HP.

    c. Suggest reasons for the changes in the fixed assets turnovers of TI and HP during the three-year period.

4.20 Calculating and Interpreting the Return on Common Share-holders' Equity and Its Components. **JCPenney** operates a chain of retail department stores, selling apparel, shoes, jewelry, and home furnishings. It also offers most of its products through catalog distribution. During fiscal Year 5, it sold **Eckerd Drugs**, a chain of retail drugstores, and used the cash proceeds, in part, to repurchase shares of its common stock. Exhibit 4.27 presents selected data for JCPenney for fiscal Year 3, Year 4, and Year 5.

REQUIRED

    a. Calculate the rate of ROA for fiscal Year 3, Year 4, and Year 5. Disaggregate ROA into the profit margin for ROA and total assets turnover components. The income tax rate is 35%.

    b. Calculate the rate of ROCE for fiscal Year 3, Year 4, and Year 5. Disaggregate ROCE into the profit margin for ROCE, assets turnover, and capital structure leverage components.

    c. Suggest reasons for the changes in ROCE over the three years.

    d. Compute the ratio of ROCE to ROA for each year.

    e. Calculate the amount of net income available to common stockholders derived from the use of financial leverage with respect to creditors' capital, the amount derived from the use of preferred shareholders' capital, and the amount derived from common sharehold-ers' capital for each year.

    f. Did financial leverage work to the advantage of the common shareholders in each of the three years? Explain.

Exhibit 4.27

Selected Data for JCPenney
(amounts in millions)
(Problem 4.20)

	Year Ended January 31,		
	Year 5	Year 4	Year 3
Sales	$18,424	$17,786	$17,633
Net income (loss)	524	(928)	405
Interest expense	279	271	245
Preferred stock dividend	12	25	27
Income tax rate	35%	35%	35%

January 31:	Year 5	Year 4	Year 3	Year 2
Total assets	$14,127	$18,300	$17,787	$18,048
Preferred stock	0	304	333	363
Total common shareholders' equity	4,856	5,121	6,037	5,766

4.21 Interpreting the Return on Common Shareholders' Equity and Its Components.

LO 4-3, LO 4-4

Selected financial data for **Georgia-Pacific Corporation**, a forest products and paper firm, appear in Exhibit 4.28.

Exhibit 4.28

Selected Data for Georgia-Pacific Corporation (Problem 4.21)

	Year 4	Year 3	Year 2	Year 1	Year 0
ROCE	10.8%	6.5%	(4.2)%	(9.1)%	7.4%
ROA	4.8%	3.7%	1.5%	0.8%	3.3%
Profit margin for ROA	5.8%	4.6%	1.7%	0.9%	3.3%
Profit margin for ROCE	3.2%	1.6%	(0.9)%	(1.9)%	1.6%
Assets turnover	0.8	0.8	0.9	0.9	1.0
Capital structure leverage	4.1	4.9	5.4	5.3	4.8
Growth rate in sales	0.0%	(13.5)%	(9.2)%	13.4%	24.1%

REQUIRED

a. In which years did financial leverage work to the advantage of the common shareholders? In which years did it work to their disadvantage? Explain.

b. Identify possible reasons for the changes in the capital structure leverage ratio during the five-year period.

4.22 Calculating and Interpreting the Return on Common Shareholders' Equity and Earnings per Common Share.

LO 4-1, LO 4-3, LO 4-4

Selected data for **General Mills** for 2007, 2008, and 2009 appear below (amounts in millions).

	2009	2008	2007
Net income	$1,304.4	$1,294.7	$1,144.0
Weighted-average number of common shares outstanding	331.9	333.0	346.5
Average common shareholders' equity	$5,695.3	$5,767.4	$5,545.5

REQUIRED

a. Compute the rate of ROCE for 2007, 2008, and 2009.

b. Compute basic EPS for 2007, 2008, and 2009.

c. Interpret the changes in ROCE versus EPS over the three-year period.

4.23 Interpreting Several Measures of Profitability.

LO 4-1, LO 4-2, LO 4-3, LO 4-4

Selected data for **The Hershey Company** for 2010–2012 appear in Exhibit 4.29.

REQUIRED

a. Compute ROA and its decomposition for 2010–2012. Assume a tax rate of 35%.

b. Compute ROCE and its decomposition for 2010–2012.

c. Interpret the trends in reported net income, EPS, ROA, and ROCE over the three-year period.

Exhibit 4.29

Selected Data for The Hershey Company
(amounts in millions except per-share data)
(Problem 4.23)

	2012	2011	2010
Sales	$6,644,252	$6,080,788	$5,671,009
Interest expense	95,569	92,183	96,434
Net income	628,962	509,799	435,994
Diluted EPS	2.89	2.74	2.21
Minority interest in net income	12,950	5,817	8,183
Total assets	4,754,839	4,407,094	4,272,732
Total shareholders' equity	1,048,373	880,943	937,601
Noncontrolling interests in subsidiaries	11,624	23,626	35,285

LO 4-1, LO 4-2, LO 4-3, LO 4-4

4.24 Calculating and Interpreting Profitability Ratios. Hasbro is a leading firm in the toy, game, and amusement industry. Its promoted brands group includes products from Playskool, Tonka, Milton Bradley, Parker Brothers, Tiger, and Wizards of the Coast. Sales of toys and games are highly variable from year to year depending on whether the latest products meet consumer interests. Hasbro also faces increasing competition from electronic and online games. Hasbro develops and promotes its core brands and manufactures and distributes products created by others under license arrangements. Hasbro pays a royalty to the creator of such products. In recent years, Hasbro has attempted to reduce its reliance on license arrangements, placing more emphasis on its core brands. Hasbro also has embarked on a strategy of reducing fixed selling and administrative costs in an effort to offset the negative effects on earnings of highly variable sales. Exhibit 4.30 presents the balance sheets for Hasbro for the

Exhibit 4.30

Hasbro
Balance Sheets
(amounts in millions)
(Problem 4.24)

	December 31,			
	Year 4	Year 3	Year 2	Year 1
ASSETS				
Cash	$ 725	$ 521	$ 496	$ 233
Accounts receivable	579	607	555	572
Inventories	195	169	190	217
Prepayments	219	212	191	346
Total Current Assets	$1,718	$1,509	$1,432	$1,368

(Continued)

years ended December 31, Years 1 through 4. Exhibit 4.31 presents the income statements and
Exhibit 4.32 presents the statements of cash flows for Years 2 through 4.

Exhibit 4.30 (Continued)

Other assets	1,316	1,454	1,498	1,765
Total Assets	$3,241	$3,163	$3,143	$3,369
LIABILITIES AND SHAREHOLDERS' EQUITY				
Accounts payable	$ 168	$ 159	$ 166	$ 123
Short-term borrowing	342	24	223	36
Other current liabilities	639	747	578	599
Total Current Liabilities	$1,149	$ 930	$ 967	$ 758
Long-term debt	303	687	857	1,166
Other noncurrent liabilities	149	141	128	92
Total Liabilities	$1,601	$1,758	$1,952	$2,016
Common stock	$ 105	$ 105	$ 105	$ 105
Additional paid-in capital	381	398	458	455
Retained earnings	1,721	1,567	1,430	1,622
Accumulated other comprehensive income (loss)	82	30	(47)	(68)
Treasury stock	(649)	(695)	(755)	(761)
Total Shareholders' Equity	$1,640	$1,405	$1,191	$1,353
Total Liabilities and Shareholders' Equity	$3,241	$3,163	$3,143	$3,369

Source: Hasbro, Inc., Form 10-K for the Fiscal Years Ended 2001–2004.

Exhibit 4.31

Hasbro
Income Statements
(amounts in millions)
(Problem 4.24)

	For the Year Ended December 31,		
	Year 4	Year 3	Year 2
Sales	$ 2,998	$ 3,139	$ 2,816
Cost of goods sold	(1,252)	(1,288)	(1,099)
Selling and administrative expenses:			
Advertising	(387)	(364)	(297)
Research and development	(157)	(143)	(154)
Royalty expense	(223)	(248)	(296)
Other selling and administrative	(687)	(799)	(788)

(Continued)

Exhibit 4.31 (Continued)

Interest expense	(32)	(53)	(78)
Income tax expense	(64)	(69)	(29)
Net Income	$ 196	$ 175	$ 75

Source: Hasbro, Inc., Form 10-K for the Fiscal Years Ended 2002–2004.

Exhibit 4.32

Hasbro
Statements of Cash Flows
(amounts in millions)
(Problem 4.24)

	For the Year Ended December 31,		
	Year 4	**Year 3**	**Year 2**
OPERATIONS			
Net income	$196	$ 175	$ 75
Depreciation and amortization	146	164	184
Addbacks and subtractions, net	17	68	(67)
(Increase) Decrease in accounts receivable	76	(13)	34
(Increase) Decrease in inventories	(16)	35	39
(Increase) Decrease in prepayments	29	8	185
Increase (Decrease) in accounts payable and other current liabilities	(90)	17	23
Cash Flow from Operations	$358	$ 454	$ 473
INVESTING			
Property, plant, and equipment acquired	$ (79)	$ (63)	$ (59)
Other investing transactions	(6)	(2)	(3)
Cash Flow from Investing	$ (85)	$ (65)	$ (62)
FINANCING			
Increase in common stock	$ 3	$ 40	$ 3
Decrease in short-term borrowing	(7)	—	(15)
Decrease in long-term borrowing	(58)	(389)	(127)
Acquisition of common stock	—	(3)	—
Dividends	(37)	(21)	(21)
Other financing transactions	7	9	12
Cash Flow from Financing	$ (69)	$(364)	$(148)
Change in Cash	$204	$ 25	$ 263
Cash—Beginning of year	521	496	233
Cash—End of Year	$725	$ 521	$ 496

Source: Hasbro, Inc., Form 10-K for the Fiscal Years Ended 2002–2004.

REQUIRED

a. Exhibit 4.33 presents profitability ratios for Hasbro for Year 2 and Year 3. Calculate each of these financial ratios for Year 4. The income tax rate is 35%.

b. Analyze the changes in ROA and its components for Hasbro over the three-year period, suggesting reasons for the changes observed.

c. Analyze the changes in ROCE and its components for Hasbro over the three-year period, suggesting reasons for the changes observed.

Exhibit 4.33			
Hasbro **Financial Statement Ratio Analysis** **(Problem 4.24)**			
	Year 4	**Year 3**	**Year 2**
Profit margin for ROA		6.7%	4.5%
Assets turnover		1.0	0.9
ROA		6.6%	3.9%
Profit margin for ROCE		5.6%	2.7%
Capital structure leverage		2.4	2.6
ROCE		13.5%	5.9%
Cost of goods sold/Sales		41.0%	39.0%
Advertising expense/Sales		11.6%	10.5%
Research and development expense/Sales		4.6%	5.5%
Royalty expense/Sales		7.9%	10.5%
Other selling and administrative expense/Sales		25.4%	28.0%
Income tax expense (excluding tax effects of interest expense)/Sales		2.8%	2.0%
Accounts receivable turnover		5.4	5.0
Inventory turnover		7.2	5.4
Fixed assets turnover		15.2	12.5

4.25 Calculating and Interpreting Profitability Ratios. Abercrombie & Fitch

LO 4-1, LO 4-2, LO 4-3, LO 4-4

sells casual apparel and personal care products for men, women, and children through retail stores located primarily in shopping malls. Its fiscal year ends January 31 of each year. Financial statements for Abercrombie & Fitch for fiscal years ending January 31, Year 3, Year 4, and Year 5 appear in Exhibit 4.34 (balance sheets), Exhibit 4.35 (income statements), and Exhibit 4.36 (statements of cash flows). These financial statements reflect the capitalization of operating leases in property, plant, and equipment and long-term debt, a topic discussed in Chapter 6. Exhibit 4.37 (page 312) presents financial statement ratios for Abercrombie & Fitch for Years 3 and 4. Selected data for Abercrombie & Fitch appear here.

Exhibit 4.34

Abercrombie & Fitch
Balance Sheets
(amounts in millions)
(Problem 4.25)

| | January 31, | | | |
	Year 5	Year 4	Year 3	Year 2
ASSETS				
Cash	$ 350	$ 56	$ 43	$ 188
Marketable securities	—	465	387	51
Accounts receivable	26	7	10	21
Inventories	248	201	169	130
Prepayments	28	24	20	15
Total Current Assets	$ 652	$ 753	$ 629	$ 405
Property, plant, and equipment, net	1,560	1,342	1,172	947
Other assets	8	1	1	—
Total Assets	$2,220	$2,096	$1,802	$1,352
LIABILITIES AND SHAREHOLDERS' EQUITY				
Accounts payable	$ 84	$ 58	$ 79	$ 32
Short-term borrowing	54	33	—	—
Other current liabilities	276	220	193	132
Total Current Liabilities	$ 414	$ 311	$ 272	$ 164
Long-term debt	872	713	629	581
Other noncurrent liabilities	265	214	165	12
Total Liabilities	$1,551	$1,238	$1,066	$ 757
Common stock	$ 1	$ 1	$ 1	$ 1
Additional paid-in capital	140	139	143	141
Retained earnings	1,076	906	701	520
Treasury stock	(548)	(188)	(109)	(67)
Total Shareholders' Equity	$ 669	$ 858	$ 736	$ 595
Total Liabilities and Shareholders' Equity	$2,220	$2,096	$1,802	$1,352

Source: Abercrombie & Fitch Co., Form 10-K for the Fiscal Years Ended 2002–2005.

REQUIRED

a. Calculate the ratios in Exhibit 4.37 for Year 5. The income tax rate is 35%.

b. Analyze the changes in ROA for Abercrombie & Fitch during the three-year period, suggesting possible reasons for the changes observed.

c. Analyze the changes in ROCE for Abercrombie & Fitch during the three-year period, suggesting possible reasons for the changes observed.

Exhibit 4.35

Abercrombie & Fitch
Income Statements
(amounts in millions)
(Problem 4.25)

	For the Year Ended January 31,		
	Year 5	Year 4	Year 3
Sales	$ 2,021	$1,708	$1,596
Cost of goods sold	(1,048)	(936)	(893)
Selling and administrative expenses	(562)	(386)	(343)
Interest expense	(63)	(54)	(48)
Interest income	5	4	4
Income tax expense	(137)	(131)	(121)
Net Income	$ 216	$ 205	$ 195
	Year 5	Year 4	Year 3
Square feet of retail space (in thousands)	5,590	5,016	4,358
Number of employees	48,500	30,200	22,000
Growth rate in sales	18.3%	7.0%	16.9%
Comparable store sales increase	2.0%	(9.0%)	5.0%

Source: Abercrombie & Fitch Co., Form 10-K for the Fiscal Years Ended 2003–2005.

Exhibit 4.36

Abercrombie & Fitch
Statements of Cash Flows
(amounts in millions)
(Problem 4.25)

	For the Year Ended January 31,		
	Year 5	Year 4	Year 3
OPERATIONS			
Net income	$ 216	$ 205	$ 195
Depreciation and amortization	106	90	76
Addbacks and subtractions, net	13	56	49
(Increase) Decrease in inventories	(34)	(27)	(34)
Increase (Decrease) in current liabilities	125	19	60
Cash Flow from Operations	$ 426	$ 343	$ 346

(Continued)

Exhibit 4.36 (Continued)

INVESTING

Property, plant, and equipment acquired	$ (185)	$ (160)	$ (146)
Marketable securities sold	4,779	3,771	2,419
Marketable securities purchased	(4,314)	(3,849)	(2,729)
Other investing transactions	—	—	5
Cash Flow from Investing	$ (280)	$ (238)	$ (451)

FINANCING

Increase in short-term borrowing	$ 20	$ 4	$ 4
Increase in common stock	49	20	—
Acquisition of common stock	(435)	(116)	(43)
Dividends	(46)	—	—
Cash Flow from Financing	$ (412)	$ (92)	$ (39)
Change in Cash	$ 294	$ 13	$ (144)
Cash—Beginning of year	56	43	188
Cash—End of Year	$ 350	$ 56	$ 43

Source: Abercrombie & Fitch Co., Form 10-K for the Fiscal Years Ended 2003–2005.

Exhibit 4.37

Abercrombie & Fitch
Financial Statement Ratio Analysis
(Problem 4.25)

	Year 5	Year 4	Year 3
Profit margin for ROA		14.1%	14.2%
Assets turnover		0.9	1.0
ROA		12.3%	14.3%
Profit margin for ROCE		12.0%	12.2%
Capital structure leverage		2.4	2.4
ROCE		25.7%	29.3%
Cost of goods sold/Sales		54.8%	56.0%
Selling and administrative expense/Sales		22.6%	21.5%
Interest revenue/Sales		0.2%	0.3%
Income tax expense (excluding tax effects of interest expense)/Sales		8.8%	8.6%
Accounts receivable turnover		200.9	103.0
Inventory turnover		5.1	6.0
Fixed assets turnover		1.4	1.5
Sales per store		$2,440,000	$2,673,367
Sales per square foot		$ 340.51	$ 366.22
Sales per employee		$ 56,556	$ 72,545

4.26 Analyzing the Profitability of a Service Firm. Kelly Services (Kelly)

LO 4-1, LO 4-2, LO 4-3, LO 4-4

places employees at clients' businesses on a temporary basis. It segments its services into (1) commercial, (2) professional and technical, and (3) international. Kelly recognizes revenues for the amount billed to clients. Kelly includes the amount it pays to temporary employees in cost of services sold. It includes the compensation paid to permanent employees that administer its offices in selling and administrative expenses. The latter expense also includes data processing costs relating to payroll records for all employees, rent, taxes, and insurance on office space. Amounts receivable from clients appear in accounts receivable, and amounts payable to permanent and temporary employees appear in current liabilities.

The temporary personnel business offers clients flexibility in adjusting the number of workers to meet changing capacity needs. Temporary employees are typically less costly than permanent workers because they have fewer fringe benefits. However, temporary workers generally are not as well trained as permanent workers and have less loyalty to clients.

Barriers to entry in the personnel supply business are low. This business does not require capital for physical facilities (most space is rented), does not need specialized assets (most temporary employees do not possess unique skills; needed data processing technology is readily available), and operates with little government regulation. Thus, competition is intense and margins tend to be thin.

Exhibit 4.38 presents selected profitability ratios and other data for Kelly Services, the largest temporary personnel supply firm in the United States. Note that the data in Exhibit 4.38 reflect the capitalization of operating leases in property, plant, and equipment and long-term debt, a topic discussed in Chapter 6.

Exhibit 4.38

Profitability Ratios and Other Data for Kelly Services (Problem 4.26)

	Year 4	Year 3	Year 2
Profit margin for ROA	0.6%	0.3%	0.6%
Assets turnover	3.8	3.5	3.5
ROA	2.2%	0.9%	2.1%
Profit margin for ROCE	0.4%	0.1%	0.4%
Capital structure leverage	2.1	2.0	1.9
ROCE	3.3%	0.8%	2.9%
Revenues	100.0%	100.0%	100.0%
Compensation of temporary employees/Revenues	84.0%	83.9%	82.9%
Selling and administrative expense/Revenues	15.1%	15.7%	16.1%
Income tax expense/Revenues	0.3%	0.2%	0.4%
Accounts receivable turnover	7.2	7.1	7.3
Fixed assets turnover	16.0	14.0	12.9
Sales mix data:			
Commercial	46.7%	49.3%	51.9%
Professional and technical	20.7	20.7	21.4
International	32.6	30.0	26.7
Total	100.0%	100.0%	100.0%

(Continued)

Exhibit 4.38 (Continued)			
Segment profit margin:			
Commercial	5.1%	4.4%	5.6%
Professional and technical	6.0%	5.9%	5.8%
International	0.8%	0.0%	0.5%
Number of offices	2,600	2,500	2,400
Number of permanent employees	8,400	7,900	8,200
Number of temporary employees, approximate	700,000	700,000	700,000
Growth rate in revenues	15.2%	6.9%	(4.7%)
Per-office data:			
Revenues	$1,916,923	$1,730,000	$1,690,417
Net income	$ 8,077	$ 2,000	$ 7,500
Permanent employees	3.2	3.2	3.4
Temporary employees	269	280	292
Per-permanent-employee data:			
Revenues	$ 593,333	$ 547,468	$ 494,756
Net income	$ 2,500	$ 633	$ 2,195
Temporary employees	83.3	88.6	85.4
Per-temporary-employee data:			
Revenues	$ 7,120	$ 6,177	$ 5,796
Net income	$ 30	$ 7	$ 26

REQUIRED

Analyze the changes in the profitability of Kelly Services during the three-year period in as much depth as permitted by the data provided.

4.27 Analyzing the Profitability of Two Hotels. Starwood Hotels

(Starwood) owns and operates many hotel properties under well-known brand names, including Sheraton, W, Westin, and St. Regis. Starwood focuses on the upper end of the lodging industry. **Choice Hotels** (Choice) is primarily a franchisor of several hotel chains, including Comfort Inn, Sleep Inn, Clarion, EconoLodge, and Rodeway Inn. Choice properties represent primarily the midscale and economy segments of the lodging industry. Exhibit 4.39 (page 315) presents selected profitability ratios and other data for Starwood, and Exhibit 4.40 (page 315) presents data for Choice. (Note that ROCE is not meaningful for Choice because of negative common shareholders' equity due to open market share repurchases, not accumulated deficits. As of the end of 2008, Choice had repurchased over one-third of all common shares issued: 34,640,510 out of 95,345,362 shares.) One of the closely followed metrics in the lodging industry is occupancy rate, which gives an indication of the capacity utilization of available hotel rooms. A second measure is the ADR (average daily rate), which measures the amount actually collected for an average room per night. Finally, REVPAR (revenue per available room) also is an important measure, which measures period-to-period growth in revenues per room for comparable properties (adjusted for properties sold or closed or otherwise not comparable across years). The interaction of occupancy rate and ADR is REVPAR.

Exhibit 4.39

Profitability Ratios and Other Data for Starwood Hotels
(Problem 4.27)

	2008	2007	2006
Sales growth	(4.0%)	2.9%	0.0%
Profit margin for ROA	7.8%	10.4%	19.8%
Assets turnover	0.61	0.65	0.55
ROA	4.8%	6.8%	10.9%
Profit margin for ROCE	5.6%	8.8%	17.4%
Capital structure leverage	5.23	3.72	2.65
ROCE	17.8%	21.3%	25.4%
Number of hotels	942	925	871
Number of rooms	285,000	282,000	266,000
Rooms per hotel	303	305	305
Occupancy rate	71.1%	72.7%	71.2%
Revenue per available room night	$ 168.93	$ 171.01	$ 136.33
Average daily rate	$ 237.45	$ 235.18	$ 191.56

Exhibit 4.40

Profitability Ratios and Other Data for Choice Hotels
(Problem 4.27)

	2008	2007	2006
Sales growth	4.2%	14.0%	13.1%
Profit margin for ROA	16.7%	19.6%	22.6%
Assets turnover	1.95	1.95	1.90
ROA	32.6%	38.2%	42.9%
Profit margin for ROCE	15.6%	18.1%	20.9%
Capital structure leverage	(2.23)	(2.88)	(2.48)
ROCE	N/M*	N/M*	N/M*
Number of hotels	4,716	4,445	4,211
Number of rooms	373,884	354,139	339,441
Rooms per hotel	79	80	81
Occupancy rate	55.3%	57.9%	58.4%
Revenue per available room night	$ 40.98	$ 41.75	$ 40.13
Average daily rate	$ 74.11	$ 72.07	$ 68.71

*N/M: Not meaningful due to negative common shareholders' equity

REQUIRED

Analyze the changes and the differences in the profitability of these two hotel chains to the deepest levels available given the data provided. Compare and contrast the ROAs and ROCEs of both companies. Do the results match your prior expectations given the type of lodging for which each company specializes?

4.28 Analyzing the Profitability of Two Rental Car Companies.

Select data for **Avis** and **Hertz** for 2012 follow. Based only on this information and ratios that you construct, speculate on similarities and differences in the operations and financing decisions of the two companies based on similarities and differences in the ratios.

	Avis Budget Group	Hertz Global Holdings
Sales	$ 7,357	$ 9,021
Interest expense	268	650
Net income	290	243
Average total assets	14,078	20,480
Average shareholders' equity	585	2,371

4.29 Analyzing the Profitability of Two Restaurant Chains.

Analyzing the profitability of restaurants requires consideration of their strategies with respect to owner-ship of restaurants versus franchising. Firms that own and operate their restaurants report the assets and financing of those restaurants on their balance sheets and the revenues and operating expenses of the restaurants on their income statements. Firms that franchise their restaurants to others (that is, franchisees) often own the land and buildings of franchised restaurants and lease them to the franchisees. The income statement includes fees received from franchisees in the form of license fees for using the franchiser's name; rent for facilities and equipment; and various fees for advertising, menu planning, and food and paper products used by the franchisee. The revenues and operating expenses of the franchised restaurants appear on the financial statements of the franchisees.

Exhibit 4.41 presents profitability ratios and other data for **Brinker International**, and Exhibit 4.42 presents similar data for **McDonald's**. Brinker operates chains of specialty sit-down restaurants in the United States under the names of Chili's, Romano's Macaroni Grill, On the Border, Maggiano's Little Italy, and Corner Bakery Cafe. Its restaurants average approximately 7,000 square feet. Brinker owns and operates approximately 81% of its restaurants. McDonald's operates chains of fast-food restaurants in the United States and other countries under the names of McDonald's, Boston Market, Chipotle Mexican Grill, and Donatos Pizza. Its restaurants average approximately 2,800 square feet. McDonald's owns and operates approximately 29% of its restaurants. It also owns approximately 25% of the restaurant land and buildings of franchisees. The financial ratios and other data in Exhibits 4.41 and 4.42 reflect the capitalization of operating leases in property, plant, and equipment and long-term debt, a topic discussed in Chapter 6.

REQUIRED

a. Suggest reasons for the changes in the profitability of Brinker during the three-year period.
b. Suggest reasons for the changes in the profitability of McDonald's during the three-year period.
c. Suggest reasons for differences in the profitability of Brinker and McDonald's during the three-year period.

Exhibit 4.41

**Profitability Ratios and Other Data for
Brinker International (dollar amounts in thousands)
(Problem 4.29)**

	Year 4	Year 3	Year 2
Profit margin for ROA	5.1%	6.2%	6.5%
Assets turnover	1.4	1.3	1.3
ROA	7.1%	8.4%	8.8%
Profit margin for ROCE	4.1%	5.1%	5.2%
Capital structure leverage	2.5	2.3	2.3
ROCE	14.1%	15.8%	16.1%
Cost of goods sold/Revenues	81.2%	80.9%	81.0%
Selling and administrative expenses/Revenues	10.9%	9.8%	9.1%
Income tax expense (excluding tax effects of interest expense)/Revenues	2.8%	3.1%	3.4%
Accounts receivable turnover	100.2	106.0	101.3
Inventory turnover	97.1	115.5	95.5
Fixed assets turnover	1.7	1.6	1.6
Revenues per restaurant	$2,516	$2,343	$2,277
Operating income per restaurant	$ 129	$ 145	$ 148
Fixed assets per restaurant	$1,476	$1,493	$1,506
Percentage of restaurants owned and operated	80.1%	81.7%	81.9%
Growth in revenues	12.8%	13.8%	16.7%
Growth in number of restaurants	5.3%	10.6%	10.9%

Exhibit 4.42

**Profitability Ratios and Other Data for
McDonald's (dollar amounts in thousands)
(Problem 4.29)**

	Year 4	Year 3	Year 2
Profit margin for ROA	15.1%	12.2%	10.0%
Assets turnover	0.6	0.5	0.5
ROA	8.5%	6.7%	5.3%
Profit margin for ROCE	12.0%	8.8%	6.4%
Capital structure leverage	2.6	2.8	2.9
ROCE	17.4%	13.5%	9.8%
Cost of goods sold/Revenues	65.8%	66.7%	66.7%
Selling and administrative expenses/Revenues	12.6%	14.4%	17.0%
Income tax expense (excluding tax effects of interest expense)/Revenues	6.5%	6.7%	6.3%

(Continued)

Exhibit 4.42 (Continued)			
Accounts receivable turnover	25.7	21.6	17.7
Inventory turnover	90.9	94.8	94.2
Fixed assets turnover	0.7	0.6	0.6
Revenues per restaurant	$ 605	$ 551	$ 495
Operating income per restaurant	$ 91	$ 67	$ 50
Fixed assets per restaurant	$ 881	$ 856	$ 795
Percentage of restaurants owned and operated	29.2%	28.8%	28.9%
Growth in revenues	11.2%	11.3%	3.6%
Growth in number of restaurants	1.4%	0.1%	3.4%

INTEGRATIVE CASE 4.1

Starbucks

Part A

Integrative Case 1.1 introduced the industry economics of coffee shops and the business strategy of **Starbucks** to compete in this industry. Exhibit 1.26 presents balance sheets for Starbucks for the years ending 2009–2012. Exhibit 1.27 presents its income statements and Exhibit 1.28 presents the statement of cash flows for the same years. Exhibit 1.29 presents common-size balance sheets and Exhibit 1.30 presents common-size income statements for Starbucks. Before beginning preparation of Integrative Case 4.1, we recommend that you review Integrative Case 1.1 in Chapter 1.

Part A of Integrative Case 4.1 analyzes changes in the profitability of Starbucks.

REQUIRED

a. Exhibit 4.43 presents profitability ratios for Starbucks for fiscals 2010 and 2011. Using the financial statement data in Exhibits 1.26 and 1.27, compute the values of these ratios for fiscal 2012. The income tax rate is 35%. For accounts receivable turnover, use only specialty revenues for the numerator, because the accounts receivable are primarily related to licensing and food service operations, not the retail operations. Use cost of sales, including occupancy costs, for the numerator of the inventory turnover, because Starbucks does not disclose separately the cost of products sold (the appropriate numerator) and occupancy costs.

b. What are the most important reasons for Starbucks' ROA fluctuation during the three-year period? Analyze the financial ratios to the maximum depth possible with the information given. Using the nomenclature from the schematic in Exhibit 4.21 (page 298), Exhibit 4.44 (page 320) provides information for analyzing profitability at Level 1, Level 2, and Level 3. Exhibit 4.44 presents additional information for Starbucks at a business segment level to permit analysis at Level 4. Differences between the sum of segment expenses and total expenses reflect corporate-level expenses not allocated to the individual segments. Additionally, if necessary, access Starbuck's annual report or form 10-K, which you should be able to access at the company's investor relations website.

c. What are the most important reasons for Starbucks' ROCE fluctuation during the three-year period?

Exhibit 4.43			
Starbucks **Financial Statement Ratio Analysis** **(Integrative Case 4.1, Part A)**			
	2012	**2011**	**2010**
Profit margin for ROA		10.9%	9.1%
Assets turnover		1.70	1.79
ROA		18.5%	16.2%
Profit margin for ROCE		10.6%	8.8%
Capital structure leverage		1.71	1.78
ROCE		30.9%	28.1%
Cost of sales/Operating revenues		42.0%	41.2%
Store operating expenses/Operating revenues		30.7%	32.4%
Other operating expenses/Operating revenues		3.4%	2.6%
Depreciation and amortization expense/Operating revenues		4.5%	4.8%
General and administrative expense/Operating revenues		6.4%	6.6%
Restructuring charge/Operating revenues		0.0%	0.5%
Income from equity investees/Operating revenues		1.5%	1.4%
Interest revenue/Operating revenues		1.1%	0.5%
Income tax expense (excluding tax effects of interest expense)/Operating revenues		4.9%	4.7%
Accounts receivable turnover		6.0	6.1
Inventory turnover		6.5	7.3
Fixed asset turnover		4.9	4.3

Part B

Part B of Integrative Case 4.1 compares the profitability of **Starbucks** with **Panera Bread Company**. Although Starbucks and Panera Bread Company are not direct competitors in terms of the principal food products offered, they compete in the sense of offering a relaxed café experience. Whereas the products of Starbucks center on coffee and related beverages, Panera Bread Company emphasizes freshly baked bread and pastries. Panera Bread Company also sells sandwiches, soups, and similar lunch and light dinner products that build on their bread offerings, as well as coffee and other beverages. The average size of a Panera Bread Company retail outlet is typically larger than that of Starbucks. Both Starbucks and Panera Bread Company own some of their retail stores and franchise or license rights to use their names and products to other parties that own and operate other retail stores. Panera Bread Company prepares fresh dough daily in various regional facilities to use in company-owned stores and to sell to franchisees. Unlike Starbucks, it has not expanded beyond the United States.

Exhibit 4.45 (page 321) presents profitability ratios for Panera Bread Company for 2010–2012, and Exhibit 4.46 (pages 321–322) presents segment profitability and other data. The format of Exhibit 4.45 is similar to that of Exhibit 4.43. However, due to less detailed disclosures by Panera, Exhibit 4.46 does not contain specific cost structures for Panera's operating segments, similar to what was available from Starbucks and presented in Exhibit 4.44. The proportions of

Exhibit 4.44

Starbucks
Segment Profitability Data
(Integrative Case 4.1, Parts A and B)

	Americas			EMEA			China/Asia Pacific			Channel Development		
	2012	2011	2010	2012	2011	2010	2012	2011	2010	2012	2011	2010
Total net revenues	$ 9,936	$ 9,065	$ 8,489	$ 1,141	$ 1,047	$ 953	$ 721	$ 552	$ 407	1,292	861	707.4
Common-Size Income Statements												
Total net revenues	100.0%	100.0%	100.0%	100.0%	100.0%	100.0%	100.0%	100.0%	100.0%	100.0%	100.0%	100.0%
Cost of sales including occupancy costs	39.1%	38.8%	38.4%	52.3%	50.7%	49.5%	50.3%	51.1%	52.4%	64.0%	56.7%	54.2%
Store operating expenses	34.5%	35.1%	36.3%	32.5%	31.3%	34.0%	16.5%	15.1%	15.7%	0.0%	0.0%	0.0%
Other operating expenses	0.8%	0.8%	0.7%	2.9%	3.5%	3.8%	6.5%	6.5%	7.4%	14.8%	17.6%	16.3%
Depreciation and amortization expenses	3.9%	4.3%	4.6%	5.0%	5.1%	5.3%	3.2%	3.3%	3.9%	0.1%	0.3%	0.5%
General and administrative expenses	0.7%	0.7%	0.7%	6.3%	6.2%	6.1%	5.3%	6.0%	6.7%	0.7%	0.8%	0.6%
Restructuring charges	0.0%	0.0%	0.3%	0.0%	0.0%	2.6%	0.0%	0.0%	0.0%	0.0%	0.0%	0.0%
Total operating expenses	79.1%	79.7%	81.1%	99.1%	96.7%	101.3%	81.8%	81.9%	86.1%	79.6%	75.3%	71.7%
Income from equity investees	0.0%	0.0%	0.0%	0.0%	0.6%	0.7%	17.0%	16.8%	17.9%	6.6%	8.8%	10.0%
Segment profit margin	20.9%	20.3%	18.9%	0.9%	3.8%	−0.6%	35.1%	35.0%	31.8%	27.0%	33.4%	38.3%
Segment asset turnover	4.5	4.9	4.6	2.4	2.6	2.0	1.1	1.0	0.9	14.6	15.7	13.1
Segment ROA	94.3%	100.0%	87.4%	2.2%	10.1%	−1.2%	38.6%	35.8%	29.3%	392.5%	526.1%	500.9%
Stores owned	7,857	7,623	7,580	882	872	847	666	512	439	N/A.	N/A	N/A
Stores licensed	5,046	4,776	5,044	987	862	807	2,628	2,334	2,141	N/A	N/A	N/A
Total stores	12,903	12,399	12,624	1,869	1,734	1,654	3,294	2,846	2,580			
Total revenues/Total stores	$770,053	$731,107	$672,410	$610,647	$603,691	$576,421	$219,004	$194,062	$157,868			
Operating income/Total stores	$160,769	$148,585	$127,281	$ 5,564	$ 23,241	$ (3,325)	$ 76,958	$ 67,850	$ 50,233			
Assets/Total stores	$170,425	$148,552	$145,588	$250,080	$229,642	$287,666	$199,332	$189,740	$171,318			
Total revenues increase	9.6%	6.8%	643.8%	9.0%	9.8%	32.2%	30.6%	35.6%	−68.5%			
Comparable stores sales increase[a]	8%	8%	7%	0	3%	5%	15%	22%	11%			

[a]Comparable stores represent stores open at least 13 months.

Exhibit 4.45

Panera Bread Company
Financial Statement Ratio Analysis
(Integrative Case 4.1, Part B)

	2012	2011	2010
Sales growth	16.9%	18.1%	14.0%
Profit margin for ROA	8.2%	7.5%	7.3%
Assets turnover	1.86	1.87	1.75
ROA	15.2%	14.0%	12.7%
Profit margin for ROCE	8.1%	7.5%	7.3%
Capital structure leverage	1.55	1.56	1.48
ROCE	23.5%	21.7%	18.7%
Cost of goods sold/Revenues	70.4%	70.6%	69.5%
Fresh dough and other product cost of sales to franchises/Revenues	6.2%	6.4%	7.2%
Depreciation and amortization expense/Revenues	4.3%	4.4%	4.5%
General and administrative expenses/Revenues	5.5%	6.2%	6.6%
Pre-opening expenses/Revenues	0.4%	0.4%	0.3%
Income tax expense (excluding tax effects of interest expense)/Revenues	5.2%	4.6%	4.5%
Accounts receivable turnover	30.2	39.2	46.2
Inventory turnover	81.6	82.0	80.5
Fixed asset turnover	4.0	3.9	3.6

Exhibit 4.46

Panera Bread Company Segment
Profitability Data
(Integrative Case 4.1, Part B)

	2012	2011	2010
Total revenue mix	100%	100%	100%
Net revenues:			
Company-operated retail	95.6%	87.4%	85.7%
Licensing	5.2%	5.1%	5.6%
Foodservice and other	−0.8%	7.5%	8.8%
Total net revenues	100.0%	100.0%	100.0%
Operating profit:			
Company-operated retail	19.3%	16.8%	16.2%
Licensing	4.9%	4.7%	5.2%
Foodservice and other	0.9%	1.1%	1.6%

(Continued)

Exhibit 4.46 (Continued)			
Segment asset turnover:			
Company-operated retail	2.3	2.3	2.3
Licensing	9.9	12.4	12.9
Foodservice and other	2.5	5.8	5.2
Segment ROA:			
Company-operated retail	47.1%	45.0%	42.9%
Licensing	927.8%	1148.3%	1203.7%
Foodservice and other	29.5%	42.0%	49.9%
Stores owned	809	740	662
Stores licensed	843	801	791
Total stores	1,652	1,541	1,453
Revenues/Stores owned	$2,322,967	$2,152,636	$1,995,713
Revenues/Stores licensed	$ 121,087	$ 115,846	$ 108,970
Total revenues/Total stores	$1,190,345	$1,182,370	$1,061,589
Operating income/Total stores	$ 171,305	$ 142,701	$ 123,993
Assets/Total stores	$ 767,653	$ 666,659	$ 636,326
Total revenues increase	7.9%	18.1%	N/A
Comparable stores sales increase	5.8%	1.9%	N/A

general and administrative expenses not allocated to divisions for Panera Bread Company are similar to the corresponding percentages for Starbucks (suggesting they are not material enough to specifically factor into the analysis).

REQUIRED

a. Both Starbucks and Panera have larger than average ROA. However, Panera's ROA has typically been below that of Starbucks. What are the likely reasons for the relative levels of ROA between Panera and Starbucks? Analyze the data to the maximum depth permitted by the information given and speculate on economic explanations for what the analysis indicates.

b. Panera's ROCE also has typically been below that of Starbucks, but by a large margin. Why?

CASE 4.2

Profitability and Risk Analysis of Walmart Stores

Part A

Walmart Stores (Walmart) is the world's largest retailer. It employs an "everyday low price" strategy and operates stores as three business segments: Walmart Stores U.S., International, and Sam's Club.

1. **Walmart Stores U.S.:** This segment represented 63.7% of all 2008 sales and operates stores in three different formats: Discount stores (approximately 108,000 square feet), Supercenters (approximately 186,000 square feet), and Neighborhood Markets (approximately 42,000 square feet). Each format carries a variety of clothing, housewares, electronic equipment,

pharmaceuticals, health and beauty products, sporting goods, and similar items, and Super-centers including a full-line supermarket.[38] Walmart U.S. Stores are in all 50 states, Discount stores are in 47 states, Supercenters are in 48 states, and Neighborhood Markets are in 16 states. Customers also can purchase many items through the company's website at http://www.walmart.com.

2. **International:** The International segment includes wholly owned subsidiaries in Argentina, Brazil, Canada, Japan, Puerto Rico, and the United Kingdom; majority-owned subsidiaries in five countries in Central America, Chile, and Mexico; and joint ventures in India and China. The merchandising strategy for the International segment is similar to that of the Walmart U.S. segment.

3. **Sam's Clubs:** Sam's Clubs are membership club warehouses that operate in 48 states. The average Sam's Club is approximately 133,000 square feet, and customers can purchase many items through the company's website at http://www.samsclub.com. These warehouses offer bulk displays of brand name merchandise, including hardgoods, some softgoods, institutional-size grocery items, and certain private-label items. Gross margins for Sam's Clubs stores are lower than those of the U.S. and International segments.

Walmart uses centralized purchasing through its home office for substantially all of its merchandise. It distributes products to its stores through regional distribution centers. During fiscal 2008, the proportion of merchandise channeled through its regional distribution centers was as follows:

Walmart Discount Stores, Supercenters, and Neighborhood Markets	81%
Sam's Club (non-fuel)	65%
International	74%

Exhibit 4.47 sets out various operating data for Walmart for 2006–2008. Exhibit 4.48 presents segment data. Exhibit 4.49 (page 325) presents comparative balance sheets for Walmart for 2005–2008 (an extra year to enable average balance computations when

Exhibit 4.47

Walmart Stores
Operating Data
(Case 4.2, Part A)

	Fiscal Year		
	2008	**2007**	**2006**
Walmart Discount Stores, Supercenters, and Neighborhood Markets (U.S.)			
Number	3,656	3,550	3,443
Square footage (millions)	589.3	566.6	540.4
Sales per square foot	$433.98	$422.75	$418.75
Operating income per square foot	$ 31.84	$ 30.91	$ 30.76

(Continued)

[38]Walmart's fiscal year ends at the end of January of each year. Despite Walmart's convention of referring to its year ending January 31, 2009, as its fiscal 2009, we follow the common practice of referring to it as 2008 because 11 of the 12 months fall within 2008. This same convention holds true for Carrefour and Target in Part B of this case.

Exhibit 4.47 (Continued)

International			
Number	3,615	3,098	2,734
Square footage (millions)	251.8	222.6	188.4
Sales per square foot	$391.76	$406.20	$383.04
Operating income per square foot	$ 19.62	$ 21.23	$ 18.76
Sam's Club (Domestic)			
Number	602	591	579
Square footage (millions)	79.9	78.2	76.3
Sales per square foot	$586.41	$567.23	$544.98
Operating income per square foot	$ 20.15	$ 20.69	$ 19.40
Domestic Comparable Store Sales Increase	3.5%	1.6%	2.0%

Exhibit 4.48

Walmart Stores
Segment Profitability Analysis
(Case 4.2, Part A)

	Fiscal Year		
	2008	**2007**	**2006**
Sales Mix			
Walmart Discount Stores, Supercenters, and Neighborhood Markets	63.7%	64.0%	65.6%
International	24.6	24.1	22.3
Sam's Club	11.7	11.9	12.1
	100.0%	100.0%	100.0%
Walmart Discount Stores, Supercenters, and Neighborhood Markets			
Operating profit margin	7.3%	7.3%	7.3%
Assets turnover	3.0	2.8	2.9
ROA	22.2%	20.8%	21.0%
International			
Operating profit margin	5.0%	5.2%	5.5%
Assets turnover	1.6	1.5	1.4
ROA	8.2%	7.6%	7.8%
Sam's Club			
Operating profit margin	3.4%	3.6%	3.6%
Assets turnover	3.8	3.8	3.6
ROA	13.0%	13.8%	12.9%

Exhibit 4.49

Walmart Stores
Balance Sheets
(amounts in millions)
(Case 4.2, Part A)

	2008	2007	2006	2005
ASSETS				
Cash and cash equivalents	$ 7,275	$ 5,492	$ 7,373	$ 6,193
Marketable securities				
Accounts receivable—net	3,905	3,642	2,840	2,575
Inventories	34,511	35,159	33,685	31,910
Prepaid expenses and other current assets	3,063	2,760	2,690	2,468
Current assets of discontinued segments	195	967	—	679
Total Current Assets	$ 48,949	$ 48,020	$ 46,588	$ 43,825
Long-term investments	—	—	—	1,884
Property, plant, & equipment—at cost	131,161	127,992	115,190	100,929
Accumulated depreciation	(35,508)	(31,125)	(26,750)	(23,064)
Goodwill and nonamortizable intangibles	18,827	18,627	16,165	14,613
Total Assets	$163,429	$163,514	$151,193	$138,187
LIABILITIES AND EQUITIES				
Accounts payable—trade	$ 28,849	$ 30,344	$ 28,090	$ 25,101
Current accrued liabilities	18,112	15,725	14,675	13,274
Notes payable and short-term debt	1,506	5,040	2,570	3,754
Current maturities of long-term debt	6,163	6,229	5,713	4,879
Income taxes payable	760	1,140	706	1,817
Total Current Liabilities	$ 55,390	$ 58,478	$ 51,754	$ 48,825
Long-term debt	34,549	33,402	30,735	30,096
Deferred tax liabilities—noncurrent	6,014	5,087	4,971	4,630
Total Liabilities	$ 95,953	$ 96,967	$ 87,460	$ 83,551
Noncontrolling interest	$ 2,191	$ 1,939	$ 2,160	$ 1,465
Common stock + Paid-in capital	4,313	3,425	3,247	3,013
Retained earnings	63,660	57,319	55,818	49,105
Accum. other comprehensive income (loss)	(2,688)	3,864	2,508	1,053
Total Shareholders' Equity	$ 65,285	$ 64,608	$ 61,573	$ 53,171
Total Liabilities and Equities	$163,429	$163,514	$151,193	$138,187

Source: Walmart Stores, Inc., Form 10-K for the Fiscal Years Ended 2005–2008.

necessary), Exhibit 4.50 (page 326) presents comparative income statements for 2006–2008, and Exhibit 4.51 (pages 326–327) presents comparative statements of cash flows for 2006–2008. Exhibit 4.52 (pages 327–328) presents selected financial statement ratios for Walmart for 2006–2008. The statutory income tax rate is 35%.

Exhibit 4.50

Walmart Stores
Income Statements
(amounts in millions)
(Case 4.2, Part A)

	2008	2007	2006
Revenues	$ 405,607	$ 378,476	$ 348,368
Cost of goods sold	(306,158)	(286,350)	(263,979)
Gross Profit	$ 99,449	$ 92,126	$ 84,389
Selling, general, and administrative expenses	(76,651)	(70,174)	(63,892)
Operating Profit	$ 22,798	$ 21,952	$ 20,497
Interest income	284	309	280
Interest expense	(2,184)	(2,103)	(1,809)
Income Before Tax	$ 20,898	$ 20,158	$ 18,968
Income tax expense	(7,145)	(6,889)	(6,354)
Noncontrolling interest in earnings	(499)	(406)	(425)
Income (loss) from discontinued operations	146	(132)	(905)
Net Income (Computed)	$ 13,400	$ 12,731	$ 11,284
Other comprehensive income items	(6,552)	1,356	1,575
Comprehensive Income	$ 6,848	$ 14,087	$ 12,859

Source: Walmart Stores, Inc., Form 10-K for the Fiscal Years Ended 2006–2008.

Exhibit 4.51

Walmart Stores
Statements of Cash Flows
(amounts in millions)
(Case 4.2, Part A)

	2008	2007	2006
Net income	$ 13,400	$ 12,731	$ 11,284
Add back depreciation and amortization expenses	6,739	6,317	5,459
Deferred income taxes	581	(8)	89
(Increase) Decrease in accounts receivable	(101)	(564)	(214)
(Increase) Decrease in inventories	(220)	(775)	(1,274)
Increase (Decrease) in accounts payable	(410)	865	2,132
Increase (Decrease) in other current liabilities	2,036	1,034	588
Other addbacks to net income			
Other subtractions from net income	(146)	132	860
Other operating cash flows	1,268	910	1,311
Net Cash Flows from Operations	$ 23,147	$ 20,642	$ 20,235

(Continued)

Exhibit 4.51 (Continued)

Proceeds from sales of property, plant, and equipment	$ 714	$ 957	$ 394
Property, plant, and equipment acquired	(11,499)	(14,937)	(15,666)
Investments sold	781		267
Investments acquired		(95)	
Other investment transactions	(1,576)	(1,338)	(68)
Other	838	(257)	610
Net Cash Flows from Investing Activities	$(10,742)	$(15,670)	$(14,463)
Increase in short-term borrowing		$ 2,376	
Decrease in short-term borrowing	$ (3,745)		$ (1,193)
Increase in long-term borrowing	6,566	11,167	7,199
Decrease in long-term borrowing	(5,739)	(9,066)	(6,098)
Share repurchases—treasury stock	(3,521)	(7,691)	(1,718)
Dividend payments	(3,746)	(3,586)	(2,802)
Other financing transactions	267	(622)	(510)
Net Cash Flows from Financing Activities	$ (9,918)	$ (7,422)	$ (5,122)
Effects of exchange rate changes on cash	(781)	252	97
Net Change in Cash	$ 1,706	$ (2,198)	$ 747
Cash and Cash Equivalents, Beginning of Year*	$ 5,492	$ 7,373	$ 6193

*The amounts do not reconcile with the balance sheet presentation because Walmart reclassified cash and equivalents applicable to discontinued operations.

Source: Walmart Stores, Inc., Form 10-K for the Fiscal Years Ended 2006–2008.

Exhibit 4.52

Walmart Stores
Financial Ratio Analysis
(Case 4.2, Part A)

	Fiscal Year		
	2008	**2007**	**2006**
Profitability Ratios			
ROA	9.3%	9.3%	9.5%
Profit margin for ROA	3.7%	3.9%	4.0%
Assets turnover	2.5	2.4	2.4
Cost of goods sold/Sales	75.5%	75.7%	75.8%
Selling and administrative expense/Sales	18.9%	18.5%	18.3%
Interest expense (net of taxes)/Sales	0.3%	0.4%	0.3%
Income tax expense (excluding tax effects of interest expense)/Sales	2.0%	2.0%	2.0%

(Continued)

Exhibit 4.52 (Continued)			
Accounts receivable turnover	107.5	116.8	128.7
Inventory turnover	8.8	8.3	8.0
Fixed assets turnover	4.2	4.1	4.2
ROCE	20.4%	20.4%	21.2%
Profit margin for ROCE	3.3%	3.4%	3.5%
Capital structure leverage	2.5	2.4	2.4
Risk Ratios			
Current ratio	0.88	0.82	0.90
Quick ratio	0.20	0.16	0.20
Accounts payable turnover	10.3	9.9	10.0
Cash flow from operations to current liabilities ratio	40.7%	37.5%	40.2%
Long-term debt ratio	34.6%	34.1%	33.3%
Total liabilities/Total assets ratio	58.7%	59.3%	57.8%
Cash flow from operations to total liabilities ratio	24.0%	22.4%	23.7%
Interest coverage ratio	10.6	10.5	11.0

REQUIRED

a. What are the likely reasons for the changes in Walmart's rate of ROA during the three-year period? Analyze the financial ratios to the maximum depth possible.

b. What are the likely reasons for the changes in Walmart's rate of ROCE during the three-year period?

   Note: Requirements c and d require coverage of material from Chapter 5.

c. How has the short-term liquidity risk of Walmart changed during the three-year period?

d. How has the long-term solvency risk of Walmart changed during the three-year period?

Part B

Part A of Case 4.2 analyzed the profitability and risk of **Walmart Stores** for its fiscal years 2006, 2007, and 2008. Part B of this case compares the profitability and risk ratios of Walmart and two other leading discount retailers, **Carrefour** and **Target**, for their 2006–2008 fiscal years.

Carrefour

Carrefour, headquartered in France, is Europe's largest retailer and the second largest retailer in the world. Sales in 2008 totaled €86,967 million (approximately $118,000 million). Carrefour is organized by geographic region (France, Europe excluding France, Asia, and Latin America). Each segment is organized according to store formats, which include the following (2008 number of stores and sales mix percentages in parentheses):

Hypermarkets (203; 62%): Offer a wide variety of household and food products at competitively low prices under the Carrefour store brand

Supermarkets (590; 22%): Sell traditional grocery products under the Champion, Norte, GS, and GB supermarkets and other store brands

Hard Discount Stores (842; 11%): Offer a limited variety of food products in smaller stores than those of hypermarkets and supermarkets at aggressively low prices under the Dia, Ed, and Minipreco store brands

Other activities (9; 5%): Includes convenience stores and wholesale stores, the latter targeted at business customers, under the SHOPI, Marche Plus, 8 A Huit, Express, Contact, and Proxi store brands

Carrefour derived approximately 44% of its 2008 sales in France, 37% in Europe excluding France, 12% in Latin America, and 7% in Asia.

Target

Target Corporation, headquartered in the United States, operates two reportable segments: retail and credit card. The retail segment includes all merchandising operations, including large-format general merchandise and food discount stores as well as an online business at http://www.target .com. Target stores offer a wide variety of clothing, household, electronics, sports, toy, and entertainment products at discount prices. Target stores attempt to differentiate themselves from Walmart's discount stores by pushing trendy merchandising with more brand-name products. Target emphasizes customer service, referring to its customers as "guests" and focusing on the theme of "Expect More, Pay Less." Target Corporation attempts to differentiate itself from competitors by providing wider aisles and a less cluttered store appearance. At the end of fiscal 2008, Target Corporation operated 1,682 stores and 34 distribution centers. The credit card segment offers branded proprietary credit cards under the names Target Visa and the Target Card. For 2008, total revenues were $64,948 million, consisting of retail sales of $62,884 million and credit card revenues of $2,064 million.

Exhibits 4.53 and 4.54 (page 330) present profitability ratios for Carrefour, Target, and Walmart for their 2006–2008 fiscal years. Exhibit 4.55 (page 331) presents risk ratios for the three firms. Exhibit 4.56 (page 332) presents selected other data for these firms. The financial

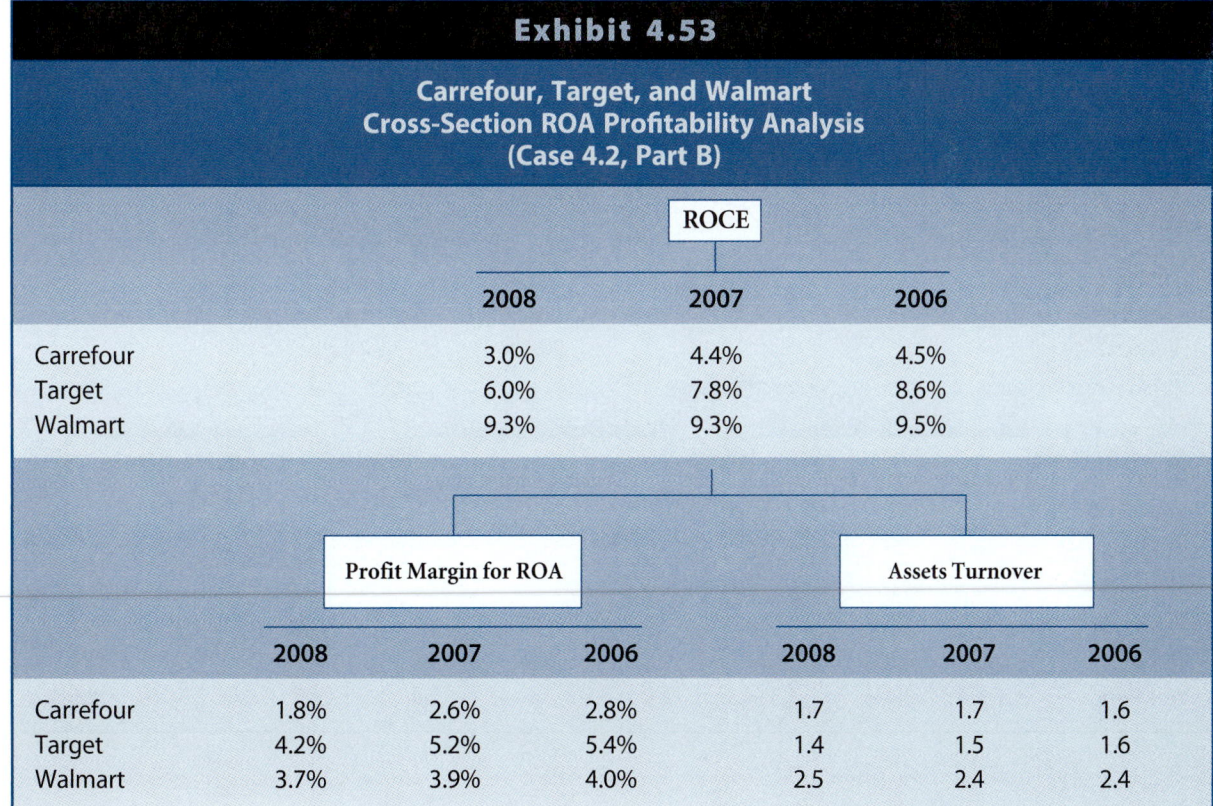

Exhibit 4.53

**Carrefour, Target, and Walmart
Cross-Section ROA Profitability Analysis
(Case 4.2, Part B)**

ROCE

	2008	2007	2006
Carrefour	3.0%	4.4%	4.5%
Target	6.0%	7.8%	8.6%
Walmart	9.3%	9.3%	9.5%

	Profit Margin for ROA			Assets Turnover		
	2008	**2007**	**2006**	**2008**	**2007**	**2006**
Carrefour	1.8%	2.6%	2.8%	1.7	1.7	1.6
Target	4.2%	5.2%	5.4%	1.4	1.5	1.6
Walmart	3.7%	3.9%	4.0%	2.5	2.4	2.4

(Continued)

Exhibit 4.53 (Continued)

	Carrefour			Target			Walmart		
	2008	2007	2006	2008	2007	2006	2008	2007	2006
Sales	100.0%	100.0%	100.0%	100.0%	100.0%	100.0%	100.0%	100.0%	100.0%
Other revenues	1.4	1.4	1.3	3.3	2.1	2.8	1.1	1.1	1.0
Cost of goods sold	(79.0)	(78.6)	(78.6)	(70.2)	(69.8)	(69.7)	(76.3)	(76.5)	(76.6)
Selling and administrative	(19.2)	(18.7)	(18.6)	(26.1)	(24.7)	(24.3)	(19.1)	(18.7)	(18.5)
Income taxes	(0.9)	(1.0)	(1.1)	(2.1)	(2.9)	(3.0)	(1.8)	(1.8)	(1.8)
Profit margin for ROA*	1.8%	2.6%	2.8%	4.2%	5.2%	5.4%	3.7%	3.9%	4.0%
Receivables turnover	27.4	23.3	21.7	7.8	8.6	9.8	107.5	116.8	128.7
Inventory turnover	10.0	10.0	9.9	6.5	6.6	6.7	8.8	8.3	8.0
Fixed assets turnover	5.9	5.8	5.7	2.5	2.7	2.9	4.2	4.1	4.2

*Amounts do not sum because profit margin for ROA is reduced by taxes on operating profits, which do not equal total taxes reported on the income statement.

Exhibit 4.54

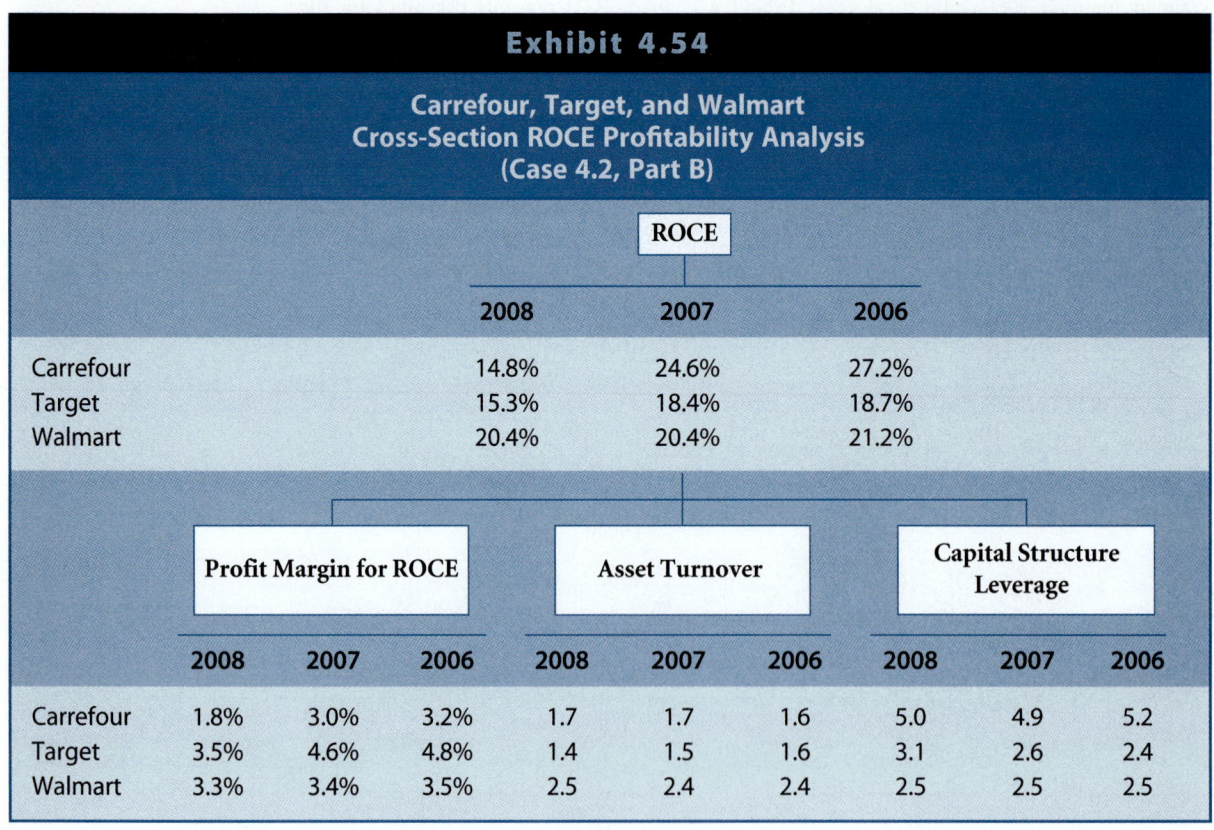

**Carrefour, Target, and Walmart
Cross-Section ROCE Profitability Analysis
(Case 4.2, Part B)**

ROCE			
	2008	2007	2006
Carrefour	14.8%	24.6%	27.2%
Target	15.3%	18.4%	18.7%
Walmart	20.4%	20.4%	21.2%

	Profit Margin for ROCE			Asset Turnover			Capital Structure Leverage		
	2008	2007	2006	2008	2007	2006	2008	2007	2006
Carrefour	1.8%	3.0%	3.2%	1.7	1.7	1.6	5.0	4.9	5.2
Target	3.5%	4.6%	4.8%	1.4	1.5	1.6	3.1	2.6	2.4
Walmart	3.3%	3.4%	3.5%	2.5	2.4	2.4	2.5	2.5	2.5

Exhibit 4.55

Carrefour, Target, and Walmart Cross-Section Risk Analysis for (Case 4.2, Part B)

	Carrefour			Target			Walmart		
	2008	2007	2006	2008	2007	2006	2008	2007	2006
Short-Term Liquidity									
Current ratio	0.70	0.65	0.66	1.66	1.60	1.32	0.88	0.82	0.90
Quick ratio	0.39	0.36	0.37	0.85	0.89	0.63	0.20	0.16	0.20
Cash flow from operations/ Average current liabilities	14.1%	14.2%	13.1%	39.7%	36.0%	47.0%	40.7%	37.5%	40.2%
Days receivables	24	27	29	47	48	49	3	3	3
Days inventory	37	39	37	55	58	57	42	44	45
Days payable	92	95	99	52	56	59	35	37	37
Long-Term Solvency									
Long-term debt ratio	46.5%	41.3%	41.8%	56.1%	49.7%	35.7%	34.6%	34.1%	33.3%
Total liabilities/Total assets ratio	79.0%	77.3%	77.9%	68.9%	65.6%	58.1%	58.7%	59.3%	57.8%
Cash flow from operations/ Average total liabilities	9.9%	10.2%	9.4%	14.9%	16.2%	22.9%	24.0%	22.4%	23.7%
Interest coverage ratio	6.4	8.4	9.1	5.9	9.6	10.0	10.6	10.5	11.0

Exhibit 4.56

Carrefour, Target, and Walmart
Selected Other Financial Data
(Case 4.2, Part B)

	2008	2007	2006
Growth Rate in Sales			
Carrefour	5.9%	6.8%	5.2%
Target	2.3%	6.2%	12.9%
Walmart	9.4%	7.2%	8.6%
Number of Stores			
Carrefour	15,430	14,991	12,547
Target	1,682	1,591	1,488
Walmart	7,873	7,239	6,756
Square Footage (000's)			
Carrefour	192,801	181,900	164,350
Target	222,588	207,945	192,064
Walmart	921,000	867,400	805,100
Sales per Square Foot			
Carrefour	€ 451	€ 452	€ 468
Target	$ 283	$ 296	$ 301
Walmart	$ 440	$ 436	$ 433
Sales per Store			
Carrefour	€ 5,636,215	€ 5,479,855	€ 6,127,919
Target	$ 37,386,445	$ 38,636,706	$ 38,896,505
Walmart	$ 51,518,735	$ 52,282,912	$ 51,564,239
Square Feet per Store			
Carrefour	12,495	12,134	13,099
Target	132,335	130,701	129,075
Walmart	116,982	119,823	119,168
Fixed Assets per Square Foot			
Carrefour	€ 77	€ 81	€ 84
Target	$ 116	$ 116	$ 112
Walmart	$ 104	$ 112	$ 110
Sales per Employee			
Carrefour	€ 175,589	€ 167,636	€ 168,503
Target	$ 179,157	$ 167,954	$ 164,426
Walmart	$ 193,146	$ 180,227	$ 183,352
Exchange Rate			
U.S. dollars per euro (€)	$ 1.4097	$ 1.4728	$ 1.3200

statements include the present value of commitments under all leases in property, plant, and equipment and in long-term debt.

REQUIRED

a. Walmart and Target follow somewhat different strategies. Walmart consistently has a higher ROA compared to Target. Using information in Exhibits 4.53 and 4.56, suggest reasons for these differences in operating profitability.

b. Walmart and Carrefour follow similar strategies. Walmart consistently outperforms Carrefour on ROA. Using information in Exhibits 4.53 and 4.56, suggest reasons for these differences in operating profitability.

c. Refer to Exhibit 4.54. Which firm appears to have used financial leverage most effectively in enhancing the rate of ROCE? Explain your reasoning.
   Note: Requirements d and e require coverage of material from Chapter 5.

d. Refer to Exhibit 4.55. Rank-order these firms in terms of their short-term liquidity risk. Do any of these firms appear unduly risky as of the end of fiscal 2008? Explain.

e. Refer to Exhibit 4.55. Rank-order these firms in terms of their long-term liquidity risk. Do any of these firms appear unduly risky as of the end of fiscal Year 4? Explain.

Risk Analysis

LEARNING OBJECTIVES

LO 5-1	Describe the information that U.S. GAAP and IFRS require firms to disclose about their *risk exposures* and risk management activities.
LO 5-2	Define *financial flexibility* and use an innovative decomposition of return on common equity to assess financial flexibility.
LO 5-3	Apply analytical tools to assess working capital management and *short-term liquidity risk.*
LO 5-4	Explain the benefits and risks of financial leverage and apply analytical tools for assessing *long-term solvency risk.*
LO 5-5	Use risk analysis tools in assessing *credit risk.*
LO 5-6	Apply predictive statistical models to assess *bankruptcy risk.*
LO 5-7	Explain the distinction between *firm-specific risks,* as measured by various financial statement ratios, and *systematic risk,* as measured by market equity beta, and relations between these types of risks.

Chapter Overview

The concept of risk means different things to different people, because the potential consequences of risk differ across different contexts and stakeholders. As a result, there are numerous definitions of risk. A general definition is that risk is some measure of exposure to a specified type of loss. The key to this general definition is what loss is specified. For example, equity investors make investment decisions based on the *expected return* from equity investments relative to the *risks* that such investments will fail to generate the expected level of returns, or worse, lose money. Similarly, lenders make lending decisions based on the expected return in the form of interest revenue relative to the risks of the borrower defaulting on repayments. The analysis of risk is central to any decision to commit economic resources to a project or an investment.

This chapter describes disclosures required by U.S. GAAP and IFRS to inform financial statement users about *specific* risks that can affect a firm and how the firm manages those risks. For example, we consider the following specific risks in this chapter: short-term liquidity, long-term solvency, credit risk, bankruptcy risk, and systematic risk. In Chapter 6, where we introduce the idea of analyzing the quality of firms' accounting information, we also introduce accounting fraud risk. These are all measures of risk that are related due to their relation to external investors and creditors. This chapter also demonstrates financial statement ratios that are useful in analyzing various types of risk, and we supplement these with statistical risk prediction models and other analytical tools. Information about risk appears in numerous places in a firm's annual report, such as the notes to the financial statements, the MD&A, the balance sheet, the income statement, and the statement of cash flows. In this chapter, we discuss how to use this collective information to examine risks faced by a firm. We demonstrate financial statement analysis techniques to assess the following types of risk:

- Financial flexibility
- Short-term liquidity risk
- Long-term solvency risk
- Credit risk
- Bankruptcy risk
- Market equity risk

As discussed in Chapter 4, firms use financial leverage to increase returns to equity shareholders. When firms obtain funds from borrowing and invest those funds in assets that generate a higher return than the after-tax cost of the borrowing, the common shareholders benefit. While capital structure leverage enhances the return to the common shareholders, it involves risk. Therefore, the analysis of profitability discussed in that chapter is linked to the analysis of risk discussed in this chapter by an examination of *financial flexibility*. Financial flexibility is the ability of a firm to obtain debt financing conditional on its current leverage and profitability of its operating assets.

The risk associated with leverage arises because satisfying future debt retirements requires cash payments. Exhibit 5.1 relates the factors affecting a firm's ability to generate cash with its need to use cash. Many financial statement analysis techniques designed to assess risk focus on a comparison of the supply of cash and the demand for cash. For example, risk analysis using financial statement information can examine *short-term liquidity risk,* which is the near-term ability to generate cash to meet working capital needs and debt service requirements, as well as *long-term solvency risk*, which is the longer-term ability to generate cash internally or externally to satisfy plant capacity and debt repayment needs.

Financial statement information also enables assessments of two closely related types of firm-specific risk: credit risk and bankruptcy risk. *Credit risk* concerns a firm's ability to make ongoing interest and principal payments on borrowings as they come due. *Bankruptcy risk*, on the other hand, relates to the likelihood that a firm will ultimately be forced to file for bankruptcy and perhaps subsequently liquidate due to a combination of insufficient profitability and cash flows and high debt service costs. Analysts view these two types of risk as states of financial distress that fall along a continuum of increasing gravity as shown in Exhibit 5.2

Exhibit 5.1

Framework for Financial Statement Analysis of Risk

Activity	Ability to Generate Cash	Need to Use Cash	Financial Statement Analysis Performed
Operating	Profitability of goods and services sold	Working capital requirements	Short-term liquidity risk
Investing	Sales of existing plant assets or investments	Plant capacity requirements	Long-term solvency risk
Financing	Borrowing capacity	Debt service requirements	

Exhibit 5.2

Severity of Various Events to a Firm's Investors

Firm			
Not Severe	**Less Severe**	**More Severe**	**Very Severe**
Stretching out trade payables	Failing to make a required interest payment on time Restructuring debt	Defaulting on a principal payment on debt Filing for bankruptcy	Liquidating the firm

Analysts concerned with the economic loss of amounts lent to or invested in a firm would examine a firm's position on this financial distress continuum. We demonstrate how analysts can use tools of short-term liquidity and long-term solvency risk in assessing credit risk and bankruptcy risk.

Less than 5% of publicly traded firms experience financial distress as defined by one of the five states in Exhibit 5.2 spanning Less Severe to Very Severe. The other 95% of firms that are reasonably financially healthy utilize borrowings to finance future expansion or unforeseen investment opportunities, which is captured by the notion of financial flexibility described earlier. Thus while examination of liquidity, solvency, credit, and bankruptcy risk is sometimes very important, analysts are more often interested in the financial flexibility of a firm to strategically utilize leverage through borrowing to enhance the returns to the firm's common equity investors.

The preceding types of risk do not encompass the full range of risks that equity investors must consider as the residual risk bearers of firms. Therefore, to value firms, investors also assess elements of risk inherent in investing in common shares of a firm relative to the risks that are common to all firms. For example, investors consider systematic (nondiversifiable) risk and use it to explain differences in expected rates of return on common stocks. Economic theory teaches that differences in risk relate to differences in expected returns. Studies of this risk/return relation use market equity beta as one measure of *market equity risk*. Market equity beta measures the covariability of a firm's returns with an index of returns of all securities in the equity capital market. Research and practice show that market equity betas increase with financial leverage. We briefly discuss the research relating financial statement data and market equity beta later in this chapter but elaborate on it more fully in Chapters 11–14. Our primary interest in this chapter is in contrasting market risk with the other risks discussed.

As will become clear, all six of these elements of risk are interrelated. Firms use financial flexibility and leverage to achieve higher returns for equity investors, but doing so involves financial risk. Analysts evaluate short-term liquidity and long-term solvency risk and assess both credit risk and bankruptcy risk. Some of the factors affecting long-term solvency risk and financial flexibility also affect market equity risk.

We illustrate the analyses of various dimensions of risk using the financial statements of **PepsiCo** in Appendix A. As we did in Chapter 4, we will compare financial ratios across years for PepsiCo. Additional insights are attained through comparison of the ratios for PepsiCo with average industry ratios or with those of PepsiCo's competitors (for example, **Coca-Cola**).

LO 5-1

Describe the information that U.S. GAAP and IFRS require firms to disclose about their *risk exposures* and risk management activities.

Disclosures Regarding Risk and Risk Management

The sources and types of risk a firm faces are numerous and often interrelated. In the United States, the SEC requires firms to identify risks they face prominently as "Item 1A. Risk Factors" on their Form 10-K. In paragraph 229.503(c) of Regulation S-K, the SEC states the following:

> Where appropriate, provide under the caption "Risk Factors" a discussion of the most significant factors that make the offering speculative or risky. This discussion must be concise and organized logically. Do not present risks that could apply to any issuer or any offering. Explain how the risk affects the issuer or the securities being offered.

Examples of such risks include the following:

Source	Type or Nature
Firm-specific	Ability to attract, retain, and motivate employees
	Dependence on one or few customers
	Dependence on one or few suppliers
	Environmental or political scrutiny
	Litigation
Industry	Availability and price of raw materials or other production inputs
	Competition
	Technology
	Regulation
	Labor wages and supply
Domestic	Political environment
	Recessions
	Inflation or deflation
	Interest rate volatility
	Demographic shifts
International	Exchange rate volatility
	Host government regulations and posturing
	Political unrest or asset expropriation

Most of these risks are unavoidable, and firms must continually monitor each one to ensure that appropriate actions are taken to minimize the impacts of detrimental events or changes in circumstances. The focus in this chapter, however, is on how to assess the financial consequences of these types of risk using disclosures and data from financial reports. Various financial reporting standards and financial market regulations require firms to discuss in notes to the financial statements or in regulatory filings how important elements of risk affect a particular firm and how the firm manages these risks. For non-U.S. companies that list securities in the United States, a required Form 20-F includes "Item 3D. Risk Factors." Capital market regulators around the world generally require companies to file similar reports. For example, in France, companies file a Registration Document annually with the Autorité des Marchés Financiers (AMF) and in Singapore, companies file an Annual Return and Audited Accounts with the

Accounting and Corporate Regulatory Authority (ACRA). We use the disclosures available in **PepsiCo**'s Form 10-K under "Item 1A. Risk Factors," as well as disclosures in Note 10, "Financial Instruments" (Appendix A), and the discussion under the heading "Our Business Risks" in PepsiCo's MD&A (Appendix B) to illustrate information that firms provide about risk, including commodity price risk, interest rate risk, and foreign exchange risk.

Firm-Specific Risks

Like all companies, **PepsiCo** is subject to numerous firm-specific risks that are driven by the nature of the business, competition, supplier relationships, customers, and overall firm strategy. Within Item 1A of Form 10-K, PepsiCo identifies almost twenty different risks related to its business, and the following are several excerpts:

- *Our financial performance could be adversely affected if we are unable to grow our business in emerging and developing markets or as a result of unstable political conditions, civil unrest or other developments and risks in the markets where our products are sold.*
- *Disruption of our supply chain could have an adverse impact on our business, financial condition and results of operations.*
- *If we are unable to hire or retain key employees or a highly skilled and diverse workforce, it could have a negative impact on our business.*
- *Our borrowing costs and access to capital and credit markets may be adversely affected by a downgrade or potential downgrade of our credit ratings.*
- *A portion of our workforce belongs to unions. Failure to successfully renew collective bargaining agreements, or strikes or work stoppages could cause our business to suffer.*

Although many of the disclosures PepsiCo provides seem general and applicable to any company, each is discussed in more detail in later sections of the company's Form 10-K. For example, in discussing the effects of disruptions in raw materials supplies, PepsiCo gives the following detail:

> *We and our business partners use various raw materials and other supplies in our business. The principal ingredients we use include apple, orange and pineapple juice and other juice concentrates, aspartame, corn, corn sweeteners, flavorings, flour, grapefruit and other fruits, oats, oranges, potatoes, raw milk, rice, seasonings, sucralose, sugar, vegetable and essential oils and wheat. Our key packaging materials include plastic resins, including polyethylene terephthalate (PET) and polypropylene resin used for plastic beverage bottles and film packaging used for snack foods, aluminum used for cans, glass bottles, closures, cardboard and paperboard cartons. Fuel and natural gas are also important commodities for us due to their use in our facilities and in the trucks delivering our products.*

The identification and discussion of firm-specific risks provides a useful bridge between understanding a company's industry, business strategy, and profitability and identifying specific risks that may have an impact on the company's ability to grow, be profitable, and ultimately create value for debt and equity stakeholders. Of the firm-specific risks identified above, some are quantifiable and subject to required disclosures in the footnotes to financial statements. The remaining discussion in this section focuses on examples of such disclosures.

Commodity Prices

Changes in the prices of raw materials used to manufacture products affect future profitability (favorably or unfavorably) unless the firm can pass along price increases to customers, engage in fixed-price contractual arrangements with suppliers, or hedge with commodity futures contracts. For example, some firms attempt to manage this risk by engaging in a purchase commitment with suppliers to purchase certain quantities at a specified price over a particular period of time. Alternatively, a firm might acquire a futures contract or another hedging instrument to neutralize the risk of changes in prices. PepsiCo discloses the following with respect to commodity price risk in Note 10:

> We are subject to commodity price risk because our ability to recover increased costs through higher pricing may be limited in the competitive environment in which we operate. This risk is managed through the use of fixed-price purchase orders, pricing agreements and derivatives. In addition, risk to our supply of certain raw materials is mitigated through purchases from multiple geographies and suppliers. We use derivatives, with terms of no more than three years, to economically hedge price fluctuations related to a portion of our anticipated commodity purchases, primarily for agricultural products, metals and energy ....
>
> Our open commodity derivative contracts that qualify for hedge accounting had a face value of $507 million as of December 29, 2012 and $598 million as of December 31, 2011. Our open commodity derivative contracts that do not qualify for hedge accounting had a face value of $853 million as of December 29, 2012 and $630 million as of December 31, 2011.

Note 10 tabulates the fair values of all financial assets and liabilities, including derivative contracts on commodities, foreign exchange rates, and interest rates. Chapter 9 discusses the accounting for commodity derivative contracts in detail, including what types of contracts qualify for hedge accounting treatment. However, at this point, it is important to understand that the footnote reveals that at the end of 2012, PepsiCo had $466 million as the fair value of derivative contracts classified as assets, and only $247 million classified as liabilities. Thus, overall it appears that PepsiCo's derivative contracts are in a net favorable position at the end of 2012. Under "Market Risks" in the MD&A (Appendix B, which can be found online at the book's companion website at www.cengagebrain.com), PepsiCo states that, if commodity prices declined 10% at the end of 2012, PepsiCo's unrealized net losses on commodity derivative instruments (that qualify for hedge accounting) would have increased by $49 million, and realized losses (for derivatives that do not qualify for hedge accounting) would have increased by $85 million. Disclosures like these are helpful as you assess the relative exposure faced by PepsiCo of a specific risk. For example, the combined $134 million exposure—assuming a 10% decrease in commodity prices—is approximately 1.6% of income before income taxes of $8,304 million.

Foreign Exchange

Changes in foreign exchange rates can affect a firm in multiple ways, including:

- the amounts a firm pays to acquire raw materials from suppliers abroad.
- the amounts received for products sold to customers abroad.

- the amount of cash a firm receives when it collects an account receivable, a loan receivable, or another receivable denominated in a currency other than its own.
- the amount of cash a firm pays when it settles an account payable, a loan payable, or another payable denominated in a currency other than its own.
- the amount of cash a firm collects when it receives remittances from a foreign branch or dividends from a foreign subsidiary.
- the cash-equivalent value of assets invested abroad and liabilities borrowed abroad in the event the firm liquidates the foreign unit.

Firms often use forward foreign exchange contracts to hedge some or all of these risks. Chapter 8 discusses the effect of exchange rate changes on reporting the operations of foreign units, and Chapter 9 discusses forward contracts used to hedge such risks.

PepsiCo states the following in Note 10:

Our operations outside of the U.S. generate 49% of our net revenue, with Russia, Mexico, Canada, the United Kingdom and Brazil comprising approximately 25% of our net revenue. As a result, we are exposed to foreign currency risks.

Additionally, we are also exposed to foreign currency risk from foreign currency purchases and foreign currency assets and liabilities created in the normal course of business. We manage this risk through sourcing purchases from local suppliers, negotiating contracts in local currencies with foreign suppliers and through the use of derivatives, primarily forward contracts with terms of no more than two years. Exchange rate gains or losses related to foreign currency transactions are recognized as transaction gains or losses in our income statement as incurred.

PepsiCo also discloses that foreign currency derivatives had a face value of $2.8 billion at the end of 2012, considerably more than the amount of commodity derivatives. For foreign currency derivatives that qualify for hedge accounting, a 10% unfavorable change in exchange rates would have increased unrealized losses by $134 million for 2012. This amount, which is equal to the commodity exposure only by coincidence, also equals approximately 1.6% of income before income taxes.

Interest Rates

Changes in interest rates can affect:

- the value of investments in bonds, investment securities, loans, or receivables with fixed interest rates.
- the value of liabilities with fixed interest rates.
- the returns a firm generates from pension fund investments.

Firms often use interest rate swaps to hedge, or neutralize, the risk of interest rate changes. As Chapter 7 discusses, locking in a fixed rate insulates the principal amount from interest rate changes, but it exposes the fair value of the principal. Locking in a variable rate protects the fair value of the principal but induces volatility in the cash flows for interest payments. Firms, especially financial institutions, also hedge some interest rate risk by matching investments in fixed-interest-rate assets with fixed-rate liabilities of equivalent amounts and duration.

PepsiCo discloses the following in Note 10:

We centrally manage our debt and investment portfolios considering investment opportunities and risks, tax consequences and overall financing strategies. We use various interest rate derivative instruments including, but not limited to, interest rate swaps, cross-currency interest rate swaps, Treasury locks and swap locks to manage our overall interest expense and foreign exchange risk. These instruments effectively change the interest rate and currency of specific debt issuances. Certain of our fixed rate indebtedness has been swapped to floating rates. The notional amount, interest payment and maturity date of the interest rate and cross-currency swaps match the principal, interest payment and maturity date of the related debt. Our Treasury locks and swap locks are entered into to protect against unfavorable interest rate changes relating to forecasted debt transactions.

The MD&A (Appendix B) indicates that a one percentage point increase in interest rates would have increased net interest expense by $9 million for 2012, which is approximately 1% of realized interest expense ($9/$899).

Other Risk-Related Disclosures

The particular elements of risk that firms include in their risk management disclosures depend on the types of risks to which a firm is exposed, and many of the financial statement footnotes include qualitative discussions or quantitative indicators of such risks. For example, PepsiCo discloses in Note 7, "Pension, Retiree Medical and Savings Plans," the effect that a 1% change in the assumed health care cost trend rate would have on service cost and interest cost components of retiree medical expense and the associated benefit liability. The required disclosures in Note 6, "Stock-Based Compensation," enable financial statement users to assess the impact of different assumptions underlying the valuation of stock options. Similarly, information in Note 5, "Income Taxes," indicates that in determining the income tax provision, the company assesses the risk of a tax position being sustained on audit based on the technical merits of the position. Finally, Note 9, "Debt Obligations and Commitments," (Appendix A) indicates that long-term contractual commitments, other than long-term debt, are *not* recorded on the balance sheet, which is useful to know when assessing various liquidity and credit risks, discussed later in this chapter.

Firms now disclose considerably more information for you to use in assessing the effect of various risks on a firm. Increasingly, standard setters and regulators are requiring firms to disclose the sensitivity of reported amounts to changes in various variables and assumptions, like those mentioned above. The disclosed information increases in value as analysts and other users of financial statements become familiar with the new reporting.

LO 5-2

Define *financial flexibility* and use an innovative decomposition of return on common equity to assess financial flexibility.

Analyzing Financial Flexibility by Disaggregating ROCE

Financial flexibility represents the ability of a firm to strategically use debt financing to increase returns to investments by common shareholders. As demonstrated in Chapter 4, firms that borrow funds and invest those funds in assets that generate a higher return than the after-tax cost of the borrowing create value for the common shareholders. Common shareholders benefit with increasing proportions of debt in the capital structure *as long as the firm maintains a rate of return on assets above the after-tax cost rate of the debt*. Therefore, financial leverage can *enhance* the return to common shareholders. In this section we present a method for decomposing ROCE that enables you to gauge the firm's financial flexibility, and thus the extent to which a firm can (or cannot) strategically use debt to generate greater returns for shareholders. This section provides a linkage between the analysis of profitability in the prior chapter and the analysis of risk in this chapter.

From Chapter 4, the disaggregation of ROCE into components of profit margin for ROCE (assets turnover and capital structure leverage) is as follows:

ROCE	=	**Profit Margin for ROCE**	×	**Assets Turnover**	×	**Capital Structure Leverage**
$\dfrac{\text{Net Income Attributable to Common Shareholders}}{\text{Average Common Shareholders' Equity}}$	=	$\dfrac{\text{Net Income Attributable to Common Shareholders}}{\text{Sales}}$	×	$\dfrac{\text{Sales}}{\text{Average Total Assets}}$	×	$\dfrac{\text{Average Total Assets}}{\text{Average Common Shareholders' Equity}}$

Higher leverage generally suggests greater financial risk. Some of these risks are discussed in the following sections on (1) short-term liquidity risk, (2) long-term solvency risk, (3) credit risk, and (4) bankruptcy risk. These risks are primarily attributable to the costs of borrowing, reflected by interest expense for long-term debt and the requirement to make debt payments in cash when they come due.

The disaggregation of ROCE suggests that common equity shareholders benefit from increasing leverage (that is, the third term in the ROCE disaggregation). However, there are two offsetting effects of increasing leverage. First, increasing leverage assumes the firm can deploy the financing proceeds into assets that maintain the current levels of profitability and turnover (that is, the first and second terms). This deployment is surely not instantaneous and further depends on the firm's ability to scale up operations without experiencing diminishing returns, market saturation, and other strategic roadblocks. Second, increasing leverage increases interest expense, which reduces profit margins (that is, the first term in the disaggregation). Thus, increasing leverage has potential benefits and risks.

A shortcoming of the standard disaggregation of ROCE is the inability to directly gauge the extent to which a firm can strategically increase leverage to increase returns to common shareholders without offsetting profitability. We refer to this as *financial flexibility*. To gauge a firm's financial flexibility, we can disaggregate ROCE to *separate the operating and financing impacts* on ROCE. The alternative disaggregation discussed next requires that we first reformulate the balance sheet and income statement into operating and financing groupings.[1]

Exhibit 5.3 presents the standard balance sheet equation in which assets are equal to liabilities plus equity. Each of these amounts is decomposed into primary components.

---

[1]This alternative disaggregation of ROCE is sometimes referred to as the "Penman decomposition," following pioneering work by Stephen H. Penman in articulating the operating and financing activities of firms. For a more detailed discussion, see Chapter 11 of Stephen H. Penman, *Financial Statement Analysis and Security Valuation* (New York: McGraw-Hill Irwin), 2004.

- Assets = Operating Assets + Financial Assets
- Liabilities = Operating Liabilities + Financial Liabilities (including Preferred Equity)
- Equity = Common Equity

The important task is to designate assets and liabilities as either *operating* or *financing*. Operating assets and liabilities are those that are necessary for the actual operations of the company, whereas financial assets and liabilities represent sources of capital that provide the funding for net operating assets. For example, operating assets include:

- Cash for liquidity
- Accounts receivable
- Prepaid assets
- Inventory
- Property, plant, and equipment
- Intangible assets
- Deferred income taxes
- Other assets

Financial assets include:

- Excess cash
- Investment securities intended to retire debt
- Restricted cash for debt covenants
- Bond sinking funds
- Other designated assets

Similarly, operating liabilities include:

- Accounts payable
- Accrued liabilities
- Deferred income taxes
- Other liabilities

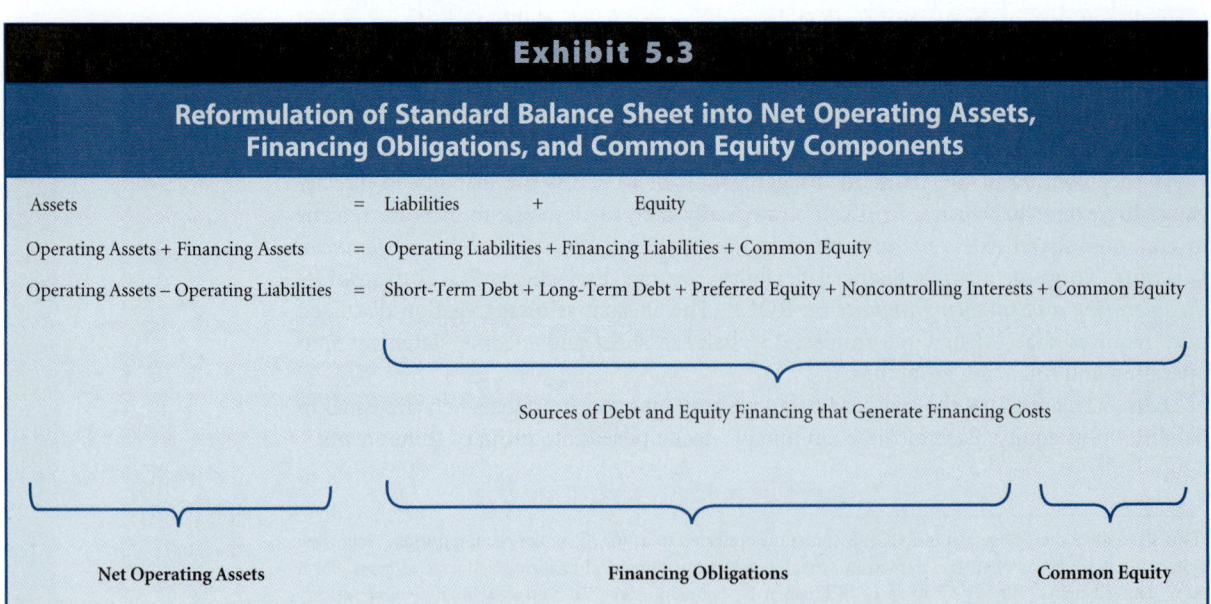

Exhibit 5.3

Reformulation of Standard Balance Sheet into Net Operating Assets, Financing Obligations, and Common Equity Components

Assets	= Liabilities + Equity
Operating Assets + Financing Assets	= Operating Liabilities + Financing Liabilities + Common Equity
Operating Assets − Operating Liabilities	= Short-Term Debt + Long-Term Debt + Preferred Equity + Noncontrolling Interests + Common Equity

Sources of Debt and Equity Financing that Generate Financing Costs

Net Operating Assets   **Financing Obligations**   **Common Equity**

Financial liabilities include:

- Short-term debt
- Notes payable
- Bonds payable
- Mortgages
- Capital leases
- Preferred equity
- Noncontrolling interests

We treat noncontrolling interests similar to preferred equity (that is, a financing obligation), consistent with the treatment of noncontrolling interests in accounting standards for business combinations. However, some analysts make the argument that noncontrolling interests should be netted against operating assets. Either approach can be justified so long as consistent treatment is used for noncontrolling interest on the income statement (discussed below).

The reformulated balance sheet equation is as follows:

$$\text{Net Operating Assets} = \text{Financing Obligations} + \text{Common Equity}$$

The primary change of this financial statement reformulation is that operating liabilities—both current and noncurrent—are netted against operating assets, leaving pure financing obligations and common equity on the right side of the equation. Also, noncontrolling interests and preferred equity are included in financing obligations to be distinct from common equity. The equation still balances, but the totals differ from the standard balance sheet equation due to the netting of operating assets and liabilities.

All firms maintain some financial assets, which include cash, marketable equity securities, and short-term investments. These financial assets must be allocated to operating versus financing categories, depending on their purpose. This allocation requires that you make a judgment call. Some financial assets are necessary elements of the firm's day-to-day operating liquidity (such as the cash and marketable securities necessary to conduct business each day and to meet cash flow requirements over different seasons and business cycles). In addition, some financial assets may be held for strategic purposes (such as investments in affiliate firms). These types of financial assets are directly related to the operations of the firm, and for most firms they comprise all or the vast majority of financial assets. However, by contrast, some firms will also hold some amounts of financial assets that are specifically intended to be part of the financial structure of the firm. These financial assets might include bond sinking funds, restricted cash (for debt covenants), and/or excess cash and marketable securities (above the amounts needed for liquidity) that the firm intends to use to retire debt. Such *financial* assets should be netted against financing obligations, which yield *net* financing obligations (similar to how operating liabilities are netted against operating assets to yield net operating assets).

A challenging judgment is how to treat cash. Some cash is necessary as part of working capital, and hence should be treated as an operating asset. However, firms can hold *excess cash.* There is no magic formula for computing excess cash, and any estimation of excess cash must consider possible reasons a firm holds what appears to be excess cash. For example, in 2004, investors criticized **Microsoft** for holding excess cash. At the end of 2004, cash and short-term investments amounted to over $60 billion, relative to total assets of $94 billion. Microsoft subsequently paid a $3-per-share special dividend, totaling $33 billion, and announced a plan to buy back up to $30 billion of outstanding common stock. It was difficult to quantify how much excess cash Microsoft held in 2004, but any approximation would have resulted in *negative* net financing obligations for Microsoft (which had no short- or long-term debt). *Negative* net financing obligations are not a problem as long as the partition of the income statement, discussed below, is done consistently with the allocation of assets and liabilities to operating and financing components.

To be consistent, we do the same for the income statement. For each line item, you designate it as either an operating or financing component of reported profitability. Once the reformulation of the balance sheet is done, the allocation of line items on the income statement to either operating or financing activities is straightforward. Any item designated as a financing asset or liability should have a corresponding 'flow' amount on the income statement, most commonly interest income (for financing assets) or interest expense (for financing liabilities). Also, note that the designation of preferred equity as a financing liability means that preferred dividends are a financing cost. Similarly, because noncontrolling interests are designated as a financing liability, the deduction for income attributable to noncontrolling interests is designated as a financing cost.

The reformulated balance sheets for **PepsiCo** for 2009–2012 are shown in Exhibit 5.4. Assuming that PepsiCo holds no financial assets intended for financing purposes (such as

Exhibit 5.4

Reformulated Balance Sheets for PepsiCo
(amounts in millions)

	2012	2011	2010	2009
OPERATING ASSETS				
Cash and cash equivalents	$ 6,297	$ 4,067	$ 5,943	$ 3,943
Short-term investments	322	358	426	192
Accounts and notes receivable, net	7,041	6,912	6,323	4,624
Inventories	3,581	3,827	3,372	2,618
Prepaid expenses and other current assets	1,479	2,277	1,505	1,194
Property, plant and equipment, net	19,136	19,698	19,058	12,671
Amortizable intangible assets, net	1,781	1,888	2,025	841
Goodwill	16,971	16,800	14,661	6,534
Other nonamortizable intangible assets	14,744	14,557	11,783	1,782
Investments in noncontrolled affiliates	1,633	1,477	1,368	4,484
Other assets	1,653	1,021	1,689	965
LESS: OPERATING LIABILITIES				
Accounts payable and other current liabilities	(11,903)	(11,757)	(10,923)	(8,127)
Income taxes payable	(371)	(192)	(71)	(165)
Other liabilities	(6,543)	(8,266)	(6,729)	(5,591)
Deferred income taxes	(5,063)	(4,995)	(4,057)	(659)
Net Operating Assets	$ 50,758	$ 47,672	$ 46,373	$ 25,306

(Continued)

Exhibit 5.4 (Continued)

FINANCING OBLIGATIONS				
Short-term obligations	$ 4,815	$ 6,205	$ 4,898	$ 464
Long-term debt obligations	23,544	20,568	19,999	7,400
Preferred stock, no par value	41	41	41	41
Repurchased preferred stock	(164)	(157)	(150)	(145)
Noncontrolling Interests	105	311	312	638
Financing Obligations	$ 28,341	$ 26,968	$ 25,100	$ 8,398
COMMON EQUITY				
Common stock, par value	$ 26	$ 31	$ 31	$ 30
Capital in excess of par value	4,178	4,461	4,527	250
Retained earnings	43,158	40,316	37,090	33,805
Accumulated other comprehensive loss	(5,487)	(6,229)	(3,630)	(3,794)
Treasury stock	(19,458)	(17,875)	(16,745)	(13,383)
Common Equity	$ 22,417	$ 20,704	$ 21,273	$ 16,908
Total Financing Obligations and				
Common Equity	$ 50,758	$ 47,672	$ 46,373	$ 25,306

a bond sinking fund), we classify PepsiCo's cash and cash equivalents and short-term investments as operating assets. As a result of this choice, PepsiCo's operating assets are the same as total assets. Current and noncurrent liabilities are netted against operating assets, resulting in net operating assets of $50,758 million for 2012. Note that total assets as reported (Appendix A) are $74,638 million for 2012.

Exhibit 5.5 presents the reformulated income statements for PepsiCo for 2010--2012. They demonstrate the straightforward identification of costs associated with financing for PepsiCo, including primarily interest expense and preferred dividends. All other amounts are elements of operating profit.[2] Operating profits are reduced by a provision for income taxes, generating the revised measure of profitability—NOPAT (net operating profit after taxes). Finance texts sometimes refer to this construct as EBIAT (earnings before interest after tax), which is the same as NOPAT with consistent treatment of operating and financing activities and proper treatment of taxes (discussed next).[3]

Note how the reformulated income statement allocates PepsiCo's provision for income taxes (from PepsiCo's as-reported income statement, Appendix A) to operating

---

[2]Chapter 4 emphasized that judgment could be exercised in the preparation of profitability ratios. The exposition there used adjusted net income based on a subjective assessment of nonrecurring components of reported profitability. For purposes here, we revert to the amounts reported in the 2012 financial statements without adjustment for nonrecurring components; doing so would complicate the exposition here. Further, we deliberately use net income available to common shareholders, which requires that preferred dividends and the component of net income attributable to noncontrolling interests be deducted from net income as shown on the income statement in Appendix A.

[3]NOPAT is more common than EBIAT. A simple online search of each term indicates approximately forty times as many results for NOPAT. Further, many of the search results for EBIAT relate to surnames, not the profitability construct.

Exhibit 5.5

Reformulated Income Statements for PepsiCo
(amounts in millions)

	2012	2011	2010
Net revenue	$ 65,492	$ 66,504	$ 57,838
Cost of sales	(31,291)	(31,593)	(26,575)
Selling, general, and administrative expenses	(24,970)	(25,145)	(22,814)
Other operating charges	(119)	(133)	(117)
Operating Profit	$ 9,112	$ 9,633	$ 8,332
Bottling equity income	0	0	735
Interest income	92	58	69
Adjusted Income Before Income Taxes	$ 9,204	$ 9,691	$ 9,136
Provision for income taxes at effective rate	(2,316)	(2,602)	(2,102)
Net Operating Profit After Taxes (NOPAT)	$ 6,888	$ 7,089	$ 7,034
FINANCING EXPENSE			
Interest expense × (1 − Effective tax rate)	$ (673)	$ (626)	$ (695)
Preferred dividends	(1)	(1)	(1)
Net income attributable to noncontrolling interests	(36)	(19)	(18)
Net Financing Expense (After Tax)	$ (710)	$ (646)	$ (714)
Net Income to Common Shareholders	$ 6,178	$ 6,443	$ 6,320
Effective tax rate	25.2%	26.9%	23.0%

and financing activities. For 2012, PepsiCo's total reported tax provision is $2,090 million (Appendix A), but Exhibit 5.5 indicates a provision on adjusted income before income taxes of $2,316 million. The higher provision in Exhibit 5.5 is due to the removal of financing expense from income before income taxes. The tax benefit of interest expense reduces *effective* interest expense from $899 million (Appendix A) to $673 million, as shown in Exhibit 5.5. The difference of $226 ($899 − $673) is the difference between the reported tax provision of $2,090 million and the adjusted provision in Exhibit 5.5 of $2,316, and reflects the benefits accruing to common shareholders from using debt and tax-deductible interest. Preferred dividends are not tax-deductible, so no tax adjustment is necessary. Also note the following:

NOPAT − Net Financing Expense (after taxes) = Net Income Available to Common Shareholders

If we had categorized PepsiCo's short-term investments as a financing asset, this asset would have been netted against PepsiCo's financing obligations in Exhibit 5.4. Accordingly, to be consistent with the treatment on the balance sheet, interest revenues (after tax) pertaining to the short-term investments would have been netted against interest expense (after tax) to compute net financing expense (after tax) in Exhibit 5.5. The reformulated balance sheets would still balance, with different totals, and the reformulated income statements would still reflect the same net income available to common, but the allocation to operating and financing components would differ. The same argument holds true for the treatment of noncontrolling interests. We treat noncontrolling interests as part of financing obligations (Exhibit 5.3), therefore we also include the share of net income attributable to noncontrolling interests in net financing expense.

With these new financial statement classifications, Exhibit 5.6 demonstrates the algebraic disaggregation of ROCE into operating and financing components. The result is an alternative disaggregation of ROCE:

$$ROCE = \text{Operating ROA} + (\text{Leverage} \times \text{Spread})$$

Operating ROA is the rate of return the firm generates on its *net* operating assets (NOPAT/Net Operating Assets). Operating ROA is the rate of return available to *all* sources of financing, including debt, preferred equity, and common equity. It is different from the definition of ROA discussed in Chapter 4, primarily because the denominator is net operating assets (as opposed to total assets).[4]

In addition to operating ROA, the right side of the new ROCE equation consists of two other factors: leverage and spread. As noted in Exhibit 5.6, leverage is captured by the total financial obligations divided by common equity, which is commensurate with the standard debt-to-equity ratio, except that preferred equity and noncontrolling interests are included in financial obligations. Spread is the difference between operating ROA and the net borrowing rate, which is the combined effective rate of interest and preferred dividends. Put simply, the greater the spread between the firm's operating ROA and net borrowing rate, the more beneficial incremental borrowing will be for the firm's common equity shareholders.

The intuition of the new ROCE equation is that returns to common equity shareholders increase with:

- Increases in the rate of return on the firm's net operating assets
- Increases in leverage
- Decreases in the after-tax cost of debt and preferred equity

Incidentally, note that similar to ROA, operating ROA can be further disaggregated simply by dividing and multiplying by sales:

$$\text{Operating ROA} = \frac{\text{NOPAT}}{\text{Average Net Operating Assets}}$$

$$= \frac{\text{NOPAT}}{\text{Sales}} \times \frac{\text{Sales}}{\text{Average Net Operating Assets}}$$

---

[4]An easy way to understand how the classification of financial statement amounts can vary while still resulting in components that combine mathematically to ROCE is to consider reformulated financial statements where all assets and all liabilities are categorized as operating. Thus, short- and long-term debt, preferred stock (if any), and minority interest are netted against assets to compute net operating assets. By definition, this equals common equity. Then to be consistent with this treatment in reformulation of the income statement, all interest expense, preferred dividends, and minority interest would be categorized as operating items. The result would be net income available to common shareholders. The alternative disaggregation of ROCE into Operating ROA + (Leverage × Spread) would reduce to ROCE = Operating ROA, where Operating ROA = Net Income Available to Common/Common Equity. This would not accomplish much, but the point of this exercise is to emphasize the mathematical equivalence of this ROCE decomposition regardless of how assets or liabilities are reformulated.

Exhibit 5.6

Algebra Demonstrating the Disaggregation of Return on Common Equity (ROCE)

$$\text{ROCE} = \frac{\text{Net Income Available to Common Shareholders}}{\text{Common Equity}}$$

$$= \frac{\text{NOPAT} - \text{Net Financing Expense (after tax)}}{\text{Common Equity}}$$

$$= \frac{\text{NOPAT}}{\text{Net Operating Assets}} \times \frac{\text{Net Operating Assets}}{\text{Common Equity}} - \frac{\text{Net Financing Expense (after tax)}}{\text{Financing Obligations}} \times \frac{\text{Financing Obligations}}{\text{Common Equity}}$$

$$= \frac{\text{NOPAT}}{\text{Net Operating Assets}} \times \frac{\text{Common Equity} + \text{Financing Obligations}}{\text{Common Equity}} - \frac{\text{Net Financing Expense (after tax)}}{\text{Financing Obligations}} \times \frac{\text{Financing Obligations}}{\text{Common Equity}}$$

$$= \frac{\text{NOPAT}}{\text{Net Operating Assets}} \times \left(1 + \frac{\text{Financing Obligations}}{\text{Common Equity}}\right) - \frac{\text{Net Financing Expense (after tax)}}{\text{Financing Obligations}} \times \frac{\text{Financing Obligations}}{\text{Common Equity}}$$

$$= \text{Operating ROA} \times \left(1 + \frac{\text{Financing Obligations}}{\text{Common Equity}}\right) - \frac{\text{Net Financing Expense (after tax)}}{\text{Financing Obligations}} \times \frac{\text{Financing Obligations}}{\text{Common Equity}}$$

$$= \text{Operating ROA} + \left(\text{Operating ROA} \times \frac{\text{Financing Obligations}}{\text{Common Equity}}\right) - \left[\frac{\text{Net Financing Expense (after tax)}}{\text{Financing Obligations}} \times \frac{\text{Financing Obligations}}{\text{Common Equity}}\right]$$

$$= \text{Operating ROA} + \frac{\text{Financing Obligations}}{\text{Common Equity}} \times \left[\text{Operating ROA} - \frac{\text{Net Financing Expense (after tax)}}{\text{Financing Obligations}}\right]$$

$$= \text{Operating ROA} + [\text{Leverage} \times (\text{Operating ROA} - \text{Net Borrowing Rate})]$$

$$= \text{Operating ROA} + \text{Leverage} \times \text{Spread}$$

Operating ROA is thus the product of profit margin for operating ROA and net operating assets turnover in the same way that ROA is the product of profit margin for ROA and total assets turnover.

Financial flexibility is the ability of a company to use debt financing to strategically take advantage of investment opportunities that arise or to respond to unforeseen expenditures that surface in the normal course of business. For example, a company with extremely high levels of debt, high borrowing rates, low profitability, or insufficient cash flows to satisfy operating or financing obligations has low financial flexibility. In contrast, a company with unused lines of credit, low borrowing rates, high profitability and high cash flows relative to operating and financing obligations has high financial flexibility.

In addition to ready access to capital, the concept of "spread" is important to fully understanding financial flexibility. Spread reflects the difference between the rate of return on the operating assets (for example, 15%) and the borrowing rate on financial obligations (for example, 8%). Larger spread means the company can obtain capital at a borrowing rate and deploy that capital into operating assets that generate a rate of return that covers the borrowing costs, and any excess is retained by the common equity investors.

Incremental increases in leverage are likely associated with increased borrowing costs, both in terms of nominal borrowing costs and marginally higher borrowing rates. For example, second mortgages on properties generally carry higher interest rates than first mortgages. Similarly, increases in debt or preferred equity incrementally increase the net borrowing rate, which decreases spread, lowering the incremental benefits of increasing leverage. Nevertheless, firms with a large spread may face strategic roadblocks in deploying capital that leads to diminishing rates of return, which dominates any increasing cost of debt or preferred equity. Thus, firms that generate very high operating ROA relative to the cost of borrowing can likely increase the level of borrowings—with either debt or preferred equity—and thus are characterized as having greater financial flexibility. Financial flexibility also is associated with lower short-term and long-term solvency risk, discussed in the next two sections.

To illustrate the disaggregation of ROCE into operating ROA, leverage, and spread, Exhibit 5.7 uses the amounts from the financial statements in Exhibits 5.4 and 5.5 to compute ROCE. For comparison, Exhibit 5.7 presents the standard and alternative decompositions of ROCE. Of course, both computations produce the same ROCE.

The alternative ROCE decomposition reveals that **PepsiCo** generates a significant spread between operating ROA and the net borrowing rate. For 2010, 2011, and 2012, Operating ROA is 14.0%, 15.1%, and 19.6%, respectively. PepsiCo's operations clearly utilize the operating assets very profitably. The net borrowing rates were 2.6% in 2012, 2.5% in 2011, and 4.3% in 2010. Therefore, PepsiCo's spread between operating ROA and the net borrowing rate was 11.4% in 2012 (14.0% operating ROA − 2.6% net borrowing rate), 12.6% in 2011, and 15.4% in 2010. An interpretation of PepsiCo's spread in 2012 is that for every dollar PepsiCo currently borrows and deploys in operating assets, it generates 14.0¢ in operating profit after tax, whereas the borrowing triggers only 2.6¢ in net borrowing costs (after tax), resulting in 11.4¢ accruing directly to common equity shareholders. *This is the essence of the strategic use of leverage by equity investors*.

The large spread generated by PepsiCo indicates that the company enjoys a high level of financial flexibility. Creditors are relatively comfortable lending money to companies that generate rates of returns on assets that far exceed debt service costs. However, the trends shown in Exhibit 5.7 suggest that PepsiCo is increasing its leverage significantly. PepsiCo's leverage was only 0.88 in 2010, but has climbed to 1.28 in 2012.

Exhibit 5.7

Computations of ROCE Decomposition Using Standard and Alternative Approaches for PepsiCo 2010–2012 (reported amounts, dollar amounts in millions)

Standard ROCE Decomposition		Calculation for 2012	2012	2011	2010
Profit Margin for ROCE	Net Income to Common/Sales	$6,171/$65,492	9.4%	9.7%	10.9%
× Assets Turnover	Sales/Average Total Assets	$65,492/[0.5($74,638 + $72,882)]	0.89	0.94	1.07
× Capital Structure Leverage	Average Total Assets/(Average Common Equity–Noncontrolling Interests)	[0.5($74,638 + $72,882)]/[0.5($22,417 + $20,704)]	3.42	3.36	2.83
= ROCE	Net Income to Common/Average Common Equity	$6,171/[0.5($22,417 + $20,704)]	28.6%	30.7%	33.1%

Alternative ROCE Decomposition			2012	2011	2010
Net Margin for Operating ROA	NOPAT/Sales	$6,887/$65,492	10.5%	10.7%	12.2%
× Net Operating Assets Turnover	Sales/Average Net Operating Assets	$65,492/[0.5($50,758 + $47,672)]	1.33	1.41	1.61
= Operating ROA	NOPAT/Average Net Operating Assets	$6,887/[0.5($50,758 + $47,672)]	14.0%	15.1%	19.6%
+ Leverage	Average Financing Obligations/Average Common Equity	[0.5($28,341 + $26,968)]/[0.5($22,417 + $20,704)]	1.28	1.24	0.88
× Spread	Operating ROA – Net Borrowing Rate [Net Financing Expense (after tax)/Average Financing Obligations]	14.0% – 2.6%	11.4%	12.6%	15.4%
= ROCE	Operating ROA + (Leverage × Spread)	14.0% + (1.28 × 11.4%)	28.6%	30.7%	33.1%
Net Borrowing Rate	Net Financing Expense (after tax)/Average Financing Obligations	$710/[0.5(28,341 + 26,968)]	2.6%	2.5%	4.3%

For 2012, the leverage and spread components suggest PepsiCo earned an incremental 14.6% in returns for shareholders by using leverage. Alternately stated, financial leverage of 1.28 indicates PepsiCo has $1.28 of borrowed capital for every $1.00 of equity. Further, on each dollar of leverage invested in operating assets, PepsiCo earned 11.4% more than the borrow costs, thereby significantly increasing returns to shareholders.

Therefore, the alternative ROCE decomposition reveals that PepsiCo's ROCE in 2012 of 28.6% is the result of an operating ROA of 14.0% plus leverage of 1.28 times the spread of 11.4% [28.6% = 14.0% + (1.28 × 11.4%)]. In comparison to 2010, this decomposition reveals that PepsiCo's 2012 operating ROA has fallen to 71.4% of its level in 2010 (14.0%/19.6%), but ROCE has fallen somewhat less to 86.4% (28.6%/33.1%) of its 2010 level, largely due to the strategic use of financial leverage that generates returns to common shareholders in compensation for taking on financial risk through leverage.

Both approaches to the decomposition of ROCE indicate decreases in margins, decreases in turnover, and increases in leverage from 2010 to 2012. However, the alternative ROCE decomposition provides additional insights about the nature of the change in leverage that are masked in the traditional ROCE decomposition at the top of Exhibit 5.7. For the alternative ROCE decomposition in the bottom part of Exhibit 5.7, the increase in leverage is more dramatic, especially between 2010 and 2011 when it rose 41% (1.24/0.88); under the standard ROE decomposition, capital structure leverage only increased 19% between 2010 and 2011 (3.36/2.83). The difference is that in our alternative ROCE decomposition, we obtain additional information by focusing specifically on interest-bearing liabilities as leverage, and quantifying spread as a gauge of financial flexibility.

Indeed, Appendix A shows that total liabilities are $52,239 million at the end of 2012, but only $28,359 million are actually interest-bearing financing obligations ($4,815 million short-term obligations + $23,544 million long-term debt obligations). The other liabilities treated as leverage in the standard decomposition of ROCE include accounts payable of $11,903 million, other noncurrent liabilities of $6,543 million, and deferred income tax liabilities of $5,063 million. Although these amounts are important for gauging long-term solvency risk, they are not direct sources of financing that trigger incremental borrowing costs.

Quick Check

- Financial flexibility represents the ability of a firm to strategically use debt financing to increase returns to investments by common shareholders.
- An alternative decomposition of ROCE requires the reformulation of financial statements into operating and financing components, which highlights the benefits available to common shareholders through the use of leverage.
- Firms with large spreads—return on net operating assets minus the net after-tax borrowing rate—stand to benefit from leverage. PepsiCo, for example, generates large returns on net operating assets and so has a large degree of financial flexibility.
- The analysis of financial flexibility provides a natural link between profitability analysis discussed in the previous chapter and the analysis of numerous risks, discussed next.

Analyzing Short-Term Liquidity Risk

LO 5-3

Apply analytical tools to assess working capital management and *short-term liquidity risk.*

Short-term liquidity is the firm's ability to satisfy payment obligations to suppliers, employees, and creditors for short-term borrowings, the current portion of long-term debt, and other short-term liabilities. Thus, the analysis of short-term liquidity risk requires an understanding of the operating cycle of a firm. Consider a typical manufacturing firm that acquires raw materials on account, promising to pay suppliers within 30–60 days. The firm then combines the raw materials, labor, and other inputs to produce a product. It pays for some of these costs at the time of incurrence and delays payment of other costs. At some point, the firm sells the product to a customer, probably on account. It then collects the customer's account and pays suppliers and others for purchases on account.

If a firm (1) can delay all cash outflows to suppliers, employees, and others until it receives cash from customers and (2) receives more cash than it must disburse, the firm will not likely encounter short-term liquidity problems. Most firms, however, cannot time their cash inflows and outflows precisely, especially firms in the start-up or growth phase. Employees may require weekly or semimonthly payments, whereas customers may delay payments for 30 days or more. Firms may experience rapid growth and need to produce more units of product than they sell during a period. Even if perfectly timed, the cash outflows to support the higher level of production in this period can exceed customers' cash inflows this period from the lower level of sales of prior periods. Firms that operate at a net loss for a period often find that the completion of the operating cycle results in a net cash outflow instead of a net cash inflow. As an extreme example, consider a single malt Scotch whiskey distillery that incurs significant cash outflows for grains and other ingredients, distills the whiskey, and then ages it in wooden barrels for many years before finally generating cash inflows from sales to customers.

Of course, long-term leverage can trigger short-term liquidity problems. For example, a firm may assume a relatively high percentage of long-term debt in its capital structure. This level of debt usually requires periodic interest payments and may also require repayments of principal. For some firms, especially financial, real estate, and energy firms, interest expense is among the largest single costs. The operating cycle must generate sufficient cash not only to supply operating working capital needs, but also to service debt.

Financially healthy firms frequently bridge temporary cash flow gaps in their operating cycles with short-term borrowing. Such firms issue commercial paper or obtain three- to six-month bank loans. Most firms maintain lines of credit with their banks to obtain cash quickly for working capital needs. Financial statement footnotes usually disclose the amount of the line of credit and the level of borrowing used on that line during the year, as well as any financial covenant restrictions imposed by the line of credit agreements. **PepsiCo,** for example, discloses the following in Note 9 "Debt Obligations and Commitments" (Appendix A):

> *In the second quarter of 2012, we extended the termination date of our four-year unsecured revolving credit agreement (Four-Year Credit Agreement) from June 14, 2015 to June 14, 2016 and the termination date of our 364-day unsecured revolving credit agreement (364-Day Credit Agreement) from June 12, 2012 to June 11, 2013. Funds borrowed under the Four-Year Credit Agreement and the 364-Day Credit Agreement may be used for general corporate purposes of PepsiCo and its subsidiaries, including, but not limited to, working capital, capital investments and acquisitions.*

Unfortunately, PepsiCo does not quantify the credit available under these credit agreements, but these are often filed separately with regulators. It is important to note available but untapped borrowing capacity when assessing the overall financial risk profile of a firm. These amounts represent potential increases in financial risk, but at the same time, they provide the firm with beneficial financial flexibility (as discussed in the previous section).

A simple way to quickly grasp short-term liquidity issues is to examine common-size balance sheets, as discussed in Chapter 1. Common-size balance sheets provide a basic quantification of the relative amounts invested in various types of assets versus liabilities. For example, Exhibit 1.17 shows that PepsiCo maintains 25.1% of its assets as current relative to a slightly smaller 22.9% of assets financed through current liabilities. We discuss six financial statement ratios for assessing short-term liquidity risk:

1. Current ratio
2. Quick ratio
3. Operating cash flow to current liabilities ratio
4. Accounts receivable turnover
5. Inventory turnover
6. Accounts payable turnover

Current Ratio

The current ratio equals current assets divided by current liabilities. It indicates the amount of cash available at the balance sheet date plus the amount of other current assets the firm expects to turn into cash within one year of the balance sheet date (from collection of receivables and sale of inventory) relative to obligations coming due during the period. Large current ratios indicate substantial amounts of current assets are available to repay obligations coming due within the next year. Small ratios, on the other hand, indicate that current assets may not be sufficient to repay short-term obligations.

The current ratio for **PepsiCo** at the end of 2012 is as follows:

$$\text{Current Ratio} = \frac{\text{Current Assets}}{\text{Current Liabilities}}$$

$$1.10 = \frac{\$18,720}{\$17,089}$$

The current ratio for PepsiCo was 0.96 at the end of 2011. Thus, PepsiCo experienced an increasing current ratio during the 2012, consistent with an improvement of its cash and near-cash assets relative to current liabilities.

Banks, suppliers, and others that extend short-term credit to a firm generally prefer a current ratio in excess of 1.0, but current ratios are not evaluated in isolation and are assessed in the context of other factors affecting a firm's liquidity. They typically evaluate the appropriate level of a firm's current ratio based on the length of the firm's operating cycle, the expected cash flows from operations, the extent to which the firm has noncurrent assets that could be used for liquidity if necessary, the extent to which the firm's current liabilities do not require cash outflows (such as liabilities for deferred revenues), and similar factors. Prior to the 1980s, the average current ratios for most industries exceeded 2.0. As interest rates increased in the early 1980s, firms attempted to stretch their accounts payable and use suppliers to finance a greater portion of their working capital needs (that is, receivables and inventories). Also, firms increasingly instituted just-in-time inventory systems that reduced the amount of raw materials and finished goods inventories. As a consequence of these two factors, current ratios began moving in the direction of 1.0. Current ratios hovering around this level, or even just below 1.0, are now common. Although this directional movement suggests an increase in short-term liquidity risk, most investors view this level of risk as tolerable.

Wide variation exists in current ratios across firms and industries, as evident in the descriptive statistics on current ratios in Appendix D. Therefore, you should consider several additional interpretive issues when evaluating the current ratio:

■ An increase of equal amounts in current assets and current liabilities (for example, purchasing inventory on account) results in a decrease in the current ratio when the ratio is greater than 1.0 before the transaction but an increase in the current ratio when it is less than 1.0 before the transaction. Similar interpretive difficulties arise when current assets and current liabilities decrease by equal amounts. With current ratios for many firms now in the neighborhood of 1.0, this concern with the current ratio has greater significance.

■ For certain firms, a very high current ratio is not desirable and may accompany poor business conditions, whereas a very low or decreasing ratio may be a sign of financial health, and may accompany profitable operations. For example, during a recession, firms may encounter difficulties in selling inventories and collecting receivables, causing the current ratio to increase to higher levels due to the growth in receivables and inventory. In a boom period, the reverse can occur.

■ A firm with a very strong ability to generate large and stable amounts of cash flows from operations may function very effectively with a low current ratio, whereas a firm with slow or volatile cash flows from operations may prefer to carry a higher current ratio.

■ The current ratio is susceptible to window dressing; that is, management can take deliberate steps prior to the balance sheet date to produce a better current ratio than is the normal or average ratio for the period. For example, toward the end of the period, a firm may accelerate purchases of inventory on account (if the current ratio is less than 1.0) or delay such purchases (if the current ratio is greater than 1.0) in an effort to improve the current ratio. Alternatively, a firm may collect loans previously made to officers, classified as noncurrent assets, and use the proceeds to reduce current liabilities.

Despite these interpretive issues with the current ratio, you will find widespread use of the current ratio as a measure of short-term liquidity risk. Empirical studies (discussed later in this chapter) of bond default, bankruptcy, and other conditions of financial distress have found that the current ratio has strong predictive power for costly financial outcomes.

Quick Ratio

A variation of the current ratio is the quick ratio, also called the acid-test ratio, computed by including in the numerator only those current assets the firm could convert *quickly* into cash, often interpreted as within 90 days. The numerator customarily includes cash, marketable securities and other short-term investments, and receivables. However, you should study the facts in each case before deciding whether to include receivables and exclude inventories. Some businesses can convert their inventory into cash more quickly (for example, a firm that carries a large amount of readily salable commodities in inventory) relative to other businesses (for example, an equipment manufacturer such as **John Deere** that provides long-term financing for its customers' purchases).

Assuming we include accounts receivable but exclude inventories, **PepsiCo**'s quick ratio at the end of 2012 is as follows:

$$\text{Quick Ratio} = \frac{\text{Cash and Cash Equivalents} + \text{Short-Term Investments} + \text{Accounts Receivable}}{\text{Current Liabilities}}$$

$$0.80 = \frac{\$6,297 + \$322 + \$7,041}{\$17,089}$$

The quick ratio for PepsiCo was 0.62 at the end of 2011. Unless inventory turnovers have changed dramatically, the comparative trends in the quick ratio and the current ratio correlate highly. That is, you obtain similar information about improving or deteriorating short-term liquidity risk by examining either ratio. Note that the current and quick ratios for PepsiCo follow the same upward trend. However, the increase in the quick ratio is more pronounced. In 2012, current assets increased 7.3%, whereas current liabilities decreased 5.9%. On the other hand, the sum of cash, marketable securities, and accounts receivable increased 20.5% in 2012, leading to the increase in these amounts relative to current liabilities. Thus, the discrepancy between the current ratio and quick ratio for PepsiCo is due to changes in less liquid current assets. Indeed, the balance sheet indicates that PepsiCo decreased both inventory and prepaid expenses and other current assets in 2012.

The quick ratio is subject to some of the same interpretive issues as the current ratio. That is, analysts interpret quick ratios in the context of the many other factors that affect the firm's liquidity, including the firm's ability to generate cash flows from operations. Appendix D again reveals significant variation in quick ratios across firms and industries.

Operating Cash Flow to Current Liabilities Ratio

Rather than use balance sheet-based metrics like the current or quick ratio, you can use more direct indicators of a firm's ability to generate cash in the near term, such as ratios based on cash flow from operations. An intuitive measure is the ratio of cash flow from operations to current liabilities, which captures cash generated over a period, relative to the level of liabilities due within one year. Because the numerator of this ratio uses amounts for a period of time, the denominator typically uses an average of current liabilities for the same period. This ratio for **PepsiCo** for 2012 is as follows:

$$\text{Operating Cash Flow to Current Liabilities Ratio} = \frac{\text{Cash Flow from Operations}}{\text{Average Current Liabilities}}$$

$$0.48 = \frac{\$8,479}{0.5(\$17,089 + \$18,154)}$$

The ratio was 0.41 for 2011. A ratio of 0.40 or more is common for a typical healthy manufacturing or retailing firm.[5] PepsiCo exhibits an operating cash flow to current liabilities ratio well above 0.40 and the trend in 2012 is positive. Thus, PepsiCo does not display much short-term liquidity risk in terms of operating cash flows relative to current liabilities.

---

[5]Cornelius Casey and Norman Bartczak, "Cash Flow—It's Not the Bottom Line," *Harvard Business Review* (July–August 1984), pp. 61–66.

Working Capital Turnover Ratios

Our final three measures capture the rate of activity in working capital accounts to calibrate the cash-generating ability of operations and the short-term liquidity risk of a firm:

$$\text{Accounts Receivable Turnover} = \frac{\text{Sales}}{\text{Average Accounts Receivable}}$$

$$\text{Inventory Turnover} = \frac{\text{Cost of Goods Sold}}{\text{Average Inventories}}$$

$$\text{Accounts Payable Turnover} = \frac{\text{Purchases}}{\text{Average Accounts Payable}}$$

Chapter 4 discussed the accounts receivable and inventory turnovers, which are components of *total* assets turnover, as measures of profitability. These same ratios are used here as measures of the speed with which firms sell inventories and turn accounts receivable into cash. The accounts payable turnover indicates the speed at which a manufacturing or retailing firm pays for purchases of raw materials and inventories on account. Firms typically do not disclose the amount of raw materials or inventory purchases, but this amount can be easily computed. Recall that the inventory account primarily reflects the following:

$$\text{Ending Inventory} = \text{Beginning Inventory} + \text{Purchases} - \text{Cost of Goods Sold}$$

Thus, you can approximate purchases as follows:[6]

$$\text{Purchases} = \text{Cost of Goods Sold} + \text{Ending Inventory} - \text{Beginning Inventory}$$

Note that Purchases is used to generically capture retailing firms' purchase of inventory or manufacturing firms' purchase of raw materials and production costs.

These turnover ratios are often stated in terms of the number of days each balance sheet item (that is, receivables, inventories, and accounts payable) is outstanding. To do so, divide 365 days by each turnover metric.[7] Mathematically equivalent, but more intuitive, you can divide the balance sheet amount by the appropriate flow variable converted to a daily average. For example, the days accounts receivable outstanding can be calculated equivalently as 365/Accounts Receivable Turnover or, more intuitively, as Average Accounts Receivable/(Sales/365).

Exhibit 5.8 presents the calculation of these three turnover ratios and the related number of days for **PepsiCo** for 2012. PepsiCo combines accounts payable and other current liabilities on its balance sheet. Note 14, "Supplemental Financial Information" (Appendix A), disaggregates this combined amount into its various elements and reports the amounts for accounts payable separately. We use the amounts for accounts payable from Note 14 to compute the accounts payable turnover. Recall a finer point mentioned in Chapter 4 that we should only use credit sales and exclude cash sales for the accounts receivable turnover; this is not relevant for a company like PepsiCo, but would be for firms with a mix of commercial and retail sales, like **Starbucks**. For

---

[6]The accounts payable turnover ratio will be skewed upward if cost of goods sold includes a high proportion of costs (such as depreciation and labor) that do not flow through accounts payable. This bias is more of a concern for manufacturing firms than for retailing firms and is more of an issue in cross-sectional comparisons than in time-series analyses.

[7]If one wants to be technically correct, you should use 364 days in leap years or 371 days in a 53-week year for firms that use 52/53-week years.

Exhibit 5.8

Working Capital Activity Ratios for PepsiCo for 2012
(dollar amounts in millions)

Accounts Receivable Turnover

$$\frac{\$65,495}{0.5(\$7,074 + \$6,912)} = 9.4 \text{ times per year}$$

Days Accounts Receivable Outstanding

$$\frac{365}{9.4} = 39 \text{ days}$$

Inventory Turnover

$$\frac{\$31,291}{0.5(\$3,581 + \$3,827)} = 8.4 \text{ times per year}$$

Days Inventory Held

$$\frac{365}{8.4} = 44 \text{ days}$$

Accounts Payable Turnover

$$\frac{\$33,393}{0.5(\$4,451 + \$4,083)} = 7.8 \text{ times per year}$$

Days Accounts Payable Outstanding

$$\frac{365}{7.8} = 47 \text{ days}$$

PepsiCo, of the $11,903 million total accounts payable and other current liabilities at the end of 2012, only $4,451 million relate to accounts payable; the remainder includes accrued marketplace spending, accrued compensation and benefits, dividends payable, and other current liabilities.

The number of days firms hold inventory until sale plus the number of days firms hold accounts receivable until collection indicates the total number of days from the production or purchase of inventory until collection of cash from the sale of inventory to customers. This combined number of days indicates the length of time for which the firm must obtain financing for its primary working capital assets. The number of days accounts payable are outstanding indicates the working capital financing the firm obtained from suppliers. The difference between the total number of days for which the firm requires financing for its working capital and the number of days for which it obtains financing from suppliers indicates the additional days for which it must obtain financing. This difference is known as the *cash-to-cash cycle* (also known as the cash operating cycle), and it quantifies the length of time between cash outlays that ultimately result in cash collections. We depict these relations here.

Days of Working Capital Financing Required:

| Days Inventory Held | Days Accounts Receivable Outstanding |

Days of Working Capital Financing Provided:

| Days Account Payable Outstanding | Days of Working Capital Financing Needed from Other Sources |

Exhibit 5.9 shows the net number of days of financing needed from other sources for PepsiCo for 2010, 2011, and 2012. PepsiCo's days accounts payable outstanding is slightly higher than its days inventory held, indicating that it has likely strategically utilized supplier financing for its inventory. The net days financed from other sources approximates the days accounts receivable were outstanding. Like most companies, PepsiCo used short-term borrowing to finance part of the net days of needed financing.

Exhibit 5.9

Net Number of Days of Working Capital Financing Needed from Other Sources for PepsiCo

Year	Days Accounts Receivable Outstanding	+	Days Inventory Held	−	Days Accounts Payable Outstanding	=	Days Other Financing Required
2010	35		41		(45)		31
2011	36		42		(45)		33
2012	39		43		(50)		32

In general, the shorter the number of days of needed financing, the larger the cash flow from operations to average current liabilities ratio. A small number of net days indicates relatively little need to finance accounts receivable and inventories (that is, the firm sells inventory quickly and receives cash from customers soon after sale) or aggressive use of credit from suppliers to finance these current assets (that is, the firm delays paying cash to suppliers). Both scenarios enhance cash flow from operations in the numerator of this ratio. Furthermore, firms with a shorter number of days of financing required from other sources are less dependent on short-term borrowing from banks and other financial institutions. Such borrowing increases current liabilities in the denominator of the operating cash flow to current liabilities ratio, thereby lowering this ratio.

As an example of a company with extremely favorable working capital requirements, Exhibit 5.10 shows the working capital financing investments for **Amazon.com, Inc.,** a

Exhibit 5.10

Net Number of Days of Working Capital Financing Needed from Other Sources for Amazon.com, Inc., 2010–2012 (amounts in millions)

	2012	2011	2010
Sales	$61,093	$48,077	$34,204
Cost of goods sold	$52,390	$41,864	$29,459
Purchases	$53,429	$43,654	$30,490
Accounts receivable	$ 3,364	$ 2,571	$ 1,587
Inventory	$ 6,031	$ 4,992	$ 3,202
Accounts payable	$13,318	$11,145	$ 8,051
Days receivables outstanding	18	16	14
Days inventory held	38	36	33
Days accounts payable outstanding	(84)	(80)	(82)
Days other financing required	(27)	(29)	(35)

well-known large online retailer of books, electronic media, and numerous other products. Due to low levels of accounts receivable and inventory and extended accounts payable, Amazon has a *negative* value for days of other financing required. Not surprisingly, Amazon does not require any short-term debt financing. The only other liabilities Amazon has at the end of 2012 are (1) accrued expenses of $5,684 million, (2) long-term debt of $3,084 million, and (3) other long-term liabilities of $2,277 million (relative to total assets of $32,555 million). At the other extreme, a jeweler like **Tiffany & Co.** has a very long cash operating cycle with over 500 days of inventory.

Quick Check

- Short-term liquidity risk ratios are helpful to determine a firm's near-term ability to meet cash flow requirements for operations and current liabilities.
- Analysis of profitability and cash flow levels is an integral part of understanding short-term liquidity risk.

- Profitable firms that generate significant cash flows are characterized as having financial flexibility.
- The availability of credit agreements with banks also indicates financial flexibility.

Analyzing Long-Term Solvency Risk

LO 5-4

Explain the benefits and risks of financial leverage and apply analytical tools for assessing *long-term solvency risk.*

As discussed above in the context of financial flexibility, financial leverage enhances ROCE when firms borrow funds and invest those funds in assets that generate a higher return than the after-tax cost of borrowing. Common shareholders benefit with increasing proportions of debt in the capital structure as long as the firm maintains ROA in excess of the after-tax cost of the debt. However, increasing the proportion of debt in the capital structure increases the risk that the firm cannot pay interest and repay the principal on the amount borrowed. That is, as credit and bankruptcy risk increases, and the incremental cost of borrowing is also likely to increase. The analysis of long-term solvency risk highlights a firm's ability to make interest and principal payments on long-term debt and similar obligations as they come due.

A firm's ability to generate earnings over a period of years is the best indicator for assessing long-term solvency risk. Profitable firms generate sufficient cash from operations, but also are able to obtain needed cash from creditors or equity investors. Therefore, the measures of profitability discussed in Chapter 4 in the context of analyzing ROA and ROCE are also useful in assessing long-term solvency risk. Additionally, analysis of long-term solvency risk must begin with an assessment of the level of and trends in financial flexibility and with an analysis of short-term liquidity risk, already discussed. Three measures are used in examining long-term solvency risk:

1. Debt ratios
2. Interest coverage ratios
3. Operating cash flow to total liabilities ratio

Debt Ratios

Debt ratios measure the relative amount of liabilities, particularly long-term debt, in a firm's capital structure. The higher a debt ratio, the greater is the long-term solvency risk. The capital structure leverage ratio discussed in Chapter 4, one of the disaggregated components of ROCE, is one version of a debt ratio. Similarly, the assessment of financial flexibility discussed earlier in the chapter provides another computation of leverage. Several additional variations in debt ratios exist, including the following four common measures:

$$\text{Liabilities to Assets Ratio} = \frac{\text{Total Liabilities}}{\text{Total Assets}}$$

$$\text{Liabilities to Shareholders' Equity Ratio} = \frac{\text{Total Liabilities}}{\text{Total Shareholders' Equity}}$$

$$\text{Long-Term Debt to Long-Term Capital Ratio} = \frac{\text{Long-Term Debt}}{\text{Long-Term Debt} + \text{Total Shareholders' Equity}}$$

$$\text{Long-Term Debt to Shareholders' Equity Ratio} = \frac{\text{Long-Term Debt}}{\text{Total Shareholders' Equity}}$$

The debt ratios for **PepsiCo** at the end of 2012 are as follows:

$$\text{Liabilities to Assets Ratio} = \frac{\$52,239}{\$74,638} = 0.70$$

$$\text{Liabilities to Shareholders' Equity Ratio} = \frac{\$52,239}{\$22,399} = 2.33$$

$$\text{Long-Term Debt to Long-Term Capital Ratio} = \frac{\$23,544}{\$23,544 + \$22,399} = 0.51$$

$$\text{Long-Term Debt to Shareholders' Equity Ratio} = \frac{\$23,544}{\$22,399} = 1.05$$

Exhibit 5.11 shows the debt ratios for **PepsiCo** at the end of 2010, 2011, and 2012. The median firm has a liabilities to equity ratio of approximately 1, and hence a liabilities to assets ratio of approximately 0.5. PepsiCo's debt ratios are somewhat higher than these, which is to be expected given PepsiCo's size, profitability, and strong capacity for debt financing. The debt ratios involving total liabilities exhibit a slight decrease from 2010 to the end of 2012. The same is true for the long-term debt ratios, although the pattern is more steadily decreasing. This is consistent with the insights generated in the previous discussion of trends in financial flexibility for PepsiCo.

Exhibit 5.11

Debt Ratios for PepsiCo at the End of 2010–2012

	2012	2011	2010
Liabilities to assets ratio	0.70	0.71	0.68
Liabilities to shareholders' equity ratio	2.33	2.49	2.17
Long-term debt to long-term capital ratio	0.51	0.50	0.48
Long-term debt to shareholders' equity ratio	1.05	0.98	0.93

Note the high correlations between changes in the two debt ratios involving total liabilities over time and in the two long-term debt ratios over time. These results are not surprising because they use overlapping financial statement data. Generally, you can select one of these ratios without losing much information based on an armada of similar ratios. Because different debt ratios exist, you should use caution when reading financial periodicals and discussing debt ratios with others, because variations in definitions are pervasive. For example, a liabilities to shareholders' equity ratio greater than 1.0 (that is, more liabilities than shareholders' equity) is not unusual, but a liabilities to assets ratio or a long-term debt to long-term capital ratio greater than 1.0 is highly unusual (because it requires a negative shareholders' equity).

In addition to computing debt ratios, you may gather information from the financial statement footnote on long-term debt. The note includes information on the types of debt a firm has issued and their interest rates and maturity dates. In certain situations, it is necessary to access public filings of debt contracts to monitor the firm's closeness to debt covenants. PepsiCo's Note 9, "Debt Obligations and Commitments" (Appendix A) provides information about the schedule of long-term debt obligations as well as significant issuances. During 2012, PepsiCo issued over $5 billion of senior notes payable, with the proceeds being used for "general corporate purposes, including the repayment of commercial paper."

In an effort to appear less risky and to lower their cost of financing or perhaps to avoid violating debt covenants in existing borrowing arrangements, some firms attempt to structure financing in a manner that keeps debt off the balance sheet. For example, companies often structure leases to qualify as operating leases instead of capital leases to minimize reported long-term debt. You should recognize the possibility of such actions when interpreting debt ratios and perhaps adjust the reported amounts, as illustrated for leases in Chapter 7 and several other arrangements in Chapter 6. PepsiCo provides a separate schedule in Note 9 of long-term contractual commitments, which includes several off-balance sheet items, such as operating leases, purchasing commitments, and marketing commitments. The total of these three items is $6,131 million at the end of 2012.

Interest Coverage Ratios

Interest coverage ratios indicate the number of times a firm's income or cash flows could cover interest charges. For example, one common approach to the interest coverage ratio divides net income before interest expense and income taxes by interest expense. This income-based interest coverage ratio for **PepsiCo**, using the amounts reported for net income and income tax expense for 2012, is as follows:[8]

$$\text{Interest Coverage Ratio (Net Income Basis)} = \frac{\substack{\text{Net Income} + \text{Interest Expense} + \text{Income Tax Expense} \\ + \text{ Net Income Attributable to Noncontrolling Interests}}}{\text{Interest Expense}}$$

$$10.2 = \frac{\$6,178 + \$899 + \$2,090 + \$36}{\$899}$$

---

[8]Increased precision suggests that the denominator include total interest cost for the year, not just the amount recognized as interest expense. If a firm self-constructs fixed assets, it must capitalize a portion of its interest cost each year and add it to the cost of the self-constructed assets. The analyst probably should apply this refinement of the interest coverage ratio only to electric utilities, which engage in heavy borrowing to construct their capital-intensive plants.

The interest coverage ratio for PepsiCo was 11.3 in 2011 and 10.1 in 2010. PepsiCo's reported profitability increased then decreased slightly across the three-year period (see the discussion in Chapter 4) while its debt levels increased, but the interest coverage ratio stayed within a relatively stable range. Analysts typically view coverage ratios of less than 2.0 as indicators of solvency risk. By this measure, PepsiCo exhibits very low long-term solvency risk.

Sometimes firms are able to capitalize interest as part of the cost basis of tangible assets. You should be aware of significant interest capitalization when examining net borrowing costs. Similarly, if a firm must make other required periodic payments (such as pensions or leases), you could include these amounts in the calculation as well. If so, the ratio is referred to as the *fixed charges coverage ratio*.

One criticism of the interest and the fixed charges coverage ratios as measures of long-term solvency risk is that they use earnings rather than cash flows in the numerator. Firms pay interest and other fixed charges with cash, not earnings. Notwithstanding the merits of earnings relative to cash flows as a summary performance measure (discussed in Chapters 2 and 3), you can create cash-flow-based variations of these coverage ratios by using cash flow from operations (before interest and income taxes) in the numerator. When the value of the ratios based on earnings is relatively low (that is, less than approximately 2.0), you might also want to examine the cash-flow based alternatives.

To illustrate, cash flow from operations for PepsiCo for 2012 was $8,479 million. Note 14, "Supplemental Financial Information" (Appendix A), indicates that PepsiCo paid $1,074 million for interest and $1,840 million for income taxes during 2012. The calculation of the interest coverage ratio using cash flows is as follows:

$$\text{Interest Coverage Ratio (Cash Flow Basis)} = \frac{\text{Cash Flow from Operations} + \text{Payments for Interest and Income Taxes}}{\text{Cash Payments for Interest}}$$

$$10.6 = \frac{\$8,479 + \$1,074 + \$1,840}{\$1,074}$$

Operating Cash Flow to Total Liabilities Ratio

Standard debt ratios such as the liabilities to assets ratio give no recognition to the ability of a firm to generate cash flow from operations to service debt. The ratio of cash flow from operations to average total liabilities overcomes this deficiency. This cash flow ratio is similar to the one used in assessing short-term liquidity, but the denominator includes all liabilities (current and noncurrent).

The operating cash flow to total liabilities ratio for 2012 for **PepsiCo** is as follows:

$$\text{Operating Cash Flow to Total Liabilities Ratio} = \frac{\text{Cash Flow from Operations}}{\text{Average Total Liabilities}}$$

$$0.16 = \frac{\$8,479}{0.5(\$52,239 + \$51,983)}$$

The ratio for PepsiCo was 0.17 in 2011 and 0.25 in 2010. A ratio of 0.20 or more is common for a financially healthy company.[9] Thus, PepsiCo appears to be right in the range of financially healthy companies, consistent with our findings with the other long-term solvency ratios.

---

[9]Casey and Bartczak, *op. cit.*

Analyzing Credit Risk

LO 5-5

Use risk analysis tools in assessing *credit risk*.

Credit risk is the likelihood that a firm will be unable to repay periodic interest and all principal borrowed. Credit risk analysis is a holistic approach to assessing the credit worthiness of a borrower. To assess credit risk, lenders will start with the short-term liquidity and long-term solvency ratios already discussed in the chapter. However, in addition, lenders will also consider other factors, such as the following:

- Circumstances leading to the need for the loan
- Firm's credit history
- Firm's cash flows
- Firm's assets that may be used as collateral
- Firm's capacity for debt
- Contingencies
- Character of management
- Communication
- Conditions or covenants

This list is neither an exhaustive catalog of such factors nor a mandatory list of factors that must be examined, but provides a context within which you can consider various firms.

Circumstances Leading to Need for the Loan

The reason a firm needs to borrow affects the riskiness of the loan and the likelihood of repayment. Consider the following examples.

Example 1: **W. T. Grant Company**, a discount retail chain, filed for bankruptcy in 1975. Its bankruptcy has become a classic example of how poorly designed and implemented controls can lead a firm into financial distress. (See Case 3.3 in Chapter 3.) Between 1968 and 1975, Grant experienced increasing difficulty collecting accounts receivable from credit card customers. To finance the buildup of its accounts receivable, Grant borrowed short-term funds from commercial banks. However, Grant failed to fix the credit extension and cash collection problems with its receivables. As a result, the bank loans simply kept Grant in business in an ever-worsening credit situation. Lending to satisfy cash-flow needs related to an unsolved problem or difficulty can be highly risky.

Example 2: **Toys"R"Us** purchases toys, games, and other entertainment products in September and October in anticipation of heavy demand during the holiday season. It typically pays its suppliers within 30 days for these purchases but does not collect cash from customers until December, January, or later. To finance its inventory, Toys

"R"Us borrows short term from its banks. It repays these loans with cash collected from customers. Lending to satisfy cash-flow needs related to ongoing seasonal business operations is generally relatively low risk. Toys"R"Us has an established brand name and predictable demand. Although some risk exists that the products offered will not meet customer preferences in a particular year, Toys"R"Us offers a sufficiently diverse product line that the likelihood of failure to collect sufficient cash is low.

Example 3: **Texas Instruments** designs and manufactures semiconductors for use in computers and other electronic products. Assume that Texas Instruments wants to develop new semiconductors and needs to borrow funds to finance the design and development effort. Such a loan would likely be relatively high-risk. Technological change occurs rapidly in semiconductors, which could make obsolete any semiconductors developed by Texas Instruments. In addition, expenditures on design and development of semiconductors would not likely result in assets that could serve as collateral for the loan.

Quick Check

■ Lending to established firms for ongoing operating needs and capital expenditures presents the lowest credit risk.

■ Lending to firms experiencing operating problems, lending to emerging businesses, and lending to support investments in intangible assets typically carry higher risks.

Credit History

Lenders like to see that a firm has borrowed in the past and successfully repaid the loans. Young firms sometimes shy away from borrowing to avoid constraints that such borrowing may impose. However, such firms often find that an inadequate credit history precludes them from borrowing later when they need to do so. On the other hand, developing a poor credit history early on can doom a firm to failure because of the difficulty of overcoming initial impressions.

Cash Flows

Lenders prefer that firms generate sufficient cash flows to pay interest and repay principal (collectively referred to as *debt service*) on a loan rather than having to rely on selling the collateral, consistent with the ratios we examined earlier in the chapter. Tools for studying the cash-generating ability of a firm include examining the statement of cash flows for recent years, computing various cash flow financial ratios, and studying cash flows in projected financial statements.

Statement of Cash Flows

An examination of a firm's statement of cash flows for the most recent three or four years will indicate whether a firm is experiencing potential cash flow problems. We discussed cash flows in detail in Chapter 3. Some of the indicators of potential cash flow problems, if observed for several years in a row, include:

■ Growth in accounts receivable and inventories exceed the growth rate in sales.
■ Increases in accounts payable or other liabilities routinely exceed the increase in inventories or sales.

- Persistent negative cash flow from operations exist because of net losses or substantial increases in net working capital (current assets minus current liabilities).
- Capital expenditures substantially exceed cash flow from operations. Although you should expect such an excess for a rapidly growing, capital-intensive firm, the negative excess cash flow (cash flow from operations minus capital expenditures) indicates a firm's continuing need for external financing to sustain that growth.
- Reductions in capital expenditures occur over time. Although such reductions conserve cash in the near term, they might signal that a firm expects declines in future sales, earnings, and operating cash flows.
- Sales of marketable securities are in excess of purchases of marketable securities. Such sales provide cash immediately but might signal the inability of a firm's operations to provide adequate cash flow to finance working capital and long-term investments. Such sales, however, may not indicate cash flow problems if the firm temporarily invested excess cash that it now plans to use to make a corporate acquisition or to acquire fixed assets.
- A reduction or elimination of dividend payments or stock repurchases occurs. Although such actions conserve cash in the near term, dividend reductions or omissions and cessation of share repurchase plans can provide a negative signal about a firm's future prospects.
- Available (previously established) revolving lines of credit are fully utilized. Full utilization of letters of credit might suggest that a firm's cash flows have become insufficient for operating purposes.

Although none of these indicators by themselves represents conclusive evidence of cash flow problems, they do signal the need to obtain explanations from management to see whether an emerging cash flow problem does exist. Just as analysts must understand a firm's industry and strategy to effectively analyze profitability, lenders must follow the same analysis steps.

Cash Flow Financial Ratios

Previous sections of this chapter discussed two cash flow ratios that may signal a cash flow problem: (1) operating cash flow to current liabilities ratio and (2) operating cash flow to total liabilities ratio.

Cash Flows in Projected Financial Statements

Projected financial statements represent forecasted income statements, balance sheets, and statements of cash flows for some number of years in the future. Lenders may require potential borrowers to prepare such statements (which are rarely made publicly available) to demonstrate the borrower's ability to repay the loan with interest as it comes due. A credit analyst privy to such forecasts should question each of the important assumptions (such as sales growth, cost structure, or capital expenditures plans) underlying these projected financial statements. Chapter 10 illustrates the preparation of projected, or forecasted, financial statements.

Collateral

A fourth consideration when assessing credit risk is the availability and value of collateral for a loan. If a company's cash flows are insufficient to pay interest and repay the principal when due, the lender has the right to take possession of any collateral pledged in support of the loan. The following are commonly collateralized assets: marketable securities; accounts receivable; inventories; property, plant, and equipment; and intangibles.

Marketable Securities

Marketable equity securities representing less than a 20% ownership appear on the balance sheet at market value. You can assess whether the market value of securities pledged as collateral exceeds the unpaid balance of a loan. Marketable securities representing 20% or more of another entity generally appear on the balance sheet using the equity method (See Chapter 8). Determining whether the market value of such securities adequately covers the unpaid balance of a loan is more difficult.

Accounts Receivable

A lender should assess whether the current value of accounts receivable is sufficient to cover the unpaid portion of a loan collateralized by accounts receivable. Determining whether the book value of accounts receivable accurately reflects their market value involves an examination of changes in the provision for uncollectible accounts relative to sales, the balance in allowance for uncollectible accounts relative to gross accounts receivable, the amount of accounts written off as uncollectible relative to gross accounts receivable, and the number of days accounts receivable are outstanding.

Inventories

Inventory represents valuable collateral to a lender only if it is salable for sufficient cash flows in the event of the borrower's distress. You should examine changes in the inventory turnover ratio; in the cost of goods sold to sales percentage; and in the mix of raw materials, work-in-process, and finished goods inventories to identify possible inventory obsolescence problems.

Property, Plant, and Equipment

Firms often pledge fixed assets as collateral for long-term borrowing. Determining the market values of such assets is difficult using reported financial statement information because of the use of acquisition cost valuations. Market values of unique firm-specific assets are particularly difficult to ascertain. Clues indicating market value declines include restructuring charges, asset impairment charges, and recent sales of such assets at a loss.

Intangibles

Intangibles such as brands, customer lists, and other assets generally do not serve well as collateral for borrowing because lenders cannot easily repossess the intangible (that is, sever it from all other assets or capabilities of the firm) in the event of a loan default. However, in some limited situations, intangibles can serve as collateral for borrowing. For example, rights owned by airlines to landing and gate slots at airports can be transferred to lenders in the event of loan default and resold to cover unpaid balances on a loan.

Capacity for Debt

Closely related to a firm's cash-generating ability and available collateral is a firm's capacity to assume additional debt, discussed earlier as financial flexibility. The cash flows and the collateral represent the means to repay the debt. Most firms do not borrow up to the limit of their debt capacity, and lenders like to see a "margin of safety." In addition to the factors discussed as part of financial flexibility, footnote disclosures highlight the amount of unused credit lines, which provide additional, direct evidence of capacity for debt.

Debt Ratios

Earlier, we described several ratios that relate the amount of long-term debt or total liabilities to shareholders' equity or total assets as measures of the proportion of liabilities in the capital structure. In general, the higher the debt ratios, the higher the credit risk and the lower the unused debt capacity of the firm. When measuring debt ratios, you must be careful to consider possible off-balance-sheet obligations (such as operating lease commitments or underfunded pension or health care benefit obligations).

Interest Coverage Ratio

As discussed earlier, the number of times interest payments are covered by operating income before interest and income taxes serves as a gauge of the margin of safety provided by operations to service debt. When the interest coverage ratio falls below approximately 2, the credit risk is generally considered high.

Contingencies

The credit standing of a firm can change abruptly if current uncertainties turn out negatively for the firm. Thus, you should assess the likelihood that contingent outcomes occur. The following are examples:

- Is the firm a defendant in a major lawsuit involving its principal products, its technological advantages, its income tax returns, or other core endeavors that could change its profitability and cash flows in the future? Most large firms are continually engaged in lawsuits as a normal part of their business, and most related losses are insured. Negative legal judgments are likely to have a more pronounced effect on smaller firms, however, because they have less of a resource base with which to defend themselves and to sustain such losses and may not carry adequate insurance.
- Has the firm sold receivables with recourse or served as guarantor on a loan by a subsidiary, joint venture, special-purpose entity, or corporate officer that, if payment is required, will consume cash flows otherwise available to service other debt obligations?
- Is the firm exposed to making payments related to derivative financial instruments that could adversely affect future cash flows if interest rates, exchange rates, or other prices change significantly in an unexpected direction? (See the discussions of derivatives in Chapters 7 and 9.)
- Is the firm dependent on one or a few key employees, contracts or license agreements, or technologies, the loss of which could substantially affect the viability of the business?

Obtaining answers to such questions requires you to read the notes to the financial statement carefully and to ask astute questions of management, attorneys, and others.

Character of Management

An intangible that can offset to some extent otherwise weak signals about the creditworthiness of a firm is the character of its management. Has the management team successively weathered previous operating problems and challenges that could have bankrupted most firms? Has the management team delivered in the past on projections regarding sales levels, cost reductions, new product development, and similar operating targets? Lenders also are more comfortable lending to firms in which management has a substantial portion of its personal wealth invested in the firm's common equity.

Communication

Developing relationships with lenders requires effective communication at the outset and on an ongoing basis. If lenders are unfamiliar with the business or its managers, efforts must be directed at communicating the nature of the firm's products and services and the strategies the firm pursues to gain competitive advantage. Throughout the term of a loan, borrowing firms are frequently required to communicate regularly with lenders. Lenders do not like surprises, so they monitor the firm's profitability and financial position, much like we have done earlier in this chapter.

Conditions or Covenants

Lenders often place restrictions, or constraints, on a firm to protect their interests. These are referred to in the banking industry as covenants. Such restrictions might include minimum or maximum levels of certain financial ratios. For example, the current ratio cannot fall below 1.2 and the long-term debt to shareholders' equity ratio cannot exceed 75%. Firms also may be precluded from paying dividends, repurchasing common stock, or taking on new financing with rights senior to existing lenders in the event of bankruptcy. Violation of such covenants could result in the need to repay loans immediately, higher interest rates, or other burdensome restrictions.

LO 5-6

Apply predictive statistical models to assess *bankruptcy risk.*

Analyzing Bankruptcy Risk

This section discusses the analysis of bankruptcy risk by using information in the financial statements.

The Bankruptcy Process

During the recession of 2008–2009, a staggering number of large, well-known firms filed for bankruptcy, including **IndyMac Bancorp** (July 2008), **Lehman Brothers** (September 2008), **Washington Mutual** (September 2008), **Circuit City** (November 2008), **Tribune Group** (December 2008), **Saab Automobile** (February 2009), **Chrysler** (April 2009), **General Motors** (June 2009), **Eddie Bauer** (June 2009), **The Jolt Company** (September 2009), and **Simmons Bedding** (November 2009). Subsequently, many more typically healthy firms filed for bankruptcy, including the publisher of this book. Most firms that file for bankruptcy in the United States file under Chapter 11 of the National Bankruptcy Code. Under Chapter 11, firms have six months in which to present a plan of reorganization to the court. After that period elapses, creditors, employees, and others can file their plans of *reorganization*. One such plan might include immediately selling the assets of the business and paying creditors the amounts due. The court decides which plan provides the fairest treatment for all parties concerned. While the firm is in bankruptcy, creditors cannot demand payment of their claims. The court oversees the execution of the reorganization. When the court determines that the firm has executed the plan of reorganization successfully and appears to be a viable entity, the firm is released from bankruptcy. In contrast to Chapter 11, a Chapter 7 filing entails an immediate sale, or liquidation, of the firm's assets and a distribution of the proceeds to the various claimants in the order of priority.

Firms typically file for bankruptcy when they have insufficient cash to pay creditors' claims coming due. If such firms did not file for bankruptcy, creditors could exercise their right to take possession of any collateral pledged to secure their lending and effectively begin liquidation of the firm. In an effort to keep assets intact and operating activities functioning and to allow time for the firm to reorganize, the firm files for bankruptcy. In recent years, some firms have filed for bankruptcy for reasons other than insufficient liquid resources to pay creditors. Some firms have filed for bankruptcy to avoid labor contracts or retirement obligations, because the firms considered them too costly. Other firms facing potentially costly litigation have filed for bankruptcy as a means of forcing the contending party to negotiate a settlement.

Models of Bankruptcy Prediction

Empirical studies of bankruptcy attempt to distinguish the financial characteristics of firms that file for bankruptcy from those that do not. The objective is to develop a model that predicts which firms will likely file for bankruptcy within one or more years. These models use financial statement ratios and other data.

Univariate Bankruptcy Prediction Models

Early research on bankruptcy prediction in the mid-1960s used univariate analysis. Univariate models examine the relation between a particular financial statement ratio and bankruptcy. Multivariate models, discussed next, combine several financial statement ratios to determine whether the set of ratios together can improve bankruptcy prediction. Beaver[10] studied 29 financial statement ratios for the five years preceding bankruptcy using a sample of 79 bankrupt and 79 nonbankrupt firms. The objective was to identify the ratios that best differentiated between these two groups of firms and to determine how many years prior to bankruptcy the differences in the ratios emerged. The six ratios with the best discriminating power (and the nature of the risk that each ratio measures) were as follows:

1. Net Income plus Depreciation, Depletion, and Amortization/Total Liabilities (long-term solvency risk)[11]
2. Net Income/Total Assets (profitability)

---

[10]William Beaver, "Financial Ratios as Predictors of Failure," *Empirical Research in Accounting: Selected Studies, 1966,* supplement to *Journal of Accounting Research* (1966), pp. 71–102.

[11]This ratio is similar to the operating cash flow to total liabilities ratio discussed earlier in this chapter except that the numerator of Beaver's ratio does not include changes in working capital accounts. Published "funds flow" statements at the time of Beaver's study defined funds as working capital (instead of cash).

3. Total Debt/Total Assets (long-term solvency risk)
4. Net Working Capital/Total Assets (short-term liquidity risk)
5. Current Assets/Current Liabilities (short-term liquidity risk)
6. Cash, Marketable Securities, Accounts Receivable/Operating Expenses Excluding Depreciation, Depletion, and Amortization (short-term liquidity risk)[12]

Note that this list includes profitability, short-term liquidity risk, and long-term solvency risk ratios. Beaver's best predictor was net income plus depreciation, depletion, and amortization divided by total liabilities. Exhibit 5.12 summarizes for each of the five years preceding bankruptcy the success of this ratio in correctly predicting firms that go bankrupt. The predictive accuracy increased as bankruptcy approached, but was close to 80% for as early as five years preceding bankruptcy.

The error rates deserve particular attention, however. A Type I error is classifying a firm as nonbankrupt when it ultimately goes bankrupt. A Type II error occurs when a firm is classified as bankrupt and ultimately survives. A Type I error is more costly to an investor because of the likelihood of losing the full amount invested. A Type II error costs the investor the opportunity cost of earnings from funds invested. Note in Exhibit 5.12 that the Type I error rates are much higher than the Type II error rates in Beaver's study. When the net income before depreciation, depletion, and amortization to total liabilities ratio is used to predict bankruptcy four years prior to bankruptcy, 47% of the predictions that firms would be nonbankrupt turned out to be incorrect, whereas only 3% of the predictions that firms would be bankrupt turned out to be incorrect.

Because univariate analysis helps identify factors related to bankruptcy, it is a useful step in the initial development of predictors of bankruptcy risk. However, in the assessment of risk, univariate analysis does not provide a means of measuring the relative importance of individual financial statement ratios or of combining them. For example,

Exhibit 5.12

Classification Accuracy and Error Rates for Bankruptcy Prediction Based on Net Income before Depreciation, Depletion, and Amortization/Total Liabilities

Years Prior to Bankruptcy	Proportion Correctly Classified	Error Rate	
		Type I	Type II
5	78%	42%	4%
4	76%	47%	3%
3	77%	37%	8%
2	79%	34%	8%
1	87%	22%	5%

Source: William Beaver, "Financial Ratios as Predictors of Failure," *Empirical Research in Accounting: Selected Studies, 1966,* supplement to *Journal of Accounting Research* (1966), p. 90. Reprinted by permission of Wiley-Blackwell.

---

[12]This ratio, referred to as the *defensive interval*, indicates the proportion of a year that a firm could continue to operate by paying cash operating expenses with cash and near-cash assets.

does a firm with a high current ratio and a high debt-to-assets ratio have more bankruptcy risk than a firm with a low current ratio and a low debt-to-assets ratio? The analyst also must subjectively judge the level of each financial ratio that signals a high probability of bankruptcy.

Bankruptcy Prediction Models Using Multiple Discriminant Analysis (MDA)

During the late 1960s and throughout the 1970s, deficiencies of univariate analysis led researchers to use MDA, a multivariate statistical technique, to develop bankruptcy prediction models. Researchers typically selected a sample of bankrupt firms and matched them with healthy firms of approximately the same size in the same industry. This matching procedure attempts to control factors for size and industry so you can examine the impact of other factors that might explain bankruptcy. You can then calculate a large number of financial statement ratios expected a priori to explain bankruptcy. Using these financial ratios as inputs, an MDA model selects the subset (usually four to six ratios) that best discriminates between bankrupt and nonbankrupt firms. The resulting MDA model includes a set of coefficients that, when multiplied by the particular financial statement ratios and then summed, yields a multivariate score that is the basis of predicting the likelihood of a firm going bankrupt. You can then examine the pattern of Type I and Type II errors and choose a cutoff that distinguishes firms with a high probability of bankruptcy from those with a low probability. Researchers usually develop the MDA model on an estimation sample and apply the resulting model to a separate holdout, or prediction, sample to check on the general applicability and predictability of the model.

Perhaps the best-known MDA bankruptcy prediction model is Altman's Z-score.[13] Altman used data for manufacturing firms to develop the model. Following is the calculation of the Z-score:

$$\text{Z-score} = 1.2\left(\frac{\text{Net Working Capital}}{\text{Total Assets}}\right) + 1.4\left(\frac{\text{Retained Earnings}}{\text{Total Assets}}\right)$$

$$+ 3.3\left(\frac{\text{Earnings before Interest and Taxes}}{\text{Total Assets}}\right) + 0.6\left(\frac{\text{Market Value of Equity}}{\text{Book Value of Liabilities}}\right)$$

$$+ 1.0\left(\frac{\text{Sales}}{\text{Total Assets}}\right)$$

Each ratio captures a different dimension of profitability or risk as follows:

1. Net Working Capital/Total Assets: The proportion of total assets comprising relatively liquid net current assets (current assets minus current liabilities). This ratio serves as a measure of short-term liquidity risk.
2. Retained Earnings/Total Assets: Accumulated profitability and relative age of a firm.
3. Earnings before Interest and Taxes/Total Assets: A variant of ROA. This ratio measures current profitability.

---

[13]Edward Altman, "Financial Ratios, Discriminant Analysis, and the Prediction of Corporate Bankruptcy," *Journal of Finance* (September 1968), pp. 589–609.

4. Market Value of Equity/Book Value of Liabilities: A form of the debt-to-equity ratio but it incorporates the market's assessment of the value of the firm's shareholders' equity. Therefore, this ratio measures long-term solvency risk and the market's overall assessment of the profitability and risk of the firm.

5. Sales/Total Assets: This is the total assets turnover ratio discussed in Chapter 4 and indicates the ability of a firm to use assets to generate sales.

In applying this model, Altman found that Z-scores of less than 1.81 indicated a high probability of bankruptcy, while Z-scores higher than 3.00 indicated a low probability of bankruptcy. Scores between 1.81 and 3.00 were in the gray area.

We can convert the Z-score into a more intuitive probability of bankruptcy using the normal density function in Excel.[14] A Z-score of 3.00 translates into a probability of bankruptcy of 2.75%. A Z-score of 1.81 translates into a probability of bankruptcy of 20.90%. Thus, Z-scores that correspond to probabilities of less than 2.75% indicate low probability of bankruptcy, probabilities between 2.75% and 20.90% are in the gray area, and probabilities above 20.90% are in the high probability area. These probability levels cannot be interpreted in the usual way. Altman had to trade off Type I and Type II errors when specifying the cutoff points for ranges of low probability, gray area, and high probability.

Altman obtained a 95% correct prediction accuracy rate one year prior to bankruptcy, with a Type I error rate of 6% and a Type II error rate of 3%. The correct prediction rate two years before bankruptcy was 83%, with a Type I error rate of 28% and a Type II error rate of 6%. As with Beaver's study, the more costly Type I error rate is larger than the Type II error rate.

Exhibit 5.13 shows the calculation of Altman's Z-score for **PepsiCo** for 2012. We use the originally reported amounts for PepsiCo instead of the adjusted amounts that eliminate nonrecurring items, because Altman developed his model using originally reported amounts. Not surprisingly, PepsiCo's Z-score of 3.33 clearly indicates a low probability of bankruptcy. FSAP computes Altman's Z-scores and the corresponding probabilities of bankruptcy (Appendix C).

The principal strengths of MDA are as follows:

- It incorporates multiple financial ratios simultaneously.
- It provides the appropriate coefficients for combining the independent variables.
- It is easy to apply once the initial model has been developed.

The principal criticisms of MDA are as follows:

- As in univariate applications, the researcher cannot be sure that the MDA model includes all relevant discriminating financial ratios. Most early studies, for example, used only accrual-basis income statement and balance sheet data and did not augment those data with cash flow data. MDA selects the best ratios from those provided, but that set does not necessarily provide the best explanatory power.
- As in univariate applications, the researcher must subjectively judge the value of the cutoff score that best distinguishes bankrupt from nonbankrupt firms, taking into consideration the levels and costs of Type I and Type II errors.

---

[14]The formula in Excel is =NORMSDIST(1–Z score). Altman developed his model so that higher positive Z-scores mean lower probability of bankruptcy; thus, computing the probability of bankruptcy requires that the normal density function be applied to 1 minus the Z-score. The website for this book (www.cengagebrain.com) contains an Excel spreadsheet for computing Altman's Z-score and the probability of bankruptcy. FSAP also computes these values.

Exhibit 5.13

Altman's Z-Score for PepsiCo, 2012 (dollar amounts in millions)

Ratio	Weight	Score
Net Working Capital/Total Assets ($18,720 − $17,089)/$74,638	1.2	0.0262
Retained Earnings/Total Assets $43,158/$74,638	1.4	0.8095
Earnings before Interest and Taxes/Total Assets ($6,214 + $899 + $2,090)/$74,638	3.3	0.4069
Market Value of Equity/Book Value of Liabilities ($68.43 × 1,544)/$52,239	0.6	1.2135
Sales/Total Assets $65,492/$74,638	1.0	0.8775
Z-Score		3.3336

- The development and application of the MDA model requires firms to disclose the information needed to compute each financial ratio. Firms excluded because they do not provide the necessary data may bias the MDA model.
- MDA assumes that each of the financial ratios for bankrupt and nonbankrupt firms is normally distributed. Firms experiencing financial distress often display unusually large or small ratios that can skew the distribution away from normal. In addition, the researcher cannot include dummy variables (for example, 0 if financial statements are audited and 1 if they are not audited). Dummy variables are not normally distributed.
- MDA requires that the variance-covariance matrix of the explanatory variables be the same for bankrupt and nonbankrupt firms.[15]

Bankruptcy Prediction Models Using Logit Analysis

A third stage in the methodological development of bankruptcy prediction research was the move during the 1980s and early 1990s to using logit analysis instead of MDA. Logit does not require that the data display the underlying statistical properties described previously for MDA.

The use of logit analysis to develop a bankruptcy prediction model follows a procedure that is similar to that of MDA: (1) initial calculation of a large set of financial ratios, (2) reduction of the set of financial ratios to a subset that best

---

[15]For an elaboration of these criticisms, see James A. Ohlson, "Financial Ratios and the Probabilistic Prediction of Bankruptcy," *Journal of Accounting Research* (Spring 1980), pp. 109–131, and Mark E. Zmijewski, "Methodological Issues Related to the Estimation of Financial Distress Prediction Models," *Journal of Accounting Research*, Supplement (1984), pp. 59–82.

predicts bankrupt and nonbankrupt firms, and (3) estimation of coefficients for each included variable.

The logit model defines the probability of bankruptcy as follows:

$$\text{Probability of Bankruptcy for a Firm} = \frac{1}{1 + e^{-y}}$$

where e equals approximately 2.718282. The exponent y is a multivariate function that includes a constant and coefficients for a set of explanatory variables (that is, financial statement ratios that discriminate bankrupt and nonbankrupt firms).

Ohlson[16] and Zavgren[17] used logit analysis to develop bankruptcy prediction models. Their models use different financial statement ratios than Altman's model, and they are somewhat more complex to apply. We do not discuss their models in depth here, but interested readers can consult the research cited. Despite the shortcomings of discriminant models, Altman's Z-score model is still the most widely referenced and the one emphasized in this chapter.

Application of Altman's Bankruptcy Prediction Model to W. T. Grant Company

W. T. Grant Company (Grant), one of the largest retailers in the United States at the time, filed for bankruptcy in October 1975. Case 3.3 in Chapter 3 includes financial statement data for Grant for its fiscal years ended January 31, 1967 through 1975. Exhibit 5.14 shows the calculation of Altman's Z-score for each of these fiscal years using amounts from Exhibits 3.38 and 3.39 of Case 3.3.

Altman's model shows a low probability of bankruptcy prior to the 1973 fiscal year, a move into the gray area in 1973 and 1974, and a high probability of bankruptcy in 1975. The absolute levels of these Z-scores are inflated because Grant was a retailer, whereas Altman developed the model using manufacturing firms. Retailing firms typically have a faster assets turnover than do manufacturing firms. In this case, the trend of the Z-score is more meaningful than its absolute level. Note that the Z-score declined steadily beginning in the 1970 fiscal year. With a few exceptions in individual years, each of the five components also declined steadily.[18]

Other Methodological Issues in Bankruptcy Prediction Research

Bankruptcy prediction research has addressed several other methodological issues.

1. **Equal Sample Sizes of Bankrupt and Nonbankrupt Firms.** The proportion of bankrupt firms in the economy is substantially smaller than the proportion of nonbankrupt firms. The matched-pairs research design common in most studies overfits the MDA and logit models toward the characteristics of bankrupt firms.

---

[16]Ohlson, *op. cit.*

[17]Christine V. Zavgren, "Assessing the Vulnerability to Failure of American Industrial Firms: A Logistic Analysis," *Journal of Business Finance and Accounting* (Spring 1985), pp. 19–45.

[18]The solution to the Grant case indicates that prior to its 1975 fiscal year, Grant failed to provide adequately for uncollectible accounts. The effect of this action was to overstate the net working capital/assets, retained earnings/assets, and EBIT/assets components of the Z-score; understate the sales/assets component; and probably overstate the overall Z-score.

Exhibit 5.14

Application of Altman's Bankruptcy Prediction Models to W. T. Grant

Fiscal Year	1968	1969	1970	1971	1972	1973	1974	1975
Altman's Z-Score Model								
Net Working Capital/Assets	0.54353	0.51341	0.44430	0.37791	0.44814	0.36508	0.38524	0.19390
Retained Earnings/Assets	0.43738	0.42669	0.41929	0.38511	0.34513	0.31023	0.25712	0.04873
EBIT/Assets	0.41358	0.44611	0.44228	0.38848	0.27820	0.26029	0.25470	(0.63644)
Market Value Equity/Book Value Liabilities	0.86643	1.01740	0.95543	0.89539	0.69788	0.50578	0.10211	0.01730
Sales/Assets	1.77564	1.76199	1.71325	1.67974	1.57005	1.58678	1.54797	1.62802
Z-score	4.03656	4.16560	3.97455	3.72663	3.33940	3.02816	2.54714	1.25151
Probability of Bankruptcy Range	Low	Low	Low	Low	Low	Gray	Gray	High
Probability of Bankruptcy	0.12%	0.07%	0.15%	0.32%	0.97%	2.13%	6.09%	40.07%

This overfitting is not necessarily a problem if the objective is to identify characteristics of bankrupt firms. However, it will likely result in classifying too many nonbankrupt firms as bankrupt (a Type II error) when the model is applied to the broader population of firms. Researchers (such as Ohlson in the study cited previously) have addressed this criticism by using a proportion of nonbankrupt firms that more closely reflects the population of firms.

2. **Matching Bankrupt and Nonbankrupt Firms on Size and Industry Characteristics.** This matching precludes consideration of either of these factors as possible explanatory variables for bankruptcy. Yet compared to larger firms, small firms may experience greater difficulty obtaining needed funds. Industry membership, particularly for cyclical industries, may be an important factor in explaining bankruptcy. Some researchers select a random sample of nonbankrupt firms. Another approach is to develop the MDA or logit models for each industry. Platt,[19] for example, developed models for 16 two-digit SIC industries. The explanatory variables and their coefficients varied across the industries. Platt and Platt[20] normalized the financial ratios of each firm by relating them to the corresponding average industry ratio of the firm's industry. They found that normalized financial ratios increased the classification accuracy of their sample to 90%, versus 78% based on a model of nonnormalized ratios.

3. **Use of Accrual versus Cash Flow Variables.** Until the mid-1980s, most bankruptcy research used accrual-basis balance sheet and income statement ratios or ratios from the "funds flow" statement, which defined funds as working capital. The transition to a cash definition of funds in the statement of cash flows led researchers to add cash flow variables to bankruptcy prediction models. Casey and Bartczak,[21] among others, found that adding cash flow from operations/current liabilities and cash flow from operations/total liabilities did not significantly add explanatory power to models based on accrual-basis amounts. However, other researchers have found contrary results, suggesting that the use of cash flow variables may enhance bankruptcy prediction.[22]

4. **Stability in Bankruptcy Prediction Models over Time.** A final methodological issue in bankruptcy prediction research concerns the stability of the bankruptcy prediction models over time with regard to the explanatory variables included and their coefficients. Bankruptcy laws and their judicial interpretation change over time. The frequency of bankruptcy filings changes as economic conditions change. Changes occur in the mix of industry concentration of firms. New financing vehicles emerge (for example, redeemable preferred stock or debt and equity securities with various option rights) that previous MDA or logit models did not consider in their formulation. To apply these models in practical settings, you should update them periodically.

[19]Harlan D. Platt, "The Determinants of Interindustry Failure," *Journal of Economics and Business* (1989), pp. 107–126.

[20]Harlan D. Platt and Marjorie B. Platt, "Development of a Class of Stable Predictive Variables: The Case of Bankruptcy Prediction," *Journal of Business, Finance, and Accounting* (Spring 1990), pp. 31–51.

[21]Casey and Bartczak, *op. cit.*

[22]For a summary of this research, see Michael J. Gombola, Mark E. Haskins, J. Edward Ketz, and David D. Williams, "Cash Flow in Bankruptcy Prediction," *Financial Management* (Winter 1987), pp. 55–65.

Begley, Ming, and Watts[23] applied Altman's MDA model and Ohlson's logit model to a sample of bankrupt and nonbankrupt firms in the 1980s, a later period than that used by Altman and Ohlson. Begley, Ming, and Watts found that the Type I and Type II error rates increased substantially relative to those in the original studies. They then reestimated the coefficients for each model using data for a portion of their 1980s sample. The coefficients on the liquidity ratios increased and the coefficients on the debt ratio decreased relative to those in the original studies. When they applied the original and reestimated coefficients to the 1980s sample, they observed a reduction in Type II errors but found no improvement in Type I errors for the Altman model. For the Ohlson model, they found that a reduction in Type II errors was offset by an equal increase in Type I errors. Thus, the revised coefficients result in fewer errors in classifying nonbankrupt firms as bankrupt, but similar or worse errors occur in classifying bankrupt firms as nonbankrupt.

Synthesis of Bankruptcy Prediction Research

The preceding sections of this chapter discussed bankruptcy prediction models. Similar streams of research relate to commercial bank lending,[24] bond ratings,[25] corporate restructurings,[26] and corporate liquidations.[27] Although the statistical models and relevant financial statement ratios vary among the numerous studies, certain commonalities do appear. This section summarizes the factors that explain bankruptcy most consistently across various studies.

Investment Factors

The following two factors relate to the asset side of the balance sheet:

1. ***Relative Liquidity of a Firm's Assets.*** The probability of financial distress decreases as the relative liquidity of a firm's assets increases. Firms with relatively large proportions of current assets tend to experience less financial distress than firms with fixed assets or intangible assets as the dominant assets. Greater asset liquidity means that the firm has or will soon generate the necessary cash to meet creditors' claims.

2. ***Rate of Assets Turnover.*** The returns from any asset investment are ultimately realized in cash. Firms acquire fixed assets or create intangibles to produce a salable product (inventory) or to create a desired service. Goods or services are often sold on account (accounts receivable) and later collected in cash. The faster assets turn over, the more quickly they generate cash. Commonly used financial ratios for this factor are total assets turnover, accounts receivable turnover, and inventory turnover.

---

[23]Joy Begley, Jin Ming, and Susan Watts, "Bankruptcy Classification Errors in the 1980s: An Empirical Analysis of Altman's and Ohlson's Models," *Review of Accounting Studies* 1, No. 4 (1996), pp. 267–284.

[24]Edward Altman, *Corporate Financial Distress and Bankruptcy,* 2nd ed., (New York: John Wiley & Sons, 1993), pp. 245–266.

[25]George E. Pinches and Kent A. Mingo, "A Multivariate Analysis of Industrial Bond Ratings," *Journal of Finance* (March 1973), pp. 1–18.

[26]James E. Seward, "Corporate Restructuring and Reorganization," *Handbook of Modern Finance,* ed. Dennis Logue, (New York: Warren, Gorham & Lamont, 1993), pp. E8–1 to E8–36.

[27]Cornelius J. Casey, Victor McGee, and Clyde P. Stickney, "Discriminating between Reorganized and Liquidated Firms in Bankruptcy," *Accounting Review* (April 1986), pp. 249–262.

Financing Factors

The following two factors relate to the liability side of the balance sheet:

1. *Relative Proportion of Total Debt in the Capital Structure.* Firms experience bankruptcy because they are unable to pay liabilities as they come due. The higher the proportion of total liabilities in the capital structure, the higher the probability that firms will experience bankruptcy. Firms with lower proportions of debt tend to have unused borrowing capacity that they can use in times of difficulty. Commonly used ratios include total liabilities/total assets and total liabilities/shareholders' equity.

2. *Relative Proportion of Short-Term Debt in the Capital Structure.* This factor has a similar rationale to that described previously except that the earlier maturity of short-term debt increases the risk of bankruptcy. A commonly used ratio for this factor is current liabilities/total assets.

Operating Factors

The following two factors relate to the operating activities of a firm:

1. *Relative Level of Profitability.* Profitable firms ultimately generate positive cash flows. Also, compared to unprofitable firms, profitable firms are usually able to borrow funds more easily. Firms with low or negative profitability must often rely on available cash or additional borrowing to meet financial commitments as they come due. Research has demonstrated that most bankruptcies initiate with one or several consecutive years of poor operating performance. Firms with unused debt capacity can often borrow for a year or two until the operating difficulties reverse. A combination of weak profitability and high debt ratios usually triggers financial distress. Commonly used financial ratios for profitability are net income/assets, income before interest and taxes/assets, net income/sales, and cash flow from operations/assets.

2. *Variability of Operations.* Firms that experience variability in their operations (for example, from cyclical sales patterns) exhibit a greater likelihood of bankruptcy than do firms with low variability. During the down times in the cycle, such firms often struggle to obtain financing to meet financial commitments and maintain operating levels.

Other Possible Explanatory Variables

Three other factors examined in bankruptcy research warrant discussion.

1. *Size.* Studies of bankruptcy have increasingly identified size as an important explanatory variable. Larger firms generally have access to a wider range of financing sources and more flexibility to redeploy assets than do smaller firms. Most studies measure size using total assets.

2. *Growth.* Studies of bankruptcy often include some measure of growth (for example, growth in sales, assets, or net income) as a possible explanatory variable. However, it is difficult to conclude much about its relative importance. The mixed results may relate in part to ambiguity in how growth relates to bankruptcy. Rapidly growing firms often need external financing to cover cash shortfalls from operations and to permit acquisitions of fixed assets. These firms often display financial ratios typical of a firm in financial difficulty (that is, high debt ratios and weak profitability). Yet their growth potential provides access to capital that allows them to survive. Firms in the late maturity or early decline phase of their life cycle may

experience slow (or even negative) growth but display healthy financial ratios. In these circumstances, future profitability can be low and as a result, the probability of future financial difficulty will be high.

3. ***Qualified Audit Opinion.*** Several studies have examined the information value of a qualified audit opinion in predicting bankruptcy.[28] The qualified audit opinion exhibits similar predictive accuracy to that of the models based on financial ratios. This result is not surprising if auditors use bankruptcy prediction models in deciding whether to issue a qualified opinion.

Some Final Thoughts

Bankruptcy prediction research represents an effort to integrate traditional financial statement analysis with statistical modeling. The models developed by Altman, Ohlson, and Zavgren rely on data that are decades old and are based on business activities and bankruptcy laws that differ from those currently encountered. Nevertheless, security analysts and academic researchers continue to use these models and they appear relatively robust despite the numerous limitations discussed previously.[29]

Measuring Systematic Risk

LO 5-7

Explain the distinction between *firm-specific risks*, as measured by various financial statement ratios, and *systematic risk*, as measured by market equity beta, and relations between these types of risks.

Firms face additional risks besides credit and bankruptcy risk. Recessions, inflation, changes in interest rates, foreign currency fluctuations, rising unemployment, and similar economic factors affect all firms, but in varying degrees depending on the nature of their operation. The investor in a firm's common stock must consider these dimensions of risk when making investment decisions. Differences in expected rates of return between investment alternatives should relate to differences in such risk. In this section, we briefly discuss how equity markets are used to obtain a broader measure of risk. Then we briefly relate this market measure of risk to financial statement information.

Studies of market rates of return have traditionally used the CAPM (capital asset pricing model). The research typically regresses the rate of returns on a particular firm's common shares [dividends plus (minus) capital gains (losses)/beginning-of-period share price] over some period of time on the excess of the returns of all common stocks over the risk-free rate. The regression takes the following form:

$$\text{Returns on Common Stock of a Particular Firm} = \text{Risk-Free Interest Rate} + \text{Market Beta} \times \left(\text{Market Return} - \text{Risk-Free Interest Rate}\right) + \text{Error}$$

The beta coefficient measures the covariability of a firm's returns with the returns of a diversified portfolio of all shares traded on the market (in excess of the risk-free interest rate). Firms with a market beta of 1.0 experience covariability of returns equal to the average covariability of the stock market as a whole. Firms with a beta greater than 1.0 experience greater covariability than the average. Firms with a beta less than 1.0

---

[28]William Hopwood, James C. McKeown, and Jane F. Mutchler, "A Reexamination of Auditor versus Model Accuracy within the Context of the Going-Concern Opinion Decision," *Contemporary Accounting Research* (Spring 1994), pp. 409–431.

[29]One study models bankruptcy prediction as an option pricing valuation using market values. The authors compare the prediction accuracy of this market-based model with the Altman and Ohlson models and find that their model has better prediction accuracy. However, using either the Altman or Ohlson model in addition to the option pricing model adds to the prediction accuracy. See Stephen A. Hillegeist, Donald P. Cram, Elizabeth K. Keating, and Kyle G. Lundstedt, "Assessing the Probability of Bankruptcy," *Review of Accounting Studies* (March 2004), pp. 5–34.

experience less covariability than the average firm. For example, a beta of 1.20 suggests 20% greater covariability; a beta of 0.80 suggests 20% less covariability.

Beta is a measure of the *systematic* (or *undiversifiable*) *risk* of the firm. The market, through the pricing of a firm's shares, rewards shareholders for bearing systematic risk. Elements of risk that are not systematic are referred to as unsystematic risk. Unsystematic risk factors include diversifiable firm-specific risks such as specific product obsolescence; labor strikes; loss of a lawsuit; and damages from fire, weather, or natural disaster. By constructing a diversified portfolio of securities, the investor can eliminate the effects of unsystematic risk on the returns to the portfolio as a whole. Thus, market pricing should provide no returns for the assumption of nonsystematic risk.

Several firm-specific factors are intuitively related to a firm's market beta, including:

- Operating leverage
- Financial leverage
- Variability of sales

Each of these factors causes the earnings of a particular firm to vary over time, and due to the association between earnings and stock prices, these factors are associated with a firm's market beta.

Operating leverage refers to the extent of fixed operating costs in the cost structure. Costs such as depreciation and amortization do *not* vary with the level of sales. Other costs, such as insurance and executive and administrative salaries and benefits, may vary somewhat with the level of sales, but they remain relatively fixed for any particular period. The presence of fixed operating costs leads to variations in operating earnings that are greater than contemporaneous variations in sales. Likewise, financial leverage (discussed earlier in the chapter) adds a fixed cost for interest and creates the potential for earnings to vary at a greater rate than sales vary. Thus, both operating and financial leverage create variations in earnings when sales vary but firms cannot simultaneously alter the level of fixed costs.

Research has shown a link between changes in earnings and changes in stock prices.[30] Thus, operating leverage, financial leverage, and variability of sales should result in fluctuations in the market returns for a particular firm's common shares. The average returns for all firms in the market should reflect the average level of operating leverage, financial leverage, and sales variability of these firms. Therefore, the market beta for a particular firm reflects its degree of variability relative to the average firm. Chapters 11 and 14 discuss more fully the relation between financial statement information and market beta and the use of market beta in the valuation of firms.

Summary

An effective analysis of risk requires you to consider a wide range of factors (for example, government regulations and posturing, industry competition, technological change, the quality of management, competitors' actions, profitability, and financial reporting risk). This chapter examines those dimensions of risk that have financial consequences and impact the financial statements.

This chapter began with a discussion of financial flexibility, which is an extension of profitability analysis, but with an emphasis on partitioning the firm's financial

---

[30]Ray Ball and Philip Brown, "An Empirical Evaluation of Accounting Income Numbers," *Journal of Accounting Research* (Autumn 1968), pp. 159–178.

statements into operating and financing components. With an understanding of how leverage can be strategically used to increase returns available to shareholders, we then examined the analysis of financial risk associated with the use of leverage along the following three dimensions:

1. *With respect to time frame:* We examined the analysis of a firm's ability to pay liabilities coming due the next year (short-term liquidity risk analysis) and its ability to pay liabilities coming due over a longer term (long-term solvency risk analysis). The financial ratios examined a firm's need for cash and other liquid resources relative to amounts coming due within various time frames.

2. *With respect to the degree of financial distress:* We emphasized the need to consider risk as falling along a continuum from low risk to high risk of financial distress. Firms with a great deal of financial flexibility fall on the low side of this continuum. Firms at risk for missing credit payment deadlines fall on the low- to medium-risk side of this continuum. Firms in danger of bankruptcy fall on the medium- to high-risk side of this continuum.

3. *With respect to covariability of returns with other securities in the market:* We briefly highlighted the use of market equity beta as an indicator of systematic risk with the market, which is affected by the types of risk analyzed in this chapter.

Analysts and academic researchers refer to the first two dimensions of risk as unsystematic, or firm-specific, risk. They refer to the third dimension of risk as systematic risk. Common factors come into play in all three settings of risk analysis. Fixed costs related to operations or to financing constrain the flexibility of a firm to adapt to changing economic, business, and firm-specific conditions. The profitability and cash-generating ability of a firm allow it to operate within its constraints or to change the constraints in some desirable direction. If the constraints are too high or the capabilities to adapt are too low, a firm faces the risk of financial distress. Firms facing potential financial distress are more likely to manipulate earnings and accounting information as we discuss in Chapter 6.

Questions, Exercises, Problems, and Cases

Questions and Exercises

5.1 Interpreting Risk Disclosures. Obtain the latest Form 10-K for **Facebook, Inc.** (www.investor.fb.com). Locate and describe the significant risks the company identifies. Are any of these unexpected based on your previous familiarity with the company?

LO 5-1

5.2 Interpreting the Alternative Decomposition of ROCE with Negative Net Financial Obligations. Suppose an analyst reformulates financial statements to prepare the alternative decomposition of ROCE for a firm with no debt. The analyst determines that the company holds excess cash as large marketable equity securities. The result will be net financial obligations that are negative. Assume that operating ROA is positive and large. How will this affect the decomposition of ROCE = Operating ROA + (Leverage × Spread)? How do you interpret the net borrowing rate for this firm?

LO 5-2

5.3 Relation between Current Ratio and Operating Cash Flow to Current Liabilities Ratio. A firm has experienced an increasing current ratio but a decreasing operating cash flow to current liabilities ratio during the last three years. What is the likely explanation for these results?

LO 5-3

LO 5-3 **5.4 Relation between Current Ratio and Quick Ratio.** A firm has experienced a decrease in its current ratio but an increase in its quick ratio during the last three years. What is the likely explanation for these results?

LO 5-3 **5.5 Relation between Working Capital Turnover Ratios and Cash Flow from Operations.** While a firm's sales and net income have been steady during the last three years, the firm has experienced a decrease in its accounts receivable and inventory turnovers and an increase in its accounts payable turnover. What is the likely direction of change in cash flow from operations? How would your answer be different if sales and net income were increasing?

LO 5-4 **5.6 Effect of Transactions on Debt Ratios.** A firm had the following values for the four debt ratios discussed in the chapter:

> Liabilities to Assets Ratio: less than 1.0
> Liabilities to Shareholders' Equity Ratio: equal to 1.0
> Long-Term Debt to Long-Term Capital Ratio: less than 1.0
> Long-Term Debt to Shareholders' Equity Ratio: less than 1.0

> **a.** Indicate whether each of the following independent transactions increases, decreases, or has no effect on each of the four debt ratios.
>>   **(1)** The firm issued long-term debt for cash.
>>   **(2)** The firm issued short-term debt and used the cash proceeds to redeem long-term debt (treat as a unified transaction).
>>   **(3)** The firm redeemed short-term debt with cash.
>>   **(4)** The firm issued long-term debt and used the cash proceeds to repurchase shares of its common stock (treat as a unified transaction).
> **b.** The text states that analysts need not compute all four debt ratios each year because the debt ratios are highly correlated. Does your analysis in Requirement a support this statement? Explain.

LO 5-4 **5.7 Interest Coverage Ratio as a Measure of Long-Term Solvency Risk.** Identify the assumptions underlying the interest coverage ratio needed to make it an appropriate measure for analyzing long-term solvency risk.

LO 5-3 **5.8 Interest Coverage Ratio as a Measure of Short-Term Liquidity Risk.** In what sense is the interest coverage ratio more a measure for assessing short-term liquidity risk than it is a measure for assessing long-term solvency risk?

LO 5-3, LO 5-4 **5.9 Interpreting Operating Cash Flow to Current and Total Liabilities Ratios.** Empirical research cited in the text indicates that firms with an operating cash flow to current liabilities ratio exceeding 0.40 portray low short-term liquidity risk. Similarly, firms with an operating cash flow to total liabilities ratio exceeding 20% portray low long-term solvency risk. What do these empirical results suggest about the mix of current and noncurrent liabilities for a financially healthy firm? What do they suggest about the mix of liabilities versus shareholders' equity financing?

LO 5-6 **5.10 Interpreting Altman's Z-score Bankruptcy Prediction Model.** Altman's bankruptcy prediction model places a coefficient of 3.3 on the earnings before interest and taxes divided by total assets variable but a coefficient of only 1.0 on the sales to total assets variable. Does this mean that the earnings variable is 3.3 times as important in predicting bankruptcy as the assets turnover variable? Explain.

5.11 Market Equity Beta in Relation to Systematic and Non-systematic Risk. LO 5-7 Market equity beta measures the covariability of a firm's returns with all shares traded on the market (in excess of the risk-free interest rate). We refer to the degree of covariability as systematic risk. The market prices securities so that the expected returns should compensate the investor for the systematic risk of a particular stock. Stocks carrying a market equity beta of 1.20 should generate a higher return than stocks carrying a market equity beta of 0.90. Nonsystematic risk is any source of risk that does not affect the covariability of a firm's returns with the market. Some writers refer to nonsystematic risk as firm-specific risk. Why is the characterization of nonsystematic risk as firm-specific risk a misnomer?

5.12 Levels versus Changes in Altman's Bankruptcy Prediction Model. LO 5-7 Altman's bankruptcy risk model utilizes the values of the variables at a particular point in time (balance sheet variables) or for a period of time (income statement values). An alternative would be to use changes in balance sheet or income statement amounts. Why might the levels of values in Altman's model be more appropriate than changes for predicting bankruptcy?

Problems and Cases

5.13 Calculating and Interpreting Risk Ratios. LO 5-3, LO 5-4 Refer to the financial statement data for **Hasbro** in Problem 4.24 in Chapter 4. Exhibit 5.15 presents risk ratios for Hasbro for Year 2 and Year 3.

Exhibit 5.15			
Risk Ratios for Hasbro **(Problem 5.13)**			
	Year 4	Year 3	Year 2
Current ratio		1.6	1.5
Quick ratio		1.2	1.1
Operating cash flow to current liabilities ratio		0.479	0.548
Days accounts receivable outstanding		68	73
Days inventory held		51	68
Days accounts payable outstanding		47	49
Net days of working capital financing needed		72	91
Liabilities to assets ratio		0.556	0.621
Liabilities to shareholders' equity ratio		1.251	1.639
Long-term debt to long-term capital ratio		0.328	0.418
Long-term debt to shareholders' equity ratio		0.489	0.720
Operating cash flow to total liabilities ratio		0.245	0.238
Interest coverage ratio		5.6	2.3

REQUIRED

  a. Calculate the amounts of these ratios for Year 4.
  b. Assess the changes in the short-term liquidity risk of Hasbro between Year 2 and Year 4 and the level of that risk at the end of Year 4.

c. Assess the changes in the long-term solvency risk of Hasbro between Year 2 and Year 4 and the level of that risk at the end of Year 4.

LO 5-3, LO 5-4 **5.14 Calculating and Interpreting Risk Ratios.** Refer to the financial statement data for **Abercrombie & Fitch** in Problem 4.25 in Chapter 4. Exhibit 5.16 presents risk ratios for Abercrombie & Fitch for fiscal Year 3 and Year 4.

Exhibit 5.16

Risk Ratios for Abercrombie & Fitch (Problem 5.14)

	Year 5	Year 4	Year 3
Current ratio		2.4	2.3
Quick ratio		1.7	1.6
Operating cash flow to current liabilities ratio		1.177	1.587
Days accounts receivable outstanding		2	4
Days inventory held		72	61
Days accounts payable outstanding		26	22
Net days of working capital financing needed		48	43
Liabilities to assets ratio		0.591	0.592
Liabilities to shareholders' equity ratio		1.443	1.448
Long-term debt to long-term capital ratio		0.454	0.461
Long-term debt to shareholders' equity ratio		0.831	0.855
Operating cash flow to total liabilities ratio		0.298	0.380
Interest coverage ratio		7.2	7.6

REQUIRED

a. Compute the amounts of these ratios for fiscal Year 5.
b. Assess the changes in the short-term liquidity risk of Abercrombie & Fitch between fiscal Year 3 and fiscal Year 5 and the level of that risk at the end of fiscal Year 5.
c. Assess the changes in the long-term solvency risk of Abercrombie & Fitch between fiscal Year 3 and fiscal Year 5 and the level of that risk at the end of fiscal Year 5.

LO 5-3, LO 5-4 **5.15 Interpreting Risk Ratios.** Refer to the profitability ratios of **Coca-Cola** in Problem 4.26 in Chapter 4. Exhibit 5.17 presents risk ratios for Coca-Cola for 2006–2008. As we did within the chapter for PepsiCo, we utilize Coca-Cola's footnote disclosures to extract the amount of trade accounts payable included within the line item accounts payable and accrued expenses.

REQUIRED

a. Assess the changes in the short-term liquidity risk of Coca-Cola between 2006 and 2008.
b. Assess the changes in the long-term solvency risk of Coca-Cola between 2006 and 2008.
c. Compare the short-term liquidity ratios of Coca-Cola with those of PepsiCo discussed in the chapter. Which firm appears to have more short-term liquidity risk? Explain.
d. Compare the long-term solvency ratios of Coca-Cola with those of PepsiCo discussed in the chapter. Which firm appears to have more long-term solvency risk? Explain.

Exhibit 5.17

Risk Ratios for Coca-Cola
(Problem 5.15)

	2008	2007	2006
Current ratio	0.9	0.9	0.9
Quick ratio	0.6	0.6	0.6
Operating cash flow to current liabilities ratio	0.578	0.647	0.636
Days accounts receivable outstanding	37	37	37
Days inventory held	71	68	68
Days accounts payable outstanding	44	38	40
Net days of working capital financing needed	64	67	65
Liabilities to assets ratio	0.495	0.497	0.435
Liabilities to shareholders' equity ratio	0.979	0.990	0.771
Long-term debt to long-term capital ratio	0.120	0.131	0.072
Long-term debt to shareholders' equity ratio	0.136	0.151	0.078
Operating cash flow to average total liabilities ratio	0.364	0.414	0.456
Interest coverage ratio	17.0	17.3	29.9

5.16 Computing and Interpreting Risk and Bankruptcy Prediction Ratios for a Firm That Declared Bankruptcy. Delta Air Lines, Inc., is one

LO 5-6

of the largest airlines in the United States. It has operated on the verge of bankruptcy for several years. Exhibit 5.18 presents selected financial data for Delta Air Lines for each of the five years ending December 31, 2000, to December 31, 2004. Delta Air Lines filed for bankruptcy on September 14, 2005. We recommend that you create an Excel spreadsheet to compute the values of the ratios and the Altman's Z-score in Requirements a and b, respectively.

REQUIRED

a. Compute the value of each the following risk ratios.
   (1) Current ratio (at the end of 2000–2004)
   (2) Operating cash flow to current liabilities ratio (for 2001–2004)
   (3) Liabilities to assets ratio (at the end of 2000–2004)
   (4) Long-term debt to long-term capital ratio (at the end of 2000–2004)
   (5) Operating cash flow to total liabilities ratio (for 2001–2004)
   (6) Interest coverage ratio (for 2000–2004)
b. Compute the value of Altman's Z-score for Delta Air Lines for each year from 2000–2004.
c. Using the analyses in Requirements a and b, discuss the most important factors that signaled the likelihood of bankruptcy of Delta Air Lines in 2005.

5.17 Alternative ROCE Decomposition. VF Corporation is an apparel

LO 5-2

company that owns recognizable brands like Timberland, Vans, Reef, and 7 For All Mankind. Exhibit 5.19 and 5.20 present balance sheets and income statements, respectively, for 2011–2012. (VF Corporation previously had noncontrolling interests, which were acquired during 2011. Nevertheless, there is a negative balance at the end of 2011, presumably pertaining to

Exhibit 5.18

Financial Data for Delta Air Lines, Inc.
(amounts in millions, except per-share amounts)
(Problem 5.16)

	For Year Ended December 31,				
	2004	**2003**	**2002**	**2001**	**2000**
Sales	$15,002	$14,087	$13,866	$13,879	$15,657
Net income (loss) before interest and taxes	$(3,168)	$(432)	$(1,337)	$(1,365)	$1,829
Interest expense	$824	$757	$665	$499	$380
Net income (loss)	$(5,198)	$(773)	$(1,272)	$(1,216)	$828
Current assets	$3,606	$4,550	$3,902	$3,567	$3,205
Total assets	$21,801	$25,939	$24,720	$23,605	$21,931
Current liabilities	$5,941	$6,157	$6,455	$6,403	$5,245
Long-term debt	$12,507	$11,040	$9,576	$7,781	$5,797
Total liabilities	$27,320	$26,323	$23,563	$19,581	$16,354
Retained earnings (deficit)	$(4,373)	$844	$1,639	$2,930	$4,176
Shareholders' equity	$(5,519)	$(384)	$1,157	$4,024	$5,577
Cash flow provided by operations	$(1,123)	$142	$225	$236	$2,898
Common shares outstanding	139.8	123.5	123.4	123.2	123.0
Market price per share	$7.48	$11.81	$12.10	$29.26	$50.18

Source: Delta Airlines, Inc., Forms 10-K for the Fiscal Years Ended June 2000–2004.

losses absorbed or currency adjustments. The noncontrolling interests will only affect your calculations through the use of average balances of financing obligations where noncontrolling interests should be allocated.)

REQUIRED

a. Compute ROCE for 2012 under the traditional calculation discussed in Chapter 4.
b. Compute ROCE for 2012 using the alternative decomposition, highlighting each component (NOPAT, leverage, spread). HINT: First, allocate individual line items on the balance sheet and income statement to operating and financing activities. Then compute each of the following for 2012:
 (1) Net operating assets
 (2) Net financing obligations
 (3) Common equity
 (4) NOPAT
 (5) Net financing expense (after tax)
 (6) Operating ROA
 (7) Leverage
 (8) Net borrowing rate
 (9) Spread

Exhibit 5.19

VF Corporation
Consolidated Balance Sheets
(amounts in thousands)
(Problem 5.17)

	December	
	2012	2011
ASSETS		
Current assets		
Cash and equivalents	$ 597,461	$ 341,228
Accounts receivable, net	1,222,345	1,120,246
Inventories	1,354,158	1,453,645
Deferred income taxes	140,515	106,717
Other current assets	135,104	166,108
Total current assets	3,449,583	3,187,944
Property, plant and equipment	828,218	737,451
Intangible assets	2,917,058	2,958,463
Goodwill	2,009,757	2,023,460
Other assets	428,405	405,808
Total assets	$9,633,021	$9,313,126
LIABILITIES AND STOCKHOLDERS' EQUITY		
Current liabilities		
Short-term borrowings	$ 12,559	$ 281,686
Current portion of long-term debt	402,873	2,744
Accounts payable	562,638	637,116
Accrued liabilities	754,142	744,486
Total current liabilities	1,732,212	1,666,032
Long-term debt	1,429,166	1,831,781
Other liabilities	1,346,018	1,290,138
Commitments and contingencies		
Stockholders' equity		
Preferred Stock, par value $1, shares authorized, 25,000,000; no shares outstanding in 2012 and 2011	—	—
Common Stock, stated value $1; shares authorized, 300,000,000; 110,204,734 shares outstanding in 2012 and 110,556,981 in 2011	110,205	110,557
Additional paid-in capital	2,527,868	2,316,107
Accumulated other comprehensive income (loss)	(453,895)	(421,477)
Retained earnings	2,941,447	2,520,804
Total equity attributable to VF corporation	5,125,625	4,525,991
Noncontrolling interests	—	(816)
Total stockholders' equity	5,125,625	4,525,175
Total liabilities and stockholders' equity	$9,633,021	$9,313,126

Source: VF Corporation, Form 10-K for the Fiscal Year Ended December 2012.

Exhibit 5.20

VF Corporation
Consolidated Statements of Income
(amounts in thousands)
(Problem 5.17)

	Year Ended December		
	2012	**2011**	**2010**
Net sales	$10,766,020	$9,365,477	$7,624,599
Royalty income	113,835	93,755	77,990
Total revenues	10,879,855	9,459,232	7,702,589
Costs and operating expenses			
Cost of goods sold	5,817,880	5,128,602	4,105,201
Marketing, administrative and general expenses	3,596,708	3,085,839	2,574,790
Impairment of goodwill and intangible assets	—	—	201,738
	9,414,588	8,214,441	6,881,729
Operating income	1,465,267	1,244,791	820,860
Interest income	3,353	4,778	2,336
Interest expense	(93,605)	(77,578)	(77,738)
Other income (expense), net	46,860	(7,248)	4,754
Income before income taxes	1,421,875	1,164,743	750,212
Income taxes	335,737	274,350	176,700
Net income	1,086,138	890,393	573,512
Net (income) loss attributable to noncontrolling interests	(139)	(2,304)	(2,150)
Net income attributable to VF Corporation	$ 1,085,999	$ 888,089	$ 571,362

Source: VF Corporation, Form 10-K for the Fiscal Year Ended December 2012.

LO 5-3, LO 5-4, LO 5-6

5.18 Computing and Interpreting Risk and Bankruptcy Prediction Ratios for a Firm That Was Acquired. Sun Microsystems, Inc., develops, manufactures, and sells computers for network systems. Exhibit 5.21 presents selected financial data for Sun Microsystems for each of the five years ending June 30, 2005, to June 30, 2009. The company did not go bankrupt, but instead was acquired in 2010 by **Oracle**. We recommend that you create an Excel spreadsheet to compute the values of the ratios and the Altman's Z-score in Requirements a and b, respectively.

REQUIRED

a. Compute the value of each of the following risk ratios.
   (1) Current ratio (at the end of 2005–2009)
   (2) Operating cash flow to current liabilities ratio (for 2006–2009)
   (3) Liabilities to assets ratio (at the end of 2005–2009)
   (4) Long-term debt to long-term capital ratio (at the end of 2005–2009)
   (5) Operating cash flow to total liabilities ratio (for 2006–2009)
   (6) Interest coverage ratio (for 2005–2009)

Exhibit 5.21

Select Financial Data for Sun Microsystems, Inc.
(amounts in millions, except per-share amounts)
(Problem 5.18)

	For Year Ended June 30,				
	2009	**2008**	**2007**	**2006**	**2005**
Sales	$11,449	$13,880	$13,873	$13,086	$11,070
Net income (loss) before interest and taxes	$(2,166)	$640	$622	$(620)	$(150)
Interest expense	$17	$30	$39	$55	$34
Net income (loss)	$(2,234)	$403	$473	$(864)	$(107)
Current assets	$6,864	$7,834	$9,328	$8,460	$7,191
Total assets	$11,232	$14,340	$15,838	$15,082	$14,190
Current liabilities	$5,621	$5,668	$5,451	$6,165	$4,766
Long-term debt	$695	$1,265	$1,264	$575	$1,123
Total liabilities	$7,927	$8,752	$8,659	$8,738	$7,516
Retained earnings	$(2,055)	$430	$189	$(257)	$1,387
Shareholders' equity	$3,305	$5,588	$7,179	$6,344	$6,674
Cash flow provided by operations	$457	$1,329	$958	$567	$279
Common shares outstanding	752	752	884	876	852
Market price per share	$9.22	$10.88	$20.76	$16.60	$14.92

Source: Sun Microsystems, Inc., Forms 10-K for the Fiscal Years Ended June 2005–2009.

b. Compute the value of Altman's Z-score for Sun Microsystems for each year from 2005–2009.
c. Using the analyses in Requirements a and b, discuss the most important factors that signal the likelihood of bankruptcy of Sun Microsystems in 2010.

5.19 Computing and Interpreting Bankruptcy Prediction Ratios. LO 5-6

Exhibit 5.22 presents selected financial data for **Best Buy Co., Inc.**, and **Circuit City Stores, Inc.**, for fiscal 2008 and 2007. Best Buy and Circuit City operate as specialty retailers offering a wide range of consumer electronics, service contracts, product repairs, and home installation. Competition from **Walmart**, **Costco**, and Internet retailers put downward pressure on prices and margins. In November 2008, Circuit City filed Chapter 7 bankruptcy. In the media, Circuit City's bankruptcy was largely blamed on its poor treatment of employees. In early 2007, Circuit City laid off 3,400 high-paid salespersons, or approximately 8% of its workforce, which left inexperienced, low-paid workers in charge of customer service. Customer service quality plummeted, which was especially harmful for a retail business providing expensive electronic items, warranty products, and installation services.

REQUIRED

a. Compute Altman's Z-score for Best Buy and Circuit City for 2007 and 2008.
b. How did the bankruptcy risk of Best Buy change between 2007 and 2008? Explain.
c. How did the bankruptcy risk of Circuit City change between 2007 and 2008? Explain.

Exhibit 5.22

Select Financial Data for Best Buy and Circuit City
(amounts in thousands, except per-share amounts)
(Problem 5.19)

	Best Buy		Circuit City	
	For Year Ended March 1,		For Year Ended Feb. 28,	
	2008	2007	2008	2007
Sales	$40,023	$35,934	$11,744	$12,430
Net income (loss) before interest and taxes	$2,290	$2,161	$(352)	$22
Net income (loss)	$1,407	$1,377	$(321)	$(10)
Current assets	$7,342	$9,081	$2,440	$2,884
Total assets	$12,758	$13,570	$3,746	$4,007
Current liabilities	$6,769	$6,301	$1,606	$1,714
Total liabilities	$8,274	$7,369	$2,243	$2,216
Retained earnings	$3,933	$5,507	$981	$1,336
Common shares outstanding	411	481	169	171
Market price per share	$42.00	$44.97	$4.38	$18.47

Source: Best Buy Co., Inc., Form 10-K for the Fiscal Year Ended March 1, 2008, and Circuit City Stores, Inc., Form 10-K for the Fiscal Year Ended February 28, 2008.

d. As noted, Circuit City filed Chapter 7 bankruptcy in November 2008. Using the analysis from Requirements b and c, would you have predicted Circuit City or Best Buy to file bankruptcy in 2008? Explain.

 LO 5-6

5.20 Applying and Interpreting Bankruptcy Prediction Models.

Exhibit 5.23 presents selected financial data for ABC Auto, and XYZ Comics, for fiscal Year 5 and Year 6. ABC Auto manufactures automobile components that it sells to automobile manufacturers. Competitive conditions in the automobile industry in recent years have led automobile manufacturers to put pressure on suppliers such as ABC Auto to reduce costs and selling prices. XYZ Comics creates and sells comic books, trading cards, and other youth entertainment products and licenses others to use fictional characters created by XYZ Comics in their products. Youth readership of comic books and interest in trading cards have been declining steadily in recent years. XYZ Comics recognized a significant asset impairment charge in fiscal Year 6.

REQUIRED

a. Compute Altman's Z-score for ABC Auto and XYZ Comics for fiscal Year 5 and Year 6.

b. How did the bankruptcy risk of ABC Auto change between fiscal Year 5 and Year 6? Explain.

<table>
<tr><td></td><td colspan="2">**ABC Auto**</td><td colspan="2">**XYZ Comics**</td></tr>
<tr><td></td><td>**Year 6**</td><td>**Year 5**</td><td>**Year 6**</td><td>**Year 5**</td></tr>
</table>

Exhibit 5.23

Select Financial Data for ABC Auto and XYZ Comics (amounts in thousands, except per-share amounts) (Problem 5.20)

	ABC Auto		XYZ Comics	
	Year 6	**Year 5**	**Year 6**	**Year 5**
Sales	$824,835	$631,832	$745,400	$828,900
Net income (loss) before interest and taxes	$(11,012)	$40,258	$(370,200)	$25,100
Net income (loss)	$(68,712)	$6,921	$(464,400)	$(48,400)
Current assets	$156,226	$195,417	$399,500	$490,600
Total assets	$617,705	$662,262	$844,000	$1,226,310
Current liabilities	$163,384	$176,000	$345,800	$318,100
Total liabilities	$648,934	$624,817	$999,700	$948,100
Retained earnings	$(184,308)	$(115,596)	$(350,300)	$114,100
Common shares outstanding	7,014	6,995	101,810	101,703
Market price per share	$85.00	$100.50	$1.625	$10.625

   c. How did the bankruptcy risk of XYZ Comics change between Year 5 and Year 6? Explain.

   d. Which firm is more likely to file for bankruptcy during fiscal Year 7? Explain using the analyses from Requirement b.

5.21 Applying and Interpreting Bankruptcy Prediction Models.

Exhibit 5.24 presents selected financial data for **The Tribune Company** and **The Washington Post Company** for fiscal 2006 and 2007. The Washington Post Company is an education and media company. It owns, among others, Kaplan, Inc.; Cable ONE Inc.; *Newsweek* magazine; and Washington Post Media. The Tribune Company is a media and entertainment company, which also is diversified, owning the *Chicago Tribune*, the *Los Angeles Times*, television and radio affiliates such as The CW Network and WGN, and the Chicago Cubs. The Tribune Company filed for bankruptcy in December 2008.

LO 5-6

REQUIRED

   a. Compute Altman's Z-score for Tribune Company and Washington Post for fiscal 2006 and 2007.

   b. How did the bankruptcy risk of Tribune Company change between fiscal 2006 and 2007? Explain.

   c. How did the bankruptcy risk of Washington Post change between fiscal 2006 and 2007? Explain.

   d. The Tribune Company filed Chapter 7 bankruptcy in December 2008. Using the analysis from Requirements b and c, would you have predicted The Tribune Company or The Washington Post Company to file bankruptcy? Explain.

Exhibit 5.24

Select Financial Data for The Tribune Company and The Washington Post Company (amounts in millions, except per-share amounts) (Problem 5.21)

	Tribune		Washington Post	
	2007	**2006**	**2007**	**2006**
Sales	$5,063	$5,444	$4,180	$3,905
Net income (loss) before interest and taxes	$619	$1,085	$505	$544
Net income (loss)	$87	$594	$289	$324
Current assets	$1,385	$1,346	$995	$935
Total assets	$13,150	$13,401	$6,005	$5,381
Current liabilities	$2,190	$2,549	$1,013	$812
Total liabilities	$16,664	$9,081	$2,543	$2,222
Retained earnings (deficit)	$(3,474)	$3,138	$4,330	$4,120
Common shares outstanding	239	307	10	10
Market price per share	$45.04	$58.69	$759.25	$711.53

Source: The Tribune Company, Form 10-K for the Fiscal Year Ended December 30, 2007, and The Washington Post Company, Form 10-K for the Fiscal Year Ended December 30, 2007.

 5.22 Reformulating Financial Statements, Preparing an Alternative Decomposition of ROCE, and Assessing Financial Flexibility. Exhibit 5.25 presents balance sheets for 2007 and 2008 for **Whole Foods Market, Inc.;** Exhibit 5.26 presents income statements for 2006–2008.

REQUIRED

a. Prepare the standard decomposition of ROCE into margin, turnover, and leverage. Use average balances for balance sheet amounts.

b. Assume that all cash is operating cash (that is, no excess cash). Also assume that deferred lease liabilities are operating. Prepare the alternative decomposition of ROCE by computing NOPAT, net financing expense (after tax), operating profit margin, net operating assets turnover, operating ROA, leverage, and spread for 2008. Use average balances for balance sheet amounts.

c. Use the same assumptions as in Requirement b, except that all cash is a financing asset (that is, all cash is excess cash) and deferred lease liabilities are a financing obligation. Prepare the alternative decomposition of ROCE by computing NOPAT, net financing expense (after tax), operating profit margin, net operating assets turnover, operating ROA, leverage, and spread for 2008. Use average balances for balance sheet amounts.

d. Does the different treatment of financial assets and liabilities affect inferences you draw from the decomposition of ROCE? Explain.

Exhibit 5.25

Whole Foods Market, Inc.
Balance Sheets
(amounts in thousands)
(Problem 5.22)

	2008	2007
ASSETS		
Cash and cash equivalents	$ 31,151	$ 2,310
Accounts receivable and other receivables	115,424	270,263
Merchandise inventories	327,452	288,112
Prepaid expenses and other current assets	68,150	40,402
Deferred income taxes	80,429	66,899
Total Current Assets	$ 622,606	$ 667,986
Property and equipment, net of accumulated depreciation and amortization	1,900,117	1,666,559
Goodwill	659,559	668,850
Intangible assets, net of accumulated amortization	78,499	97,683
Deferred income taxes	109,002	104,877
Other assets	10,953	7,173
Total Assets	$ 3,380,736	$ 3,213,128
LIABILITIES AND SHAREHOLDERS' EQUITY		
Current installments of long-term debt and capital lease obligations	$ 380	$ 24,781
Accounts payable	183,134	225,728
Accrued payroll, bonus and other benefits due team members	196,233	181,290
Other current liabilities	286,430	340,551
Total Current Liabilities	$ 666,177	$ 772,350
Long-term debt and capital lease obligations, less current installments	928,790	736,087
Deferred lease liabilities	199,635	152,552
Other long-term liabilities	80,110	93,335
Total Liabilities	$ 1,874,712	$ 1,754,324
Common stock, no par value, 300,000 shares authorized; 140,286 and 143,787 shares issued, 140,286 and 139,240 shares outstanding in 2008 and 2007, respectively	$1,066,180	$1,232,845
Common stock in treasury, at cost	—	(199,961)
Accumulated other comprehensive income	422	15,722
Retained earnings	439,422	410,198
Total Shareholders' Equity	$ 1,506,024	$ 1,458,804
Total Liabilities and Shareholders' Equity	$ 3,380,736	$ 3,213,128

Source: Whole Foods Market, Inc., Form 10-K for the Fiscal Year Ended September 28, 2008.

Exhibit 5.26

Whole Foods Market, Inc.
Income Statements
(amounts in thousands)
(Problem 5.22)

	2008	2007	2006
Sales	$7,953,912	$6,591,773	$5,607,376
Cost of goods sold and occupancy costs	5,247,207	4,295,170	3,647,734
Gross Profit	$2,706,705	$2,296,603	$1,959,642
Direct store expenses	2,107,940	1,711,229	1,421,968
General and administrative expenses	270,428	217,743	181,244
Pre-opening expenses	55,554	59,319	32,058
Relocation, store closure and lease termination	36,545	10,861	5,363
Operating Income	$ 236,238	$ 297,451	$ 319,009
Interest expense	(36,416)	(4,208)	(32)
Investment and other income	6,697	11,324	20,736
Income before income taxes	$ 206,519	$ 304,567	$ 339,713
Provision for income taxes	91,995	121,827	135,885
Net Income	$ 114,524	$ 182,740	$ 203,828

Source: Whole Foods Market, Inc., Form 10-K for the Fiscal Year Ended September 28, 2008.

LO 5-2, LO 5-3, LO 5-4, LO 5-6

INTEGRATIVE CASE 5.1

Starbucks

Exhibit 5.27 presents risk ratios for **Starbucks** for 2010 and 2011. Exhibits 1.26, 1.27, and 1.28 in Chapter 1 present the financial statements for Starbucks.

REQUIRED

a. Compute the values of each of the ratios in Exhibit 5.27 for Starbucks for 2012. Starbucks had 749.3 million common shares outstanding at the end of fiscal 2012, and the market price per share was $50.71. For days accounts receivable outstanding, use only specialty revenues in your calculations, because accounts receivable are primarily related to licensing and food service operations, not the retail operations.

b. Interpret the changes in Starbucks risk ratios during the three-year period, indicating areas of concern.

Exhibit 5.27

Starbucks
Risk Ratios
(Integrative Case 5.1)

	2012	2011	2010
Current ratio		1.83	1.55
Quick ratio		1.17	0.98
Operating cash flow to current liabilities ratio		0.84	1.01
Days accounts receivable outstanding		61	60
Days inventory held		56	50
Days accounts payable outstanding		28	23
Net days of working capital financing needed		89	87
Liabilities to assets ratio		0.40	0.42
Liabilities to shareholders' equity ratio		0.68	0.73
Long-term debt to long-term capital ratio		0.11	0.13
Long-term debt to shareholders' equity ratio		0.13	0.15
Interest coverage ratio		47.9	54.3
Operating cash flow to total liabilities ratio		0.57	0.65
Altman's Z-score		9.094	7.577
Probability of bankruptcy		0.0%	0.0%

CASE 5.2

LO 5-5

Massachusetts Stove Company—Bank Lending Decision

Massachusetts Stove Company manufactures wood-burning stoves for the heating of homes and businesses. The company has approached you, as chief lending officer for the Massachusetts Regional Bank, seeking to increase its loan from the current level of $93,091 as of January 15, Year 12, to $143,091. Jane O'Neil, chief executive officer and majority stockholder of the company, indicates that the company needs the loan to finance the working capital required for an expected 25% annual increase in sales during the next two years, including to pay suppliers and provide funds for expected nonrecurring legal and retooling costs.

The company's woodstoves have two distinguishing characteristics: (1) the metal frame of the stoves includes inlaid soapstone, which increases the intensity and duration of the heat provided by the stoves and enhances their appearance as an attractive piece of furniture and (2) a catalytic combustor, which adds heating potential to the stoves and reduces air pollution.

The company manufactures wood-burning stoves in a single plant in Greenfield, Massachusetts. It purchases metal castings for the stoves from foundries in Germany and Belgium. The soapstone comes from a supplier in Canada. These purchases are denominated in U.S. dollars. The catalytic combustor is purchased from a supplier in the United States. The manufacturing process is essentially an assembly operation. The plant employs an average of eight workers. The two keys to quality control are structural airtightness and effective operation of the catalytic combustor.

The company rents approximately 60% of the 25,000-square-foot building it uses for manufacturing and administrative activities. This building also houses the company's factory showroom. The remaining 40% of the building is not currently rented.

The company's marketing of woodstoves follows three channels:

1. Wholesaling of stoves to retail hardware stores. This channel represents approximately 20% of the company's sales in units.
2. Retail direct marketing to individuals in all 50 states. This channel utilizes (a) national advertising in construction and design magazines and (b) the sending of brochures to potential customers identified from personal inquiries. This channel represents approximately 70% of the company's sales in units. The company is the only firm in the industry with a strategic emphasis on retail direct marketing.
3. Retailing from the company's showroom. This channel represents approximately 10% of the company's sales in units.

The company offers three payment options to retail purchasers of its stoves:

1. Full payment: Check, money order, or charge to a third-party credit card is used to pay in full.
2. Layaway plan: Monthly payments are made over a period not exceeding one year. The company ships the stove after receiving the final payment.
3. Installment financing plan: The company has a financing arrangement with a local bank to finance the purchase of stoves by credit-approved customers. The company is liable if customers fail to repay their installment bank loans.

The imposition of strict air emission standards by the Environmental Protection Agency (EPA) has resulted in a major change in the woodstove industry. By December 31, Year 9, firms were required by EPA regulations to demonstrate that their woodstoves met or surpassed specified air emission standards. These standards were stricter than industry practices accommodated at the time, and firms had to engage in numerous company-sponsored and independent testing of their stoves to satisfy EPA regulators. As a consequence, the number of firms in the woodstove industry decreased from more than 200 in the years prior to Year 10 to approximately 35 by December 31, Year 11.

The company received approval for its Soapstone Stove I in Year 11, after incurring retooling and testing costs of $63,001. It capitalized these costs in the Property, Plant, and Equipment account. It depreciates these costs over the five-year EPA approval period. A second stove, Soapstone Stove II, is currently undergoing retooling and testing. For this stove, the company incurred costs of $19,311 in Year 10 and $8,548 in Year 11 and has received preliminary EPA approval. It anticipates additional design, tooling, and testing costs of approximately $55,000 in Year 12 and $33,000 in Year 13 to obtain final EPA approval.

The company holds an option to purchase the building in which it is located for $608,400. The option also permits the company to assume the unpaid balance on a low-interest-rate loan on the building from the New England Regional Industrial Development Authority. The interest rate on this loan is adjusted annually and equals 80% of the bank prime interest rate. The unpaid balance on the loan exceeds the option price and will result in a cash transfer to the company from the owner of the building at the time of transfer. The company exercised its option in Year 9, but the owner of the building refused to comply with the option provisions. The company sued the owner. The case has gone through the lower court system in Massachusetts and is currently under review by the Massachusetts Supreme Court. The company incurred legal costs totaling $68,465 through Year 11 and anticipates additional costs of approximately $45,000 in Year 12. The lower courts have ruled in favor of the company's position on all of the major issues in the case. The company expects the

Massachusetts Supreme Court to concur with the decisions of the lower courts when it renders its final decision in the spring of Year 12. The company has held discussions with two prospective tenants for the building's 10,000 square feet that Massachusetts Stove Company does not use in its operations.

Jane O'Neil owns 51% of the company's common stock. The remaining stockholders include John O'Neil (chief financial officer and father of Jane O'Neil), Mark Forest (vice president of manufacturing), and four independent local investors.

To assist in the loan decision, the company provides you with financial statements (see the first three columns of Exhibits 5.28–5.30 on pages 400–402) and notes for the three years ending December 31, Year 9, Year 10, and Year 11. These financial statements were prepared by John O'Neil, chief financial officer, and are not audited. The company also provides you with projected financial statements for Year 12 and Year 13 (see the last two columns of Exhibits 5.28–5.30) to demonstrate its need for the loan and its ability to repay. The loan requested involves an increase in the current loan amount from $93,091 to $143,091. The company will pay monthly interest and repay the $50,000 additional amount borrowed by December 31, Year 13. Exhibit 5.31 (page 403) presents financial statement ratios for the company.

The assumptions underlying the projected financial statements are as follows:

- *Sales:* Sales are projected to increase 25% annually during the next two years, after increasing 17.7% in Year 10 and 21.9% in Year 11. The increase reflects continuing market opportunities related to the company's strategic emphasis on retail direct marketing and to the expected continuing contraction in the number of competitors in the industry.

- *Cost of Goods Sold:* Most manufacturing costs vary with sales. The company projects cost of goods sold to equal 51% of sales in Year 12 and 49% of sales in Year 13, having declined from 69.2% of sales in Year 9 to 53.9% of sales in Year 11. The reductions resulted from a higher proportion of retail sales in the sales mix (which have a higher gross margin than wholesale sales), a more favorable pricing environment in the industry (fewer competitors), a switch to lower-cost suppliers, and more efficient production.

- *Selling and Administrative Expenses:* The company projects these costs to equal 41% of sales, having increased from 26.7% of sales in Year 9 to 40.9% of sales in Year 11. The increases resulted from a heavier emphasis on retail sales, which require more aggressive marketing than wholesale sales.

- *Legal Expenses:* The additional $45,000 of legal costs represents the best estimate by the company's attorneys.

- *Interest Expense:* Interest expense has averaged approximately 6% of short- and long-term borrowing during the last three years. The projected income statement assumes a continuation of the 6% average rate.

- *Income Tax Expense:* The company has elected to be taxed as a Subchapter S corporation, which means that the net income of the firm is taxed at the level of the individual shareholders, not at the corporate level. Thus, the pro forma financial statements include no income tax expense. The firm operated at a net loss for several years prior to Year 11, primarily because of losses of a lawn products business that it acquired ten years ago. The company discontinued the lawn products business in Year 10.

- *Cash:* The projected amounts for cash represent a plug to equate projected assets with projected liabilities and shareholders' equity. Projected liabilities include the requested loan during Year 12 and its repayment at the end of Year 13.

- *Accounts Receivable:* Days accounts receivable outstanding, calculated on the average accounts receivable balances, will be 11 days in Year 12 and Year 13.

■ *Inventories:* Days inventory held, calculated on the average inventory balances, will be 155 days in Year 12 and Year 13.

■ *Property, Plant, and Equipment:* Capital expenditures for Year 12 include a $55,000 cost for retooling the Soapstone Stove II and $7,500 for other equipment; for Year 13, they include $33,000 for retooling the Soapstone Stove II and $14,500 for other equipment. The projected balance excludes the cost of acquiring the building, its related debt, the cash received at the time of transfer, and rental revenues from leasing the unused 40% of the building to other businesses.

■ *Accumulated Depreciation:* This is continuation of the historical relation between depreciation expense and the cost of property, plant, and equipment.

■ *Other Assets:* A new financial reporting standard no longer requires amortization of intangibles after Year 11.

■ *Accounts Payable:* Days accounts payable outstanding, based on the average accounts payable balances, will be 97 days in Year 12 and 89 days in Year 13. The decrease in days payable reflects the ability to pay suppliers more quickly with the proceeds of the increased bank loan.

■ *Notes Payable:* Notes payable is projected to increase by the amount of the bank loan in Year 12 and to decrease by the loan repayment at the end of Year 13.

■ *Other Current Liabilities:* The large increase at the end of Year 11 resulted from a major promotional offer in the fall of Year 11, which increased the amount of deposits by customers. The projected amounts for Year 12 and Year 13 represent more normal expected levels of deposits.

■ *Long-Term Debt:* Long-term borrowing represents loans from shareholders to the company. The company does not plan to repay any of these loans in the near future.

■ *Retained Earnings:* The change each year represents net income or net loss from operations. The company does not pay dividends.

■ *Statement of Cash Flows:* Amounts are taken from the changes in various accounts on the actual and projected balance sheets.

Exhibit 5.28

Massachusetts Stove Company
Income Statements
(Case 5.2)

	Actual			Projected	
	Year 9	**Year 10**	**Year 11**	**Year 12**	**Year 13**
Sales	$ 665,771	$ 783,754	$ 955,629	$1,194,535	$1,493,170
Cost of goods sold	(460,797)	(474,156)	(514,907)	(609,213)	(731,653)
Selling and administrative	(177,631)	(290,719)	(390,503)	(489,760)	(612,200)
Legal (Note 1)	(28,577)	(30,092)	(9,796)	(45,000)	—
Interest	(25,948)	(24,122)	(23,974)	(26,510)	(26,510)
Income tax (Note 2)	—	—	—	—	—
Net Income (Loss)	$ (27,182)	$ (35,335)	$ 16,449	$ 24,052	$ 122,807

Exhibit 5.29

Massachusetts Stove Company
Balance Sheets
(Case 5.2)

December 31	Actual				Projected	
	Year 8	Year 9	Year 10	Year 11	Year 12	Year 13
ASSETS						
Cash	$ 3,925	$ 11,707	$ 8,344	$ 37,726	$ 11,289	$ 6,512
Accounts receivable	94,606	54,772	44,397	31,964	40,035	49,964
Inventories	239,458	208,260	209,004	225,490	291,924	329,480
Total Current Assets	$ 337,989	$ 274,739	$ 261,745	$ 295,180	$ 343,248	$ 385,956
Property, plant, and equipment, at cost	$ 258,870	$ 316,854	$ 362,399	$ 377,784	$ 440,284	$ 487,784
Accumulated depreciation	(205,338)	(228,985)	(250,189)	(274,347)	(302,502)	(333,694)
Property, plant, and equipment, net	$ 53,532	$ 87,869	$ 112,210	$ 103,437	$ 137,782	$ 154,090
Other assets	$ 17,888	$ 17,888	$ 17,594	$ 17,006	$ 17,006	$ 17,006
Total Assets	$ 409,409	$ 380,496	$ 391,549	$ 415,623	$ 498,036	$ 557,052
LIABILITIES AND SHAREHOLDERS' EQUITY						
Accounts payable	$ 148,579	$ 139,879	$ 189,889	$ 160,905	$ 198,206	$ 176,915
Notes payable—banks (Note 3)	152,985	140,854	125,256	93,091	143,091	93,091
Other current liabilities (Note 4)	13,340	11,440	23,466	62,440	33,500	41,000
Total Current Liabilities	$ 314,904	$ 292,173	$ 338,611	$ 316,436	$ 374,797	$ 311,006
Long-term debt (Note 3)	248,000	269,000	268,950	298,750	298,750	298,750
Total Liabilities	$ 562,904	$ 561,173	$ 607,561	$ 615,186	$ 673,547	$ 609,756
Common stock	$ 2,000	$ 2,000	$ 2,000	$ 2,000	$ 2,000	$ 2,000
Additional paid-in capital	435,630	435,630	435,630	435,630	435,630	435,630
Accumulated deficit	(591,125)	(618,307)	(653,642)	(637,193)	(613,141)	(490,334)
Total Shareholders' Equity	$(153,495)	$(180,677)	$(216,012)	$(199,563)	$(175,511)	$ (52,704)
Total Liabilities and Shareholders' Equity	$ 409,409	$ 380,496	$ 391,549	$ 415,623	$ 498,036	$ 557,052

Exhibit 5.30

Massachusetts Stove Company
Statements of Cash Flows
(Case 5.2)

	Actual			Projected	
	Year 9	Year 10	Year 11	Year 12	Year 13
OPERATIONS					
Net income (loss)	$(27,182)	$(35,335)	$ 16,449	$ 24,052	$122,807
Depreciation and amortization	23,647	21,204	24,158	28,155	31,192
(Increase) Decrease in accounts receivable	39,834	10,375	12,433	(8,071)	(9,929)
(Increase) Decrease in inventories	31,198	(744)	(16,486)	(66,434)	(37,556)
Increase (Decrease) in accounts payable	(8,700)	50,010	(28,984)	37,301	(21,291)
Increase (Decrease) in other current liabilities	(1,900)	12,026	38,974	(28,940)	7,500
Cash Flow from Operations	$ 56,897	$ 57,536	$ 46,544	$(13,937)	$ 92,723
INVESTING					
Fixed assets acquired	$(57,984)	$(45,545)	$(15,385)	$(62,500)	$ (47,500)
Other investing	—	294	588	—	—
Cash Flow from Investing	$(57,984)	$(45,251)	$(14,797)	$(62,500)	$ (47,500)
FINANCING					
Increase (Decrease) in short-term borrowing	$(12,131)	$(15,598)	$(32,165)	$ 50,000	$ (50,000)
Increase (Decrease) in long-term borrowing	21,000	(50)	29,800	—	—
Cash Flow from Financing	$ 8,869	$(15,648)	$ (2,365)	$ 50,000	$ (50,000)
Change in Cash	$ 7,782	$ (3,363)	$ 29,382	$(26,437)	$ (4,777)
Cash—beginning of year	3,925	11,707	8,344	37,726	11,289
Cash—End of Year	$ 11,707	$ 8,344	$ 37,726	$ 11,289	$ 6,512

Notes to Financial Statements

Note 1: The company has incurred legal costs to enforce its option to purchase the building used in its manufacturing and administrative activities. The case is under review by the Massachusetts Supreme Court, with a decision expected in the spring of Year 12.

Note 2: The company is not subject to income tax because it has elected Subchapter S tax status.

Note 3: The notes payable to banks are secured by machinery and equipment, shares of common stock of companies traded on the New York Stock Exchange owned by two shareholders, and personal guarantees of three shareholders. The long-term debt consists of unsecured loans from three shareholders.

Exhibit 5.31

Massachusetts Stove Company
Profitability and Risk Ratios
(Case 5.2)

	Actual			Projected	
	Year 9	Year 10	Year 11	Year 12	Year 13
Profit margin for ROA	(0.2%)	(1.4%)	4.2%	4.2%	10.0%
Assets turnover	1.7	2.0	2.4	2.6	2.8
Return on assets	(0.3%)	(2.9%)	10.0%	11.1%	28.3%
Cost of goods sold/Sales	69.2%	60.5%	53.9%	51.0%	49.0%
Selling and administrative expenses/Sales	26.7%	37.1%	40.9%	41.0%	41.0%
Legal expense/Sales	4.3%	3.8%	1.0%	3.8%	—
Interest expense/Sales	3.9%	3.1%	2.5%	2.2%	1.8%
Days accounts receivable outstanding	41	23	15	11	11
Days inventory held	177	161	154	155	155
Days accounts payable outstanding	122	127	122	96	89
Fixed assets turnover	9.4	7.8	8.9	9.9	10.2
Current ratio	0.9	0.8	0.9	0.9	1.2
Quick ratio	0.2	0.2	0.2	0.1	0.2
Operating cash flow to current liabilities ratio	0.187	0.182	0.142	(0.040)	0.270
Liabilities to assets ratio	1.475	1.552	1.480	1.352	1.095
Long-term debt to shareholders' equity ratio	0.707	0.687	0.719	0.600	0.536
Operating cash flow to total liabilities ratio	0.101	0.098	0.076	(0.022)	0.145
Interest coverage ratio	0.0	(0.5)	1.7	1.9	5.6

Note 4: Other current liabilities include the following:

	Year 8	Year 9	Year 10	Year 11
Customer deposits	$11,278	$ 9,132	$20,236	$59,072
Employee taxes withheld	2,062	2,308	3,230	3,368
	$13,340	$11,440	$23,466	$62,440

REQUIRED

Would you make the loan to the company in accordance with the stated terms? Explain. In responding, consider the reasonableness of the company's projections, positive and negative factors affecting the industry and the company, and the likely ability of the company to repay the loan. (Excel spreadsheet for this case is available at www.cengagebrain.com.)

LO 5-6

CASE 5.3

Fly-by-Night International Group: Can This Company Be Saved?

Douglas C. Mather, founder, chair, and chief executive of Fly-by-Night International Group (FBN), lived the fast-paced, risk-seeking life that he tried to inject into his company. Flying the company's Learjets, he logged 28 world speed records. Once he throttled a company plane to the top of Mount Everest in three and a half minutes.

These activities seemed perfectly appropriate at the time. Mather was a Navy fighter pilot in Vietnam and then flew commercial airlines. In the mid-1970s, he started FBN as a pilot training school. With the defense buildup beginning in the early 1980s, Mather branched out into government contracting. He equipped the company's Learjets with radar jammers and other sophisticated electronic devices to mimic enemy aircraft. He then contracted his "rent-an-enemy" fleet to the Navy and Air Force for use in fighter pilot training. The Pentagon liked the idea, and FBN's revenues grew to $55 million in the fiscal year ending April 30, Year 14. Its common stock, issued to the public in Year 9 at $8.50 a share, reached a high of $16.50 in mid-Year 13. Mather and FBN received glowing write-ups in *Business Week* and *Fortune*.

In mid-Year 14, however, FBN began a rapid descent. Although still growing rapidly, its cash flow was inadequate to service its debt. According to Mather, he was "just dumbfounded. There was never an inkling of a problem with cash."

In the fall of Year 14, the board of directors withdrew the company's financial statements for the year ending April 30, Year 14, stating that there appeared to be material misstatements that needed investigation. In December of Year 14, Mather was asked to step aside as manager and director of the company pending completion of an investigation of certain transactions between Mather and the company. On December 29, Year 14, NASDAQ (over-the-counter stock market) discontinued quoting the company's common shares. In February, Year 15, following its investigation, the board of directors terminated Mather's employment and membership on the board.

Exhibits 5.32–5.34 present the financial statements and related notes of FBN for the five years ending April, Year 10, through April, Year 14. The financial statements for Year 10 to Year 12 use the amounts originally reported for each year. The amounts reported on the statement of cash flows for Year 10 (for example, the change in accounts receivable) do not precisely reconcile to the amounts on the balance sheet at the beginning and end of the year because certain items classified as relating to continuing operations on the balance sheet at the end of Year 9 were reclassified as relating to discontinued operations on the balance sheet at the end of Year 10. The financial statements for Year 13 and Year 14 represent the restated financial statements for those years after the board of directors completed its investigation of suspected material misstatements that caused it to withdraw the originally issued financial statements for fiscal Year 14. Exhibit 5.35 (page 408) lists the members of the board of directors. Exhibit 5.36 (page 408) presents profitability and risk ratios for FBN.

REQUIRED

Study these financial statements and notes and respond to the following questions:
- **a.** What evidence do you observe from analyzing the financial statements that might signal the cash flow problems experienced in mid-Year 14?
- **b.** Can FBN avoid bankruptcy during Year 15? What changes in the design or implementation of FBN's strategy would you recommend? To compute Altman's Z-score, use the low-bid market price for the year to determine the market value of common shareholders' equity.

Fly-by-Night International Group
Comparative Balance Sheets
(amounts in thousands)
(Case 5.3)

				April 30,			
	Year 14	Year 13	Year 12	Year 11	Year 10	Year 9
ASSETS						
Cash	$ 159	$ 583	$ 313	$ 142	$ 753	$ 192
Notes receivable	—	—	—	1,000	—	—
Accounts receivable	6,545	4,874	2,675	1,490	1,083	2,036
Inventories	5,106	2,514	1,552	602	642	686
Prepayments	665	829	469	57	303	387
Net assets of discontinued businesses	—	—	—	—	1,926	—
Total Current Assets	$ 12,475	$ 8,800	$ 5,009	$ 3,291	$ 4,707	$ 3,301
Property, plant, and equipment	$106,529	$76,975	$24,039	$17,809	$37,250	$17,471
Less accumulated depreciation	(17,231)	(8,843)	(5,713)	(4,288)	(4,462)	(2,593)
Net	$ 89,298	$68,132	$18,326	$13,521	$32,788	$14,878
Other assets	$ 470	$ 665	$ 641	$ 1,112	$ 1,566	$ 1,278
Total Assets	$102,243	$77,597	$23,976	$17,924	$39,061	$19,457
LIABILITIES AND SHAREHOLDERS' EQUITY						
Accounts payable	$ 12,428	$ 6,279	$ 993	$ 939	$ 2,285	$ 1,436
Notes payable	—	945	140	1,021	4,766	—
Current portion of long-term debt	60,590	7,018	1,789	1,104	2,774	1,239
Other current liabilities	12,903	12,124	2,423	1,310	1,845	435
Total Current Liabilities	$ 85,921	$26,366	$ 5,345	$ 4,374	$11,670	$ 3,110
Long-term debt	—	41,021	9,804	6,738	20,041	9,060
Deferred income taxes	—	900	803	—	1,322	1,412
Other noncurrent liabilities	—	—	226	—	248	—
Total Liabilities	$ 85,921	$68,287	$16,178	$11,112	$33,281	$13,582
Common stock	$ 34	$ 22	$ 21	$ 20	$ 20	$ 20
Additional paid-in capital	16,516	5,685	4,569	4,323	3,611	3,611
Retained earnings	(29)	3,802	3,208	2,469	2,149	2,244
Treasury stock	(199)	(199)	—	—	—	—
Total Shareholders' Equity	$ 16,322	$ 9,310	$ 7,798	$ 6,812	$ 5,780	$ 5,875
Total Liabilities and Shareholders' Equity	$102,243	$77,597	$23,976	$17,924	$39,061	$19,457

Exhibit 5.33

Fly-by-Night International Group
Comparative Income Statements
(amounts in thousands)
(Case 5.3)

	For the Year Ended April 30,				
	Year 14	Year 13	Year 12	Year 11	Year 10
CONTINUING OPERATIONS					
Sales	$54,988	$36,597	$20,758	$19,266	$31,992
EXPENSES					
Cost of services	$38,187	$26,444	$12,544	$ 9,087	$22,003
Selling and administrative	5,880	3,020	3,467	2,989	4,236
Depreciation	9,810	3,150	1,703	2,798	3,003
Interest	5,841	3,058	1,101	2,743	2,600
Income taxes	(900)	379	803	671	74
Total Expenses	$58,818	$36,051	$19,618	$18,288	$31,916
Income—continuing operations	$ (3,830)	$ 546	$ 1,140	$ 978	$ 76
Income—discontinued operations	—	47	(400)	(659)	(171)
Net Income	$ (3,830)	$ 593	$ 740	$ 319	$ (95)

Notes to Financial Statements

1. Summary of Significant Accounting Policies

Consolidation. The consolidated financial statements include the accounts of the company and its wholly owned subsidiaries. The company uses the equity method for subsidiaries that are not majority owned (50% or less) and eliminates significant intercompany transactions and balances.

Inventories. Inventories, which consist of aircraft fuel, spare parts, and supplies, appear at lower of FIFO cost or market.

Property and Equipment. Property and equipment appear at acquisition cost. The company capitalizes major inspections, renewals, and improvements, while it expenses replacements, maintenance, and repairs that do not improve or extend the life of the respective assets. The company computes depreciation of property and equipment using the straight-line method.

Contract Income Recognition. Contractual specifications (such as revenue rates, reimbursement terms, and functional considerations) vary among contracts; accordingly, the company recognizes guaranteed contract income (guaranteed revenue minus related direct costs) as it logs flight hours or on a straight-line monthly basis over the contract year, whichever method better reflects the economics of the contract. The company recognizes income from discretionary hours flown in excess of the minimum guaranteed amount each month as it logs such discretionary hours.

Income Taxes. The company recognizes deferred income taxes for temporary differences between financial and tax reporting amounts.

Exhibit 5.34

Fly-by-Night International Group
Comparative Statements of Cash Flows
(amounts in thousands)
(Case 5.3)

	For the Year Ended April 30,				
	Year 14	Year 13	Year 12	Year 11	Year 10
OPERATIONS					
Income—continuing operations	$ (3,830)	$ 546	$ 1,140	$ 978	$ 76
Depreciation	9,810	3,150	1,703	2,798	3,003
Other adjustments	1,074	1,817	1,119	671	74
Changes in working capital:					
(Increase) Decrease in receivables	(1,671)	(2,199)	(1,185)	(407)	403
(Increase) Decrease in inventories	(2,592)	(962)	(950)	40	19
(Increase) Decrease in prepayment	164	(360)	(412)	246	36
Increase (Decrease) in accounts payable	6,149	5,286	54	(1,346)	359
Increase (Decrease) in other current liabilities	779	9,701	1,113	(535)	596
Cash Flow from Continuing Operations	$ 9,883	$ 16,979	$ 2,582	$ 2,445	$ 4,566
Cash flow from discontinued operations	—	(77)	(472)	(752)	(335)
Net Cash Flow from Operations	$ 9,883	$ 16,902	$ 2,110	$ 1,693	$ 4,231
INVESTING					
Sale of property, plant, and equipment	$ 259	$ 3	$ 119	$ 18,387	$ 12
Acquisition of property, plant, and equipment	(33,035)	(52,960)	(6,573)	(2,424)	(20,953)
Other	(1,484)	78	1,017	(679)	30
Net Cash Flow from Investing	$(34,260)	$(52,879)	$(5,437)	$ 15,284	$(20,911)
FINANCING					
Increase in short-term borrowing	$ —	$ 805	$ —	$ —	$ 4,766
Increase in long-term borrowing	43,279	42,152	5,397	5,869	14,739
Issue of common stock	12,266	191	428	—	—
Decrease in short-term borrowing	(945)	—	(881)	(3,745)	—
Decrease in long-term borrowing	(30,522)	(7,024)	(1,647)	(19,712)	(2,264)
Acquisition of common stock	—	(198)	—	—	—
Other	(125)	321	201	—	—
Net Cash Flow from Financing	$ 23,953	$ 36,247	$ 3,498	$(17,588)	$ 17,241
Change in Cash	$ (424)	$ 270	$ 171	$ (611)	$ 561
Cash—beginning of year	583	313	142	753	192
Cash—End of Year	$ 159	$ 583	$ 313	$ 142	$ 753

Exhibit 5.35

Fly-by-Night International Group
Members of the Board of Directors
(Case 5.3)

Charles A. Barry, USAF (Ret.), Executive Vice President of Wicks and Associates, Inc., a management consulting firm
Thomas P. Gilkey, Vice President, Marketing
Lawrence G. Hicks, Secretary and General Counsel
Michael S. Holt, Vice President, Finance, and Chief Financial Officer
Gordon K. John, Executive Vice President and Chief Operating Officer
Douglas C. Mather, Chair of the Board, President and Chief Executive Officer
Edward F. O'Hara, President of the O'Hara Companies, which manufactures aircraft products
E. William Shapiro, Professor of Law, Emory University

Exhibit 5.36

Profitability and Risk Ratios for FBN
(Case 5.3)

	Year 14	Year 13	Year 12	Year 11	Year 10
Profit margin for ROA	(0.1%)	6.9%	9.0%	14.5	5.6%
Assets turnover	0.6	0.7	1.0	0.7	1.1
ROA	0.0%	5.0%	8.9%	9.8%	6.1%
Cost of goods and services/Sales	69.4%	72.3%	60.4%	47.2%	68.8%
Selling and administrative/Sales	10.7%	8.3%	16.7%	15.5%	13.2%
Depreciation expense/Sales	17.8%	8.6%	8.2%	14.5%	9.4%
Income tax expense (excluding tax effects of interest)/Sales	2.1%	4.0%	5.7%	8.3%	3.0%
Interest expense/Sales	10.6%	8.4%	5.3%	14.2%	8.1%
Days accounts receivable outstanding	38	38	37	24	18
Days accounts payable outstanding	84	48	26	65	31
Fixed assets turnover	0.7	0.8	1.3	0.8	1.3
Profit margin for ROCE	(7.0%)	1.5%	5.5%	5.1%	0.2%
Capital structure leverage	7.0	5.9	2.9	4.5	5.0
ROCE	(29.9%)	6.4%	15.6%	15.5%	1.3%
Current ratio	0.2	0.3	0.9	0.8	0.4
Quick ratio	0.1	0.2	0.6	0.6	0.2
Operating cash flow to current liabilities ratio	0.176	1.071	0.531	0.305	0.618
Liabilities to assets ratio	0.840	0.880	0.675	0.620	0.852
Long-term debt to long-term capital ratio	0.000	0.815	0.557	0.497	0.776
Operating cash flow to total liabilities ratio	0.128	0.402	0.189	0.112	0.195
Interest coverage ratio	0.2	1.3	2.8	1.6	1.1

2. Transactions with Major Customers

The company provides contract flight services to three major customers: the U.S. Air Force, the U.S. Navy, and the Federal Reserve Bank System. These contracts have termination dates in Year 16 or Year 17. Revenues from all government contracts as a percentage of total revenues were as follows: Year 14, 62%; Year 13, 72%; Year 12, 73%; Year 11, 68%; and Year 10, 31%.

3. Segment Data

During Year 10, the company operated in the following five business segments:

Flight Operations—Business. Provides combat readiness training to the military and nightly transfer of negotiable instruments for the Federal Reserve Bank System, both under multiyear contracts.

Flight Operations—Transport. Provides charter transport services to a variety of customers.

Fixed-Base Operations. Provides ground support operations (fuel and maintenance) to commercial airlines at several major airports.

Education and Training. Provides training for nonmilitary pilots.

Aircraft Sales and Leasing. Acquires aircraft that the company then resells or leases to various firms.

The company discontinued the Flight Operations—Transport and Education and Training segments in Year 11. It sold most of the assets of the Aircraft Sales and Leasing segment in Year 11.

Segment revenue, operating profit, and asset data for the various segments are as follows (amounts in thousands):

	April 30,				
	Year 14	**Year 13**	**Year 12**	**Year 11**	**Year 10**
Revenues					
Flight Operations—Business	$ 44,062	$31,297	$16,026	$11,236	$10,803
Flight Operations—Transport	—	—	—	—	13,805
Fixed-Base Operations	9,597	4,832	4,651	3,911	3,647
Education and Training	—	—	—	—	542
Aircraft Sales and Leasing	1,329	468	81	4,119	3,195
Total	$ 54,988	$36,597	$20,758	$19,266	$31,992
Operating Profit					
Flight Operations—Business	$ 5,707	$ 4,863	$ 3,455	$ 2,463	$ 849
Flight Operations—Transport	—	—	—	—	(994)
Fixed-Base Operations	(2,041)	1,362	1,038	174	332
Education and Training	—	—	—	—	12
Aircraft Sales and Leasing	1,175	378	(15)	1,217[b]	2,726[a]
Total	$ 4,841	$ 6,603	$ 4,478	$ 3,854	$ 2,925
Assets					
Flight Operations—Business	$ 85,263	$64,162	$17,738	$11,130	$13,684
Flight Operations—Transport	—	—	—	—	1,771
Fixed-Base Operations	16,544	13,209	5,754	5,011	4,784
Education and Training	—	—	—	—	1,789
Aircraft Sales and Leasing	436	226	438	1,262	18,524
Total	$102,243	$77,597	$23,930	$17,403	$40,552

[a]Includes a gain of $1.2 million on the sale of aircraft
[b]Includes a gain of $2.6 million on the sale of aircraft

4. Discontinued Operations

Income from discontinued operations consists of the following (amounts in thousands):

Year 13

Income from operations of Flight Operations—Transport ($78), net of income taxes of $31	$ 47

Year 12

Loss from write-off of airline operations certificates in Flight Operations—Transport business	$(400)

Year 11

Loss from operations of Flight Operations—Transport ($1,261) and Education and Training ($172) segments, net of income tax benefits of $685	$(748)
Gain on disposal of Education and Training business, net of income taxes of $85	89
Total	$(659)

Year 10

Loss from operations of Charter Tour business, net of income tax benefits of $164	$(171)

5. Related-Party Transactions

On April 30, Year 11, the company sold most of the net assets of the Aircraft Sales and Leasing segment to Interlease, Inc., a Georgia corporation wholly owned by the company's majority stockholder, whose personal holdings at that time represented approximately 75% of the company.

Under the terms of the sale, the sales price was $1,368,000, of which the buyer paid $368,000 in cash and gave a promissory note for the remaining $1,000,000. The company treated the proceeds received in excess of the book value of the net assets sold of $712,367 as a capital contribution due to the related-party nature of the transaction. FBN originally acquired the assets of the Aircraft Sales and Leasing segment during Year 10.

On September 29, Year 14, FBN's board of directors established a Transaction Committee to examine certain transactions between the company and Douglas Mather, FBN's chair, president, and majority stockholder. These transactions appear here.

Certain Loans to Mather. In early September, Year 13, the board of directors authorized a $1 million loan to Mather at the company's cost of borrowing plus $1/8$%. On September 19, Year 13, Mather tendered a $1 million check to the company in repayment of the loan. On September 22, Year 13, at Mather's direction, the company made an additional $1 million loan to him, the proceeds of which Mather apparently used to cover his check in repayment of the first $1 million loan. The Transaction Committee concluded that the board of directors did not authorize the September 22, Year 13, loan to Mather, nor was any director other than Mather aware of the loan at the time. The company's Year 13 Proxy Statement, dated September 27, Year 13, incorrectly stated that "as of September 19, Year 13, Mather had repaid the principal amount of his indebtedness to the company." Mather's $1 million loan remained outstanding until it was canceled in connection with the ESOP (employee stock ownership plan) transaction discussed next.

ESOP Transaction. On February 28, Year 14, the company's ESOP acquired 100,000 shares of the company's common stock from Mather at $14.25 per share. FBN financed the purchase. The ESOP gave the company a $1,425,000 unsecured demand note. To complete the transaction, the company canceled a $1,000,000 promissory note from Mather and paid the remaining $425,000 in cash. The Transaction Committee determined that the board of directors did not authorize the $1,425,000 loan to the ESOP, the cancellation of Mather's $1,000,000 note, or the payment of $425,000 in cash.

Eastwind Transaction. On April 27, Year 14, the company acquired four Eastwind aircraft from a German company. FBN subsequently sold these aircraft to Transreco, a corporation owned by Douglas Mather, for a profit of $1,600,000. In late September and early October, Transreco sold these four aircraft at a profit of $780,000 to unaffiliated third parties. The Transactions Committee determined that none of the officers or directors of the company were aware of the Eastwind transaction until late September, Year 14.

On December 12, Year 14, the company announced that Mather had agreed to step aside as chair and director and take no part in management of the company pending resolution of the matters presented to the board by the Transactions Committee. On February 13, Year 15, the company announced that it had entered into a settlement agreement with Mather and Transreco resolving certain of the issues addressed by the Transactions Committee. Pursuant to the agreement, the company will receive $211,000, the bonus paid to Mather for fiscal Year 14, and $780,000, the gain recognized by Transreco on the sale of the Eastwind aircraft. Also pursuant to the settlement, Mather will resign all positions with the company and waive his rights under his employment agreement to any future compensation or benefits to which he might otherwise have a claim.

6. Long-Term Debt

Long-term debt consists of the following (amounts in thousands):

| | April 30, | | | | |
	Year 14	**Year 13**	**Year 12**	**Year 11**	**Year 10**
Notes payable to banks:					
Variable rate	$ 44,702	$30,495	$ 2,086	$ 2,504	$ 3,497
Fixed rate	13,555	14,679	6,292	3,562	1,228
Notes payable to finance companies:					
Variable rate	—	—	1,320	1,737	10,808
Fixed rate	—	—	—	—	325
Capitalized lease obligations	2,333	2,865	1,295	—	5,297
Other	—	—	600	39	1,660
Total	$ 60,590	$48,039	$11,593	$ 7,842	$22,815
Less current portion	(60,590)	(7,018)	(1,789)	(1,104)	(2,774)
Net long-term debt	$ —	$41,021	$ 9,804	$ 6,738	$20,041

Substantially all of the company's property, plant, and equipment serve as collateral for this debt. The borrowings from bank and finance companies contain restrictive covenants, the most restrictive of which appear in the following table:

	Year 14	**Year 13**	**Year 12**	**Year 11**	**Year 10**
Liabilities/Tangible net worth	<2.5	<3.0	<4.2	<5.5	<6.7
Tangible net worth	>$20,000	>$5,800	>$5,400	>$5.300	>$5,100
Working capital	>$5,000	—	—	—	—
Interest coverage ratio	>1.15	—	—	—	—

As of April 30, Year 14, the company is in default of its debt covenants. It is also in default with respect to covenants underlying its capitalized lease obligations. As a result, lenders have the right to accelerate repayment of their loans. Accordingly, the company has classified all of its long-term debt as a current liability.

The company has entered into operating leases for aircraft and other equipment. The estimated present value of the minimum lease payments under these operating leases as of April 30 of each year is as follows:

Year 14	$2,706
Year 13	3,142
Year 12	3,594
Year 11	3,971
Year 10	4,083

7. Income Taxes

Income tax expense consists of the following:

	Year Ended April 30,				
	Year 14	**Year 13**	**Year 12**	**Year 11**	**Year 10**
Current					
Federal	$ —	$ —	$ —	$—	$ —
State	—	—	—	—	—
Deferred					
Federal	$(845)	$380	$685	$67	$(85)
State	(55)	30	118	4	(5)
Total	$(900)	$410	$803	$71	$(90)

The cumulative tax loss and tax credit carryovers as of April 30 of each year are as follows:

April 30,	Tax Loss	Tax Credit
Year 14	$10,300	$250
Year 13	5,200	280
Year 12	1,400	300
Year 11	2,100	450
Year 10	4,500	750

The deferred tax provision results from temporary differences in the recognition of revenues and expenses for income tax and financial reporting. The sources and amounts of these differences for each year are as follows:

	Year 14	**Year 13**	**Year 12**	**Year 11**	**Year 10**
Depreciation	$ —	$ 503	$ 336	$(770)	$ 778
Aircraft modification costs	—	1,218	382	982	703
Net operating losses	(900)	(1,384)	290	—	(1,729)
Other	—	73	(205)	(141)	158
Total	$(900)	$ 410	$ 803	$ 71	$ (90)

A reconciliation of the effective tax rate with the statutory tax rate is as follows:

	Year 14	Year 13	Year 12	Year 11	Year 10
Federal taxes at statutory rate	(35.0)%	35.0%	34.0%	34.0%	(34.0)%
State income taxes	(2.5)	3.0	3.0	3.0	(3.0)
Effect of net operating loss and investment credits	16.5	—	(7.2)	(29.9)	—
Other	2.0	2.9	22.2	11.1	(12.0)
Effect tax rate	(19.0)%	40.9%	52.0%	18.2%	(49.0)%

8. Market Price Information

The company's common stock trades on the NASDAQ National Market System under the symbol FBN. Trading in the company common stock commenced on January 10, Year 10. High- and low-bid prices during each fiscal year are as follows:

Fiscal Year	High Bid	Low Bid
Year 14	$16.50	$9.50
Year 13	14.63	6.25
Year 12	11.25	3.25
Year 11	4.63	3.00
Year 10	5.25	3.25

On December 29, Year 14, the company announced that NASDAQ had decided to discontinue quoting the company's common stock because of the company's failure to comply with NASDAQ's filing requirements.

Ownership of the company's stock at various dates appears as follows:

	April 30,				
	Year 14	Year 13	Year 12	Year 11	Year 10
Douglas Mather	42%	68%	72%	75%	75%
Public	48	23	24	25	25
Company ESOP	10	9	4	—	—
	100%	100%	100%	100%	100%
Common shares outstanding (000's)	3,357.5	2,222.8	2,095.0	2,000.0	2,000.0

Accounting Quality

LO 6-1 Describe the concept of quality of accounting information, including the attributes of economic content and earnings persistence.

LO 6-2 Describe the characteristics of balance sheet quality and earnings quality.

LO 6-3 Define earnings management and describe the conditions under which managers might be likely to engage in it.

LO 6-4 Identify the different types of liabilities, how judgment can affect liability recognition and measurement, and how off-balance-sheet financing can affect accounting quality.

LO 6-5 Identify how asset recognition and measurement rules and judgments can affect accounting quality.

LO 6-6 Evaluate the effects on profitability assessment and earnings persistence of various items that occur infrequently but can have a large impact on reported financial statements.

LO 6-7 Assess accounting quality by partitioning earnings into its accrual and cash flow components.

LO 6-8 Compute the Beneish Manipulation Index to assess the likelihood of earnings manipulation.

LO 6-9 Explain the effect of two sets of accounting rules (IFRS and U.S. GAAP) on worldwide financial comparability.

Chapter Overview

Chapters 4 and 5 provide tools for analyzing the profitability and risk of a firm using financial statement data. We presume that reported financial statement data

- accurately portrays the economic effects of a firm's decisions and actions during the current period.
- appropriately characterizes the firm's financial position at the end of the period.
- is informative about the firm's likely future profitability and risk.

If the presumption is incorrect, the data is low quality and it may need to be adjusted to obtain better insight. This chapter discusses accounting quality as it relates to analyzing a firm's profitability and risk and forecasting its future financial statements. We also

- describe earnings management both within and outside the limits of U.S. GAAP or IFRS (e.g., fraudulent reporting) and managers' incentives to engage in it.
- discuss the effects of a number of accounting issues on balance sheet and earnings quality, including judgment in the recognition and measurement of liabilities and assets and the impact on reported earnings of various types of non-recurring events.

■ demonstrate two useful tools for assessing earnings management and manipulation.
■ consider the effects of having two sets of accounting standards, U.S. GAAP and IFRS, on the financial analyst's task.

LO 6-1

Describe the concept of quality of accounting information, including the attributes of economic content and earnings persistence.

Accounting Quality

Financial reporting abuses by companies such as **HealthSouth**, **AIG**, **Adelphia**, **Enron**, **WorldCom**, **Parmalat**, **Ahold**, **Satayam**, and **Global Crossing** are rare but dramatic examples of why it is so important to assess the quality of accounting information. These firms reported accounting information that misrepresented their underlying economics and earnings potential. In addition, it is important to realize that even correctly applied accounting rules may, on occasion, fail to indicate future earnings potential and limit the balance sheet's usefulness in assessing financial position and risk.

We frame our discussion of accounting quality by focusing on the following accounting quality issues that are central to analysis and valuation:

■ Accounting information should be a fair and complete representation of the firm's economic performance, financial position, and risk.
■ Accounting information should provide relevant information to forecast the firm's expected future earnings and cash flows.

Our notion of *accounting quality* encompasses the economic information contained in the income statement, the balance sheet, the statement of cash flows, notes to the financial statements, and MD&A (management's discussion and analysis). Each of these financial statements and supplemental disclosures integrates and articulates with the others, and each aids financial statement users in the assessment of profitability, risk, and value.

Our view of accounting quality is broader than accounting *conservatism*, which is sometimes construed as an attribute of reporting quality. Because conservative accounting numbers are biased, they are not, in their own right, high quality for purposes of financial statement analysis and valuation. Conservatism is simply a prudent response by accountants and managers when faced with uncertainty in measuring the economic effects of transactions, events, and commercial arrangements.

Our approach to accounting quality is also broader and more demanding than merely asking whether the firm used U.S. GAAP or IFRS and received an unqualified opinion from the independent auditor. We instead apply a rigorous test to reported financial statements to determine whether they provide users with useful information that is relevant and reliable for understanding the firm's financial position, performance, and risk, and that aids the projection of the firm's future earnings and cash flows.

High Quality Reflects Economic Reality

Conceptually, accounting amounts may reflect three elements:

■ Economics
■ Measurement error (or noise)
■ Bias

High-quality accounting information portrays fairly and completely the economic effects of a firm's decisions and actions and paints an accurate economic portrait of the firm's financial position, performance, and risk. That is, high-quality accounting information maximizes economic content and minimizes measurement error and bias.

Measurement errors occur when managers, in good faith, make estimates that turn out to be wrong. Accounting standards require managers to make many (often difficult) estimates each period, such as the collectability of receivables, the fair values of financial assets, pension liabilities, and many others. Given the high degree of uncertainty in some of these estimates, some measurement errors are inevitable. Good faith, well-informed estimates yield small measurement errors in directions that are not predictable. The errors tend to cancel out over time and across the many estimates that managers must make in a given year, yielding high-quality accounting numbers. *Bias* occurs when managers apply biased accounting standards (for example, standards that require asset write-downs and do not permit asset write-ups) and when managers take advantage of the estimation process to report overly optimistic (and less often pessimistic) accounting numbers. Neutral application of accounting standards to reduce bias yields high-quality accounting numbers.[1]

Quality in Financial Statements and Disclosures

The following paragraphs decompose the accounting-related portion of a 10K SEC filing into its major parts and define how each part can achieve high accounting quality.

Balance Sheet. A high-quality balance sheet portrays the economic resources that can be reasonably expected to generate future economic benefits (and the claims on those resources) at a point in time. Balance sheet quality is low if assets are misrepresented or liabilities are omitted.

Income Statement. A high-quality income statement includes

- all revenues the firm earned during the period and can reasonably expect to collect.
- the costs of all resources consumed, including resources consumed in the production process to generate revenues (that is, costs directly related to revenues, such as cost of sales).
- resources consumed during the period as a function of time that indirectly relate to revenues (such as fixed administrative costs and interest expenses).
- the effects of any gains or losses from other transactions and events of that period.

Accounting quality is low if net income

- includes revenues the firm did not earn during the period or may not be able to collect.
- fails to include expenses or losses of the period.
- includes expenses or losses that are attributable to other periods.
- misclassifies or disguises key income items.

The Statement of Cash Flows. A high-quality statement of cash flows

- summarizes the cash flow implications of the firm's performance and changes in the firm's financial position over a period of time.
- reports significant non-cash investing and financing activities in an accompanying note.
- appropriately classifies cash flows into operating, investing, and financing activities in sufficient detail for the analyst to understand why cash flows change each period.

---

[1]Some level of bias (for example, conservative accounting standards) may be preferred by creditors.

Notes to the Financial Statements. High-quality notes to the financial statements

- provide additional information that enhances the users' understanding of the accounting methods used and the judgments and estimates the firm's managers made in measuring and reporting accounting amounts and changes in those amounts.
- provide a useful quantitative disaggregation and explanation of financial statement amounts.

Management's Discussion and Analysis. A high-quality MD&A section in Form 10-K and the annual report

- enhances these disclosures with qualitative discussions of operations and risks.[2]
- provides an in-depth qualitative and unbiased context to the quantitative data reported in the financial statements.

Management's Role in Quality

Achieving high accounting quality begins with management. Managers' choices and estimates within U.S. GAAP or IFRS should be determined by firms' underlying economic circumstances, including conditions in their industry, competitive strategy, and technology. For example, U.S. GAAP and IFRS allow two methods of accounting for leases—the operating lease method and the capital lease method—to reflect differences in the economics of these leasing arrangements.[3] Thus, to obtain quality accounting information, management should select the accounting principles that best portray the economics of their activities from the set permitted.

Even when managers select the most appropriate accounting principles or methods, they still must make numerous estimates in applying those principles. Virtually all accounting amounts require some degree of estimation. For example, firms use up the services of buildings and equipment at different rates over time, so accounting standards allow managers to estimate useful lives. Given that managers have discretion in choosing their accounting principles in some cases and must make estimates in applying those accounting principles in most cases, firms should disclose sufficient information in the financial statements and notes to permit users to assess the economic appropriateness of those choices. Thus, informative disclosures are an essential element of quality accounting information.

Standard Setters' Role in Quality

Accounting standard setters establish principles to provide firms with guidance and rules for measuring and reporting the economic effects of firms' activities, performance, and financial position in order to achieve high-quality accounting. Standard setters also establish principles to provide auditors with a common basis for auditing the fairness of firms' reporting and to provide financial statement users with a comparable and understandable set of principles for firms' accounting. Standard setters recognize, however, that measuring the economic effects of firms' activities, performance, and financial

---

[2]See Appendix B, which can be found online at the book's companion website at www.cengagebrain.com, for **PepsiCo**'s MD&A discussions of key assumptions; critical accounting policies, risks, liquidity, and capital resources; and estimates made by the firm.

[3]Chapter 7 discusses accounting for leases in detail.

position often requires judgment, estimation, and subjectivity. As the degree of subjectivity increases, so does the potential for firms to report accounting information that includes unintentional measurement error or intentional bias to portray the firm in a light most favorable to the firm or its managers. Standard setters often react to this potential for intentional bias or unintentional estimation error when establishing principles by making trade-offs between accurately reflecting economic reality and obtaining reliable accounting information. Thus, quality accounting information maximizes relevance and economic faithfulness, which are subject to the constraints of the reliability of the measurements.

Finally, in some cases, standard setters have removed accounting method choice, resulting in accounting principles that do not faithfully portray underlying circumstances for all firms all of the time. For example, **PepsiCo** cannot recognize its valuable brand name as an asset because U.S. GAAP views internally-developed intangible assets as very difficult to value reliably in the absence of a market-based, arms-length transaction. **Apple**, **Google**, and **Eli Lilly** rely heavily on investments made in R&D and have proven technologies, patents, and intellectual property that can be traced to R&D expenditures. Yet because U.S. GAAP is concerned with the lack of reliable measurements for such assets, U.S. GAAP does not permit companies like these to capitalize these resources that are critical to their economic position and performance. That is, companies can faithfully apply U.S. GAAP or IFRS and still produce lower-quality financial statements.

Analysts Role in Quality

The analyst may conclude that the reported financial statements for a particular firm fall short on accounting quality. In these cases, the analyst might adjust reported amounts to enhance the accounting quality before using them to assess operating performance, financial position, or risk. For example, the analyst might judge that an accelerated depreciation rather than a straight-line method more accurately reflects the economic decline in service potential of a building or machine, or that a higher bad debts provision is necessary to measure likely uncollectible accounts. In this chapter, we discuss, at a general level, these choices and the types of adjustments the analyst might make to reported amounts to enhance the quality of accounting information.[4]

Quick Check

Users of financial statements should consider the following when evaluating the quality of accounting information:

- Economic faithfulness of accounting recognition, measurements, and classifications
- Reliability of the measurements
- When accounting choices exist in U.S. GAAP or IFRS, how the firm's choices fit its activities
- Reasonableness of the estimates made in applying U.S. GAAP or IFRS
- Adequacy of disclosures and credibility of qualitative discussions
- When accounting choices do not exist in U.S. GAAP or IFRS, how the rules fit the firm's underlying economic conditions

---

[4]Chapters 7–9 go into greater detail.

High Quality Leads to the Ability to Assess Earnings Persistence over Time

In the preceding section, we described the first key quality of accounting information, to faithfully measure and report current period financial performance and financial position. The second key quality of financial accounting information is the extent to which it measures and reports earnings that are likely to persist into the future versus earnings that are more likely to be transitory and not recur in the future. Considering these two qualities together yields the following four combinations:

■ *Earnings are very informative about current performance and tell you that current performance will persist.* This constitutes high quality on both dimensions (for example, a big jump in sales and earnings this period because of new products that will continue to be successful for a long time). Or, *earnings are very informative about current performance and tell you that the current level of earnings performance will not persist.* Again, this constitutes high quality on both dimensions. For example, the firm realizes an unexpected gain (or loss) this year but clearly classifies and reports it as nonrecurring; there is no ambiguity because the gain is informative in that it will not likely affect future earnings.

■ *Earnings are informative about current performance but not informative (that is, does not reduce uncertainty) about the future.* In this case, we have high information quality for the current period but low information quality for the future. For example, a firm experiences a sudden drop in cost of goods sold due to an unexpected reduction in the cost of raw materials inventory. The cost of goods sold measure is relevant and reliable for the current period performance, but this year's greater income does not help you forecast whether the raw material price decrease is relatively permanent and thus whether earnings will persist.

■ *Earnings are not informative about current period performance but are informative about the persistence of future earnings.* Here we have low current period information quality but high information quality for the long run. For example, earnings this period include expenses for pre-opening costs for new stores; the new stores are operational and are expected to be profitable in the future.

■ *Earnings are neither informative about current performance nor future performance.* This combination of low quality on both dimensions is relatively rare. An example would be the fraudulent reporting of a sale on credit. Current earnings are misstated, and prospects for continued earnings and sales growth are also misleading.

Earnings and Valuation

As Chapters 10–14 illustrate, firm value depends on predictions of future payoffs to investors: dividends, free cash flows, and earnings. To link our discussion about current period earnings and expected future earnings to valuation, consider the following four scenarios. In each case, we assume that the analyst has adjusted or restated reported earnings amounts to achieve the desired level of economic information content about current period and future period performance.

Scenario 1: Earnings for the current period are high-quality, are in line with expectations, and do not suggest any changes in expected future earnings. You should not expect to observe a change in the market price of the equity securities. Market prices likely already reflect the expected earnings levels.

Earnings are informative in the sense that they signal the market that its prior expectations have been met and there are no surprises that trigger a change in expectations for the future.

Scenario 2: Earnings for the current period differ from expectations, and the new earnings level is expected to persist.

A firm may have introduced a successful new product during the period, and the market had not fully anticipated the success of the new product in pricing the equity security. The new product should enhance earnings for a number of years in the future. The market price of the security should increase for the realized additional earnings of the current period and for the present value of the expected additional earnings in the future. Earnings are informative if they signal the portion of the current period's earnings due to the new product and the additional earnings in the future as a result of the persistence of this new earnings stream.

Consider a second example. A firm unexpectedly loses a patent infringement lawsuit. As a consequence, the firm is enjoined from selling a key line of products that generate substantial profits for the firm and is required to pay immediate damages. The market value of the firm's equity securities should decline as a result of the damages paid. In addition, the level of expected earnings for the future will decline relative to those previously anticipated, which means that the market value of the firm's equity securities also should decline to reflect the present value of the lower expected future profits. Earnings are informative if they signal the amount of the immediate economic loss and the persistent negative effect on future earnings.

Scenario 3: Earnings for the current period differ from expectations, but expected future earnings do not change.

Because a local government corrects a processing error, a firm receives an unexpected rebate on property taxes previously paid. The market value of the firm's equity securities should increase as a result of the rebate. Because expected future earnings do not change, there should be no further market price reaction for the equity securities. Earnings are informative if they disclose the amount of the rebate and signal its one-time nature.

Scenario 4: Earnings for the current period do not differ from expectations, but expected future earnings do change.

At the end of the current period, a manufacturing firm replaces a piece of equipment with a new piece of equipment that has an identical cost but is more efficient. The new piece of equipment adds to the firm's productive capacity and will reduce manufacturing costs, increasing expected earnings for future periods. The acquisition of the equipment should not materially affect the market value of the firm's equity securities; however, the market value should increase for the present value of the higher expected future earnings. Earnings are informative if they disclose sufficient information for the analyst to forecast the increase in expected future earnings.

- Accounting quality is a broad concept encompassing all of the financial statements, notes, and supplemental disclosures and discussion.
- High quality accurately reflects economic reality and earnings persistence.

- High-quality past earnings and current earnings allow the analyst to develop informed expectations of future earnings and assess firm value.

Quick Check

LO 6-2

Describe the characteristics of balance sheet quality and earnings quality.

Earnings Quality versus Balance Sheet Quality

Given that accounting quality is a property of all financial statements, it is useful to distinguish between the concept of earnings quality (an income statement concept) and the concept of balance sheet quality. While earnings quality permits an accurate assessment of current performance and a foundation for predicting future performance, balance sheet quality permits an accurate assessment of key descriptions of risk: liquidity, financial flexibility, and solvency. The ratios used to measure each element of risk require proper measurement and inclusion of assets and liabilities.[5] The ratios' descriptive power suffers when balance sheet quality is low.

Earnings and Balance Sheet Quality Are Linked by Financial Statement Articulation

As discussed in Chapters 2 and 3, financial statements articulate. One can measure how balance sheet assets and liabilities change and reflect that change (with few exceptions) on the income statement as revenues and expenses. Alternatively, one can measure revenues and expenses on the income statement using revenue recognition rules and expense recognition conventions and then reflect the associated changes in assets and liabilities on the balance sheet. A good example of the option to start with either statement and then reflect the effect on the other statement is given by conceptual alternatives in the accounting for machinery depreciation. Conceptually, one could measure and report the fair value of the remaining service potential of machinery on the balance sheet, reflecting any service potential decline as an expense on the income statement. Or, one could use an expense recognition convention designed to systematically allocate the original cost of the machine to depreciation expense on the income statement, reflecting the depreciation as a reduction of the book value of the machine asset on the balance sheet. Whatever the choice, judgment, or estimate used by management to account for machinery, the effects of the accounting will be reflected in both the income statement and the balance sheet. Thus, an unrealistic estimate, bad judgment, or unjustifiable choice can affect both balance sheet quality and earnings quality.

Earnings and Balance Sheet Quality Can Differ Due to the Different Objectives of the Income Statement and the Balance Sheet

The strong correspondence of earnings and balance sheet quality created by financial statement articulation is affected to some extent by the fact that, in financial statement analysis, balance sheets and income statements can be used for different objectives. Thus, it is possible that accounting standards and management choices leading to, say, a high-quality balance sheet might have no effect or even a negative effect on earnings quality. Continuing with the machinery example, fair valuing a machine on the balance sheet might result in a high-quality balance sheet in that the machine asset is not based on an outdated historical cost. Given that balance sheet values are useful in credit analysis, fair value gives a better picture of the liquidity, financial flexibility, and solvency of a company. However, changes in machine fair value reflected on the income statement might be caused by outside forces that are less controllable by management and less predictive of future performance. If the fair value changes are a transitory (i.e., not a

---

[5]See Chapter 5 for a detailed discussion of these ratios.

persistent) indicator of future performance, the prediction of future earnings for valuation purposes would be more difficult. Earnings quality remains high, however, if the firm adequately discloses the transitivity of the change in fair value. But, fair values have to be estimated, which creates greater exposure to unintentional error or bias.

Another example is provided by management's choice of whether to use the last-in, first-out (LIFO) or first-in, first-out (FIFO) inventory method. If inventory acquisition prices have been rising over time, measuring the balance sheet inventory amount using LIFO yields out-of-date costs on the balance sheet. LIFO assumes that recently purchased inventory (at higher acquisition prices) are sold first and that inventory purchased in previous periods (at lower acquisition prices) remain in inventory. Thus, balance sheet inventory is reported at older costs that understate the future cash flow potential from selling the inventory. Balance sheet quality is impaired because the balance sheet does not capture liquidity adequately. However, gross margins on the income statement are equal to a recent selling price minus a recent acquisition cost, and thus capture economic content and yield a more persistent earnings number. These are characteristics of a high-quality income statement. If management chose to use the FIFO method under these circumstances, then liquidity measurement would be improved on the balance sheet, but income statement quality might suffer.[6]

Earnings Management

LO 6-3

Define earnings management and describe the conditions under which managers might be likely to engage in it.

High-quality accounting occurs when managers measure and report firm performance and financial position with very little measurement error or bias. However, management's influence over accounting practice can result in *earnings management*, low accounting quality, and the need to adjust financial data to better reflect its economic information content. Earnings management connotes different things to different users of the term. Healy and Wahlen provide the following definition of earnings management:

> Earnings management occurs when managers use judgment in financial reporting and in structuring transactions to alter financial reports to either mislead some stakeholders about the underlying economic performance of the company or to influence contractual outcomes that depend on reporting accounting numbers.[7]

Note that the definition includes managers' choices, judgments, and estimates that are necessary but that mask the underlying economic performance of a firm.

In addition, structuring transactions may also be used as an earnings management tool. For example, managers might delay maintenance to increase reported income. This is often referred to as *real earnings management* because, although no estimates or judgments were involved, a real decision to delay maintenance was undertaken to influence a decision maker's understanding of the earnings signal for future profitability.

---

[6]In Chapter 9, we describe the disclosure of the LIFO Reserve in financial statement notes and show how an analyst can use this information to achieve high quality in both financial statements.

[7]Paul M. Healy and James M. Wahlen, "A Review of the Earnings Management Literature and Its Implications for Standard Setting," *Accounting Horizons* (December 1999), pp. 365–383. Another useful definition is provided in Katherine Schipper, "Commentary: Earnings Management," *Accounting Horizons* (December 1989), pp. 91–102: "a purposeful intervention in the external financial reporting process, with the intent of obtaining some private gain (as opposed to, say, merely facilitating the neutral operation of the process) ...."

Detecting earnings management is difficult, because managers can exercise judgment in financial reporting in many ways. Moreover, earnings management is often intended to create the appearance of fundamental economic growth (for example, increasing sales and earnings).

Incentives to Practice Earnings Management

Managers may engage in earnings management if choices and estimates allowed in U.S. GAAP or IFRS benefit them personally or if doing so leads to benefits for the firm and its stakeholders. Examples of reasons for earnings management are:

- Managing earnings upward might increase the manager's compensation under compensation contracts based on earnings or stock prices.
- Managing earnings upward might enhance job security for senior management by influencing the outcomes of transactions that affect corporate control, such as proxy fights and takeovers.
- Managing earnings upward might allow the firm to obtain debt financing at a lower cost by appearing more profitable or less risky, avoid violation of debt covenants, or influence the effects of other binding constraints from accounting-based contracts.
- Managing earnings upward might influence short-term share price performance and increase the economic benefits to the firm from engaging in initial public and seasoned equity offerings and using firm shares in acquisitions.
- Managing earnings upward prior to managers' sale of their personal ownership interests (insider selling) might increase share prices and maximize manager gains from the sale.
- Managing earnings upward might influence stock prices positively (or delay stock price declines) by meeting or beating the market's expectations for earnings, managers' own earnings forecasts, and prior period's earnings, and might also maintain a smooth earnings time-series to cause the firm to appear less risky.
- Managing earnings downward might discourage entry into the industry by potential competitors.
- Managing earnings downward might reduce the probability of antitrust actions against the firm or other regulatory interventions or political interference related to tax issues, capital requirements (e.g., for banks, thrifts, and insurers), and import relief.
- Managing earnings downward might suppress stock prices and thus yield favorable terms when taking a company private.
- Managing earnings downward prior to managers' insider share purchases might decrease share prices and maximize manager gains from future share sales.
- Managing earnings downward might cause negative current consequences but will create opportunities to reverse earnings management in future periods.

Deterrents to Earnings Management

Managers may be deterred from engaging in earnings management for the following reasons:

- Capital markets and regulators such as the SEC penalize firms identified as flagrant earnings managers.
- Firms and managers who are perceived as practicing aggressive earnings management will lose their reputation for being honest and trustworthy among capital

market participants and stakeholders. When it is revealed that a firm has managed earnings, its stock price usually falls dramatically and firm managers are often punished or fired.

■ Legal consequences can result from aggressive earnings management and fraud.

■ Securities regulations and stock exchanges require annual audits by independent accountants. Auditors can monitor particularly aggressive actions taken by management to influence earnings, although an auditor's power to thwart actions taken within the bounds of U.S. GAAP or IFRS is limited.

■ The ongoing scrutiny of financial analysts and investors serves as a check on earnings management. Security analysts typically follow several firms in an industry and have a sense of the corporate reporting "personalities" and strategies of various firms. The frequency, timeliness, and quality of management's communications with shareholders and analysts signal the forthrightness of management and the likelihood of earnings being highly managed.[8]

Although deterrents exist, the existence of incentives to practice earnings management indicates that you are best served by increasing your analysis of accounting quality when these incentives are present.

Accounting Quality in the Liability Recognition and Measurement Area

A high-quality balance sheet is extremely important in assessing financial flexibility (i.e., the debt capacity of the firm for funding new projects) and financial risk. Given that financial flexibility and risk are closely tied to proper recognition, measurement, and classification of liabilities, we begin our discussion with a consideration of what balance sheet liabilities should capture. Financial reporting recognizes a liability if it satisfies the following criteria:

■ The obligation involves a probable future sacrifice of economic benefits—a future transfer of cash, goods, or services; the forgoing of a future cash receipt; or the transfer of equity shares—at a specified or determinable date. The firm can measure with reasonable precision the cash-equivalent value of the resources needed to satisfy the obligation.

■ The firm has a present obligation (not a possible future obligation) and little or no discretion to avoid the transfer.

■ The transaction or event that gave rise to the obligation has already occurred.[9]

While the criteria for liability recognition may appear straightforward and subject to unambiguous interpretation, unfortunately, this is often not the case. Various obligations of an enterprise fall along a continuum with respect to how well they satisfy these criteria. Exhibit 6.1 classifies obligations into six groups.

LO 6-4

Identify the different types of liabilities, how judgment can affect liability recognition and measurement, and how off-balance-sheet financing can affect accounting quality.

---

[8]Mark H. Lang and Russell J. Lundholm, "Corporate Disclosure Policy and Analyst Behavior," *Accounting Review* (October 1996), pp. 467–492.

[9]Financial Accounting Standards Board, *Statement of Financial Accounting Concepts No. 6*, "Elements of Financial Statements" (1985). Financial Accounting Standards Board, *Statement of Financial Accounting Standards No. 150*, "Accounting for Certain Financial Instruments with Characteristics of both Liabilities and Equity," (2008) requires certain obligations settled in equity shares to be classified as liabilities; *FASB Codification Topic 480*.

Exhibit 6.1

Classification of Accounting Liabilities by Degree of Uncertainty

Most Certain ← → Least Certain

Obligations with Fixed Payment Dates and Amounts	Obligations with Fixed Payment Amounts but Estimated Payment Dates	Obligations for Which the Firm Must Estimate Both Timing and Amount of Payment	Obligations Arising from Advances from Customers on Unexecuted Contracts and Agreements	Obligations under Mutually Unexecuted Contracts	Contingent Obligations*
Notes Payable	Accounts Payable	Warranties Payable	Rental Fees Received in Advance	Purchase Commitments	Unsettled Lawsuits
Interest Payable	Salaries Payable				Financial Instruments with Off-Balance-Sheet Risk
Bonds Payable	Taxes Payable	Insurance Claims	Subscription Fees Received in Advance	Employment Commitments	Loan Guarantees

Recognized as Accounting Liabilities

Not Generally Recognized as Accounting Liabilities

*If an obligation meets certain criteria for a loss contingency, firms must recognize this obligation as a liability. See the discussion later in this chapter.

Obligations with Fixed Payment Dates and Amounts

The obligations that most clearly satisfy the liability recognition criteria are those with fixed payment dates and amounts (typically set by contract). Most obligations arising from borrowing arrangements (classified as financing activities) fall into this category. The borrowing agreement specifies the timing and amount of interest and principal payments.

However, even with payment dates and amounts set by contract, long-term liabilities require the choice of an interest rate. At the date of the original transaction, the appropriate interest rate is the effective interest rate implied by the cash transfer from the lender. However, revaluations of long-term liabilities (i.e., fair value measurements) are required for the notes to the financial statements, and managers may choose to use fair value as a basis for reporting in the balance sheet (with changes in fair value affecting the income statement).[10] To the extent possible, you should ascertain how those fair value measurements were determined by thoroughly reading the long-term debt note and the note describing accounting policy. If fair value is determined by reference to market prices or based on market prices of similar instruments (which implies a market-determined interest rate), then management discretion is minimized, and accounting quality is likely higher. If interest rates are firm-estimated, then material changes in long-term liability fair values require greater scrutiny because using too high of an assumed discount rate reduces liability fair values.[11]

In Note 10, **PepsiCo** reports that debt obligations in its December 29, 2012 Consolidated Balance Sheet with a book value of $28.359 billion ($23,544 million long-term + $4,815 million short-term) had a fair value of $30.5 billion on the same date. PepsiCo bases the fair values on prices of similar instruments in the marketplace.

Obligations with Fixed Payment Amounts but Estimated Payment Dates

Most current operating liabilities fall into this category. Oral agreements, written agreements, or legal statutes fix the amounts payable to suppliers, employees, and government agencies. Firms normally settle these obligations within a few months after incurring them. The firm can estimate the settlement date with sufficient accuracy to warrant recognizing a liability.

Aside from concerns over outright fraudulent attempts to hide liabilities, the lack of an interest rate assumption in measuring these liabilities, their short-run nature, and the tendency for amounts to be fixed by contract causes few quality concerns. For example, **PepsiCo** reports that it has $838 million Dividends payable at December 29, 2012, in its Note 14 to the Consolidated Financial Statements.

Obligations with Estimated Payment Dates and Amounts

Obligations in this group require estimation because the firm cannot identify the specific future recipients of cash, goods, or services at the time the obligation becomes a liability. In addition, the firm cannot precisely compute what amount of resources it will transfer in the future or when the transfers will occur. For example, when a firm sells products under a warranty agreement, it promises to replace defective parts or perform certain repair services for a specified period of time. At the time of sale, the firm can neither identify the specific customers who will receive warranty benefits nor ascertain

---

[10]*FASB Codification Topic 825*; International Accounting Standards Board, *International Accounting Standard 39*, "Financial Instruments: Recognition and Measurement."

[11]Because most companies report liability fair values only in the notes to financial statements, this issue primarily affects note quality as it relates to balance sheet quality. Interestingly, increases in a firm's own risk increase discount rates and decrease liability fair values, making the firm look less risky if fair values are used in ratio analysis. **Barclays** reported a £2.7 billion dollar gain from downward revaluation of its own debt in its 2011 IFRS-based financial statements.

the timing or amounts of customers' claims. Past experience, however, often provides the necessary information for estimating the likely proportion of customers who will make claims and the probable average amount of their claims. As long as the firm can reasonably estimate the probable amount of the obligation, it satisfies the first criterion for liability recognition. Both balance sheet and earnings quality are similarly affected by this category of liability. Managers must judge if and when future resource outflows will occur. They must also estimate the cost of satisfying the obligations.

High-quality note disclosure assists your quality assessment task. Quite often, firms report estimates, realizations, and estimate changes in their notes. For example, **Harley Davidson** reports estimated motorcycle repair expenses under its warranties, how much repair expense actually incurred to fix motorcycles, and changes in the balance of the warranty obligation going forward due to historical repair experience and any new warranty issues discovered. Insurance companies also provide detailed note disclosures of estimated obligations under insurance contracts and their loss experiences.

Analysts should study these notes carefully, with a particular eye on unexpected changes in this type of liability. Managers can manipulate earnings by under-reserving to meet or beat street earnings expectations or over-reserving when earnings are high to permit under-reserving in future periods. Current period over-reserving followed by future period opportunistic under-reserving is an example of establishing and using "cookie jar reserves."

Obligations Arising from Advances from Customers on Unexecuted Contracts and Agreements

A firm sometimes receives cash from customers in advance for goods or services it will provide at a future time. Many types of revenues involve prepayments from customers, such as airfares, subscriptions, insurance premiums, membership dues, and license fees, among others, which create service obligations for firms. Revenue recognition usually requires that the firm deliver the goods or provide the services before recognizing revenue.[12] The important balance sheet and earnings quality issue is whether revenue has been recognized too early, in which case balance sheet quality is impaired by an understatement of liabilities and earnings quality is impaired by an overstatement of revenue. Therefore, you should study the accounting policy on revenue recognition and decide whether the policy makes sense in light of the economics of the industry and corporate operating strategy.

Best Buy describes revenue recognition relating to its gift cards in its 2012, 10-K Note 1 (Critical Accounting Policies) as follows (amounts in millions of dollars):

> We recognize revenue from gift cards when: (i) the gift card is redeemed by the customer, or (ii) the likelihood of the gift card being redeemed by the customer is remote ("gift card breakage"), and we determine that we do not have a legal obligation to remit the value of unredeemed gift cards to the relevant jurisdictions. We determine our gift card breakage rate based upon historical redemption patterns. Based on our historical information, the likelihood of a gift card remaining unredeemed can be determined 24 months after the gift card is issued. At that time, we recognize breakage income for those cards for which the likelihood of redemption is deemed remote and we do not have a legal obligation to remit the value of such unredeemed gift cards to the relevant

---

[12]We analyze revenue recognition in great detail in Chapter 9.

jurisdictions. Gift card breakage income is included in revenue in our Consolidated Statements of Earnings. Gift card breakage income was as follows in fiscal 2012, 2011, and 2010:

	2012	2011	2010
Gift card breakage income	$54	$51	$41

Obligations under Mutually Unexecuted Contracts

Mutually unexecuted contracts arise when two entities agree to transfer resources but *neither* entity has yet made a transfer. For example, **Starbucks** may agree to purchase green coffee beans from its suppliers over the next two years. A baseball organization may agree to pay its "franchise" player a certain sum as compensation for services the player will render over the next five years. A bank may agree to provide lines of credit to its business customers in the event these firms need funds in the future. Both parties have exchanged promises, but neither party has transferred resources. Thus, no accounting liability arises at the time of the exchange of promises. A liability arises only when one party or the other transfers resources. This category of obligation, called *executory contracts,* differs from the preceding two, in which the contracts or agreements are partially executed. With warranty agreements, a firm receives cash but has not fulfilled its warranty obligation. With advances from customers, a firm receives cash but has not provided the required goods or services.

U.S. GAAP and IFRS generally do not require firms to recognize as accounting liabilities obligations under mutually unexecuted contracts. If the amounts involved are material, the firm must disclose the nature of the obligation and its amount in notes to the financial statements. You might conclude, however, that these obligations create sufficient risk for the firm to justify adjusting the reported financial statements to include such obligations.

Purchase commitments are one kind of mutually unexecuted contract bearing such risk. In a purchase commitment, a firm promises to make a future fixed price payment for a future delivery of inventory. Because payment has not been made and inventory has not been delivered, the contract is not recorded as a liability. The firm, however, bears the risk of changes in the fair value of the inventory reflected in the market price it would pay to acquire the inventory if it did not have the contract in place. You can read the required financial statement note on commitments that will show the expected cash flows under purchase commitments. Further, under U.S. GAAP, the firm must report a loss on purchase commitments if the price to acquire inventory on the open market as of the balance sheet date falls below the fixed price in the contract.

Due to the desire to minimize fluctuations in raw material acquisition costs, purchase commitments are common. Although not recorded as a liability on its balance sheet, **PepsiCo** reports $1,738 million in purchase commitments as of December 29, 2012 (Note 9 to its Consolidated Financial Statements).

Contingent Obligations

An event whose future outcome is unknown may create an obligation for the future transfer of resources. For example, a firm may be a defendant in a lawsuit, the outcome of which depends on the results of legal proceedings. Or a firm may guarantee loans of a subsidiary, the outcome of which depends on the future solvency of the subsidiary.

Or an insurer may promise to pay certain amounts or reimburse certain expenses if particular future events occur. Obligations such as these are *contingent* on future events.

Contingent obligations may or may not trigger recognition of accounting liabilities. Financial reporting requires firms to recognize an estimated loss from a contingency (called a *loss contingency*) and a related liability only if both of the following conditions are met:

- Information available prior to the issuance of the financial statements indicates that it is probable that an asset has been impaired or that a liability has been incurred.
- The firm can estimate the amount of the loss with reasonable precision.[13]

For the first criterion, clear guidance as to what probability cutoff defines *likely* or *probable* does not exist. The FASB has stated that "probable is used with its usual general meaning, rather than in a specific accounting or technical sense, and refers to that which can be expected or believed on the basis of available evidence or logic but is neither certain or proved."[14]

For the second criterion, the concept of *reasonably estimable* is not defined in precise terms. If the firm can narrow the amount of the loss to a reasonable range, however large, the firm has achieved sufficient precision to justify recognition of a liability. The amount to be reported is the most likely estimate within the range. If no amount within the range is more likely than another, the firm should use the amount at the lower end of the range. As might be suspected, the contingent liability estimates are fraught with measurement error, and possibly managerial bias, rendering lower balance sheet and earnings quality.

Closely related to the concept of a loss contingency is a *guarantee*. For example, one firm may guarantee the repayment of another entity's borrowing in the event the other entity cannot repay the loan at maturity. As another example, a firm may sell a portion of its accounts receivable to another entity, promising to reimburse the other entity if uncollectible accounts exceed a specified amount. The need to make future cash payments is contingent on future events. U.S. GAAP requires firms to recognize the fair value of the guarantee as a liability.[15] Measuring this fair value involves estimating the likelihood, timing, and amount that might be payable. However, a guarantee can have a fair value even when the likelihood of making a future payment is low. A guarantee by a financially strong firm of a financially weaker firm's debt will reduce the weaker firm's cost of borrowing. The guarantor recognizes a receivable and a liability for the fair value of the benefit it granted to the borrower. The obligation to reimburse a purchaser of accounts receivable for excess uncollectibles likely increases the amount the buyer pays the seller for the receivables. Recognizing the fair value of this guarantee as a liability affects the amount of gain or loss the seller recognizes on the sale of the receivables. In addition to recognizing the fair value of guarantees as liabilities, firms must disclose the maximum amount that could become payable and any available collateral that the guarantor could recover in the event it must execute the guarantee.

Guarantees are contractual. Their disclosure provides you with a clear indication of potential liabilities of the guarantor if default occurs. In addition to these explicit

---

[13]*FASB Codification Topic 450.*

[14]*Statement of Financial Accounting Concepts No. 6* (1985). Although the FASB has not defined *probable*, practice demands that firms and auditors define it. Currently, most firms and auditors appear to use *probable* to mean at least 80%–85% likelihood.

[15]*FASB Codification Topic 460.*

guarantees, you should use the knowledge gained in the strategy analysis step to consider whether a firm will assist a strategic partner with financing even if it is not legally liable for the strategic partner's debt. For example, prior to consolidating their bottling affiliates, both **PepsiCo** and **Coca-Cola** held large, but not controlling, stakes in their affiliates. It is likely that both firms would consider extending financing to a strategically important bottler that was experiencing financial difficulties.

Off-Balance-Sheet Financing Arrangements

Investors and lenders often use the proportion of debt in a firm's capital structure as a measure of risk and therefore as a factor in establishing the cost of funds.[16] Other things being equal, firms prefer to obtain funds without showing a liability on the balance sheet in the hope that future lenders or investors will ignore the risks associated with such financing. Firms sometimes structure innovative financing arrangements in ways that may not satisfy the criteria for the recognition of a liability, often transacting on situations where financial reporting treats the obligation (if any) as an executory contract or a contingency. The principal aim of such arrangements is to reduce the amount shown as liabilities on the balance sheet. Firms accomplish off-balance-sheet financing using a variety of approaches, including leases, the sale of receivables, product financing arrangements, use of another entity, use of joint ventures, and take-or-pay contracts.

Leases

The most common and potentially largest source of off-balance-sheet financing is the use of operating leases. Lease accounting is complex and will be discussed in detail in Chapter 7. However, at this point, it is useful to understand the effect of operating lease treatment on balance sheet quality. In a typical lease, lessors deliver a long-lived productive asset (delivery van, building, etc.) to a lessee in exchange for the lessee's noncancelable promise to pay cash to the lessor over the lease term. Leases may be treated as operating or capital:

- In an operating lease, the lessee does not record the asset received in property, plant, and equipment, and does not record the present value of the promised lease payments in long-term debt.
- Capital leases treat the transaction as the issuance of long-term debt to acquire a long-term asset.

The balance sheet quality issues are that operating leases substantially understate reported long-term, interest bearing-liabilities and property, plant, and equipment, which leads you to understate long-term solvency risk ratios and overstate return on assets. Retailers such as **Macy's** and **Finish Line**, restaurants such as **Starbucks**, and airlines such as **Delta** and **AirFrance/KLM** are heavy users of operating leases.[17]

Sale of Receivables

Firms sometimes sell their receivables as a means of obtaining financing or use a special purpose entity (an SPE) to issue securities backed by the receivables (for example, mortgage-backed securities issued by financial institutions or their SPEs). Exhibit 6.2

---

[16]Chapter 5 discusses various ratios for measuring risk, and Chapter 11 describes techniques for using a firm's capital structure to compute the weighted average cost of capital.

[17]In Chapter 7, we illustrate a method to adjust operating to capital leases.

Exhibit 6.2

Obtaining Financing by Transferring Receivables to an SPE

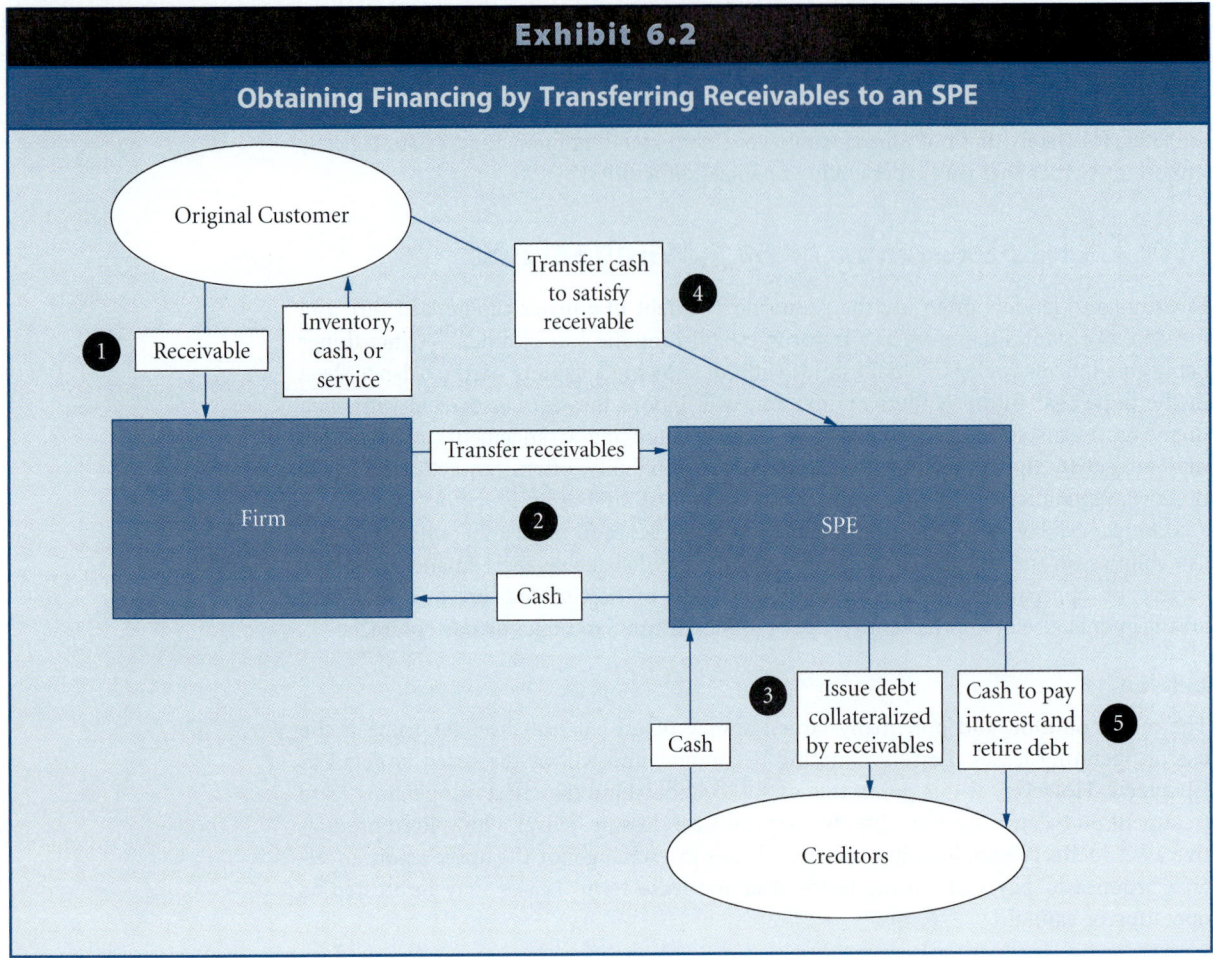

illustrates the use of an SPE to accomplish the sale of receivables. In transaction 1, the firm sells inventory, lends cash, or provides services to an original customer. Rather than wait for customer payment, the firm transfers the receivables to the SPE in exchange for cash (transaction 2). The SPE obtains the cash it transfers to the firm from creditors by issuing debt (transaction 3). The debt is collateralized by the receivables. In transaction 4, the original customer pays off the receivables to the SPE, and in transaction 5, the SPE uses the cash to pay interest and principal to creditors. If collections from customers are not sufficient to repay the amount borrowed plus interest, the transferring firm may have to pay the difference; that is, the lender has recourse against the borrowing firm.[18]

The question arises as to whether the recourse provision creates an accounting liability. Some argue that the arrangement is similar to a collateralized loan. The firm should leave the receivables on its books and recognize a liability in the amount of the cash received in transaction 2. Others argue that the firm has sold an asset; it should

---

[18]To understand the same transaction without using an SPE, replace the SPE with the Creditors and eliminate transactions 3 and 5.

recognize a liability only if it is probable that collections from customers will be insufficient and the firm will be required to repay some portion of the amount received.

The FASB and IASB provide accounting rules to guide the decision of whether to classify a transfer of receivables as a sale or a loan.[19] For example, U.S. GAAP requires that firms recognize transfers of receivables as sales only if the transferor surrenders control of the receivables. Firms surrender control only if all of the following conditions are met:

- The assets transferred (that is, receivables) have been isolated from the selling ("transferor") firm; that is, neither the transferor nor a creditor of the selling firm could access the receivables in the event of the seller's bankruptcy.
- The buying ("transferee") firm obtains the right to pledge or exchange the transferred assets, and no condition both constrains the transferee from taking advantage of its right and provides more than a trivial benefit to the transferor.
- The selling firm does not maintain effective control over the assets transferred through (a) an agreement that both entitles and obligates it to repurchase the assets or (b) the ability to unilaterally cause the transferee to return specific assets.

The principal refinement to the concept of an accounting liability is in identification of which party enjoys the economic benefits and sustains the economic risk of the assets (receivables in this case). If the selling (borrowing) firm controls the economic benefits/risks, the transaction is a collateralized loan. If the arrangement transfers these benefits/risks to the buying (lending) firm, the transaction is a sale.

Product Financing Arrangements

Product financing arrangements occur when a firm (sponsor) does either of the following:

- Sells inventory to another entity and, in a related transaction, agrees to repurchase the inventory at specified prices over specified times
- Arranges for another entity to purchase inventory items on the firm's behalf and, in a related transaction, agrees to purchase the inventory items from the other entity

The first arrangement is similar to the sale of receivables with recourse except that greater certainty exists that the inventory transaction will require a future cash outflow. The second arrangement is structured to appear as a purchase commitment. In this case, however, the sponsoring firm usually creates an SPE for the sole purpose of acquiring the inventory. The sponsoring firm usually guarantees the debt incurred by the SPE in acquiring the inventory.

Exhibit 6.3 illustrates the use of an SPE to accomplish the product financing arrangement. In transaction 1, the SPE acquires inventory from a supplier by issuing a note payable. The firm also agrees to purchase the inventory from the SPE in the future, which is a purchase commitment (transaction 2). Because it is executory, the firm records neither the inventory nor the promise to pay for it. The firm generally guarantees the note or the SPE uses the purchase commitment as evidence of lower lending risk.

---

[19]*FASB Codification Topic 860;* Financial Accounting Standards Board, *Statement of Financial Accounting Standards No. 156,* "Accounting for Servicing of Financial Assets" (2006); International Accounting Standards Board, *International Accounting Standard No. 39,* "Financial Instruments: Recognition and Measurement" (revised 2003).

Exhibit 6.3

Product Financing Arrangement Using an SPE

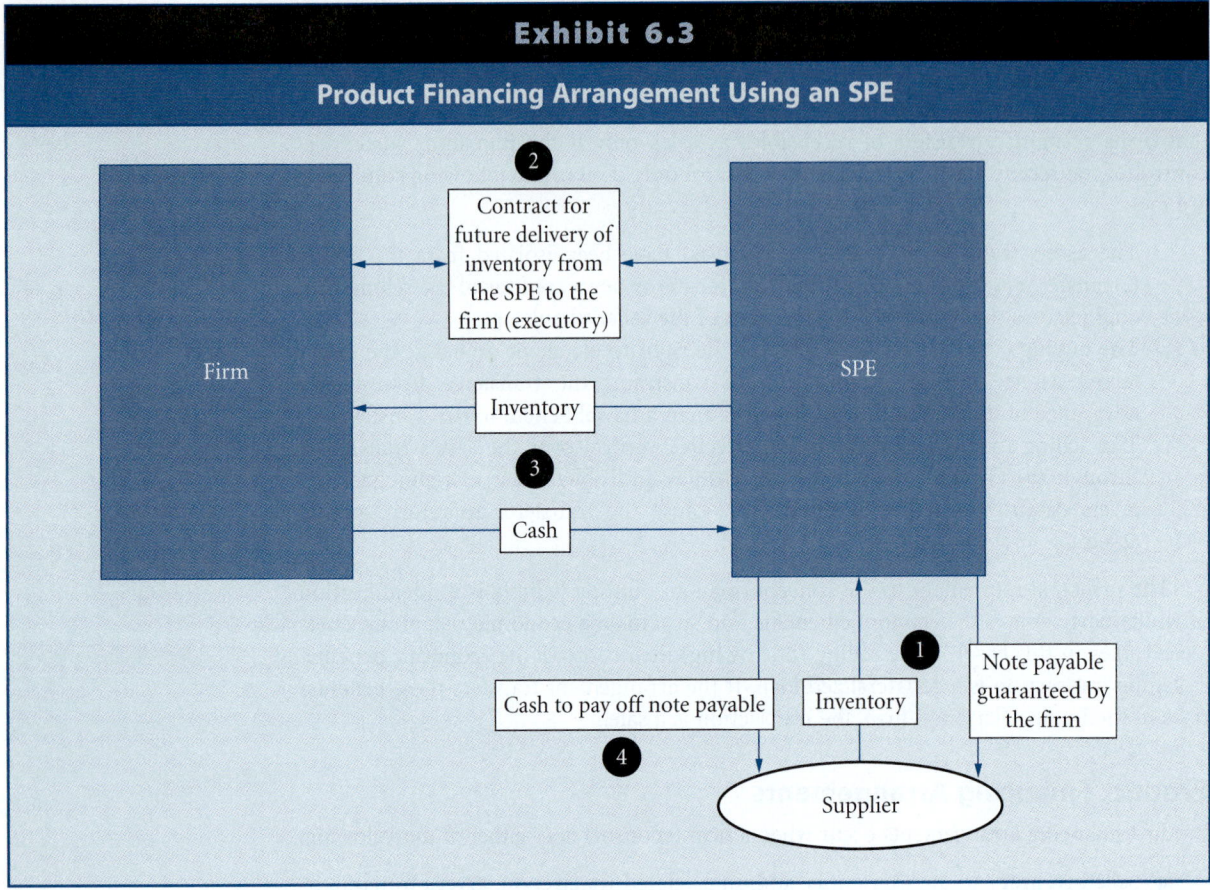

The firm purchases the inventory from the SPE with cash (transaction 3) which is then sent by the SPE to the supplier to pay off the note payable and interest.

Financial reporting requires that firms recognize product financing arrangements as liabilities if they meet two conditions:

- The arrangement requires the sponsoring firm to purchase the inventory, substantially identical inventory, or processed goods of which the inventory is a component at specified prices.
- The payments made to the other entity cover all acquisition, holding, and financing costs.[20]

The second criterion requires that the sponsoring firm recognize a liability whenever it incurs the economic risks (such as changing costs or interest rates) of purchasing and holding inventory, even though it may not physically control the inventory or have a legal obligation to the supplier of the inventory. Thus, as with sales of receivables with recourse, a firm recognizes a liability when it controls the determination of which party enjoys the economic benefits and incurs the economic risks of the asset involved. It also recognizes an asset of equal amount, usually inventory.

---

[20]*FASB Codification Topic 470.*

Use of Another Entity to Obtain Financing

Firms often use other entities to obtain asset financing in a way that permits neither the asset nor its financing to appear on the firm's balance sheet. Instead, they appear on the balance sheet of the other entity.

Suppose, for example, a firm needs additional manufacturing capacity but does not want to borrow funds to build the extra plant assets. Instead, it commits to purchase a certain amount of output from an unaffiliated company at a specified cost that covers operating and debt-service costs. The unaffiliated company takes the purchase commitment to a financial institution and obtains a loan. The unaffiliated company uses the loan proceeds to construct the needed capacity. The new plant assets and the loan appear on the balance sheet of the unaffiliated company. The purchase commitment is a mutually unexecuted contract of the firm initially needing the additional manufacturing capacity. Recall that firms do not recognize executory contracts as liabilities.

Alternatively, the firm can accomplish the same result using an affiliated company, one over which the firm has a greater degree of influence than an unaffiliated one. The debt will not appear on the balance sheet if the firm is not required to prepare consolidated financial statements with the affiliated company. Consolidated statements aggregate the separate financial statements of two or more entities under the control of one of the entities. The debt will appear on the consolidated balance sheet as long as it appears on the balance sheet of any one entity in the consolidated group.[21] To avoid consolidation, the firm needing the financing must not effectively *control* the entity obtaining the financing.

One way firms have avoided consolidation is to set up a joint venture with another entity, with each entity owning 50% of the common stock. In this case, neither firm controls the joint venture. U.S. GAAP currently does not require either firm to prepare consolidated financial statements with the joint venture. Another way firms have avoided consolidation is to set up an *SPE (special-purpose entity)*, also known as a *VIE (variable interest entity)*.[22] The SPE obtains financing and either (1) constructs or acquires the asset desired by the firm attempting to keep debt off its balance sheet or (2) purchases the particular asset from this firm. In both cases, the asset held by the SPE serves as collateral for the loan. The lender to the SPE will likely require some commitment from the firm that sets up the SPE to ensure repayment of the loan. The commitment may take the form of a noncancelable purchase commitment or a loan guarantee. The key to avoiding consolidation is that effective control of the SPE must not reside primarily with the firm setting it up. The SPE must have economic substance of its own, and other parties—the lender or other equity owners—must be the primary beneficiaries of the SPE. The diagram of this type of arrangement is similar to Exhibit 6.3, except that, in transaction 1, the SPE obtains financing from a creditor and then constructs the productive asset and produces inventory in house.

Central to the bankruptcy of **Enron**, for example, was the misuse of SPEs to hold off-balance-sheet derivative instruments, securities, and other assets (such as power plants in India and Nigeria) while also keeping the related financing for these instruments and securities off the balance sheet. Enron did not consolidate these SPEs, maintaining that it did not control them. Later revelations showed that Enron had

---

[21]Chapter 8 discusses consolidated financial statements more fully.

[22]Chapter 8 discusses the accounting for SPEs.

effective control, requiring Enron to restate its previously issued financial statements. The restatements increased assets and liabilities on the balance sheet and eliminated gains that Enron recognized on the "sale" of the assets to the SPEs.

Research and Development Financing Arrangements

When a firm borrows funds to conduct R&D, it recognizes a liability at the time of borrowing and recognizes expenses as it incurs R&D costs. Firms have engaged in innovative means of financing aimed at keeping liabilities off the balance sheet and effectively excluding R&D expenses from the income statement. For example, assume that two pharmaceutical firms form a joint venture to develop, manufacture, and market new products. Because joint ventures are owned equally by the two entities in each case, neither firm consolidates the financial statements of the joint venture with its own financial statements; instead, both report their share of ownership in the joint venture as an investment. Any liabilities of the joint venture appear only on the financial statements of the joint venture, not on either firm's balance sheet. Likewise, the R&D expense of the joint venture appears on neither firm's income statement.

Firms can also use other arrangements besides joint ventures. Although the structures vary somewhat across firms, they generally operate as follows (as illustrated in Exhibit 6.4):

- The sponsoring firm contributes either preliminary R&D work or rights to future products to a partnership in exchange for a general interest in the partnership (transaction 1.)
- It obtains limited partners (often corporate directors or officers) who contribute cash for their partnership interests (transaction 2).
- The sponsoring firm conducts R&D work for the partnership for a fee (transaction 3). The sponsoring firm usually performs the R&D on a best-efforts basis, with no guarantee of success. The sponsoring firm recognizes amounts received from the partnership for R&D services as revenues. The amount of revenue generally equals or exceeds the R&D costs it incurs.
- The rights to any resulting products usually reside in the partnership. However, the partnership agreement usually constrains the returns and risks of the limited partners. The sponsoring firm can often acquire the limited partners' interests in the partnership if valuable products emerge. The sponsoring firm may have to guarantee certain minimum royalty payments to the partnership or agree to purchase the partnership's rights to the product.

In arrangements such as these, a primary objective of the sponsoring firm involves obtaining financing for its R&D work without having to recognize a liability. Criteria exist for when firms must recognize such financing arrangements as liabilities.[23] The sponsoring firm must recognize a liability under either of the following conditions:

- The contractual agreement requires the sponsoring firm to repay any of the funds provided by the other parties regardless of the outcome of the R&D.
- Surrounding conditions indicate that the sponsoring firm bears the risk of failure of the R&D work even though the contractual agreement does not obligate it to repay the other parties. For example, if a sponsoring firm guarantees the debt of the partnership, must make minimum royalty payments to the partnership, or must acquire the partnership's interest in any product, the sponsoring firm will bear the risk of the R&D work.

---

[23]*FASB Codification Topic 730.*

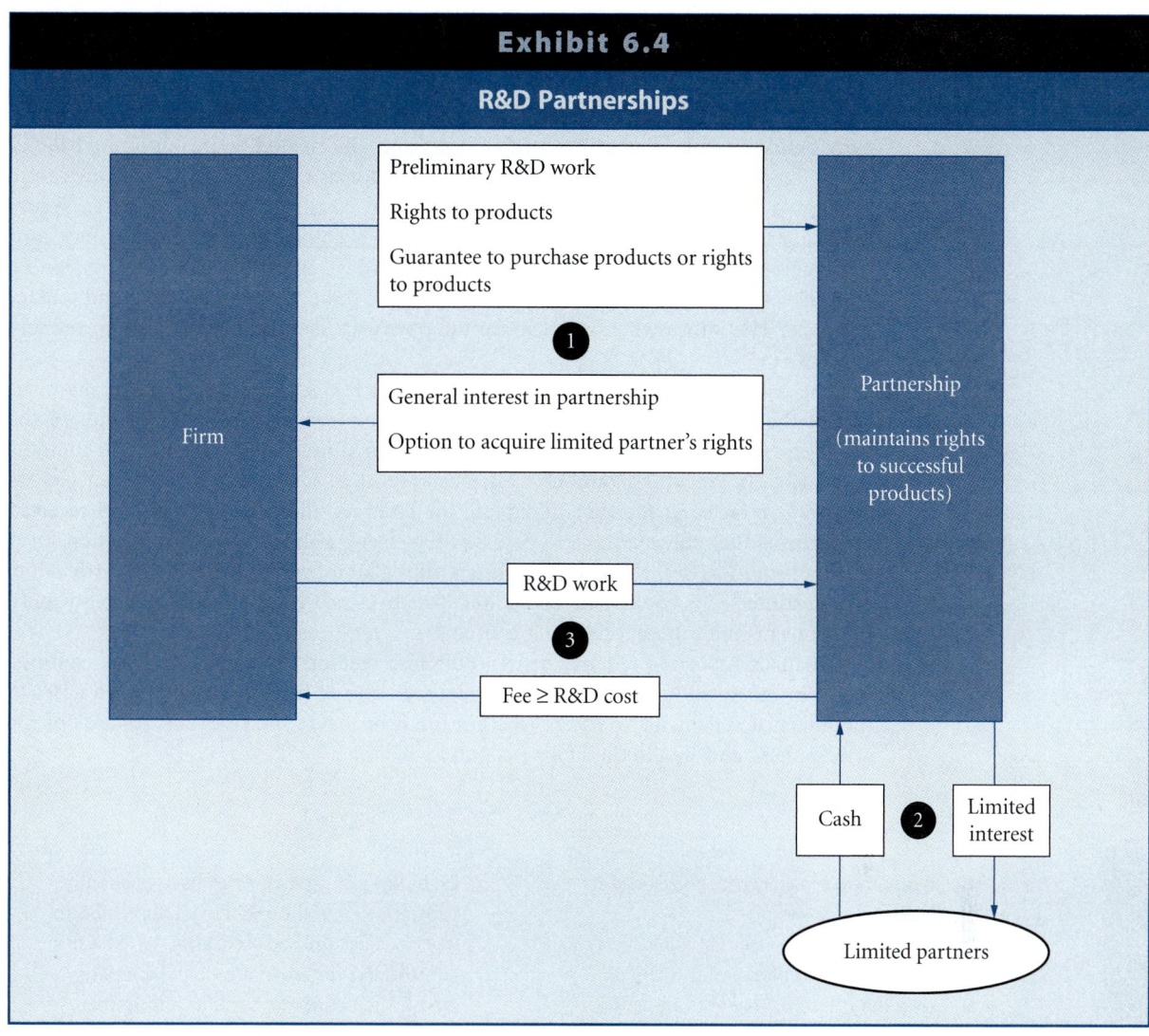

As with the off-balance-sheet financing arrangements involving receivables and inventories discussed previously, firms recognize liabilities when they bear the risk associated with the asset or product involved in the financing of a joint venture for R&D.[24]

Take-or-Pay or Throughput Contracts

A take-or-pay contract is an agreement in which a purchaser agrees to pay specified amounts periodically to a seller for products or services. A throughput contract is

---

[24]A study of firms that conduct their research and development through limited partnerships found that the stock market appears to consider the call option that firms have on research findings in the valuation of the firm. The author calls for improved disclosure of these arrangements instead of recognition of a liability in the balance sheet. See Terry Shevlin, "The Valuation of R&D Firms with R&D Limited Partnerships," *Accounting Review* (January 1991), pp. 1–21.

similar to a take-or-pay contract except that the "product" purchased is transportation or processing services.

To understand the rationale for such arrangements, consider the following case. Suppose two petroleum companies need additional refining capacity. If either company builds a refinery, it will record an asset and any related financing on its balance sheet. Suppose instead that the two companies form a joint venture to construct a refinery. The joint venture obtains financing and constructs the refinery. To secure financing for the joint venture, the two petroleum companies sign take-or-pay contracts agreeing to make certain payments to the joint venture each period for refining services. The payments are sufficient to cover all of the refinery's operating and financing costs. The joint owners must make the payments even if they acquire no refinery services.

The economic substance of this arrangement is that each petroleum company owns half of the refinery and is obligated for half of the financing. The legal status of the arrangement is that the two firms have simply signed noncancelable purchase commitments (that is, executory contracts). Financial reporting treats these arrangements as executory contracts. At the time of signing the contract, the firms have not yet received any benefits that obligate them to pay. As they receive benefits or incur obligations over time, a liability arises. If one or the other entity guarantees the debt of the partnership, the guarantee is a contingent obligation, which is not recognized as a liability until future events indicate that payment is probable.

Financial reporting requires firms to disclose take-or-pay and throughput commitments in the notes.[25] You should examine disclosures of these commitments in notes to the financial statements to assess whether the firm incurs the risks and rewards of the arrangement and should therefore recognize a liability.

Quick Check

- Financial reporting typically recognizes events when an exchange takes place.
- Financial reporting recognizes liabilities when a firm incurs an obligation to sacrifice resources in the future for benefits already received.
- Financial reporting has typically not recognized mutually unexecuted contracts as liabilities because the parties have merely exchanged promises to perform in the future.
- Financial reporting does not generally require the recognition of contingent obligations as liabilities because some future obligating event must occur to establish the existence of a liability.

- Exchanges of promises can have economic substance even though a legal obligation to pay does not immediately arise. When a firm controls the determination of which party enjoys the economic benefits and/or incurs the economic risks from an asset, the firm should recognize the asset and its related financial obligations.
- The FASB and IASB closely monitor reporting issues related to off-balance-sheet commitments of firms, but continue to be challenged because of the ever-changing nature of business financing arrangements and the flexible and fluid organizational arrangements that firms create.[26]

---

[25]*FASB Codification Topic 440.*

[26]Specific IFRS rules relating to off-balance-sheet financing are rare. However, guidelines may be found in IASB, *SIC Interpretation 12, "Consolidating Special Purpose Entities"* (1998).

Asset Recognition and Measurement

A high-quality balance sheet reflects asset values in a way that promotes a proper assessment of liquidity risk and, when considered relative to properly recognized liabilities, helps gauge financial risk.[27] Further, as we learned in Chapter 4, profitability analysis (i.e., ROA) and the efficiency element of profitability analysis (i.e., various asset turnover ratios) critically depend on proper asset recognition and measurement. Chapters 8 and 9 discuss different kinds of assets and their varying characteristics in detail. Here, we focus on a more general understanding of how application of asset measurement rules and management discretion can affect balance sheet quality and earnings quality.

LO 6-5

Identify how asset recognition and measurement rules and judgments can affect accounting quality.

Current Assets

Ratios that measure short-term liquidity risk depend on the proper measurement and reporting of cash, short-term investments, accounts receivable, and inventories.

Cash

Cash usually does not have significant measurement problems. Even cash amounts in foreign currencies can be readily estimated and measured in their U.S. dollar (or corporate home country currency) amounts. However, inclusion of cash as a current asset requires that it be available to satisfy current obligations, and you should carefully read the notes to the financial statements to ascertain whether there are any restrictions on the company's use of cash for that purpose. Cash restricted for longer-term disbursements (e.g., bond sinking funds, plant expansions, etc.) should be reported as noncurrent.

Short-Term Investments

Short-term investments are usually measured with readily available market values and thus are of less concern relative to measurement issues in accounting for accounts receivable and inventories.

Accounts Receivable

Accounts receivable are initially measured at the fair value of the exchange in a credit sale or service arrangement. At the balance sheet date, accounts receivable are adjusted downward by management's estimate of the amount of uncollectible accounts arising from customer defaults or customer returns. Accounting quality for receivables is thus determined by the company's revenue recognition policy and the quality of management's uncollectible account estimation. If revenue is recognized too early or if it is recognized fraudulently, then accounts receivable will be overstated on the balance sheet. If the revenue comes from a product sale, then inventory is understated as well. Thus, the numerator of the current ratio (a key liquidity ratio) is overstated by the amount of the profit margin on the sale. Further, accounts receivable are overstated if management underestimates uncollectible accounts.

Because balance sheets and income statements articulate, low-quality accounts receivable measurement also affects earnings quality. Aggressive recognition of receivables from sales and services will lead to overstated revenues and likely overstated net income. Underestimating uncollectible accounts receivable will give rise to understated bad debt expense and likely overstated income.

---

[27]See Chapter 5 for the various risk-related ratios.

Inventory

Inventory is initially recorded at the original cost incurred to obtain the inventory. There are two primary asset measurement issues for inventory that affect accounting quality. The first is the choice of inventory method. LIFO is a popular method for inventory valuation under U.S. GAAP (but not allowed under IFRS).[28] LIFO assumes that goods purchased more recently (generally at a higher cost) are sold first. LIFO generally yields higher earnings quality because most recent costs are matched with most recent revenues, earnings better capture the economist's definition of income (based on replacement costs of goods sold), and earnings tend to be more persistent. However, LIFO results in far more conservative estimates of inventory value on the balance sheet because only older costs are reflected in the inventory valuation. Other methods, such as FIFO or average cost, yield balance sheet inventory valuations that are closer to fair value obtained from selling the inventory (i.e., future cash inflow), and thus enable a better assessment of liquidity.

The second inventory measurement issue that affects accounting quality arises from the financial reporting requirement that companies annually assess whether inventory costs reflected as assets exceed their market value due to obsolescence, unfavorable supply and demand conditions, or some other economic phenomenon that causes the inventory to decline in value. If so, then the inventory must be written down to market value under the lower-of-cost-or-market rule, triggering an associated loss on the income statement. Management judgments play a large role in the amount and timing of these write-downs and thus, accounting quality can be impaired.[29]

Noncurrent Assets

Recognition and measurement rules for noncurrent assets have major implications for accounting quality. The following general process describes the accounting for most noncurrent assets:

- A noncurrent asset is initially recognized when a past transaction or event enables a firm to control probable benefits of the asset.
- A noncurrent asset is initially measured at the fair value sacrificed to obtain the asset or the fair value of the asset obtained if more clearly determinable.
- Changes in noncurrent assets must be evaluated to ensure that periodic income captures any value declines.

The accounting rules for noncurrent assets are complex and vary greatly across asset classes.[30] At this point, we consider how the aforementioned parts of the process can yield accounting quality problems in more general terms.

Control

The initial recognition of a noncurrent asset emphasizes acquiring control of an asset and its future economic benefits. The issue here concerns the difference between control

---

[28]Chapter 9 discusses LIFO in greater detail.

[29]Another complicated inventory issue affecting accounting quality discussed in Chapter 9 is a LIFO layer liquidation. Such liquidations are transitory and can seriously affect estimates of future earnings unless adjusted by the analyst.

[30]We discuss noncurrent assets in detail in Chapters 8 and 9, where we reconsider the effects of management judgments, estimates, and incentives on accounting quality.

and ownership. This distinction is critical for SPEs.[31] Historically, the assets of SPEs had not been reported as part of the sponsoring entity's balance sheet because the sponsoring entity's ownership of voting common equity shares was minimal. However, recent rules require SPEs to be consolidated as part of a firm's balance sheet if the firm exerts control in some way over the SPE or the firm is the substantial beneficiary of asset benefits held by the SPE. These new rules improve balance sheet quality.

Probability

Initial recognition of a noncurrent asset also requires that the future economic benefits are probable. Management judgment of what is probable is a potential source of low accounting quality. You should read the accounting policy note to understand what costs are capitalized as part of property, plant, and equipment and intangible assets. Often, standard setters don't give companies a choice, prohibiting capitalization of items such as R&D and marketing costs as noncurrent assets. On one hand, this improves balance sheet quality by limiting management judgment in some cases. On the other hand, balance sheet quality can be reduced by keeping valuable assets such as brands and intellectual property from research off of the balance sheet.

Fair Value

In an arm's-length exchange of regularly traded assets, the initial fair value measurement is generally easy to determine. However, unique transactions can be difficult to measure and value and thus can lead to low accounting quality. Consider, for example, a company that provides unique consulting or design services in exchange for a long-term note receivable. The note receivable should be reported initially as a noncurrent asset at its fair value. However, if the services are unique and have no established market value, accountants directly determine the fair value of the note and use it as a basis to record the transaction. The fair value is determined by contractual cash inflows (i.e., periodic interest and final maturity value) and an interest rate that is appropriate for the risk level of the note. Considerable management judgment might be necessary in this situation, and errors in judgment, whether intentional or not, could yield a low-quality note valuation. Because financial statements articulate, service revenue is also valued too high or too low if the note is valued too high or too low, and earnings quality is compromised. Companies have controls in place and auditors have incentives to make sure that these transactions are recorded in a reasonable, unbiased way. However, you should also identify if substantial amounts of revenues or asset acquisitions are a result of unique transactions and how the company accounts for these transactions.

Changes in Value

On an ongoing basis, long-lived productive assets such as buildings and equipment must be depreciated over estimated useful lives to an estimated salvage value using a depreciation method. Changing useful life estimates without having an economic reason changes depreciation expense, possibly in a way that could help a company achieve an earnings target. Biased or opportunistic management estimates of depreciation can lead to low earnings quality.[32]

---

[31]We discuss SPEs further in Chapter 9.

[32]Chapter 8 presents methods of detecting whether depreciation estimates are opportunistic.

When a firm acquires assets such as property, plant, and equipment and intangible assets, it assumes that those assets will generate future benefits. This does not always turn out to be the case, however. The development of new technologies by competitors, changes in government regulations, changes in demographic trends, and other factors may reduce the future benefits originally anticipated from the assets. In an attempt to improve balance sheet quality in the accounting for real noncurrent assets (as opposed to financial assets), standard setters have created a set of tests for asset impairment. The general process is to estimate whether the fair value of a noncurrent asset has declined below its recorded book value. If so, balance sheet quality is improved by writing down the value of the asset and representing the asset at its lower probable future economic benefits. Earnings quality, especially as it relates to earnings persistence, often suffers when noncurrent asset impairment losses are included in current period income from continuing operations, and if those losses should have been recorded in prior periods, the quality of those earnings will have turned out to be low as well. Again, high-quality disclosure can increase earnings quality. If the notes to the income statement clearly designate the nature of the write-down so that analysts can assess when the asset decline occurred and its likely persistence, earnings quality remains high.

The FASB cites the following events or circumstances as examples that may signal recoverability problems for a long-lived asset or group of assets:

- A significant decrease in the market price of a long-lived asset
- A significant adverse change in the extent or manner in which a long-lived asset is being used or in its physical condition
- A significant adverse change in legal factors or in the business climate that could affect the value of a long-lived asset, including an adverse action or assessment by a regulator
- An accumulation of costs significantly in excess of the amount originally expected for the acquisition or construction of a long-lived asset
- A current-period operating or cash flow loss combined with a history of operating or cash flow losses or a projection or forecast that demonstrates continuing losses associated with the use of a long-lived asset
- A current expectation that, more likely than not,[33] a long-lived asset will be sold or otherwise disposed of significantly before the end of its previously estimated useful life[34]

What is particularly noteworthy about this list is that a firm, in effect, must recognize impairment when it anticipates that assets previously acquired will no longer provide the future benefits initially anticipated. This is a valuable disclosure to consider when you attempt to assess a firm's past strategic decisions.

Firms must include impairment losses in income before taxes from continuing operations. Asset impairments do not warrant presentation in a separate section of the income statement, such as that given for discontinued operations or extraordinary gains

---

[33]The term *more likely than not* refers to a level of likelihood that is more than 50%.

[34]*FASB Codification Topic 360 (-10-35-21)*; Also, see Hugo Nurnberg and Nelson Dittmar, "Reporting Impairments of Long-Lived Assets: New Rules and Disclosures," *Journal of Financial Statement Analysis* (Winter 1997), pp. 37–50. The article includes examples of how these impairment indicators are applied by firms in the oil and gas, restaurant, retail food, and service-related industries.

or losses (discussed later). However, alternative methods for reporting the losses include a separate line item on the income statement or a detailed note that describes what line items on the income statement include the impairment losses.

- Choices, estimates, judgments, and promulgated accounting standards play an important role in asset and liability measurement and hence the ability of the balance sheet to accurately reflect liquidity risk, solvency risk, and financial flexibility.

- Given the articulation between the balance sheet and income statement, balance sheet quality almost always affects earnings quality.

Specific Events and Conditions That Affect Earnings Persistence

LO 6-6

Evaluate the effects on profitability assessment and earnings persistence of various items that occur infrequently but can have a large impact on reported financial statements.

In this section, we turn our attention to a set of specific conditions and transactions that affect earnings quality, primarily with respect to earnings persistence. To provide a framework for our discussion, Exhibit 6.5 presents a hypothetical income statement that shows the reporting of special items (in capital letters) if they receive separate line-item treatment on the income statement.

Exhibit 6.5	
XYZ Company **Statement of Comprehensive Income**	
Sales revenue	X
Cost of goods sold	(X)
Selling and administrative expenses	(X)
Operating Income	X
GAINS (LOSSES) FROM PERIPHERAL ACTIVITIES	(X)
RESTRUCTURING CHARGES AND IMPAIRMENT LOSSES	(X)
Interest income	X
Interest expense	(X)
Income before Income Taxes	X
Income tax expense	(X)
Income from Continuing Operations	X
INCOME FROM DISCONTINUED OPERATIONS, NET OF TAXES	X
EXTRAORDINARY GAINS (LOSSES) NET OF TAXES	(X)
Net Income	X
OTHER COMPREHENSIVE INCOME, NET OF TAXES	X
Comprehensive Income	X

Gains and Losses from Peripheral Activities

Firms often enter into transactions that are peripheral to their core operations but generate gains and losses that must be reported on the income statement. For example, to create, manufacture, and market products, firms generally need to invest in assets such as buildings and equipment. When a firm decides to sell and replace such assets, the sale usually results in a gain or loss. Similar to restructuring charges, gains and losses from activities peripheral to the primary activities of a firm are included in income from continuing operations. You should search for such items and decide whether to exclude them when assessing current profitability and forecasting future earnings. Because gains and losses tend to be generated from sales of long-term assets or extinguishment of long-term liabilities, it is not clear that the change in asset or liability value is related to the current period. For example, a gain on a sale of a building might have been the result of an economic gain from appreciation in a prior period. Or, depreciation in prior years might have been too high because of an unrealistically low useful life estimate. In either case, including the gain to assess current period profitability is not warranted.

Firms report peripheral gains and losses on a *pretax* basis. Income tax expense includes any tax effects of the gain or loss. If you decide to eliminate the gain or loss from income from continuing operations, you also must eliminate the related tax effect from income tax expense using specific information disclosed about the tax effects or using the statutory rate if the firm does not disclose specific information about the tax effects.

Gains and losses can be recurring, material, and a part of corporate strategy. For example, Exhibit 6.6 shows how **Singapore Airlines** reported surplus (gains) on disposal of aircraft, spare parts, and spare engines over 2003–2008. Singapore Airlines maintains a reputation for flying newer, technologically advanced aircraft, which results in the use of aircraft for fewer years than other airlines. Thus, the sale of aircraft and spare parts is a significant portion of Singapore Airlines's profitability and should be treated as recurring when forecasting future earnings.

Restructuring Charges and Impairment Losses

Firms may decide to remain in a segment of their business but elect to make major changes in the strategic direction or level of operations of that business.[35] In many of these cases, firms record a restructuring charge against earnings for the cost of implementing the decision, which might include terminating or transferring employees, closing down certain types of operations, or substantially changing production and sales processes. Employee-related costs from downsizing or employee retraining and reassignment typically make up a substantial portion of restructuring costs. Restructuring plans also tend to trigger the asset impairments discussed in the earlier section on accounting quality related to noncurrent assets.

The treatment of restructuring charges in analyzing profitability and assessing earnings persistence is important because recessionary conditions often induce firms to include restructuring charges in their reported earnings for the current period. Whether the recessionary conditions are expected to persist will have a bearing on forecasting

---

[35]If the firm decides to abandon a business segment or component altogether, the reporting policies discussed later for discontinued operations apply. In many cases, however, firms are not abandoning current areas of business, but are "restructuring" them to improve profitability.

Exhibit 6.6

Summary of Singapore Airlines Aircraft Disposal Gains (Singapore dollar amounts in millions)

Fiscal Year	Surplus on Disposal	Pretax Income	Percentage of Pretax Income
2003–2004	$102.7	$ 820.9	12.5%
2004–2005	$215.2	$1,829.4	11.7%
2005–2006	$115.7	$1,662.1	6.9%
2006–2007	$237.9	$2,284.6	10.4%
2007–2008	$ 60.6	$1,198.6	5.0%

earnings in the future. Further, restructurings are expected to yield operating efficiencies or strategic benefits, and thus, may be associated with lower future expenses and higher future revenues. Consistent with this value-added characteristic of restructurings, announcements of restructurings are typically associated with stock price increases.

Interpreting a particular firm's restructuring charge is difficult because firms vary in their treatment of these items, as follows.

- Firms that apply accounting principles conservatively (for example, use relatively short lives for depreciable assets, immediately expense expenditures for repairs of equipment, or use shorter amortization lives for intangible assets) have smaller amounts to write off as restructuring charges than those that are less conservative.
- Firms that sidestep proper financial reporting treatment by spreading out restructuring charges to minimize the impact of the restructuring charge on annual earnings often must take restructuring charges for several years to provide adequately for restructuring costs.
- Firms that maximize the amount of the restructuring charge in a particular year communicate the "bad news" all at once (referred to as the "big bath" approach) and reduce or eliminate the need for additional restructuring charges in the future. If the restructuring charge later turns out to have been too large, income from continuing operations in a later period includes a restructuring credit that increases reported earnings.

The prevalence of restructuring charges in recent years has prompted standard setters to address these measurement and reporting issues. Although differences between U.S. GAAP and IFRS often caused differences in the timing of the charges in past years, recent revisions to *IAS 19* effective January 1, 2013, substantially align the two sets of rules related to restructurings.[36] The basic rules are that firms record a *restructuring liability* on the balance sheet and the associated *restructuring charge* (an expense) on the income statement when these two conditions are present:

- Management has committed to the restructuring plan and has informed employees of termination benefits.
- Restructuring costs meet the definition of a liability.

---

[36]*FASB Codification Topic 420;* International Accounting Standards Board, *International Accounting Standard 37,* "Provisions, Contingent Assets and Contingent Liabilities" (1998); International Accounting Standards Board, *International Accounting Standard 19* (Revised), "Employee Benefits" (2011).

To illustrate the reporting of restructuring charges, consider the disclosures provided by **Iomega Corporation** (now a wholly owned subsidiary of **EMC Corporation**) which sells data storage products to consumer and corporate customers. Iomega is a leading manufacturer of portable data storage solutions, including drives and disks, which are used for sharing, transporting, sorting, and backing up critical information. Employee compensation and associated costs represent one of the largest expenses for Iomega. Other significant expenses include the cost of leased space and depreciation of furniture and fixtures. Iomega provided an extensive note on the composition of its restructuring charges for 2003 and 2004, including amounts for employee severance packages, lease termination fees, and furniture write-offs. Exhibit 6.7 presents excerpts from Iomega's Note 5, "Restructuring Charges/Reversals."

Note that Iomega does not disclose the tax savings resulting from the charges for either year. These tax savings are deferred tax assets until the related restructuring liabilities are paid and a deduction is taken on the corporate tax return. Also note that the firm discloses the cash component of the charges for 2004 but not for 2003. The restructuring charges for Iomega also appear to be recurring in nature. Although not reported here, Iomega had a restructuring charge in 2002 as well. Thus, when forecasting future profitability, you can include them (and related estimated tax effects) in income from continuing operations. Iomega continued to show restructuring charges in future years. It reported $5.7 million in 2005 and $3.0 million in 2006. Iomega did not report a restructuring charge in 2007, the year prior to EMC Corporation acquiring it.

Discontinued Operations

When a firm decides to exit a particular component of its business, it classifies that business as a discontinued operation. This classification provides analysts and other financial statements users with information to distinguish the effects of continuing versus

---

Exhibit 6.7

Excerpts from Iomega Corporation's Note 5

2004 Restructuring Actions. During 2004, the Company recorded $3.7 million of restructuring charges for the 2004 restructuring actions, including $2.6 million of cash charges for severance and benefits for 108 regular and temporary personnel worldwide (approximately 19% of the Company's worldwide workforce) who were notified by September 26, 2004 that their positions were being eliminated, $0.7 million of cash charges for lease termination costs and $0.4 million of non-cash charges related to excess furniture. All of the $3.7 million of restructuring charges recorded during 2004 are being shown as restructuring expenses as a component of operating expenses. None of these restructuring charges were allocated to any of the business segments.

2003 Restructuring Actions. The $14.5 million of charges for the 2003 restructuring actions included $6.5 million for severance and benefits for 198 regular and temporary personnel worldwide, or approximately 25% of the Company's worldwide workforce, $3.0 million to exit contractual obligations, $2.6 million to reimburse a strategic supplier for its restructuring expenses, $1.8 million for lease termination costs and $0.6 million related to excess furniture.

Source: Iomega Corporation, Form 10-K for the Fiscal Year Ended December 31, 2004.

discontinuing operations on current period performance and provides a basis for forecasting future income from the continuing operations of the firm. U.S. GAAP stipulates that a discontinued business is either a separable business or a component of the firm with clearly distinguishable operations and cash flows.[37] The degree to which a particular divested component operationally integrates with ongoing businesses is likely to vary across firms depending on their organizational structures and operating policies. Thus, the gain or loss from the sale of a business might appear in income from continuing operations for one firm (that is, the divested business is operationally integrated) and in discontinued operations for another firm (that is, the divested business is not operationally integrated).

IFRS rules are more restrictive as to what constitutes a discontinued operation.[38] Only disposals of a major line of business or geographic area qualify. For example, if a restaurant chain with a total of 20 restaurants sold three underperforming restaurants with independent cash flows and the chain had no continuing involvement in the operations of the sold restaurants (for example, through franchise agreements), the sale might qualify as a discontinued operation under U.S. GAAP but not under IFRS.[39]

A firm reports the net income or loss from operating the discontinued business between the beginning of the reporting period and the disposal date as a separate item in the discontinued operations section of the income statement (net of tax effects). Firms also report the gain or loss on disposal (net of tax effects) in this same section of the income statement, often labeled "Income, Gains, and Losses from Discontinued Operations." Most U.S. firms include three years of income statement information in their income statements. A firm that decides to divest a business during the current year includes the net income or loss of this business as discontinued operations for the current year and in comparative income statements for the preceding two years. (Previously, the firm reported the latter income in continuing operations in the income statements originally prepared for those two years.) If final sale has not occurred as of the end of the period, the remaining assets held for sale are assessed for impairment and an impairment loss (net of tax) is included as part of the discontinued operations disclosure. The assets and liabilities of the discontinued operations are isolated and receive separate disclosure on the balance sheet or in notes that support the balance sheet.

Exhibit 6.8 illustrates the reporting of discontinued operations for **Bowne & Co.**, one of the largest printers of financial documents in the United States. During 2004, Bowne decided to sell its document-related outsourcing business to **Williams Lea, Inc.**

Note that Bowne presents the income from operating the discontinued businesses separately from the gain on disposal, each net of tax effects. The magnitude of discontinued operations in 2004, net of tax, transforms a small loss from continuing operations into a modest positive net income. Bowne reports the amount of assets and

---

[37]The most recent U.S. GAAP ruling on discontinued operations, Financial Accounting Standards Board, *Statement of Financial Accounting Standards No. 144,* "Accounting for the Impairment or Disposal of Long-Lived Assets" (2001), maintained the basic provisions of Accounting Principles Board, *Opinion No. 30,* "Reporting the Results of Operations" (1973) for presenting discontinued operations, but broadened the presentation to include more disposal transactions. *FASB Codification Topic 360.*

[38]International Accounting Standards Board, *International Financial Reporting Standard 5,* "Noncurrent Assets Held for Sale and Discontinued Operations" (2004).

[39]The FASB and IASB continue to jointly deliberate discontinued operations treatment, although as of early 2013, the project appears to have been assigned a lower priority relative to deliberations on revenue recognition, financial instruments, leasing, and financial statement presentation.

Exhibit 6.8

Bowne & Co.
Selected Information Related to Discontinued Operations
(amounts in thousands)

	2004	2003
INCOME STATEMENT		
Revenue	$ 899,011	$ 847,636
Expenses:		
Cost of revenue	(574,264)	(536,166)
Selling and administrative	(266,034)	(247,977)
Depreciation	(32,121)	(35,466)
Amortization	(2,713)	(2,478)
Gain on sale of building	896	—
Restructuring, integration, and asset impairment charges	(14,644)	(23,076)
Operating (Loss) Income	$ 10,131	$ 2,473
Interest expense	(10,709)	(11,389)
Loss on extinguishment of debt	(8,815)	—
Other expense, net	(118)	(1,367)
Loss from Continuing Operations before Income Taxes	$ (9,511)	$ (10,283)
Income tax benefit (expense)	1,313	729
Loss from Continuing Operations	$ (8,198)	$ (9,554)
Discontinued Operations:		
Income from discontinued operations, net of tax	$ 4,150	$ 1,805
Gain on sale of discontinued operations, net of tax	31,552	—
Net Income from Discontinued Operations	$ 35,702	$ 1,805
Net Income (Loss)	$ 27,504	$ (7,749)
CONDENSED CONSOLIDATED BALANCE SHEETS		
Assets held for sale, noncurrent	—	$ 106,898
Other assets (details not provided)	—	620,927
Total Assets	$ 648,811	$ 727,825
Liabilities held for sale, noncurrent	—	$ 3,882
Other liabilities and shareholders' equity	—	723,943
Total Liabilities and Shareholders' Equity	$ 648,811	$ 727,825
CONDENSED CONSOLIDATED STATEMENTS OF CASH FLOWS		
Cash Flows from Operating Activities:		
Loss from continuing operations	$ (8,198)	$ (9,554)
Depreciation and amortization	34,834	37,944
Asset impairment charges	518	2,198
Gain on sale of building	(896)	—
Loss on extinguishment of debt	8,815	—
Changes in other assets and liabilities, net of non-cash transactions	(2,404)	(10,339)
Net Cash Provided by Operating Activities	$ 32,669	$ 20,249

(Continued)

Exhibit 6.8 (Continued)		
Cash Flows from Investing Activities (details omitted)	$ 148,200	$ (21,117)
Cash Used in Financing Activities (details omitted)	(97,784)	(10,872)
Net Cash Used in Discontinued Operations	(20,123)	(4,131)
Net increase (decrease) in cash and cash equivalents	$ 62,962	$ (15,871)
Cash and cash equivalents—Beginning of period	17,010	32,881
Cash and cash equivalents—End of period	$ 79,972	$ 17,010

Source: Bowne & Co., Form 10-K for the Fiscal Years Ended December 31, 2003 and 2004.

liabilities related to discontinued operations on its balance sheet each year. When assessing Bowne's sustainable profitability, one should exclude income from discontinued operations from the numerator of the return on assets ratio and exclude the related assets from the denominator as well.

Interestingly, Exhibit 6.8 indicates that Bowne also eliminated the effect of discontinued operations from the calculation of cash flow from operations and classified all of the cash flows related to discontinued operations in a separate section of the statement of cash flows after financing activities. Because cash flow from operations contains no amounts related to discontinued operations, you can use it when computing cash flow ratios (for example, cash flow from operations to average current liabilities) without making additional adjustments. If the firm had not excluded the cash flow effects of discontinued operations from cash flow from operations, you should do so.

For most firms, income from discontinued operations represents a source of earnings that does not persist. Thus, in most cases, you should exclude income from discontinued operations from forecasts of future earnings, focusing instead on income from continuing operations.[40]

Extraordinary Gains and Losses

The income statement can include extraordinary gains and losses. To be classified as extraordinary, an income item must meet the following two criteria:[41]

- Unusual in nature
- Infrequent in occurrence

A firm applies these criteria in the context of its own operations and to similar firms in the same industry, taking into consideration the environment in which the entities operate. Thus, an item might be extraordinary for some firms but not for others.

---

[40]For some firms that regularly pursue a strategy to acquire firms and subsequently sell them, income from discontinued operations is an ongoing source of profitability, and you might decide to include this income in forecasts of future earnings. Also, some firms might continue to engage in significant changes in strategy in order to focus on a smaller core of profitable operations, reporting additional discontinued operations in the process. Such was the case for Bowne. It reported additional discontinued operations before being acquired by **RR Donnelley** in 2010. Expectations about whether discontinued operations will continue to occur are best developed in the industry and strategy analysis stages of the analysis process.

[41]*FASB Codification Topic 225.*

Extraordinary item treatment is rare. Losses from the events of September 11 and Hurricane Katrina were not treated as extraordinary. In the case of the September 11 events, standard setters believe that a reliable separation of event-related losses and non-event losses was not possible and thus prohibited extraordinary item treatment. Katrina was not considered to be unusual in nature and infrequent in occurrence given that hurricanes occur regularly in the Gulf Coast region. However, extraordinary items are still reported occasionally. The Mount St. Helens eruption (first eruption in 130 years) was considered extraordinary. **Verizon Communications Inc.** reported a 2007 extraordinary item for Venezuela's nationalization of one of its unconsolidated affiliates.

Firms reporting under IFRS isolate and describe material, unusual items. However, IFRS does not allow the term *extraordinary* to appear on the face of or in the notes to the financial statements.[42]

Other Comprehensive Income Items

U.S. GAAP and IFRS require firms to revalue certain assets and liabilities each period even though firms have not yet realized the value change in a market transaction. As discussed in Chapter 2, the recognition and valuation of these assets and liabilities do not immediately affect net income and retained earnings. Instead, these unrealized gains and losses are reported as other comprehensive income for the period and are included within accumulated other comprehensive income or loss in the shareholders' equity section of the balance sheet.

Under current U.S. GAAP, four balance sheet items receive this accounting treatment:[43]

- Fair value gains and losses on investment securities deemed available for sale
- Fair value gains and losses on derivatives held as cash flow hedges
- Certain adjustments to pensions and other postemployment benefits obligations
- Foreign currency adjustments for assets and liabilities in certain foreign operations

IFRS also permits upward revaluations of tangible fixed assets used in operations.

You must decide whether to include the unrealized gains and losses when assessing earnings persistence and predicting future profitability:

- These gains and losses are more likely to be part of future earnings when:
  - they closely relate to ongoing operating activities.
  - measuring the amount of the gain or loss is relatively objective (i.e., when active markets exist to indicate the amount of the value changes).
- These gains and losses are less likely to be part of future earnings when:
  - they are not directly related to the firm's ongoing operating activities.
  - the amount of gain or loss that firms ultimately realize when they sell the assets or settle the liabilities will likely differ from the amount reported each period and might reverse in future years prior to disposal or settlement.
  - measuring the amount of the gain or loss on certain types of assets can be subjective because they are not traded in active markets.

---

[42]International Accounting Standards Board, *International Accounting Standard 1*, "Presentation of Financial Statements" (revised 2003).

[43]Chapters 7–9 discuss the accounting for each of these items in great detail.

Changes in Accounting Principles

Firms occasionally change the accounting principles used to generate financial statements. Sometimes standard setters mandate the changes. Regardless of the source of the change, firms following U.S. GAAP must report amounts for the current and prior years as if the new accounting principle had been applied all along (termed *retrospective treatment*). The rationale for this reporting is that it results in net income amounts for the current and prior periods measured using the same accounting principles the firm intends to use in future periods, thereby enhancing the information content of reported earnings in forecasting future earnings. This treatment is in line with IFRS.[44]

Firms need not restate prior-year earnings retrospectively if it is impracticable to determine the period-specific effects of the change or the cumulative effect of the change. In this case, firms must apply the new accounting policy to the balances of assets and liabilities as of the earliest period for which retrospective application is practicable and to make a corresponding adjustment to retained earnings for that period. When it is impracticable for an entity to determine the cumulative effect of applying a change in accounting principle to *all* prior periods to which it relates, firms must apply the new accounting principle as if it were made prospectively from the start of the year of the change.

For example, if a firm switches from the FIFO cost-flow assumption to the LIFO cost-flow assumption for inventories and cost of goods sold, typically it is impracticable to reconstruct the effects of the accounting change on prior years. In this case, the change to the LIFO cost-flow assumption will be applied prospectively (that is, in current and future years) at the start of the year in which the accounting change takes place.

Firms may choose retrospective treatment on a voluntary basis as well. For example, Exhibit 6.9 presents **Apple Inc.**'s Form 10-K/A to amend its 2009 Form 10-K. In the amendment, Apple explains the financial statement effects when it applied new required accounting methods to account for the iPhone and Apple TV. Prior accounting methods required Apple to defer all revenues and expenses related to sales of iPhone and Apple TV and recognize these revenues and expenses on a straight-line basis over the expected product life because Apple had promised the possibility of free future upgrades and features. The justification for deferral is typically that revenue has not been earned. New standards require Apple to recognize revenue and expenses relating to existing delivered hardware and software at the time of sale and to defer the estimated fair value of the right to receive free future upgrades and features. Apple had a choice of applying the new standards prospectively (in current and future periods) or retrospectively (adjust prior years' results and then use the new standard in current and future periods). Apple chose retrospective application to enhance comparability. Note the huge amounts involved. Adoption of the new standards increased Apple's revenue by $6.4 billion in 2009, $5.0 billion in 2008, and $483 million in 2007.

Changes in Accounting Estimates

As discussed earlier in this chapter, application of accounting standards requires firms to make many estimates. Examples include the amount of uncollectible accounts receivable, the useful lives for fixed assets and intangible assets, the percentage-of-completion

---

[44]*FASB Codification Topic 250*; International Accounting Standards Board, *International Accounting Standard 8*, "Accounting Policies, Change in Accounting Estimates, and Errors" (revised 2003).

Exhibit 6.9

Excerpt from Apple's Explanation of Change in Revenue Recognition Method

Under the historical accounting principles, the Company was required to account for sales of both iPhone and Apple TV using subscription accounting because the Company indicated it might from time-to-time provide future unspecified software upgrades and features for those products free of charge. Under subscription accounting, revenue and associated product cost of sales for iPhone and Apple TV were deferred at the time of sale and recognized on a straight-line basis over each product's estimated economic life. This resulted in the deferral of significant amounts of revenue and cost of sales related to iPhone and Apple TV. Costs incurred by the Company for engineering, sales, marketing and warranty were expensed as incurred. As of September 26, 2009, based on the historical accounting principles, total accumulated deferred revenue and deferred costs associated with past iPhone and Apple TV sales were $12.1 billion and $5.2 billion, respectively.

The new accounting principles generally require the Company to account for the sale of both iPhone and Apple TV as two deliverables. The first deliverable is the hardware and software delivered at the time of sale, and the second deliverable is the right included with the purchase of iPhone and Apple TV to receive on a when-and-if-available basis future unspecified software upgrades and features relating to the product's software. The new accounting principles result in the recognition of substantially all of the revenue and product costs from sales of iPhone and Apple TV at the time of sale. Additionally, the Company is required to estimate a standalone selling price for the unspecified software upgrade right included with the sale of iPhone and Apple TV and recognizes that amount ratably over the 24-month estimated life of the related hardware device. For all periods presented, the Company's estimated selling price for the software upgrade right included with each iPhone and Apple TV sold is $25 and $10, respectively. The adoption of the new accounting principles increased the Company's net sales by $6.4 billion, $5.0 billion and $572 million for 2009, 2008 and 2007, respectively. As of September 26, 2009, the revised total accumulated deferred revenue associated with iPhone and Apple TV sales to date was $483 million; revised accumulated deferred costs for such sales were zero.

The Company had the option of adopting the new accounting principles on a prospective or retrospective basis. Prospective adoption would have required the Company to apply the new accounting principles to sales beginning in fiscal year 2010 without reflecting the impact of the new accounting principles on iPhone and Apple TV sales made prior to September 2009. Accordingly, the Company's financial results for the two years following adoption would have included the impact of amortizing the significant amounts of deferred revenue and cost of sales related to historical iPhone and Apple TV sales. The Company believes prospective adoption would have resulted in financial information that was not comparable between financial periods because of the significant amount of past iPhone sales; therefore, the Company elected retrospective adoption. Retrospective adoption required the Company to revise its previously issued financial statements as if the new accounting principles had always been applied. The Company believes retrospective adoption provides the most comparable and useful financial information for financial statement users, is more consistent with the information the Company's management uses to evaluate its business, and better reflects the underlying economic performance of the Company. Accordingly, the Company has revised its financial statements for 2009, 2008 and 2007 in this Form 10-K/A to reflect the retrospective adoption of the new accounting principles. There was no impact from the retrospective adoption of the new accounting principles for 2006 and 2005. Those years predated the Company's introduction of iPhone and Apple TV.

Source: Apple Corporation, Form 10-K/A for the Fiscal Year Ended September 26, 2009.

rate for a long-term project, the return rate for warranties, and interest, compensation, and inflation rates for pensions, health care, and other retirement benefits. Firms periodically change these estimates. The amounts reported in prior years for various revenues and expenses will differ from the amounts suggested by the new estimates. Standard setters view making and revising estimates as an integral and ongoing part of applying accounting principles. They are concerned about the credibility of financial statements if firms restate their prior financial statements each time they change an accounting estimate. Therefore, current accounting standards require firms to account for changes in estimates by using the new estimates in the current year and in future years.

Because new estimates alone can change current period income, you should attempt to determine whether estimate changes are significant. However, often you must infer the impact of changes in estimates. For example, Chapter 8 will provide a formula for computing average useful lives of depreciable assets. If you detect an increase in average useful lives in a year in which reported earnings barely exceeded expectations, you could recompute depreciation expense using the prior year's average useful life to detect whether the depreciation difference drove the increase in current period earnings. Likewise, you can monitor changes in estimated bad debts expense by reviewing the ratio of bad debts expense to sales. Whenever possible, you should compare the pattern of estimated to realized amounts to assess the extent of management's changes in estimates and to determine whether trends will continue.

You must remember that estimates change over time for legitimate reasons. One of the main determinants of the value of accrual-based financial statements is that the amounts of reported assets and liabilities can reflect management's beliefs. Again, knowledge of a company's industry economics and strategy allows for a more informed judgment of whether an estimate change is warranted.

You must also decide whether to use the financial statement data as originally reported for each year or as restated to reflect the new conditions. Because the objective of most financial statement analysis is to evaluate the past as a guide for projecting the future, the logical response is to use the restated data.

However, you encounter difficulties when using restated data. In their annual reports, most companies include balance sheets for two years and income statements and statements of cash flows for three years. You can calculate ratios and perform other analyses based on balance sheet data (such as current assets/current liabilities or long-term debt to shareholders' equity) on a consistent basis for only two years. You can calculate ratios based on data from the income statement (for example, cost of goods sold/sales) or from the statement of cash flows (for example, cash flow from operations/capital expenditures) for three years at most on a consistent basis. However, many important ratios and other analyses rely on data from the balance sheet and either the income statement or the statement of cash flows. For example, the rate of return on common shareholders' equity equals net income to common shareholders divided by average common shareholders' equity. The denominator of this ratio requires two years of balance sheet data. Thus, it is possible to calculate comparable ratios based on average restated data from the balance sheet and one of the other two financial statements for only one year under the new conditions. You could obtain balance sheet amounts for prior years from earlier annual reports, but reliance on the earlier reports results in comparing restated income statement or statement of cash flow data with non-restated balance sheet data for those earlier years. You should evaluate the likely magnitude of the effect of the restatement on ratios using prior years' data. **Apple Inc.**'s 10-K/A restated revenues and net income for the years 2009, 2008, and 2007. Also, Apple disclosed that the restatement effects on earlier years were immaterial due to limited revenues from iPhone sales prior to 2007.

When a firm provides sufficient information so that you can restate prior years' financial statements using reasonable assumptions, you should use retroactively restated financial statement data. When the firm does not provide sufficient information to do the restatements, you should use the amounts as originally reported for each year. To interpret the resulting ratios, attempt to assess how much of the change in the ratios results from the new reporting condition and how much relates to other factors. Clearly, restatements can create significant interpretation issues when analyzing historical financial data.

Accounting Classification Differences

While accounting quality is primarily a firm-specific concept, a related concern arises when you wish to compare two firms that use different accounting classifications for the same economic item. For example, consider two luxury goods retailers, **Coach** and **Tiffany**. Coach includes shipping and handling expense (for shipping products to retail locations and to customers) in selling, general, and administrative expenses, while Tiffany includes it in cost of goods sold. This creates a source of difference in their gross margins. If the amounts of shipping and handling expense are disclosed, then analysts can adjust SG&A and cost of goods sold. If the amounts are not disclosed, the analyst must take the difference into account when making profitability comparisons.

The account classification issue is exacerbated when comparing firms in different countries. Exhibit 6.10 presents the 2009 consolidated income statement of the Finnish company **Stora Enso**, prepared in accordance with IFRS. Stora Enso is a global paper, packaging, and wood products company that produces newsprint and book paper, magazine paper, fine paper, consumer board, industrial packaging, and wood products. Stora Enso's sales totaled EUR 8.9 billion in 2009. The company has approximately 27,000 employees in more than 35 countries worldwide.

Typical of the financial statements for a non-U.S. company, Stora Enso classifies expenses by source instead of function. For example, a U.S. paper company includes as operating expenses cost of goods sold, SG&A (selling, general, and administrative) expenses, possibly some other gains and losses, restructuring charges, and impairments. Wages and salary costs and depreciation costs are allocated to cost of goods sold and SG&A expenses. Cost of goods sold includes the costs allocated to inventory sold that period, such as wages and depreciation (that is, manufacturing overhead) costs, as well as materials costs. Wages, salaries, and depreciation not related to production appear in SG&A. In contrast, Stora Enso does not make those allocations. For example, "Personnel expenses" are listed, but one does not know the portion of those expenses that would be included in inventory and therefore included in cost of goods sold in the U.S. company. Likewise, Stora Enso reports "Depreciation, amortisation, and impairment charge," which is different from what is done in the U.S. reporting approach. Instead of cost of goods sold, Stora Enso reports "Materials and services" and "Changes in inventories of finished goods and work in progress." An analyst estimating cost of goods sold would have to include these two accounts, an estimated portion of personnel expenses to be included in inventory, and an estimated portion of depreciation to be included in inventory.

When you can easily and unambiguously reclassify accounts, the reclassified data should serve as the basis for analysis. If the reclassifications require numerous assumptions, you should make them as precisely as possible or avoid making them and note the differences in account classification for further reference when interpreting the financial statement analysis.

Exhibit 6.10

Stora Enso
Consolidated Income Statement
(amounts in millions)

EUR million	Year Ended 31 December		
	2009	2008	2007
Continuing Operations			
Sales	**8 945.1**	**11 028.8**	**11 848.5**
Other operating income	172.8	120.2	88.4
Change in inventories of finished goods and work in progress	(200.5)	(76.1)	81.0
Change in net value of biological assets	(3.3)	(18.2)	7.5
Materials and services	(5 464.3)	(6 815.7)	(7 051.5)
Freight and sales commissions	(833.6)	(1 127.1)	(1 133.9)
Personnel expenses	(1 349.6)	(1 669.1)	(1 712.9)
Other operating expenses	(833.1)	(752.6)	(761.9)
Share of results in equity accounted investments	111.8	7.6	341.3
Depreciations, amortisation and impairment changes	(1 152.9)	(1 422.4)	(1 529.6)
Operating (Loss)/Profit	**(607.6)**	**(726.6)**	**176.9**
Financial income	209.3	356.7	161.9
Financial expense	(488.5)	(523.9)	(318.6)
(Loss)/Profit before Tax	**(886.8)**	**(893.8)**	**20.2**
Income tax	8.6	214.8	(7.4)
Net (Loss)/Profit for the Year from Continuing Operations	**(878.2)**	**(679.0)**	**12.8**
Discontinued Operations Profit/(Loss) after Tax for the Year	—	4.3	(225.2)
Net (Loss) for the Year from Total Operations	**(878.2)**	**(674.7)**	**(212.4)**

Source: Stora Enso, Annual Report for the Fiscal Year Ended December 31, 2009.

Tools in the Assessment of Accounting Quality

In the preceding sections, we identified areas of potential low accounting quality and suggested how you might read the financial statements and notes in order to identify low accounting quality and make necessary adjustments to profitability and risk assessment. In the next two sections, we present two additional tools that can be used to assess accounting quality. The first is a partition of earnings into its cash flow and accrual components to gain a better understanding of the persistence of earnings. The second tool is a model to assess the likelihood of financial statement manipulation.

LO 6-7

Assess accounting quality by partitioning earnings into its accrual and cash flow components.

Partitioning Earnings into Operating Cash Flow and Accrual Components

Operating cash inflows and outflows are easy to identify and measure. However, accrual accounting requires a consideration of changes in non-cash assets and liabilities to measure earnings. Non-cash assets and liabilities are called accruals. Earnings are the sum of cash flow and accrual changes. For example, if a firm performs a service for $1,000, collecting $700 in cash and a $300 account receivable from a customer and promising to pay an employee $200 in wages, the firm's earnings equal $800:

Income statement:	Service revenue	$1,000
	Wages expense	(200)
	Earnings	$ 800

Alternatively, earnings can be expressed as the sum of a cash component and an accrual component:

Balance sheet effects:	Increase in cash from sale (cash component)		$700
	Increase in accruals (accrual component)		
	Increase in accounts receivable	$ 300	
	Increase in wages payable	(200)	100
	Earnings		$800

Accrual accounting is superior to cash accounting on the dimensions of capturing economic content and predicting future cash flows. The $100 net increase in accruals is a prediction of future cash flows. Next period, the firm will collect the $300 accounts receivable in cash and pay the $200 wages payable in cash, yielding a net inflow of $100 in cash.

Analyzing Patterns in Accruals

If managers attempt to manage reported earnings, they will typically do so through accruals estimates. Even if managers do not introduce bias into the financial statements, the accrual component of net income will exhibit a persistence that differs from the operating cash flow component of net income. To further clarify what is meant by "accruals," Exhibit 6.11 provides a schematic of a statement of cash flows and identifies accruals.

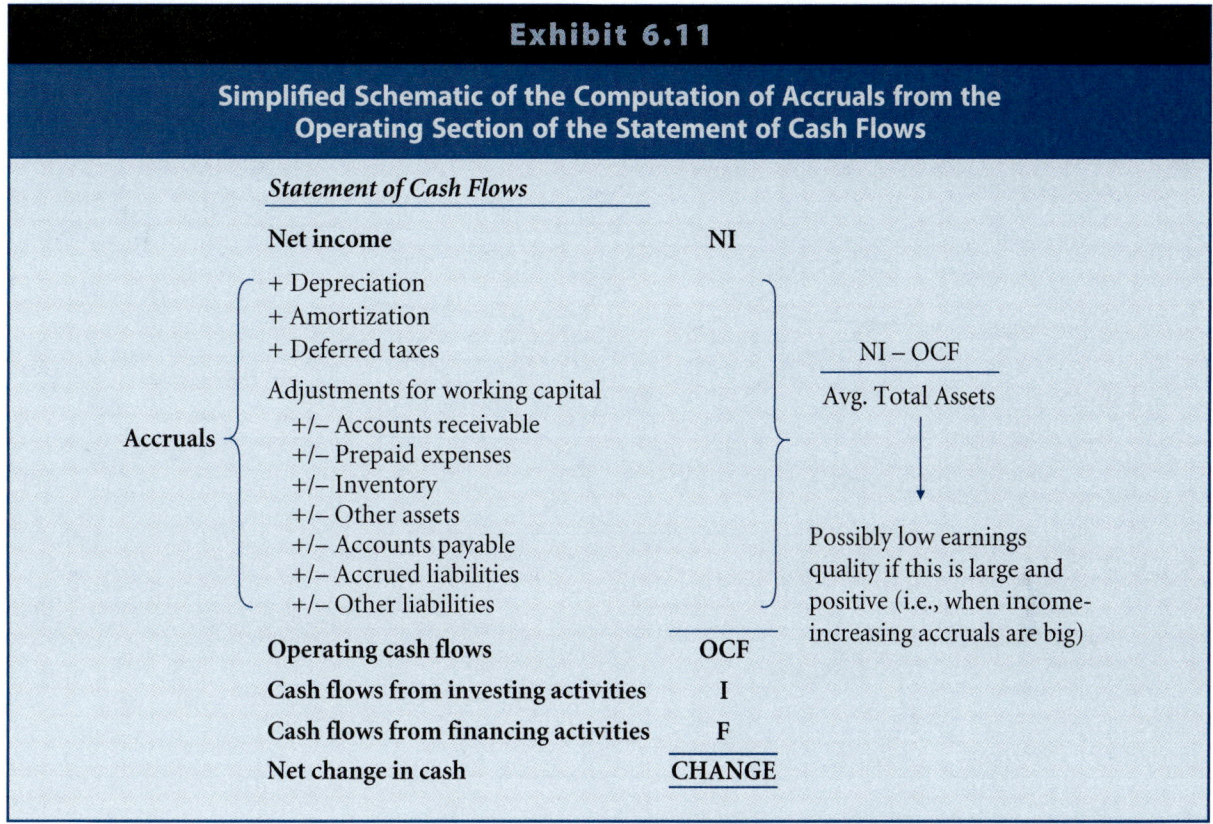

Accruals are the adjustments that reconcile cash flows from operations and net income. They are components of earnings because they map underlying economics into reported profitability. Investors who fixate on net income or operating cash flows without understanding the relation between the two may make erroneous inferences regarding the persistence of cash flows or earnings.

Sloan examined the relation between net income and operating cash flows by focusing on the behavior of net income conditional on the magnitude of accruals.[45] He defines the accrual component of current earnings as net income minus operating cash flows, and then scales the amount by dividing by the average of beginning and ending total assets so that firms can be compared regardless of their size. He then ranked firms based on this measure of accruals. He plotted net income (scaled by average total assets) for five years before and after the year in which he measured the accruals.

Exhibit 6.12 provides the plots for the decile of firms with the lowest (most negative) accruals and the decile of firms with the highest (most positive) accruals. The top line on the graph indicates that in the ranking year, firms with the highest current accruals have very high income. Moreover, this high income represents a spike relative to the previous five years. More importantly, it represents a spike that reverses almost entirely

---

[45]Richard G. Sloan, "Do Stock Prices Fully Reflect Information in Accruals and Cash Flows about Future Earnings?" *The Accounting Review* (1996), pp. 289–315.

Exhibit 6.12

Patterns of Earnings Surrounding High and Low Accruals

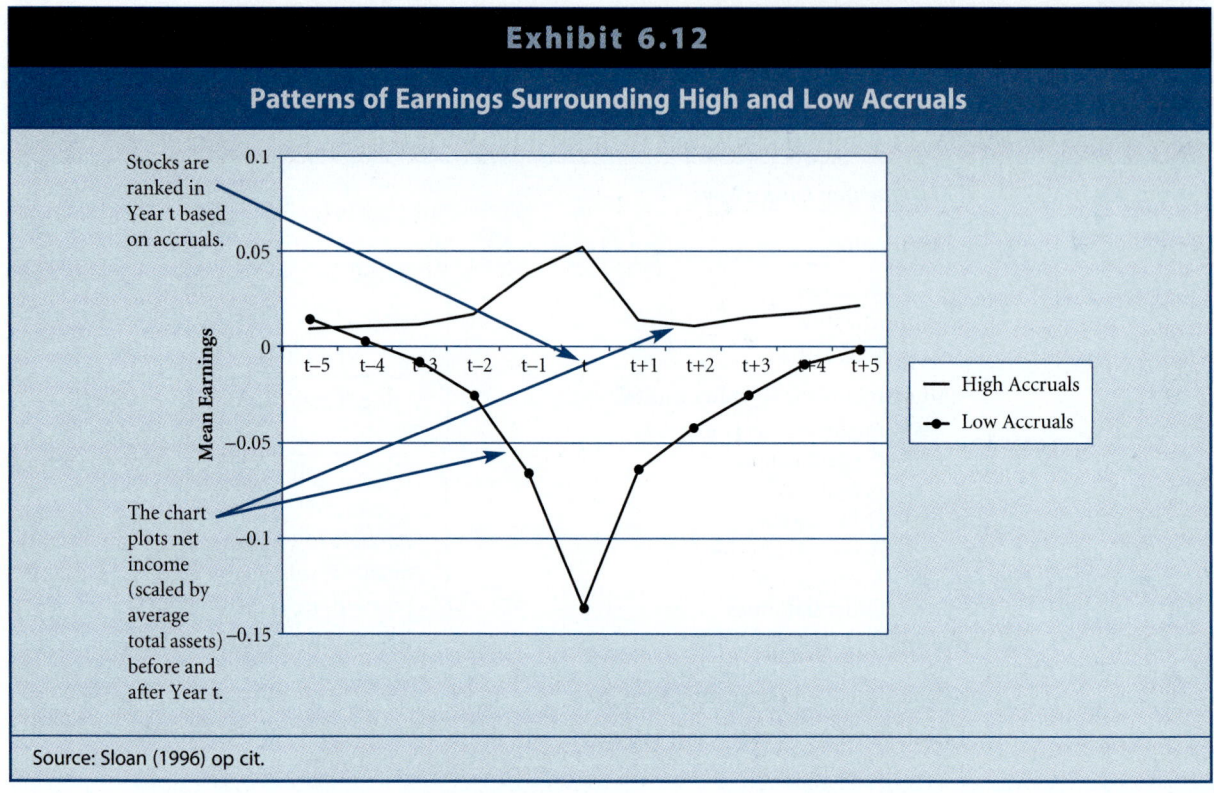

Stocks are ranked in Year t based on accruals.

The chart plots net income (scaled by average total assets) before and after Year t.

Mean Earnings

— High Accruals
— Low Accruals

Source: Sloan (1996) op cit.

in the next year. On the other side, firms with the most negative current accruals report net income that is extremely low relative to prior years, but this decline turns around over the following years. When net income is high relative to operating cash flows, we describe the firm as having recorded "*income-increasing*" accruals; when net income is low relative to operating cash flows, we describe the firm as having recorded "*income-decreasing*" accruals. Non-working capital accruals (e.g., depreciation) tend to be more persistent than working capital accruals (e.g., accounts receivable, accounts payable, inventory), which tend to go up and down and generally fluctuate around zero for mature firms.

The patterns of net income in Exhibit 6.12 indicate that when net income is high because of large income-increasing accruals (such as increases in accounts receivable and decreases in payables), the reversal of these accruals generates predictable decreases in the level of earnings in future years. The same is true for income-decreasing accruals (such as decreases in receivables and increases in payables). This should be intuitive. For example, if a firm generates a spike in sales made on credit, this increases accounts receivable and recognized sales. In the following year, the firm will have to generate incremental sales to maintain the level (or growth) in sales, which is difficult to do if the prior year's high levels were unusual or transitory. The statement of cash flows highlights the evolution of receivables by quantifying period-to-period changes in the balance. If a firm with a high increase in sales made on credit does not replenish these with more sales, the statement of cash flows in the following period will indicate a decrease in receivables. Although the collection of cash will contribute to cash flows from operations, net income will tend to fall because of the relative reduction in sales due to the non-replenishment of prior-period credit sales. Ultimately, declines in earnings are strongly associated with declines in security prices.

If investors neglect to examine the components of net income, they may fail to appreciate the fact that large earnings driven by large *income-increasing* accruals are less persistent. Similarly, they might fail to appreciate that low earnings driven by large *income-decreasing* accruals also are less persistent and generally reverse with improved earnings in future periods. If enough investors fail to fully appreciate the relation between components of current earnings and future earnings, the result may be mispricing a firm's common stock. Indeed, this describes the pattern of stock returns for the firms shown in Exhibit 6.12.

Total accruals divided by average total assets can be thought of as an inverse measure of earnings quality: the higher the measure, the lower the earnings quality in the sense that reported earnings may not be as persistent in the future and will likely decline. The lack of persistence might be due to low earnings quality in the sense that managers introduced bias into accruals, which will have to reverse under double-entry accounting, or it might be due to the tyranny of mean reversion whereby shocks like large increases in credit sales or big decreases in expenses are not sustainable. Increasingly, investors and the financial press are focusing on the link between accruals and earnings quality. For example, in an article profiling **Microsoft**'s 2009 second-quarter earnings announcement, TheStreet.com stated:

> Companies that report lukewarm results on poor earnings quality are prime candidates to miss estimates by a wide margin in future quarters due to the reversal of accruals.[46]

Exhibit 6.13 plots one- and two-year-ahead future stock returns for a ranking of firms by the sign and magnitude of accruals (scaled by average total assets) shown in Exhibit 6.12. Decile 1 consists of the 10% of firms with the highest income-increasing accruals. Decile 10 consists of the 10% of firms with the largest income-decreasing accruals. The stock returns plotted in Exhibit 6.13 are the average stock return for all firms in the decile, where each firm's return is first adjusted for the return of a portfolio of similarly sized firms. Thus, the returns are referred to as "abnormal" returns. Positive abnormal returns indicate that the firm's stock price performed much better than similar-sized firms, and negative abnormal returns indicate worse performance than similar-sized firms. Exhibit 6.13 indicates that in the first year after firms are ranked based on the magnitude of their accruals, the firms with the highest income-increasing accruals experience the worst stock returns and firms with the highest income-decreasing accruals experience the best stock returns. The plots show a similar ranking of stock returns in the second year after stocks are ranked based on accruals, but the effect diminishes somewhat. Overall, these patterns of returns are consistent with investors, on average, not realizing how important the accrual components of reported earnings are in helping them form expectations of future earnings and, as a consequence, in predicting future stock returns. As firms report quarterly results in years subsequent to large income-increasing or income-decreasing accruals, investors gradually see the turnaround in earnings that is shown in Exhibit 6.12. As this occurs, stock prices gradually adjust to the investors' revised expectations of future earnings.

---

[46]David MacDougall, "Analyst's Toolkit: Don't Hate on Microsoft," *TheStreet.com* (July 29, 2009).

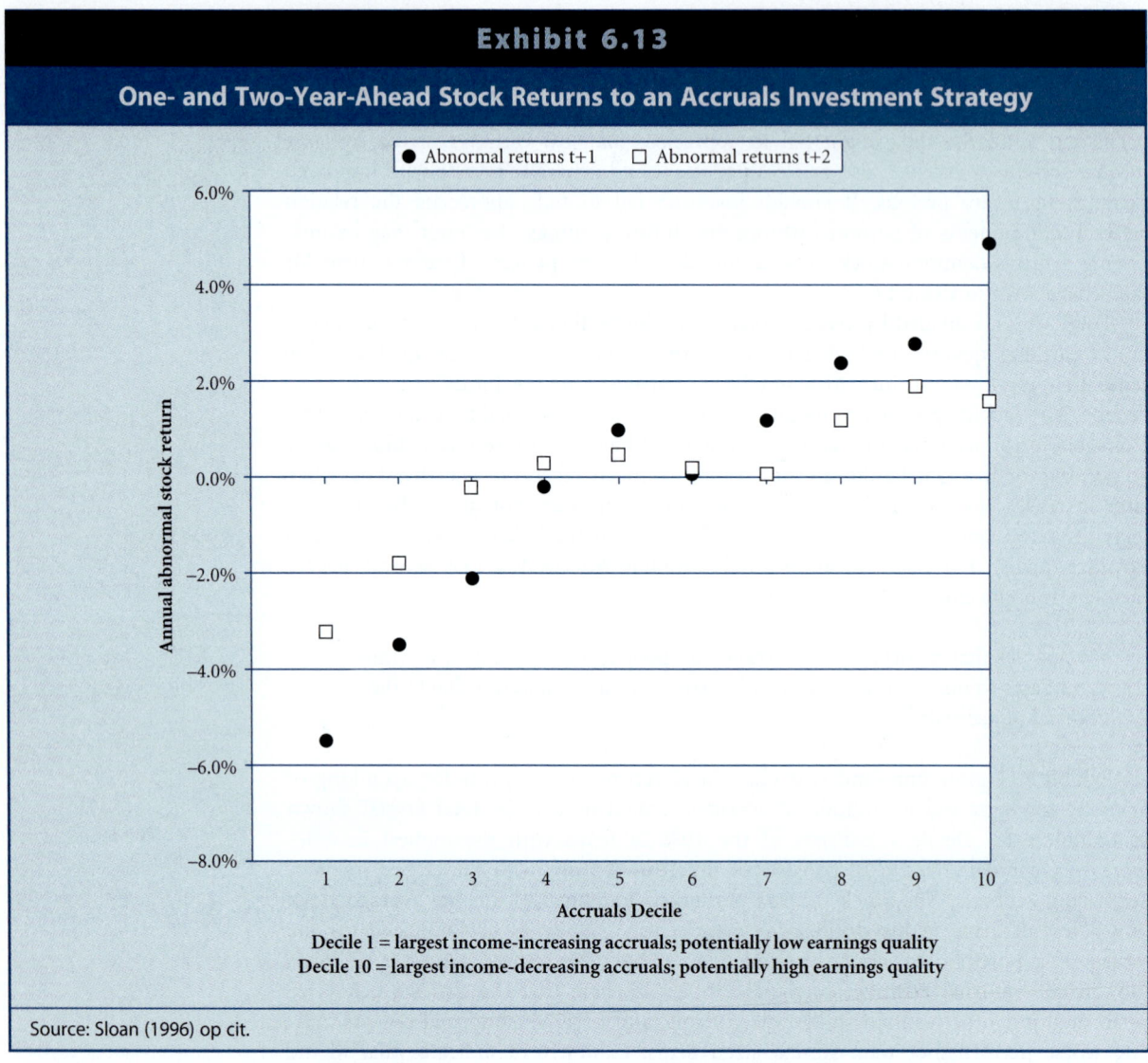

Exhibit 6.13

One- and Two-Year-Ahead Stock Returns to an Accruals Investment Strategy

● Abnormal returns t+1   □ Abnormal returns t+2

Decile 1 = largest income-increasing accruals; potentially low earnings quality
Decile 10 = largest income-decreasing accruals; potentially high earnings quality

Source: Sloan (1996) op cit.

Do Analysts Recognize These Earnings Patterns?

Analysts ought to be familiar with financial statements and be adept at understanding when earnings are temporarily high or low due to large income-increasing or income-decreasing accruals. Exhibit 6.14 provides evidence from a study by Bradshaw, Richardson, and Sloan consistent with analysts failing to understand the patterns of earnings shown in Exhibit 6.12.[47] The plot shows analysts' forecast errors for the 12 months subsequent to the ranking of firms based on accruals (as shown in Exhibit 6.12). Forecast errors are computed as the analysts' forecast of earnings per share (EPS) for a firm minus the actual reported EPS, and this difference is scaled by stock price per share so that forecast errors can be averaged across firms regardless of the level of EPS. The

---

[47]Mark T. Bradshaw, Scott A. Richardson, and Richard G. Sloan, "Do Analysts and Auditors Use Information in Accruals?" *Journal of Accounting Research* (June 2001), pp. 45–74.

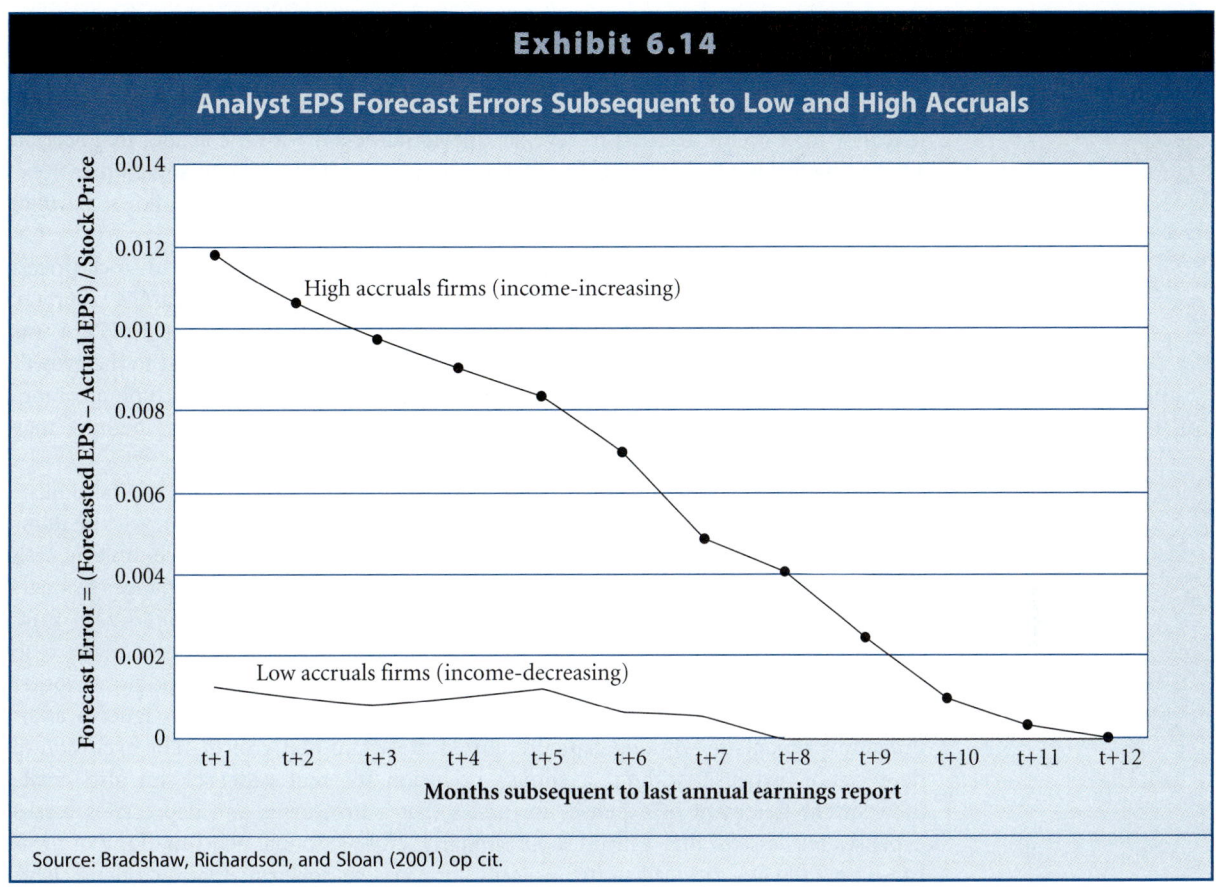

Exhibit 6.14

Analyst EPS Forecast Errors Subsequent to Low and High Accruals

High accruals firms (income-increasing)

Low accruals firms (income-decreasing)

Forecast Error = (Forecasted EPS – Actual EPS) / Stock Price

Months subsequent to last annual earnings report

Source: Bradshaw, Richardson, and Sloan (2001) op cit.

exhibit displays the average forecast errors for the highest deciles of income-increasing and income-decreasing accrual firms.

It is clear that for firms with the highest income-increasing accruals (and hence, high earnings), analysts tend to extrapolate those high earnings into the future (in the first several months), but gradually realize that the high earnings reported in the previous year are not repeating in the subsequent year. Eventually, the analysts walk down their forecasts to the amount reported, but it takes the entire 12-month period subsequent to the announcement of the previous year's earnings for them to get it right. As was shown in Exhibit 6.13, during this time, the firms' stock prices are falling as well due to the same phenomenon whereby investors are walking down their expectations and valuations from elevated levels driven by the high earnings composed of income-increasing accruals in the previous year.[48]

The patterns of earnings, stock returns, and analysts' forecasts shown in Exhibits 6.12–6.14 suggest that investors who utilize the statement of cash flows to identify circumstances in which earnings are supported by accruals that tend to reverse will have an advantage over other investors, including professional analysts.

---

[48]Note that analysts are typically optimistic in their forecasts early in a year. This optimistic bias early in a fiscal year results in the forecasts for the firms with the lowest earnings (driven by large income-decreasing accruals) being optimistic, but not nearly to the extent that they are for the income-increasing accrual firms.

A Caveat: The Relative Quality of Cash Flows, EBITDA, and Earnings

Given our previous discussion of earnings management, earnings manipulation, and the tendency for extreme accruals to reverse, one could be left with the feeling that accrual accounting yields earnings numbers that are quite deficient relative to some other measure of performance such as cash flows or a measure to approximate cash flows: *earnings before interest, taxes, depreciation, and amortization* (EBITDA).

Some analysts champion EBITDA as a measure more closely related to stock prices. These analysts view EBITDA as an approximation of a cash-based measure of pretax operating earnings. Prior to the availability of the statement of cash flows, EBITDA was a "quick and dirty" calculation for cash flows, which certainly contributed to the growth of its popularity. However, cash flows from operations or operating income are more complete measures of operating performance that are easier to calculate because they are reported directly in the financial statements.

More importantly, EBITDA excludes four significant non-working capital adjustments. The exclusion of depreciation and amortization adjusts net income for the items that, for most firms, are the largest non-working capital adjustments in computing cash flow from operations. If a firm is not growing rapidly, adjustments for changes in operating working capital accounts should be relatively small and vary around zero from year to year. The presumption in such cases is that EBITDA roughly approximates cash flow from operations. However, EBITDA can differ significantly depending on other activities of the firm. For example, for rapidly growing firms, EBITDA ignores additional investments in working capital required to sustain that growth. The exclusion of depreciation expense, without a similar exclusion for rent expense, can also create inconsistent treatment of expenses for assets that a firm owns and depreciates versus expenses for "assets" that a firm leases. Similarly, cross-sectional benchmarking of firms based on EBITDA can lead to inconsistent comparisons for firms that own depreciable assets relative to those that lease assets.

The exclusion of interest expense provides a measure of earnings independent of financing costs. The exclusion of interest in computing EBITDA has an element of logic if the analyst is interested in EBITDA as a crude measure of the firm's ability to cover the costs of leverage or if the analyst uses EBITDA for enterprise valuation using a discount rate or earnings multiple that incorporates the cost of both debt and equity capital. However, as emphasized in Chapter 4, analysts must be careful not to confuse measures of profitability at the enterprise level (e.g., ROA) versus those at the common equity level (e.g., ROE). Finally, the rationale for the exclusion of income taxes is not at all clear. Firms that generate positive earnings must pay income taxes just as they must pay suppliers, employees, and other providers of goods and services. It is difficult to construct a cogent argument for why tax expense should be ignored in the assessment of a firm's profitability.

Academic research has examined the correlation between market rates of return on common stock and (1) net income, (2) cash flow from operations, and (3) EBITDA.[49] The results of these studies indicate that stock returns are more highly correlated with net income than with either cash flow from operations or EBITDA. For example, Chapter 2 discussed research by Dechow, who examined the relative ability of cash flows and net

---

[49]Mary E. Barth, Donald P. Cram, and Karen K. Nelson, "Accruals and the Prediction of Future Cash Flows," *Accounting Review* (January 2001), pp. 27–58.

income to explain stock returns. Her study confirms that as the measurement window increases (she aggregated firm performance measures over several years), cash flows and net income become similar in their association with stock returns. Dechow showed that over long windows such as five years, both aggregate cash flows and aggregate earnings capture economics well and are closely associated with changes in stock prices. It is over short horizons (such as a quarter or a year) that net income is more closely associated with changes in stock price. Moreover, the primary conclusion supported by many studies, including Dechow's, is that "earnings better reflect firm performance than cash flows, in firms with more volatile operating, investment and financing activities."[50] Also, refer again to Exhibit 1.14 in Chapter 1, which shows that the spread in abnormal returns between increases and decreases in earnings averages 35.6%, whereas the spread between positive and negative changes in cash flows from operations is only 15.0%.

These findings are not surprising given that net income is a bottom-line measure of profitability that does not omit working capital adjustments which have information content for future cash flows. Further, if net income is negative in a given period, it is generally indicative of poor performance and value destruction. On the other hand, if cash flow from operations is negative, it is ambiguous and may reflect very good performance and value creation (for example, start-up and growth firms). In the same manner that operating cash flows omits important elements of performance, EBITDA excludes expenses that are value-relevant for profitable, capital-intensive, or leveraged firms.

Given that operating income, net income, and cash flow from operations are required disclosures, you might wonder why analysts often use EBITDA as an approximation of these measures. As noted, EBITDA not only ignores four important costs of conducting business, but also ignores changes in operating working capital accounts that can fluctuate depending on growth, operating cycles, and managerial discretion, all crucial to the assessment of firm profitability and valuation. A better measure of the cash flows of a firm can be directly obtained from the statement of cash flows.

A Model to Detect the Likelihood of Fraud

LO 6-8

Compute the Beneish Manipulation Index to assess the likelihood of earnings manipulation.

Accounting research has examined potential conditions that could enable (or possibly signal the likelihood of) fraudulent reporting. Dechow, Sloan, and Sweeney[51] examined the governance characteristics of firms subject to accounting and auditing enforcement actions by the SEC (i.e., formal charges of manipulation). They found that such firms have weak corporate governance structures, including the absence of an audit committee within their board of directors, the appointment of the founder of the company as the CEO (chief executive officer), the appointment of the CEO as chairperson of the board, and the domination of the board by insiders (employees, consultants, or individuals otherwise closely associated with the firm). The SEC enforcement actions led to declines in stock prices by an average of 9%, increases in the bid-ask spread,[52] increases

---

[50]Patricia M. Dechow, "Accounting Earnings and Cash Flows as Measures of Firm Performance: The Role of Accounting Accruals," *Journal of Accounting and Economics* (1994), p. 7.

[51]Patricia M. Dechow, Richard G. Sloan, and Amy P. Sweeney, "Causes and Consequences of Earnings Manipulation: An Analysis of Firms Subject to Enforcement Actions by the SEC," *Contemporary Accounting Research* (Spring 1996), pp. 1–36.

[52]Bid-ask spread is the difference between the highest stock price that a buyer is willing to pay and the lowest price for which a seller is willing to sell.

in the dispersions in analyst earnings forecasts, and increases in short interest,[53] each of which likely increased the firms' cost of capital. Nevertheless, governance is neither a solution nor a well-defined concept. For example, the World Council for Corporate Governance awarded **Satyam** its coveted Golden Peacock Award for Corporate Governance in 2008, shortly before it was uncovered that the company had perpetrated one of the largest financial reporting frauds in corporate history.

Messod D. Beneish developed both a twelve- and an eight-factor model to identify the financial characteristics of firms likely to engage in earnings manipulation:[54]

- The twelve-factor model relies on a combination of financial statement items and changes in stock prices for a firm's shares.
- The eight-factor model uses only financial statement items.

Beneish developed the models using data for firms subject to SEC enforcement actions related to fraudulent accounting reports.

Developing these models involves identifying characteristics of firms likely to manipulate earnings, selecting financial statement ratios or other measures of these characteristics, and then using probit regressions to select the significant factors and the appropriate coefficient for each factor.[55] The general approach is to estimate a probit regression equation to obtain coefficients on factors associated with earnings manipulation, and then use those coefficients along with a firm's measured factors to calculate a manipulation score, which we will denote y. A probit model converts y into a probability using a standardized normal distribution and a specified prior probability of earnings manipulation. The command NORMSDIST in Excel®, when applied to a particular value of y, converts it to the appropriate probability value. Positive coefficients increase the probability of earnings manipulation.

Beneish's eight factors and the rationale for their inclusion are discussed below. Note that some of these factors attempt to capture the existence of earnings manipulation (e.g., *DSRI*), whereas other factors attempt to capture the existence of heightened incentives managers might face that might lead to earnings manipulation (e.g., *GMI*).

1. **Days' Sales in Receivables Index (DSRI).** This index relates the ratio of accounts receivable at the end of the current year as a percentage of sales for the current year to the corresponding amounts for the preceding year. A large increase in accounts receivable as a percentage of sales might indicate an overstatement of accounts receivable and sales during the current year to boost earnings. Such an increase also might result from a change in the firm's credit policy (for example, liberalizing credit terms).

2. **Gross Margin Index (GMI).** This index relates gross margin (that is, sales minus cost of goods sold) as a percentage of sales last year to the gross margin as a percentage of sales for the current year. A decline in the gross margin percentage will

---

[53]Short interest is the number of shares investors have sold short but not yet covered or closed out. It represents market sentiment about whether a stock's price will fall.

[54]Messod D. Beneish, "Detecting GAAP Violations: Implications for Assessing Earnings Management among Firms with Extreme Financial Performance," *Journal of Accounting and Public Policy* (1997), pp. 271–309. For an instructional case applying this model to an actual company, see Christine I. Wiedman, "Instructional Case: Detecting Earnings Manipulation," *Issues in Accounting Education* (February 1999), pp. 145–176. Also see Messod D. Beneish, "A Note on Wiedman's (1999) Instructional Case: Detecting Earnings Manipulation," *Issues in Accounting Education* (May 1999), pp. 369–370. Messod D. Beneish, "The Detection of Earnings Manipulation," Financial Analyst Journal (September/October 1999), pp. 24–36.

[55]This process is similar to the approaches for identifying predictors of bankruptcy, described in Chapter 5.

result in an index greater than 1.0. Firms with weaker profitability this year are more likely to engage in earnings manipulation.

3. ***Asset Quality Index (AQI).*** Asset quality refers to the proportion of total assets comprising assets other than (1) current assets; (2) property, plant, and equipment; and (3) investments in securities. The remaining assets include intangibles for which future benefits are less certain than for current assets and property, plant, and equipment. The AQI equals the proportion of these potentially lower quality assets during the current year relative to the preceding year. An increase in the proportion might suggest an increased effort to capitalize and defer costs the firm should have expensed.

4. ***Sales Growth Index (SGI).*** This index equals sales of the current year relative to sales of the preceding year. Growth does not necessarily imply manipulation. However, growing companies usually rely on external financing more than do mature companies. The need for low-cost external financing might motivate managers to manipulate sales and earnings. Growing companies are often young and tend to have less-developed governance practices to monitor managers' manipulation efforts.

5. ***Depreciation Index (DEPI).*** This index equals depreciation expense as a percentage of net property, plant, and equipment before depreciation for the preceding year relative to the corresponding percentage for the current year. A ratio greater than 1.0 indicates that the firm has slowed the rate of depreciation, perhaps by lengthening depreciable lives, thereby increasing earnings.

6. ***Selling and Administrative Expense Index (SAI).*** This index equals selling and administrative expenses as a percentage of sales for the current year to the corresponding percentage for the preceding year. An index greater than 1.0 might suggest increased marketing expenditures that would lead to increased sales in future periods. Firms not able to sustain the sales growth might be induced to engage in earnings manipulation. An alternative interpretation is that an index greater than 1.0 suggests that the firm has not taken advantage of capitalizing various costs; instead, it has expensed them. Firms attempting to manipulate earnings would defer costs, and the index value would be less than 1.0. If this latter explanation is descriptive, the coefficient on this variable will be negative. Thus, the interpretation of this component of Beneish's fraud model is conditional.

7. ***Leverage Index (LVGI).*** This index equals the proportion of total financing comprising current liabilities and long-term debt for the current year relative to the proportion for the preceding year. An increase in the proportion of debt likely subjects a firm to a greater risk of violating debt covenants and the need to manipulate earnings to avoid the violation.

8. ***Total Accruals to Total Assets (TATA).*** Total accruals equals the difference between income from continuing operations and cash flow from operations. Dividing total accruals by total assets at the end of the year scales total accruals across firms and across time. Beneish used this variable as an indicator of the extent to which earnings result from accruals instead of from cash flows. A large excess of income from continuing operations over cash flow from operations indicates that accruals play a large part in measuring income. Accruals can serve as a means of manipulating earnings.

Beneish developed a weighted probit model that takes the proportion of earnings manipulations into account and an unweighted probit model. We illustrate the unweighted model in this section and FSAP uses the unweighted model to compute

Beneish's Manipulation Index and the corresponding probabilities of earnings manipulation. The unweighted model tends to classify more nonmanipulating firms as manipulators (higher Type II error), but lowers the most costly Type I error rate. The value of y is computed as follows:

$$y = -4.840 + (0.920 \times DSRI) + (0.528 \times GMI) + (0.404 \times AQI) + (0.892 \times SGI)$$
$$+ (0.115 \times DEPI) - (0.172 \times SAI) - (0.327 \times LVGI) + (4.670 \times TATA)$$

The coefficient on SAI is negative, suggesting that a lower selling and administrative expense to sales percentage in the current year relative to the preceding year increases the likelihood that the firm engaged in earnings manipulation to boost earnings. The coefficient on the leverage variable also is negative. A decrease in the proportion of debt in the capital structure may suggest decreased ability to obtain funds from borrowing and the need to engage in earnings manipulation to portray a healthier firm. The coefficients on the SAI and $LVGI$ variables were not statistically significant. However, one cannot interpret the sign or statistical significance of a coefficient in a multivariate model independent of the other variables in the model; so these factors must be included.

Application of Beneish's Model to Sunbeam Corporation

We illustrate the application of Beneish's probit model to **Sunbeam Corporation**'s financial statements. Sunbeam manufactures countertop kitchen appliances and barbecue grills. Its sales growth and profitability slowed considerably in the mid-1990s, and the firm experienced market price declines for its common stock. The firm hired Al Dunlap in mid-1996 as CEO. Known as "Chainsaw Al," he had developed a reputation for dispassionately cutting costs and strategically redirecting troubled companies. Dunlap laid off half the workforce, closed or consolidated more than half of Sunbeam's factories, and divested several businesses in 1996 and 1997. He also announced major growth initiatives centering on new products and corporate acquisitions.

The reported results for 1997 showed significant improvement over 1996. Sales increased 18.7% while gross margin increased from 8.5% to 28.3%. The stock price more than doubled between the announcement of Dunlap's hiring in mid-1996 and the end of 1997.

The turnaround appeared to proceed according to plan until the firm announced earnings for the first quarter of 1998, seven quarters into the turnaround effort. To the surprise of analysts and the stock market, Sunbeam reported a net loss for the quarter. Close scrutiny by analysts and the media suggested that Sunbeam might have manipulated earnings in 1997. The SEC instituted a formal investigation into this possibility in mid-1997. Sunbeam responded in October 1998 by restating its financial statements from the fourth quarter of 1996 to the first quarter of 1998. The restatements revealed that Sunbeam had engaged in various actions that boosted earnings for 1997. The actions included the following:

- Sunbeam instituted "early buy" and "bill and hold" programs in 1997 to encourage retailers to purchase inventory from Sunbeam during the last few months of 1997. Sunbeam did not adequately provide for returns and canceled transactions, resulting in an overstatement of sales and net income for 1997.
- Sunbeam overstated a restructuring charge in the fourth quarter of 1996 for expenses that should have appeared on the income statement for 1997.
- Sunbeam understated bad debt expense for 1997.

Exhibit 6.15

Application of Beneish's Earnings Manipulation Model to Sunbeam Corporation

Value of Variable Before Applying Coefficient	Originally Reported		Restated	
	1996	**1997**	**1996**	**1997**
Days' sales in receivables index	1.020	1.167	1.020	0.982
Gross margin index	2.403	0.300	2.303	0.393
Asset quality index	0.912	0.928	0.912	0.919
Sales growth index	0.968	1.187	0.968	1.090
Depreciation index	0.752	1.284	0.752	1.290
Selling and administrative expense index	1.608	0.516	1.665	0.632
Leverage index	1.457	0.795	1.457	0.917
Total accruals/Total assets	(0.196)	0.117	(0.208)	0.055
Beneish's manipulation y value	(2.983)	(1.827)	(3.101)	(2.388)
Probability of manipulation	0.143%	3.386%	0.096%	0.848%

Note: The amounts in this table are rounded to three decimal places.

Exhibit 6.15 shows the application of Beneish's earnings manipulation model to the originally reported financial statement amounts and the restated amounts for 1996 and 1997.[56]

Selecting the cutoff probability that signals earnings manipulation involves trade-offs between Type I and Type II errors in a manner similar to that of Beaver's bankruptcy prediction tests discussed in Chapter 5:

- A Type I error involves failing to identify a firm as an income manipulator when it turns out to be one.
- A Type II error involves identifying a firm as an income manipulator when it turns out not to be one.

The Type I error is more costly to the investor than a Type II error. The cutoff probability depends on the analyst's view of the relative cost of the Type I error compared to a Type II error. That is, how much more costly is it to classify an actual earnings manipulator as a nonmanipulator than to classify an actual nonmanipulator as a manipulator? A Type I error can result in an investor losing *all* of the investment in a firm when the manipulation comes to light. In contrast, misclassifying an actual nonmanipulator results only in a forgone investment opportunity, the amount being the return that could have been earned had an investment been made in the firm. However, the investor presumably invested the funds in another firm. Thus, as with bankruptcy prediction, the Type I error is more costly. If a particular investment makes up a small proportion of an investor's diversified portfolio of investments, a Type I error is less costly than if the investment comprises a more significant proportion of a less diversified

---

[56]The website for this book contains an Excel spreadsheet called Beneish's Manipulation Index for use in calculating the probability of earnings manipulation using Beneish's probit model. This spreadsheet is adapted from one prepared by Professor Christine I. Wiedman (see Wiedman 1999, *op. cit*). FSAP also computes Beneish's Manipulation Index and the corresponding probability of earnings manipulation.

portfolio of investments. The cutoff probabilities for various relative mixtures of Type I and Type II error costs follow.

Cost of Type I Error Relative to Type II Error	Cutoff Probability
10:1	6.85%
20:1	3.76%
30:1	3.76%
40:1 or higher	2.94%

Exhibit 6.15 indicates that the probability of manipulation for Sunbeam for 1996 is 0.143% based on its originally reported amounts. This probability level falls well below the cutoff probabilities listed previously for all mixtures of Type I and Type II errors; therefore, it does not suggest earnings manipulation. On the other hand, the probability for 1997 jumps to 3.386%. Under the assumption of a 40:1 Type I to Type II cost relation, you would conclude that Sunbeam is a manipulator. An examination of changes in the individual variables between 1996 and 1997 signals the nature of the manipulation that might have occurred. The total accruals to total assets index increased significantly. Sunbeam reported a significant increase in income from continuing operations from a net loss of $196.7 million in 1996 to a net profit of $123.1 million in 1997, but cash flow from operations turned from $13.3 million in 1996 to a negative $8.2 million in 1997. Buildups of accounts receivable and inventories are major reasons for the negative cash flow from operations in 1997. The days' sales in receivables index increased between these two years, consistent with the buildup of receivables related to the early buy-and-bill and hold programs. The sale growth index also increased, consistent with the aggressive recognition of revenues. The depreciation index increased between the two years, but the firm's financial statements and notes provide no obvious explanation to suggest manipulation. The gross margin index improved significantly between the two years, moderating the increased probability of earnings manipulation. However, this improvement is misleading because of failure to provide adequately for returns and canceled transactions.

Exhibit 6.15 indicates that the probabilities of manipulation based on the restated data are below the cutoff points for 1996 and 1997. The most important difference between the reported and restated probabilities arises for 1997. The downward restatement of income from continuing operations results in fewer accruals, moderating the influence of this variable on the manipulation index. Interestingly, the model would not indicate that Sunbeam was an earnings manipulator if it had reported accurately to begin with (that is, reported the restated data). Initially reporting the restated data, however, would likely have decreased Sunbeam's stock price, which Dunlap presumably wanted to avoid.

The recent revelations of corporate reporting abuses add to the importance of assessing whether firms have intentionally manipulated earnings. Academic research on earnings manipulation is at an early stage of development. The data in the studies discussed previously deal with reporting violations prior to the mid-1990s. The business environment since that time has changed dramatically, particularly for technology-based companies. Additional research in this area might be expected in coming years.

The assessment of earnings manipulation risk is not restricted to the construction of financial ratios. Also relevant are qualitative factors that might change the incentives of managers to incur the potential costs of manipulating earnings, such as an increase in compensation based on stock options, an expectation of growth, or extensive related-party transactions.

Financial Reporting Worldwide

LO 6-9

Explain the effect of two sets of accounting rules (IFRS and U.S. GAAP) on worldwide financial comparability.

Thus far, we have identified many accounting quality and comparability issues. The concerns discussed in the chapter to this point apply equally to firms that follow reporting systems employed outside of the United States, such as IFRS. However, important additional concerns also exist in comparing financial data for firms that operate in different countries.

Cross-national analysis of firms entails a two-step approach:

1. Achieve comparability of the reporting methods and accounting principles employed by the firms under scrutiny.
2. Understand corporate strategies, institutional structures, and cultural practices unique to the countries in which the firms operate.

Beginning in 2005, the financial statements of firms in the European Community were required to conform to IFRS pronouncements. In addition, the convergence of IFRS and U.S. GAAP will be central to achieving worldwide conformity of financial reporting. The IASB and FASB pledged to use their best efforts to make existing U.S. and IASB standards fully compatible as soon as practicable and to coordinate their future work programs to ensure that once achieved, compatibility is maintained. For example, the "Projects" section of the FASB website (fasb.org) indicates projects that are being jointly addressed by the IASB and FASB.

Firms headquartered outside of the United States that have debt or equity securities traded in U.S. capital markets are required to file a Form 10-K using U.S. GAAP or a Form 20-F report with the SEC each year. In past years, Form 20-F had to include a reconciliation of shareholders' equity and net income as reported under IFRS (or standards of the firm's local country) with U.S. GAAP. With this information, the analyst could convert the financial statements of a non-U.S. firm to achieve comparable accounting principles with U.S. firms.

Preparation of the reconciliation—essentially requiring a foreign filer in the United States to maintain two sets of financial records—is a costly endeavor and a potential deterrent to companies interested in listing on U.S. exchanges. Thus, the SEC recently relaxed the reporting requirements of non-U.S. filers and now accepts financial reports prepared in accordance with IFRS as legislated by the IASB without reconciliation to U.S. GAAP. SEC Final Rule No. 33-8879 provides U.S. investors with two sets of accounting principles—IFRS and U.S. GAAP. The elimination of the reconciliation is a controversial issue, because research suggests that material differences between IFRS and U.S. GAAP remain and eliminating the reconciliation diminishes the relevant information set available to investors in the United States and around the world.[57]

Exhibit 6.16 presents the Form 20-F reconciliations for **Ericsson**, a Swedish cell phone manufacturer. Ericsson provides extensive discussion of each reconciling item in its Form 20-F filing in Note 32, "Reconciliation to Accounting Principles Generally Accepted in the United States." In fact, the note is more than five pages long.

Achieving comparability in reporting is important to the analysis of multinational firms, but the data must be carefully interpreted. Analysis of multinational firms is complicated by the fact that the environments in which the firms operate may vary

---

[57]Not all firms domiciled in non-U.S. locations use IFRS. Many are required to file financial statements using home-country standards or IFRS modified for local laws and preferences, and thus would be required to reconcile to U.S. GAAP if listed on U.S. exchanges.

Exhibit 6.16

Ericsson
Form 20-F Reconciliations
(amounts in millions)

	2003	2002	2001
Adjustments to Shareholders' Equity			
Reported shareholders' equity	SEK 60,481	SEK 73,607	SEK 68,587
Capitalization of software	6,409	11,652	16,502
Capitalization of interest expense	133	172	211
Pensions	(299)	440	99
Goodwill	2,700	1,064	—
Hedging	3,509	2,744	(2,196)
Restructuring costs	1,442	217	1,458
Sale-leaseback	(1,381)	(2,063)	(2,176)
Deferred taxes	(3,347)	(4,021)	(4,487)
Other	316	(609)	(197)
Stockholders' equity according to U.S. GAAP	SEK 69,963	SEK 83,203	SEK 77,801
Adjustments to Net Income			
Reported net loss	SEK (10,844)	SEK (19,013)	SEK (21,264)
Restructuring costs	1,225	(1,240)	(1,642)
Capitalization of software			
Development costs	(5,153)	(4,940)	(2,135)
Goodwill amortization	1,636	1,064	—
Pensions	(840)	459	1,006
Hedging	1,603	2,884	(2,233)
Sale-leaseback	682	113	(815)
Deferred income taxes	533	966	2,042
Other	561	(211)	638
Net income according to U.S. GAAP	SEK (10,597)	SEK (19,918)	SEK (24,403)

Source: Ericsson, Form 20-F for the Fiscal Year Ended December 31, 2003.

extensively across countries. A firm may implement operational strategies in its home country that it cannot implement in other countries. Institutional arrangements, such as significant alliances with banks and extensive intercorporate holdings, may be common in one country but not in another. Cultural characteristics may exist in one country that affect how firms do business in that country—with those same characteristics foreign to other business settings.[58]

---

[58]See Don Herrmann, Tatsuo Inoue, and Wayne Thomas, "Are There Benefits to Restating Japanese Financial Statements According to U.S. GAAP?" *Journal of Financial Statement Analysis* (Fall 1996), pp. 61–73, for an example of environmental factors that must be considered in order to effectively interpret foreign financial statements even after adjusting them to be comparable to U.S. GAAP.

Summary

The financial analysis framework discussed in Chapters 1–5 and the discussion of forecasting and valuation presented in Chapters 10–14 assume that a firm's reported financial statement data accurately reflect the economic effects of a firm's decisions. Another assumption is that the financial data are informative about the firm's likely future profitability and risk. This chapter develops the concept of accounting quality as the basis for assessing the information content of reported financial statement data and for adjusting that data before assessing a firm's profitability and risk or forecasting or valuing the firm.

We discuss earnings management, liability and asset measurement and reporting quality, and the conditions that can trigger low accounting quality. The concepts of accounting quality and earnings management often are linked in discussions of the need to adjust financial data to better reflect its economic information content. In Chapters 7–9, we illustrate the financial reporting for financing, investing, and operating activities and we examine accounting quality in greater detail.

Questions, Exercises, Problems, and Cases

Questions and Exercises

6.1 Concept of Earnings Quality. The concept of accounting quality has several dimensions, but two characteristics often dominate: the accounting information should be a fair representation of performance for the reporting period, and it should provide relevant information to forecast expected future earnings. Provide a specific example of poor accounting quality that would hinder the forecasting of expected future earnings.

`LO 6-1`

6.2 Balance Sheet Quality and Earnings Quality. How are balance sheet quality and earnings quality related? Provide a specific example of a management judgment, estimate, or choice that could decrease both balance sheet and earnings quality. Be specific as to how the judgment decreased quality in each of the two financial statements. Give a different example of how a management judgment, estimate, or choice could increase balance sheet quality, but potentially impair earnings quality.

`LO 6-2`

6.3 Concept of Earnings Management. Define earnings management. Discuss why it is difficult to discern whether a firm does in fact practice earnings management.

`LO 6-3`

6.4 Own Debt Profits. Most economists describe three determinants of the interest rates on a borrower's debt: a real interest rate, which is a charge for using capital; an adjustment for expected inflation to insure that debt is repaid in dollars having the same purchasing power; and an adjustment for the borrower's credit risk, which is intended to compensate the lender for the possibility that the borrower will default. Certain companies book gains and losses on their own debt on the income statement due to a revaluation of debt to fair value. For example, if expectations for inflation were to rise, the appropriate interest rate to charge borrowers would rise above the contractual historical interest rate initially used to value and record the debt. If the debt is adjusted to fair value (i.e., rediscounted at the new higher interest rate), the debt book value falls, and because a liability has decreased, a gain is recorded on the income statement. The counterparty to the debt (e.g., the lender) records a loss. These adjustments can be extremely large for banks. For example, **Citi**'s 2011 third quarter net income

`LO 6-5, LO 6-6`

was $3.7 billion, which included a $1.9 billion gain from revaluing its own debt (before tax) in revenues and income. In Citi's case, the gain was driven from a widening in its credit-default swap spreads, which is an indication of its higher probability of default on its obligations and derivative contracts. How should an analyst view gains on the revaluation of a company's own debt due to changes in its credit risk? How would a debtor realize such gains (i.e., how does such a gain affect cash flows)? Is the gain a persistent component of earnings?

LO 6-4, LO 6-5   **6.5 Incentives to Manage the Balance Sheet.** Assume that a corporation needs to enter the private debt market to raise funds for plant expansion. The corporation expects debt covenants to place restrictions on the levels of its current ratio and total-liabilities-to-assets ratio. Considering the accounts that comprise these ratios, give examples of accounting estimates, accounting judgments, and structured transactions that the lender should examine closely.

LO 6-3   **6.6 Incentives to Manage Earnings Upward.** Identify conditions that would lead an analyst to expect that management might attempt to manage earnings upward.

LO 6-3   **6.7 Incentives to Manage Earnings Downward.** Identify conditions that would lead an analyst to expect that management might attempt to manage earnings downward.

LO 6-6   **6.8 Criteria to Identify Nonrecurring Items.** The chapter discusses eight items that occur infrequently but that can have a large impact on financial statements. What criteria should an analyst employ to assess whether to include or eliminate items from the financial statements related to these topics?

LO 6-6   **6.9 Restating Earnings for Litigation Loss. Rock of Ages, Inc.,** is the largest integrated granite quarrier, manufacturer, and retailer of finished granite memorials in North America. The firm reported a net loss for 2004 of $3.2 million. In 2004, the firm reported a pretax litigation settlement loss of $6.5 million, and management stated that, in its opinion, the litigation settlement loss did not reflect the current year's operations because it was the first year in five years that the firm reported such a loss. (Rock of Ages' exclusion of an item from the calculation of net income is an example of what the financial press calls "reporting pro forma earnings.") Calculate pro forma earnings for 2004 excluding the settlement costs and speculate on management's reasoning as to why it believes that pro forma earnings is a better measure of performance for Rock of Ages. State any assumptions you make in your calculations.

LO 6-6   **6.10 Reporting Impairment and Restructuring Charges. Checkpoint Systems** is a leading provider of source tagging, handheld labeling systems, retail merchandising systems, and bar-code labeling systems. In a press release, Checkpoint stated the following:

> GAAP reported net loss for the fourth quarter of 2004 was $29.3 million, or $0.78 per diluted share, compared to net earnings of $4.5 million, or $0.13 per diluted share, for the fourth quarter 2003. Excluding impairment and restructuring charges, net of tax, the Company's net income for the fourth quarter 2004 was $0.30 per diluted share, compared to $0.27 per diluted share in the fourth quarter 2003.

Calculate the amount of the impairment and restructuring charges Checkpoint reported in 2004 and 2003. Discuss why the firm reported earnings both including and excluding impairment and restructuring charges.

6.11 Concept of a Peripheral Activity. Firms often enter into transactions that are peripheral to their core operations but generate gains and losses that must be reported on the income statement. Provide an example in which a gain generated from the sale of an equity security may be labeled a peripheral activity by one firm but is considered a core activity by another firm.

LO 6-6

6.12 Reporting Impairment Charges. Financial accounting rules require firms to assess whether they will recover carrying amounts of long-lived assets and, if not, to write down the assets to their fair value and recognize an impairment loss in income from continuing operations. Impairment charges often appear as a separate line item on the income statement of companies that experience reductions in the future benefits originally anticipated from the long-lived assets. Conduct a search to identify a firm (other than those given in this chapter) that has recently reported an impairment charge. Discuss how the firm (a) reported the charge on the income statement, (b) determined the amount of the charge, and (c) used cash related to the charge.

LO 6-6

6.13 Effect of Alternative Accounting Standards on Financial Statement Analysis. **Nestlé Group**, a multinational food products firm based in Switzerland, recently issued its financial statements. The auditor's opinion attached to the financial statements stated the following: "In our opinion, the financial statements for the year ended 31 December 2012 comply with Swiss law and the Company's Articles of Incorporation. In the notes to its financial statements, Nestlé's states that its financial reports are prepared using IFRS standards. One of Nestlé's competitors is **PepsiCo**, which prepares financial reports following U.S. GAAP. Describe the necessary steps an analyst should consider to develop comparable accounting data when conducting a profitability and risk analysis of these two firms.

LO 6-9

6.14 Accounting for Loss Contingencies. Loss contingencies may or may not give rise to accounting liabilities. Financial reporting requires firms to recognize a loss contingency when two criteria are met. Describe the two criteria and provide an example in which applying the criteria would trigger booking the loss contingency as an accounting liability.

LO 6-4

6.15 Securitization of Receivables. Firms such as **Deere & Company** and **Macy's, Inc.**, often sell their receivables as a means of obtaining financing. Should firms selling receivables remove the receivables from the balance sheet, or should the receivables remain on the balance sheet? Should the firms recognize a liability in the amount of the cash received for the receivables? Describe the applicable criteria to determine whether the transfer of receivables can be recorded as a sale.

LO 6-4

Problems and Cases

6.16 Achieving Off-Balance-Sheet Financing. *(Adapted from materials by R. Dieter, D. Landsittel, J. Stewart, and A. Wyatt)* Diviney Company wants to raise $50 million cash but for various reasons does not want to do so in a way that results in a newly recorded liability. The firm is sufficiently solvent and profitable, so its bank is willing to lend up to $50 million at the prime interest rate. Diviney's financial executives have devised six different plans, described in the following sections.

LO 6-4

TRANSFER OF RECEIVABLES WITH RECOURSE

Diviney will transfer to Condon Company its long-term accounts receivable, which call for payments over the next two years. Condon will pay an amount equal to the present value of the receivables, minus an allowance for uncollectibles, as well as a discount, because it is paying now but will collect cash later. Diviney must repurchase from Condon at face value any receivables that become uncollectible in excess of the allowance. In addition, Diviney may repurchase any of the receivables not yet due at face value minus a discount specified by formula and based on the prime rate at the time of the initial transfer. (This option permits Diviney to benefit if an unexpected drop in interest rates occurs after the transfer.) The accounting issue is whether the transfer is a sale (in which Diviney increases Cash, reduces Accounts Receivable, and recognizes expense or loss on transfer) or merely a loan collateralized by the receivables (in which Diviney increases Cash and increases Notes Payable at the time of transfer).

PRODUCT FINANCING ARRANGEMENT

Diviney will transfer inventory to Condon, which will store the inventory in a public warehouse. Condon may use the inventory as collateral for its own borrowings, the proceeds from which will be used to pay Diviney. Diviney will pay storage costs and will repurchase the entire inventory within the next four years at contractually fixed prices plus interest accrued for the time elapsed between the transfer and later repurchase. The accounting issue is whether the inventory is sold to Condon, with later repurchases treated as new acquisitions for Diviney's inventory, or whether the transaction is merely a loan, with the inventory remaining on Diviney's balance sheet.

THROUGHPUT CONTRACT

Diviney wants a branch line of a railroad built from the main rail line to carry raw material directly to its plant. It could, of course, borrow the funds and build the branch line itself. Instead, it will sign an agreement with the railroad to ship specified amounts of material each month for ten years. Even if Diviney does not ship the specified amounts of material, it will pay the agreed shipping costs. The railroad will take the contract to its bank and, using it as collateral, borrow the funds to build the branch line. The accounting issue is whether Diviney should increase an asset for future rail services and increase a liability for payments to the railroad. The alternative is to make no accounting entry except when Diviney makes payments to the railroad.

CONSTRUCTION PARTNERSHIP

Diviney and Mission Company will jointly build a plant to manufacture chemicals that both need in their production processes. Each will contribute $5 million to the project, called Chemical. Chemical will borrow another $40 million from a bank, with Diviney being the only guarantor of the debt. Diviney and Mission are each to contribute equally to future operating expenses and debt service payments of Chemical, but in return for its guaranteeing the debt, Diviney will have an option to purchase Mission's interest for $20 million four years hence. The accounting issue is whether Diviney should recognize a liability for the funds borrowed by Chemical. Because of the debt guarantee, debt service payments ultimately will be Diviney's responsibility. Alternatively, the debt guarantee would be treated as a commitment merely to be disclosed in the notes to Diviney's financial statements.

RESEARCH AND DEVELOPMENT PARTNERSHIP

Diviney will contribute a laboratory and preliminary findings about a potentially profitable gene-splicing discovery to a partnership, called Venture. Venture will raise funds by selling the remaining interest in the partnership to outside investors for $2 million and borrowing $48 million from a bank, with Diviney guaranteeing the debt. Although Venture will operate under Diviney's management, it will be free to sell the results of its further discoveries and development efforts to anyone, including Diviney. Diviney is not obligated to purchase any of Venture's output. The accounting issue is whether Diviney would recognize the liability.

HOTEL FINANCING

Diviney owns and operates a profitable hotel. It could use the hotel as collateral for a conventional mortgage loan. Instead, it considers selling the hotel to a partnership for $50 million cash. The partnership will sell ownership interests to outside investors for $5 million and borrow $45 million from a bank on a conventional mortgage loan, using the hotel as collateral. Diviney guarantees the debt. The accounting issue is whether Diviney would record the liability for the guaranteed debt of the partnership.

REQUIRED

Discuss the appropriate treatment of each proposed arrangement from the viewpoint of the auditor, who must apply U.S. GAAP in deciding whether the transaction will result in a liability to be recorded or whether note disclosure will suffice. Does U.S. GAAP reporting result in an accurate portrayal of the economics of the arrangement in each case? Explain.

6.17 Accounting Scandals. Recent years have witnessed some of the most significant accounting scandals in history. For each scandal listed in Exhibit 6.17, identify how balance sheet quality and earnings quality were impaired.

`LO 6-5`

Exhibit 6.17	
Accounting Scandals **(Problem 6.17)**	
Scandal	**Alleged Accounting Wrongdoing**
Waste Management (1988; waste management industry)	Falsely increased the useful lives of long-lived tangible assets
Enron (2001; energy)	Underreported balance sheet long-term debt
WorldCom (2002; telecommunications)	Capitalized rather than expensed expenditures to maintain transmission lines
AIG (2003; health care)	Booked debt as revenue
Lehman Brothers (2008; financial services)	Sold toxic assets (i.e., financial investments) to other banks with a buyback agreement, removing the toxic assets from its books
Saytam (2009; IT and accounting services)	Created fictitious revenue recognition journal entries

6.18 Adjusting for Unusual Income Statement and Classification Items.
`LO 6-6`

Henry Company is a marketer of branded foods to retail and foodservice channels. Exhibit 6.18 presents Henry's income statements for Year 10, Year 11, and Year 12.

Notes to the financial statements reveal the following information:

1. **Gain on sale of a portion of the branded product line.** In Year 10, Henry completed the sale of a portion of one of its branded product lines for $735 million. The transaction resulted in a pretax gain of $464.5 million. The sale did not qualify as a discontinued operation. Henry did not disclose the tax effect of the gain reported in Exhibit 6.18.
2. **Extraordinary loss.** In Year 11, Henry experienced an extraordinary loss when a subsidiary was expropriated during a military coup in a previously stable country. The loss was $17 million, net of income taxes of $10 million.

Exhibit 6.18

Henry Company
Income Statement
(amounts in millions)
(Problem 6.18)

	Year 12	Year 11	Year 10
Sales	$ 9,431	$ 8,821	$ 8,939
Gain on sale of branded product line	—	—	465
Cost of goods sold	(6,094)	(5,884)	(5,789)
Selling and administrative expenses	(1,746)	(1,955)	(1,882)
Interest income	27	23	25
Interest expense	(294)	(333)	(270)
Other income (expense)	(45)	1	(25)
Income before Income Taxes and Cumulative Effect of Accounting Changes	$ 1,279	$ 673	$ 1,463
Income tax expense	(445)	(178)	(573)
Income before Extraordinary Item	$ 834	$ 495	$ 890
Extraordinary loss (net of taxes)	—	(17)	—
Net Income	$ 834	$ 478	$ 890

3. **Sale and promotion costs.** In Year 11, Henry changed the classification of certain sale and promotion incentives provided to customers and consumers. In the past, Henry classified these incentives as selling and administrative expenses (see Exhibit 6.18), with the gross amount of the revenue associated with the incentives reported in sales. Beginning in Year 11, Henry changed to reporting the incentives as a reduction of revenues. As a result of this change, the firm reduced reported revenues by $693 million in Year 12, $610 million in Year 11, and $469 million in Year 10. The firm stated that selling and administrative expenses were "correspondingly reduced such that net earnings were not affected." Exhibit 6.18 already reflects the adjustments to sales revenues and selling and administrative expenses for Years 10 through 12.
4. **Tax rate.** The U.S. federal statutory income tax rate was 35% for each of the years presented in Exhibit 6.18.

REQUIRED

a. Discuss whether you would adjust for each of the following items when using earnings to forecast the future profitability of Henry:
   (1) Gain on sale of a portion of the branded product line
   (2) Extraordinary loss
b. Indicate the adjustment you would make to Henry's net income for each item in Part a.
c. Discuss whether you believe the reclassification adjustments made by Henry for the sale and promotion incentive costs (Item 3) are appropriate.
d. Prepare a common-size income statement for Year 10, Year 11, and Year 12 using the amounts in Exhibit 6.18. Set sales equal to 100%.
e. Repeat Requirement d after making the income statement adjustments in Requirement b.
f. Assess the changes in the profitability of Henry during the three-year period.

6.19 Unusual Income Statement Items. Vulcan Materials Company, a `LO 6-6` member of the S&P 500 Index, is the nation's largest producer of construction aggregates, a major producer of asphalt mix and concrete, and a leading producer of cement in Florida. Exhibit 6.19 presents Vulcan's summarized income statement.

In Note 2 to the consolidated financial statements, "Discontinued Operations," Vulcan describes a June 2005 sale of substantially all assets of its Chemicals business, known as Vulcan Chemicals, to **Basic Chemicals**, a subsidiary of **Occidental Chemical Corporation**. Basic Chemicals assumed certain liabilities relating to the chemicals business, including the obligation to monitor and remediate all releases of hazardous materials at or from the Wichita, Geismar, and Port Edwards plant facilities. The decision to sell the chemicals business was based on Vulcan's desire to focus its resources on the construction materials business. The amounts reported as discontinued operations are not revenues and expenses from Vulcan operating the

Exhibit 6.19

Vulcan Materials Company Summarized Income Statement (amounts in thousands) (Problem 6.19)			
	2008	**2007**	**2006**
Total revenues	$3,651,438	$3,327,787	$3,342,475
Cost of revenues	2,901,726	2,376,884	2,410,571
SG&A	342,584	289,604	264,276
Goodwill impairment	252,664	—	—
Loss (gain) on sale of property, plant & equipment and businesses, net	(94,227)	(58,659)	(5,557)
Other operating (income) expense, net	(411)	5,541	(21,904)
Total operating expenses, net	3,402,336	2,613,370	2,647,386
Operating earnings	249,102	714,417	695,089
Other income (expense), net	(4,357)	(5,322)	28,541
Interest income	3,126	6,625	6,171
Interest expense	(172,813)	(48,218)	(26,310)
Earnings from continuing operations before income taxes	75,058	667,502	703,491
Provision for income taxes	(76,724)	(204,416)	(223,313)
Earnings from continuing operations	(1,666)	463,086	480,178
Discontinued operations (Note 2):			
Loss from results of discontinued operations	(4,059)	(19,327)	(16,624)
Income tax benefit	1,610	7,151	6,660
Loss on discontinued operations, net of income taxes	(2,449)	(12,176)	(9,964)
Net earnings (loss)	$ (4,115)	$ 450,910	$ 470,214

Source: Vulcan Materials Company, Form 10-K for the Fiscal Years Ended December 31, 2008, 2007, and 2006.

discontinued segment. Instead, the amounts represent a continual updating of the amount payable by the segment buyer. The receivable held by Vulcan from the sale is dependent on the levels of gas and chemical prices through the end of 2012. Vulcan classifies this financial instrument as a derivative contract that must be marked to market. The derivative does not hedge an existing transaction; therefore, its value changes are reflected in income as part of discontinued operations. As of 2008, Vulcan reported that final gains on disposal (if any) would occur after December 31, 2008.

Goodwill impairment relates to Vulcan's cement segment. Vulcan explains the need for the impairment as arising from the need to increase discount rates due to disruptions in credit markets as well as weak levels of construction activity.

REQUIRED

a. Discuss the appropriate treatment of the following when forecasting future earnings of Vulcan Materials: (1) goodwill impairment; (2) discontinued operations; and (3) loss (gain) on sale of property, plant, and equipment and businesses (net).

b. Prepare common-size income statements for Vulcan Materials. Interpret changes in profit margin over the three-year period in light of the special items.

 6.20 Implications of a Goodwill Impairment Charge for Future Cash Flow and Profitability. **Northrop Grumman Corporation** is a leading global security company that provides innovative systems products and solutions in aerospace, electronics, information systems, shipbuilding, and technical services to government and commercial customers worldwide. In an early 2009 press release, Northrop reported that it would record a non-cash, after-tax charge of between $3.0 billion and $3.4 billion for impairment of goodwill in its 2008 fourth-quarter income statement. As a result of the charge, Northrop reported net losses for the fourth quarter and all of 2008.

Northrop explained how it determined the impairment as follows: "The company performed its required annual testing of goodwill as of Nov. 30, 2008 using a discounted cash flow analysis supported by comparative market multiples to determine the fair value of its businesses versus their book values. Testing as of Nov. 30, 2008 indicated that book values for Shipbuilding and Space Technology exceeded the fair values of these businesses .... This non-cash charge does not impact the company's normal business operations."

REQUIRED

a. Explain how a company computes a goodwill impairment. Describe the usefulness of discounted cash flow and comparative market multiples in the computation of an impairment.

b. Explain the consequences of a goodwill impairment for the assessment of (1) current period profitability as measured by ROA, (2) future earnings projections, and (3) future period profitability as measured by ROA.

 6.21 Restructuring Charges at Intel. **Intel Corporation**'s consolidated income statement appears in Exhibit 6.20.

Note 15, which follows, explains the source of the restructuring charges, the breakdown of the charges into employee-related costs and asset impairments, and the balance of the accrued restructuring liability account.

Exhibit 6.20

Intel Corporation
Consolidated Income Statement
(amounts in millions, except per share amounts)
(Problem 6.21)

	2008	2007	2006
Net revenue	$37,586	$38,334	$35,382
Cost of sales	16,742	18,430	17,164
Gross margin	20,844	19,904	18,218
Research and development	5,722	5,755	5,873
Marketing, general and administrative	5,458	5,417	6,138
Restructuring and asset impairment charges	710	516	555
Operating expenses	11,890	11,688	12,566
Operating income	8,954	8,216	5,652
Gains (losses) on equity method investments, net	(1,380)	3	2
Gains (losses) on other equity investments, net	(376)	154	212
Interest and other, net	488	793	1,202
Income before taxes	7,686	9,166	7,068
Provision for taxes	2,394	2,190	2,024
Net income	$ 5,292	$ 6,976	$ 5,044
Basic earnings per common share	$ 0.93	$ 1.20	$ 0.87

Source: Intel Corporation, Form 10-K for the Fiscal Year Ended December 27, 2008.

Note 15: Restructuring and Asset Impairment Charges

The following table summarizes restructuring and asset impairment charges by plan for the three years ended December 27, 2008:

(in millions)	2008	2007	2006
2008 NAND plan	$ 215	$ —	$ —
2006 efficiency program	495	516	555
Total restructuring and asset impairment charges	$710	$516	$555

We may incur additional restructuring charges in the future for employee severance and benefit arrangements, and facility-related or other exit activities. Subsequent to the end of 2008, management approved plans to restructure some of our manufacturing and assembly and test operations, and align our manufacturing and assembly and test capacity to current market conditions. These actions, which are expected to take place beginning in 2009, include closing two assembly and test facilities in Malaysia, one facility in the Philippines, and one facility in China; stopping production at a 200mm wafer fabrication facility in Oregon; and ending production at our 200mm wafer fabrication facility in California.

2008 NAND PLAN

In the fourth quarter of 2008, management approved a plan with Micron to discontinue the supply of NAND flash memory from the 200mm facility within the IMFT manufacturing network. The agreement resulted in a $215 million restructuring charge, primarily related to the IMFT 200mm supply agreement. The restructuring charge resulted in a reduction of our investment in IMFT of $184 million, a cash payment to Micron of $24 million, and other cash payments of $7 million.

2006 EFFICIENCY PROGRAM

The following table summarizes charges for the 2006 efficiency program for the three years ended December 27, 2008:

(in millions)	2008	2007	2006
Employee severance and benefit arrangements	$ 151	$ 289	$ 238
Asset impairments	344	227	317
Total	**$495**	**$516**	**$555**

The following table summarizes the restructuring and asset impairment activity for the 2006 efficiency program during 2007 and 2008:

(in millions)	Employee Severance and Benefits	Asset Impairments	Total
Accrued restructuring balance as of December 30, 2006	$ 48	$ —	$ 48
Additional accruals	299	227	526
Adjustments	(10)	—	(10)
Cash payments	(210)	—	(210)
Non-cash settlements	—	(227)	(227)
Accrued restructuring balance as of December 29, 2007	$ 127	$ —	$ 127
Additional accruals	167	344	511
Adjustments	(16)	—	(16)
Cash payments	(221)	—	(221)
Non-cash settlements	—	(344)	(344)
Accrued restructuring balance as of December 27, 2008	$ 57	$ —	$ 57

We recorded the additional accruals, net of adjustments, as restructuring and asset impairment charges. The remaining accrual as of December 27, 2008 was related to severance benefits that we recorded within accrued compensation and benefits.

From the third quarter of 2006 through the fourth quarter of 2008, we incurred a total of $1.6 billion in restructuring and asset impairment charges related to this program. These charges included a total of $678 million related to employee severance and benefit arrangements for approximately 11,900 employees, and $888 million in asset impairment charges.

REQUIRED

a. Based on your reading of the note, how would you treat Intel's restructuring charges in the assessment of current profitability and the prediction of future earnings?

b. Why is the balance of the "accrued restructuring" limited to employee-related costs?

c. Describe the effect on net income of each entry in the "accrued restructuring balance" account reconciliation. (For example, what is the effect of "Additional accruals" on net income?)

d. How do U.S. GAAP and IFRS differ on the rules used to compute the restructuring charge?

6.22 Interpreting the Statement of Cash Flows. Sunbeam Corporation

manufactures and sells a variety of small household appliances, including toasters, food processors, and waffle grills. Exhibit 6.21 presents a statement of cash flows for Sunbeam for Year 5, Year 6, and Year 7. After experiencing decreased sales in Year 5, Sunbeam hired Albert Dunlap in Year 6 to turn the company around. The restructuring effort involved firing employees and cutting costs aggressively. Most of these restructuring efforts took place during Year 6. The market expected significantly improved results in Year 7. Reported sales increased 18.7% between Year 6 and Year 7, and net income improved. However, subsequent revelations showed that almost half of the sales increase resulted from fraudulent early recognition of revenues in the fourth quarter of Year 7 that the firm should have recognized in the first quarter of Year 8. Growth in revenues as originally reported for Years 5, 6, and 7 was −2.6%, −3.2%, and 18.7%, respectively.

Exhibit 6.21			
Sunbeam Corporation **Statement of Cash Flows** **(amounts in millions)** **(Problem 6.22)**			
	Year 7	**Year 6**	**Year 5**
OPERATIONS			
Net income (loss)	$ 109.4	$(228.3)	$ 50.5
Depreciation and amortization	38.6	47.4	44.2
Restructuring and asset impairment charges	—	283.7	—
Deferred income taxes	57.8	(77.8)	25.1
Other additions	13.7	46.2	10.8
Other subtractions	(84.6)	(27.1)	(21.7)
(Increase) Decrease in accounts receivable	(84.6)	(13.8)	(4.5)
(Increase) Decrease in inventories	(100.8)	(11.6)	(4.9)
(Increase) Decrease in prepayments	(9.0)	2.7	(8.8)
Increase (Decrease) in accounts payable	(1.6)	14.7	9.2
Increase (Decrease) in other current liabilities	52.8	(21.9)	(18.4)
Cash Flow from Operations	$ (8.3)	$ 14.2	$ 81.5
INVESTING			
Fixed assets acquired	$ (58.3)	$ (75.3)	$(140.1)
Sale of businesses	91.0	—	65.3
Acquisitions of businesses	—	(.9)	(33.0)
Cash Flow from Investing	$ 32.7	$ (76.2)	$(107.4)

(Continued)

Exhibit 6.21 (Continued)

FINANCING			
Increase (Decrease) in short-term borrowing	$ 5.0	$ 30.0	$ 40.0
Increase in long-term debt	—	11.5	—
Issue of common stock	26.6	9.2	9.8
Decrease in long-term debt	(12.2)	(1.8)	(5.4)
Acquisition of common stock	—	—	(13.0)
Dividends	(3.4)	(3.3)	(3.3)
Other financing transactions	.5	(.4)	(.2)
Cash Flow from Financing	$ 16.5	$ 45.2	$ 27.9
Change in Cash	$ 40.9	$ (16.8)	$ 2.0
Cash—Beginning of year	11.5	28.3	26.3
Cash—End of Year	$ 52.4	$ 11.5	$ 28.3

Source: Sunbeam Corporation, Form 10-K for the Fiscal Year Ended December 28, 1997.

REQUIRED

a. Using the information provided and the statement of cash flows for Year 5 in Exhibit 6.21, identify any signals before the turnaround effort that Sunbeam was experiencing operating difficulties and was in need of restructuring.

b. Using information in the statement of cash flows for Year 6, identify indicators of the turnaround efforts and any relations between cash flows that trouble you.

c. Using information in the statement of cash flows for Year 7, indicate any signals that the firm might have engaged in aggressive revenue recognition and had not yet fixed its general operating problems.

LO 6-8

6.23 Applying and Interpreting the Earnings Manipulation Model. Exhibit 6.22 presents selected financial statement data for **Enron Corporation** as originally reported for 1997, 1998, 1999, and 2000. In 2001, Enron restated its financial statements for earlier years because it reported several items beyond the limits of U.S. GAAP.

Exhibit 6.22

Enron Corporation
Financial Statement Data
(amounts in millions)
(Problem 6.23)

	2000	1999	1998	1997
Accounts receivable	$ 10,396	$ 3,030	$ 2,060	$ 1,697
Current assets	30,381	7,255	5,933	4,669
Property, plant, and equipment, net	11,743	10,681	10,657	9,170
Total assets	65,503	33,381	29,350	23,422
Current liabilities	28,406	6,759	6,107	4,412
Long-term debt	8,550	7,151	7,357	6,254

(Continued)

Exhibit 6.22 (Continued)

Sales	$100,789	$40,112	$31,260	$20,273
Cost of goods sold	94,517	34,761	26,381	17,311
Selling and administrative expenses	3,184	3,045	2,473	1,406
Income from continuing operations	979	1,024	703	105
Cash flow from operations	4,779	1,228	1,640	501
Depreciation expense	485	565	563	480

Source: Enron Corporation, Form 10-K for the Fiscal Years Ended December 31, 1997, 1998, 1999, and 2000.

REQUIRED

a. Use Beneish's earnings manipulation model to compute the probability that Enron engaged in earnings manipulation for 1998, 1999, and 2000.

b. Identify the major reasons for the changes in the probability of earnings manipulation during the three-year period.

6.24 Using Originally Reported versus Restated Data. Prior to Year 8,

LO 6-9

Cooper Corporation engaged in a wide variety of industries, including weapons manufacturing under government contracts, information technologies, commercial aircraft manufacturing, missile systems, coal mining, material service, ship management, and ship financing. During Year 8, Cooper sold its information technologies business. During Year 9, Cooper sold its commercial aircraft manufacturing business. During Year 9, it also announced its intention to sell its missile systems, coal mining, material service, ship management, and ship financing businesses. These strategic moves left Cooper with only its weapons manufacturing business. Financial statements for Cooper for Year 9 as reported, Year 8 as restated in the Year 9 annual report for discontinued operations, and Year 8 as originally reported appear in Exhibit 6.23 (balance sheet), Exhibit 6.24 (income statement), and Exhibit 6.25 (statement of cash flows).

Exhibit 6.23

Cooper Corporation
Balance Sheet
(amounts in millions)
(Problem 6.24)

	Year 9 as Reported	Year 8 as Restated in Year 9 Annual Report	Year 8 as Originally Reported
ASSETS			
Cash and cash equivalents	$ 513	$ 507	$ 513
Marketable securities	432	307	307
Accounts receivable	64	99	444
Contracts in process	1,550	1,474	2,606
Net assets of discontinued businesses	767	1,468	—
Other current assets	329	145	449
Total Current Assets	$ 3,655	$ 4,000	$ 4,319

(Continued)

Exhibit 6.23 (Continued)

Property, plant, and equipment, net	$ 322	$ 372	$1,029
Other assets	245	300	859
Total Assets	$4,222	$4,672	$6,207
LIABILITIES AND SHAREHOLDERS' EQUITY			
Accounts payable and accruals	$ 553	$ 642	$2,593
Current portion of long-term debt	145	450	516
Other current liabilities	1,250	1,174	—
Total Current Liabilities	$1,948	$2,266	$3,109
Long-term debt	38	163	365
Other noncurrent liabilities	362	263	753
Total Liabilities	$2,348	$2,692	$4,227
Common stock	$ 42	$ 55	$ 55
Additional paid-in capital	—	25	25
Retained earnings	2,474	2,651	2,651
Treasury stock	(642)	(751)	(751)
Total Shareholders' Equity	**$1,874**	**$1,980**	**$1,980**
Total Liabilities and Shareholders' Equity	$4,222	$4,672	$6,207

Exhibit 6.24

Cooper Corporation
Income Statement
(amounts in millions)
(Problem 6.24)

	Year 9 as Reported	Year 8 as Restated in Year 9 Annual Report	Year 8 as Originally Reported
Continuing Operations			
Sales	$ 3,472	$ 3,322	$ 8,751
Operating costs and expenses	(3,297)	(3,207)	(8,359)
Interest income (expense), net	25	4	(34)
Other expense, net	27	(27)	(27)
Earnings before Income Taxes	$ 227	$ 92	$ 331
Income tax credit	21	114	43
Income from Continuing Operations	$ 248	$ 206	$ 374
Discontinued Operations			
Earnings from operations	$ 193	$ 299	$ 131
Gain on disposal	374	—	—
Net Income	$ 815	$ 505	$ 505

Exhibit 6.25

Cooper Corporation
Statement of Cash Flows
(amounts in millions)
(Problem 6.24)

	Year 9 as Reported	Year 8 as Restated in Year 9 Annual Report	Year 8 as Originally Reported
OPERATIONS			
Income from continuing operations	$ 248	$ 206	$ 374
Depreciation and amortization	56	140	303
(Increase) Decrease in accounts receivable	35	4	(91)
(Increase) Decrease in contracts in process	(76)	(83)	237
(Increase) Decrease in other current assets	(6)	8	13
Increase (Decrease) in accounts payable and accruals	(66)	51	262
Increase (Decrease) in other current liabilities	11	(41)	(469)
Cash flow from continuing operations	$ 202	$ 285	$ 629
Cash flow from discontinued operations	288	324	44
Cash Flow from Operations	$ 490	$ 609	$ 673
INVESTING			
Proceeds from sale of discontinued operations	$ 1,039	$ 184	$ 184
Capital expenditures	(18)	(29)	(82)
Purchase of marketable securities	(125)	(307)	(307)
Other	32	3	56
Cash Flow from Investing	$ 928	$(149)	$(149)
FINANCING			
Issue of common stock	$ 57	$ —	$ —
Repayment of debt	(454)	(11)	(61)
Purchase of common stock	(960)	—	—
Dividends	(55)	(42)	(42)
Other	—	—	(17)
Cash Flow from Financing	$(1,412)	$ (53)	$(120)
Change in Cash	$ 6	$ 407	$ 404
Cash—Beginning of Year	507	100	109
Cash—End of Year	$ 513	$ 507	$ 513

REQUIRED

a. Refer to Exhibit 6.23. Why does the restated amount for total assets for Year 8 of $4,672 million differ from the originally reported amount of $6,207 million?

b. Refer to Exhibit 6.24. Why are the originally reported and restated net income amounts for Year 8 the same (that is, $505 million) when each of the individual revenues and expenses decreased on restatement?

c. Refer to Exhibit 6.25. Why is the restated amount of cash flow from operations for Year 8 of $609 million less than the originally reported amount of $673 million?

d. If the analyst wanted to analyze changes in the structure of assets and equities between Year 8 and Year 9, which columns and amounts in Exhibit 6.23 would he or she use? Explain.

e. If the analyst wanted to analyze changes in the operating profitability between Year 8 and Year 9, which columns and amounts in Exhibit 6.24 would he or she use? Explain.

f. If the analyst wanted to use cash flow ratios to assess short-term liquidity and long-term solvency risk, which columns and amounts in Exhibit 6.25 would he or she use? Explain.

INTEGRATIVE CASE 6.1

Starbucks

Exhibits 1.26–1.28 of Integrative Case 1.1 (Chapter 1) present the financial statements for **Starbucks** for 2009–2012. The following presents the majority of the items Starbucks discusses in its first note to the financial statements, "Summary of Significant Accounting Policies":

Note 1: Summary of Significant Accounting Policies

Estimates and Assumptions

Preparing financial statements in conformity with accounting principles generally accepted in the United States of America ("GAAP") requires management to make estimates and assumptions that affect the reported amounts of assets, liabilities, revenues and expenses. Examples include, but are not limited to, estimates for asset and goodwill impairments, stock-based compensation forfeiture rates, future asset retirement obligations, and inventory reserves; assumptions underlying self-insurance reserves and income from unredeemed stored value cards; and the potential outcome of future tax consequences of events that have been recognized in the financial statements. Actual results and outcomes may differ from these estimates and assumptions.

Fair Value

Fair value is the price we would receive to sell an asset or pay to transfer a liability (exit price) in an orderly transaction between market participants. For financial instruments and investments that we record or disclose at fair value, we determine fair value based upon the quoted market price as of the last day of the fiscal period, if available. If a quoted market price is not available for identical assets, we determine fair value based upon the quoted market price of similar assets or using a variety of other valuation methodologies. We determine fair value of our auction rate securities using an internally developed valuation model, using inputs that include interest rate curves, credit and liquidity spreads, and effective maturity.

The carrying value of cash and cash equivalents approximates fair value because of the short-term nature of these instruments. The fair value of our long-term debt is estimated based on the quoted market prices for the same or similar issues or on the current rates offered to us for debt of the same remaining maturities.

We measure our equity and cost method investments at fair value on a nonrecurring basis when they are determined to be other-than temporarily impaired. Fair values are determined using available quoted market prices or discounted cash flows.

Allowance for Doubtful Accounts

Allowance for doubtful accounts is calculated based on historical experience, customer credit risk and application of the specific identification method. As of September 30, 2012, October 2, 2011, and October 3, 2010, the allowance for doubtful accounts was $5.6 million, $3.3 million, and $3.3 million respectively.

Inventories

Inventories are stated at the lower of cost (primarily moving average cost) or market. We record inventory reserves for obsolete and slow-moving inventory and for estimated shrinkage between physical inventory counts. Inventory reserves are based on inventory obsolescence trends, historical experience and application of the specific identification method. As of September 30, 2012, October 2, 2011, and October 3, 2010, inventory reserves were $22.6 million, $19.5 million, and $18.1 million, respectively.

Property, Plant and Equipment

Property, plant and equipment are carried at cost less accumulated depreciation. Depreciation of property, plant and equipment, which includes assets under capital leases, is provided on the straight-line method over estimated useful lives, generally ranging from 2 to 15 years for equipment and 30 to 40 years for buildings. Leasehold improvements are amortized over the shorter of their estimated useful lives or the related lease life, generally 10 years. For leases with renewal periods at our option, we generally use the original lease term, excluding renewal option periods, to determine estimated useful lives. If failure to exercise a renewal option imposes an economic penalty to us, we may determine at the inception of the lease that renewal is reasonably assured and include the renewal option period in the determination of the appropriate estimated useful lives. The portion of depreciation expense related to production and distribution facilities is included in cost of sales including occupancy costs on the consolidated statements of earnings. The costs of repairs and maintenance are expensed when incurred, while expenditures for refurbishments and improvements that significantly add to the productive capacity or extend the useful life of an asset are capitalized. When assets are retired or sold, the asset cost and related accumulated depreciation are eliminated with any remaining gain or loss recognized in net earnings.

Goodwill

We test goodwill for impairment on an annual basis during our third fiscal quarter, or more frequently if circumstances, such as material deterioration in performance or a significant number of store closures, indicate reporting unit carrying values may exceed their fair values. When evaluating goodwill for impairment, we first perform a qualitative assessment to determine if the fair value of the reporting unit is more likely than not greater than the carrying amount. If not, we calculate the implied estimated fair value of the reporting unit. If the carrying amount of goodwill exceeds the implied estimated fair value, an impairment charge to current operations is recorded to reduce the carrying value to the implied estimated fair value.

As a part of our ongoing operations, we may close certain stores within a reporting unit containing goodwill due to underperformance of the store or inability to renew our lease, among other reasons. We abandon certain assets associated with a closed store including leasehold improvements and other non-transferable assets. Under GAAP, when a portion of a reporting unit that constitutes a business is to be disposed of, goodwill associated with the business is included in the carrying amount of the business in determining any loss on disposal. Our evaluation of whether the portion of a reporting unit being disposed of constitutes a business occurs on the date of abandonment. Although an operating store meets the accounting defini-tion of a business prior to abandonment, it does not constitute a business on the closure date because the remaining assets on that date do not constitute an integrated set of assets that are capable of being conducted and managed for the purpose of providing a return to investors. As a result, when closing individual stores, we do not include goodwill in the calculation of any loss on disposal of the related assets. As noted above, if store closures are indicative of potential impairment of goodwill at the reporting unit level, we perform an evaluation of our reporting unit goodwill when such closures occur. During Fiscal 2012 and fiscal 2011 we recorded no impairment charges and recorded $1.6 million in fiscal 2010.

Other Intangible Assets

Other intangible assets consist primarily of trademarks with indefinite lives, which are tested for impairment annually or more frequently if events or changes in circumstances indicate that the asset might be impaired. Definite-lived intangible assets, which mainly consist of contract-based patents and copyrights, are amortized over their estimated useful lives, and are tested for impairment when facts and circumstances indicate that the carrying values may not be recover-able. Based on the impairment tests performed, there was no impairment of other intangible assets in fiscal 2012, 2011, and 2010.

Long-lived Assets

When facts and circumstances indicate that the carrying values of long-lived assets may not be recoverable, we evaluate long-lived assets for impairment. We first compare the carrying value of the asset to the asset's estimated future cash flows (undiscounted). If the estimated future cash flows are less than the carrying value of the asset, we calculate an impairment loss based on the asset's estimated fair value. The fair value of the assets is estimated using a discounted cash flow model based on forecasted future revenues and operating costs, using internal projec-tions. Property, plant and equipment assets are grouped at the lowest level for which there are identifiable cash flows when assessing impairment. Cash flows for company-operated store assets are identified at the individual store level. Long-lived assets to be disposed of are reported at the lower of their carrying amount, or fair value less estimated costs to sell.

We recognized net impairment and disposition losses of $31.7 million, $36.2 million, and $67.7 million in fiscal 2012, 2011, and 2010, respectively, primarily due to underperforming company-operated stores. Depending on the underlying asset that is impaired, these losses may be recorded in any one of the operating expense lines on the consolidated statements of earn-ings: for retail operations, the net impairment and disposition losses are recorded in store oper-ating expenses and for all other operations, these losses are recorded in cost of sales including occupancy costs, other operating expenses, or general and administrative expenses.

Insurance Reserves

We use a combination of insurance and self-insurance mechanisms, including a wholly owned captive insurance entity and participation in a reinsurance treaty, to provide for the potential liabilities for certain risks, including workers' compensation, healthcare benefits, general liability, property insurance, and director and officers' liability insurance. Liabilities associated with the risks that are retained by us are not discounted and are estimated, in part, by considering historical claims experience, demographic, exposure and severity factors, and other actuarial assumptions.

Revenue Recognition

Consolidated revenues are presented net of intercompany eliminations for wholly owned sub-sidiaries and investees controlled by us and for licensees accounted for under the equity method, based on our percentage ownership. Additionally, consolidated revenues are recognized net of any discounts, returns, allowances and sales incentives, including coupon redemptions and rebates.

Company-operated Stores Revenues

Company-operated store revenues are recognized when payment is tendered at the point of sale. Retail store revenues are reported net of sales, use or other transaction taxes that are collected from customers and remitted to taxing authorities.

Licensed Stores Revenues

Licensed stores revenues consist of product sales to licensed stores, as well as royalties and other fees paid by licensees to use the Starbucks brand. Sales of coffee, tea and related products are generally recognized upon shipment to licensees, depending on contract terms. Shipping charges billed to licensees are also recognized as revenue, and the related shipping costs are included in cost of sales including occupancy costs on the consolidated statements of earnings.

Initial nonrefundable development fees for licensed stores are recognized upon substantial performance of services for new market business development activities, such as initial business, real estate and store development planning, as well as providing operational materials and functional training courses for opening new licensed retail markets. Additional store licensing fees are recognized when new licensed stores are opened. Royalty revenues based upon a percentage of reported sales and other continuing fees, such as marketing and service fees, are recognized on a monthly basis when earned.

CPG, Foodservice and Other Revenues

CPG, foodservice and other revenues primarily consist of domestic and international sales of packaged coffee and tea as well as a variety of ready-to-drink beverages and single-serve coffee and tea products to grocery, warehouse club and specialty retail stores, sales to our national foodservice accounts, and revenues from sales of products to and license revenues from manufacturers that produce and market Starbucks and Seattle's Best Coffee branded products through licensing agreements. Sales of coffee, tea, ready-to-drink beverages and related products to grocery and warehouse club stores are generally recognized when received by the customer or distributor, depending on contract terms. We maintain a sales return allowance to reduce packaged goods revenues for estimated future product returns based on historical patterns. Revenues are recorded net of sales discounts given to customers for trade promotions and payments to customers for product placement in our customers' stores.

Revenues from sales of products to manufacturers that produce and market Starbucks and Seattle's Best Coffee branded products through licensing agreements are generally recognized when the product is received by the manufacturer or distributor. License revenues from manufacturers are based on a percentage of sales and are recognized on a monthly basis when earned. National foodservice account revenues are recognized when the product is received by the customer or distributor.

Stored Value Cards

Revenues from our stored value cards, primarily Starbucks Cards, are recognized when redeemed or when the likelihood of redemption, based on historical experience, is deemed to be remote. Outstanding customer balances are included in deferred revenue on the consolidated balance sheets. There are no expiration dates on our stored value cards, and we do not charge any service fees that cause a decrement to customer balances. While we will continue to honor all stored value cards presented for payment, management may determine the likelihood of redemption to be remote for certain cards due to long periods of inactivity. In these circumstances, if management also determines there is no requirement for remitting balances to government agencies under unclaimed property laws, card balances may then be recognized in the consolidated statements of earnings, in net interest income and other. For the fiscal years ended September 30, 2012, October 2, 2011, and October 3, 2010, income recognized on unredeemed stored value card balances was $65.8 million, $46.9 million, and $31.2 million, respectively. In fiscal 2012, we recognized additional income associated with unredeemed gift cards due to a recent court ruling relating to state unclaimed property laws.

Customers in the US, Canada, and the UK who register their Starbucks Card are automatically enrolled in the My Starbucks Reward program and earn points ("Stars") with each purchase. Reward program members receive various benefits depending on the number of Stars earned in a 12-month period. The value of Stars earned by our program members towards free product is included in deferred revenue and recorded as a reduction in revenue at the time the Stars are earned, based on the value of Stars that are projected to be redeemed.

Marketing & Advertising

Our annual marketing expenses include many components, one of which is advertising costs. We expense most advertising costs as they are incurred, except for certain production costs that are expensed the first time the advertising campaign takes place.

Annual marketing expenses totaled $277.9 million, $244.0 million, and $198.7 million in fiscal 2012, 2011, and 2010, respectively. Included in these costs were advertising expenses, which totaled $182.4 million, $141.4 million, and $176.2 million in fiscal 2012, 2011, and 2010, respectively.

Store Preopening Expenses

Costs incurred in connection with the start-up and promotion of new store openings are expensed as incurred.

Operating Leases

We lease retail stores, roasting, distribution and warehouse facilities, and office space under operating leases. Most lease agreements contain tenant improvement allowances, rent holidays, lease premiums, rent escalation clauses and/or contingent rent provisions. For purposes of recognizing incentives, premiums and minimum rental expenses on a straight-line basis over the terms of the leases, we use the date of initial possession to begin amortization, which is generally when we enter the space and begin to make improvements in preparation of intended use.

For tenant improvement allowances and rent holidays, we record a deferred rent liability on the consolidated balance sheets and amortize the deferred rent over the terms of the leases as reductions to rent expense on the consolidated statements of earnings.

For premiums paid upfront to enter a lease agreement, we record a deferred rent asset on the consolidated balance sheets and then amortize the deferred rent over the terms of the leases as additional rent expense on the consolidated statements of earnings.

For scheduled rent escalation clauses during the lease terms or for rental payments commencing at a date other than the date of initial occupancy, we record minimum rental expenses on a straight-line basis over the terms of the leases on the consolidated statements of earnings.

Certain leases provide for contingent rents, which are determined as a percentage of gross sales in excess of specified levels. We record a contingent rent liability on the consolidated balance sheets and the corresponding rent expense when specified levels have been achieved or when we determine that achieving the specified levels during the fiscal year is probable.

When ceasing operations in company-operated stores under operating leases, in cases where the lease contract specifies a termination fee due to the landlord, we record such expense at the time written notice is given to the landlord. In cases where terms, including termination fees, are yet to be negotiated with the landlord, we will record the expense upon signing of an agreement with the landlord. In cases where the landlord does not allow us to prematurely exit the lease, but allows for subleasing, we estimate the fair value of any sublease income that can be generated from the location and expense the present value of the excess of remaining lease payments to the landlord over the projected sublease income at the cease-use date.

Asset Retirement Obligations

We recognize a liability for the fair value of required asset retirement obligations ("ARO") when such obligations are incurred. Our AROs are primarily associated with leasehold improvements, which, at the end of a lease, we are contractually obligated to remove in order to comply with the lease agreement. At the inception of a lease with such conditions, we record an ARO liability and a corresponding capital asset in an amount equal to the estimated fair value of the obligation. The liability is estimated based on a number of assumptions requiring management's judgment, including store closing costs, cost inflation rates and discount rates, and is accreted to its projected future value over time. The capitalized asset is depreciated using the same depreciation convention as leasehold improvement assets. Upon satisfaction of the ARO conditions, any difference between the recorded ARO liability and the actual retirement costs incurred is recognized as an operating gain or loss in the consolidated statements of earnings. As of September 30, 2012 and October 2, 2011, our net ARO asset included in property, plant and equipment was $8.8 million and $11.8 million, respectively, and our net ARO liability included in other long-term liabilities was $42.6 million and $50.1 million, respectively.

Income Taxes

We compute income taxes using the asset and liability method, under which deferred income taxes are provided for the temporary differences between the financial statement carrying amounts and the tax basis of our assets and liabilities. We routinely evaluate the likelihood of realizing the benefit of our deferred tax assets and may record a valuation allowance if, based on all available evidence, we determine that some portion of the tax benefit will not be realized. We recognize the tax benefit from an uncertain tax position only if it is more likely than not that the tax position will be sustained on examination by the relevant taxing authorities, based on the technical merits of our position. The tax benefits recognized in the financial statements from such a position are measured based on the largest benefit that has a greater than 50% likelihood of being realized upon ultimate settlement. Starbucks recognizes interest and penalties related to income tax matters in income tax expense.

REQUIRED

a. Given your knowledge of Starbucks' key success and risk factors, use the note information presented above to evaluate Starbucks' accounting quality.

b. If you believe that Starbucks' accounting policy does not yield measurements of assets and liabilities that reflect economic reality and a measurement of net income that is predictive of future earnings, suggest any changes that you would make to assets, liabilities, and earnings to improve accounting quality. (At this point in your learning process, if you do not have specific numerical adjustments to propose, at least describe potential journal entries you would make to change the financial statements, if any, and what information you might need to make those entries.)

c. Evaluate whether your proposed adjustments are necessary for (1) credit analysis, (2) equity valuation, and (3) management evaluation.

CASE 6.2

Citi: A Very Bad Year

Citigroup Inc. (Citi) is a leading global financial services company with over 200 million customer accounts and operations in more than 140 countries. Its operating units Citicorp and Citi Holdings provide a broad range of financial products and services to consumers, governments, institutions, and corporations. Services include investment banking, consumer and corporate banking and credit, securities brokerage, and wealth management.

Citi reported a net loss of $27,684 million, or $5.59 per share in 2008. Exhibit 6.26 presents Citigroup's consolidated statements of income for 2006–2008.

Exhibit 6.26

Citigroup Inc.
Consolidated Statements of Income
(amounts in millions, except per share amounts)
(Case 6.2)

| | Citigroup Inc. and Subsidiaries | | |
| | Year ended December 31 | | |
	2008	2007	2006
Revenues			
Interest revenue	$106,655	$121,429	$ 93,611
Interest expense	52,963	76,051	55,683
Net interest revenue	$ 53,692	$ 45,378	$ 37,928
Commissions and fees	$ 11,227	$ 20,706	$ 18,850
Principal transactions	(22,188)	(12,086)	7,990
Administration and other fiduciary fees	8,560	9,132	6,903
Realised gains (losses) from sales of investments	(2,061)	1,168	1,791
Insurance premiums	3,221	3,062	2,769
Other revenue	342	11,135	10,096
Total non-interest revenues	$ (899)	$ 33,117	$ 48,399
Total revenues, net of interest expense	$ 52,793	$ 78,495	$ 86,327
Provisions, for credit losses and for benefits and claims			
Provision for loan losses	$ 33,674	$ 16,832	$ 6,320
Policyholder benefits and claims	1,403	935	967
Provision for unfunded lending commitments	(363)	150	250
Total provisions for credit losses and for benefits and claims	$ 34,714	$ 17,917	$ 7,537

(Continued)

Exhibit 6.26 (Continued)			
Operating expenses			
Compensation and benefits	$ 32,440	$ 33,892	$ 29,752
Net occupancy	7,125	6,648	5,794
Technology/communication	4,897	4,511	3,741
Advertising and marketing	2,292	2,803	2,471
Restructuring	1,766	1,528	—
Other operating	22,614	10,420	8,543
Total operating expenses	$ 71,134	$ 59,802	$ 50,301
Income (loss) from continuing operations before income taxes and minority interest	$ (53,055)	$ 776	$ 28,489
Provision (benefit) for income taxes	(20,612)	(2,498)	7,749
Minority interest, net of taxes	(349)	285	289
Income (loss) from continuing operations	$ (32,094)	$ 2,989	$ 20,451
Discontinued operations			
Income from discontinued operations	$ 1,478	$ 925	$ 1,177
Gain on sale	3,139	—	219
Provision (benefit) for income taxes and minority interest, net of taxes	207	297	309
Income from discontinued operations, net of taxes	$ 4,410	$ 628	$ 1,087
Net income (loss)	$ (27,684)	$ 3,617	$ 21,518
Basic earnings per share[1]			
Income (loss) from continuing operations	$ (6.42)	$ 0.60	$ 4.17
Income from discontinued operations, net of taxes	0.83	0.13	0.22
Net income (loss)	$ (5.59)	$ 0.73	$ 4.39
Weighted average common shares outstanding	5,265.4	4,905.8	4,887.3
Diluted earnings per share[1]			
Income (loss) from continuing operations	$ (6.42)	$ 0.59	$ 4.09
Income from discontinued operations, net of taxes	0.83	0.13	0.22
Net income (loss)	$ (5.59)	$ 0.72	$ 4.31
Adjusted weighted average common shares outstanding	$ 5,795.1	$ 4,995.3	$4,986.1

[1]Diluted shares used in the diluted EPS calculation represent basic shares for 2009 due to the net loss. Using actual diluted shares would result in anti-dilution.

Source: Citigroup Inc., Form 10-K for the Fiscal Years Ended December 31, 2008, 2007, and 2006.

Excerpts from Financial Statement Notes:

The following excerpts were disclosed in the notes to Citigroup's 2008 financial statements:

3. Discontinued Operations

Sale of Citigroup's German Retail Banking Operations

On December 5, 2008, Citigroup sold its German retail banking operations to Credit Mutuel for Euro 5.2 billion, in cash plus the German retail bank's operating net earnings accrued in 2008 through the closing. The sale resulted in an after-tax gain of approximately $3.9 billion including the after-tax gain on the foreign currency hedge of $383 million recognised during the fourth quarter of 2008.

The sale does not include the corporate and investment banking business or the Germany-based European data center.

The German retail banking operations had total assets and total liabilities as of November 30, 2008, of $15.6 billion and $11.8 billion, respectively.

Results for all of the German retail banking businesses sold, as well as the net gain recognized in 2008 from this sale, are reported as *Discontinued Operations* for all periods presented.

Summarized financial information for *Discontinued Operations*, including cash flows, related to the sale of the German retail banking operations is as follows:

in millions of dollars	2008	2007	2006
Total revenues, net of interest expense	**$6,592**	$2,212	$2,126
Income from discontinued operations	**$1,438**	$ 652	$ 837
Gain on sale	**3,695**	—	—
Provision for income taxes and minority interest, net of taxes	**426**	214	266
Income from discontinued operations, net of taxes	**$4,707**	$ 438	$ 571

in millions of dollars	2008	2007	2006
Cash flows from operating activities	**$ (4,719)**	$ 2,227	$ 2,246
Cash flows from investing activities	**18,547**	(1,906)	(3,316)
Cash flows from financing activities	**(14,226)**	(213)	1,147
Net cash provided by (used in) discontinued operations	**$ (398)**	$ 108	$ 77

CitiCapital

On July 31, 2008, Citigroup sold substantially all of CitiCapital, the equipment finance unit in *North America*. The total proceeds from the transaction were approximately $12.5 billion and resulted in an after-tax loss to Citigroup of $305 million. This loss is included in *Income from discontinued operations* on the Company's Consolidated Statement of Income for the second quarter of 2008. The assets and liabilities for CitiCapital totaled approximately $12.9 billion and $0.5 billion, respectively, at June 30, 2008.

This transaction encompassed seven CitiCapital equipment finance business lines, including Healthcare Finance, Private Label Equipment Finance, Material Handling Finance, Franchise Finance, Construction Equipment Finance, Bankers Leasing, and CitiCapital Canada. CitiCapital's Tax Exempt Finance business was not part of the transaction and was retained by Citigroup.

CitiCapital had approximately 1,400 employees and 160,000 customers throughout North America.

Results for all of the CitiCapital businesses sold, as well as the net loss recognized in 2008 from this sale, are reported as *Discontinued operations* for all periods presented.

Summarized financial information for *Discontinued operations,* including cash flows, related to the sale of CitiCapital is as follows:

in millions of dollars	2008	2007	2006
Total revenues, net of interest expense	**$ 24**	$991	$1,162
Income (loss) from discontinued operations	**$ 40**	$273	$ 313
Loss on sale	**(506)**	—	—
Provision (benefit) for income taxes and minority interest, net of taxes	**(202)**	83	86
Income (loss) from discontinued operations, net of taxes	**$(264)**	$190	$ 227

in millions of dollars	2008	2007	2006
Cash flows from operating activities	**$(287)**	$(1,148)	$ 2,596
Cash flows from investing activities	**349**	1,190	(2,664)
Cash flows from financing activities	**(61)**	(43)	3
Net cash provided by (used in) discontinued operations	**$ 1**	$ (1)	$ (65)

Sale of the Asset Management Business

On December 1, 2005, the Company completed the sale of substantially all of its Asset Management business to Legg Mason, Inc. (Legg Mason).

On January 31, 2006, the Company completed the sale of its Asset Management business within Bank Handlowy (an indirect banking subsidiary of Citigroup located in Poland) to Legg Mason. This transaction, which was originally part of the overall Asset Management business sold to Legg Mason on December 1, 2005, was postponed due to delays in obtaining local regulatory approval. A gain from this sale of $18 million after-tax and minority interest ($31 million pretax and minority interest) was recognized in the first quarter of 2006 in *Discontinued operations.*

During March 2006, the Company sold 10.3 million shares of Legg Mason stock through an underwritten public offering. The net sale proceeds of $ 1.258 billion resulted in a pretax gain of $24 million in *ICG.*

In September 2006, the Company received from Legg Mason the final closing adjustment payment related to this sale. This payment resulted in an additional after-tax gain of $51 million ($83 million pretax), recorded in *Discontinued operations.*

Sale of the Life Insurance and Annuities Business

On July 1, 2005, the Company completed the sale of Citigroup's Travelers Life & Annuity and substantially all of Citigroup's international insurance businesses to MetLife, Inc. (MetLife).

During the first quarter of 2006, $15 million of the total $657 million federal tax contingency reserve release was reported in *Discontinued operations* as it related to the Life Insurance and Annuities business sold to MetLife.

In July 2006, Citigroup recognized an $85 million after-tax gain from the sale of MetLife shares. This gain was reported in income from continuing operations in *ICG.*

In July 2006, the Company received the final closing adjustment payment related to this sale, resulting in an after-tax gain of $75 million ($ 115 million pretax), which was recorded in *Discontinued operations.*

In addition, during the third quarter of 2006, a release of $42 million of deferred tax liabilities was reported in *Discontinued operations* as it related to the Life Insurance & Annuities business sold to MetLife.

In December 2008, the Company fulfilled its previously agreed upon obligations with regard to its remaining 10% economic interest in the long-term care business that it had sold to the predecessor of Genworth Financial in 2000. Under the terms of the 2005 sales agreement of Citi's Life Insurance and Annuities business to MetLife, Citi agreed to reimburse MetLife for certain liabilities related to the sale of the long-term-care business to Genworth's predecessor. The assumption of the final 10% block Genworth at December 31, 2008, resulted in a pretax loss of $50 million ($33 million after-tax), which has been reported in *Discontinued operations.*

Combined Results for Discontinued Operations

The following is summarized financial information for the German retail banking operations, CitiCapital, Life Insurance and Annuities business, Asset Management business, and TPC:

in millions of dollars	2008	2007	2006
Total revenues, net of interest expense	**$6,616**	$3,203	$3,507
Income from discontinued operations	**$1,478**	$ 925	$1,177
Gain on sale	**3,139**	—	219
Provision (benefit) for income taxes, and minority interest, net of taxes	**207**	297	309
Income from discontinued operations, net of taxes	**$4,410**	$ 628	$1,087

Cash Flows from Discontinued Operations			
in millions of dollars	2008	2007	2006
Cash flows from operating activities	**$ (5,006)**	$1,079	$ 4,842
Cash flows from investing activities	**18,896**	(716)	(5,871)
Cash flows from financing activities	**(14,287)**	(256)	1,150
Net cash provided by (used in) discontinued operations	**$ (397)**	$ 107	$ 121

5. Interest Revenue and Expense

For the years ended December 31, 2008, 2007, and 2006, respectively, interest revenue and expense consisted of the following:

in millions of dollars	2008	2007	2006
Interest revenue			
Loan interest, including fees	**$ 62,336**	$ 63,201	$52,086
Deposits with banks	**3,119**	3,113	2,240
Federal funds sold and securities purchased under agreements to resell	**9,175**	18,354	14,199
Investments, including dividends	**10,718**	13,423	10,340
Trading account assets[1]	**17,489**	18,507	11,865
Other interest	**3,818**	4,831	2,881
Total interest revenue	**$106,655**	$121,429	$93,611

(Continued)

Interest expense

Deposits	**$ 20,271**	$ 28,402	$21,336
Federal funds purchased and securities loaned or sold under agreements to repurchase	**11,330**	23,028	17,448
Trading account liabilities[1]	**1,277**	1,440	1,119
Short-term borrowings	**4,039**	7,071	4,632
Long-term debt	**16,046**	16,110	11,148
Total interest expense	**$ 52,963**	$ 76,051	$55,683
Net interest revenue	**$ 53,692**	$ 45,378	$37,928
Provision for loan losses	**33,674**	16,832	6,320
Net interest revenue after provision for loan losses	**$ 20,018**	$ 28,546	$31,608

[1]Interest expense on *Trading account facilities* of *ICG* is reported as a reduction of interest revenue from *Trading account assets*.

6. Commissions and Fees

Commissions and fees revenue includes charges to customers for credit and bank cards, including transaction-processing fees and annual fees; advisory and equity and debt underwriting services; lending and deposit-related transactions, such as loan commitments, standby letters of credit and other deposit and loan servicing activities; investment management-related fees, including brokerage services and custody and trust services; and insurance fees and commissions.

The following table presents commissions and fees revenue for the years ended December 31:

in millions of dollars	2008	2007	2006
Investment banking	**$ 2,284**	$ 5,228	$ 4,093
Credit cards and bank cards	**4,517**	5,036	5,191
Smith Barney	**2,836**	3,265	2,958
ICG trading-related	**2,322**	2,706	2,464
Checking-related	**1,134**	1,108	911
Transaction Services	**1,423**	1,166	859
Other Consumer	**1,211**	649	279
Nikko Cordial-related[1]	**1,086**	834	—
Loan servicing[2]	**(1,731)**	560	660
Primerica	**415**	455	399
Other *ICG*	**747**	295	243
Other	**(141)**	71	58
Corporate finance[3]	**(4,876)**	(667)	735
Total commissions and fees	**$11,227**	$20,706	$18,850

[1](Commissions and fees for Nikko Cordial have not been detailed due to unavailability of the information.

[2]Includes fair value adjustments on mortgage servicing assets. The mark-to-market on the underlying economic hedges of the MSRs is included in *Other revenue*.

[3]Includes write-downs of approximately $4.9 billion in 2008 and $1.5 billion in 2007, net of underwriting fees, on funded and unfunded highly leveraged finance commitments, recorded at fair value and reported as loans held for sale in *Other assets*. Write-downs were recorded on all highly leveraged finance commitments where there was value impairment, regardless of funding date.

7. Principal Transactions

Principal transactions revenue consists of realized and unrealized gains and losses from trading activities. Not included in the table below is the impact of net interest revenue related to trading activities, which is an integral part of trading activities' profitability. The following table presents principal transactions revenue for the years ended December 31:

in millions of dollars	2008	2007	2006[1]
Institutional Clients Group			
Fixed income[2]	**$ (6,455)**	$ 4,053	$5,593
Credit products[3]	**(21,614)**	(21,805)	(744)
Equities[4]	**(394)**	682	866
Foreign exchange[5]	**2,316**	1,222	693
Commodities[6]	**667**	686	487
Total *ICG*	**$(25,480)**	$(15,162)	$6,895
Consumer Banking/Global Cards[7]	**1,616**	1,364	504
Global Wealth Management[7]	**836**	1,315	680
Corporate/Other	**840**	397	(89)
Total principal transactions revenue	**$(22,188)**	$(12,086)	$7,990

[1]Reclassified to conform to the current period's presentation.

[2]Includes revenues from government securities and corporate debt, municipal securities, preferred stock, mortgage securities, and other debt instruments. Also includes spot and forward trading of currencies and exchange-traded and over-the-counter (OTC) currency options, options on fixed income securities, interest rate swaps, currency swaps, swap options, caps and floors, financial futures, OTC options, and forward contracts on fixed income securities. Losses in 2008 reflect the volatility and dislocation in the credit and trading markets.

[3]Includes revenues from structured credit products such as North America and Europe collateralized debt obligations, In 2007 and 2008, losses recorded were related to subprime-related exposures in *ICG's* lending and structuring business and exposures to super senior CDOs.

[4]Includes revenues from common, preferred and convertible preferred stock, convertible corporate debt, equity-linked notes, and exchange-traded and OTC equity options and warrants.

[5]Includes revenues from foreign exchange spot, forward, option and swap contracts, as well as translation gains and losses.

[6]Primarily includes the results of Phibro LLC, which trades crude oil, refined oil products, natural gas, and other commodities.

[7]Includes revenues from various fixed income, equities and foreign exchange transactions.

10. Restructuring

In the fourth quarter of 2008, Citigroup recorded a pretax restructuring expense of $1.797 billion pre-tax related to the implementation of a Company-wide re-engineering plan. This initiative will generate headcount reductions of approximately 20,600. The charges related to the 2008 Re-engineering Projects Restructuring Initiative are reported in the Restructuring line on the Company's Consolidated Statement of Income and are recorded in each segment.

In 2007, the Company completed a review of its structural expense base in a Company-wide effort to create a more streamlined organization, reduce expense growth, and provide investment funds for future growth initiatives. As a result of this review, a pretax restructuring charge of $1.4 billion was recorded in *Corporate/Other* during the first quarter of 2007. Additional net charges of $151 million were recognized in subsequent quarters throughout 2007 and a net release of $31 million in 2008 due to a change in estimates. The charges related to the 2007 Structural Expense Review Restructuring Initiative are reported in the Restructuring line on the Company's Consolidated Statement of Income.

The primary goals of the 2007 Structural Expense Review and Restructuring, and the 2008 Re-engineering Projects and Restructuring Initiatives were:

- eliminate layers of management/improve workforce management;
- consolidate certain back-office, middle-office and corporate functions;
- increase the use of shared services;
- expand centralized procurement; and
- continue to rationalize operational spending on technology.

The implementation of these restructuring initiatives also caused certain related premises and equipment assets to become redundant. The remaining depreciable lives of these assets were shortened, aid accelerated depreciation charges began in the second quarter of 2007 and fourth quarter of 2008 for the 2007 and 2008 initiatives, respectively, in addition to normal scheduled depreciation.

19. Goodwill and Intangible Assets

Goodwill

The changes in goodwill during 2007 and 2008 were as follows:

in millions of dollars	Goodwill
Balance at December 31, 2006	$33,264
Acquisition of GFU	865
Acquisition of Quilter	268
Acquisition of Nikko Cordial[1]	892
Acquisition of Grupo Cuscatlán	921
Acquisition of Egg	1,471
Acquisition of Old Lane	516
Acquisition of BISYS	872
Acquisition of BOOC	712
Acquisition of ATD	569
Sale of Avantel	(118)
Foreign exchange translation, smaller acquisitions and other	821
Balance at December 31, 2007	**$41,053**
Sale of German retail bank	$ (1,047)
Sale of CitiCapital	(221)
Sale of Citigroup Global Services Limited	(85)
Purchase accounting adjustments—BISYS	(184)
Purchase of the remaining shares of Nikko Cordial—net of purchase accounting adjustments	287
Acquisition of Legg Mason Private Portfolio Group	98
Foreign exchange translation	(3,116)
Impairment of goodwill	(9,568)
Smaller acquisitions, purchase accounting adjustments and other	(85)
Balance at December 31, 2008	**$27,132**

In the following press release, Citi further describes the source of the goodwill impairment:

Citi Announces Fourth Quarter Goodwill Impairment of $9.6 Billion[59]

Results in Additional Net Loss of $9.0 Billion for 2008

New York — Citi announced today that it recorded a pre-tax goodwill impairment charge of approximately $9.6 billion ($8.7 billion after-tax) in the fourth quarter of 2008. Citi had previously announced in its fourth quarter earnings press release (January 16, 2009) that it was continuing to review its goodwill to determine whether a goodwill impairment had occurred as of December 31, 2008, and this charge is the result of that review and testing. The goodwill impairment charge was recorded in North America Consumer Banking, Latin America Consumer Banking, and EMEA Consumer Banking, and resulted in a write-off of the entire amount of goodwill allocated to those reporting units. The charge does not result in a cash outflow or negatively affect the Tier 1 or Total Regulatory Capital ratios, Tangible Common Equity or Citi's liquidity position as of December 31, 2008.

In addition, Citi recorded a $374 million pre-tax charge ($242 million after-tax) to reflect further impairment evident in the intangible asset related to Nikko Asset Management at December 31, 2008.

The primary cause for both the goodwill and the intangible asset impairments mentioned above was the rapid deterioration in the financial markets, as well as in the global economic outlook generally, particularly during the period beginning mid-November through year-end 2008. This deterioration further weakened the near term prospects for the financial services industry.

Giving effect to these charges, Net Income (Loss) from Continuing Operations for 2008 was $(32.1) billion and Net Income (Loss) was $(27.7) billion, resulting in Diluted Earnings per Share of $(6.42) and $(5.59) respectively.

A complete description of Citi's goodwill impairment testing as of December 31, 2008 and the related charges will be included in Citi's Form 10-K to be filed with the Securities and Exchange Commission on or before March 2, 2009.

REQUIRED

Consider the following items reported in Citi's Consolidated Statement of Income:

- Principal transactions
- Realized (gain) losses from sales of investments
- Provision for loan losses
- Restructuring
- Other operating expenses (which presumably includes the goodwill impairment)
- Discontinued operations

Discuss whether you would eliminate all or part of each item when assessing current profitability and forecasting the future earnings of Citi. If so, what adjustments would you make to the financial statements (assuming a tax rate of 35%)?

---

[59]Press release found at: http://www.citigroup.com/citi/press/2009/090227b.htm. Reprinted by permission.

CASE 6.3

Arbortech: Apocalypse Now

Arbortech, a designer, manufacturer, and marketer of PC cards for computers, printers, tele-communications equipment, and equipment diagnostic systems, was the darling of Wall Street during Year 6. Its common stock price was the leading gainer for the year on the New York Stock Exchange. Its bubble burst during the third quarter of Year 7 when revelations about seriously misstated financial statements for prior years became known. This case seeks to identify signals of the financial shenanigans and to assess the likelihood of the firm's future survival.

Industry and Products

Digital computing and processing have expanded now include a broad array of mobile applications, including tablets, laptops, cell phones, digital cameras, and medical and automobile diagnostic equipment. A PC card is a rugged, lightweight, credit-card-sized device inserted into a dedicated slot in these products that provides programming, processing, and storage capabilities provided on hard drives in conventional desktop computers. The PC card has a high shock and vibration tolerance, low power consumption, a smaller size (relative to previous technologies), and a high access speed. At the time, the market for PC cards was one of the fastest growing segments of the electronics industry.

Arbortech designs PC cards for four principal industries: (1) communications (routers, cell phones, and local-area networks), (2) transportation (vehicle diagnostics and navigation), (3) mobile computing (handheld data collection terminals and notebook computers), and (4) medical (blood gas analysis systems and defibrillators). The firm targets its engineering and product development, all of which it conducts in-house, to these four industry groups. It works closely with original equipment manufacturers (OEMs) to design PC cards that meet specific needs of products aimed at these four industries. Arbortech also conducts its manufacturing in-house, which allows it to respond quickly to changing requirements and schedules of these OEMs. The firm markets its products using its own sales force.

In Year 4, Arbortech was incorporated in Delaware. The firm made its initial public offering of common stock (1 million shares) on April 19, Year 4, at a price of $5.625 per share. Each common share issued included a redeemable common stock purchase warrant that permitted the holder to purchase one share of the firm's common stock for $7.20. Prior to its initial public offering, Arbortech obtained a $550,000 bridge loan during Year 4, which it repaid with proceeds from the initial public offering. Holders of the stock purchase warrants exercised their options during Year 5 and Year 6. The firm obtained equity capital during Year 5 as a result of a private placement of its common stock at $5.83 a share. It issued additional shares to the public during Year 6 at $18 a share. Its stock price was $5.25 on June 30, Year 4; $22.625 on June 30, Year 5; $29.875 on June 30, Year 6; and $52 on December 31, Year 7.

Arbortech maintained a line of credit throughout Year 4 to Year 6 with a major Boston bank to finance its accounts receivables and inventories. The borrowing was at the bank's prime lending rate. Substantially all of the assets of the firm collateralized this borrowing.

The firm's chief executive officer, Daniel James, also is its major shareholder. The firm maintains an employment agreement with James under which it pays his compensation to a Swiss executive search firm, which then pays James.

Beginning in Year 6, Arbortech made minority investments in five corporations engaged in technology development, four of which the firm accounts for using the cost method and one of which it accounts for using the equity method. Products developed by these companies could conceivably use PC cards. Arbortech also advanced amounts to some of these companies using interest-bearing notes.

Exhibits 6.27–6.29 present Arbortech's financial statements for the fiscal years ended June 30, Year 4, Year 5, and Year 6, based on the amounts originally reported for each year. Exhibit 6.30 presents selected financial statement ratios based on these reported amounts.

Exhibit 6.27

Arbortech
Balance Sheets as Originally Reported
(amounts in thousands)
(Case 6.3)

	Year 6	Year 5	Year 4	Year 3
ASSETS				
Cash	$ 6,182	$ 970	$ 981	$ —
Marketable securities	4,932	—	—	—
Accounts receivable	12,592	3,932	1,662	730
Inventories	18,229	8,609	3,371	2,257
Other current assets	6,256	1,932	306	234
Total Current Assets	$48,191	$15,443	$6,320	$3,221
Investments in securities	2,472	—	—	—
Property, plant, and equipment, net	4,698	1,323	669	208
Other assets	421	1,433	601	666
Total Assets	$55,782	$18,199	$7,590	$4,095
LIABILITIES AND SHAREHOLDERS' EQUITY				
Accounts payable	$ 3,494	$ 3,571	$ 616	$1,590
Notes payable	4,684	1,153	—	980
Current portion of long-term debt	336	103	—	—
Other current liabilities	614	765	516	457
Total Current Liabilities	$ 9,128	$ 5,592	$1,132	$3,027
Long-term debt	367	162	—	—
Deferred tax liability	242	—	39	24
Total Liabilities	$ 9,737	$ 5,754	$1,171	$3,051
Common stock	$ 165	$ 110	$ 90	$ 60
Additional paid-in capital	38,802	10,159	5,027	146
Retained earnings	7,078	2,176	1,302	838
Total Shareholders' Equity	$46,045	$12,445	$6,419	$1,044
Total Liabilities and Shareholders' Equity	$55,782	$18,199	$7,590	$4,095

Exhibit 6.28

Arbortech
Income Statements as Originally Reported
(amounts in thousands)
(Case 6.3)

	Year 6	Year 5	Year 4
Sales	$ 37,848	$12,445	$ 8,213
Other revenues	353	10	9
Cost of goods sold	(23,636)	(6,833)	(4,523)
Selling and administrative	(4,591)	(3,366)	(1,889)
Research and development	(1,434)	(752)	(567)
Interest	(370)	(74)	(495)*
Income taxes	(3,268)	(556)	(284)
Net Income	$ 4,902	$ 874	$ 464

*Includes the cost of factoring receivables and interest on bridge financing obtained and repaid during the year.

Exhibit 6.29

Arbortech
Statements of Cash Flows as Originally Reported
(amounts in thousands)
(Case 6.3)

	Year 6	Year 5	Year 4
OPERATIONS			
Net income	$ 4,902	$ 874	$ 464
Depreciation	645	337	193
Other addbacks and subtractions, net	1,159	(5)	219
Working capital provided by operations	$ 6,706	$ 1,206	$ 876
(Increase) Decrease in accounts receivables	(8,940)	(2,433)	(981)
(Increase) Decrease in inventories	(9,620)	(5,238)	(1,115)
(Increase) Decrease in other current assets	(836)	(2,406)	(71)
Increase (Decrease) in accounts payable	(76)	2,955	(974)
Increase (Decrease) in other current liabilities	(152)	251	87
Cash Flow from Operations	$(12,918)	$(5,665)	$(2,178)
INVESTING			
Sale of investments	$ 3,981	$ —	$ —
Acquisition of fixed assets	(3,899)	(862)	(525)
Acquisitions of investments	(11,186)	—	—
Other investing transactions	(2,800)	—	—
Cash Flow from Investing	$(13,904)	$ (862)	$ (525)

(Continued)

Exhibit 6.29 (Continued)

FINANCING			
Increase in short-term borrowing	$ 3,531	$ 1,153	$ 550
Increase in long-term borrowing	691	320	—
Increase in common stock	28,064	5,099	4,663
Decrease in short-term borrowing	—	—	(1,529)
Decrease in long-term borrowing	(252)	(56)	—
Cash Flow from Financing	$ 32,034	$ 6,516	$ 3,684
Net Change in Cash	$ 5,212	$ (11)	$ 981
Cash—Beginning of year	970	981	—
Cash—End of Year	$ 6,182	$ 970	$ 981

Exhibit 6.30

Arbortech
Financial Ratios Based on Originally Reported Amounts
(Case 6.3)

	Year 6	Year 5	Year 4
Profit margin for ROA	13.6%	7.4%	9.6%
Assets turnover	1.0	1.0	1.4
ROA	13.9%	7.2%	13.5%
Profit margin for ROCE	13.0%	7.0%	5.6%
Capital structure leverage	1.3	1.4	1.6
ROCE	16.8%	9.3%	12.4%
Cost of goods sold/Sales	62.4%	54.9%	55.1%
Selling and administrative/Sales	12.1%	27.0%	23.0%
Research and development/Sales	3.8%	6.0%	6.9%
Income tax expense (excluding tax effects of interest expense)/Sales	9.0%	4.7%	5.5%
Accounts receivable turnover	4.6	4.4	6.9
Inventory turnover	1.8	1.1	1.6
Fixed assets turnover	12.6	12.5	18.7
Current ratio	5.3	2.8	5.6
Quick ratio	2.6	0.9	2.3
Days accounts payable	39	63	71
Operating cash flow to current liabilities ratio	(1.755)	(1.685)	(1.047)
Long-term debt to long-term capital ratio	0.008	0.013	—
Liabilities to assets ratio	0.175	0.316	0.154
Operating cash flow to total liabilities ratio	(1.668)	(1.636)	(1.032)
Interest coverage ratio	23.1	20.3	2.5

Financial Statement Irregularities

On February 10, Year 7, after receiving information regarding various accounting and reporting irregularities, the board of directors fired James and relieved the chief financial officer of his duties. The board formed a special committee of outside directors to investigate the purported irregularities, obtaining the assistance of legal counsel and the firm's independent accountants. On February 21, Year 7, the New York Stock Exchange announced the suspension of trading in the firm's common stock. The stock was delisted on April 25, Year 7. On February 14, Year 7, the major Boston bank providing working capital financing notified the firm that the firm had defaulted on its line of credit agreement. Although this bank subsequently extended the line of credit through July 31, Year 7, it increased the interest rate significantly above prime. Arbortech decided to seek a new lender.

The investigation by the board's special committee revealed the following accounting and reporting irregularities:

- Recording of invalid sales transactions: The firm created fictitious purchase orders from regular customers using purchase order forms from legitimate purchase transactions. The firm then purportedly shipped empty PC card housings to these customers at bogus addresses. James apparently paid the accounts receivable underlying these sales with his personal funds.
- Recording of revenues from bill and hold transactions: The firm kept its books open beyond June 30 each year and recorded as sales of each year products that were shipped in July and should have been recorded as revenues of the next fiscal year.
- Manipulation of physical counts of inventory balances and inclusion of empty PC card housings in finished goods inventories.
- Failure to write down inventories adequately for product obsolescence.
- Inclusion of certain costs in property, plant, and equipment that the firm should have expensed in the period incurred.
- Inclusion in advances to other technology companies of amounts that represented pre-paid license fees. The firm should have amortized these fees over the license period.
- Failure to provide adequately for uncollectible amounts related to advances to other technology companies.
- Failure to write down or write off investments in other technology companies when their market value was less than the cost of the investment.

Exhibits 6.31–6.33 present Arbortech's restated financial statements for the fiscal years ending June 30, Year 4, Year 5, and Year 6, after correcting for the irregularities. These exhibits also present the financial statements for the nine months ended March 30, Year 7. The firm decided during February of Year 7 to change its fiscal year to a March year-end. Exhibit 6.34 presents selected financial ratios based on the restated financial statements.

REQUIRED

a. Using information in the financial statements as originally reported in Exhibits 6.27–6.29, compute the value of Beneish's manipulation index for fiscal Year 5 and Year 6.

b. Using information from Requirement a and the financial ratios in Exhibit 6.30, indicate possible signals that Arbortech might have been manipulating its financial statements.

c. Describe the effect of each of the eight accounting irregularities on the balance sheet, income statement, and statement of cash flows.

d. Using information in the restated financial statements in Exhibits 6.31–6.33, the financial ratios in Exhibit 6.34, and the information provided in this case, as a commercial banker,

Exhibit 6.31

Arbortech
Balance Sheets Using Restated Data
(amounts in thousands)
(Case 6.3)

	Year 7	Year 6	Year 5	Year 4	Year 3
ASSETS					
Cash	$ 57	$ 6,182	$ 970	$ 981	$ —
Marketable securities	—	4,932	—	—	—
Accounts receivable	5,571	11,260	2,802	1,280	730
Inventories	7,356	8,248	2,181	1,581	2,257
Other current assets	14,229	6,395	2,284	839	669
Total Current Assets	$ 27,213	$ 37,017	$ 8,237	$4,681	$3,656
Investments in securities	20,332	1,783	—	—	—
Property, plant, and equipment, net	3,087	2,033	923	399	243
Other assets	566	299	390	123	172
Total Assets	$ 51,198	$ 41,132	$ 9,550	$5,203	$4,071
LIABILITIES AND SHAREHOLDERS' EQUITY					
Accounts payable	$ 4,766	$ 3,025	$ 3,303	$ 772	$1,590
Notes payable	10,090	4,684	1,153	—	980
Current portion of long-term debt	671	336	103	—	—
Other current liabilities	7,117	811	562	116	457
Total Current Liabilities	$ 22,644	$ 8,856	$ 5,121	$ 888	$3,027
Long-term debt	—	367	162	—	—
Total Liabilities	$ 22,644	$ 9,223	$ 5,283	$ 888	$3,027
Common stock	$ 177	$ 165	$ 110	$ 90	$ 60
Additional paid-in capital	82,240	42,712	10,843	5,059	146
Retained earnings	(53,630)	(10,968)	(6,686)	(834)	838
Foreign currency adjustment	(233)	—	—	—	—
Total Shareholders' Equity	$ 28,554	$ 31,909	$ 4,267	$4,315	$1,044
Total Liabilities and Shareholders' Equity	$ 51,198	$ 41,132	$ 9,550	$5,203	$4,071

would you be willing to offer Arbortech a line of credit as of July 31, Year 7? If so, provide the conditions that would induce you to offer such a line of credit.

e. Exhibit 6.35 presents the values of Altman's Z-score for fiscal Year 4, Year 5, and Year 6 based on the originally reported amounts and the restated amounts. Compute the value of Altman's Z-score for the fiscal year ended March 31, Year 7. Although this is not technically correct, use the income amounts for the nine-month period ending March 31, Year 7. Based on the amounts in the proposed settlement of the class-action lawsuits, the value of the common equity on March 31, Year 7, is $50,068,568.

f. Can Arbortech avoid bankruptcy as of mid-Year 7? Explain. Why doesn't the Altman model signal the financial difficulties earlier?

Exhibit 6.32

Arbortech
Income Statements Using Restated Data
(amounts in thousands)
(Case 6.3)

	Nine Months Ended March 31:	Year Ended June 30:		
	Year 7	Year 6	Year 5	Year 4
Sales	$ 28,263	$ 33,412	$ 8,982	$ 7,801
Other revenues	67	353	10	9
Cost of goods sold	(24,453)	(29,778)	(11,575)	(6,508)
Selling and administrative	(7,318)	(3,803)	(2,442)	(2,083)
Research and development	(1,061)	(1,434)	(753)	(567)
Loss on investments	(14,096)[a]	(2,662)[a]	—	—
Investigation costs	(3,673)[b]	—	—	—
Provision for settlement of shareholder litigation	(20,000)[c]	—	—	—
Interest	(391)	(370)	(74)	(495)
Income taxes	—[d]	—[d]	—[d]	171
Net Income (Loss)	$(42,662)	$ (4,282)	$ (5,852)	$(1,672)

[a]Write-offs of advances (and write-downs or write-offs of investments) in technology companies.

[b]Legal, accounting, and related costs of investigating misstatements of financial statements.

[c]Estimated cost of class-action lawsuits arising from misstatements of financial statements. Arbortech reached an agreement on June 18, Year 7, to pay the plaintiffs $1,475,000 in cash (included in accounts payable on the March 31, Year 7 balance sheet) and common stock of $18,525,000 (included in additional paid-in capital on the March 31, Year 7 balance sheet). The common stock portion of the settlement represents 37% of the common stock of Arbortech.

[d]Arbortech incurred net losses for income tax purposes and maintains a valuation allowance equal to the balance in deferred tax assets.

Exhibit 6.33

Arbortech
Statements of Cash Flows Using Restated Data
(amounts in thousands)
(Case 6.3)

	Nine Months Ended March 31,	Year Ended June 30,		
	Year 7	Year 6	Year 5	Year 4
OPERATIONS				
Net loss	$(42,662)	$ (4,282)	$(5,852)	$(1,672)
Depreciation and amortization	831	471	281	176
Other addbacks and subtractions, net	28,812	2,005	224	352
Working capital provided by operations	$(13,019)	$ (1,806)	$(5,347)	$(1,144)
(Increase) Decrease in accounts receivable	5,289	(8,883)	(1,693)	(599)
Increase (Decrease) in inventories	454	(6,067)	(600)	676
(Increase) Decrease in other current assets	$ (8,092)	$ (5,213)	$(1,932)	$ (176)
Increase (Decrease) in accounts payable	6,572	(9)	3,072	(818)
Increase (Decrease) in other current liabilities	—	(20)	(96)	(340)
Cash Flow from Operations	$ (8,796)	$(21,998)	$(6,596)	$(2,401)
INVESTING				
Sale of investments	$ 32,182	$ 3,981	$ —	$ —
Acquisition of fixed assets	(2,074)	(1,459)	(583)	(332)
Acquisition of investments	(38,892)	(11,186)	—	—
Cash Flow from Investing	$ (8,784)	$ (8,664)	$ (583)	$ (332)
FINANCING				
Increase in short-term borrowing	$ 5,406	$ 3,531	$ 1,153	$ 550
Increase in long-term borrowing	250	691	320	—
Increase in capital stock	4,060	28,813	5,099	4,663
Decrease in short-term borrowing	—	—	—	(1,529)
Decrease in long-term borrowing	(282)	(252)	(56)	—
Proceeds from related-party transaction	2,021	3,091	652	30
Cash Flow from Financing	$ 11,455	$ 35,874	$ 7,168	$ 3,714
Change in Cash	$ (6,125)	$ 5,212	$ (11)	$ 981
Cash—Beginning of year	6,182	970	981	—
Cash—End of Year	$ 57	$ 6,182	$ 970	$ 981

Exhibit 6.34

Arbortech
Financial Ratios Based on Restated Data
(Case 6.3)

	Year 7*	Year 6	Year 5	Year 4
Profit margin for ROA	(150.0%)	(12.1%)	(64.6%)	(17.2%)
Assets turnover	0.6	1.3	1.2	1.7
ROA	(91.9%)	(15.9%)	(78.7%)	(29.0%)
Profit margin for ROCE	(150.9%)	(12.8%)	(65.2%)	(21.4%)
Capital structure leverage	1.5	1.4	1.7	1.7
ROCE	(141.1%)	(23.7%)	(136.4%)	(62.4%)
Cost of goods sold/Sales	86.5%	89.1%	128.9%	83.4%
Selling and administrative/Sales	25.9%	11.4%	27.2%	26.7%
Research and development/Sales	3.8%	4.3%	8.4%	7.3%
Special provisions/Sales	133.6%	8.0%	—	—
Accounts receivable turnover	3.4	4.8	4.4	7.8
Inventory turnover	3.1	5.7	6.2	3.4
Fixed assets turnover	11.0	22.6	13.6	24.3
Current ratio	1.2	4.2	1.6	5.3
Quick ratio	0.3	2.5	0.7	2.6
Days accounts payable	60	32	61	74
Operating cash flow to current liabilities ratio	(0.558)	(3.148)	(2.195)	(1.227)
Long-term debt to long-term capital ratio	—	0.011	0.037	—
Liabilities to assets ratio	0.442	0.224	0.553	0.171
Operating cash flow to total liabilities ratio	(0.552)	(3.033)	(2.138)	(1.227)
Interest coverage ratio	(108.1)	(10.6)	(78.1)	(2.7)

*Amounts based on a nine-month fiscal year.

Exhibit 6.35					
Arbortech **Altman's Z-Score** **(Case 6.3)**					
	Originally Reported Data			**Restated Data**		
	Year 6	**Year 5**	**Year 4**	**Year 6**	**Year 5**	**Year 4**
Net working capital/Total assets	0.8403	0.6496	0.8203	0.8216	0.3915	0.8748
Retained earnings/Total assets	0.1776	0.1674	0.2402	(0.3733)	(0.9801)	(0.2244)
Income before interest and taxes/ Total assets	0.5052	0.2727	0.5404	(0.3139)	(1.9966)	(0.8550)
Market value of equity/Book value of liabilities	15.3089	13.1911	8.0700	16.1620	14.3672	10.6419
Sales/Total assets	0.6785	0.6838	1.0821	0.8123	0.9405	1.4993
Z-score	17.5105	14.9646	10.7530	17.1088	12.7225	11.9366

Financing Activities

LEARNING OBJECTIVES

LO 7-1 Describe the financial statement reporting of investments by owners (equity issuances) and distributions to owners (dividends and share repurchases).

LO 7-2 Explain the accounting for share-based compensation (stock options, stock appreciation rights, and restricted stock).

LO 7-3 Identify the components of other comprehensive income.

LO 7-4 Apply financial reporting principles to long-term and short-term debt (bonds, notes payable, leases, and troubled debt).

LO 7-5 Explain the accounting for and financial reporting of hybrid securities.

LO 7-6 Describe how operating and capital leases affect financial statements, and make adjustments required to convert operating leases to capital leases.

LO 7-7 Explain how economic effects of derivatives used to hedge changes in long-term debt interest rates are reported in financial statements.

LO 7-8 Identify significant likely changes in the financial reporting standards for debt and leases.

Chapter Overview

Chapter 6 examined the concept of accounting quality. In this and the next two chapters, we describe certain accounting issues in more depth so that you can understand the accounting procedures used by management to, hopefully, best represent the economics of the business. In this chapter, we examine the accounting issues related to financing activities, focusing on the right side of the balance sheet which conveys the results of raising equity capital from investors and debt capital from creditors. We will also examine the effects of financing activities on income and cash flows. Firms engage in financing activities to raise the capital necessary to engage in investing activities (the acquisition of productive and investment assets), which we cover in . Having deployed external capital into productive assets, firms engage in their primary operating activities, which we discuss in . Throughout Chapters 7–9, we identify the choices made by management and the principles established by standard setters that lead to published financial statements. Because of the rapid pace with which accounting is moving toward common standards for financial reporting, we cover both U.S. GAAP and IFRS. Many of the accounting principles are similar under U.S. GAAP and IFRS, but we note significant differences.[1]

To preview the focus in this chapter on financing activities, refer to **PepsiCo**'s December 29, 2012, consolidated balance sheet (Appendix A). PepsiCo reports $74,638

---

[1]We provide codification numbers from the FASB's Codification Project, which represents authoritative guidance in the United States as of July 1, 2009. We also refer to specific accounting standards by the IASB.

million of total assets, virtually all of which PepsiCo uses in its operations. The primary claims against these assets are $52,239 million of creditor claims (that is, total liabilities), of which $23,544 million and $4,815 million are classified as long-term and short-term debt obligations, respectively, and $22,399 million in equity claims (that is, total common shareholders' equity). This chapter focuses on the balance sheet claims represented by long-term and short-term debt obligations, as well as residual claims represented by shareholders' equity.

We begin with equity financing activities, which include raising capital by issuing common stock and preferred stock, the return of capital to shareholders via dividends and share repurchases, and the use of equity (and equity appreciation) to compensate employees via stock options, stock appreciation rights, and restricted stock plans. Then we discuss the effects on shareholders' equity of net income and other comprehensive income. The second section of the chapter deals with debt financing activities. We examine the accounting for and reporting of notes payable and bonds, troubled debt, hybrid securities, and liabilities that are not reflected in financial statements (off-balance-sheet financing), including operating leases and their effective capitalization for cross-sectional comparability and risk-analysis purposes. We also discuss the use of derivatives to hedge interest rate risk on long-term debt. We conclude with a look at likely major changes in the financial reporting of debt and leases that are under standard-setter deliberation as of the writing of this text.

LO 7-1

Describe the financial statement reporting of investments by owners (equity issuances) and distributions to owners (dividends and share repurchases).

Equity Financing

Corporations raise a substantial amount of cash by issuing shares of common stock and by deploying the funds received into profitable operations. The amount of shareholders' equity reported in the balance sheet (the *book value* of shareholders' equity) is the investment base for return-on-equity calculations used in profitability analysis (Chapter 4), the measure of owner financing in risk analysis (Chapter 5), and the measure of the value of net assets in place used in residual income-based equity valuation (Chapters 13 and 14). The three primary events that change the book value of shareholders' equity are:

- Investments by shareholders, usually net cash received by the company at equity issue date.
- Distributions to shareholders, usually in the form of periodic cash dividend payments to investors and/or share repurchases.
- Profitable operating and investing activities, primarily consisting of net income but also "other comprehensive income."

The following sections discuss the accounting and financial statement disclosures related to these events.[2]

---

[2]*FASB Codification Topic 505* describes applicable U.S. GAAP on shareholders' equity accounting. Equity financing is an example of the scarcity of formal IFRS guidance. Other than standards on disclosure (International Accounting Standards Board, *International Accounting Standards 1,* "Presentation of Financial Statements") and share-based payment (International Accounting Standards Board, *International Financial Reporting Standard 2,* "Share-Based Payment"), international standards are basically silent on how to account for shareholders' equity transactions.

Investments by Shareholders: Common Equity Issuance

The general principle of accounting for common equity issues is to record the equity claim on the balance sheet at the *fair value* of what the corporation initially receives from the investor. If the issuing firm cannot reliably measure fair value of what it receives, it uses the fair value of the equity issued to record the transaction. As long as the fair value of one side of the exchange is determinable, the fair value of the other side of the transaction is implied under the assumption that unrelated parties exchange equal fair values in arm's-length transactions.

Most commonly, an equity investor transfers cash to the corporation to secure an equity interest. However, the investor could transfer assets (such as property) to or perform services for the corporation in return for an equity interest. Instead of issuing common stock to the investor, the corporation could issue other types of equity interests: preferred stock, options to purchase common stock, or stock rights.[3] In any event, the fair-value rule applies. The fair value received is split between two contributed capital accounts: common stock (par value) and additional paid-in capital (amount of fair value received that exceeds par value). Additional paid-in capital is generally referred to as *share premium* in many non-U.S. jurisdictions. The partition of proceeds into the par and additional paid-in capital accounts is not significant from an analysis viewpoint because par value is declared by the board of directors and has no economic meaning. In fact, some firms issue "no par" common stock.[4]

Common shareholders' equity is the residual interest in the corporation, which equals the assets remaining after all liabilities are paid. Because common shareholders bear both residual upside and downside risk, they generally have control, as evidenced by the right to vote. However, contractual relationships between the firm and other parties can limit common shareholder control. For example, effective control can be obtained through contracts to acquire all of a firm's output or to use all of a firm's productive capacity or through rights to obtain control of productive capacity through purchase at a later date. These types of contracts are common in the area of SPEs (special-purpose entities), which were discussed in Chapter 6. Also, to protect their claims on assets, debtholders often require firms to enter into debt covenants, which are contracts to restrict common shareholder control of certain operating and financing decisions such as expansion, dividend payment, and additional borrowings.

Corporations sometimes also issue *preferred stock*. Issuing preferred stock involves a trade-off between maintaining corporate control (preferred stock does not have voting

---

[3]Common shareholders normally possess a preemptive right that enables them to maintain a proportional ownership when the corporation issues additional stock. When a corporation issues stock rights, it receives nothing from investors in return (no effect on financial statements). The issuance of rights is nothing more than a formal recognition of a right that already existed. When investors exercise their stock rights, the resulting issuance of common stock is reported as an issue of stock for cash. Another type of stock right sometimes issued by a company as a takeover defense, stock purchase rights, allows current shareholders to purchase an additional number of shares in the event that an outside party acquires or attempts to acquire a substantial equity stake in the company.

[4]Generally, fair value is measured at the date on which common shares are issued. Under some circumstances (discussed in this and later chapters), the fair value received might be measured on two dates: an earlier date when the first part of a two-part transaction occurs (for example, date of issue of warrants, convertible preferred stock, and stock options) and then a later date when the corporation receives cash (for example, when options or warrants are exercised). Also, on occasion, individuals and governments donate assets to a corporation. Although the corporation issues nothing in return, existing shareholders have greater equity because of the donation. The basis for recording a donation is the fair value of the donated asset.

rights) and creating a class of shareholders with preference above common equity share-holders in all asset distributions, including dividends. Accounting for the initial issue of preferred stock is no different than accounting for the issue of common stock. The fair-value rule applies when a firm issues preferred stock. Preferred stock (at par) is normally reported before common stock in the shareholders' equity section because preferred shareholders have priority over common shareholders in corporate liquidations. In addition to the preference in dividends and distribution, preferred stock dividends may accumulate if not declared and paid (the cumulative right). These *dividends in arrears* must be declared and paid before common stock dividends are declared and paid and must be disclosed in the notes to the financial statements. Preferred stock may be convertible into common shares (a positive feature for investors) or callable at scheduled dates or at the firm's discretion (a negative feature for investors). The call options that can exist on preferred stock raise the larger issue (discussed in a later section) of whether certain types of preferred stock should be designated as debt rather than equity.

To illustrate basic shareholders' equity accounting, assume that a company raises capital through the following series of equity issues:

1. Issues 100,000 shares of $1 par value common stock for $5 per share.
2. Receives land in exchange for 28,000 shares of $1 par common stock. The equity investor purchased the land for $85,000. Similar land has recently sold for $150,000.
3. Issues 5,000 shares of $10 par value preferred stock for $75,000.

Exhibit 7.1 summarizes the financial statement effects of the transactions. (Let APIC = additional paid-in capital.) Dollar amounts indicate the effects of each transaction on the

Exhibit 7.1: Accounting for Common and Preferred Share Issuances

	Assets		=	Liabilities	+	Shareholders' Equity			
						CC		AOCI	RE
1.	Cash	+500, 000				Common Stock +100,000 APIC +400,000			

Cash		500,000	
Common Stock			100,000
APIC			400,000

	Assets		=	Liabilities	+	Shareholders' Equity			
						CC		AOCI	RE
1.	Cash	+150, 000				Common Stock +28,000 APIC +122,000			

Land		150,000	
Common Stock			28,000
APIC			122,000

	Assets		=	Liabilities	+	Shareholders' Equity			
						CC		AOCI	RE
3.	Cash	+75,000				Preferred Stock +50,000 APIC +25,000			

Cash		75,000	
Preferred Stock			50,000
APIC			25,000

financial statement elements (that is, on assets, liabilities, or a subelement of shareholders' equity: contributed capital = CC, accumulated other comprehensive income = AOCI, or retained earnings = RE). The applicable journal entry follows each financial statement effect template entry and shows the effects of each transaction on specific accounts.

Shareholders' equity is increased by the fair value of the asset (cash) contributed to the corporation in Transaction 1. In Transaction 2, the fair value of the land contributed to the company is a readily determinable $150,000 (cash price of similar land), and this amount becomes the basis for measurement of the transaction. However, often fair values of non-cash asset (for example, land) are harder to obtain and may require the corporation to rely on an estimate of the fair value of common shares issued (for example, share price in an active market if available). Note that contributed capital is divided into par value and additional paid-in capital amounts when preferred or common shares are issued.

Cash flow effects of these financing activities are reported in the financing section of the statement of cash flows as sources of cash. The issue of stock for land is reported in a separate schedule of "significant investing and financing activities that do not affect cash" that accompanies the statement of cash flows.

Refer to **PepsiCo**'s consolidated balance sheet (Appendix A). In the shareholders' equity section, PepsiCo discloses that it has *issued* 1,866 million shares of common stock (out of 3,600 million shares *authorized* for issue by the board of directors) and repurchased 322 million shares that it holds in the *treasury*, a net of 1,544 million shares *outstanding*, with a par value of 1 2/3¢ per share. (1,544 million × 1 2/3¢ per share is approximately equal to $26 million.) The December 29, 2012, balance in capital in excess of par (that is, additional paid-in capital) implies that issue prices over time for common stock and possibly options and warrants (discussed later) have exceeded par value by $4,178 million. PepsiCo reports $41 in preferred stock, but does not use a separate additional paid-in capital account because the preferred stock has no par value. PepsiCo reports in Note 12 that the preferred stock was issued for an employee stock ownership program established by its Quaker subsidiary. Each of the 186,533 shares outstanding as of December 29, 2012, is convertible into 4.9625 shares of PepsiCo common stock at the option of the holder. PepsiCo also may call the preferred shares at $78 per share plus accrued and unpaid dividends. We examine the financial statement effects of conversions and calls later in this chapter.

Distributions to Shareholders: Dividends

Net income is accumulated through time in retained earnings, which is reported as part of shareholders' equity on the balance sheet. Dividend distributions reduce retained earnings. They are simply a transfer to shareholders of a portion of what they already own—the increase over time in the net assets of the firm recognized as net income. The portion of net income retained by the firm represents reinvestments by shareholders.

The declaration of dividends is formalized by three important dates because of the administrative complexity of identifying shareholders of record at any given point in time.

- On the date on which the board of directors declares a dividend, called the *date of declaration,* the firm incurs a legal liability to distribute the dividend.
- The recipients of the dividend will be the owners of the stock as of a specific future date, called the *date of record.*
- On the *date of payment,* the dividend distribution occurs.

Typically, these three dates are several weeks apart.

Corporations generally pay dividends in cash. However, corporations can also pay dividends with

- interest-bearing promissory notes (scrip dividends).
- investments in other corporations' stock (property dividends).
- corporate assets, such as property (dividends in kind).

For cash, scrip, and in-kind dividends, the retained earnings component of share-holders' equity is reduced by the fair value of the item distributed on the date of declara-tion and a liability is recorded. Dividends decrease the net assets of a corporation, and this decrease is reported in the statement of shareholders' equity. The date of record has no impact on the corporation's accounting. No change in equity occurs on the date of payment because both assets (cash or property) and liabilities (dividends payable) decrease (that is, no change in *net* assets). If dividends are declared but not paid by year-end, a (nonoperating) liability for dividends payable appears in the current liabil-ities section of the balance sheet.[5]

In many jurisdictions (especially non-U.S. countries), the balance of retained earn-ings represents the limit for dividend payments. However, payments to shareholders that exceed the balance in retained earnings, called *liquidating dividends*, can occur. If the dividend is greater than the retained earnings balance, in most jurisdictions, the increment must be used to decrease contributed capital. A liquidating dividend is a return of the original investment by shareholders (that is, their original contribution to the firm when they purchased common shares).

Stock Dividends and Stock Splits

On occasion, corporations distribute additional shares of their own stock to current stockholders in the form of *stock dividends*. Unlike other forms of dividends, stock divi-dends do *not:*

- involve a transfer of assets to investors.
- result in a change in total shareholders' equity.
- change the proportional ownership of shareholders.
- change investor wealth.

The effects of stock dividends and splits on retained earnings and contributed cap-ital are determined by accounting rules and jurisdictional legal requirements. In small stock dividends (distributions of less than 20–25% of common shares), the fair value of shares issued is transferred out of retained earnings and into contributed capital. U.S. GAAP is ambiguous with respect to midrange dividends (20–100%), and fre-quently, laws of the state of incorporation determine the accounting treatment. How-ever, in most cases (and consistent with SEC guidance), midrange stock dividends are treated as a transfer of the par value of shares among shareholders' equity accounts (that is, from retained earnings to contributed capital or within contributed capital accounts).

Most large distributions that are greater than or equal to 100% are in the form of a *stock split*. Suppose a company wanted to double the number of shares outstanding and therefore halve the price of its stock. This could be accomplished by issuing a 100% stock dividend or a 2-for-1 stock split. Similar to midrange stock dividends, accounting

---

[5]IFRS (*IAS* 1) requires disclosure of proposed but not yet approved dividends and post-year-end declared dividends.

for a large stock dividend depends on appropriate state law. Most of the time, the par value of the shares is transferred to common stock from either retained earnings or additional paid-in capital. Firms may also wish to reduce the number of shares outstanding using a *reverse stock split*. For example, in a 1-for-2 reverse stock split, the number of shares outstanding is reduced by 50% and the stock price per share doubles. In the past, firms have engaged in reverse stock splits to meet minimum share price requirements to be listed on organized exchanges and to attract institutional investors that may have policies prohibiting the acquisition of shares traded below a threshold price.

In a stock split, U.S. GAAP does not require an amount to be shifted from retained earnings to contributed capital, but state laws may allow an amount to be shifted from either retained earnings or additional paid-in capital to common stock. Accounting rules require that the par value of individual shares be adjusted so that the total par value after the stock split is the same as the total par value before the split. Therefore, in a 2-for-1 split of 50,000 shares of $10 par value stock, a company issues an additional 50,000 shares and reduces par value to $5 on all 100,000 shares.

From an analysis viewpoint, it is important to remember that:

- the accounting for stock dividends and splits simply reallocates amounts *within* shareholders' equity.
- the total amount of shareholders' equity remains unchanged, because assets have not been disbursed from the corporation (that is, cash has not been paid out).
- increasing the number of shares outstanding does proportionately decrease per-share amounts for earnings, book value, and cash flow.

To illustrate the accounting for stock dividends and splits, assume that Mystic, Inc., reports the following in its 2012 financial statements:

- Common stock, $3 par, 2,263 million shares outstanding
- Average share price during 2012: approximately $20
- Common dividends paid during 2012: $0.20 per share

Exhibit 7.2 shows the financial statement effects of the following events. (Assume the events are independent.)

1. Mystic declares and pays a dividend of $452.6 million (2,263 million shares × $0.20 per share). Assume that the dividends are declared and then paid at a later date.
2. Mystic distributes a property dividend by giving common shareholders common shares of another company that it carries as a short-term investment in marketable securities. The securities have a fair value of $2.0 million and an original cost of $1.8 million. Mystic uses mark-to-market accounting for these securities and declares the dividend at some time after the securities have been marked to market.
3. Mystic distributes a 10% stock dividend (10% × 2,263 million shares outstanding = 226.3 million shares; 226.3 million shares × $3 = $678.9 million par value; 226.3 million shares × $20 market price = $4,526 million fair value).
4. Mystic distributes a 100% stock dividend (2,263 million additional shares; 2,263 × $3 = $6,789 million par value).
5. Mystic declares a 2-for-1 stock split.
6. Mystic declares a 1-for-2 reverse stock split.

Exhibit 7.2: Accounting for Stock Dividends and Splits (amounts in millions)

Declaration:

	Assets	=	Liabilities	+	Shareholders' Equity		
					CC	AOCI	RE
1.			Dividends Payable +452.6				Retained Earnings −452.6

| Retained Earnings | | | | 452.6 | | | |
| Dividends Payable | | | | | | 452.6 | |

Date of record: No entry

Payment:

	Assets	=	Liabilities	+	Shareholders' Equity		
					CC	AOCI	RE
1.	Cash −452.6		Dividends Payable +452.6				

| Dividends Payable | | | | 452.6 | | | |
| Cash | | | | | | 452.6 | |

	Assets	=	Liabilities	+	Shareholders' Equity		
					CC	AOCI	RE
2.	Investments −2.0						Retained Earnings −2.0

| Retained Earnings | | | | 2.0 | | | |
| Investments | | | | | | 2.0 | |

	Assets	=	Liabilities	+	Shareholders' Equity		
					CC	AOCI	RE
3.					Common Stock +678.9 APIC +3,847.1		Retained Earnings −4,526.0

Retained Earnings				4,526.0			
Common Stock						678.9	
APIC						3,847.1	

	Assets	=	Liabilities	+	Shareholders' Equity		
					CC	AOCI	RE
4.					Common Stock +6,789.3		Retained Earnings −6,789.3

| Retained Earnings | | | | 6,789.3 | | | |
| Common Stock | | | | | | 6,789.3 | |

5. Memorandum entry only to note that the number of shares outstanding doubles to 4,526.2 million and the par value decreases to $1.50 per share.
6. Memorandum entry only to note that number of shares outstanding falls in half to 1,131.6 million and the par value doubles to $6 per share.

Note that dividends distributed in the form of assets (that is, cash and property; Transactions 1 and 2) decrease shareholders' equity (the sum of the last three columns). Dividends distributed in the form of common stock (Transactions 3 and 4) generate a rearrangement of shareholders' equity but no change in total shareholders' equity. Likewise, stock splits (Transactions 5 and 6) have no effect on total shareholders' equity or the balance of any account in shareholders' equity. Cash outflow for cash dividends is reported in the financing section of the statement of cash flows.[6]

Refer to **PepsiCo**'s 2012 consolidated statement of common shareholders' equity. In the reconciliation of retained earnings, PepsiCo reports cash dividends declared in

[6]Transaction 3 and 4 assume that Mystic declares a stock dividend and distributes the dividend in the same period. If a financial statement reporting date intervenes, "stock dividend distributable" will be reported as a contra-equity account instead of a reduction in retained earnings as shown in the template.

2012 on common stock ($3,312 million), on preferred stock ($1 million), and on RSUs, or restricted stock units, ($23 million), yielding total reduction of retained earnings due to a dividend declaration of $3,366 million. PepsiCo's consolidated statement of cash flows reports $3,305 million cash dividends paid in the financing activities section. The excess of dividends declared over dividends paid as of the balance sheet date ($61 million) is reflected as an increase in the nonoperating liability "Dividends payable."

Distributions to Shareholders: Share Repurchases

For several reasons, corporations may distribute cash to shareholders and reduce shareholders' equity via *share repurchases*. For example, employee compensation plans often grant options to acquire common stock. To service the possible exercise of options, companies may repurchase shares to have a supply of their own stock on hand or, alternatively, to offset the dilution of existing shareholders' proportional ownership from share issuances under the option exercises. Corporations also might repurchase stock simply to shift the mix of debt and equity financing or to signal to investors that corporate management believes the stock is undervalued because investors have underestimated potential future earnings or cash flows. Finally, fewer shares outstanding mean less dilution of voting power. This may be particularly important if the firm is facing a takeover attempt, for example.

Share repurchases reduce equity, and the effects on the statement of cash flows are simple. Using cash to reduce equity is a cash outflow reported as a financing activity. Similarly, the effects on the income statement are simple: there are no effects. The reduction of equity is a distribution to owners, a transaction that does not affect income. Balance sheet effects of share repurchases depend on whether the shares of stock are retired or held as treasury stock for eventual reissue. If the shares are retired, the amounts originally recorded in the common stock (that is, par value) and the additional paid-in capital accounts are removed. **Microsoft** and **Starbucks** are examples of companies that repeatedly engage in large share repurchases and the retirement of the purchased shares, either by choice or because state law requires the retirement. The typical case is that the cash paid to retire the shares exceeds the amount at which the shares were originally issued. This excess is treated as a dividend, and like regular cash dividends, it is removed from retained earnings. Less typical is the case in which the amount paid to buy back the shares is less than the original issue price. In this case, additional paid-in capital is increased as if the shareholders left amounts in the firm as a permanent capital contribution.

If firms repurchase stock for reissue at a later date, the stock is referred to as *treasury stock*. Two acceptable methods are used to account for treasury stock: the cost method and the par method. Because the par method is rarely used, we focus our discussion on the cost method. The cost method was designed under the assumption that any treasury stock acquired would be reissued.

Using cash to acquire stock to be held in the treasury decreases shareholders' equity. The treasury stock acquired is not an asset of the corporation. A corporation cannot own itself. The payment of cash to owners is a distribution to owners. Under the cost method, this distribution is shown as an increase in a contra-equity account called Treasury Stock. The increase in contra-equity is equivalent to a decrease in equity. Under the cost method, the Treasury Stock account is usually shown at the bottom of the shareholders' equity section. Subsequent treasury share reissues reduce the treasury stock contra-equity account and increase (or decrease) additional paid-in capital if the subsequent reissue price is greater than (less than) the cost of the treasury stock.

No gain or loss is recorded because the reissue of treasury stock is, in concept, identical to the original issue of common stock (cash invested, common stock issued).

Refer to the common shareholders' equity section of **PepsiCo**'s consolidated balance sheet (Appendix A). PepsiCo reports a subtraction in the equity section for (in millions) "Repurchased common stock, in excess of par value (332 and 301 shares, respectively)" of $19,458 million and $17,870 million at the ends of 2012 and 2011, respectively. In past years' financial statements, PepsiCo has reported treasury stock at cost as a single subtraction in the shareholders' equity section, an approach consistent with the fact that it uses the cost method to account for treasury shares. In this current set of financial statements, however, PepsiCo has split up the cost amount between par value and cost over par value to accomplish the disclosure. Both its past and current approaches effectively subtract the cost of treasury stock from the section.

PepsiCo's consolidated statement of common shareholders' equity explains the change between years. Additional share repurchases total $3,219 million. This amount is a cash outflow to reduce equity capital, so it also is reported in the financing activities section of PepsiCo's consolidated statement of cash flows. In fact, it is the second-largest single cash outflow for 2012, and when added to dividends paid, represents $6,324 million in cash returned to equity holders. Treasury stock is often reissued when stock options are exercised, a topic discussed in the next section.

LO 7-2

Explain the accounting for share-based compensation (stock options, stock appreciation rights, and restricted stock).

Equity Issued as Compensation: Stock Options

Firms develop compensation plans to attract, retain, and motivate employees. Many of these plans include cash compensation that is fixed or that varies with levels of employee performance, often defined by an accounting-based income measure (such as return on equity) or stock returns. In a typical compensation arrangement, firms give employees the right, or option, to acquire shares of common stock at a fixed price. If share prices increase over time, employees can exercise their option to purchase shares at a price that is less than the market price of the shares. These arrangements are referred to as *stock options*, and their use skyrocketed during the 1990s and early 2000s. Firms in the technology sector have used options as a dominant component of their employee compensation packages.[7]

Stock options permit employees to purchase shares of common stock at a price usually equal to (or just above) the market price of the stock at the time the firm grants the stock option. Employees exercise these stock options at a later time if the stock price increases above the stock option exercise price. Corporations grant stock options because they have characteristics that align the interests of the employees with those of the shareholders. Clearly, an increase in stock price benefits shareholders, which is the same way stock options reward employees. Unlike compensation in the form of salaries, however, stock options do not require firms to use cash during the period in which the stock options are granted. In addition, the ability of a corporation to attract and retain employees is enhanced when firms offer equity incentives such as stock options as part of the compensation package. Employees with unvested stock options have an incentive to continue their employment with the company until they can exercise their options.

An understanding of the accounting for stock-based compensation requires understanding several key parameters:

- The *grant date* is the date a firm gives a stock option to employees.
- The *vesting date* is the first date employees can exercise their stock options.

[7]Due to more recent concerns about excessive executive compensation, the use of stock options has declined to some degree. However, many companies still use stock option plans for incentive compensation.

- Employees cannot exercise options before the vesting date or after the end of the option's life.
- To enhance employee retention and increase motivation during the vesting period, firms usually structure stock option plans so that a period of time elapses between the grant date and the vesting date.
- Firms may preclude employees from exercising the option for one or more years, or they may set an exercise price so high that employees would not want to exercise the option until the stock price increases.

- The *exercise date* is the date employees elect to exchange the options plus cash for shares of common stock.
- The *exercise price* is the price specified in the stock option contract for purchasing the common stock.
- The *market price* is the price of the stock as it trades in the market.
- In theory, the value of a stock option has two elements: (1) the benefit realized on the exercise date because the market price of the stock exceeds the exercise price (the *benefit element*) and (2) the length of the period during which the holder can exercise the option (the *time-value element*).

The amount of the benefit element is not known until the exercise date. In general, stock options with exercise prices less than the current market price of the stock (described as *in the money*) have a higher value than stock options with exercise prices exceeding the current market price of the stock (described as *out of the money*).

The time-value element of an option results from the benefit it provides its holder if the market price of the stock increases during the exercise period. The greater the market price of the stock exceeds the exercise price during the exercise period, the greater the benefit to the option holder. This time-value element of an option will have more value the longer the exercise period, the more volatile the market price of the stock, the lower the dividend yield, and the lower the discount rate. Note that a stock option may have an exercise price that exceeds the current market price (zero value for the benefit element) but still have value because of the possibility that the market price will exceed the exercise price on the exercise date (positive value for the time-value element). As the expiration date of the option approaches, the value of the time-value element approaches zero.

Fair value is the basis for stock option accounting.[8] Firms must measure the fair value of stock options on the date of grant. Because the value of employee stock options typically cannot be measured with an observable value established by trading in an active market, most firms will estimate the fair value of the options with the Black-Scholes model or a lattice model (for example, the binomial model). A detailed discussion of option valuation models can be found in the finance literature and is beyond the scope of this text. However, any model employed must incorporate a variety of factors, including the exercise price of the option, the term of the option, the current market price of each share of underlying stock, expected stock price volatility, dividends, and the risk-free interest rate.[9]

---

[8]*FASB Codification Topic 718.* The promulgation of FASB *Statement No. 123 (Revised 2004)* represents a convergence with international standards. International Accounting Standards Board, *International Financial Reporting Standard 2,* "Share-Based Payment."

[9]For an elaboration on the history of options pricing, see Fischer Black and Myron Scholes, "The Pricing of Options and Corporate Liabilities," *Journal of Political Economy* (May/June 1973), pp. 637–654. A critique of the reliability of various valuation models can be found in American Accounting Association's Financial Accounting Standards Committee, "Response to the FASB's Exposure Draft on Share-Based Payment: An Amendment of FASB *Statements No. 123* and *No. 95,*" *Accounting Horizons* (June 2005), pp. 101–114.

Once the firm estimates the fair value of stock options as of the grant date, it must recognize this amount as compensation expense ratably over the period in which an employee provides services (commonly, the vesting period) and disclose the effects of the stock option grants on total compensation expense, the methodology (model) used to value the stock options, and the key assumptions made to estimate the value of the stock options.

Illustration of Accounting for Stock Options

Assume that an Internet-based company decides to conserve cash and align management incentives with shareholders' incentives by compensating managers with 9,000 options to purchase $1 par value common stock for $10 per share. The current stock price is $10 per share. The vesting period is three years, and the options can be exercised during the following seven years. Using an appropriate options pricing model, the company values the options at $2 each.

Exhibit 7.3 illustrates the financial statement effects of these transactions:

1. Grant date
2. Recognition of compensation expense for each of the three years in the vesting period
3. Exercise of an option when a share of common stock is trading at $18
4. Expiration of an option
5. Revocation of an option early in the third year of the vesting period when a manager leaves the firm

The options' fair value is $18,000 ($2 per option × 9,000 options). No financial statement effects occur at the grant date because the manager has yet to provide service to the firm. The $18,000 fair value is allocated over the three-year vesting period, $6,000 per year, as an increase in compensation expense (a decrease in net income, which is also a decrease in retained earnings). Rather than accepting cash compensation, the manager accepts an option to acquire an equity interest; therefore APIC from stock options increases shareholders' equity. Note that the net effect of Transaction 2 on total shareholders' equity (the sum of the last three columns) is zero (retained earnings decreases, but APIC increases).

Exercise of an option (Transaction 3) involves a transfer of the stock option plus a $10 exercise price from the manager to the corporation. Through the effects on three shareholders' equity accounts, total shareholders' equity increases by $10, the fair value of the cash received. Note that the cash received is not equal to the fair value of the common equity, which is trading at $18. The amount reflected in the equity accounts after this transaction is posted is $1 in common stock and $11 in additional paid-in capital. Thus, common stock issued is recorded at $12, which equals the fair value of the cash surrendered ($10) plus the grant date estimate of the fair value of the option ($2).[10]

In a stock option expiration (Transaction 4), the capital contributed to the firm by the manager's employment is reclassified as a permanent contribution to shareholders' equity. If a manager fails to perform the three years of service, the option is revoked (Transaction 5). The amount of the compensation expense related to revoked options is removed from compensation expense of the current period. This treatment is an example of a change in estimate handled prospectively. The firm estimated that compensation expense was $6,000 per year based on the expected three-year service of

---

[10]If previously acquired treasury shares rather than new shares are issued, treasury stock is reduced by the amount of the original acquisition cost and APIC is used to record the remainder of the equity increase.

Exhibit 7.3: Accounting for Stock Options

1. No entry at grant date. (The contract is executory.) However, the fair value of the options is measured at the grant date. Fair value = 9,000 options × $2 per option = $18,000.

Years 1, 2, and 3:

	Assets	=	Liabilities	+	Shareholders' Equity		
					CC	AOCI	RE
2.					APIC—Stock Options +6,000		Compensation Expense −6,000

Each year		
Compensation Expense	6,000	
APIC—Stock Options		6,000

Exercise:

	Assets	=	Liabilities	+	Shareholders' Equity		
					CC	AOCI	RE
3.	Cash +10				Common Stock +1 APIC +11 APIC—Stock Options −2		

Cash	10	
APIC—Stock Options	2	
Common Stock		1
APIC		11

Expiration:

	Assets	=	Liabilities	+	Shareholders' Equity		
					CC	AOCI	RE
4.					APIC—Expired Options +2 APIC—Stock Options −2		

APIC—Stock Options	2	
APIC—Expired Options		2

Revocation:

	Assets	=	Liabilities	+	Shareholders' Equity		
					CC	AOCI	RE
5.					APIC—Stock Options −2		Compensation Expense +2

APIC—Stock Options	2	
Compensation Expense		2

employees. If an employee leaves the firm and an option is revoked, estimates must be revised *going forward.* Prior period adjustments to expenses are not made.[11]

Option events create two cash flows. The exercise of an option increases cash from equity issues and is reported as a financing activity. Although not shown in the preceding template, the corporation will receive a tax deduction at the date the manager exercises the option, equal to the market price at the exercise date minus the exercise price. (The manager will be taxed on this same amount because it is compensation.) The tax savings is treated as a financing cash inflow.

---

[11]We assume that the forfeiture was unexpected. If forfeitures are expected, then the original estimate of compensation expense should be lower, and the treatment we show should be used for unexpected additional forfeitures. Also, we reduced compensation expense by the entire amount of the option (instead of the two-thirds already recognized as compensation expense) assuming that the last year's worth of the compensation expense allocation would be unaffected. An alternative would be to reduce compensation expense by $2 × 2/3 and reduce the $6,000 compensation expense for Year 3 by the same amount.

Options "Overhang"

The existence of unexercised options and the expected future issuance of shares create a potentially dilutive effect on firm value. When options are exercised, firms receive cash equal to the exercise price, but must transfer shares to the option holder to satisfy the exercise. The exercise price is often considerably less than the market price of a share, so additional cash, which would have been free cash flow to current shareholders, must be used to buy back outstanding shares from the market. Alternatively, the firm could issue new shares, but again, this has a dilutive effect on value per share for existing shareholders.

Option overhang can be significant, especially for technology firms that tend to compensate with options. Defining options overhang in terms of the ratio of outstanding options to outstanding shares, **Cisco**'s options overhang was slightly under 10% as of the end of 2012, but exceeded 20% five years earlier. Cisco's option overhang was reduced by substantial exercises and open market share repurchases to satisfy the exercises.

The potential cash flow consequences of options overhang to existing shareholders measured by the difference between current market price and the exercise price (i.e., the intrinsic value of the options) is disclosed in the notes to the financial statements. For example, in Note 6, **PepsiCo** discloses that the intrinsic values of exercisable stock options and restricted stock units as of December 29, 2012, are $567.7 million and $815.0 million, respectively.

You should be aware of the potential of options overhang to adversely affect firm value. The intrinsic values presented above are not exact estimates of net cash outflows which could be less if the options are not vested and which will be less due to the tax deduction to the firm when the employee exercises.

LO 7-2

Explain the accounting for share-based compensation (stock options, stock appreciation rights, and restricted stock).

Alternative Share-Based Compensation: Restricted Stock and RSUs

Exercising stock options can create a cash flow problem for employees. The employee must pay the exercise price and may have to pay taxes on compensation in order to acquire the stock, which he or she may want to hold rather than sell. An alternative share-based compensation program eliminates a manager's need to pay the exercise price. At the grant date, the manager could be given shares of stock rather than options (far fewer shares than options because the fair value of a share is usually greater than the fair value of an option to purchase the stock), which cannot be traded until after a vesting period (*restricted stock*).[12] Or the manager could receive nontradable rights for a number of shares of stock once the vesting period is completed (called *restricted stock units*, or RSUs).

To illustrate the accounting for restricted stock, assume that an Internet-based company decides to compensate managers by giving them 1,000 shares of $1 par value common stock when the market price is $10 per share. The vesting period is two years, and the stock cannot be traded until after the vesting period. Exhibit 7.4 illustrates the financial statement effects of the following transactions:

1. Grant date
2. Recognition of compensation expense at the end of each of the two years in the vesting period

---

[12]The descriptor *restricted* simply means that the stock granted is generally restricted from being traded until it vests; the holder of restricted shares is usually entitled to dividends and voting rights.

Exhibit 7.4: Accounting for Restricted Stock

Grant Date:

	Assets	=	Liabilities	+	Shareholders' Equity		
					CC	AOCI	RE
1.					Common Stock +1,000 APIC +9,000 Deferred Compensation −10,000		
	Deferred Compensation				10,000		
	Common Stock				1,000		
	APIC				9,000		

Years 1 and 2:

	Assets	=	Liabilities	+	Shareholders' Equity		
					CC	AOCI	RE
2.					Deferred Compensation +5,000		Compensation Expenses −5,000
	Each Year:						
	Compensation Expense				5,000		
	Deferred Compensation				5,000		

In contrast to an option grant, the common stock is issued at the grant date, so an entry recognizes the existence of the common stock (Transaction 1). Note that no change in net assets occurred, so total shareholders' equity does not change. The amount of compensation is more reliably measured (relative to an option) given that the fair value of the stock is more easily measured by reference to market prices. During the vesting period, as managers earn the compensation under the restricted stock plan (Transaction 2), retained earnings is decreased by the net income effect of compensation expense and deferred compensation, a contra-equity account, is decreased. The net effect of the second transaction is a shift of amounts out of retained earnings in to contributed capital. Again, no change in assets or liabilities occurred, so no change in total shareholders' equity is recognized.

The decrease in stock option use in recent years has been offset by an increase in the use of restricted stock plans and cash settlement plans. Once the FASB disallowed the use of the previously acceptable intrinsic value method to value stock options (usually at $0), the primary benefit of using stock options for compensation—no expense on the income statement—disappeared. As a consequence, the use of restricted stock became more common, and although there are some tax ramifications to the employee, a primary benefit to the employee of restricted stock grants relative to option grants is that options can expire worthless but restricted stock almost always has a nonzero value.

Alternative Share-Based Compensation: Cash-Settled Share-Based Plans

LO 7-2

Explain the accounting for share-based compensation (stock options, stock appreciation rights, and restricted stock).

The number, complexity, and diversity of share-based compensation plans do not permit a comprehensive treatment in any given textbook. However, the stock option, restricted stock, and RSU plans illustrated in this chapter represent the large majority of share-based compensation plans.

In recent years, a number of firms have created compensation plans that provide cash compensation to employees based on share-price appreciation. These plans, often called *stock appreciation rights* plans, are cash-settled plans and, accordingly, do not result in increases in the contributed capital portion of shareholders' equity pursuant to a distribution of an option or a share of common stock. Conceptually, cash-settled share appreciation plans are similar to compensating employees with cash bonuses for output (for example, exceeding sales quotes or earnings targets). The key difference is that the firm relies on the stock market's assessment of the value of the firm to determine the amount of the cash payment.

The essence of the accounting for cash-settled compensation plans is an increase in an operating liability for the estimated cash payments to the employee and a corresponding increase in compensation expense. For example, **SAP AG**'s IFRS-based financial statements describe the workings of its STAR plan and note that "As our STAR plans are settled in cash, rather than by issuing equity instruments, a liability is recorded for such plans based on the current fair value of the STAR awards at the reporting date."

Note 6, "Stock-Based Compensation" (Appendix A), describes the stock options **PepsiCo** granted to employees and members of the company's board of directors. The PepsiCo LTIP (long-term incentive plan) is typical of plans offered by many firms. PepsiCo options generally have ten-year terms and three-year vesting periods. In a subsection of Note 6, "Stock-Based Compensation—Method of Accounting and Our Assumptions" (Appendix A), PepsiCo states, "We account for our employee stock options under the fair value method of accounting using a Black-Scholes valuation model to measure stock option expense at the date of grant." PepsiCo also uses RSUs and a new plan based on the achievements of earnings targets and stock prices (PepsiCo equity performance units or "PEPUnits") to compensate executives. Stock-based compensation for 2012 ($278 million) is relatively small for PepsiCo when compared to its total expenses for 2012 of more than $56 billion, as shown on its consolidated income statement. However, this is not the case for some firms, particularly technology-based firms.

PepsiCo reports four line items in its 2012 consolidated statement of cash flows that relate to share-based compensation arrangements. In the financing activities section, cash proceeds from the exercise of stock options totaled $1,122 million, which by any measure is a substantial increase in equity financing. The financing activities section also includes the tax benefits from the deduction afforded PepsiCo when employees exercise their options, $124 million in 2012. Because stock option-based compensation is an operating expense that reduces net income (and the tax savings increases net income), two line items exist in the operating activities section as well. Under the indirect method of preparing this section, stock-based compensation expense is a non-cash expense; thus, $278 million is added back to net income. Also, although the excess tax benefits are a source of cash, the source is not considered an operating activity by rule; thus, the $124 million tax benefits are deducted to arrive at operating cash flows.

Quick Check

- Although there are many kinds of capital transactions with owners, each involves the exchange of something of value (cash, property, services, labor, etc.) for a right to the item of value (for example, a share of common stock or an option to acquire it).
- Fair value is the basis for recording each of the transactions.

- When the item of value is transferred to the firm, such as cash to purchase shares or labor to acquire stock options, owners' equity increases. When the item of value is transferred to the owner, such as cash to pay dividends or to reacquire shares, owners' equity decreases.

Net Income, Retained Earnings, Accumulated Other Comprehensive Income, and Reserves

LO 7-3

Identify the components of other comprehensive income.

In addition to contributed capital, earned capital not distributed in dividends is available to finance investing and operating activities. The following sections describe the reporting of earned capital.

Net Income and Retained Earnings

Many of the financing events examined so far—equity issues, share buybacks, and cash dividends—are transactions with shareholders that change shareholders' equity directly. Profitable investing and operating activities also lead to increases in shareholders' equity via increases in net assets reported as net income on the income statement. Through the accounting closing process, net income is reflected as an increase in retained earnings on the statement of shareholders' equity, which supports the balance in retained earnings reported on the balance sheet.

PepsiCo's 2012 consolidated statement of shareholders' equity reconciles the balance of retained earnings at the beginning of 2012 ($40,316 million) to its balance at the balance sheet date, December 29, 2012, ($43,158 million). Net income of $6,178 million causes retained earnings (and thus, shareholders' equity) to increase. Dividends declared on common stock, preferred stock, and RSUs decrease retained earnings.

Accumulated Other Comprehensive Income

Another component of shareholders' equity, *AOCI (accumulated other comprehensive income),* is a consequence of standard setters allowing certain asset and liability revaluations (called *other comprehensive income*) to bypass the income statement and be reported directly in shareholders' equity (as opposed to the treatment of items in net income, which first appear on the income statement and then are reflected as an increase in shareholders' equity via retained earnings).[13] Chapter 3 introduced the comprehensive income concept. This chapter provides a brief discussion of the items comprising AOCI, with subsequent chapters discussing the detailed accounting and reporting. Under U.S. GAAP, four items are disclosed as part of AOCI, and IFRS adds a fifth item:

- *Unrealized gains and losses from investments in available-for-sale securities.* Other comprehensive income arises when firms experience unrealized fair value gains or losses on securities deemed available for sale (described in detail in Chapter 8). Each year, a firm will recognize in the statement of comprehensive income the net change in unrealized fair value gains or losses on available-for-sale securities, which are reported cumulatively in AOCI. When the firm sells the securities, it eliminates the unrealized gain or loss account and recognizes a realized gain or loss in measuring net income.

---

[13]*FASB Codification Topic 220;* International Accounting Standards Board, *International Accounting Standard 1,* "Presentation of Financial Statements."

- *Unrealized gains and losses from translation of foreign financial statements during the consolidation process.* U.S. firms with foreign operations usually translate the financial statements of their foreign entities into U.S. dollars each period using the exchange rate at the end of the period (also discussed in detail in Chapter 8). Changes in the exchange rate cause an unrealized foreign currency gain or loss. Firms do not recognize this gain or loss in measuring net income each period; instead, they recognize foreign currency translation gains and losses in the statement of comprehensive income, and accordingly increase or decrease AOCI in shareholders' equity. Presumably, using AOCI to capture such unrealized gains and losses minimizes the impact of the volatility of foreign currency exchange rates on reported profits while reflecting current values of assets and liabilities. If exchange rates reverse or the firm disposes of the foreign unit, it eliminates the unrealized foreign currency adjustment from AOCI and, in the case of a disposal, recognizes a gain or loss in net income.
- *Unrealized gains and losses from certain hedging activities.* Illustrated in a latter part of this chapter and again in Chapter 9, changes in the fair value of cash flow hedges are also reported as other comprehensive income and accumulated in other comprehensive income on the balance sheet. When the hedged cash flows occur and generate an income statement effect, an offsetting portion of the AOCI is reclassified into current net income.
- *Unrealized gains and losses from changes in certain pension assets and liabilities.* Pension accounting (discussed in detail in Chapter 9) is driven by changes in two key economic amounts, the pension liability, which is the present value of all future expected pension payments to retirees, and the pension asset, which is the fair value of cash and securities set aside to make those payments. *Expected* changes in the liability, determined by the discount rate used to compute the liability's present value and the service credits earned during the period by current employees, and *expected* changes in the asset, determined by the expected return on asset investments, are reflected in current period net income through pension expense. *Unexpected* changes in the asset and liability, driven by changes in the discount rate, actual returns on assets, and changes in other actuarial assumptions such at mortality rates, are treated as unrealized gains and losses and reported in AOCI. They are amortized to current period net income over time.
- *Unrealized gains and losses from revaluations of long-lived operational assets (IFRS).* IFRS permits periodic revaluations of fixed assets and intangible assets to their current market value (discussed in Chapter 8). Increased valuation of assets leads to an increase in a revaluation reserve account included in the shareholders' equity section of the balance sheet (similar to AOCI). Depreciation or amortization of the revalued assets may appear fully on the income statement each period as an expense or may be split between the income statement (depreciation or amortization based on acquisition cost) and a reduction in the revaluation reserve (depreciation or amortization based on the excess of current market value over acquisition cost).

Given that total shareholders' equity is the same regardless of whether the unrealized gain or loss immediately affects net income or affects another shareholders' equity account (AOCI) and later affects net income, your primary concern with other comprehensive income is the appropriateness of revaluing the associated asset or liability and delaying recognition of its income effect. To the extent that the changes in AOCI are transitory (it is, after all, difficult to predict future changes in interest rates, market returns, and exchange rates), the amounts should be excluded from predictions of future earnings. However, you should consider whether management can control the timing of reclassifications of AOCI to current income. We consider this issue in the context of trading securities in Chapter 8.

Fluctuations in comprehensive income and AOCI reflect risks. The fluctuations are quantifications of the effect on value of the firms' exposures to interest rate, market return, exchange rate, and commodity price risk. A look at a firms' comprehensive income through time confirms that comprehensive income is generally far more volatile than net income.

Reserves

In some countries, local GAAP permits certain income items to bypass the income statement and, instead, increase or decrease a shareholders' equity account directly (similar to AOCI under U.S. GAAP and IFRS). A practice in some countries is to create a reserve account by reducing retained earnings. For example, a firm might decrease retained earnings and increase a shareholders' equity account titled Reserve for Contingencies or Retained Earnings Appropriated for Contingencies. When firms later resolve the contingency, they charge the cost against the reserve account rather than include it in expenses. Therefore, these costs bypass the income statement and usually result in an overstatement of reported earnings. Note that this use of reserves does not misstate total shareholders' equity because all of the affected accounts (retained earnings, reserve accounts, and expense accounts) are components of shareholders' equity. Thus, your primary concern with these reserves is assessing whether the reported net income that excludes these items is an appropriate representation of firm profitability and a reliable base for estimating future earnings. You can study the shareholders' equity portion of the balance sheet to ascertain whether firms have used reserve accounts to avoid sending legitimate expenses through the income statement. Reserves of this type had been particularly common in the German home-country standards-based reporting system prior to the adoption of IFRS.

Refer to the common shareholders' equity section of **PepsiCo**'s consolidated balance sheet (Appendix A). At December 29, 2012, PepsiCo reports retained earnings of $43,158 million and an accumulated other comprehensive loss of $5,487 million. The retained earnings balance represents accumulated (over the life of PepsiCo) increases in net assets of the company, *which were reported in net income*, minus dividends declared. The accumulated other comprehensive loss represents decreases in net assets of the company from asset and liability revaluations, *which were not reported in net income*. PepsiCo's consolidated statement of common shareholders' equity describes how accumulated other comprehensive loss changed during 2012 from a beginning accumulated loss of $6,229 million to the ending accumulated loss of $5,487 million reported in the balance sheet. This *decrease* in accumulated other comprehensive loss (that is, a current year gain) is the difference between 2012 net income ($6,214 million) and 2012 comprehensive income ($6,920 million). PepsiCo shows this reconciliation in a consolidated statement of comprehensive income.[14] The gain that PepsiCo recognize in comprehensive income in 2012 is largely a consequence of a currency translation gain ($737 million). During 2011, comprehensive income ($3,844 million) was considerably smaller than net income ($6,443 million) because of foreign currency translation and pension-related losses. One argument for recognizing such gains and losses in other comprehensive income and in the Accumulated Other Comprehensive Income/Loss account is that these types of revaluations of assets and liabilities tend to be transitory; that is, they have the potential to reverse over time. You should examine the behavior of accumulated other comprehensive income through time to see whether including elements of other comprehensive income in current income would aid in the assessment of the risk of the firm and in the prediction of future income.

---

[14]IFRS (IAS 1) also require a schedule of other comprehensive income.

Summary and Interpretation of Equity

Common shareholders' equity represents the book value of equity investor claims. Dividing common shareholders' equity by the number of common shares outstanding yields *book value per share*. Securities markets determine the *market price per share* of common stock, by the interaction of supply and demand for shares. The ratio of book and market value, called the *market-to-book ratio,* is as follows:

$$\text{Market-to-Book Ratio} = \text{Market Price per Share}/\text{Book Value per Share}$$

Market-to-book ratios that are exactly equal to one imply the market value and the accounting value of equity are the same. In many cases, market-to-book ratios are greater than one for two primary reasons. First, the conservatism of accounting (as a result of accounting standards themselves or management's application of accounting standards) leads to book values of individual assets that are typically equal to or less than their fair values (but not greater than their fair values). For example, if a company's operations include a great deal of R&D (research and development) which is expensed immediately under U.S. GAAP, the unrecorded economic assets created by such expenditures causes book value per share to be lower than fair value. Second, future growth opportunities increase market price per share but have not been reflected in accounting measurements of book value.

For book value to be recognized in financial statements, U.S. GAAP and IFRS require that transactions have taken place or that unresolved future events can be estimated reliably. Therefore, book value of shareholders' equity tends to lag market value. Chapters 13 and 14 describe a valuation approach that relates book value to market value through the expectations of future accounting earnings not yet embedded in book value.

Quick Check

- Changes in shareholders' equity result from transactions with owners (issuances of stock and distributions such as dividends and share buybacks).
- Changes in shareholders' equity also result from transactions with non-owners, which are reflected in one of the two parts of comprehensive income, either net income or other comprehensive income.

- Financing strategy drives the changes in shareholders' equity from transactions with owners.
- Operating and investing strategies drive profitability and the changes in shareholders' equity from transactions with non-owners.

LO 7-4

Apply financial reporting principles to long-term and short-term debt (bonds, notes payable, leases, and troubled debt).

Debt Financing

As discussed in Chapter 5, the use of debt to finance investments and operations levers up the return on common equity, which can benefit common shareholders. However, the use of debt also has its risks and costs. Debt increases solvency risk, and therefore the required return to common shareholders (that is, the cost of equity capital) is increasing in the amount of debt in a corporation's capital structure. Further, net income is reduced by interest charges on debt. Accordingly, the financial reporting and analysis of debt is critical to understanding the profitability and risk of a firm.

In this section, we address the accounting for traditional debt financing activities that receive balance sheet recognition, including the issue of long-term notes and bonds, debt reduction, accounting for troubled debt, and the issue and conversion of hybrid securities, as well as other financing activities which may or may not result in balance sheet recognition (sales of receivables and operating leases). We give special attention to lease financing, and we show how you can adjust financial statements to incorporate off-balance-sheet lease financing in the assessment of financial risk.

Financing with Long-Term Debt

As illustrated in Chapters 4 and 5, profitable firms can use leverage to increase the rate of return on common equity. The primary source of leverage for most firms is the issuance of long-term debt in the form of notes payable (primarily to banks and other financial institutions), bonds payable (to any type of bondholder, including open-market debt investors), and leases (entered into with property owners, equipment dealers, or finance companies). Debt issuance is evidenced by a bond indenture, promissory note, or lease agreement. These documents will specify:

- promises to pay principal amounts at specified dates.
- promises to pay cash interest (or in the case of leases, lease payments) of specified amounts at specified dates.
- call provisions.
- descriptions of property pledged as security.
- whether the debt is convertible to another claim and at what rate the conversion will occur.
- covenants and restrictions that specify sinking fund requirements, working capital restrictions, dividend payment restrictions, restrictions on the issuance of new debt, and other restrictions.

This section illustrates the accounting for long-term debt using notes payable. Accounting for bonds payable is similar except for the possibility that bonds may be traded in more active markets, thus having more readily determinable fair values. As discussed in the following sections, fair value of financial instruments is a required disclosure in the notes to the financial statements and an optional measurement for recognition in the financial statements. Note 9, "Debt Obligations and Commitments" (Appendix A), indicates that **PepsiCo** uses a number of long-term interest-bearing notes to raise capital. Assume that on January 1, 2013, PepsiCo issues a $100 million promissory note to a bank. The note matures in five years on January 1, 2018, and pays 5% interest once a year on January 1. The bank transfers $95.79 million (rounded) to PepsiCo.

PepsiCo's cash flows over the life of the note are as follows (in millions):

Cash inflow at issue		$ 95.79
Annual cash outflows (interest payments):		
Face amount of note	$100.00	
Coupon or stated interest rate	×5%	
Annual cash interest payment	$ 5.00	
Years	×5	
Total interest payments		(25.00)
Cash outflow at retirement date		(100.00)
Net cash outflow		$ (29.21)

The $29.21 million net cash outflow represents the total interest cost on the note. Accrual accounting recognizes the interest cost on the note over the five-year period in an economically meaningful way.

By paying less than $100 million for the note, the bank will earn a return that is greater than the 5% stated interest rate. That is, this investment is sufficiently risky such that the yield or effective interest rate should be higher than 5%, and therefore, the bank "discounts" the note. *Effective interest,* also known as the *yield, yield-to-maturity,* or *rate of return,* is a function of the risk characteristics of the transaction. It is the economic return on the transaction to creditors and the economic cost to debtors. In contrast, *cash interest* is determined by the *coupon rate* or *stated rate* of interest multiplied by the face value of the debt. The stated rate of interest is negotiated in a note or private bond placement or simply presented to potential buyers in a public bond issuance.[15]

A number of factors determine the effective interest rate. A portion of any effective interest rate contains compensation for the use of the lender's funds. While the funds are on loan, alternative, possibly more profitable opportunities may become available. Also, the effective interest rate will reflect expected inflation, which causes future dollars to have less purchasing power. In addition, if the loan is denominated in a foreign currency, relative changes in economic conditions across countries could result in an unfavorable transformation of foreign currency into the dollar. Finally, firm-specific liquidity and solvency risk (as discussed in Chapter 5) explains differences in effective interest rates.

You solve for a loan's effective rate of return (i) using the following formula:

$$\text{Present Value} = \sum_{n=1}^{t} \frac{\text{Cash Interest}}{(1+i)^n} + \frac{\text{Maturity Value}}{(1+i)^t}$$

$$\$95.79 \text{ million} = \sum_{n=1}^{5} \frac{\$5 \text{ million}}{(1+i)^n} + \frac{\$100 \text{ million}}{(1+i)^5}$$

Solving for i results in a yield of 6%.[16]

PepsiCo must use the effective interest method to account for the note. The effective interest amortization table is presented in Exhibit 7.5. Amounts in the Cash Interest column are obtained by multiplying the face value of the debt by the stated interest rate of 5%, and amounts in the Effective Interest column are obtained by multiplying the beginning of the period book value of note (previous row) by the 6% effective interest rate charged by the bank. The difference between them is the amortization of the discount.

The beginning book value of $95.79 million represents the amount lent to PepsiCo on 1/1/13. In 2013, PepsiCo incurs a 6% interest charge on its $95.79 million initial borrowing, $5.75 million of effective interest expense. Essentially, the debt has grown by $5.75 million. Because PepsiCo pays only $5 million in cash interest to the bank, the difference between the effective interest expense reported on the income statement and cash interest paid [shown in the Amortization column ($0.75 million)] increases the book value of the debt. Note that the amount of effective interest expense increases each period because the amount owed increases each period as PepsiCo incurs a constant

---

[15]If the effective rate of interest and the stated rate of interest are equal, computing the present value of the note will yield a present value equal to the face value of the note. When the debt holder pays the face value to acquire a bond or note, the bond or note is said to be "issued at par."

[16]Using a financial calculator to solve for i involves setting n (number of annual interest payments) = 5, payment (annual cash interest payment) = $5 million, present value = $95.79 million, and future value = $100 million.

		Exhibit 7.5		
		Effective Interest Amortization Table **(amounts in millions)**		
Date	**5% Cash Interest**	**6% Effective Interest Expense**	**Amortization**	**Book Value of Note**
1/1/13				$ 95.79
12/31/13	$ 5.00	$ 5.75	$0.75	96.54
12/31/14	5.00	5.79	0.79	97.33
12/31/15	5.00	5.84	0.84	98.17
12/31/16	5.00	5.89	0.89	99.06
12/31/17	5.00	5.94	0.94	100.00
	$25.00	$29.21		

6% economic interest charge on the debt. The annual increase in the debt is paid off as part of the $100 million maturity payment. Exhibit 7.6 shows the financial statement effects of these transactions and events.

Financial Reporting of Long-Term Debt

On the balance sheet, bonds and notes payable are reported at the present value of future cash flows using the historical effective rate of interest at the issue date. Note that the effective interest amortization table provides the book values of the note at each year end. At December 31, 2017, the $100 million maturity value must be reclassified as a current liability because funds will be disbursed within one year of the balance sheet date (actually, the next day). A reclassification of a large note payable from long-term to current may have a material adverse impact on working capital (current assets minus current liabilities) and the current ratio (current assets divided by current liabilities). In practice, this potential adverse impact is alleviated two ways. First, a firm may set up a sinking fund in liquid assets (because of debt covenants or as part of the firm's cash management policy) to be used to repay the debt. The sinking fund and debt classifications will have countervailing effects on working capital.[17]

Another means of avoiding the reclassification of long-term debt to a current liability is to enter into a refinancing agreement. If the firm has the intent and ability to refinance the debt on a long-term basis, U.S. GAAP allows the obligation to remain in the long-term classification at the balance sheet date (with appropriate footnote disclosure). Auditors will investigate whether the ability to refinance is present by searching for a refinancing agreement with a lender or for evidence that actual refinancing has taken place before the financial statements are issued.[18]

The statement of cash flows reports the net proceeds of debt issues, interest payments, and maturity payments. Under both U.S. GAAP and IFRS, cash flows relating to principal amounts of debt are reported as financing activities. Under U.S. GAAP, the

---

[17]Firms must provide note disclosure of sinking fund and bond retirement payments for each of the next five years after the balance sheet date. *FASB Codification Topic 440.*

[18]*FASB Codification Topics 440 and 470.*

Exhibit 7.6: Accounting for Notes Payable

1/1/13 Signing:

Assets		=	Liabilities		+	Shareholders' Equity		
						CC	AOCI	RE
Cash	+95.79		Note Payable	+95.79				

Cash	95.79	
Note Payable		95.79

12/31/13 Year-End Interest Accrual:

Assets	=	Liabilities		+	Shareholders' Equity			
					CC	AOCI	RE	
		Note Payable	+0.75				Interest Expense	−5.75
		Interest Payable	+5.00					

Interest Expense	5.75	
Note Payable		0.75
Interest Payable		5.00

1/1/14 Interest Payment Date:

Assets		=	Liabilities		+	Shareholders' Equity		
						CC	AOCI	RE
Cash	+5.00		Interest Payable	−5.00				

Interest Payable	5.00	
Cash		5.00

12/31/14 Year-End Interest Accrual:

Assets	=	Liabilities		+	Shareholders' Equity			
					CC	AOCI	RE	
		Note Payable	+0.79				Interest Expense	−5.79
		Interest Payable	+5.00					

Interest Expense	5.79	
Note Payable		0.79
Interest Payable		5.00

1/1/15 Interest Payment Date:

Assets		=	Liabilities		+	Shareholders' Equity		
						CC	AOCI	RE
Cash	+5.00		Interest Payable	−5.00				

Interest Payable	5.00	
Cash		5.00

12/31/15 Year-End Interest Accrual:

Assets	=	Liabilities		+	Shareholders' Equity			
					CC	AOCI	RE	
		Note Payable	+0.84				Interest Expense	−5.84
		Interest Payable	+5.00					

Interest Expense	5.84	
Note Payable		0.84
Interest Payable		5.00

cash flow portion of interest expense is included as an operating cash outflow because interest expense reduces net income, which is reported as a source of cash flow from operating activities under the indirect method. Under the indirect method, this is achieved by adjustments to net income for the portions of interest expense that are not cash flows. That is, interest payable increases must be added back in the operating cash flow section. Further, amortizations of bond discounts (premiums) increase (decrease) interest expense but are not cash outflows (inflows). Amortization of bond discounts (premiums) are added back (subtracted) in the operating section as well.[19]

Many companies disclose cash interest payments in the notes to the financial statements or in a supplementary schedule provided with the cash flow statement. PepsiCo discloses cash paid for interest in Note 14. Under IFRS, cash payments for interest can be reported as an operating or financing cash outflow. Under both U.S. GAAP and IFRS, the income statement reports interest expense as a nonoperating charge.

Fair Value Disclosure and the Fair Value Option

Long-term notes and bonds are financial instruments; therefore, firms must disclose the fair values in the notes to the financial statements.[20] In referring back to Exhibit 7.5, the December 31, 2015, book value of the note payable is $98.17 million. This amount is referred to as *amortized cost* because it represents the original "cost" of the debt, $95.79 million, adjusted for the amortization of the bank's discount for 2013–2015. The amount also represents the present value of the remaining cash flows (two more $5 million interest payments and one final $100 million principal payment) at the historical 6% effective rate of interest.

$$\$98.17 \text{ million} = \sum_{n=1}^{2} \frac{\$5 \text{ million}}{(1 + 0.06)^n} + \frac{\$100 \text{ million}}{(1 + 0.06)^2}$$

If the market's required rate of interest has changed since the original signing date of the note, the fair value of the debt will change as well. Suppose the market requires a 7% return on PepsiCo's note at December 31, 2015. The fair value of the note would then be:

$$\$96.38 \text{ million} = \sum_{n=1}^{2} \frac{\$5 \text{ million}}{(1 + 0.07)^n} + \frac{\$100 \text{ million}}{(1 + 0.07)^2}$$

PepsiCo would report the amortized cost of $98.17 million on the face of the balance sheet (probably in a group with other long-term debt) and the fair value of $96.38 million in the notes to the financial statements.

Recently, both the FASB and IASB passed a rule allowing firms the option of using fair value as the basis for balance sheet reporting of financial liabilities (and financial assets) instead of amortized cost.[21] If PepsiCo were to adopt the *fair value option* for this

---

[19]As discussed in Chapter 8, some interest can be capitalized when self-constructing an asset, which also causes a difference between interest expense and interest paid. Capitalized interest is a cash outflow in the investment activities section of the cash flow statement, reported as part of capital expenditures.

[20]*FASB Codification Topic 825*; International Accounting Standards Board, *International Financial Reporting Standard 7*, "Financial Instruments: Disclosures."

[21]Financial Accounting Standards Board, *Statement of Financial Accounting Standards No.159*, "The Fair Value Option for Financial Assets and Financial Liabilities" (2008); *FASB Codification Topic 825*; International Accounting Standards Board, *International Financial Reporting Standard 39*, "Financial Instruments: Recognition and Measurement."

debt, it would report $96.38 million of notes payable on the face of the balance sheet and an unrealized gain on remeasurement of long-term debt equal to $1.79 million ($98.17 million − $96.38 million) on the income statement (see Exhibit 7.7). The standards are silent on how to recognize interest expense on this new long-term-debt basis. However, using the effective interest method (as described previously) with the new market rate and new book value would be consistent with current practice. Firm must choose whether to elect the fair value option or not with the inception of each new financing instrument, and be consistent over the life of the instrument. Firms do not have to be consistent from one instrument to the next, so some firms may have some financing instruments reported on the balance sheet at amortized cost and other instruments reported at fair value.

Measuring Fair Value

The challenge that companies face in providing fair value disclosures is obtaining reliable data. Historically, standard setters have eschewed fair value measurement in favor of reliable historical data obtained from arm's-length transactions between the company and outside parties. Recently, however, the potential relevance of fair value data in decision making has been judged to outweigh potential measurement reliability issues, especially when the item being measured is a financial asset or financial liability and the company can provide information on the level of likely data reliability. For example, you may wish to use debt fair value estimates in weighted average cost of capital computations if the fair value differs significantly from book value.

Authoritative guidance identifies a hierarchy of inputs for fair value measurements, which were introduced in the discussion of fair value in Chapter 2. Level 1 inputs provide the most reliable measure and should be used if possible, followed by Level 2 and then Level 3. The level used for each asset or liability measurement must be disclosed. If multiple levels are used for a measurement, the least reliable level having a significant influence on the measurement must be disclosed. **PepsiCo**'s Note 10 discloses that PepsiCo uses a Level 2 basis for determining the fair value of its long-term debt. PepsiCo reports the fair value of its debt obligations as of December 29, 2012, and December 31, 2011, at $30.5 billion and $29.8 billion, respectively, based upon prices of similar instruments in the market place. The book value of debt obligations reported on the balance sheet was $28.359 billion and $26.773 billion at the same dates, suggesting a decrease in interest rates since original debt issue (that is, discounting fixed cash flows at lower interest rates increases the debt's present value). PepsiCo has not chosen the fair value option for debt. As a result, approximately $2.1 billion in unrealized loss (the current period excess of debt fair value over book value) does not appear in PepsiCo's 2012 income.

While few question the relevance of fair value measurement, many worry about the reliability of Level 2 and Level 3 estimates of fair values. While the quoted market prices of Level 1 valuations have intuitive appeal, the reliability of a Level 1 valuation is compromised if the market from which it comes is not "orderly." The market for mortgage-backed securities in 2008–2009 exhibited a volatility that caused some to question its orderliness.

Exhibit 7.7: Accounting for Revaluation of Notes Payable

12/31/15 Year-End Remeasurement at Fair Value:

Assets	=	Liabilities		+	Shareholders' Equity		
					CC	AOCI	RE
		Note Payable	−1.79				Unrealized Gain +1.79
Note Payable		1.79					
Unrealized Gain					1.79		

Reducing Debt

Outstanding debt can be reduced by paying off the principal when the debt matures. Alternatively, debt can be retired earlier through open-market purchase of traded debt, exercising call options (if available), or through conversion (if available). The difference between the amounts used to extinguish the debt and the book value of the debt at the time of extinguishment is reported as a realized gain or loss on the income statement. Cash flows used to reduce debt are reported as cash outflows from financing activities in the statement of cash flows. *In-substance defeasance* of debt, transferring or pledging assets to an irrevocable trust to satisfy debt while remaining contingently obligated, used to be another popular way of removing debt from the balance sheet. U.S. GAAP and IFRS (IAS 39) now prohibit de-recognition of debt via in-substance defeasance.

Accounting for Troubled Debt

The financial crisis of the late 2000s found many firms struggling to make debt payments. Many firms ended up declaring bankruptcy or renegotiating the terms of outstanding debt obligations. This section examines how the debtor accounts for the restructuring of troubled debt.[22] From the debtor's perspective, two situations exist for handling troubled debt: settlement and modification of terms.

The *settlement* of troubled debt results in an economic gain to the debtor because the creditor accepts less than the book value of the debt to settle the debt. If a non-cash asset is transferred to settle the debt (for example, a collateral asset), the non-cash asset must be adjusted to fair value prior to its transfer, with the resulting gain or loss reported in income. A gain on debt settlement is recognized as the difference between the book value of the debt settled (principal plus any accrued interest) and the fair value of the non-cash asset or cash transferred to retire the debt. Alternatively, debt could be settled by issuing capital stock. In this case, the stock issue is recorded at its fair value and the gain to the debtor is the excess of the book value of the debt relative to the fair value of the stock issued.

Instead of accepting an asset or common stock to retire the debt, a creditor might *modify the terms* of the debt (for example, reducing the payments or lengthening the amount of time to pay), hoping a debtor will be able to perform under less stringent debt service requirements. Under U.S. GAAP, if terms are modified, the debtor must compare the total (undiscounted) future cash flows of the restructured debt to the current book value of the debt. If the total restructured future cash flows remain greater than the book value of the debt, the debtor will make no adjustment to book value (that is, record no gain). Future recognition of interest expense will follow the effective interest method using a new interest rate that discounts the total restructured future cash flows to the current book value.

Alternatively, if the total undiscounted restructured future cash flows are less than the book value of the debt, the debtor will reduce the book value of the debt to equal the total of the new restructured future cash flows, recording a gain in the process.

---

[22]U.S. GAAP for the debtor is found in *FASB Codification Topic 470*. We address creditor accounting for troubled debt in Chapter 8. In a troubled debt restructuring, a creditor makes concessions to a debtor experiencing financial difficulties. Recently, the FASB issued "A Creditor's Determination of Whether a Restructuring is a Troubled Debt Restructuring," *Accounting Standards Update No. 2011-02* (Norwalk, CT: FASB 2011), which clarifies that a concession involves the creditor receiving restructured cash flows that are lower than original contractual cash flows and that financial difficulties means that it is probable that the debtor will not pay some or all of the original contractual cash flows. IFRS ("Financial Instruments: Recognition and Measurement," *International Accounting Standard No. 39*, as amended effective January 1, 2011) requires similar identification of a restructuring except that, under IFRS, objective evidence of a loss event leading to the expected impairment is required.

Future interest expense will not be recognized because all future cash flows represent the repayment of principal; that is, the discount rate is assumed to be zero. This accounting is conservative because future cash flows must fall significantly before the debtor actually recognizes a gain. The result of the conservative accounting is to minimize any gains recognized by debtors who experience difficulty and must restructure debt agreements. The existing conservative accounting rules for troubled debt are subject to frequent (and deserved) criticism because they ignore the present value of future restructured cash flows for determining book values of troubled debt and gains from debt restructuring, and they often result in subsequent recognition of interest expense based on an unrealistic interest rate assumption.

We contrast U.S. GAAP and IFRS treatment of troubled debt from the debtor's perspective with the following example. Assume that Tribune Co. owes Bank of America $2,000,000 on a 5-year, 8% note originally issued at par. After one year of making scheduled payments, Tribune faces financial difficulty. At the end of the second year, Tribune owes Bank of America $2,000,000 plus $160,000 of accrued but unpaid interest. Bank of America restructures the note by forgiving the $160,000 interest payable, reducing the note principal to $1,800,000, and reducing the interest rate to 7%.

Under U.S. GAAP, Tribune compares the gross (that is, undiscounted) future cash outflows under the restructured debt to the current book value of the debt as follows:

Undiscounted future cash flows of restructured debt:

New principal	$1,800,000	
New interest ($1,800,000 × 7% × 3 remaining years)	378,000	$2,178,000

Current book value of debt:

Old principal	$2,000,000	
Old accrued interest	160,000	$2,160,000

Because undiscounted future cash flows exceed the current book value of the debt, Tribune does not record a gain. Future interest expense is accounted for using the effective interest method and an effective interest rate that equates the future cash flows with the present value (that is, current book value) of the debt.

$$\$2,160,000 = \sum_{n=1}^{3} \frac{\$126,000}{(1+i)^n} + \frac{\$1,800,000}{(1+i)^3}$$

Solving for i yields a very small interest rate of 0.0029%.

Instead, if Bank of America reduced the principle to $1,700,000, Tribune would make the following comparison:

Undiscounted future cash flows of restructured debt:

New principal	$1,700,000	
New interest ($1,700,000 × 7% × 3 remaining years)	357,000	$2,057,000

Current book value of debt:

Old principal	$2,000,000	
Old accrued interest	160,000	$2,160,000

Because undiscounted future cash flows are less than the current book value of debt, Tribune reduces the book value of the debt to $2,057,000 and records a gain of $103,000 ($2,160,000 − $2,057,000). Future interest expense does not exist (that is, the effective rate is set equal to zero) because the future cash flows are now equal to the present value (that is, the reduced book value).

Under IFRS, Tribune would compare the present value of future cash flows under the restructured debt (instead of the undiscounted cash flows as under U.S. GAAP) to the book value of the debt. Return to the original example where Bank of America reduced the principal to $1,800,000. The present value calculation uses the historical effective interest rate of 8% as follows:

Present value of future cash flows (using a financial calculator):

FV = $1,800,000, PMNT = $1,800,000 × 7% =		
$126,000, i = 8%, n = 3		$1,753,612
Current book value of debt:		
Old principal	$2,000,000	
Old accrued interest	160,000	$2,160,000

IFRS uses a "10 percent rule" to determine whether a gain is recognized. Because the present value of $1,753,612 is 23.2% below the book value of $2,160,000 (that is, greater than 10% below book value), Tribune recognizes a gain. The *amount of the* gain is equal to the amount by which the *fair value* of the debt is below the current book value. Computing fair value of the restructured debt's cash flows requires the use of a current market rate of interest instead of the historical rate of 8%. For example, because of Tribune's financial difficulties, assume that a more appropriate current rate of interest for Tribune is 12%. Discounting the same cash flows using a 12% rate yields a present value of $1,583,835. Therefore, Tribune would report the book value of this restructured debt at $1,583,835 and record a gain of $576,165 ($2,160,000 − $1,583,835) in net income. Under IFRS, Tribune will recognize future interest expense using the 12% effective interest rate so that the new book value is correctly amortized to the new maturity value by the maturity date.

If the present value of the restructured cash flows at the historical rate is within 10% of the book value of the debt, Tribune does not recognize a gain. Income effects are similar to the effects under U.S. GAAP when no gain is recognized. Because IFRS uses the economically sound present value approach to determine the magnitude of the settlement and U.S. GAAP uses the more conservative undiscounted future cash flows approach, the magnitude of the new book value of the restructured debt will be lower and the gain recognition will be larger under IFRS.

Hybrid Securities

LO 7-5

Explain the accounting for and financial reporting of hybrid securities.

Ambiguities arise in the measurement and classification of certain debt and preferred stock securities issued to raise capital because the securities have option features that have both debt and equity characteristics (for example, convertible bonds). These securities are referred to as *hybrid securities* or *compound financing instruments*. For example, firms often issue preferred stock that is subject to certain rights of redemption in either cash or common shares after some period of time.[23] The classification of preferred stock

---

[23]The following discussion is based on *FASB Codification Topic 480*; Securities and Exchange Commission *Accounting Series Release No. 268*, "Presentation in Financial Statements of Redeemable Preferred Stock"; And International Accounting Standards Board, *International Accounting Standard 32*, "Financial Instruments: Presentation" (as amended effective January 1, 2011).

as debt or equity depends on who holds the power to trigger redemption and whether the firm reports under U.S. GAAP or IFRS. If redemption will occur at a specific time or upon a specific event (for example, death of the holder), both U.S. GAAP and IFRS treat the preferred stock as a liability. This situation is typically referred to as *mandatorily redeemable preferred stock.* If the redemption is at the option of the issuing firm (that is, the preferred stock is callable), U.S. GAAP and IFRS will treat the preferred stock as equity. If redemption is at the holder's discretion (that is, the preferred stock is "putable"), U.S. GAAP will require that the stock be disclosed between debt and equity (the so-called "mezzanine" disclosure) and IFRS will require disclosure as a liability.

Convertible preferred stock is similar to preferred stock except that the holder has the option to exchange the convertible preferred stock for common stock under some preagreed exchange ratio. For example, a holder of 1,000 shares of $100 par, 7% convertible preferred stock may have the right to exchange each share of convertible preferred for five shares of $10 par common stock. Convertible preferred stock is treated as preferred stock at the date of issue. (Equity increases by the fair value of the consideration received at the issue date.) If converted to common stock, the recorded amounts are simply shifted from preferred stock to common stock.

Convertible debt may, at the creditor's option, be converted into common shares at a pre-specified exchange rate. The creditor holds (1) debt with a stated interest rate and maturity date and (2) an option to exchange the debt for equity. However, the debt and option features do not trade separately in secondary markets. While holding the convertible debt, the creditor receives interest payments, a feature of debt. Also, the debtholder has the ability to exchange the debt for equity, an equity-like feature. Under U.S. GAAP, accountants have historically recorded convertible debt as a financial liability and recorded interest expense. The option to exchange the debt for equity is not valued and recorded. IFRS differs in that the debt and equity features are recorded separately to the extent that the separate components can be reliably estimated at fair value.

Under both U.S. GAAP and IFRS, most companies use the *book value method* to record conversion. The book value method is based on the idea that the conversion is a culmination of the original transaction. Whatever amounts are recorded in debt (and in equity under IFRS) are simply shifted to shareholders' equity when the debt is converted into equity. Both U.S. GAAP and IFRS allow the use of the *market value method,* under which the market value of the common stock determines the basis of the conversion transaction. This approach is rarely used because it generates potentially large losses.

We illustrate the accounting for hybrid securities. The December 31, 2008, Consolidated Balance Sheet of **Digital River, Inc.,** reports 1.25%, 20-year convertible senior notes originally issued in 2004 at a par value of $195 million. Each $1,000 of note principal may be converted into 22.6948 shares of Digital River $0.01 par value common stock, a conversion price of $44.063 per share. Exhibit 7.8 shows the financial statement effects under both U.S. GAAP and IFRS of the following transactions:

1. Recording of the original issue. For the IFRS treatment, assume that Digital River would have borrowed at 4% if it did not offer a conversion privilege.
2. Recognition of one year's interest effect.
3. Conversion of the notes assuming a share of Digital River trades at $50 and the book value method.

U.S. GAAP treats the entire convertible note issue proceeds of Transaction 1 as debt. Under IFRS, the proceeds are allocated between the fair values of the notes (debt) and the conversion options on the notes (equity). If Digital would have paid 4% interest on

Exhibit 7.8: Accounting for Hybrid Securities (amounts in millions)

U.S. GAAP:

	Assets	=	Liabilities	+	Shareholders' Equity		
					CC	AOCI	RE
1.	Cash +195.00		Notes Payable +195.00				

Cash	195.00	
Note Payable		195.00

IFRS:

	Assets	=	Liabilities	+	Shareholders' Equity		
					CC	AOCI	RE
1.	Cash +195.00		Notes Payable +122.12		APIC—Notes Payable +72.88		

Cash	195.00	
Notes Payable		122.12
APIC—Notes Payable		72.88

U.S. GAAP:

	Assets	=	Liabilities	+	Shareholders' Equity		
					CC	AOCI	RE
2.	Cash −2.4375						Interest Expense −2.4375

Interest Expense	2.4375	
Cash		2.4375

IFRS:

	Assets	=	Liabilities	+	Shareholders' Equity		
					CC	AOCI	RE
2.	Cash −2.4375		Notes Payable +2.4473				Interest Expense −4.8848

Interest Expense	4.8848	
Notes Payable		2.4473
Cash		2.4375

U.S. GAAP:

	Assets	=	Liabilities	+	Shareholders' Equity		
					CC	AOCI	RE
3.			Notes Payable −195.0000		Common Stock +0.0443 APIC +194.9557		

Notes Payable	195.0000	
Common Stock		0.0443
APIC		194.9557

IFRS:

	Assets	=	Liabilities	+	Shareholders' Equity		
					CC	AOCI	RE
3.			Notes Payable −124.5273		APIC—Notes Payable −72.8800 Common Stock +0.0443 APIC +197.3630		

Notes Payable	124.5273	
APIC—Notes Payable	72.8800	
Common Stock		0.0443
APIC		197.3630

the notes issued without the conversion option, the fair value of the notes could be approximated by discounting the notes' contractual cash flows at 4%. The present value of $195 million received in 20 years and a contractual cash interest payment of $2.4375 million ($195 million × 1.25%) each period for 20 years equals $122.12 million. Thus, the note payable is recorded at $122.12 million and the remainder of the proceeds ($195 million – $122.12 million = $72.88 million) is classified as equity. The account Additional Paid-in Capital—Note Payable would be reported in the shareholders' equity section as part of additional paid-in capital.

U.S. GAAP records the $2.4375 million annual payment as interest expense in Transaction 2. The cash interest and effective interest are equal because Digital River issued the notes payable at par. Under IFRS treatment, the notes were discounted at the effective interest rate of 4%. Therefore, the effective interest of $4.8848 million ($122.12 million beginning note book value times 4% effective interest rate) does not equal the contractual cash interest, and the note payable discount ($2.4473 million) is amortized.[24]

The book value method (Transaction 3) is based on the idea that the conversion is a culmination of a transaction to issue equity. The amounts recorded as debt are simply shifted to shareholders' equity when the debt is converted into equity. Under U.S. GAAP, the original issue was recorded as debt. Therefore, the $195 million is removed from notes payable. The common shares issued at conversion total 4,425,486, which is computed by multiplying the 22.6948 contractual conversion rate per $1,000 of note principal by 195,000 notes ($195 million divided by $1,000 per note). The common stock account is increased by the par value of those shares ($0.01 × 4,425,486 shares), and the rest is treated as additional paid-in capital. Under IFRS, the original issue was treated as part debt (recorded as notes payable) and part equity (recorded as additional paid-in capital—notes payable). Upon conversion, the amounts are shifted into common stock (at par) and additional paid-in capital. The amount shifted out of notes payable is equal to its original issue price from Transaction 1 plus the increase in notes payable from the amortization of the note in Transaction 2.

Bonds issued with detachable warrants provide a good example of where debt and equity features may be more easily separated (and are separated under both U.S. GAAP and IFRS). Typically, after issuance, the bonds and detachable warrants are traded separately in secondary markets. When purchasing bonds with detachable warrants, an investor is buying a debt instrument (the bond) and the option to acquire equity at a fixed price (the stock warrants). Because the debt and equity features trade separately after issuance, accountants allocate the purchase price of the bond with detachable warrants between the bond and the stock warrants on the basis of the two instruments' relative fair market values. As a simple example, assume that bonds with a face value of $1,000,000 plus detachable warrants are issued for $975,000. Assume that immediately after issue, the bonds trade for $900,000 and the warrants trade for $100,000. Accountants would allocate 90% ($900,000 value of the bonds/$1,000,000 value of bonds plus warrants) of the $975,000 value received to the bonds ($975,000 × 90% = $877,500) and 10% to the warrants ($975,000 × 10% = $97,500).

---

[24]As is the case with any long-term debt, accrual of interest expense at the effective rate increases the amount owed by Digital River and contractual cash payments decrease the amount owed. Given that the effective interest is greater than the cash payment, Digital River's debt has increased as evidenced by the increase in notes payable.

Transfers of Receivables

Firms sometimes transfer their receivables as a means of obtaining financing or use an SPE to issue securities backed by the receivables (for example, mortgage-backed securities issued by financial institutions or their SPEs). If collections from customers are not sufficient to repay the amount borrowed plus interest, the transferring firm may have to pay the difference; that is, the lender may have recourse against the borrowing firm.[25]

Does the recourse provision create an accounting liability? Some argue that the arrangement is similar to a collateralized loan. The firm should leave the receivables on its books and recognize a liability for the cash received. Others argue that the firm has sold an asset; it should recognize a liability only if it is probable that collections from customers will be insufficient and the firm will be required to repay some portion of the amount received.

To illustrate the accounting for the transfer of receivables, assume that Sears transfers $1,000,000 of installment receivables to a bank in exchange for $950,000. Sears is liable to the bank for uncollectible receivables (a "with recourse" transfer), and the estimated fair value of the recourse obligation is $20,000. Exhibit 7.9 shows the financial statement effects if reported as a borrowing and if reported as a sale.

In the "borrowing" transaction, Sears does not surrender control of the receivables (that is, does not meet the FASB's three conditions to record a sale). Therefore, Sears keeps the accounts receivable on its books and records the receipt of cash and the incurrence of a liability (loan payable). In the "sale" transaction, Sears removes the accounts receivable from the balance sheet because Sears no longer controls the accounts receivable. Sears also records the expected cash outflow to satisfy the recourse provisions of the agreement should customers fail to pay. Because net assets decrease by $50,000 and liabilities increase by $20,000, Sears records a loss on sale of $70,000, which is reported on the income statement and reduces retained earnings.

Exhibit 7.9: Accounting for a Transfer of Receivables

Borrowing:

	Assets		=	Liabilities		+	Shareholders' Equity		
							CC	AOCI	RE
1.	Cash	+950,000		Loan Payable	+950,000				
	Cash				950,000				
	Loan Payable						950,000		

Sale:

	Assets		=	Liabilities		+	Shareholders' Equity			
							CC	AOCI	RE	
	Cash	+950,000		Recourse Liability	+20,000				Loss on Sale	−70,000
	Accounts Receivable	−1,000,000								
	Cash				950,000					
	Loss on Sale				70,000					
	Accounts Receivable						1,000,000			
	Recourse Liability						20,000			

---

[25]The contract of sale will specify whether the purchaser has recourse or whether the sale has taken place on a without-recourse basis, in which case the purchaser assumes all risk of collection.

LO 7-6

Describe how operating and capital leases affect financial statements, and make adjustments required to convert operating leases to capital leases.

Leases

Many firms acquire rights to use assets through leases. For example, a company might agree to lease computer equipment for 3 years, an office suite for 5 years, or an entire building for 40 years, promising to pay a fixed periodic fee for the duration of the lease. Leasing provides benefits to lessees (the users of the leased assets) such as the following:

- Ability to shift the tax benefits from depreciation and other deductions from a lessee that has little or no taxable income (such as an airline) to a lessor, or owner of the asset, that has substantial taxable income. The lessee negotiates with the lessor to share some of the benefits of these tax deductions through lower lease payments.
- Flexibility to change capacity as needed without having to purchase or sell assets.
- Ability to reduce the risk of technological obsolescence, relative to outright ownership, by maintaining the flexibility to shift to technologically more advanced assets.
- Ability to finance the acquisition of an asset using lessor financing when alternative sources of financing are unavailable or more costly.

These potential benefits of leasing to lessees do not come without a cost. When the lessor assumes the risks of ownership, it requires the lessee to make larger lease payments than if the lessee faces these risks. Which party bears the risks is a matter of negotiation between lessor and lessee.

Promising to make an irrevocable series of lease payments commits the firm just as surely as a bond indenture or a mortgage, and the accounting is similar in many cases.[26] This section examines two methods of accounting for long-term leases: the operating lease method and the capital (sometimes called finance) lease method.[27] The illustrations show the accounting by the lessee, the user of the leased asset.

To illustrate these two methods, suppose Myers Company wants to acquire a computer that has a three-year life and that Myers Company can pay 10% per year to borrow money for three years. The computer manufacturer is willing to sell the equipment for $45,000 or to lease it for three years. Myers Company is responsible for property taxes, maintenance, and repairs of the computer whether it leases or purchases the computer.

Assume that Myers Company signs a lease on January 1, Year 1, and must make payments on the lease on December 31, each year. (In practice, lessees usually make lease payments in advance, but the assumption of year-end payments simplifies the computations.) The lessor sets the lease payments to return the $45,000 principal and 10% interest in three equal end-of-year payments. Similar to bond and note calculations, the payment is the amount that solves the following equation:

$$\$45,000 = \sum_{n=1}^{3} \frac{\text{Payment}}{(1 + 0.10)^n}$$

---

[26]Lease disclosures often use the term *noncancelable leases* to capture the contractual lease commitments of the lessee. Under noncancelable leases, the lessee typically can cancel the lease after incurring a severe penalty.

[27]*FASB Codification Topic 840*; International Accounting Standards Board, *International Accounting Standard 17*, "Leases" (revised 2003).

Solving this equation for the payment using a financial calculator ($i = 0.10$, $n = 3$, future value $= 0$, present value $= \$45,000$) yields an annual payment of $\$18,095$.

Operating Lease Method

In an operating lease, the owner, or lessor, transfers only the rights to use the property to the lessee for a specified period of time. At the end of the lease period, the lessee returns the property to the lessor. For example, car rental companies lease cars by the day or week. If the lessee neither assumes the risks nor enjoys the rewards of ownership, the lessee should treat the lease as an operating lease. Accounting gives no recognition to the signing of an operating lease. (That is, the lessee reports neither the leased asset nor a lease liability on its balance sheet; the lease is simply a mutually unexecuted contract). Over the life of the lease, the lessee recognizes rent expense in measuring net income each year. The effect on the financial statements of Myers Company each year (ignoring income taxes) if it treats the lease as an operating lease appears in Exhibit 7.10.

The total income statement effect over the three years is the sum of the rent expense ($\$54,285$), which also equals the total cash outflow from lease payments.

Capital Lease Method

In leasing arrangements in which the lessee assumes the risks and enjoys the rewards of ownership, the lease contract is considered a capital lease. In a capital lease, the lessee recognizes the signing of the lease as the simultaneous acquisition of a long-term asset and the incurring of a long-term liability for lease payments. Lessees recognize two expense items each year on capital leases. First, the lessee must depreciate the leased asset over the time period it uses the asset (that is, the lease term or the asset's economic useful life if the asset is expected to remain with the lessee after the lease term expires). Assuming that Myers Company uses straight-line depreciation, it recognizes depreciation expense of $\$15,000$ ($\$45,000/3$) each year. Second, as shown in the amortization schedule in Exhibit 7.11, the lease payment made each year is part interest expense and part reduction of the liability itself.

The effects of (1) the signing of the capital lease on January 1, Year 1, and the recognition of (2) depreciation and (3) interest for each year appear in Exhibit 7.12.

The leased asset and liability are shown on the balance sheet as of the signing of the lease. Then in each year, the effective interest method is used to account for the lease liability as was illustrated earlier for a note payable, and the leased asset is depreciated. Notice that in the capital lease method, the total expense over the three years is $\$54,285$, comprising $\$45,000$ for depreciation expense and $\$9,285$ for interest expense. This total expense is the same as that recognized under the operating lease method described previously ($\$18,095 \times 3 = \$54,285$). The capital lease method recognizes expenses sooner

Exhibit 7.10: Operating Lease Treatment

12/31/Year 1, Year 2, and Year 3:

Assets			=	Liabilities		+	Shareholders' Equity		
							CC	AOCI	RE
Cash		−18,095							Rent Expense −18,095
Rent Expense					18,095				
Cash							18,095		

Exhibit 7.11

Lease Amortization Table

Date	Payment	10% Effective Interest Expense	Amortization	Book Value of Lease Liability
1/1/Year 1				$45,000
12/31/Year 1	$18,095	$4,500	$13,595	31,405
12/31/Year 2	18,095	3,141	14,954	16,451
12/31/Year 3	18,095	1,644	16,451	0
	$54,285	$9,285	$45,000	

Exhibit 7.12: Capital Lease Treatment

1/1/Year 1 Signing:

Assets		=	Liabilities		+	Shareholders' Equity		
						CC	AOCI	RE
Leased Asset	+45,000		Lease Liability	+45,000				

Leased Asset   45,000
   Leased Liability   45,000

12/31/Year 1 Payment:

Assets		=	Liabilities		+	Shareholders' Equity		
						CC	AOCI	RE
Cash	−18,095		Lease Liability	−13,595				Interest Expense −4,500

Interest Expense   4,500
Lease Liability   13,595
   Cash   18,095

12/31/Year 1 Depreciation:

Assets		=	Liabilities		+	Shareholders' Equity		
						CC	AOCI	RE
Leased Asset (Net)	−15,000							Depreciation Expense −15,000

Depreciation Expense   15,000
   Leased Asset (Net)   15,000

12/31/Year 2 Payment:

Assets		=	Liabilities		+	Shareholders' Equity		
						CC	AOCI	RE
Cash	−18,095		Leased Liability	−14,954				Interest Expense −3,141

Interest Expense   3,141
Lease Liability   14,954
   Cash   18,095

12/31/Year 2 Depreciation:

Assets		=	Liabilities		+	Shareholders' Equity		
						CC	AOCI	RE
Leased Asset (Net)	−15,000							Depreciation Expense −15,000

Depreciation Expense   15,000
   Leased Asset (Net)   15,000

Exhibit 7.12 (Continued)

12/31/Year 3 Payment:

Assets		=	Liabilities		+	Shareholders' Equity		
						CC	AOCI	RE
Cash	−18,095		Lease Liability	−16,451				Interest Expense	−1,644

Interest Expense	1,644	
Lease Liability	16,451	
Cash		18,095

12/31/Year 3 Depreciation:

Assets		=	Liabilities		+	Shareholders' Equity		
						CC	AOCI	RE
Leased Asset (Net)	−15,000							Depreciation Expense	−15,000

Depreciation Expense	15,000	
Leased Asset (Net)		15,000

than the operating lease method does. But once the lease terminates, total expense equals the cash expenditure under both methods. The capital lease method recognizes both the asset and the liability on the balance sheet.[28]

Choosing the Accounting Method

When a lessee treats a lease as a capital lease, it recognizes an asset and a liability, thereby increasing total liabilities and making the company appear riskier. Given a choice, most lessees prefer not to show the asset and a related liability on the balance sheet. For this reason, lessees prefer an operating lease to an installment purchase or a capital lease. Lessees also prefer to recognize expenses for financial reporting later rather than sooner. These preferences have led a number of lessees to structure asset acquisitions so that the financing takes the form of an operating lease, thereby achieving off-balance-sheet financing.

U.S. GAAP provides detailed rules for accounting for long-term leases. The lessor and lessee must account for a lease as a capital lease if the lease meets any one of four conditions.[29] These conditions attempt to identify which party, the lessor or the lessee, bears most of the risk related to the asset under lease. When the lessor bears most of the risk, the lease is an operating lease. When the lessee bears most of the risk, the lease is a capital lease.

A lease is a capital lease if it meets any one of the following conditions:

- If it extends for at least 75% of the asset's total expected economic life (that is, the lessee uses the asset for most of its life).
- If it transfers ownership to the lessee at the end of the lease term (that is, the lessee bears the risk of changes in the residual value of the asset at the end of the lease term).
- If it seems likely the lessor will transfer ownership to the lessee because of a "bargain purchase" option (that is, the lessee again bears the residual value risk; a bargain purchase option gives the lessee the right to purchase the asset for a price

---

[28]The fair value option is not allowed for assets and liabilities reported under capital leases.

[29]*FASB Codification Topic 840.*

less than the expected fair market value of the asset when the lessee exercises its option).

■ The present value of the contractual minimum lease payments equals or exceeds 90% of the fair market value of the asset at the time of signing.[30]

The first three conditions are relatively easy to avoid in lease contracts if lessors and lessees prefer to treat a lease as an operating lease instead of a capital lease. The most difficult of the four conditions to avoid is the fourth. When the present value of the contractual minimum lease payments equal or exceed 90% of the fair market value of the asset at the time of signing, the lessor has less than or equal to 10% of the asset's value at risk to an uncertain residual value at the end of the lease term. Therefore, the lease transfers the major risks and rewards of ownership from the lessor to the lessee. In economic substance, the lessee has acquired an asset and has agreed to pay for it under a long-term contract, which the lessee recognizes as a liability. When the present value of the minimum lease payments is less than 90% of the fair market value of the asset at the time of signing, the lessor bears the major risks and rewards of ownership and the lease is an operating lease.

Firms often report both operating and capital leases because certain lease agreements meet one or more of these conditions while others do not. As an example of the significance of leasing activities, consider a typical firm in the airline industry that leases many of its aircraft and ground facilities. In Note 8 to its December 31, 2011, consolidated financial statements, **Southwest Airlines** provides schedules of capital and operating lease commitments, as shown in Exhibit 7.13. Southwest Airlines also reports $3,751 million of combined long-term debt and current maturities of long-term debt in its December 31, 2011, consolidated balance sheet. Note that the capitalized lease payments are not a large portion of Southwest's long-term debt. Southwest's commitments under operating leases (gross future cash flows of $5,583 million) are more substantial, representing an important off-balance-sheet cash flow commitment of the firm.

Converting Operating Leases to Capital Leases

Lease commitments by lessees accounted for as operating leases do not appear as assets or liabilities on the balance sheet and, if you believe these obligations are essentially financial commitments, can cause you to understate the short-term liquidity or long-term solvency risk of the firm. In cross-sectional comparisons of different firms, you may want to treat all leases as capital leases with the objective of making all firms more comparable in terms of assets and liabilities. Restating the financial statements of lessees in this way provides a more conservative measure of total liabilities.

To illustrate the conversion of operating to capital leases, refer to **PepsiCo**'s operating lease disclosures in Note 9, "Debt Obligations and Commitments" (Appendix A). Exhibit 7.14 summarizes PepsiCo's information on operating lease commitments. The second column shows PepsiCo's commitments on noncancelable operating leases net of sublease revenues at December 29, 2012. PepsiCo reports aggregate payments for 2014–2015 and

---

[30]IFRS criteria are similar, although as is often the case with IFRS, the criteria do not provide "bright-line" percentages such as 75% or 90%. Instead, judgment is relied upon to implement the following: (1) Does ownership transfer from the lessor to the lessee at the end of the lease? (2) Is there a bargain purchase option? (3) Does the lease extend for the major portion of the asset's useful life? (4) Does the present value of the minimum lease payments equal substantially all of the asset's fair value? (5) Is the leased asset specialized for use by the lessee?

Exhibit 7.13

Southwest Airline
Excerpts from December 31, 2011, 10-K
(amounts in millions)

Note 8 (partial). Total rental expense for operating leases, both aircraft and other, charged to operations in 2011, 2010 and 2009 was $847 million, $631 million, and $596 million, respectively.... Future minimum lease payments under capital leases and noncancelable operating leases and capital leases with initial or remaining terms in excess of one year at December 31, 2011 were:

	Capital leases	Operating leases
2012	$ 6	$ 640
2013	6	717
2014	6	642
2015	6	579
2016	6	489
Thereafter	26	2,516
Total minimum lease payments	$56	$5,583
Less amount representing interest	14	
Present value of minimum lease payments	$42	
Less current portion	3	
Long-term portion	$39	

2016–2017. We assume the payments are evenly distributed. To convert these operating lease cash payments to a capital lease, you must discount the lease commitments to present value. The discount rate you should use is the lessee's incremental borrowing rate for secured debt with similar risk to that of the leasing arrangement. PepsiCo's interest expense (see the income statement) as a percentage of average short- and long-term borrowing for 2012 (see the balance sheet) is 3.3% {$899/[0.5($4,815 + $23,544 + $6,205 + $20,568)]}. We assume a 4% rate to compute the present value of operating lease commitments.

Exhibit 7.14 illustrates the lease capitalization process. The present value of each cash flow equals the cash flow times a present value factor. Each factor in the column is obtained from a present value table or by the formula $1/(1 + i)^n$. For example, 2014's factor of $0.92455 = 1/(1 + 0.04)^2$. To discount payments in 2018 and beyond, you needs to know the years and amounts in which PepsiCo will pay the $620 million. Presuming that payments will continue at the same amount as the $181 million payment in 2017, PepsiCo will pay the remaining $620 million in less than four periods ($620/$181 < 4). Given the decline in payments over the years shown in Exhibit 7.14, we assume that the remainder is spread over four periods, yielding a payment of $155 million per year ($620 million/4 years). The $462.4 million present value is obtained by computing the present value of an annuity of $155 million for four periods at 4% to yield a present value at the end of 2017 and then discounting that amount for five additional periods at 4%. The present value of all of PepsiCo's operating lease payments is $1,768.7 million.

Exhibit 7.14
PepsiCo, Inc. **Operating Lease Disclosures; Summarized** **from December 29, 2012, Annual Report** **(amounts in millions)**

Year	Operating Lease Commitments	Present Value Factor at 6%	Present Value
2013	$ 445	0.96153	$ 427.9
2014	317	0.92455	293.1
2015	317	0.88899	281.8
2016	181	0.85480	154.7
2017	181	0.82192	148.8
2018 and beyond	620	—	462.4[41]
	$2,061		$ 1,768.7

[41]Present value of an annuity of $155 million for four periods at 4%, then that present value discounted back five periods at 4%.

To approximate what leased assets and liabilities would have existed if capital lease treatment had been used, you add the $1,768.7 million lease to property, plant, and equipment; the $427.9 million present value of the 2013 lease payments to short-term debt; and the $1,340.8 ($1,768.7 − $427.9) million present value of lease payments in 2014 and beyond to long-term debt on the December 29, 2012, balance sheet. Certain ratios could be affected substantially by the operating lease capitalization. For example, PepsiCo's ratio of long-term debt to shareholders' equity based on reported amounts is 105.0% ($23,544/$22,417). Adding the long-term portion of the capital lease liability of $1,340.8 million to the numerator changes the ratio to 111.0% ($23,544 + $1,340.8)/ $22,417). While this increase is not large for PepsiCo, greater increases are often found when the adjustment is made for retailers, restaurant chains, and airlines. For time-series analysis of PepsiCo, similar calculations would be necessary for at least two previous years.

If you convert operating leases to capital leases on the balance sheet for comparison purposes across firms, you also should convert the income statement from the operating to the capital lease method by

- eliminating rent expense.
- including depreciation expense on the capitalized asset.
- including interest expense on the lease obligation.

In general, if the average lease is in the first half of its life, total expenses under the capital lease method tend to exceed total expenses under the operating lease method; so adjusted income will tend to be less than reported income. If the average lease is in the last half of its life, total expenses under the capital lease method tend to be less than under the operating lease method; so adjusted income tends to be greater than reported income. The two expense amounts are approximately equal at the midlife point. The average operating lease for PepsiCo appears to be near the midpoint of its life. You reach this conclusion by comparing the operating lease payment in 2013 ($445 million), which would be treated as rent expense for an operating lease, to the following rough approximations for expenses under a capital lease:

$$\text{Depreciation Expense} = \$1,768.7 \text{ million asset}/7 \text{ years remaining lease life}^{31}$$
$$= \$252.67 \text{ million}$$

$$\text{Interest Expense} = \$1,768.7 \text{ million lease liability} \times 4\,\%$$
$$= \$70.75 \text{ million}$$

The sum of depreciation expense and interest expense (capital lease treatment) is $323.42 million, which is less than the $445.0 million in rent expense (operating lease treatment). PepsiCo's Note 4, "Property, Plant, and Equipment and Intangible Assets" (Appendix A), shows that accumulated depreciation on depreciable property, plant, and equipment is about one-half of property, plant, and equipment, confirming the estimate that remaining asset lives are approximately at the midpoint of total useful life.

Therefore, constructive capitalization of the operating leases would increase net income by the difference between these two expenses ($121.58 million) times one minus the statutory tax rate, or $79.03 million [$121.58 million $\times$ (1 – 0.35)]. This amount is slightly more than 1% of PepsiCo's 2012 net income of $6,178 million. The effects on other commonly used performance measures are more pronounced. Because EBITDA excludes depreciation, interest, and tax expenses (and therefore any adjustments for these items when operating leases are effectively capitalized), it increases by the full $445.0 million when rent expense is excluded. Similarly, because operating income excludes interest expense, it increases by the excluded rent expense minus the included depreciation expense, a net increase of $192.3 million.

Often, balance sheet restatements are more significant than income statement restatements. Consequently, you usually can ignore restatements of the income statement, particularly if the emphasis is assessment of a firm's credit risk, as discussed in Chapter 5. However, note that even for firms with leases at the midlife point, where the income statement effect may be immaterial, the effect on the balance sheet can be substantial.[32]

You could restate the statement of cash flows for the capitalization of operating leases. Under the operating lease method, the lease payment for the year is an operating use of cash. Its inclusion as a subtraction in computing net income results in reporting its negative cash flow effect in the operating section of the statement of cash flows. Under the capital lease method, a portion of the cash payment represents a repayment of the lease liability, a financing use of cash instead of an operating use of cash. You

---

[31]Using a weighted average approach, we calculated the approximately seven years (7.02) as follows: If the rent payments are equal over the 2013–2021 period, it would be reasonable to assume that all leased assets are going to be used over the nine-year period. However, the rent payments decline, implying that some assets are used up and, thus, off-lease. Working backwards in the schedule, $155 million of cash flow appears in each year, $26 million additional cash flow ($155 + $26 = $181) in cash flow appears in the first five years, $136 million additional cash flow appears for the first three years ($181 + $136 = $317), and $128 million additional cash flow ($317 + $128 = $445) appears in 2013. Therefore 67.7% of the cash flows related to assets in use for nine years ($155 per year $\times$ 9 years = $1,395 out of a total of $2,061), 6.3% of the cash flows related to assets in use for five years ($26 per year $\times$ 5 years = $130 out of a total of $2,061), and so on. Weighting a nine-year life by 67.6%, a five-year life by 6.3%, and so on, yields an average useful life of 7.02 years.

[32]For an alternative procedure for converting operating leases into capital leases, see Eugene A. Imhoff, Jr., Robert C. Lipe, and David W. Wright, "Operating Leases: Impact of Constructive Capitalization," *Accounting Horizons* (March 1991), pp. 51–63. In this study, the authors found that capitalizing operating leases decreased the rate of return on assets 34% for high-lease firms and 10% for low-lease firms and increased the debt-to-equity ratio 191% for high-lease firms and 47% for firms.

should reclassify this portion of the cash payment from the operating section to the financing section of the statement of cash flows. You also could reduce net income for depreciation expense on the capitalized lease assets, but this amount appears as an add-back to net income for a non-cash expense. Thus, the net effect of depreciation expense on operating cash flows is zero.

It is clear from the discussion that footnote disclosures allow the financial analyst to capitalize operating leases effectively, but with some error. A number of assumptions and estimates (sometimes rough) must be employed, and these assumptions may not be valid for all firms in all industries. As a result, credit rating agencies such as Moody's and Fitch have developed methodologies with the objectives of standardization and simplicity. For example, some analysts estimate the lease liability and leased asset to be capitalized simply using an "8X" rule. That is, a simple method of computing the capitalized liability and asset is to multiply the amount of annual rent expense times eight. Because this "8X" heuristic is based on specific assumptions (e.g., a 9% interest rate and an asset life of 15 years or a 4% interest rate and an asset life of 4 years, both of which yield a present value factor of approximately 8 for a $1 annuity), Moody's uses a modified approach that takes into account industry differences in useful lives and the "seasoning" (that is, age) of the leased assets. Thus, for any given firm, a factor of 5X, 6X, 8X, or greater might be applied, with firms with long-lived assets such as airlines, shipping, and public utilities receiving the highest factor. Fitch also uses the 8X heuristic, a present value approach if sufficient data exists, and individual analysis about the validity of the approach for a given firm.[33]

Virtually all firms have some amount of commitment under operating leases. The change in debt ratios for some firms is relatively minor, as is the case for PepsiCo. For other firms, particularly airlines and retail stores, the effect can be significant. Even for firms for which the effect is relatively small, adding the effect of capitalizing operating leases to the effect of other off-balance-sheet obligations can result in a combined material effect. Thus, you should examine the effect of leases when assessing the risk and accounting quality of a firm's financial statements. You should also consider the effects of off-balance-sheet leases when determining capital structure weights and debt costs for the weighted average cost of capital calculations used in enterprise valuation.

Quick Check

- Proper measurement and reporting of long-term debt is crucial for an accurate assessment of long-term solvency risk.
- Long-term debt is initially reported at fair value, which is, in theory, the present value of future cash outflows discounted at a rate of interest commensurate with the issuer's risk.
- Interest expense is based on the effective interest rate determined by the economics of the transaction while cash interest is determined by the stated rate of interest in the note agreement or bond indenture.

- Some operating-type leases are structured in a way that avoids long-term debt reporting. Standard setters are currently deliberating a new standard that will limit the use of the operating lease treatment and thus will improve long-term debt reporting.
- Long-term debt other than capital leases may be reported at fair value subsequent to the date of issue.
- Long-term debt is a financial instrument for which note reporting of fair value is required.

---

[33]Moody's Approach to Global Standard Adjustments in the Analysis of Financial Statements for Non-Financial Corporations — Part I, *Standardized Adjustments to Enable Global Consistency for US and Canadian GAAP Issuers* (March 2005); "Capitalization of Operating Leases by Credit Rating Agencies," *ELT* (February 2007).

The Use of Derivatives to Hedge Interest Rate Risk

LO 7-7

Explain how economic effects of derivatives used to hedge changes in long-term debt interest rates are reported in financial statements.

Long-term borrowing subjects firms to the risk of interest rate changes. *Derivative instruments* can help a firm mitigate interest rate (and other types of) risks. This section discusses the nature, use, accounting, and reporting of derivative instruments, with a primary focus on the use of derivatives to hedge interest rate risk.[34] To facilitate this discussion, we use the following two scenarios:

Scenario 1: Firm A gives a note payable to a supplier on January 1, 2013, to acquire manufacturing equipment. The note has a face value of $100,000 and bears a fixed interest rate of 8% per year. Interest is payable annually on December 31, and the note matures on December 31, 2015. Firm A has the option of repaying the note prior to maturity. The prepayment will be based on the fair value of the note on the prepayment date, which is based on prevailing market interest rates on that date. Firm A is concerned that the value of the note will increase if interest rates decrease and that it will have to pay more than $100,000 if it decides to repay the note early.

Scenario 2: Firm B gives a note payable to a supplier on January 1, 2013, to acquire manufacturing equipment. The note has a face value of $100,000 and bears interest at the prime lending rate. Assume that the prime lending rate is 8% on January 1, 2013. The supplier will reset the interest rate each December 31 to establish the interest charge for the next calendar year. Interest is payable on December 31 of each year, and the note matures on December 31, 2015. Firm B is concerned that interest rates will increase to more than 8% during the term of the note and negatively affect its cash flows.

Nature and Use of Derivative Instruments

A derivative is a financial instrument that *derives* its value from some other financial instrument or observable market prices, such as stock prices, interest rates, currency exchange rates, commodity prices, and the like. For example, an option to purchase a share of stock (an option contract) derives its value from the market price of the stock. A commitment to purchase a certain amount of foreign currency in the future (a forward contract) derives its value from changes in the exchange rate for that currency. Firms typically use derivative instruments (option, forward, and swap contracts) to hedge the risk of losses from changes in market prices, interest rates, foreign exchange rates, and commodity prices. The general idea is that changes in the value of the derivative instrument offset changes in the value of an asset or a liability or changes in future cash flows, thereby neutralizing the economic loss.

Refer to Scenario 1. Firm A wants to neutralize the effect of changes in the market value of the note payable caused by changes in market interest rates. It engages in one type of derivative instrument, a swap contract, with a notional value of $100,000 with its bank. In effect, the swap allows Firm A to swap its fixed-interest-rate obligation for a variable-interest-rate obligation. That is, in the swap contract, Firm A agrees to pay the bank a variable rate of interest on $100,000, and in exchange the bank will pay Firm A

---

[34]U.S. GAAP and IFRS have similar derivative accounting rules. *FASB Codification Topics 815 and 825;* International Accounting Standards Board, *International Accounting Standard 39,* "Financial Instruments: Recognition and Measurement" (revised 2003); International Accounting Standards Board, *International Financial Reporting Standard 7,* "Financial Instruments: Disclosures," (2005).

a fixed rate of interest (8%). The market value of the note will remain at $100,000 as long as the variable interest rate in the swap is the same as the variable rate used by the supplier to revalue the note while it is outstanding. The swap causes Firm A's interest payments to vary as the variable interest rate changes, but it locks the value of the note payable at $100,000.

Refer to Scenario 2. Firm B wants to protect its future cash flows against increases in the variable interest rate to more than the initial 8% rate. It also engages in a swap contract with a notional value of $100,000 with its bank. In effect, the swap allows Firm B to swap its variable-interest-rate obligation for a fixed-interest-rate obligation. That is, in the swap contract, Firm B agrees to pay the bank a fixed rate of 8% interest on $100,000, and in exchange the bank will pay Firm A a variable rate of interest. The swap fixes the firm's annual interest expense and cash expenditure to 8% of the $100,000 note, which eliminates Firm B's risk of interest rate increases. By engaging in the swap, however, Firm B cannot take advantage of decreases in interest rates to less than 8%, which it could have done with its variable-rate note. In this example, the swap locks in Firm B's interest payments on the note, but the value of the note to the supplier will vary as the variable interest rate changes.

Banks and other financial intermediaries structure derivatives for a fee to suit the needs of their customers. Thus, the nature and complexity of derivatives vary widely. We focus our discussion to the interest rate swap contracts in the two scenarios to illustrate the accounting and reporting of derivatives. Consider the following elements of a derivative:

- A derivative has one or more *underlyings*. An underlying is the specified item to which the derivative applies, such as an interest rate, a commodity price, a foreign exchange rate, or another variable. Interest rates are the underlying in the two scenarios.
- A derivative has one or more *notional amounts*. A notional amount is the number of units (dollar amounts, foreign currency units, bushels, barrels, gallons, shares, or other units) specified in a contract. The $100,000 face value of the note is the notional amount in the two scenarios.
- A derivative may or may not require an initial investment. The firm usually acquires a derivative by exchanging promises with a *counterparty*, such as a commercial or investment bank. The acquisition of a derivative is usually an exchange of promises, a mutually unexecuted contract.
- Derivatives typically require, or permit, *net settlement*. For example, Firm A in Scenario 1 will pay the supplier the 8% interest established in the fixed-rate note. If the variable interest rate used in the swap contract decreases to 6%, the counterparty bank will pay Firm A an amount equal to 2% (8% − 6%) of the notional amount of the note, $100,000. Paying interest of 8% to the supplier and receiving cash of 2% from the counterparty results in net interest cost of 6%. If the variable interest rate increases to 10%, Firm A still pays the supplier interest of 8% as specified in the original note. It would then pay the counterparty bank an additional 2% (10% − 8%), resulting in total interest expense equal to the variable rate of 10%.

Accounting for Derivatives

Derivatives are reported as assets or liabilities depending on the rights and obligations under the contract. The swap contracts in Scenarios 1 and 2 may be assets or liabilities depending on the level of interest rates. A later section discusses the initial valuation of these assets and liabilities.

Firms must revalue the derivatives to fair value each period. In addition to increasing or decreasing the derivative asset or liability, the revaluation amount also affects net income immediately, or other comprehensive income immediately and net income later (depending on U.S. GAAP and IFRS requirements discussed shortly). Recall from Chapter 2 that other comprehensive income is a temporary shareholders' equity account that reports changes during an accounting period in the recorded amounts of certain assets and liabilities, such as derivatives. Firms close the amount of other comprehensive income at the end of the period to the Accumulated Other Comprehensive Income (AOCI) account, a permanent shareholders' equity account. Whether the income effect is reported in net income or other comprehensive income depends on the nature of the hedge for which a firm acquires a derivative. Under U.S. GAAP and IFRS, there are three classifications of derivatives:

- Speculative investments
- Fair value hedges
- Cash flow hedges

Firms typically classify derivatives as fair value hedges or cash flow hedges. Firms must choose to designate each derivative as one or the other depending on their general hedging strategy and purpose in acquiring the particular derivative instrument.

Speculative Investment

Firms that acquire derivatives for reasons other than hedging a specific risk classify the derivative as a *speculative investment*. Firms must revalue derivatives held as speculative investments to fair value each period and recognize the resulting gain or loss in net income.

Fair Value Hedges

Derivative instruments acquired to hedge exposure to changes in the fair values of assets or liabilities are *fair value hedges*. Fair value hedges are of two general types: hedges of a *recognized* asset or liability and hedges of an *unrecognized* firm commitment.[35] Firm A in Scenario1 entered into the interest swap agreement to neutralize the effect of changes in interest rates on the market value of its notes payable, a hedge of a recognized liability. Therefore, this derivative instrument is a fair value hedge.

Cash Flow Hedges

Derivative instruments acquired to hedge exposure to variability in expected future cash flows are *cash flow hedges*. Cash flow hedges are of two general types: hedges of cash flows of an *existing* asset or liability and hedges of cash flows of *forecasted* transactions.[36] Firm B in Scenario 2 entered into the interest swap agreement to neutralize changes in cash flows for interest payments on its variable-rate notes payable, a hedge of an existing liability. Therefore, this derivative instrument is a cash flow hedge.

---

[35]We discuss the hedge of an unrecognized firm commitment in Chapter 9.

[36]We discuss the hedge of a forecasted transaction in Chapter 9.

In summary:

Scenario	Type of Hedge	Derivative Instrument Used
1	Fair Value—Liability	Swap Contract—Variable for Fixed Rate
2	Cash Flow—Interest Payments	Swap Contract—Fixed for Variable Rate

Treatment of Derivatives and Hedging Gains and Losses

For a derivative financial instrument classified as a *fair value hedge*, U.S. GAAP and IFRS require firms to recognize the derivative as an asset or liability in the amount of the gain and loss from changes in the fair value of the derivative and to recognize the fair value gain or loss in net income each period while the firm holds the financial instrument. U.S. GAAP and IFRS also require firms to revalue the asset or liability that is hedged to fair value and to recognize a corresponding loss or gain. If the hedge is fully effective, the gain (loss) on the derivative financial instrument will precisely offset the loss (gain) on the asset or liability hedged. The net effect on earnings is zero. If the hedge is not fully effective, the net gain or loss increases or decreases net income.

U.S. GAAP and IFRS require firms to include gains and losses from changes in the fair value of a derivative financial instrument classified as a *cash flow hedge* in other comprehensive income each period to the extent that the financial instrument is "highly effective" in neutralizing the risk. Firms must include the ineffective portion currently in net income. Financial reporting rules give general guidelines but leave the meaning of "highly effective" to professional judgment. The firm removes the accumulated amount in other comprehensive income related to a particular derivative instrument and transfers it to net income periodically during the life of the derivative instrument or at the time of settlement, depending on the type of derivative instrument used.

The logic for the different treatment of gains and losses from changes in fair value of derivative financial instruments is as follows. In a fair value hedge of a recognized asset or liability, the hedged asset (or liability) and its related derivative generally appear on the balance sheet. The firm revalues the hedged asset (or liability) and its related derivative to fair value each period, and reports the gain or loss on the hedged asset (or liability) as well as the loss or gain on the derivative in net income. Net income therefore includes the net gain or loss based on the effectiveness of the hedge in neutralizing the risk. In a cash flow hedge of an anticipated transaction, the hedged cash flow commitment does not yet appear on the balance sheet but the derivative instrument does. When a gain or loss occurs on the derivative, it is recognized as an asset or liability on the balance sheet, but there is no asset or liability on the balance sheet yet in which to recognize the corresponding change in fair value. Therefore, the change in the fair value is recognized in AOCI. For this reason, the firm classifies the corresponding gain or loss on the derivative instrument in other comprehensive income and later reclassifies the gain or loss to net income when it records the actual transaction.

Illustrations of Accounting for Derivatives

The next two sections illustrate the accounting for the derivatives using the two interest rate swap scenarios.

Fair Value Hedge: Interest Rate Swap to Convert Fixed-Rate Debt to Variable-Rate Debt (Scenario 1 involving Firm A)

Exhibit 7.15 presents the financial statement effects and journal entries for transactions from January 1, 2013, to December 31, 2015. The following paragraphs explain the accounting for the note and the associated derivative.

Exhibit 7.15: Fair Value Hedge: Interest Rate Swap to Convert Fixed-Rate Debt to Variable-Rate Debt

Assets	=	Liabilities	+	Total Shareholders' Equity		
				CC	AOCI	RE
January 1, 2013 Equipment +100,000		Notes Payable +100,000				
Equipment Notes Payable		100,000		100,000		
December 31, 2013 *Interest Expense on Note:* Cash −8,000 *Revaluation of Note:* *Revaluation of Swap Contract:* Swap Contract +3,667		Notes Payable +3,667				Interest Expense −8,000 Loss on Revaluation of Notes Payable −3,667 Gain on Revaluation of Swap Contract +3,667
Interest Expense Cash Loss on Revaluation of Notes Payable Notes Payable Swap Contract Gain on Revaluation of Swap Contract		8,000 3,667 3,667		8,000 3,667 3,667		
December 31, 2014 *Interest Expense on Note:* Cash −8,000 *Interest Revenue on Swap Contract Asset:* Swap Contract +220 *Cash Receipt from Counterparty:* Cash +2,000 Swap Contract −2,000 *Revaluation of Note:* *Revaluation of Swap Contract:* Swap Contract −1,887		Notes Payable −1,780 Notes Payable −3,705 Swap Contract +1,818				Interest Expense −6,220 Interest Revenue +220 Gain on Revaluation of Notes Payable +3,705 Loss on Revaluation of Swap Contract −3,705
Interest Expense Notes Payable Cash Swap Contract Interest Revenue Cash Swap Contract Notes Payable Gain on Revaluation of Notes Payable Loss on Revaluation of Swap Contract Swap Contract		6,220 1,780 220 2,000 3,705 3,705		8,000 220 2,000 3,705 3,705		

(*Continued*)

Exhibit 7.15 (Continued)

December 31, 2015						
Interest Expense on Note:						
Cash	−8,000	Notes Payable	+1,818		Interest Expense	−182
Interest Expense on						
Swap Contract Liability:						
		Swap Contract	+182			
Cash Payment to Counterparty:					Interest Expense	−182
Cash	−2,000	Swap contract	−2,000			
Repayment of the Note:						
Cash	−100,000	Notes Payable	−100,000			

Interest Expense	9,818	
Notes Payable		1,818
Cash		8,000
Interest Expense	182	
Swap Contract		182
Swap Contract	2,000	
Cash		2,000
Notes Payable	100,000	
Cash		100,000

- Firm A issues the note to the supplier on January 1, 2013, in exchange for the equipment and enters into the swap contract on the same date. The swap contract is a mutually unexecuted contract on January 1, 2013. The variable interest rate on this date is 8%, the same as the fixed rate for the note to the equipment supplier. The swap contract has a fair value of zero on this date. Thus, Firm A makes no entry to record the swap contract.

- On December 31, 2013, Firm A makes the required interest payment of $8,000 (0.08 × $100,000) on the note for 2013 and reduces net income by the amount of the interest expense.

- Assume interest rates decline during 2013 to 6%. On December 31, the counterparty with whom Firm A entered into the swap contract resets the interest rate to 6% for 2014. Firm A must restate the note payable to fair value and record the change in the market value of the swap contract caused by the decline in the interest rate. The present value of the remaining cash flows on the note payable (two cash interest payments of $8,000 and one $100,000 maturity value received in two years) when discounted at 6% is $103,667. Firm A records the $3,667 increase in the note's fair value and recognizes a Loss on Revaluation of Note Payable on the income statement in the same amount. Unless the fair value option discussed earlier has been chosen, firms typically do not revalue financial instruments, such as this note payable, to market value when interest rates change. They continue to account for the financial instruments using the interest rate at the time of the initial recording of the financial instrument in the accounts. However, when a firm hedges a financial instrument, it must recognize changes in fair values. It must likewise recognize changes in the fair value of the swap contract.

- The decline in interest rates to 6% means that Firm A will save $2,000 each year in interest payments because it entered into the swap contract. The present value of a $2,000 annuity for two periods at 6% is $3,667. Thus, the value of the swap contract increased from zero at the beginning of 2013 to $3,667 at the end of the year. Firm A records the increase in the fair value of the swap contract as an asset and recognizes a $3,667 gain on revaluation of swap contract on the income statement. The loss from the revaluation of the note payable exactly offsets the gain from the revaluation of the swap contract, indicating that the swap contract was fully effective (that is, the loss on revaluation of note payable is 100% offset by the gain on revaluation of swap contract) in hedging the interest rate risk.

Firm A follows a similar process at December 31, 2014:

- Firm A records interest expense on the note payable using the effective interest method to compute interest expense for the year. The effective interest rate for 2014 is 6%, and the (new, post-revaluation) book value of the note payable at the beginning of the year is $103,667. Therefore, interest expense is $6,220 (0.06 × $103,667). The cash payment of $8,000 is the amount set forth in the original borrowing arrangement with the equipment supplier. Because more cash than interest expense is paid, notes payable decreases by the difference, $1,780. (This is a premium amortization.)

- Firm A records an increase in the swap contract asset due to the passage of time of $220 (0.06 × $3,667) and the associated interest income. Recall that the swap contract was originally valued using present value; thus, its present value increases by the amount of interest each year. Interest expense (net) as a result of the two entries is $6,000 ($6,220 interest expense − $220 interest income), which is the variable rate for 2014 of 6% times the $500,000 face value of the note.

- Firm A receives $2,000 under the swap contract with its counterparty because the interest rate decreased from 8% to 6% [$100,000 × (0.08 − 0.06)], which also reduces the swap contract asset by $2,000. In a sense, the $2,000 cash received from the counterparty reimburses Firm A for paying interest at 8% on the note, whereas the swap contract provides that the firm benefits when interest rates decline, in this case to 6%.

- Assume interest rates increased during 2014 to 10%, so the bank resets the interest rate in the swap agreement to 10% for 2015. Firm A must revalue the note payable and the swap contract for changes in fair value. The present value of the remaining payments on the note (one cash interest payment of $8,000 and one maturity payment of $100,000 one year hence) at 10% is $98,182. The book value of the note payable before revaluation is $101,887 ($103,667 − $1,780 amortization). The entry to revalue the note payable reduces the note payable by $3,705 ($101,887 − $98,182), which is shown as a gain on revaluation of note payable on the income statement. The fair value of the swap contract decreases. Firm A must now pay an additional $2,000 in interest in 2015 because of the swap contract. Thus, the swap contract becomes a liability instead of an asset. When discounted at 10%, the present value of $2,000 is a $1,818 swap contract liability. The book value of the swap contract asset before revaluation is $1,887 ($3,667 + $220 − $2,000). The entry to revalue the swap contract from a $1,887 asset to a $1,818 liability results in a $3,705 loss on revaluation of swap contract reflected on the income statement. The gain on revaluation of the note exactly offsets the loss on revaluation of the swap contract, so the swap contract hedges the change in interest rates.

Following a similar process at December 31, 2015:

- Firm A records interest expense of $9,818 (0.10 × $98,182), increasing notes payable by $1,818 (a discount amortization), when it pays $8,000 (0.08 × $100,000) in cash.

- Firm A also recognizes interest expense of $182 (0.10 × $1,818) due to the passage of time on the swap contract liability. (Recall that when the swap contract was an asset, interest revenue was generated by the passage of time.) Interest expense (net) after these two effects is $10,000 ($9,818 interest expense + $182 interest expense), which equals the variable interest rate of 10% times the face value of the note.

- Firm A must pay the counterparty an extra 2% because the variable interest rate of 10% exceeds the fixed interest rate of 8%. Thus, cash and the swap contract liability decrease by $2,000.
- Firm A also repays the note and closes out the swap contract. The swap contract account has a zero balance on December 31, 2015, after the preceding entries ($1,818 + $182 – $2,000) are made, so the firm does not need to make additional entries to close out this account.

In summary, note that net income reflects the variable interest rate each year: 8% for 2013, 6% for 2014, and 10% for 2015. The note payable and the swap contract net to $100,000 at the end of each year.

Quick Check

The following summarizes the accounting for a fair value hedge of an existing asset or liability:

- The hedged asset or liability already appears on the books. Its valuation depends on U.S. GAAP's required accounting for the particular asset or liability (for example, lower of cost or market for inventories and present value of future cash flows for long-term receivables and payables).
- The firm recognizes the derivative as an asset on the date of acquisition to the extent it makes an initial investment. Otherwise, if the derivative is an exchange of mutually unexecuted promises, no amount appears on the balance sheet for the derivative.

- At the end of each period, the firm revalues the hedged asset or liability to fair value and includes the resulting gain or loss in net income.
- At the end of each period, the firm revalues the derivative instrument to fair value and includes the resulting loss or gain in net income.
- The firm shows the hedged asset and liability and its related derivative separately on the balance sheet.
- The firm removes the hedged asset or liability and its related derivative from the accounts at the time of settlement (for example, at the time of interest payments).

Cash Flow Hedge: Interest Rate Swap to Convert Variable-Rate Debt to Fixed-Rate Debt (Scenario 2 involving Firm B)

In Scenario 2, Firm B wants to hedge the risk of changes in interest rates on its cash payments for interest. It enters into a swap contract with a counterparty to convert its variable-rate note payable to a fixed-rate note. Firm B designates the swap contract as a cash flow hedge. The note has a $100,000 face value and an initial variable interest rate of 8%, which the counterparty resets to 6% for 2014 and 10% for 2015. The note matures on December 31, 2015. Exhibit 7.16 presents the financial statement template for this derivative contract.

- On January 1, 2013, Firm B records the issue of the note to acquire the equipment as before.
- On December 31, 2013, Firm B records the $8,000 cash interest outflow and $8,000 interest expense for 2013.
- The fair value of the note in this case, unlike Scenario 1, will not change as interest rates change because the note carries a variable interest rate. However, the fair

Exhibit 7.16: Cash Flow Hedge: Interest Rate Swap to Convert Variable-Rate Debt to Fixed-Rate Debt

Assets	=	Liabilities	+	Total Shareholders' Equity		
				CC	AOCI	RE
January 1, 2013 Equipment +100,000		Notes Payable +100,000				
Equipment 100,000 Notes Payable 100,000						
December 31, 2013 *Interest Expense on Note:* Cash −8,000 *Revaluation of Swap Contract*		Swap Contract +3,667			OCI—Swap Contract −3,667	Interest Expense −8,000
Interest Expense 8,000 Cash 8,000 Loss on Revaluation of Swap Contract (OCI) 3,667 Swap Contract 3,667						
December 31, 2014 *Interest Expense on Note:* Cash −6,000 *Interest "Expense" (OCI) on Swap Contract Liability:* *Cash Payment to Counterparty:* Cash −2,000 *Reclassification of a Portion of Other Comprehensive Income:* *Revaluation of Swap Contract:* Swap Contract +1,181		Swap Contract +220 Swap Contract −2,000 Swap Contract −1,887			OCI—Swap Contract −220 OCI—Swap Contract +2,000 OCI—Swap Contract +3,705	Interest Expense −6,000 Interest Expense −2,000
Interest Expense 6,000 Cash 6,000 OCI—Swap Contract 220 Swap Contract 220 Swap Contract 2,000 Cash 2,000 Interest Expense 2,000 OCI—Swap Contract 2,000 Swap Contract 3,705 OCI—Swap Contract 3,705						
December 31, 2015 *Interest Expense on Note:* Cash −10,000 *Interest "Revenue" (OCI) on Swap Contract Asset:* Swap Contract +182 *Cash Receipt from Counterparty:* Cash +2,000 Swap Contract −2,000 *Reclassification of a Portion of Other Comprehensive Income:* *Repayment of the Note:* Cash −100,000		Notes payable −100,000			OCI—Swap Contract +182 OCI—Swap Contract −2,000	Interest Expense −10,000 Interest Expense +2,000

(Continued)

Exhibit 7.16 (Continued)

Interest Expense	10,000	
Cash		10,000
Swap Contract	182	
OCI—Swap Contract		182
Cash	2,000	
Swap Contract		2,000
OCI—Swap Contract	2,000	
Interest Expense		2,000
Notes Payable	100,000	
Cash		100,000

value of the swap contract does change, and becomes a liability. The fair value on December 31, 2013, after the counterparty resets the interest rate to 6%, is $3,667. This amount is the present value of the $2,000 that Firm B will pay the counterparty on December 31, 2014 and 2015, if the interest rate remains at 6%. The swap contract (initially valued at $0) is now a liability of $3,667 due to the interest rate change. The loss from the upward revaluation of the swap contract liability does not immediately affect net income on a cash flow hedge. Instead, it reduces other comprehensive income. Other comprehensive income is closed into (and thus, is an element of) AOCI, a shareholders' equity account.

- The book value of the note payable of $100,000 plus the book value of the swap contract of $3,667 is $103,667. This amount is the present value of the expected cash flows under the fixed-rate note and swap contract combined, discounted at 6%.
- On December 31, 2014, Firm B pays the (now) $6,000 interest on the variable-rate note and recognizes interest expense.
- Firm B also must increase the book value of the swap contract liability by $220 (0.06 × $3,667) for the passage of time. Note that the interest charge does not immediately affect net income; instead, it decreases other comprehensive income.
- Firm B pays the counterparty the $2,000 [$100,000 × (0.08 – 0.06)] required by the swap contract and reduces the swap contract liability. Because the swap contract hedged cash flows related to interest rate risk during 2014, Firm B reclassifies a portion of other comprehensive income, $2,000 [$100,000 × (0.08 – 0.06)], to net income. At this point, the swap contract liability account has a balance of $1,887 ($3,667 + $220 – $2,000). Accumulated other comprehensive income related to this transaction also has been reduced to a debit balance (that is a net subtraction from shareholders' equity) of $1,887. Interest expense on the income statement is $8,000 ($6,000 + $2,000).
- Restating the interest rate on December 31, 2014, for the year 2015 to 10% changes the value of the swap contract from a liability to an asset. The present value of the $2,000 that Firm B will receive from the counterparty at the end of 2015 when discounted at 10% is $1,818. Firm B revalues the swap contract by reducing the swap contract liability by $1,887 and increasing the swap contract asset by $1,818. Removing the liability and recognizing the asset increases 2014 other comprehensive income by $3,705. At this point, other comprehensive income for 2014 is $5,485 ($2,000 + $3,705 – $220), which increases accumulated other comprehensive income from its $3,667 debit balance at the end of 2013 to a $1,818 credit balance at the end of 2014. This credit balance equals the balance in the swap contract asset account.
- On December 31, 2015, Firm B pays the (now) 10% interest on the loan and recognizes interest expense. Firm B also increases the book value of the swap contract

asset and increases other comprehensive income by $182 (0.10 × $1,818) for the passage of time. The swap contract requires the counterparty to pay the firm $2,000 under the swap contract, which reduces the swap contract asset by $2,000.

- Because the swap contract hedged cash flows related to interest rate risk during 2015, Firm B reclassifies $2,000 of other comprehensive income to net income by reducing interest expense. Thus, interest expense (net) for 2015 is $8,000 ($10,000 – $2,000).
- Finally, Firm B repays the note on December 31, 2015, and closes out the swap contract account. This account has a balance of zero on December 31, 2015 ($1,818 + $182 – $2,000). Thus, Firm B does not need to make an entry. If the swap contract had been highly but not perfectly effective in neutralizing the interest rate risk, accumulated other comprehensive income would have a balance related to the swap contract, which Firm B would reclassify to net income at this point.

In summary, note that interest expense is $8,000 each year, the fixed rate of 8% that Firm B obtained by entering into the swap contract. The amounts in other comprehensive income reflect changes in the fair value of the swap contract. The swap contract begins and ends with a zero value.

Quick Check

The following summarizes the accounting for a cash flow hedge associated with an existing asset or liability:[37]

- The hedged asset or liability already appears on the books. Its valuation depends on U.S. GAAP's required accounting for the particular asset.
- The firm recognizes the derivative as an asset on the date of acquisition to the extent that it makes an initial investment. Otherwise, if the derivative consists of mutually unexecuted promises, no amount appears on the balance sheet for the derivative.
- At the end of each period, the firm revalues the derivative instrument to fair value and recognizes a corresponding asset or liability. It also includes the resulting loss or gain in other comprehensive income.

- The firm reclassifies gains and losses from other comprehensive income to net income when the gain or loss on the hedged future cash flow occurs. If the derivative is not highly effective in neutralizing the gain or loss on the future cash flow, the firm must reclassify the ineffective portion to net income immediately and not wait until the cash flow occurs.
- The firm shows the derivative separately on the balance sheet. Also, it shows the cumulative amount of net fair value changes for the derivative in AOCI.
- The firm removes the hedged asset or liability and its related derivative from the accounts at the time of settlement (for example, at the time of the future cash flows for interest payments).

Summary of Derivative Examples

Firms record changes in the market value of all derivatives each reporting period. Changes in the value of derivatives and the related asset, liability, or commitment for fair value hedges flow through to net income immediately. Changes in the value of derivatives related to cash flow hedges initially increase or decrease other comprehensive income. They affect net income in the same period when the cash flows they hedge

---

[37]As we note previously, cash flow hedging also occurs for future anticipated transactions (e.g., a future inventory or equipment purchase). Hedging activities related to these planned transactions that are not currently recognized as assets and liabilities are discussed further in Chapters 8 and 9.

affect net income. Although this section does not illustrate separately the accounting for derivatives held as speculative investments because of their infrequent usage, the accounting is the same as for fair value hedges.

Disclosures Related to Derivative Instruments

Firms must disclose the book value and the fair value of financial instruments. Financial instruments impose on one entity a right to receive cash and an obligation on another entity to pay cash. Financial instruments include accounts receivable, notes receivable, notes payable, bonds payable, forward contracts, swap contracts, and most derivatives. Fair value is the current amount at which two willing parties exchange the instrument for cash. In addition, firms must disclose the following with respect to derivatives:

- Firms must describe their risk management strategy and how particular derivatives help accomplish their hedging objectives. The description should distinguish between derivative instruments designated as fair value hedges, cash flow hedges, and all other derivatives.
- For fair value and cash flow hedges, firms must disclose the net gain or loss recognized in earnings resulting from the hedges' ineffectiveness (that is, not offsetting the risk hedged) and the line item on the income statement that includes this net gain or loss.
- For cash flow hedges, firms must describe the transactions or events that will result in reclassifying gains and losses from other comprehensive income to net income and the estimated amount of such reclassifications during the next 12 months.
- Firms must disclose the net amount of gains and losses recognized in earnings because a hedged firm commitment no longer qualifies as a fair value hedge or because a hedged forecasted transaction no longer qualifies as a cash flow hedge.[38]

PepsiCo's Derivatives Disclosures

PepsiCo uses derivatives to hedge commodity prices, foreign exchange rates, and interest rates. PepsiCo describes its use of derivatives in Note 10, "Financial Instruments" (Appendix A). With respect to the hedging of interest rate risk discussed in this chapter, PepsiCo states the following:

> Certain of our fixed rate indebtedness has been swapped to floating rates. The notional amount, interest payment and maturity date of the interest rate and cross-currency swaps match the principal, interest payment and maturity date of the related debt … The notional amounts of the interest rate derivative instruments outstanding as of December 29, 2012 and December 31, 2011 were $8.1 billion and $8.3 billion, respectively. For those interest rate derivative instruments that qualify for cash flow hedge accounting, any ineffectiveness is recorded immediately. Ineffectiveness was not material for all periods

---

[38]U.S. GAAP requires qualitative disclosures about objectives and strategies for using derivatives, quantitative disclosures about fair value amounts of and gains and losses on derivative instruments, and disclosures about credit-risk-related contingent features in derivative agreements. *FASB Codification Topic 815.*

presented. During the next 12 months, we expect to reclassify net losses of $23 million related to these hedges from accumulated other comprehensive loss into net income. As of December 29, 2012, approximately 27% of total debt, after the impact of the related interest rate derivative instruments, was exposed to variable rates, compared to 38% as of December 31, 2011.

Firms must report the impact on earnings of certain changes in each of the major risk factors to which the earnings are subject. Firms typically disclose this information in their management discussion and analysis of operations. PepsiCo discusses (Appendix B) the effect on earnings of changes in commodity prices, foreign exchange rates, and interest rates. This information permits the analyst to assess the extent and effectiveness of hedging activities on each of these risks. For 2012, PepsiCo states that "Assuming year-end 2012 variable rate debt and investment levels, a 1-percentage-point increase in interest rates would have increased net interest expense by $9 million in 2012."

Accounting Quality Issues and Derivatives

Firms must mark derivatives to fair value each period. Fair values are usually reliable and easy to obtain when active, established markets exist for derivatives, as is the case for many forward contracts and interest and currency swaps. When firms engage in derivative transactions for which active markets do not exist, questions arise about the reliability of the fair values. **Enron**, for example, purchased and sold derivatives on the price and availability of broadband services. Broadband services were an emerging market at the time, with Enron one of only a few firms engaging in this type of derivative trading. Enron also held billions of dollars of notional value in derivatives for long-forward sales and purchases of various energy commodities, including oil, natural gas, and electricity, with some as far as 25 years in the future. Enron was the largest market maker (and one of the only market makers) for such derivatives, which were not widely traded.

A second accounting quality concern involves the classification of derivatives as fair value hedges versus cash flow hedges. In some cases, firms can classify exchange and commodity contracts as fair value hedges or cash flow hedges. Gains and losses on cash flow hedges affect earnings later than those on fair value hedges. When gains and losses on cash flow hedges substantially exceed the gains and losses on fair value hedges included in earnings, the analyst must at least question the firm's classification of its hedges.

When firms use derivatives to manage risks effectively, the net gain or loss each period should be relatively small. Large and varying amounts of gains or losses usually signal an ineffective use of derivatives.

Expected Rule Changes in Accounting for and Reporting of Debt Financing

LO 7-8

Identify significant likely changes in the financial reporting standards for debt and leases.

As of the writing of this text, the financial community continues to wait for the outcome of joint FASB and IASB deliberations in several areas, including the accounting for and reporting of debt financing. Important projects nearing completion are likely to significantly affect accounting practice. Although it is not yet possible to specify the new accounting rules, preliminary discussions provide some glimpse of likely future changes.

Joint FASB and IASB deliberations continue on a major financial instruments project, including financial instruments that have characteristics of equity. Likely outcomes of these related projects are:

- Standardized definitions of financial assets classes and how the financial assets in those classifications will be measured and reported (we will discuss these likely rule changes when we cover investments in Chapter 8).
- Recognition of financial liabilities (discussed in this chapter) at amortized cost with the fair value option rarely allowed, but fair values disclosed on the face of the balance sheet. It is interesting to note that elimination of the fair value option for financial liabilities would remove the counterintuitive result of gains on own debt when interest rates rise.
- U.S. GAAP changes in the way convertible debt is recorded. It appears that U.S. GAAP will separate the debt and equity components of convertible debt to match IFRS rules.
- A convergence of U.S. GAAP and IFRS treatments of troubled debt restructurings.

The long-awaited jointly issued lease standard appears to be nearing completion. On May 16, 2013, the lease standard draft was re-exposed with the expectation that (after comments are collected and re-deliberations occur) a final standard will be issued in 2014, effective in 2017 (with retroactive restatements to 2015). In this chapter, we illustrated the effective capitalization of operating leases and how the capitalization affects the balance sheet and the income statement. Under the expected rule change, you will not have to perform this task. Except for short-term leases, the present value of minimum lease payments (a measure of "usage rights") will be recorded on the balance sheet as a financial liability and an operating asset, thus removing the off-balance-sheet financing issue related to operating leases. The income statement effects will depend on whether the leased asset is property (such as land, office buildings, and integral equipment) or "other than property" (such as copiers, aircraft, delivery vans, etc.). The proposed standards favor income statement recognition of amortization/depreciation and interest expense for "other than property" leases, much like the methods illustrated in this chapter for capital leases. The proposed standards favor a straight-line recognition of lease expense for property leases. The rationale for the different income statement recognition approaches lies with standard setters' beliefs that property leases involve less consumption of the asset during the lease term. Accordingly, the lessor sets lease payments to provide a return *on* investment rather than a return *on* and *of* investment as in the case of "other than property" leases in which the asset is substantially consumed.

We recommend that you continue to monitor the FASB and IASB deliberations on these and other issues.

Summary

This chapter explores various accounting issues related to measuring the financing activities of the firm. Both profitability analysis and risk analysis are affected by management's choice between interest-bearing debt and shareholders' equity to finance the acquisition of operating capacity. The proper measurement and reporting of liabilities enables you to understand the risk of investing in the firm's debt and equity instruments, and the existence of off-balance-sheet arrangements complicates the analysis.

This chapter focuses primarily on the set of liabilities arising from transactions with lending institutions that generate notes and bonds payable. Typically, these liabilities are generated to raise funds for investments in long-term assets used in operations. The next chapter (Chapter 8) examines the accounting issues surrounding these long-term assets. Chapter 9 returns to measuring and reporting liabilities generated from operating activities, such as accounts payable, provisions, deferred tax liabilities, and pension liabilities.

Questions, Exercises, Problems, and Cases

Questions and Exercises

7.1 Common Equity Transactions. Describe the directional effect (increase, decrease, or no effect) of each transaction on the components of the book value of common shareholders' equity shown in the chart below.

LO 7-1, LO 7-2

  a. Issuance of $1 par value common stock at an amount greater than par value
  b. Donation of land by a governmental unit to a corporation
  c. Cash dividend declared
  d. Previously declared cash dividend paid
  e. Property dividend declared and paid
  f. Large stock dividend declared and issued
  g. Small stock dividend declared and issued
  h. 2-for-1 stock split announced and issued
  i. Stock options granted
  j. Recognition of compensation expense on stock options
  k. Stock options exercised
  l. Stock options expired
  m. Treasury stock acquired (company uses the cost method)
  n. Treasury stock in Transaction m reissued at an amount greater than original acquisition price
  o. Treasury stock in Transaction m reissued at an amount less than the original acquisition price
  p. Restricted stock issued (grant date)
  q. Recognition of compensation expense related to restricted stock
  r. Granting of stock appreciation rights to be settled with cash
  s. Recognition of compensation expense on stock appreciation rights
  t. Reacquisition and retirement of common stock at an amount greater than original issue price

Item	Common Stock	Additional Paid-in Capital	Deferred Compensation	Retained Earnings (use * to indicate income statement effect)	Treasury Stock at Cost	Total Common Shareholders' Equity
a.						
b.						
c.						
...						

LO 7-1

7.2 Common Equity Issue. Assume that a start-up manufacturing company raises capital through a series of equity issues.

a. Using the financial statement template below, summarize the financial statement effects of the following transactions. Identify the account affected and use plus and minus signs to indicate the increases and decreases in the specific element of the balance sheet (assets, liabilities, components of shareholders' equity).

(1) Issues 100,000 shares of $1 par value common stock for $10 per share.

(2) Receives land in exchange for 10,000 shares of $1 par common stock when the common stock is trading in the market at $15 per share. The land has no readily determinable market value.

Assets	=	Liabilities	+	Shareholders' Equity		
				CC	AOCI	RE
Journal entry:						

b. In each case, how does the company measure the transaction? What measurement attribute is used?

LO 7-1

7.3 Dividends. Following is the shareholders' equity section of All-Wood Doors on a day its common stock is trading at $130 per share.

Common stock ($2 par value, 40,000 shares issued and outstanding)	$ 80,000
Additional paid-in capital on common stock	1,600,000
Retained earnings	3,000,000

a. Use the financial statement template below to show the financial statement effects of the following dividend events. (Assume that the events are independent.)

(1) Cash dividend declaration and payment of $1 per share

(3) Property dividend declaration and payment of shares representing a short-term investment in Screen Products, Ltd., with a fair value of $10,000

(3) 10% stock dividend

(4) 100% stock dividend

(5) 3-for-1 stock split

(6) 1-for-2 reverse stock split

Assets	=	Liabilities	+	Shareholders' Equity		
				CC	AOCI	RE
Journal entry:						

b. Which events changed the book value of common equity? Under what conditions will these events lead to future increases and decreases in ROE?

LO 7-1, LO 7-4, LO 7-5

7.4 Cash Flow Effects of Equity and Debt Financing. Identify where the cash flow effect of each of the following transactions is reported in the statement of cash flows: operating, investing, or financing section. State the direction of each change. State *None* if there is no cash flow effect.

a. Issuance of stock for cash

b. Issuance of stock for land

c. Acquisition of treasury stock

d. Reissuance of treasury stock

e. Declaration of a cash dividend

f. Payment of a cash dividend previously declared

g. Declaration and issuance of a large stock dividend

h. Declaration and issuance of a small stock dividend

i. Granting of stock options

j. Exercise of stock options

k. Granting of RSUs

l. Issuance of long-term notes payable

m. Issuance of convertible bonds

n. Conversion of convertible bonds to common stock

o. Payment of interest on bonds

p. Retirement of bonds at book value

q. Retirement of bonds at a gain

r. Retirement of bonds at a loss

7.5 Accounting for a Note Payable. Assume that on December 31, 2013, The Coca-Cola Company borrows money from a consortium of banks by issuing a $900 million promissory note. The note matures in four years on December 31, 2017, and pays 3% interest once a year on December 31. The consortium transfers $867.331 million (rounded) to Coca-Cola, implying that the bank expects a 4% return on the note.　**LO 7-4**

a. Use the template below to show the financial statement effects of (1) the December 31, 2013, issue, (2) the December 31, 2014, interest payment and interest expense accrual, and (3) the December 31, 2015, interest payment and interest expense accrual.

| | Assets | = | Liabilities | + | Shareholders' Equity | | |
					CC	AOCI	RE
Journal entry:							

b. Assume that events involving foreign operations have increased the risk of The Coca-Cola Company to the point where creditors expect a 5% return on the note as of December 31, 2015. What amounts would Coca-Cola report for long-term debt (1) on the face of its December 31, 2015, balance sheet and (2) in the notes to the financial statements?

c. In addition to the information in Requirement b, assume that The Coca-Cola Company has chosen the fair value option for the reporting of this note. What amounts would Coca-Cola report for long-term debt (1) on the face of its December 31, 2015, balance sheet and (2) and on the income statement with respect to the note's fair value change?

7.6 Accounting For Troubled Debt: Settlement. Assume that Circuit City owes Synovus Bank $1,000, 000 on a 4-year, 7% note originally issued at par. After one year of making scheduled payments, Circuit City faces financial difficulty. At the end of the second year, Circuit City owes Synovus $1,000,000 plus $70,000 of accrued but unpaid interest. Circuit City settles the debt by paying $700,000 in cash and transferring investments to Synovus. Circuit City recently purchased the investments for $120,000 and carried them on the books at that amount. The investments are worth $135,000 at the date of the debt settlement. Use the template below to show the financial statement effects of the debt settlement.　**LO 7-4**

| | Assets | = | Liabilities | + | Shareholders' Equity | | |
					CC	AOCI	RE
Journal entry:							

7.7 Accounting for Troubled Debt: Modification of Terms. Assume that Great Beef Co. owes Bank of America $5,000, 000 on a 3-year, 9% note originally issued at　 **LO 7-4**

par. After one year of making scheduled payments, the firm faces financial difficulty. At the end of the second year, Great Beef owes Bank of America $5,000,000 plus $450,000 of accrued but unpaid interest. (Assume that the financial difficulty has increased the riskiness of Great Beef Co. to the point where it would have to pay 15% to borrow money.)

   a. Assume that Bank of America restructures the note by forgiving the $450,000 interest payable, reducing the note principal to $4,500,000, and reducing the interest rate to 6%. Show the financial statement effects at the date of restructuring using the template below assuming that Great Beef Co. uses:

   (1) U.S. GAAP
   (2) IFRS

Assets	=	Liabilities	+	Shareholders' Equity		
				CC	AOCI	RE
Journal entry:						

   b. Assume that Bank of America restructures the note by forgiving the $450,000 interest payable, reducing the note principal to $4,800,000, and reducing the interest rate to 7%. Show the financial statement effects at the date of restructuring using the template below assuming that Great Beef Co. uses:

   (1) U.S. GAAP
   (2) IFRS

Assets	=	Liabilities	+	Shareholders' Equity		
				CC	AOCI	RE
Journal entry:						

   c. Comment on the differences between the two systems. Which reporting system better represents the underlying economics of the debt restructuring? Will U.S. GAAP supplemental disclosures provide similar information? Explain.

LO 7-1, LO 7-4, LO 7-5

7.8 Redeemable Preferred Stock. Determine and compare the financial reporting (debt versus equity classification) of redeemable preferred stock with the following characteristics under U.S. GAAP and IFRS.

   a. Redemption will occur at a specific time or upon a specific event (for example, death of the holder).
   b. Redemption is at the option of the issuing firm; that is, the preferred stock is "callable."
   c. Redemption is at the holder's discretion; that is, the preferred stock is "putable."

LO 7-1, LO 7-4, LO 7-5

7.9 Convertible Preferred Stock. Assume that John Deere Co. issues 2,000 shares of $100 par, 6% convertible preferred stock for $105 per share. Shareholders have the right to exchange each share of convertible preferred stock for five shares of $10 par common stock. Use the template below to show the financial statement effects of the following events.

   a. Issuance of the preferred stock
   b. Declaration and payment of the cash dividend on the preferred stock
   c. Conversion of the preferred stock to common stock when the market value of the common stock is $29 per share

Assets	=	Liabilities	+	Shareholders' Equity		
				CC	AOCI	RE
Journal entry:						

7.10 Convertible Debt under IFRS and U.S. GAAP. `LO 7-5`

ARTL Company issued 3%, 10-year convertible bonds on January 1, 2013, at their par value of $500 million. Each $1,000 bond is convertible into 40 shares of ARTL's $1 par value common stock. Use the template below to show the financial statement effects under U.S. GAAP and IFRS of the following transactions.

a. Original issue (For the IFRS treatment, assume that ARTL would have borrowed at 8% if it did not offer a conversion privilege.)

b. Recognition of one year's interest effect

c. Conversion of the bonds when a share of ARTL common stock trades at $30

| | | | | | Shareholders' Equity | | |
	Assets	=	Liabilities	+	CC	AOCI	RE
Journal entry:							

7.11 Bonds Issued with Detachable Warrants. `LO 7-5`

Assume that Motorola, Inc., issues bonds with a face value of $10,000,000 for $9,200,000. The bonds have detachable warrants that may be traded in for shares of common stock. Assume that immediately after issue, bonds with warrants detached trade for $9,000,000; the warrants, for $400,000. Use the template below to show the financial statement effects at the date of issue.

| | | | | | Shareholders' Equity | | |
	Assets	=	Liabilities	+	CC	AOCI	RE
Journal entry:							

7.12 Effect of Capital and Operating Leases on the Financial Statements. `LO 7-6`

All leases for financial reporting purposes are treated as either capital (finance) leases or operating leases. The effects of the two reporting techniques on the financial statements differ substantially. From the perspective of the lessee, prepare a chart that lists the line items reported on the (a) income statement, (b) balance sheet, and (c) statement of cash flows under each reporting technique.

7.13 Nature of Reserve Accounts. `LO 7-1`

The use of the term *reserve* in the title of a financial statement account is not acceptable in the United States, primarily because its purpose is often too vague. However, informal use of the term by chief financial officers, analysts, and the media is common when they are discussing various aspects of *acceptable* accrual accounting techniques employed by U.S. firms. Provide several examples of financial statement accounts that are often loosely referred to as reserves. What is typically common about all financial statement accounts that are informally referred to as reserves?

7.14 Accounting for Stock-Based Compensation. `LO 7-2`

Historically, technology firms have been the most aggressive users of stock-based compensation in the form of stock options granted to almost all employees of the firms. What is the rationale for offering stock options as compensation? Why has this form of compensation been particularly popular with technology firms in the past?

7.15 Valuation of Derivatives. `LO 7-7`

Financial reporting classifies derivatives as (a) speculative investments, (b) fair value hedges, or (c) cash flow hedges. However, firms revalue all derivatives to market value each period regardless of the firm's reason for acquiring the derivatives. In addition to increasing or decreasing the derivative asset or liability, the revaluation amount either affects net income immediately or it affects other comprehensive income immediately and net income later. For each type of derivative, describe where firms report the revaluation amount on the financial statements.

Problems and Cases

7.16 Accounting for Securitization of Receivables. Ford Motor Credit Company discloses the following information with respect to finance receivables (amounts in millions).

December 31:	2004	2003
Finance Receivables	$146,451	$152,276
Securitized Receivables Sold	$ (35,600)	$ (46,900)
Finance Receivables on Balance Sheet	$110,851	$105,376
Retained Interest in Securitized Receivables Sold	$ 9,166	$ 12,569

Notes to Financial Statements

The Company periodically sells finance receivables in securitization transactions to fund operations and to maintain liquidity. The securitization process involves the sale of interest-bearing securities to investors, the payment of which is secured by a pool of receivables. In many securitization transactions, the Company surrenders control over certain of its finance receivables by selling these assets to SPEs. SPEs then securitize the receivables by issuing certificates representing undivided interests in the SPEs' assets to outside investors and to the Company (retained interest). These certificates entitle the holder to a series of scheduled cash flows under present terms and conditions, the receipt of which is dependent upon cash flows generated by the related SPEs' assets. The cash flows on the underlying receivables are used to pay principal and interest on the debt securities as well as transaction expenses.

In each securitization transaction, the Company retains certain subordinated interests in the SPE, which are the first to absorb credit losses on the sold receivables. As a result, the credit quality of certificates held by outside investors is enhanced. However, the investors and the trusts have no recourse against the Company beyond the trust assets. The Company also retains the servicing rights to the sold receivables and receives a servicing fee. While servicing the sold receivables for the SPE, the Company applies the same servicing policies and procedures that it applies to its own receivables and maintains a normal relationship with its financing customers.

Source: Ford Motor Credit Company, Form 10-K for the Fiscal Year Ended December 31, 2004.

REQUIRED

a. Applying the criteria for the sale of receivables, justify Ford Motor Credit's treatment of the securitization of finance receivables on December 31, 2003 and 2004, as a sale instead of a collateralized loan.

b. Assume that the receivables disclosed as securitized on December 31, 2003, had been initially securitized on that day. Give the journal entry that Ford Motor Credit would have made to securitize these receivables, assuming that it securitized the receivables at no gain or loss.

c. Assume that Ford Motor Credit decided to consolidate its receivables securitization structure in 2004 and to start accounting for it as secured borrowings. Give the journal entry that the company would make on December 31, 2004, to account for this change, assuming that it recognized no gain or loss on this event.

d. Most firms prefer to report the securitization of receivables as a sale. The alternative is to view the arrangement as a collateralized loan with the receivables remaining on the firm's balance sheet. Speculate on why firms prefer to report the securitization of receivables as a sale.

7.17 Accounting for Off-Balance-Sheet Financing. On June 24, Year 4, a [LO 7-4] major airline entered into a revolving accounts receivable facility (Facility) providing for the sale of $489 million of a defined pool of accounts receivable (Receivables) through a wholly owned subsidiary to a trust in exchange for a senior certificate in the principal amount of $300 million (Senior Certificate) and a subordinate certificate in the principal amount of $189 million (Subordinate Certificate). The subsidiary retained the Subordinate Certificate, and the company received $300 million in cash from the sale of the Senior Certificate to a third party. The principal amount of the Subordinate Certificate fluctuates daily depending on the volume of Receivables sold and is payable to the subsidiary only to the extent that the collections received on the Receivables exceed amounts due on the Senior Certificate. The full amount of the allowance for doubtful accounts related to the Receivables sold has been retained, as the company has substantially the same credit risk as if the Receivables had not been sold. Under the terms of the Facility, the company is obligated to pay fees that approximate the purchaser's cost of issuing a like amount of commercial paper plus certain administrative costs.

REQUIRED

The airline's management requests your advice on the appropriate accounting for this transaction. How would you respond?

7.18 Effect of Capitalizing Operating Leases on Balance Sheet Ratios. Some retailing companies own their own stores or acquire their premises under capital [LO 7-6] leases. Other retailing companies acquire the use of store facilities under operating leases, contracting to make future payments. An analyst comparing the capital structure risks of retailing companies may want to adjust reported financial statement data to put all firms on a comparable basis. Certain data from the financial statements of **Gap Inc.** and **Limited Brands** follow (amounts in millions).

Balance Sheet as of January 31, 2009	Gap Inc.	Limited Brands
Current liabilities	$2,158	$1,255
Long-term debt	0	2,897
Other noncurrent liabilities	1,019	946
Shareholders' equity	4,387	1,874
Total	$7,564	$6,972
Minimum Payments under Operating Leases		
2009	$1,069	$ 478
2010	927	455
2011	712	416
2012	520	373
2013	386	341
After 2013	1,080	1,334
Total	$4,694	$3,397

REQUIRED

a. Compute the present value of operating lease obligations using an 8% discount rate for Gap Inc. and Limited Brands as of January 31, 2009. Assume that all cash flows occur at the end of each year. Also assume that the minimum lease payment each year after 2013 equals $360 million per year for three years for Gap Inc. and $333.5 million for four years for Limited Brands. (This payment scheduling assumption can be obtained by assuming that the payment amount for 2013 continues until the aggregate payments after 2013 have been made, rounding the number of years upward, and then assuming level payments for that number of years. For Gap Inc.: $1,080/$386 = 2.8 years. Rounding up to three years creates a three-year annuity of $1,080/3 years = $360 million per year.)

b. Compute each of the following ratios for Gap, Inc. and Limited Brands as of January 31, 2009, using the amounts originally reported in their balance sheets for the year.

(1) Liabilities to Assets Ratio = Total Liabilities/Total Assets

(2) Long-Term Debt to Long-Term Capital Ratio = Long-Term Debt/(Long-Term Debt + Shareholders' Equity)

c. Repeat Requirement b but assume that these firms capitalize operating leases.

d. Comment on the results from Requirements b and c.

 7.19 Stock-Based Compensation. Exhibit 7.17 includes a footnote excerpt from the annual report of **The Coca-Cola Company** for 2004. The beverage company offers stock options to key employees under plans approved by stockholders.

Exhibit 7.17

The Coca-Cola Company
Stock Option Disclosures
(Problem 7.19)

Note—Stock-Based Compensation (partial footnote disclosure)

Our Company currently sponsors stock option plans. Effective January 1, 2002, our Company adopted the preferable fair value recognition provisions of Statement of Financial Accounting Standards ("SFAS") No. 123, "Accounting for Stock-Based Compensation." The fair values of the stock awards are determined using a single estimated expected life. The compensation expense is recognized on a straight-line basis over the vesting period. The total stock-based compensation expense, net of related tax effects, was $254 million in 2004, $308 million in 2003, and $267 million in 2002.

	2004	2003	2002
Stock-Based Compensation Expense, pretax[a]	$ 345	$ 422	$ 365
Number of Options Granted[b]	31	24	29
Average Option Price per Share	$ 41.63	$ 49.67	$ 44.69
Average Market Price per Share at Time of Grant	$ 41.63	$ 49.67	$ 44.69
Fair Value of Option Granted per Share	$ 8.84	$ 13.49	$ 13.10
Vesting Period of Options Granted, years	1–4	1–4	1–4
Life of Options, years	10	10	10
Option Valuation Assumptions for Black-Scholes Model[b]			
Risk-Free Interest Rate	3.8%	3.5%	3.4%
Dividend Yield	2.5%	1.9%	1.7%
Stock Volatility	23.0%	28.1%	30.2%
Expected Option Life, years	6.0	6.0	6.0
Number of Options Exercised[a]	5	4	3
Average Option Exercise Price	$ 35.54	$ 26.96	$ 31.09

[a]Amounts in millions.

[b]Weighted averages.

Source: The Coca-Cola Company, Form 10-K for the Fiscal Year Ended December 31, 2004.

REQUIRED

Review Exhibit 7.17 and answer the following questions.

a. Coca-Cola reports both pretax and after-tax stock-based compensation in its notes to the financial statements. What is the tax savings for 2002, 2003, and 2004 that Coca-Cola generates from the stock-based compensation provided to its employees? Speculate on what income statement line item includes this tax savings as well as what income statement line item includes the stock-based compensation expense. (The income statement is not provided in this problem.)

b. The average option price per share and market price per share at time of grant is equal each year ($44.69 for 2002, $49.67 for 2003, and $41.63 for 2004). Discuss why Coca-Cola structured the stock option grants this way each year.

c. What are the likely reasons that the fair value of options granted per share increased from 2002 to 2003 and then decreased from 2003 to 2004?

d. Coca-Cola does not report the market price of its stock at the time employees exercised options (3 million in 2002, 4 million in 2003, and 5 million in 2004), but in each year the end-of-year market price is substantially higher than the average option exercise price reported in Exhibit 7.17. Discuss why Coca-Cola is willing to sell shares of its stock to employees at a price (option exercise price) much lower than the firm could obtain for shares sold on the market (market price at time of exercise).

e. Coca-Cola employs the Black-Scholes valuation model for valuing stock option grants. Speculate on the directional effects of the key assumptions made in applying the Black-Scholes options pricing model. That is, which assumptions will result in a higher fair value for stock options and which will result in a lower fair value? Why?

7.20 Stock-Based Compensation. Eli Lilly and Company produces pharmaceu   LO 7-2
tical products for humans and animals. Exhibit 7.18 includes a footnote excerpt from the annual report of Lilly for the period ending December 31, 2004.

REQUIRED

Review Exhibit 7.18 and answer the following questions.

a. Lilly's statement of cash flows (not provided in this problem) includes an addback for stock-based compensation in calculating cash flows from operations of $108.2 million for 2004 and $25.2 million for 2003. Why does Lilly add stock-based compensation back to net income?

b. Refer to Requirement a. Lilly's statement of cash flows includes a cash inflow in the section on cash flows from financing activities of $12.5 million for 2004 and $46.5 million for 2003. The amounts are labeled "Issuance of common stock under stock plans." Who provided these cash inflows to Lilly? In general terms, how are the amounts determined?

c. Lilly states in the note: "Stock options are granted to employees at exercise prices equal to the fair market value of our stock at the dates of grant." Discuss why Lilly structured the stock option grants this way.

d. The note reports $397.5 million of remaining unrecognized compensation cost related to nonvested stock options. What portion of this amount will be reported as compensation expense in the second quarter ending June 30, 2004? Does this amount represent total stock-based compensation expense for the quarter?

e. In the past, firms were required to report pro forma earnings per share, taking into consideration stock-based compensation. Current financial reporting requires stock-based compensation to be reported in the income statement, and thus included in the calculations of reported earnings per share. Many firms also present non-GAAP earnings numbers before deducting the effects of stock compensation as a supplemental disclosure in their annual reports (which is comparable to the reported earnings number under the

Exhibit 7.18

Eli Lilly and Company
Stock Option Disclosures
(Problem 7.20)

Note—Stock-Based Compensation (partial footnote disclosure)

We adopted Statement of Financial Accounting Standards No. 123 (revised 2004), Share-Based Payment (SFAS 123R), effective January 1, 2004. SFAS 123R requires the recognition of the fair value of stock-based compensation in net income. Stock options are granted to employees at exercise prices equal to the fair market value of our stock at the dates of grant. Generally, options fully vest three years from the grant date and have a term of 10 years. We recognize the stock-based compensation expense over the requisite service period of the individual grantees, which generally equals the vesting period.

We recognized compensation cost in the amount of $108.2 million and $25.2 million in the first quarter of 2004 and 2003, respectively, as well as related tax benefits of $32.8 million and $8.8 million, respectively.

Beginning with the 2004 stock option grant, we utilized a lattice-based option valuation model for estimating the fair value of the stock options. The lattice model allows the use of a range of assumptions related to volatility, risk-free interest rate, and employee exercise behavior. Expected volatilities utilized in the lattice model are based on implied volatilities from traded options on our stock, historical volatility of our stock price, and other factors. Similarly, the dividend yield is based on historical experience and our estimate of future dividend yields. The risk-free interest rate is derived from the U.S. Treasury yield curve in effect at the time of grant. The model incorporates exercise and post-vesting forfeiture assumptions based on an analysis of historical data. The expected life of the 2004 grants is derived from the output of the lattice model.

The weighted-average fair values of the options granted in the first quarter of 2004 were $16.06 per option, determined using the following assumptions:

Dividend Yield	2.0%
Weighted-Average Volatility	27.8%
Range of Volatilities	27.6%–30.7%
Risk-Free Interest Rate	2.5%–4.5%
Weighted-Average Expected Life	7.2 years

As of March 31, 2004, the total remaining unrecognized compensation cost related to non-vested stock options amounted to $397.5 million which will be amortized over the weighted-average remaining requisite service period of 2 years.

Source: Elli Lilly and Company, Form 10-K for the Fiscal Year Ended December 31, 2004.

older rules). Why do companies do this? Which earnings number is more meaningful, net income or this non-GAAP measure?

7.21 Stock-Based Compensation—Vesting and Valuation Models.
Exhibits 7.17 and 7.18 provide footnote excerpts to the financial reports of **The Coca-Cola Company** and **Eli Lilly and Company** that discuss the stock option grants given to the employees of the two firms. Each firm uses options extensively to reward employees for their performance.

REQUIRED

Review Exhibits 7.17 and 7.18 and answer the following questions.

    a. Explain the concept of vesting. Discuss why firms typically include a vesting feature in the stock-based compensation plans that they offer to their employees.

b. What are the vesting characteristics of the two plans discussed in the exhibits? What effect do they have on stock-based compensation expense using the fair value method?

c. For each firm, (1) what is the life of the options granted, (2) how does option life relate to the vesting period, and (3) why might the weighted-average *expected* life of the options be less than the full life of the options?

d. The Coca-Cola Company uses the Black-Scholes valuation model for estimating the fair value of the stock options, whereas Eli Lilly and Company utilizes a lattice-based option valuation model. Both valuation techniques are permitted by U.S. GAAP. Perform an Internet search to determine which valuation model is more commonly used by the largest publicly held firms. Speculate on why this is the case.

7.22 Interpreting Stock Option Disclosures. Exhibit 7.19 summarizes the information disclosed by a large conglomerate regarding its stock option plans for Years 2–4. Assume an income tax rate of 35%.

LO 7-2

REQUIRED

a. The average option price per share and market price per share at time of grant is equal in each year ($27.37 for Year 2, $31.19 for Year 3, and $32.26 for Year 4). Speculate on why the company structured the stock option grants this way in each year.

b. What are the likely reasons that the fair value of options granted per share increased from Year 2 to Year 3?

c. Compute the amount that the company received from the exercise of stock options each year versus the amount it would have received if it had issued the same number of shares on the market.

d. Refer to your answer to Requirement c. Discuss why the company is willing to sell shares of its stock to employees at a price (average option exercise price) much lower than the firm could obtain for shares sold on the market (average market price at time of exercise).

Exhibit 7.19			
Stock Options (Problem 7.22)			
	Year 4	**Year 3**	**Year 2**
Number of options granted[a]	27.141	8.261	46.928
Average option price per share	$ 32.26	$ 31.19	$ 27.37
Average market price per share at time of grant	$ 32.26	$ 31.19	$ 27.37
Fair value of option granted per share	$ 8.33	$ 9.44	$ 7.73
Vesting period of options granted, years	1–5	1–5	1–5
Option valuation assumptions:			
Discount rate	4.0%	3.5%	3.5%
Volatility	27.7%	34.7%	33.7%
Dividend yield	2.5%	2.5%	2.7%
Expected option life, years	6.0	6.0	6.0
Number of options exercised (in millions)	43.110	43.829	29.146
Average option exercise price	$ 10.54	$ 9.45	$ 9.45
Average market price at time of exercise	$ 32.68	$ 27.59	$ 31.86

e. Refer again to your answer to Requirement c. Compute the effect of stock-based compensation on net income for each year, assuming that stock option compensation expense equaled the difference between the market price and the exercise price of options exercised.

f. Discuss the strengths and weaknesses of each of the following approaches to recognizing the cost of stock options: (1) no expense as long as the option price equals the market price on the date stock options are granted, (2) expense in the year of the grant equal to value of options granted, and (3) expense in the year of exercise equal to the benefit realized by employees from purchasing shares for less than market value.

LO 7-7	**7.23 Hedging Interest Rate Risk Part A.** Floral Delivery, Inc. (FD) acquired a fleet of vans on January 1, 2013, by issuing a $500,000, 4-year, 4% fixed rate note, with interest payable annually on December 3. FD has the option to repay the note prior to maturity at the note's fair value. FD engages in a contract with the bank to swap its fixed-interest-rate obligation for a variable-interest-rate obligation; the variable rate in the swap is intended to track the variable rate used by the supplier to revalue the note while it is outstanding. The swap causes FD's interest payments to vary as the variable interest rate changes, but it locks the value of the note payable at $100,000, and thus qualifies the swap as a hedge of value changes in an existing liability. Under the terms of the swap, the counterparty (the bank) resets the interest rate each December 31. Assume that the interest rate is reset to 3% at December 31, 2013, and to 5% at December 31, 2014. Interest rates remain steady from that date forward.

REQUIRED

Use the financial template to record the financial statement effects of these transactions and events through December 31, 2015.

Part B.

REQUIRED

Repeat Part A assuming that the 4% interest rate is variable and that the supplier resets the interest rate each December 31 to establish the interest charge for the next calendar year. In this case, FD wants to protect its future cash flows against increases in the variable interest rate to more than the initial 4% rate, so it contracts with the bank to swap its variable-interest-rate obligation for a fixed-interest-rate obligation. The swap fixes the firm's annual interest expense and cash expenditure to 4% of the $500,000 note. FD designates the swap contract as a cash flow hedge.

LO 7-4, LO 7-6

INTEGRATIVE CASE 7.1

Starbucks

Starbucks' consolidated balance sheet as of September 30, 2012, reports $549.6 million in long-term debt and $5,046.2 million in total shareholders' equity. Therefore, the long-term debt to long-term capital ratio, defined as Long-Term debt/(Long-Term Debt + Shareholders' Equity), is 9.71%.

In the MD&A and notes to the financial statements, Starbucks also reports additional information relative to its reported debt and equity:

Fair value of the $549.6 million, 6.25% senior notes (based on a Level 2 valuation; Note 4)	$ 674 million
Average market value per share for common stock during the 4th quarter of fiscal 2012 (MD&A)	$48.67
Shares outstanding at the balance sheet date (balance sheet)	749.3 million

In addition, as is common practice for fast-food and retail coffee shop chains, Starbucks leases some or all of its retail space under operating leases. Note 10 to Starbuck's consolidated financial statements for the fiscal year ending September 30, 2012, provides the following future operating lease commitments of Starbucks as of the end of the fiscal year (amounts in millions).

Fiscal Year Ending in:	
2013	$ 787.9
2014	728.5
2015	640.4
2016	531.5
2017	403.4
Thereafter	968.5
Total lease payments	$4, 060.2

REQUIRED

a. Compute the present value of operating lease obligations using a 6.25% discount rate. Assume that all cash flows occur at the end of each year. Also assume that the minimum lease payments after 2017 occur evenly over a five-year period.

b. Recompute the long-term debt to long-term capital ratio assuming that Starbucks capitalizes operating leases and reports the long-term portion as part of long-term debt.

c. Recompute the long-term debt to long-term capital ratio assuming that the long-term portion of operating leases are treated as long-term debt and using market values of long-term debt and equity.

d. Comment on the results from Requirements b and c. What additional insights do these alternative calculations provide?

e. Starbucks reports an expense labeled "Cost of Sales including Occupancy Costs" on its income statement. Speculate why Starbucks reports cost of sales and occupancy (operating lease payments) costs as a combined amount on the income statement.

CASE 7.2

LO 7-1, LO 7-2

Oracle Corporation: Share-Based Compensation Effects/Statement of Shareholders' Equity

A sales-based ranking of software companies provided by **Yahoo! Finance** on November 5, 2008, places **Oracle Corporation** third behind sales leaders **Microsoft Corporation** and **IBM Software**. Typical of high-tech companies in the software industry, Oracle Corporation uses share-based compensation plans extensively to motivate its employees. In Note 11 of its May 31, 2008, annual report, Oracle states that it settles employee stock options exercises primarily with newly issued common shares.

As indicated by the selected data from Oracle's May 31, 2008, consolidated balance sheet in Exhibit 7.20, Oracle finances operations using substantially more common shareholder's equity than it does long-term debt. However, Oracle's long-term debt to shareholders' equity ratio of 44.5% is substantially larger than that of major U.S. competitor Microsoft Corporation and major foreign competitor **SAP AG**, both of which report almost no long-term

Exhibit 7.20

Oracle Corporation
May 31, 2008 Consolidated Balance Sheet
(in millions of dollars)
(Case 7.2)

	May 31,	
	2008	**2007**
Non-current notes payable and other non-current borrowings	$10,235	$ 6,235
Stockholders' equity		
Common stock, $0.01 par value and additional paid-in capital— authorized: 11,000 shares; outstanding: 5,150 shares and 5,107 shares as of May 31, 2008 and 2007	$12,446	$10,293
Retained earnings	9,961	6,223
Accumulated other comprehensive income	618	403
Total stockholders' equity	$23,025	$16,919

Source: Oracle Corporation, Form 10-K for the Fiscal Year Ended May 31, 2008.

financial debt. Exhibit 7.21 presents the consolidated statement of shareholders' equity for 2008. Exhibit 7.22 presents portions of financial statement Notes 10 and 11.

REQUIRED

a. Compute Oracle's long-term debt to shareholders' equity ratio for May 31, 2008 and 2007. Identify the increases in shareholders' equity in 2008 from share-based compensation plans. Calculate the long-term debt to shareholders' equity ratio that would have occurred had Oracle not implemented the stock repurchase plan. Comment on the potential effect on future ROE of Oracle's financing strategy.

b. Retained earnings increases because of net income and decreases because of dividends declared. Why, then, did Oracle decrease retained earnings when it repurchased common stock?

c. Of the first five changes listed in the shareholders' equity section, one of them, the common stock repurchase, clearly represents a cash outflow. Identify the cash flow effects of the other four items. Where will each cash flow effect be reported in the statement of cash flows?

d. Oracle engages in many transactions with non-owners (that is, customers, suppliers, and the government) that increase net assets. For example, Oracle's foreign subsidiaries perform services on credit with unrelated third-party customers. The accounts receivable generated by the transactions are denominated in a foreign currency and thus are reported on the foreign subsidiaries balance sheet in that foreign currency. The consolidation process causes the subsidiary's accounts receivable to be added to the parent company's (Oracle's) accounts receivable and reported on Oracle's Consolidated Balance Sheet. Assuming that the foreign currency strengthens relative to the U.S. dollar, how does Oracle's Consolidated Statement of Shareholders' Equity capture the increases in accounts receivable described in this example transaction?

e. Using the foreign currency translation gain of $300 million as a context, present an argument for including the gain on Oracle's income statement and an argument for excluding the gain as Oracle does under U.S. GAAP.

f. Under Oracle's Employee Stock Purchase Plan, employees can purchase common shares at 95% of their fair values. Will Oracle report a loss on this transaction? Why or why not?

Exhibit 7.21

**Oracle Corporation
Consolidated Statements of Stockholders' Equity at May 31, 2008
(in millions of dollars)
(Case 7.2)**

	Comprehensive Income	Common Stock and Additional Paid-in Capital		Retained Earnings	Accumulated Other Comprehensive Income	Total
		Number of Shares	Amount			
Balances as of May 31, 2007		5,107	$10,293	$ 6,223	$403	$16,919
Common stock issued under stock award plans		137	1,229			1,229
Common stock issued under stock purchase plans		3	59			59
Assumption of stock award in conjunction with acquisitions			240			240
Stock-based compensation			367			367
Repurchase of common stock		(97)	(214)	(1, 786)		(2,000)
Tax benefits from stock plans			472			472
Adjustment to retained earnings upon adoption of FIN 48				3		3
Net unrealized loss on defined benefit plan assets, net of tax	$ (9)				(9)	(9)
Foreign currency translation	300				300	300
Net unrealized losses on derivative financial instruments, net of tax	(77)				(77)	(77)
Net unrealized gain on marketable securities, net of tax	1				1	1
Net income	5,521			5,521		5,521
Comprehensive income	$5,736					
Balances as of May 31, 2008		5,150	$12,446	$ 9,961	$618	$23,025

Source: Oracle Corporation, Form 10-K for the Fiscal Year Ended May 31, 2008.

Exhibit 7.22

Oracle Corporation
Portions of Notes 10 and 11
(Case 7.2)

10. Stockholders' Equity (partial)

Stock Repurchases

Our Board of Directors has approved a program for Oracle to repurchase shares of our common stock to reduce the dilutive effect of our stock option and stock purchase plans. In April 2007, our Board of Directors expanded our repurchase program by $4.0 billion and as of May 31, 2008, $2.2 billion was available for share repurchases pursuant to our stock repurchase program. We repurchased 97.3 million shares for $2.0 billion (including 1.1 million shares for $24 million that were repurchased but not settled), 233.5 million shares for $4.0 billion and 146.9 million shares for $2.1 billion in fiscal 2008, 2007 and 2006, respectively.

Our stock repurchase authorization does not have an expiration date and the pace of our repurchase activity will depend on factors such as our working capital needs, our cash requirements for acquisitions, our debt repayment obligations (as described above), our stock price, and economic and market conditions. Our stock repurchases may be affected from time to time through open market purchases or pursuant to a Rule 10b5-1 plan. Our stock repurchase program may be accelerated, suspended, delayed or discontinued at any time.

11. Employee Benefit Plans (partial)

Stock-based Compensation Plans

Stock Option Plans

… In connection with certain of our acquisitions, including PeopleSoft, BEA, Siebel and Hyperion, we assumed all of the outstanding stock options and other stock awards of each acquiree's respective stock plans. These stock options and other stock awards generally retain all of the rights, terms and conditions of the respective plans under which they were originally granted. As of May 31, 2008, options to purchase 77 million shares of common stock and 1 million shares of restricted stock were outstanding under these plans.

Tax Benefits from Option Exercises

We settle employee stock option exercises primarily with newly issued common shares and may, on occasion, settle employee stock option exercises with our treasury shares. Total cash received as a result of option exercises was approximately $1.2 billion, $873 million and $573 million for fiscal 2008, 2007 and 2006, respectively. The aggregate intrinsic value of options exercised was $2.0 billion, $986 million and $594 million for fiscal 2008, 2007 and 2006, respectively. In connection with these exercises, the tax benefits realized by us were $588 million, $338 million and $169 million for fiscal 2008, 2007 and 2006, respectively. The adoption of Statement 123(R) required us to change our cash flow classification of certain tax benefits received from stock option exercises beginning in fiscal 2007. Of the total tax benefits received, we classified excess tax benefits from stock-based compensation of $454 million and $259 million as cash flows from financing activities rather than cash flows from operating activities for fiscal 2008 and 2007, respectively.

Employee Stock Purchase Plan

We have an Employee Stock Purchase Plan (Purchase Plan). Starting with the April 1, 2005 semi-annual option period, we amended the Purchase Plan such that employees can purchase shares of common stock at a price per share that is 95% of the fair value of Oracle stock as of the end of the semi-annual option period. As of May 31, 2008, 81 million shares were reserved for future issuances under the Purchase Plan. During fiscal 2008, 2007 and 2006, we issued 3 million, 3 million and 6 million shares, respectively, under the Purchase Plan.

Source: Oracle Corporation, Form 10-K for the Fiscal Year Ended May 31, 2008.

CASE 7.3

Long-Term Solvency Risk: Southwest and Lufthansa Airlines

The first decade of the 21st century witnessed a flurry of losses, bankruptcies, acquisitions, and strategic partnerships in the airline industry. The heavily levered firms in the industry are particularly susceptible to increases in fuel prices, economic changes that affect travel, and safety concerns. These conditions require you to have a strong understanding of the long-term solvency risk of firms in the airline industry.

Two of the larger liabilities of airlines relate to promises to provide free flights to customers (frequent-flyer programs) and promises to make cash payments under flight equipment and ground facilities agreements. The former liability is captured in the total liabilities to assets ratio. The latter promise is captured in the total liabilities to assets ratio and in the long-term debt to shareholders' equity ratio, but only if the promises are treated as long-term debt.

Exhibits 7.23–7.28 present the income statements, balance sheets, and other key information for U.S. airline **Southwest**, which prepares financial statements under U.S. GAAP, and German airline **Lufthansa**, which prepares financial statements under IFRS.

REQUIRED

a. Using the information in the exhibits, provide a comprehensive and detailed comparison of the long-term solvency risk of Southwest to Lufthansa as of December 31, 2008, and as of December 31, 2007. (Ignore tax effects. Deferred taxes are covered in Chapter 8 on operating activities.)

(1) Consider the following ratios in your analysis:

$$\text{Liabilities to Assets Ratio} = \text{Total Liabilities/Total Assets}$$

$$\text{Long-Term Debt to Shareholders' Equity Ratio} = \text{Long-Term Debt/} \\ \text{Total Shareholders' Equity}$$

$$\text{Operating Cash Flow to Average Total Liabilities Ratio} = \text{Operating Cash Flow/} \\ \text{Average Total Liabilities}$$

$$\text{Interest Coverage Ratio (cash basis)} = \text{(Operating Cash Flow} + \text{Interest Paid} + \\ \text{Taxes Paid)/Interest Paid}$$

(2) Compute the ratios using financial information (a) as reported and (b) after capitalization of operating leases. (Hint: Adjusting operating cash flow for assumed lease capitalization requires the removal of rent paid from operating cash flows and the inclusion of interest paid in operating cash flows. Use rent expense and interest expense to approximate rent paid and interest paid, respectively.

b. An analyst who compares the debt ratios of firms under U.S. GAAP and IFRS must consider key differences in the two sets of standards related to convertible debt and troubled debt restructurings. In general, which system would most likely yield lower debt and higher equity? Explain.

Exhibit 7.23

Southwest Airlines Co.
Consolidated Balance Sheet
(in millions, except share data)
(Case 7.3)

	December 31	
	2008	**2007**
ASSETS		
Current assets:		
Cash and cash equivalents	$ 1, 368	$ 2, 213
Short-term investments	435	566
Accounts and other receivables	209	279
Inventories of parts and supplies, at cost	203	259
Fuel derivative contracts	—	1,069
Deferred income taxes	365	—
Prepaid expenses and other current assets	313	57
Total current assets	2,893	4,443
Property and equipment, at cost:		
Flight equipment	13,722	13,019
Ground property and equipment	1,769	1,515
Deposits on flight equipment purchase contracts	380	626
	15,871	15,160
Less allowance for depreciation and amortization	4,831	4,286
	11,040	10,874
Other assets	375	1,455
	$14,308	$16,772
LIABILITIES AND STOCKHOLDERS' EQUITY		
Current liabilities:		
Accounts payable	$ 668	$ 759
Accrued liabilities	1,012	3,107
Air traffic liability	963	931
Current maturities of long-term debt	163	41
Total current liabilities	2,806	4,838
Long-term debt less current maturities	3,498	2,050
Deferred income taxes	1,904	2,535
Deferred gains from sale and leaseback of aircraft	105	106
Other deferred liabilities	1,042	302
Commitments and contingencies		
Stockholders' equity:		
Common stock, $1.00 par value: 2,000,000,000 shares authorized;		
807,611,634 shares Issued in 2008 and 2007	808	808
Capital in excess of par value	1,215	1,207
Retained earnings	4,919	4,788
Accumulated other comprehensive income (loss)	(984)	1,241

Exhibit 7.23 (Continued)

Treasury stock, at cost: 67,619,062 and 72,814,104 shares in 2008 and 2007, respectively	(1,005)	(1,103)
Total stockholders' equity	4,953	6,941
See accompanying notes.	$14,308	$16,772

Source: Southwest Airlines Co., Form 10-K for the Fiscal Year Ended December 31, 2008.

Exhibit 7.24

Southwest Airlines Co.
Consolidated Statement of Income
(in millions, except per-share amounts)
(Case 7.3)

	Years Ended December 31,		
	2008	**2007**	**2006**
OPERATING REVENUES:			
Passenger	$10,549	$9,457	$8,750
Freight	145	130	134
Other	329	274	202
Total operating revenues	11,023	9,861	9,086
OPERATING EXPENSES:			
Salaries, wages, and benefits	3,340	3,213	3,052
Fuel and oil	3,713	2,690	2,284
Maintenance materials and repairs	721	616	468
Aircraft rentals	154	156	158
Landing fees and other rentals	662	560	495
Depreciation and amortization	599	555	515
Other operating expenses	1,385	1,280	1,180
Total operating expenses	10,574	9,070	8,152
OPERATING INCOME	449	791	934
OTHER EXPENSES (INCOME):			
Interest expense	10	119	128
Capitalized interest	(25)	(50)	(51)
Interest income	(26)	(44)	(84)
Other (gains) losses, net	92	(292)	151
Total other expenses (income)	171	(267)	144
INCOME BEFORE INCOME TAXES	278	1,058	790
PROVISION FOR INCOME TAXES	100	413	291
NET INCOME	$ 178	$ 645	$ 499
NET INCOME PER SHARE, BASIC	$ .24	$ .85	$ .63
NET INCOME PER SHARE, DILUTED	$ .24	$ .84	$ .61

Source: Southwest Airlines Co., Form 10-K for the Fiscal Year Ended December 31, 2008.

Exhibit 7.25

Southwest Airlines Co.
Additional Data from December 31, 2008 10K Filing
(Case 7.3)

From Consolidated Statement of Cash Flows (in millions):	2008	2007
Net cash provided by (used in) operating activities	$(1,521)	$2,845
Interest paid	$ 100	$ 63
Income taxes	$ 71	$ 94

From 2008 Note 8 (Leases)

... Total rental expense for operating leases, both aircraft and other, charged to operations in 2008, 2007, and 2006 was $527 million, $469 million, and $433 million, respectively. The majority of the Company's terminal operations space as well as 82 aircraft were under operating leases at December 31, 2008. Future minimum lease payments under capital leases and noncancelable operating leases with initial or remaining terms in excess of one year at December 31, 2008, are provided in the following table.

in millions	Capital Leases	Operating Leases
2009	$16	$ 376
2010	15	324
2011	12	249
2012	—	203
2013	—	152
After 2013	—	728
Total minimum lease payments	43	$2,032
Less amount representing interest	4	
Present value of minimum lease payments	39	
Less current portion	14	
Long-term portion	$25	

From 2007 Note 8 (Leases)

... Total rental expense for operating leases, both aircraft and other, charged to operations in 2007, 2006, and 2005 was $469 million, $433 million, and $409 million, respectively. The majority of the Company's terminal operations space as well as 86 aircraft were under operating leases at December 31, 2007. Future minimum lease payments under capital leases and noncancelable operating leases with initial or remaining terms in excess of one year at December 31, 2007, are provided in the following table.

in millions	Capital Leases	Operating Leases
2008	$16	$ 400
2009	17	335
2010	15	298
2011	12	235
2012	—	195
After 2012	—	876
Total minimum lease payments	60	$2,339

Exhibit 7.25 (Continued)

Less amount representing interest	8
Present value of minimum lease payments	52
Less current portion	13
Long-term portion	$39

Source: Southwest Airlines Co., Form 10-K for the Fiscal Year Ended December 31, 2008.

Exhibit 7.26

Lufthansa
Consolidated Balance Sheet as of 31 December 2008
(Case 7.3)

Assets

in €m	Notes	31.12.2008	31.12.2007
Intangible assets with indefinite useful life*	17)	821	797
Other intangible assets	18)	261	252
Aircraft and reserve engines	19) 22)	8,764	8,380
Repairable spare parts for aircraft		669	586
Property, plant and other equipment	20) 22)	1,931	1,773
Investment property	21)	3	3
Investments accounted for using the equity method	23)	298	323
Other equity investments	24) 25)	790	777
Non-current securities	24) 25)	509	298
Loans and receivables	24) 26)	475	399
Derivative financial instruments	24) 27)	339	368
Accrued income and advance payments	30)	15	22
Effective income tax receivables	14)	72	79
Deferred claims for income tax rebates	14)	28	19
Non-current assets		**14,975**	**14,076**
Inventories	28)	581	511
Trade receivables and other receivables	24) 29)	3,015	3,448
Derivative financial instruments	24) 27)	213	481
Accrued income and advance payments	30)	119	110
Effective income tax receivables		130	62
Securities	24) 31)	1,834	1,528
Cash and cash equivalents	24) 32)	1,444	2,079
Assets held for sale	33)	97	25
Current assets		**7,433**	**8,244**
Total assets		**22,408**	**22,320**

(Continued)

Exhibit 7.26 (Continued)

Shareholders' equity and liabilities

In €m	Notes	31.12.2008	31.12.2007
Issued capital	34) 35)	1,172	1,172
Capital reserve	36)	1,366	1,366
Retained earnings	36)	3,140	2,063
Other neutral reserves	36)	579	589
Net profit for the period	36)	599	1,655
Equity attributable to shareholders of Deutsche Lufthansa AG		6,856	6,845
Minority interests		63	55
Shareholders' equity		**6,919**	**6,900**
Pension provisions	37)	2,400	2,461
Other provisions	38)	291	349
Borrowings	39) 40)	3,161	3,098
Other financial liabilities	41)	51	55
Advance payments received, accruals and deferrals and other non-financial liabilities	42)	64	66
Derivative financial instruments	27) 39)	118	371
Deferred income tax liabilities	14)	813	749
Non-current provisions and liabilities		**6,898**	**7,149**
Other provisions	38)	1,873	1,686
Borrowings	39) 40)	420	247
Trade payables and other financial liabilities	39) 43)	3,626	3,959
Liabilities from unused flight documents		1,693	1,546
Advance payments received, accruals and deferrals and other non-financial liabilities	44)	388	289
Derivative financial instruments	27) 39)	492	481
Actual income tax liabilities		99	51
Provisions and liabilities included in disposal groups	45)	—	12
Current provisions and liabilities		**8,591**	**8,271**
Total shareholders' equity and liabilities		**22,408**	**22,320**

*Incl. goodwill.

Source: Lufthansa Group, Annual Report for the Fiscal Year Ended December 31, 2008.

Exhibit 7.27

Lufthansa
Consolidated Income Statement for the 2008 Financial Year
(Case 7.3)

in €m	Notes	2008	2007
Traffic revenue	3)	19,998	17,568
Other revenue	4)	4,872	4,852
Total revenue		**24,870**	**22,420**
Changes in inventories and work performed by the enterprise and capitalised	5)	178	119
Other operating income	6)	1,969	1,571
Cost of materials and services	7)	−13,707	−11,553
Staff costs	8)	−5,692	−5,498
Depreciation, amortisation and impairment	9)	−1,289	−1,204
Other operating expenses	10)	−4,946	−4,269
Profit from operating activities		**+ 1,383**	**+ 1,586**
Result of equity investments accounted for using the equity method	11)	−22	+ 223
Result from other equity investments	11)	+ 42	+131
Interest income	12)	202	177
Interest expense	12)	−374	−371
Other financial items	13)	−427	−133
Financial result		**−579**	**+27**
Profit before income taxes		**+804**	**+ 1,613**
Income taxes	14)	−195	−356
Profit from continuing operations		**+609**	**+ 1, 257**
Profit from the discontinued Leisure Travel segment	15)	—	+503
Profit after income taxes		**+609**	**+ 1, 760**
Minority interests		−10	−105
Net profit attributable to shareholders of Lufthansa AG		**+599**	**+ 1, 655**
Basic earnings per share in €	16)	1.31	+ 3.61
Diluted earnings per share in €	16)	1.30	+ 3.60

Source: Lufthansa Group, Annual Report for the Fiscal Year Ended December 31, 2008.

Exhibit 7.28

Lufthansa
Additional Data from December 31, 2008 Annual Report
(Case 7.3)

From Consolidated Statement of Cash Flows (In €m):	2008	2007
Net cash provided by (used in) operating activities	2,473	2,862
Net interest paid	172	194
Income taxes	123	274

12) Net interest

Net Interest

In €m	2008	2007
Income from other securities and financial loans	11	13
Other interest and similar income	191	164
Interest income	**202**	**177**
Interest expenses on pensions obligations	−119	−154
Interest expense on other provisions	−16	−9
Interest and other similar expenses	−239	−208
Interest expenses	**−374**	**−371**
	−172	−194

Operating leases

In addition to the finance leases, a large number of leases have been signed which, on the basis of their economic parameters, are qualified as operating leases, i.e. the leased asset is deemed to belong to the lessor. As well as 106 additional aircraft on operating leases, these are mainly aircraft leased as part of the Lufthansa Regional concept and leases for buildings.

The operating leases for aircraft have a term of between one and nine years. These agreements generally end automatically after the term has expired, but there is sometimes an option for extending the agreement.

The leases for buildings generally run for up to 25 years. The fixtures at the airports in Frankfurt and Munich are leased for 30 years.

The following payments are due in the years ahead (amounts in millions; p.a. denotes per annum):

in €m	2009	2010−2013	from 2014
Aircraft	209	343	—
Various buildings	213	872	215 p.a.
Other leases	70	273	56 p.a.
	492	**1,488**	**271 p.a.**
Payments from sub-leasing	9	13	1 p.a.

In the previous year the following figures were given for operating leases:

in €m	2008	2009−2012	from 2013
Aircraft	196	418	—
Various buildings	236	920	227 p.a.
Other leases	80	306	65 p.a.
	512	**1,644**	**292 p.a.**
Payments from sub-leasing	14	13	2 p.a.

Source: Lufthansa Group, Annual Report for the Fiscal Year Ended December 31, 2008.

Investing Activities

LEARNING OBJECTIVES

LO 8-1 Describe the accounting and reporting for a firm's investments in tangible and intangible productive assets, including the initial decision to capitalize or expense them.

LO 8-2 Discuss the exercise of judgment used in the allocation of costs through the depreciation and amortization process.

LO 8-3 Apply the rules for testing the impairment of different categories of long-lived assets, including goodwill.

LO 8-4 Describe the accounting and reporting for investments in debt securities, including the fair value and amortized cost methods, and investments in equity securities, including the fair value, equity, and consolidation methods.

LO 8-5 Describe variable-interest entities, sometimes referred to as special-purpose entities, and explain the need for the primary beneficiary to consolidate them.

LO 8-6 Translate subsidiary financial statements denominated in a foreign currency to facilitate consolidation with a U.S. parent.

Chapter Overview

In Chapter 7 we discussed the financial reporting for financing activities, which are the primary sources of capital for investing and operating activities. In this chapter, we discuss the financial reporting for investing activities. Once a firm obtains financing, it must invest the proceeds effectively to generate returns that cover the costs of the financing.

Investing activities create assets, and thus, the accounting for investments directly affects the denominator for the return on assets computations discussed in Chapters 4 and 5. Also, forecasted future financial statements depend heavily on forecasted investing activities, especially investments in operating assets such as property, plant, and equipment.

Investing activities fall into two broad categories:

- Investments in *long-lived operating assets* (which include long-lived tangible fixed assets such as land, buildings, and equipment; intangible assets such as patents, brand names, customer lists, and goodwill; and natural resources such as oil reserves and timberlands).
- Investments in the *securities* of other firms (including stock and bond investments).[1]

Firms also make tactical and operating investments in net working capital. Because working capital assets (for example, accounts receivable and inventory) and working capital liabilities (for example, accounts payable and other current liabilities) are generated by and used in day-to-day normal revenue-generating activities, these investments are discussed with operating activities in Chapter 9.

---

[1]Because a significant subset of stock investments are controlling investments in foreign subsidiaries, we discuss the translation of foreign subsidiary financial statements denominated in a foreign currency in this chapter as well.

To illustrate the scope of this chapter, refer to the Assets section of **PepsiCo**'s 2012 consolidated balance sheet in Appendix A. PepsiCo shows short-term investments (in the current assets section) and many assets listed as noncurrent assets (that is, property, plant, and equipment, net; amortizable intangible assets, net; goodwill; other nonamortizable intangible assets; and investments in noncontrolled affiliates). Collectively, these assets sum to $54,587 million, or more than 73% of PepsiCo's $74,638 million total assets at December 29, 2012. Also, the fact the PepsiCo's statements are "consolidated" means that in all of its financial statements, PepsiCo includes the assets, liabilities, revenues, expenses, and cash flows of its subsidiaries.

Because this chapter focuses on a major portion of a company's assets, it is useful to revisit the definition of *assets* discussed in Chapter 1 prior to consideration of the two major classifications of assets created by investing activities. An asset has four characteristics (the first three form the definition of an asset and the fourth is necessary for measurement):

1. Provides probable future benefits
2. Is obtained/controlled by the entity
3. Is a result of past transactions and events
4. Can be reliably measured (at acquisition cost or fair value)[2]

For many long-lived productive assets, such as machinery, determining whether the item acquired is an asset and measuring its cost are not difficult tasks. However, some transactions present challenges. For example, certain expenditures might fail the probable future benefits test, such as those related to research and development, marketing and brand-building activities, and exploration for natural resources. Also, as discussed later in the chapter, consideration of the "control" characteristic will determine which assets are recognized in the financial statements of the investor in an intercompany investment. Finally, the availability of reliable fair value information will drive the measurement for many financial assets.

LO 8-1

Describe the accounting and reporting for a firm's investments in tangible and intangible productive assets, including the initial decision to capitalize or expense them.

Investments in Long-Lived Operating Assets

Refer to **PepsiCo**'s Note 4, "Property, Plant and Equipment and Intangible Assets" in Appendix A in which PepsiCo provides the detail to support the following long-lived operating assets reported in its consolidated balance sheet at December 29, 2012:

- $19,136 million in property, plant and equipment, net
- $1,781 million in amortizable intangible assets, net
- $31,715 million in nonamortizable intangible assets (including goodwill)

---

[2]Financial Accounting Standards Board, *Statement of Financial Accounting Concepts No. 5*, "Recognition and Measurement in Financial Statements of a Business Enterprise," (1984); Financial Accounting Standards Board, *Statement of Financial Accounting Concepts No. 6*, "Elements of Financial Statements," (1985). Currently, the IFRS definition of an asset is very similar to the U.S. GAAP definition. As of the writing of this text, the FASB and IASB continue work on Phase B of its Conceptual Framework project, which will finalize convergent definitions of financial statement items. Tentatively, the new definition of assets deemphasizes past transactions and events and expected future benefits in favor of determining whether the entity has, at present, an economic resource that (a) is separable from the entity by sale, license, or another potential type of exchange or (b) is arising from a contractual or legal right. This definition is consistent with standard setters' beliefs that more assets and liabilities should be measured at fair value. The separability of the asset and the contractual or legal right definitions directly permit or enhance the ability to measure an asset's fair value.

The individual amounts in Note 4 provide a good summary of the accounting issues of interest to a financial statement analyst, as follows:

- PepsiCo uses the first part of the note to explain the $19,136 million reported as the *net book value* of its *tangible asset* property, plant, and equipment on the balance sheet. PepsiCo reports $36,162 million as the cost of acquiring the property, plant, and equipment, and then subtracts accumulated depreciation of $17,026 million to date. The annual depreciation expenses (that sum over time to equal accumulated depreciation) are reflected each year in PepsiCo's net income. For 2012, PepsiCo reports $2,489 million of depreciation expense.

- In the second part of the note, PepsiCo repeats this description of acquisition cost and accumulated amortization for a second type of long-lived operating asset, *amortizable intangible assets* with definite useful lives. PepsiCo recognizes amortization expense of $119 million in 2012 net income.

- In the last part of the note, PepsiCo reconciles the ending and beginning balances of the components of a third type of long-lived operating asset, *nonamortizable intangible assets*—perpetual brands, franchise rights, and goodwill. Because these assets have been judged to have indefinite lives, they are not amortized but instead are assessed annually for impairment. If impaired, the carrying amounts are written down to fair value. As a result, PepsiCo recognizes no amortization expense for these assets in net income in 2012. As Note 4 indicates, PepsiCo did record impairment charges on nonamortizable assets of $23 million and $14 million in 2012 and 2011, respectively.

Each of the following sections identifies an important issue in financial statement analysis and refers back to Note 4. The section headings are in the form of analysts' questions. The answers determine accounting quality in the long-lived asset investments area. We also consider how the answers affect an analyst's ability to conduct profitability and risk analysis and to forecast future financial statements.

Are the Acquisition Costs Assets or Expenses?

The initial effects on financial statements depend on whether the acquisition costs can be capitalized and recognized as an asset (i.e., the four conditions for asset recognition and measurement are met) or not, and thus recognized as an expense. If the acquisition costs are initially capitalized, subsequent cost allocation decreases the long-lived asset over its useful life, and the consumption of the cost is treated as an expense. The remaining book value of the asset (its *adjusted acquisition cost*) is reported on the balance sheet. If the initial cost is deemed to be an expense, the amount of consideration given will be expensed immediately and no balance sheet asset will exist.

Because of the very different effects of capitalizing and expensing acquisition costs on balance sheets and income statements, your analysis of the quality of accounting for acquisition costs must focus on several related questions: Are capitalized acquisition costs justified? Were assets created, or should the costs be expensed? Are the firm's capitalization policies clear and in line with competitors and economic reality? Were some economic assets created even though accounting rules require expense treatment? To inform your analysis, we examine issues related to the financial reporting of expenditures incurred in activities relating to real assets (tangible and intangible). We consider:

- property, plant, and equipment.
- research and development costs.
- software development costs.
- subsequent expenditures to enhance or maintain property, plant, and equipment.
- costs of self-construction.
- costs of acquiring intangible assets.
- costs of acquiring natural resources.

Accounting for the Acquisition of Property, Plant, and Equipment: General Rule

In many cases, it is clear that the costs to acquire a piece of property, plant, and equipment will yield future benefits; thus, asset recognition is warranted. The general rule for recognizing the acquisition of an asset is that it should be recorded at the fair value of what has been sacrificed to acquire the asset (whether it be cash, debt, or equity shares) and to prepare the asset for its intended use (including costs to ship, temporarily store, insure, set up, test, and calibrate).

Cash used to acquire property, plant, and equipment is reported as a cash outflow in the investing activities section of the statement of cash flows. If property, plant, and equipment is acquired using debt or equity (both of which are non-cash transactions), the investing activity will be reported as a significant non-cash investing and financing activity in a separate schedule. **PepsiCo** reports annual capital spending of between $2.7 and $3.3 billion over 2010–2012 in its consolidated statement of cash flows (Appendix A). In addition, acquisition of the intangible "manufacturing and distribution rights from DPSG" represents an additional $2.8 billion in 2010. These investments in tangible and intangible real assets utilize a significant portion of the $8.4–$8.9 billion annual net cash provided by operating activities over the same three-year period.

Accounting for Research and Development Costs

R&D (research and development) is an important activity for many firms. However, because of the inherent uncertainty in determining whether R&D activities will produce sufficient and reliably measurable future economic benefits to warrant being capitalized as an asset, U.S. GAAP requires firms to expense immediately all internal R&D costs.[3] Externally acquired R&D from purchasing patents or licenses can be capitalized because the arm's-length transaction between two market participants provides a reliable measure of acquisition cost and is an indicator of the existence of future economic benefits. For industries with high R&D expenditures, such as the research-intensive biotechnology industry, the U.S. GAAP requirement to expense internal R&D costs rather than capitalize them is especially noteworthy, because a major asset never appears on the balance sheet.

A further complication in analyzing R&D activities arises from firms using different strategies to carry out R&D activities. For example, compare the different strategies of

---

[3]*FASB Codification Topic 730.* Long-lived assets, such as buildings, computers, and lab equipment, used in multiple R&D projects are initially capitalized; then the depreciation of the assets is assigned to R&D expense.

Biogen Idec and **Amgen, Inc.** Biogen Idec has leading products and capabilities in neurology, hemophilia, and immunology. Revenues for 2012 exceed $5.5 billion. Biogen Idec principally develops drug-related products *internally* in its research laboratories, and discovers and develops drugs for human health care through genetic engineering. In describing its accounting policy on R&D costs, Biogen Idec states:

> Research and development expenses consist of upfront fees and milestones paid to collaborators and expenses incurred in performing research and development activities including compensation and benefits, facilities expenses, overhead expenses, clinical trial and related clinical manufacturing expenses, fees paid to clinical research organizations (CROs), and other outside expenses. Research and development expenses are expensed as incurred.[4]

The firm's 2012 R&D expense was approximately 24% of sales. In accordance with U.S. GAAP, the firm showed no asset on its balance sheet related to this in-house research activity. Biogen Idec also engages in *acquisitions* of other technology companies, in which it acquires established technologies, patent rights, and R&D work that is in process. Because these acquisitions are transactions with outside parties, Biogen reports a $1,039.6 million intangible asset on its balance sheet for established core technologies and patent rights and the fair value of in-process R&D of $330 million, which included $219 from a single acquisition of Stomedix in 2012.[5]

Amgen Inc. is a leading human therapeutics company, generating over $17 billion in revenues in 2012 from a number of top-selling products. The firm follows a strategy of *internal* development of biotechnology and *external* development through a series of joint ventures, licensing relationships, and partnerships. Amgen contributes preliminary research findings to obtain its interest in these joint ventures and partnerships. The other participants provide funding to continue development of this preliminary research. In some cases, Amgen contracts with the joint venture or partnership to perform the continued development in its own laboratories. In this case, Amgen receives a fee each period in an amount approximately equal to the R&D costs incurred in conducting the research (resulting in no net R&D cost). In other cases, the joint venture or partnership entity conducts the research, in which case Amgen may show no R&D expense on its books. Amgen generally maintains a right of first refusal for any products developed, in which case it must pay the owners of the joint venture a periodic royalty. Amgen's R&D expense for 2012 was 20.3% of sales.

Although these firms have similarly (large) R&D expenses as a percentage of sales, Amgen's expense ratio does not capture the extent of its R&D activities, and its balance sheet might not capture the possibility of future cash inflows from using the future technologies in production. Amgen reports no R&D asset although it is a company that, in the past, has turned R&D assets into successful products and future cash flows. Further, its R&D expenses do not adequately capture its R&D activities because many of those activities are performed by its joint ventures and not shown as R&D expense on Amgen's income statement. Biogen's R&D expense captures its own R&D efforts to a greater extent and its balance sheet captures significantly more R&D activity cash flow potential because it is allowed to capitalize its fair value estimates of established core technologies and in-process R&D.

---

[4]Note 1 to 12/31/2012 Biogen Idec Inc. 10K.

[5]Capitalization of the fair value of in-process R&D obtained in a merger or acquisition is now required. *FASB Codification Topic 805* reflects the 2007 rule change for U.S. GAAP, and International Accounting Standards Board, *International Financial Reporting Standard 3*, "Business Combinations" (2007) describes the IFRS rule.

You could address this issue by choosing a single method to account for all R&D expenditures and modify financial statements by capitalizing and subsequently amortizing all expenditures on R&D that have future service potential, whether a firm incurs the R&D cost internally or purchases in-process or completed technology externally, and immediately expense all R&D costs that are not likely to have future service potential. This approach would also require the consolidation of the firm's share of the assets, liabilities, revenues, and expenses of R&D joint ventures or partnerships. Unfortunately, you would quickly discover that the inherent uncertainty about future benefits that led accounting standard setters to require all internal R&D expenditures to be expensed creates difficulties in judging future service potential from financial statement disclosures alone. Reliance on firm disclosures of scientific and other information outside the financial reporting model is necessary. Also, the consolidation of joint ventures also might prove to be difficult because only some R&D joint venture data will be present in notes to the financial statements.

Even when modification of the financial statements is not possible because of lack of data, you should be aware of the effects of the R&D expensing rule on profitability analysis. The effects on ROA are countervailing between numerator and denominator. Missing assets understate total assets in the denominator. The numerator of ROA, net income (adjusted), is understated when all R&D is classified as current expense and is overstated when the amortization of R&D assets from prior successful R&D efforts is excluded. When R&D expenditures are growing, the net effect on the numerator will be understatement because current R&D expenses exceed the amortizations. A mature firm may reach a steady state where current R&D expense equals total amortization, which would have taken place if R&D had been capitalized. If that happens, the ROA numerator would be unaffected, but the denominator would still be understated due to the omission of the R&D asset. IFRS rules mitigate the likely overstatement of ROA because research costs are expensed and product development costs (the costs incurred after the research yields a product or process that is technologically feasible) are capitalized.[6]

In general, capitalization and amortization (relative to immediate expensing) results in a smoother income series and thus produces net income that is theoretically easier to predict. Although managers and others view R&D as a necessary investing activity, statement of cash flow reporting treats R&D as an operating activity because it does not result in a balance sheet asset. R&D reduces current period net income and thus reduces current period cash flows from operating activities.

Accounting for Software Development Costs

U.S. GAAP treats the cost of developing computer software somewhat differently than it treats R&D costs. Firms must expense all internally incurred costs of developing computer software until such development achieves the "technological feasibility" of a product. Thereafter, the firm must capitalize and subsequently amortize additional development costs.[7] U.S. GAAP defines technological feasibility as "completion of a detailed program design or, in its absence, completion of a working model." Clearly, determining when a software development project achieves technological feasibility requires significant judgment by managers and other personnel. For example, **IBM**'s R&D expense includes costs for conceptual formulation of software products as well as amortization of software costs previously capitalized for products that had reached the

---

[6]International Accounting Standards Board, *International Accounting Standard 38,* "Intangible Assets" (1998).

[7]*FASB Codification Topic 985.* These rules on costs of computer software relate to software to be sold, leased, or otherwise marketed, not to software created for internal use that is capitalized and amortized.

technological feasibility stage. In contrast, **Adobe Systems**, whose Acrobat® and Reader® products are well known, develops new software internally and through aggressive external acquisitions of other software companies. Adobe also expenses initial software development costs incurred internally as R&D expense and capitalizes those costs related to developing software deemed technological feasible. In addition, it capitalizes the cost of software acquired in corporate acquisitions if the software has achieved technological feasibility. **Microsoft** appears to capitalize only a very small portion of the development costs of subsequent generations of Windows® or Office because of the lateness of the point at which it believes that technological feasibility is reached, which is after most development costs have been incurred. Fortunately, because of the very rapid pace of technology development where software and tech products have short life cycles of only a few years, the differences between capitalization and immediate expensing are getting much shorter and much less significant.

Subsequent Expenditures for Enhancement or Improvements

Subsequent to acquiring long-lived operating assets, firms make additional expenditures to enhance or improve them. Proper accounting is to capitalize (that is, add to the asset's book value) expenditures that increase the service life or potential (in either quantity or quality) of an asset beyond that originally anticipated. Firms should expense immediately expenditures for repairs and maintenance that merely maintain the originally expected service potential. For example, replacing tires on a delivery truck does not qualify as a capital expenditure because the original useful life was determined with the assumption that tires would be replaced regularly. However, if a refrigeration unit was added to the cargo area of the truck to add the capability to transport perishable cargo, the expenditure would be capitalized because the quality of service was improved beyond original expectations.

Maintenance costs can be significant. **American Airlines**, one of the largest airlines in the world, follows a rigorous maintenance program for all of its aircraft. In its 2012 10-K, American Airlines reports more than $1 billion of maintenance and repairs in operating expenses.

Management judgment in the subsequent expenditures area creates ample opportunity for earnings management. Remember that the capitalization versus expensing choice has immediate effects on the income statement. One way to increase earnings is to (incorrectly) classify routine maintenance and repair costs as capital expenditures. Investors must rely on management integrity and auditor monitoring as protection against self-interested managers manipulating earnings through biased application of the judgment necessary in many settings. Strong corporate governance and auditor reporting of internal control weaknesses assist the assessment of accounting quality.

Costs of Self-Construction

A company might choose to self-construct plant and equipment because it wants to save costs or because no external supplier is available. **Walmart Stores, Inc.,** for example, might construct its own stores. The cost of a self-constructed asset equals the fair value of all necessary costs incurred to produce it, including materials, labor, and overhead. For example, self-construction projects frequently use existing equipment and do not create the need for additional expenditures on equipment, plant management supervision, and property taxes. But these fixed costs are necessary for the construction to occur, and both U.S. GAAP and IFRS require an allocation of part of the fixed overhead cost to self-construction costs. If internal expenditures exceed the cost of acquiring the asset externally, the amount recorded in the self-constructed asset's account will be limited to the cost of external purchase and the excess of costs incurred over the external fair value is recorded as a loss of the period. This process ensures that an asset is not recorded initially at an amount greater than its fair value.

As a general rule, interest costs on debt are treated as an expense of the period, as illustrated in Chapter 7. However, both U.S. GAAP and IFRS have an exception to this rule for interest incurred during the self-construction of a long-lived productive asset intended for the company's own use.[8] Interest on incremental debt used to finance asset construction is a valid and often necessary cost of constructing an asset. By capitalizing interest on self-constructed assets, the firm better captures the fair value sacrificed to acquire the asset. The capitalized interest cost becomes part of the asset's historical cost (depreciation basis) and, hence, annual depreciation expense.

Costs of Acquiring Natural Resources

Oil fields, timber tracts, and mineral deposits are examples of natural resources. Three types of costs incurred in connection with natural resources are as follows:

- Acquisition costs
- Exploration costs
- Development costs[9]

Acquisition Costs. Acquisition costs include the costs of acquiring the natural resources and the costs associated with returning the resource site to an acceptable condition after the resources have been obtained. Often, the natural resource is attached to land that is salvageable at the end of production. If that is the case, the initial cost is separated into two accounts, with the portion of cost attributable to land reported separately in a "land" or "property" account. All other costs of acquisition are capitalized as part of the "natural resources" account and reported in the property, plant, and equipment section with the other productive, operational assets.

Frequently, a natural resource asset is subject to *reclamation cost* or *restoration costs* at the end of the life of a project. For example, at the end of a coal strip mine's productive life, the mine operator incurs substantial costs to fill in the mine and return the land to its original contour. The need to incur costs to reclaim a natural resource is an example of an *ARO (asset retirement obligation)*. The fair value of the obligation (usually determined by discounting expected future reclamation costs) is capitalized and amortized over the life of the related natural resource asset.[10]

Exploration Costs. Exploration costs are incurred to discover the existence and exact location of a natural resource. For example, a petroleum manufacturer acquires an oil field (acquisition cost) and then drills to discover oil. The costs of engaging in the

---

[8]Interest costs also may be capitalized on construction of certain types of inventory (discussed in Chapter 9). *FASB Codification Topic 835*; International Accounting Standards Board, *International Accounting Standard 23 (revised 2007)*, "Borrowing Costs."

[9]*FASB Codification Topics 930 and 932*; International Accounting Standards Board, *International Financial Reporting Standard 6*, "Exploration for and Evaluation of Mineral Resources" (2004). IFRS cost classifications are slightly different from U.S. GAAP classifications. IFRS requires a clear and consistent accounting policy in the natural resource area involving judgment as to whether costs are capitalized or expensed. Given that the U.S. GAAP rules described in this section yield asset measurements that can be justified by reasonable judgment and permit some choice in the capitalization versus expensing decision, one can conclude that U.S. GAAP and IFRS treatments are not likely to yield variations in natural resource valuations that are greater than the variations in valuations that occur in U.S. GAAP.

[10]*FASB Codification Topic 410*; International Accounting Standards Board, *International Accounting Standard 16*, "Property, Plant and Equipment" (1998).

drilling activity, including supplies, labor, and machinery depreciation charges, are exploration costs. The accounting for exploration costs has emerged as one of the most controversial topics in accounting history. At the center of the controversy is the determination of whether the costs of unsuccessful exploration activities are assets or expenses. The following two schools of thought on that issue have emerged:

- *Successful efforts* (exploration costs of successful wells are capitalized as assets, but unsuccessful wells are expensed)
- *Full costing* (exploration costs of successful and unsuccessful wells are assets)

The successful efforts approach maintains that if six wells are drilled and two produce oil, then the exploration costs of the two successful wells are capitalized in the natural resources account and the costs of the four unsuccessful wells are expensed. This argument is rational because only the successful wells yield probable future economic benefits (that is, the sale of oil) and, hence, should be called assets.

The full costing approach capitalizes exploration costs for all six wells as part of the natural resources account. The argument is that it was necessary to drill all of the wells in order to discover oil. The cost of exploring all six locations is deemed a necessary investment to generate future economic benefits. Therefore, all costs are capitalizable. This argument also is rational, and it has precedence in other areas of accounting. The costs of producing defective or spoiled inventory, for example, are included as part of the cost of producing good inventory if it is necessary to destroy or spoil some goods in the production of good output. For example, the rapid filling of beverage bottles involves some waste; however, the cost of the wasted beverage is capitalized as part of beverage inventory.

Because reasonable arguments can be made to support both the successful efforts and the full costing approaches, either method may be used to account for natural resource exploration costs. Managers choose the method they believe is best for their company. Firms in the same industry frequently choose different approaches, and the resulting financial statements can be difficult to compare across firms. Many financial statement users complained about the lack of comparability brought about by the availability of two such different accounting methods for the same transaction. Currently, the successful efforts method tends to be used by larger producers, while full costing tends to be used by smaller producers. Accordingly, you should consider the differential treatment of exploration costs when comparing the profitability and risk of small and large firms in the extractive industry. Firms disclose their method choice in the accounting policies note to the financial statements.

Development Costs.
Once the natural resource has been acquired and exploration has determined the location of deposits, the natural resource must be developed. Development costs are both tangible (for example, heavy equipment to drill and transport the resource) and intangible (for example, the costs of drilling wells and constructing mine shafts). Tangible development costs are capitalized as part of the equipment (or another property, plant, and equipment) account. Intangible development costs are capitalized as part of the natural resources account because the costs are not separable from the natural resource; for example, the costs associated with drilling a specific oil well cannot be moved to another well site.[11]

---

[11]The accounting system captures costs incurred with respect to natural resources, including additional costs incurred to protect the environment. Some costs are incurred to minimize the environmental risk. For example, in the aftermath of the *Exxon Valdez* oil spill, double-hull oil tankers, which are more expensive to produce than single-hull tankers, are now used to transport Alaskan crude oil. The direct cost to Exxon to clean up the oil spill and indirect costs associated with tarnishing **Exxon**'s reputation were substantial.

Summing acquisition costs, exploration costs (of successful efforts or all efforts depending on the method used), and intangible development costs yields the capitalized natural resource asset. Costs are expensed as the natural resource is consumed. Depletion expense represents an estimate of the percentage amount of consumption.

Costs of Acquiring Intangible Assets

Intangible assets include trade and brand names, trademarks, patents, copyrights, franchise rights, customer lists, and goodwill. Under both U.S. GAAP and IFRS, firms expense the cost of *internally* developing intangibles in the period incurred. The rationale for immediate expensing of such costs is the difficulty and uncertainty in ascertaining whether a particular expenditure results in a future benefit (an asset) or not (an expense). Thus, although **PepsiCo** spends millions of dollars each year promoting its products, and brand names such as Pepsi and Frito-Lay® represent valuable economic "assets" of the firm, PepsiCo is not permitted to recognize an asset for the expenditures made to internally develop and maintain its brand names. The rationale for not recognizing the value of intangible assets such as brand names is that the error in estimating such valuations and management incentives to misuse discretion over the capitalization of such costs are so great as to offset the relevance of such estimates in the financial statements.

Firms capitalize the costs to acquire intangible assets from others because the existence of an external market transaction provides a reliable measure of its value. PepsiCo acquired many of its brands over the years through acquisitions. The third part of Note 4, "Property, Plant and Equipment and Intangible Assets" to PepsiCo's 2012 financial statements (Appendix A) shows that total capitalized brands totals $4,839 million.

Because intangible assets, by definition, involve an inherently high degree of uncertainty regarding future economic benefits, most analysts prefer immediate expensing of all intangible assets.[12] Some analysts remove from the balance sheet any R&D costs, software development costs, and goodwill reported as assets before performing financial analysis. They argue that (1) the quality of earnings information improves because the ability to manage earnings is reduced and (2) the quality of balance sheet information improves because the balance sheet is cleansed of "soft" assets lacking physical substance. Some analysts also remove the costs of the intangible assets from retained earnings, as if intangible acquisition costs had been expensed over time. (Often the term *tangible equity* is used to describe the remaining shareholders' equity.) The financial analysis must be interpreted carefully, however, because the analyst may understate a firm's asset base by eliminating these assets—as is the case with PepsiCo's asset base, because PepsiCo's balance sheet does not recognize brand names such as Pepsi and Frito-Lay® (among other important intangibles owned by the firm). Further, as discussed in more detail later in this chapter, many intangibles acquired in a business combination receive balance sheet recognition because they have fair values accruing from a contractual right and may be separated and either leased or sold by the firm.

Goodwill

The most common setting for intangible asset recognition is in corporate acquisitions, where acquiring firms must allocate the purchase price to the assets acquired and liabilities assumed. Acquiring firms usually allocate the purchase price to the fair values of identifiable, tangible assets (inventories, land, and equipment) and liabilities first. They

---

[12]For a stable or moderate-growth firm, the expense each year from immediate expensing is approximately the same as the expense from capitalizing expenditures and subsequently amortizing them.

then allocate any excess purchase price to the fair values of specifically identifiable intangible assets such as patents, customer lists, and trade names, with the remainder allocated to goodwill. *Goodwill* is a residual and effectively represents all intangibles that are not specifically identifiable. **PepsiCo**'s Note 4 reports $16,971 million goodwill as of December 29, 2012.

How should you treat goodwill that appears on a firm's balance sheet? One approach is to follow financial reporting rules and view goodwill like any other productive asset of the firm. The justification is that the initial valuation of goodwill arose from an arm's-length investment in another corporate entity and represents valuable resources that accountants cannot identify and measure separately. You should include these resources in the asset base on which management is expected to generate a reasonable return. If these valuable resources are not likely to last forever, amortization of their cost over some number of years is appropriate.

Another approach is to eliminate goodwill from assets and to subtract its amount from retained earnings or other common shareholders' equity accounts. The justification for this approach is that the amount allocated to goodwill from a corporate acquisition may occur simply because the firm paid too much and may not necessarily indicate the presence of resources with future service potential. Subtracting the amount allocated to goodwill from retained earnings suggests that the excess purchase price is a loss for the firm. Immediate subtraction of goodwill from retained earnings treats goodwill arising from an acquisition similar to goodwill developed internally. Later in this chapter, we discuss corporate acquisitions, and we address goodwill in more detail at that point.

Quick Check

- Firms capitalize costs to acquire and maintain long-lived tangible and intangible assets if future benefits are probable and reasonably estimated; otherwise, the costs are expensed.
- Management conveys information to investors and analysts about whether they believe these costs will result in future economic benefits by their capitalization decision. However, management discretion can also lead to manipulated financial statements by capitalization decisions that ignore economic reality.

- In some cases, standard setters have removed management discretion and required expense treatment for certain investing activities. A consequence is that valuable assets may be omitted from the firm's balance sheet.
- It is important to understand the firm's capitalization policy, the unique types of assets they possess, and why their capitalization policy might differ from industry norms.

What Choices Are Managers Making to Allocate Acquisition Costs to the Periods Benefited?

LO 8-2

Discuss the exercise of judgment used in the allocation of costs through the depreciation and amortization process.

Cost allocation includes the processes of depreciation (for tangible fixed assets), amortization (for limited-life intangible assets), and depletion (for natural resources). When allocating acquisition costs to the periods benefited, managers must: (1) choose an allocation method, (2) estimate useful life, and (3) estimate salvage value. Also, throughout the life of a long-lived asset, the book value must be tested for reasonableness relative to economic values, which may result in revaluing the asset downward for impairment (U.S. GAAP and IFRS) or upward for appreciation (an option under IFRS). Such assessments often require a significant amount of judgment and estimation.

Given the magnitude of long-lived assets on most balance sheets and the importance of understanding accounting judgments available to managers, the following subsections discuss these choices and estimates to help you answer the following questions:

- Are useful lives and salvage values reasonable given the economic service and value of the assets?
  - Are they in line with competitors?
  - Can changes in average useful life estimates be explained by strategy or economic reality, or do the useful life changes appear to be opportunistic?
- Are depreciation methods consistent with the expected economic lives of the assets?
  - Are they similar to useful lives used by competitors with similar assets?
  - Are methods frequently changed?

Useful Life for Long-Lived Tangible and Limited-Life Intangible Assets

Physical wear and tear and technological obsolescence affect the projection of the total useful life and salvage value. Managers have an opportunity to convey information to the firm's stakeholders about their expectations of the future usefulness of long-lived assets. However, the estimation process also provides an opportunity to introduce bias into reported earnings. For example, a manager wanting to report higher earnings could bias the estimated useful lives or salvage values of assets upward, which would result in lower annual depreciation expense.

Unfortunately, the disclosures that firms make about depreciable lives are usually not very helpful in assessing a firm's aggressiveness in lengthening or shortening depreciable lives to manage earnings. The problems include the aggregated nature of the disclosures, the fact that firms usually disclose broad ranges of useful lives for asset categories, and the rare disclosure of expected salvage values. For example, we demonstrate the process of estimating average lives for long-lived assets from note disclosures using **PepsiCo**'s financial disclosures. PepsiCo's Note 4, "Property, Plant and Equipment and Intangible Assets" (Appendix A), reports average useful lives of depreciable and amortizable assets, as follows:

Land and improvements	10–34 years
Buildings and improvements	15–44 years
Machinery and equipment, including fleet and software	5–14 years
Acquired franchise rights	56–60 years
Reacquired franchise rights	1–14 years
Brands	5–40 years
Other identifiable intangibles	10–24 years

Because most U.S. firms use the straight-line depreciation method for financial reporting purposes, you can estimate the average useful life of depreciable (and amortizable) assets by dividing average depreciable cost (gross, assuming zero salvage value) by depreciation expense for the year. The calculations for PepsiCo for 2007–2012 are presented in Exhibit 8.1.

Exhibit 8.1

Calculation of PepsiCo's Average Useful Life for PP&E and Intangible Assets
(amounts in millions)

FYE	PP&E (Excluding Construction in Progress)	Depreciation Expense	Depreciable Life Estimate	Intangible Assets	Amortization Expense	Amortizable Life Estimate
2007	$19,912	$1,304		$1,820	$ 58	
2008	20,779	1,422	14.31	1,771	64	28.05
2009	23,471	1,500	14.75	1,970	63	29.69
2010	31,121	2,124	12.85	3,269	117	22.39
2011	33,314	2,476	13.01	3,220	133	24.39
2012	34,425	2,489	13.61	3,199	119	26.97

Depreciable Life Estimate = [(Current Year PP&E + Prior Year PP&E) × 0.5]/Depreciation Expense

Amortizable Life Estimate = [(Current Year Intangible Assets + Prior Year Intangible Assets) × 0.5]/Amortization Expense

In 2012, the average useful life estimates are 13.6 years for property, plant, and equipment and almost 27.0 years for amortizable intangible assets. Comparing these estimates to the estimates calculated for 2007 (14.3 and 28.5 years, respectively) shows that PepsiCo's total useful lives used in depreciation and amortization computations have decreased over the five-year period. If PepsiCo had used 14.3 years life for the depreciation computation in 2012, depreciation expense would have been $2,368.5 million {[($34,425 + $33,314) × 0.5]/14.3 years} instead of $2,489 million reported in 2012. The $120.5 million pretax difference is 1.45% of the $8,304 million pretax income in 2012 (slightly less than 1% of net income assuming a 35% tax rate). This might be considered material, but it represents a *lower* reported net income. Generally, estimate changes on long-lived assets leading to lower reported earnings are of less concern unless the firm in question regularly disposes of the assets (which PepsiCo does not, as evidenced by rare disclosure of material gains or losses from asset sales over time). You should however be concerned when firms increase depreciation rates over time and also engage in frequent long-lived asset sales resulting in gains. This is an example of creating "cookie jar" reserves (see Chapter 6) and using them later to manage earnings.

Even with such aggregated data, you can gain insight by comparing the average useful life of depreciable assets across firms. Firms with similar asset composition (such as direct competitors) should have similar useful lives; if not, you should assess why they differ. Possibly one firm's strategy causes a particular asset to have a shorter useful life. For example, an airline choosing a shorter useful life (e.g., **Singapore Airlines**) might do so because its strategy requires it to fly newer planes, and thus, its aircraft have shorter useful lives. You also need to question firms that report dramatic changes in the useful lives of depreciable assets over time.[13] Is the change because of assumption

---

[13]When a firm changes a useful life or salvage value estimate, it handles the change prospectively. That is, it simply depreciates the remaining book value over the remaining useful life. *FASB Codification Topic 250.* International Accounting Standards Board, *International Accounting Standard 16,* "Property, Plant and Equipment" (1998).

changes in the useful lives of the assets, has the composition of the firm's assets changed over time, or has the firm made the strategic decision to use assets differently? The change over time in the depreciation rates for PepsiCo is not unexpected given the substantial acquisition activity of PepsiCo during this period and the likely change in the composition of both tangible and intangible assets. Firms choosing useful lives that accurately (and consistently) represent the period of time they expect to be able to use the assets report the highest-quality accounting data for depreciable assets.

Both U.S. GAAP and IFRS allow managers to classify certain intangible assets (such as perpetual brands and goodwill reported by PepsiCo in Note 4) as having an indefinite life; therefore, they are not amortized. These nonamortizable intangibles are assessed for impairment (discussed in a later section).

Cost Allocation (Depreciation/Amortization/ Depletion) Method

Firms may allocate the acquisition costs over the useful life of the asset using *any* systematic and rational method. The allocation of cost is charged to depreciation expense (for tangible fixed assets), amortization expense (for intangibles), or depletion expense (for natural resources) and is reported on the income statement.[14]

Most firms write off tangible long-lived assets evenly over their useful lives (straight-line method). Some firms write off larger amounts during the early years and smaller amounts in later years (accelerated depreciation methods). Nearly all firms amortize intangible assets using the straight-line method. Firms generally deplete natural resources using the straight-line method or in proportion to the amount of natural resources consumed (for example, number of board feet of lumber harvested relative to an estimate of the total amount of board feet of lumber in a forest). Regardless of the cost allocation method chosen, the total depreciation over an asset's life generally does not exceed acquisition costs (except in rare cases when firms revalue such assets to current fair values). Thus, the various depreciation methods differ only in the timing of expense, not in its total amount over time.

Virtually all U.S. firms use accelerated depreciation methods for tax reporting purposes based on depreciable lives specified in the income tax law, which are usually shorter than the depreciable lives that firms use for financial reporting purposes. In countries where tax laws heavily influence financial reporting (such as Germany, France, and Japan), many firms use accelerated depreciation methods for both financial and tax reporting. Thus, comparisons of U.S. to foreign firms require an assessment of the effects of different depreciation methods and assumptions. To increase comparability, you can restate reported U.S. amounts to an accelerated basis or convert reported amounts for other countries to a straight-line basis.

You can place U.S. firms on an accelerated depreciation basis using information in the income tax note. As Chapter 2 described, firms must report in notes to the financial statements the portion of the deferred tax liability that is attributable to book versus tax depreciation timing differences at the beginning and end of the year.

To illustrate, **PepsiCo**'s Note 5, "Income Taxes" (Appendix A), reports that the portion of its deferred tax liability attributable to property, plant, and equipment was $2,424 million on December 29, 2012, and $2,466 million on December 31, 2011. A decrease in a deferred tax liability relating to differences in expensing procedure for

---

[14]If the long-lived asset is used in production, the depreciation/amortization/depletion is initially added to inventory as a product cost and then expensed as cost of goods sold when the inventory is sold.

book and tax purposes indicates that PepsiCo depreciated fixed assets faster for book purposes than for tax purposes in the current year. (This is a rare occurrence for a growing firm). If you want to compare PepsiCo's profitability and risk to another company (foreign or otherwise) that uses accelerated methods of depreciation, you must convert key amounts for PepsiCo, including the asset PP&E (net) and net income, to an accelerated depreciation method basis or convert those amounts for the comparable firm to a straight-line basis. The following computations demonstrate the former approach, converting PepsiCo's amounts to an accelerated depreciation basis. (PepsiCo discloses a 35% federal statutory tax rate in Note 5.)

Conversion of PP&E (net) to an accelerated basis (amounts in millions):

PP&E (net) as reported at December 29, 2012, using book depreciation method		$19,136.0
Excess accumulated depreciation over time using tax method:		
Deferred tax liability related to excess depreciation (measured originally by multiplying the excess	$2,424.0	
depreciation by the tax rate) ÷ tax rate	÷0.35	(6,925.7)
PP&E (net) using tax depreciation method		$12,210.3

Because PepsiCo measures the deferred tax liability of $2,424.0 million by multiplying the excess tax depreciation over time by 35%, the excess accumulated tax depreciation over time ($6,925.7 million) can be obtained by dividing the deferred tax liability amount by 35%.

The lower current depreciation expense using the tax method would have resulted in greater net income as follows:

Decrease in deferred tax liability during the year ($2,466 − $2,424)	$42.0	
÷ tax rate	÷0.35	$120.0
Increase in tax expense ($120.0 × 0.35)		(42.0)
Increase in 2012 net income if tax depreciation method is used		$ 78.0

This latter computation relies on the idea that income is affected by the *change* in the deferred tax liability amount ($42.0 million), which, when divided by the tax rate, represents the lower tax depreciation expense if an accelerated method is used. If PepsiCo had used the tax method, it would have had a higher pretax income and, hence, a higher tax expense of $42.0 million. Thus, changing PepsiCo's book depreciation to a tax-based method would increase 2012 net income by $78.0 million, approximately 1.3%.

When Will the Long-Lived Assets Be Replaced?

Forecasting future financial statements requires expectations of future tangible asset acquisitions for replacement of existing production or service capacity and growth in capacity. Although you must rely on knowledge of industry conditions and firm strategy to estimate capital expenditure growth, you can make two computations to gain a better understanding of when existing long-lived assets must be replaced. Because the amount of accumulated depreciation depends on the number of years for which depreciation has been taken, the *average age of depreciable assets* equals the amount of accumulated depreciation divided by depreciation expense. Based on **PepsiCo**'s Note 4, "Property, Plant and Equipment and Intangible Assets" (Appendix A), disclosures, ($17,026/$2,489) equals 6.8 years average age. Also, the *proportion of depreciable assets consumed* equals total accumulated depreciation divided by acquisition cost. For PepsiCo, $17,026/$34,425 = 49.4%. In the same vein, you also can estimate the *remaining useful life* by dividing net depreciable PP&E by annual depreciation expense. For PepsiCo, ($34,425 − $17,026)/$2,489 equals 7.0 years average remaining life. You can track average age and proportion consumed through time and compare them to competitors' numbers to ascertain whether assets are getting older on average and whether they are at a point where large capital expenditures are necessary to replace them. Also, the combination of older assets with high proportion consumed provides an indication that the firm is in a later stage of average product life cycle.

When older assets are taken out of service and scrapped, any remaining book value must be removed from the accounts and reported as a realized loss on disposal in operating income. Cash inflows from sales of long-lived assets are reported in the investing section of the statement of cash flows. Assets also may be traded in for newer assets. Both U.S. GAAP and IFRS require firms to record the new asset acquired at fair value with resulting gains and losses on trade-ins reported in net income. An exception to this rule occurs if the transaction lacks commercial substance, in which case the acquired asset is recorded at the book value of the assets surrendered (including the traded-in asset) and liabilities assumed with no recognition of gain or loss.[15]

Quick Check

- Managers must choose depreciation, amortization, and depletion methods to allocate the acquisition costs of limited-life tangible and intangible operational assets to the periods benefited.
- They must also estimate useful lives and salvage values. Managers can use these estimates to convey their beliefs or to manipulate financial statements.

- You should consider the consequences of changes in methods or different methods across firms when performing ratio analysis.
- If long-lived assets are material to the firm's balance sheet, changes in useful life estimates can have material effects on the income statement through depreciation and amortization expense. You should examine whether any changes in estimates are material and consistent with economic conditions.

LO 8-3

Apply the rules for testing the impairment of different categories of long-lived assets, including goodwill.

What Is the Relation between the Book Values and Market Values of Long-Lived Assets?

Firms report long-lived operational assets at acquisition costs minus the accumulated depreciation to date (adjusted acquisition cost). The use of acquisition-cost-based

---

[15]*FASB Codification Topic 845;* International Accounting Standards Board, *International Accounting Standard 16,* "Property, Plant and Equipment" (revised 1998). A lack of commercial substance is evidenced by relatively little change in the cash flows to the firm after it replaces the asset. This provision exists to remove the past abuse of asset trading rules in which two firms trade nearly identical assets with book values below their fair values simply to record the gain on the difference between fair and book value rather than for any commercial reason.

reporting rests on the presumption that such amounts are more objectively measurable than the fair values of fixed assets. Difficulties encountered in determining fair values include:

1. the absence of active markets for many used fixed assets, particularly those specific to a particular firm's needs.
2. the need to identify comparable assets currently available in the market to value assets in place.
3. the need to make assumptions about the effect of technological and other improvements when using the prices of new assets currently available on the market in the valuation process.

Nevertheless, accounting standards require firms to determine whether the net book values of long-lived assets are not overstated relative to the economic reality of market values. In particular, accounting standards are concerned with how long-lived asset values must be tested for impairments and written down if impairment losses have occurred (an application of conservatism).

To understand how accounting measurement rules affect your analysis of the profitability of a firm and your expectations of future profitability, you should develop answers to the following questions:

- Are asset impairment charges consistent with the firm's economic environment?
- Are the charges transitory or do they occur frequently?
- Are asset impairment charges or IFRS upward revaluations based on reliable fair value estimates?

To sharpen your ability to make these judgments, the following sections examine the U.S. GAAP and IFRS standards related to reporting long-lived assets when book values and market values differ. The next three sections deal with three basic types of long-lived operating assets: (1) long-lived assets subject to depreciation and amortization (land is in this category even though it is not depreciated), (2) intangible assets not subject to amortization because of indefinite lives, and (3) goodwill. Then, a fourth section addresses upward revaluations of long-lived assets under IFRS.

Impairment of Long-Lived Assets Subject to Depreciation and Amortization

The development of new technologies by competitors, changes in government regulations, changes in demographic trends, and other external factors may reduce the future benefits originally anticipated from long-lived assets. Firms are required to assess whether conditions exist implying that the carrying amounts of fixed assets are not recoverable, and if they are not, firms are to write down the assets to their fair values and recognize impairment losses in income from continuing operations.[16]

U.S. GAAP defines a carrying amount (that is, the book value at the moment of the impairment test) as not being recoverable if it is greater than the sum of the *undiscounted* cash flows expected from the asset's use and disposal. If an impairment charge is to be recorded because the asset's carrying amount is not recoverable, the charge equals the amount by which the carrying value exceeds the asset's fair value. Under U.S. GAAP,

---

[16]*FASB Codification Topic 360;* International Accounting Standards Board, *International Accounting Standard 36,* "Impairment of Assets."

although the firm uses undiscounted future cash flows to decide whether an impairment charge is necessary, fair value is used to determine the actual impairment charge. Fair value is defined using the three-level FASB designation described in Chapter 2. Because of the difficulty of observing values of the same or similar assets in organized markets, firms often must estimate fair values by computing the present (*discounted*) value of expected cash flows from using the fixed asset (Level 3 inputs used in a valuation approach applying present value techniques, like those presented in Chapter 12).

In requiring firms to use undiscounted cash flows to test for impairment of long-lived tangible assets, U.S. standard setters reasoned that a loss had not occurred if the firm could recover in future cash flows an amount equal to or larger than the current book value. Accounting theorists and practitioners question the logic of using undiscounted, instead of discounted, cash flows in testing for impairment. In some cases, the economic value of the long-lived asset may decline below its carrying value but the firm would recognize no impairment because the *undiscounted* future cash flows from the asset exceed its carrying value.

IFRS uses rules that are more theoretically defensible. Firms are required to determine whether an impairment has occurred and to measure impairment by comparing the book value of the long-lived asset to the greater of (1) the fair value of the assets minus estimated costs to *sell* the asset or (2) the value of the asset *in use* (which is the present value of estimated future cash flows from using the asset).

Differences in U.S. GAAP and IFRS Impairment of Long-Lived Assets

To illustrate the differences between U.S. GAAP and IFRS, assume that a real estate company owns an apartment building that originally cost $20 million, with a current carrying amount of $15 million. The company originally expected to collect rents of $1.67 million each year for 30 years before selling the apartment complex for $8 million. Deteriorating neighborhood conditions, however, have caused the company to reassess the future rentals, especially given a recent appraisal that set a fair value for the apartment building at $10 million. The company now estimates that it will receive rentals of $1.35 million per year for 15 years and then will sell the building for $5 million. The company uses an 8% discount rate to compute the present value for this investment. Costs to sell are estimated at $300,000.

U.S. GAAP Treatment: Because total undiscounted future cash flows of $25.25 million [($1.35 × 15) + $5] exceed the carrying value of $15 million, the real estate company reports no impairment loss. In essence, the firm has suffered an economic loss but will not report any loss for financial reporting. If the total undiscounted future cash flows in this illustration were estimated to fall below the carrying value of $15 million, the real estate company would compute an impairment loss as the difference between the carrying value and the fair market value of the apartment building (in this case, $10 million). The company would report the impairment loss of $5 million in income from continuing operations, and the apartment building would be recorded at the new carrying value of $10 million.

IFRS Treatment: Under IFRS, the greater of the asset's value in use and fair value from sale is identified first. Value in use is $13.1 million, obtained by using the 8% discount rate to compute the present value of a 15-year annuity of $1.35 million cash inflow plus the present value of $5 million received at the end of Year 15. The value from a sale is $9.7 million, the $10 million fair value minus $0.3 million in disposal costs. The larger of the two, $13.1 million, is then compared to the carrying value of $15 million, triggering a $1.9 million impairment. The company would report an impairment loss of $1.9 million in income from continuing operations, and the apartment building would be recorded at the new carrying value of $13.1 million.

Impairment of Intangible Assets Not Subject to Amortization

For intangibles *not requiring* amortization (that is, intangible assets with an indefinite life), firms must test for asset impairment annually—or more frequently if events and circumstances indicate that the asset may be impaired. Unlike the impairment test for depreciable assets and amortizable intangible assets, U.S. GAAP defines impairment of intangible assets not subject to amortization as occurring when the fair value of the intangible asset is below its carrying amount. This approach is more defendable from a theoretical viewpoint because fair value is more closely related to discounted cash flows than to the undiscounted cash flows used in the impairment tests for limited-life assets. IFRS impairment tests for intangible assets not subject to amortization mirror its tests for depreciable and amortizable assets.

Impairment of Goodwill

The U.S. GAAP and IFRS goodwill impairment tests are similar. Both sets of standards view goodwill as not being separable from other assets and therefore require the impairment test to be conducted at the unit level. U.S. GAAP (FASB Codification Topic 350) defines a *reporting unit* as a segment or a component of a segment that is a business with separate financial information that management regularly reviews. IFRS (IAS 36) defines a *cash generating unit* as "the smallest identifiable group of assets that generates cash inflows that are largely independent of the cash inflows from other assets or groups of assets." The impairment test is basically a simulation of a transaction between the firm and an outsider in an organized market to acquire the unit.

Example: Impairment of Goodwill

To illustrate goodwill impairment, assume that Cabrera Co. acquires Golf Tech, Inc., on January 1, 2014, by paying $1,000,000 in cash. At the date of acquisition, the price is allocated as follows:[17]

Price paid	$1,000,000
Fair value of Golf Tech's long-lived tangible assets	(400,000)
Fair value of a brand name with an indefinite useful life	(100,000)
Goodwill	$ 500,000

---

[17]In an acquisition, the fair value transferred by the acquirer ($1,000,000 in this example) is assigned to the assets acquired, which are recorded at their fair values. The excess is recorded as goodwill. The acquisition process is discussed in greater detail later in the chapter.

One year later on December 31, 2014, Cabrera estimates the fair value of the Golf Tech unit to be $800,000. The book and fair values of Golf Tech's long-lived tangible assets are $400,000, and the fair value of the brand name is $70,000.

U.S. GAAP Treatment: Firms following U.S. GAAP would first apply impairment tests to its non-goodwill assets. The fair value of the brand name has declined by $30,000. Therefore, a $30,000 intangible asset impairment charge is reported by reducing the carrying value of the intangible asset to $70,000. The second step in the process is to compare the carrying amount of the unit to the unit's fair value, as follows:

Fair value of Golf Tech unit at 12/31/14		$800,000
Carrying values of Golf Tech assets at 12/31/14:		
Long-lived tangible assets	$400,000	
Brand name (after its reduction to fair value)	70,000	
Goodwill	500,000	
Carrying value of Golf Tech unit at 12/31/14		$970,000

If the fair value of the unit exceeds the carrying value, goodwill is deemed not to be impaired. However, in this example, the carrying value exceeds the fair value of the unit, so Cabrera must measure the amount of goodwill impairment by simulating a reacquisition. The fair value of the unit is compared to the fair value of the identifiable assets to yield an implied goodwill, as follows:

Fair value of Golf Tech unit at 12/31/14		$ 800,000
Fair values of Golf Tech's assets other than goodwill at 12/31/14:		
Long-lived tangible assets	$400,000	
Brand name	70,000	(470,000)
Implied goodwill at 12/31/14		$ 330,000

Goodwill is written down from $500,000 to $330,000, and a $170,000 impairment loss is reflected in operating income. Exhibit 8.2 shows the brand name and goodwill impairment charges, which total $200,000.[18]

Exhibit 8.2: Goodwill Impairment under U.S. GAAP

Assets		=	Liabilities	+	Total Shareholders' Equity		
					CC	AOCI	RE
Brand Name	−30,000						Impairment
Goodwill	−170,000						Losses −200,000
Impairment Losses			200,000				
Brand Name					30,000		
Goodwill					170,000		

---

[18]*FASB Codification Topic 350* describes the financial reporting for intangibles. In 2012, the FASB amended U.S. GAAP to allow firms to first assess qualitative factors to determine whether it is necessary to perform the quantitative impairment test. It is deemed not necessary if qualitative factors may it more likely than not that fair value remains above book value. ASU 2012-02, "Testing Indefinite-Lived Intangible Assets for Impairment."

Note that the new carrying amounts for individual assets are as follows:

Long-lived tangible assets	$400,000
Brand name ($100,000 – $30,000 impairment)	70,000
Goodwill ($500,000 – $170,000 impairment)	330,000
Total new carrying value	$800,000

IFRS Treatment: Under IFRS, the recoverable amount of the assets is compared to their original carrying amounts. For long-lived tangible assets and brand names, the recoverable amount is the higher of fair value in use or from sale (less disposal costs). For goodwill, the recoverable amount is the implied goodwill of $330,000 computed in the same way as previously illustrated for the U.S. GAAP treatment.

	Original Carrying Amount	Recoverable Amount
Long-lived tangible assets	$ 400,000	$400,000
Brand name	100,000	70,000
Goodwill	500,000	330,000
Total	$1,000,000	$800,000

The financial statement effects are the same as those shown in Exhibit 8.2. These amounts support the write-down of brand name and goodwill by $30,000 and $170,000, respectively.

It is clear from the example above that managers (and their valuation consultants) make several estimates of future cash flows or fair values to support a goodwill impairment charge. You should consider several issues when assessing current profitability and predicting future earnings. First, the relatively unpredictable and volatile goodwill impairment charge has replaced the inherently certain and constant goodwill amortization charge. You should examine a firm's past goodwill impairment charges as well as the reasonableness of prices paid in recent acquisitions to forecast whether additional impairments are likely. Second, you should attempt to determine whether the goodwill impairment charge is indicative of management paying too much for the acquisition, poor management performance in operating the unit, or uncontrollable external factors. Finally, the substantial estimation involved in goodwill impairments permits earnings management.

Impairment Shortly after Acquisition

The impairment of goodwill can occur shortly after an acquisition. In 2008, **Nike** acquired **Umbro**. Exhibit 8.3 provides an excerpt from Nike's June 2009 10-K:

Note that Nike uses a combination of models (discounted cash flow analysis and market comparables) because it argues that these models are used by market participants. Also note the assumptions to develop the projections used in the discounted cash flow analysis, the use of a weighted-average discount rate, and the sensitivity analysis performed. Return to this example after studying financial statement forecasts and valuations covered in Chapters 10–14.

Exhibit 8.3

Excerpts from Nike's Reporting of Umbro Impairment

In accordance with FAS 142 "Goodwill and Other Intangible Assets," the Company performs annual impairment tests on goodwill and intangible assets with indefinite lives in the fourth quarter of each fiscal year, or when events occur or circumstances change that would, more likely than not, reduce the fair value of a reporting unit or intangible assets with an indefinite life below its carrying value. As a result of a significant decline in global consumer demand and continued weakness in the macro-economic environment, as well as decisions by Company management to adjust planned investment in the Umbro brand, the Company concluded that sufficient indicators of impairment existed to require the performance of an interim assessment of Umbro's goodwill and indefinite lived intangible assets as of February 1, 2009. Accordingly, the Company performed the first step of the goodwill impairment assessment for Umbro by comparing the estimated fair value of Umbro to its carrying amount, and determined there was a potential impairment of goodwill as the carrying amount exceeded the estimated fair value. Therefore, the Company performed the second step of the assessment which compared the implied fair value of Umbro's goodwill to the book value of goodwill. The implied fair value of goodwill is determined by allocating the estimated fair value of Umbro to all of its assets and liabilities, including both recognized and unrecognized intangibles, in the same manner as goodwill was determined in the original business combination.

The Company measured the fair value of Umbro by using an equal weighting of the fair value implied by a discounted cash flow analysis and by comparisons with the market values of similar publicly traded companies. The Company believes the blended use of both models compensates for the inherent risk associated with either model if used on a stand-alone basis, and this combination is indicative of the factors a market participant would consider when performing a similar valuation .... The assessments of the Company resulted in the recognition of impairment charges of $199.3 million and $181.3 million related to Umbro's goodwill and trademark, respectively, during the third quarter ended February 28, 2009. A deferred tax benefit of $54.5 million was recognized as a result of the trademark impairment charge. In addition to the above impairment analysis, the Company determined an equity investment held by Umbro was impaired, and recognized a charge of $20.7 million related to the impairment of this investment. These charges are included in the Company's "Other" category for segment reporting purposes.

The discounted cash flow analysis calculated the fair value of Umbro using management's business plans and projections as the basis for expected cash flows for the next twelve years and a 3% residual growth rate thereafter. The Company used a weighted average discount rate of 14% in its analysis, which was derived primarily from published sources as well as our adjustment for increased market risk given current market conditions. Other significant estimates used in the discounted cash flow analysis include the rates of projected growth and profitability of Umbro's business and working capital effects. The market valuation approach indicates the fair value of Umbro based on a comparison of Umbro to publicly traded companies in similar lines of business. Significant estimates in the market valuation approach include identifying similar companies with comparable business factors such as size, growth, profitability, mix of revenue generated from licensed and direct distribution and risk of return on investment.

Holding all other assumptions constant at the test date, a 100 basis point increase in the discount rate would reduce the adjusted carrying value of Umbro's net assets by 12%.

If a company reports an impairment of any kind, net income is reduced. However, impairments are not cash outflows. Accordingly, impairments, if any, are added back to net income in the operating section of the statement of cash flows. Impairments that reflect management's beliefs and that are not opportunistically timed are informative to investors and analysts about future cash flows.

IFRS Treatment of Upward Asset Revaluations

Under U.S. GAAP, upward revaluations of long-lived assets are not permitted. However, IFRS gives firms the option to revalue upward both intangible and tangible long-lived assets.[19] Firms must choose the class of asset to which revaluations will apply and then perform the revaluations on a regular basis. The choice is irrevocable, and the fair value of nonfinancial assets in active markets is difficult to obtain. The significant cost associated with obtaining reliable measurements often exceeds the benefits of presenting a relevant asset valuation on the balance sheet. The fact that many firms choose not to exercise the upward revaluation option is a testimony to the time and effort required for its implementation.

When fair value remains above original acquisition cost, upward and downward revaluations are reported as other comprehensive income and are accumulated in the shareholders' equity section of the balance sheet. The account typically used in the other comprehensive income classification is "Revaluation Surplus." If fair value is less than or equal to cost, reversals of previous downward revaluations (that were reported as losses on the income statement) are treated as gains on the income statement.

To illustrate the IFRS treatment, assume that a French company following IFRS has vineyard land originally costing €2,000,000. At the next four year-ends, the land is worth the following:

2013:	€2,500,000
2014:	€2,300,000
2015:	€1,900,000
2016:	€2,000,000

Exhibit 8.4 shows the effects of upward and downward revaluations of the asset.

Fair value increases above original acquisition cost in 2013, causing an upward revaluation of the land and an increase in comprehensive income (OCI) but not net income. The increase is recognized in accumulated other comprehensive income in the shareholders' equity section. In 2014, the land is revalued downward, causing a partial reversal in the accumulated unrealized gains. Such reversals of previously unrealized gains are reported as losses in other comprehensive income and reduce accumulated other comprehensive income on the balance sheet as long as fair value is greater than original acquisition cost. In 2015, fair value falls below original acquisition cost, causing a reversal of the remainder of the accumulated unrealized gains in accumulated other comprehensive income via the recognition in other comprehensive income of €300,000 unrealized loss and recognition in net income of €100,000 unrealized loss. The land recovers its value in 2016, and the reversal of the 2015 unrealized loss reported in net income is reported in 2016 net income as an unrealized gain.[20]

---

[19]International Accounting Standards Board, *International Accounting Standard 16,* "Property, Plant and Equipment" (1998).

[20]A final category of long-lived assets exists that is unique to IFRS. Biological assets are living plants and animals that will be transformed into items for sale, agricultural produce, or additional biological assets. For example, in the production of wine, the vintner has vines that produce grapes that ultimately produce wine. The vines are the biological asset. Unless fair value is clearly unreliable, biological assets are reported at fair value less estimated disposal costs at each balance sheet date, with all value changes reflected in current net income. International Accounting Standards Board, *International Accounting Standard 41,* "Agriculture" (2001).

Exhibit 8.4: Upward Asset Revaluations under IFRS

Assets	=	Liabilities	+	Total Shareholders' Equity		
				CC	AOCI	RE
2013: Land +500,000					Unrealized Gains +500,000	
2014: Land −200,000					Unrealized Gains −200,000	
2015: Land −400,000					Unrealized Gains −300,000	Unrealized Losses −100,000
2016: Land +100,000						Unrealized Gains +100,000

2013:
Land   500,000
   Unrealized Gains (OCI)   500,000

2014:
Unrealized Gains (OCI)   200,000
   Land   200,000

2015:
Unrealized Gains (OCI)   300,000
Unrealized Losses (NI)   100,000
   Land   400,000

2016:
Land   100,000
   Unrealized Gains (NI)   100,000

Quick Check

- Book and fair values of long-lived tangible and intangible assets diverge over time due to changes in economic conditions and from depreciation methods that focus on cost allocation rather than measuring asset fair value declines.
- Firms must assess whether fair values have declined below book values and recognize impairments. Impairments that reflect changes in management's beliefs about an asset's future cash flows and that are not timed opportunistically are informative to investors and analysts.
- You should remember that fair values are often difficult to obtain for real assets.
- IFRS impairment rules differ from U.S. GAAP rules and are more closely related to economic conditions.

Summary

An understanding of the firm's accounting policy in the long-lived asset area is important when a firm invests heavily in tangible and intangible long-lived assets. The choices that managers make can convey a wealth of information to financial statement users, but this freedom also permits managers to bias or manipulate the financial statements. Pay particular attention to changes in estimates used in the depreciation and amortization process and the reasons for and timing of asset impairment charges and gains and losses on sales of long-lived assets. These sometimes discretionary management decisions shift earnings among periods and bias long-lived asset balance sheet valuations.

James intends to hold the Oden, Miller, Haslem, and Allen shares as trading securities while holding the Wade and Bosh shares as available-for-sale securities for an indefinite period. James does not have significant influence with any of the companies. During 2013 and 2014, James received $25,000 and $20,000, respectively, in dividends from the stock investments. James sold the investment in Allen Company in 2014 for $62,000. At the end of 2013 and 2014, market values were as follows:[22]

	2013	2014
Oden	$ 30,000	$55,000
Miller	20,000	23,000
Haslem	10,000	10,000
Allen	63,000	0
Total	$123,000	$88,000
Wade	$ 25,000	$20,000
Bosh	30,000	22,000
Total	$ 55,000	$42,000

Because James has no significant influence with the investee companies, James accounts for these investments using the market method. Exhibit 8.5 analyzes the costs and fair values of the two portfolios of investments in trading and available-for-sale securities at each balance sheet date.

In the current assets section of the balance sheet, investments in trading securities are reported at their December 31, 2013, and December 31, 2014, fair values of $123,000 and $88,000, respectively. In the long-term investments section, the investments in available-for-sale securities also are reported at fair values as of December 31, 2013, and December 31, 2014, at $55,000 and $42,000, respectively. The year-to-year fluctuations in the trading security fair values, a $19,000 unrealized loss in 2013 and a $28,000 unrealized gain in 2014, are reported in the income statement. In contrast, the unrealized gain of $5,000 in 2013 and the unrealized loss of $13,000 in 2014 on revaluations of available-for-sale securities are reported as other comprehensive income on the statement of comprehensive income. The cumulative adjustment from cost to fair value is reported in the accumulated other comprehensive income section of the owners' equity section. Dividend income of $25,000 and $20,000 is also reported in 2013 and 2014, respectively.

In Exhibit 8.5, the costs and fair values of the investment in Allen trading securities do not factor into the analysis in 2014 because the securities were sold. A realized loss

---

[22]Note that in this example, James holds three of the trading securities over a two-year period. By definition, a trading security is held for a short period of time (for example, 90 days). A security that is held for two years should not be classified as trading. However, the purpose of this problem is to compare and contrast the accounting for trading and available-for-sale equity security investments. Accordingly, the trading securities are artificially held over two periods so that you can compare and contrast the accounting for trading and available-for-sale equity security investments.

Exhibit 8.5

Application of Market Method to Trading Securities
(amounts in thousands)

	December 31, 2013		December 31, 2014	
Trading Securities:	Cost	Fair Value	New Basis	Fair Value
Oden	$ 50	$ 30	$ 30	$55
Miller	20	20	20	23
Haslem	12	10	10	10
Allen	60	63	—	—
Totals	$142	$123	$ 60	$88
(Loss) Gain reported on income statement as unrealized	$ (19)		$ 28	
Available-for-Sale Securities:				
Wade	$ 30	$ 25	$ 30	$20
Bosh	20	30	20	22
Totals	$ 50	$ 55	$ 50	$42
Unrealized gain (loss) reported on balance sheet in shareholders' equity as accumulated other comprehensive income	$ 5		$ (8)	
Change from prior year reported in other comprehensive income as unrealized gain (loss)	$ 5		$(13)	

occurred on that sale, computed by comparing the new basis (that is, the fair value at the end of 2013) to the selling price, as follows:

Sales price	$ 62,000
December 31, 2013 basis of Allen Company securities	(63,000)
Realized loss on sale	$ (1,000)

The realized loss is recognized in net income in 2014.

The statement of cash flows reports the initial investments in the trading securities as cash outflows in the operating activities section because the majority of firms that invest in trading securities are financial firms that make the investments for operating purposes. The initial investments in available-for-sale securities are reported as cash outflows in the investing activities section. Dividends received are also reported as cash inflows in the operating section under U.S. GAAP. IFRS permits the reporting of dividend receipts in the operating or investing section of the cash flow statement.

Exhibit 8.6 summarizes the financial statement effects and shows the journal entries that would be made to account for the investments in trading and available-for-sale securities.

Exhibit 8.6: Financial Statement Effects of Trading and Available-for-Sale Securities

Assets	=	Liabilities	+	Total Shareholders' Equity		
				CC	AOCI	RE
2013 Purchase of Investments: Trading Securities +142,000 AFS Securities +50,000 Cash −192,000						
2013 Dividend Receipts: Cash +25,000						Dividend Revenue +25,000

*12/31/2013 Adjustments to
 Fair Value:*
 Trading Securities   −19,000
 AFS Securities   +5,000
					Cumulative Unrealized
					  Loss/Gain on Adjustment
					  of AFS Securities to
					  Fair Value (OCI) +5,000
						Unrealized Loss
						  on Adjustment of
						  Trading Securities
						  to Fair Value −19,000

2014 Dividend Receipts: Cash +20,000						Dividend Revenue +20,000

*2014 Sale of Allen Company
 Securities:*
 Cash   +62,000
 Trading Securities   −63,000
						Realized Loss on
						  Sale of Trading
						  Securities −1,000

*12/31/2014 Adjustments to
 Fair Value:*
 Trading Securities   +28,000
 AFS Securities   −13,000
					Cumulative Unrealized
					  Loss/Gain on Adjustment
					  of AFS Securities to
					  Fair Value (OCI) −13,000
						Unrealized Gain
						  on Adjustment of
						  Trading Securities
						  to Fair Value +28,000

2013 Purchase of Investments:		
Trading Securities	142,000	
AFS Securities	50,000	
Cash		192,000
2013 Dividend Receipts:		
Cash	25,000	
Dividend Revenue		25,000
12/31/2013 Adjustments to Fair Value:		
Unrealized Loss on Adjustment of Trading		
Securities to Fair Value	19,000	
Trading Securities		19,000
AFS Securities	5,000	
Cumulative Unrealized Loss/Gain on Adjustment		
of AFS Securities to Fair Value		5,000
2014 Dividend Receipts:		
Cash	20,000	
Dividend Revenue		20,000
2014 Sale of Allen Company Securities:		
Cash	62,000	
Realized Loss on Sale of Trading Securities	1,000	
Trading Securities		63,000
12/31/2014 Adjustments to Fair Value:		
Trading Securities	28,000	
Unrealized Gain on Adjustment of Trading		
Securities to Fair Value		28,000
Cumulative Unrealized Loss/Gain on Adjustment		
of AFS Securities to Fair Value	13,000	
AFS Securities		13,000

Security Classification and Potential Earnings Management

The reporting of unrealized gains and losses on available-for-sale securities in owners' equity rather than income has the advantage of deferring short-term value fluctuations on longer-term transactions. Keeping these gains and losses out of current income is a reasonable approach because the intent is not to liquidate in the short run. However, earnings management opportunities are created by the special treatment afforded available-for-sale securities: "winners" can be sold, and "losers" can be held in the portfolio. This allows realized gains to be reported as income, while unrealized losses as a component of owners' equity are deferred. For example, suppose a company made two recent investments in available-for-sale equity securities. Both were purchased for $10,000. Investment A has appreciated to $11,000 during the current period, and Investment B has declined in fair value to $9,500. If the company wanted to report more income during the current period, Investment A could be sold at a gain of $1,000. Otherwise, the $1,000 would be disclosed as an unrealized gain in the shareholders' equity section. Similar discretion to generate a loss exists with respect to Investment B. Comprehensive income would reflect both the unrealized gain and the unrealized loss, and would not be affected by attempts to manipulate reported net income. Available-for-sale security gains and losses, realized or unrealized, are part of comprehensive income.

The different treatment given to unrealized gains and losses on available-for-sale securities in net income versus other comprehensive income creates the need to *recycle* realized gains and losses through net income when an available-for-sale security is sold. Extending our example, assume that the portfolio of available-for-sale securities is sold during 2015 for $42,000, the portfolio's fair value at December 31, 2014. At that date, the portfolio had a cost of $50,000 and the accumulated comprehensive loss reported in shareholders' equity was $8,000 to reflect the downward valuation of the portfolio. When the portfolio is sold, the loss of $8,000 is realized and reported in (recycled through) net income and then included in retained earnings. The accumulated other comprehensive loss of $8,000 is removed from shareholders' equity by being reversed through OCI in 2015. Therefore, the unrealized fair value gains and losses flow through accumulated other comprehensive income (described in Chapter 2 as a temporary "holding tank") until they are realized in cash, at which time they flow through net income (and ultimately into retained earnings). Because the realized loss is reported in net income and the decrease in the accumulated other comprehensive loss also is reported in other comprehensive income, the two income effects cancel each other, avoiding double counting in comprehensive income. In other words, comprehensive income reflects fair value gains and losses in the available-for-sale portfolio when they occur during the first two years, not when the securities are sold.

Held-to-Maturity Investments in Debt Securities

Debt securities do not convey voting rights, so controlling influence is not an issue. Therefore, accounting for debt securities classified as trading and available for sale parallels the rules for investments in equity securities. Interest revenue determined using the effective interest method illustrated in Chapter 7 is reported on the income statement, and debt amortization is added back to net income in the case of a discount in the operating section of the statement of cash flows (amortization of a premium is deducted from net income in the operating section). At each reporting date, the debt securities are marked to market (that is, reported at fair value).

In contrast, *held-to-maturity* debt securities are investments for which managers have the intent and ability to hold to maturity. (Note that "maturity" does not necessarily imply a long-term holding period. If a held-to-maturity debt security is due to mature within one year, it is reported as a current asset.) While intent is quite subjective, ability is less subjective. If, for example, a company has a large liability coming due before the debt investment matures, the investment may have to be liquidated in order to extinguish the liability. Thus, the matching of maturities of assets and liabilities central to financial management is important in documenting the ability to hold to maturity. Held-to-maturity debt investments are reported at amortized cost at each balance sheet date. Standard setters have concluded that short-run fluctuations in market value are less relevant in predicting the level of cash flows, because the debt security will not be sold before it matures. Accordingly, held-to-maturity debt securities are *not* marked to market on the balance sheet, but fair values are *disclosed* in the notes.

PepsiCo reports $322 million of short-term investments in the current assets section of its December 29, 2012 consolidated balance sheet (Appendix A). Note 10, "Financial Instruments" (Appendix A), provides a list of all of PepsiCo's financial assets, but it does not provide a direct explanation of the composition of the $322 million included in short-term investments. It does show that the portion of short-term investments held in index funds has a fair value of $79 million (Level 1). The consolidated statement of comprehensive income reports an $18 million unrealized gain on these securities, net of tax.

"Other than Temporarily Impaired" Securities

As you have learned in the preceding sections, declines in fair values of available-for-sale and held-to-maturity investments are not reflected in net income until they are realized through the sale or maturity of the security. This accounting is driven by the assumptions that fair value declines might reverse for available-for-sale securities, and the investor will hold the debt securities to maturity and collect the interest and maturity value.

If managers of the firm determine that the securities are "other than temporarily impaired," the securities must be written down to fair value with the unrealized loss reported in net income of the period. For this reason, in each period, managers must test whether securities that have experienced unrealized losses are "other than temporarily impaired." Firms disclose how long "temporarily" impaired securities have remained impaired and often discuss the reasons for management's belief that interest and maturity values of debt securities will be collected.

Exhibit 8.7 provides an example of this disclosure for **Qualcomm Incorporated**, a company that develops, manufactures, and markets digital wireless telecommunications products and services. Qualcomm describes its accounting for marketable securities in the notes accompanying its 2012 Form 10-K.

Exhibit 8.7

Qualcomm Incorporated Excerpts from the Accounting Policy and Marketable Securities Notes, 2012 Form 10-K

At each balance sheet date, the Company assesses available-for-sale securities in an unrealized loss position to determine whether the unrealized loss is other than temporary. The Company considers factors including: the significance of the decline in value compared to the cost basis; underlying factors contributing to a decline in the prices of securities in a single asset class; how long the market value of the security has been less than its cost basis; the security's relative performance versus its peers, sector or asset class; expected market volatility, the market and economy in general; analyst recommendations and price targets; views of external investment managers; news or financial information that has been released specific to the investee; and the outlook for the overall industry in which the investee operates.

(Continued)

Exhibit 8.7 (Continued)

Available-for-sale securities were comprised as follows (in millions):

	Cost	Unrealized Gains	Unrealized Losses	Fair Value
September 28, 2012				
Equity securities	$ 2,599	$ 628	$(14)	$ 3,213
Debt securities	17,714	573	(19)	18,268
	$20,313	$1,201	$(33)	$21,481

The following table shows the gross unrealized losses and fair values of the Company's investments in individual securities that have been in a continuous unrealized loss position deemed to be temporary for less than 12 months and for more than 12 months, aggregated by investment category (in millions):

	Less than 12 months		More than 12 months	
	Fair Value	Unrealized Losses	Fair Value	Unrealized Losses
Corporate bonds and notes	$ 723	$ (8)	$256	$ (9)
Mortgage- and asset-backed securities	143	(1)	7	—
Auction rate securities	—	—	115	(1)
Common and preferred stock	105	(5)	9	—
Equity funds	64	(4)	36	(5)
	$1,035	$(18)	$423	$(15)

Qualcomm has investments in both debt and equity securities classified as available for sale. Qualcomm uses the note disclosure to indicate the unrealized gains and losses on these securities. If these gains and losses are temporary, they will reverse. Qualcomm divides the securities into two groups based on the amount of time for which losses they consider temporary have persisted for more than 12 months. In assessing the quality of accounting information, you must decide whether to include any change in the unrealized holding gain or loss on available-for-sale securities in earnings for the period. The principal argument for excluding such amounts is that the unrealized gain or loss may likely reverse or may not be realized for many years, if ever. The principal argument for including the change in earnings relates to the fact that regardless of whether it is realized, the gain or loss has economic significance and therefore has a bearing on evaluation of the firm's investment performance. The various disclosures of investment gains and losses are particularly important for financial services firms such as banks and insurers, because performance and management of their investment portfolios are critically important to the profitability and risk of such firms and because of the sheer magnitude of the numbers. For example, during the recent financial crisis, **Citigroup, Inc.**'s 2008 annual report disclosed 2008 unrealized losses on available-for-sale securities totaling $10,118 million. Although this amount appears in Citigroup's comprehensive income, it is not part of its $27,684 million net loss for 2008. Insurance giant **AIG** also reported a 2008 net unrealized loss on available-for-sale securities of $8,722 million.

- The accounting for minority, passive investments is driven by the lack of a firm's influence generally associated with relatively small equity share holdings or holdings of nonvoting financial instruments such as debt.
- The accounting is also influenced by management's intent to trade the security, hold it as available for sale, or hold it to maturity. Unless held to maturity, minority, passive investments are marked to market at the end of each reporting period.

- Value fluctuations are always a part of comprehensive income, but appear as part of net income only for trading securities.
- You should be assess whether sales of available-for-sale securities are timed opportunistically (e.g., to generate a gain to meet or beat street earnings expectations).

Minority, Active Investments

Firms often acquire shares of another corporation to exert significant influence over that company's activities. This significant influence is usually at a broad policy-making level through representation on the other corporation's board of directors. Because of wide dispersion of ownership of most publicly held corporations, and the fact that many shareholders do not vote their shares, firms can exert significant influence (but not out-right control) over another corporation with ownership of less than a majority of the voting stock. In general, investments of between 20% and 50% of the voting stock of another company are generally deemed minority, active investments unless evidence indicates that the acquiring firm cannot exert significant influence, other circumstances give the investor firm control over the investee, or the investing firm is deemed the VIE's primary beneficiary.

U.S. GAAP and IFRS require firms to account for minority, active investments, gen-erally those for which ownership is between 20% and 50%, using the *equity method*.[23] Under the equity method, the firm owning shares in another firm recognizes as income (loss) each period its share of the net income (loss) of the other firm. See, for example, the income statement of **PepsiCo** (Appendix A), which reports "Bottling equity income" of $734 million in 2010. At that time, this represented PepsiCo's share of the earnings from 20–50%-owned bottling affiliates. The investor treats dividends received from the investee as a return of investment, not as income. Although PepsiCo acquired the remaining shares of its bottlers and now consolidates them, it still has equity method investments reported on the balance sheet as "Investments in Noncontrolled Affiliates" of $1,633 million at December 29, 2012. This balance sheet account repre-sents PepsiCo's original investment in the affiliates plus the accumulated amount of equity income it has recognized over time minus the dividends it has received from the affiliates.

Illustration of the Equity Method for Minority, Active Investments

On January 1, 2013, Lake Co. bought 40% of Pond Co. common stock at a cost of $500,000. Pond Co.'s net assets have a book value of $1,000,000. Assume that the indi-vidual fair values of identifiable net assets are equal to the book values of Pond's assets except for a building that has a fair value that is $150,000 above book value. The

---

[23]*FASB Codification Topic 323;* International Accounting Standards Board, *International Accounting Standard 28,* "Investments in Associates" (1989).

building has an estimated remaining useful life of ten years. During 2013, Pond's net income is $50,000 and it pays $30,000 in dividends.

Lake Co. paid $500,000 to acquire 40% of Pond Co., which implies that $460,000 was paid for identifiable net assets and $40,000 for unidentifiable assets, as follows:

Price paid	$ 500,000
Fair value of identifiable net assets acquired ($1,150,000 × 40%)	(460,000)
Unidentifiable asset acquired (implied goodwill)	$ 40,000

If Lake were to use the market method, the investment in Pond Co. would be marked to market at year-end. Further, $12,000 in dividend revenue ($30,000 × 40%) would be reported on the income statement. Under the equity method, however, the investee's income, rather than the distribution of dividends, triggers the investor's income recognition. Lake's investment income is determined as follows:

Investee earnings ($50,000 × 40%)	$20,000
Excess building depreciation ($150,000 × 40%/10 years)	(6,000)
Investment revenue	$14,000

The investee (Pond Co.) calculated its $50,000 income by basing depreciation charges on the book values of its assets. Under the equity method, the investor (Lake) records its pro rata share of investee income of $20,000 ($50,000 × 40%). However, from Lake's point of view, the resources committed to generating 40% of Pond's revenues are greater than 40% of Pond's costs because Lake paid $60,000 extra for the appreciated building when it purchased the 40% interest. Allocation of the cost of that extra investment also must be reflected in income measurement (hence, the $6,000 additional depreciation expense).

The Investment in Pond Co. account is reported in the long-term investments section of the balance sheet at the original cost plus increases in the investment from the investee's income less decreases in the investment from dividend distribution, as follows:

Investment in Pond (original cost) at January 1, 2013	$500,000
Lake's adjusted share of Pond's earnings	14,000
Lake's share of Pond's dividends ($30,000 × 40%)	(12,000)
Investment in Pond reported at December 31, 2013	$502,000

Exhibit 8.8 summarizes the financial statement effects for Lake Company of its equity method investment in Pond.

Although Lake's net income includes an increment of $14,000 from investment revenue, it received only $12,000 of cash dividends. Therefore, the operating activities section of Lake's statement of cash flows will report a $14,000 subtraction from net income for this non-cash component of income, as well as a $12,000 cash inflow from dividends (or alternately, a net $2,000 deduction for undistributed earnings of affiliates).

Minority, active investments are *related parties*. Sales to and purchases from related parties, including any receivable and payable relationships, must be disclosed in the

Exhibit 8.8: Financial Statement Effects for Lake Company (Equity Method of Accounting for Minority, Active Investments)

Assets	=	Liabilities	+	Total Shareholders' Equity		
				CC	AOCI	RE
Acquisition of Investment:						
Investment in Pond +500,000						
Cash −500,000						
Dividends Received:						
Investment in Pond −12,000						
Cash +12,000						
Recognition of Pond's Earnings:						
Investment in Pond +14,000						Equity in Affiliate Earnings +14,000

Acquisition of Investment:			
Investment in Pond	500,000		
Cash		500,000	
Dividends Received:			
Cash	12,000		
Investment in Pond		12,000	
Recognition of Share of Pond's Earnings:			
Investment in Pond	14,000		
Equity in Affiliate Earnings		14,000	

notes to the financial statements.[24] Related-party transactions with minority, active investments are not eliminated from the investor's financial statements. However, profit lodged in inventory from intercompany sales or purchases must be eliminated by reducing both equity in net income of the affiliate and the Investment in Affiliate account. Assume that Lake sold inventory costing $75 to Pond for $100. Pond holds $10 of the inventory at year-end. Lake must eliminate $1 profit because, based on the gross margin percentage of 25% ($25 profit/$100 selling price), the $10 inventory contains $2.50 in profit and Lake owns 40% of Pond ($2.50 × 40% = $1).[25]

■ When a firm can significantly influence the decisions of an investee's management, equity method accounting is required.

■ The equity method recognized the income effects of the investment when the investee earns income, not when the investee remits dividends to the firm.

Quick Check

Majority, Active Investments

When one investor firm owns more than 50% of the voting stock of another company, the investor firm generally has control. This control may occur at both a broad policy-making level and a day-to-day operational level. The majority investor in this case is the *parent,* and the majority-owned company is the *subsidiary.* Financial reporting requires

---

[24]*FASB Codification Topic 850;* International Accounting Standards Board, *International Accounting Standard 24,* "Related Party Disclosures" (revised 2003); and International Accounting Standards Board, *International Accounting Standard 1,* "Presentation of Financial Statements" (revised 2007).

[25]Companies also may choose the fair value option to report minority, active investments, recording all gains and losses from revaluation in operating income.

combining, or *consolidating*, the financial statements of majority-owned companies with those of the parent (unless for legal or other reasons the parent cannot exercise control).[26]

Purpose of Consolidated Statements

A consolidation of the financial statements of the parent and each of its subsidiaries presents the results of operations, financial position, and changes in cash flows of an affiliated group of companies under the control of a parent, essentially as if the group of companies were a single entity. The parent and each subsidiary are legally separate entities, but they operate as one centrally controlled economic entity. Consolidated financial statements generally provide more useful information to the shareholders of the parent corporation than do separate financial statements of the parent and each subsidiary.

In general, consolidated financial statements also provide more useful information than does the equity method used to account for minority, active investments. The parent, because of its voting interest, can effectively control the use of the subsidiary's assets, financial leverage, dividend policy, and strategies. Consolidation of the individual assets, liabilities, revenues, and expenses of both the parent and the subsidiary provides a more complete and realistic picture of the operations and financial position of the whole economic entity.

It is common practice in the United States to present only the consolidated statements in published annual reports. In some cases, firms do report separate financial statements for consolidated subsidiaries. For example, large conglomerates such as **General Electric** and **Ford** report separate financial statements for their finance subsidiaries.

Corporate Acquisitions and Consolidated Financial Statements Illustrated

Corporate acquisitions occur when one corporation acquires a majority ownership interest in another corporation. Current standards are the result of a joint project between the FASB and IASB on business combinations.[27] This section deals with two types of business combinations: (1) *statutory mergers* that result when one entity acquires all of the assets and liabilities of another entity and places the acquired assets and liabilities on its books and (2) *acquisitions* of between 51% and 100% of the common stock of an acquired entity, where the acquired entity continues to operate as a separate legal entity with separate financial records.[28] Both types of business combinations

---

[26]*FASB Codification Topics 805 and 810;* International Accounting Standards Board, *International Accounting Standard 28,* "Investments in Associates" (1989); International Accounting Standards Board, *International Accounting Standard 27,* "Consolidated and Separate Financial Statements" (revised 2003); International Accounting Standards Board, *International Financial Reporting Standard 3,* "Business Combinations" (revised 2008); and International Accounting Standards Board, *Standing Interpretations Committee Interpretation 12,* "Special Purpose Entities" (1998).

[27]The FASB Codification incorporates Financial Accounting Standards Board, *Statement No. 141R* (which requires the acquisition method for business combinations) replaces *Statement No. 141,* which required firms to account for all corporate acquisitions using the purchase method. For many years prior to the issuance of *Statement No. 141,* U.S. GAAP required firms to use one of two methods to account for corporate acquisitions: a version of the purchase method or the pooling-of-interests method. Most firms preferred to account for corporate acquisitions as pooling of interests rather than as purchases because of the positive effect on earnings subsequent to the acquisition. Pooling, however, has not been an allowable method for some time.

[28]A parent company may prefer to operate as a group of legally separate corporations rather than as a single legal entity. For example, separate operations isolate subsidiary financial and legal risk from the parent, permit a firm doing business in many states and countries to more efficiently contend with overlapping and inconsistent taxation, regulations, and legal requirements, and might improve incentive alignment between managers and investors when appreciation of stock in a focused firm can be part of the compensation formula.

use the *acquisition method* and have the same financial statement effects. However, acquisitions of over 50% are active, majority investments as described in the preceding section and thus require the preparation of consolidation worksheets to support consolidated financial statements.

To illustrate merger and acquisition accounting, assume that, on December 31, 2013, Parent Company issues 100,000 shares of its common stock to acquire 100% of the common stock of Sub Company. In addition, Parent agrees to pay former Sub Company shareholders an additional $500,000 in cash if certain earnings projections are achieved over the next two years. Based on probabilities of achieving the earnings projections, Parent estimates the fair value of this promise to be $300,000. Parent pays $20,000 in legal fees and $25,000 in stock issue costs to effect the acquisition. Parent also incurs $10,000 in internal costs related to management's time to complete the transaction. Parent's shares have a fair value of $30 per share at the date of acquisition. Exhibit 8.9 provides the book values of Parent Company and the book and fair values of Sub Company at the date of acquisition.

Statutory Merger. To record the acquisition assuming that Sub Company is dissolved (a statutory merger), the acquisition method is applied to this business combination using the following three steps:

1. *Measure the fair value of the consideration transferred to acquire Sub.* A key concept underlying the acquisition method is measurement of the transaction at the fair value transferred by Parent. Parent chose to issue common stock with a fair value of $3,000,000 (10,000 shares × $30 fair value per share) and to incur a liability (the contingent consideration obligation) with a fair value of $300,000. Parent also incurred $55,000 in related legal costs, internal costs, and stock issue costs. Because accounting standards define fair value as the price received to sell an asset or the price paid to transfer a liability in an orderly transaction between market participants at the measurement date, standard setters concluded that the fair value of the transaction is the net proceeds from the stock issue, $2,975,000 ($3,000,000 − $25,000 costs to issue), plus the fair value of the stock issue costs, $25,000, plus the fair value of the liability assumed, $300,000, which sum to $3,300,000. (Alternatively, just add the fair value of the stock issued to the fair value of the liability assumed because stock issue costs appear as an addition to and subtraction from fair value.) The legal costs of $20,000 and the internal costs of $10,000 are expenses of the period and are not considered part of the acquisition price.

2. *Measure the fair values of the identifiable assets acquired, liabilities assumed, and noncontrolling interests (if any).* In arriving at the $3,300,000 acquisition price, Parent estimated the value of the net assets of Sub Company whether or not they were recorded on Sub's books. The information provided in Exhibit 8.9 indicates that cash, accounts payable, and notes payable had acquisition date fair values equal to their book values. The equality of book and fair values for short-term monetary assets and liabilities (that is, assets and liabilities with fixed cash flows set by contract) is common. Also, with the advent of the fair value option, the likelihood that book values and fair values will be identical increases. Parent estimates the fair value of receivables to be $450,000, which is $50,000 less than book value, an indication that Parent believes that Sub has under-reserved for potential uncollectible accounts. Parent estimates that Sub's nonmonetary assets, inventory, and property, plant, and equipment have fair values that are greater than their book values. The acquirer must recognize separately from goodwill any intangible

Exhibit 8.9

Date of Acquisition Book and Fair Values for Parent Company and Sub Company

	Parent Company Book Values at 12/31/13	Sub Company Book Values at 12/31/13	Sub Company Fair Values at 12/31/13
Cash	$ 900,000	$ 400,000	$ 400,000
Receivables	1,400,000	500,000	450,000
Inventory	1,700,000	1,200,000	1,400,000
PP&E (net)	14,000,000	1,600,000	2,000,000
Customer lists	0	0	100,000
Unpatented technology	0	0	200,000
In-process R&D	0	0	300,000
Total Assets	**$ 18,000,000**	**$ 3,700,000**	**$ 4,850,000**
Accounts payable	$ (600,000)	$ (400,000)	$ (400,000)
Notes payable	(5,100,000)	(2,100,000)	(2,100,000)
Total Liabilities	**$ (5,700,000)**	**$(2,500,000)**	**$(2,500,000)**
Common stock ($1 par)	$ (200,000)	$ (100,000)	
Additional paid-in capital	(4,400,000)	(500,000)	
Retained earnings	(3,700,000)	(300,000)	
Revenues	(9,000,000)	(2,000,000)	
Expenses	5,000,000	1,700,000	
Total Shareholders' Equity	**$(12,300,000)**	**$(1,200,000)**	

Liabilities and shareholders' equity accounts are in parentheses to indicate that they are claims against assets; that is, they are credits for those interpreting the worksheet from the accountant's traditional debit/credit approach. Revenues, gains, and net income are in parentheses to indicate that their signs are opposite those of expenses and losses; again, they are credits in the traditional debit/credit framework.

assets that arise from legal or contractual rights or that can be sold or otherwise separated from the acquired enterprise. The FASB has identified a nonexhaustive list of possible identifiable intangible assets other than goodwill that meet the criteria for recognition as assets. (See Exhibit 8.10.) Parent identifies three such intangible assets that are not recorded on Sub's books. Sub has customer lists with fair values of $100,000, unpatented technology that has a fair value of $200,000, and in-process R&D that has a fair value of $300,000. These assets have no book value because Sub engaged in internal marketing, advertising, and R&D activities to create them, and, by rule, expensed them previously.

3. *Assign any excess consideration to goodwill or record a gain from a bargain purchase.* The difference between the fair value given by the acquirer and the fair values of the individual identifiable assets is goodwill. In this example, Parent gave $3,300,000 to acquire net assets of Sub that had a fair value of $2,350,000 ($4,850,000 fair value assets − $2,500,000 fair value liabilities). Therefore, goodwill is the difference, $950,000 ($3,300,000 − $2,350,000). The parties, in their

Exhibit 8.10

Examples of Intangible Assets that Meet the Criteria of Recognition Separately from Goodwill

Marketing-Related Intangible Assets
Trademarks, trade names[CL]
Service marks, collective marks, certification marks[CL]
Trade dress (unique color, shape, or package design)[CL]
Newspaper mastheads[CL]
Internet domain names[CL]
Noncompetition agreements[CL]

Customer-Related Intangible Assets
Customer lists[S]
Order or production backlog[S]
Customer contracts and related customer relationships[S]
Noncontractual customer relationships[S]

Artistic-Related Intangible Assets
Plays, operas, and ballets[CL]
Books, magazines, newspapers, and other literary works[CL]
Musical works such as compositions, song lyrics, advertising jingles[CL]
Pictures and photographs[CL]
Video ad audiovisual material, including motion pictures, music videos, television programs[CL]

Contract-Based Intangible Assets
Licensing, royalty, standstill agreements[CL]
Advertising, construction, management, service, or supply contracts[CL]
Lease agreements[CL]
Construction permits[CL]
Franchise agreements[CL]
Operating and broadcast rights[CL]
Use rights such as landing, drilling, water, air, mineral, timber cutting, and route authorities[CL]
Servicing contracts such as mortgage servicing contracts[CL]
Employment contracts[CL]

Technology-Based Intangible Assets
Patented technology
Computer software and mask works[CL]
Unpatented technology[S]
Databases, including title plants[S]
Trade secrets, including secret formulas, processes recipes[CL]

Source: *SFAS 141 and SFAS 141R.*
[CL]indicates that the assets meet the *Contractual/Legal* criterion. (The asset also might meet the separability criterion, but that is not necessary for recognition.)
[S]indicates that the asset does not meet the contractual/legal criterion but does meet the *Separability* criterion.

negotiation, assign an enterprise value to Sub that exceeds the sum of the fair values of identifiable assets. Goodwill represents the superior expected profitability of Sub's operations that exceeds what one would expect from Sub's assets.

If Parent acquired Sub at a bargain, the fair value given would have been less than the fair values of the individual identifiable assets. Bargain purchases rarely occur given the rational behavior of owners. However, they do exist, often because of some unusual circumstance that requires a quick liquidation of a company, such as the death of an owner or forced liquidation due to bankruptcy or other financial distress. If a bargain purchase occurs, the acquirer has an economic gain equal to the fair value received less the fair value given. The gain is reported on the acquirer's income statement. During the recent financial crisis, a number of healthy banks recognized gains on bargain purchases of distressed banks (and often the acquisitions were assisted by the FDIC). In 2008, for example, **J. P. Morgan Chase & Co.** acquired **Washington Mutual**, recognizing a $1.9 billion gain from the bargain purchase.

Exhibit 8.11 shows the effects of the acquisition and the journal entry to record the acquisition on Parent's books at December 31, 2013. Parent records the fair value of assets

Exhibit 8.11: Financial Statement Effects of a Merger (Acquisition Date)

Assets		=	Liabilities		+	Total Shareholders' Equity		
						CC	AOCI	RE
Primary Consideration:								
Cash	+400,000		Accounts Payable	+400,000		Common		
Receivables	+450,000		Notes Payable	+2,100,000		Stock +100,000		
Inventory	+1,400,000		Contingent			APIC +2,900,000		
PP&E	+2,000,000		Performance					
Customer Lists	+100,000		Obligation	+300,000				
Unpatented								
Technology	+200,000							
In-Process R&D	+300,000							
Goodwill	+950,000							
Legal and Management Costs:								
Cash	−30,000							Operating
								Expenses −30,000
Stock Issue Costs:								
Cash	−25,000					APIC −25,000		
Primary Consideration:								
Cash			400,000					
Receivables			450,000					
Inventory			1,400,000					
PP&E			2,000,000					
Customer Lists			100,000					
Unpatented Technology			200,000					
In-Process R&D			300,000					
Goodwill			950,000					
Accounts Payable						400,000		
Notes Payable						2,100,000		
Contingent Performance Obligation						300,000		
Common Stock						100,000		
APIC						2,900,000		
Legal and Management Costs:								
Operating Expenses			30,000					
Cash						30,000		
Stock Issue Costs:								
APIC			25,000					
Cash						25,000		

and liabilities received from Sub and the fair values of consideration given to Sub's shareholders (the contingent performance obligation and the common stock issued). Note that identifiable intangible assets, in-process R&D, and goodwill are recorded at their fair values, even though their original book values on Sub's books were zero. Given that many firms expensed in-process R&D in the past, the change in U.S. GAAP and IFRS to the current acquisition accounting standards is a significant change for firms acquiring technology-intensive firms. Legal costs and management time related to the combination are expensed as part of operating expenses. Stock issue costs reduce the proceeds of the issue and thus are treated as a reduction of additional paid-in capital.

Because Sub's assets and liabilities now appear on Parent's books and Sub no longer exists as a separate legal entity, Parent does not have to prepare consolidated financial statements.

Acquisition. If the terms of the business combination cause Sub to continue as a separate legal entity (an acquisition), the date of acquisition journal entry differs from the entry used to record a statutory merger. Exhibit 8.12 shows the effects of the

Exhibit 8.12: Financial Statement Effects of an Acquisition (Acquisition Date)

Assets	=	Liabilities	+	Total Shareholders' Equity		
				CC	**AOCI**	**RE**
Primary Consideration:						
Investment in Sub +3,300,000		Contingent Performance Obligation +300,000		Common Stock +100,000 APIC +2,900,000		
Legal and Management Costs:						
Cash −30,000						Operating Expenses −30,000
Stock Issue Costs:						
Cash −25,000				APIC −25,000		
Primary Consideration:						
Investment in Sub		3,300,000				
Contingent Performance Obligation				300,000		
Common Stock				100,000		
APIC				2,900,000		
Legal and Management Costs:						
Operating Expenses		30,000				
Cash				30,000		
Stock Issue Costs:						
APIC		25,000				
Cash				25,000		

acquisition and the journal entry to record the acquisition on Parent's books if Sub continues as a separate legal entity. In an acquisition, Parent records a single account, "Investment in Sub," to represent its interest in the fair values of Sub. The remaining entries are identical to the entries for a merger.

Because Sub's assets and liabilities do not appear on Parent's books and Parent controls Sub, Parent must prepare consolidated financial statements to reflect the substance of the entity over its legal form. The following schedule is a review of why Parent paid $3,300,000 to acquire Sub's shares. The fair value allocation schedule shows three components present in the $3,300,000 acquisition price. The first two are (1) the book value of Sub and (2) the amounts by which individual identifiable assets exceed their book values. The sum of the first two components equals the fair value of the identifiable assets of Sub. The third component is goodwill.

Fair value allocation schedule (date of acquisition):

Fair value of consideration transferred by Parent		$ 3,300,000
Book value of Sub (total shareholders' equity from Exhibit 8.9)		(1,200,000)
Excess		$ 2,100,000
Allocation to differences between fair value and book value at acquisition:		
Receivables ($450,000 − $500,000)	$ (50,000)	
Inventory ($1,400,000 − $1,200,000)	200,000	
PP&E ($2,000,000 − $1,600,000)	400,000	
Customer lists ($100,000 − $0)	100,000	
Unpatented technology ($200,000 − $0)	200,000	
In-process R&D ($300,000 − $0)	300,000	(1,150,000)
Allocated to goodwill		$ 950,000

Preparing Consolidated Statements at the Date of Acquisition

Exhibit 8.13 presents the worksheet necessary to consolidate Parent and Sub at the date of acquisition. The primary objective of the worksheet is to replace the Investment in Sub account with the aforementioned three components in the account.

Exhibit 8.13

Date of Acquisition Consolidation Worksheet (December 31, 2013)

	Parent (adjusted for the acquisition) effects)	Sub	Eliminations	Consolidated
INCOME STATEMENT				
Revenues	$ (9,000,000)	—	—	$ (9,000,000)
Expenses	5,030,000	—	—	5,030,000
Net Income	$ (3,970,000)	—	—	$ (3,970,000)
BALANCE SHEET				
Cash	$ 845,000	$ 400,000		$ 1,245,000
Receivables	1,400,000	500,000	$ (50,000)	1,850,000
Inventory	1,700,000	1,200,000	200,000	3,100,000
PP&E (net)	14,000,000	1,600,000	400,000	16,000,000
Investment in Sub	3,300,000	—	(3,300,000)	—
Customer lists	—	—	100,000	100,000
Unpatented technology	—	—	200,000	200,000
In-process R&D	—	—	300,000	300,000
Goodwill	—	—	950,000	950,000
Total Assets	$ 21,245,000	$ 3,700,000	$(1,200,000)	$ 23,745,000
Accounts payable	$ (600,000)	$ (400,000)	—	$ (1,000,000)
Notes payable	(5,100,000)	(2,100,000)	—	(7,200,000)
Contingent performance obligation	(300,000)	—	—	(300,000)
Common stock	(300,000)	(100,000)	$ 100,000	(300,000)
Additional paid-in capital	(7,275,000)	(500,000)	500,000	(7,275,000)
Retained earnings, Dec. 31, 2013	(7,670,000)	(600,000)	600,000	(7,670,000)
Total Liabilities and Shareholders' Equity	$(21,245,000)	$(3,700,000)	$ 1,200,000	$(23,745,000)

Revenues, gains, and net income are in parentheses to indicate that their signs are opposite those of expenses and losses; that is, they are credits for those interpreting the worksheet from the accountant's traditional debit/credit approach. Liabilities and shareholders' equity accounts are in parentheses to indicate that they are claims against assets; again, they are credits in the traditional debit/credit framework.

1. In the Eliminations column, "Investment in Sub" is removed so that, after the row is summed, the account does not appear in the Consolidated column. From a consolidated viewpoint, the combined Parent and Sub entity does not have an investment in Sub separate from the entity's ownership of all of Sub's assets. Because Parent will add the individual assets and liabilities of Sub into the consolidated totals, maintaining the Investment in Sub account would be double-counting.

2. All of the individual assets and liabilities from Sub Company's own financial statements are added to Parent's individual assets and liabilities by summing each row to obtain the consolidated total. Sub's shareholders' equity accounts are eliminated because no outside ownership of Sub's shares exists. These steps accomplish the objective of having the first component of the acquisition price, *book value of Sub*, appear in the consolidated totals.

3. The remainder of the eliminations add the second (*differences between fair and book values of Sub's identifiable net assets*) and third (*goodwill*) components of the acquisition price into the consolidated totals.

The consolidated assets and liabilities appearing in Parent's consolidated financial statements are equal to the sum of Parent's book values and Sub's fair values as remeasured at the acquisition date. Sub's income statement amounts are not part of the consolidation process because the consolidated entity has not yet engaged in operations. The elimination entries are worksheet entries only. They are not entered in the financial records of Parent or Sub. Therefore, the consolidation worksheet must be prepared each reporting period.

A Note on Acquisition Reserves

Use of the acquisition method often entails establishing specific "acquisition reserves" at the time one company acquires another company because the acquiring company may not know the potential losses inherent in the acquired assets or the potential liabilities of the acquired company.[29] Acquisition reserve accounts increase a liability or reduce an asset. The acquiring company will allocate a portion of the purchase price to various types of acquisition reserves (for example, estimated losses on long-term contracts and estimated liabilities for unsettled lawsuits). An acquiring company has up to one year after the date of acquisition to revalue these acquisition reserves as new information becomes available. After that, the acquisition reserve amounts remain in the accounts and absorb losses as they occur. That is, the acquiring firm charges actual losses against the specific acquisition reserves established, instead of against income, to measure the expected loss.

To illustrate, assume that an acquired company has an unsettled lawsuit for which the acquiring company anticipates a $10 million pretax loss will ultimately result. It allocates $10 million to an acquisition reserve (estimated liability from lawsuit). The acquiring firm would presumably pay less for this company because of the potential liability. Assume that settlement of the lawsuit occurs three years after the date of the acquisition for $8 million (pretax). The accountant offsets the $8 million loss against the $10 million reserve instead of against net income for the year. Furthermore, the accountant reverses the $2 million remaining in the acquisition reserve, increasing net income in the year of the settlement.

---

[29]Chapter 7 discusses the various types of reserve accounts that appear in financial statements. In the title of an account in the United States, the term *reserve* is generally unacceptable unless it includes a descriptor as to its purpose. U.S. firms generally use more precise titles for reserve accounts, such as allowance for uncollectible accounts and estimated warranty liability.

Acquisition reserves can affect assessments of the quality of accounting information, and regulators carefully monitor their use (and abuse). When used properly, an acquisition reserve is an accounting mechanism that helps ensure that the assets and liabilities of an acquired company reflect market values. However, given the estimates required in establishing such reserves, management has some latitude in managing earnings.

Consolidated Financial Statements Subsequent to Date of Acquisition

Subsequent to acquisition, the consolidation process must take into account the operating activities of both firms. Therefore, in addition to a consolidated balance sheet, we have consolidation of all of the financial statements. To illustrate the consolidation process one year later, refer to the original data in Exhibit 8.9 that listed differences between Sub's fair values and book values at the date of acquisition and assume that PP&E, customer lists, unpatented technology, and in-process R&D have remaining useful lives of ten years. Exhibit 8.14 presents the consolidated worksheet one year later on December 31, 2014. To focus on eliminations and the meaning of the resulting

Exhibit 8.14

Consolidation Worksheet One Year after Date of Acquisition

	Parent 12/31/14	Sub 12/31/14	Eliminations	Consolidated 12/31/14
INCOME STATEMENT				
Revenues	(P)	(S)		(P) + (S)
Cost of goods sold	P	S	$ 200,000	P + S + $200,000
Bad debts expense	P	S	($50,000)	P + S − $50,000
Depreciation expense	P	S	40,000	P + S + $40,000
Amortization expense	P	S	10,000	
			20,000	P + S + $60,000
			30,000	
Equity in Sub's earnings	(P)		P[a]	$0
Net Income	(P)	(S)	S	(P)
BALANCE SHEET				
Cash	P	S		P + S
Receivables	P	S		P + S
Inventory	P	S		P + S
PP&E (net)	P	S	$ 360,000	P + S + $360,000
Investment in Sub	P		(P)[b]	$0
Customer lists	P		$ 90,000	P + S + $90,000
Unpatented technology	P		$ 180,000	P + S + $180,000
In-process R&D	P		$ 270,000	P + S + $270,000
Goodwill			$ 950,000	$950,000
Total Assets	P	S	$1,850,000	P + S + $1,850,000

(Continued)

Exhibit 8.14 (Continued)

Accounts payable	(P)	(S)		(P) + (S)
Notes payable	(P)	(S)		(P) + (S)
Contingent performance obligation	(P)	(S)		(P) + (S)
Common stock	(P)	(S)	S^c	(P)
Additional paid-in capital	(P)	(S)	S^c	(P)
Retained earnings, 12/31/14	(P)	(S)	S^c	(P)
Total Liabilities and Shareholders' Equity	(P)	(S)	S	(P) + (S's liabilities)

[a]To eliminate S's net income adjusted for amortizations of the excesses of fair values over book values.
[b]To eliminate equity method balance equal to original investment + S's net income adjusted for amortizations of the excesses of fair values over book values – S's dividends paid.
[c]To eliminate S's shareholders' equity.

Revenues, gains, and net income are in parentheses to indicate that their signs are opposite those of expenses and losses; that is, they are credits for those interpreting the worksheet from the accountant's traditional debit/credit approach. Liabilities and shareholders' equity accounts are in parentheses to indicate that they are claims against assets; again, they are credits in the traditional debit/credit framework.

consolidated numbers, we use P and S for Parent and Sub's own financial statement amounts, respectively. In the passages that follow, we also describe the differences between consolidation at acquisition and consolidation subsequent to acquisition.

1. In the Eliminations column, "Investment in Sub" is removed so that, after the row is summed, it does not appear in the Consolidated column. "Investment in Sub" includes the original investment plus Parent's equity in Sub's earnings for the period (all of Sub's earnings because of 100% ownership adjusted for amortizations of the differences between fair and book value) minus Parent's share of Sub's dividends (again, all of Sub's dividends because of 100% ownership).

2. Parent adds all of the individual assets and liabilities from Sub's financial statements to Parent's individual assets and liabilities by summing each row to obtain the consolidated total. Parent eliminates Sub's shareholders' equity accounts because no outside ownership of Sub's shares exists. These steps accomplish the objective of having the first component of the acquisition price, book value of Sub, appear in the consolidated totals. Sub's assets, liabilities, and owners' equity reflect the book value of Sub at the date of acquisition plus the changes in assets and liabilities from Sub's activities during the year. The changes in assets and liabilities reflected in Sub's income are based on the book value of Sub's assets and liabilities. For example, Sub charges cost of goods sold for the book value of inventory when inventory is sold, not the fair value established at the date of acquisition.

3. A set of adjustments adds the second component (differences between fair and book values of Sub's identifiable net assets) and the third component (goodwill) of acquisition price into the consolidated totals. Exhibit 8.15 supports the entries in the Elimination column. At the date of acquisition, we deducted $50,000 from receivables in the consolidated worksheet to reflect the lower receivable fair value. Assuming that Parent was correct in believing that the receivables would not be

Exhibit 8.15

Differences between Fair and Book Values of Identifiable Assets One Year after Acquisition

Date of Acquisition Differences	Charged (Credited) to Expense	Balance One Year Later
Receivables: ($50,000)	($50,000) reduction of bad debt expense	$ 0
Inventory: $200,000	$200,000 increase in cost of goods sold	$ 0
PP&E: $400,000	$400,000/10 years = $40,000 increase in depreciation expense	$ 360,000
Customer lists: $100,000	$100,000/10 years = $10,000 increase in amortization expense	$ 90,000
Unpatented technology: $200,000	$200,000/10 years = $20,000 increase in amortization expense	$ 180,000
In-process R&D: $300,000	$300,000/10 years = $30,000 increase in amortization expense	$ 270,000
Allocated to goodwill: $950,000	$0 unless impaired	$ 950,000
Net effects	Decrease income by $250,000	Increase assets by $1,850,000

collected (that is, customers defaulted), Sub has shown a larger bad debt expense on its own financial statements due to the unexpected (from its viewpoint) customer defaults in the current year. As Exhibit 8.15 shows, the consolidated worksheet in Exhibit 8.14 reduces bad debts expense by $50,000 and makes no adjustment to accounts receivable. The allocation of all of the fair value/book value acquisition date differences to expenses and none to the asset will occur when an item (accounts receivable in this case) is a current asset. Given that inventory also is a current asset (that is, the inventory is sold in less than a year), Exhibit 8.15 allocates all of the acquisition date $200,000 fair value excess to cost of goods sold and none to inventory. As noted in Item 2 above, Sub based cost of goods sold on book value when it sold the inventory. Parent uses the worksheet to adjust cost of goods sold to the consolidated point of view. The remaining items in Exhibit 8.15 are long-term; therefore, if the items are depreciable or amortizable, a portion of the acquisition date excess fair value will be allocated to expense based on the item's estimated remaining useful life, with the remainder allocated to the asset. Goodwill is not amortized; so the full amount is reflected in the Elimination column as an adjustment to the asset.

4. Equity in Sub's earnings is eliminated. The one-line consolidation of Sub has been converted to an item-by-item income statement consolidation through addition of revenues and expenses of Parent and Sub across columns.

We use the letters *P* and *S* instead of numbers in the financial statements of Parent and Sub, respectively, one year later to concentrate on what appears in the Consolidated column subsequent to the date of acquisitions. "Investment in Sub" and "Equity in Sub's earnings" do not appear. The consolidated assets and liabilities appearing in Parent's consolidated financial statements are equal to the sum of Parent's book values and Sub's fair values as measured at the acquisition date and are adjusted for Parent's expensing of a portion of the fair value/book value differences to calculate net income on a consolidated basis. Note that in the case of 100% ownership, consolidated net income is simply P's net income under the equity method. Individual revenues and expenses replace the summary of S's income in the Equity in Sub's earnings account, which is already in Parent's net income because of its use of the equity method.

Related-Party Transactions

Several additional transactions must be considered in the preparation of consolidated financial statements. Transactions between the parent and the subsidiary affect their individual financial statements but should not affect the consolidated financial statements. Additional eliminations should be made for:

- Intercompany loans and receivables and the interest expense and revenues from those arrangements. Parents often provide loans to subsidiaries, and the subsidiary's accounting system will show a payable and accrued interest expense on its own books. Similarly, the parent will show a receivable and accrued interest revenue.
- Intercompany sales and purchases and the profits lodged in ending inventory. An earlier section of this chapter discussed investments in affiliates (minority, active investments). Recall that intercompany sales and purchases are disclosed as related-party transactions but are not eliminated. An example also was provided of how profits lodged in inventory on such sales must be eliminated. In the preparation of consolidated financial statements, the intercompany sales and purchases also must be eliminated because the purchases and sales were not with a party outside the consolidated entity.
- Intercompany payables and receivables as a result of intercompany sales and purchases. For example, if the parent company purchases inventory from the subsidiary company on credit, the subsidiary will recognize receivables that include payables from the parent.

Other extremely complex transactions that occur between parents and subsidiaries are beyond the scope of this text. However, the guiding principle in the preparation of consolidated financial statements is the need to view the substance of transactions from the consolidated entity's point of view.

What Are Noncontrolling Interests?

If an investing firm owns less than 100% of the voting shares of another firm, a *noncontrolling interest* will exist. Many companies use the term *minority interest* to describe the noncontrolling interest in their financial statements. The noncontrolling interest, which may be widely held, is entitled to a pro rata portion of net assets, earnings, and dividends. Recent accounting standards have drastically changed accounting for noncontrolling interests. In the past, an acquisition of less than 100% resulted in only a partial remeasurement of the acquired firm's assets and liabilities to fair value. For example, in a 70% acquisition, land with a book value of $100 and fair value of $110 would be remeasured and reported at $107 in the consolidated financial statements. The parent's interest in the land would be based on fair value, $77 ($110 × 70%), and the noncontrolling interest would be based on book value, $30 ($100 × 30%). Under current standards (the acquisition method), the basis for recording the acquisition transaction is the fair value of the acquired firm. Therefore, land is remeasured to its fair value of $110, with a pro rata share allocated to parent and noncontrolling interests. The measurement of noncontrolling interests also extends to goodwill, which puts both controlling and noncontrolling interests at full fair value. However, under IFRS, firms have an option (on a transaction-by-transaction basis) to assign to noncontrolling interests only their pro rata share of differences between fair value and book value of identifiable assets and liabilities, but not goodwill.

Prior to the issuance of the current accounting standards, noncontrolling interests received disclosure on the balance sheet between liabilities and shareholders' equity ("mezzanine" disclosure). Under current accounting standards, noncontrolling interests are a component of shareholders' equity.

To illustrate an acquisition of less than 100%, Exhibit 8.16 presents the separate financial statements at December 31, 2015, of Power Company and its 80%-owned subsidiary, Small Technologies. Two years earlier, on January 1, 2014, Power acquired 80% of the common shares of Small for $3,900 in cash (all amounts in millions). Small's 2014 net income was $350, but Small paid no dividends in that year. Small's 2015 income was $450, and it paid $250 dividends on common stock during 2015.

Shortly after the date of acquisition, Small common stock traded at a share price that was close to the share price Power paid in the acquisition. Because this condition

---

Exhibit 8.16

Power Company and Small Technologies Financial Statements at December 31, 2015

	Power Company	Small Technologies
Revenues	$ (4,550)	$(2,150)
Cost of goods sold	1,720	1,000
Depreciation expense	300	100
Amortization expense	500	375
Interest expense	350	225
Equity in subsidiary earnings	(320)	0
Net Income	$ (2,000)	$ (450)
Cash	$ 2,600	$ 2,000
Short-term investments	1,030	225
Land	1,520	1,475
Equipment (net)	1,950	800
Investment in Small Technologies	4,260	0
Patented technologies	4,400	2,700
Total Assets	$ 15,760	$ 7,200
Long-term liabilities	$ (5,410)	$(2,950)
Common stock	(4,350)	(1,150)
Retained earnings	(6,000)	(3,100)
Total Liabilities and Shareholders' Equity	$(15,760)	$(7,200)

Revenues, gains, and net income are in parentheses to indicate that their signs are opposite those of expenses and losses; that is, they are credits for those interpreting the worksheet from the accountant's traditional debit/credit approach. Liabilities and shareholders' equity accounts are in parentheses to indicate that they are claims against assets; again, they are credits in the traditional debit/credit framework.

indicated the lack of a control premium, the fair value of Small Technologies was computed as $4,875 ($3,900 acquisition price ÷ 80%). Recording the acquisition at $4,875 (the acquisition method based on fair value) rather than $3,900 (the purchase method) causes the noncontrolling interest to reflect fair value as well.[30]

Exhibit 8.17 presents Power's allocation of Small's fair value at the date of acquisition, updated through the current balance sheet date, December 31, 2015. One year of excess fair value amortization must be reflected in consolidated net income each year, and the balance sheet amounts have accumulated two years of amortization as of December 31, 2015. For example, patented technologies had a fair value that exceeded Small's book value by $600. If the estimated life is 20 years, patent amortization expense on a consolidated basis must be increased by $30 in a given year. After two years have passed, the consolidated balance sheet reports the excess fair value at $540.

Exhibit 8.18 traces Power Company's equity method accounting for Small. Power paid $3,900 at the acquisition date (1/1/14), increased the investment account to recognize its equity in Small's earnings (percent ownership times Small's earnings, adjusted for the excess amortizations from Exhibit 8.17), and decreased the investment when it received its share of Small's dividends. The $320 equity in Small's earnings for 2015 appears in Power's own income statement, and the $4,260 investment in Small Technologies appears on Power's own December 31, 2015 balance sheet. The noncontrolling interest computations follow the same process, yielding a noncontrolling interest in 2015 net income of $80 and a noncontrolling interest in the net assets of Small of $1,065 at December 31, 2015.

Exhibit 8.19 presents the consolidation worksheet at December 31, 2015. The eliminations have been coded to facilitate the explanation. The consolidation process for less than 100% ownership follows the same process as illustrated for 100% ownership, with

Exhibit 8.17

Power Company's Fair Value Allocation at the Date of Acquisition of Small Technologies

	Allocation of Fair Values	Estimated Life	Charged (Credited) to Expense Each Year	Balance on December 31, 2015
Small fair value at acquisition date	$ 4,874			
Small book value at acquisition date	(3,700)			
Fair value in excess of book value	$ 1,175			
Land (not depreciated)	300	NA	$ 0	$300
Equipment	(50)	10	(5)	(40)
Patented technologies	600	20	30	540
Long-term liabilities	200	8	25	150
Goodwill	$ 125	Indefinite	0	125
			$50	

---

[30]If Small common stock trades at a lower amount than the per-share price paid by Power, a control premium exists. The fair value of the acquisition (and, hence, the fair value assigned to the noncontrolling interest) would be based on the price paid by Power plus the lower fair value of the remaining noncontrolling shares.

Exhibit 8.18

Investor Interests in Small Technologies
(in millions)

	Power Company Controlling Interest (80%)		Noncontrolling Interest (20%)	
Acquisition date fair value (1/1/14) = $4,875		$3,900		$ 975
2014 net income of Small = $350	$280		$ 70	
Annual excess amortizations = $50 (Exhibit 8.17)	(40)		(10)	
Equity in Small's earnings for 2014		240		60
Investment in Small Technologies (12/31/14)		$4,140		$1,035
2015 net income of Small = $450	$360		$ 90	
Annual excess amortizations = $50 (Exhibit 8.17)	(40)		(10)	
Equity in Small's earnings for 2015		320		80
Dividends paid by Small in 2015 = $250		(200)		(50)
Investment in Small Technologies (12/31/15)		$4,260		$1,065

Exhibit 8.19

Consolidation Worksheet at December 31, 2015
(in millions)

	Power	Small	Eliminations		Consolidated
Revenues	$ (4,550)	$(2,150)			$ (6,700)
Cost of goods sold	1,720	1,000			2,720
Depreciation expense	300	100	C	$ (5)	395
Amortization expense	500	375	C	30	905
Interest expense	350	225	C	25	600
Equity in subsidiary earnings	(320)	0	D	320	0
Net Income	$ (2,000)	$ (450)			
Consolidated net income					$ (2,080)
Noncontrolling interest in net income			E	80	80
Net income to controlling interest					$ (2,000)
Cash	$ 2,600	$ 2,000			$ 4,600
Short-term investments	1,030	225			1,255
Land	1,520	1,475	C	300	3,295
Equipment (net)	1,950	800	C	(40)	2,710
Investment in Small Technologies	4,260	0	A	(4,260)	0
Patented technologies	4,400	2,700	C	540	7,640
Goodwill			C	125	125
Total Assets	$ 15,760	$ 7,200			$ 19,625

(Continued)

Exhibit 8.19 (Continued)

Long-term liabilities	$ (5,410)	$(2,950)		150	$ (8,210)
Common stock	(4,350)	(1,150)	B	1,150	(4,350)
Noncontrolling interests			E	(1,065)	(1,065)
Retained earnings	(6,000)	(3,100)	B	3,100	(6,000)
Total Liabilities and Shareholders' Equity	$(15,760)	$ 7,200		$ 0	$(19,625)

Revenues, gains, and net income are in parentheses to indicate that their signs are opposite those of expenses and losses; that is, they are credits for those interpreting the worksheet from the accountant's traditional debit/credit approach. Liabilities and shareholders' equity accounts are in parentheses to indicate that they are claims against assets; again, they are credits in the traditional debit/credit framework.

the addition of recognizing the noncontrolling interest in net income and net assets computed in Exhibit 8.18. The eliminations are as follows:

A = Elimination of the Investment in Small Technologies account
B = Elimination of Small's shareholders' equity accounts
C = Allocation of excess fair value amounts at the date of acquisition to expenses and to the balance sheet as computed in Exhibit 8.17
D = Elimination of the Equity in subsidiary earnings account
E = Recognition of an $80 noncontrolling claim on consolidated net income and of noncontrolling equity of $1,065

The noncontrolling equity interest of $1,065 should be reported as a component of shareholders' equity. As noted in Chapter 4, if the denominator of the ROA computation includes all assets (as it typically does), the numerator should be calculated *before* the allocation of consolidated net income to the noncontrolling interest. A tax effect adjustment is not necessary because the noncontrolling interest is in after-tax net income.

Corporate Acquisitions and Income Taxes

Most corporate acquisitions involve a transaction between the acquiring corporation and the *shareholders* of the acquired corporation. Although the board of directors and management of the acquired company are usually deeply involved in discussions and negotiations, the acquisition usually takes place with the acquiring corporation giving some type of consideration to the shareholders of the acquired corporation in exchange for their stock. From a legal viewpoint, the acquired corporation remains a legally separate entity that has simply had a change in the makeup of its shareholder group.

The income tax treatment of corporate acquisitions follows these legal entity notions. In many acquisitions, the acquired company does not restate its assets and liabilities for tax purposes to reflect the amount that was paid by the acquirer to shareholders for their shares of common stock. Instead, the tax basis of assets and liabilities of the acquired company before the acquisition carries over after the acquisition (termed a *nontaxable reorganization* by the Internal Revenue Code).

The preceding examples ignored the tax effects to focus on the acquisition and consolidation process. However, the following illustrates how deferred taxes would be recognized on a given difference between fair and book values. Assume that inventory had a book value of $70 and a fair value of $80; the tax rate is 35%. In the fair value allocation at the date of acquisition (and in the elimination entries during consolidation) inventory is increased by $10 and a deferred tax liability is increased by $3.50 ($10 × 35%). The deferred tax liability is accrued at the date of acquisition to recognize the increase in tax liability when the inventory is sold in the future. If during the next year the subsidiary sells the inventory at its $80 fair value, the subsidiary will have a pretax profit (for book purposes) and a taxable income (for tax purposes) of $10. However, the consolidated financial statements recognize no profit on the sale because of two counterbalancing effects: the subsidiary shows a $10 pretax profit, but the $10 additional cost of goods sold (the $10 extra paid by the parent to acquire the inventory) is recognized through the elimination process. Accordingly, consolidated pretax profit on the transaction is zero; thus, consolidated income tax expense is zero. However, the tax basis of the inventory has not been "stepped up" to $80 at the date of acquisition. Therefore, the subsidiary must pay taxes of $3.50 when the inventory is sold (the reversal of the deferred tax liability).

Consolidation of Unconsolidated Affiliates and Joint Ventures

In some cases, firms have joint ventures or minority-owned affiliates that comprise strategically important components integral to the operations of the firm but that are not consolidated. To get a more complete picture of the economic position and performance of the firm, you may want to assess the firm after consolidating all important minority-owned affiliates. For example, firms frequently work together in joint ventures to carry out their business activities. These companies do not consolidate the financial statements of the joint ventures with their financial statements, but instead use the equity method to account for the joint ventures because they are not majority-owned by the firm.

The procedure to consolidate unconsolidated affiliates and joint ventures follows the consolidated worksheet illustrated earlier. Basically, you eliminate the investment account, add the assets and liabilities of the affiliate or joint venture to the parent's assets and liabilities, adjust the assets and liabilities for any unamortized differences between the affiliate or joint venture's book and fair values (if that information is available in the notes to the parent's financial statements), and recognize the noncontrolling interest in net assets.

Proportionate consolidation is an alternative to full consolidation. Under proportionate consolidation, the investor's *share* of the affiliate's assets and liabilities appears in separate sections on the asset and liabilities sides of the balance sheet, with the equity investment account eliminated, and no noncontrolling interest is recognized. This alternative is particularly appealing for firms that enter into joint ventures in which ownership of the venture is split equally between two firms. Under U.S. GAAP, firms account for investments in joint ventures using the equity method because these investments fall between minority, active investments and majority, active investments. IFRS permits use of proportionate consolidation for joint ventures, arguing that proportionate consolidation better captures the economics of transactions in which joint control is present.

Primary Beneficiary of a Variable-Interest Entity

LO 8-5

Describe variable-interest entities, sometimes referred to as special-purpose entities, and explain the need for the primary beneficiary to consolidate them.

Control achieved by ownership of more than 50% of voting shares justifies the preparation of consolidated financial statements. However, firms can have far less than 50% ownership in an entity but still be the primary beneficiary of the entity's operations and achieve control over the entity's decision-making process by contractual relationships. Special-purpose or variable-interest entities (VIEs) were part of the massive fraud infamously perpetrated by **Enron**, and such arrangements now tend to conjure up images of corporate malfeasance. However, companies may establish VIEs for legitimate business purposes. VIEs can take the form of a corporation, partnership, trust, or any other legal structure used for business purposes. Examples include entities that administer real estate leases, R&D agreements, and energy-related foreign exchange contracts. Often VIEs hold financial assets (such as accounts or loans receivable), real estate, or other property. The VIE may be passive and simply carry out a function on behalf of one or more firms (administering a commercial real estate lease, for example), or it may actively engage in some activity on behalf of one or more firms (such as conducting R&D activities). VIEs can be quite large and significant relative to the sponsoring firms. For example, in 2004, **The Walt Disney Company** announced that it would consolidate VIEs Euro Disney and Hong Kong Disneyland. The Walt Disney Company owned slightly more than 40% of each affiliate.

One of the primary benefits of the VIE is low-cost financing of asset purchases. For example, a sponsoring firm can create a VIE by using minimal amounts of equity investment, some debt investment, and probably some guarantee of VIE debt or other loss protection to outside investors. The VIE could acquire an asset and lease it to the sponsoring firm. Isolation of the asset from the sponsor's operations, the collateral presented by the asset, and sponsor debt guarantees motivate lenders to provide a lower interest rate loan to the VIE to acquire the asset.

Because of the low level of equity investment, the sponsoring firm would not consolidate a VIE under the percentage of ownership criterion. However, the sponsoring firm might possess the rights of a typical equity investor via contractual control of a VIE's operating, investing, and financing activities and may bear losses and reap profits as if it were an equity investor.

When Is an Entity Classified as a VIE?

A firm's investment in another entity is classified as a VIE investment if either of the following conditions exist:[31]

- The total equity investment at risk is not sufficient to permit the entity to finance its activities without additional subordinated financial support from other parties, including equity holders. The presumption is that an equity investment of less than 10% of the entity's total assets is not sufficient to permit the entity to finance its activities without additional support. However, entities that are holding high-risk assets, engaging in high-risk activities, or exposed to risks beyond their reported assets and liabilities may be required to have more than a 10% investment.

---

[31]*FASB Codification Topics 810 and 860.*

- The equity-investing firms lack any one of the following three characteristics of a controlling financial interest:
  - The direct or indirect ability to make decisions about the entity's activities through voting rights or similar rights. Contractual arrangements with the subordinated providers of funds usually restrict the ability of the equity-investing firms to make decisions about the entity's activities.
  - The obligation to absorb the expected losses of the entity if they occur. The subordinated providers of funds absorb some of the expected losses.
  - The right to receive the expected residual returns of the entity if they occur. The subordinated providers of funds have a claim on some of the expected residual returns.

Which Entity Should Consolidate the VIE?

If a firm has a relationship with an entity deemed to be a VIE, it must ascertain whether it is the primary beneficiary of the VIE. If it is, it must consolidate the VIE's assets, liabilities, revenues, expenses, and noncontrolling interests. The firm is the primary beneficiary if it has:

- the direct or indirect ability to make decisions about the entity's activities.
- the obligation to absorb the entity's expected losses if they occur.
- the right to receive the entity's expected residual returns if they occur.

These criteria recognize that contractual rights can cause a sponsoring firm to have *variable interests* similar to those possessed by traditional equity owners. Examples of variable interests and links to potential losses and returns are as follows:

- Participation rights (entitling holders to the VIE's residual profits)
- Asset purchase options (entitling holders to benefit from increases in fair values, often versus bargain repurchase rights)
- Guarantees of debt (the maker of the guarantee must stand ready to repay a VIE's liabilities if the VIE cannot)
- Subordinated debt instruments (the subordinated creditor provides the cash flow to pay senior debt when the VIE cannot)
- Lease residual value guarantees (the maker of the guarantee covers losses when a leased assets value falls below its expected residual value)

The presence of these variable interests leads to control in the absence of equity ownership. Therefore, consolidation of the VIE is appropriate because the primary beneficiary controls the net assets of the VIE. Consolidation of a VIE follows the same process as that illustrated for majority, active investments.

If material to the financial statements, the primary beneficiary must disclose:

- the nature, purpose, size, and activities of the VIE.
- the carrying amount and classification of the consolidated assets that represent collateral for the VIE's obligations.
- the status of VIE creditors' recourse (if any) to the assets of the primary beneficiary.

Firms holding significant variable interest in a VIE must disclose:

- the nature of its involvement with the VIE and the start of that involvement.
- the nature, purpose, size, and activities of the VIE.
- the investing firm's maximum exposure to loss given its involvement with the VIE.

Ford Motor Company describes its VIEs in Note 12 of its 2012 10-K. For each VIE, Ford describes whether or not it is the primary beneficiary and the basis for its conclusion.

As diagrammed in Exhibit 8.20, Ford Motor Company's finance subsidiary, Ford Credit, sponsors (that is, creates) a VIE with a minimal amount of equity investment. The VIE's balance sheet shows relatively small amounts of cash. The VIE needs to acquire assets of some kind to carry out its operations; therefore, it must attract capital from other parties. When a potential capital provider (for example, bank, insurer, or equity investor) assesses the risk of the VIE, Ford Motor Company's risk is not an issue. The VIE is a legally separate entity from Ford Motor Company. The term used to describe this status is *bankruptcy remote*. Because of bankruptcy remote status, the VIE should be able to obtain better financing terms. The VIE will determine its capital structure based on the risk of cash flows from the assets it acquires to carry on its stated purpose. In the case of Ford's financial services, the VIEs acquire customer receivables from Ford Credit and securitize the receivables. That is, the VIEs issue rights to investors to the cash flows from receivable collection. The cash it collects from investors upon selling the secured interests is transferred back to Ford Credit as payment for the receivables acquired. Customers pay cash on their receivables to Ford Credit, and Ford Credit delivers scheduled cash payments to the VIEs' investors.

The benefit to Ford Motor Company of this arrangement is clear: Ford quickly converts its receivables to cash, and Ford Credit can offer more financing to stimulate future sales. This benefit comes at a cost, because investors in the VIE demand a return on their investment. The bankruptcy remote status of the VIE will help incent VIE investors to accept a lower return, but the investors often require more guarantees that Ford Credit will share in the risk that the securitized receivables will not generate sufficient cash flows. Because Ford Motor Company is the primary beneficiary of the VIE, it appropriately consolidates the VIE.

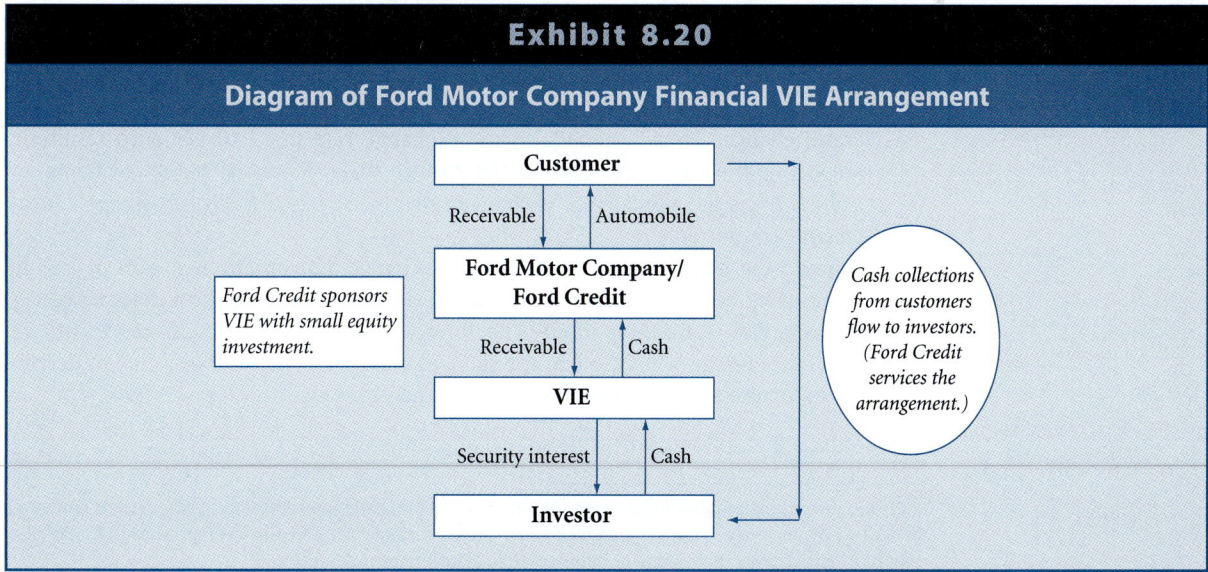

Exhibit 8.20

Diagram of Ford Motor Company Financial VIE Arrangement

LO 8-6

Translate subsidiary financial statements denominated in a foreign currency to facilitate consolidation with a U.S. parent.

Foreign Currency Translation

Firms headquartered in a particular country often have substantial operations outside of that country. For example, in Note 1, "Basis of Presentation and Our Divisions" (Appendix A), **PepsiCo** indicates that it generates approximately 49% of its net revenues internationally (defined as outside the United States).[32] For some firms (such as **Coca-Cola**), international sales dominate even though the firm is headquartered in the United States. U.S. parent companies must translate the financial statements of foreign branches and subsidiaries into U.S. dollars before preparing consolidated financial statements for shareholders and creditors. This section describes and illustrates the translation methodology and discusses the implications of the methodology for interpreting financial statement disclosures.[33]

The following general issues arise in translating the financial statements of a foreign branch or subsidiary:

■ Should the firm translate individual financial statement items using the exchange rate at the time of the transaction (referred to as the *historical exchange rate)* or the exchange rate during or at the end of the current period (referred to as the *current exchange rate)*? Financial statement items that firms translate using the historical exchange rates appear in the financial statements at the same U.S. dollar equivalent amount each period regardless of changes in the exchange rate. For example, land acquired in France for €10,000 when the exchange rate was $1.05 per euro appears on the balance sheet at $10,500 each period. Financial statement items that firms translate using the current exchange rate appear in the financial statements at a different U.S. dollar amount each period when exchange rates change. Thus, a change in the exchange rate to $1.40 per euro results in reporting the land at $14,000 in the balance sheet. Financial statement items for which firms use the current exchange rate give rise to a *foreign exchange adjustment* each period.

■ Should the firm recognize the foreign exchange adjustment as a gain or loss in measuring net income each period as it arises, or should the firm defer its recognition until a future period? The foreign exchange adjustment represents an unrealized gain or loss, much the same as changes in the market value of derivatives, marketable securities, inventories, and other assets.

The sections that follow address these two questions.

---

[32]Financial reporting requires firms to disclose segment data by geographic location (foreign versus domestic) as well as by reportable operating segments and major customers. *FASB Codification Topic 280.* PepsiCo reports extensive geographic segment information in Note 1 (Appendix A).

[33]Other than terminology and other relatively minor implementation differences, IFRS and U.S. GAAP are similar in the foreign currency translation area.

Functional Currency Concept

Central to the translation of foreign currency items under U.S. GAAP is the *functional currency concept.*[34] Determination of the functional currency drives the accounting for translating the financial statements of foreign entities of U.S. firms into U.S. dollars. Foreign entities (whether branches or subsidiaries) are of two general types:

- A self-contained and integrated unit in a particular foreign country. The functional currency for these operations is the currency of that foreign country. The rationale is that management of the foreign unit likely makes operating, investing, and financing decisions based primarily on economic conditions in that foreign country, with secondary concern for economic conditions, exchange rates, and similar factors in other countries.
- A direct and integral component or extension of the parent company's operations. The functional currency for these operations is the U.S. dollar. The rationale is that management of the foreign unit likely makes decisions from the perspective of a U.S. manager concerned with the impact of decisions on U.S. dollar amounts even though day-to-day transactions of the entity are usually conducted in the foreign currency.

U.S. GAAP identifies characteristics for determining whether the currency of the foreign unit or the U.S. dollar is the functional currency. Exhibit 8.21 summarizes these characteristics. The operating characteristics of a particular foreign operation may provide mixed signals regarding which currency is the functional currency. Managers must exercise judgment in determining which functional currency best captures the economic effects of a foreign entity's operations and financial position. As a later section discusses, managers may structure certain financing or other transactions to influence the identification of the functional currency. Once a firm determines the functional currency of a foreign entity, it must use that currency consistently over time unless changes in economic circumstances clearly indicate that a change in the functional currency be made.

There is one exception to the guidelines in Exhibit 8.21. If the foreign entity operates in a highly inflationary country, U.S. GAAP considers its currency too unstable to serve as the functional currency, and the firm must use the U.S. dollar instead. A highly inflationary country is one that has experienced cumulative inflation of at least 100% over a three-year period. Some developing nations fall within this exception and pose particular problems for U.S. parent companies. In its 2012 10-K, **PepsiCo** discloses that, although it generally designates the functional currency to be the currency of its foreign subsidiary, it designates the U.S. dollar as its functional currency for Venezuela due to its highly inflationary environment.

Translation Methodology—Foreign Currency Is Functional Currency

When the functional currency is the currency of the foreign unit, U.S. GAAP requires firms to use the *all-current translation method.* The rationale for this method is that the firm's investment in the foreign unit is for the long term; therefore, short-term changes

---

[34]*FASB Codification Topics 220 and 830.*

Exhibit 8.21

Factors for Determining Functional Currency of a Foreign Unit of a U.S.-Based Firm

	Functional Currency Is:	
	Foreign Currency	**U.S. Dollar**
Cash flows of foreign entity	Receivables and payables denominated in foreign currency and not usually remitted to parent currently	Receivables and payables denominated in U.S. dollars and readily available for remittance to parent
Sales prices	Influenced primarily by local competitive conditions and not responsive on a short-term basis to exchange rate changes	Influenced by worldwide competitive conditions and responsive on a short-term basis to exchange rate changes
Cost factors	Foreign unit obtains labor, materials, and other inputs primarily from its own country	Foreign unit obtains labor, materials, and other inputs primarily from the United States.
Financing	Financing denominated in currency of foreign unit or generated internally by the foreign unit	Financing denominated in U.S. dollars or ongoing fund transfers by the parent
Relations between parent and foreign unit	Low volume of intercompany transactions and little operational interrelations between parent and foreign unit	High volume of intercompany transactions and extensive operational interrelations between parent and foreign unit

in exchange rates should not affect periodic net income. Under the all-current translation method,:

- translate revenues and expenses at the average exchange rate during the period.
- translate balance sheet items at the end-of-the-period exchange rate.
- include the resulting "translation adjustment" (the amount needed to balance the balance sheet) as a component of other comprehensive income rather than net income.
- recognize the cumulative amount in the translation adjustment account in net income when measuring any gain or loss in the case of a sale or disposal of a foreign unit.

The "translation adjustment" reported by a firm can include a second component in addition to the effect of exchange rate changes on the parent's equity investment in foreign subsidiaries or branches. Firms can hedge their investment in foreign operations using forward contracts, currency swaps, or other derivative instruments. As part of the translation adjustment, firms report the change in fair value of a derivative that qualifies as a hedge of the net investment in a foreign entity.[35] In this sense, the foreign currency

---

[35]*FASB Codification Topic 815*. However, if the foreign currency hedge does not qualify as a hedge of the net investment, the criteria established in this standard for fair value and cash flow hedges are applied to determine the appropriate accounting. See Chapter 7 for a discussion of the accounting for derivatives used in fair value and cash flow hedging activities.

hedge is treated similar to a cash flow hedge (discussed and illustrated in Chapter 7) in that the change in the fair value of the hedge appears in other comprehensive income. The difference is that firms do not separately disclose the change in the fair value of the hedge, but rather embed it in the translation adjustment, which also captures the effect of exchange rate changes on the parent's equity investment in the foreign entity.

Illustration—Foreign Currency Is Functional Currency

Exhibit 8.22 illustrates the all-current method for a foreign unit *during its first year of operations*. The exchange rate was $1.0:1FC (FC = one unit of a foreign currency such as a euro or Singapore dollar) on January 1, $2.0:1FC on December 31, and $1.5:1FC on

Exhibit 8.22			
Illustration of Transition Methodology When the Foreign Currency Is the Functional Currency			
	Foreign Currency		**U.S. Dollars**
BALANCE SHEET			
ASSETS			
Cash	FC 10	$2.0:1FC	$ 20.0
Receivables	20	$2.0:1FC	40.0
Inventories	30	$2.0:1FC	60.0
Fixed assets (net)	40	$2.0:1FC	80.0
Total Assets	FC 100		$ 200.0
LIABILITIES AND SHAREHOLDERS' EQUITY			
Accounts payable	FC 40	$2.0:1FC	$ 80.0
Bonds payable	20	$2.0:1FC	40.0
Total Liabilities	FC 60		$ 120.0
Common stock	FC 30	$1.0:1FC	$ 30.0
Retained earnings	10		12.5[a]
Accumulated other comprehensive income— unrealized translation adjustment	—		37.5[b]
Total Shareholders' Equity	FC 40		$ 80.0
Total Liabilities and Shareholders' Equity	FC 100		$ 200.0
INCOME STATEMENT			
Sales	FC 200	$1.5:1FC	$ 300.0
Realized transaction gain	2[c]	$1.5:1FC	3.0[c]
Unrealized transaction gain	1[d]	$1.5:1FC	1.5[d]
Cost of goods sold	(120)	$1.5:1FC	(180.0)
Selling & administrative expense	(40)	$1.5:1FC	(60.0)
Depreciation expense	(10)	$1.5:1FC	(15.0)
Interest expense	(2)	$1.5:1FC	(3.0)
Income tax expense	(16)	$1.5:1FC	(24.0)
Net Income	FC 15		$ 22.5

(Continued)

Exhibit 8.22 (Continued)

[a]Retained earnings, January 1	FC 0.0		$ 0.0
Plus net income	15.0		22.5
Less dividends	(5.0)	$2.0:1FC	$ (10.0)
Retained Earnings, December 31	FC 10.0		$ 12.5
[b]**Net Asset Position, January 1**	FC 30.0	$1.0:1FC	$ 30.0
Plus net income	15.0		22.5
Less dividends	(5.0)	$2.0:1FC	$ (10.0)
Net Asset Position, December 31	FC 40.0		$ 42.5
	∟⟶	$2.0:1FC	80.0
Unrealized Translation "Gain"			$ 37.5

[c]The foreign unit had receivables and payables denominated in a currency other than its own. When it settled these accounts during the period, the foreign unit made a currency conversion and realized a transaction gain of FC2.

[d]The foreign unit has receivables and payables outstanding that will require a currency conversion in a future period when the foreign unit settles the accounts. Because the exchange rate changed while the receivables/payables were outstanding, the foreign unit reports an unrealized transaction gain for financial reporting.

---

average during the year. Thus, the foreign currency increased in value relative to the U.S. dollar during the year. The translation process is as follows:

- The firm translates all assets and liabilities on the balance sheet at the exchange rate on December 31.
- The firm translates common stock at the exchange rate on the date of issuance.
- The firm translates all revenues and expenses of the foreign unit at the average exchange rate. The foreign unit realized a transaction gain during the year and recorded it in current income. In addition, the translated amounts for the foreign unit include an unrealized transaction gain arising from exposed accounts that are not yet settled. (These *transactions* gains and losses are covered in Chapter 9.)
- The firm takes translated net income and dividends to determine translated retained earnings. Note (a) to Exhibit 8.22 shows the computation of translated retained earnings. The foreign unit paid the dividend on December 31.
- The firm uses the translation adjustment account to reflect the cumulative effects of the exchange rate translations on this investment. The amount is determined as shown in note (b) to Exhibit 8.22.

Note b shows the calculation of the translation adjustment. By investing $30 in the foreign unit on January 1 and allowing the $22.5 of earnings to remain in the foreign unit throughout the year while the foreign currency was increasing in value relative to the U.S. dollar, the parent has a potential exchange gain of $37.5. It reports this amount as a component of other comprehensive income on the statement of comprehensive income.

Translation Methodology—U.S. Dollar Is Functional Currency

When the functional currency is the U.S. dollar, firms must use the *monetary/nonmonetary translation method*. The underlying premise of the monetary/nonmonetary method is that the translated amounts reflect amounts that the firm would have reported if it had originally made all measurements in U.S. dollars. To implement this underlying premise, it is necessary to distinguish between monetary items and nonmonetary items and translate each item at the appropriate exchange rate:

- A monetary item is an account whose nominal maturity amount does not change as the exchange rate changes.
- From a U.S. dollar perspective, monetary items give rise to exchange gains and losses because the number of U.S. dollars required to settle the fixed foreign currency amounts fluctuates over time with exchange rate changes.
- Monetary items include cash, marketable securities, receivables, accounts payable, other accrued liabilities, and short-term and long-term debt.
- Firms translate monetary items using the *end-of-the-period exchange rate* and recognize translation gains and losses.
- These translation gains and losses increase or decrease net income each period whether or not the foreign unit must make an actual currency conversion to settle the monetary item. The rationale for the recognition of unrealized translation gains and losses in net income is that the foreign unit will likely make a currency conversion in the near future to settle monetary assets and liabilities or to convert foreign currency into U.S. dollars to remit a dividend to the parent. These activities are consistent with foreign units that operate as extensions of the U.S. parent.
- Nonmonetary items include inventories, fixed assets, common stock, revenues, and expenses.
- Firms translate nonmonetary items using the *historical exchange rate* in effect when the foreign unit initially made the measurements underlying these accounts.
  - Inventories and cost of goods sold translate at the exchange rate when the foreign unit acquired the inventory items.
  - Fixed assets and depreciation expense translate at the exchange rate when the foreign unit acquired the fixed assets.
  - Most revenues and operating expenses other than cost of goods sold and depreciation translate at the average exchange rate during the period.
  - The objective is to state these accounts at their U.S. dollar-equivalent historical cost amounts. In this way, the translated amounts reflect the U.S. dollar perspective that is appropriate when the U.S. dollar is the functional currency.

Illustration—U.S. Dollar Is Functional Currency

Exhibit 8.23 shows the application of the monetary/nonmonetary method to the data considered in Exhibit 8.22. Net income again includes both realized and unrealized transaction gains and losses. Net income under the monetary/nonmonetary translation method also includes a $22.5 translation loss.

As note (b) to Exhibit 8.23 shows, the firm was in a net monetary liability position during a period when the U.S. dollar decreased in value relative to the foreign currency. The translation loss arises because the U.S. dollars required to settle these foreign-denominated net liabilities at the end of the year exceed the U.S. dollar amount required to settle the net liability position before the exchange rate changed.

The organizational structure and operating policies of a particular foreign unit determine its functional currency. The two acceptable choices and the corresponding translation methods were designed to capture the different economic and operational relationships between a parent and its foreign affiliates. However, firms have some latitude in deciding the functional currency (and therefore the translation method) for each

Exhibit 8.23

Illustration of Translation Methodology When the U.S. Dollar Is the Functional Currency

	Foreign Currency		U.S. Dollars
BALANCE SHEET			
ASSETS			
Cash	FC 10	$2.0:1FC	$ 20.0
Receivables	20	$2.0:1FC	40.0
Inventories	30	$1.5:1FC	45.0
Fixed assets (net)	40	$1.0:1FC	40.0
Total Assets	FC 100		$ 145.0
Liabilities and Shareholders' Equity			
Accounts payable	FC 40	$2.0:1FC	$ 80.0
Bonds payable	20	$2.0:1FC	40.0
Total Liabilities	FC 60		$ 120.0
Common stock	FC 30	$1.0:1FC	$ 30.0
Retained earnings	10		(5.0)[a]
Total Shareholders' Equity	FC 40		$ 25.0
Total Liabilities and Shareholders' Equity	FC 100		$ 145.0
INCOME STATEMENT			
Sales	FC 200	$1.5:1FC	$ 300.0
Realized transaction gain	2	$1.5:1FC	3.0
Unrealized transaction gain	1	$1.5:1FC	1.5
Unrealized translation loss	—		(22.5)[b]
Cost of goods sold	(120)	$1.5:1FC	(180.0)
Selling & administrative expense	(40)	$1.5:1FC	(60.0)
Depreciation expense	(10)	$1.0:1FC	(10.0)
Interest expense	(2)	$1.5:1FC	(3.0)
Income tax expense	(16)	$1.5:1FC	(24.0)
Net Income	FC 15		$ 5.0
[a]**Retained earnings, January 1**	FC 0		$ 0.0
Plus net income	15		5.0
Less dividends	(5)	$2.0:1FC	(10.0)
Retained Earnings, December 31	FC 10		$ (5.0)

[b]Income for financial reporting includes any unrealized translation gain or loss for the period. The net monetary position of a foreign unit during the period serves as the basis for computing the translation gain or loss. The foreign unit was in a net monetary liability position during a period when the U.S. dollar decreased in value relative to the foreign currency. The translation loss arises because the U.S. dollars required to settle the net monetary liability position at the end of the year exceed the U.S. dollars required

(Continued)

Exhibit 8.23 (Continued)

to settle the obligation at the time the firm initially recorded the transactions that gave rise to change in net monetary liabilities during the period. The calculations appear below.

	Foreign Currency		U.S. Dollars
Net Monetary Position, January 1	FC 0.0	—	$ 0.0
Plus:			
Issue of common stock	30.0	$ 1.0:1FC	30.0
Sales for cash and on account	200.0	$ 1.5:1FC	300.0
Settlement of exposed receivable/payable at a gain	2.0	$ 1.5:1FC	3.0
Unrealized gain on exposed receivable/payable	1.0	$ 1.5:1FC	1.5
Less:			
Acquisition of fixed assets	(50.0)	$ 1.0:1FC	(50.0)
Acquisition of inventory	(150.0)	$ 1.5:1FC	(225.0)
Selling & administrative costs incurred	(40.0)	$ 1.5:1FC	(60.0)
Interest cost incurred	(2.0)	$ 1.5:1FC	(3.0)
Income taxes paid	(16.0)	$ 1.5:1FC	(24.0)
Dividend paid	(5.0)	$ 2.0:1FC	(10.0)
Net Monetary Liability Position, December 31	FC (30.0)		$ (37.5)
	⟶	$ 2.0:1FC	−(60.0)
Unrealized Translation Loss			$ 22.5

foreign unit. In many cases, signals about the appropriate functional currency will be mixed and firms will have latitude to select among them. Actions that management might consider to swing the balance of factors toward use of the foreign currency as the functional currency include the following:

- *Decentralize decision making to the foreign unit.* The greater the degree of autonomy of the foreign unit, the more likely its currency will be the functional currency. The U.S. parent company can design effective control systems to monitor the activities of the foreign unit while permitting the foreign unit to operate with considerable freedom.
- *Minimize remittances/dividends.* The greater the degree of earnings retention by the foreign unit, the more likely its currency will be the functional currency. The parent may obtain cash from a foreign unit indirectly rather than directly through remittances or dividends. For example, a foreign unit with mixed signals about its functional currency might, through loans or transfer prices for goods or services, send cash to another foreign unit whose functional currency is clearly its own currency. This second foreign unit can then remit it to the parent. Other possibilities for inter-unit transactions are acceptable as well to ensure that *some* foreign currency rather than the U.S. dollar is the functional currency.

Most U.S. firms with foreign operations use the foreign currency as the functional currency. When the U.S. dollar is chosen as the functional currency, it is most often because the subsidiary is in a highly inflationary country, where firms must use the

U.S. dollar as the functional currency. Thus, it appears that firms prefer the all-current translation method, in large part because they can exclude unrealized foreign currency "gains and losses" from earnings each period and experience fewer earnings surprises due to exchange rate fluctuations.

The question to consider when assessing earnings quality is whether to include the change in the foreign currency translation account in earnings or leave it as a component of other comprehensive income. The principal argument for excluding it is that the unrealized gains or losses may well reverse in the long term and, in any case, may not be realized for many years. The principal arguments for including it in earnings are that (1) management has purposely chosen the foreign currency as the functional currency to avoid including such gains or losses in earnings, not because the firm allows its foreign units to operate as independent units, and (2) the change in the foreign currency translation adjustment represents the current period's portion of the eventual net gain or loss that *will* be realized. When using earnings to value a firm, Chapter 13 suggests that earnings should include all recognized value changes regardless of whether U.S. GAAP includes them in net income or other comprehensive income.

A study examining the valuation relevance of the translation adjustment regressed market-adjusted returns on (1) earnings excluding exchange gains and losses, (2) transaction exchange gains and losses included in earnings, and (3) changes in the translation adjustment reported as a component of comprehensive income.[36] The study found that the coefficient on the translation adjustment was statistically significant but smaller than that on earnings excluding all exchange gains and losses, suggesting that the market considers the translation adjustment relevant for security valuation but less persistent than earnings excluding gains and losses. Given this finding, the FASB's decision to require firms to report the translation adjustment change as a *separate and distinct* component of comprehensive income appears to be helpful for investors.

The functional currency for **PepsiCo**'s foreign subsidiaries is generally the currency of the foreign unit. As a result, PepsiCo reports the currency translation adjustment in other comprehensive income. PepsiCo's consolidated statement of comprehensive income (Appendix A) reconciles from net income reported on the income statement to comprehensive income attributable to PepsiCo for 2010–2012. Note that net income over the three-year period is relatively stable. This is not the case for comprehensive income, which is more volatile. In each year, the largest other comprehensive income item is the currency translation adjustment: $299 million gain in 2010, a $1,463 million loss in 2011 (which is more than 20% of net income for the year), and a $737 million gain in 2012, which is more than 10% of net income for the year. The consolidated balance sheet (Appendix A) reports that accumulated other comprehensive loss is $5,487 million at December 29, 2012. Note 13, "Accumulated Other Comprehensive Loss Attributable to PepsiCo" (Appendix A), discloses that the December 29, 2012, accumulated other comprehensive income balance includes $1,946 million of cumulative translation losses through time. Given that PepsiCo's shareholders' equity is $22,417, it is clear that the cumulative translation loss is material. Over time, the value of PepsiCo's net asset positions in foreign subsidiaries has declined due to the falling value of foreign currency relative to the U.S. dollar. This amount is unrealized; PepsiCo has not liquidated its investment in the subsidiaries.

---

[36]Billy S. Soo and Lisa Gilbert Soo, "Accounting for the Multinational Firm: Is the Translation Process Valued by the Stock Market?" *The Accounting Review* (October 1995), pp. 617–637.

In its MD&A, PepsiCo discloses that remeasurement of the net monetary assets of its Venezuelan business has resulted in a net after-tax charge against net income of $120 million in 2010 (roughly 1.5% of net income in 2010 before taking the charge). In February 2013, the Venezuelan government devalued the Bolivar further, and PepsiCo expects another $100 million dollar after-tax charge against net income in the first quarter of 2013.

Interpreting the Effects of Exchange Rate Changes on Operating Results

In addition to understanding the effects of the foreign currency translation method on a firm's financial statements, you should consider how changes in exchange rates affect changes in sales levels, sales mix, and net income. For example, assume that a firm generated sales of $10,000 in the United States and FC2,000 in a particular foreign country during Year 1. The exchange rate between the U.S. dollar and the foreign currency was $2.0:1FC during Year 1. The FC2,000 of sales translates into $4,000 of foreign sales, resulting in a mix of 71.4% domestic sales and 28.6% foreign sales. For illustration, assume that domestic sales for Year 2 are $10,000 and foreign sales are FC2,000. Also assume first that the U.S. dollar increases in value relative to the foreign currency during Year 2, with an average exchange rate of $1.8:1FC. The FC2,000 of foreign sales translates into $3,600, resulting in a mix of 73.5% domestic sales and 26.5% foreign sales. Alternatively, assume that the U.S. dollar decreases in value during Year 2, with an average exchange rate of $2.4:1FC. The FC2,000 of foreign sales translates into $4,800, resulting in a mix of 67.6% domestic sales and 32.4% foreign sales. Without considering the effects of changes in selling price and volume, changes in exchange rates affect the level and mix of domestic versus foreign sales.

	Exchange Rate	Domestic Sales	Foreign Sales	Total Sales	Sales Domestic	Mix Foreign
Year 1	$2.0:FC1	$10,000	$4,000[a]	$14,000	71.4%	28.6%
Year 2	$1.8:FC1	$10,000	$3,600[b]	$13,600	73.5%	26.5%
Year 2	$2.4:FC1	$10,000	$4,800[c]	$14,800	67.6%	32.4%

[a]FC2,000 × $2.0:FC1 = $4,000
[b]FC2,000 × $1.8:FC1 = $3,600
[c]FC2,000 × $2.4:FC1 = $4,800

Changes in exchange rates also affect profit margins and rates of return. The profit margin for a firm is a weighted average of the profit margins of its domestic and foreign units, for which the weights are the sales mix percentages. Changes in exchange rates affect the sales mix proportions (in addition to any effects on the amount for foreign-source earnings) and thereby the firm's overall profit margin.

In **PepsiCo**'s MD&A section accompanying its 2012 Annual Report (Appendix B, which can be found online at the book's companion website at www.cengagebrain.com), PepsiCo discusses the effects of exchange rates on the sales of its various divisions. For some of the divisions, foreign exchange rate fluctuations (and acquisitions) explain major portions of the compound growth rate for sales. In Chapter 10, we predict PepsiCo's future sales. To perform this analysis, we analyze the effects of exchange rates on sales.

- During the consolidation process, firms must translate foreign subsidiary financial statements into U.S. dollars. The translation results in an unrealized gain or loss for the period.
- If the foreign currency is the functional currency, the unrealized gains and losses are reported in other comprehensive income and accumulated

in accumulated other comprehensive income in the shareholders' equity section of the balance sheet.
- If the U.S. dollar is the functional currency, the unrealized gains and losses are reported in net income.

Summary

Investing activities create the capacity for operations. Firms invest in assets for their own operations. Their balance sheets report the balances of property, plant, and equipment; intangible assets (including goodwill); and natural resources. Firms also invest in the operations of other firms. Their balance sheets report passive investments in marketable debt and equity securities; active equity method investments in affiliates; and because they are the consolidated with entities they control, the individual assets, liabilities, revenues, and expenses of majority investments in subsidiaries and VIEs for which they are the primary beneficiary.

Firms undertake investing activities on behalf of the claimants to the firm's assets—debtholders, preferred shareholders, controlling interests in shareholders' equity, and noncontrolling interests in shareholders' equity. Management's goal is to generate returns on these investments through operating activities. The next chapter examines the operating process and presents the accounting and reporting for operating activities.

Questions, Exercises, Problems, and Cases

Questions and Exercises

LO 8-1

8.1 Capitalization versus Expensing Decision. When a firm incurs costs on an item to be used in operations, management must decide whether to treat the cost as an asset or an expense. Assume that a company used cash to acquire machinery expected to contribute to the generation of revenues over a three-year period and the company erroneously expensed the cost to acquire the machine.

   a. Describe the effects on ROA of the error over the three-year period.
   b. Explain how the error would affect the statement of cash flows.

LO 8-1

8.2 Self-Constructed Assets. Assume that a company needs to acquire a large special-purpose materials handling facility. Given that no outside vendor exists for this type of facility and that the company has available engineering, management, and productive capacity, the company borrows funds and builds the facility itself. Identify the costs to construct this facility that should be capitalized as assets.

LO 8-1

8.3 Natural Resources. The three types of costs incurred in oil production are acquisition costs (costs to acquire the oil fields, minus the cost of the land, plus the present value of future cash flows necessary to restore the site), exploration costs (costs of drilling), and development costs (pipes, roads, and so on, to extract and transport the oil to refineries). Should each of these costs be capitalized or expensed? Explain.

8.4 Research and Development Costs. U.S. GAAP requires firms to expense immediately all internal expenditures for R&D costs. Alternatively, U.S. GAAP could require firms to capitalize and subsequently amortize all internal expenditures on R&D that have future potential. Why have standard setters chosen not to allow the capitalization alternative? How would analysts be better served if U.S. GAAP required capitalization of R&D costs?

`LO 8-1`

8.5 Capitalization of Software Development Costs. In practice, very few firms capitalize costs of developing computer software. However, U.S. GAAP requires that firms capitalize (and subsequently amortize) development costs once the "technological feasibility" stage of a product is reached. Review the Adobe Systems illustration in the chapter (page 597) and discuss why the firm does not capitalize any software development costs.

`LO 8-1`

8.6 Testing for Goodwill Impairment. Goodwill is an intangible asset that firms report on their balance sheets as a result of acquiring other firms. Goodwill generally has an indefinite life and should not be amortized, but should be tested for impairment at least annually. Describe the procedures prescribed by U.S. GAAP and IFRS to test for goodwill impairment. How do these procedures differ from the procedure followed for testing the impairment of a patent, which is an intangible asset with a definite life?

`LO 8-3`

8.7 Earnings Management and Depreciation Measurement. Earnings management entails managers using judgment and reporting estimates in such a way as to alter reported earnings to their favor.
   a. Discuss the three factors that must be estimated in measuring depreciation.
   b. Provide an illustration as to how each of these factors can be employed to manage earnings.

`LO 8-2`

8.8 Corporate Acquisitions and Goodwill. Not every acquisition results in goodwill reported in the consolidated balance sheet. Describe the valuation procedures followed by the acquiring firms to determine whether any goodwill should be recorded as a result of an acquisition and the circumstances that could lead to no recognition of goodwill in an acquisition.

`LO 8-1`

8.9 Corporate Acquisitions and Acquisition Reserves. Often the application of the acquisitions method entails establishing one or more acquisition reserves. Define an acquisition reserve, provide several examples of such reserves, and discuss how the quality of accounting information can be diminished as a result of misusing acquisition reserves.

`LO 8-4`

8.10 Accounting for Available-for-Sale and Trading Marketable Equity Securities. Firms invest in marketable securities for a variety of reasons. One of the most common reasons is to temporarily invest excess cash. Securities that qualify for the available-for-sale reporting classification are accounted for differently from those that qualify for the trading reporting classification. Describe the similarity between the reporting for the two classifications. Also describe the differences in reporting between the two classifications.

`LO 8-4`

8.11 Equity Method for Minority, Active Investments. U.S. GAAP requires firms to account for equity investments in which ownership is between 20% and 50% using the equity method. Ace Corporation owns 35% of Spear Corporation during 2014. Spear

`LO 8-4`

Corporation reported net income of $100.4 million for 2014 and declared and paid dividends of $25 million during the year.

  a. Calculate the equity income that Ace Corporation reports in 2014 related to its ownership in Spear Corporation.
  b. What does Ace Corporation report in its statement of cash flows for 2014 related to its ownership in Spear Corporation?
  c. Assuming that Ace Corporation's balance sheet account, Investment in Spear Corporation, is $1,100 million at the beginning of 2014, what is the balance in the account at the end of 2014? Support your answers with calculations.

LO 8-5

8.12 Consolidation of Variable-Interest Entities. Some accounting theorists propose that firms should consolidate any entity in which they have a "controlling financial interest." Typically, the percentage of equity ownership that one firm has in another entity determines whether consolidation is appropriate, with greater than 50% ownership requiring consolidation. Why is the percentage of ownership criterion often *not* appropriate for judging whether a VIE should be consolidated? What criterion is used to determine whether a VIE should be consolidated?

LO 8-6

8.13 Choice of a Functional Currency. Choosing the functional currency is a key decision for translating the financial statements of foreign entities of U.S. firms into U.S. dollars. Qing Corporation, a U.S. firm that sells car batteries, formed a wholly owned subsidiary in Mexico to manufacture components needed in the production of the batteries. Approximately 50% of the subsidiary's sales are to Qing Corporation. The subsidiary also sells the components it manufactures to independent third parties, and these sales are denominated in Mexican pesos. Financing for the manufacturing plants in Mexico is denominated in U.S. dollars, but labor contracts are denominated in both dollars and pesos. All material contracts are denominated in Mexican pesos. Senior managers of the subsidiary are employees of Qing Corporation who have been transferred to the subsidiary for a tour of international service. Is the functional currency of the subsidiary the peso or the U.S. dollar? Explain your reasoning.

LO 8-6

8.14 Foreign Currency as Functional Currency. Identify the exchange rates used to translate income statement and balance sheet items when the foreign currency is defined as the functional currency. Discuss the logic for the use of the exchange rates you identified.

Problems and Cases

LO 8-2

8.15 Analyzing Disclosures Regarding Fixed Assets. Exhibit 8.24 presents selected financial statement data for three chemical companies: **Monsanto Company**, **Olin Corporation**, and **NewMarket Corporation**. (NewMarket was formed from a merger of Ethyl Corporation and Afton Chemical Corporation.)

REQUIRED

  a. Compute the average total depreciable life of assets in use for each firm.
  b. Compute the average age to date of depreciable assets in use for each firm at the end of the year.
  c. Compute the amount of depreciation expense recognized for tax purposes for each firm for the year using the amount of the deferred taxes liability related to depreciation timing differences.
  d. Compute the amount of net income for the year for each firm assuming that depreciation expense for financial reporting equals the amount computed in Requirement c for tax reporting.

Exhibit 8.24

Three Chemical Companies
Selected Financial Statement Data on Depreciable Assets
(amounts in millions)
(Problem 8.15)

	NewMarket Corporation	Monsanto Company	Olin Corporation
Depreciable assets at cost:			
Beginning of year	$752	$4,611	$1,796
End of year	777	4,604	1,826
Accumulated depreciation:			
Beginning of year	584	2,331	1,301
End of year	611	2,517	1,348
Net income	33	267	55
Depreciation expense	27	328	72
Deferred tax liability relating to depreciable assets:			
Beginning of year	13	267	83
End of year	9	256	96
Income tax rate	35%	35%	35%
Depreciation method for financial reporting	Straight-line	Straight-line	Straight-line
Depreciation method for tax reporting	Accelerated	Accelerated	Accelerated

Sources: NewMarket Corporation, Form 10-K for the Fiscal Year ended December 31, 2004; Monsanto Company, Form 10-K for the Fiscal Year ended August 31, 2004; and Olin Corporation, Form 10-K for the Fiscal Year ended December 31, 2004.

e. Compute the amount each company would report for property, plant, and equipment (net) at the end of the year if it had used accelerated (tax reporting) depreciation instead of straight-line depreciation.

f. What factors might explain the difference in average total life of the assets of NewMarket Corporation and Olin Corporation relative to the assets of Monsanto Company?

g. What factors might explain the older average age for depreciable assets of NewMarket Corporation and Olin Corporation relative to Monsanto Company?

8.16 Asset Impairments. Nonrelated scenarios for Hammerhead Paper Company and Sterling Company follow:

`LO 8-3`

Scenario 1: Hammerhead Paper Company owns a press used in the production of fine paper products. The press originally cost $2,000,000, and it has a current carrying amount of $1,200,000. A decrease in the demand for fine paper products has caused the company to reassess the future cash flows from using the machine. The company now estimates that it will receive cash flows of $160,000 per year for 12 years. The company uses a 10% discount rate to compute the present value for this investment. A similar machine recently sold for $1,000,000 in the secondhand market. Hammerhead estimates that it would cost $50,000 to sell the machine.

REQUIRED

 a. Compute the amount of Hammerhead's press impairment, if any, under U.S. GAAP and IFRS.

Scenario 2: Sterling Co. acquires Vineyard Aging, Inc., on January 1, 2014, by paying $2,000,000 in cash. At the date of acquisition, the price is allocated as follows:

Price paid	$ 2,000,000
Fair value of Vineyard's identifiable assets	(1,600,000)
Goodwill	$ 400,000

One year later on December 31, 2014, Sterling estimates the fair value of the unit to be $1,800,000. The carrying value of Vineyard's identifiable assets is $1,500,000 after impairment tests are applied.

REQUIRED

 b. Compute the amount of Sterling's goodwill impairment, if any.
 c. How is the goodwill impairment reflected in the financial statements?

8.17 Upward Revaluations under IFRS. Bed and Breakfast (B&B), an Italian company operating in the Tuscany region, follows IFRS and has made the choice to remeasure long-lived assets at fair value. B&B purchased land in 2013 for €150,000. At December 31 of the next four years, the land is worth €160,000 in 2013, €155,000 in 2014, €140,000 in 2015, and €145,000 in 2016.

REQUIRED

 a. Describe how B&B will reflect the changes in the land's value in each of its annual financial statements.
 b. Assume that the asset was a building with a ten-year remaining useful life as of the end of 2013. After writing the building upward to €160,000, how much should B&B charge to depreciation expense in 2013?

8.18 Application of *Statement No. 115* for Investments in Marketable Equity Securities. **SunTrust Banks, Inc.,** owns a large block of **The Coca-Cola Company** (Coke) common stock that it has held for many years. SunTrust indicates in a note to its financial statements that all equity securities held by the bank, including its investment in Coke stock, are classified as available for sale. In its 2006 Form 10-K, SunTrust reports the following information for its Coke investment (amounts in thousands):

Coke common stock investment, market value on December 31, 2006	$2,324,826
Coke common stock investment, market value on December 31, 2005	1,945,622
Net income for 2006	2,109,742

REQUIRED

 a. Calculate the effect of the change in the market value of SunTrust's investment in Coke's common stock on SunTrust's 2006 (1) net income and (2) shareholders' equity. Ignore taxes.
 b. How would your answer to Requirement a differ if SunTrust classified its investment in Coke's common stock as a trading security?
 c. Does the value reported on SunTrust's balance sheet for the investment in Coke's stock differ depending on the firm's reason for holding the stock (that is, whether it is classified as available for sale versus trading by management)? Explain.

8.19 Effect of an Acquisition on the Date of Acquisition Balance Sheet.

Lexington Corporation acquired all of the outstanding common stock of Chalfont, Inc., on January 1, 2013. Lexington gave shares of its no par common stock with a market value of $504 million in exchange for the Chalfont common stock. Chalfont will remain a legally separate entity after the exchange, but Lexington will prepare consolidated financial statements with Chalfont each period. Exhibit 8.25 presents the balance sheets of Lexington and Chalfont on January 1, 2013, just prior to the acquisition. The market value of Chalfont's fixed assets exceeds their book value by $80 million. Chalfont owns a copyright with a market value of $50 million. Chalfont is a defendant in a lawsuit that it expects to settle during 2013 at a cost of $30 million. The firm carries no insurance against such lawsuits. Lexington plans to establish an acquisition reserve for this lawsuit.

REQUIRED

a. Prepare a schedule that shows the allocation of the consideration given to individual assets and liabilities under the acquisition method. Ignore deferred tax effects.

b. Prepare a consolidated balance sheet for Lexington and Chalfont on January 1, 2013. Show your supporting calculations for any amount that is not simply the sum of the amounts for Lexington and Chalfont from their separate financial records.

Exhibit 8.25

Lexington Corporation and Chalfont, Inc.
Balance Sheets
January 1, 2013
(amounts in millions)
(Problem 8.19)

	Lexington Corporation	Chalfont, Inc.
Cash	$ 100	$ 30
Accounts receivable	240	90
Fixed assets (net)	1,000	360
Copyright	—	—
Deferred tax asset	40	—
Goodwill	—	—
Total Assets	**$1,380**	**$480**
Accounts payable and accruals	$ 240	$ 80
Long-term debt	480	100
Deferred tax liability	160	—
Other noncurrent liabilities	120	—
Common stock	320	100
Retained earnings	60	200
Total Liabilities and Shareholders' Equity	**$1,380**	**$480**

8.20 Effect of an Acquisition on the Postacquisition Balance Sheet and Income Statement. Ormond Co. acquired all of the outstanding common stock of Daytona Co. on January 1, 2014. Ormond Co. gave shares of its common stock with a fair value of $312 million in exchange for 100% of the Daytona Co. common stock. Daytona Co. will remain a legally separate entity after the exchange, but Ormond Co. will prepare consolidated financial statements with Daytona Co each period. Exhibit 8.26 presents the balance sheets of Ormond Co. and Daytona Co. on January 1, 2014, just after the acquisition. The following information applies to Daytona Co.:

1. The market value of Daytona Co.'s fixed assets exceeds their book value by $50 million.
2. Daytona Co. owns a patent with a market value of $40 million.
3. Daytona Co. is a defendant in a lawsuit that it expects to settle during 2014 at a cost of $25 million. The firm carries no insurance against such lawsuits. If permitted, Ormond Co. wants to establish an acquisition reserve for this lawsuit.
4. Daytona Co. has an unrecognized and unfunded retirement health care benefits obligation totaling $20 million on January 1, 2014.

REQUIRED

a. Prepare a consolidated balance sheet for Ormond Co. and Daytona Co. on January 1, 2014. Ignore deferred tax effects. (A consolidated worksheet is not required, but recommended.)

Exhibit 8.26

Ormond Co. and Daytona Co.
Balance Sheets on January 1, 2014
(amounts in millions)
(Problem 8.20)

	Ormond Co.	Daytona Co.
Cash	$ 25	$ 15
Accounts receivable	60	40
Investment in Daytona	312	—
Fixed assets (net)	250	170
Patent	—	—
Deferred tax asset	10	—
Goodwill	—	—
Total Assets	$657	$225
Accounts payable & accruals	$ 60	$ 40
Long-term debt	120	60
Deferred tax liability	40	—
Other noncurrent liabilities	30	—
Common stock	392	50
Retained earnings	15	75
Total Liabilities and Shareholders' Equity	$657	$225

b. Exhibit 8.27 presents income statements and balance sheets taken from the separate-company books at the end of 2014. The following information applies to these companies:

- The fixed assets of Daytona Co. had an average remaining life of five years on January 1, 2014. The firms use the straight-line depreciation method.
- The patent of Daytona Co. had a remaining life of ten years on January 1, 2014.
- Daytona Co. settled the lawsuit during 2014 and expects no further liability.
- Daytona Co. will amortize and fund its retirement health care benefits obligation over 20 years. It included $1 million in operating expenses during 2014 related to amounts unrecognized and unfunded as of January 1, 2014.
- The test for goodwill impairment indicates that no impairment charge is necessary for 2014.

Prepare a consolidated income statement for 2014 and a consolidated balance sheet on December 31, 2014. (A consolidated worksheet is not required, but it will be illustrated in the solution.)

Exhibit 8.27

Ormond Co. and Daytona Co.
Income Statement and Balance Sheet for 2014
(in millions)
(Problem 8.20)

	Ormond Co.	Daytona Co.
Income Statement for 2014		
Sales	$ 600	$ 450
Equity in earnings of Daytona Co.	30	—
Operating expenses	(550)	(395)
Interest expense	(10)	(5)
Loss on lawsuit	—	(20)
Income tax expense	(28)	(12)
Net Income	$ 42	$ 18
Balance Sheet on December 31, 2014		
Cash	$ 45	$ 25
Accounts receivable	80	50
Investment in Daytona Co.	339	—
Fixed assets	280	195
Patent	—	—
Deferred tax asset	15	—
Goodwill	—	—
Total Assets	$ 759	$ 270
Accounts payable and accruals	$ 90	$ 55
Long-term debt	140	75
Deferred tax liability	50	—
Other noncurrent liabilities	40	—
Common stock	392	50
Retained earnings	47	90
Total Liabilities and Shareholders' Equity	$ 759	$ 270

LO 8-5

8.21 Variable-Interest Entities. **Molson Coors Brewing Company** (Molson Coors) is the fifth-largest brewer in the world. It is one of the leading brewers in the United States and Canada; the company's brands include Coors, Molson Canadian, Carling, and Killian's Irish Red. Molson and Adolph Coors Brewing Company merged in early 2005. In the final annual report of Adolph Coors Brewing Company for the year ended December 26, 2004, sales exceeded 32 million barrels (1 U.S. barrel equals 31 gallons). Coors reported $4.3 billion of net sales for 2004.

The firm invests in various entities to carry out its brewing, bottling, and canning activities. The investments take the legal form of partnerships, joint ventures, and limited liability corporations, among other arrangements. The firm states in its 2004 annual report, issued under the Molson Coors name, that each of these arrangements has been tested to determine whether it qualifies as a VIE.

The following excerpt is taken from the firm's note on VIEs in its 2004 annual report:

> Note 3. Variable-Interest Entities. Once an entity is determined to be a VIE, the party with the controlling financial interest, the primary beneficiary, is required to consolidate it. We have investments in VIEs, of which we are the primary beneficiary. Accordingly, we have consolidated three joint ventures in 2004, effective December 29, 2003, the first day of 2004. These include Rocky Mountain Metal Container (RMMC), Rocky Mountain Bottle Company (RMBC) and Grolsch (UK) Limited (Grolsch). The impacts to our balance sheet include the addition of net fixed assets of RMMC and RMBC totaling approximately $65 million, RMMC debt of approximately $40 million, and Grolsch net intangibles of approximately $20 million (at current exchange rates). The most significant impact to our cash flow statement for the year ended December 26, 2004, was to increase depreciation expense by approximately $13.2 million and cash recognized on initial consolidation of the entities of $20.8 million. Our partners' share of the operating results of the ventures is eliminated in the minority interests line of the Consolidated Statements of Income.

Molson Coors also provides additional information in its annual report on each of the consolidated joint ventures, as follows:

1. RMBC is a joint venture with Owens-Brockway Glass Container, Inc., in which we hold a 50% interest. RMBC produces glass bottles at a glass-manufacturing facility for use at the Golden, Colorado brewery. Under this agreement, RMBC supplies our bottle requirements and Owens-Brockway has a contract to supply the majority of our bottle requirements not met by RMBC. In 2003 and 2002, the firm's share of pretax joint venture profits for the venture, totaling $7.8 million and $13.2 million, respectively, was included in cost of goods sold on the consolidated income statement.

2. RMMC, a Colorado limited liability company, is a joint venture with Ball Corporation in which we hold a 50% interest. RMMC supplies the firm with substantially all of the cans for our Golden, Colorado brewery. RMMC manufactures the cans at our manufacturing facilities, which RMMC operates under a use and license agreement. In 2003 and 2002, the firm's share of pretax joint venture profits (losses), totaling $0.1 million and ($0.6) million, respectively, was included in cost of goods sold on the consolidated income statement. As stated previously, on consolidation of RMMC, debt of approximately $40 million was added to the balance sheet. As of December 26, 2004, Coors is the guarantor of this debt.

3. Grolsch is a joint venture between CBL and Royal Grolsch N.V. in which we hold a 49% interest. The Grolsch joint venture markets Grolsch branded beer in the United Kingdom and the Republic of Ireland. The majority of the Grolsch branded beer is produced by

CBL under a contract brewing arrangement with the joint venture. CBL and Royal Grolsch N.V. sell beer to the joint venture, which sells the beer back to CBL (for onward sale to customers) for a price equal to what it paid plus a marketing and overhead charge and a profit margin. In 2003 and 2002, the firm's share of pretax profits for this venture, totaling $3.6 million and $2.0 million, respectively, was included in cost of goods sold on the consolidated income statement. As stated previously, on consolidation, net fixed assets of approximately $4 million and net intangibles of approximately $20 million were added to our balance sheet.

REQUIRED

a. Describe the operational purpose of the three VIEs consolidated by Molson Coors.

b. Molson Coors is the primary beneficiary for three investments that the firm identified as VIEs. What criteria did Molson Coors apply to determine that the firm is the primary beneficiary for these three investments?

c. For each investment, Molson Coors reports the income statement impact as a reduction of cost of goods sold on the consolidated income statement. What is the rationale for reporting the impact this way on the income statement?

d. The firm states, "Our partners share of the operating results of the ventures is eliminated in the minority interests line of the Consolidated Statements of Income." Define *minority interests* as it appears on the income statement. Discuss why Molson Coors subtracts it to calculate consolidated net income.

e. RMBC, RMMC, and Grolsch are consolidated with the financial statements of Molson Coors because the three investments qualify as VIEs as defined in *Interpretation No. 46* and the firm determined that it is the primary beneficiary for the investments. Explain what reporting technique Molson Coors would use to account for the investments if, in fact, they did not qualify as VIEs. What would be the impact on the balance sheet? What would be the impact on the income statement? What would be the impact on the statement of cash flows?

f. The firm reports that the depreciation expense on the statement of cash flows for 2004 increased by approximately $13.2 million as a result of consolidating the VIEs. Why did consolidating the VIEs increase depreciation expense?

8.22 Accounting for a Merger under the Acquisition Method. On

`LO 8-4`

December 31, 2014, Pace Co. paid $3,000,000 to Sanders Corp. shareholders to acquire 100% of the net assets of Sanders Corp. Pace Co. also agreed to pay former Sanders shareholders $200,000 in cash if certain earnings projections were achieved over the next two years. Based on probabilities of achieving the earnings projections, Pace estimated the fair value of this promise to be $150,000. Pace paid $10,000 in legal fees and incurred $10,000 in internal cash costs related to management's time to complete the transaction. Exhibit 8.28 provides the book and fair values of Sanders Corp. at the date of acquisition.

REQUIRED

a. Record the merger using the financial statement effects template or journal entries.

b. How would the financial effects *change* if the cash paid was $2,000,000?

8.23 Consolidation Subsequent to the Date of Acquisition. Exhibit

`LO 8-4`

8.29 presents the separate financial statements at December 31, 2015, of Prestige Resorts and its 80%-owned subsidiary Booking, Inc. Two years earlier on January 1, 2014, Prestige acquired 80% of the common shares of Booking for $1,170 million in cash. Booking's 2014

Exhibit 8.28

Sanders Corp. Book and Fair Values as of December 31, 2014
(Problem 8.22)

	Sanders Corp. Book Values at 12/31/14	Sanders Corp. Fair Values at 12/31/14
Cash	$ 400,000	$ 400,000
Receivables	500,000	500,000
Inventory	1,200,000	1,600,000
PP&E (net)	1,600,000	2,000,000
Unpatented technology	0	300,000
In-process R&D	0	200,000
Total Assets	$ 3,700,000	$ 5,000,000
Accounts payable	$ (400,000)	$ (400,000)
Notes payable	(2,100,000)	(2,200,000)
Total Liabilities	$(2,500,000)	$(2,600,000)
Common stock ($1 par)	$ (100,000)	
Additional paid-in capital	(500,000)	
Retained earnings	(300,000)	
Revenues	(2,000,000)	
Expenses	1,700,000	
Total Shareholders' Equity	$(1,200,000)	

Revenues, gains, and net income are in parentheses to indicate that their signs are opposite those of expenses and losses; that is, they are credits for those interpreting the worksheet from the accountant's traditional debit/credit approach. Liabilities and shareholders' equity accounts are in parentheses to indicate that they are claims against assets; again, they are credits in the traditional debit/credit framework.

Exhibit 8.29

Prestige Resorts and Booking, Inc. Financial Statements
at December 31, 2015 (in millions)
(Problem 8.23)

	Prestige Resorts	Booking, Inc.
Revenues	$(1,365)	$ (645)
Cost of goods sold	516	300
Depreciation expense	90	30
Amortization expense	150	112.5
Interest expense	105	67.5
Equity in subsidiary earnings	(96)	0
Net Income	$ (600)	$ (135)

(Continued)

Exhibit 8.29 (Continued)

Cash	$ 780	$ 600
Short-term investments	309	67.5
Land	456	442.5
Equipment (net)	585	240
Investment in Small Technologies	1,278	0
Customer lists	1,320	810
Total Assets	$ 4,728	$ 2,160
Long-term liabilities	$(1,623)	$ (885)
Common stock	(1,305)	(345)
Retained earnings	(1,800)	(930)
Total Liabilities and Shareholders' Equity	$(4,728)	$(2,160)

Revenues, gains, and net income are in parentheses to indicate that their signs are opposite those of expenses and losses; that is, they are credits for those interpreting the worksheet from the accountant's traditional debit/credit approach. Liabilities and shareholders' equity accounts are in parentheses to indicate that they are claims against assets; again, they are credits in the traditional debit/credit framework.

net income was $105 million, and Booking paid no dividends in 2014. Booking's 2015 income was $135 million, and it paid $75 million dividends on common stock during 2015. Booking's pre- and postacquisition stock prices do not support the existence of a control premium. Exhibit 8.30 shows the allocation of fair value at the date of acquisition, January 1, 2014. Exhibit 8.31 traces Prestige Resorts' equity method accounting for Booking, Inc. Ignore deferred tax effects.

Exhibit 8.30

Allocations of Fair Value (in millions) (Problem 8.23)

	Allocation of Fair Values	Estimated Life	Charged (Credited) to Expense Each Year	Balance on December 31, 2015
Booking fair value at acquisition date	$ 1,462.5			
Booking book value at acquisition date	(1,110.0)			
Fair value in excess of book value	$ 352.5			
Land (not depreciated)	(90)	NA		
Equipment	15	10		
Customer lists	(180)	20		
Long-term liabilities (lower fair value)	(60)	8		
Goodwill	$ 37.5	Indefinite		

Exhibit 8.31

Investor Interests in Booking, Inc. (in millions)
(Problem 8.23)

	Prestige Properties (80% controlling interest)	Noncontrolling Interest (20%)
Acquisition date fair value (1/1/14) = $1,462.5	$1,170	
2014 net income of Booking = $105	$ 84	
Annual excess amortizations = $15	(12)	_____
Equity in Booking's earnings for 2014	72	_____
Investment in Booking, Inc. (12/31/14)	$1,242	
2015 net income of Booking = $135	$108	
Annual excess amortizations = $15	(12)	_____
Equity in Booking's earnings for 2015	96	
Dividends paid by Booking in 2015 = $75	(60)	_____
Investment in Booking, Inc. (12/31/15)	$1,278	_____

REQUIRED

a. Complete Exhibit 8.30 to show income effects and balance sheet adjustments to be reflected in the December 31, 2015, Eliminations column of the consolidated worksheet.

b. Complete Exhibit 8.31 to trace the noncontrolling interests in Booking, Inc.'s earnings and net assets.

c. Prepare a worksheet to consolidate Prestige and Booking at December 31, 2015.

 8.24 Calculating the Translation Adjustment under the All-Current Method and the Monetary/Nonmonetary Method. Foreign Sub is a wholly owned subsidiary of U.S. Domestic Corporation. U.S. Domestic Corporation acquired the subsidiary several years ago. The financial statements for Foreign Sub for 2014 in its own currency appear in Exhibit 8.32.

Exhibit 8.32

Foreign Sub
Financial Statement Data
(Problem 8.24)

	December 31	
	2013	2014
Cash	FC 100	FC 150
Accounts receivable	300	350
Inventories	350	400
Land	500	700
Total Assets	FC1,250	FC 1,600

(Continued)

Exhibit 8.32 (Continued)

Accounts payable	FC 150	FC 250
Long-term debt	200	300
Common stock	500	600
Retained earnings	400	450
Total Liabilities and Equities	FC1,250	FC 1,600

	For 2010
Sales	FC 4,000
Cost of goods sold	(3,200)
Selling and administrative expenses	(400)
Income taxes	(160)
Net Income	FC 240
Dividend declared and paid on December 31	(190)
Increase in Retained Earnings	FC 50

The exchange rates between the U.S. dollar and the foreign currency of the subsidiary

December 31, 2013	$10.0:1FC
Average, 2014	$ 8.0:1FC
December 31, 2014	$ 6.0:1FC

On January 1, 2014, Foreign Sub issued FC100 of long-term debt and FC100 of common stock in the acquisition of land costing FC200. Operating activities occurred evenly over the year.

REQUIRED

a. Assume that the currency of Foreign Sub is the functional currency. Compute the change in the cumulative translation adjustment for 2014. Indicate whether the change increases or decreases shareholders' equity.

b. Assume that the U.S. dollar is the functional currency. Compute the amount of the translation gain or loss for 2014. Indicate whether the amount is a gain or loss.

8.25 Translating the Financial Statements of a Foreign Subsidiary; Comparison of Translation Methods. Stebbins Corporation established a wholly owned Canadian subsidiary on January 1, Year 1, by contributing US$500,000 for all of the subsidiary's common stock. The exchange rate on that date was C$1:US$0.90 (that is, one Canadian dollar equaled 90 U.S. cents). The Canadian subsidiary invested C$500,000 in a building with an expected life of 20 years and rented it to various tenants for the year. The average exchange rate during Year 1 was C$1:US$0.85, and the exchange rate on December 31, Year 1, was C$1:US$0.80. Exhibit 8.33 shows the amounts taken from the books of the Canadian subsidiary at the end of Year 1, measured in Canadian dollars.

LO 8-6

Exhibit 8.33

Canadian Subsidiary
Financial Statements
Year 1
(Problem 8.25)

Balance Sheet as of December 31, Year 1

ASSETS

Cash	C$ 77,555
Rent receivable	25,000
Building (net)	475,000
	C$577,555

LIABILITIES AND EQUITY

Accounts payable	C$ 6,000
Salaries payable	4,000
Common stock	555,555
Retained earnings	12,000
	C$577,555

Income Statement for Year 1

Rent revenue	C$125,000
Operating expenses	(28,000)
Depreciation expense	(25,000)
Translation exchange loss	—
Net Income	C$ 72,000

Retained Earnings Statement for Year 1

Balance, January 1, Year 1	C$ —
Net income	72,000
Dividends	(60,000)
Balance, December 31, Year 1	C$ 12,000

REQUIRED

a. Prepare a balance sheet, an income statement, and a retained earnings statement for the Canadian subsidiary for Year 1 in U.S. dollars assuming that the Canadian dollar is the functional currency. Include a separate schedule showing the computation of the translation adjustment account.

b. Repeat Requirement a assuming that the U.S. dollar is the functional currency. Include a separate schedule showing the computation of the translation gain or loss.

c. Why is the sign of the translation adjustment for Year 1 under the all-current translation method and the translation gain or loss for Year 1 under the monetary/nonmonetary translation method the same? Why do their amounts differ?

d. Assuming that the firm could justify either translation method, which method would the management of Stebbins Corporation likely prefer for Year 1? Why?

8.26 Translating the Financial Statements of a Foreign Subsidiary; Second Year of Operations. LO 8-6

Refer to Problem 8.25 for Stebbins Corporation for Year 1, its first year of operations. Exhibit 8.34 shows the amounts for the Canadian subsidiary for Year 2. The average exchange rate during Year 2 was C$1:US$0.82, and the exchange rate on December 31, Year 2, was C$1:US$0.84. The Canadian subsidiary declared and paid dividends on December 31, Year 2.

REQUIRED

a. Prepare a balance sheet, an income statement, and a retained earnings statement for the Canadian subsidiary for Year 2 in U.S. dollars, assuming that the Canadian dollar is the functional currency. Include a separate schedule showing the computation of the translation adjustment for Year 2 and the change in the translation adjustment account.

b. Repeat Requirement a assuming that the U.S. dollar is the functional currency. Include a separate schedule showing the computation of the translation gain or loss.

Exhibit 8.34

Canadian Subsidiary Financial Statements Year 2 (Problem 8.26)

Balance Sheet

ASSETS

Cash	C$116,555
Rent receivable	30,000
Building (net)	450,000
	C$596,555

LIABILITIES AND EQUITY

Accounts payable	C$ 7,500
Salaries payable	5,500
Common stock	555,555
Retained earnings	28,000
	C$596,555

Income Statement

Rent revenue	C$150,000
Operating expenses	(34,000)
Depreciation expense	(25,000)
Translation exchange gain	—
Net Income	C$ 91,000

Retained Earnings Statement

Balance, January 1, Year 2	C$ 12,000
Net income	91,000
Dividends	(75,000)
Balance, December 31, Year 2	C$ 28,000

c. Why is the sign of the translation adjustment for Year 2 under the all-current translation method and the translation gain or loss under the monetary/nonmonetary translation method the same? Why do their amounts differ?

d. Assuming that the firm could justify either translation method, which method would management of Stebbins Corporation likely prefer for Year 2? Why?

LO 8-6

8.27 Identifying the Functional Currency. Alpha Computer Systems (ACS) designs, manufactures, sells, and services networked computer systems; associated peripheral equipment; and related network, communications, and software products.

Exhibit 8.35 presents geographic segment data. ACS conducts sales and marketing operations outside the United States, principally through sales subsidiaries in Canada, Europe, Central and South America, and the Far East; by direct sales from the parent corporation; and through various representative and distributorship arrangements. The company's international manufacturing operations include plants in Canada, the Far East, and Europe. These manufacturing

Exhibit 8.35

Alpha Computer Systems
Geographic Segment Data
(amounts in thousands)
(Problem 8.27)

	Year 3	Year 4	Year 5
Revenues			
United States Customers	$ 4,472,195	$ 5,016,606	$ 5,810,598
Intercompany	1,354,339	1,921,043	2,017,928
Total	$ 5,826,534	$ 6,937,649	$ 7,828,526
Europe Customers	$ 2,259,743	$ 3,252,482	$ 4,221,631
Intercompany	82,649	114,582	137,669
Total	$ 2,342,392	$ 3,367,064	$ 4,359,300
Canada, Far East, Americas Customers	$ 858,419	$ 1,120,356	$ 1,443,217
Intercompany	577,934	659,204	912,786
Total	$ 1,436,353	$ 1,779,560	$ 2,356,003
Eliminations	$(2,014,922)	$(2,694,829)	$ (3,068,383)
Net Revenue	$ 7,590,357	$ 9,389,444	$11,475,446
Income			
United States	$ 342,657	$ 758,795	$ 512,754
Europe	405,636	634,543	770,135
Canada, Far East, Americas	207,187	278,359	390,787
Eliminations	(126,771)	(59,690)	(38,676)
Operating Income	$ 828,709	$ 1,612,007	$ 1,635,000
Interest Income	116,899	122,149	143,665
Interest Expense	(88,079)	(45,203)	(37,820)
Income before Income Taxes	$ 857,529	$ 1,688,953	$ 1,740,845

(Continued)

Exhibit 8.35 (Continued)			
Assets			
United States	$ 3,911,491	$ 4,627,838	$ 5,245,439
Europe	1,817,584	2,246,333	3,093,818
Canada, Far East, Americas	815,067	843,067	1,293,906
Corporate Assets (temporary cash investments)	2,035,557	1,979,470	2,057,528
Eliminations	(1,406,373)	(1,289,322)	(1,579,135)
Total Assets	$ 7,173,326	$ 8,407,386	$10,111,556

plants sell their output to the company's sales subsidiaries, the parent corporation, or other manufacturing plants for further processing.

ACS accounts for intercompany transfers between geographic areas at prices representative of unaffiliated-party transactions.

Sales to unaffiliated customers outside the United States, including U.S. export sales, were $5,729,879,000 for Year 5, $4,412,527,000 for Year 4, and $3,179,143,000 for Year 3, which represented 50%, 47%, and 42%, respectively, of total operating revenues. The international subsidiaries have reinvested substantially all of their earnings to support operations. These accumulated retained earnings, before elimination of intercompany transactions, aggregated $2,793,239,000 at the end of Year 5, $2,070,337,000 at the end of Year 4, and $1,473,081,000 at the end of Year 3.

The company enters into forward exchange contracts to reduce the impact of foreign currency fluctuations on operations and the asset and liability positions of foreign subsidiaries. The gains and losses on these contracts increase or decrease net income in the same period as the related revenues and expenses; for assets and liabilities, in the period in which the exchange rate changes.

REQUIRED

Discuss whether ACS should use the U.S. dollar or the currencies of its foreign subsidiaries as its functional currency.

INTEGRATIVE CASE 8.1

Starbucks

Part I—Accounting Policy

Presented below are excerpts from Note 1 to **Starbucks'** September 30, 2012, consolidated financial statements in which Starbucks describes accounting policy for long-lived assets.

Excerpts from Note 1: "Summary of Significant Accounting Policies"

Property, Plant and Equipment

Property, plant and equipment are carried at cost less accumulated depreciation. Depreciation of property, plant and equipment, which includes assets under capital leases, is provided on the straight-line method over estimated useful lives, generally ranging from 2 to 15 years for equipment and 30 to 40 years for buildings. Leasehold improvements are amortized over the shorter of their estimated useful lives or the related lease life, generally 10 years. For leases with renewal periods at the Company's option, we generally use the original lease term, excluding renewal option periods, to determine estimated useful lives. If failure to exercise a renewal option imposes an economic penalty to us, we may determine at the inception of the lease that renewal is reasonably assured and include the renewal option period in the determination of appropriate estimated useful lives. The portion of depreciation expense related to production and distribution facilities is included in cost of sales including occupancy costs on the consolidated statements of earnings. The costs of repairs and maintenance are expensed when incurred, while expenditures for refurbishments and improvements that significantly add to the productive capacity or extend the useful life of an asset are capitalized. When assets are retired or sold, the asset cost and related accumulated depreciation are eliminated with any remaining gain or loss reflected in net earnings.

Goodwill

We test goodwill for impairment on an annual basis during our third fiscal quarter, or more frequently if circumstances, such as material deterioration in performance or a significant number of store closures, indicate reporting unit carrying values may exceed their fair values. When evaluating goodwill for impairment, we first perform a qualitative assessment to determine if the fair value of the reporting unit is more likely than not greater than the carrying amount. If not, we calculate the implied estimated fair value of the reporting unit. If the carrying amount of goodwill exceeds the implied estimated fair value, an impairment charge to current operations is recorded to reduce the carrying value to the implied estimated fair value.

As a part of our ongoing operations, we may close certain stores within a reporting unit containing goodwill due to underperformance of the store or inability to renew our lease, among other reasons. We abandon certain assets associated with a closed store including leasehold improvements and other nontransferable assets. Under GAAP, when a portion of a reporting unit that constitutes a business is to be disposed of, goodwill associated with the business is included in the carrying amount of the business in determining any loss on disposal. Our evaluation of whether the portion of a reporting unit being disposed of constitutes a business occurs on the date of abandonment. Although an operating store meets the accounting definition of a business prior to abandonment, it does not constitute a business on the closure date because the remaining assets on that date do not constitute an integrated set of assets that are capable of being conducted and managed for the purpose of providing a return to investors. As a result, when closing individual stores, we do not include goodwill in the calculation of any loss on disposal of the related assets. As noted above, if store closures are indicative of potential impairment of goodwill at the reporting unit level, we perform an evaluation of our reporting unit goodwill when such closures occur. During Fiscal 2012 and fiscal 2011 we recorded no impairment charges and recorded $1.6 million in fiscal 2010.

Other Intangible Assets

Other intangible assets consist primarily of trademarks with indefinite lives, which are tested for impairment annually or more frequently if events or changes in circumstances indicate that the asset might be impaired. Definite-lived intangible assets, which mainly consist of contract-based patents and copyrights, are amortized over their estimated useful lives, and are tested for impairment when facts and circumstances indicate that the carrying values may not be recoverable. Based on the impairment tests performed, there was no impairment of other intangible assets in fiscal 2012, 2011, and 2010.

Long-lived Assets

When facts and circumstances indicate that the carrying values of long-lived assets may not be recoverable, we evaluate long-lived assets for impairment. We first compare the carrying value of the asset to the asset's estimated future cash flows (undiscounted). If the estimated future cash flows are less than the carrying value of the asset, we calculate an impairment loss based on the asset's estimated fair value. The fair value of the assets is estimated using a discounted cash flow model based on forecasted future revenues and operating costs, using internal projections. Property, plant and equipment assets are grouped at the lowest level for which there are identifiable cash flows when assessing impairment. Cash flows for company-operated store assets are identified at the individual store level. Long-lived assets to be disposed of are reported at the lower of their carrying amount, or fair value less estimated costs to sell.

We recognized net impairment and disposition losses of $31.7 million, $36.2 million, and $67.7 million in fiscal 2012, 2011, and 2010, respectively, primarily due to underperforming company-operated stores. Depending on the underlying asset that is impaired, these losses may be recorded in any one of the operating expense lines on the consolidated statements of earnings: for retail operations, the net impairment and disposition losses are recorded in store operating expenses and for all other operations, these losses are recorded in cost of sales including occupancy costs, other operating expenses, or general and administrative expenses.

Asset Retirement Obligations

We recognize a liability for the fair value of required asset retirement obligations ("ARO") when such obligations are incurred. Our AROs are primarily associated with leasehold improvements, which, at the end of a lease, we are contractually obligated to remove in order to comply with the lease agreement. At the inception of a lease with such conditions, we record an ARO liability and a corresponding capital asset in an amount equal to the estimated fair value of the obligation. The liability is estimated based on a number of assumptions requiring management's judgment, including store closing costs, cost inflation rates and discount rates, and is accreted to its projected future value over time. The capitalized asset is depreciated using the same depreciation convention as leasehold improvement assets. Upon satisfaction of the ARO conditions, any difference between the recorded ARO liability and the actual retirement costs incurred is recognized as an operating gain or loss in the consolidated statements of earnings. As of September 30, 2012 and October 2, 2011, our net ARO asset included in property, plant and equipment was $8.8 million and $11.8 million, respectively, and our net ARO liability included in other long-term liabilities was $42.6 million and $50.1 million, respectively.

Source: Starbucks Corporation, Form 10-K for the Fiscal Year ended September 30, 2012.

REQUIRED

a. Leasehold improvements are substantial costs incurred by Starbucks to outfit, remodel, and improve leased retail outlets. Why does Starbucks capitalize and amortize leasehold improvements? Does its policy for determining useful lives in the presence of a lease renewal option yield high-quality accounting numbers? How would Starbucks account for the leasehold improvement costs remaining at the end of a lease it had expected to renew but did not?

b. Starbucks has an ARO related to the leasehold improvements. Describe how Starbucks recognizes the ARO initially in the balance sheet. Then describe how Starbucks recognizes changes in the ARO-related asset and ARO liability in the income statement over time. How is income affected when Starbucks actually spends cash to return a leased property to its original condition? If Starbucks spends more cash than reflected in the ARO liability, how will it account for the difference?

    c. How would the first two sentences of the Long-lived Assets section of Note 1 appear if Starbucks followed IFRS? Which system do you believe provides the best quality accounting for long-lived asset impairment?

    d. The second paragraph of the Long-Lived assets section of the note describes how Starbucks reflects impairment charges in the income statement. Which line item would you prefer that Starbucks use to report the charges? Why?

Part II—Business Combinations

Starbucks prepares consolidated financial statements. Presented below are excerpts from Notes 1 and 2, and a major portion of Note 8 from Starbucks' fiscal 2012 consolidated financial statements.

Excerpts from Note 1: Summary of Significant Accounting Policies

Principles of Consolidation

The consolidated financial statements reflect the financial position and operating results of Starbucks, including wholly owned subsidiaries and investees that we control. Investments in entities that we do not control, but have the ability to exercise significant influence over operating and financial policies, are accounted for under the equity method. Investments in entities in which we do not have the ability to exercise significant influence are accounted for under the cost method. Intercompany transactions and balances have been eliminated.

Foreign Currency Translation

Our international operations generally use their local currency as their functional currency. Assets and liabilities are translated at exchange rates in effect at the balance sheet date. Income and expense accounts are translated at the average monthly exchange rates during the year. Resulting translation adjustments are recorded as a component of accumulated other comprehensive income on the consolidated balance sheets.

Excerpts from Note 2: Acquisitions

On July 3, 2012, we acquired 100% ownership interest in Bay Bread, LLC and its La Boulange bakery brand (collectively "La Boulange"), to elevate our core food offerings and build a premium, artisanal bakery brand. We acquired La Boulange for a purchase price of approximately $100 million in cash. The following table summarizes the allocation of the purchase price to the fair values of the assets acquired and liabilities assumed on the closing date (in millions):

	Fair Value at July 3, 2012
Property, plant and equipment	$18.1
Intangible assets	24.3
Goodwill	58.7
Other current and noncurrent assets	5.1
Current liabilities	(6.4)
Total cash paid	$99.8

The assets acquired and liabilities assumed are included in our Americas operating segment. Other current assets acquired primarily include cash, trade receivables, and inventory. In addition, we assumed various current liabilities primarily consisting of accounts payable and accrued payroll related liabilities. The intangible assets acquired as part of the transaction include the La Boulange trade name and proprietary recipes and processes. The La Boulange trade name was valued at $9.7 million and determined to have an indefinite life while the intangible asset relating to the proprietary recipes and processes was valued at $14.6 million and will be amortized over a period of 10 years. The $58.7 million of goodwill is deductible for income tax purposes and was allocated to our Americas operating segment.

Source: Starbucks Corporation, Form 10-K for the Fiscal Year ended September 30, 2012.

REQUIRED

a. How does the concept of fair value drive the accounting for acquisitions?

b. What method will Starbucks use to translate its foreign subsidiaries' financial statements so that they can be consolidated? Will Starbucks report gains and losses on the translation in net income?

c. At the date of acquisition, it is likely that the La Boulange trade name and proprietary recipes and processes had book values near $0. One year later, what amounts will be shown in Bay Bread's own financial statements for:

- Trade name
- Proprietary recipes and processes
- Goodwill

One year later, what amounts will be shown in Starbucks' consolidated financial statements for:

- Trade name
- Proprietary recipes and processes
- Goodwill
- Depreciation and amortization expense

Part III—Depreciation and Useful Lives

Presented below is a portion of Note 7 to Starbucks' 2012 consolidated financial statements.

Excerpts from Note 7: Supplemental Balance Sheet Information *(in millions)*

Property, Plant and Equipment, net	September 30, 2012	October 2, 2011
Land	$ 46.2	$ 44.8
Buildings	225.2	218.5
Leasehold improvements	3,957.6	3,617.1
Store equipment	1,251.0	1,101.8
Roasting equipment	322.8	295.1
Furniture, fixtures and other	836.2	757.8
Work in progress	264.1	127.4
Property, plant and equipment, gross	$ 6,903.1	$ 6,163.1
Less accumulated depreciation and amortization	(4,244.2)	(3,808.1)
Property, plant and equipment, net	$ 2,658.9	$ 2,355.0

Source: Starbucks Corporation, Form 10-K for the Fiscal Year ended September 30, 2012.

REQUIRED

a. Estimate the average total estimated useful life of depreciable property, plant, and equipment. Starbucks reports $580.6 million of depreciation and amortization in the statement of cash flows, of which $4.5 million relates to amortization of limited-life intangible assets. Does the estimate reconcile with stated accounting policy on useful lives for property, plant, and equipment? Explain.

b. How should an analyst interpret fluctuations in this estimate for a given company over time? How should an analyst interpret differences in this estimate between a company and its competitors?

c. Estimate the average age of depreciable assets, the percentage of PP&E that has been used up, and the remaining useful life. How might an analyst use this information?

CASE 8.2

Disney Acquisition of Marvel Entertainment

In August 2009, **The Walt Disney Company** announced that it would acquire **Marvel Entertainment, Inc.,** in a $4 billion cash and common stock deal. On a per-share basis, the consideration given by Disney to Marvel shareholders represents a 29% premium over Marvel's share price at the date of acquisition. Disney acquires the more than 5,000 characters in Marvel's library, including Iron Man, Spider-Man, X-Men, Captain America, and the Fantastic Four. Exhibit 8.36 presents the condensed consolidated balance sheet of Marvel at the end of its June 30, 2009 second quarter.

Exhibit 8.36

Marvel Entertainment, Inc.
Condensed Consolidated Balance Sheets
(unaudited)
(in thousands, except per-share amounts)

	June 30 2009	December 31 2008
ASSETS		
Current assets:		
Cash and cash equivalents	$ 81,039	$ 105,335
Restricted cash	38,220	12,272
Short-term investments	—	32,975
Accounts receivable, net	29,471	144,487
Inventories, net	13,473	11,362
Income tax receivable	206	2,029
Deferred income taxes, net	25,497	34,072
Prepaid expenses and other current assets	9,164	5,135
Total current assets	$ 197,070	$ 347,667

(Continued)

Exhibit 8.36 (Continued)

Fixed assets, net	$ 4,194	$ 3,432
Film inventory, net	192,068	181,564
Goodwill	346,152	346,152
Accounts receivable, non-current portion	7,010	1,321
Income tax receivable, non-current portion	5,906	5,906
Deferred income taxes, net—non-current portion	17,046	13,032
Deferred financing costs	3,320	5,810
Restricted cash, non-current portion	42,274	31,375
Other assets	5,489	455
Total assets	$ 820,529	$ 936,714
LIABILITIES AND EQUITY		
Current liabilities:		
Accounts payable	$ 2,860	$ 2,025
Accrued royalties	89,912	76,580
Accrued expenses and other current liabilities	33,826	40,635
Deferred revenue	67,468	81,335
Film facility	—	204,800
Total current liabilities	$ 194,066	$ 405,375
Accrued royalties, non-current portion	806	10,499
Deferred revenue, non-current portion	93,696	48,939
Film facility, non-current portion	—	8,201
Income tax payable	66,522	59,267
Other liabilities	10,680	8,612
Total liabilities	$ 365,770	$ 540,893
Commitments and contingencies	—	—
Marvel Entertainment, Inc. stockholders' equity:		
Preferred stock, $.01 par value, 100,000,000 shares authorized, none issued	—	—
Common stock, $.01 par value, 250,000,000 shares authorized, 134,681,030 issued and 77,997,619 outstanding in 2009 and 134,397,258 issued and 78,408,082 outstanding in 2008	$ 1,347	$ 1,344
Additional paid-in capital	752,438	750,132
Retained earnings	628,628	555,125
Accumulated other comprehensive loss	(4,574)	(4,617)
Total Marvel Entertainment, Inc. stockholders' equity before treasury stock	$1,377,839	$1,301,984
Treasury stock, at cost, 56,683,411 shares in 2009 and 55,989,176 shares in 2008	(921,700)	(905,293)
Total Marvel Entertainment, Inc. stockholders' equity	$ 456,139	$ 396,691
Noncontrolling interest in consolidated Joint Venture	(1,380)	(870)
Total equity	$ 454,759	$ 395,821
Total liabilities and equity	$ 820,529	$ 936,714

Source: Marvel Entertainment, Inc., Quarterly Reports, June 30, 2009, and December 31, 2008.

REQUIRED

a. From a strategic perspective, discuss why you believe Disney would make this acquisition.

b. Assuming that the assets and liabilities of Marvel approximate their individual fair values at the date of acquisition, compute goodwill.

c. This is a 100% acquisition. What role does the 29% premium play in the computation of goodwill? If this were a less than 100% acquisition, how would the 29% premium affect the computation of the noncontrolling interest?

d. Disney will record a decrease in its cash and an increase in its shareholders' equity totaling $4 billion at the date of acquisition. Contrast the rest of the financial statement effects on Disney's own records and on its consolidated balance sheet between two scenarios: Marvel is dissolved (a merger) and Marvel continues to exist as a separate legal entity (an acquisition).

e. It is unlikely that the assets and liabilities of Marvel as shown in the condensed quarterly balance sheet approximate their individual fair values at the date of acquisition. Indeed, some of Marvel's most valuable resources might not be recognized on their balance sheet. As a result, the entire excess acquisition price is not likely to be assigned to goodwill. Identify items that are likely to receive a portion of the allocation based on the differences between their book values and fair values.

Operating Activities

LO 9-1 Discuss and apply the criteria for the recognition of *revenues* from operating activities, as well as the related assets, liabilities, and cash flows.

LO 9-2 Discuss and apply the criteria for the recognition of *expenses* from operating activities, as well as the related assets, liabilities, and cash flows.

LO 9-3 Use the financial statement and note information for corporate *income taxes* to analyze the firm's tax strategies.

LO 9-4 Identify the effects of *pensions and other postemployment benefits* on the financial statements.

LO 9-5 Explain how firms use *derivative instruments* to hedge currency and commodity risk from operating transactions.

Chapter Overview

The results of a firm's operating activities are reported in the operating income section of the income statement (on an accrual basis) and in the operating cash flows section of the statement of cash flows (on a cash basis). Also, the balance sheet reflects a number of working capital and longer-term assets and liabilities generated for or by operations. **PepsiCo**'s consolidated statement of income (Appendix A) reports operating profit for the year ended December 29, 2012, of $9,112 million. That amount is comprised of $65,492 million in net revenue minus $31,291 million in cost of sales; $24,970 million in selling, general, and administrative expense (often called SG&A); and $119 million amortization of intangible assets. After other income and expenses and the provision for income taxes of $2,090 million, PepsiCo reports net income for the fiscal year 2012 of $6,214 million.

PepsiCo's consolidated statement of cash flows (Appendix A) shows net cash provided by operating activities of $8,479 million for the year ended December 29, 2012, a measure of current-period operating success on a cash basis. Like most firms, PepsiCo uses the indirect method to derive cash flow from operations and thus begins the section with net income of $6,214 million. PepsiCo then adjusts for all of the non-cash income items (such as depreciation and amortization expenses) as well as cash flows triggered by changes in operating assets and liabilities (that is, working capital). The operating activities section prepared using the indirect method reconciles the two measures of operating results: accrual-basis net income and cash-basis cash flow from operations. Alternatively stated, the operating section 'undoes' the effects of accruals on reported net income to reveal the underlying cash flows.

Most of the assets and liabilities in PepsiCo's consolidated balance sheet are generated by or used in operations. Chapter 7 examined the liabilities generated by financing activities: short-term and long-term debt obligations. Chapter 8 examined the operating assets generated by investing activities: short-term investments; property, plant, and equipment; amortizable intangible assets; goodwill; other nonamortizable intangible assets; and investments in noncontrolled affiliates. This chapter examines the remainder of the assets and liabilities generated for or by operations: working capital assets (other than short-term investments) found in the current assets section; working capital liabilities (other than short-term debt obligations) found in the current liabilities section; income-tax-related liabilities, including income taxes payable and deferred income taxes; and pension-related and other postemployment-benefits-related liabilities.

We follow the organization of the income statement to explain operating activities. We begin the chapter with the important topic of revenue recognition and the related working capital items created by delayed receipt of cash (accounts receivable) and accelerated receipt of cash (deferred revenues). Then we examine the accounting and reporting for the major income statement expenses, including cost of sales (along with a consideration of the working capital items inventory and accounts payable), selling, general, and administrative (SG&A) expenses (including working capital accounts such as prepaid and accrued expenses), income tax expenses (and current and deferred taxes payable), and compensation expenses (including pensions and other postemployment benefits obligations). We conclude with the accounting for derivatives used to hedge the foreign currency and commodity risks associated with operating activities.

LO 9-1

Discuss and apply the criteria for the recognition of *revenues* from operating activities, as well as the related assets, liabilities, and cash flows.

Revenue Recognition

The income statement begins with a listing of revenues from sales and services. As discussed in Chapter 10, financial statement forecasting begins with a projection of future revenues, and many expense, asset, and liability forecasts are conditional on projected revenues. Therefore, understanding how and when firms recognize revenues is a crucial part of accounting analysis. The following sections discuss the current criteria for revenue recognition and practical application of the criteria. Financial statements through the end of 2014 (and possibly later) are based on current financial accounting and reporting standards. As of the writing of this text, a major joint IASB/FASB project on revenue recognition is nearing completion. The new standards outlined in this project will apply to financial statements *no earlier than* reporting periods beginning after January 1, 2015 (i.e., December 31, 2015, for firms having a calendar-year reporting period). The revenue recognition project's goal is a single set of standards to guide the kinds of revenue recognition decisions that we discuss in the following sections.

Criteria for Revenue Recognition

Revenue recognition is primarily a question of timing. One of the most important financial reporting decisions firms must make is *when* to recognize revenue. IFRS and U.S. GAAP criteria for revenue recognition are similar but not identical. Under U.S. GAAP (FASB-issued SFAC No. 5 guidance), revenue recognition occurs when a firm has done both of the following:

1. Provided all or a substantial portion of the product to be delivered or the services to be performed. The firm has completed what it needs to do to earn the revenue.
2. Received an asset (such as cash, a receivable that the firm is reasonably certain it will collect, or some other asset) or satisfied a liability (such as an advance from a customer or a deferred revenue) with a value the firm can measure with reasonable precision.[1]

---

[1]Financial Accounting Standards Board, *Statement of Financial Accounting Concepts No. 5*, "Recognition and Measurement in Financial Statements of Business Enterprises" (1984).

A typical firm recognizes revenue at the time of sale, when it delivers goods or services to customers. At this point, a firm has completed production of the goods or creation of the services and has delivered them to a customer, satisfying the first criterion. The benefit a firm obtains from providing goods or services is the cash, receivable, or other consideration that the firm expects to receive. If the customer promises to pay cash in the future, the firm examines the credit standing of the customer and assesses the likelihood of receiving the cash. The second criterion is satisfied so long as the firm can reasonably predict the amount of cash it will collect or can assess the value of the asset it has received or the value of the liability that has been satisfied.

The Securities and Exchange Commission (SEC) also considers revenue recognition to be critically important to accurate performance reporting and profit measurement. Accordingly, the SEC issued SAB 104, which outlines the following four conditions for revenue recognition:

1. There is pervasive evidence that an arrangement exists.
2. Delivery has occurred or services have been performed.
3. The seller's price to the buyer is fixed or determinable.
4. Collectibility is reasonably assured.[2]

Although worded differently, the SAB 104 criteria are only slightly more restrictive than the two criteria provided by the FASB *Statement of Financial Accounting Concepts No. 5*. The primary difference is the first criterion, the pervasive evidence that an arrangement exists. Evidence of such an arrangement includes a formal contract with a customer stating the buyer's and seller's responsibilities and risks, as well as terms and timing of cash flows. However, less formal relationships between buyer and seller that imply these conditions also may be judged as pervasive evidence, including prior business dealings and common business practices.

U.S. GAAP also has a substantial amount of industry- and transaction-specific guidance (for example, franchise, real estate, and motion picture revenue recognition) that is summarized in the FASB's Codification. On the other hand, IFRS guidance is nearly all general. With respect to the sale of goods, IFRS provides the following five criteria for revenue recognition:

1. The seller has transferred to the buyer the significant risks and rewards of ownership of the goods.
2. The seller has not retained either effective control or the kind of involvement that is associated with ownership.
3. The amount of revenue can be measured reliably.
4. It is probable that the seller will obtain the economic benefits associated with the transaction.
5. The costs incurred or to be incurred can be measured reliably.[3]

For service revenue, IFRS replaces the first two criteria with the criterion that the stage of completion of services can be measured reliably. Again, although worded differently, the IFRS criteria are consistent with U.S. GAAP, and revenue recognition is generally consistent under the two sets of standards. However, one must realize that even subtle differences in wording of U.S. GAAP compared with the IFRS's "principles-based approach" could lead to differences in revenue recognition. Consider, for example, the

---

[2]Securities and Exchange Commission, *Staff Accounting Bulletin No. 104, 17 CFR Part 211* (December 2003).

[3]International Accounting Standards Board, *International Accounting Standard 18,* "Revenue" (1993).

SEC's requirement that "the seller's price to the buyer is fixed or determinable" versus the IFRS's requirement that "the amount of revenue can be reasonably measured." Under the SEC's requirement, a sale involving contingent consideration (payments to the seller based on some future event) would not be recognized as revenue until the contingency is removed. Under IFRS, a high probability of contingency removal is considered reliable and revenue recognition can occur earlier.

The complexity and variety in commercial arrangements between sellers and customers in today's business environment has heightened the importance of understanding a firm's business model and its relation to the revenue recognition principles chosen for reporting. Businesses with sales that include future performance obligations, sales that involve a barter exchange of services between firms, and sales that bundle several products and services are just a few examples in which the selection and application of revenue recognition principles can have a dramatic effect on the amount and timing of reported revenue.

The notes to the financial statements identify the significant accounting policies employed for recognizing revenues. For example, **PepsiCo** discloses its revenue recognition policy in Note 2 to the financial statements, "Our Significant Accounting Policies—Revenue Recognition" (Appendix A), and in the first section of MD&A, "Our Critical Accounting Policies—Revenue Recognition" (Appendix B, which can be found online at the book's companion website at www.cengagebrain.com). PepsiCo recognizes revenue when it ships its products or delivers them to the customer. The straightforward revenue recognition policies are not surprising given the short-term nature of PepsiCo's products (food and beverages).

Application of Revenue Recognition Criteria

Applying the revenue recognition principles to actual business settings is not always as straightforward as it is for companies such as PepsiCo. To demonstrate the complexities often involved in applying these principles, consider the examples that follow.

- *Bundled deliverables in leases.* **Xerox Corporation** typically manufactures copiers and either sells them to customers or leases them to customers under multi-year leases. If Xerox sells a copier to a creditworthy customer, it recognizes revenue from the sale of the copier at the time of delivery. When Xerox leases copiers to customers, the length of the leases often approximates the useful life of the copiers. Thus, the arrangement is equivalent to a sale of the copier, with Xerox providing financing to the customer signing the lease. The accounting becomes complex, however, because the lease contract usually entails bundled monthly payments that cover not just use of the copier by the customer over the life of the lease, but also maintenance services, photocopying supplies (paper and toner cartridges) up to certain maximum usage, and financing costs. The revenue recognition question is *when* Xerox should recognize revenue from the four services covered in the lease: (1) copier use, (2) maintenance, (3) supplies, and (4) financing.

    When the transaction is *not* an outright sale, but rather a lease arrangement that involves a bundled periodic lease payment, Xerox must unbundle the monthly payment to ascertain the proportion of revenue related to each component of this bundled transaction. If the leasing arrangement is equivalent in economic substance to a sale, Xerox must determine (1) how much revenue the firm should recognize up front for manufacturing the copier and providing its use to the customer over its entire life and (2) how much the firm should allocate to the remaining three categories of the arrangement and recognize over time. In fact,

Xerox does make these allocations, but, in the past, the SEC accused Xerox of allocating too much of the monthly payment to the sale of the copiers and too little to maintenance, supplies, and financing. The result was an acceleration of revenues and earnings that authorities contended was too aggressive. Xerox accordingly restated its earnings.

- *Uncertain revenue timing.* Founded in 1810, the **Hartford Financial Services Group** is one of the largest investment and insurance companies in the United States. Hartford is a leading provider of (1) life insurance and group and employee benefits, (2) automobile and homeowners insurance, and (3) business insurance. Hartford's automobile insurance unit receives cash from both premiums and investments each period. It invests in readily marketable securities for the most part so it can measure objectively the changes in the market value of its investments. Measuring the amount of revenue each period while the automobile insurance policy is outstanding presents few difficulties because of the (generally) one-year policy coverage period. In contrast, Harford's life insurance revenue recognition timing is more complex. In a term policy (five years, for example), it makes sense to recognize revenue over the five-year period. In a whole life policy, premium recognition timing depends on the expected life of the policyholder. Further, straight-line revenue recognition over a whole life policy may not make sense because the probability of death increases over time. Another issue is whether firms like Hartford should recognize as revenue the interest and dividend income from investments as well as realized and unrealized gains and losses from changes in the market value of investments. Common practice in the insurance industry is to recognize interest and dividend income as well as realized and unrealized gains and losses on investments each year in computing net income.[4]

- *Bundled service deliverables.* **MicroStrategy, Inc.,** is a software and consulting firm in the information technology sector. The firm specializes in tailoring proprietary software to analyze large databases of clients. Clients often sign two- or three-year contracts with the firm that cover customizing the software to the specific needs of the client and then licensing (as opposed to selling) the use of the software for the length of the contract. The contracts often require MicroStrategy to train the client's personnel to use the software to mine large databases and to assist the client in designing reports and analyses based on this data mining. The contracts establish key deliverables, together with a schedule for the payment of fees over the life of the contract. Assuming reasonable assurance of the collectibility of fees from the client, the important revenue recognition issue is *when* MicroStrategy meets the substantial performance criterion for revenue recognition. The situation is complicated because MicroStrategy provides (1) a license to use its proprietary software tailored to the client's needs and (2) a consulting service to ensure that client personnel produce value-added reports and analyses. What proportion of the contract relates to the software, and what proportion relates to the consulting services? How precise are the deliverables requirements, which determine when MicroStrategy has completed the process to earn the revenue?

  In the past, MicroStrategy recognized approximately 50% of the amount of the total contract as revenue at the time the contract was signed. The firm

---

[4]Expense recognition is equally complicated for whole life contracts because the pattern of expense recognition requires actuarial calculations of expected life, investment returns, and similar factors. Life insurance companies increase a liability account each period, often called Policyholder Reserves, for the amount of expense recognized. They reduce this account when they pay insurance claims.

concluded that it had substantially performed about half of what it promised to the customer at the contract signing date. The SEC disagreed with this assessment, however, and concluded that 50% was far too aggressive and represented an inappropriate acceleration of revenue. MicroStrategy scaled back the amount of revenue it recognized at the contract signing date to approximately 10% and restated past financial statements. The news of the need to restate previously reported earnings led to a substantial drop in MicroStrategy's stock price.

■ *Gross versus net: Online advertising.* **AOL**, formerly the Internet services division of AOL Time Warner (it was spun off as a separate company in December 2009), generates subscription revenues from subscribers to its online services, as well as advertising revenues for advertisements it places on various websites. In the past, AOL entered into an advertising arrangement with **eBay**. Under the arrangement, AOL located firms that wanted to advertise on the eBay website. AOL sold the advertising space to various companies and remitted a portion of this amount to eBay. AOL bore no credit risk if the firms failed to pay for the advertising space. AOL guaranteed the sale of a minimum amount of advertising space each month. Failure to sell the minimum space required AOL to make payments to eBay. AOL booked the amount to be received from the various companies as revenues and the amount paid to eBay as an expense. In turn, eBay booked the net amount received from AOL as revenue.

The accounting issue for this revenue stream is whether AOL is a principal or an agent in purchasing and selling advertising space. The revenue recognition described above considers AOL a principal because it entails booking the full revenue and expense. However, U.S. GAAP requires a firm to assume substantial product risk if it is to be considered a principal, which would not characterize the AOL–eBay arrangement if AOL is highly likely to sell sufficient advertising space each month to cover the minimum obligation to eBay. AOL bears little risk of unsold advertising space. Thus, it serves as an agent, which requires that only the *net* amount be recognized as revenue. The net amount would be the amount collected from purchasers of advertising minus the amount AOL remits to eBay. The distinction is an important one because, although there is no effect on bottom-line net income, the magnitude of revenues reported as a principal is substantially higher than that reported as an agent. Revenues often are a driver for assessing firms, particularly technology and Internet firms such as AOL.

■ *Gross versus net: Online sales.* **Priceline.com**'s business model, allowing customers to "name their price" when booking hotel rooms, generates similar revenue recognition questions. Should Priceline recognize the price of the hotel room as revenue (a practice known as grossing up) and the cost of the hotel room charged by the hotel to Priceline as cost of goods sold? Or should Priceline record only the difference between the price and the hotel cost as its fee revenue? The latter approach is probably the better measure of Priceline's revenue because recording the full revenue and full cost assumes that Priceline consumed an asset (the right to stay in a hotel room for a night) that caused the expense, cost of goods sold. However, Priceline did not bear the risk of ownership of this asset. In fact, Priceline's only significant risk is its contention that it is "the merchant of record" in the transaction. The SEC does not permit the grossing up of revenue for agents, but controversy continues to surround revenue recognition in business models such as Priceline's.

■ *Gross versus net: Efficient inventory management.* Although the revenue-generating models of AOL and Priceline are unique, the grossing up of revenue also can be seen in more traditional situations where efficient inventory management practices exist. For example, if **Dell Inc.** receives an order and has its supplier ship inventory directly to the customer, as it often does, should Dell record the grossed-up revenue and associated cost of goods sold for the cost of the inventory that it has probably not even purchased at the time the customer's order was received? Should the French retailer **Carrefour** gross up revenues when it sells items on its floor that it does not purchase until the point of sale? If you want to compare ratios such as gross margin percentages across firms and forecast sales growth, you must read the notes to the financial statements carefully to understand the revenue recognition practices of firms and industries. Dell Inc. and Carrefour never bore risks of holding inventory because neither had title to the goods before the sale. However, both companies bear the risks of product performance and the risks of re-sale if the products are returned. They are the merchants of record and should probably not be treated as agents.

■ *Swaps of production capacity.* **Global Crossing**, **Qwest Communications**, and other telecommunications companies have created worldwide fiber-optics networks in past years. Companies in the industry typically enter into long-term leases for the use of the networks developed by other companies in the industry. For example, Global Crossing might create a fiber-optics network in India, Qwest Communications might create a similar network in China, and each in turn might lease part of the capacity of the networks to each other. The leases often give the lessee an indefeasible right of use to the capacity, essentially a legal transfer of title to the capacity. Each company books the "sale" of the legal rights to the capacity as revenue in the year it signs the leases. The company treats the "purchase" of the legal rights to the capacity as a capital expenditure, much like the purchase of a long-lived asset. The revenue recognition issue is whether these firms satisfy the revenue recognition criterion that requires receipt of an asset with a measurable cash-equivalent value when they swap legal rights to capacity. In contrast to the manufacture and sale of physical equipment, these situations simply involve the sale of legal rights to use capacity. If the capacity is already in place, the "manufacturing" activity is complete. As long as there are no significant restrictions on the ability of the buyer to use the capacity purchased, the purchaser of the capacity receives an asset: the right to use capacity of the other firm in the future. You must consider at least two other issues, however. First, is the seller of the capacity likely to exist for the full period of the contract and be in a position to provide the services? Financial difficulties that firms in the telecommunications industry experienced in recent years make this an important consideration. Second, how should the firms establish the value of the contract? Given that contracts often entail the swapping of promises to provide capacity in the future with no cash changing hands, it is difficult to determine their true value. The SEC decided that the capacity swap accounting inflated profits and assets for these telecommunication giants. Both firms were required to restate their balance sheets and income statements to remove the effects of the swap accounting profits.

The preceding examples illustrate the difficulty of applying general principles for recognizing revenues. You need to increase the usual degree of healthy skepticism when analyzing reported financial data when the activities of the firms or industries under scrutiny involve heightened levels of uncertainty or subjectivity. In recent years, the SEC has emphasized the importance of investors understanding revenue recognition practices and initiated a stepped-up enforcement of firms' providing clear and complete descriptions of their revenue recognition practices.

Revenue Recognition at the Time of Sale (Delivery)

For most firms, revenue recognition occurs at the point of product or service delivery. On the balance sheet, cash or accounts receivable increases for the amount of the sale. If returns are allowed and can be reliably estimated, the sales revenue and associated accounts receivable are reported net of the expected returns.[5] The recognition of revenue at the time of sale (delivery) is so common that you may neglect to assess whether this timing is appropriate for a particular firm. However, firms may attempt to increase reported earnings by accelerating the timing of revenues or estimating the collectible amounts too aggressively. Consider the following three conditions, each of which is a signal that revenue recognition at the time of sale may be too early: (1) large and volatile amounts of uncollectible accounts receivable, (2) unusually large amounts of returned goods, and (3) excessive warranty expenditures. Each of these conditions should bear a reasonably stable relation to revenues over time. Unusual year-to-year fluctuations should raise questions about the appropriateness of revenue recognition at the time of sale.

Recognizing revenues at the time of sale suffers from an even more fundamental problem at times: to accelerate revenue recognition, some firms may alter their definition of *sale*. Does the receipt of firm customer orders for goods held in inventory constitute a sale? Or does the sale depend on physical delivery of the product and transfer of legal title to the customer? Is completion of custom-produced goods sufficient to recognize revenue, or is physical delivery necessary? In an effort to achieve sales targets for a period, firms sometimes record sales earlier than physical delivery. Revenues must not be recognized until the earnings process is substantially complete, which would suggest that revenues should not be recognized until the firm has delivered control and legal title of the products to customers.

Some firms, eager to report higher sales revenues or sales revenue increases, might be inclined to violate revenue recognition rules by recording sales based merely on an indication of interest in a product by a customer. The pressure that sales personnel face can lead to such a violation of the revenue recognition criteria. A related earnings management strategy is to accelerate the shipment of product and the recognition of sales revenues to closely related customers (such as dealerships, franchisees, and affiliates) at the end of the year and then understate the likely sales returns by those customers (a practice known as channel-stuffing). Even more aggressive, some firms create artificial sales invoices and ship and store the goods in a remote or independently owned warehouse, hoping an independent auditor will not detect them.

Revenues are at the core of a firm's ability to generate and report profits and to grow and prosper. Firms that strive to achieve very aggressive sales growth objectives and firms experiencing declining sales growth relative to other firms in the industry are most likely to be tempted to manage earnings by stretching the revenue recognition rules. Although this type of earnings management eventually catches up with the firm, it is precisely in these situations that a firm's sustainable earnings are likely to be declining.

Delaying Revenue Recognition When Substantial Performance Remains

Cash is often collected from customers but the revenue recognition criteria have not been met, usually because the selling firm has not met some or all of its obligations to

---

[5]*FASB Codification Topic 605* provides explicit guidance. IFRS does not. If the amount of returns cannot be reliably estimated, revenue recognition is delayed until the return privilege expires.

the buyer. The earlier example of insurance premiums being paid in advance, with revenues being recognized over the life of the policy is a case in point. Many other examples exist in which customers pay in advance of receiving goods or services and revenue recognition must be delayed until the revenues have been earned. Delayed revenue recognition typically arises with sales of gift cards redeemable for products (at **Starbucks** or **Nordstrom**, for instance), subscriptions, airfares, and memberships. For example, **Sam's Club** (a division of **Walmart** that offers discount warehouse shopping) collects an annual membership fee and promises to let customers shop at Sam's Club stores for one year. When it sells an annual membership, Walmart records the increase in cash, but must delay revenue recognition until Sam's Club meets its obligation to members over time. Walmart records a liability (often called deferred revenue, unearned revenue, or advances from customers) for the full amount of the membership fee. Each month of the annual membership period, Walmart removes one-twelfth of the liability and recognizes one-twelfth of the fee as revenue. At year-end, the portion of the membership fee that has not yet been earned is reported as a liability on Walmart's balance sheet; it will be earned as revenue during the next fiscal year.

Software firms such as **MicroStrategy** and **Microsoft** bundle product and services. For example, Microsoft bundles Windows® software, telephone support, and future upgrades. U.S. GAAP and IFRS require the selling price to be allocated to the individual elements of the bundle based on their relative fair values.[6] Delivery of each item or performance of each service triggers revenue recognition equal to the fair value of the element in the bundle. Microsoft, for example, uses the straight-line method to recognize revenue on promised services in its software over the time period of the promise, reporting the remainder of the promised but undelivered service as "unearned revenues."

When analyzing liquidity, you should take into account that deferred or unearned revenue liabilities can sometimes be large, but they are not cash-settled obligations; they are settled with the performance of services. For Starbucks, for example, the deferred revenue liability at the end of 2012 was $510 million, or 23% of the company's total current liabilities. Starbucks satisfies this liability by delivering coffee to card-holding customers.

Income Recognition under Long-Term Contracts

This section describes methods that recognize income earlier than the completion of a long-term contract (a common practice among long-term contractors) or upon completion of a long-term contract (a common practice when firms face high uncertainty regarding the future costs of the long-term contract or the collectibility of cash).

The operating cycle for a long-term contractor (such as a commercial or industrial building contractor, an aerospace manufacturer, or a ship builder) differs from that of a typical manufacturing firm in three important respects:

- The period of construction (production) may span many accounting periods.
- Contractors identify customers and agree to build customized projects for the customers for a contract price and terms agreed upon in advance of construction (or at least in the early stages).
- Customers often make periodic payments of the contract price as work progresses.

The operating activities of long-term contractors often satisfy the criteria for the recognition of revenue during the period of construction and prior to completion.

---

[6]See FASB *Codification Topic 605* for guidance. IFRS guidance is less specific but similar in spirit.

The existence of a contract indicates that the contractor has identified a buyer and the contractor and buyer have agreed on the scope of the construction project and a price. The contractor collects cash in advance or concludes, based on an assessment of the customer's credit standing, that it will receive cash equal to the contract price after construction is complete. Although the contract may obligate the contractor to perform substantial future services, the contractor should be able to estimate the cost of these services with reasonable precision. In agreeing to a contract price, the contractor should have some confidence in the estimates of the total costs it will incur on the contract.

Percentage-of-Completion Method

Many long-term contractors meet the criteria for revenue recognition during the construction process, such as when they complete certain construction milestones and are entitled to invoice the customer for payments for partial completion. When contractors meet the criteria for revenue recognition as construction progresses, they can recognize revenue using the percentage-of-completion method. Under this method, contractors recognize a portion of the total contract price, based on the degree of completion of the work during the period, as revenue for the period. They base this proportion on engineers' or architects' estimates of the degree of completion or on the ratio of costs incurred to date to the total expected costs for the contract. The actual schedule of cash collections is *not* a determining factor in measuring the amount of revenue recognized each period under the percentage-of-completion method. Even if a contractor expects to collect the entire contract price at the completion of construction, it still uses the percentage-of-completion method as long as it can make reasonable estimates as construction progresses of the amount of cash it will collect and of the costs it will incur. As contractors recognize portions of the contract price as revenues, they recognize corresponding proportions of the total estimated costs of the contract as expenses.

To illustrate the percentage-of-completion method, assume that a firm agrees to construct a bridge for $5,000,000. Estimated costs are as follows: Year 1, $1,500,000; Year 2, $2,000,000; Year 3, $500,000. Thus, the expected gross margin from the contract is $1,000,000 ($5,000,000 − $1,500,000 − $2,000,000 − $500,000). The firm bills the customer (and collects) $2,000,000 in Year 1, $2,000,000 in Year 2, and $1,000,000 in Year 3. Assuming that the contractor bases the degree of completion on the percentage of total costs incurred to date and that it incurs actual costs as anticipated, revenues and expenses from the contract are as follows:

Year	Degree of Completion	Revenues	Expenses	Gross Margin
1	$1,500,000/$4,000,000 = 37.5%	$1,875,000	$1,500,000	$ 375,000
2	$2,000,000/$4,000,000 = 50.0%	2,500,000	2,000,000	500,000
3	$500,000/$4,000,000 = 12.5%	625,000	500,000	125,000
	Totals	$5,000,000	$4,000,000	$1,000,000

Notice that the cash amounts collected are not the amounts used for revenues. Rather, the income statement effect is to recognize pro rata revenues, expenses, and gross margins based on the degree of completion, thus providing a better measure of the operating success of the contractor each period during the contract. Exhibit 9.1 provides

Exhibit 9.1: Long-Term Construction Accounting

	Assets	=	Liabilities	+	Total Shareholders' Equity		
					CC	AOCI	RE
1.	*Year 1:* Cash −1,500,000 Contracts in Progress + 1,500,000						
	Contracts in Progress 1,500,000 Cash				1,500,000		

2.	Accounts
	  Receivable +2,000,000
	Accounts
	  Receivable −2,000,000
	Cash +2,000,000
			Progress Billings +2,000,000				

	Accounts Receivable 2,000,000
	  Progress Billings
	Cash 2,000,000
	  Accounts Receivable
					2,000,000
					
					2,000,000		

3.	Contracts
	  in Progress +375,000
							Contract
							  Revenue +1,875,000
							Contract
							  Expense −1,500,000

	Contracts in Progress 375,000 Contract Expense 1,500,000 Contract Revenue				1,875,000		
4.	*Year 2:* Cash −2,000,000 Contracts in Progress +2,000,000						
	Contracts in Progress 2,000,000 Cash				2,000,000		

5.	Accounts
	  Receivable +2,000,000
	Accounts
	  Receivable −2,000,000
	Cash +2,000,000
			Progress Billings +2,000,000				

	Accounts Receivable 2,000,000
	  Progress Billings
	Cash 2,000,000
	  Accounts Receivable
					2,000,000
					
					2,000,000		

6.	Contracts
	  in Progress + 500,000
							Contract
							  Revenue +2,500,000
							Contract
							  Expense −2,000,000

	Contracts in Progress 500,000 Contract Expense 2,000,000 Contract Revenue				2,500,000		
7.	*Year 3:* Cash −500,000 Contracts in Progress +500,000						
	Contracts in Progress 500,000 Cash				500,000		

8.	Accounts
	  Receivable +1,000,000
	Accounts
	  Receivable −1,000,000
	Cash +1,000,000
			Progress Billings +1,000,000				

	Accounts Receivable 1,000,000
	  Progress Billings
	Cash 1,000,000
	  Accounts Receivable
					1,000,000
					
					1,000,000		

(Continued)

Exhibit 9.1 (Continued)

9.	Contracts in Progress	+125,000						Contract Revenue	+625,000
								Contract Expense	−500,000

Contracts in Progress		125,000	
Contract Expense		500,000	
Contract Revenue			625,000

a more detailed look at the financial statement impacts of the following underlying transactions in this example:

Year 1

1. Incur $1,500,000 costs. (Assume that all costs are paid in cash.)
2. Bill customer for $2,000,000. Collect cash in full.
3. Recognize $1,875,000 of revenue and $1,500,000 of expenses using the percentage-of-completion method.

Year 2

4. Incur $2,000,000 costs. (Assume that all costs are paid in cash.)
5. Bill customer for $2,000,000. Collect cash in full.
6. Recognize $2,500,000 of revenue and $2,000,000 of expenses using the percentage-of-completion method.

Year 3

7. Incur $500,000 costs. (Assume that all costs are paid in cash.)
8. Bill customer for $1,000,000. Collect cash in full.
9. Recognize $625,000 of revenue and $500,000 of expenses using the percentage-of-completion method.

The two primary balance sheet accounts that are unique in the long-term contracts area are the liability account *Progress Billings* and the asset account *Contracts in Process*. Contractors report actual contract costs on the balance sheet in a Contracts in Process account (Transactions 1, 4, and 7), which is an asset that represents future economic benefits (the project being constructed). It is measured as the accumulated costs and gross margin on construction to date, which totals over the life of the contract to the contract price (gross margin added in Transactions 3, 6, and 9). When the contractor invoices the customer for progress payments, the contractor increases Accounts Receivable and an account called Progress Billings, which is a liability account (Transactions 2, 5, and 8). Progress billings is a liability because the customer is billed for promised work at the contract price and the contractor is obligated to deliver the asset under construction to the customer upon completion. The net amount of these two accounts (contracts in progress minus progress billings) is disclosed as a net obligation (if more has been billed than work performed) or as a net asset (if more work has been performed than billed). For example, at the end of Year 2, Contracts in Progress totals $4,375,000 ($1,500,000 + $375,000 + $2,000,000 + $500,000), and Progress Billings totals $4,000,000 ($2,000,000 + $2,000,000). Therefore, the Year 2 balance sheet reports contracts in progress in excess of billings of $375,000 as an asset. Upon completing the project at the end of Year 3, Contracts in Progress and Progress Billings will have equal balances and will be closed out.

Actual costs on contracts seldom coincide precisely with expectations. As new information on expected total costs becomes available, contractors must adjust reported income in current and future periods rather than retroactively restating income of prior periods. Assume that actual costs incurred in Year 2 for the contract were $2,200,000 instead of $2,000,000 and that total expected costs on the contract increase to $4,200,000. Revenue, expense, and gross margin from the contract are as follows:

Year	Cumulative Degree of Completion	Revenue	Expense	Margin
1	$1,500,000/$4,000,000 = 37.5%	$1,875,000	$1,500,000	$375,000
2	$3,700,000/$4,200,000 = 88.1%	2,530,000[a]	2,200,000	330,000
3	$4,200,000/$4,200,000 = 100.0%	595,000[b]	500,000	95,000
		$5,000,000	$4,200,000	$800,000

[a]$(0.881 \times \$5,000,000) - \$1,875,000 = \$2,530,000$
[b]$\$5,000,000 - \$1,875,000 - \$2,530,000 = \$595,000$

The unexpected costs are a *change in estimate*. Therefore, Year 2 revenue is cumulative revenue recognized to date based on the new estimate of costs minus past cumulative revenue recognition based on the old cost estimate.

If it appears that the contractor will ultimately realize a loss on completion of a contract, the contractor must recognize the loss in full as soon as it becomes evident. For example, if at the end of Year 2 the contractor expects to realize a loss of $200,000 on the total contract, it must recognize a loss of $575,000 in Year 2. The $575,000 amount offsets the income of $375,000 recognized in Year 1 plus a loss of $200,000 anticipated on the overall contract.

Completed-Contract Method

Under U.S. GAAP, when the contract price, costs, or degree of completion are not reasonably estimable, long-term contractors postpone the recognition of revenue until they complete the construction project. Such firms use the completed-contract method of recognizing revenue. If the firm in our original example had used the completed-contract method, it would have recognized no revenue or expense from the contract during Year 1 or Year 2. It would recognize contract revenue of $5,000,000 and contract expenses of $4,000,000 in Year 3. Note that total gross margin is $1,000,000 under both the percentage-of-completion and completed-contract methods, equal to cash inflows of $5,000,000 minus cash outflows of $4,000,000. However, if the contractor anticipates a loss on a contract, it recognizes the loss as soon as the loss becomes evident, even if the contract is incomplete.

IFRS does not permit the use of the completed-contract method if the percentage-of-completion method cannot be used for the reasons given above. Instead, firms must use the cost-recovery method, which we illustrate in a subsequent section.

Choice of Reporting Method by Long-Term Contractors

A contractor should not use the percentage-of-completion method when there is substantial uncertainty regarding the total costs it will incur to complete the project. If the contractor cannot estimate the total costs, it cannot estimate the percentage of total costs incurred as of a given date and thereby the percentage of services already rendered and the amount of revenue that can be recognized. It also will be unable to estimate the total income from the contract prior to its completion.

In some cases, contractors use the completed-contract method because the contracts are of such short duration (such as a few months) that earnings reported with the percentage-of-completion and the completed-contract methods are not significantly different. In these cases, the lower costs of implementing the completed-contract method justify its use. Contractors also use the completed-contract method when they have not obtained a specific buyer during the construction phase, as is sometimes the case in the construction of residential housing. These cases require future selling efforts. Substantial uncertainty may exist regarding the ultimate contract price and the amount of cash that the contractor will receive.

Not surprisingly, contractors must use the percentage-of-completion method for income tax purposes. Although most firms would prefer to use the completed-contract method for tax purposes, thereby delaying the recognition of income and payment of income taxes, the Internal Revenue Code does not permit this method.

The preceding examples illustrate the dramatic level of estimation and uncertainty involved with income recognition for long-term contractors. Sometimes a project can take a number of years to complete. In some cases, contractors work with hundreds of subcontractors. Renegotiating contracts several times during the course of a large contract is commonplace. Analysts estimating persistent earnings using historical data for firms that construct and sell long-term projects must consider these and other firm factors, including the volume of projects currently under way, the success in completing projects on time and within budget, the length of typical projects, the types of projects undertaken, and the nature of the customer (if that information is available). Long-term construction firms usually address many of these factors in the analysis of operations found in the annual report and Form 10-K filing. Because (1) the time period between cash inflows and outflows for these firms is so long and (2) a large degree of estimation is needed to measure revenues and expenses, the potential for earnings management is high. When evaluating firms in the construction, aircraft, and defense-related industries, for example, you must be particularly sensitive to this fact.

Revenue Recognition When Cash Collectibility Is Uncertain

In many cases, the seller has completed delivery of the product or service to the customer but allows the customer to pay over a long period of time. Determining a reliable estimate of the amount of cash the firm will ultimately receive from customers can be difficult. This may occur because the future financial condition of the customer is highly uncertain or because the customer may have the right to return the items purchased, thereby avoiding the obligation to make cash payments. This uncertainty regarding future cash inflows may prevent the selling firm from measuring (at the time of sale) the present value of the cash it expects to receive, thereby failing to fulfill the second criterion for revenue recognition: being able to reliably measure the value of the asset received in a revenue transaction.

Given the difficulty in estimating cash inflows in these situations, the opportunity to manage earnings may cloud management's best intentions to measure earnings accurately. The uncertainty of future cash flows also affects assessments of earnings persistence. As an example, in hindsight, it is now very clear that the future cash collections associated with homes that were sold and financed with subprime mortgages in the mid-2000s were far more uncertain and riskier than expected.

When future cash collections are uncertain and cannot be reliably estimated, the firm must delay revenue recognition and recognize revenue only at the time it collects cash using either the installment method or the cost-recovery method. The installment and cost-recovery methods exist as prudent and conservative approaches to the problem of revenue recognition when cash collection is uncertain. Your task is twofold: (1) understand the installment and cost-recovery method accounting and (2) judge whether a firm recognizing revenue using the time-of-sale method should be using one of these more conservative methods because the level of cash inflow uncertainty is high. We address these tasks next.

Installment Method

Under the installment method, a firm recognizes revenue as it collects portions of the selling price in cash. At the same time, it recognizes proportionate amounts of the cost of the goods or services sold as an expense. For example, assume that a firm makes a $100 sale of merchandise costing $60. The buyer agrees to pay (ignoring interest) $20 each month for five months. The firm recognizes revenue of $20 each month as it receives cash. Likewise, it recognizes cost of goods sold of $12 ($20/$100 × $60) each month. By the end of five months, the firm recognizes total income of $40 [5 × ($20 − $12)].

Land development companies, which typically sell undeveloped land and promise to develop it over several future years, sometimes use the installment method. The buyer makes a nominal down payment and agrees to pay the remainder of the purchase price in installments over 10, 20, or more years. In these cases, future development of the land is a significant aspect of the earnings process. Also, substantial uncertainty often exists as to the ultimate collectibility of the installment notes, particularly those not due until many years in the future. The customer can always elect to stop making payments, losing the right to own the land.

Cost-Recovery Method

When firms experience substantial uncertainty about cash collection (or if they are under IFRS and cannot use the percentage-of-completion method), they can use the cost-recovery method of income recognition, which is a very conservative method of income recognition up until the point of cost recovery, after which it becomes an anti-conservative, or aggressive, method of income recognition. The cost-recovery method matches the costs of generating revenues dollar for dollar with cash receipts until the firm recovers all such costs. The firm will not recognize revenue until it receives cash, and then it will recognize matching amounts of expenses in each period until full cost recovery occurs. Only when cumulative cash receipts exceed total costs will a firm begin to show profit on the income statement. Once full cost recovery occurs, the firm will recognize further cash receipts from the customer as revenues, with no further costs to match with those revenues.

To illustrate the cost-recovery method, refer to the previous example relating to the sale of merchandise for $100. During each of the first three months, the firm would recognize revenue of $20 and expense of $20. By the end of the third month, the total costs have been recovered because cumulative cash receipts of $60 exactly equal the cost of the merchandise sold. During the fourth and fifth months, the firm would recognize revenue of $20 each month, but without an offsetting expense. For the five months as a whole, total income is again $40 (equal to cash inflow of $100 minus cash outflow of $60) but the income recognition pattern differs from that of the installment method.

Comprehensive Illustration of Income Recognition Methods for Installment Sales

Technor Computer Corporation (TCC) sold a computer costing $16,000,000 to the city of Boston for $20,000,000 on January 1, Year 1. The city of Boston agreed to make five annual payments of $5,548,195 on December 31, Year 1, to December 31, Year 5. Panel A of Exhibit 9.2 shows an amortization table for the note receivable underlying this transaction. The five payments of $5,548,195 each when discounted at 12% have a present value equal to the $20,000,000 selling price. Thus, 12% is the interest rate implicit in the note. TCC recognizes interest revenue using the effective interest method illustrated in Chapter 7.

In addition to interest revenue on the note, TCC recognizes gross margin on the sale. Panel B shows the revenue, expense, and gross margin under three income recognition methods. The time-of-sale method rests on the premise of a high probability that the city of Boston will pay the amounts due on the note. Receiving immediate recognition are $20,000,000 revenue, $16,000,000 costs, and $4,000,000 gross margin.

If substantial uncertainty exists regarding cash collectibility of the notes, TCC should use the installment method or the cost-recovery method. The installment method recognizes revenues equal to collections of the $20,000,000 principal amount of the note as shown in Panel A (that is, the portion of each cash payment made by the city that does not represent interest). Each year's expense is 80% ($16,000,000/ $20,000,000) of the revenue recognized. Under the cost-recovery method, TCC recognizes no income until Year 5, when cumulative cash receipts exceed the $16,000,000 cost of manufacturing the computer.

Note that at the end of five years, cumulative gross margin is identical for all three income recognition methods. Only the *timing* of revenue and income recognition differs. The timing is driven by when the note receivable collection has reached a sufficiently high probability of collection.

Investment in Working Capital: Accounts Receivable and Deferred Revenues

Revenues typically generate cash inflows, but they are not necessarily equal in a given period. From the examples given previously in this chapter, it is clear that cash inflows often occur after revenue is recognized, resulting in a working capital asset, accounts receivable, or before revenue is recognized, resulting in a working capital liability, deferred revenues (also called unearned revenues or advances from customers). Cash flows from operations are delayed with accounts receivable but are accelerated with deferred revenues.

PepsiCo reports $7,041 million in accounts and notes receivable at December 29, 2012, on its consolidated balance sheet, which is 9.4% of its total assets. Note 14, "Supplemental Financial Information" (Appendix A), indicates that the majority of the receivables are "trade receivables," which means that they have been generated by sales. Note 14 also describes the composition of current liabilities but shows no separate amount for deferred revenues. Given PepsiCo's operating model, it is unlikely that cash is received before revenue is recorded. Accordingly, PepsiCo's 2012 consolidated statement of cash flows shows a $250 million deduction for an increase in accounts and notes receivable when reconciling net income to cash flows from operations.

Exhibit 9.2

Illustration of Income Recognition Methods from Installment Sales

Panel A: Amortization Schedule for Note Receivable

Year	Note Receivable, January 1	Interest Revenue at 12%	Cash Payment Received	Repayment of Principal	Note Receivable, December 31
1	$20,000,000	$2,400,000	$ 5,548,195	$ 3,148,195	$16,851,805
2	16,851,805	2,022,217	5,548,195	3,525,978	13,325,827
3	13,325,827	1,599,099	5,548,195	3,949,096	9,376,731
4	9,376,731	1,125,208	5,548,195	4,422,987	4,953,744
5	4,953,744	594,451	5,548,195	4,953,744	0
Total		$7,740,975	$27,740,975	$20,000,000	

Panel B: Income Recognition from Sale of Computer

Year	Time-of-Sale Method			Installment Method			Cost-Recovery Method		
	Revenue	Expense	Gross Margin	Revenue	Expense	Gross Margin	Revenue	Expense	Gross Margin
1	$20,000,000	$16,000,000	$4,000,000	$ 3,148,195	$ 2,518,556	$ 629,639	$ 3,148,195	$ 3,148,195	$ 0
2	0	0	0	3,525,978	2,820,782	705,196	3,525,978	3,525,978	0
3	0	0	0	3,949,096	3,159,277	789,819	3,949,096	3,949,096	0
4	0	0	0	4,422,987	3,538,390	884,597	4,422,987	4,422,987	0
5	0	0	0	4,953,744	3,962,995	990,749	4,953,744	953,744	4,000,000
Total	$20,000,000	$16,000,000	$4,000,000	$20,000,000	$16,000,000	$4,000,000	$20,000,000	$16,000,000	$4,000,000

In contrast, retail coffee and fast-food franchisers typically have both receivables and deferred revenues. **TCBY Enterprises Inc.**, for example, has point-of-sale revenues (retail sales of yogurt and ice cream products), receivables (royalties from licensees and product sales to affiliates), and deferred revenues (gift cards and up-front license payments from licensees).

The IASB and FASB's Revenue Recognition Project

As mentioned at the beginning of this chapter, the FASB and IASB are nearing completion of a joint project on revenue recognition. The core principle of the proposed new revenue guidance is as follows: "An entity should recognize revenue to depict the transfer of promised goods or services to customers in an amount that reflects the consideration to which the entity expects to be entitled in exchange for those goods or services."[7] In addition to the typical transfer of goods or services, the proposed guidance applies to the sale of nonfinancial assets, such as property, plant, and equipment and intangible assets, but it does not apply to leases, insurance, financial instruments, or certain nonmonetary exchanges. Entities will apply the finalized new standard retrospectively, and it will likely cause a restatement of prior years' earnings.

To apply the core principle, five steps are required:

1. *Identify the contract with a customer.* The contract can be oral, written, or simply implied by an entity's customary business practices as long as it creates enforceable rights and obligations. This may require a considerable amount of judgment to determine the entity's contracts with customers, especially when the firm's sales arrangements are complex, such as when the "customers" are collaborators and partners.

2. *Identify the separate performance obligations in the contract.* This is a significant part of the new guidance, which requires a firm to identify whether a given good or service is "distinct," and thus accounted for separately, or indistinct, and thus combined with other promised goods or services until the firm is able to identify a bundle of goods or services that is distinct. A good or service is distinct if either of the following criteria is met:
   - The entity regularly sells the good or service separately.
   - The customer can benefit from the good or service either on its own or together with other resources that are readily available to the customer.

   A good or service is not considered distinct if it is part of an interrelated bundle that the entity has combined and modified or customized for the customer to fulfill the contract. It is not difficult to imagine that two companies in the same industry might interpret these requirements differently and thus recognize revenues differently.

3. *Determine the transaction price.* When determining the transaction price, an entity would consider the effects of all of the following:
   - If payment from the customer is variable (rather than fixed), the expected (i.e., probability-weighted) or most likely (i.e., outcome with the highest probability) variable consideration amount, depending on which one it expects to

---

[7]*Revenue from Contracts with Customers: Proposed Accounting Standards Update (Revised)*, Financial Accounting Standards Board, January 4, 2012. This section draws heavily from the structure and language of the exposure draft summary.

better predict the amount of consideration. This guidance will require a great deal of judgment. In addition, it is likely that firms will have to defend their experience with a particular contingency that determines variable consideration outcomes.

- The time value of money if the contract has a significant financing component (only if contract completion will be beyond one year).
- Non-cash consideration, either directly measured at fair value or, if not reasonably estimated, indirectly measured by reference to the standalone selling price of the goods or services promised to the customer in exchange for the consideration.
- Consideration payable to the customer, which should be treated as a reduction of the transaction price unless the payment is in exchange for a distinct good or service.

Customer credit risk (that is, collectibility) is not to be considered when determining the transaction price. Firms are to follow current standards to recognize bad debt expense, but in a departure from current practice, it will be reported as a separate line item immediately following the revenue line item. Deducting bad debt expense from revenue will redefine the gross profit margin.

4. *Allocate the transaction price to the separate performance obligations in the contract.* After observing the standalone selling price of each separate performance obligation, or estimating it if it is not observable, the firm should allocate the transaction price on a relative standalone selling price basis.

5. *Recognize revenue when (or as) the entity satisfies a performance obligation.* Satisfaction occurs when (or as) the customer obtains control of the good or service. Firms must estimate whether performance obligations are satisfied by transferring control of a good or service *over time*. If not, then the performance obligation is satisfied *at a point in time*. The FASB's proposal outlines a number of criteria for determining when performance obligations are satisfied over time, such as when the entity's performance creates or enhances an asset that the customer controls. If the performance is satisfied over time, revenue is measured by the progress toward complete satisfaction of that performance obligation either using output or input methods. For example, the progress on road construction could be measured by considering the miles of pavement installed (an output measure) or cost incurred to date to install the pavement (an input measure). If the performance is at a point in time, revenue recognition is based on indicators of the transfer of control that include the following:

- The entity has a present right to payment for the asset.
- The customer has legal title to the asset.
- The entity has transferred physical possession of the asset.
- The customer has the significant risks and rewards of ownership of the asset.
- The customer has accepted the asset.

The above is a summary of the thought process involved under the new proposed guidance. The proposed guidance includes implementation guidance on specified topics (for example, repurchase agreements, consignment arrangements, and bill-and-hold arrangements) to help an entity determine when control of a promised good or service is transferred to a customer and guidance on how and when to recognize onerous performance obligations and the costs of acquiring sales contracts.

There are two clear general implications of the new guidance. First and foremost, the standard improves revenue recognition under both U.S. GAAP and IFRS, and it more closely aligns the two sets of standards. U.S. GAAP has many bright line rules for revenue recognition in different business models. The proposed guidance is a judgment-based unified standard that would replace the majority of these bright line rules. Second, the volume of disclosures will increase significantly. The proposed guidance will require disclosures about the contracts, the basis for judgments about the performance obligations and their satisfaction, and many other related items.

LO 9-2

Discuss and apply the criteria for the recognition of *expenses* from operating activities, as well as the related assets, liabilities, and cash flows.

Expense Recognition

When engaging in operating activities, firms consume assets and incur liabilities and, thus, incur operating expenses. The next several sections discuss the general criteria for expense recognition and apply the criteria to explain how firms recognize the various operating expenses reported on the income statement.

Criteria for Expense Recognition

Both U.S. GAAP and IFRS require the recognition of expenses under the accrual basis of accounting as follows:

1. Costs *directly* associated with revenues must be recognized as expenses in the period when a firm recognizes the revenues.
2. Costs *not directly* associated with revenues must be recognized as expenses in the period when a firm consumes the services or benefits of the costs in operations.

Most of the costs of manufacturing can be directly linked or reliably allocated to particular products. When the products are sold, the firm recognizes revenue and these directly linked expenses, referred to as *product* costs. Other costs (rent, insurance and property taxes, salaries of corporate officers and staff, and depreciation and amortization on tangible and intangible assets that are not part of the manufacturing process) are related to doing business in a particular period and bear only an indirect relation to revenues generated during the period. Such costs become expenses in the period in which the firm consumes the benefits of these types of services. Accountants refer to such costs as *period* costs.

Because a large proportion of the expenses that firms report on the income statement associate directly with revenue recognized and because another large proportion of the expenses relate to doing business during the reporting period, income statements provide generally reliable assessments of firms' economic performance each period. However, certain period expenses are more susceptible to management control than others. Expenditures that are somewhat discretionary and reported on the income statement as period costs are prime candidates for managing earnings. You should carefully monitor bad debts expense, advertising, R&D, and maintenance expenditures, as examples, to discern whether substantive reasons exist for changes in the levels of these expenditures (especially relative to sales) or whether the changes are intended to manage earnings. For example, if a firm's earnings in a period just barely meet or beat the consensus analyst forecast and discretionary expenses suddenly decrease for no apparent reason, managers might be cutting these expenses to meet or beat that period's earnings target.

Similar to revenue recognition, firms must identify in notes to the financial statements the significant policies employed for recognizing expenses. For example, refer to **PepsiCo**'s Note 2 to the consolidated financial statements (Appendix A). PepsiCo describes its accounting policies for sales incentives and other marketplace spending, distribution costs, software costs, commitments and contingencies, R&D, and other expenses.

Cost of Sales

For most retail and manufacturing firms, cost of sales represents the single largest expense reported on the income statement. Retailers accumulate the net costs of inventory purchases (invoice cost minus purchase discounts and purchase returns plus freight costs paid by the purchaser) in the inventory account. Manufacturers accumulate the same costs in raw materials inventory. Then as the raw materials are used in production, the raw materials costs are assigned to work-in-process inventory along with production-related labor, supplies, and overhead costs (including depreciation on production-related property, plant, and equipment). As products are finished, the costs are transferred to finished goods inventory. Finally, as products are sold, inventory costs are reported as cost of goods sold.

Firms selling relatively high dollar value items such as automobiles, airplanes, and real estate can ascertain from the accounting records the specific cost of each item sold. They recognize revenue when each item is sold and then recognize the specific cost of each item sold as cost of goods sold.

In most cases, however, firms cannot identify the cost of the specific items sold. Sometimes inventory items are so similar and their unit costs so small that firms cannot justify economically the cost of designing an accounting system to keep track of specific unit costs. To measure cost of goods sold in these cases, firms must make some assumption about the flow of costs. Three cost-flow assumptions exist:

- Weighted average
- First-in, first-out (FIFO)
- Last-in, first-out (LIFO)

Note that these assumptions about cost flows and do not necessarily reflect the physical flow of units. For example, a grocery store could use either method to account for its milk inventory, even though they would certainly sell the oldest milk first. Also note that many firms use a combination of cost-flow assumptions for different items of inventory in different subsidiaries or business segments or in different countries.

With the introduction of cost-flow assumptions into the reporting system, however, comes the possibility of earnings management and varying degrees of earnings quality. Analyzing earnings quality in the context of inventory accounting requires understanding the implications of the reporting options available to management.

Weighted Average

The weighted-average cost-flow assumption simply determines the weighted-average cost of all inventory units available for sale during the period (units in beginning inventory plus units purchased), then it assigns that cost to each unit sold and to each unit in ending inventory. When inventory turns over rapidly, purchases during the current period receive a heavy weight in the weighted-average unit cost.

FIFO

FIFO assigns the cost of the earliest purchases to the units sold and the cost of the most recent purchases to ending inventory. FIFO results in a balance sheet amount for ending inventory that is closest to current replacement cost. The cost of goods sold can be somewhat out of date, however, because FIFO recognizes costs of goods sold based on the costs of beginning inventory and the earliest purchases during the year. When inventory costs are rising, FIFO leads to the highest reported net income (lowest cost of goods sold) and the highest balance sheet value for inventory of the three methods, and when inventory costs fall, FIFO leads to the smallest net income and the lowest balance sheet value of inventory.

LIFO

LIFO assigns the cost of the most recent purchases to the cost of goods sold and the earliest purchases to inventory. LIFO results in amounts for cost of goods sold that closely approximate current replacement costs. Balance sheet amounts, however, can contain the cost of inventory acquisitions made many years previously. During periods of rising inventory costs, LIFO generally results in the highest cost of goods sold and the lowest net income of the three cost-flow assumptions. For this reason, firms usually prefer LIFO for income tax purposes. If a firm chooses a LIFO cost-flow assumption for tax purposes, the income tax law requires the firm to use LIFO for financial reporting to shareholders. IFRS does not permit the use of LIFO.

LIFO Liquidation

One exception to the generalization that LIFO produces the lowest net income during periods of rising prices occurs when a firm sells more units during a period than it purchases (referred to as a *LIFO layer liquidation*). In this case, LIFO assigns the cost of all current period purchases plus the costs assigned to the liquidated LIFO layers to the cost of goods sold. During periods of rising prices, the liquidated layers of LIFO inventory may be at much lower costs than current costs, which can cause costs of goods sold to be relatively low and net income to be relatively high. When firms experience LIFO liquidations, two cash flow effects likely occur. First, firms have delayed purchasing inventory items, thereby delaying a cash outflow. Second, firms increase taxable income and the required cash outflow for taxes. In Note 7, "Inventory," to its December 31, 2008 consolidated financial statements, **General Motors Corporation** (GM) reported a LIFO reserve of $1,233 million. GM also reported a LIFO layer liquidation as follows:

> In 2008 and 2007, U.S. LIFO eligible inventory quantities were reduced. This reduction resulting in a liquidation of LIFO inventory quantities carried at lower costs prevailing in prior years as compared with the cost of 2008 and 2007 purchases, the effect of which decreased automotive cost of sales by approximately $355 million and $100 million in 2008 and 2007, respectively.

If GM's LIFO layer liquidation is a transitory event, then GM's current period profits are not indicative of future earnings.

Characteristics of LIFO Adopters

Researchers have examined the characteristics of firms that do and do not adopt LIFO. Although these research studies do not always show consistent results, the following factors appear related to the decision to adopt LIFO:[8]

---

[8]For a review of these studies, see Frederick W. Lindahl, "Dynamic Analysis of Inventory Accounting Choice," *Journal of Accounting Research* (Autumn 1989), pp. 201–226, and Nicholas Dopuch and Morton Pincus, "Evidence on the Choice of Inventory Accounting Methods: LIFO versus FIFO," *Journal of Accounting Research* (Spring 1988), pp. 28–59.

Firms Following U.S. GAAP. IFRS does not permit the use of LIFO, but U.S. and non-U.S. domiciled firms that follow U.S. GAAP for consolidated reporting are permitted to use LIFO. Some of these firms have subsidiaries that are domiciled in countries that follow IFRS, so they may be prohibited from using LIFO for the inventory of those subsidiaries even though they use LIFO for inventory in the subsidiaries in U.S. GAAP jurisdictions.

Direction and Rate of Factor Price Changes for Inventory Items. Firms experiencing rapidly increasing factor prices for raw materials, labor, or other product costs obtain greater tax benefits from LIFO than firms that experience smaller factor price increases or that experience price decreases. Although adopting LIFO implies future tax savings (good news), it also implies higher expected future factor prices for inventory (bad news).

Variability in the Rate of Inventory Growth. LIFO adopters show more variable rates of inventory growth before adopting LIFO than do firms that remain on FIFO. The variability of inventory growth declines after LIFO is adopted. Because LIFO tends to match more recent inventory costs with sales than does FIFO or weighted average (these methods sometimes use costs that are 6–15 months old relative to current replacement costs), LIFO tends to result in less variability in the gross margin percentage over the business cycle. Firms with variable rates of inventory growth (perhaps because of cyclicality in their industry) can more easily accomplish an income-smoothing reporting objective using LIFO than if they use FIFO or average cost. Income smoothing is achieved by creating additional LIFO layers to match against sales through additional end-of-period purchases.

Tax Savings Opportunities. LIFO adopters tend to adopt LIFO to provide future tax savings. LIFO adopters also realize larger tax savings in the year of adoption than in the surrounding years, suggesting that the decision is in part motivated by tax rather than financial reporting considerations.

Industry Membership. Firms in certain industries are more likely to adopt LIFO. Because firms in a particular industry face similar factor price changes and variability in their inventory growth rates, those firms are likely to make similar choices of cost-flow assumptions.

Asset Size. Larger firms are more likely to adopt LIFO than are smaller firms. LIFO increases record-keeping costs relative to FIFO, both in the year of adoption and in subsequent years. To absorb the adoption and ongoing record-keeping costs of LIFO, larger firms realize larger amounts of tax savings than do smaller firms.

One hypothesis examined in this research is the relation between LIFO adoption and managerial compensation. Because LIFO usually results in lower earnings, managerial compensation of LIFO adopters would likely be less than compensation of non-LIFO adopters or include a lower component of compensation based on earnings. Studies have found no difference in managerial compensation of LIFO and non-LIFO adopters, although adopters had a smaller earnings component to their compensation.

Conversion from LIFO to FIFO

If a firm reports current costs on the income statement under LIFO, its balance sheet amount for ending inventory might contain some very old costs relative to FIFO that is an approximation of "current cost" inventory. If LIFO inventory valuation results in low out-of-date inventory values, the balance sheet amounts for inventory reflect poor accounting information quality and provide potentially misleading information to users of financial statements (although costs of goods sold under LIFO may more closely reflect replacement cost and reflect high accounting quality). The SEC requires firms using LIFO to disclose in notes to the financial statements the amounts by which LIFO inventories differ from the amounts the firm would recognize for inventories under FIFO. Analysts sometimes refer to the difference in ending inventory valuation between LIFO and FIFO as the *LIFO reserve.* From this disclosure, it is possible to restate a LIFO firm's income and inventory to a FIFO basis. In this way, you can place firms using LIFO on a basis more comparable to that of firms using FIFO.

PepsiCo reports inventories on the balance sheet (Appendix A) of $3,581 million and $3,872 million at the end of 2012 and 2011, respectively. Note 14, "Supplemental Financial Information" (Appendix A), indicates that PepsiCo uses LIFO for only 3% of its inventories and costs of goods sold. The firm indicates that the differences between the FIFO and LIFO methods for valuing inventories are immaterial for both 2012 and 2011.

Firms with long inventory holding periods often have significant LIFO reserves. **Nucor Corporation**, a primarily North American steel manufacturer, was incorporated in 1958. Exhibit 9.3 shows selected annual report data from Nucor's December 31, 2012, Form 10-K. Nucor uses the LIFO inventory method for much of its inventory.

To convert Nucor Corporation to FIFO, we use balance sheet amounts based on LIFO for beginning and ending inventory and the income statement amount for cost of sales to infer purchases during the period. Then, to convert the beginning inventory, ending inventory, and cost of sales to the FIFO basis, we use the information from the financial statement note that provides the amount by which beginning and ending inventories would be larger under FIFO. The notes to Nucor's financial statements

Exhibit 9.3

Nucor Corporation
Selected Financial Statement Information
(amounts in thousands)

Balance Sheet	December 31, 2012	December 31, 2011
Inventories	$2,323,641	$1,987,257
Current assets (including inventory)	5,661,364	6,708,081
Current liabilities	2,029,568	2,396,059

Income Statement	2012	
Sales	$19,429,273	
Cost of sales	17,915,735	
Gross margin	1,513,538	
Net income	504,619	

indicate that the FIFO basis beginning and ending inventories are $607,200 thousand and $763,200 thousand higher, respectively, than the amounts reported on the balance sheets under LIFO. The conversion to FIFO is as follows:

(amounts in thousands)	LIFO Basis (as Reported)	Adjustments	FIFO Basis
Sales (*a*)	$19,429,273		$19,429,273
Beginning inventory	$ 1,987,257	$ 763,200	$ 2,750,457
Purchases	18,252,119		18,252,119
Goods available for sale	$20,239,376		$21,002,576
Ending inventory	(2,323,641)	(607,200)	(2,930,841)
Cost of sales	$17,915,735	$(156,000)	$18,071,735
Gross margin (*b*)	$ 1,513,538		$ 1,357,538

In periods of rising input prices, FIFO yields a higher cost of sales and therefore a lower gross margin percentage (*b*/*a*):

$$\text{Gross margin percentage as reported under LIFO} = 7.79\%$$
$$\text{Gross margin percentage on a FIFO basis} = 6.99\%$$

Net income (as reported under LIFO) is $504,619 thousand. To adjust net income to a FIFO basis, deduct the increase in cost of sales times one minus the tax rate to obtain a $101,400 thousand decrease in net income [−$156,000 × (1 − 0.35)], which is 20% of reported net income. Adjusted net income would therefore have been $403,219 thousand if Nucor had used FIFO.

The calculation of the inventory turnover ratio (cost of sales/average inventory), a measure that indicates the efficiency with which a firm manages its inventory, is as follows:

$$\text{As reported under LIFO: } \$17,915,735/[0.5 \times (\$1,987,257 + \$2,323,641)] = 8.31$$
$$\text{On a FIFO basis: } \$18,071,735/[0.5 \times (\$2,750,457 + \$2,930,841)] = 6.36$$

The dramatic difference in the inventory turnover ratio under LIFO and FIFO reflects the many years that have elapsed since Nucor adopted LIFO. The current (FIFO) cost of its inventory is much larger than its book (LIFO) value. The inventory turnover ratio based on LIFO amounts gives a poor indication of the actual turnover of inventory items because it divides a cost of goods sold amount reflecting current costs by an average inventory amount reflecting older costs. The inventory turnover ratio under FIFO provides a better indication of the turnover of inventory items because it divides a cost of goods sold reflecting relatively current costs by an average inventory reflecting relatively recent costs. Although the trend in the inventory turnover ratio for most firms is likely to be similar under LIFO and FIFO, cross-sectional comparisons are inappropriate if one firm uses LIFO and the other firm uses FIFO. This example illustrates the tradeoff that can exist between balance sheet and earnings quality. As we discussed earlier, while LIFO may not be the best method for valuing inventory on the balance sheet, it does produce a high quality earnings number by reflecting current costs in cost of goods sold.

The inventory cost-flow assumption also affects the current ratio (current assets/ current liabilities), a measure commonly used to assess short-term liquidity risk that was introduced in Chapter 5, as follows:

(amounts in thousands)	2012	2011
Current assets (as reported)	$5,661,364	$6,708,081
Adjust inventory to FIFO	607,200	763,200
Current assets (FIFO)	$6,268,564	$7,471,281
Current liabilities	$2,029,568	$2,396,059
Current ratio (as reported)	2.78	2.80
Current ratio (FIFO)	3.09	3.12

Nucor's current ratio would be higher in each year if it used FIFO.

Reporting Changes in the Fair Value of Inventory

FIFO, LIFO, and weighted average are methods for assigning acquisition costs to ending inventory and cost of sales. For many firms, market values of inventory will likely differ from acquisition costs at balance sheet reporting dates. Under both U.S. GAAP and IFRS, firms are required to follow the conservative lower-of-cost-or-market method to report inventory at each balance sheet date.[9] Increases in market value are not reflected in the financial statements until the inventory is sold. If market value has increased and firms are able to pass the market value increases on to customers by increasing selling price, sales of inventory will realize higher gross profits and greater amounts of cash or accounts receivable. This effect should occur relatively quickly because inventory is a current asset.

Under U.S. GAAP and IFRS, when inventory market values decline below cost, the losses must be reflected in the financial statements as decreases in inventory and increases in cost of goods sold or, if material, as a separate income statement line item for the loss on decline in inventory market value. Subsequent recoveries in market value are not reflected under U.S. GAAP, but they are under IFRS. Write-downs of inventory in the current period due to market decline are intended to appropriately reflect the value of inventory on the balance sheet and to yield a normal gross margin on a subsequent period's sale. That is, sales price in the subsequent period will be lower due to the market decline, and cost of goods sold in the subsequent period will be lower by the same amount because cost of goods sold is determined by the (now lower) cost of the inventory.

Accounting Quality: Cost of Sales and Inventory

To assess the quality of accounting information with respect to cost of sales and inventory, you should consider the following:

- The inventory cost-flow assumption chosen by management
- Price variation and the speed at which inventory turns over
- Any liquidation of LIFO inventory layers
- Any physical deterioration or obsolescence of inventory
- The financing of inventory acquisitions

---

[9]*FASB Codification Topic 330;* International Accounting Standards Board, *International Accounting Standard 2,* "Inventories." One difference between U.S. GAAP and IFRS is the definition of *market.* Under U.S. GAAP, *market* is defined as the cost to replace the inventory (replacement cost), while under IFRS, *market* is defined as the selling price of the inventory minus estimated costs of disposal (net realizable value). U.S. GAAP substitutes net realizable value for replacement cost if net realizable value is less than replacement cost. Therefore, under either set of standards, inventory will not be reported at greater than its net realizable value.

Choice of Cost-Flow Assumption. Because LIFO generally matches the most recent acquisition costs against revenues in measuring earnings, LIFO-based earnings generally provide the best measure of sustainable earnings. A firm must replace goods sold if it is to continue operating, and the most recent cost of the items purchased serves as the best predictor of their replacement costs. A FIFO cost-flow assumption matches older acquisition costs with current revenues, and a weighted-average cost-flow assumption provides results between LIFO and FIFO. Researchers examining the relation between market returns on equity securities and earnings based on LIFO versus FIFO cost of goods sold found that earnings numbers based on LIFO explain more of the cross-sectional variation in returns than do earnings numbers based on FIFO.[10]

Although LIFO generally provides a higher-quality income statement, FIFO generally provides a higher-quality balance sheet. This is because the inventory values under LIFO can be considerably less than replacement or current costs, which FIFO values approximate. However, a firm cannot use LIFO for measuring cost of goods sold on the income statement and FIFO for measuring inventory on the balance sheet. Firms using LIFO must disclose the difference between the FIFO and LIFO costs of inventories. As illustrated in an earlier section, with this information, you can convert inventory on the balance sheet to an amount more closely approximating current economic value.

Rapid Inventory Turnover and Price Stability. The tax savings-related preference for LIFO is tempered significantly when (1) inventory turns over quickly or (2) acquisition costs of inventory items do not vary much. LIFO, FIFO, and weighted-average cost-flow assumptions yield approximately the same amounts for cost of goods sold if inventory turns over roughly four or more times each year or if inventory does not turn over quickly but prices are so stable that the choice of the cost-flow assumption is of little consequence.

Liquidation of LIFO Inventory Layers. When firms dip into LIFO layers, they must report the amount by which cost of goods sold was reduced (the usual case) and earnings were increased. This is a classic example of lower quality of earnings despite higher reported profits. When using earnings of the current period to estimate sustainable earnings, you should eliminate the effect of the dip into old LIFO layers from the current period's earnings. You also should understand the reason why inventory levels were depleted. For example, inventory could have been depleted because of excess customer demand or a strategic choice to liquidate inventory.

Obsolete or Damaged Inventory. As noted earlier in the discussion of the lower-of-cost-or-market rule, when the current value of inventories declines below acquisition cost because of obsolescence, physical deterioration, or theft (particularly among retailers), firms must write down their inventories to reflect the decline. You need to rely on management and the auditors to determine when inventory is overvalued, but good gauges include whether competitors are also recognizing write-downs and whether new product or technology introductions have occurred to reduce the value of existing inventory. Another signal comes from industry-wide publications addressing the demand for the firm's products.

---

[10]Ross Jennings, Paul J. Simko, and Robert B. Thompson II, "Does LIFO Inventory Accounting Improve the Income Statement at the Expense of the Balance Sheet?" *Journal of Accounting Research* (Spring 1996), pp. 85–109.

Inventory Financing Arrangements. Firms often need substantial amounts of cash early in their operating cycle to finance the purchase of raw materials. Firms may finance these purchases with suppliers through short-term borrowing agreements that appear on the balance sheet as accounts payable. However, firms sometimes obtain financing for their inventories in a manner that avoids reporting a liability on the balance sheet. For example, a firm might create a legal trust with the sole purpose of purchasing raw materials that the firm needs in its operations. The trust purchases the raw materials on account from various suppliers. The firm later purchases the needed raw materials from the trust at agreed-upon prices and reimburses the trust for the cost of carrying the raw materials until the firm needs them. The supplier is willing to sell to the trust on account because of the firm's purchase commitment.

The economic substance of such an arrangement is that the firm has purchased raw materials on account, yet no accounts payable appear on the financial statements of the firm. Current financial reporting rules sometimes allow the firm to leave the implicit inventory and the accounts payable off the balance sheet, thereby lowering its debt levels and increasing its inventory and accounts payable turnover ratios. You should examine the notes to the financial statements for significant purchase commitments and consider adding them to inventories and accounts payable.

A firm may also outsource a substantial portion of its manufacturing with commitments to acquire the finished inventory or components to be used to finish the inventory. For example, in its 2012 10-K, **Apple** disclosed that it

> … utilizes several outsourcing partners to manufacture sub-assemblies for the Company's products and to perform final assembly and testing of finished products … Consistent with industry practice, the Company acquires components through a combination of purchase orders, supplier contracts, and open orders based on projected demand information. As of September 29, 2012, the Company had outstanding off-balance sheet third-party manufacturing commitments and component purchase commitments of $21.1 billion.

Investment in Working Capital: Inventory and Accounts Payable

Combining **PepsiCo**'s two largest working capital assets (receivables and inventory) yields $10,622 million of working capital investments at December 29, 2012, roughly 14% of total assets. To offset the effect of having cash invested in inventory pending sale and collection of cash, firms delay payments to suppliers, employees, and taxing authorities as long as possible. PepsiCo's current liabilities section shows $11,903 million for accounts payable and other current liabilities at the same date, of which $4,451 million (an amount larger than its inventory balance) belongs to accounts payable, as per Note 14.

SG&A Costs

While costs like sales commissions vary directly with sales, most of the SG&A costs generally bear a less direct relation with sales. SG&A expenses reported on the income statement as part of operating profit represent the consumption of assets and incurrence of liabilities to carry on corporate functions other than production, such as advertising, marketing, sales, administration, accounting, information systems, and credit functions. The sections that follow describe the accounting and reporting of SG&A expenses.

Advertising and Marketing Costs

Many firms in the consumer products industry have large expenditures for advertising and marketing. Although these expenditures are undertaken with the expectation that they will create value, quantifying the value is difficult. Thus, both U.S. GAAP and IFRS require immediate expensing of these costs. As discussed in detail in Chapter 8, these expenditures fail to meet the definition of an asset. Prepayments for advertising (such as prepayments for commercial time on broadcast media such as television and radio or prepayments for advertising space in publications) create working capital assets (usually titled prepaid expenses). Delays in paying suppliers and service providers for advertising and marketing costs also create working capital liabilities (usually reported as accrued expenses). PepsiCo's Note 14 reports a material liability for marketplace (marketing-related) spending that increased from 2011 to 2012.

Although material for a company such as PepsiCo, these expenses are often not disclosed separately on the face of the income statement. However, PepsiCo discloses in Note 2, "Our Significant Accounting Policies" (Appendix A), that advertising and other marketing activities totaled $3.7 billion in 2012, $3.5 billion in 2011, and $3.4 billion in 2010, and it is reported as a part of SG&A expenses on the income statement.

Compensation

Wages, salaries, payroll taxes, bonuses, commissions, and fringe benefits are capitalized as part of inventory if incurred in the production process and then expensed as part of cost of goods sold when the inventory is sold. If compensation costs are related to the selling, advertising, marketing, or administrative functions, they are reported as compensation expenses within SG&A. Again, Note 14 reports a working capital liability (accrued compensation) for compensation arising from delayed payments to employees and Note 6, "Stock-Based Compensation" (Appendix A), provides detailed information on stock-based compensation.

Depreciation, Depletion, and Amortization

Recall that depreciation, amortization, and depletion of long-lived productive assets are allocations of the costs of assets to the periods benefited. If the long-lived assets are used in production, the allocated costs are capitalized as part of inventory. If not, the allocated costs are expensed as part of SG&A. The materiality of these expenses requires that they be disclosed in the notes to the financial statements. Also, depreciation, depletion, and amortization typically represent the largest addbacks to net income in the operating section of the statement of cash flows.

Credit Policy

In an effort to increase sales, most firms allow customers to delay payment. If cash collection is not highly likely, the sale should not be recorded in the first place. However, even if cash collection is generally likely to occur at an individual customer level, at a portfolio level some customers will not pay. Also, customers' ability to pay can change in the period between the initial sale and dates of scheduled cash payments.

Accounts receivable must be reported on the balance sheet at the amount of cash that is expected to be realized (that is, the *net realizable value*). Net realizable value reporting requires an estimate, at each balance sheet date, of the two causes of uncollectible receivables: sales returns and bad debts.

If sales returns are small in dollar amount and infrequent, they are recorded as incurred by simultaneously reducing sales and accounts receivable. If sales returns are material, they should be accounted for using the *allowance method*. Basically, the expected returns are estimated and reported as a subtraction from sales revenue in the income statement ("estimated sales returns") and as a subtraction from accounts receivable on the balance sheet ("allowance for sales returns"). For example, if a company had $1,000 of credit sales of which $200 was collected in the period and the company estimated $50 in sales returns, the company reports $950 in "net sales" and $750 in accounts receivable. Note that sales returns are a direct reduction in sales, not an SG&A expense.

Bad debts also are accounted for using the allowance method. The proper balance in the "allowance for doubtful accounts" is typically determined by a percentage of ending accounts receivable, or an aging of accounts receivable. By determining the allowance using the aging method, the firm uses its historical experience with past bad debts and its expectations going forward to estimate the proportion of accounts receivable that will not be collected based on the length of time receivables have been outstanding. The likelihood an account will not be collected increases with its age. For example, experience may show that bad debts arise from 1% of receivables less than 60 days old, from 5% of the receivables that are between 61 and 180 days old, and 40% of receivables that are more than 180 days old. At the end of each period, the firm estimates the necessary balance in the allowance for doubtful accounts. The necessary adjustment to increase the allowance for doubtful accounts is recognized as bad debts expense (often called provision for bad debts), which is reported as a component of SG&A expenses.[11]

Under U.S. GAAP, an analogous treatment is given to receivables with maturity dates beyond one year, such as notes receivable. These receivables are initially reported at their present value. Then at each balance sheet date, an allowance for uncollectible notes (often referred to as an allowance or reserve for loan losses) is established. Actual loan impairments are written off against the allowance for loan losses, much like the procedure for bad debts. In contrast, under IFRS, notes receivable balance sheet reporting follows the fair value reporting rules for investments illustrated in Chapter 8.

Time series and cross-sectional analyses of accounts receivable, bad debt expense, and sales can alert you to possible revenue and expense manipulation. If a firm experiences a substantial increase in the number of days accounts receivable are outstanding, it is possible that the company has intentionally extended credit to additional groups to generate sales or that the company has entered different product markets that have different payment practices. However, it is also possible that customers are taking longer to pay their invoices because they are experiencing financial difficulties (suggesting that more bad debt expense should be accrued or that future additional sales to the same parties are less likely) or, in the extreme, the customers are not paying because they don't exist (i.e., sales are fraudulent). Examining the income statement ratio of bad debt expense to sales and the balance sheet ratio of allowance for doubtful accounts to accounts receivable can detect inadequate recognition of bad debt exposure.

Warranty Expense

Another method of increasing sales is to guarantee the performance of the product sold. Estimated costs under warranties must be accrued in the period in which the guaranteed goods are sold by increasing a warranty obligation and increasing warranty expense (a portion of SG&A expense). Then as warranty claims arise, the costs of servicing the warranty claims reduce the estimated warranty obligation. As in the case of bad debts expense, accounting quality is compromised if inappropriate or inconsistent amounts represent opportunistic bias.

---

[11]If the new revenue recognition rules pass, bad debt expense will be deducted from sales at the top of the income statement, and will no longer be part of SG&A expenses.

Operating Profit

Sales revenue minus cost of sales and SG&A expenses yields operating profit before income taxes. From this amount, firms deduct "other" revenues and expenses from financing and investing activities (primarily interest income and interest expense), including equity in the earnings of affiliates. Finally, income tax expense is subtracted to obtain net income.

Income Taxes

LO 9-3

Use the financial statement and note information for corporate *income taxes* to analyze the firm's tax strategies.

Income taxes are a significant operating expense. Chapter 2 provides an introduction to income taxes and illustrates the accounting that leads to income tax expense and deferred tax assets and liabilities. You may wish to review it at this time. In this section, we focus on the income tax note to the financial statements to illustrate how to assess a firm's income tax position and understand more about the difference between accrual accounting and tax accounting (which is often similar to cash accounting).

Required Income Tax Disclosures

The income tax note is a rich source of information. This section describes four required and useful disclosures:

- Components of the provision for income taxes (i.e., income tax expense)
- Reconciliation of income taxes at the statutory rate with the provision for income taxes
- Components of deferred tax assets and liabilities
- Information regarding uncertain tax positions and related reserves

We analyze each disclosure using **PepsiCo**'s income tax disclosures in Note 5, "Income Taxes," to its financial statements (Appendix A). To facilitate our discussion, we reproduce portions of Note 5 in each section.

Components of Income Tax Expense

Exhibit 9.4 shows PepsiCo's disclosure of income before taxes and the components of income tax expense. First, PepsiCo partitions income before taxes by income source—U.S. and foreign. Note that foreign income is larger in every year presented. The shift in income source has potentially significant tax implications given that foreign tax rates are often lower than U.S. tax rates. The next portion of the disclosure shows the provision for income taxes (i.e., the $2,090 million reported on PepsiCo's 2012 consolidated income statement shown as the sum of the 2012 column) partitioned by taxing jurisdiction—U.S. federal, foreign, and state—and by whether the component of income tax expense is current or deferred.

PepsiCo's average, or effective, tax rates for the three years on total income before taxes (total provision for income taxes ÷ total income before taxes) are as follows:

2010:	$1,894/$8,232 = **23.0%**
2011:	$2,372/$8,834 = **26.8%**
2012:	$2,090/$8,304 = **25.2%**

Exhibit 9.4

PepsiCo
Portion of Tax Note 5 from 2012 10-K
(Income before Taxes and Income Tax Expense)
(amounts in millions)

Note 5—Income Taxes

		2012	2011	2010
Income before income taxes				
U.S.		$3,234	$3,964	$4,008
Foreign		5,070	4,870	4,224
		$8,304	$8,834	$8,232
Provision for income taxes				
Current:	U.S. Federal	$ 911	$ 611	$ 932
	Foreign	940	882	728
	State	153	124	137
		2,004	1,617	1,797
Deferred:	U.S. Federal	154	789	78
	Foreign	(95)	(88)	18
	State	27	54	1
		86	755	97
		$2,090	$2,372	$1,894

The average tax rate increased over the three-year period, and it varied quite a bit. We can further analyze the source of the rate differences by using the U.S. (federal + state) and foreign partitions:

	U.S. Federal and State	**Foreign**
2010:	($932 + $137 + $78 + $1)/$4,008 = **28.6%**	($728 + $18)/$4,224 = **17.7%**
2011:	($611 + $124 + 789 + 54)/$3,964 = **39.8%**	($882 − $88)/$4,870 = **16.3%**
2012:	($911 + $153 + $154 + $27)/$3,234 = **38.5%**	($940 − $95)/$5,070 = **16.7%**

It is clear that PepsiCo derives a substantial source of net profitability by generating its income in lower tax jurisdictions. In general U.S. tax rules require U.S. companies to pay taxes on earnings regardless of the jurisdiction in which the earnings were generated. An exception exists, however, for foreign earnings that are reinvested rather than repatriated to the United States in the form of dividends. In a latter part of the note, PepsiCo presents a short section on undistributed international earnings in which it states:

> As of December 29, 2012, we had approximately $32.2 billion of undistributed international earnings. We intend to continue to reinvest earnings outside the U.S. for the foreseeable future and, therefore, have not recognized any U.S. tax expense on these earnings.

Reconciliation of Income Taxes at Statutory Rate with Income Tax Expense

U.S. firms are also required to disclose why the average tax rates shown previously differ from the statutory federal tax rate on income before taxes. Firms can express reconciling items in dollar amounts or in percentage terms. Exhibit 9.5 presents **PepsiCo**'s tax rate reconciliation.

Sometimes the reconciliation is presented using percentages, as PepsiCo does, and sometimes the reconciliation is presented using the dollar values of tax effects. The initial assumption in this reconciliation is that all income is subject to taxes at a rate equal to the U.S. federal statutory rate. This is a reasonable assumption given the general tendency for the United States to tax all income regardless of where it is earned. State and local income taxes generally trigger increases in firms' average tax rates beyond the federal statutory tax rate (net of their U.S. federal tax benefit because they are deductible). In PepsiCo's case, state taxes increased the average tax rate for PepsiCo by between 1.1% and 1.4%.

As we learned in the previous section, the primary driver of PepsiCo's relatively low average tax rates during these three years is lower tax rates on PepsiCo's income from foreign operations. It is noteworthy, however, that the benefit of these lower tax rates appears to be dwindling (a −9.4% adjustment in 2010 but only a −6.9% adjustment in 2012). The increasing tax rates abroad and an increasing proportion of income derived from abroad suggest a continuing increase in the combined average tax rate that could hurt future profitability unless the firm takes counteractions. Some of this foreign tax benefit reduction is likely beyond PepsiCo's control, especially if it is simply caused by

Exhibit 9.5			
PepsiCo **Portion of Tax Note 5 from 2012 10-K** **(Tax Rate Reconciliation)**			
	2012	**2011**	**2010**
U.S. Federal statutory tax rate	35.0%	35.0%	35.0%
State income tax, net of U.S. Federal tax benefit	1.4	1.3	1.1
Lower taxes on foreign results	(6.9)	(8.7)	(9.4)
Tax benefit related to tax court decision	(2.6)	—	—
Acquisitions of PBG and PAS	—	—	(3.1)
Other, net	(1.7)	(0.8)	(0.6)
Annual tax rate	25.2%	26.8%	23.0%

foreign jurisdictions raising tax rates. But, you might assess whether PepsiCo's tax strategy will shift income from higher to lower tax jurisdictions by

- physically shifting operations (for example, manufacturing or marketing).
- adjusting transfer prices or cost allocations to shift income.
- shifting borrowing between jurisdictions or shifting financing between debt and equity in a given jurisdiction to maximize the tax benefits of interest deductions.

While the federal, state, and foreign components are generally permanent, many items in the tax rate reconciliation are transitory. In 2012, PepsiCo's average tax rate is lower as a result of resolving open tax issues relating to an audit of its financial instruments classification. The 2.6% reduction in the average tax rate is quite large relative to a 35% statutory rate. Also, PepsiCo reports a 3.1% reduction in the tax rate in 2010 due to its acquisition of the remaining interests in its bottling affiliates. As explained in PepsiCo's MD&A, "Our Financial Results, Items Affecting Comparability" (Appendix B), PepsiCo recorded a gain when it purchased the remaining shares of its affiliate bottlers because the fair value of its previous interest was greater than what it had recorded in its Investments in Bottling Affiliates account. IRS rules regarding this type of acquisition treats most of the gain as nontaxable.

Finally, there are some minor reductions in the tax rate in each year labeled "Other, net." It is likely that these include permanent differences that are never taxable or deductible (e.g., municipal bond interest, tax fines and penalties, etc.) and thus (as discussed in Chapter 2) have no impact on income tax expense.

When you assess profitability, be sure to consider whether a portion of profitability is driven by a transitory event such as an acquisition or resolution of an audit. When predicting future provisions for income taxes, you should determine the expected future tax rate by analyzing the tax rate reconciliation over time. Generally, the more persistent portion of the rate is obtained by summing federal and state rates minus the foreign tax benefit.

Components of Deferred Tax Assets and Liabilities

Firms must also disclose the components of deferred tax assets and the deferred tax liabilities. The components describe the *cumulative* extent to which accrual accounting differs from the cash-flow-based tax treatments for many items over time. Exhibit 9.6 presents **PepsiCo**'s disclosure in Note 5 of the components of deferred tax assets and liabilities.

In the following subsections, we discuss several of these specific components, paying particular attention to the components that you would commonly see in the tax note disclosure.

Investment in Noncontrolled Affiliates. PepsiCo owns less than a controlling interest in some affiliates and uses the equity method to account for its investments. PepsiCo recognizes its share of the earnings of the investee each year and includes it in income. This income is taxed only when PepsiCo receives a dividend from the affiliate. Deferred tax liabilities related to the future dividend receipts from these investments totaled $48 million and $41 million at the end of 2012 and 2011, respectively. In past years when PepsiCo had not yet acquired the remainder of the equity interest in its bottlers, this temporary difference was large and the amount was rising. Now it is relatively small.

Property, Plant, and Equipment. Firms claim depreciation deductions on their tax returns using accelerated methods over periods shorter than the expected useful lives of depreciable assets. Most firms depreciate assets for financial reporting using the straight-line method over the expected useful lives of such assets. Thus, the book bases of depreciable assets will likely exceed their tax bases. Depreciation expense for

Exhibit 9.6

PepsiCo
Components of Deferred Tax Assets and Liabilities from 2012 10-K
(amounts in millions)

	2012	2011	2010
Deferred tax liabilities			
Investments in noncontrolled affiliates	$ 48	$ 41	
Debt guarantee of wholly owned subsidiary	828	828	
Property, plant and equipment	2,424	2,466	
Intangible assets other than nondeductible goodwill	4,388	4,297	
Other	260	184	
Gross deferred tax liabilities	7,948	7,816	
Deferred tax assets			
Net carryforwards	1,378	1,373	
Stock-based compensation	378	429	
Retiree medical benefits	411	504	
Other employee-related benefits	672	695	
Pension benefits	647	545	
Deductible state tax and interest benefits	345	339	
Long-term debt obligations acquired	164	223	
Other	863	822	
Gross deferred tax assets	4,858	4,930	
Valuation allowances	(1,233)	(1,264)	
Deferred tax assets, net	3,625	3,666	
Net deferred tax liabilities	$ 4,323	$ 4,150	

tax reporting in future years will be less than the amounts for financial reporting, giving rise to a liability for future tax payments. The deferred tax liability relating to depreciable assets is very large, consistent with good tax planning to defer taxes. The liability remained relatively constant for PepsiCo, suggesting that depreciable assets are slightly past the midpoint in useful life when the temporary differences begin to reverse and possibly that PepsiCo is experiencing a slower growth rate in capital expenditures.

Intangible Assets Other Than Nondeductible Goodwill. PepsiCo indicates in its Note 4, "Property, Plant and Equipment and Intangible Assets" (Appendix A), that it amortizes definite-lived intangibles other than goodwill over periods ranging from 5–40 years. The reporting of a deferred tax liability for these items suggests that PepsiCo writes off these intangibles more quickly for tax purposes, which lowers the current tax liability but increases a future tax liability. This is the largest source of deferred tax liabilities for PepsiCo.

Net Carryforwards. The first and largest deferred tax asset component is net carryforwards. A firm may operate for both financial and tax reporting at a net loss for the year. The firm can carry back this net loss to offset taxable income of the two preceding years and receive a refund for income taxes paid in those years. The firm recognizes the refund as an income tax credit in the year of the net loss. If the firm has no positive taxable income in the two preceding years against which to carry back the net loss or if the net loss exceeds the taxable income of those years, the firm can carry forward the net loss up to 20 years. This carryforward provides future tax benefits in that it can offset positive taxable incomes and thereby reduce income taxes otherwise payable. The benefits of the NOL carryforward give rise to a deferred tax asset.

PepsiCo recognizes a deferred tax asset for the future saving in taxes when it is able to offset NOLs previously incurred against the positive income of future periods. The deferred tax asset is $1,378 million at the end of 2012. PepsiCo also describes in the Note 5 narrative that this represents $10.4 billion of loss carryforwards and describes when the loss carryforwards will expire.

Stock-Based Compensation.

For financial reporting, PepsiCo records its stock-based compensation expense by determining option values on the date of the grant of stock options and then recognizing the expense over the vesting period. For tax reporting, the expense is recognized later, when the stock options are exercised by employees. Upon exercise, U.S. tax law permits firms to deduct the difference between market price and exercise price of the shares being issued. PepsiCo has deferred tax assets of $378 million related to stock-based compensation at the end of 2012.

Retiree Medical, Other Employee-Related, and Pension Benefits.

For financial reporting purposes, firms recognize postretirement and pension expenses each year as employees render services. For tax reporting, firms receive a deduction when the firm contributes cash to funds to support these benefits. Because of the limits to tax deductions for contributions, pensions are often underfunded and postretirement benefits are almost always underfunded. The balance sheet liability to make future contributions is much larger than the tax-basis liability (which is equal to zero). Thus, the future tax deductions for contributions to satisfy the liability result in current deferred tax assets. These assets as of 2012 are $411 million, $672 million, and $647 million for retiree medical, other employee, and pension benefits, respectively.

Other Common Deferred Tax Asset Components.

PepsiCo either does not have or reports as "other" some deferred tax asset components that you are likely to find common among other firms. These include:

- **Uncollectible Accounts Receivable.** Firms estimate uncollectible accounts in the year of sale for financial reporting but cannot recognize bad debt expense for tax purposes until an actual customer's account becomes uncollectible. Thus, the book value of accounts receivable will be less than its tax basis. The difference represents the future tax deductions for bad debt expense. These future tax-benefits times the tax rate give rise to a deferred tax asset.
- **Warranties.** Firms expense estimated warranty costs over the period of warranty coverage for financial reporting but cannot deduct warranty expense for tax reporting until the firm makes actual expenditures to provide warranty services. Thus, the book value of the warranty liability (a positive amount) will exceed the tax basis of the warranty liability (zero because the income tax law does not permit recognition of a warranty liability). The difference represents the future tax deductions for warranty expense, and hence, gives rise to a deferred tax asset.
- **Impairment and Restructuring Charges.** Firms write down intangible and tangible assets to recognize impairments and record liabilities related to restructuring. They cannot deduct these items for tax purposes until the firm makes actual expenditures. The future tax deductions give rise to a deferred tax asset.

Deferred Tax Asset Valuation Allowances. Firms must recognize a valuation allowance for any deferred tax assets they are not likely to realize as tax benefits so that deferred tax assets will be reported at the most likely net realizable value. PepsiCo's valuation allowance is similar in amount to the deferred tax asset for NOL carryforwards each year, suggesting that the valuation allowance likely relates to these items. PepsiCo is profitable and paying taxes, so the net loss is related to subsidiaries. The net loss of the subsidiary can offset only net income of that subsidiary in a later year. NOLs generally are not transferable between subsidiaries because the tax law treats the subsidiaries as different taxable entities. If a company such as PepsiCo is generally very profitable and paying taxes but the subsidiary is not, both now and in the future, the deferred tax assets associated with NOL carryforwards may go unused and a valuation allowance is appropriate.

The deferred tax valuation allowance is a tax reserve that leads to greater tax expense and thus lower net income on a dollar-per-dollar basis. That is, unlike other nontax asset or liability changes that generally affect net income by the change amount multiplied by one minus the tax rate, the reserve change affects income tax expense directly. Any large change in this reserve has magnified effects on net income and should be investigated further.

Information Regarding Uncertain Tax Positions and Related Reserves

Financial reporting standards require that firms report reserves for the tax benefits of uncertain tax positions. For example, assume a firm takes a tax deduction or excludes income when filing its corporate return. The firm is uncertain about whether its position will be supported in the event of an audit by the IRS or other taxing authority. If it is more likely than not that the tax position would be upheld in the audit or subsequent litigation and appeal, then the firm is allowed to recognize the benefit as a reduction of tax expense. Otherwise, a reserve must be established. PepsiCo states in Note 5 that it has $2,425 million in such reserves reported in income taxes payable and other liabilities as a result of open tax audits in the United States, Mexico, United Kingdom, Canada, and Russia. Exhibit 9.7 presents the required reconciliation of the beginning and ending balances of the reserve:

Exhibit 9.7		
PepsiCo **Portion of Tax Note 5 from 2012 10-K (Tax Reserve)** **(amounts in millions)**		
	2012	**2011**
Balance, beginning of year	**$2,167**	**$2,022**
Additions for tax positions related to the current year	275	233
Additions for tax positions from prior years	161	147
Reductions for tax positions from prior years	(172)	(46)
Settlement payments	(17)	(156)
Statute of limitations expiration	(3)	(15)
Translation and other	14	(18)
Balance, end of year	**$2,425**	**$2,167**

The reserve increased by $145 million in 2011 and by $258 million in 2012. This would not be surprising if net income increased in both years, but it did not. In 2012, PepsiCo's net income decreased by $265 million. As in the case of the deferred tax asset valuation allowance, this tax reserve increase leads to greater tax expense and thus lower net income on a dollar-per-dollar basis. The change in reserve alone explains nearly all of the decline in PepsiCo's net income. This gives you an idea of the magnitude of these reserves and their materiality and why you want to pay close attention to how a tax reserve changes during a period.

Quick Check

- The income statement reports the amount of income tax expense. You can compute the relation between income tax expense and income before taxes, resulting in a firm's *average tax rate*. The income tax note explains the major reasons why the average tax rate differs from the statutory federal tax rate. Most differences between average and statutory tax rates are transitory and thus do not affect the prediction of future periods' net income. However, shifts between domestic and foreign operations may create persistent tax rate changes.
- The income tax note indicates the mix of currently payable and deferred taxes and the extent to which a firm has delayed or accelerated the payment of income taxes. It also indicates the components of deferred tax assets and liabilities, which you can tie to the analysis of various other transactions of the firm (such as intercorporate investments and pension and retiree medical obligations).
- Accounting quality can be compromised in the process by which tax reserves are estimated. The dollar-for-dollar nature of tax reserves, the estimation required in their measurement, and the magnitude of tax rates combine to cause reserves to be a potentially material part of a company's profitability.

LO 9-4

Identify the effects of *pensions and other postemployment benefits* on the financial statements.

Pensions and Other Postretirement Benefits

In addition to salaries, bonuses, wages, vacation time, and share-based compensation, most employers provide benefits to employees when they retire. This section deals with pension benefits. Later, we provide a brief summary of similar financial reporting for other postretirement benefits such as health care.[12]

To provide for retiree pension benefits, employers sponsor *defined contribution plans* or *defined benefit plans*. In a *defined contribution plan,* employers promise to place a certain percentage of an employee's earnings into an investment vehicle as specified by the employee. During the past decade, more employers have begun to offer defined contribution plans, typically 401(k) plans. The employer makes a cash contribution to an investment account each year based on a percentage of the employee's salary. The employer's obligation under the plan is satisfied once the funds are placed into the investment account. The employer does not guarantee a given benefit payment when the employee retires. Instead, the fund balance at retirement depends on the investing success of the investment company and the employee's allocation of the contribution across different types of investments. The accounting for a defined contribution plan is straightforward. Because of the plan contract, the employee's current service generates

---

[12]Standards on pensions and postemployment benefits are: *Codification Topics 715 and 958;* International Accounting Standards Board, *International Accounting Standard 19,* "Employees Benefits" (revised 1998).

the employer's obligation to make periodic payments, and the employer records pension expense for the amount of the defined contribution obligation.

In a *defined benefit plan,* employers incur the obligation to provide a pension payment to employees throughout the employee's retirement period. The final obligation is determined by the terms of a pension plan, which are negotiated by employers and employees. Normally, many factors affect the determination of the final obligation, including the length of the employee's service to the company, expected employee longevity, status at retirement, and final pay. The intricacies of determining the obligation and assigning pension cost to particular periods create complex accounting.

Normally, a corporation hires a third-party trustee, usually an insurance company or another financial services company, to administer such plans. Each year the employer makes an annual contribution to the trustee, which is invested in plan assets (usually a portfolio of cash, debt, and equity securities) managed by the trustee. The trustee keeps records of the plan's obligations to individual employees and makes pension payments to eligible employees. The remaining discussion of pensions relates to understanding the accounting for these more complex defined benefit plans.

The Economics of Pension Accounting in a Defined Benefit Plan

The underlying economic explanation of defined benefit pension plans involves understanding and comparing two key amounts: *pension obligations* and *pension assets.*

Pension Obligation (Liability)

In a typical defined benefit arrangement, employees are promised a lump-sum payment or periodic monthly payments when they retire based on some plan formula. A typical plan formula considers the number of years of employee service, a credit for each year of annual service (usually expressed as a percentage of final salary), and final salary at retirement date. For example, assume that a pension plan is governed by the following formula:

Annual Benefits = Annual Credit × Years of Service × Salary at Retirement Date

If the annual credit is 1%, the interpretation of the formula is that for each year of service, an employee's annual retirement benefit increases by 1% of the salary at retirement date. An employee who worked 30 years under the plan would retire at 30% of final salary. The PBO (*projected benefit obligation*) is the actuarially determined present value of estimated retirement payments calculated according to the benefit formula (using expected future salary levels) to be paid to employees because employees have worked and earned benefits until the current date. The discount (interest) rate used for the present value computation is called the settlement rate, which represents the current market rate at which an outside party would effectively settle the obligation.

Pension Assets

To have the funds available to make pension payments when due, employers accumulate pension assets by setting aside funds for that purpose (self-administration of the plan) or by making cash payments to a plan trustee with the expectation that the trustee will invest the cash and increase the fund by generating returns on the investments. If the employer self-administers the plan, it is referred to as an unfunded plan. If a plan trustee is used, the plan is considered a funded plan. Unless otherwise noted, we assume that all plans are administered by a third-party trustee. The employer and third-party trustee, in consultation with an actuary, make decisions about payments to the trustee based on an assumption about the expected long-term rate of return on plan assets.

Pension fund assets are measured at their fair market value (FMV) at the end of each year. Employers use the year-end FMV or an average FMV over a period of time, usually five years (the average is referred to as the *market-related fair value*), in financial reporting. Determining the fair value of the assets in the fund usually is not a problem because prudent investing of fund assets generally yields funds comprised of cash and widely held, often-traded securities.

The Economic Status of the Plan

The economic status of the plan is determined by comparing the two amounts: the PBO and the FMV of plan assets:

If PBO > FMV of plan assets, the plan is underfunded, resulting in a *net obligation*.
If PBO < FMV of plan assets, the plan is overfunded, resulting in a *net asset*.

The economic status of the plan is reflected on the balance sheet. Underfunded plans are recognized as net liabilities on the firm's balance sheet, whereas overfunded plans are net assets. If a firm has several different plans (across employee groups, subsidiaries, countries, etc.), then the net funded status is determined for each one separately. Plans with net asset status and plans with net obligation status are accumulated and reported separately.

What Changes the Economic Status of the Plan during the Year?

Other than funding (that is, payments by the firm to the trustee), changes in the economic status of the plan are reported in comprehensive income.

What Changes PBO (That Is, the Pension Plan Liability)? Five events have the potential of changing the PBO during a given period: service cost, interest on PBO, prior service cost, liability (actuarial) gains and losses, and benefit payments to retirees.

1. Employees earn benefits in the current year (*service cost*).
   By working one additional year, employees earn an increase in future benefits. The actuarially determined present value of the increase in future benefits represents an increase in the employer's pension liability. This liability increase is called service cost.
2. Time passes (*interest on PBO*).
   PBO represents the present value of future benefits payable to retirees. As time passes without the liability being extinguished, the liability accumulates interest at the settlement interest rate. That is, the long-term liability PBO grows at a rate of interest equal to the settlement interest rate. The liability increase due to the passage of time is called interest cost.
3. Plan amendments grant retroactive benefits (*prior service cost*).
   From time to time, employers and employees negotiate and decide to change the pension plan benefit formula. Usually, the negotiation leads to increased retirement benefits, which are applied retroactively. Recall the pension plan formula example described earlier. Now assume that the employer amends the pension plan agreement to increase the annual credit from 1% to 2%. If the amendment is retroactive, the employee now is entitled to an annual benefit equal to 60% of final salary. This sudden increase in retirement payments translates into a sudden increase in PBO because PBO is the actuarially determined present value of the estimated

future retirement payments. The increase in PBO from amending a pension plan and retroactively granting benefits is defined as prior service cost. Employers often justify the sudden increase in the liability with the argument that the current employee group benefiting from the retroactive amendment represents a more loyal workforce with a higher morale. These conditions translate into a future economic benefit for the employer over the remaining service life of the affected group.

4. Actuarial assumptions about future retirement payments change [*liability (actuarial) gains and losses*].

   Each period the actuary estimates PBO using the most current assumptions about items such as interest rates, mortality, pay increases, and job classifications. If experience during the period indicates that assumptions should be changed, the actuary recomputes the PBO based on the new assumptions. The resulting increase or decrease in PBO is referred to as a liability (actuarial) gain or loss. For example, if new information becomes available that employees are estimated to live longer after retirement than previously thought, increased future retirement payments will occur, and consequently, PBO increases. The unexpected increase in PBO is a liability loss. Other changes in plan assumptions could lead to decreased PBO, which would be classified as a liability gain.

5. Retirement benefits are paid (*benefit payments*).

   Actually paying retirement benefits to retired employees reduces the PBO.

What Changes the FMV of Pension Plan Assets? Three events may change the FMV of pension plan assets during a given period: employer cash payments to the pension plan, actual return on plan assets, and retirement benefits payments.

1. Employer cash payments are made to the plan trustee (*employer contributions*). Funding the plan by making a cash contribution to the pension plan increases the FMV of pension plan assets. Within certain boundaries, company management decides how much cash to contribute to the pension plan each year. The U.S. federal government mandates minimum funding amounts for defined benefit pension plans, which become the minimum company contribution amounts. Internal Revenue Service regulations allow only a certain amount to be tax deductible, which most firms treat as the maximum company contribution amount. Firms normally make a pension plan contribution between these minimum and maximum amounts. Note that this contribution amount reduces the obligation to retired employees, the PBO.

2. There are actual returns on invested plan assets (*return on plan assets*). The pension plan trustee invests the cash contributed by the employer in stocks, bonds, and other assets, which earn a return (for example, dividends or interest) and experience changes in market value. The change in the FMV of plan assets during the period, adjusted for employer contributions and benefit payments, leads to the computation of an *actual return* on plan assets. If the return is positive, the FMV of the assets increased during the period. But the return can be negative as well. The actual return on plan assets can be thought of as being comprised of two components: expected return and unexpected return.

   - The *expected return on plan assets*, which is always positive, is based on long-run expected rates of return on diversified portfolios of assets similar to those of the pension fund.
   - The *unexpected return on plan assets* is based on deviations of actual rates of return from expected rates (*asset gains and losses*).

For example, if a company expects a 10% return and the actual return is 9%, the two components of actual return are an expected return of 10% and a plan asset loss of 1%. The PBO increases due to accruing interest at the settlement rate. Similarly, the FMV of plan assets increases based on the expected return. The PBO increases or decreases if the settlement rate (or other assumptions) turns out to be different than expected. The FMV of plan assets also increases (a gain) or decreases (a loss) if the actual return turns out to be higher or lower than expected.

3. Retirement benefits are paid (*benefit payments*).

   Finally, actually paying retirement benefits to retired employees reduces the FMV of available plan assets. Note that this amount also reduces the obligation to retired employees, the PBO.

Reporting the Income Effects in Net Income and Other Comprehensive Income

Each non-cash change in PBO and the FMV of plan assets is given (1) immediate recognition as a part of pension expense of the current period or (2) delayed recognition as part of other comprehensive income.

Type of Change in Pension Plan	Treatment
Changes in PBO:	
Service cost	Increase pension expense
Interest cost on PBO	Increase pension expense
Prior service cost	Decrease other comprehensive income
Liability gains/losses on PBO	Increase/decrease other comprehensive income
Changes in FMV of plan assets:	
Actual return on plan assets (two components):	
Expected return on plan assets	Decrease pension expense
Asset gains/losses	Increase/decrease other comprehensive income

Items receiving immediate recognition in net income are service cost, interest cost, and expected return on plan assets. Immediate recognition of service cost and interest on PBO increases pension expense because both represent an increase in the PBO liability. The expected return on plan assets is always positive. Because it represents an increase in the FMV of plan assets, it decreases pension expense.[13]

Prior service cost is generally an increase in the PBO liability, and it is recognized as a decrease in other comprehensive income. However, prior service cost is recognized in net income over time through an amortization process. The recognition of

---

[13]We use the terms *pension expense* and *net pension cost* interchangeably. This is not always correct because a cost can be an expense or an asset depending on whether economic benefits are expected to exist beyond the current period. We have abstracted from the idea that pension cost can be part of inventory (for example, if it is the pension of a direct laborer) to make the discussion easier. However, if pension cost is deemed to be part of inventory, it is not reported as pension expense; instead, it is allocated to inventory as a product cost and then becomes part of cost of goods sold when the inventory is sold.

prior service cost in net income over time is consistent with the idea that prior service costs generate employee goodwill, with the benefits of such goodwill realized over the remaining service period of the employees to whom the retroactive benefits were granted. Recognition of gains and losses on pension liabilities and assets is delayed because of a smoothing objective inherent in the accounting for pensions. A primary argument in support of this objective is that most gains and losses are transitory fluctuations for which current recognition should not be given. The rules for the specific delayed recognition of gains and losses are complex, and we discuss them subsequently in the chapter. The basic idea is that only if transitory gains and losses become very large are they amortized and reflected in net income. However, in the period in which they occur, all liability gains and losses are reflected in other comprehensive income.

The sum of the amounts currently recognized in net income is reported as pension expense on the income statement. To strengthen your understanding of pension expense computation and to illustrate the balance sheet and note presentations, we consider the following simplified example.

Pension Expense Calculation with Balance Sheet and Note Disclosures

On January 1, 2013, Moreno Co. adopted a defined benefit pension plan, at which time both its PBO and FMV of plan assets equaled zero. In early 2014, Moreno granted retroactive benefits of $100,000 to employees who have an average remaining service period of ten years from that date. Moreno decided to fund the plan at the end of each year by sending $60,000 to a plan trustee. Service cost is $50,000 each year. Moreno earns 10% on investments and can settle the obligation by purchasing an annuity with a 7% interest rate. To simplify this first example, assume (1) that actual and expected returns on plan assets are equal (that is, no asset gains or losses) and (2) that actual and expected PBO are equal (that is, no liability gains or losses). Our goal is to prepare financial statement disclosures for 2013–2015.

To compute many of the pension disclosures, it is necessary to reconcile PBO and FMV of plan assets. Exhibit 9.8 shows the reconciliations for Moreno Co.

In 2013, PBO began at $0 and increased $50,000 due to employees' current service. Because there was no beginning PBO, it did not grow due to the passage of time; thus, interest cost on PBO is $0. No other changes in PBO occurred in 2013. (Two possible other changes intentionally not considered in this example are liability gains/losses and payments to retired employees.) The FMV of plan assets began at zero, no return was earned on the $0 investment, and $60,000 was contributed to the plan trustee at the end of the year. (Again, by construction of the example, no payments were made to retirees.) Comparing PBO and FMV of plan assets at 12/31/13, we see that Moreno contributed $10,000 more than the pension plan obligation to employees. Thus, the plan is overfunded by $10,000. That is, the pension plan is in a $10,000 net asset position, which will be reported on Moreno's balance sheet as of 12/31/13.

In 2014, the situation changes substantially. Again, service cost of $50,000 increases PBO. But now the $50,000 beginning PBO accrues interest at the 7% settlement rate such that PBO goes up by an additional $3,500 (interest cost on PBO). Also, 2014 is the year in which Moreno granted retroactive benefits in a plan amendment causing PBO to increase $100,000 for prior service cost. Therefore, at December 31, 2014, PBO is

Exhibit 9.8

Moreno Co.
Reconciliation of Pension Liability and Assets

Changes in PBO		2013		2014		2015
PBO, 1/1		$ 0		$ 50,000		$203,500
Service cost		50,000		50,000		50,000
Interest cost on PBO:						
Beginning PBO balance	$0		$50,000		$203,500	
Settlement rate	×0.07		× 0.07		× 0.07	
Interest cost		0		3,500		14,245
Prior service cost		0		100,000		0
PBO, 12/31		$50,000		$203,500		$267,745

Changes in FMV of Plan Assets		2013		2014		2015
FMV of plan assets, 1/1		$ 0		$ 60,000		$126,000
Expected return on plan assets:						
Beginning balance	$0		$60,000		$126,000	
Long-term expected return						
on plan assets	×0.10		× 0.10		× 0.10	
Expected return		0		6,000		12,600
Contributions		60,000		60,000		60,000
FMV of plan assets, 12/31		$60,000		$126,000		$198,600

$203,500. Moreno did not choose to immediately fund the prior service cost PBO increase. The FMV of plan assets increased only by the 10% return on the beginning plan assets plus the annual end-of-period payment of $60,000 to the trustee. Therefore, at December 31, 2014, Moreno is in a net liability position of $77,500, which can be found by comparing the $203,500 PBO to the $126,000 FMV of plan assets. This will be reported as a liability on Moreno's 2014 balance sheet. Under certain laws, severe underfunding of a plan can trigger a legal requirement to purchase insurance on the plan. Even if underfunding does not trigger legal actions, it can trigger employee disenchantment, and represents a formidable headwind for the firm's future earnings and cash flows.

The events that change PBO and FMV of plan assets in 2015 are similar. However, interest on PBO ($14,245) now exceeds the actual return on plan assets ($12,600). When this occurs, an employer would have to fund at a rate higher than annual service cost to keep the underfunded position (that is, net obligation) from growing.

Income Statement Effects

Service cost, interest on PBO, and expected return on plan assets received immediate recognition as part of pension expense on Moreno's books. Prior service cost and gains and losses receive delayed recognition by initially recognizing the increase in PBO in other comprehensive income and then recycling it through net income by amortizing the beginning balances over the average remaining service period of employees.

Computation of Net Pension Expense	2013	2014	2015
Service cost	$50,000	$50,000	$ 50,000
Interest on PBO	0	3,500	14,245
Expected return on assets	0	(6,000)	(12,600)
Amortization of PSC*	0	0	10,000
Amortization of gain/loss	0	0	0
Net pension expense	$50,000	$47,500	$ 61,645

*Assumes that the December 31, 2014, prior service cost is amortized beginning in 2015. The amount is amortized over average remaining service life of the workforce at December 31, 2014, which is assumed to be ten years.

Note that amortization of prior service cost is $0 in 2013, $0 in 2014 (because there was no beginning balance to amortize), and $10,000 in 2015 ($100,000 prior service cost/10 years). The amortization of prior service cost will continue for nine more years.

Net pension expense is reflected in the income statement in each of the three years. For merchandising firms, it appears as an operating expense. For manufacturing firms, the portion that pertains to employees involved in manufacturing inventory is capitalized as part of inventory and then expensed as a portion of cost of goods sold when the inventory is sold.

Exhibit 9.9 presents the previous discussion within the financial statement effects template. In 2013, an increase in the pension liability occurs that causes $50,000 in pension expense. Funding increases the pension asset by $60,000. In 2014, the plan amendment increases the pension liability by the $100,000 prior service cost. Prior service cost

Exhibit 9.9: Financial Statement Effects of Pension Accounting

Assets		=	Liabilities		+	Total Shareholders' Equity		
						CC	AOCI	RE
2013								
Record Pension Expense:			Pension Liability	+50,000				Pension Expense −50,000
Record Cash Payment:								
Cash	−60,000							
Pension Asset	+60,000							
Pension Expense				50,000				
Pension Liability						50,000		
Pension Asset				60,000				
Cash						60,000		
2014								
Record Plan Amendment:			Pension Liability	+100,000			OCI −100,000	
Record Pension Expense:			Pension Liability	+53,500				Pension Expense −47,500
Pension Asset	+6,000							
Record Cash Payment:								
Cash	−60,000							
Pension Asset	+60,000							

(Continued)

Exhibit 9.9 (Continued)

OCI		100,000				
Pension Liability			100,000			
Pension Expense		47,500				
Pension Asset		6,000				
Pension Liability			53,500			
Pension Asset		60,000				
Cash			60,000			

2015						
Record Pension Expense:						
Pension Asset +12,600	Pension Liability +64,245			OCI +10,000	Pension Expense −61,645	
Record Cash Payment:						
Cash −60,000						
Pension Asset +60,000						

Pension Expense		61,645	
Pension Asset		12,600	
OCI			10,000
Pension Liability			64,245
Pension Asset		60,000	
Cash			60,000

receives delayed recognition (that is, it is not reflected in current pension expense). Instead, other comprehensive income is reduced. The remainder of the changes in the pension liability (increase of $53,500) and pension asset (increase of $6,000) is from events receiving immediate recognition in pension expense (increase of $47,500). Again, funding increases the pension asset further ($60,000 increase). In 2015, similar events occur to change the pension asset and liability. In addition, the prior service cost is amortized to pension expense by removing $10,000 from other comprehensive income.

In the notes, Moreno will disclose the components of the net periodic pension expense, as shown in the table illustrating the pension expense computations on page 725. Additional required disclosures reconcile beginning PBO to ending PBO and beginning FMV of plan assets to ending FMV of plan assets.

Note Disclosures: Reconciliations of PBO and FMV of Plan Assets	2013	2014	2015
January 1, PBO	$ 0	$ 50,000	$203,500
Service cost	50,000	50,000	50,000
Interest cost	0	3,500	14,245
Prior service cost	0	100,000	0
Benefit payments	0	0	0
December 31, PBO	$ 50,000	$203,500	$267,745
January 1, FMV of plan assets	$ 0	$ 60,000	$126,000
Company contributions	60,000	60,000	60,000
Benefit payments	0	0	0
Actual return on plan assets	0	6,000	12,600
December 31, FMV of plan assets	$ 60,000	$126,000	$198,600
Net pension liability (asset)	$(10,000)	$ 77,500	$ 69,145

Gain and Loss Recognition

To this point, we have assumed that all actual and expected amounts are equal. Gains and losses occur when expectations turn out to be different than realizations. That is:

Expected PBO $\neq$ Actual PBO, which results in liability gains or losses

Expected FMV $\neq$ Actual FMV, which results in asset gains or losses

Pension plan accounting defers both asset and liability gains and losses. The net deferred gain/loss amount is amortized only if it becomes very large. The FASB set an arbitrary amount, called the *corridor* amount, as the threshold for deferred gain or loss amortization. The *corridor* is defined as 10% of the greater of actual PBO or actual FMV. The logic behind this treatment is simple. Gains and losses are deviations from expectations. If expectations are unbiased, gains and losses will offset over time and the net gain or loss should fluctuate around zero. If, however, the gains and losses do not offset over time, the accumulated gains or losses will become large, with *large* defined as exceeding the corridor. The FASB prescribes amortization only if the balance becomes larger than the corridor. The decision to amortize net deferred gains or losses is made each year, and that decision is independent of any decision made in prior years. Also, the decision is made based upon *beginning-of-the-year balances* (that is, using prior year-end balances for net deferred gain or loss, PBO, and FMV). The financial statement effects of amortizing a net loss are identical to the effects of amortizing prior service cost. Amortizing a net gain decreases other comprehensive income and increases net income via a reduction in pension expense.

Impact of Actuarial Assumptions

Firms must disclose in notes to the financial statements the assumptions made with respect to

- the discount rate used to compute the pension benefit obligation.
- the expected rate of return on pension investments (including the pension plan investment guidelines that form the basis for establishing the expected rate of return).
- the rate of compensation increase, which affects the amount of the PBO.

The amount of the pension benefit obligation is inversely related to the discount rate. U.S. GAAP specifies that firms should use a long-term government bond rate as the discount rate. Thus, firms should not vary significantly with respect to the discount rate used. However, even small differences in the discount rate can materially affect the size of the pension benefit obligation.

Firms use different expected rates of return on pension investments, in part because of different mixtures of investments in their pension portfolios. For example, a firm with equal proportions of debt and equity should have a lower expected return (and lower risk) than a firm that invests fully in equities. **PepsiCo** discloses in Note 7 that its expected return on investments of plan assets is 7.8% for all three years presented. PepsiCo reports that its target allocation is for the plan assets to be invested 40% in fixed income securities, 33% in U.S. equity, 22% in international equity, and 5% in real estate. PepsiCo also provides a detailed analysis of how it determined the fair values of the plan assets. This disclosure is useful for two reasons. First, you can examine the reliability of the fair values. For each investment listed, PepsiCo labels the fair value as Level 1, 2, or 3, and provides more detail on the source of information used in the valuation. For example, under U.S. plan assets, you will find "Government securities." The disclosure indicates that the $1,287 million is a Level 2 valuation "based on quoted bid prices for comparable securities in the marketplace and broker/dealer quotes that are not observable." Note that very few plan assets are invested in Level 3 assets.

Second, the disclosure allows an assessment of whether target allocations are being achieved. For example, at the end of 2011, the fair values of investments in fixed income securities of both U.S. and international plan assets totaled $4,606 million out of total plan assets of $11,293 million. This proportion is 40.8%. A similar computation yields 39.5% at the end of 2012. Therefore, PepsiCo is near its target allocation of 40% in fixed income securities.

These transparent disclosures of target and actual investment allocations exist because of concerns that firms may use different expected rates of return in an effort to manage earnings. The assumed long-term rate of return on pension assets impacts the analysis of pensions in several ways. First, if the firm cannot generate returns, on average, equal to this rate, the firm will need to contribute additional assets in the future. Second, the expected return on pension investments reduces pension expense each period and increases earnings. Firms must amortize any combined difference between expected and actual returns and liability gains and losses if the accumulated gains and losses exceed the corridor, so a deficiency resulting from expecting too high a level of returns shows up slowly in pension expense.

The problem also exists with the assumed rate of compensation increases, which is determined by management and thus not as externally verifiable as the discount rate for the PBO and the expected return on plan assets. The amount of the pension benefit obligation is directly related to the assumed rate of compensation increases. Firms have incentives to use a lower rather than higher assumed rate of compensation increases, both to lower their PBO and to create lower expectations among employees about future compensation increases. You should compare a firm's assumptions over time with other firms to evaluate the firm's level of aggressiveness in making assumptions.

Other Postretirement Benefits

Employers provide postretirement benefits other than pensions to employees as well as to employees' spouses and dependents. These benefits may include medical and hospitalization coverage, college tuition assistance, and life insurance coverage. As in the case of pensions, current employee service triggers these promises, and the expected obligation for these benefits can be computed as the actuarially determined present value of future payments.

A good understanding of postretirement benefits accounting can be obtained by adopting the same framework for expense recognition, balance sheet presentation, and note reconciliation as that discussed for pensions. However, there are two major differences. First, many companies simply pay these benefits when retirees make claims and do not fund a portfolio of plan assets dedicated to pay for other postretirement benefits, because government regulations do not specify minimum funding for postretirement benefits other than pensions. As a result, the FMV of postretirement plan assets is zero for many companies. Second, there are two additional required disclosures for postretirement benefits other than pensions: (1) the assumed health care cost trend rate(s) used in actuarial computations and (2) the effects of a one-percentage-point increase and decrease in the assumed health care cost trend rate on the accumulated postretirement benefit obligation for health care benefits and on the aggregate of the service and interest cost components of the net periodic postretirement health care benefit cost.

Signals about Earnings Persistence

Large swings in the market values of investments can impact pension expense and earnings significantly. Although firms use long-term expected returns on investments to compute the expected return on assets each period, they apply this rate to the market value of assets in the pension portfolio. When market values increase, as they did in the early to late 1990s, many firms found that their pension expenses became pension income. During this period, some firms' pension income was a substantial portion of their increased earnings. In the stock market downturn that followed, companies recognized pension expense rather than pension income, exacerbating the downward pressure on earnings from weakened economic conditions. When using earnings of the current period to forecast earnings in the future, you should recognize the impact of changing stock prices on the measurement of pension expense.

PepsiCo's Pensions and Other Postemployment Benefits

Note 7 to **PepsiCo**'s consolidated financial statements presents pension (for U.S. and international) and other postemployment benefits information. The first major schedule shows that the projected benefit liability (PBO) on U.S. plans at the beginning of 2012 was $11,901 million and increased to $12,886 million. PBO increased due to service cost ($407 million), interest cost on the beginning PBO ($534 million), a plan amendment that increased the past benefits of employees ($15 million), and an unfavorable change in the actuarial assumptions used to estimate the PBO ($932 million). PBO decreased due to payments to retired employees ($278). Also, plans will be terminated or curtailed occasionally. PepsiCo reports a settlement/curtailment in 2012, the payment of which decreased PBO ($633 million). Also, an employee group occasionally negotiates a special termination benefit when terminating plan coverage. PepsiCo reports an increase in the PBO due to such an event ($8 million). PepsiCo provides similar descriptions of PBO changes from international plans and retiree medical plans in the remaining columns. A substantial difference is the large foreign currency adjustment that increases the PBO liability when the plans are translated to U.S. dollars ($102 million).

PepsiCo explains the changes in the fair value of plan assets in the next part of the schedule. U.S. plan assets began 2012 at a fair value of $9,072. The actual return on plan assets increased that amount by $1,282 million, a 14.1% return that was substantially higher than expected (PepsiCo discloses a 7.8% long-run expected return on plan assets). PepsiCo contributed $1,368 million to the plan assets and used $278 million of plan assets to pay benefits and another $627 million for the settlement/curtailment and special termination benefits. By year-end, PepsiCo was in a net liability position because plan assets were only $10,817 million as compared to a PBO of $12,886 million. The difference, $2,069 million, is reported primarily as a part of other noncurrent liabilities on the balance sheet ($2,018 million in other liabilities in the long-term section of the balance sheet and the remainder in current liabilities according to Note 7).

Again, the remaining columns provide similar descriptions of changes in the fair value of plan assets for international plans and retiree medical plans. The large foreign currency adjustment that increased the PBO liability by $102 million also increased the fair value of plan assets by $86 million.

Pepsi next reports that most of these changes are included in other comprehensive income for the period and as accumulated other comprehensive income on the balance sheet. In total, $4,333 million of decreases in comprehensive income over time from U.S. plans and $1,093 million from international plans have not been reflected on the income statement. The combined total is nearly 98.9% of the $5,487 accumulated comprehensive loss reported as a component of shareholders' equity as of December 29, 2012. The majority of this amount is accumulated net unfavorable, unexpected changes in the assumptions underlying the computation of the PBO and fair value of plan assets ($4,212 million for U.S. and $1,096 million for international plans, respectively). To appreciate how quickly this large of a loss can accumulate, one need only consider PepsiCo's disclosure of the increases and decreases in the net loss in 2012 and 2011 for U.S. and international plans. In the row entitled "Change in discount rate," $776 and $1,710 million loss has occurred for U.S. plans in 2012 and 2011, respectively, and $188 and $302 million loss has occurred for international plans in 2012 and 2011, respectively. The sum of these four losses incurred in only two years is $2,976 million, approximately 56% of the losses accumulated over time. Therefore, in only two years, falling interest rates led to a lower discount rate assumption to compute the present value of future pension benefits (i.e., the PBO) and a nearly $3 billion loss reported as part of accumulated other comprehensive income.

PepsiCo continues by disclosing how it calculated the pension expense recognized in net income. Pension expense is increased by service cost ($407 million) and interest cost ($534 million). It is decreased by the *expected* return on plan assets ($796 million), which you will recall was much smaller than the actual return on plan assets. Prior service cost, initially reflected in other comprehensive income, is recycled to pension expense via amortization ($17 million), and the amount of loss initially reflected in other comprehensive income has become so large that it exceeds the corridor and must be recycled to pension expense via amortization ($259 million). Settlement/curtailments ($185 million) and special termination benefits ($8) also received immediate recognition in pension expense.

PepsiCo's disclosures highlight the income-smoothing nature of pension accounting. Imagine the effect on net income of the period if all of the actual gain on plan assets were included in current net income instead of added to other comprehensive income or all of the loss from decreases in the discount rate were recognized in income. The justification for this treatment is the transitory nature of security market movements and the long-run nature of PepsiCo's obligations to retired employees. However, because actuarial gains and losses, unexpected returns on plan assets, and unamortized prior service costs are part of comprehensive income (along with unrealized gains and losses on available-for-sale securities, foreign currency translation gains and losses, and certain derivative gains and losses) and current comprehensive income affects other accumulated comprehensive income, shareholders' equity is not smoothed by pension accounting.

Quick Check

- Pensions and other postemployment benefits have two key economic amounts: the present value of expected payments to retirees and the fair value of assets that have been set aside to make those payments.
- Non-cash expected changes in these two economic amounts are accumulated into pension expense.

- Non-cash unexpected changes are reported as other comprehensive income and accumulated other comprehensive income. The amounts either reverse or are recycled through pension expense in later periods.
- The difference between the two key economic amounts is reported as either a net asset or a net liability in the balance sheet.

Use of Derivative Instruments to Hedge Foreign Currency and Commodity Price Risk

LO 9-5

Explain how firms use *derivative instruments* to hedge currency and commodity risk from operating transactions.

Firms engage in many transactions that subject them to the risks associated with changes in interest rates, foreign currency exchange rates, and commodity prices. In the context of Chapter 7's look at financing activities, we discussed accounting for derivatives in general and illustrated the use of one type of derivative, an interest rate swap, to hedge interest rate risk. At this point, you may wish to review that discussion. In this chapter on operating activities, we illustrate three common uses of derivatives in operations:

- a forward contract to hedge *foreign currency risk* on an *existing asset or liability* resulting from exporting or importing goods (a contract that does not qualify for hedge accounting treatment)
- a forward contract to hedge *foreign currency risk* on an *unrecognized firm commitment* (which qualifies as a *fair value hedge*)
- a forward contract to hedge the *commodity price risk* inherent in a *forecasted future transaction* (which qualifies as a *cash flow hedge*).

Hedging Foreign Currency Risk: Existing Asset or Liability

In Chapter 8, we learned the process by which firms *translate* subsidiary financial statements denominated in a foreign currency and how the resulting unrealized translation gains and losses are reported. The unrealized translation gains and losses are intended to measure the risk of owning a subsidiary with assets and liabilities denominated in a currency that fluctuates in value relative to the U.S. dollar.[14] Firms are also exposed to currency risk if they import or export goods and the contracts are denominated in a foreign currency.

To illustrate this risk, how it can be hedged, and the financial reporting implications, we use the example of an importer. Suppose Worldwide Style, Inc., a U.S. retail firm with a December 31 year-end, purchases inventory on December 5, 2013, for €100,000 from an Italian supplier. The euro-denominated invoice is payable on April 5, 2014. On December 5, 2013, to protect against the possibility that euros may be more costly to buy on April 5, 2014, Worldwide Style locks in the future exchange rate by entering into a forward contract to buy €100,000 on April 5, 2014. Spot (i.e., current) and forward rates expressed at the number of U.S. dollars per euro at important measurement dates are as follows:

December 5, 2013:   Spot rate = 1.40   Forward rate for April 5, 2014 = 1.44
December 31, 2013:   Spot rate = 1.45   Forward rate for April 5, 2014 = 1.50
April 5, 2014:   Spot rate = Forward rate = 1.52

Exhibit 9.10 presents the financial statement template to record these transactions.[15]

---

[14]This risk can also be hedged, but we do not cover the hedging of net investments in subsidiaries in this text.

[15]Future payables and receivables and thus hedging contracts should be discounted to take the time value of money into account. We ignore the complex discounting issue in our presentation. For short duration contracts, the difference between gross and discounted amounts is generally immaterial.

Exhibit 9.10: Hedging Foreign Currency Risk on an Existing Liability

Assets	=	Liabilities	+	Shareholders' Equity		
				CC	AOCI	RE
December 5, 2013						
Purchase:						
Inventory +140,000		Accounts Payable +140,000				
Forward Contract:						
Receivable from		Payable to Dealer +144,000				
Dealer +144,000						
Inventory		140,000				
Accounts Payable				140,000	(1.40 spot rate × €100,000)	
Receivable from Dealer		144,000				
Payable to Dealer				144,000	(1.44 forward rate × €100,000)	
December 31, 2013						
Remeasure Payable:						
		Accounts Payable +5,000				Exchange Loss −5,000
Remeasure Forward:						
Receivable from Dealer +6,000						Exchange Gain +6,000
Exchange Loss		5,000		[(1.45 − 1.40) increase in spot rate × €100,000]		
Accounts Payable				5,000		
Receivable from Dealer		6,000				
Exchange Gain				6,000	[(1.50 − 1.44) increase in forward rate × €100,000]	
April 5, 2014						
Remeasure Payable:						
		Accounts Payable +7,000				Exchange Loss −7,000
Remeasure Forward:						
Receivable from Dealer +2,000						Exchange Gain +2,000
Settle Forward:						
Cash −144,000		Payable to Dealer −144,000				
Foreign Currency +152,000						
Receivable from						
Dealer −152,000						
Settle Payable:						
Foreign Currency −152,000		Accounts Payable −152,000				
Exchange Loss		7,000		[(1.52 − 1.45) increase in spot rate × €100,000]		
Accounts Payable				7,000		
Receivable from Dealer		2,000				
Exchange Gain				2,000	[(1.52 − 1.50) increase in forward rate × €100,000]	
Payable to Dealer		144,000				
Cash				144,000		
Foreign Currency		152,000				
Receivable from Dealer				152,000		
Accounts Payable		152,000				
Foreign Currency				152,000		

- At December 5, 2013, the purchase is recorded at the spot rate, thus establishing the cost of inventory at its fair value. The forward contract is generally not recorded because it is executory. However, we show a journal entry for it because doing so makes it easier to learn the foreign currency fluctuation effects. The receivable from the dealer and the payable to the dealer are measured at the forward rate. Because the contract is executory, no asset or liability related to the forward contract will be reported.
- As you look at the December 5, 2013, financial statement effects, realize that the inventory purchase is complete, and subsequent exchange rate fluctuations will only affect the fair value of the open accounts payable. Also, the payable to dealer has been fixed at $144,000, and subsequent exchange rate fluctuations will only

affect the fair value of the receivable from the dealer. Therefore, Worldwide Style has two exposures to risk, one liability and one asset, and each must be subsequently remeasured at key dates. The $4,000 cost of transferring foreign currency risk to the dealer is the difference between the final cash outflow of $144,000 to the dealer and the $140,000 fair value of the inventory.

- At the December 31, 2013, financial statement date, the accounts payable and the receivable from dealer must be remeasured. Spot rates have increased, meaning that it will take more U.S. dollars to pay the euro-denominated invoice. Accordingly, the accounts payable is increased by the increase in the spot rate, and a $5,000 exchange loss is recognized. Forward rates have also increased, meaning that the euros to be received from the dealer are more valuable. Accordingly, the value of the receivable from the dealer is increased by the increase in the forward rate, and a $6,000 exchange gain is recognized. The $6,000 is reported as an asset from a forward contract. The exchange losses and gains are reported in net income.

- Settlement occurs on April 5, 2014. First, we remeasure the accounts payable and receivable from the dealer at the prevailing spot rate (1.52), which triggers additional exchange losses and gains. Worldwide Style pays the dealer the fixed $144,000 and removes the payable to the dealer. The dealer transfers €100,000 (now worth $152,000 = 1.52 × €100,000) to Worldwide, which removes the receivable from the dealer. Worldwide transfers the €100,000 to the Italian supplier to satisfy the accounts payable.

- Summing the exchange gains and losses yields a net loss of $4,000. As we established earlier, this is the difference between the spot and the forward rates at the date of the initial purchase and it represents the cost of shifting the risk to the foreign exchange dealer.

The example is generalizable to exporters who sell inventory and enter forward contracts to exchange the foreign currency-denominated receivables for a fixed amount of U.S. dollars. Also, in our example, the forward rate was a premium and rates moved upward. The example is also generalizable to the case of forward discounts and alternative rate movements.

Hedging Foreign Currency Risk: Unrecognized Foreign Currency Commitment

Firms also enter into commitments to purchase inventory in the future at a set price. If the price is denominated in a foreign currency, the firm bears the risk of foreign currency fluctuations. A firm can enter into a forward contract to hedge this currently unrecognized foreign currency commitment. If the commitment is probable, identifiable, and the commitment specifies prices and quantities, then the transaction qualifies as a fair value hedge (the fair value in question is the fair value of the inventory asset).

To illustrate this transaction, we change the prior example in one way. Rather than purchasing the inventory on December 5, 2013, Worldwide Style enters into a commitment to purchase and pay for the inventory on April 5, 2014. Exhibit 9.11 illustrates the accounting.

Exhibit 9.11: Hedging Foreign Currency Risk: Unrecognized Foreign Currency Commitment

Assets	=	Liabilities	+	Shareholders' Equity		
				CC	AOCI	RE
December 5, 2013						
Forward Contract:						
Receivable from		Payable to Dealer +144,000				
Dealer +144,000						
Receivable from Dealer		144,000				
Payable to Dealer				144,000 [1.44 forward rate × €100,000]		
December 31, 2013						
Remeasure Purchase Commitment:		Purchase Commitment +5,000				Exchange Loss −5,000
Remeasure Forward:						
Receivable from						Exchange Gain +6,000
from Dealer +6,000						
Exchange Loss		5,000		[(1.45 − 1.40) increase in spot rate × €100,000]		
Purchase Commitment				5,000		
Receivable from Dealer		6,000				
Exchange Gain				6,000 [(1.50 − 1.44) increase in forward rate × €100,000]		
April 5, 2014						
Remeasure Purchase Commitment:		Purchase Commitment +7,000				Exchange Loss −7,000
Remeasure Forward:						
Receivable from Dealer +2,000						Exchange Gain +2,000
Settle Forward:						
Cash −144,000		Payable to Dealer −144,000				
Foreign Currency +152,000						
Receivable from						
Dealer −152,000						
Settle Payable:						
Foreign Currency −152,000						
Inventory +140,000		Purchase Commitment −12,000				
Exchange Loss		7,000		[(1.52 − 1.45) increase in spot rate × €100,000]		
Purchase Commitment				7,000		
Receivable from Dealer		2,000				
Exchange Gain				2,000 [(1.52 − 1.50) increase in forward rate × €100,000]		
Payable to Dealer		144,000				
Cash				144,000		
Foreign Currency		152,000				
Receivable from Dealer				152,000		
Inventory		144,000				
Purchase Commitment		12,000				
Foreign Currency				152,000		

- At December 5, 2013, the purchase commitment is not recorded because it is an executory contract. Also, the forward contract generally is not recorded because it is executory. However, we again show a journal entry to demonstrate the foreign currency fluctuation effects. The receivable from the dealer and the payable to the dealer are measured at the forward rate. Because the contract is executory, no asset or liability related to the forward contract is reported.
- As in our prior example, at the December 31, 2013, financial statement date, the purchase commitment and the receivable from the dealer must be remeasured. All entries are identical to our prior example except for one account title. Accounts payable does not yet exist in a purchase commitment. Therefore, we increase the purchase commitment (a liability) when we recognize the $5,000 exchange loss.
- Settlement occurs on April 5, 2014. First, we remeasure the purchase commitment and the receivable from the dealer. The forward is settled as before, giving

Worldwide €100,000. The entries to record these facts are as in our prior example. The only entry that differs is the entry in which Worldwide transfers €100,000 (now worth $152,000) to the Italian supplier to make the committed purchase. At this point, Inventory of $140,000 is recorded. The remaining $12,000 satisfies the full purchase commitment liability that has been accrued.

■ All exchange gains and losses of fair value hedges are recognized in net income.

Hedging Commodity Price Risk: Forecasted Future Transaction

Finally, we consider a different kind of hedging commonly used in operations to mitigate commodity price risk. To illustrate the hedging of a forecasted future transaction, assume that Jittery Joe's Coffee brews its own coffee from Arabica beans. On December 1, 2013, Jittery Joe estimates that it will need to acquire 10,000 pounds of beans during February 2014, at which time it intends brew and sell the coffee. Jittery Joe would like to fix the price at which it can buy the coffee, so it enters into a futures contract fixing the price for February delivery at $1.20 per pound. It acquired the futures contract to protect its future cash margins from bean price increases. Even though the purchase has not been made, it is probable. This contract is a hedge involving a forecasted transaction and Jittery Joe's designates the derivative instrument as a cash flow hedge. Exhibit 9.12 illustrates the accounting for this hedge assuming the forward price of coffee beans on December 31, 2013, for February 2014 delivery is $1.22 per pound.

■ At December 1, 2013, the futures contract is not recorded because it is an executory contract.

■ At December 31, 2013, the futures contract has become more valuable by $200 [($1.22 − 1.20) × 10,000 pounds] because it fixes Jittery Joe's purchase price at $1.20 when, without the contract, the purchase price would have been $1.22. The gain is reported in other comprehensive income.

Exhibit 9.12: Hedging Commodity Price Risk: Forecasted Future Transaction

Assets		=	Liabilities		+	Shareholders' Equity		
						CC	AOCI	RE
December 1, 2013								
No entry for forward contract								
December 31, 2013								
Remeasure Contract:								
Futures Contract	+200						Unrealized Holding Gain +200	
Futures Contract				200				
Unrealized Holding Gain (OCI)						200	[($1.22 − 1.20) increase in price × 10,000 pounds]	
February 2014								
Acquire Inventory:								
Cash	−12,200							
Inventory	+12,200							
Settle Futures Contract:								
Cash	+200							
Futures Contract	−200							
Inventory				12,200				
Cash							12,200	
Cash				200				
Futures Contract							200	

- Settlement occurs in February 2014. (We assumed no further price movements. If price movements would have occurred, we would first remeasure the futures contract before settling it.) Jittery Joe acquires the inventory at $1.22 \times 10,000 = $12,200. The futures contract is settled net, providing $200 in cash.
- Later, when the inventory is sold, the unrealized holding gain on the futures contract will be recycled to the income statement by reducing cost of goods sold by $200. Thus, the net margin is based on a $12,000 cost of goods sold ($12,200 − 200). The hedge is effective.

Summary

Operating profitability is the key driver of firm value. This chapter examined the accounting and reporting issues surrounding operating activities. Our discussion of operating profitability followed the generally occurring order of the income statement. We began with a study of revenue recognition and followed with discussions of the major expense categories: cost of sales, SG&A expense, and income tax expense. These operating activities require investments in working capital. Accordingly, we examined issues surrounding inventory and accounts receivable reporting and the reporting of many working capital assets and liabilities that arise when accrual measurement and cash flow timing do not coincide. Finally, we considered the financial statement effects of pensions and derivatives, two areas in which the reporting of profitability is divided between current recognition on the income statement and delayed recognition in other comprehensive income.

Questions, Exercises, Problems, and Cases

Questions and Exercises

LO 9-1

9.1 Delayed Revenue Recognition. Software companies often bundle upgrades and technical support services with their software. Assume that a software company promises to automatically deliver upgrades for two years when a customer purchases software costing $100. Describe how the software company should determine the amount of revenue to recognize at the date of sale and subsequent to the date of sale.

LO 9-1

9.2 Revenue Recognition. Revenues are at the core of a firm's ability to grow and prosper; thus, they are central to the analysis of a firm's profitability. Although the time-of-sale method is the most common technique employed to recognize revenues, in some instances, a strong argument can be made for recognizing revenue before the product has been completed and delivered. Discuss circumstances in which this scenario is appropriate.

LO 9-1

9.3 Long-Term Contract Profit Recognition. Three alternative revenue recognition methods are available to long-term contractors when cash inflows are probable: percentage of completion, completed contract, and cost recovery. Assuming that the contract price is known, discuss the appropriate method under U.S. GAAP and IFRS under two alternative scenarios: (a) the proportion of work performed and the proportion of work remaining until completion can be reliably determined and (b) no reliable basis exists for determining the total amount of work necessary to complete the project. (Note: Because percentage of completion is generally estimated by comparing the costs to date to expected total costs, the inability to estimate the total amount of work to be performed creates the inability to estimate percent complete reliably.)

LO 9-1, LO 9-2

9.4 Working Capital. Identify the working capital accounts related to (a) revenues recognized and deferred, (b) cost of goods sold, (c) employee salary and wages, and (d) income tax expense. For each account, indicate whether an increase in the working capital asset or liability would be an addition or subtraction when reconciling from net income to cash flows from operations.

9.5 Expense Recognition. Provide three examples of expense recognition justified by (a) a direct relation with revenue (cause and effect) and (b) an indirect relation with revenue (the consumption of an asset or an increase in a liability during a period in which revenue is recognized).

`LO 9-2`

9.6 Accounts Receivable. Using the following key, identify the effects of the following transactions or conditions on the various financial statement elements: I = increases; D = decreases; NE = no effect.

`LO 9-1, LO 9-2`

	Assets	Liabilities	Shareholders' Equity	Net Income
a. A credit sale				
b. Collection of a portion of accounts receivable				
c. Estimate of bad debts				
d. Write-off of a specific uncollectible account				

9.7 Inventory Costing and Valuation. The acquisition cost of inventory remaining at the end of a period is measured using LIFO, FIFO, or average cost.

`LO 9-2`

   a. Rank cost of goods sold, gross profit, and ending inventory from highest to lowest under the three cost-flow assumptions when input prices are rising.

   b. How should differences between acquisition cost and the market value of inventory be reported on the balance sheet under IFRS and U.S. GAAP?

9.8 LIFO Layer Liquidation. What is a LIFO layer liquidation? How does it affect the prediction of future earnings?

`LO 9-2`

9.9 Effect of Weighted-Average Cost-Flow Assumption on Inventory. The weighted-average cost-flow assumption is a common technique used to value inventory and determine cost of goods sold. It falls between LIFO and FIFO as to the differential effect on inventory and cost of goods sold amounts, although normally it is more like FIFO than LIFO in its effect on the balance sheet. Why?

`LO 9-2`

9.10 Reconcile PBO/FMV of Plan Assets. Given the following information, compute December 31, 2014, projected benefit obligation (PBO) and fair market value (FMV) of plan assets for Lee Company.

`LO 9-2`

Prior service cost granted in a 2014 plan amendment	$110,000
Interest on PBO	70,000
Actual return on plan assets	100,000
Service cost	80,000
Contribution sent to plan trustee	60,000
Benefit payments to retirees	20,000
Liability loss (gain)	(30,000)
FMV of plan assets, January 1, 2014	750,000
PBO, January 1, 2014	800,000

What amount of asset or liability will be reported on the balance sheet at December 31, 2014?

LO 9-4

9.11 Financial Statement Effects of Pension Plan Events. Using the following key, identify the effects of the following transactions or conditions on the various financial statement elements: I = increases; D = decreases; NE = no effect.

Note that the questions pertain to the employer's financial statements, not to the pension plan's financial statements. Analyze effects on the current year only.

Pension Plan Events or Conditions	Assets	Liabilities	Shareholders' Equity	Net Income
a. Employees performing current service				
b. Plan amendment grants retroactive benefits				
c. Projected benefit obligation accrues interest at the settlement rate				
d. Unexpected increases in PBO due to changes in actuarial assumptions				
e. Retired employees are paid benefits				
f. Contributions made to plan trustee				
g. Plan assets increase by expected return from investing				
h. Unexpected decrease in FMV of plan assets due to an asset loss				
i. Amortization of prior service cost				
j. Amortization of gain				

LO 9-4

9.12 Components of Pension Expense. Pension expense typically consists of five components. Answer the following questions related to each component.

a. Service cost: Is it possible for the service cost component to *reduce* pension expense for the year? Explain your answer.

b. Interest cost: Is it possible for the interest cost component to *reduce* pension expense for the year? Explain your answer.

c. Expected return on plan assets: U.S. GAAP requires firms to reduce pension expense each year by the expected, not the actual, return on investments. What is the logic employed by policy makers in reaching this decision?

d. Amortization of prior service cost: What is a prior service cost? Provide an example of a plan change that would generate an amount labeled prior service cost.

e. Amortization of actuarial gains and losses: What circumstances give rise to actuarial gains and losses?

LO 9-4

9.13 Postretirement Benefits Other Than Pensions. The notes to a firm's financial statements reveal that the obligations for postretirement health care benefits at the end of 2014 total $2.1 billion. The fair value of plan assets for these benefits at the end of 2014 is reported at zero, with an unrecognized net actuarial loss of $310 million reported for the same year. Calculate the amount of the postretirement health care benefit obligation reported by the firm at the end of 2014. Discuss what classification category (or categories) on the balance sheet would appropriately include the obligation.

Problems and Cases

9.14 Income Recognition for Various Types of Businesses. Discuss

LO 9-1, LO 9-2

when each of the following types of businesses is likely to recognize revenues and expenses.

a. A bank lends money for home mortgages.

b. A travel agency books hotels, transportation, and similar services for customers and earns a commission from the providers of these services.

c. A major league baseball team sells season tickets before the season begins and signs its players to multiyear contracts. These contracts typically defer the payment of a significant portion of the compensation provided by the contract until the player retires.

d. A producer of fine whiskey ages the whiskey 12 years before sale.

e. A timber-growing firm contracts to sell all timber in a particular tract when it reaches 20 years of age. Each year it harvests another tract. The price per board foot of timber equals the market price when the customer signs the purchase contract plus 10% for each year until harvest.

f. An airline provides transportation services to customers. Each flight grants frequent-flier miles to customers. Customers earn a free flight when they accumulate sufficient frequent-flier miles.

9.15 Measuring Income for a Software Manufacturer. DataTech (DT) is

LO 9-1, LO 9-2

a software manufacturer. It develops, markets, and supports software that helps manufacturers improve the competitiveness of their products. DT provides a detailed description of its revenue streams in its SEC 10-K filing, excerpts of which are as follows:

> We derive revenues from three primary sources: (1) software licenses, (2) maintenance services and (3) other services, which include consulting and education services. We exercise judgment and use estimates in connection with the determination of the amounts of software license and services revenues to be recognized in each accounting period.
>
> For software license arrangements that do not require significant modification or customization of the underlying software, we recognize revenue when: (1) persuasive evidence of an arrangement exists, (2) delivery has occurred (generally, FOB shipping point or electronic distribution), (3) the fee is fixed or determinable, and (4) collection is probable. Substantially all of our license revenues are recognized in this manner. Our software is distributed primarily through our direct sales force. However, our indirect distribution channel continues to expand through alliances with resellers. Revenue arrangements with resellers are recognized on a sell-through basis; that is, when we receive persuasive evidence that the reseller has sold the products to an end-user customer. We do not offer contractual rights of return, stock balancing, or price protection to our resellers, and actual product returns from them have been insignificant to date. As a result, we do not maintain reserves for product returns and related allowances.
>
> At the time of each sale transaction, we must make an assessment of the collectibility of the amount due from the customer. Revenue is only recognized at that time if management deems that collection is probable. In making this assessment, we consider customer creditworthiness and historical payment experience. At that same time, we assess whether fees are fixed or determinable and free of contingencies or significant uncertainties. If the fee is not fixed or determinable, revenue is recognized only as payments become due from the customer, provided that all other revenue recognition criteria are met. In assessing whether the fee is fixed or determinable, we consider the payment terms of the transaction and our collection experience in similar transactions without making concessions, among other factors. Our software license arrangements generally do not include customer acceptance provisions. However, if an arrangement includes an acceptance provision, we record revenue only upon the earlier of (1) receipt of written acceptance from the customer or (2) expiration of the acceptance period.

Our software arrangements often include implementation and consulting services that are sold separately under consulting engagement contracts or as part of the software license arrangement. When we determine that such services are not essential to the functionality of the licensed software and qualify as "service transactions," we record revenue separately for the license and service elements of these arrangements.

Maintenance services generally include rights to unspecified upgrades (when and if available), telephone and Internet-based support, updates and bug fixes. Maintenance revenue is recognized ratably over the term of the maintenance contract on a straight-line basis. It is uncommon for us to offer a specified upgrade to an existing product; however, in such instances, all revenue of the arrangement is deferred until the future upgrade is delivered.

When consulting qualifies for separate accounting, consulting revenues under time and materials billing arrangements are recognized as the services are performed.

Education services include on-site training, classroom training, and computer-based training and assessment. Education revenues are recognized as the related training services are provided.

REQUIRED

a. DT generates revenues from software licenses. Discuss the appropriateness of revenue recognition techniques employed by the firm for software licenses in relation to the two general criteria for revenue recognition presented in the chapter.

b. DT recognizes maintenance service revenue ratably over the term of the maintenance contract unless a specific software upgrade is promised to the customer as part of the maintenance contract. Describe the revenue recognition policy of DT for maintenance contracts that include a specific upgrade. Justify the logic for the policy.

c. DT provides educational services to its clients, such as on-site training and assessment, and recognizes revenue when the services are provided. Speculate on the criteria employed by DT to justify when the services have been provided.

d. DT states that the firm must "exercise judgment and use estimates in connection with the determination of the amounts of software license and services revenues to be recognized in each accounting period." Provide several illustrations of judgments or estimates that DT must employ for determining the amount of software license and service revenues to report each accounting period.

LO 9-1, LO 9-2   **9.16 Measuring Income for a Consultancy Firm.** Sanders Company is a technology consultancy firm. Sanders disclosures in a recent Form 10-K filing provided an extensive discussion of its revenue recognition policies, excerpts of which follow:

We recognize revenue from the provision of professional services under written service contracts with our clients. We derive a significant portion of our revenue from fixed-price, fixed-time contracts. Revenue generated from fixed-price contracts, with the exception of support and maintenance contracts, is recognized based on the ratio of labor hours incurred to estimated total labor hours. This method is used because reasonably dependable estimates of the revenues and costs applicable to various stages of a contract can be made, based on historical experience and milestones set in the contract.

Revenue generated from fixed-price support and maintenance contracts is recognized ratably over the contract term.

Certain contracts provide for revenue to be generated based upon the achievement of certain performance standards. Revenue is recognized when such performance standards are achieved.

Revenue from multiple element arrangements is accounted for under EITF Issue No. 00-21 (EITF 00-21), "Revenue Arrangements with Multiple Deliverables." For these arrangements, we evaluate all deliverables in the contract to determine whether they represent separate units of accounting. If the deliverables represent separate units of accounting, we then measure and allocate the consideration from the arrangement to the separate units, based on reliable evidence of the fair value of each deliverable. This evaluation is performed at the inception of the arrangement and as each item in the arrangement is delivered, and involves significant judgments regarding the nature of the services and deliverables being provided and whether these services and deliverables can reasonably be divided into the separate units of accounting.

REQUIRED

a. Sanders recognizes revenues based on the provisions of the written service contracts generated for each client. The primary types of contracts are (1) fixed-price, fixed-time contracts; (2) support and maintenance contracts; and (3) performance standards contracts. Discuss the criteria used to recognize revenue for each type of contract and the difficulties in applying the criteria.

b. Discuss the appropriateness of the revenue recognition techniques employed by Sanders in relation to the general revenue recognition criterion of "substantial portion of services has been provided" as discussed in the text of this chapter.

c. As detailed earlier, some contracts have multiple-element arrangements with separate deliverable components. Discuss the criteria used to distinguish among multiple components of the contract. Also speculate on how the firm recognizes revenue when the contract cannot be separated into distinct deliverable components.

9.17 Measuring Income for a Long-Haul Transport Firm. Canadian National Railway Company

`LO 9-1, LO 9-2`

(CN) spans Canada and mid-America and provides freight transport services from the Atlantic Ocean to the Pacific Ocean and to the Gulf of Mexico. It is currently the largest private rail system in Canada and was privatized by the Canadian government when it was considered one of the worst rail transport companies in North America. CN has been a success story since its privatization and is now considered one of the strongest and most efficient rail freight transport companies. Its success is partly due to a fundamental change in the way it offers freight services to customers. CN runs what the firm refers to as a *scheduled railroad*. Similar to rail passenger service, as much as possible CN maintains a fixed operating schedule and a fixed freight-car fleet movement across the continent. Thus, customers know what shipment options are available to them and know with a high degree of accuracy when shipments will arrive at designated locations.

Typically, a customer contracts a fixed fee with CN to ship its freight from the point of origination (for example, the Port of Halifax) to the point of destination (for example, the Port of Vancouver). CN provides the entire transport (that is, CN does not contract out a portion of the shipment to other rail transport companies), and the length of time taken to deliver the freight depends on the distance and the type of service (fast delivery versus normal delivery, for example) purchased by the customer. In a recent annual report, CN succinctly states its policy on recognizing revenue: "Freight revenues are recognized on services performed by the Company, based on the percentage of complete service method. Costs associated with movements are recognized as the service is performed."

REQUIRED

Discuss the appropriateness of the revenue recognition techniques employed by CN for recognizing freight revenues.

9.18 Measuring Income from Long-Term Contracts.

`LO 9-1, LO 9-2`

On January 1, 2014, assume that Turner Construction Company agreed to construct an observatory for Dartmouth College for $120 million. Dartmouth College must pay $30 million upon signing and $30 million at the end of 2014, 2015, and 2016. Expected construction costs are $10 million for 2014,

$60 million for 2015, and $30 million for 2016. Assume that these cash flows occur at the end of each year. Also assume that an appropriate interest rate for this contract is 10%. Amortization schedules for the deferred cash flows follow.

	Amortization Schedule for Cash Received (amounts in thousands)				
Year	**Balance Jan. 1**	**Interest Revenue**	**Payment**	**Reduction in Principal**	**Balance Dec. 31**
2014	$74,606	$7,460	$30,000	$22,540	$52,066
2015	52,066	5,207	30,000	24,793	27,273
2016	27,273	2,727	30,000	27,273	0

	Amortization Schedule for Cash Disbursed (amounts in thousands)				
Year	**Balance Jan. 1**	**Interest Expense**	**Payment**	**Reduction in Principal**	**Balance Dec. 31**
2014	$81,217	$8,122	$10,000	$ 1,878	$79,339
2015	79,339	7,934	60,000	52,066	27,273
2016	27,273	2,727	30,000	27,273	0

REQUIRED

a. Indicate the amount and nature of income (revenue and expense) that Turner would recognize during 2014, 2015, and 2016 if it uses the completed-contract method. Ignore income taxes.
b. Repeat Requirement a using the percentage-of-completion method.
c. Repeat Requirement a using the installment method.
d. Indicate the balance in the Construction in Process account on December 31, 2014, 2015, and 2016, (just prior to completion of the contract) under the completed-contract and the percentage-of-completion methods.

LO 9-1, LO 9-2 **9.19 Interpreting Financial Statement Disclosures Relating to Income Recognition. Deere & Company** manufactures agricultural and industrial equipment and provides financing services for its independent dealers and their retail customers. In Note 2 to its October 31, 2012, 10K, Deere discloses the following revenue recognition policy:

Sales of equipment and service parts are recorded when the sales price is determinable and the risks and rewards of ownership are transferred to independent parties based on the sales agreements in effect. In the U.S. and most international locations, this transfer occurs primarily when goods are shipped. In Canada and some other international locations, certain goods are shipped to dealers on a consignment basis under which the risks and rewards of ownership are not transferred to the dealer. Accordingly, in these locations, sales are not recorded until a retail customer has purchased the goods. In all cases, when a sale is recorded by the company, no significant uncertainty exists surrounding the purchaser's obligation to pay. No right of return exists on sales of equipment ... Financing revenue is recorded over the lives of related receivables using the interest method ...

REQUIRED

a. Using the criteria for revenue recognition, justify Deere's timing of revenue recognition for its equipment sales. Consider why recognition of revenue earlier or later than the time of shipment to dealers would not be more appropriate.

b. Describe briefly how the balance sheet accounts of Deere & Company listed here would change if it recognized revenues during the period of production using the percentage-of-completion method. You do not need to give amounts, but indicate the likely direction of the change and describe the computation of its amount.
- Accounts and Notes Receivable
- Inventories
- Retained Earnings

c. Respond to Requirement b assuming that Deere & Company recognized revenue using the installment method.

9.20 LIFO and FIFO Cost-Flow Assumptions for Inventory. A large   `LO 9-2`
manufacturer of truck and car tires recently changed its cost-flow assumption method for inventories at the beginning of 2014. The manufacturer has been in operation for almost 40 years, and for the last decade it has reported moderate growth in revenues. The firm changed from the LIFO method to the FIFO method and reported the following information (amounts in millions):

| | December 31 | |
	2013	2014
Inventories at FIFO cost	$ 788.1	$ 861.7
Excess of FIFO cost over LIFO cost	(429.0)	(452.4)
Cost of goods sold (FIFO)	—	4,150.8
Cost of goods sold (LIFO)	—	4,417.1

REQUIRED

Calculate the inventory turnover ratio for 2014 using the LIFO and FIFO cost-flow assumption methods. Explain why the costs assigned to inventory under LIFO at the end of 2013 and 2014 are so much less than they are under FIFO.

9.21 Reconcile PBO/FMV of Plan Assets; Compute Pension   `LO 9-4`
Expense. The following information relates to a firm's pension plan.

Prior service cost due to 2013 amendment	$ 60,000
PBO, January 1, 2013	1,000,000
FMV, January 1, 2013	1,200,000
Settlement interest rate	7%
Expected return on plan assets	9%
Actual return on plan assets	8%
Liability loss (gain)	(40,000)
Contribution to plan trustee (made at end of year)	100,000
Service cost	115,000
Payments to retired employees	30,000

REQUIRED

a. Compute the December 31, 2013, PBO and FMV of pension assets.
b. Compute 2013 pension expense.
c. Use the financial statements effects template to show the effects on the 2013 financial statements.

LO 9-5
9.22 Accounting for Forward Foreign Exchange Contract as a Fair Value Hedge.
Lynn Construction enters into a firm purchase commitment for equipment to be delivered on June 30, 2013, for a price of 10,000 GBP. It simultaneously signs a forward foreign exchange contract for 10,000 GBP. The forward rate on June 30, 2013, for settlement on June 30, 2014, is $1.64 per GBP. Lynn designates the forward foreign exchange contract as a fair value hedge of the firm commitment.

REQUIRED

    a. U.S. GAAP and IFRS do not require Lynn to record the purchase commitment or the forward foreign exchange contract on the balance sheet as a liability and an asset on June 30, 2013. What is the logic for this accounting?

    b. On December 31, 2013, the forward foreign exchange rate for settlement on June 30, 2011, is $1.73 per GBP. Using the financial statement effects template, show the financial statement effects of recording the change in the value of the purchase commitment and the change in the value of the forward contract for 2013. Ignore discounting.

    c. On June 30, 2014, the spot foreign exchange rate is $1.75 per GBP. Show the financial statement effects of recording the change in the value of the purchase commitment and the change in the value of the forward contract due to changes in the exchange rate during the first six months of 2014.

    d. Show the financial statement effects of the June 30, 2014, purchase of 10,000 GBP with U.S. dollars and acquisition of the equipment.

    e. Show the financial statement effects on June 30, 2014, to settle the forward foreign exchange contract.

    f. How would the effects in Requirements b–e differ if Lynn had chosen to designate the forward foreign exchange contract as a cash flow hedge instead of a fair value hedge?

    g. Suggest a scenario that would justify Lynn treating the forward foreign exchange contract as a fair value hedge and a scenario that would justify the firm treating the contract as a cash flow hedge.

LO 9-5
9.23 Accounting for Forward Commodity Price Contract as a Cash Flow Hedge.
Kentucky Gold (KG) holds 10,000 gallons of whiskey in inventory on October 31, 2013, that costs $225 per gallon. KG contemplates selling the whiskey on March 31, 2014, when it completes the aging process. Uncertainty about the selling price of whiskey on March 31, 2014, leads KG to acquire a forward contract on whiskey. The forward contract does not require an initial investment of funds. KG designates the forward commodity contract as a cash flow hedge of an anticipated transaction. The forward price on October 31, 2013, for delivery on March 31, 2014, is $320 per gallon.

REQUIRED

    a. Using the financial statement effects template, show the financial statement effects, if any, that KG would have on October 31, 2013, when it acquires the forward commodity price contract.

    b. On December 31, 2013, the end of the accounting period for KG, the forward price of whiskey for March 31, 2014, delivery is $310 per gallon. Show the financial statement effects of recording the change in the value of the forward commodity price contract. Ignore the discounting of cash flows in this part and in the remainder of the problem.

    c. Show the financial statement effects of the December 31, 2013, decline in value of the whiskey inventory.

    d. On March 31, 2014, the price of whiskey declines to $270 per gallon. Show the financial statement effects of revaluing the forward contract.

e. Show the financial statement effects on March 31, 2014, to reflect the decline in value of the inventory.

f. Show the financial statement effects on March 31, 2014, to settle the forward contract.

g. Assume that KG sells the whiskey on March 31, 2014, for $270 a gallon. Show the financial statement effects of recording the sale and recognizing the cost of goods sold.

h. How would the effects in Requirements b–g differ if KG had chosen to designate the forward commodity price contract as a fair value hedge instead of a cash flow hedge?

i. Suggest a scenario that would justify treating the forward commodity price contract as a fair value hedge and a scenario that would justify treating it as a cash flow hedge.

9.24 Interpreting Derivatives Disclosures. Excerpts from the disclosures on derivatives made by a large beverage manufacturer in Year 4 appear below:

LO 9-5

Our Company uses derivative financial instruments primarily to reduce our exposure to adverse fluctuations in interest rates and foreign exchange rates, and, to a lesser extent, in commodity prices and other market risks. When entered into, the Company formally designates and documents the financial instrument as a hedge of a specific underlying exposure, as well as the risk management objectives and strategies for undertaking the hedge transaction. The Company formally assesses, both at the inception and at least quarterly thereafter, whether the financial instruments that are used in hedging transactions are effective at offsetting changes in either the fair value or cash flows of the related underlying exposures. Our Company does not enter into derivative financial instruments for trading purposes.

Our Company monitors our mix of fixed-rate and variable-rate debt. This monitoring includes a review of business and other financial risks. We also enter into interest rate swap agreements to manage these risks. These contracts had maturities of less than one year on December 31, Year 4. The fair value of our Company's interest rate swap agreements was approximately $6 million at December 31, Year 4. The Company estimates the fair value of its interest rate management derivatives based on quoted market prices. Interest rate swap agreements are accounted for as fair value hedges. During Year 4, there has been no ineffectiveness related to fair value hedges.

We enter into forward exchange contracts to hedge certain portions of forecasted cash flows denominated in foreign currencies. These contracts had maturities up to one year on December 31, Year 4. The purpose of our foreign currency hedging activities is to reduce the risk that our eventual U.S. dollar net cash inflows resulting from sales outside the United States will be adversely affected by changes in exchange rates. We designate these derivatives as cash flow hedges. During Year 4, we decreased accumulated other comprehensive income by $76 million ($46 million after tax) for changes in the fair value of cash flow hedges. The amount recorded in earnings for the ineffective portion of cash flow hedges during Year 4 was not significant. We also reclassified net losses of $86 million ($52 million after tax) from accumulated other comprehensive income to earnings. The accumulated net loss on cash flow derivatives on December 31, Year 4, is $56 million ($34 million after tax). The carrying and fair value of foreign exchange contracts on December 31, Year 4, is $39 million.

We monitor our exposure to financial market risks using value-at-risk models. Our value-at-risk calculations use a historical simulation model to estimate potential future losses in the fair value of our derivatives and other financial instruments that could occur as a result of adverse movements in foreign currency and interest rates. We examined historical weekly returns over the previous 10 years to calculate our value at risk. The average value at risk represents the simple average of quarterly amounts over the past year. According to our interest rate value-at-risk calculations, we estimate with 95% confidence that an adverse move in interest rates over a one-week period would not have a material impact on our consolidated financial statements for Year 4. Similar calculations for adverse movements in foreign exchange rates indicate a maximum impact on earnings over a one-week period of $17 million. Net income for Year 4 was $4,847 million.

REQUIRED

   a. The company indicates that it "formally specifies the risk management objectives and strategies for undertaking the hedge transactions." Identify the risk management objectives and describe how the particular derivative accomplishes these objectives with respect to interest rate swap agreements.

   b. Repeat Requirement a for forward exchange contracts.

   c. What is the rationale for the company's designation of the interest rate swaps as fair value hedges and the forward exchange contracts as cash flow hedges?

   d. Why does the company assess both initially and at least quarterly the effectiveness of these hedging instruments?

   e. Compute the amount that the company initially recorded on its books for foreign exchange contracts outstanding on December 31, Year 4. What events will cause the carrying value of these contracts at any later date to differ from the amounts initially recorded?

   f. For Year 4, the company reports a $76 million net loss from changes in the value of cash flow hedges. What does the disclosure that the company recognized a net loss instead of a net gain suggest about the direction of changes in exchange rates between the U.S. dollar and the foreign currencies underlying the foreign exchange contracts? Will the forward exchange contracts likely appear on the company's balance sheet as assets or liabilities? Explain.

   g. Justify the company's treatment of the $76 million net loss from changes in the value of cash flow hedges during Year 4 as a decrease in accumulated other comprehensive income instead of an ineffective cash flow hedge that should be included in earnings.

   h. The gains and losses from changes in the fair value of foreign exchange contracts are taxed in the period of settlement. Will the tax effects of the $76 million pretax loss for Year 4 affect current taxes payable or deferred taxes? If the answer to the previous question is deferred taxes, will it affect deferred tax assets or deferred tax liabilities? Explain.

   i. Describe the likely event that will cause the company to reclassify amounts from accumulated other comprehensive income to earnings.

   j. Assess the effectiveness of the company's management of risk changes from interest and foreign exchange rates for Year 4.

 9.25 Interpreting Income Tax Disclosures. Disclosures related to income taxes for **The Coca-Cola Company** (Coca-Cola) for 2006–2008 appear in Exhibit 9.13.

REQUIRED

   a. Why are Coca-Cola's average tax rates so low?

   b. Is it likely that Coca-Cola has recognized a net asset or a net liability on its balance sheet for pension and other postretirement benefit plans? Explain your reasoning.

   c. Coca-Cola discloses that the valuation allowance on deferred tax assets relates primarily to net operating loss carryforwards. Assume for purposes of this question that Coca-Cola had recognized a valuation allowance each year exactly equal to the deferred tax assets recognized for net operating loss carryforwards. Indicate the effect on income tax expense and income tax payable in the year Coca-Cola initially recognizes the net operating loss carryforwards.

   d. Refer to Requirement c. Indicate the effect on income tax expense and income tax payable in the year Coca-Cola benefits from the net operating loss carryforwards.

   e. Interpret Coca-Cola's recognition of net deferred tax liabilities, instead of deferred tax assets, for equity investments in 2008.

Exhibit 9.13

The Coca-Cola Company
Income Tax Reconciliation and Components of Deferred Taxes
(amounts in millions)
(Problem 9.25)

	2008	2007	2006
Income Tax Reconciliation			
U.S. Statutory Tax Rate	35.0%	35.0%	35.0%
State Taxes, Net of Federal Tax Benefit	0.8	0.6	0.7
Foreign Earnings Taxes at Lower Rates	(14.3)	(10.8)	(11.4)
Equity Income or Loss	0.2	(1.3)	(0.6)
Other Operating Charges	0.7	0.5	0.6
Other	(0.5)	(0.0)	(1.5)
Average Tax Rate	21.9%	24.0%	22.8%

Components of Deferred Taxes on December 31:	2008	2007	
Deferred Tax Assets			
Property, Plant and Equipment	$ 33	$ 45	
Trademarks and Other Intangible Assets	79	76	
Equity Method Investments	339	238	
Other Liabilities	447	845	
Benefit Plans	1,171	881	
Net Operating Loss Carryforwards	494	554	
Other	532	266	
Total Deferred Tax Assets (Gross)	$ 3,095	$ 2,905	
Valuation Allowance	(569)	(611)	
Total Deferred Tax Assets (Net)	$ 2,526	$ 2,294	
Deferred Tax Liabilities			
Property, Plant and Equipment	$ (667)	$ (670)	
Trademarks and Other Intangible Assets	(1,974)	(1,925)	
Equity Method Investments	(267)	(841)	
Other Liabilities	(101)	(90)	
Other	(229)	(383)	
Total Deferred Tax Liabilities	$(3,238)	$(3,909)	
Net Deferred Tax Assets (Liability)	$ (712)	$(1,615)	

Source: The Coca-Cola Company, Form 10-K for the Fiscal Year ended December 31, 2008.

f. Why does Coca-Cola report tax effects of equity income and investments in the income tax reconciliation and in deferred tax liabilities?

g. Interpret Coca-Cola's recognition of deferred tax liabilities, instead of deferred tax assets, for intangible assets.

INTEGRATIVE CASE 9.1

Starbucks

REQUIRED

Starbucks generates revenues in many different ways. In addition to owning its own stores, it licenses other companies to sell Starbucks brewed and ground coffees, teas, and other products.

a. For each of the following customers, describe how Starbucks should recognize revenue and the working capital accounts that would likely be created by the revenue recognition approach. (For Items 1–5, ignore sales tax.)

(1) Cash customer purchasing coffee at a Starbucks-owned retail store

(2) Customer adding cash balance to her Starbucks card

(3) Customer at Starbucks-owned retail store paying for coffee with a Starbucks card

(4) Other businesses that purchase Starbucks' products on credit

(5) Licensed stores

(6) Customer remitting sales taxes to Starbucks when purchasing coffee

b. Starbucks' "gold-level" customers purchase 15 cups of coffee and then receive a free 16th cup of coffee. How should Starbucks account for this customer loyalty program? (Assume that the selling price for a cup of coffee is $2.20 and that the direct inventory cost per cup is $1.50.)

CASE 9.2

Arizona Land Development Company

Joan Locker and Bill Dasher organized the Arizona Land Development Company (ALDC) on January 2, Year 1. They contributed land with a market value of $300,000 and $100,000 cash for all of the common stock of the corporation. The land served as the initial inventory of property sold to customers.

ALDC sells undeveloped land, primarily to individuals approaching retirement. Within nine years from the date of sale, ALDC promises to develop the land so that it is suitable for the construction of residential housing. ALDC makes all sales on an installment basis. Customers pay 10% of the selling price at the time of sale and remit the remainder in equal installments over the next nine years.

ALDC estimates that development costs will equal 50% of the selling price of the land and that development work will take nine years to complete from the date of sale. Actual development costs have coincided with expectations. The firm incurs 10% of the development costs at the time of sale and incurs the remainder evenly over the next nine years.

ALDC remained a privately held firm for its first six years. Exhibits 9.14–9.16 present the firm's income statement, balance sheet, and statement of cash flows, respectively, for Year 1–Year 6. ALDC recognizes income from sales of undeveloped land at the time of sale. The amount shown for sales each year in Exhibit 9.14 represents the gross amount ALDC ultimately expects to collect from customers for land sold in that year. The amount shown for estimated development costs each year is the gross amount ALDC ultimately expects to disburse to develop land sold in that year. The firm treats selling expenses as a period expense. It is subject to a 34% income tax rate. ALDC uses the installment method of income recognition for income tax purposes.

Exhibit 9.14

Arizona Land Development Company
Income Statements
Income Recognition at Time of Sale—No Discounting of Cash Flows
(Case 9.2)

	Year 1	Year 2	Year 3	Year 4	Year 5	Year 6
Sales	$ 650,000	$ 900,000	$1,500,000	$ 2,500,000	$1,200,000	$ 400,000
Less:						
Cost of land inventory sold	(65,000)	(90,000)	(150,000)	(250,000)	(120,000)	(40,000)
Estimated development costs	(325,000)	(450,000)	(750,000)	(1,250,000)	(600,000)	(200,000)
Gross Profit	$ 260,000	$ 360,000	$ 600,000	$ 1,000,000	$ 480,000	$ 160,000
Selling expenses	(65,000)	(90,000)	(150,000)	(250,000)	(120,000)	(40,000)
Net Income before Taxes	$ 195,000	$ 270,000	$ 450,000	$ 750,000	$ 360,000	$ 120,000
Income taxes:						
Current	—	—	(9,778)	(26,091)	(73,009)	(94,902)
Deferred	(66,300)	(91,800)	(143,222)	(228,909)	(49,391)	54,102
Net Income	$ 128,700	$ 178,200	$ 297,000	$ 495,000	$ 237,600	$ 79,200

Exhibit 9.15

Arizona Land Development Company
Balance Sheets
Income Recognition at Time of Sale—No Discounting of Cash Flows
(Case 9.2)

	Year 1	Year 2	Year 3	Year 4	Year 5	Year 6
ASSETS						
Cash	$100,000	$ 132,500	$ 100,222	$ 126,631	$ 131,122	$ 273,720
Notes receivable	520,000	1,175,000	2,220,000	3,915,000	4,320,000	3,965,000
Land inventory	235,000	145,000	95,000	45,000	125,000	185,000
Total Assets	$855,000	$1,452,500	$2,415,222	$4,086,631	$4,576,122	$4,423,720
LIABILITIES AND SHAREHOLDERS' EQUITY						
Estimated development cost liability	$260,000	$ 587,500	$1,110,000	$1,957,500	$2,160,000	$1,982,500
Deferred income taxes	66,300	158,100	301,322	530,231	579,622	525,520
Common stock	400,000	400,000	400,000	500,000	500,000	500,000
Retained earnings	128,700	306,900	603,900	1,098,900	1,336,500	1,415,700
Total Liabilities and Shareholders' Equity	$855,000	$1,452,500	$2,415,222	$4,086,631	$4,576,122	$4,423,720

Exhibit 9.16

Arizona Land Development Company
Statements of Cash Flows
Income Recognition at Time of Sale—No Discounting of Cash Flows
(Case 9.2)

	Year 1	Year 2	Year 3	Year 4	Year 5	Year 6
OPERATIONS						
Net income	$ 128,700	$ 178,200	$ 297,000	$ 495,000	$ 237,600	$ 79,200
(Increase) Decrease in notes receivable	(520,000)	(655,000)	(1,045,000)	(1,695,000)	(405,000)	355,000
(Increase) Decrease in land inventory	65,000	90,000	50,000	50,000	(80,000)	(60,000)
Increase (Decrease) in estimated development cost liability	260,000	327,500	522,500	847,500	202,500	(177,500)
Increase (Decrease) in deferred income taxes	66,300	91,800	143,222	228,909	49,391	(54,102)
Cash Flow from Operations	$ 0	$ 32,500	$ (32,278)	$ (73,591)	$ 4,491	$ 142,598
FINANCING						
Common stock issued	—	—	—	100,000	—	—
Change in Cash	$ 0	$ 32,500	$ (32,278)	$ 26,409	$ 4,491	$ 142,598

ALDC contemplates making its initial public offering of common stock early in Year 7. The firm asks you to assess whether its income recognition method, as reflected in Exhibits 9.14–9.16, accurately reflects its operating performance and financial position. To assist you, the firm has prepared financial statements following three other income recognition methods as described next.

Income Recognition at Time of Sale but with Discounting of Future Cash Flows to Present Value

Exhibits 9.17–9.19 present the financial statements that use this income recognition method. This method discounts future cash inflows from customers and future cash outflows for development work to their present values. The gross profit recognized at the time of sale equals the present value of cash inflows net of the present value of cash outflows. One might view this gross profit as the current cash-equivalent value of the gross profit the firm will ultimately realize over the nine-year period. This method reports the increase in the present value of cash

	Exhibit 9.17					
	Arizona Land Development Company **Income Statements** **Income Recognition at Time of Sale—With Discounting of Cash Flows** **(Case 9.2)**					
	Year 1	**Year 2**	**Year 3**	**Year 4**	**Year 5**	**Year 6**
Sales	$ 411,336[a]	$ 569,543	$ 865,737	$1,442,895	$ 759,390	$ 253,130
Less:						
Cost of land inventory sold	(65,000)	(90,000)	(150,000)	(250,000)	(120,000)	(40,000)
Estimated development costs	(205,668)[b]	(284,771)	(432,869)	(721,448)	(379,695)	(126,565)
Gross Profit	$ 140,668	$ 194,772	$ 282,868	$ 471,447	$ 259,695	$ 86,565
Selling expenses	(65,000)	(90,000)	(150,000)	(250,000)	(120,000)	(40,000)
Interest revenue	41,560[c]	96,293	196,609	361,257	411,130	400,899
Interest expense	(20,780)[d]	(48,147)	(98,304)	(180,628)	(205,566)	(200,449)
Net Income before Taxes	$ 96,448	$ 152,918	$ 231,173	$ 402,076	$ 345,259	$ 247,015
Income taxes:						
Current			(9,778)	(26,091)	(73,009)	(94,902)
Deferred	(32,792)	(51,992)	(68,821)	(110,615)	(44,379)	10,917
Net Income	$ 63,656	$ 100,926	$ 152,574	$ 265,370	$ 227,871	$ 163,030

[a]Represents the present value of $65,000 received on January 1, Year 1, plus the present value of a series of $65,000 cash inflows on December 31, Year 1 to Year 9, discounted at 12%.

[b]Represents the present value of $32,500 paid on January 1, Year 1, plus the present value of a series of $32,500 cash outflows on December 31, Year 1 to Year 9, discounted at 12%.

[c]12% × ($411,336 − $65,000) = $41,560.

[d]12% × ($205,668 − $32,500) = $20,780.

Exhibit 9.18

Arizona Land Development Company
Balance Sheets
Income Recognition at Time of Sale—With Discounting of Cash Flows
(Case 9.2)

	Year 1	Year 2	Year 3	Year 4	Year 5	Year 6
ASSETS						
Cash	$100,000	$ 132,500	$ 100,222	$ 126,631	$ 131,122	$ 273,720
Notes receivable	322,896[a]	743,732	1,351,078	2,350,230	2,725,750	2,624,779
Land inventory	235,000	145,000	95,000	45,000	125,000	185,000
Total Assets	$657,896	$1,021,232	$1,546,300	$2,521,861	$2,981,872	$3,083,499
LIABILITIES AND SHAREHOLDERS' EQUITY						
Estimated development cost liability	$161,448[b]	$ 371,866	$ 675,539	$1,175,115	$1,362,876	$1,312,390
Deferred income taxes	32,792	84,784	153,605	264,220	308,599	297,682
Common stock	400,000	400,000	400,000	500,000	500,000	500,000
Retained earnings	63,656	164,582	317,156	582,526	810,397	973,427
Total Liabilities and Shareholders' Equity	$657,896	$1,021,232	$1,546,300	$2,521,861	$2,981,872	$3,083,499

[a]$411,336 − $65,000 + $41,560 − $65,000 = $322,896 [see Notes (a) and (c) to Exhibit 9.17].
[b]$205,668 − $32,500 + $20,780 − $32,500 = $161,448 [see Notes (b) and (d) to Exhibit 9.17].

inflows as time passes as interest revenue each year and the increase in the present value of cash outflows as interest expense. Thus, this income recognition method results in the reporting of two types of income: a gross profit from the selling of land and interest from delayed cash flows. The computations of present values underlying the financial statements in Exhibits 9.17–9.19 rest on the following assumptions:

1. ALDC makes all sales on January 1 of each year. It receives 10% of the gross selling price at the time of sale and pays 10% of the gross development costs immediately.
2. The firm receives 10% of the gross selling price from customers and pays 10% of the gross development costs on December 31 of each year, beginning with the year of sale.
3. The interest rates used in discounting are as follows:

Sales In:	Interest Rate
Year 1	12%
Year 2	12%
Year 3	15%
Year 4	15%
Year 5	12%
Year 6	12%

Exhibit 9.19

Arizona Land Development Company
Statements of Cash Flows
Income Recognition at Time of Sale—With Discounting of Cash Flows
(Case 9.2)

	Year 1	Year 2	Year 3	Year 4	Year 5	Year 6
OPERATIONS						
Net income	$ 63,656	$ 100,926	$ 152,574	$ 265,370	$ 227,871	$163,030
(Increase) Decrease in notes receivable	(322,896)	(420,836)	(607,346)	(999,152)	(375,520)	100,971
(Increase) Decrease in land inventory	65,000	90,000	50,000	50,000	(80,000)	(60,000)
Increase (Decrease) in estimated development cost liability	161,448	210,418	303,673	499,576	187,761	(50,486)
Increase (Decrease) in deferred income taxes	32,792	51,992	68,821	110,615	44,379	(10,917)
Cash Flow from Operations	$ 0	$ 32,500	$ (32,278)	$ (73,591)	$ 4,491	$142,598
FINANCING						
Common stock issued	—	—	—	100,000	—	—
Change in Cash	$ 0	$ 32,500	$ (32,278)	$ 26,409	$ 4,491	$142,598

Income Recognition Using the Installment Method—With Discounting of Cash Flows

Exhibits 9.20–9.22 present the financial statements following this income recognition method. ALDC uses this income recognition method for tax reporting.

Income Recognition Using the Percentage-of-Completion Method

Exhibits 9.23–9.25 (pages 756–758) present the financial statements that use this income recognition method. The presumption underlying this method is that ALDC is primarily a developer of real estate and that its income should reflect its development activity, not its sales activity. The difference between the contract price and the total estimated costs of the land and development work represents the total income from development of the land. The percentage-of-completion method uses actual costs incurred to date as a percentage of estimated total costs to determine the degree of completion each period. Multiplying this percentage times the contract price yields sales revenue each year. Multiplying this percentage times the total expected costs yields cost of goods sold.

Exhibit 9.20

Arizona Land Development Company
Income Statements
Income Recognition Using Installment Method—With Discounting of Cash Flows
(Case 9.2)

	Year 1	Year 2	Year 3	Year 4	Year 5	Year 6
Sales	$ 88,440[a]	$148,707	$ 258,391	$ 443,744	$ 383,868	$ 354,101
Cost of goods sold	(58,195)	(97,852)	(172,963)	(297,634)	(254,699)	(235,427)
Gross Profit	$ 30,245	$ 50,855	$ 85,428	$ 146,110	$ 129,169	$ 118,674
Selling expenses	(65,000)	(90,000)	(150,000)	(250,000)	(120,000)	(40,000)
Interest revenue	41,560[b]	96,293	196,609	361,257	411,130	400,899
Interest expense	(20,780)[c]	(48,147)	(98,304)	(180,628)	(205,566)	(200,449)
Net Income before Taxes	$(13,975)	$ 9,001	$ 33,733	$ 76,739	$ 214,733	$ 279,124
Income taxes:						
Current	—[d]	—[d]	(9,778)[d]	(26,091)	(73,009)	(94,902)
Deferred	4,751	(3,060)	(1,691)	—	—	—
Net Income	$ (9,224)	$ 5,941	$ 22,264	$ 50,648	$ 141,724	$ 184,222

[a]Exhibit 9.17 indicates that the total gross profit from land sold in Year 1 is $140,668. The present value of the amounts that ALDC will receive from customers is $411,336 (see Exhibit 9.17). Thus, for each dollar of the $411,336 collected, the firm recognizes 34.2 cents ($140,668/$411,336) of gross profit. During Year 1, ALDC collects $130,000 from sales of land made in Year 1 ($65,000 on January 1 and $65,000 on December 31). However, only $23,440 ($65,000 − $41,560) of the December 31 payment represents payment of a portion of the $411,336 selling price. The remainder ($41,560) represents interest. Thus, the gross profit recognized in Year 1 is $30,245 [0.342 × ($65,000 + $23,440)].

[b]See Note (c) to Exhibit 9.17.

[c]See Note (d) to Exhibit 9.17.

[d]ALDC carries forward the $13,975 loss in Year 1 to offset taxable income in future years ($9,001 in Year 2 and $4,974 in Year 3).

Exhibit 9.21

Arizona Land Development Company
Balance Sheets
Income Recognition Using Installment Method—With Discounting of Cash Flows (Case 9.2)

	Year 1	Year 2	Year 3	Year 4	Year 5	Year 6
ASSETS						
Cash	$100,000	$132,500	$ 100,222	$ 126,631	$ 131,122	$ 273,720
Notes receivable	212,473[a]	489,392	899,298	1,573,113	1,818,107	1,749,245
Land inventory	235,000	145,000	95,000	45,000	125,000	185,000
Deferred tax asset	4,751	1,691	—	—	—	—
Total Assets	$552,224	$768,583	$1,094,520	$1,744,744	$2,074,229	$2,207,965
LIABILITIES AND SHAREHOLDERS' EQUITY						
Estimated development cost liability	$161,448[b]	$371,866	$ 675,539	$1,175,115	$1,362,876	$1,312,390
Deferred income taxes	—	—	—	—	—	—
Common stock	400,000	400,000	400,000	500,000	500,000	500,000
Retained earnings	(9,224)	(3,283)	18,981	69,629	211,353	395,575
Total Liabilities and Shareholders' Equity	$552,224	$768,583	$1,094,520	$1,744,744	$2,074,229	$2,207,965

[a]The derivation of this amount is as follows:

	Notes Receivable—Gross	Deferred Gross Profit	Notes Receivable—Net
January 1, Year 1	$411,336	$140,668	$270,668
Less cash received, January 1, Year 1	(65,000)	—	(65,000)
Plus interest revenue, Year 1	41,560	—	41,560
Less cash received, December 31, Year 1	(65,000)	—	(65,000)
Gross profit recognized, Year 1	—	(30,245)	30,245
Totals	$322,896	$110,423	$212,473

[b]See Note (b) to Exhibit 9.18.

Exhibit 9.22

Arizona Land Development Company
Statements of Cash Flows
Income Recognition Using Installment Method—With Discounting of Cash Flows
(Case 9.2)

	Year 1	Year 2	Year 3	Year 4	Year 5	Year 6
OPERATIONS						
Net income (loss)	$ (9,224)	$ 5,941	$ 22,264	$ 50,648	$ 141,724	$184,222
(Increase) Decrease in notes receivable	(212,473)	(276,919)	(409,906)	(673,815)	(244,994)	68,862
(Increase) Decrease in land inventory	65,000	90,000	50,000	50,000	(80,000)	(60,000)
(Increase) Decrease in deferred tax asset	(4,751)	3,060	1,691	—	—	—
(Increase) Decrease in estimated development cost liability	161,448	210,418	303,673	499,576	187,761	(50,486)
Cash Flow from Operations	$ 0	$ 32,500	$ (32,278)	$ (73,591)	$ 4,491	$142,598
FINANCING						
Common stock issued	—	—	—	100,000	—	—
Change in Cash	$ 0	$ 32,500	$ (32,278)	$ 26,409	$ 4,491	$142,598

Exhibit 9.23

Arizona Land Development Company
Income Statements
Income Recognition Using Percentage-of-Completion Method
(Case 9.2)

	Year 1	Year 2	Year 3	Year 4	Year 5	Year 6
Sales	$ 216,667[a]	$ 354,167	$ 629,167	$1,087,500	$ 862,500	$ 695,833
Cost of goods sold	(130,000)[a]	(212,500)	(377,500)	(652,500)	(517,500)	(417,500)
Gross Profit	$ 86,667[a]	$ 141,667	$ 251,667	$ 435,000	$ 345,000	$ 278,333
Selling expenses	(65,000)	(90,000)	(150,000)	(250,000)	(120,000)	(40,000)
Net Income before Taxes	$ 21,667	$ 51,667	$ 101,667	$ 185,000	$ 225,000	$ 238,333
Income taxes:						
Current	—	—	(9,778)	(26,091)	(73,009)	(94,902)
Deferred	(7,367)	(17,567)	(24,789)	(36,809)	(3,491)	13,869
Net Income	$ 14,300	$ 34,100	$ 67,100	$ 122,100	$ 148,500	$ 157,300

[a]Land sold under contract in Year 1 had a contract price of $650,000 and estimated contract cost of $390,000 ($65,000 + $325,000) (see Exhibit 9.14). ALDC incurred development costs of $130,000 ($65,000 for land + $32,500 on January 1, Year 1 + $32,500 on December 31, Year 1) during Year 1. Thus, the percentage of completion as of the end of Year 1 is 33.3% ($130,000/$390,000). Sales are 33.3% of $650,000 and cost of goods sold is 33.3% of $390,000.

Exhibit 9.24

Arizona Land Development Company
Balance Sheets
Income Recognition Using Percentage-of-Completion Method
(Case 9.2)

	Year 1	Year 2	Year 3	Year 4	Year 5	Year 6
ASSETS						
Cash	$ 100,000	$ 132,500	$ 100,222	$ 126,631	$ 131,122	$ 273,720
Contracts in process	216,667[a]	570,834	1,200,001	2,287,501	3,150,001	3,845,834
Less progress billings	(130,000)[b]	(375,000)	(830,000)	(1,635,000)	(2,430,000)	(3,185,000)
Contracts in process, net	$ 86,667	$ 195,834	$ 370,001	$ 652,501	$ 720,001	$ 660,834
Land inventory	235,000	145,000	95,000	45,000	125,000	185,000
Total Assets	$ 421,667	$ 473,334	$ 565,223	$ 824,132	$ 976,123	$ 1,119,554
LIABILITIES AND SHAREHOLDERS' EQUITY						
Deferred income taxes	$ 7,367	$ 24,934	$ 49,723	$ 86,532	$ 90,023	$ 76,154
Common stock	400,000	400,000	400,000	500,000	500,000	500,000
Retained earnings	14,300	48,400	115,500	237,600	386,100	543,400
Total Liabilities and Shareholders' Equity	$ 421,667	$ 473,334	$ 565,223	$ 824,132	$ 976,123	$ 1,119,554

[a]Accumulated costs of $130,000 + gross profit recognized in Year 1 of $86,667 (see Note (a) to Exhibit 9.23).
[b]Down payment of $65,000 received on January 1, Year 1, plus $65,000 installment payment received on December 31, Year 1.

Exhibit 9.25

Arizona Land Development Company
Statements of Cash Flows
Income Recognition Using Percentage-of-Completion Method
(Case 9.2)

	Year 1	Year 2	Year 3	Year 4	Year 5	Year 6
OPERATIONS						
Net income	$ 14,300	$ 34,100	$ 67,100	$ 122,100	$ 148,500	$ 157,300
(Increase) Decrease in contracts in process	(216,667)	(354,167)	(629,167)	(1,087,500)	(862,500)	(695,833)
Increase (Decrease) in progress billings	130,000	245,000	455,000	805,000	795,000	755,000
(Increase) Decrease in land inventory	65,000	90,000	50,000	50,000	(80,000)	(60,000)
Increase (Decrease) in deferred income taxes	7,367	17,567	24,789	36,809	3,491	(13,869)
Cash Flow from Operations	$ 0	$ 32,500	$ (32,278)	$ (73,591)	$ 4,491	$ 142,598
FINANCING						
Common stock issued	—	—	—	100,000	—	—
Change in Cash	$ 0	$ 32,500	$ (32,278)	$ 26,409	$ 4,491	$ 142,598

REQUIRED

a. For each of the four income recognition methods illustrated in Exhibits 9.14–9.25, show the supporting calculations for each of the following items for Year 2:

(1) Sales for Year 2

(2) Cost of goods sold for Year 2

(3) Gross profit for Year 2

(4) Notes Receivable on December 31, Year 2, under the first three income recognition methods and the contracts in process account on December 31, Year 2, under the fourth income recognition method

(5) Estimated development costs liability on December 31, Year 2, under the first three income recognition methods and the progress billings account on December 31, Year 2, under the fourth income recognition method

b. Evaluate each of the four income recognition methods described in the case relative to the criteria for revenue and expense recognition. Which method best portrays the operating performance and financial position of ALDC? Discuss your reasoning.

c. Which income recognition method is ALDC likely to prefer when reporting to shareholders?

d. Why did ALDC choose the installment method for tax reporting?

e. With respect to maximizing cumulative reported earnings, the four income recognition methods rank-order as follows:

(1) Income recognition at time of sale—no discounting of cash flows

(2) Income recognition at time of sale—with discounting of cash flows

(3) Income recognition using the percentage-of-completion method

(4) Income recognition using the installment method—with discounting of cash flows

What is the reason behind this rank ordering?

f. The difference in cumulative reported earnings between any two income recognition methods equals the difference in notes receivable or contracts in process (net) minus the difference in the estimated development cost liability minus the difference in the deferred income taxes liability. What is the rationale behind this relation?

g. Why is the amount shown on the income statement for "current" income taxes the same in each year for all four income recognition methods but the amount of total income tax expenses (current plus deferred) in each year is different across income recognition methods?

h. Given that net income each year differs across the four income recognition methods, why is the amount of cash provided by operations the same? Under what conditions would a firm report different amounts of cash flow from operations for different income recognition methods?

CASE 9.3

LO 9-4

Coca-Cola Pensions

In its December 31, 2008, Consolidated Financial Statements, **The Cola-Cola Company** (Coca-Cola) reports a substantial shift in its net pension liability ($1,328 million) relative to December 31, 2007 ($85 million).

REQUIRED

a. Given a portion of Coca-Cola's Note 16 reconciliations provided below, write a memorandum explaining the change in the net pension liability. (Do not assume that the reader knows what items such as *service cost* mean.)

(amounts in millions)	**2008**
Benefit obligation at the beginning of the year	$3,517
Service cost	114
Interest cost	205
Foreign currency exchange rate changes	(141)
Amendments	(13)
Actuarial loss (gain)	125
Benefits paid*	(199)
Settlements/curtailments	(4)
Special termination benefits	11
Other	3
Benefit obligation at the end of the year	**$3,618**
Fair value of plan assets at beginning of year	$3,428
Actual return on plan assets	(961)
Employer contributions	96
Foreign currency exchange rate changes	(118)
Benefits paid*	(155)
Settlements/curtailments	(3)
Other	3
Fair value of plan assets at the end of the year	**$2,290**

*Some pension plans are "unfunded," meaning that the company does not hire an independent trustee and send the funds to the trustee for investment, but, instead, pays retirees out of company rather than trustee pension fund assets. Coca-Cola paid $44 million out of company assets to retirees who are covered by unfunded plans.

Source: The Coca-Cola Company, Form 10-K for the Fiscal Year ended December 31, 2008.

b. For each item in the reconciliation, explain whether the effect on the PBO and the fair value of plan assets is reflected in current period pension expense or as a change in other comprehensive income.

c. Provide a general justification for keeping some PBO and fair value of plan asset changes out of current period net income.

d. In the same note, Coca-Cola indicates that it changed a key assumption during the period. The expected rate of increase in compensation levels was decreased by 1%. What effect does this assumption change have on the pension liability (PBO) and current and future pension expense?

Forecasting Financial Statements

LO 10-1 Explain how the first four steps of the analytical framework of this text have provided you with the necessary foundation for forecasting.

LO 10-2 List and describe the general forecasting principles and the seven steps of the forecasting framework.

LO 10-3 Build forecasts of future balance sheets, income statements, and statements of cash flows by applying the seven-step forecasting framework to project:
  a. revenues.
  b. operating expenses.
  c. operating assets and liabilities.
  d. financial leverage, capital structure, and financial income items.
  e. taxes, net income, dividends, and retained earnings.
  f. a balance sheet that balances.
  g. cash flows.

LO 10-4 Understand how and when to use shortcut forecasting techniques.

LO 10-5 Test the validity of your forecast assumptions and results.

LO 10-6 Test the sensitivity of your forecasts to variations in critical assumptions and parameters.

LO 10-7 Develop forecast models that are flexible and comprehensive, allowing you to respond quickly and effectively when a company announces important new information.

Chapter Overview

Thus far, the preceding nine chapters of this text have drawn on the disciplines of accounting, finance, economics, and strategy. These chapters have demonstrated the first four steps of the analysis and valuation framework. They describe how to analyze: (1) the economics of a firm's industry, (2) the competitive advantages and risks of the firm's strategy, (3) the information content and quality of the firm's accounting, and (4) the firm's financial performance and risk. The next five chapters cover the two culminating steps of the framework: (5) forecasting the future operating, investing, and financing activities of the firm, and then (6) valuing the firm.

In this chapter, we shift our focus to the future, because the value of an investment is a function of its *expected future payoffs* conditional on the *risks inherent in those payoffs*. You will use your knowledge about a firm's industry, strategy, accounting quality, past and current profitability, and risk, to develop unbiased expectations about the firm's future operating, investing, and financing activities. Then you will capture those expectations in forecasts of future financial statements—income statements, balance sheets, and statements of cash flows. The purpose in building financial statement forecasts is to develop unbiased expectations for a firm's future earnings, cash flows, and dividends that you can use to estimate the firm's share value. You also can use financial statement forecasts in a wide array of decision contexts, such as strategic planning, credit analysis, corporate management, and mergers and acquisitions.

The financial statement forecasts we develop in this chapter we will then use in subsequent chapters to derive and value the future payoffs to the firm's common equity shareholders. Chapter 11 describes how to estimate risk-based costs of capital and then demonstrates the classical dividends-based valuation model, which is the theoretical foundation for other approaches to firm valuation. Chapter 12 demonstrates valuation models using expected future free cash flows. Chapter 13 implements valuation models that rely on expected future earnings. Chapter 14 demonstrates valuation approaches that rely on comparable companies and market-based multiples, such as price-earnings ratios and market-to-book ratios. Chapter 14 also illustrates some advanced valuation techniques, including computing price differentials and reverse engineering share prices.

Introduction to Forecasting

LO 10-1

Explain how the first four steps of the analytical framework of this text have provided you with the necessary foundation for forecasting.

Analysts must develop realistic expectations for the outcomes of a firm's future business activities. To develop these expectations, analysts *forecast* expected future income statements, balance sheets, and statements of cash flows. Financial statement forecasts are integrated projections of a firm's future operating, investing, and financing activities. These activities will determine the firm's future profitability, growth, financial position, cash flows, and risk. Financial statement forecasts are important tools because you can derive expectations of future payoffs to equity shareholders—earnings, cash flows, and dividends—which are the fundamental bases for share value.

Financial statement forecasts also are important tools in many other decision contexts. Credit risk decisions require expectations for future cash flows available to make required interest and principal payments. Managers' decisions about firm strategy, customer or supplier relationships, mergers or acquisitions, divestitures of divisions or subsidiaries, and even whether a firm presents a good employment opportunity, all depend on expectations for future payoffs and the risks of those payoffs.

Developing forecasts is in many ways the most difficult step of the six-step framework of this text because it requires you to confront a high degree of uncertainty, and forecast errors can prove very costly. Optimistic forecasts can lead you to overestimate future earnings and cash flows or underestimate risk and therefore overstate the value of the firm. Pessimistic or conservative forecasts can lead you to understate future earnings and cash flows or overstate risk and consequently miss valuable investment opportunities. As an analyst, you need to develop *realistic*—unbiased and objective, not optimistic or conservative—expectations of future earnings and cash flows that enable you to make well-informed investment decisions.

Superior forecasting has the potential to help you pick stocks that will generate superior returns. As Chapter 1 discussed, empirical research results from Nichols and Wahlen (2004) show that firms that generated increases in annual earnings also experienced stock returns that exceeded the market average by roughly 19% per year, whereas firms that generated decreases in annual earnings experienced stock returns that were roughly 16% below the average market return.[1] You should consider these results encouraging, because they suggest that by increasing your ability to forecast future changes in annual earnings, you will have a greater potential to distinguish future winning stocks from losing stocks.

Accounting researchers also have investigated whether financial statement ratios like those described in this text can be used to accurately predict future changes in earnings. For example, Ou and Penman (1989) built prediction models based on regressions of future earnings changes on a set of financial statement ratios.[2] Their prediction models estimate the probability of an earnings increase one year ahead. They conduct out-of-sample tests and find that their probability estimates correctly predict whether one-year-ahead earnings will increase or decrease for roughly 67% of their observations. They also show that taking hypothetical long (short) positions in shares of firms with a high (low) probability of an earnings increase resulted in average market-adjusted returns of roughly 8% per year during their study period. This study and subsequent related studies indicate that fundamental analysis of financial statement ratios can produce more accurate forecasts of future earnings and profitable investment decisions.

The first four steps of the analytical framework of this text have provided you with the necessary foundation for forecasting. To maximize your ability to develop reliable forecasts of financial statements and to avoid costly forecast errors, your expectations should reflect: (1) the economics of the industry, (2) the competitive advantages and risks of the firm's strategy, (3) the quality of the firm's accounting, and (4) the drivers of the firm's profitability and risk. These four steps inform you about the critical risk and success factors of the firm and the key drivers of the firm's profitability and risk. The critical factors that are the focal points of the firm's strategy, accounting quality, profitability, and risk are the most important building blocks for forecasting a firm's future financial statements.

This chapter first outlines general forecasting principles, describes a seven-step process for forecasting financial statements, and offers several practical coaching tips on forecasting. The chapter then applies each of the steps to PepsiCo, developing forecasts for income statements, balance sheets, and statements of cash flows for the next five years. The chapter then describes techniques to enhance the reliability of forecasts, including sensitivity analysis, iteration, and validity checks. The chapter also describes some shortcut forecasting techniques and the conditions under which such shortcuts are more reliable and less likely to result in forecast errors.

---

[1] D. Craig Nichols and James M. Wahlen, "How Do Earnings Numbers Relate to Stock Returns? A Review of Classic Accounting Research with Updated Evidence," *Accounting Horizons* 18 (December 2004), pp. 263–286. This study uses data from 1988 to 2001 to replicate the seminal findings in Ray Ball and Philip Brown, "An Evaluation of Accounting Income Numbers," *Journal of Accounting Research* (Autumn 1968), pp. 159–178; Roger Kormendi and Robert Lipe, "Earnings Innovations, Earnings Persistence, and Stock Returns," *Journal of Business* 60 (1987), pp. 323–345; and Victor Bernard and Jacob Thomas, "Post-Earnings Announcement Drift: Delayed Price Response or Risk Premium?," *Journal of Accounting Research* (1989 Supplement), pp. 1–48.

[2] See Jane Ou and Stephen Penman, "Financial Statement Analysis and the Prediction of Stock Returns," *Journal of Accounting and Economics* (November 1989), pp. 295–330. For examples of other studies in this area, see Jeffery Abarbanell and Brian Bushee, "Abnormal Stock Returns to a Fundamental Analysis Strategy," *The Accounting Review* 73 (January 1998), pp. 19–46; Stephen Penman and X. J. Zhang, "Modeling Sustainable Earnings and P/E Ratios With Financial Statement Information," 2010 working paper, Columbia University; and James Wahlen and Matthew Wieland, "Can Financial Statement Analysis Beat Consensus Analysts' Recommendations?" *Review of Accounting Studies* (March 2011), pp. 89–115.

LO 10-2

List and describe the general forecasting principles and the seven steps of the forecasting framework.

Preparing Financial Statement Forecasts

In this section we first describe general principles of building forecasts, and then a seven-step forecasting procedure, along with some practical forecasting tips. We also briefly describe how to use FSAP to build financial statement forecasts.

General Forecasting Principles

Several key principles of forecasting deserve mention at the outset.

- **Forecasts should project the firm's future operating, investing, and financing activities; projected future financial statements measure those activities.** You should focus on *projecting the firm's future business activities*. For example, when will a manufacturer invest in a new production plant, how much will that plant produce, and how will it be financed? The financial statements measure the projected effects of the firm's future business activities.
- **The objective of forecasting is to produce reliable and realistic expectations of future earnings, cash flows, and dividends, which determine the future payoffs to investment.** To maximize reliability and avoid costly forecast errors, your financial statement forecasts should provide *unbiased* and *objective* predictions of the firm's future operating, investing, and financing activities. Firm managers tend to be optimistic, and accountants tend to be conservative. Ideally, your forecasts should be neither optimistic nor conservative; instead they should be accurate and realistic.
- **Forecasts should avoid wishful thinking.** That is, do not create forecasts based on strategies you *hope* the firm will pursue or think the firm *should* pursue. Instead, your forecasts should capture the strategies you believe the firm *actually will execute and achieve* in the future.
- **Financial statement forecasts should be comprehensive.** The financial statement forecasts should *include all expected future operating, investing, and financing activities*. For example, suppose an analyst takes a quick-and-dirty approach and simply uses the prior year's sales growth rate to extrapolate expected future sales and then projects expected future earnings by assuming a constant profit margin. This approach fails to consider all of the elements that will determine future profitability, which can cause the earnings forecasts to be incomplete, erroneous, and misleading. By assuming a constant profit margin, the analyst ignores important considerations, such as whether the cost of goods sold and operating expenses will increase more quickly or more slowly than sales.
- **Financial statement forecasts must be internally consistent.** Forecasts of financial statements should rely on the *additivity* within financial statements and the *articulation* across the three primary financial statements to avoid internal inconsistencies and to reduce the possibility of errors from inconsistent assumptions. To capture the many complex relations among operating, investing, and financing activities, financial statement forecasts should add up and articulate with each other. The income statement should measure profit or loss appropriately for each period by including all revenues, expenses, gains, and losses each period. The balance sheet should capture all of the elements of financial position and should balance. The statement of

cash flows should reflect all cash inflows and outflows implied by the income statement and all changes in the firm's balance sheet. Forecasts of each of the financial statements will impact and be impacted by each of the other statements.

■ **Financial statement forecast assumptions must have external validity.** Forecast assumptions should pass the test of *common sense*. You should impose reality checks on your forecast assumptions. For example, do your sales growth forecast assumptions appropriately reflect the firm's strategy and the competitive conditions in the industry, including market demand and price elasticity for the firm's products, as well as the firm's productive capacity? You should benchmark the external validity of your forecast assumptions by comparing them to industry averages and to the firm's past performance and strategies.

Seven-Step Forecasting Game Plan

Exhibit 10.1 summarizes the following seven-step process, which provides you with a logical, sequential process for forecasting future financial statements:

1. Project revenues from selling products and delivering services to customers.
2. Project operating expenses (for example, cost of goods sold and selling, general, and administrative expenses) and derive projected operating income.
3. Project the operating assets (for example, cash; marketable securities; receivables; inventory; property, plant, and equipment; intangible assets) that will be necessary to support the level of operations projected in Steps 1 and 2. Also project the operating liabilities that will be triggered by these activities (for example, accounts payable and accrued expenses).
4. Project the financial liabilities, financial assets, and common equity capital (for example, short-term and long-term debt, any excess cash or investment securities available to service debt or equity claims, and common shareholders' equity except for retained earnings) that will be necessary to finance the net operating assets projected in Step 3. In addition, determine the interest expense that will be triggered by the financing liabilities and any interest and investment income from financial assets.
5. Project nonrecurring gains or losses (if any) and derive projected income before tax. Subtract the projected provision for income taxes to derive projected net income. Subtract expected dividends from net income to project the change in retained earnings. Also project other comprehensive income items, if any.
6. At this point the projected balance sheet will likely not balance, so you will have to determine how the firm will likely use its financial flexibility to balance the balance sheet. For example, if projected assets exceed projected liabilities and equities, it indicates the firm will need to raise capital through additional short- or long-term debt or equity issuances. Alternately, if projected liabilities and equities exceed projected total assets, it indicates the firm will be able to pay down debt, increase dividends, or repurchase stock. Steps 4, 5, and 6 must be repeated until the balance sheet is in balance.
7. Derive the projected statement of cash flows from the projected income statement and the changes in the projected balance sheet amounts.

Exhibit 10.1

The Seven-Step Process for Preparing Financial Statement Forecasts

Balance Sheet

Assets

Cash
Marketable Securities
Accounts Receivable
Inventories
Other Current Assets
Property, Plant, and Equipment
Intangible Assets

Short-Term Investments
Long-Term Investments

Total Assets =

Investing Activities
Net Capital Expenditures on Property, Plant, and Equipment
Purchases or Sales of Investments
Other Investing Transactions

Cash Flow from Investing

Liabilities and Shareholders' Equity

Accounts Payable
Accrued Expenses
Income Taxes Payable
Pension and Retirement Benefit Obligations
Deferred Taxes

Short-Term and Long-Term Debt
Contributed Equity Capital

Retained Earnings
Accumulated Other Comprehensive Income

Total Liabilities and Shareholders' Equity

Financing Activities
Changes in Short-Term and Long-Term Debt
Issues or Repurchases of Common Equity
Dividend Payments
Other Financing Transactions

Cash Flow from Financing

STEP 1: Project Operating Revenues

STEP 2: Project Operating Expenses and Derive Operating Income

STEP 3: Project Operating Assets and Liabilities

STEP 4: Project Financial Leverage, Financial Assets, Common Equity Capital, and Financial Income Items

STEP 5: Project Nonrecurring Items, Provisions for Income Taxes, Net Income, Dividends, Changes in Retained Earnings, and Other Comprehensive Income Items

STEP 6: Balance the Balance Sheet

STEP 7: Derive Cash Flows from Operating, Investing, and Financing Activities

Statement of Cash Flows

Income Statement and the Change in Retained Earnings

Sales Revenues
Other Operating Revenues

Operating Expenses:
– Cost of Goods Sold
– Selling, General, and Administrative Expense
– Other Operating Expenses
= **Operating Income**

– Interest Expense
+ Interest Income

– Income Taxes
= **Net Income**
– Dividends
= **Change in Retained Earnings**

Operating Activities
Net Income
Depreciation Expense
Other Adjustments
Changes in Receivables
Changes in Inventories
Changes in Other Current Assets
Changes in Payables
Changes in Accrued Expenses

Cash Flow from Operations

Throughout this book we demonstrate how you can gain additional insights about a firm by evaluating the operating, investing, and financing activities of the firm. The economic, strategic, and financial analysis techniques in Chapters 1 through 5 emphasize how to analyze operating, investing, and financing activities as integrated drivers of the profitability and risk of the firm. The accounting analysis techniques in Chapters 6 through 9 demonstrate how to assess the accounting quality of the financing, investing, and operating activities of the firm. We carry this perspective into the forecasting and valuation techniques in Chapters 10 through 14. In this chapter, the seven-step forecasting procedure begins with projecting the operating activities that occur in the normal day-to-day operations of producing and selling goods and services. Those activities involve accounts such as cash, receivables, inventory, payables, accrued expenses, and taxes. Projecting the firm's investing activities involves forecasting the acquisition and use of long-lived productive resources such as property, plant, and equipment and intangible assets, as well as financial resources such as short-term and long-term investment securities. The projected financing activities determine the financial capital structure of the firm. They typically involve financial liabilities such as short-term and long-term debt (notes, mortgages, bonds, and capital leases), in addition to preferred and common stock, and dividend payments.

Coaching Tips for Implementing the Seven-Step Forecasting Game Plan

- **Integrated and interdependent steps.** You should consider these seven steps as integrated and interdependent tasks that are not necessarily sequential or linear. The order in which you implement these steps and the amount of emphasis you place on each step will depend on the integration of the firm's operating, investing, and financing activities. For example, your forecasts of revenues for a retail or restaurant chain may first require forecasts of the number of new stores that will be open. Your sales forecasts for a manufacturer may depend on building a new plant, which may depend on obtaining long-term financing.

- **Forecast amounts must articulate among the three financial statements.** Most forecast amounts affect all three financial statements because they represent complex, interrelated business activities. For example, sales forecasts will affect the revenues on the income statement, receivables on the balance sheet, and operating cash flows on the statement of cash flows. As another example, the ending balance in retained earnings on the balance sheet should reflect the beginning balance plus net income from the income statement minus dividends from the statement of cash flows. Property, plant, and equipment on the balance sheet will be affected by capital expenditures from the statement of cash flows and depreciation expense, which affects both the income statement and the statement of cash flows. Net cash flow on the statement of cash flows must equal the change in cash on the balance sheet.

- **Financial flexibility, iterations, and circularity.** Your financial statement forecasts must balance, so you will require at least one flexible financial account and an iterative and circular process. Firms must rely on flexible financial accounts—financial assets, financial liabilities, equity capital, and dividends—that can expand or contract with the firm's supply and demand for capital. For example, a firm with growth opportunities that requires capital may need to raise cash by issuing short-term or long-term debt or equity shares. A mature cash-cow firm may generate substantial amounts of excess cash and use it to pay down debt, invest in financial assets, pay dividends, or repurchase common shares. Therefore, you must identify what financial flexibility the firm has and how it will use it. Then you must adjust these flexible financial accounts as necessary to match the firm's future financial capital structure with the firm's future operations and investments. Thus, producing a set of financial statement forecasts will require several iterations and a degree of circularity. For example, your first pass through a set of financial statement forecasts may reveal that the firm must increase long-term debt to finance future capital expenditures. Increased long-term debt, however, will increase interest expense, which will cause net income to fall. As a consequence, retained earnings will fall; so the firm may have to increase long-term debt a bit more. You must repeat this process until the balance sheet balances and articulates with the income statement and the statement of cash flows.[3]

- **Garbage in, garbage out.** The quality of your forecasts—and the quality of your investment decisions based on these forecasts—will depend on the quality of your forecast assumptions. You should thoughtfully justify each assumption, especially the most important assumptions that reflect the critical risk and success factors of the firm's strategy. In addition, you should reality check the assumptions by analyzing the forecasted financial statements using ratios and common-size and rate-of-change financial statements. These analytical tools (discussed in Chapters 1, 4, and 5) may reveal that certain assumptions are unrealistic or inconsistent.

- **Sweat the big stuff, not the little stuff.** You should devote thoughtful time and effort to developing the most important forecast assumptions—those that reflect the critical business activities that will determine the future growth, profitability, and risk of the business. For example, for most firms, forecasts of revenues, key operating expenses, important assets (property, plant, and equipment), and the debt-equity structure deserve a good amount of your thoughtful attention. However, some of the accounts in a set of financial statements are not critical to the risk or success of the business. As such, you should be efficient, making simple reasonable assumptions about these noncritical accounts, and do not get bogged down in "analysis-paralysis."

- **Conduct sensitivity analysis on the financial statement forecasts.** Some assumptions have more significant consequences than others, and sensitivity analyses will help you assess the extent to which forecast results depend on key assumptions. You should test, for example, variation in earnings and cash flows across different sales growth scenarios, comparing across the most likely, optimistic, and pessimistic growth rate assumptions.

The subsequent sections of this chapter illustrate the seven-step forecasting procedure using **PepsiCo**'s 2012 financial statements as a base. In this chapter we analyze and use PepsiCo's financial statement data for 2010 through 2012 to carefully develop forecast assumptions and to compute financial statement forecasts for PepsiCo for 2013

---

[3]Most computer spreadsheet software facilitates iterative and circular computations. For example, in Excel, under Excel Options, the Formulas page contains a box you can check to enable iterative calculations, so the spreadsheet will automatically compute iteratively (for example, 1,000 times) until the computations converge to a specified maximum change.

through 2017, which we label Year +1 through Year +5 to denote that they are forecasts of activities we expect to occur one year ahead through five years ahead.[4]

Using FSAP to Prepare Forecasted Financial Statements

FSAP, the financial statement analysis package introduced in Chapter 1, contains a Forecasts spreadsheet that you can use to prepare financial statement forecasts. The website for this text (www.cengagebrain.com) contains a blank FSAP template and the FSAP PepsiCo file for easy downloading and use. If you have not previously designed an Excel spreadsheet to prepare financial statement forecasts, you should do so *before* using the Forecasts spreadsheet in FSAP. The proper design of a spreadsheet and the preparation of forecasted financial statements provide excellent learning experiences to enhance and solidify your understanding of the relations among various financial statement items. Once you become comfortable with using spreadsheets for forecasting financial statements, using the Forecasts spreadsheet in FSAP will save you time.

The Forecasts spreadsheet in FSAP is a general and adaptable template for forecasting financial statements. In addition, FSAP contains a Forecast Development spreadsheet that you can use to compute various detailed forecast assumptions. To illustrate the use of the Forecasts template and the Forecast Development spreadsheet, we incorporate in FSAP the specific forecast assumptions we make for PepsiCo in this chapter, including the Forecasts spreadsheet with explicit financial statement forecast assumptions through Year +5, and the Forecast Development spreadsheet with various supporting computations. FSAP also contains instructions and user guides.

All financial statement amounts throughout this chapter appear in millions. The spreadsheets take all computations to multiple decimal places. Because we express all amounts in millions, some minor rounding differences will arise and make it appear as though various totals disagree with the sum of the individual items that make up the total.

Step 1: Project Revenues

The principal business activities of most firms involve generating revenues by selling products or delivering services. Therefore, most analysts commonly begin the process of forecasting financial statements by projecting revenues from the principal business activities of the firm. Analysts frequently use the expected future level of revenues as a basis for deriving many other amounts in the financial statement forecasts.[5]

LO 10-3a

Build forecasts of future balance sheets, income statements, and statements of cash flows by applying the seven-step forecasting framework to project:
a. revenues.

---

[4]Previous chapters also have analyzed data from the most recent three years to evaluate PepsiCo's current profitability, risk, and accounting quality. In forecasting financial statements that extend one to five years or more into the future, it is often helpful for the analyst to draw on a longer time series of historical data to evaluate a firm's long-term trends. This is particularly helpful for mature and stable firms. For firms in the introduction or growth phase of the life cycle, or for firms that have recently experienced significant mergers or divestitures, a long time series of historical data may not be available or may not permit reliable comparisons with current period data.

[5]Revenue forecasts are particularly important because they have crucial impacts on the projected income statements, balance sheets, and cash flows. You should utilize as much relevant information as possible in developing reliable revenue forecast assumptions. You can often find useful information for forecasts in company disclosures, competitors' financial statements and disclosures, industry data, and regional- and country-specific economic data. This chapter seeks to illustrate the techniques of using such information in developing forecasts, while also being concise and efficient for you, the reader.

Revenues are determined by sales volumes (quantities) and prices. Some firms report sales volumes (for example, automobile manufacturers report numbers of vehicles sold and beverage makers report gallons or cases sold), enabling you to assess volume and price separately as drivers of past revenues and predictors of future revenues. Some firms report volume-related measures that you can use to forecast revenues, such as the number of stores for retailers and restaurant chains or the number of passenger and revenue seat miles for airlines. When you perform the industry analysis in the first step of the financial statement analysis process, you will discover industry-wide conditions that will influence your volume forecasts. For a stable firm in a mature industry (for example, consumer foods), you might conclude that the firm will not significantly gain or lose market share, but that sales volume will grow with the population in the firm's geographic markets. For a firm that has increased its production capacity in an industry with high anticipated growth (for example, biotechnology or tablet computers), you can use the industry growth rate coupled with the expansion in the firm's capacity to project sales volume increases.

When projecting *prices*, you should consider factors specific to the firm and its industry that will affect demand and price elasticity, such as excess or constrained capacity, raw material surpluses or shortages, substitute products, and technological changes in products or production methods. Capital-intensive firms, such as manufacturers of paper products or computer chips, may require several years to add new capacity. If the firm competes in a capital-intensive industry that you expect will operate near capacity for the next few years, price increases will be more likely. On the other hand, if the firm competes in a capital-intensive industry with excess capacity, price increases will be less likely. Further, a capital-intensive firm with excess capacity in a competitive industry may face high exit barriers and thus may experience future price decreases. A firm in transition from the high-growth to the mature phase of its life cycle or a firm with significant technological improvements in its production processes (for example, some portions of the computer industry or cell phone industry) might expect increases in sales volume but decreases in prices. If a firm has established a competitive brand name or unique characteristics for its products, it may have a greater potential to maintain or increase prices than a competitor with generic products.

When projecting revenues, you also should consider economy-wide factors such as the expected rate of inflation and changes in foreign currency exchange rates. As discussed in Chapter 8, a parent company adds the revenues and expenses of controlled subsidiaries to its income statement during the consolidation process. If the financial statements of the subsidiary are denominated in a foreign currency that has appreciated relative to the currency used to prepare the parent company's financial statements, the translation and consolidation process will increase reported revenues due to the foreign exchange rate increase, thus leading to a higher revenue growth unrelated to volume or pricing increases. In addition, you also should factor the effects of corporate transactions such as acquisitions and divestitures into revenue forecasts. Acquisitions typically increase revenues, whereas divestitures of subsidiaries usually reduce revenues.

If revenues have grown at a reasonably steady rate in prior periods and nothing indicates that economic, industry, or firm-specific factors will change significantly, you can project that the historical growth rate will persist into the future. If the firm's historical revenue growth rate has been affected by changes in foreign exchange rates or by a major acquisition or divestiture, you should adjust for these effects when making projections. Projecting revenues for a cyclical firm (for example, heavy machinery manufacturers, property-casualty insurers, and investment banks) involves an additional degree of difficulty. For cyclical firms, the historical growth rates for revenues often exhibit wide variations in both direction and amount over the business cycle. For such firms, you can project revenue growth rates that vary with the stages of the business cycle, assuming you can correctly identify the business's current point in the cycle and how quickly it will progress to the next stages.

It is challenging to project future revenues for firms that depend heavily on new product discovery to generate growth (such as pharmaceutical firms conducting research to discover new drugs, technology firms developing breakthrough new products, or oil and gas firms exploring for new reserves) because of the inherent uncertainty in the discovery and development process. In those cases, analysts often rely heavily on firms' disclosures about the research and development pipeline. In addition, analysts often seek help from scientists, doctors, or technology experts who can provide knowledgeable advice on the likelihood of the future success of the firm's research and product development efforts.

This discussion reinforces how forecasting depends heavily on the first four steps of the analysis process. Projecting a firm's future business activities, such as revenues, relies heavily on understanding the economic and competitive forces of the industry, the competitive strategy of the firm, the quality of the firm's accounting, and the drivers of the firm's profitability and risk.

Projecting Revenues for PepsiCo

Earlier chapters indicated that the consumer foods industry in the United States is mature. Industry revenues have grown recently at the growth rate for the general population, approximately 2% per year. Some consumer foods companies have achieved higher growth rates through corporate acquisitions, international expansion, and entry into related markets such as restaurants. **PepsiCo** has defied these industry averages, generating a compounded rate of growth in net revenues of 6.4% between 2010 and 2012.

In PepsiCo's 2012 Annual Report, the MD&A section titled "Results of Operations—Division Review" discloses information about revenues and operating profits for each of PepsiCo's six operating divisions (also called segments), which it organizes into four business units, grouped by product and geography. The largest business unit in terms of revenues is PepsiCo Americas Foods, which consists of three divisions: Frito-Lay North America (FLNA; snack foods), Quaker Foods North America (QFNA: cereals, rice, pasta, and dairy), and Latin America Foods (LAF; snack foods). The second-largest business unit in terms of revenues is PepsiCo Americas Beverages (PAB; beverages in North America and Latin America). The third largest unit is PepsiCo Europe (beverage, food, and snack businesses in all of Europe and South Africa), while the smallest unit is PepsiCo Asia, Middle East, and Africa (AMEA; beverage, food, and snack food businesses throughout the region, excluding South Africa).

For each division, PepsiCo discloses overall revenue growth rates as well as revenue growth rates attributable to volume, pricing, foreign exchange rates, acquisitions and divestitures, and a 53rd week of business in fiscal year 2011 (fiscal 2012 and 2010 only contained 52 weeks). The data for PepsiCo's revenue drivers appear in Exhibit 10.2. These data reveal significant differences in the drivers of growth across the six segments. For example, all of the divisions have managed to generate revenue growth from effective net pricing; however, the Quaker Foods North America division has been

Exhibit 10.2

PepsiCo
Revenue Growth Analysis by Division
(dollar amounts in millions)

	2010	2011	2012
PepsiCo Total Net Revenue Amounts	$57,838	$66,504	$ 65.492
Annual growth rates		15.0%	−1.5%
Compound annual growth rate			6.4%
Frito-Lay North America (FLNA)	$12,573	$13,322	$ 13,574
Overall growth rates		6.0%	1.9%
Growth in volume		2.0%	−1.0%
Growth from effective net pricing		2.0%	4.8%
Impact of foreign currency translation		0.0%	0.0%
53rd week effect		1.9%	−1.9%
Quaker Foods North America (QFNA)	$ 2,656	$ 2,656	$ 2,636
Overall growth rates		0.0%	−0.8%
Growth in volume		−5.0%	−1.0%
Growth from effective net pricing		2.1%	2.1%
Impact of foreign currency translation		1.0%	0.0%
53rd week effect		1.9%	−1.9%
Latin America Foods (LAF)	$ 6,315	$ 7,156	$ 7,780
Overall growth rates		13.3%	8.7%
Growth in volume and impact of acquisitions, net		3.5%	6.0%
Growth from effective net pricing		5.9%	11.6%
Impact of foreign currency translation		2.0%	−7.0%
53rd week effect		1.9%	−1.9%
PepsiCo Americas Beverages (PAB)	$20,401	$22,418	$ 21,408
Overall growth rates		9.9%	−4.5%
Growth in volume and impact of acquisitions, net		6.0%	−7.5%
Growth from effective net pricing		1.0%	4.9%
Impact of foreign currency translation		1.0%	0.0%
53rd week effect		1.9%	−1.9%
Europe	$ 9,602	$13,560	$ 13,441
Overall growth rates		41.2%	−0.9%
Growth in volume and impact of acquisitions, net		36.0%	2.0%
Growth from effective net pricing		0.3%	6.0%
Impact of foreign currency translation		3.0%	−7.0%
53rd week effect		1.9%	−1.9%

(Continued)

Exhibit 10.2 (Continued)			
	2010	2011	2012
Asia, Middle East, & Africa (AMEA)	$ 6,291	$ 7,392	$ 6,653
Overall growth rates		17.5%	−10.0%
Growth in volume and impact of acquisitions, net		10.0%	−9.0%
Growth from effective net pricing		3.6%	3.9%
Impact of foreign currency translation		2.0%	−3.0%
53rd week effect		1.9%	−1.9%

experiencing declining sales volumes. Revenue growth in the Latin America Foods and Europe divisions has been most affected by swings in foreign currency translation rates. The PepsiCo Americas Beverages, Europe, and AMEA divisions have all experienced swings in revenue growth through acquisitions and divestitures. By analyzing the drivers of revenue growth at the division level, we can develop more accurate forecasts for PepsiCo's revenue growth in each division and, in turn, for PepsiCo's total revenues.

Frito-Lay North America Revenue Growth

The Frito-Lay North America segment generates revenues from manufacturing and selling snack foods in the United States and Canada. In PepsiCo's 2012 Annual Report, the MD&A section titled "Results of Operations—Division Review" discloses that this segment generated 1.9% revenue growth in 2012 and 6.0% growth in 2011, implying a compound annual growth rate of 3.9% between 2010 and 2012 {computed as $3.9\% = [(1.019 \times 1.060)^{(0.5)}] - 1.0$}. PepsiCo discloses that Frito-Lay North America's 6.0% growth rate in 2011 resulted from the combination of a 2% increase in volume, a 2% increase in effective net pricing, and a 53rd week of business [which contributes roughly 1.9% growth over 2010, which only consisted of 52 weeks; computed as $1.9\% = (53 \div 52) - 1$]. In 2012, the division's 1.9% revenue growth rate was the result of the combination of a 1% decline in volume, a 4.8% increase in effective net pricing, less a 1.9% decline relative to 53 weeks in 2011. The price increases likely reflect the overall strength of the Frito-Lay brand in the relatively price-competitive snack foods markets.

Based on the underlying strength of Frito-Lay's core brands and its continuing ability to develop and introduce successful new products, we expect that sales volume will exhibit 1.0% growth per year into the future. We expect that future price increases will be limited to 2.0% per year because of the competitive and mature nature of the snack foods industry in North America. We project foreign exchange rates and acquisitions will not likely have a material persistent effect on this division's future sales. These assumptions produce an annual sales growth rate of 3.0% (that is, $1.030 = 1.010 \times 1.020$).

In Year +4, PepsiCo's fiscal year (which ends on the last Saturday of December each year) will again contain 53 weeks. To capture this effect in our revenue forecasts for Frito-Lay North America in Year +4, we project an overall sales growth rate of 5.0% (that is, $1.050 = 1.010 \times 1.020 \times 53/52$). In Year +5, PepsiCo will revert to a normal 52-week year, so the sales growth rate relative to Year +4 will be only 1.1% (that is, $1.011 = 1.010 \times 1.020 \times 52/53$). PepsiCo will not encounter another 53-week fiscal year for several years in the future, so we ignore the effects on our sales forecasts beyond Year +5.

The revenue projections and growth rates for Frito-Lay North America over the first five years of the forecast horizon are as follows (allow for rounding):

2012 actual	$13,574	
Year +1 forecast	$13,984	+3.0%
Year +2 forecast	$14,406	+3.0%
Year +3 forecast	$14,841	+3.0%
Year +4 forecast	$15,584	+5.0%
Year +5 forecast	$15,751	+1.1%

Quaker Foods North America Revenue Growth

The Quaker Foods North America division sells cereals, rice, pasta, dairy and other branded products. It is a very stable division in a mature and competitive industry. Quaker experienced a slight decline in revenues over Years 2010 to 2012. In 2011, Quaker's revenue growth was flat, the result of a 5.0% decline in sales volume, partially offset by a 2.1% increase driven by effective net pricing, a 1.0% increase from favorable foreign currency exchange rates, and a 1.9% increase from the 53rd-week effect. From 2011 to 2012, Quaker experienced a 0.8% decline in revenues, resulting from a 1.0% decline in sales volume, a 1.9% decline because of the 53rd week in 2011, partially offset by a 2.1% increase driven by effective net pricing.

Looking ahead, we expect this division to continue to experience a 1.0% decline in sales volume, offset by 1.0% price increases. We do not expect foreign currency exchange rates and acquisitions to have a material effect on this division's future sales. Thus, we will expect the Quaker division to generate zero revenue growth, on average (that is, $1.000 = 0.990 \times 1.010$). In Year +4, we expect Quaker to generate a 1.9% revenue growth due to the 53rd week (that is, $1.019 = 0.990 \times 1.010 \times 53/52$). In Year +5, after reversing the 53rd-week effect, we expect Quaker to experience a 1.9% decline in revenues (that is, $0.981 = 0.990 \times 1.010 \times 52/53$). Revenue forecast amounts and growth rates for the Quaker Foods North America division over the five-year forecast horizon are as follows:

2012 actual	$2,636	
Year +1 forecast	$2,636	+0.0%
Year +2 forecast	$2,636	+0.0%
Year +3 forecast	$2,636	+0.0%
Year +4 forecast	$2,686	+1.9%
Year +5 forecast	$2,635	−1.9%

Latin America Foods Revenue Growth

The Latin America Foods division sells snacks, cereals, and breakfast foods throughout Latin America. It grew revenues at an impressive compound annual rate of 11.0% from 2010 to 2012. From 2010 to 2011, this division's revenue growth was the result of a 3.5% increase in sales volume, 5.9% increase driven by effective net pricing, a 2.0% increase from favorable foreign exchange rates, and 1.9% from the 53rd-week effect. Growth from 2011 to 2012, however, tells a very different story. In 2012, the division experienced a strong 6.0% growth in sales volume, an even stronger 11.6% increase driven by effective net pricing, but was hampered by a 7.0% decrease in sales from unfavorable foreign exchange rates and a 1.9% decline relative to the 53 weeks in 2011.

We project that this segment will maintain fairly strong growth of 4.0% in volume and 4.0% in price increases due to the strength of its brands in this region. Therefore, we expect the Latin America Foods division to generate an 8.2% revenue growth rate (that is, $1.082 = 1.040 \times 1.040$) each year. In Year +4, we expect this division to generate a 10.2% revenue growth due to the effect of the 53rd week (that is, $1.102 = 1.040 \times 1.040 \times 53/52$). In Year +5, after reversing the 53rd-week effect, we expect this division to experience 6.1% growth (that is, $1.061 = 1.040 \times 1.040 \times 52/53$). Revenue forecast amounts and growth rates for the Latin America Foods division over the five-year forecast horizon are as follows:

2012 actual	$ 7,780	
Year +1 forecast	$ 8,415	+8.2%
Year +2 forecast	$ 9,101	+8.2%
Year +3 forecast	$ 9,844	+8.2%
Year +4 forecast	$10,852	+10.2%
Year +5 forecast	$11,516	+6.1%

PepsiCo Americas Beverages Revenue Growth

The PepsiCo Americas Beverages segment manufactures and sells a wide variety of fountain syrups, concentrates, and finished goods beverages including carbonated and noncarbonated soft drinks, juices, water, tea, and coffee in the United States, Canada, and Latin America. This segment experienced highly variable growth, with revenues increasing nearly 10% in 2011, and declining by 4.5% in 2012. The segment's revenue growth in 2011 was driven largely by volume growth, acquisitions, effective net pricing, and the 53rd-week effect. The revenue decline in 2012 was largely the result of divestitures, declining volumes, and the reversal of the 53rd-week effect, partially offset by a 4.9 increase driven by effective net pricing.

Going forward, we expect that PepsiCo Americas Beverage unit will bounce back to sustain 1.0% growth in sales volume in the future because it has a deep and broad portfolio of branded products that span the beverages market (for example, carbonated soft drinks, sports drinks, juices, waters, coffees, and teas). We also expect that the 4.9% price growth in 2012, which exceeded the rate of inflation in North America during that same period, is unsustainable and that PepsiCo will generate and sustain only 2.0% growth in prices in the future, closer to the economy-wide inflation rate. We also expect minimal impact on future revenues from foreign exchange and acquisitions. Together, these assumptions create an annual revenue growth rate of 3.0% ($1.030 = 1.010 \times 1.02$).

Including the 53rd-week effect, the revenue growth rate will increase to 5.0% in Year +4 (that is, $1.050 = 1.01 \times 1.02 \times 53/52$), and revert to only 1.1% in Year +5 (that is, $1.011 = 1.01 \times 1.02 \times 52/53$). Revenue forecast amounts and growth rates for the PepsiCo Americas Beverages segment over the five-year forecast horizon are as follows:

2012 actual	$21,408	
Year +1 forecast	$22,055	+3.0%
Year +2 forecast	$22,721	+3.0%
Year +3 forecast	$23,407	+3.0%
Year +4 forecast	$24,577	+5.0%
Year +5 forecast	$24,842	+1.1%

Europe Revenue Growth

During 2010 to 2012, the PepsiCo Europe segment was the fastest-growing segment in the company. This division sells PepsiCo foods, snacks, and beverages throughout the United Kingdom, Europe, Russia, the former Soviet states, and South Africa. PepsiCo discloses that net revenue growth in the Europe division during 2011 was 41.2%, largely fueled by a major acquisition in Russia, combined with sales volume increases, favorable foreign currency rates, and the 53rd-week effect. Revenues in the Europe division declined slightly, −0.9%, in 2012. This decline was driven by a 7.0 decrease due to unfavorable foreign exchange rates, particularly declines in the value of the Russian ruble and the euro relative to the U.S. dollar (PepsiCo's revenues in rubles and euros translated into fewer U.S. dollars), as well as a 1.9% decline due to the reversal of the 53rd week in 2011. Together, these more than offset a 2.0 increase due to acquisitions and a 6.0 growth driven by effective net pricing.

Based on the track record of PepsiCo's Europe division, we expect a 2.0% growth in sales volume in the future. We also expect the division to sustain 2.0% growth in prices into the future. We assume that unfavorable foreign currency movements are not likely to persist over the next five years. With these assumptions, we forecast average revenue growth of 4.0% for the Europe division (that is, $1.040 = 1.020 \times 1.020$). Including the 53rd-week effect, the sales growth rate should jump to 6.0% for Year +4 (that is, $1.060 = 1.020 \times 1.020 \times 53/52$) and then fall back to 2.1% in Year +5 (that is, $1.021 = 1.02 \times 1.02 \times 52/53$). Revenue amounts and growth rates for PepsiCo's Europe division over the five-year forecast horizon are as follows:

2012 actual	$13,441	
Year +1 forecast	$13,984	+4.0%
Year +2 forecast	$14,549	+4.0%
Year +3 forecast	$15,137	+4.0%
Year +4 forecast	$16,051	+6.0%
Year +5 forecast	$16,385	+2.1%

Asia, Middle East, and Africa Revenue Growth

PepsiCo's AMEA division, which sells PepsiCo foods, snacks, and beverages throughout these regions, experienced highly variable revenue growth from 2010 to 2012. In 2011, this division experienced a 17.5% jump in revenues, which included volume growth of 10.0%, effective net pricing of 3.6%, foreign exchange rate effects of 2.0%, and 1.9% from the 53rd week effect. During 2012, AMEA revenues decreased by 10.0% relative to 2011, a consequence of a 17.0% decline in revenues as a result of divestitures, an 8.0% increase from sales volume, a 3.0% decline from unfavorable foreign exchange rates, a 1.9% decline from the reversal of the 53rd-week effect in 2011, partially offset by a 3.9% increase driven by effective net pricing.

The AMEA division is clearly difficult to predict because of this volatility in revenue growth. We expect the AMEA division to sustain 5.0% growth from sales volume increases and possible future acquisitions, augmented with 2.0% growth in prices. It is difficult to predict persistent favorable or unfavorable foreign currency movements over the next five years. With these assumptions, we project average annual revenue growth of 7.1% for the AMEA division (that is, $1.071 = 1.050 \times 1.020$). After including the 53rd-week effect, the revenue growth rate will be 9.2% in Year +4 (that is, $1.092 = 1.050 \times 1.020 \times 53/52$) and only 5.1% Year +5 (that is, $1.051 = 1.05 \times 1.02 \times 52/53$).

Revenue amounts and growth rates for PepsiCo's AMEA division over the five-year forecast horizon are as follows:

2012 actual	$6,653	
Year +1 forecast	$7,125	+7.1%
Year +2 forecast	$7,631	+7.1%
Year +3 forecast	$8,173	+7.1%
Year +4 forecast	$8,922	+9.2%
Year +5 forecast	$9,375	+5.1%

Combined Revenue Growth

The following table combines the revenue forecasts for each of the six divisions of PepsiCo. The table presents the projected revenue amounts for each segment, PepsiCo's total net revenues, and annual growth rates for each year through Year +5.

Revenue Forecasts for PepsiCo by Division

	2012	Year +1	Year +2	Year +3	Year +4	Year +5
Frito-Lay North America (FLNA)	$13,574	$13,984	$14,406	$14,841	$15,584	$15,751
Quaker Foods North America (QFNA)	2,636	2,636	2,635	2,635	2,686	2,635
Latin America Foods (LAF)	7,780	8,415	9,101	9,844	10,852	11,516
PepsiCo Americas Beverages (PAB)	21,408	22,055	22,721	23,407	24,577	24,842
Europe	13,441	13,984	14,549	15,137	16,051	16,385
Asia, Middle East & Africa (AMEA)	6,653	7,125	7,631	8,173	8,922	9,375
PepsiCo Total Revenues	$65,492	$68,198	$71,044	$74,037	$78,672	$80,503
Overall growth rates		4.1%	4.2%	4.2%	6.3%	2.3%

The Forecasts spreadsheet in FSAP gives you the opportunity to input specific forecast parameters (such as revenue growth rates) for Year +1 through Year +5, as well as general forecast parameters for Year +6 and beyond. For Years +1 through +5, we will enter the revenue growth rates and amounts shown above. The forecast parameters for Year +6 and beyond represent general forecast assumptions over the long-run horizon. We assume PepsiCo will sustain a 3.0% revenue growth rate in Year +6 and beyond, consistent with expected long-run growth in the economy and expected long-run inflation that together will average 3.0% per year.[6]

You can use the Forecast Development spreadsheet in FSAP to develop detailed revenues forecasts, capturing the key drivers of the firm's growth. We have done that here by analyzing and forecasting PepsiCo's revenue growth drivers separately for each division and then aggregating those forecasts into total revenue forecasts through Year +5. Appendix C illustrates how we used the spreadsheet to develop the revenue forecasts for PepsiCo.

---

[6]It is reasonable and common for analysts to expect that long-run growth rates will average 3.0% in years following Year +5, However, the analyst interested in greater forecast accuracy may want to use longer forecast horizons (for example, ten years) before adopting a single linear long-run growth rate.

LO 10-3b

Build forecasts of future balance sheets, income statements, and statements of cash flows by applying the seven-step forecasting framework to project:
b. operating expenses.

Step 2: Project Operating Expenses

The procedure for projecting operating expenses depends on the degree to which they have fixed or variable components. If certain operating expenses vary directly with sales and if you anticipate no changes in the relation between these expenses and sales, you can project these future operating expenses using common-size income statement percentages. You can project the future operating expense amounts by either multiplying projected sales by the appropriate common-size percentage or by projecting those operating expenses to grow at the same rate as sales.

If you determine that operating expenses reflect cost structures that will not change linearly with sales (for example, the firm may experience economies of scale as sales increase or may face expenses that remain relatively fixed even if sales decrease), then using the common-size income statement approach can result in operating expense projections that are too high or too low. Unfortunately, firms rarely disclose the fixed versus variable components of their expense structure. Thus, you must estimate the contribution of fixed versus variable expenses to the total amounts reported.

Many expenses have both a fixed portion and a portion that varies with sales. For example, a firm's cost of sales might include components that are fixed periodic costs such as rent and depreciation and costs that vary directly with product sales such as direct labor and materials. Selling, general, and administrative expenses often include fixed components for items such as salaries, rent, insurance, and other corporate overhead expenses but variable components that vary directly with sales, such as sales commissions. A possible clue for the existence of fixed costs is the stability of the ratio of the percentage change in an expense relative to the percentage change in sales. Changes in this ratio over time may be due to the existence of fixed costs.

When sales grow at faster rates than costs of goods sold or selling, general, and administrative expenses, it often indicates the presence of fixed costs. You can estimate the variable cost as a percentage of sales for a particular expense by dividing the amount of the change in the expense item by the corresponding amount of the change in sales for the same period. You can then multiply sales by the variable-cost percentage to estimate the total variable cost. Subtracting the variable cost from the total cost yields an estimate of the fixed cost for that particular item. Using this approach, you can project a particular future expense with two components: a fixed component and a component that varies with sales. For a firm that is particularly dependent on property, plant, and equipment, you may need to create a separate schedule to forecast capital expenditures that lead projected future sales, and forecast depreciation expense amounts that lag capital expenditures on property, plant, and equipment (demonstrated later in this chapter).[7]

When projecting operating expenses as a percentage of sales, you should keep in mind that an expense as a percentage of sales can change over time:

- *Expenses can change, even if sales remain constant.* For example, you may expect an expense to decrease relative to sales over time if the firm will drive down costs by creating operating efficiencies or new production technologies. Alternately, you might expect an expense to increase relative to sales if the firm will face increasing input costs that it cannot pass along to customers by raising prices.

---

[7]Sometimes more advanced approaches may be necessary, such as using regression analysis to estimate fixed versus variable components of expenses. For example, an analyst might use time-series data to estimate the relation, $COGS = \alpha + \beta \times Sales + \varepsilon$. The estimated intercept, α, is an estimate of the fixed costs, and the variable cost proportion would be reflected by the slope coefficient, β.

- *Sales can change, even if expenses remain constant.* For example, you may expect that the firm will hold expenses (such as cost of goods sold) relatively steady but will face increased competition for market share and therefore may be forced to lower sales prices, causing the expected expense-to-sales ratio to increase. Alternately, you might expect that sales will increase, but because of fixed costs in the production process, expenses will remain fairly steady.
- *Sales and expenses can change simultaneously and in the same direction.* If you expect both sales and operating expenses to increase (or decrease) simultaneously, the net result on the projected expense-to-sales percentage will depend on which of the two effects is proportionally greater.
- *Sales and expenses can change simultaneously but in opposite directions.* For example, if you expect sales to increase while operating expenses decrease (as might occur for a firm in transition from the start-up phase to the growth phase of its life cycle), or vice versa (sales decrease while operating expenses increase, as might occur for a firm in distress), the net result on the projected expense-to-sales percentage will depend on the relative magnitudes of the two effects.

In projecting the future relations between revenues and expenses, it is essential to evaluate the firm's strategies with respect to future growth, shifts in product/portfolio mix, changes in the mix of fixed and variable expenses, competitive pressure on pricing, and many other factors that will impact expected future revenues and expenses.

Projecting Cost of Goods Sold

The common-size income statement data discussed in Chapter 1 and 4 (and presented in the Analysis spreadsheet of FSAP) indicate that **PepsiCo**'s cost of goods sold as a percent of sales has steadily increased from 45.9% in 2010 to 47.8% in 2012. In the MD&A section of the annual report, PepsiCo provides very little discussion to explain this negative trend other than to mention strategic investments and rising raw material commodity costs as contributing factors across virtually all six divisions.

PepsiCo's cost of goods sold as a percentage of sales has been increasing despite the prior observation that PepsiCo's recent sales growth in 2011 and 2012 has been driven more by effective net pricing than sales volume increases. With costs held constant, sales price increases should translate into decreasing cost of goods sold percentages. Given this recent performance, you might question whether PepsiCo will be able to improve its performance and reduce the cost of goods sold percentage in the future by cutting costs.[8]

In recent years, PepsiCo has generated its fastest rates of sales growth in the Latin America Foods division, the Europe division, and the AMEA division, which generate the lowest operating profit margins of PepsiCo's six divisions (as disclosed in the 2012 Annual Report MD&A section titled "Results of Operations—Division Review"). Therefore, PepsiCo is generating more sales growth from lower profit margin divisions, which partially explains why the cost of goods sold has been increasing as a percentage of sales. Given that our sales forecasts project that the Latin America Foods, Europe, and the AMEA divisions will become increasingly larger proportions of PepsiCo's total sales in

---

[8]PepsiCo's main competitor in the beverage business, **Coca-Cola**, exhibits lower but rising cost of goods sold percentages, from 36.1% in 2010, to 39.1% in 2011, to 39.7% in 2012. While the two companies are direct global competitors, their cost structures likely differ because of differences in their business models. Coca-Cola is primarily a beverage company, whereas PepsiCo's sales include a high proportion of snack foods and breakfast foods, in addition to beverages.

the future, we expect PepsiCo's future cost of goods sold percentage to increase over the five-year forecast horizon. Ideally, PepsiCo would disclose costs of goods sold by division and we could vary projected future costs of goods sold across each division. However, PepsiCo only discloses cost of goods sold aggregated across all divisions. Given this analysis, we predict that PepsiCo's cost of goods sold will increase gradually from 47.9% of sales in Year +1 to 48.3% in Year +5 and beyond. The cost of goods sold forecasts through Year +5 are as follows:

	Revenues	Percentage of Revenues	Cost of Goods Sold
Year +1 forecast	$68,198	47.9%	$32,667
Year +2 forecast	$71,044	48.0%	$34,101
Year +3 forecast	$74,038	48.1%	$35,612
Year +4 forecast	$78,672	48.2%	$37,920
Year +5 forecast	$80,504	48.3%	$38,883

Projecting Selling, General, and Administrative Expenses

As disclosed in the 2012 Annual Report MD&A section titled "Our Financial Results," PepsiCo has been implementing a program to control costs by creating incremental efficiencies in selling, general, and administrative (SG&A) expenses. The common-size income statement data reveal that PepsiCo's SG&A expenses varied from 39.4% of revenues in 2010, down to 37.8% in 2011, and then up to 38.1% in 2012.[9] In light of this, it is likely that PepsiCo will continue to experience minor variations in SG&A expenses as a percentage of revenues, and therefore we project SG&A expenses will be on average roughly 38.1% of revenues in the future.

The projected amounts for SG&A expenses through Year +5 are as follows:

	Revenues	Percentage of Revenues	SG&A Expenses
Year +1 forecast	$68,198	38.1%	$25,984
Year +2 forecast	$71,044	38.1%	$27,068
Year +3 forecast	$74,038	38.1%	$28,208
Year +4 forecast	$78,672	38.1%	$29,974
Year +5 forecast	$80,504	38.1%	$30,672

As the title of this expense account implies, SG&A expenses encompass a wide range of operating expenses. In Note 2, "Our Significant Accounting Policies" (Appendix A), PepsiCo discloses that in 2012, SG&A expenses include $3,700 million in advertising and marketing expenses; $9,100 million in shipping and handling expenses; $552 million in R&D expenses; and amounts for compensation and employee benefits, rent, and various other expenses. If you expect these individual expense items to be driven by factors other than sales growth, or if you expect the proportionate composition of these

---

[9]On this dimension, PepsiCo was outperformed by its rival Coca-Cola, which experienced SG&A expenses of 37.6% of sales in 2010, 37.4% in 2011, and 36.9% in 2012.

expenses to change relative to future sales, then you should project the items individually and sum them to obtain total SG&A expense projections.

Projecting Other Operating Expenses

In 2010 through 2012, PepsiCo recognized expenses for amortization of intangible assets amounting to $117 million, $133 million, and $119 million, respectively, each of which are roughly equivalent to 0.2% of revenues. These expenses represent amortization of intangibles such as franchise rights, brands, and trademarks with limited useful lives (ranging from 1 to 60 years). The net book value of PepsiCo's amortizable intangible assets amounts to $1,781 million on the 2012 balance sheet. In Note 4, "Property, Plant and Equipment and Intangible Assets" (Appendix A), PepsiCo provides helpful disclosures indicating that it expects amortization expense for these intangible assets to be $110 million in Year +1, $95 million in Year +2, $86 million in Year +3, $78 million in Year +4, and $72 million in Year +5, based on 2012 foreign exchange rates and the assumption of no additional investments in amortizable intangible assets over that period. Therefore, we use these amounts as our forecasts for PepsiCo's amortization expense and to reduce the net book value of the amortizable intangible asset account balance each year.

U.S. GAAP does not require amortization of goodwill or other intangible assets deemed to have indefinite useful lives. Goodwill ($16,971 million) and other nonamortizable intangible assets ($14,744 million) represent roughly 95% of PepsiCo's total intangible assets on the 2012 balance sheet. In our forecasts, we include no amortization expenses or impairment losses for these nonamortizable intangibles.

Projecting Nonrecurring Income Items

As discussed in prior chapters, it is not uncommon for firms' reported income statements to include other nonrecurring gains or losses that are part of operations, unusual gains or losses that are peripheral to operations, and income from discontinued segments. For example, as disclosed in the 2012 Annual Report MD&A section titled "Our Financial Results—Items Affecting Comparability," PepsiCo recognized restructuring and impairment charges amounting to $279 million, all of which was included in SG&A expenses. In addition, in 2012 PepsiCo included mark-to-market gains on commodity derivatives of $65 million; merger integration charges of $11 million; restructuring charges of $150 million associated with a divestiture (Tingyi); as well as pension lump sum settlement charges of $195 million. Absent these charges and gains, SG&A expenses would have been slightly lower, 37.3% of sales in 2012. In the same disclosure, PepsiCo also reported various restructuring charges, merger and integration charges, mark-to-market gains and losses, and inventory fair value adjustments in 2011 and in 2010. That disclosure also highlighted the effects of the 53rd week on reported revenues and income for fiscal 2011.

PepsiCo also disclosed in the 2012 Annual Report MD&A section, titled "Market Risks," that in the first quarter of 2013 it will take an after-tax charge of over $100 million reflecting the decline in the value of PepsiCo's Venezuelan bolivar-denominated net monetary assets following the devaluation of the Venezuelan bolivar relative to the US dollar. PepsiCo took a $120 million charge for a similar devaluation of Venezuelan operations in 2010, and included that charge in SG&A expense.

As previous chapters discussed, you must determine whether items such as these are likely to persist in the future; if so, include them in the financial statement forecasts. Although it is very difficult to predict specific future amounts of nonrecurring items for PepsiCo, such as restructuring charges or merger integration charges, because of their past frequency it is very likely that PepsiCo will continue to experience such charges in the future (such as the impending Venezuelan bolivar devaluation loss). We assume that our projections of future costs of goods sold and SG&A expenses will implicitly include these charges in 2012. In addition, we will explicitly include the effects of the 53rd week of operations in our revenue and expense forecasts for Year +4 and Year +5.

Projecting Operating Income

The revenue forecasts, together with the projected costs of goods sold, SG&A expenses, and amortization of intangible assets, lead to the following projected amounts of operating income for PepsiCo for Years +1 through +5:

	Year +1	Year +2	Year +3	Year +4	Year +5
Revenues	$ 68,198	$ 71,044	$ 74,038	$ 78,672	$ 80,504
Cost of goods sold	−32,667	−34,101	−35,612	−37,920	−38,883
Gross profit	$ 35,531	$ 36,943	$ 38,426	$ 40,752	$ 41,621
Gross profit margin	(52.1%)	(52.0%)	(51.9%)	(51.8%)	(51.7%)
SG&A expenses	−25,984	−27,068	−28,208	−29,974	−30,672
Amortization of intangible assets	−110	−95	−86	−78	−72
Operating income	$ 9,438	$ 9,780	$ 10,131	$ 10,700	$ 10,877
Operating profit margin	(13.8%)	(13.8%)	(13.7%)	(13.6%)	(13.5%)

Exhibit 10.3 (pages 784–785) presents the complete forecasts of PepsiCo's income statements, as well as comprehensive income and the change in retained earnings for Years +1 through +5. The exhibit also presents forecast amounts for Year +6, assuming PepsiCo will grow at a constant rate of 3%. The format of this exhibit mirrors the format of the Forecasts spreadsheet in FSAP. In later sections of this chapter, we discuss the projections of interest income, interest expense, income tax expense, net income, comprehensive income, and the change in retained earnings, after projecting PepsiCo's balance sheet.

LO 10-3c

Build forecasts of future balance sheets, income statements, and statements of cash flows by applying the seven-step forecasting framework to project:
c. operating assets and liabilities.

Step 3: Project Operating Assets and Liabilities on the Balance Sheet

In this section, we describe how the operating activities projected for the income statement will give rise to future operating assets and liabilities on the balance sheet. We demonstrate how to develop forecasts using various drivers of growth in different assets and liabilities, allowing the mix of assets and liabilities to change as the business evolves over time.

Techniques to Project Operating Assets and Liabilities

To develop forecasts of individual operating assets and liabilities, you must first determine the underlying operating activities that drive them. For some types of assets, such as inventory and property, plant, and equipment, asset growth typically *leads* future sales growth. Growth for other types of assets, such as accounts receivable, typically *lags* sales growth. Certain operating liabilities will be determined by operating assets (such as accounts payable arising from inventory purchases), whereas others will be determined by operating expenses (such as liabilities for accrued expenses).

After determining the types of business activities that are likely to drive future operating assets and liabilities, you can adopt a number of techniques to forecast the future balance sheet amounts. You might project certain types of assets and liabilities using a growth rate, such as the expected growth in sales, for assets and liabilities that vary linearly with sales. For example, you might project the firm's future accounts receivable will grow at the same rate of sales. You might choose to project future amounts for operating assets and liabilities using turnover rates, such as projecting future inventory and payables using the corresponding turnover ratios. For some types of assets and liabilities, you might project future growth rates based on past growth trends or expected shifts in the firm's strategy. For example, perhaps the firm plans to hold larger amounts of cash than it has held in the past in order to increase its liquidity. In other cases, the firm may have a strategy of maintaining certain types of assets and liabilities at relatively steady proportions of total assets, in which case you might project future amounts using the expected future common-size percentages. This approach would work, for example, if the firm maintains a target percentage of total assets in cash. In some instances, asset and liability amounts can be projected based on large future transactions. For instance, if a firm is expected to borrow a large amount of cash next year in order to invest it in acquiring another firm or in constructing a new plant, you might project a large increase in cash next year after the borrowing and a large decrease the following year after the investment.

Analysts often use techniques based on the turnover ratios demonstrated in Chapter 4 to forecast operating assets and liabilities that may be driven by revenues, such as cash; accounts receivable; inventories; property, plant, and equipment; and accounts payable. Using turnover ratios produces reasonable forecasts of average and year-end account balances if the firm generates revenues evenly throughout the year and if the forecasted account varies reliably with revenues. However, you should not use a turnover-based forecast if the firm will experience substantially different future growth rates in revenues and the forecasted account, or if the relation between them varies unpredictably over time.

A less desirable feature that can result from using a sales-turnover forecasting approach is that if the firm has exhibited volatility in historical amounts, it can trigger volatility in forecast amounts as well. To illustrate, suppose you expect that sales will remain constant at $12,167 per year over the next five years. Suppose also that you expect the firm will hold roughly 30 days of sales in cash and that it currently has a cash balance of $800. Using the cash turnover rate of 30 days' sales, you would project the firm will maintain an average cash balance of $1,000 ($12,167/365 × 30).

Exhibit 10.3

PepsiCo
Actual and Forecast Statements of Net Income and Comprehensive Income
(amounts in millions; allow for rounding)

Actual and forecast amounts in bold; below the actual amounts (only) we report historical common-size and rate-of-change percentages; below the forecast amounts (only) we report the forecast assumptions and brief explanations.

	Actuals			Forecasts					
Year	2010	2011	2012	Year +1	Year +2	Year +3	Year +4	Year +5	Year +6
INCOME STATEMENT									
Revenues	**$57,838**	**$66,504**	**$65,492**	**$68,198**	**$71,044**	**$74,038**	**$78,672**	**$80,504**	**$82,919**
common size	100.0%	100.0%	100.0%						
rate of change		15.0%	−1.5%	4.1%	4.2%	4.2%	6.3%	2.3%	
				(See Forecast Development worksheet for details of revenues forecasts.)					
Cost of goods sold	**−26,575**	**−31,593**	**−31,291**	**−32,667**	**−34,101**	**−35,612**	**−37,920**	**−38,883**	**−40,050**
common size	−45.9%	−47.5%	−47.8%	−47.9%	−48.0%	−48.1%	−48.2%	−48.3%	
rate of change		18.9%	−1.0%						
				(Assume slowly increasing cost of goods sold as a percent of sales.)					
Gross profit	**31,263**	**34,911**	**34,201**	**35,531**	**36,943**	**38,426**	**40,752**	**41,621**	**42,869**
common size	54.1%	52.5%	52.2%	52.1%	52.0%	51.9%	51.8%	51.7%	51.7%
rate of change		11.7%	−2.0%	3.9%	4.0%	4.0%	6.1%	2.1%	
Selling, general and administrative expenses	**−22,814**	**−25,145**	**−24,970**	**−25,984**	**−27,068**	**−28,208**	**−29,974**	**−30,672**	**−31,592**
common size	−39.4%	−37.8%	−38.1%	−38.1%	−38.1%	−38.1%	−38.1%	−38.1%	
rate of change		10.2%	−0.7%						
				(Assume steady SG&A expense as a percent of sales.)					
Amortization of intangible assets	**−117**	**−133**	**−119**	**−110**	**−95**	**−86**	**−78**	**−72**	**−74**
common size	−0.2%	−0.2%	−0.2%						
rate of change		13.7%	−10.5%						
				(Amounts based on PepsiCo disclosures in Note 4.)					
Operating profit	**8,332**	**9,633**	**9,112**	**9,438**	**9,780**	**10,131**	**10,700**	**10,877**	**11,203**
common size	14.4%	14.5%	13.9%	13.8%	13.8%	13.7%	13.6%	13.5%	13.5%
rate of change		15.6%	−5.4%	3.6%	3.6%	3.6%	5.6%	1.6%	
Interest income	**68**	**57**	**91**	**61**	**56**	**58**	**61**	**63**	**65**
common size	0.1%	0.1%	0.1%	1.0%	1.0%	1.0%	1.0%	1.0%	1.0%
rate of change		−16.2%	59.6%	(Assume 1.0% interest earned on avg. balance in cash and marketable securities.)					

Year	Actuals			Forecasts					
	2010	2011	2012	Year +1	Year +2	Year +3	Year +4	Year +5	Year +6
Interest expense	−903	−856	−899	−1,049	−1,087	−1,136	−1,196	−1,248	−1,286
common size	−1.6%	−1.3%	−1.4%	−3.65%	−3.65%	−3.65%	−3.65%	−3.65%	
rate of change		−5.2%	5.0%	(Weighted-average interest rate on financial liabilities.)					
Income from equity affiliates	735	0	0	0	0	0	0	0	0
common size	1.3%	0.0%	0.0%						
rate of change		−100.0%	0.0%						
Income before tax	8,232	8,834	8,304	8,450	8,749	9,053	9,565	9,691	9,982
common size	14.2%	13.3%	12.7%	12.4%	12.3%	12.2%	12.2%	12.0%	12.0%
rate of change		7.3%	−6.0%	1.8%	3.5%	3.5%	5.7%	1.3%	3.0%
Income tax expense	−1,894	−2,372	−2,090	−2,281	−2,362	−2,444	−2,583	−2,617	−2,695
common size	−3.3%	−3.6%	−3.2%	−27.0%	−27.0%	−27.0%	−27.0%	−27.0%	−27.0%
rate of change		25.2%	−11.9%	(Assume effective income tax rate equal to that of past two years.)					
Net income	6,338	6,462	6,214	6,168	6,387	6,609	6,983	7,075	7,287
common size	11.0%	9.7%	9.5%	9.0%	9.0%	8.9%	8.9%	8.8%	8.8%
rate of change		2.0%	−3.8%	−0.7%	3.5%	3.5%	5.7%	1.3%	3.0%
Net income attributable to noncontrolling interests	−18	−19	−36	−10.5	−10.5	−10.5	−10.5	−10.5	−11
common size	0.0%	0.0%	−0.1%	10.0%	10.0%	10.0%	10.0%	10.0%	
rate of change		5.6%	89.5%	(Assume noncontrolling interests earn a 10% rate of return.)					
Net income attributable to common shareholders	6,320	6,443	6,178	6,158	6,377	6,598	6,972	7,064	7,276
common size	10.9%	9.7%	9.4%	9.0%	9.0%	8.9%	8.9%	8.8%	8.8%
rate of change		1.9%	−4.1%	−0.3%	3.6%	3.5%	5.7%	1.3%	3.0%
Other comprehensive income items	146	−2,618	706	0	0	0	0	0	0
common size	0.3%	−3.9%	1.1%	0.0%	0.0%	0.0%	0.0%	0.0%	
rate of change		−1893.2%	−127.0%	(Assume random walk with a mean of zero.)					
Comprehensive income attributable to PepsiCo	$6,484	$3,844	$6,920	$6,158	$6,377	$6,598	$6,972	$7,064	$7,276
common size	11.2%	5.8%	10.6%	9.0%	9.0%	8.9%	8.9%	8.8%	8.8%
rate of change		−40.7%	80.0%	−11.0%	3.6%	3.5%	5.7%	1.3%	3.0%

To compute the year-end cash balance from the average cash balance, you multiply the average by two and then subtract the beginning balance [Ending = (Average × 2) − Beginning]. Applying this approach, the projected year-end cash balances would be as follows:

	Annual Sales Forecasts	Average Sales per Day	Days' Sales in Cash	Average Cash Balance	Beginning Cash Balance	Ending Cash Balance
Year +1	$12,167	$33.33	30	$1,000	$ 800	$1,200
Year +2	$12,167	$33.33	30	$1,000	$1,200	$ 800
Year +3	$12,167	$33.33	30	$1,000	$ 800	$1,200
Year +4	$12,167	$33.33	30	$1,000	$1,200	$ 800
Year +5	$12,167	$33.33	30	$1,000	$ 800	$1,200

Notice that, because the firm held a smaller-than-average-cash balance at the start of the forecast period ($800), the forecast will have to compensate and project a larger-than-average cash balance ($1,200) at the end of Year +1. The forecast model will then have to compensate again in Year +2, and project a smaller-than-average year-end balance ($800). The relatively small balance at the beginning of Year +1 triggers a relatively large balance at the end of Year +1, which in turn triggers a relatively small balance at the end of Year +2, and so on. Exhibit 10.4 depicts this type of sawtooth pattern of variability.

In certain contexts, this type of variability is a realistic outcome of volatility in the firm's operating environment (such as seasonality or cyclicality). Volatile forecasts that reflect seasonality or cyclicality are preferable in contexts in which the analyst is concerned about whether a firm will violate certain contractual constraints, such as debt covenants or regulatory capital requirements. In other contexts, you may prefer smooth forecasts that mitigate the variability in this pattern. Smooth forecasts are often preferable in contexts where you expect random fluctuations around a generally smooth average growth trend over time. Analysts also often prefer smooth growth

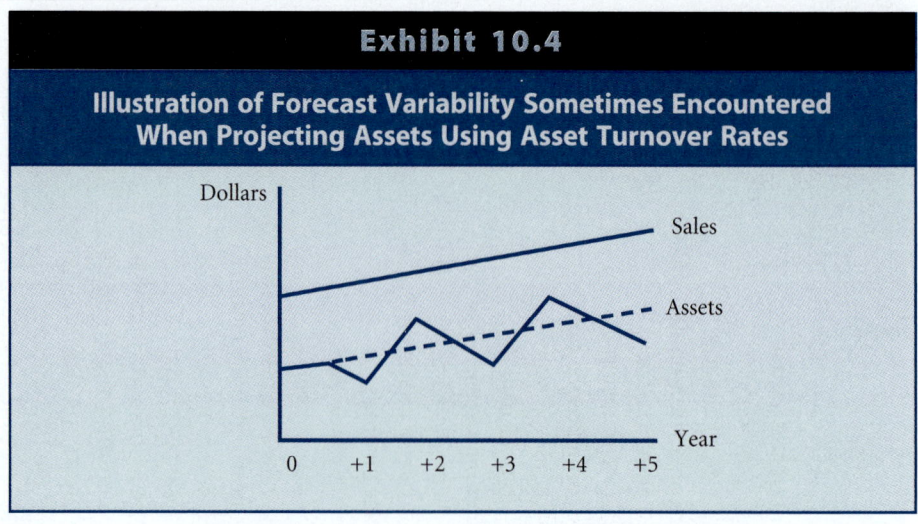

Exhibit 10.4

Illustration of Forecast Variability Sometimes Encountered When Projecting Assets Using Asset Turnover Rates

forecasts because these forecasts tend to be easier to present and explain to an audience.

A number of techniques exist for you to produce smooth forecasts. One such technique is to project the ending balances to equal the projected average balances. In the example, one would simply assume that the projected ending balance in cash each year will equal the average balance ($1,000), which would produce smooth forecasts.

Another forecast smoothing technique involves using turnover ratios to project the ending balance in the forecast account at the end of the forecast horizon (say, Year +5). First, determine the average annual rate of growth that would be necessary over that horizon to reach that ending balance amount, then project each year-end balance using this growth rate. Using a simple example, if the cash balance is $800 now and is projected to be $1,200 at the end of Year +5, that implies an average annual growth rate of 8.45%, so we could use that growth rate to project a smooth pattern of cash balances for Year +1 through Year +5. Alternately, if one expects the ending cash balance to vary directly with sales, then one can simply project growth in cash balances using the expected growth rates in sales. In choosing among forecasting techniques, you must trade off the objectives of achieving forecast precision and minimizing forecast error while avoiding unnecessary computational complexity.

In the sections that follow, we project individual operating assets and liabilities for **PepsiCo** using a combination of forecast drivers, including common-size percentages, growth rates, and asset turnovers. Exhibit 10.5 provides a preview of the projected balance sheets for PepsiCo for Year +1 through Year +5, which we developed using the Forecasts spreadsheet in FSAP. The exhibit also presents forecast amounts for Year +6, assuming PepsiCo will grow at a constant rate of 3%.

Projecting Cash and Cash Equivalents

The Analysis spreadsheet in FSAP computes the average turnover of cash through revenues each year, so we use that turnover ratio to project **PepsiCo**'s ending cash balances during the forecast horizon. Like all firms, PepsiCo needs a certain amount of cash on hand for day-to-day liquidity.[10] PepsiCo's cash holdings have varied between 2010 and 2012. During 2010, PepsiCo had average cash balances of roughly 31.2 days of sales, whereas in 2011 and 2012, average cash balances were roughly 27.5 days and 28.9 days of sales, respectively (computed as 365 days divided by the ratio of revenues to the average balance in cash; in 2012, 28.9 days = 365/{$65,492/[($4,067 + $6,297)/2]}. We assume that PepsiCo will maintain ending cash balances equivalent to 28 days of sales in the future.

To apply this approach, we use our forecasts of revenues and the projected number of days' sales in cash to compute the ending balance in cash each year. The Year +1 revenue forecast is $68,198 million, or an average of $186.8 million per day. We project PepsiCo will hold 28 days of sales in cash at the end of Year +1, for a cash balance of $5,232 million.

---

[10]The forecasts assume that PepsiCo uses cash for day-to-day operating liquidity purposes, so cash is treated as an element of working capital. Some firms maintain excess cash balances far beyond what is needed for daily liquidity. For such firms, cash may be forecasted in two separate components: cash necessary for liquidity and excess cash. For these firms, the excess cash can serve as the flexible financial account used to balance the balance sheet and should be considered a financial asset.

Exhibit 10.5

PepsiCo
Actual and Forecast Balance Sheets
(amounts in millions; allow for rounding)

The actual and forecast amounts are in bold. Below the actual amounts (only), we report historical common-size and rate-of-change percentages. Below the forecast amounts (only), we report the forecast assumptions and brief explanations.

	Actuals			Forecasts					
	2010	2011	2012	Year +1	Year +2	Year +3	Year +4	Year +5	Year +6
BALANCE SHEET ASSETS:									
Cash and cash equivalents	**$5,943**	**$4,067**	**$6,297**	**$5,232**	**$5,450**	**$5,680**	**$6,035**	**$6,176**	**$6,361**
common size	8.7%	5.6%	8.4%	28.0	28.0	28.0	28.0	28.0	
rate of change		−31.6%	54.8%	(Assume ending cash balances equal to 28 days of sales.)					
Marketable securities	**426**	**358**	**322**	**293**	**267**	**243**	**221**	**201**	**207**
common size	0.6%	0.5%	0.4%	−9.0%	−9.0%	−9.0%	−9.0%	−9.0%	
rate of change		−16.0%	−10.1%	(Assume 9.0% decline, consistent with trend since 2010.)					
Accounts and notes receivable—net	**6,323**	**6,912**	**7,041**	**7,287**	**7,591**	**7,911**	**8,406**	**8,602**	**8,860**
common size	9.3%	9.5%	9.4%	39.0	39.0	39.0	39.0	39.0	
rate of change		9.3%	1.9%	(Assume ending accounts receivable equals 39 days of sales.)					
Inventories	**3,372**	**3,827**	**3,581**	**3,938**	**4,158**	**4,391**	**4,727**	**4,900**	**5,047**
common size	4.9%	5.3%	4.8%	44.0	44.5	45.0	45.5	46.0	
rate of change		13.5%	−6.4%	(Assume continued increase in ending inventory, consistent with recent trend.)					
Prepaid expenses and other current assets	**1,505**	**2,277**	**1,479**	**1,540**	**1,604**	**1,672**	**1,777**	**1,818**	**1,873**
common size	2.2%	3.1%	2.0%	4.1%	4.2%	4.2%	6.3%	2.3%	
rate of change		51.3%	−35.0%	(Assume growth with SG&A expenses, which grow with sales.)					
Current Assets	**17,569**	**17,441**	**18,720**	**18,290**	**19,070**	**19,896**	**21,166**	**21,697**	**22,348**
common size	25.8%	23.9%	25.1%	24.1%	24.3%	24.5%	24.8%	24.9%	24.9%
rate of change		−0.7%	7.3%	−2.3%	4.3%	4.3%	6.4%	2.5%	3.0%

	Actuals			Forecasts					
	2010	2011	2012	Year +1	Year +2	Year +3	Year +4	Year +5	Year +6
Investments in noncontrolled affiliates	1,368	1,477	1,633	1,764	1,905	2,057	2,222	2,399	2,471
common size	2.0%	2.0%	2.2%	8.0%	8.0%	8.0%	8.0%	8.0%	
rate of change		8.0%	10.6%	(Assume 8.0% growth, consistent with past two years.)					
Property, plant and equipment—at cost	33,041	35,140	36,162	39,162	42,572	46,126	49,902	53,766	55,379
common size	48.5%	48.2%	48.4%						
rate of change		6.4%	2.9%	(PP&E assumptions—see schedule in Forecast Development spreadsheet.)					
Accumulated depreciation	−13,983	−15,442	−17,026	−19,760	−22,732	−25,953	−29,437	−33,190	−34,186
common size	−20.5%	−21.2%	−22.8%						
rate of change		10.4%	10.3%	(See depreciation schedule in Forecast Development spreadsheet.)					
Amortizable intangible assets (net)	2,025	1,888	1,781	1,671	1,576	1,490	1,412	1,340	1,380
common size	3.0%	2.6%	2.4%	−110	−95	−86	−78	−72	
rate of change		−6.8%	−5.7%	(Assume amortization per PepsiCo disclosures in Note 4.)					
Goodwill	14,661	16,800	16,971	17,672	18,410	19,185	20,386	20,861	21,487
common size	21.5%	23.1%	22.7%	4.1%	4.2%	4.2%	6.3%	2.3%	
rate of change		14.6%	1.0%	(Assume growth with sales.)					
Other nonamortizable intangible assets	11,783	14,557	14,744	15,353	15,994	16,668	17,711	18,124	18,667
common size	17.3%	20.0%	19.8%	4.1%	4.2%	4.2%	6.3%	2.3%	
rate of change		23.5%	1.3%	(Assume growth with sales.)					
Other assets	1,689	1,021	1,653	1,721	1,793	1,869	1,986	2,032	2,093
common size	2.5%	1.4%	2.2%	4.1%	4.2%	4.2%	6.3%	2.3%	
rate of change		−39.6%	61.9%	(Assume growth with sales.)					
Total Assets	$68,153	$72,882	$74,638	$75,873	$78,587	$81,338	$85,348	$87,029	$89,640
common size	100.0%	100.0%	100.0%	100.0%	100.0%	100.0%	100.0%	100.0%	100.0%
rate of change		6.9%	2.4%	1.7%	3.6%	3.5%	4.9%	2.0%	3.0%

(Continued)

Exhibit 10.5 (Continued)

	Actuals			Forecasts					
	2010	**2011**	**2012**	**Year +1**	**Year +2**	**Year +3**	**Year +4**	**Year +5**	**Year +6**
LIABILITIES:									
Accounts payable	$3,865	$4,083	$4,451	$4,524	$4,701	$4,910	$5,241	$5,350	$5,511
common size	5.7%	5.6%	6.0%	50.0	50.0	50.0	50.0	50.0	
rate of change		5.6%	9.0%	(Assume a 50-day payment period consistent with prior year.)					
Current accrued expenses	7,058	7,674	7,452	7,760	8,084	8,424	8,952	9,160	9,435
common size	10.4%	10.5%	10.0%	4.1%	4.2%	4.2%	6.3%	2.3%	
rate of change		8.7%	-2.9%	(Assume growth with SG&A expenses, which grow with sales.)					
Notes payable and short-term debt	4,898	6,205	4,815	4,943	5,169	5,402	5,722	5,892	6,069
common size	7.2%	8.5%	6.5%	2.7%	4.6%	4.5%	5.9%	3.0%	
rate of change		26.7%	-22.4%	(Assume growth that is 1.0% faster than total assets growth.)					
Income taxes payable	71	192	371	379	393	407	427	435	448
common size	0.1%	0.3%	0.5%	0.5%	0.5%	0.5%	0.5%	0.5%	
rate of change		170.4%	93.2%	(Assume a constant 0.5% of total assets.)					
Current Liabilities	15,892	18,154	17,089	17,606	18,347	19,143	20,341	20,837	21,463
common size	23.3%	24.9%	22.9%	23.2%	23.3%	23.5%	23.8%	23.9%	23.9%
rate of change		14.2%	-5.9%	3.0%	4.2%	4.3%	6.3%	2.4%	
Long-term debt obligations	19,999	20,568	23,544	24,169	25,275	26,413	27,979	28,810	29,674
common size	29.3%	28.2%	31.5%	2.7%	4.6%	4.5%	5.9%	3.0%	
rate of change		2.8%	14.5%	(Assume growth that is 1.0% faster than total assets growth.)					
Long-term accrued liabilities	6,729	8,266	6,543	6,813	7,098	7,397	7,860	8,043	8,284
common size	9.9%	11.3%	8.8%	4.1%	4.2%	4.2%	6.3%	2.3%	
rate of change		22.8%	-20.8%	(Assume growth with SG&A expenses, which grow with sales.)					
Deferred tax liabilities—noncurrent	4,057	4,995	5,063	5,159	5,344	5,531	5,804	5,918	6,095
common size	6.0%	6.9%	6.8%	6.8%	6.8%	6.8%	6.8%	6.8%	
rate of change		23.1%	1.4%	(Assume a constant 6.8% of total assets.)					
Total Liabilities	46,677	51,983	52,239	53,748	56,064	58,484	61,984	63,608	65,516
common size	68.5%	71.3%	70.0%	70.8%	71.3%	71.9%	72.6%	73.1%	73.1%
rate of change		11.4%	0.5%	2.9%	4.3%	4.3%	6.0%	2.6%	

	Actuals			Forecasts					
	2010	2011	2012	Year +1	Year +2	Year +3	Year +4	Year +5	Year +6
SHAREHOLDERS' EQUITY:									
Preferred stock	−109	−116	−123	0	0	0	0	0	0
common size	−0.2%	−0.2%	−0.2%	0.0	0.0	0.0	0.0	0.0	
rate of change		6.4%	6.0%	(Assume preferred stock retired.)					
Common stock + Additional paid in capital	4,558	4,487	4,204	4,249	4,401	4,555	4,779	4,874	5,020
common size	6.7%	6.2%	5.6%	5.6%	5.6%	5.6%	5.6%	5.6%	
rate of change		−1.6%	−6.3%	(Assume steady percent of total assets.)					
Retained earnings	37,090	40,316	43,158	45,866	48,735	51,705	54,842	58,021	59,762
common size	54.4%	55.3%	57.8%						
rate of change		8.7%	7.0%	(Add net income and subtract dividends; see dividends forecast below.)					
Accum. other comprehensive income (loss)	−3,630	−6,229	−5,487	−5,487	−5,487	−5,487	−5,487	−5,487	−5,487
common size	−5.3%	−8.5%	−7.4%	0.0	0.0	0.0	0.0	0.0	
rate of change		71.6%	−11.9%	(Add other comprehensive income items from income statement)					
Treasury stock and other equity adjustments	−16,745	−17,870	−19,458	−22,608	−25,231	−28,023	−30,875	−34,092	−35,279
common size	−24.6%	−24.5%	−26.1%	−3,144	−2,618	−2,786	−2,846	−3,211	
rate of change		6.7%	8.9%	(Treasury stock repurchases, net of treasury stock reissues.)					
Total Common and Preferred Shareholders' Equity	21,164	20,588	22,294	22,020	22,418	22,749	23,260	23,316	24,015
common size	31.1%	28.2%	29.9%	29.0%	28.5%	28.0%	27.3%	26.8%	
rate of change		−2.7%	8.3%	−1.2%	1.8%	1.5%	2.2%	0.2%	
Noncontrolling interests	312	311	105	105	105	105	105	105	108
common size	0.5%	0.4%	0.1%	0.0	0.0	0.0	0.0	0.0	
rate of change		−0.3%	−66.2%	(Assume noncontrolling interests remain constant; all earnings distributed.)					
Total Equity	21,476	20,899	22,399	22,125	22,523	22,854	23,365	23,421	24,123
common size	31.5%	28.7%	30.0%	29.2%	28.7%	28.1%	27.4%	26.9%	
rate of change		−2.7%	7.2%	−1.2%	1.8%	1.5%	2.2%	0.2%	
Total Liabilities and Equities	$68,153	$72,882	$74,638	$75,873	$78,587	$81,338	$85,348	$87,029	$89,640
common size	100.0%	100.0%	100.0%	100.0%	100.0%	100.0%	100.0%	100.0%	100.0%
rate of change	2.4%	6.9%	2.4%	1.7%	3.6%	3.5%	4.9%	2.0%	3.0%

The projected balances in cash and cash equivalents on the projected PepsiCo balance sheets follow (allow for rounding):

	Cash and Cash Equivalents			
	Annual Revenue Forecasts	Average Revenue per Day	Days Revenues in Cash	Ending Cash Balance
Year +1	$68,198	$186.8	28	$5,232
Year +2	$71,044	$194.6	28	$5,450
Year +3	$74,038	$202.8	28	$5,680
Year +4	$78,672	$215.5	28	$6,035
Year +5	$80,504	$220.6	28	$6,176

For the three primary financial statement forecasts to articulate with each other, the change in the cash balance on the projected balance sheet each year must agree with the change in cash on the projected statement of cash flows. Later in the chapter, we demonstrate how to build the implied statement of cash flows.

Projecting Marketable Securities

During 2010 through 2012, **PepsiCo**'s marketable securities balances (also commonly referred to as short-term investments) have been trending steadily down, declining at an average rate of roughly 9% per year. It appears PepsiCo primarily manages its liquidity through its fairly large cash balances rather than through its very small amounts of marketable securities. Going forward, we assume that PepsiCo will continue this trend, and ending marketable securities balances will shrink by 9% per year. The projected balances follow:

	Marketable Securities		
	Beginning Balance	Growth Rate	Ending Balance
Year +1	$322	−9.0%	$293
Year +2	$293	−9.0%	$267
Year +3	$267	−9.0%	$243
Year +4	$243	−9.0%	$221
Year +5	$221	−9.0%	$201

As described shortly, we also include on the forecasted income statements the future interest income that we expect the cash and marketable securities to generate.

Projecting Accounts Receivable

Chapter 4's analysis of **PepsiCo**'s accounts receivable turnover ratios revealed that PepsiCo's collection period has grown over the last three years, from an average of 35 days during 2010, to 36 days in 2011, and 39 days in 2012. (In 2012, for example, 39 days = 365/{$65,492/[($6,912 + $7,041)/2]}). We project accounts receivable by assuming that PepsiCo will maintain an average 39-day collection period into the future, turning over accounts receivable approximately 9.4 times a year (365/39). As we demonstrated earlier for our projections of cash, we will simply use the average turnover rate to project PepsiCo's ending accounts receivable. The projected amounts are as follows (allow for rounding):

	Accounts Receivable			
	Annual Sales Forecasts	**Average Sales per Day**	**Days' Sales in Accounts Receivable**	**Ending Balance**
Year +1	$68,198	$186.8	39	$7,287
Year +2	$71,044	$194.6	39	$7,591
Year +3	$74,038	$202.8	39	$7,911
Year +4	$78,672	$215.5	39	$8,406
Year +5	$80,504	$220.6	39	$8,602

Projecting Inventories

Chapter 4's analysis of **PepsiCo**'s inventory turnover ratios revealed that PepsiCo has experienced gradually longer inventory turnover rates of 41 days in 2010, 42 days in 2011, and 43 days in 2012. Because of this trend in PepsiCo's inventory management, and because of PepsiCo's increasing growth and emphasis in the Latin America, Europe, and AMEA regions, we project PepsiCo's inventory turnover days continue to gradually increase, reaching 46 days by Year +5. The projected year-end inventory amounts follow:

	Inventories			
	Cost of Goods Sold	**Cost of Goods Sold Per Day**	**Inventory Turnover Days**	**Ending Balance**
Year +1	$32,667	$ 89.50	44.0	$3,938
Year +2	$34,101	$ 93.43	44.5	$4,158
Year +3	$35,612	$ 97.57	45.0	$4,391
Year +4	$37,920	$103.89	45.5	$4,727
Year +5	$38,883	$106.53	46.0	$4,900

For some firms, such as retail chains, inventory is a large proportion of total assets. For such firms, you should link inventory forecasts to projections of the number of stores that will be operating in future years (or even more specifically, to the number of square feet of retail space). For retail firms that operate large big-box stores (**Walmart** or **Costco**, for example), inventory projections may grow stepwise because each new store will require millions of dollars of additional inventory. Retail chains with seasonal sales will strive to have new stores (and thus new inventory) in place before heavy selling seasons (such as the back-to-school season for casual clothing and the Christmas season for toys); thus, analysts link inventory forecasts to projections of new stores in advance of these heavy selling seasons.

Projecting Prepaid Expenses and Other Current Assets

Prepaid expenses and other current assets represent items such as prepaid rent, advertising, and insurance. These items often vary in relation to the level of operating activity, such as sales, advertising, production, new stores or restaurants, and total assets. In the case of **PepsiCo**, we will simply assume prepaid expenses and other current assets will grow in the future at the same rate as revenues. The projected amounts are as follows:

	2012	Prepaid Expenses and Other Current Assets				
	2012	**Year +1**	**Year +2**	**Year +3**	**Year +4**	**Year +5**
Revenue growth rates		+4.1%	+4.2%	+4.2%	+6.3%	+2.3%
Projected amounts	$1,479	$1,540	$1,604	$1,672	$1,777	$1,818

Projecting Investments in Noncontrolled Affiliates

Prior to 2010, these investments were very substantial and important to **PepsiCo**, amounting to over 10% of total assets. In 2009 alone, PepsiCo recognized $365 million in income from its investments in these equity affiliates, reported on a separate line of the income statement. These affiliates represented major investments in PepsiCo's primary bottlers, particularly The Pepsi Bottling Group (PBG) and Pepsi Americas (PAS). However, during 2010 PepsiCo completed acquisitions of all of the remaining outstanding shares of these companies and began reporting them on a consolidated basis.

As of 2011 and 2012, PepsiCo's investments in noncontrolled affiliates represent its interests in joint ventures with **Unilever** and **Starbucks**, among others. These noncontrolled affiliates now amount to only about 2% of PepsiCo's total assets. PepsiCo's share of the income from these investments is no longer reported on a separate line of the income statement and is instead simply aggregated with SG&A expense (thereby reducing the reported amount for SG&A). These investments grew at a rate of 8.0% in 2011 and 10.6% in 2012.

We assume that investments in noncontrolled affiliates will continue to grow 8.0% per year over the five-year forecast horizon. We also assume that PepsiCo's share of the income from these affiliates is implicitly included as an offset to SG&A expense.[11] The projected investment amounts are as follows (allow for rounding):

	2012	Investments in Noncontrolled Affiliates				
	2012	**Year +1**	**Year +2**	**Year +3**	**Year +4**	**Year +5**
Growth rates		+ 8.0%	+ 8.0%	+ 8.0%	+ 8.0%	+ 8.0%
Ending balance	$1,633	$1,764	$1,905	$2,057	$2,222	$2,399

Projecting Property, Plant, and Equipment

PepsiCo's fixed-assets turnover ratio has declined a bit from 3.6 in 2010 to 3.4 in 2012 (computed for 2012 as 3.4 = $65,492/[($19,136 + $19,698)/2]). This declining fixed-assets turnover indicates PepsiCo is not utilizing its fixed assets as efficiently as it had in

---

[11]For the analyst who needs greater forecast precision, the projections of future balances in Investments in Noncontrolled Affiliates should follow the accounting methods for equity method investments. As such, the balances should grow with the firm's proportionate share of the net income of the affiliate minus dividends received from the affiliate each period, and should increase with additional investments and decrease with dispositions of investments in such affiliates.

the past. This is primarily a consequence of the decline in PepsiCo's net revenues from $66.5 billion in 2011 to $65.5 billion in 2012, resulting in lower fixed asset efficiency.

In the 2012 Annual Report, PepsiCo's MD&A section describing "Our Liquidity and Capital Resources" discloses that management expects "2013 net capital spending to be approximately $3.0 billion, within our long-term capital spending target of less than or equal to 5% of net revenue." Given this guidance, we assume that net capital spending in Year +1 will be $3.0 billion, which amounts to 4.4% of projected revenues of $68,198 million. Given PepsiCo's guidance and stable history of capital spending, we also assume that capital spending in Year +2 and beyond will average 4.8% of revenues. We include these net capital expenditures in our projected balance sheets by increasing PP&E, and we include them as cash outflows in the investing section of our projected statements of cash flows. Also, we assume these amounts reflect net capital expenditures, after proceeds from sales of PP&E (which tend to be minor amounts for PepsiCo). The projected amounts for capital expenditures follow:

	Property, Plant, and Equipment		
Year	Annual Revenue Forecasts	Capital Spending (% of Revenues)	Capital Spending
+1	$68,198	4.4%	$3,000
+2	$71,044	4.8%	$3,410
+3	$74,038	4.8%	$3,554
+4	$78,672	4.8%	$3,776
+5	$80,504	4.8%	$3,864

PepsiCo's existing PP&E will continue to depreciate as PepsiCo uses these assets in its operations. In addition, PepsiCo's capital expenditures on new PP&E will trigger a new layer of depreciation expense each year. PepsiCo discloses in Note 4, "Property, Plant and Equipment and Intangible Assets" (Appendix A), that it uses the straight-line depreciation method for financial statement purposes. Note 4 in PepsiCo's financial statements does not disclose information related to salvage values, but an analyst might assume that PepsiCo depreciates PP&E to zero salvage value. Based on this assumption, we estimate the average useful life that PepsiCo uses for depreciation by taking the average amount in PP&E at acquisition cost and dividing it by depreciation expense for that year. In 2012, for depreciation purposes PepsiCo used an average useful life of 14.32 years {[($36,162 + $35,140)/2]/$2,489}. We assume that PepsiCo will continue to use a 14.32-year average useful life for depreciation.[12]

---

[12]PepsiCo discloses that 2012 depreciation expense equals $2,489 million in Note 4, "Property, Plant and Equipment and Intangible Assets." In that note, PepsiCo also discloses that PP&E includes land, which is not depreciable (although land improvements are depreciable), and construction in progress, which is not yet depreciable but will be in the future. The analyst interested in slightly greater precision should exclude these amounts from the useful-life computation and the depreciation expense projections. Also note that on PepsiCo's Statement of Cash Flows for 2012 (Appendix A), PepsiCo adds back $2,689 million in depreciation and amortization expense to net income, which consists of $2,489 million of depreciation expense and $200 million of amortization expense. We use the depreciation expense disclosed in Note 4 ($2,489 million) to avoid confounding the estimate of the depreciable useful life with amortization expense. Notice that the total PP&E increased by $1,022 million, which is less than the $2,619 million in net capital expenditures in 2012. Also notice that the increase in accumulated depreciation during 2012 was only $1,584 million (from $15,442 million to $17,026 million), an amount significantly less than depreciation expense. These differences arise because PepsiCo sold (or wrote off as impaired) PP&E assets that had accumulated depreciation; so the costs of these assets and their respective accumulated depreciation amounts were removed from the accounts.

In computing depreciation expense for Year +1, we need to forecast two components. The first component is depreciation on the $36,162 million of existing PP&E as of the beginning of Year +1, which will be $2,525 million ($36,162/14.32 years). The second component is depreciation on the Year +1 capital expenditures of $3,000 million, which will be $209 million ($3,000/14.32 years). Together, total depreciation expense in Year +1 will be $2,734 million ($2,525 + $209), and accumulated depreciation will grow by this amount of depreciation. In Year +2, depreciation expense will be $2,972 million, which consists of those two components plus a third component to reflect depreciation expense of $238 million ($3,410/14.32 years) on Year + 2 capital expenditures on PP&E, and so on. The projected amounts for depreciation expense are as follows:

	Depreciable Bases	Depreciation Expense				
		Depreciation Amounts per Year (assuming 14.32 year life):				
		Year +1	Year +2	Year +3	Year +4	Year +5
Existing PP&E	$36,162	$2,525	$2,525	$2,525	$2,525	$2,525
Capital spending Year +1	$ 3,000	209	209	209	209	209
Capital spending Year +2	$ 3,410		238	238	238	238
Capital spending Year +3	$ 3,554			248	248	248
Capital spending Year +4	$ 3,776				264	264
Capital spending Year +5	$ 3,864					270
Total depreciation expense		$2,734	$2,972	$3,220	$3,484	$3,754

Like most firms, PepsiCo does not report depreciation expense as a separate line item on the income statement, but it allocates depreciation expense to cost of goods sold and SG&A expense based on whether the underlying assets are being used in production or sales and administration. Therefore, in our projections we do not include these amounts of depreciation expense separately in the income statement and assume these amounts are included in our projections of cost of goods sold and SG&A expense. However, we do add depreciation expense back to net income in our projected statement of cash flows, discussed in a later section of this chapter. The projected amounts for capital expenditures; property, plant, and equipment; depreciation expense; and accumulated depreciation are as follows (allow for rounding):

	Property, Plant, and Equipment				
Year	Capital Spending	Ending Balance (at Cost)	Depreciation Expense	Accumulated Depreciation	Ending Balance (Net)
2012 actual		$36,162		$(17,026)	$19,136
+1	$3,000	$39,162	$2,734	$(19,760)	$19,402
+2	$3,410	$42,572	$2,972	$(22,732)	$19,840
+3	$3,554	$46,126	$3,220	$(25,953)	$20,173
+4	$3,776	$49,902	$3,484	$(29,437)	$20,465
+5	$3,864	$53,766	$3,754	$(33,191)	$20,575

When forecasting fixed assets for capital-intensive firms (such as manufacturing firms or utility companies) or firms for which fixed-asset growth is a critical driver of future sales growth and earnings (for example, new stores for retail chains or restaurant chains), PP&E is typically a large proportion of total assets and has a material impact on the analysts' forecasts. For such firms, analysts often invest considerable time and effort in developing detailed forecasts of capital expenditures, PP&E, and depreciation expense. In FSAP, the Forecast Development spreadsheet includes a model for forecasting capital expenditures, PP&E, depreciation expense, and accumulated depreciation. The FSAP output (Appendix C) demonstrates the use of this model to compute the preceding forecasts for PepsiCo.

Projecting Amortizable Intangible Assets

Amortizable intangible assets for **PepsiCo** include primarily acquired franchise rights and brands, trademarks, and other identifiable intangible assets with limited useful lives that PepsiCo obtained through acquisitions of other companies. As discussed previously, PepsiCo amortizes these assets ratably over their estimated useful lives (ranging from 1–60 years). The net book value of PepsiCo's amortizable intangible assets amounts to $1,781 million on the 2012 balance sheet (only 2.4% of total assets). In 2010, the balance in amortizable intangible assets more than doubled as a consequence of PepsiCo acquiring and consolidating its bottlers, PBG and PAS. In 2011 and 2012, the balance in amortizable intangible assets has decreased each year primarily because of amortization, with only very minor amounts of additional investment. In Note 4, "Property, Plant and Equipment and Intangible Assets" (Appendix A), PepsiCo discloses the amount of amortization expense it expects on these intangible assets over the next five years, which we include under the heading "Amortization of Intangible Assets" on the projected income statements. We assume the amortizable intangible asset amounts will continue to decrease by the amounts of amortization expense that PepsiCo disclosed. Consistent with the past two years, we also assume that PepsiCo will not acquire any additional amortizable intangible assets; instead, it will acquire goodwill and nonamortizable intangible assets, which we discuss next.

Projecting Goodwill and Nonamortizable Intangible Assets

The majority of **PepsiCo**'s intangible assets involve goodwill ($16,971 million) and other nonamortizable intangible assets (primarily brands, $14,744 million) with indefinite lives. These intangible assets arise when PepsiCo acquires other companies. These accounts recognize the portion of the acquisition price that PepsiCo allocates to intangible assets such as goodwill and brands. Not surprisingly, these accounts jumped dramatically from a combined $8.3 billion in 2009 to $26.4 billion in 2010, as a consequence of PepsiCo acquiring and consolidating its two primary bottlers, PBG and PAS. U.S. GAAP and IFRS do not require firms to amortize these assets because they have indefinite useful lives, but U.S. GAAP and IFRS do require firms to test their values annually for impairment and to write the carrying values down to fair value if deemed impaired. Thus far, PepsiCo has deemed it necessary to recognize only very minor impairment losses on its goodwill and brand assets ($23 million in 2012 and $14 million in 2011 on certain brands in Europe). Had we forecasted sales declines and negative operating income, this might indicate possibly impaired intangible assets, but the strong sales growth and operating income assumptions imply that future impairment losses are unlikely.

Acquiring other companies with valuable goodwill, brand names, and products is a key element of PepsiCo's strategy. Such acquisitions help PepsiCo create new sales growth, expand its product portfolio, and enter new markets around the world. In 2011, PepsiCo increased the goodwill and nonamortizable intangible assets accounts by a total of $5.6 billion (primarily because it acquired WBD, a Russian subsidiary). In 2012, PepsiCo increased those accounts by an additional net amount of $358 million (divestitures triggered a $171 million reduction but foreign currency translation gains added $529 million). It seems likely that PepsiCo will continue to pursue the strategy of making acquisitions, but in the absence of inside information, it is very difficult to forecast specific acquisitions. Thus, we will assume that PepsiCo's goodwill and nonamortizable intangible assets will grow at the same rate as sales. We will also assume that no future impairment charges will be necessary for these assets. The projected amounts are as follows (allow for rounding):

	Goodwill and Nonamortizable Intangible Assets				
	Beginning Balances		Revenue Growth Rates	Ending Balances	
	Goodwill	Nonamortizable Intangibles		Goodwill	Nonamortizable Intangibles
Year +1	$16,971	$14,744	4.1%	$17,672	$15,353
Year +2	$17,672	$15,353	4.2%	$18,410	$15,994
Year +3	$18,410	$15,994	4.2%	$19,185	$16,668
Year +4	$19,185	$16,668	6.3%	$20,386	$17,711
Year +5	$20,386	$17,711	2.3%	$20,861	$18,124

Projecting Other Noncurrent Assets

In Note 14, "Supplemental Financial Information" (Appendix A), **PepsiCo** discloses that other noncurrent assets consist of noncurrent receivables, deferred marketplace spending, pension assets, other investments, and others. For PepsiCo, these amounts have fluctuated widely over the past three years. For example, other assets amounted to $1,689 million at the end of 2010; $1,021 million at the end of 2011; and $1,653 million at the end of 2012. In the absence of more information to forecast other asset amounts specifically, we assume that other noncurrent assets will grow at the same rate as revenues each year. The projected amounts are as follows:

	Other Assets		
	Beginning Balance	Revenue Growth Rates	Ending Balance
Year +1	$1,653	4.1%	$1,721
Year +2	$1,721	4.2%	$1,793
Year +3	$1,793	4.2%	$1,869
Year +4	$1,869	6.3%	$1,986
Year +5	$1,986	2.3%	$2,032

Projecting Assets That Vary as a Percentage of Total Assets

In some circumstances, you may need to project individual asset amounts that will vary as a percentage of total assets, particularly for firms that maintain a steady proportion of total assets invested in specific types of assets. For example, suppose **PepsiCo**'s strategy is to maintain 7.0% of total assets in cash for liquidity purposes. (Note: We have already projected the future cash balances we will use for PepsiCo; this discussion is for illustration purposes only.) Suppose our projected amounts for Year +1 for all of the individual assets other than cash are as follows:

Marketable securities	$ 293
Accounts receivable	7,287
Inventories	3,938
Prepaid expenses and other current assets	1,540
Long-term investments	1,764
Property, plant, and equipment, net	19,402
Amortizable intangible assets	1,671
Goodwill	17,672
Nonamortizable intangible assets	15,353
Other noncurrent assets	1,721
Subtotal of assets	$70,641

The $70,641 million subtotal represents 93.0% (1.00 – 0.07) of total assets. Therefore, projected total assets should equal $75,959 ($70,641/0.93). Thus, in this hypothetical example, the ending cash balance would equal $5,317 (0.07 × $75,959).

Note that this approach to forecasting introduces some circularity into the projected financial statements; the cash balance is a function of total assets, which is a function of the cash balance. This forecast approach is not unrealistic, nor does it create a problem for the computations. A later subsection of this chapter discusses how to solve for code-termined variables in financial statement forecasts.

Projecting Accounts Payable

PepsiCo reports accounts payable and other current liabilities on a single line on its balance sheet, amounting to $11,903 million at the end of 2012. Note 14, "Supplemental Financial Information" (Appendix A), discloses that $4,451 million of that total is attributable to accounts payable, and the remainder ($7,452 million) is attributable to accrued liabilities for marketplace spending, compensation and benefits, dividends, and other expenses. Future credit purchases of inventory and PepsiCo's payment policy to its suppliers will likely drive accounts payable, whereas accrued expenses will likely grow with future selling, general, and administrative expenses. Therefore, we forecast accounts payable and accrued expenses separately.

PepsiCo's days payable was 45 days in 2010 and 2011, but it jumped to 50 days in 2012. We assume that PepsiCo will continue to maintain an accounts payable period of 50 days in the future. To forecast future accounts payable balances, we begin by forecasting inventory purchases on account (which drive payables). We rely on our prior forecasts of PepsiCo's cost of goods sold and add the changes in the inventory balances to compute inventory purchases, which will flow through accounts payable. We then project ending balances in accounts payable, assuming 50 days payable periods, as follows (allow for rounding):

			Accounts Payable				
	Cost of Goods Sold	Add: Ending Inventory	Less: Beginning Inventory	Equals: Inventory Purchases	Purchases per Day	Payables Period	Ending Balance
Year +1	$32,667	$3,938	$3,581	$33,024	$ 90.5	50 days	$4,524
Year +2	$34,101	$4,158	$3,938	$34,321	$ 94.0	50 days	$4,701
Year +3	$35,612	$4,391	$4,158	$35,845	$ 98.2	50 days	$4,910
Year +4	$37,920	$4,727	$4,391	$38,256	$104.8	50 days	$5,241
Year +5	$38,883	$4,900	$4,727	$39,056	$107.0	50 days	$5,350

Projecting Other Current Accrued Liabilities

As discussed in the prior section, Note 14, "Supplemental Financial Information" (Appendix A), discloses that at the end of 2012, **PepsiCo**'s accrued liabilities for marketplace spending, compensation and benefits, dividends, and other expenses amount to $7,452 million. Our forecasts of income for PepsiCo assumed that SG&A expenses would remain a steady percentage of revenues, and therefore grow proportionately with revenues. We therefore forecast that other current accrued liabilities will grow with SG&A expenses, which grow with revenues (allow for rounding).

	Other Current Accrued Liabilities		
	Beginning Balance	SG&A Expense Growth Rate	Ending Balance
Year +1	$7,452	4.1%	$7,760
Year +2	$7,760	4.2%	$8,084
Year +3	$8,084	4.2%	$8,424
Year +4	$8,424	6.3%	$8,952
Year +5	$8,952	2.3%	$9,160

Projecting Current Liabilities: Income Taxes Payable

PepsiCo's current liabilities include a separate line item for income taxes payable. Income taxes payable varies with the income tax provision on the income statement, but income taxes payable also varies with tax payments, settlements of tax disputes, mergers and acquisitions, changes in deferred tax assets and liabilities, and other elements that are difficult to predict with confidence. PepsiCo's income taxes payable has varied within a narrow range between 0.1% and 0.5% of total assets over 2010–2012.

We simply assume that PepsiCo's income taxes payable will average 0.5% of total assets in the future. The projected amounts are as follows:

| | Income Taxes Payable | | |
	Total Assets	As a Percentage of Total Assets	Balance
Year +1	$75,873	0.5%	$379
Year +2	$78,587	0.5%	$393
Year +3	$81,338	0.5%	$407
Year +4	$85,348	0.5%	$427
Year +5	$87,029	0.5%	$435

Projecting Other Noncurrent Liabilities

Other noncurrent liabilities are accrued liabilities for expenses that relate to pension obligations, health care obligations, long-term compensation, and other operating and administrative activities. We therefore project other noncurrent liabilities will grow with SG&A expenses, which we assume grow with revenues (allow for rounding):

| | Other Noncurrent Liabilities | | |
	Beginning Balance	SG&A Expense Growth Rate	Ending Balance
Year +1	$6,543	4.1%	$6,813
Year +2	$6,813	4.2%	$7,098
Year +3	$7,098	4.2%	$7,397
Year +4	$7,397	6.3%	$7,860
Year +5	$7,860	2.3%	$8,043

Projecting Deferred Income Taxes

PepsiCo's Note 5, "Income Taxes" (Appendix A), indicates that deferred taxes relate to a variety of operating items (for example, property, plant, and equipment; and intangible assets). During 2010, the deferred tax liability jumped from $659 million to $4,057 million, largely a result of PepsiCo's acquiring and consolidating the bottlers, PBG and PAS. In 2011 and 2012, PepsiCo's deferred income tax liability remained a relatively steady 6.8% of total assets. We project that deferred tax liabilities will remain at that proportionate level of total assets in future years. The amounts are as follows:

| | Deferred Income Taxes | | |
	Total Assets	As a Percentage of Total Assets	Ending Balance
Year +1	$75,873	6.8%	$5,159
Year +2	$78,587	6.8%	$5,344
Year +3	$81,338	6.8%	$5,531
Year +4	$85,348	6.8%	$5,804
Year +5	$87,029	6.8%	$5,918

LO 10-3d

Build forecasts of future
balance sheets, income
statements, and statements
of cash flows by applying the
seven-step forecasting
framework to project:
d. financial leverage, capital
structure, and financial
income items.

Step 4: Project Financial Leverage, Financial Assets, Common Equity Capital, and Financial Income Items

After completing forecasts of the operating assets and liabilities of the balance sheet, we must now project any financial assets the firm will hold, and the financial debt and shareholders' equity amounts that will be necessary to finance the firm's operating and investing activities. In addition, we project the effects of financing on net income by projecting future interest income, interest expense, and other elements of financial income.

For firms that maintain a particular capital structure over time, you can use the common-size balance sheet percentages to project amounts of debt and equity capital. If the firm has a target capital structure that consists of stable proportions of liabilities and equity (for instance, a firm might have a target capital structure of 60% liabilities and 40% equities), you can use these common-size percentages and the projected amounts of total assets to project future totals of liabilities and equities.

Alternatively, you can project debt capital and shareholders' equity accounts by projecting potential future changes in the financial leverage strategy of the firm. For instance, in recent years, interest rates on corporate debt have been at historically low levels, so many firms are taking on more financial leverage by recapitalizing with greater amounts of short- and long-term debt and using this debt financing to reduce shareholders' equity through repurchases of common shares and increased dividends. In other cases, you may need to project how a firm will alter its capital structure as a result of a merger, acquisition, or divestiture transaction.

In this section, we forecast debt and equity by projecting the financial leverage strategy of **PepsiCo**, changing the expected debt and equity amounts over time. Each account is discussed next.

Projecting Financial Assets

You must assess the firm's business activities and financial strategy to determine the extent to which the firm uses financial assets for operating liquidity purposes versus financial purposes. Most firms use financial assets, such as cash, short-term and long-term investment securities, to accomplish one or all of the following:

- manage seasonal swings in operating liquidity.
- provide a financial cushion for future uncertainties.
- have financial flexibility to take advantage of profitable opportunities when they arise.

As such, for these firms it makes sense to forecast financial assets as part of the liquidity and operating activities of the firm. For example, **PepsiCo**'s 2012 balance sheet recognizes cash, short-term investments (marketable securities) and investments in noncontrolled affiliates. As discussed previously, PepsiCo uses cash and short-term investments to provide liquidity for operating activities, and the investments in noncontrolled affiliates represent PepsiCo's investments in non-consolidated joint ventures. Therefore, we included these types of financial assets in our projections of PepsiCo's operating activities.

By contrast, some firms hold excess cash and/or short-term or long-term investments that are not needed for operating liquidity purposes, and are instead intended for future financial purposes, such as debt retirement, corporate acquisitions, repurchasing shares, or paying dividends. When forecasting the future financial capital structure for firms like these, you must project the future financial assets that represent financial savings that can be used for debt retirement or other financial purposes. Suppose, for example, a firm had issued bonds to finance plant and equipment and the bond indenture agreement required the firm to maintain a bond sinking fund (a reserve of cash or securities to be used for future bond retirement). The cash and securities in the sinking fund would represent financial assets intended for debt retirement and should be projected with the firm's financial structure rather than as part of the firm's operating activities. As of the 2012 balance sheet, PepsiCo does not report any short-term or long-term investment securities for debt retirement purposes. Because PepsiCo is not likely to need future reserves of investment securities for debt retirement, we will not forecast them.

Projecting Short-Term and Long-Term Debt

As of the end of 2012, **PepsiCo** was utilizing a total of $28,359 million in short-term and long-term borrowings to help finance its assets. The common-size balance sheet data for PepsiCo (Chapter 1) show that short-term and long-term debt obligations have become increasingly larger proportions of total assets. From 2009 to 2010, the proportion of total debt in PepsiCo's capital structure jumped considerably, from 19.7% of total assets to 36.5%, following the acquisitions of their primary bottlers. Since 2010, the proportion of total debt has continued to increase slightly, to 36.7% in 2011, and then to 38.0% in 2012. The common-size balance sheet data for PepsiCo indicate that short-term debt has ranged from 7.2% of total assets in 2010, to 8.5% in 2011, to 6.5% in 2012. Long-term debt has ranged from 29.3% of total assets in 2010, to 28.2% in 2011, to 31.5% in 2012.

PepsiCo's 2012 consolidated balance sheet (Appendix A) recognizes $4,815 million of short-term obligations. Note 9, "Debt Obligations and Commitments," reveals that short-term debt obligations includes $2,901 million of current maturities of long-term debt, $1,101 million of commercial paper, and $813 million of other short-term borrowings.[13] Note 9 also discloses that at the end of 2012, PepsiCo has $23,544 million in long-term debt obligations (a total of $26,445 million minus the $2,901 million maturing in 2013).

PepsiCo's statement of cash flows for 2012 (Appendix A) indicates the firm generated approximately $8.5 billion of net cash flow from operating activities and used $3.0 billion for investing activities. In terms of financing activities in 2012, PepsiCo used $3.3 billion in cash to pay dividends and $3.2 billion to repurchase common stock, after raising nearly $3.5 billion (net) from issuing long-term debt and paying down roughly $1.5 billion (net) in short-term debt. Clearly, PepsiCo generates a lot of cash from its operating activities and is choosing to increase its debt obligations in order to return more cash to shareholders through dividends and share repurchases.

---

[13]Firms can classify current maturities of long-term debt as long-term debt if the firm has the intent and ability to refinance on a long-term basis.

PepsiCo appears to be shifting its financial leverage strategy to recapitalize by issuing greater amounts of long-term debt while paying larger dividends and repurchasing more common equity shares. In fact, as disclosed in Note 9, during 2012 PepsiCo issued a total of nearly $6.0 billion of new long-term debt obligations, using seven new debt issues with maturities ranging from 2015 to 2042. We assume that PepsiCo will continue to increase short-term and long-term debt obligations, which will become larger proportions of total assets, consistent with this recent trend. Therefore, we project that short-term and long-term debt will grow at rates that are 1% faster than the projected growth rates in total assets (derived from our projected amounts for total assets) in Year +1 through Year +5, thereby gradually increasing PepsiCo's projected leverage from 38% to almost 40% of total assets by Year +5. The projected amounts for short-term and long-term debt (the sum of which is total interest-bearing debt) are as follows (allow for rounding):

| | Projected Total Assets | Total Assets Growth | Short-Term and Long-Term Debt | | | |
			Projected Growth in Debt	Short-Term Debt	Long-Term Debt	Total Interest-Bearing Debt
Actual 2012	$74,638			$4,815	$23,544	$28,359
Year +1	$75,873	1.7%	2.7%	$4,943	$24,169	$29,112
Year +2	$78,587	3.6%	4.6%	$5,169	$25,275	$30,444
Year +3	$81,338	3.5%	4.5%	$5,402	$26,413	$31,815
Year +4	$85,348	4.9%	5.9%	$5,722	$27,979	$33,701
Year +5	$87,029	2.0%	3.0%	$5,892	$28,810	$34,702

In the next section we will use the preceding projected amounts for interest-bearing debt as a basis to project PepsiCo's future interest expense.

PepsiCo's outstanding long-term debt matures at varying dates extending to 2013 to 2042. Note 9, "Debt Obligations and Commitments" (Appendix A), discloses information on the amounts that mature in Year +1 through Year +5 and beyond. For analysts developing forecasts for firms that are deleveraging and retiring debt or for firms that are highly leveraged and facing a high probability of distress or bankruptcy, the schedule of future long-term debt maturities is very helpful in projecting when the firm will have to retire or refinance mature debt.

Projecting Interest Expense

We can now project our first-iteration estimate of interest expense, based on our projected balances in interest-bearing short-term and long-term debt. Note 9, "Debt Obligations and Commitments" (Appendix A), indicates that at the end of 2012, the interest rates ranged from 0.1% on commercial paper to 9.3% on other long-term borrowings. Dividing the 2012 interest expense by the average amount of interest-bearing debt outstanding during 2012 implies that **PepsiCo**'s weighted-average interest rate on long-term and short-term debt was roughly 3.3% {$899/[($23,544 + $4,815 + $20,568 + $6,205)/2]}. This average is likely to be slightly understated, however, because, as noted earlier, PepsiCo issued seven new long-term debt obligations during 2012, so it did not incur interest expense on them for the full year.

Alternatively, we can use the data disclosed in PepsiCo's Note 9 to estimate the weighted-average interest rate on total debt outstanding, as follows:

Weighted-Average Cost of Debt Capital

	Amounts	Weights	Interest Rates	Weighted-Average Rates
Notes due 2013	$ 2,891	0.102	2.3	0.234
Commercial paper	1,101	0.039	0.1	0.004
Other borrowings maturing in 2013	813	0.029	7.4	0.212
Notes due 2014	3,237	0.114	4.4	0.502
Notes due 2015	3,300	0.116	1.5	0.175
Notes due 2016	1,878	0.066	3.9	0.258
Notes due 2017	1,250	0.044	2.0	0.088
Notes due 2018–2042	13,781	0.486	4.4	2.138
Other, due 2013–2020	108	0.004	9.3	0.035
Total	**$28,359**	**1.000**		**3.647**

This alternative approach captures the interest rate weightings going forward. We therefore project interest expense using an interest rate of 3.65% on the average amount of interest-bearing debt in Year +1 through Year +5 to match the weighted-average interest rate on the outstanding debt. Using the projected amounts of total interest-bearing debt in the prior section, the projected interest expense amounts follow (allow for rounding):

	Interest Expense on Interest-Bearing Debt					
	Short-Term Debt	Long-Term Debt	Total Interest-Bearing Debt	Average Interest-Bearing Debt	Interest Rate	Interest Expense
2012	$4,815	$23,544	$28,359			$ 899
Year +1	$4,943	$24,169	$29,112	$28,735.5	3.65%	$1,049
Year +2	$5,169	$25,275	$30,444	$29,778.0	3.65%	$1,087
Year +3	$5,402	$26,413	$31,815	$31,129.5	3.65%	$1,136
Year +4	$5,722	$27,979	$33,701	$32,758.0	3.65%	$1,196
Year +5	$5,892	$28,810	$34,702	$34,201.5	3.65%	$1,248

The interest expense projections are higher than recent past interest expense amounts for PepsiCo, reflecting PepsiCo's shift in financial strategy in 2012 to greater reliance on long-term debt capital. We can now enter these "first-pass" interest expense amounts in the projected income statements. If the projected balance sheets imply that PepsiCo will need larger or smaller amounts of long-term debt to finance future asset growth, then we will need to recompute the interest expense projections to reflect different amounts of debt.

Projecting Interest Income

We can also project our first-pass estimates of **PepsiCo**'s interest income on financial assets, such as cash and short-term investments in marketable securities. In 2012, PepsiCo recognized $91 million in interest income. The average amount of cash and marketable securities during 2012 was $5,522 million [($6,297 + $322 + $4,067 + $358)/2], for an average return of 1.65 ($91/$5,522). The average rates of return PepsiCo earned on these assets were only 1.3% in 2010 and 1.0% in 2011. These rates of return reflect the very low interest rate environment present during 2010 through 2012. In addition, it is likely that PepsiCo's cash and marketable securities are very low-risk but highly liquid instruments, and therefore yield very low rates of return. At the beginning of Year +1, risk-free rates on low risk, highly liquid short-term and medium-term U.S. Treasury bonds were at or below 1.0%. Therefore, we assume PepsiCo will earn a 1.0% return on the average balances in cash and marketable securities each year. The projected amounts for interest income are as follows (allow for rounding):

	Interest Income				
	Ending Balances:				
Year	**Cash**	**Marketable Securities**	**Average Balances**	**Rate of Return**	**Interest Income**
2012	$6,297	$322			
Year +1	$5,232	$293	$6,072	1.0%	$61
Year +2	$5,450	$267	$5,621	1.0%	$56
Year +3	$5,680	$243	$5,819	1.0%	$58
Year +4	$6,035	$221	$6,089	1.0%	$61
Year +5	$6,176	$201	$6,316	1.0%	$63

If the projected balance sheets imply that PepsiCo will generate and retain larger amounts of cash and marketable securities, then we need to recompute the interest income projections to reflect additional interest-earning assets.

Projecting Equity Income from Investments in Noncontrolled Affiliates

As Chapter 8 describes, some firms make substantial investments in affiliated companies or joint ventures that enable the investor company to exert significant influence but not control over the operating and financing decisions of the investee. In such cases, the investor might own 20% to 50% of the outstanding shares of the affiliate company, but does not own enough of the shares to control the firm's activities, and therefore does not report the investment on a consolidated basis. Instead, under U.S. GAAP and IFRS, the investor company reports in income its proportionate share of the net income of the affiliate. On the balance sheet, investments in noncontrolled affiliates should increase with the firm's proportionate share of the net income of the affiliate, minus dividends received from the affiliate each period, plus or minus any additional investments or dispositions of investments in such affiliates.

To forecast future equity income from investments in noncontrolled affiliates, an analyst can project a normal rate of return and the level of investment in noncontrolled affiliates. Alternately, a more time-consuming but potentially more accurate approach would be to prepare a full set of financial statement forecasts for the noncontrolled affiliates and estimate the investor's share of expected future income. This approach is worthwhile for firms that have very large and important investments in joint ventures and affiliated companies.

Until 2010, **PepsiCo** held relatively large investments in noncontrolled affiliates, primarily bottlers, and generated a significant amount of income from these investments.

During 2009, PepsiCo recognized $365 million in equity income on these investments, with an average book value of $4,184 million [($4,484 + 3,883)/2], which implies a rate of return of roughly 8.7%. As we mentioned previously, in 2010 PepsiCo acquired 100% ownership of its primary bottlers and began to report them on a consolidated basis.

As of 2011 and 2012, PepsiCo's investments in noncontrolled affiliates represent its interests in joint ventures with **Unilever**, **Starbucks**, and others. These investments now amount to only 2% of PepsiCo's total assets. PepsiCo no longer reports its share of the income from these investments on a separate line of the income statement and instead simply aggregates this income with SG&A expense. As such, it is not possible to determine from these disclosures the amount of income or the rate of return PepsiCo generates from these investments. Given this lack of transparency, we will simply assume that equity income from noncontrolled affiliates is an implicit component of our forecasts of (net) SG&A expense.

Projecting Preferred Stock

PepsiCo has a negative amount (–$123 million) in convertible preferred stock at the end of 2012. Note 12, "Preferred Stock" (Appendix A), discloses that Quaker Foods had issued the preferred stock in 2001 and years prior as part of an employee stock ownership plan and that the shares can be redeemed by plan participants or repurchased by PepsiCo at a premium. The amount of preferred stock is negative, which is unusual, because Quaker raised $41 million by issuing the stock and to date PepsiCo has paid a total of $164 million for the shares that have been redeemed or repurchased. In Note 12, PepsiCo also discloses that the roughly 186,000 outstanding preferred shares have a fair value of $63 million at the end of 2012. We assume that all of these remaining shares will be repurchased by PepsiCo or redeemed by plan participants in Year +1 at fair value. We assume the payment of $63 million will be a special one-time liquidating dividend to buy back and retire these preferred shares. Because we forecast that all of the preferred shares will be retired, we forecast the ending balance in preferred stock to be zero at the end of Year +1. We will record the $63 million payment to retire the remaining shares as a dividend and the $123 million adjustment to zero out the negative balance in the preferred stock account with an implicit adjustment to treasury stock. (See Chapter 7 for a discussion of accounting for share retirements.)

Projecting Noncontrolling Interests

Noncontrolling interests in equity are similar to the investments in noncontrolled affiliates (described earlier), but in this case the firm is the controlling shareholder and consolidates the subsidiaries. Noncontrolling interests therefore account for the equity ownership of minority investors that own less than 50% of the shares of the subsidiary company (this is the mirror image of accounting for investments in noncontrolled affiliates).

At the end of 2012, **PepsiCo** has $105 million of equity capital from noncontrolling interest shareholders. These investors own significant but not controlling proportions of the equity in certain subsidiaries which PepsiCo controls and consolidates. We therefore need to project the future amounts of equity by projecting additional investments by or retirements of these noncontrolling equity investors as well as the proportionate share of income and dividends from these subsidiaries to these investors.

For simplicity, we assume that PepsiCo will not retire any of the noncontrolling interests, nor will it raise any additional noncontrolling equity capital. PepsiCo's consolidated statement of equity (Appendix A) shows that, in 2012, the net income attributable to noncontrolling interests amounted to $36 million, or roughly an 18% return on the average amount invested, whereas in 2011 the return was only about 6%. For simplicity, we assume these investors receive a 10% return on their investments ($10.5 million on $105 million invested), and all of this income will be distributed to them each year by the subsidiary companies. We therefore assume that, going forward, noncontrolling interests will continue to be $105 million. We therefore reduce net income in our projected income statements by $10.5 million of net income attributable to noncontrolling interests each year, with the remainder of net income attributable to PepsiCo shareholders.

Projecting Common Stock and Capital in Excess of Par Value

As Chapter 7 explains, common stock and paid-in capital accounts increase as the firm raises capital by selling common shares to investors or by issuing shares in a merger or acquisition, and these accounts decrease when the firm retires shares. The paid-in capital accounts also increase when firms award share-based compensation and bonuses, such as stock options or restricted share units, to employees, executives, and board members. Paid-in capital accounts increase (but retained earnings decreases) by the fair value of the share-based compensation expense. Subsequently, if individuals exercise stock options or convert restricted shares into unrestricted shares, then paid-in capital accounts increase by the net amount of any cash received from the individuals (such as the exercise price of the options).

PepsiCo's consolidated statement of equity (Appendix A) shows that, in 2010, PepsiCo's common stock and capital in excess of par value increased dramatically as a consequence of PepsiCo issuing roughly $4.5 billion in equity shares to acquire its primary bottlers, PBG and PAS. In 2010 through 2012, PepsiCo's paid-in capital accounts also changed because of share-based compensation awards as well as stock option exercises and restricted share conversions. The common-sized balance sheet data (Chapter 1) show that PepsiCo's paid-in capital accounts jumped from 0.7% of total assets at the end of 2009 to 6.7% at the end of 2010. That percentage has declined a bit since then, to 6.2% at the end of 2011, and 5.6% at the end of 2012. Given that PepsiCo has shifted its capital strategy to increase the proportion of long-term debt, we do not expect significant future issues of common equity. We therefore simply project common stock and capital in excess of par value to grow with total assets, remaining at 5.6% of total assets. The projected amounts for common stock and capital in excess of par value are as follows:

	Common Stock and Capital in Excess of Par Value		
	Projected Total Assets	As a Percentage of Total Assets	Ending Balance
Year +1	$75,873	5.6%	$4,249
Year +2	$78,587	5.6%	$4,401
Year +3	$81,338	5.6%	$4,555
Year +4	$85,348	5.6%	$4,779
Year +5	$87,029	5.6%	$4,874

Projecting Treasury Stock

The treasury stock account becomes *more* negative when the firm repurchases some of its outstanding common equity shares. The treasury stock account becomes *less* negative when the firm reissues treasury shares on the open market, uses them to meet stock option exercises, issues them in merger or acquisition transactions, or retires them. (See Chapter 7 for more discussion of accounting for treasury stock transactions.) For 2010 through 2012, **PepsiCo**'s statement of common shareholders' equity (Appendix A) reveals that it has repurchased roughly $10.7 billion in common shares ($5.0 billion in 2010; $2.5 billion in 2011; and $3.2 billion in 2012) to reduce the equity capital base and increase leverage. In addition, over the same period, PepsiCo reissued treasury shares to meet roughly $4.6 billion in stock option exercises and other stock-based transactions ($1.6 billion in 2010; $1.4 billion in 2011, and $1.6 billion in 2012).[14]

In PepsiCo's 2012 annual report, the MD&A section titled "Our Liquidity, Capital Resources and Financial Position" (Appendix B, which can be found online at the book's companion website at www.cengagebrain.com) discloses that during the first quarter of 2013, PepsiCo announced a new $10.0 billion share repurchase program that had been approved by the board of directors to succeed the existing share repurchase program expiring in 2013. PepsiCo will likely continue to make substantial repurchases. PepsiCo's MD&A disclosures also reveal that the firm projects that it expects to make treasury stock purchases of approximately $3.0 billion in 2013 (Year +1). For our first-iteration assumptions, we project that PepsiCo's treasury stock repurchases, net of treasury stock issued for stock compensation plans, will amount to $3.0 billion during Year +1 and will continue at this level through Year +5. (Recall that we also assumed the treasury stock account would implicitly include in Year +1 a reduction of $123 million to eliminate the negative balance in preferred stock.) We may need to reduce the projected amount of treasury stock repurchases in particular years if we determine later in our analysis that PepsiCo will not have sufficient cash flow for these repurchases, or if our equity valuation estimates indicate that the capital market has overpriced PepsiCo stock. Alternately, we may increase these projected amounts if our analysis reveals that PepsiCo will have excess future cash flow or if our valuation estimates indicate PepsiCo's shares are underpriced.

In projecting stock repurchases net of stock reissues, we assume that employees will continue to exercise stock options and other stock-based compensation awards in future years. We may need to revise this assumption later in the analysis if our equity valuation estimates indicate that PepsiCo's stock options are not likely to be "in the money." We implicitly include an expense for the fair value of stock-based compensation in the projections of selling, general, and administrative expense.

---

[14]The stock market often interprets share repurchase announcements as "good news," inferring that management, with its in-depth knowledge of the firm, believes that the capital market is underpricing the firm's stock (although, ironically, most stock repurchase plans are not completed at the announced levels). The stock market typically reacts to this positive signal by bidding up the price of the firm's shares. Stock repurchases also may be perceived favorably by capital markets participants because they represent a form of implicit dividend to individual shareholders that may be taxed at capital gains rates, which may be lower than the ordinary income tax rates on dividends (depending on the shareholders' holding period and tax status).

The projected amounts for treasury stock are as follows:

	Treasury Stock		
	Beginning Balance	**Share Repurchases, Net of Reissues**	**Ending Balance**
2012 actual	−$17,870	−$1,588	−$19,458
Year +1	−$19,458	−$3,000	−$22,458
Year +2	−$22,458	−$3,000	−$25,458
Year +3	−$25,458	−$3,000	−$28,458
Year +4	−$28,458	−$3,000	−$31,458
Year +5	−$31,458	−$3,000	−$34,458

Projecting Accumulated Other Comprehensive Income or Loss

As described in Chapters 8 and 9, the gains and losses that impact other comprehensive income items result from four specific types of asset and liability revaluations: fair value gains and losses on available-for-sale securities, foreign currency translation adjustments, adjustments to certain pension and retiree benefit obligations, and fair value gains and losses on cash flow hedges. Because economy-wide changes in interest rates and foreign exchange rates tend to be transitory and because many firms tend to hedge or mitigate exposure to such risks, it is often very difficult for an analyst to predict with confidence whether a particular firm will consistently generate persistent gains or losses from such changes over long periods of time. As such, analysts commonly forecast gains or losses from other comprehensive income items to be zero, on average.

On the consolidated statement of comprehensive income (Appendix A), **PepsiCo** reported net income of $6,214 million for 2012 but comprehensive income of $6,951 million—PepsiCo's other comprehensive income items amounted to $737 million after tax. As that statement shows, these income items were attributable primarily to foreign currency translation adjustments. In 2012, the U.S. dollar value fell against many other currencies in which PepsiCo holds net assets, which triggered the translation gains. Also in 2012, PepsiCo recognized smaller amounts for fair value losses on cash flow hedges, losses on adjustments to pension and retiree benefit plan obligations, and fair value gains on investment securities. According to PepsiCo's consolidated statement of equity (Appendix A), accumulated other comprehensive loss was −$6,229 million at the beginning of 2012, and consequently, by the end of 2012 it had become −$5,487 million.[15]

In our previous forecasts of revenues from PepsiCo's various international divisions, we assumed PepsiCo will continue to expand these international operations. However, even for the most experienced macroeconomic experts, it is difficult to forecast whether the U.S. dollar will increase or decrease in value relative to the foreign currencies PepsiCo uses in its international operations over the next five years. Also, PepsiCo might hedge or limit its exposure to foreign currency movements. Thus, we project that PepsiCo will experience neither persistent negative nor positive foreign currency

---

[15]The change in PepsiCo's accumulated balance is +$742 million, which seems inconsistent with the statement of comprehensive income reporting +$737 million in comprehensive income items for 2012. The difference can be seen in the fact that $5 million of comprehensive losses were attributed to noncontrolling equity interests.

translation adjustments in the future. This is equivalent to assuming that PepsiCo's future foreign currency translation adjustments are equally likely to be positive or negative in any given year and that, on average, they will be zero over time. In addition, it is logical to assume that PepsiCo's pension and retiree benefit plans, available-for-sale investment securities, and cash flow hedges are equally likely to generate gains or losses in any given year and that, on average, they will be zero over the next five years. Therefore, we project that accumulated other comprehensive loss will remain at its current level. Accordingly, other comprehensive income items included in comprehensive income will also be zero in future years.

Step 5: Project Provisions for Taxes, Net Income, Dividends, and Retained Earnings

LO 10-3e

Build forecasts of future balance sheets, income statements, and statements of cash flows by applying the seven-step forecasting framework to project: e. taxes, net income, dividends, and retained earnings.

Thus far we have developed forecasts of **PepsiCo**'s operating activities, including operating income as well as the operating assets and liabilities. In addition, we have projected PepsiCo's future financial liabilities, common equity capital, and financial income items including interest income, interest expense, and income from noncontrolled affiliates. In Step 5, we complete the forecasting of PepsiCo's net income and dividends, and determine the projection of PepsiCo's retained earnings. This will lead us into Step 6, in which we will determine whether we need to revisit some of our previous forecast assumptions to make our balance sheet forecasts balance.

Projecting Provisions for Income Taxes

As Chapter 9 discusses, **PepsiCo**'s Note 5, "Income Taxes" (Appendix A), shows the reconciliation between the statutory tax rate and PepsiCo's average, or effective, tax rate. The statutory U.S. federal income tax rate was 35.0% during 2010–2012. During 2012, PepsiCo experienced an increase in its average annual tax rate of roughly 1.4% from state income taxes, a decrease in its average tax rate of approximately 6.9% from lower tax rates in international tax jurisdictions, and other factors associated with a 1.7% decrease, yielding an effective tax rate of approximately 27.8%. In addition, PepsiCo also experienced tax benefits from favorable rulings in tax court, reducing the effective rate in 2012 by another 2.6%, for a net effective rate of 25.2%. In 2011 and 2010, PepsiCo experienced effective tax rates of 26.8% and 23.0%, respectively, with 2010 including a 3.1% reduction as a consequence of the acquisitions of PBG and PAS. In the absence of nonrecurring factors, PepsiCo's effective tax rates would have been 27.8% in 2012, 26.8% in 2011, and 26.1% in 2010, for an average of roughly 27.0% (which is consistent with years prior to 2010 as well). We assume that PepsiCo's average combined federal, state, and foreign income tax rate for Year +1 through Year +5 will continue to be 27.0%.

In Note 5, titled "Income Taxes," (Appendix A), PepsiCo discloses that it has reserves of $2,425 million for uncertain tax positions, accrued as part of the current liability for income taxes payable. It also discloses that "it is reasonably possible that our reserves for uncertain tax positions could decrease by approximately $1.5 billion within the next twelve months as a result of the completion of audits in various jurisdictions." If PepsiCo does obtain favorable resolution of these audits and can reduce these reserves, it will trigger a much lower income tax provision in Year +1. Given the uncertainty surrounding the outcomes of these audits, we maintain the assumption of a 27.0% effective tax rate in Year +1 but will monitor the situation and react quickly if PepsiCo provides new information.

Net Income Attributable to PepsiCo Common Shareholders

All of the elements of the income statement, including first-iteration estimates of interest expense, interest income, and income taxes, are now complete. Recall that Exhibit 10.3 presents these income statement projections. The projected amounts of net income attributable to **PepsiCo** common shareholders, the implied growth rates, and net profit margins are as follows:

Year	Net Income Attributable to Common Shareholders	Implied Percentage Growth	Implied Net Profit Margin
2012 actual	$6,178	−4.1%	9.4%
Year +1 forecast	$6,158	−0.3%	9.0%
Year +2 forecast	$6,377	3.6%	9.0%
Year +3 forecast	$6,598	3.5%	8.9%
Year +4 forecast	$6,972	5.7%	8.9%
Year +5 forecast	$7,064	1.3%	8.8%

The forecasts of net income for PepsiCo imply only modest growth in net income, similar to what PepsiCo has exhibited in recent years. The forecasts also imply a slightly lower profit margin than in 2010–2012. One contributing factor is our projection of slight increases in PepsiCo's cost of goods sold, and therefore decreases in gross profit margins in the future.

Retained Earnings

In general, retained earnings typically increases by the amount of net income and decreases for dividends declared and net losses. From 2010 to 2012, **PepsiCo**'s dividend payout rates have increased from 47.0% to 48.9% to 53.2% of net income, respectively. In the 2012 annual report, PepsiCo's MD&A section titled "Our Liquidity, Capital Resources and Financial Position" (Appendix B) discloses that PepsiCo's board of directors approved a 5.6% increase in dividend payouts, to $2.27 per share in 2013, totaling roughly $3.4 billion.[16] Relying on that disclosure, we project that PepsiCo's dividend payout policy will average 55% of net income from continuing operations in Years +1 through + 5. Therefore, forecasts of dividends to common shareholders will vary over time with net income. For example, the forecast of dividends to common shareholders in Year +1 is $3,387 million (0.55 × $6,158). This projection is very close to the $3.4 billion amount projected by PepsiCo's management.

---

[16]The capital markets generally react positively when firms announce plans to increase dividend payouts because market participants infer that this is a signal of managers' favorable private information about expectations for future sustainable earnings and cash flows. Moreover, managers are reluctant to cut or omit dividends because the market usually reacts negatively to such announcements. Thus, managers typically do not increase dividends unless they believe the increase can be sustained.

Recall that in the discussion of PepsiCo's preferred stock, we projected that PepsiCo would also reduce retained earnings by $63 million to reflect payment in Year +1 to retire the remaining outstanding preferred shares, and would reduce treasury stock to eliminate the negative $123 million balance in the preferred stock account. The implied changes in retained earnings are as follows (allow for rounding):

| | **Retained Earnings** | | | | |
	Year +1	**Year +2**	**Year +3**	**Year +4**	**Year +5**
Beginning of year balance	$43,158	$45,866	$48,735	$51,705	$54,842
Net income attributable to common shareholders	6,158	6,377	6,598	6,972	7,064
Dividends to common shareholders	(3,387)	(3,507)	(3,629)	(3,835)	(3,885)
Retirement of preferred stock	(63)	(0)	(0)	(0)	(0)
End of year balance	$45,866	$48,735	$51,705	$54,842	$58,021

Step 6: Balance the Balance Sheet

LO 10-3f

Build forecasts of future balance sheets, income statements, and statements of cash flows by applying the seven-step forecasting framework to project:
f. a balance sheet that balances.

Even though the first-pass forecasts of all amounts on the income statement and balance sheet are complete, the balance sheet does not balance because we have projected individual asset and liability accounts to capture their underlying business activities, which are not perfectly correlated. The difference between the initial projected total assets and the projected total liabilities and shareholders' equity each year represents the amount by which we must adjust a "flexible" financial account to balance the balance sheet. If the difference is a positive amount, projected assets exceed projected liability and equity claims; so the firm must raise additional debt or equity capital or reduce projected assets. If the difference is a negative amount, projected assets are less than projected liability and equity claims, in which case the firm can pay down debt, issue larger dividends, repurchase more shares, or increase investments in financial assets. The change in the difference represents the increment by which we must adjust the flexible financial account each year.

The analyst must evaluate the firm's financial flexibility and adjust the balance sheet accordingly. For some firms (for example, start-ups), financial flexibility may be in cash or marketable securities, which represent financial liquidity "safety valves." These firms often keep relatively large amounts of cash or marketable securities on the balance sheet for financial slack and use the funds when necessary to meet periodic cash requirements. For these firms, large inflows of cash (such as from a new issue of debt or equity shares) build up the cash and marketable securities accounts, and large outflows (such as for the purchase of an asset or R&D expenditures) deplete the accounts. For these firms, analysts can use cash or marketable securities as the financial flexibility account needed to balance the balance sheet after all other balance sheet amounts have been determined.

For profitable growth firms that do not have large reserves of excess cash or marketable securities, financial flexibility may be exercised through short-term or long-term debt or equity. As the firm grows and invests in increasing productive capacity, it must raise the necessary capital through borrowing or issuing equity. As the firm matures and becomes a cash cow, it will shift how it uses its financial flexibility to pay down debt and perhaps initiate or increase dividends and share repurchases. You should consider carefully what financial flexibility the firm has and is likely to use.

Balancing PepsiCo's Balance Sheets

Currently, our projections of **PepsiCo**'s total assets minus total liabilities and shareholders' equity indicate the amounts by which our balance sheets do not balance. These amounts are shown below (allow for rounding):

Projections:	Year +1	Year +2	Year +3	Year +4	Year +5
Total assets (A)	$ 75,873	$ 78,587	$ 81,338	$ 85,348	$ 87,029
Total liabilities	$ 53,748	$ 56,064	$ 58,484	$ 61,984	$ 63,608
Common stock + Additional paid-in capital	4,249	4,401	4,555	4,779	4,874
Retained earnings	45,866	48,735	51,705	54,842	58,021
Accumulated other comprehensive loss	(5,487)	(5,487)	(5,487)	(5,487)	(5,487)
Treasury stock	(22,458)	(25,458)	(28,458)	(31,458)	(34,458)
Noncontrolling interests	105	105	105	105	105
Total liabilities and shareholders' equity (L + SE)	$ 76,023	$ 78,360	$ 80,904	$ 84,765	$ 86,663
Difference [A − (L + SE)]	−$150	+ $226	+ $434	+ $583	+ $366
Change in the difference	−$150	+ $376	+ $208	+ $148	− $217
Change in the difference as a percent of total assets	−0.2%	+ 0.5%	+ 0.3%	+ 0.2%	− 0.2%

In Year +1, the first-iteration forecasts project that liabilities and equities exceed assets by $150 million (about 0.2% of total assets), so we will need an adjustment for this amount. In Year +2, the first-iteration projections indicate that assets will exceed liabilities and equities by a total of $226 million, so we need an additional adjustment of +$376 million in Year +2 (about 0.5% of total assets), and so on. We could use a number of flexible financial accounts for this adjustment each year, depending on PepsiCo's strategy for investments and capital structure. Consider the following options:

- Increase marketable securities, assuming PepsiCo will retain excess capital in marketable securities for financial flexibility.
- Reduce short-term or long-term debt, assuming PepsiCo will use its financial flexibility to reduce leverage.
- Reduce retained earnings by increasing projected dividends.
- Reduce the treasury stock account by increasing treasury stock repurchases.

PepsiCo's MD&A section titled "Our Liquidity and Capital Resources" (Appendix B) states the following for 2012:

> Management operating cash flow was used primarily to repurchase shares and pay dividends. We expect to continue to return management operating cash flow to our shareholders through dividends and share repurchases while maintaining credit ratings that provide us with ready access to global and capital credit markets.[17]

Given this disclosure and the fact that PepsiCo has clearly demonstrated its willingness and ability to pay out increasing amounts of capital to shareholders through dividends and share repurchases, we adjust share repurchases as the flexible financial account. Equivalently, we could assume that PepsiCo will distribute the excess capital to

---

[17] "Management operating cash flow" is PepsiCo's measure of cash flows from operating activities minus net capital expenditures for property, plant, and equipment.

shareholders through additional dividends rather than treasury stock repurchases. Either assumption, that PepsiCo will return the excess capital to shareholders through increased dividends and/or treasury stock repurchases, will have the same effect on total assets, total liabilities, total shareholders' equity, and net income. Therefore, in Year +1, we will increase the share repurchase forecast by $150 million, the amount necessary to balance the balance sheet. This simply means that if PepsiCo's financial performance and position during Year +1 exactly match our forecasts, then PepsiCo can increase share repurchases by $150 million to keep assets in balance with liabilities and equity. In Years +2 through +5, we will also adjust our share repurchase forecasts up or down slightly each year by the incremental amount of the necessary adjustment to balance the balance sheet (that is, $376 million in Year +2; $208 million in Year +3, and so on). The projected total amounts of share repurchases are as follows:

	Year +1	Year +2	Year +3	Year +4	Year +5
Initial projection of share repurchases	−$3,000	−$3,000	−$3,000	−$3,000	−$3,000
Financial flexible adjustment	−150	+376	+208	+148	−217
Total share repurchases	−$3,150	−$2,624	−$2,792	−$2,852	−$3,217

After adjusting our share repurchases projections as necessary to balance the balance sheet, the Treasury Stock account projections are as follows (allow for rounding):

	Treasury Stock				
	Year +1	Year +2	Year +3	Year +4	Year +5
Beginning of year	$(19,458)	$(22,608)	$(25,231)	$(28,023)	$(30,875)
Less share repurchases	(3,150)	(2,624)	(2,792)	(2,852)	(3,217)
End of year	$(22,608)	$(25,231)	$(28,023)	$(30,875)	$(34,092)

The final projections of the balance sheet total amounts, which you should verify by referring back to the projected balance sheets presented in Exhibit 10.4, are as follows (allow for rounding):

Projections:	Year +1	Year +2	Year +3	Year +4	Year +5
Total assets (A)	$ 75,873	$ 78,587	$ 81,338	$ 85,348	$ 87,029
Total liabilities	$ 53,748	$ 56,064	$ 58,484	$ 61,984	$ 63,608
Common stock + Additional paid-in capital	4,249	4,401	4,555	4,779	4,874
Retained earnings	45,866	48,735	51,705	54,842	58,021
Accumulated other comprehensive loss	(5,487)	(5,487)	(5,487)	(5,487)	(5,487)
Treasury stock	(22,608)	(25,231)	(28,023)	(30,875)	(34,092)
Noncontrolling interests	105	105	105	105	105
Total liabilities and shareholders' equity (L + SE)	$ 75,873	$ 78,587	$ 81,338	$ 85,348	$ 87,029
Difference [A − (L + SE)]	$ 0	$ 0	$ 0	$ 0	$ 0

Closing the Loop: Solving for Codetermined Variables

If we had added the excess capital to interest-earning asset accounts (for example, marketable securities or cash) or subtracted it from interest-bearing liability accounts (for example, short-term or long-term debt), the projected amounts for interest income or interest expense would have to be adjusted on the income statement. This would have created an additional set of codetermined variables in the financial statement forecasts.

For example, suppose we use long-term debt as the flexible financial account and adjust it to balance assets with liabilities and shareholders' equity. To determine the necessary adjustment to long-term debt, we must first forecast all of the other asset, liability, and shareholders' equity amounts, including retained earnings. To forecast retained earnings, we must forecast net income, which depends on interest expense on long-term debt. To determine retained earnings, we must also forecast dividends, which depend on net income. Thus, it is necessary to simultaneously solve for at least five variables.

This problem might seem intractable, but it is not because of the computational capabilities of computer spreadsheet programs such as Excel. To solve for multiple variables simultaneously in older versions of Excel, check the box to "Enable iterative calculation" and allow for up to 1,000 iterations.[18] That way, Excel will solve and resolve circular references up to 1,000 times until all calculations fall within the specified tolerance for precision. Then you can program each cell to calculate the variables needed, even if they are simultaneously determined with other variables. With FSAP, the default settings allow for iterative simultaneous computations, but some versions of Excel automatically reset the default settings. So you should follow these steps to double-check that the FSAP spreadsheet will compute codetermined variables simultaneously.

LO 10-3g

Build forecasts of future balance sheets, income statements, and statements of cash flows by applying the seven-step forecasting framework to project:
g. cash flows.

Step 7: Project the Statement of Cash Flows

The final step of the seven-step forecasting process involves projecting the statement of cash flows, which was described in Chapter 3. This is a relatively straightforward task because the statement of cash flows simply characterizes all of the changes in the balance sheet in terms of the implications for cash. Thus, we derive the implied cash flows directly from the projected changes in all of the balance sheet accounts (other than the cash account, of course), as follows:

- Increases in assets imply uses of cash.
- Decreases in assets imply sources of cash.
- Increases in liabilities and shareholders' equity imply sources of cash.
- Decreases in liabilities and shareholders' equity imply uses of cash.

---

[18]This box appears in different places in different versions of Excel. In recent versions, it appears within the Formulas menu under the Options tab under the File tab. In less recent versions, it appears within the Calculations menu under the Formulas menu.

Tips for Forecasting Statements of Cash Flows

Here are a few coaching tips for preparing forecasts of statements of cash flows:

- The statement of cash flows will not reconcile with the projected income statement and balance sheets if the balance sheets do not balance or if the income statement does not articulate with the balance sheets. (That is, net income should be included in the change in retained earnings.)
- You should *not* attempt to project future statements of cash flows from historical statements. Instead, you should simply follow the procedure we describe here in projecting *the implied statement of cash flows*. Unfortunately, unlike historical balance sheets and income statements, historical statements of cash flows *do not* provide good bases for projecting future cash flows because many of the line items on the statement of cash flows are difficult to reconcile with historical changes in balance sheet amounts. The reason is because in preparing the statement of cash flows, the accountant aggregates numerous cash flows on each line item of the statement and you may not be able to determine what amounts have been aggregated or how they relate to balance sheet accounts. For example, the accountant must report separately the net cash flow implications of a business acquisition on one line of the statement, but the business acquisition causes changes in many asset and liability accounts. In addition, the accountant may choose to disclose details of cash flows that the analyst cannot verify. For example, the accountant might disclose separately in the statement of cash flows the amounts of marketable securities purchased and sold, but the analyst cannot verify those amounts because the analyst can only observe the net change in the marketable securities balance from the beginning to the end of the year.
- We strongly recommend simply following the steps below to compute the *implied statement of cash flows* from the projected income statements and balance sheets, which you can observe and verify. The Forecasts spreadsheet in FSAP (Appendix C) is programmed to use this approach to automatically calculate implied statements of cash flows from the projected income statements and balance sheets.

Specific Steps for Forecasting Implied Statements of Cash Flows

Exhibit 10.6 presents the projected implied statement of cash flows for **PepsiCo** for Years +1 through +6. We describe the derivation of each line item next. You should verify how the projected implied statements of cash flows in Exhibit 10.6 capture the cash inflows and outflows described in each of the following line items.

- **(1) Net Income:** Use the amounts in the forecasted income statements (Exhibit 10.3).
- **(2) Depreciation Expense:** Add back the projected amount of depreciation expense included in net income and used to compute the net change in accumulated depreciation on property, plant, and equipment. The depreciation expense forecast should reconcile with the change in accumulated depreciation on the projected balance sheet (minus the decrease in accumulated depreciation from assets that were sold or retired, if any). For PepsiCo, we add back depreciation expense, which we included implicitly in our cost of goods sold and SG&A expense forecasts.
- **(3) Amortization Expense:** Add back amortization expense on amortizable intangible assets. The amount of amortization expense to add back to net income should reconcile with the change in amortizable intangible assets balance, adjusted for any new investments in those assets (which should be included as

Exhibit 10.6

PepsiCo
Actual and Forecast Statements of Cash Flows
(Actual and forecast amounts in bold. Amounts in millions; allow for rounding.)

IMPLIED STATEMENT OF CASH FLOWS	Actuals			Forecasts					line no.
	2011	2012	Year +1	Year +2	Year +3	Year +4	Year +5	Year +6	
Net Income	$ 6,462	$ 6,214	$ 6,168	$ 6,387	$ 6,609	$ 6,983	$ 7,075	$ 7,287	(1)
Add back depreciation expense (net)	1,459	1,584	2,734	2,972	3,220	3,484	3,754	996	(2)
Add back amortization expense (net)	133	119	110	95	86	78	72	74	(3)
(Increase) Decrease in receivables—net	(589)	(129)	(246)	(304)	(320)	(495)	(196)	(258)	(4)
(Increase) Decrease in inventories	(455)	246	(357)	(220)	(233)	(336)	(173)	(147)	(5)
(Increase) Decrease in prepaid expenses	(772)	798	(61)	(64)	(68)	(105)	(41)	(55)	(6)
Increase (Decrease) in accounts payable—trade	218	368	73	178	209	330	110	161	(7)
Increase (Decrease) in current accrued liabilities	616	(222)	308	324	341	527	208	275	(8)
Increase (Decrease) in income taxes payable	121	179	8	14	14	20	8	13	(9)
Net change in deferred tax assets and liabilities	938	68	96	185	187	273	114	178	(10)
Increase (Decrease) in long-term accrued liabilities	1,537	(1,723)	270	284	299	463	183	241	(11)
Net Cash Flows from Operations	9,668	7,502	9,104	9,850	10,344	11,222	11,114	8,764	
(Increase) Decrease in property, plant & equip. at cost	(2,099)	(1,022)	(3,000)	(3,410)	(3,554)	(3,776)	(3,864)	(1,613)	(12)
(Increase) Decrease in marketable securities	68	36	29	26	24	22	20	(6)	(13)
(Increase) Decrease in investment securities	(109)	(156)	(131)	(141)	(152)	(165)	(178)	(72)	(14)
(Increase) Decrease in amortizable intangible assets (net)	4	(12)	0	0	0	0	0	(114)	(15)
(Increase) Decrease in goodwill and nonamort. intangibles	(4,913)	(358)	(1,311)	(1,378)	(1,450)	(2,244)	(887)	(1,170)	(16)
(Increase) Decrease in other assets	668	(632)	(68)	(72)	(76)	(117)	(46)	(61)	(17)
Net Cash Flows from Investing Activities	(6,381)	(2,144)	(4,481)	(4,975)	(5,207)	(6,280)	(4,955)	(3,036)	

IMPLIED STATEMENT OF CASH FLOWS	Actuals		Forecasts						line
	2011	2012	Year +1	Year +2	Year +3	Year +4	Year +5	Year +6	no.
Increase (Decrease) in short-term debt	1,307	(1,390)	128	226	233	320	170	177	(18)
Increase (Decrease) in long-term debt	569	2,976	625	1,106	1,138	1,566	831	864	(19)
Increase (Decrease) in preferred stock	(7)	(7)	123	0	0	0	0	0	(20)
Increase (Decrease) in common stock + paid-in capital	(71)	(283)	45	152	154	225	94	146	(21)
Increase (Decrease) in accum. OCI	(2,599)	742	0	0	0	0	0	0	(22)
Increase (Decrease) in treasury stock and other equity adjs.	(1,125)	(1,588)	(3,150)	(2,624)	(2,792)	(2,852)	(3,217)	(1,187)	(23)
Dividends	(3,217)	(3,336)	(3,450)	(3,507)	(3,629)	(3,835)	(3,885)	(5,535)	(24)
Increase (Decrease) in noncontrolling interests	(20)	(242)	(11)	(11)	(11)	(11)	(11)	(8)	(25)
Net Cash Flows from Financing Activities	(5,163)	(3,128)	(5,689)	(4,657)	(4,907)	(4,586)	(6,018)	(5,543)	
Net Change in Cash	$(1,876)	$ 2,230	$(1,065)	$ 218	$ 230	$ 356	$ 141	$ 185	(26)

Note: We label the statements of cash flows and amounts for 2011 and 2012 as "Actuals" even though we derive them from the actual balance sheet and income statement amounts in PepsiCo's financial statements rather than from the financial statement forecasts. Appendix A presents the actual statements of cash flows for 2011 and 2012 as prepared and reported by PepsiCo according to U.S. GAAP.

cash outflows in the investing section of this statement).[19] For PepsiCo, we add back amortization expense, which we included as an operating expense on PepsiCo's income statement forecasts. For some firms, if the amount of amortization expense is not large, you can ignore adding it back to net income to compute cash flow from operating activities and simply include the net change in amortizable intangible assets in the investing section. This will slightly understate cash inflows from operations and slightly understate cash outflows for investing activities, but the two effects will offset so that net cash flow is not affected.

(4)–(9) Working Capital Accounts: Adjust net income for changes in all of the various operating current asset and current liability accounts other than cash (such as accounts receivable, inventory, accounts payable, accrued expenses, and others) appearing on the projected balance sheets.

(10), (11) Deferred Taxes and Long-Term Accrued Expenses: Adjust net income for changes in deferred taxes, noncurrent liabilities for accrued expenses, and changes in other noncurrent liabilities. These items include changes in long-term accruals for expenses that are part of operations, including deferred taxes, pension and retiree benefit obligations, warranties, and other noncurrent liabilities that appear on the projected balance sheets.

Net Cash Flows from Operations: The sum of lines (1) through (11) is the implied amount of net cash flows from operating activities.

(12) Property, Plant and Equipment: The amount on this line captures cash outflows for the projected capital expenditures included in the change in property, plant, and equipment (at cost) on the projected balance sheet in Exhibit 10.4, minus any cash proceeds from sales of property, plant, and equipment. As a check, make sure the statement of cash flows captures all of the net cash flow implications of property, plant, and equipment. To verify this, the amount of depreciation expense added back to net income *minus* cash outflows for capital expenditures *plus* cash inflows for any asset sales or retirements should equal the change in net property, plant, and equipment on the projected balance sheet.

(13), (14) Marketable Securities and Investment Securities (net): The statement of cash flows classifies net purchases and sales of marketable securities (current asset) and investment securities (noncurrent asset) as investing transactions. The net changes in these accounts on the projected balance sheets determine the cash flow amounts for these items on the statement of cash flows. Some error in the implied cash flow amount from investment securities can occur. This change should be increased (become less negative) for the excess (if any) of equity earnings over dividends received from noncontrolled affiliates (which is a non-cash increase in this asset amount). Similarly, the excess of equity earnings over dividends received also should be subtracted from net income in the operating section of the statement of cash flows. Rather than making assumptions about this relatively immaterial item (the effects of which completely offset each other), we simply treat the entire change in investments as an investing transaction. This choice means that cash flows from operating activities may be slightly overstated and cash flows from investing activities may be slightly understated by an equivalent amount but that the net change in cash each year is not affected.

---

[19]Note that you should not need to add back any amortization expense for nonamortizable intangible assets such as goodwill and brands with indefinite lives because under U.S. GAAP and IFRS, goodwill and other intangibles with indefinite lives are not amortized. Thus, no amortization expense for these assets was included in the projected income statements.

(15) Amortizable Intangible Assets: Enter the implied net cash flows from any changes in amortizable intangible assets on this line, which should include any projected cash outflows to acquire amortizable intangible assets net of any cash inflows from sales or retirements of such assets. As discussed in Item (3), amortization expense is already added back to income in the operating section of the statement of cash flows. Thus, the adjustment for cash outflows or inflows for amortizable intangible assets in the investing section of the statement should not include the effects of amortization expense. Given that amortizable intangibles are commonly shown on balance sheets net of accumulated amortization, the change in the net amortizable intangible assets account balance will reflect both effects: cash flows from investing activities and amortization expense. To isolate the cash flows from investing, you should add amortization expense back to the net change in this account balance.

(16) Goodwill and Nonamortizable Intangible Assets: Enter the implied cash flows from changes in goodwill and nonamortizable intangible assets on this line. Given that these assets are not amortized, the net change in the nonamortizable intangible assets balance on the projected balance sheets should reflect cash outflows to acquire new nonamortizable intangible assets net of any cash inflows from selling or retiring such assets. If the account balance for goodwill or nonamortizable intangible assets has declined because of an impairment charge, you should add this noncash charge back to net income in the operating section of the statement of cash flows and adjust accordingly the cash flow implications from net changes in goodwill or nonamortizable intangibles in the investing section (similar to adding back amortization expense).

(17) Other Noncurrent Assets: Enter the changes in other noncurrent assets on this line. The changes in the other noncurrent asset accounts on the projected balance sheets measure the cash outflows to acquire such assets net of any cash inflows from sales or retirements of such assets.

   Net Cash Flows from Investing Activities: The sum of lines (12) through (17) on PepsiCo's projected implied statement of cash flows measures the implied amount of net cash flows from investing activities.

(18), (19) Short-Term and Long-Term Debt: Changes in interest-bearing debt (short-term notes payable, current maturities of long-term debt, and long-term debt) on the projected balance sheets are financing activities.

(20) Noncontrolling Interests and Preferred Stock: The changes in noncontrolling interests and preferred stock on the projected balance sheets are financing activities. For PepsiCo in Year +1, the adjustment to zero out the negative balance in preferred stock appears as a cash inflow, but that effect is offset by an equivalent adjustment included as a cash outflow with share repurchases on line 24.

(21) Changes in Common Stock and Additional Paid-in Capital: These amounts represent the financing cash flows from changes in the common stock and paid-in capital accounts on the projected balance sheets.

(22) Changes in Accumulated Other Comprehensive Income: These amounts represent the changes in the accumulated other comprehensive income account that is a component of shareholders' equity on the projected balance sheets.

(23) Treasury Stock: The amounts represent the net cash flow implications of treasury stock transactions that are captured in the net change in the treasury stock account on the projected balance sheets.

(24) Dividends: Enter the projected amounts for common and preferred dividends each year (discussed earlier in the section on retained earnings in the projected balance sheets). For PepsiCo in Year $+1$, this includes the amount paid to retire outstanding preferred stock.

(25) Noncontrolling Interests: Enter the projected amounts of dividends to non-controlling interests as cash outflows, net of any cash inflows (if any) from additional investments by noncontrolling investors.

Net Cash Flows from Financing Activities: The sum of lines (18) through (25) measures the implied amount of net cash flows from financing activities.

(26) Net Change in Cash: The aggregate of the amounts of cash flows from operations, investing activities, and financing activities. This total should equal the change in cash on the projected balance sheets.

LO 10-4

Understand how and when to use shortcut forecasting techniques.

Shortcut Approaches to Forecasting

Thus far, the chapter has emphasized a methodical, detailed approach to forecasting drivers of expected future operating, investing, and financing activities that will determine future amounts for individual accounts on the income statement, balance sheet, and statement of cash flows. In some circumstances, however, you may find it necessary to forecast income statement and balance sheet totals directly without carefully considering each account. This shortcut approach has the potential to introduce forecasting error if the shortcut assumptions do not fit each account very well. On the other hand, if the firm is stable and mature in an industry in steady-state equilibrium, shortcut forecasting techniques are efficient approaches to project current steady-state conditions to the future. This section illustrates shortcut approaches for forecasting **PepsiCo**'s income statements and balance sheets.

Projected Revenues and Income Approach

Shortcut projections for total revenues and net income can be developed using **PepsiCo**'s recent revenue growth rates and net profit margins. Common-size and rate-of-change income statement data reveal that during 2010 through 2012, PepsiCo generated a compound growth rate in revenues of 6.4% and an average net profit margin of 10.0%. If we simply use these ratios to forecast revenues and net income over Years $+1$ to $+5$, the projected amounts are as follows:

Year	Revenue Growth Rates	Projected Revenues	Net Profit Margin	Projected Net Income
2012 actual		$65,492		
Year $+1$	6.4%	$69,683	10.0%	$6,968
Year $+2$	6.4%	$74,143	10.0%	$7,414
Year $+3$	6.4%	$78,888	10.0%	$7,889
Year $+4$	6.4%	$83,937	10.0%	$8,394
Year $+5$	6.4%	$89,309	10.0%	$8,931

These shortcut projections for revenues and net income are much higher than the detailed revenue and income projections developed for PepsiCo throughout this chapter (particularly those for Years $+3$ to $+5$). By forecasting individual expense amounts, the more detailed projections capture expected changes in expenses relative to revenues, whereas the shortcut approach assumes that existing relations between revenues and expenses will persist linearly into the future.

Projected Total Assets Approach

Total assets can be projected using the recent historical growth rate in total assets. Between the end of 2010 and the end of 2012, **PepsiCo**'s total assets grew at an annual 4.6% compound rate. If this growth rate continues through Year +5, total assets will increase as follows (allow for rounding):

Year	Asset Growth Rate	Projected Total Assets
2012 actual		$74,638
Year +1	4.6%	$78,108
Year +2	4.6%	$81,740
Year +3	4.6%	$85,541
Year +4	4.6%	$89,518
Year +5	4.6%	$93,680

Using historical growth rates to project total assets can result in erroneous projections if you fail to consider the link between revenue growth and asset growth. We assumed a revenue growth rate for PepsiCo of 6.4% in the shortcut approach to revenue projections but a 4.6% growth in assets, which implies a significant increase in total assets turnover from 0.88 in 2012 to 0.95 in Year +5. If this increase in total asset efficiency is not realistic, the use of these forecast procedures will lead to erroneous projections.

An alternative shortcut approach to projecting total assets uses the total assets turnover ratio, explicitly linking revenue growth and asset growth. Like before, we assume that PepsiCo's sales growth will persist at 6.4% per year, but now we also assume total assets turnover will remain at 0.88 over the next five years. The calculation of projected year-end total assets using the assets turnover ratio shortcut follows:

Year	Projected Revenues	Average Assets Turnover Ratio	Projected Year End Total Assets	Implied Percent Change in Total Assets
Year +1	$69,683	0.88	$ 79,185	6.4%
Year +2	$74,143	0.88	$ 84,253	6.4%
Year +3	$78,888	0.88	$ 89,645	6.4%
Year +4	$83,937	0.88	$ 95,382	6.4%
Year +5	$89,309	0.88	$101,488	6.4%

This approach ties the projections of total assets to projections of revenues, which is valid if the relation between total assets and revenues will remain constant and linear over the forecast horizon.

Once you project total assets, common-size balance sheet percentages provide a shortcut approach for allocating total assets to individual assets, liabilities, and shareholders' equity. In using these common-size percentages, you are assuming that the firm maintains a constant mix of assets, liabilities, and equities regardless of the level of total assets. Equivalently, you are assuming that each asset, liability, and equity account grows at the same rate as total assets, which grow at the same rate as revenues. For example, the common-size balance sheet for 2012 for PepsiCo (Chapter 1) indicates that total liabilities represent roughly 70.0% and equities represent 30.0% of total assets. If we assume that PepsiCo will maintain exactly the same proportions of debt and equity in its capital structure in future years, and if we use the projections of total assets, we can project total liabilities and shareholders' equity amounts for Years +1 through +5 as follows:

Year	Projected Year-End Total Assets	Projected Total Liabilities (70.0%)	Projected Shareholders' Equity (30.0%)
Year +1	$ 79,186	$55,430	$23,756
Year +2	$ 84,254	$58,978	$25,276
Year +3	$ 89,646	$62,752	$26,894
Year +4	$ 95,383	$66,768	$28,615
Year +5	$101,488	$71,041	$30,447

Using common-size balance sheet percentages to project individual assets, liabilities, and shareholders' equity encounters (at least) three potential shortcomings. First, the common-sized short-cut approaches do not allow you an effective mechanism to forecast major transactions that reflect disproportionate shifts in assets relative to liabilities and equities. For example, in 2010, PepsiCo acquired and consolidated its primary bottlers, causing certain assets, liabilities, and equity accounts to change dramatically, inconsistent with a constant common-size approach. Second, in using common-size percentages for forecasting, you assume the firm maintains a constant mix of assets, liabilities, and equities, and that each asset, liability, and equity account grows at the same rate as total assets, which grow at the same rate as revenues. This strong assumption may not be valid for a majority of firms, which tend to experience dynamic, nonlinear changes over time.

Third, using the common-size percentages does not permit you to change the assumptions about the future behavior of an individual asset or liability. For example, assume that PepsiCo plans to implement inventory control systems that will accelerate inventory turnover so that inventory will comprise a smaller percentage of total assets in the future than it has in the past. In such case, you will encounter difficulties adjusting the common-size balance sheet percentages to reflect the changes in inventory policies.

In general, shortcut approaches to forecasting have the benefit of greater efficiency but greater potential for error as compared to more thoughtful and deliberate forecasts of income statement and balance sheet accounts. Given that forecast errors are very costly when they lead to bad investment decisions, we strongly advocate the careful, detailed approach to projecting financial statements by forecasting the firm's future operating, investing, and financing activities using individual income statement and balance sheet accounts.

LO 10-5

Test the validity of your forecast assumptions and results.

Test the Validity of the Forecast Assumptions and Results by Analyzing Projected Financial Statements

The reasonableness of the forecast assumptions and their internal consistency can be tested by analyzing the projected financial statements using the same ratios and other analytical tools discussed in previous chapters. Exhibit 10.7 presents a ratio analysis for **PepsiCo** based on the financial statement forecasts for Year +1 to Year +5. The FSAP Forecasts spreadsheet provides these ratio computations (Appendix C).

Exhibit 10.7

PepsiCo

Financial Ratio Analysis Based on Actual and Forecast Financial Statements

	Actuals			Forecasts					
	2010	2011	2012	Year +1	Year +2	Year +3	Year +4	Year +5	Year +6
FORECAST VALIDITY CHECK DATA: GROWTH									
Revenue Growth Rates	33.8%	15.0%	−1.5%	4.1%	4.2%	4.2%	6.3%	2.3%	3.0%
Net Income Growth Rates	6.3%	1.9%	−4.1%	−0.7%	3.5%	3.5%	5.7%	1.3%	3.0%
Total Asset Growth Rates	71.0%	6.9%	2.4%	1.7%	3.6%	3.5%	4.9%	2.0%	3.0%
RETURN ON ASSETS (based on reported amounts):									
Profit Margin for ROA	12.0%	10.6%	10.4%	10.2%	10.1%	10.0%	10.0%	9.9%	9.9%
× Asset Turnover	1.1	0.9	0.9	0.9	0.9	0.9	0.9	0.9	0.9
= Return on Assets	12.8%	10.0%	9.2%	9.2%	9.3%	9.3%	9.4%	9.3%	9.3%
RETURN ON ASSETS (excluding nonrecurring items):									
Profit Margin for ROA	12.6%	11.4%	10.8%	10.2%	10.1%	10.0%	10.0%	9.9%	9.9%
× Asset Turnover	1.1	0.9	0.9	0.9	0.9	0.9	0.9	0.9	0.9
= Return on Assets	13.5%	10.8%	9.6%	9.2%	9.3%	9.3%	9.4%	9.3%	9.3%
RETURN ON COMMON EQUITY (based on reported amounts):									
Profit Margin for ROCE	10.9%	9.7%	9.4%	9.0%	9.0%	8.9%	8.9%	8.8%	8.8%
× Asset Turnover	1.1	0.9	0.9	0.9	0.9	0.9	0.9	0.9	0.9
× Capital Structure Leverage	2.8	3.4	3.4	3.4	3.5	3.5	3.6	3.7	3.7
= Return on Common Equity	33.1%	30.7%	28.6%	27.5%	28.7%	29.3%	30.4%	30.4%	30.8%

(Continued)

Exhibit 10.7 (Continued)

| | Actuals | | | Forecasts | | | | | |
	2010	2011	2012	Year +1	Year +2	Year +3	Year +4	Year +5	Year +6
RETURN ON COMMON EQUITY (excluding nonrecurring items):									
Profit Margin for ROCE	11.5%	10.6%	9.9%	9.0%	9.0%	8.9%	8.9%	8.8%	8.8%
× Asset Turnover	1.1	0.9	0.9	0.9	0.9	0.9	0.9	0.9	0.9
× Capital Structure Leverage	2.8	3.4	3.4	3.4	3.5	3.5	3.6	3.7	3.7
= Return on Common Equity	35.0%	33.5%	29.9%	27.5%	28.7%	29.3%	30.4%	30.4%	30.8%
OPERATING PERFORMANCE:									
Gross Profit/Revenues	54.1%	52.5%	52.2%	52.1%	52.0%	51.9%	51.8%	51.7%	51.7%
Operating Profit before Taxes/Revenues	14.4%	14.5%	13.9%	13.8%	13.8%	13.7%	13.6%	13.5%	13.5%
ASSET TURNOVER:									
Revenues/Avg. Accounts Receivable	10.6	10.0	9.4	9.5	9.6	9.6	9.6	9.5	9.5
COGS/Average Inventory	8.9	8.8	8.4	8.7	8.4	8.3	8.3	8.1	8.1
Revenues/Average Fixed Asset	3.6	3.4	3.4	3.5	3.6	3.7	3.9	3.9	4.0
LIQUIDITY:									
Current Ratio	1.1	1.0	1.1	1.0	1.0	1.0	1.0	1.0	1.0
Quick Ratio	0.8	0.6	0.8	0.7	0.7	0.7	0.7	0.7	0.7
SOLVENCY:									
Total Liabilities/Total Assets	68.5%	71.3%	70.0%	70.8%	71.3%	71.9%	72.6%	73.1%	73.1%
Total Liabilities/Total Equity	217.3%	248.7%	233.2%	244.1%	250.1%	257.1%	266.5%	272.8%	272.9%
Interest Coverage Ratio	10.1	11.3	10.2	9.1	9.0	9.0	9.0	8.8	8.8

Forecast growth rates for revenues are relatively smooth, which is not consistent with PepsiCo's past sales growth performance, which includes the acquisition of the primary bottlers in 2010. The forecasts of net income exhibit growth rates that are less volatile than those PepsiCo experienced in its recent past. The projected rate of ROA (return on assets) varies slightly between 9.2% in Year +1 to 9.3% in Year +5, consistent with PepsiCo's ROA in 2012. The projected ROCE (return on common equity) varies from 28.6% in 2012 up to 30.8% in Year +5. This occurs because of the projected increase in financial leverage.

The projected increase in capital structure leverage over the forecast horizon is the result of PepsiCo's strategy to increase outstanding long-term debt, a shift that began in 2007 with the net issuance of $1.6 billion in long-term debt, and jumped considerably in 2010 with a net issuance of $5.9 billion. In addition, PepsiCo has returned and will continue to return excess cash flows to shareholders through increased dividends and share repurchases. PepsiCo is expected to finance the treasury stock repurchases and dividends with cash flow from operations, which will reduce shareholders' equity relative to debt, thereby increasing the capital structure leverage ratio. The net effect of increasing the ratio of long-term debt to assets, while at the same time reducing equity by repurchasing shares and paying dividends, suggests that PepsiCo's capital structure leverage will increase. Given that PepsiCo also is expected to generate healthy profit margins, the increased capital structure leverage will generate increasingly higher returns to common equity shareholders.

The operating performance ratios, liquidity ratios, assets turnover ratios, and solvency ratios confirm that our forecast assumptions are reasonable given PepsiCo's expected future financial performance and position. Unfortunately, these ratios cannot confirm whether our forecast assumptions will turn out to be correct. These ratios do not tell us whether we have accurately and realistically captured PepsiCo's future sales growth, profitability, cash flows, and financial position. For this confirmation, only time will tell.

Sensitivity Analysis

LO 10-6

Test the sensitivity of your forecasts to variations in critical assumptions and parameters.

These financial statement forecasts can serve as the "base case" from which you can assess the impacts of variations in critical forecast assumptions for the firm. For example, with these financial statement forecasts, you can assess the sensitivity of projected net income and cash flows to key assumptions about revenue growth rates, gross profit margins, SG&A expenses, and others. Using the projected financial statements (Exhibits 10.3, 10.4, and 10.6) as the base case, you can easily assess the impact on **PepsiCo**'s profitability from a one-point increase or decrease in revenue growth or from a one-point increase or decrease in the gross profit margin.

You also can use the projected financial statements to assess the sensitivity of the firm's liquidity and leverage to changes in key assumptions. For example, you can assess the impact on PepsiCo's liquidity and solvency ratios by varying the long-term debt to assets assumptions and the interest expense assumptions. Lenders and credit analysts can use the projected financial statements to assess the conditions under which the firm's debt covenants may become binding. For example, suppose PepsiCo's long-term debt and revolving line of credit agreements contain covenants that require PepsiCo to maintain liquidity and interest coverage ratios that exceed certain minimum levels. The financial statement forecasts provide these analysts with a structured approach to assess how far net income and cash flows would need to decrease (and how much long-term debt and interest expense would need to increase) before PepsiCo would violate these debt covenants.

LO 10-7

Develop forecast models that are flexible and comprehensive, allowing you to respond quickly and effectively when a company announces important new information.

Reactions to Announcements

The projected financial statements also enable you to react quickly and efficiently to new announcements by the firm. For example, suppose in 2009 you had built a model like the one in this chapter to forecast financial statements for **PepsiCo**. Then surprisingly, PepsiCo submitted bids to acquire the majority equity interests in its two anchor bottlers. The boards of directors and management teams of the two bottlers rejected those bids. PepsiCo responded with higher bids to acquire the two bottlers, their boards deemed the bids to be acceptable, and the acquisitions were completed. Suppose that during the bidding process, you needed to project PepsiCo's financial statements, incorporating the effects of these proposed acquisitions. By having a dynamic, flexible financial statement forecast model (like the one in FSAP), you can react relatively efficiently and incorporate new information quickly into your expectations for PepsiCo's future earnings, balance sheets, and cash flows.

As an alternative example, suppose PepsiCo suddenly announces that it is reversing its recapitalization strategy, such that it will discontinue purchases of treasury stock in Year +1 (and will reissue previously acquired treasury shares as needed to meet stock options exercises), and that it intends to use this cash to reduce interest-bearing long-term debt. Our original projections included $3,000 million in treasury stock repurchases in Year +1, which must now become zero. Our projections must also change to reflect that PepsiCo will use this capital to reduce (rather than increase) long-term borrowings. We can efficiently incorporate the effects of this announcement into the projected financial statements by merely changing a couple of forecast assumptions. PepsiCo's original and revised projected ratios for Year +1 are as follows:

	Year +1 Original Projections	Year +1 Revised Projections
Net profit margin for ROA	10.2%	10.2%
ROA	9.2%	9.2%
ROCE	27.5%	25.8%
Capital structure leverage	3.4	3.2
Total liabilities/Total assets	70.8%	66.7%
Interest coverage ratio	9.1	9.6

Thus, the assumptions about the growth in treasury stock and long-term debt have significant effects on projected financial statements and ratios for PepsiCo. Various other changes in assumptions are possible. By designing a flexible spreadsheet model for projecting financial statements, you can quickly and efficiently change any one or a combination of assumptions and observe the effect on the financial statements and ratios. FSAP provides a flexible spreadsheet for forecasting.

Summary

This chapter demonstrates a seven-step procedure for developing financial statement forecasts. The preparation of financial statement forecasts requires numerous assumptions about the future operating, investing, and financing activities of the firm, including future growth rates in sales, cost behavior of various expenses, levels of investments in various working capital and fixed assets, the financial capital structure of the firm, and dividend payouts. You should carefully develop realistic expectations for these activities and capture those expectations in financial statement forecasts that provide an objective and realistic portrait of the firm in the future. You should then study the sensitivity of the financial statements to the assumptions made and to the impacts of variations in the assumptions.

After developing careful and realistic expectations for future earnings, cash flows, and dividends using financial statement projections, you can use the information to make a wide array of decisions about the firm, including evaluating the firm as a potential equity investment. The next four chapters demonstrate how to incorporate expectations for future dividends, cash flows, and earnings into estimates of firm value.

Questions, Exercises, Problems, and Cases

Questions and Exercises

10.1 Relying on Accounting to Avoid Forecast Errors. The chapter states that forecasts of financial statements should rely on the *additivity* within financial statements and the *articulation* across financial statements to avoid internal inconsistencies in forecasts. Explain how the concepts of additivity and articulation apply to financial statement forecasts. Also explain how these concepts can help you avoid potential forecast errors.

`LO 10-2`

10.2 Objective and Realistic Forecasts. The chapter encourages analysts to develop forecasts that are realistic, objective, and unbiased. Some firms' managers tend to be optimistic. Some accounting principles tend to be conservative. Describe the different risks and incentives that managers, accountants, and analysts face. Explain how these different risks and incentives lead managers, accountants, and analysts to different biases when predicting uncertain outcomes.

`LO 10-2`

10.3 Projecting Revenues: The Effects of Volume versus Price. Suppose a firm has generated 10.25% revenue growth in the past two years, consisting of 5.0% growth in sales volume compounded with 5.0% growth in prices. Describe one firm-specific strategic factor, one industry-specific factor, and one economy-wide factor that could help this firm sustain 5.0% growth in sales volume next year. Describe one firm-specific strategic factor, one industry-specific factor, and one economy-wide factor that could help this firm sustain 5.0% growth in prices next year.

`LO 10-3a`

10.4 Projecting Gross Profit: The Effects of Volume versus Price. Suppose you are analyzing a firm that is successfully executing a strategy that differentiates its products from those of its competitors. Because of this strategy, you project that next year the firm will generate 6.0% revenue growth from price increases and 3.0% revenue growth from sales volume increases. Assume that the firm's production cost structure involves strictly variable costs. (That is, the cost to produce each unit of product remains the same.) Should you project that the firm's gross profit will increase next year? If you project that the gross profit will

`LO 10-3`

increase, is the increase a result of volume growth, price growth, or both? Should you project that the firm's gross profit margin (gross profit divided by sales) will increase next year? If you project that the gross profit margin will increase, is the increase a result of volume growth, price growth, or both?

LO 10-3

10.5 Projecting Revenues, Cost of Goods Sold, and Inventory. Use the following hypothetical data for **Walgreens** in Years 11 and 12 to project revenues, cost of goods sold, and inventory for Year +1. Assume that Walgreens's Year +1 revenue growth rate, gross profit margin, and inventory turnover will be identical to Year 12. Project the average inventory balance in Year +1 and use it to compute the implied ending inventory balance.

Walgreens (data in millions)	Year 11	Year 12
Sales revenues	$53,762	$59,034
Cost of goods sold	$38,518	$42,391
Ending inventory	$ 6,791	$ 7,249

LO 10-3f

10.6 The Flexible Financial Account. The chapter describes how firms must use flexible financial accounts to maintain equality between assets and claims on assets from liabilities and equities. Chapter 1 describes how some firms progress through different life-cycle stages—from introduction to growth to maturity to decline—and how firms experience very different cash flows during different stages of the life cycle. For each life-cycle stage, identify the different types of flexible accounts that firms will be more likely to use to balance the balance sheet.

LO 10-3f

10.7 Dividends as a Flexible Financial Account. The following data for Schwartz Company represent a summary of your first-iteration forecast amounts for Year +1. Schwartz uses dividends as a flexible financial account. Compute the amount of dividends you can assume that Schwartz will pay in order to balance your projected balance sheet. Present the projected balance sheet.

	Year +1
Operating income	$ 58
Interest expense	(8)
Income before tax	$ 50
Tax provision (20.0% effective tax rate)	(10)
Net income	$ 40
Total assets	$200
Accrued liabilities	43
Long-term debt	80
Common stock, at par	20
Retained earnings (at the beginning of Year +1)	34

LO 10-3f

10.8 Long-Term Debt as a Flexible Financial Account. For this exercise, use the preceding data for Schwartz Company. Now assume that Schwartz pays common shareholders a dividend of $25 in Year +1. Also assume that Schwartz uses long-term debt as a flexible financial account, increasing borrowing when it needs capital and paying down debt when it generates excess capital. For simplicity, assume that Schwartz pays 10.0% interest expense on the ending balance in long-term debt for the year and that interest expense is tax deductible at Schwartz's average tax rate of 20.0%. Present the projected income statement and balance

sheet for Year +1. (Hint: Because of the circularity among interest expense, net income, and debt, you may need several iterations to balance the projected balance sheet and to have the projected balance sheet articulate with net income. You may find it helpful to program a spreadsheet to work the iterative computations.)

Problems and Cases

10.9 Store-Driven Forecasts. The Home Depot is a leading specialty retailer of

hardware and home improvement products and is the second-largest retail store chain in the United States. It operates large warehouse-style stores. Despite declining sales and difficult economic conditions in 20X1 and 20X2, The Home Depot continued to invest in new stores. The following table provides summary hypothetical data for The Home Depot.

The Home Depot (amounts in millions except number of stores)	20X1	20X2
Number of stores	2,234	2,274
Sales revenues	$77,349	$71,288
Inventory	$11,731	$10,673
Capital Expenditures, net	$ 3,558	$ 1,847

REQUIRED

a. Use the preceding data for The Home Depot to compute average revenues per store, capital spending per new store, and ending inventory per store in 20X2.

b. Assume that The Home Depot will add 100 new stores by the end of Year +1. Use the data from 20X2 to project Year +1 sales revenues, capital spending, and ending inventory. Assume that each new store will be open for business for an average of one-half year in Year +1. For simplicity, assume that in Year +1, Home Depot's sales revenues will grow, but only because it will open new stores.

10.10 Projecting Property, Plant, and Equipment. Intel is a global leader

in manufacturing microprocessors, which is very capital-intensive. The production processes in microprocessor manufacturing require sophisticated technology, and the technology changes rapidly, particularly with each new generation of microprocessor. As a consequence, production and manufacturing assets in the microprocessor industry tend to have relatively short useful lives. Assume the following selected information relates to Intel's property, plant, and equipment for 20X1 and 20X2:

Intel (amounts in millions)	20X1	20X2
Property, plant, and equipment, at cost	$ 46,052	$ 48,088
Accumulated depreciation	$(29,134)	$(30,544)
Property, plant, and equipment, net	$ 16,918	$ 17,544
Depreciation expense		$ 4,360
Capital expenditures, net		$ 5,200

REQUIRED

Assume that Intel depreciates all property, plant, and equipment using the straight-line depreciation method and zero salvage value. Assume that Intel spends $6,000 on new depreciable assets in Year +1 and does not sell or retire any property, plant, and equipment during Year +1.

a. Compute the average useful life that Intel used for depreciation in 20X2.
b. Project total depreciation expense for Year +1 using the following steps: (1) project depreciation expense for Year +1 on existing property, plant, and equipment at the end of 20X2; (2) project depreciation expense on capital expenditures in Year +1 assuming that Intel takes a full year of depreciation in the first year of service; and (3) sum the results of (1) and (2) to obtain total depreciation expense for Year +1.
c. Project the Year +1 ending balance in property, plant, and equipment, both at cost and net of accumulated depreciation.

LO 10-3

10.11 Identifying the Cost Structure and Projecting Gross Margins for Capital-Intensive, Cyclical Businesses. AK Steel is an integrated manufacturer of high-quality steel and steel products in capital-intensive steel mills. AK Steel produces flat-rolled carbon, stainless and electrical steel products, and carbon and stainless tubular steel products for automotive, appliance, construction, and manufacturing markets. Nucor manufactures more commodity-level steel and steel products at the lower end of the market in less capital-intensive mini-mills. The following selected hypothetical data describe sales and cost of products sold for both firms for Years 3 and 4.

($ amounts in millions)	Year 3	Year 4
AK Steel		
Sales	$4,042	$ 5,217
Cost of products sold	$3,887	$ 4,554
Gross profit	$ 155	$ 663
Gross margin	3.8%	12.7%
Nucor		
Sales	$6,266	$11,377
Cost of products sold	$5,997	$ 9,129
Gross profit	$ 269	$ 2,248
Gross margin	4.3%	19.8%

Industry analysts anticipate the following annual changes in sales for the next five years: Year +1, 5% increase; Year +2, 10% increase; Year +3, 20% increase; Year +4, 10% decrease; Year +5, 20% decrease.

REQUIRED

a. Estimate the variable cost as a percentage of sales for the cost of products sold by dividing the amount of the change in the cost of products sold by the amount of the change in sales. Then multiply the variable-cost percentage times sales to estimate the total variable cost. Subtract the variable cost from the total cost to estimate the fixed cost for cost of products sold. Follow this procedure to estimate the manufacturing cost structure (variable cost as a percentage of sales, total variable costs, and total fixed costs) for cost of products sold for both AK Steel and Nucor in Year 4.
b. Discuss the structure of manufacturing cost (that is, fixed versus variable) for each firm in light of the manufacturing process and type of steel produced.
c. Using the analysts' forecasts of sales growth rates, compute the projected sales, cost of products sold, gross profit, and gross margin (gross profit as a percentage of sales) of each firm for Year +1 through Year +5.
d. Why do the levels and variability of the gross margin percentages differ for these two firms for Year +1 through Year +5?

10.12 Identifying the Cost Structure. Sony Corporation manufactures and markets consumer electronics products. Assume the following are selected income statement data for 20X1 and 20X2 (amounts in billions of yen):

LO 10-3

	20X1	20X2
Sales	¥ 8,296	¥ 8,871
Cost of goods sold	(5,890)	(6,290)
Selling and administrative expenses	(1,788)	(1,714)
Operating income before income Taxes	¥ 618	¥ 867

REQUIRED

a. Estimate the variable cost as a percentage of sales for the cost of goods sold by dividing the amount of the change in the cost of goods sold by the amount of the change in sales. Then multiply the variable-cost percentage times sales to estimate the total variable cost. Subtract the variable cost from the total cost to estimate the fixed cost for cost of goods sold. Follow this procedure to determine the cost structure (fixed cost plus variable cost as a percentage of sales) for cost of goods sold for Sony.

b. Repeat Requirement a for selling and administrative expenses.

c. Suppose that Sony Corporation discloses that it expects sales to grow at the following rates in future years: Year +1, 12%; Year +2, 10%; Year +3, 8%; Year +4, 6%. Project sales, cost of goods sold, selling and administrative expenses, and operating income before income taxes for Sony for Year +1 to Year +4 using the cost structure amounts derived in Requirements a and b.

d. Compute the ratio of operating income before income taxes to sales for Year +1 through Year +4.

e. Interpret the changes in the ratio computed in Requirement d in light of the expected changes in sales.

10.13 Smoothing Changes in Accounts Receivable. Hasbro designs, manufactures, and markets toys and games for children and adults in the United States and in international markets. Hasbro's portfolio of brands and products contains some of the most well-known toys and games under famous brands such as Playskool, Tonka Trucks, Milton Bradley, and Parker Brothers and includes such classic games as Scrabble®, Monopoly®, and Clue®. Assume that sales during 20X2 totaled $4,022 million. Also assume that accounts receivable totaled $655 million at the beginning of 20X2 and $612 million at the end of 20X2.

LO 10-3

REQUIRED

a. Use the average balance to compute the accounts receivable turnover ratio for Hasbro for 20X2.

b. Assume that Hasbro's sales will grow at a 13.0% rate each year for Year +1 through Year +5 and that the accounts receivable turnover ratio each year will equal the ratio computed in Requirement a for 20X2. Project the amount of accounts receivable at year-end through Year +5 based on the accounts receivable turnover computed in Requirement a. Also compute the percentage change in accounts receivable between each of the year-ends through Year +5.

c. Does the pattern of growth in your projections of Hasbro's accounts receivable seem reasonable considering the assumptions of smooth growth in sales and steady turnover? Explain.

d. The changes in accounts receivable computed in Requirement b display the sawtooth pattern depicted in Exhibit 10.4. Smooth the changes in accounts receivable by computing the year-end accounts receivable balances for Year $+1$ through Year $+5$ using the compound annual growth rate in accounts receivable between the end of 20X2 and the end of Year $+1$ from Requirement b.

e. Smooth the changes in accounts receivable using the compound annual growth rate in accounts receivable between the end of 20X2 and the end of Year $+4$ from Requirement b. Apply this growth rate to compute accounts receivable at the end of Year $+1$ through Year $+5$. Why do the amounts for ending accounts receivable using the growth rate from Requirement d differ from those using the growth rate from this requirement?

f. Compute the accounts receivable turnover for 20X2 by dividing sales by the balance in accounts receivable at the end of 20X2 (instead of using average accounts receivable as in Requirement a). Use this accounts receivable turnover ratio to compute the projected balance in accounts receivable at the end of Year $+1$ through Year $+5$. Also compute the percentage change in accounts receivable between the year-ends for Year $+1$ through Year $+5$.

LO 10-3 **10.14 Smoothing Changes in Inventories. Barnes & Noble** sells books, magazines, music, and videos through retail stores and online. For a retailer like Barnes & Noble, inventory is a critical element of the business, and it is necessary to carry a wide array of titles. Inventories constitute the largest asset on Barnes & Noble's balance sheet, totaling $1,203 million at the end of 20X2 and $1,358 million at the end of 20X1. Assume that in 20X2, sales totaled $5,122 million and cost of sales totaled $3,541 million.

REQUIRED

a. Compute the inventory turnover ratio for Barnes & Noble for 20X2.

b. Over the last two years, suppose the number of Barnes & Noble retail stores has remained constant and sales have grown at a compounded annual rate of 11.6%. Assume that the number of stores will remain constant and that sales will continue to grow at an annual rate of 11.6% each year between Year $+1$ and Year $+5$. Also assume that the future cost of goods sold to sales percentage will equal that realized in 20X2 (which is very similar to the cost of goods sold percentage over the past three years). Project the amount of inventory at the end of Year $+1$ through Year $+5$ using the inventory turnover ratio computed in Requirement a. Also compute the percentage change in inventories between each of the year-ends between 20X2 and Year $+5$. Does the pattern of growth in your projections of Barnes & Noble inventory seem reasonable to you considering the assumptions of smooth growth in sales and steady cost of goods sold percentages? Explain.

c. The changes in inventories in Requirement b display the sawtooth pattern depicted in Exhibit 10.4. Smooth the changes in the inventory forecasts between 20X2 and Year $+5$ using the compound annual growth rate in inventories between the end of 20X2 and the end of Year $+5$ implied by the projections in Requirement b. Does this pattern of growth seem more reasonable? Explain.

d. Now suppose that instead of following the smoothing approach in Requirement c, you used the rate of growth in inventory during 20X2 to project future inventory balances at the end of Year $+1$ through Year $+5$. Use these projections to compute the implied inventory turnover rates. Does this pattern of growth and efficiency in inventory for Barnes & Noble seem reasonable? Explain.

LO 10-3 **10.15 Identifying Financial Statement Relations.** Partial forecasts of financial statements for Watson Corporation appear in Exhibit 10.8 (income statement), Exhibit 10.9 (balance sheet), and Exhibit 10.10 (statement of cash flows). Selected amounts have been omitted, as have all totals (indicated by XXXX).

Exhibit 10.8

Watson Corporation
Partial Income Statements
(Problem 10.15)

	Year 0 Actual	Year +1 Projected	Year +2 Projected	Year +3 Projected	Year +4 Projected
Sales	$ 46,000	$ 50,600	$ 56,672	$ 64,606	$ 74,943
Cost of goods sold	(29,900)	(32,890)	XXXX	(40,702)	(46,465)
Selling and administrative	(10,580)	(11,638)	(12,468)	(13,567)	(14,989)
Interest expense	(3,907)	(4,298)	d	(3,866)	(5,227)
Income taxes	(565)	(621)	(1,372)	(2,265)	(2,892)
Net income	$ XXXX	$ XXXX	$ XXXX	$ XXXX	$ XXXX

Exhibit 10.9

Watson Corporation
Partial Balance Sheets
(Problem 10.15)

	Year 0 Actual	Year +1 Projected	Year +2 Projected	Year +3 Projected	Year +4 Projected
ASSETS					
Cash	$ 1,200	$ 664	$ 206	$ 416	$ 1,262
Accounts receivable	8,000	8,433	8,855	10,420	12,286
Inventories	7,500	8,223	c	10,711	11,333
Fixed assets:					
Cost	110,400	120,445	126,467	f	169,895
Accumulated depreciation	(33,100)	(36,112)	(37,917)	(45,352)	(50,938)
Total Assets	$ XXXX	$ XXXX	$ XXXX	$ XXXX	$ XXXX
LIABILITIES AND SHAREHOLDERS' EQUITY					
Accounts payable	$ 2,500	$ 2,801	$ 3,107	$ 3,376	$ 3,828
Notes payable	6,500	6,852	7,195	8,467	9,982
Other current liabilities	3,300	3,630	e	4,635	5,376
Long-term debt	45,000	49,094	51,549	h	69,251
Total Liabilities	$ XXXX	$ XXXX	$ XXXX	$ XXXX	$ XXXX
Common stock	$ 15,000	$ 17,233	$ 17,539	$ 22,434	$ 24,319
Retained earnings	21,700	22,043	23,700	g	31,082
Total Shareholders' Equity	$ XXXX	$ XXXX	$ XXXX	$ XXXX	$ XXXX
Total Liabilities and Shareholders' Equity	$ XXXX	$ XXXX	$ XXXX	$ XXXX	$ XXXX

Exhibit 10.10

Watson Corporation
Partial Statements of Cash Flows
(Problem 10.15)

	Year 0 Actual	Year +1 Projected	Year +2 Projected	Year +3 Projected	Year +4 Projected
OPERATIONS					
Net income	$ 1,048	$ 1,153	$ XXXX	$ 4,206	$ 5,370
Depreciation	2,378	b	1,805	7,435	5,586
Change in accounts receivable	(394)	(433)	(422)	(1,565)	(1,866)
Change in inventories	(657)	(723)	(1,322)	(1,166)	(622)
Change in accounts payable	274	301	306	269	452
Change in other current liabilities	300	330	436	569	741
Cash Flow from Operations	$ XXXX	$ XXXX	$ XXXX	$ XXXX	$ XXXX
INVESTING					
Acquisition of fixed assets	$(9,130)	$(10,045)	$(6,022)	$(24,796)	$(18,632)
FINANCING					
Change in notes payable	$ 320	$ 3352	$ 343	$ 1,272	$ 1,515
Change in long-term debt	3,721	4,094	2,455	10,107	7,595
Change in common stock	2,029	2,233	306	4,895	1,885
Dividends	(750)	a	(891)	(1,016)	(1,178)
Cash Flow from Financing	$ XXXX	$ XXXX	$ XXXX	$ XXXX	$ XXXX
Change in Cash	$ XXXX	$ XXXX	$ XXXX	$ XXXX	$ XXXX

REQUIRED

Determine the amount of each of the following items.
- **a.** Dividends declared and paid during Year 1
- **b.** Depreciation expense for Year 1 assuming that Watson Corporation neither sold nor retired depreciable assets during Year 1
- **c.** Inventories at the end of Year 2
- **d.** Interest expense on borrowing during Year 2, with an interest rate of 7%
- **e.** Other current liabilities at the end of Year 2
- **f.** Property, plant, and equipment at the end of Year 3 assuming that Watson Corporation neither sold nor retired depreciable assets during Year 3
- **g.** Retained earnings at the end of Year 3
- **h.** Long-term debt at the end of Year 3
- **i.** The income tax rate for Year 4
- **j.** Purchases of inventories during Year 4

LO 10-3   **10.16 Preparing and Interpreting Financial Statement Forecasts.**
Walmart Stores, Inc. (Walmart) is the largest retailing firm in the world. Building on a base of discount stores, Walmart has expanded into warehouse clubs and Supercenters, which sell traditional discount store items and grocery products.

Exhibits 10.11, 10.12, and 10.13 present the financial statements of Walmart for 2010–2012. Exhibits 4.50–4.52 (Case 4.2 in Chapter 4) also present summary financial statements for Walmart, and Exhibit 4.53 presents selected financial statement ratios for Years 2010–2012. (Note: A few of the amounts presented in Chapter 4 for Walmart differ slightly from the amounts provided here because, for purposes of computing financial analysis ratios, the Chapter 4 data have been adjusted slightly to remove the effects of nonrecurring items such as discontinued operations.)

Exhibit 10.11

Walmart Stores, Inc.
Balance Sheets
(amounts in millions; allow for rounding)
(Problem 10.16)

	2010	2011	2012
Assets:			
Cash and cash equivalents	$ 7,395	$ 6,550	$ 7,781
Accounts and notes receivable—net	5,089	5,937	6,768
Inventories	36,318	40,714	43,803
Prepaid expenses and other current assets	2,960	1,774	1,588
Current assets of discontinued segments	131		
Current Assets	**$ 51,893**	**$ 54,975**	**$ 59,940**
Property, plant, and equipment—at cost	154,489	160,938	171,724
Accumulated depreciation	(46,611)	(48,614)	(55,043)
Goodwill	16,763	20,651	20,497
Other assets	4,129	5,456	5,987
Total Assets	**$ 180,663**	**$ 193,406**	**$ 203,105**
Liabilities and Equities:			
Accounts payable	$ 33,557	$ 36,608	$ 38,080
Current accrued expenses	18,701	18,180	18,808
Notes payable and short-term debt	1,031	4,047	6,805
Current maturities of long-term debt	4,991	2,301	5,914
Income taxes payable	157	1,164	2,211
Current liabilities of discontinued operations	47		
Current Liabilities	**$ 58,484**	**$ 62,300**	**$ 71,818**
Long-term debt obligations	43,842	47,079	41,417
Deferred tax liabilities–noncurrent	6,682	7,862	7,613
Redeemable noncontrolling interest	408	404	519
Total Liabilities	**$109,416**	**$117,645**	**$121,367**
Common stock + Additional paid in capital	3,929	4,034	3,952
Retained earnings	63,967	68,691	72,978
Accum. other comprehensive income (loss)	646	(1,410)	(587)
Total Common Shareholders' Equity	**$ 68,542**	**$ 71,315**	**$ 76,343**
Noncontrolling interests	2,705	4,446	5,395
Total Equity	**$ 71,247**	**$ 75,761**	**$ 81,738**
Total Liabilities and Equities	**$180,663**	**$193,406**	**$203,105**

Exhibit 10.12

Walmart Stores, Inc.
Income Statements
(amounts in millions; allow for rounding)
(Problem 10.16)

	2010	2011	2012
Revenues	$ 421,849	$ 446,950	$ 469,162
Cost of goods sold	(314,946)	(335,127)	(352,488)
Gross Profit	**$ 106,903**	**$ 111,823**	**$ 116,674**
Selling, general and administrative expenses	(81,361)	(85,265)	(88,873)
Operating Profit	**$ 25,542**	**$ 26,558**	**$ 27,801**
Interest income	201	162	187
Interest expense	(2,205)	(2,322)	(2,251)
Income before Tax	**$ 23,538**	**$ 24,398**	**$ 25,737**
Income tax expense	(7,579)	(7,944)	(7,981)
Income (Loss) from discontinued operations	1,034	(67)	
Net Income	**$ 16,993**	**$ 16,387**	**$ 17,756**
Net income attributable to noncontrolling interests	(604)	(688)	(757)
Net Income attributable to common shareholders	**$ 16,389**	**$ 15,699**	**$ 16,999**
Other comprehensive income items	716	(2,056)	823
Comprehensive Income	**$ 17,105**	**$ 13,643**	**$ 17,822**

Exhibit 10.13

Walmart Stores, Inc.
Statements of Cash Flows
(amounts in millions, allow for rounding)
(Problem 10.16)

	2010	2011	2012
Net Income	$ 16,993	$ 16,387	$ 17,756
Add back depreciation and amortization expenses	7,641	8,130	8,501
Deferred income taxes	651	1,050	(133)
(Increase) Decrease in accounts receivable	(733)	(796)	(614)
(Increase) Decrease in inventories	(3,205)	(3,727)	(2,759)
Increase (Decrease) in accounts payable	2,676	2,687	1,061
Increase (Decrease) in income taxes payable	(153)	994	981
Increase (Decrease) in other current liabilities	(280)	(935)	271
(Income) Loss from discontinued segments	(1,034)	67	—
Other operating cash flows	1,087	398	527
Net Cash Flow from Operating Activities	**$ 23,643**	**$ 24,255**	**$ 25,591**

(Continued)

Exhibit 10.13 (Continued)			
	2010	**2011**	**2012**
Proceeds from sales of property, plant, and equipment	489	580	532
Property, plant, and equipment acquired	(12,699)	(13,510)	(12,898)
Investments acquired	(202)	(3,548)	(316)
Other investment transactions	219	(131)	71
Net Cash Flow from Investing Activities	$(12,193)	$(16,609)	$(12,611)
Increase (Decrease) in short-term borrowing	503	3,019	2,754
Increase (Decrease) in long-term borrowing	7,316	466	(1,267)
Share repurchases—treasury stock	(14,776)	(6,298)	(7,600)
Dividend payments	(4,437)	(5,048)	(5,361)
Other financing activities	(634)	(597)	(498)
Net Cash Flow from Financing Activities	$(12,028)	$ (8,458)	$(11,972)
Effects of exchange rate changes on cash	66	(33)	223
Net Change in Cash	$ (512)	$ (845)	$ 1,231
Cash and cash equivalents, beginning of year	$ 7,907	$ 7,395	$ 6,550
Cash and cash equivalents, end of year	$ 7,395	$ 6,550	$ 7,781

REQUIRED (additional requirements follow on page 843)

a. Design a spreadsheet and prepare a set of financial statement forecasts for Walmart for Year +1 to Year +5 using the assumptions that follow. Project the amounts in the order presented (unless indicated otherwise) beginning with the income statement, then the balance sheet, and then the statement of cash flows. For this portion of the problem, assume that Walmart will exercise its financial flexibility with the cash and cash equivalents account to balance the balance sheet.

Income Statement Forecast Assumptions

Sales Sales grew by 3.4% in 2010, 6.0% in 2011, and 5.0% in 2012. The compound annual sales growth rate during the last three years was 5.5%. Walmart generates sales growth primarily through increasing same-store sales, opening new stores, and acquiring other retailers. In the future, Walmart will continue to grow in international markets by opening stores and acquiring other firms and in domestic U.S. markets by converting discount stores to Supercenters. In addition, despite vigorous competition, Walmart will likely continue to generate steady increases in same-store sales, consistent with its experience through 2012. Assume that sales will grow 4.0% each year from Year +1 through Year +5.

Cost of Goods Sold The percentage of costs of goods sold relative to sales increased slightly from 74.7% of sales in 2010 to 75.0% in 2011 to 75.1% in 2012. Walmart's everyday low-price strategy, its movement into grocery products, and competition will likely prevent Walmart from achieving significant reductions in this expense percentage. Assume that the cost of goods sold to sales percentage will be 75.0% for Year +1 to Year +5.

Selling and Administrative Expenses The selling and administrative expense percentage has declined slightly from 19.3% of sales in 2010 to 19.1% in 2011 to 18.9% in 2012.

Walmart has exhibited strong cost control over the years, and is likely to continue to exhibit such control. Assume that the selling and administrative expenses will continue to average 19.0% of sales for Year +1 to Year +5.

Interest Income Walmart earns interest income on its cash and cash equivalents accounts. The average interest rate earned on average cash balances was approximately 2.6% during 2012, similar to rates earned in 2010 and 2011. Assume that Walmart will earn interest income based on a 2.6% interest rate on average cash balances (that is, the sum of beginning and end-of-year cash balances divided by 2) for Year +1 through Year +5. (Note: Projecting the amount of interest income must await projection of cash on the balance sheet.)

Interest Expense Walmart uses long-term mortgages and capital leases to finance new stores and warehouses and short- and long-term debt to finance corporate acquisitions. The average interest rate on all interest-bearing debt and capital leases was approximately 4.2% during 2011 and 2012. Assume a 4.2% interest rate for all outstanding borrowing (short-term and long-term debt, including capital leases, and the current portion of long-term debt) for Walmart for Year +1 through Year +5. Compute interest expense on the average amount of interest-bearing debt outstanding each year. (Note: Projecting the amount of interest expense must await projection of the interest-bearing debt accounts on the balance sheet.)

Income Tax Expense Walmart's average income tax rate as a percentage of income before taxes has been roughly 32% during the last two years. Assume that Walmart's effective income tax rate remains a constant 32.0% of income before taxes for Year +1 through Year +5. (Note: Projecting the amount of income tax expense must await computation of income before taxes.)

Net Income Attributable to Noncontrolling Interests Noncontrolling interest shareholders in Walmart subsidiaries were entitled to a $757 million share in Walmart's 2012 net income, which amounted to roughly a 15% rate of return on investment. Assume that the portion of net income attributable to noncontrolling interests in the future will continue to amount to a 15% rate of return in Year +1 through Year +5.

Balance Sheet Forecast Assumptions

Cash We will adjust cash as the flexible financial account to equate total assets with total liabilities plus shareholders' equity. Projecting the amount of cash must await projections of all other balance sheet amounts.

Accounts Receivable As a retailer, a large portion of Walmart's sales are in cash or for third-party credit card charges, which Walmart can convert into cash within a day or two. Walmart has its own credit card that customers can use for purchases at its Sam's Club warehouse stores, but the total amount of receivables outstanding on these credit cards is relatively minor compared to Walmart's total sales. As a consequence, Walmart's receivables turnover is very steady and fast, averaging roughly five days during each of the past two years. Assume that accounts receivable will continue to turnover at the same rate and increase at the growth rate in sales.

Inventories Walmart's overall inventory efficiency has declined slightly in the past two years, in part because of the distribution of merchandise to stores worldwide. Inventory turnovers have decreased from an average of 42 days in 2011 to 44 days in 2012. Assume that ending inventory will continue to be equal to 44 days of cost of goods sold, in Year +1 to Year +5.

Prepaid Expenses Current assets include prepayments for ongoing operating costs such as rent and insurance. Assume that prepayments will grow at the growth rate in sales.

Current Assets and Liabilities of Discontinued Segments Walmart's balance sheets in 2010 and prior recognize amounts as current assets and current liabilities that are associated with discontinued segments (subsidiaries that Walmart is divesting). These operations were divested in 2011, so assume that these amounts will be zero in Year +1 through Year +5.

Property, Plant, and Equipment—At Cost Property, plant, and equipment (including assets held under capital leases) grew by roughly $12.5 billion per year in 2010 through 2012 (capital expenditures net of proceeds from selling property, plant, and equipment). The construction of new Supercenters and the acquisition of established retail chains abroad will require additional investments in property, plant, and equipment. Assume that property, plant, and equipment will continue to grow by $12.5 billion each year from Year +1 through Year +5.

Accumulated Depreciation In 2011 and 2012, Walmart depreciated property, plant, and equipment using an average useful life of approximately 19.8 years. For Year +1 through Year +5, assume that accumulated depreciation will increase each year by depreciation expense. For simplicity, compute straight-line depreciation expense based on an average 20-year useful life and zero salvage value. In computing depreciation expense each year, make sure you depreciate the beginning balance in the existing property, plant, and equipment—at cost. Also add a new layer of depreciation expense for the new property, plant, and equipment acquired through capital expenditures. Assume that Walmart recognizes a full year of depreciation on new property, plant, and equipment in the first year of service.

Goodwill and Other Assets Goodwill and other assets include primarily goodwill arising from corporate acquisitions outside the United States. Such acquisitions increase Walmart sales. Assume that goodwill and other assets will grow at the same rate as revenues. Also assume that goodwill and other assets are not amortizable.

Accounts Payable Walmart has maintained a steady accounts payable turnover, with payment periods averaging 9.5 times per year (an average turnover of roughly 38 days) during the last three years. Assume that ending accounts payable will continue to approximate 38 days of inventory purchases in Years +1 to +5. To compute the ending accounts payable balance using a 38-day turnover period, remember to add the change in inventory to the cost of goods sold to obtain the total amount of credit purchases of inventory during the year.

Accrued Liabilities Accrued liabilities relate to accrued expenses for ongoing operating activities and are expected to grow at the growth rate in selling and administrative expenses, which are expected to grow with sales.

Income Taxes Payable and Deferred Tax Liabilities—Noncurrent For simplicity, assume that income taxes payable and deferred tax liabilities—noncurrent grow at 3.0% per year in Year +1 through Year +5.

Redeemable Noncontrolling Interests Redeemable noncontrolling interests amount to investments made by third-party investors in subsidiaries that Walmart controls and consolidates. Because these noncontrolling interests are redeemable, Walmart can redeem (pay off and retire) these interests. For simplicity, assume Walmart redeems and retires these redeemable noncontrolling interests in Year +1.

Short-Term Debt, Current Maturities of Long-Term Debt, Capital Leases, and Long-Term Debt   Walmart uses short-term debt, current maturities of long-term debt, capital leases, and long-term debt to augment cash from operations to finance capital expenditures on property, plant, and equipment and acquisitions of existing retail chains outside the United States. Over the past three years, each individual amount of debt financing (short-term debt, current maturities of long-term debt, and long-term debt) have fluctuated considerably from year to year, whereas the aggregate amount of debt financing has remained fairly steady, averaging roughly 27.0% of total assets. For simplicity, assume that the total amount of short-term debt, current maturities of long-term debt, and long-term debt will continue to remain a fairly steady percentage of total assets for Year +1 through Year +5. Assume that Walmart's short-term debt, current maturities of long-term debt, and long-term debt will grow at 3.0% per year in Year +1 through Year +5, roughly consistent with the projected growth in total assets.

Common Stock and Additional Paid-in Capital   Over the past three years, Walmart's common stock and additional paid-in capital have remained a fairly steady 2.0% of total assets. (Walmart repurchases company shares on the open market and then reissues these shares to employees and executives to satisfy stock option exercises). Assume that common stock and additional paid-in capital will continue to be 2.0% of total assets for Year +1 through Year +5.

Retained Earnings   The increase in retained earnings equals net income minus dividends. In 2012, Walmart paid total dividends of $5,361 million to common shareholders, which amounted to roughly 30% of net income attributable to Walmart shareholders. Assume that Walmart will maintain a policy to pay dividends equivalent to 30% of net income attributable to Walmart shareholders in Year +1 through Year +5.

Accumulated Other Comprehensive Income   Assume that accumulated other comprehensive income will not change. Equivalently, assume that future other comprehensive income items will be zero, on average, in Year +1 through Year +5.

Noncontrolling Interests   Noncontrolling interests amount to equity investments made by third-party investors in subsidiaries that Walmart controls and consolidates. Noncontrolling interests grow each year by their proportionate share of the subsidiary's income, and these interests decrease by any dividends paid to them. We assumed for purposes of the income statement, that net income attributable to noncontrolling interests would generate a 15% rate of return for those investors. For simplicity, assume Walmart's noncontrolling interests will grow by the amount of net income attributable to these noncontrolling interests each year, and dividends paid to them will be the same amount in Year +1 to Year +5. Therefore, the amount of noncontrolling interests in equity will remain constant.

Cash   At this point, you can project the amount of cash on Walmart's balance sheet at each year-end from Year +1 to Year +5. Assume that Walmart uses cash as the flexible financial account to balance the balance sheet. The resulting cash balance each year should be the total amount of liabilities and shareholders' equity minus the projected ending balances in all non-cash asset accounts.

Statement of Cash Flows Forecast Assumptions

Depreciation Addback   Include depreciation expense, which should equal the change in accumulated depreciation.

Other Addbacks   Assume that changes in other noncurrent liabilities on the balance sheet are operating activities.

Other Investing Transactions Assume that changes in other noncurrent assets on the balance sheet are investing activities.

LO 10-3

REQUIRED (continued from page 839)

    b. If you have programmed your spreadsheet correctly, the projected amount of cash grows steadily from Year +1 to Year + 5 and the projected cash balance at the end of Year +5 is a whopping $33,511 million (allow for rounding), which is more than 12.5% of total assets. Identify one problem that so much cash could create for the financial management of Walmart.

    c. Assume that Walmart will augment its dividend policy by paying out 30% of lagged net income plus the amount of excess cash each year (if any). Assume that during Year +1 to Year +5, Walmart will maintain a constant cash balance of $7,781 million (the ending cash balance in 2012). Revise your forecast model spreadsheets to change the financial flexibility account from cash to dividends. Determine the total amount of dividends that Walmart could pay each year under this scenario. Identify one potential benefit that increased dividends could create for the financial management of Walmart.

    d. Calculate and compare the return on common equity for Walmart using the forecast amounts determined in Requirements a and c for Year +1 to Year +5. Why are the two sets of returns different? Which results will Walmart's common shareholders prefer? Why?

INTEGRATIVE CASE 10.1

Starbucks

The **Starbucks** integrative case provides you with an opportunity to apply to Starbucks the entire six-step analysis framework of this textbook. Beginning in Chapter 1 and following each chapter of the book, we use the Starbucks Integrative Case to illustrate and apply all of the tools of financial statements analysis and valuation. This portion of the integrative case relies on the analysis of Starbucks' financial statements through fiscal year 2012 and applies the seven-step forecasting procedure of this chapter to develop complete forecasts of Starbucks' financial statements through Year +5.

Exhibits 10.14 and 10.15 provide Starbucks' income statements and balance sheets for fiscal years 2010 through 2012 in dollar amounts, common-size format, and rate-of-change format. Exhibit 10.16 (see pages 847–848) presents Starbucks' statements of cash flows for fiscal years 2010 through 2012. These financial statements report the financial performance and position of Starbucks and summarize the results of Starbucks' operating, investing, and financing activities. The common-size and rate-of-change balance sheets and income statements for Starbucks highlight relations among accounts and trends over time. Exhibit 10.17 (see pages 848–849) provides sales analysis data and store operating data through fiscal year 2012, including same-store sales growth rates, new store openings, and total numbers of stores open, including a detailed breakdown of revenues and revenue growth by segment and by store-type. You may want to refer back to Exhibits 1.26–1.30 (Chapter 1) for additional financial statement data and to Exhibits 4.44 and 4.45 (Chapter 4) for a ratio analysis of Starbucks' profitability and operating segments. All of the other chapters in the text also have illustrated accounting quality issues and financial statement analysis issues for Starbucks. All of these data and analyses now come into play in this portion of the comprehensive Starbucks case, as you develop forecasts of Starbucks' future financial statements.

Exhibit 10.14

Starbucks
Income Statements in Dollar Amounts, Common-Size Percentages, and Percentage Changes
(amounts in millions, except per-share amounts)
(Integrative Case 10.1)

	2010	2011	2012
Revenues	$ 10,707	$ 11,700	$ 13,300
Cost of goods sold and occupancy expense	−4,459	−4,916	−5,813
Gross Profit	6,249	6,785	7,486
Store operating expenses	−3,551	−3,595	−3,918
Other operating expenses	−293	−393	−430
Depreciation and amortization	−510	−523	−550
General and administrative expenses	−570	−749	−801
Restructuring charge/nonrecurring gain	−53	30	0
Income from equity investees	148	174	211
Operating Profit	1,419	1,728	1,997
Interest income	50	116	94
Interest expense	−33	−33	−33
Income before Tax	1,437	1,811	2,059
Income tax expense	−489	−563	−674
Net Income	$ 948	$ 1,248	$ 1,385
Net income attributable to noncontrolling interests	−3	−2	−1
Net Income Attributable to Common Shareholders	$ 946	$ 1,246	$ 1,384
Earnings per share (basic)	$ 1.27	$ 1.66	$ 1.83
Other comprehensive income items	−8	−11	−24
Comprehensive Income	$ 940	$ 1,237	$ 1,361

	Common Size			Percentage Change		
	2010	2011	2012	2011	2012	Compound
Revenues	100.0%	100.0%	100.0%	9.3%	13.7%	11.4%
Cost of goods sold and occupancy expense	−41.6%	−42.0%	−43.7%	10.2%	18.3%	14.2%
Gross Profit	58.4%	58.0%	56.3%	8.6%	10.3%	9.5%
Store operating expenses	−33.2%	−30.7%	−29.5%	1.2%	9.0%	5.0%
Other operating expenses	−2.7%	−3.4%	−3.2%	34.0%	9.4%	21.1%
Depreciation and amortization	−4.8%	−4.5%	−4.1%	2.5%	5.2%	3.8%
General and administrative expenses	−5.3%	−6.4%	−6.0%	31.6%	6.9%	18.6%
Restructuring charge/nonrecurring gain	−0.5%	0.3%	0.0%	−156.6%	−100.0%	−100.0%
Income from equity investees	1.4%	1.5%	1.6%	17.3%	21.3%	19.3%
Operating Profit	13.3%	14.8%	15.0%	21.8%	15.6%	18.6%

(Continued)

Exhibit 10.14 (Continued)

	Common Size			Percentage Change		
	2010	2011	2012	2011	2012	Compound
Interest income	0.5%	1.0%	0.7%	130.4%	−18.6%	37.0%
Interest expense	−0.3%	−0.3%	−0.2%	1.8%	−1.8%	0.0%
Income before Tax	**13.4%**	**15.5%**	**15.5%**	**26.0%**	**13.7%**	**19.7%**
Income tax expense	−4.6%	−4.8%	−5.1%	15.2%	19.8%	17.5%
Net Income	**8.9%**	**10.7%**	**10.4%**	**31.6%**	**11.0%**	**20.8%**
Net income attributable to noncontrolling interests	0.0%	0.0%	0.0%	−14.8%	−60.9%	−42.3%
Net Income Attributable to Common Shareholders	**8.8%**	**10.6%**	**10.4%**	**31.7%**	**11.1%**	**21.0%**

Exhibit 10.15

Starbucks
Balance Sheets in Dollar Amounts, Common-Size Percentages, and Percentage Changes
(amounts in millions)
(Integrative Case 10.1)

	2010	2011	2012
ASSETS:			
Cash and cash equivalents	$ 1,164	$ 1,148	$ 1,189
Marketable securities	286	903	848
Accounts and notes receivable—net	303	387	486
Inventories	543	966	1,242
Prepaid expenses and other current assets	157	162	197
Deferred tax assets—current	304	230	239
Current Assets	**2,756**	**3,795**	**4,200**
Investments in noncontrolled affiliates	342	372	460
Property, plant and equipment—at cost	5,889	6,163	6,903
Accumulated depreciation	−3,472	−3,808	−4,244
Amoritizable intangible assets—net	417	410	386
Goodwill	262	322	399
Long-term investments	192	107	116
Total Assets	**$ 6,386**	**$ 7,360**	**$ 8,219**
LIABILITIES AND EQUITIES:			
Accounts payable	$ 283	$ 540	$ 398
Current accrued expenses	936	941	1,134
Deferred Revenue	414	449	510
Insurance Reserves	146	146	168
Current Liabilities	**1,779**	**2,076**	**2,210**

(Continued)

Exhibit 10.15 (Continued)

	2010	2011	2012
Long-term debt obligations	549	550	550
Long-term accrued liabilities	375	348	345
Total Liabilities	**2,704**	**2,973**	**3,105**
Common stock + Additional paid-in capital	146	41	40
Retained earnings	3,471	4,297	5,046
Accum. other comprehensive income	57	46	23
Total Common Shareholders' Equity	**3,675**	**4,385**	**5,109**
Noncontrolling interests	8	2	6
Total Equity	**3,682**	**4,387**	**5,115**
Total Liabilities and Equities	**$ 6,386**	**$ 7,360**	**$ 8,219**

	Common Size			Percentage Change		
	2010	2011	2012	2011	2012	Compound
ASSETS:						
Cash and cash equivalents	18.2%	15.6%	14.5%	−1.4%	3.5%	1.1%
Marketable securities	4.5%	12.3%	10.3%	215.9%	−6.0%	72.3%
Accounts and notes receivable—net	4.7%	5.3%	5.9%	27.7%	25.7%	26.7%
Inventories	8.5%	13.1%	15.1%	77.8%	28.5%	51.2%
Prepaid expenses and other current assets	2.5%	2.2%	2.4%	3.2%	21.7%	12.1%
Deferred tax assets—current	4.8%	3.1%	2.9%	−24.3%	3.6%	−11.4%
Current Assets	**43.2%**	**51.6%**	**51.1%**	**37.7%**	**10.7%**	**23.4%**
Investments in noncontrolled affiliates	5.3%	5.1%	5.6%	9.0%	23.5%	16.0%
Property, plant and equipment—at cost	92.2%	83.7%	84.0%	4.7%	12.0%	8.3%
Accumulated depreciation	−54.4%	−51.7%	−51.6%	9.7%	11.5%	10.6%
Amortizable intangible assets (net)	6.5%	5.6%	4.7%	−1.8%	−5.8%	−3.9%
Goodwill	4.1%	4.4%	4.9%	22.6%	24.1%	23.3%
Long-term investments	3.0%	1.5%	1.4%	−44.2%	8.4%	−22.2%
Total Assets	**100.0%**	**100.0%**	**100.0%**	**15.3%**	**11.7%**	**13.4%**
LIABILITIES AND EQUITIES:						
Accounts payable	4.4%	7.3%	4.8%	91.1%	−26.3%	18.7%
Current accrued expenses	14.7%	12.8%	13.8%	0.5%	20.5%	10.0%
Notes payable and short-term debt	0.0%	0.0%	0.0%	na	na	na
Current maturities of long-term debt	0.0%	0.0%	0.0%	na	na	na
Deferred Revenue	6.5%	6.1%	6.2%	8.5%	13.6%	11.0%
Insurance Reserves	2.3%	2.0%	2.0%	−0.4%	15.2%	7.1%
Current Liabilities	**27.9%**	**28.2%**	**26.9%**	**16.7%**	**6.5%**	**11.4%**
Long-term debt obligations	8.6%	7.5%	6.7%	0.0%	0.0%	0.0%
Long-term accrued liabilities	5.9%	4.7%	4.2%	−7.3%	−0.7%	−4.1%
Total Liabilities	**42.3%**	**40.4%**	**37.8%**	**10.0%**	**4.4%**	**7.2%**

(Continued)

Exhibit 10.15 (Continued)

	Common Size			Percentage Change		
	2010	2011	2012	2011	2012	Compound
Common stock + Additional paid-in capital	2.3%	0.6%	0.5%	−71.8%	−2.7%	−47.6%
Retained earnings	54.4%	58.4%	61.4%	23.8%	17.4%	20.6%
Accum. other comprehensive income	0.9%	0.6%	0.3%	−19.1%	−51.0%	−37.0%
Total Common Shareholders' Equity	**57.5%**	**59.6%**	**62.2%**	**19.3%**	**16.5%**	**17.9%**
Noncontrolling interests	0.1%	0.0%	0.1%	−68.4%	129.2%	−14.9%
Total Equity	**57.7%**	**59.6%**	**62.2%**	**19.1%**	**16.6%**	**17.9%**
Total Liabilities and Equities	**100.0%**	**100.0%**	**100.0%**	**15.3%**	**11.7%**	**13.4%**

Exhibit 10.16

Starbucks
Consolidated Statements of Cash Flows
(amounts in millions)
(Integrative Case 10.1)

	2010	2011	2012
Net Income	$ 948	$ 1,248	$1,385
Add back depreciation and amortization expenses	541	550	581
Add back stock-based compensation expense	77	145	154
Deferred income taxes	−42	106	61
Income from equity affiliates, net of dividends	−17	−33	−49
(Increase) Decrease in accounts receivable	−33	−89	−90
(Increase) Decrease in inventories	123	−422	−273
Increase (Decrease) in accounts payable	−4	228	−105
Increase (Decrease) in other current liabilities	1	−82	24
Increase (Decrease) in deferred revenues	24	36	61
Other addbacks to (subtractions from) net income	52	−52	24
Other operating cash flows	35	−23	−20
Net Cash Flow from Operating Activities	**1,705**	**1,612**	**1,750**
Property, plant and equipment acquired	−441	−415	−851
(Increase) Decrease in marketable securities	−338	−536	48
Investments acquired	−12	−56	−129
Other investment transactions	1	−13	−42
Net Cash Flow from Investing Activities	**−790**	**−1,020**	**−974**
Increase (Decrease) in short-term borrowing	0	31	−31
Increase (Decrease) in long-term borrowing	−7	−4	0
Issue of capital stock	128	235	237
Proceeds from stock option exercises	37	104	170
Share repurchases—treasury stock	−286	−556	−549

(Continued)

Exhibit 10.16 (Continued)

	2010	2011	2012
Dividend payments	−171	−390	−513
Other financing transactions	−48	−28	−59
Net Cash Flow from Financing Activities	**−346**	**−608**	**−746**
Effects of exchange rate changes on cash	−5	−1	10
Net Change in Cash	$ 564	$ −16	$ 40
Cash and cash equivalents, beginning of year	$ 600	$ 1,164	$1,148
Cash and cash equivalents, end of year	$1,164	$ 1,148	$1,189

Exhibit 10.17

Starbucks
Sales Analysis and Store Operating Data
(dollar amounts in millions; allow for rounding)
(Integrative Case 10.1)

	2010	2011	2012
Total Revenues:			
Company-operated stores	$ 8,963.5	$ 9,632.4	$ 10,534.5
Licensed stores	875.2	1,007.5	1,210.3
CPG, foodservice and other	868.7	1,060.5	1,554.7
Total revenues	$10,707.4	$11,700.4	$13,299.5
Growth rates		9.3%	13.7%
Sales by Segment and Type:			
Company-Operated Stores	$ 8,963.5	$ 9,632.4	$10,534.5
Growth rates		7.5%	9.4%
Number of company stores	8,866	9,007	9,405
Sales/Average store	$ 1.007	$ 1.078	$ 1.144
Sales growth/Average store		7.0%	6.2%
Licensing	$ 875.2	$ 1,007.5	$ 1,210.3
Growth rates		15.1%	20.1%
Number of company stores	7,992	7,996	8,661
Sales/Average store	$ 0.112	$ 0.126	$ 0.145
Sales growth/Average store		13.0%	15.3%
CPG, Foodservice, and Other	$ 868.7	$ 1,060.5	$ 1,554.7
Growth rates		22.1%	46.6%
Total revenues	$10,707.4	$11,700.4	$13,299.5
Americas			
Net new stores opened (closed) during the year:			
Company-operated	(33)	43	234
Licensed	111	(268)	270
Total	78	(225)	504

(Continued)

Exhibit 10.17 (Continued)			
	2010	**2011**	**2012**
Total stores:			
Company-operated	7,580	7,623	7,857
Licensed	5,044	4,776	5,046
Total	12,624	12,399	12,903
Revenues:			
Company-operated		$ 8,365.5	$ 9,077.0
Revenues per store/year			$ 1.173
Growth rate			8%
Licensed		$ 676.7	$ 825.8
Revenues per store/year			$ 0.168
Europe, Middle East, Africa (EMEA)			
Net new stores opened (closed) during the year:			
Company-operated	(64)	25	10
Licensed	100	79	101
Total	36	104	111
Total stores:			
Company-operated	847	872	882
Licensed	807	886	987
Total	1,654	1,758	1,869
Revenues:			
Company-operated		$ 905.5	$ 968.3
Revenues per store/year			$ 1.104
Growth rate			0%
Licensed		$ 112.2	$ 139.5
Revenues per store/year			$ 0.149
China Asia Pacific (CAP)			
Net new stores opened during the year:			
Company-operated	30	73	154
Licensed	79	193	294
Total	109	266	448
Total stores:			
Company-operated	439	512	666
Licensed	2,141	2,334	2,628
Total	2,580	2,846	3,294
Revenues:			
Company-operated		$ 361.4	$ 489.2
Revenues per store/year			$ 0.831
Growth rate			15%
Licensed		$ 190.9	$ 232.2
Revenues per store/year			$ 0.094
CPG, Foodservice, and Other			
(including Americas, EMEA, CAP)			
Revenues	$ 868.7	$ 1,060.5	$ 1,554.7
Growth rates		22.1%	46.6%

Note: Management guidance, disclosed in 2012 and again at the end of the first quarter in Year +1, indicates Starbucks is planning to open roughly 1,300 new stores during Year +1 (300 owned and 300 licensed stores in the Americas; 200 owned and 400 licensed stores in the China Asia Pacific segment; and 34 owned and 66 licensed stores in the Europe, Middle East and Africa segment). Starbucks management also indicated they expect to incur $1,200 million in capital expenditures during Year +1. Management did not provide guidance beyond Year +1.

REQUIRED

Develop complete forecasts of Starbucks' income statements, balance sheets, and statements of cash flows for Years +1 through +5. As illustrated in this chapter, develop objective and unbiased forecast assumptions for all of Starbucks' future operating, investing, and financing activities through Year +5 and capture those expectations using financial statement forecasts.

SPECIFICATIONS

  a. Build your own spreadsheets to develop and capture your financial statement forecast assumptions and data for Starbucks. Building your own financial statement forecast spreadsheets is a valuable learning experience. You can use the **PepsiCo** examples presented throughout this chapter as models to follow in building your spreadsheets. If you have already had the learning experience of building forecast spreadsheets, you can build your financial statement forecasts using the FSAP template for Starbucks that accompanies this book. If you want to start from scratch, you can download the blank FSAP template from the book's website: www.cengagebrain.com and input the accounting data for Starbucks from Exhibits 10.14–10.16 into the Data Spreadsheet.

  b. Starbucks' operating, investing, and financing activities involve primarily opening and operating company-owned retail coffee shops in the United States and around the world. Starbucks' annual reports provide useful data on the number of company-operated stores Starbucks owns, the new stores it opens each year, and the same-store sales growth rates. These data reveal that Starbucks' revenues and revenue growth rates differ significantly across different segments. Use these data, summarized in Exhibit 10.17 as a basis to forecast (1) Starbucks' future sales from existing stores, (2) the number of new company-operated stores Starbucks will open, (3) future sales from new stores, and (4) capital expenditures for new stores.

  c. Starbucks' business also involves generating revenues from licensing Starbucks stores and selling Starbucks coffee and other products through foodservice accounts, grocery stores, warehouse clubs, and so on. Use the data in Exhibits 10.17 to build forecasts of future revenues from licensing activities and foodservice and other activities.

  d. Use your forecasts of capital expenditures for new stores together with Starbucks' data on property, plant, and equipment and depreciation to build a schedule to forecast property, plant, and equipment and depreciation expense as described in the chapter for PepsiCo.

  e. Starbucks appears to use repurchases of common equity shares as the flexible financial account for balancing the balance sheet. Common equity share repurchases are similar to dividends as a mechanism to distribute excess capital to common equity shareholders. Therefore, build your financial statement forecasts using dividends as the flexible financial account.

  f. Save your forecast spreadsheets. In subsequent chapters, you will continue to use Starbucks as a comprehensive integrative case. In those chapters, you will apply the valuation models to your forecasts of Starbucks' future earnings, cash flows, and dividends to assess Starbucks' share value.

CASE 10.2

Massachusetts Stove Company: Analyzing Strategic Options[20]

The Woodstove Market

Since the early 1990s, woodstove sales have declined from 1,200,000 units per year to approximately 100,000 units per year. The decline has occurred because of (1) stringent new federal EPA regulations, which set maximum limits on stove emissions beginning in 1992; (2) stable energy prices, which reduced the incentive to switch to woodstoves to save on heating costs; and (3) changes in consumers' lifestyles, particularly the growth of two-income families.

During this period of decline in industry sales, the market was flooded with woodstoves at distressed prices as companies closed their doors or liquidated inventories made obsolete by the new EPA regulations. Downward pricing pressure forced surviving companies to cut prices, output, or both. Years of contraction and pricing pressure left many of the surviving manufacturers in a precarious position financially, with excessive inventory, high debt, little cash, uncollectible receivables, and low margins.

The shakeout and consolidation among woodstove manufacturers and, to a lesser extent, woodstove specialty retailers have been dramatic. The number of manufacturers selling more than 2,000 units a year (characterized in the industry as "large manufacturers") has declined from approximately 90 to 35 in the prior ten years. The number of manufacturers selling less than 2,000 units per year (characterized as "small manufacturers") has declined from approximately 130 to 6. Because the current woodstove market is not large enough to support all of the surviving producers, manufacturers have attempted to diversify in order to stay in business. Seeking relief, nearly all of the survivors have turned to the manufacture of gas appliances.

The Gas Appliance Market

The gas appliance market includes three segments: (1) gas log sets, (2) gas fireplaces, and (3) gas stoves. Gas log sets are "faux fires" that can be installed in an existing fireplace. They are primarily decorative and have little heating value. Gas fireplaces are fully assembled fireboxes that a builder or contractor can install in new construction or in renovated buildings and houses. They are mainly decorative and are less expensive and easier to maintain than a masonry/brick fireplace. Gas stoves are freestanding appliances with a decorative appearance and efficient heating characteristics.

The first two segments of the gas appliance market (log sets and fireplaces) are large, established, stable markets. Established manufacturers control these markets, and distribution is primarily through mass merchandisers. The third segment (gas stoves) is less than five years old. Although it is growing steadily, it has an annual volume of only about 100,000 units (almost identical to the annual volume of the woodstove market). This is the market to which woodstove manufacturers have turned for relief.

The gas stove market is not as heavily regulated as the woodstove market, and there are currently no EPA regulations governing the emissions of gas heating appliances. Gas stoves are perceived as being more appropriate for an aging population because they provide heat and ambiance but require no effort. They can be operated with a wall switch or thermostat or by

[20]The authors acknowledge the assistance of Tom P. Morrissey in the preparation of this case.

remote control. Because actual fuel cost (or cost savings) is not an issue for many buyers, a big advantage of heating with wood is no longer a consideration for many consumers. Gas stoves are sold and distributed through mass merchandisers and through natural gas or propane dealers. The gas industry has the financial, promotional, organizational, and lobbying clout to support the development of the gas stove market, attributes that the tiny woodstove industry lacks.

Unfortunately, life has not been rosy for all of the woodstove companies entering this new market. Development costs and selling costs for new products using a different fuel and different distribution system have been substantial. Improvements in gas logs and gas burners have required rapid changes in product design. In contrast, woodstove designs are fairly stable and slow to change. Competition for market share has renewed pricing pressure on gas stove producers. Companies trying to maintain their woodstove sales while introducing gas products must carry large inventories to service both product lines. Failure to forecast demand accurately has left many companies with inventory shortages during the selling season or with large inventories of unsold product at the end of the season.

Many surviving manufacturers who looked to gas stoves for salvation are now quietly looking for suitors to acquire them. A combination of excessive debt and inventory levels, together with high development and distribution costs, has made financial success highly uncertain. Continued consolidation will take place in this difficult market during the next five years.

Massachusetts Stove Company

Massachusetts Stove Company (MSC) is one of the six "small manufacturers" to survive the EPA regulation and industry meltdown. The company has just completed its sixth consecutive

Exhibit 10.18

Massachusetts Stove Company
Income Statements
(Case 10.2)

	Year Ended December 31:				
	Year 3	Year 4	Year 5	Year 6	Year 7
Sales	$1,480,499	$1,637,128	$ 2,225,745	$ 2,376,673	$ 2,734,986
Cost of goods sold	(727,259)	(759,156)	(1,063,135)	(1,159,466)	(1,380,820)
Depreciation	(56,557)	(73,416)	(64,320)	(66,829)	(72,321)
Facilities costs	(59,329)	(47,122)	(66,226)	(48,090)	(45,309)
Facilities rental income	25,856	37,727	38,702	42,142	41,004
Selling expenses	(452,032)	(563,661)	(776,940)	(874,000)	(926,175)
Administrative expenses	(36,967)	(39,057)	(46,444)	(48,046)	(111,199)
Operating Income	$ 174,211	$ 192,443	$ 247,382	$ 222,384	$ 240,166
Interest income	712	2,242	9,541	9,209	16,665
Interest expense	(48,437)	(44,551)	(47,535)	(52,633)	(42,108)
Income Before Income Taxes	$ 126,486	$ 150,134	$ 209,388	$ 178,960	$ 214,723
Income taxes	(35,416)	(42,259)	(64,142)	(45,794)	(60,122)
Net Income	$ 91,070	$ 107,875	$ 145,246	$ 133,166	$ 154,601

Exhibit 10.19

Massachusetts Stove Company
Balance Sheets
(Case 10.2)

	December 31:					
	Year 2	**Year 3**	**Year 4**	**Year 5**	**Year 6**	**Year 7**
ASSETS						
Cash	$ 50,794	$ 19,687	$ 145,930	$ 104,383	$ 258,148	$ 351,588
Accounts receivable	12,571	56,706	30,934	41,748	30,989	5,997
Inventories	251,112	327,627	347,883	375,258	409,673	452,709
Other current assets	1,368	—	—	—	—	—
Total Current Assets	$ 315,845	$ 404,020	$ 524,747	$ 521,389	$ 698,810	$ 810,294
PP&E, at cost	1,056,157	1,148,806	1,164,884	1,184,132	1,234,752	1,257,673
Accumulated depreciation	(296,683)	(353,240)	(426,656)	(490,975)	(557,804)	(630,125)
Other assets	121,483	94,000	61,500	12,200	—	—
Total Assets	$1,196,802	$1,293,586	$1,324,475	$1,226,746	$1,375,758	$1,437,842
LIABILITIES AND SHAREHOLDERS' EQUITY						
Accounts payable	$ 137,104	$ 112,815	$ 43,229	$ 60,036	$ 39,170	$ 47,809
Notes payable	25,000	12,000	—	—	—	—
Current portion of long-term debt	27,600	29,000	21,570	113,257	115,076	27,036
Other current liabilities	39,530	100,088	184,194	189,732	244,241	257,252
Total Current Liabilities	$ 229,234	$ 253,903	$ 248,993	$ 363,025	$ 398,487	$ 332,097
Long-term debt	972,446	953,491	881,415	599,408	574,332	547,296
Deferred income taxes	—	—	—	—	5,460	6,369
Total Liabilities	$1,201,680	$1,207,394	$1,130,408	$ 962,433	$ 978,279	$ 885,762
Common stock	2,000	2,000	2,000	2,000	2,000	2,000
Additional paid-in capital	435,630	435,630	435,630	435,630	435,630	435,630
Retained earnings (deficit)	(442,508)	(351,438)	(243,563)	(98,317)	34,849	189,450
Treasury stock	—	—	—	(75,000)	(75,000)	(75,000)
Total Shareholders' Equity	$ (4,878)	$ 86,192	$ 194,067	$ 264,313	$ 397,479	$ 552,080
Total Liabilities and Shareholders' Equity	$1,196,802	$1,293,586	$1,324,475	$1,226,746	$1,375,758	$1,437,842

year of slow but steady growth in revenue and profit since complying with the EPA regulations. Exhibits 10.18–10.20 present the financial statements of MSC for Year 3–Year 7. Exhibit 10.21 (see page 855) presents selected financial statement ratios.

The success of MSC in recent years is a classic case of a company staying small, marketing in a specific niche, and vigorously applying a "stick-to-your-knitting" policy. MSC is the only

Exhibit 10.20

Massachusetts Stove Company
Statements of Cash Flows
(Case 10.2)

	Year Ended December 31:				
	Year 3	Year 4	Year 5	Year 6	Year 7
OPERATIONS					
Net income	$ 91,070	$107,875	$ 145,246	$133,166	$ 154,601
Depreciation and amortization	56,557	73,416	64,320	66,829	72,321
Other addbacks	27,483	32,500	49,300	17,660	909
(Increase) Decrease in receivables	(44,135)	25,772	(10,814)	10,759	24,992
(Increase) Decrease in inventories	(76,515)	(20,256)	(27,375)	(34,415)	(43,036)
Decrease in other current assets	1,368	—	—	—	—
Increase (Decrease) in payables	(24,289)	(69,586)	16,807	(20,866)	8,639
Increase in other current liabilities	60,558	84,106	5,538	54,509	13,011
Cash Flow from Operations	$ 92,097	$233,827	$ 243,022	$227,642	$ 231,437
INVESTING					
Capital expenditures	$(92,649)	$ (16,078)	$ (19,249)	$ (50,620)	$ (22,921)
Cash Flow from Investing	$(92,649)	$ (16,078)	$ (19,249)	$ (50,620)	$ (22,921)
FINANCING					
Increase in long-term debt	$ 10,000	$ —	$ —	$ —	$ —
Decrease in short-term debt	(13,000)	(12,000)	—	—	—
Decrease in long-term debt	(27,555)	(79,506)	(190,320)	(23,257)	(115,076)
Acquisition of common stock	—	—	(75,000)	—	—
Cash Flow from Financing	$(30,555)	$ (91,506)	$(265,320)	$ (23,257)	$(115,076)
Change in Cash	$(31,107)	$126,243	$ (41,547)	$153,765	$ 93,440
Cash—Beginning of year	50,794	19,687	145,930	104,383	258,148
Cash—End of Year	$ 19,687	$145,930	$ 104,383	$258,148	$ 351,588

woodstove producer that has not developed gas products; 100% of its sales currently come from woodstove sales. MSC is the only woodstove producer that sells by mail order directly to consumers. The mail-order market has sheltered MSC from some of the pricing pressure that other manufacturers have had to bear. The combination of high entry costs and high risks make it unlikely that another competitor will enter the mail-order niche.

MSC's other competitive advantages are the high efficiency and unique features of its woodstoves. MSC equips its woodstoves with a catalytic combuster, which reburns gases emitted from burning wood. This reburning not only increases the heat generated by the stoves, but also reduces pollutants in the air. MSC offers a woodstove with inlaid soapstone. This soapstone heats up and provides warmth even after the fire in the stove has dwindled. The soapstone also adds to the attractiveness of the stove as a piece of furniture. MSC's customer base includes many middle- and upper-income individuals.

Exhibit 10.21

Massachusetts Stove Company
Financial Statement Ratios
(Case 10.2)

	Year 3	Year 4	Year 5	Year 6	Year 7
Profit Margin for ROA	8.5%	8.5%	8.1%	7.2%	6.8%
Total Assets Turnover	1.2	1.3	1.7	1.8	1.9
ROA	10.1%	10.7%	14.1%	13.1%	13.1%
Profit Margin for ROCE	6.2%	6.6%	6.5%	5.6%	5.7%
Capital Structure Leverage	30.6	9.3	5.6	3.9	3.0
ROCE	224.0%	77.0%	63.4%	40.2%	32.6%
Cost of Goods Sold/Sales	49.1%	46.4%	47.8%	48.8%	50.5%
Depreciation Expense/Sales	3.8%	4.5%	2.9%	2.8%	2.6%
Facilities Costs Net of Rental Income/Sales	2.3%	0.6%	1.2%	0.3%	0.2%
Selling Expense/Sales	30.5%	34.4%	34.9%	36.8%	33.9%
Administrative Expenses/Sales	2.5%	2.4%	2.1%	2.0%	4.0%
Interest Income/Sales	—	0.1%	0.4%	0.4%	0.6%
Interest Expense/Sales	3.3%	2.7%	2.1%	2.2%	1.5%
Income Tax Expense/Income before Taxes	28.0%	28.1%	30.6%	25.6%	28.0%
Accounts Receivable Turnover	42.7	37.4	61.2	65.3	147.9
Inventory Turnover	2.5	2.2	2.9	3.0	3.2
Fixed Assets Turnover	1.9	2.1	3.1	3.5	4.2
Current Ratio	1.59	2.11	1.44	1.75	2.44
Quick Ratio	0.30	0.71	0.40	0.73	1.08
Days Accounts Receivable	9	10	6	6	3
Days Inventory Held	146	166	126	122	114
Days Accounts Payable	51	33	16	14	11
Cash Flow from Operations/ Average Current Liabilities	38.1%	93.0%	79.4%	59.8%	63.4%
Long-Term Debt/Shareholders' Equity	1,106.2%	454.2%	226.8%	144.5%	99.1%
Cash Flow from Operations/ Average Total Liabilities	7.6%	20.0%	23.2%	23.5%	24.8%
Interest Coverage Ratio	3.6	4.4	5.4	4.4	6.1

MSC believes that profitable growth of woodstove sales beyond gross revenues of $3 million a year in the mail-order niche is unlikely. However, no one is selling gas appliances by mail order. Many of MSC's customers and prospects have asked whether MSC plans to produce a gas stove.

Management of MSC is contemplating the development of several gas appliances to sell by mail order. There are compelling reasons for MSC to do this, as well as some good reasons to be cautious.

Availability of Space MSC owns a 25,000-square-foot building but occupies only 15,000 square feet. MSC leases the remaining 10,000 square feet to two tenants. The tenants pay rent plus their share of insurance, property taxes, and maintenance costs. The addition of gas appliances to its product line would require MSC to use 5,000 square feet of the space currently rented to one of its tenants. MSC would have to give the tenant six months' notice to cancel its lease.

Availability of Capital MSC has its own internal funds for product development and inventory, as well as an unused line of credit. But it will lose interest income (or incur interest expense) if it invests these funds in development and increased inventory.

Existing Demand MSC receives approximately 50,000 requests for catalogs each year and has a mailing list of approximately 220,000 active prospects and 15,000 recent owners of woodstoves. There is anecdotal evidence of sufficient demand so that MSC could introduce its gas stoves with little or no additional marketing expense, other than the cost of printing some additional catalog pages each year. MSC's management worries about the risk of the gas stove sales cannibalizing its existing woodstove sales. Also, if the current base of woodstove sales is eroded through mismanagement, inattention, or cannibalization, attempts to grow the business through expansion into gas appliances will be self-defeating.

Vacant Market Niche No other manufacturer is selling gas stoves by mail order. Because the entry costs are high and the unit volume is small, it is unlikely that another producer will enter the niche. MSC has had the mail-order market for woodstoves to itself for approximately seven years. MSC believes that this lack of existing competition will give it additional time to develop new products. However, management also believes that a timely entry will help solidify its position in this niche.

Suppliers MSC has existing relationships with many of the suppliers necessary to manufacture new gas products. The foundry that produces MSC's woodstove castings is one of the largest suppliers of gas heating appliances in central Europe. On the other hand, MSC would be a small, new customer for the vendors that provide the ceramic logs and gas burners. This could lead to problems with price, delivery, or service for these parts.

Synergies in Marketing and Manufacturing MSC would sell gas appliances through its existing direct-mail marketing efforts. It would incur additional marketing expenses for photography, printing, and customer service. MSC's existing plant is capable of manufacturing the shell of the gas units. It would require additional expertise to assemble fireboxes for the gas units (valves, burners, and log sets). MSC would have to increase its space and the number of employees to process and paint the metal parts of the new gas stoves. The gross margin for the gas products should be similar to that of the woodstoves.

Lack of Management Experience Managing new product development, larger production levels and inventories, and a more complex business would require MSC to hire more management expertise. MSC also would have to institute a new organization structure for its more complex business and define responsibilities and accountability more carefully. Up to now, MSC has operated with a fairly loose organizational philosophy.

REQUIRED (additional requirements follow on page 857)

a. Identify clues from the financial statements and financial statement ratios for Year 3– Year 7 that might suggest that Massachusetts Stove Company is a mature business.

b. Design a spreadsheet for the preparation of projected income statements, balance sheets, and statements of cash flows for MSC for Year 8–Year 12. Also forecast the financial statements for each of these years under three scenarios: (1) best case, (2) most likely, and (3) worst case. The following sections describe the assumptions you can make.

Development Costs MSC plans to develop two gas stove models, but not concurrently. It will develop the first gas model during Year 8 and begin selling it during Year 9. It will develop the second gas model during Year 9 and begin selling it during Year 10. MSC will capitalize the development costs in the year incurred (Year 8 and Year 9) and amortize them straight line over five years, beginning with the year the particular stove is initially sold (Year 9 and Year 10). Estimated development cost for each stove are as follows:

Best Case: $100,000
Most Likely Case: $120,000
Worst Case: $160,000

Capital Expenditures Capital expenditures, other than development costs, will be as follows: Year 8, $20,000; Year 9, $30,000; Year 10, $30,000; Year 11, $25,000; Year 12, $25,000. Assume a six-year depreciable life, straight-line depreciation, and a full year of depreciation in the year of acquisition.

Sales Growth Changes in wood and gas stove sales relative to total sales of the preceding year are as follows:

| Year | Best Case | | | Most Likely Case | | | Worst Case | | |
	Wood	Gas	Total	Wood	Gas	Total	Wood	Gas	Total
8	+2%	—	+2%	−2%	—	−2%	−4%	—	−4%
9	+2%	+6%	+8%	−2%	+4%	+2%	−4%	+2%	−2%
10	+2%	+12%	+14%	−2%	+8%	+6%	−4%	+4%	+0%
11	+2%	+12%	+14%	−2%	+8%	+6%	−4%	+4%	+0%
12	+2%	+12%	+14%	−2%	+8%	+6%	−4%	+4%	+0%

Because sales of gas stoves will start at zero, the projections of sales should *use the preceding growth rates in total sales.* The growth rates shown for woodstove sales and gas stove sales simply indicate the components of the total sales increase.

Cost of Goods Sold Manufacturing costs of the gas stoves will equal 50% of sales, the same as for woodstoves.

Depreciation Depreciation will increase for the amortization of the product development costs on the gas stoves and depreciation of additional capital expenditures.

Facilities Rental Income and Facilities Costs Facilities rental income will decrease by 50% beginning in Year 9 when MSC takes over 5,000 square feet of its building now rented to another company and will remain at that reduced level for Year 10–Year 12. Facilities costs will increase by $30,000 beginning in Year 9 for facilities costs now paid by a tenant and for additional facilities costs required by gas stove manufacturing. These costs will remain at that increased level for Year 10–Year 12.

Selling Expenses Selling expenses as a percentage of sales are as follows:

Year	Best Case	Most Likely Case	Worst Case
8	34%	34.0%	34%
9	33%	33.5%	35%
10	32%	33.0%	36%
11	31%	32.5%	37%
12	30%	32.0%	38%

Administrative Expenses Administrative expenses will increase by $30,000 in Year 8, $30,000 in Year 9, and $20,000 in Year 10 and then remain at the Year 10 level in Years 11 and 12.

Interest Income MSC will earn 5% interest on the average balance in cash each year.

Interest Expense The interest rate on interest-bearing debt will be 6.8% on the average amount of debt outstanding each year.

Income Tax Expense MSC is subject to an income tax rate of 28%.

Accounts Receivable and Inventories Accounts receivable and inventories will increase at the growth rate in sales.

Property, Plant, and Equipment Property, plant, and equipment at cost will increase each year by the amounts of capital expenditures and expenditures on development costs. Accumulated depreciation will increase each year by the amount of depreciation and amortization expense.

Accounts Payable and Other Current Liabilities Accounts payable will increase with the growth rate in inventories. Other current liabilities include primarily advances by customers for stoves manufactured soon after the year-end. Other current liabilities will increase with the growth rate in sales.

Current Portion of Long-Term Debt Scheduled repayments of long-term debt are as follows: Year 8, $27,036; Year 9, $29,200; Year 10, $31,400; Year 11, $33,900; Year 12, $36,600; Year 13, $39,500.

Deferred Income Taxes Deferred income taxes relate to the use of accelerated depreciation for tax purposes and the straight-line method for financial reporting. Assume that deferred income taxes will not change.

Shareholders' Equity Assume that there will be no changes in the contributed capital of MSC. Retained earnings will change each year in the amount of net income.

REQUIRED (continued from page 857)

c. Calculate the financial statements ratios listed in Exhibit 10.21 for MSC under each of the three scenarios for Year 8–Year 12.
Note: You should create a fourth spreadsheet as part of your preparation of the projected financial statements that will compute the financial ratios.

d. What advice would you give the management of MSC regarding its decision to enter the gas stove market? Your recommendation should consider the profitability and risks of this action as well as other factors you deem relevant.

Risk-Adjusted Expected Rates of Return and the Dividends Valuation Approach

LO 11-1 Describe the general valuation model and its culminating role in the six-step analysis and valuation process that is the focus of this book.

LO 11-2 Explain the fundamental equivalence of valuation based on expected future dividends, free cash flows, and earnings.

LO 11-3 Estimate risk-adjusted expected rates of return on equity capital as well as weighted-average costs of capital, which you will use to discount future payoffs to present value.

LO 11-4 Explain the rationale and basic concepts behind the dividends-based valuation approach, including the relation between cash flows to the investor versus cash flows reinvested in the firm.

LO 11-5 After tackling some of the more advanced concepts involved in dividends valuation, demonstrate how to measure dividends, establish a forecast horizon, and value continuing dividends.

LO 11-6 Bring all of the elements together to formulate the dividends-based valuation model.

LO 11-7 Apply the dividends valuation techniques to estimate firm value.

LO 11-8 Assess the sensitivity of firm value estimates to key valuation parameters, such as discount rates and expected long-term growth rates, and make investment decisions.

Chapter Overview

The first portion of this chapter describes the equivalence among valuation approaches that are based on dividends, free cash flows, and earnings. The second portion of the chapter describes and demonstrates computing risk-adjusted expected rates of return on equity capital and weighted-average costs of capital, which we use as discount rates in the valuation process. The latter portion of this chapter describes and applies the dividends-based valuation model. We demonstrate these techniques using **PepsiCo**.

Looking further ahead, Chapter 12 presents and applies cash-flow-based valuation approaches. Chapter 13 describes and applies earnings-based valuation approaches. Chapters 11–13 discuss and illustrate the important issues that determine the conceptual and practical strengths and weaknesses of each approach. All three chapters illustrate the equivalence of these valuation approaches using the theoretical development of the models and applying these approaches to the projected dividends, cash flows, and earnings derived from the financial statements forecasts developed for PepsiCo in Chapter 10. Chapter 14 describes and applies market multiples such as price-earnings ratios and market-to-book ratios that analysts use in some circumstances to value firms.

LO 11-1

Describe the general valuation model and its culminating role in the six-step analysis and valuation process that is the focus of this book.

The General Valuation Model

Economic theory teaches that the value of an investment equals the present value of the projected future payoffs from the investment discounted at a rate that reflects the time value of money and the risk inherent in those expected payoffs. A general model for the present value of a security at time $t=0$ (denoted as V_0) with an expected life of n future periods is as follows:[1]

$$V_0 = \sum_{t=1}^{n} \frac{\text{Projected Future Payoffs}_t}{(1 + \text{Discount Rate})^t}$$

In securities markets that are less than perfectly efficient, *price* does not necessarily equal *value* for every security at all times. Therefore, it can be very fruitful to search for and analyze securities that may have prices that have deviated temporarily from their fundamental values. When buying a security, the investor pays the security's price and receives the security's value. When selling a security, the investor receives the selling price and gives up the security's value. Price is observable, but value is not; value must be estimated. Therefore, estimating the value of a security to make intelligent investment decisions is a common objective of financial statement analysis. Investors, analysts, investment bankers, corporate managers, and others engage in financial statement analysis and valuation to determine a reliable appraisal of the value of shares of common equity or the value of whole firms. The questions they typically address include the following:

- What is the value of a particular company's common stock?
- Comparing my estimate of value to the current price in the market, should I buy, sell, or hold a particular firm's common shares?
- What is a reasonable price to accept (or ask) as a seller or pay (or bid) as a buyer for the shares of a firm in an initial public offering or a corporate merger or acquisition?

Equity valuation models based on dividends, cash flows, and earnings have been the topic of many theoretical and empirical research studies. These studies provide many insights into valuation, but two very compelling general conclusions emerge and motivate the discussion and application of valuation models in this text:

- Share prices in the capital markets *generally* correlate closely with share value, but
- Share prices *do not always* equal share values, and temporary deviations of price from value occur.

First, many empirical studies demonstrate that dividends, cash flows, and earnings-based valuation models generally provide significant explanatory power for share prices

---

[1]Throughout this chapter, t refers to accounting periods. The valuation process determines an estimate of firm value, denoted V_0, when $t=0$. The period $t=1$ refers to the first accounting period being discounted to present value. Period $t=n$ is the period of the expected final, or liquidating, payoff.

observed in the capital markets.[2] Share value estimates determined from these valuation models exhibit high positive correlations with the stock prices observed in the capital markets. These correlations hold across different types of firms, during different periods of time, and across different countries. In the same vein, many empirical research studies also have shown that unexpected *changes* in earnings, dividends, and cash flows correlate closely with *changes* in stock prices.

Second, a number of empirical research studies show that valuation models also help identify when share prices in the capital markets temporarily deviate from fundamental share values. Dividends, cash flows, and earnings-based valuation models help identify when shares are temporarily overpriced or underpriced, representing potentially profitable investment opportunities. For example, Exhibit 11.1 is a graphic depiction of results from a study by Frankel and Lee (1998) in which they sorted a sample of firms each year into five portfolios based on quintiles of their estimate of value (*V*) to share price (*P*).[3] Their findings show striking differences in the average 36-month stock returns earned by their portfolios. The highest value-to-price quintile portfolio generated significantly greater average returns than the lowest value-to-price portfolio. These results should be very encouraging for those interested in developing fundamental forecasting and valuation skills for investment purposes.

Exhibit 11.1

Empirical Evidence on Portfolio Stock Returns Associated with Share Value Relative to Share Price (*V/P*)

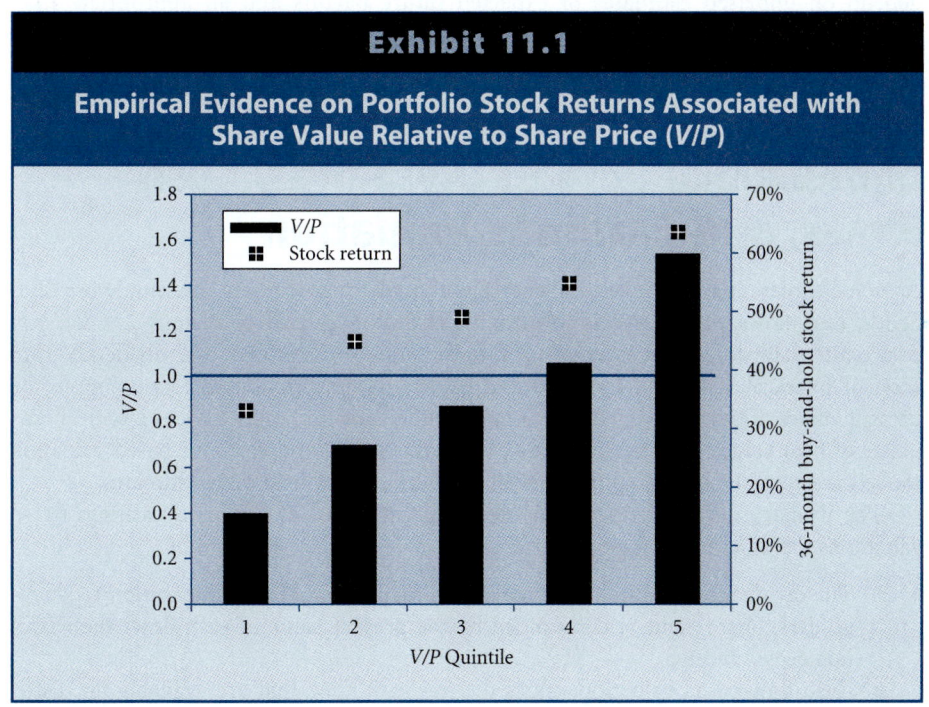

---

[2]For examples, see Craig Nichols, James Wahlen, and Matthew Wieland, "Pricing and Mispricing in the Time-Series and the Cross-Section," 2013 working paper, Indiana University; Stephen Penman and Theodore Sougiannis, "A Comparison of Dividend, Cash Flow, and Earnings Approaches to Equity Valuation," *Contemporary Accounting Research* 15, no. 3 (Fall 1998), pp. 343–383; and Jennifer Francis, Per Olsson, and Dennis Oswald, "Comparing the Accuracy and Explainability of Dividend, Free Cash Flow, and Abnormal Earnings Equity Value Estimates," *Journal of Accounting Research* 38 (Spring 2000), pp. 45–70.

[3]Richard Frankel and Charles Lee, "Accounting Valuation, Market Expectation, and Cross-Sectional Stock Returns," *Journal of Accounting and Economics* 25, Issue 3 (1998), pp. 283–319.

The six-step analysis and valuation framework that forms the structure of this book (Exhibit 1.2 in Chapter 1) is a logical sequence of steps for understanding the fundamentals of a business and for determining intelligent estimates of its value. First, we analyze the economics and competitive conditions of the industry. Second, we analyze the particular firm's strategy in light of the competitive dynamics of the industry. Third, we assess the quality of the firm's accounting and financial reporting. Fourth, we analyze the firm's profitability and risk with a set of financial ratios. Fifth, we use all of this information to project the firm's future financial statements. In the final step, we derive from projected financial statements our forecasts of future earnings, cash flows, and dividends as measures of projected future payoffs for the firm. We use these projected future payoffs as inputs to valuation models to determine the value of the firm. Reliable projections of future payoffs to the firm (the numerator in the general valuation model presented at the start of this chapter) depend on unbiased and thorough forecasts of future income statements, balance sheets, and statements of cash flows, all of which depend on reliable projections of the firm's future operating, investing, and financing activities. Assessing an appropriate risk-adjusted discount rate (the denominator in the general valuation model) requires an assessment of the inherent risk in the set of expected future payoffs. Therefore, reliable estimates of firm value depend on unbiased estimates of expected future payoffs and an appropriate risk-adjusted discount rate, all of which depend on the collective information from the six steps of the framework.

LO 11-2

Explain the fundamental equivalence of valuation based on expected future dividends, free cash flows, and earnings.

Equivalence among Dividends, Cash Flows, and Earnings Valuation

As noted earlier, analysts, investors, and capital market participants commonly use dividends, cash flows, and earnings to estimate share values and pick stocks. When you derive internally consistent forecasts of future earnings, cash flows, and dividends from a set of financial statement forecasts and use the same discount rate to compute the present values of those expected future payoffs, the valuation models yield identical estimates of firm value. That is, dividends-, free-cash-flows-, and earnings-based valuation models are complementary approaches that produce equivalent value estimates.

The primary differences between dividends-, free-cash-flows-, and earnings-based valuations are differences in perspective:

- The dividends-based valuation approach focuses on *wealth distribution* to shareholders. Share value is determined by the present value of cash flows the shareholder will receive.
- Cash-flow-based valuation values the *free cash flows* that are available for distribution to shareholders after cash is used for necessary investments in operating assets and required payments to debtholders.
- Earnings-based valuation takes the perspective that earnings measure the capital that firms create (or destroy) for common shareholders each period that will ultimately be realized in cash flows and distributed as dividends to shareholders.

Thus, the earnings-based valuation approach focuses on the firm's *wealth creation* for shareholders, the cash-flows-based approach focuses on *dividend-paying ability*, and the dividends-based approach focuses on *wealth distribution* to shareholders.

Free cash flows can be used instead of dividends as the expected future payoffs to the investor in the numerator of the general valuation model. Both approaches, if implemented with consistent assumptions, will lead to identical estimates of value. This equivalence occurs because over the life of the firm, the free cash flows into the firm will be equivalent to the cash flows paid out of the firm in dividends to shareholders.

The earnings-based valuation approach is an alternative valuation perspective, equivalent to both dividends- and free-cash-flows-based valuation. It will also yield a valuation identical to the valuation based on dividends and free cash flows as long as the forecasts of earnings, dividends, and cash flows are based on consistent assumptions. Exhibit 11.2 provides a conceptual illustration of these three approaches to firm valuation. If you apply all three of these different valuation approaches, you will gain much better insights about firm value than analysts who rely on only one approach. You will understand valuation more thoroughly across a wider array of situations when you can triangulate valuation across the dividends-, cash-flows-, and earnings-based approaches.

All four valuation chapters (Chapters 11–14) emphasize that the objective of the valuation process is not a single point estimate of value per se; instead, the objective is to determine a reliable distribution of value estimates across the relevant ranges of critical

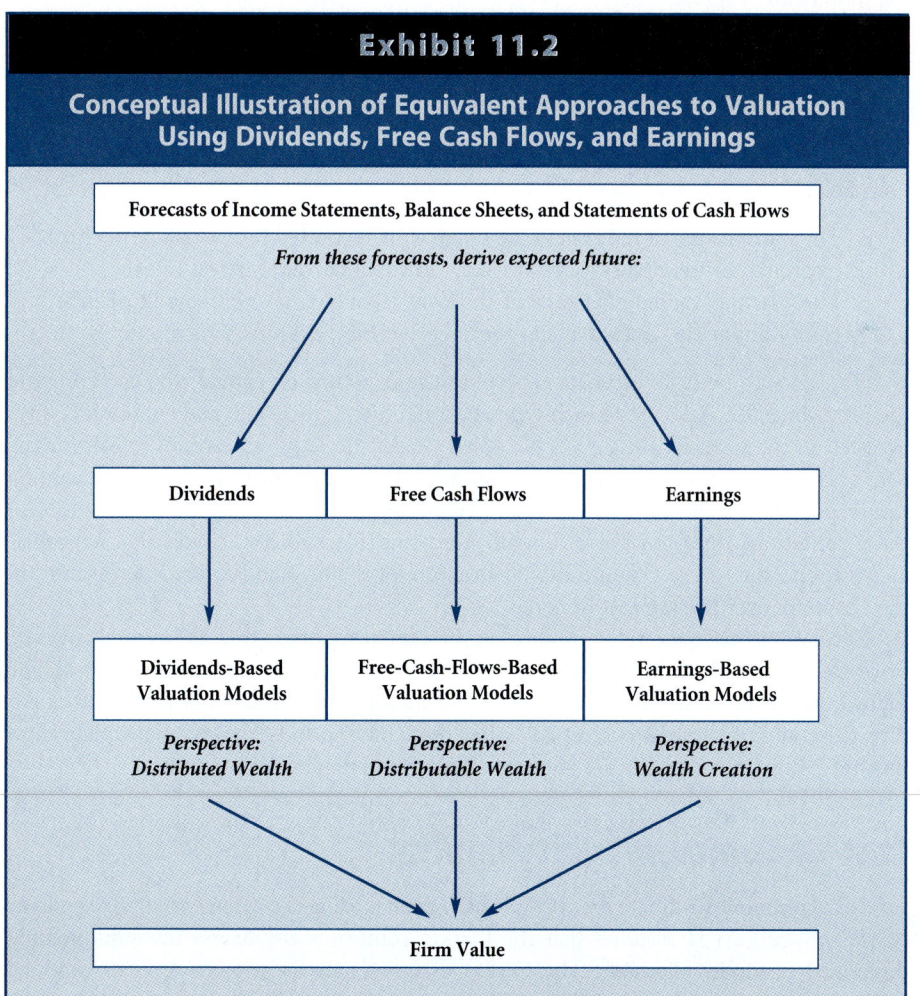

Exhibit 11.2

Conceptual Illustration of Equivalent Approaches to Valuation Using Dividends, Free Cash Flows, and Earnings

Forecasts of Income Statements, Balance Sheets, and Statements of Cash Flows

From these forecasts, derive expected future:

| Dividends | Free Cash Flows | Earnings |

| Dividends-Based Valuation Models | Free-Cash-Flows-Based Valuation Models | Earnings-Based Valuation Models |

Perspective: Distributed Wealth — *Perspective: Distributable Wealth* — *Perspective: Wealth Creation*

Firm Value

forecast assumptions and valuation parameters. By estimating share value using cash flows, earnings, and dividends, and by assessing the sensitivity of these value estimates across a distribution of relevant forecast assumptions and valuation parameters, you can determine the most likely range of values for a share, which you can then compare to the share's price in the capital market for an intelligent investment decision.

Risk-Adjusted Expected Rates of Return

We base all of the valuation approaches we describe and demonstrate in Chapters 11–14 on the general valuation model set forth at the beginning of this chapter, in which we determine firm value by discounting projected future payoffs to present value. Therefore, for all of the valuation approaches, we need a discount rate to compute the present value of all projected future payoffs. To compensate for the time value of money and risk, the discount rate should equal the required rate of return that investors demand from the firm to induce them to commit capital. When you compute the present value of payoffs (dividends, free cash flows, or earnings) to *common equity shareholders*, you should use a discount rate that reflects the risk-adjusted required rate of return on *common equity* capital.

The discount rate should be a forecast of the required rate of return on the investment and, therefore, should be conditional on the expected future riskiness of the firm and expected future interest rates in the economy over the period during which the payoffs will be generated. The historical discount rate of the firm may be a good indicator of the appropriate discount rate to apply to the firm in the future, but only if the following three conditions hold:

- The current risk of the firm is the same as the expected future risk of the firm.
- Expected future interest rates are likely to equal current interest rates.
- The existing capital structure of the firm (that is, the current mix of debt and equity financing) is the same as the expected future capital structure of the firm.

As a starting point to estimate expected rates of return on capital, you can compute the prevailing after-tax cost of each type of capital (debt, preferred, and common equity) invested in the firm. Existing costs of capital reflect the required rates of return for the firm's existing capital structure, and they are appropriate discount rates for valuing future payoffs for the firm if the three preceding conditions hold. If one or more of these conditions does not hold, you will need to project discount rates that appropriately capture the future risk and capital structure of the firm and future interest rates in the economy over the forecast horizon.

Developing discount rates using costs of capital assumes that the capital markets price capital to reflect the risk-free time value of money plus a premium for risk. The following sections describe and demonstrate techniques to estimate the firm's cost of equity, debt, and preferred stock capital. After these descriptions, the chapter explains and illustrates how to compute a weighted-average cost of capital for the firm.

Cost of Common Equity Capital

Analysts commonly estimate the cost of equity capital using the *capital asset pricing model (CAPM)*. The CAPM assumes that the market comprises risk-averse investors holding diversified portfolios of assets. The CAPM assumes that for a given level of expected return, risk-averse investors will seek to bear as little risk as possible and will mitigate risk by diversifying across the types of assets they hold in a portfolio. Therefore, the CAPM hypothesizes that in equilibrium, investors should expect to earn a rate of return on a firm's common equity capital that equals the rate of return the market requires to hold that firm's stock in a diversified portfolio of assets. In theory, the market comprises risk-averse investors who demand a rate of return that (1) compensates them for forgoing the consumption of capital (the time value of money) and (2) compensates them with a risk premium for bearing *systematic, marketwide risk* that cannot be diversified. Systematic risk arises from economy-wide factors (such as economic growth or recession, unemployment, unexpected inflation, unexpected changes in prices for natural resources such as oil and gas, unexpected changes in exchange rates, and population growth) that affect all firms to varying degrees and therefore cannot be fully diversified. Therefore, the market's required rate of return on equity capital is a function of prevailing risk-free rates of interest in the economy plus a risk premium for bearing risk, conditional on the level of nondiversifiable risk inherent in the firm's common stock.

Note that the CAPM views nonsystematic risk as factors that are diversifiable by the investor holding a broad portfolio of stocks. Nonsystematic risk factors are industry- and firm-specific, including factors such as the level of competition in an industry, the product portfolio of a particular firm, the sustainability of the firm's strategy, and the firm's ability to generate revenue growth and control expenses. A competitive equilibrium capital market, according to CAPM, does not expect a return for a firm's nonsystematic risk because such risk can be diversified away in a portfolio of stocks.

Analysts measure nondiversifiable or systematic risk as the degree of covariation between a firm's stock returns and a marketwide index of stock returns. Analysts commonly measure systematic risk using the firm's *market beta*, which is estimated as the slope coefficient from regressing the firm's stock returns on an index of returns reflecting a marketwide portfolio of stocks over a relevant period of time.[4] If a firm's market beta from such a regression is equal to 1, it indicates that, on average, the firm's stock returns covary identically with returns to a marketwide portfolio, indicating that the firm has the same degree of systematic risk as the market as a whole. If a firm's market beta is greater than 1, the firm has a greater degree of systematic risk than the market as a whole, whereas a firm with a market beta less than 1 has less systematic risk than the market as a whole.

Exhibit 11.3 reports industry median, 25th percentile, and 75th percentile market betas for a sample of 47 industries over the years 2003–2012.[5] These data depict wide variation in systematic risk across industries during this ten-year period, with industry median market betas ranging from a low of 0.58 (Beer & Liquor and Tobacco Products) to highs of 1.72 and 1.76 (Steel Works and Coal, respectively). Various financial data sources and websites regularly publish market betas for common equity in publicly traded firms. It is not uncommon to find considerable variation in market betas among the various sources. This occurs in part because of differences in the period and methodology used to estimate betas.[6]

---

[4]Researchers and analysts have developed a variety of approaches to estimate market betas. One common approach estimates a firm's market beta by regressing the firm's monthly stock returns on a marketwide index of returns (such as the S&P 500 index) over the last 60 months.

[5]Many thanks to Professor Matt Wieland for help in collecting these data.

[6]Eugene Fama and Kenneth French developed an empirical model that explains realized stock returns using three factors they found to be correlated with returns during their study period. Their model and results indicate that during their sample period (1963–1990), firms' stock returns were related to firms' market betas, market capitalizations (size), and market-to-book ratios [see Eugene F. Fama and Kenneth R. French, "The Cross Section of Expected Stock Returns," *Journal of Finance* (June 1992), pp. 427–465]. Data to implement their model can be obtained from French's website (http://mba.tuck.dartmouth.edu/pages/faculty/ken.french/data_library.html).

Exhibit 11.3

Relation between Industry and Systematic Risk over 2003–2012

Industry Name	25th percentile	Median	75th percentile
Beer & Liquor	0.39	0.58	0.79
Tobacco Products	0.43	0.58	0.72
Food Products	0.44	0.68	1.03
Candy & Soda	0.46	0.74	0.95
Banking	0.21	0.76	1.35
Utilities	0.55	0.77	1.00
Real Estate	0.26	0.77	1.42
Defense	0.54	0.84	1.32
Healthcare	0.52	0.85	1.19
Recreation	0.49	0.90	1.31
Medical Equipment	0.57	0.90	1.27
Printing and Publishing	0.55	0.93	1.32
Personal Services	0.55	0.94	1.28
Agriculture	0.51	0.94	1.30
Textiles	0.41	0.95	1.38
Consumer Goods	0.48	0.96	1.39
Insurance	0.67	0.96	1.31
Rubber and Plastic Products	0.49	0.97	1.38
Restaurants, Hotels, Motels	0.54	1.00	1.33
Precious Metals	0.68	1.01	1.51
Wholesale	0.58	1.01	1.47
Pharmaceutical Products	0.63	1.02	1.48
Entertainment	0.63	1.03	1.49
Communication	0.74	1.05	1.49
Apparel	0.58	1.09	1.41
Trading	0.65	1.09	1.54
Business Services	0.69	1.11	1.56
Measuring and Control Equipment	0.65	1.12	1.60
Shipping Containers	0.88	1.12	1.45
Aircraft	0.89	1.15	1.44
Construction Materials	0.65	1.16	1.56
Transportation	0.79	1.16	1.54
Business Supplies	0.71	1.17	1.60
Retail	0.80	1.19	1.53
Electrical Equipment	0.71	1.21	1.63
Computers	0.79	1.21	1.66
Fabricated Products	0.60	1.24	1.72
Chemicals	0.90	1.28	1.67
Petroleum and Natural Gas	0.86	1.31	1.76
Machinery	0.91	1.35	1.75

(Continued)

Exhibit 11.3 (Continued)			
Electronic Equipment	0.87	1.35	1.90
Automobiles and Trucks	0.95	1.36	1.77
Shipbuilding, Railroad Equipment	0.69	1.40	1.90
Non-Metallic and Industrial Metal Mining	0.98	1.45	1.87
Construction	1.17	1.60	1.98
Steel Works	1.25	1.72	2.11
Coal	1.16	1.76	2.11
Overall	**0.61**	**1.06**	**1.52**

The CAPM projects the expected return on common equity capital for Firm j as follows:

$$E[R_{Ej}] = E[R_F] + \beta_j \times \{E[R_M] - E[R_F]\}$$

where E denotes that the related variable is an expectation; R_{Ej} denotes required return on common equity in Firm j; R_F denotes the risk-free rate of return; β_j denotes the market beta for Firm j; and R_M denotes the required return on a diversified, marketwide portfolio of stocks (such as the S&P 500). According to the CAPM, a common equity security with no systematic risk (that is, a stock with $\beta_j = 0$) should be expected to earn a return equal to the expected rate of return on risk-free securities. Of course, most equity securities are not risk-free. The subtraction term in brackets in the preceding equation represents the average market risk premium, which is equal to the amount of return above the risk-free rate that equity investors in the capital markets require for bearing the average amount of systematic risk in the market as a whole. Therefore,

- An equity security with systematic risk equal to the average amount of systematic risk of all equity securities in the market has a market beta equal to 1, so the cost of common equity capital for such a firm should be equal to the required return on the market portfolio.
- A firm with a market beta greater than 1 has higher than average systematic risk and faces a higher cost of equity capital because the capital markets expect the firm to yield a commensurately higher return to compensate investors for bearing greater risk.
- A firm with a market beta less than 1 faces a lower cost of equity capital because the capital markets expect the firm to yield a commensurately lower return to investors for bearing less risk.

Exhibit 11.4 depicts the CAPM graphically.

You should use the market return on securities with zero systematic risk as the risk-free interest rate in the CAPM. Returns on such systematic risk-free securities (for example, U.S. Treasury securities) should exhibit no correlation with returns on a diversified marketwide portfolio of stocks. Given that equity securities have indefinitely long lives, it might seem appropriate to use the yield on long-term U.S. Treasury securities as a proxy for a risk-free rate. However, yields on long-term U.S. government securities tend to exhibit greater sensitivity to changes in inflation and interest rates; therefore, they have a greater degree of systematic risk (although the systematic risk is still quite low) compared to short-term U.S. government securities. Common practice uses the yield on intermediate-term U.S. government securities (for example, yields on ten-year

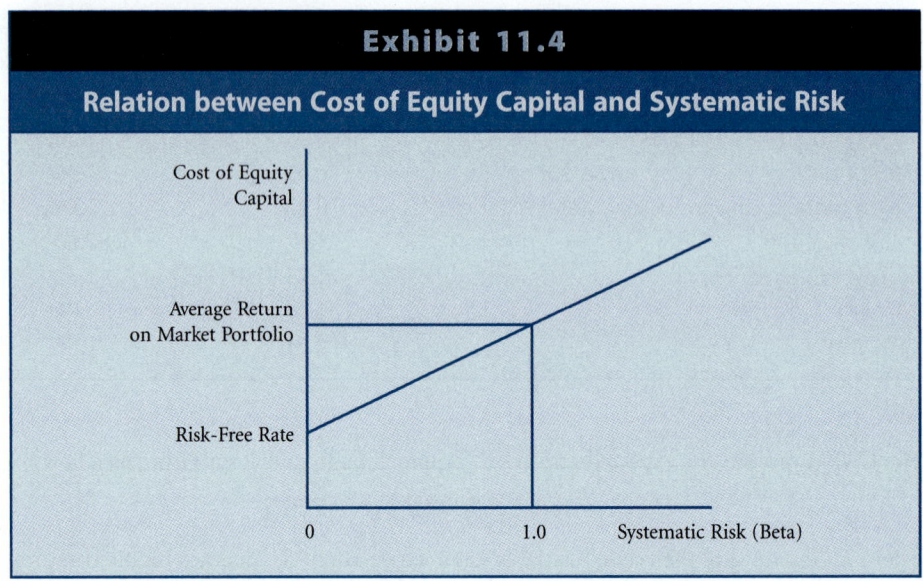

Exhibit 11.4

Relation between Cost of Equity Capital and Systematic Risk

U.S. Treasury securities) as the risk-free rate. Historically, these yields have averaged around 6% over the long run, although in recent years, they have been quite low, averaging from roughly 1%–4%.

The average realized rate of return on the market portfolio depends on the period studied. Historically, the realized rate of return on the market portfolio has varied between 9%–13%. Thus, the risk premium on the market portfolio over the risk-free rate has varied between 3%–7%. Some financial economists argue that the market risk premium varies over time with investors' demand for consumption. The economists argue that, on the margin, when the economy is healthy and growing (with low unemployment and high consumer confidence), investors' demand for additional consumption is relatively low; therefore, investors demand relatively low rates of return for postponing consumption and bearing risk. Thus, risk premia tend to be lower (perhaps 3%–4%) when economic conditions are strong. Conversely, when the economy is weak and investors face a higher degree of uncertainty, investors' demand for additional consumption is relatively high; therefore, they demand relatively high rates of return for postponing consumption and bearing risk. Thus, risk premia tend to be higher (perhaps 6%–7%) when economic conditions are weak. The theories asserting that risk premia are time-varying (and vary inversely with investors' marginal demand for consumption) seem intuitive and appear to explain risk premia observed in the capital markets quite well, but are somewhat difficult to integrate into valuations and require more empirical research.

Using the CAPM to Compute Expected Rates of Return

Suppose Firm A has a market beta of 0.60 and Firm B has a market beta of 1.40. Assume that the prevailing yields on ten-year U.S. Treasury bonds are roughly 3.0% and that the capital markets require a 5.0% risk premium for bearing an average amount of systematic risk. Applying the CAPM, we would compute the following expected rates of return for Firm A and Firm B:

$$\text{Firm A: } E[R_A] = 3.0 + (0.60 \times 5.0) = 6.0$$
$$\text{Firm B: } E[R_B] = 3.0 + (1.40 \times 5.0) = 10.0$$

Thus, the CAPM implies that investors require a 6.0% rate of return on capital invested in the equity of Firm A and a 10.0% rate of return on capital invested in the equity of

Firm B. Firm B faces a higher cost of equity capital because it has a higher degree of systematic risk. In determining the share values of Firm A and Firm B, investors should discount to present value the expected future payoffs using a 6.0% discount rate for Firm A and a 10.0% discount rate for Firm B. If investors expect Firm A and Firm B to generate equivalent payoffs (although Firm B's payoffs will be riskier), investors will assign a lower value to (and pay a lower price for) the common shares of Firm B than Firm A. The difference between the value of Firm B's shares and those of Firm A reflects the additional compensation that shareholders demand for holding the riskier Firm B shares relative to shares of Firm A. Shareholders will realize this compensation in the form of the equivalent payoffs, for which shareholders in Firm B paid a lower price than did shareholders in Firm A.

Computing the Required Rate of Return on Equity Capital for PepsiCo

At the end of 2012, different sources provided different estimates of market beta for **PepsiCo** common stock, ranging from 0.50 to roughly 1.00. Historically, PepsiCo's market beta has varied around 0.75 over time, so we will assume that PepsiCo common stock has a market beta of roughly 0.75 as of the end of 2012. At that time, U.S. Treasury bills with ten years to maturity traded with a yield of just below 3.0%, which we use as the risk-free rate. Additionally, economic conditions were improving, stock market indexes had experienced strong gains, and investors were less risk-averse than normal; so we will assume investors demanded a 6.0% market risk premium. Therefore, the CAPM indicates that PepsiCo has a cost of common equity capital of 7.50% [3.0 + (0.75 × 6.0)].

Adjusting Market Equity Beta to Reflect a New Capital Structure

Recall from the discussion in Chapter 5 that market beta reflects operating leverage, financial leverage, variability of sales and earnings, and other firm characteristics. The market beta computed using historical market price data reflects the firm's existing capital structure. In some settings, such as a leveraged buyout, firms plan to make significant changes in the financial capital structure. In such cases, you need to project what the market beta is likely to be after the firm changes the capital structure. You can "unlever" the current market beta by adjusting it to remove the effects of leverage and then "relever" it by adjusting it to reflect leverage under the new capital structure. The following formula estimates an unlevered market beta (sometimes referred to as an *asset beta*):

$$\text{Current Levered Market Beta} = \text{Unlevered Market Beta} \times$$
$$\left[1 + (1 - \text{Income Tax Rate}) \times \left(\frac{\text{Current Market Value of Debt}}{\text{Current Market Value of Equity}}\right)\right]$$

The intuition behind this formula is that current market beta reflects two components: (1) the systematic risk of the operations and assets of the firm (the unlevered beta), compounded by (2) the financial leverage of the firm (the debt-to-equity ratio), net of the tax benefit from using leverage (that is, tax savings from interest expense deductions.) Estimating the new levered beta requires two steps:

1. Solve for the unlevered beta by rearranging the preceding equation to divide the current levered market beta by the term in square brackets on the right side of the equation, as follows:

   Unlevered Market Beta = Current Levered Market Beta/[1 + (1 − Income Tax Rate) × (Current Market Value of Debt/Current Market Value of Equity)]

2. Project the new levered market beta by multiplying the unlevered beta by the term in square brackets on the right side of the equation after substituting the projected new ratio of the market value of debt to the market value of equity in place of the current ratio of the market value of debt to the market value of equity, as follows:

$$\text{New Levered Market Beta} = \text{Unlevered Market Beta} \times [1 + (1 - \text{Income Tax Rate}) \times (\text{New Market Value of Debt/New Market Value of Equity})]$$

To illustrate the effects of leverage on beta and expected rates of return, suppose a firm has a market beta of 0.9, is subject to an income tax rate of 35%, and has a market-value-of-debt-to-market-value-of-equity ratio of 60%. If the risk-free rate is 6% and the market risk premium is 7%, then according to the CAPM, the market expects this firm to generate equity returns of 12.3% [6.0% + (0.9 × 7.0%)]. The firm intends to adopt a new capital structure that will increase the debt-to-equity ratio to 140%. To project the firm's levered beta under the new capital structure, the first step is to solve for the unlevered beta, denoted X, as follows:

$$0.9 = X \times [1 + (1 - 0.35) \times (0.60/1.00)]$$
$$X = 0.9/[1 + (1 - 0.35) \times (0.60/1.00)]$$
$$X = 0.65$$

Because financial leverage is positively related to market beta, removing the effect of financial leverage reduces market beta. The unlevered beta should reflect the effects of the firm's operating risk, sales volatility, and other operating factors, but not risk related to financial leverage. The new market beta is projected to reflect the new debt-to-equity ratio as follows:

$$Y = 0.65 \times [1 + (1 - 0.35) \times (1.40/1.00)] = 1.24$$

The new capital structure will increase the leverage and therefore the systematic risk of the firm. According to the CAPM, this firm will face an equity cost of capital of 14.68% [6.0% + (1.24 × 7.0%)] under the new capital structure.

Evaluating the Use of the CAPM to Measure the Cost of Equity Capital

The use of the CAPM to calculate the cost of equity capital has been subject to various criticisms, as follows:

- Market betas for a firm should vary over time as the systematic risk of the firm changes; however, market beta estimates are quite sensitive to the time period and methodology used in their computation.
- In theory, the CAPM estimates required returns based on the stock's risk relative to a diversified portfolio of assets across the economy, but a return index for a diversified portfolio of assets that spans the entire economy does not exist. Measuring a stock's systematic risk relative to a stock market return index such as the S&P 500 Index fails to consider covariation between the stock's returns and returns on assets outside the stock market, including other financial investments (for example, U.S. government and corporate debt securities and privately held equity), real estate, and human capital.
- The market risk premium is not stable over time and is sensitive to the time period used in its calculation. Considerable uncertainty surrounds the appropriate adjustment for the market risk premium. It is not clear whether the appropriate adjustment

should be on the order of 3%, 7%, or somewhere in between.[7] As noted earlier, some financial economists now argue that the risk premium is lower in periods of economic health and growth and higher in periods of economic weakness and uncertainty, which seems plausible and consistent with observable variation in marketwide stock returns over time. However, this approach requires more research to develop practical models for measuring firm-specific time-varying risk premia.

In light of these criticisms of the CAPM and considering the crucial role of the risk-adjusted discount rate for common equity valuation, it is important to analyze the sensitivity of share value estimates across different discount rates. For example, you should estimate values for a share of common equity in a particular firm across a relevant range of discount rates for common equity by varying the market risk premium from 3% to 7%.

Chapter 14 describes techniques to reverse-engineer the implicit expected rate of return on common equity securities. Chapter 14 also describes an approach to estimate the implicit discount in share price for risk by using risk-free discount rates. These techniques do not require the assumption of an asset pricing model such as the CAPM.

Cost of Debt Capital

You should compute the after-tax cost of each component of debt capital, including short-term and long-term notes payable, mortgages, bonds, and capital lease obligations, as the yield to maturity on each type of debt times one minus the statutory tax rate applicable to income tax deductions for interest. The yield to maturity is the rate that discounts the contractual cash flows on the debt to the debt's current fair value. If the fair value of the debt is equal to face value (for example, a $1,000 debenture trades on an exchange for $1,000), the yield to maturity equals the stated interest rate on the debt. If the fair value of the debt exceeds the face value of the debt, yield to maturity is lower than the stated rate. This can occur after interest rates fall; previously issued fixed-rate debt will have a stated rate that exceeds current market yields for debt with comparable credit quality and terms. On the other hand, after interest rates rise, existing fixed-rate debt may have a stated rate that is lower than prevailing market rates for comparable debt, in which case the debt will have a fair value that is less than face value and the yield to maturity will be greater than the stated rate.

Firms disclose in notes to their financial statements the stated interest rates on their existing interest-bearing debt capital. Firms also disclose in notes the estimated fair values of their interest-bearing debt, which should reflect the present value of the debt using prevailing market yields to maturity on the debt. Together, these disclosures allow you to estimate prevailing market yields to maturity on the firm's outstanding debt.

In computing costs of debt capital, analysts typically exclude operating liability accounts (such as accounts payable, accrued expenses, deferred income tax liability, and retirement benefit obligations). Instead, analysts typically treat these items as part of the firm's operating activities rather than as part of the firm's financial capital structure.

A capitalized lease obligation will generally have an implicit after-tax cost of capital equal to the after-tax yield to maturity on collateralized borrowing with equivalent risk and maturity. Firms recognize capital lease obligations on the balance sheet as financial

---

[7]See, for example, James Claus and Jacob Thomas, "Equity Premia as Low as Three Percent? Empirical Evidence from Analysts' Earnings Forecasts for Domestic and International Stock Markets," *Journal of Finance* 56 (October 2001), pp. 1629–1666. Also see Peter Easton, Gary Taylor, Pervin Shroff, and Theodore Sougiannis, "Using Forecasts of Earnings to Simultaneously Estimate Growth and the Rate of Return on Equity Investment," *Journal of Accounting Research* 40 (June 2000), pp. 657–676.

liabilities; however, as described in Chapter 7, firms also may have significant off-balance-sheet commitments to make future payments under operating leases. If the firm has significant commitments under operating leases, you may believe it necessary to include them in the computation of the cost of debt capital. If you elect to adjust the firm's balance sheet to capitalize operating lease commitments as debt (as illustrated in Chapter 7), you should make three sets of adjustments to include the effects of operating leases on the total cost of debt capital:

1. Include the present value of operating lease commitments in calculating the fair value of various components of outstanding debt.
2. Include the discount rate used to compute the present value of the operating lease commitments as the after-tax interest rate on operating leases in the computation of the cost of debt capital. The lessor bears more risk in an operating lease than in a capital lease, so the cost of capital represented by operating leases is likely to be higher than for capital leases.
3. The cash outflows for rent payments under operating leases should be reclassified as interest and principal payments of debt when computing free cash flows. Chapter 7 discusses techniques to convert operating leases to capital leases.

The income tax rate used to compute the tax effects of interest should be the firm's tax rate applicable to interest expense deductions. For most firms, the tax rate applicable to interest expense deductions is the statutory federal tax rate, which is 35% in the United States in 2013. However, state and foreign taxes or other special tax factors may increase or decrease the combined statutory tax rate depending on where the firm raises its debt capital. Firms generally do not separately disclose statutory state or foreign tax rates, but do summarize the effect of these taxes in the income tax reconciliation found in the income tax note. To achieve greater precision, you could approximate the combined statutory tax rate applicable to interest expense deductions using the effective tax rate disclosed in the income tax footnote.

Cost of Preferred Equity Capital

The cost of preferred stock capital depends on the preference conditions. Preferred stock that has preference over common shares with respect to dividends and priority in liquidation generally sells near its par value. Therefore, its cost of capital is the dividend rate on the preferred stock. Depending on the attributes of the preferred stock, dividends on preferred stock may give rise to a tax deduction, in which case the after-tax cost of capital will be lower than the pretax cost. Preferred stock that is convertible into common stock has both preferred and common equity attributes. Its cost is a blending of the cost of nonconvertible preferred stock and common equity.

Cost of Equity Capital Attributable to Noncontrolling Interests

As described in Chapter 7, noncontrolling interests account for the equity ownership of minority investors who own less than 50% of the shares of a subsidiary company. When a firm reports equity capital attributable to noncontrolling interests in shareholders' equity on the balance sheet, it indicates that the firm is the controlling shareholder and consolidates the subsidiary. The noncontrolling interests account measures and reports the amount of equity capital that has been invested by the noncontrolling investors. The relevant cost of capital depends on the risk of this component of equity capital. In some cases, the subsidiary company may be a publicly traded firm for which you can obtain an estimate of systematic risk (e.g., beta). In those cases, you can use the CAPM to estimate the cost of capital for noncontrolling interests. For subsidiary companies that are not publicly traded, you must estimate the appropriate cost of capital using other methods. For example, if the subsidiary company has very similar risk as the consolidated firm, then it is appropriate to use the parent company's cost of equity capital.

Computing the Weighted-Average Cost of Capital

In some circumstances, you may need to determine the present value of payoffs to investment in all of the assets of a firm, not just the equity capital of the firm. Such circumstances might arise, for example, if you are considering acquiring all of the assets of a firm or considering acquiring controlling interest in a firm. If you need to determine the present value of the payoffs from investing in the total assets of the firm, or, equivalently, acquiring all of the financing claims on the firm, you should use a discount rate that reflects the weighted-average required rate of return that encompasses the debt, preferred, and common equity capital used to finance the net operating assets of the firm.

A formula for the weighted-average cost of capital (denoted as R_A) is given here:

$$R_A = [w_D \times R_D \times (1 - \textit{Income Tax Rate})] + [w_P \times R_P] + [w_E \times R_E] + [w_{NCI} \times R_{NCI}]$$

where: w denotes the weight on each type of capital
D denotes debt capital
P denotes preferred stock capital
E denotes common equity capital
NCI denotes equity capital attributable to noncontrolling interests
R denotes the cost of each type of capital
Income Tax Rate denotes the tax rate applicable to debt capital costs

The weights used to compute the weighted-average cost of capital should be the market values of each type of capital in proportion to the total market value of the financial capital structure of the firm (that is, $w_D + w_P + w_E + w_{NCI} = 1.0$). On the right side of the equation, the first term in brackets measures the weighted after-tax cost of debt capital, the second term measures the weighted cost of preferred stock capital, the third term measures the weighted cost of common equity capital, and the fourth term measures the weighted cost of capital for noncontrolling interests.

To determine the appropriate weights to use in the weighted-average cost of capital, you must first determine the market values of each type of capital (debt, preferred, common, and noncontrolling interests). Market values for debt will be observable only for firms that have issued publicly traded debt; however, U.S. GAAP and IFRS require firms to disclose the fair value of their outstanding debt capital in notes to the financial statements each year. Fair value disclosures may not be available, however, if the firm is privately owned, if it is not required to follow U.S. GAAP or IFRS, or if it is a division and does not publish its own financial statements. If market values are not observable and fair values for the firm's debt are not disclosed, you can (1) estimate the fair value of the firm's debt if sufficient data are available about the firm's credit quality and the maturity and terms of the debt or (2) rely on the book value of debt. The book value of debt can be a reliable estimate of fair value if the debt:

- is recently issued.
- bears a variable rate of interest.
- bears a fixed rate of interest but interest rates and the firm's credit quality have been stable since the debt was issued.

Because the yield to maturity on debt is inversely related to its market value, analysts sometimes approximate the cost of debt by simply using the coupon rate and the book value of debt, particularly when interest rates are stable and the market value of debt is likely to be close to book value.

If available, market prices for equity securities provide the amounts for determining the market value of equity. Market prices for equity may not be available, however, if the firm is privately owned or if it is a subsidiary of a parent firm. You can then use the book value of equity as a starting point to compute the weight of equity in the capital structure.

Over time, the weights you assign to debt, preferred, common equity, and noncontrolling interests capital may change if you expect the firm's capital structure to change over the forecast horizon. In addition, you may expect yields to maturity on debt capital and required rates of return on equity capital to change as interest rates in the economy change, the risk of the firm changes, or the firm's tax status changes. To capture these changes, you may need to project the weighted-average cost of capital *for each period* over the forecast horizon.

Computing the Weighted-Average Cost of Capital

To demonstrate how to compute the weighted-average cost of capital, suppose a firm has the following capital structure on its balance sheet:

	Book Value
Long-term bonds, 10% annual coupon, issued at par	$20,000,000
Preferred stock, 4% dividend, issued at par	5,000,000
Common equity	25,000,000
Total	$50,000,000

The market values of the securities are as follows: bonds, $22,000,000; preferred equity, $5,000,000; common equity, $33,000,000. The market has priced the bonds to yield 8.0%. (That is, 8.0% is the interest rate that discounts the annuity of contractual $2,000,000 interest payments and the $20,000,000 maturity value to the bonds' $22,000,000 fair value.) The firm's income tax rate is 35%, so the after-tax cost of debt is 5.2% [$(1 - 0.35) \times 8.0\%$]. Note that this rate is less than the coupon rate of 10% and that the market value of the debt is greater than its par value. Use of coupon rates and book values in this case would result in a higher cost of debt capital ($6.5\% = 0.65 \times 10.0\%$) but a smaller weight for debt in the weighted average. Assuming that the dividend on the preferred stock is not tax deductible, its cost is the dividend rate of 4.0% because it is selling for par value. The equity capital has a market beta of 0.9. Assuming a risk-free interest rate of 6.0% and a market premium of 7.0%, the cost of equity capital is 12.3% [$6.0\% + (0.9 \times 7.0\%)$]. The calculation of the weighted-average cost of capital is as follows:

Security	Market Value	Weight	After-Tax Cost	Weighted Average
Long-term debt	$22,000,000	37%	5.2%	1.92%
Preferred equity	5,000,000	8	4.0%	0.32
Common equity	33,000,000	55	12.3%	6.77
Total	$60,000,000	100%		9.01%

Computing the Weighted-Average Cost of Capital Iteratively

The preceding discussion reveals circular reasoning in computing weighted-average costs of capital for valuation purposes. Analysts use the market values of debt and equity to compute the weighted-average cost of capital, which is used in turn to compute the value of the debt and equity in the firm. This is circular reasoning because you need to know the market values to determine the weights but need to know the weights to determine the weighted-average cost of capital to use in estimating firm value. In practice, you can use two approaches to deal with this circularity. One approach assumes that the firm will maintain a target debt-to-equity structure in the future based on benchmarks such as the firm's past debt-to-equity ratios, the firm's stated strategy with respect to financial leverage, or industry averages. The other approach computes iteratively the weighted-average cost of capital and the value of debt and equity capital until the weights and the values converge.

Suppose that you need to compute the weighted-average cost of capital and the market value of equity for a firm for which no market or fair value data are available. Also suppose that the firm has outstanding debt with a book value of $40 million. The firm recently issued this debt, and it carries a stated rate of 8.0%, so you can assume that this is a reliable measure of the cost of debt capital. The firm faces a 35% tax rate. The book value of equity is $60 million. Similar firms in the same industry with comparable risks have a market beta of 1.2. Using the same risk-free rate and market risk premium as in the prior example, the cost of equity capital is 14.4% [6.0% + (1.2 × 7.0%)]. The first estimate of the weighted-average cost of capital is as follows:

Security	Amount	Weight	After-Tax Cost	Weighted Average
Debt	$ 40,000,000	40%	5.2%	2.08%
Common equity	60,000,000	60	14.4%	8.64
Total	$100,000,000	100%		10.72%

After using the 10.72% weighted-average cost of capital to discount the free cash flows to present value, you determine that the firm's equity value is roughly $120 million (calculations not shown). Therefore, the values and weights you used to compute the weighted-average cost of capital are inconsistent with your value estimates for equity. Your first-iteration estimates placed too much weight on debt and too little weight on equity. You should use the revised estimate of the value of equity to recompute the weighted-average cost of capital and then recompute the value of the firm. Using the revised estimates produces a weighted-average cost of capital estimate as follows:

Security	Amount	Weight	After-Tax Cost	Weighted Average
Debt	$ 40,000,000	25%	5.2%	1.30%
Common equity	120,000,000	75	14.4%	10.80
Total	$160,000,000	100%		12.10%

You should then use the revised estimate of the weighted-average cost of capital of 12.10% to recompute the value of equity once again and then iterate this process until your values of debt and equity converge with your weights of debt and equity.

Computing the Weighted-Average Cost of Capital for PepsiCo

PepsiCo's balance sheet (Appendix A) at the end of 2012 shows interest-bearing debt from short-term obligations of $4,815 million and long-term debt obligations of $23,544 million, totaling $28,359 million. Recall that Chapter 10 used information disclosed in Note 9, "Debt Obligations and Commitments" (Appendix A), to assess stated interest rates on PepsiCo's interest-bearing debt. In 2012, PepsiCo's outstanding debt carries a weighted-average interest rate of approximately 3.65%. In Note 10, "Financial Instruments" (Appendix A), PepsiCo discloses that the fair value of outstanding debt obligations at the end of 2012 is $30,500 million. Thus, PepsiCo has experienced an unrealized (and unrecognized) loss of $2,141 million ($28,359 million − $30,500 million) on its debt capital. This unrealized loss is surprising because the financing activities section of PepsiCo's statement of cash flows (Appendix A) reveals that PepsiCo issued a total of $15,450 million in new outstanding long-term debt over 2010–2012 at prevailing market rates. The unrealized loss implies that the firm's prior issues of outstanding long-term fixed-rate debt must carry stated rates of interest that now exceed prevailing market yields, which at the end of 2012 are at relatively low levels. Based on the fact that a significant portion of PepsiCo's outstanding debt obligations were recently issued, Chapter 10 projected that PepsiCo's cost of debt capital will continue to approximate 3.65% in Year +1 and beyond. We use the current fair value (as a proxy for market value) of PepsiCo's debt for weighting purposes. In Note 5, "Income Taxes" (Appendix A), PepsiCo discloses that the combined average federal, state, and foreign tax rate is 25.2% in 2012. Chapter 10 projected that PepsiCo will face average tax rates of roughly 27% in Year +1 and beyond. Therefore, we will assume the tax rate applicable to PepsiCo's interest expense deductions will be the effective 27% rate rather than the statutory federal rate of 35%. These projections imply that PepsiCo faces an after-tax cost of debt capital of 2.66% [3.65 × (1 − 0.270)].

PepsiCo also has a net *negative* balance of $123 million in preferred stock on the 2012 balance sheet. Chapter 10 projected that PepsiCo will retire the remaining outstanding preferred stock during Year +1 and not issue any additional preferred stock in future years. Therefore, we include no preferred stock in the computation of PepsiCo's weighted-average cost of capital.

PepsiCo's 2012 balance sheet also reports $105 million in equity capital attributable to noncontrolling interests. Chapter 10 projected that noncontrolling interests would earn a 10% rate of return, so we will use that as an estimate of the cost of capital for noncontrolling interests.

Recall that earlier in this chapter we used the CAPM to determine that PepsiCo faces a 7.50% cost of equity capital. At the end of 2012, PepsiCo had 1,544 million shares outstanding and a share price of $68.43, for a total market capital of common equity of $105,656 million.

Bringing these costs of debt and equity capital together, we compute PepsiCo's weighted-average cost of capital to be 6.420% as follows (allow for rounding):

Capital	Value Basis	Amount	Weight	After-Tax Cost of Capital	Weighted-Average Component
Debt	Fair	$ 30,500	22.38%	2.66%	0.596%
Common Equity	Market	105,656	77.54	7.50%	5.816
Noncontrolling Interests	Book	105	0.08	10.0%	0.008
Total		$136,261	100.00%		6.420%

This is just an initial estimate of PepsiCo's weighted-average cost of capital. As described earlier, the weighted-average cost of capital must be computed iteratively until the weights used are consistent with the present values of debt and equity capital.

In this chapter, we only use our estimate of PepsiCo's equity cost of capital to compute the dividends-based valuation model. However, in Chapter 12 we use PepsiCo's weighted-average cost of capital to compute the free-cash-flows-based valuation model. We turn next to the rationale and basic concepts of the dividends-based valuation approach.

Dividends-Based Valuation: Rationale and Basic Concepts

LO 11-4

Explain the rationale and basic concepts behind the dividends-based valuation approach, including the relation between cash flows to the investor versus cash flows reinvested in the firm.

Dividends are the most fundamental expected future payoffs to use to value shares because they represent the distribution of wealth from the firm to the shareholders. The equity shareholder invests cash to purchase the share and then receives cash in the form of dividends as the payoffs from holding the share, including the final "liquidating" dividend when the investor sells the share. In dividends-based valuation, we define *dividends* broadly to include *all* cash flows between the firm and the common equity shareholders. Therefore, in valuation, "dividends" encompass all cash flows from the firm to shareholders through periodic dividend payments, stock buy-backs, and the liquidating dividend, as well as cash flows from the shareholders to the firm when the firm issues shares (in a sense, *negative* dividends).

The rationale for using expected dividends in valuation is twofold:

1. Cash is the primary medium of exchange for consumption, which is the ultimate source of value. When individuals and firms invest cash in an economic resource, they forgo current consumption in favor of future consumption. Cash is the medium of exchange that will permit them to consume various goods and services in the future. An investment has value because of its ability to provide future cash flows. Dividends measure the cash that investors ultimately receive from investing in an equity share.
2. Dividends are paid in cash, and cash serves as a measurable common denominator for comparing the future benefits of alternative investment opportunities. One might compare investment opportunities involving a bond, a stock, or real estate, but comparing these alternatives requires a common measuring unit of their future benefits. The future cash flows derived from them serve that function.

As a practical matter, however, quarterly or annual dividend payment amounts are arbitrary, established by a dividend policy set by the firm's managers and board of directors. Periodic dividend payments typically do not vary closely with firm performance each period. Some firms do not pay any regular periodic dividends, particularly young, high-growth firms. For most firms, the final liquidating dividend plays an important role, usually representing a large proportion of firm value in a dividends-based valuation. The final liquidating dividend can arise when the firm liquidates its assets and returns all of the capital to shareholders, when another firm acquires all of the outstanding shares of the firm in a merger or acquisition transaction, or when shareholders liquidate their investment by selling shares. Therefore, to value a firm's shares using dividends, one must forecast dividends over the life of the firm (or the expected length of time the share will be held), including the final liquidating dividend (that is, the future price at which shares will be retired, acquired, or sold). Thus, the analyst faces the challenge of needing to forecast the value of shares in the future at the time of the liquidating dividend in order to value the shares today.

Dividends-Based Valuation Concepts

This section describes and illustrates key concepts in dividends-based valuation, first presenting simple examples involving a single project and then confronting conceptual measurement issues regarding dividends to the investor versus cash flows to the firm, and nominal versus real dividends. Later in the chapter, we apply this approach to a complex and realistic example involving the valuation of **PepsiCo**.

Dividends Valuation for a Single-Asset Firm

For the following examples, make these assumptions:

- The firm consists of a single asset that will generate pretax net cash flows of $2 million per year forever.
- The income tax rate is 40%.
- After making debt service payments and paying taxes, the firm pays dividends to distribute any remaining cash flows to the equity shareholders each year.

Example: Value of Common Equity in an All-Equity Firm

For this example, make the following additional assumptions:

- Equity shareholders have financed the asset entirely with $10 million of equity capital.
- The cost of equity capital is 10%.

The value of the firm to the shareholders can be determined using the present value of dividends for common equity shareholders. The dividends each year will be as follows:

Net pretax cash flow for all debt and equity capital	$2,000,000
Interest paid on debt	(0)
Income taxes (0.40 × $2,000,000)	(800,000)
Dividends for common equity shareholders	$1,200,000

The value to the shareholders of the common equity in the firm is $12,000,000 ($1,200,000/0.10). Dividing by the discount rate is appropriate because the $1,200,000 annual dividend for common equity is a *perpetuity*. This investment is worth $12,000,000 to those shareholders (a gain of $2,000,000 over their initial $10,000,000 investment).

Example: Value of Common Equity in a Firm with Debt Financing

Assume the same original facts, but now make the following additional assumptions:

- The equity shareholders finance a portion of the investment in the asset with $4 million of equity capital.
- The firm finances the remainder of the asset using $6 million of debt capital.

- This amount of debt in the firm's capital structure does not alter substantially the risk of the firm to the equity investors, so they continue to require a 10% rate of return.
- The debt is issued at par, and it is less risky than equity; so the debtholders demand interest of only 6% each year, payable at the end of each year.
- Interest expense is deductible for income tax purposes.

Again, the value of the common equity investment can be determined using the present value of dividends for common equity shareholders. The dividend to common equity is as follows:

Net pretax cash flow for all debt and equity capital	$2,000,000
Interest paid on debt (0.06 × $6,000,000)	(360,000)
Income taxes [0.40 × ($2,000,000 − $360,000)]	(656,000)
Dividends for common equity shareholders	$ 984,000

Assuming that the firm will pay this amount of dividend each year in perpetuity, the value of the common equity to the shareholders in the firm is $9,840,000 ($984,000/0.10). Note that in this example, the present value of the gain to the common equity shareholders in excess of their initial investment is $5,840,000 ($9,840,000 − $4,000,000). In this example, the gain to the shareholders is larger than in the previous example by $3,840,000 ($5,840,000 − $2,000,000) because:

- The debt capital is less expensive than the equity capital (6% rather than 10% on $6,000,000 of debt financing), creating $2,400,000 of value for equity shareholders from capital structure leverage {$6,000,000 × [(0.10 − 0.06)/0.10]}.
- The net tax savings from interest expense creates $1,440,000 of value for equity shareholders [($800,000 − $656,000)/0.10, or, alternatively, ($360,000 interest deduction × 0.40 tax rate)/0.10].
- We assume that the amount of debt in the capital structure did not alter the discount rate for equity.

Example: Value of More Risky Common Equity in a Firm with Debt Financing

Now make the same assumptions as the preceding example except assume that by changing the capital structure to 60% debt and 40% equity, the firm becomes more risky to the equity investors and they demand a 15% rate of return rather than 10%. Under these assumptions, the value of the common equity to the investors in the firm will be $6,560,000 ($984,000/0.15). Note that in this example, the present value of the gain to the common equity investors in excess of their initial investment falls to $2,560,000 ($6,560,000 − $4,000,000). Because of the increased risk, the investors demand a higher rate of return, so the value for equity investors from the net tax savings from interest expense falls to $960,000 [($800,000 − $656,000)/0.15] and the value for equity investors from capital structure leverage falls to $1,600,000 ($2,560,000 − $960,000).[8]

---

[8]The lower value to equity investors from capital structure leverage is the net result of two effects. First, the increased risk of the firm causes the equity investors to increase the discount rate from 10% to 15%, which would (if considered in isolation) cause the value of the project to fall to $8,000,000 ($1,200,000/0.15), which would imply a $2,000,000 loss on the investors' $10,000,000 investment. Second, the debt capital is less expensive than the equity capital, creating $3,600,000 of value for equity investors from capital structure leverage {[$6,000,000 × (0.15 − 0.06)]/0.15}. The net result is $1,600,000 of value to equity investors from capital structure leverage, net of the incremental effects of risk.

Dividends to the Investor versus Cash Flows to the Firm

The beginning of this chapter asserted that you can use dividends expected to be paid to the investor or the free cash flows expected to be generated by the firm (that will ultimately be paid to the investor) as equivalent approaches to measure value-relevant expected payoffs to shareholders. Will using net cash flows into the firm result in the same estimate of value as using dividends paid out of the firm? Cash flows paid to the investor via dividends and free cash flows to the firm that are available for common equity shareholders will differ each period to the extent that the firm reinvests a portion (or all) of the cash flows generated. However, if the firm generates a rate of return on reinvested free cash flow equal to the discount rate used by the investor (that is, the cost of equity capital), either set of payoffs (dividends or free cash flows) will yield the same valuation of a firm's shares at a point in time. To demonstrate this equivalence, consider the following scenarios.

Example: Dividend Policy Irrelevance with 100% Payout

A firm expects to generate free cash flows of 15% annually on invested equity capital for the rest of its life, which is likely to continue for an indefinitely long period of time into the future (until $t = n$). Equity investors in this firm require a 15% return each year, considering the riskiness of the firm. Assume that the firm pays out 100% of the free cash flows each year as dividends to the shareholders (i.e., free cash flows generated by the firm = cash dividends distributed to the shareholders each period). Thus, each dollar of capital committed by the investors has a present value of future cash flows equal to one dollar. That is, over an indefinitely long period of time into the future,

$$\$1 = \sum_{t=1}^{n} \frac{\$0.15}{(1.15)^t}$$

Example: Dividend Policy Irrelevance with Zero Payout

Assume the same facts as the prior example except that the firm pays out none of the free cash flows as a dividend. The firm retains the $0.15 free cash flow on each dollar of capital and reinvests it in projects expected to earn a 15% return per year. In this case, the investor receives no periodic dividends and receives cash only when the investor sells the shares or the firm liquidates at date $t = n$. By the terminal date, n periods in the future, each dollar of capital invested in the firm today will have earned a compound rate of return of 15%, equal to the required rate of return. In this case also, each dollar of invested capital has a present value of future cash flows equal to one dollar, exactly the same as in the full payout dividend discount example above. That is,

$$\$1 = \frac{(\$1.15)^n}{(1.15)^n}$$

Example: Dividend Policy Irrelevance with Partial Payout

Assume the same facts as the preceding example except that the firm pays out 25% of the free cash flow each period as a dividend and reinvests the other 75% in projects expected to generate a return of 15%. In this case also, each dollar of invested capital has a present value of future cash flows equal to one dollar, the same as in the two preceding examples. Conceptually,

$$\$1 = \sum_{t=1}^{n} \frac{(0.25)(\$0.15)}{(1.15)^t} + \frac{(0.75)(\$1.15)^n}{(1.15)^n}$$

These three examples illustrate the *irrelevance* of the firm's dividend policy in valuation, assuming the firm reinvests cash flows to earn the investors' required rate of return.[9]

Quick Check

- The same valuation should arise whether you discount
  - the expected dividends to the investor, or
  - the expected free cash flows to the firm that are available to pay future dividends to equity shareholders.
- Further, the same valuation should arise whether
  - the firm pays all of its cash flows as a dividend,
  - reinvests all cash flows to earn the investors' required rate of return, or
  - pays a portion of cash flows in dividends each period and reinvests the remaining cash flows to earn the investors' required rate of return.

Nominal versus Real Dividends

Changes in general price levels (that is, inflation or deflation) cause the purchasing power of the monetary unit to change over time. Should the valuation use projected nominal dividends, which include the effects of inflation or deflation, or real dividends, which filter out the effects of changes in general purchasing power?[10] The valuation of an investment in an economic resource should be the same whether nominal or real dividend amounts are used as long as the discount rate used is the nominal or real rate of return, respectively, that is consistent with the dividend measure. That is, if projected dividends are nominal and include the effects of changes in general purchasing power of the monetary unit, the discount rate should be nominal and include an inflation component. If projected dividends are real amounts that filter out the effects of general price changes, the discount rate should be a real rate of return, excluding the inflation component.

Example: Nominal versus Real Dividends

A firm owns an asset that it expects to sell one year from today for $115.5 million. The firm expects the general price level to increase 10% during this period. The real interest rate is 5%. The nominal discount rate should be 15.5% to measure the compound effects

---

[9]Merton Miller and Franco Modigliani, "Dividend Policy, Growth and the Valuation of Shares," *Journal of Business* (October 1961), pp. 411–433. Penman and Sougiannis test empirically the replacement property of dividends for future earnings and find support for the irrelevance of dividend policy in valuation. See Stephen H. Penman and Theodore Sougiannis, "The Dividend Displacement Property and the Substitution of Anticipated Earnings for Dividends in Equity Valuation," *The Accounting Review* (January 1997), pp. 1–21.

[10]Note that the issue here is not with specific price changes of a firm's particular assets, liabilities, revenues, and expenses. These specific price changes affect projections of the firm's dividends, cash flows, and earnings and should enter into the valuation of the firm. The issue is whether some portion, all, or more than all of the specific price changes represent simply an economy-wide change in the purchasing power of the monetary unit, which should not affect the value of a firm.

of the real rate of interest and inflation $[0.155 = (1.10 \times 1.05) - 1]$. Discounting nominal or real dividends, the value of the asset to the firm today is $100 million, as shown:

Nominal Dividends	$\times$	Discount Rate Including Expected Inflation	$=$	Value
$115.5 million	$\times$	$1/(1.05 \times 1.10)$	$=$	$100 million

Real Dividends	$\times$	Discount Rate Excluding Expected Inflation	$=$	Value
$115.5 million/1.10	$\times$	$1/1.05$	$=$	$100 million

Both examples derive the value of the equity of the firm by computing the present value of the dividends to common equity shareholders. As a practical matter, costs of capital and expected returns are typically quoted in nominal terms, so analysts usually find it more straightforward to discount nominal dividends using nominal discount rates.

LO 11-5

After tackling some of the more advanced concepts involved in dividends valuation, demonstrate how to measure dividends, establish a forecast horizon, and value continuing dividends.

Dividends-Based Valuation: Advanced Concepts

In this section, we explain and demonstrate three advanced concepts that are essential in dividends valuation:

1. Measuring dividends
2. Determining the forecast horizon
3. Projecting and valuing continuing dividends

In the sections that follow, we bring all of these concepts together in the dividends-based valuation model, and then apply it to value **PepsiCo**.

Measuring Dividends

An important step in this process is, of course, measuring the dividends that determine share value. The dividends-based approach values the common equity in a firm by measuring the present value of all net cash flows from the firm to the equity shareholders. Therefore, the objective in dividends valuation is to measure the present value of *total net dividends* for common equity shareholders, including *all* of the cash flows the shareholders will receive from holding the shares.

Total net dividends encompass cash flows from the firm to common equity shareholders through periodic (quarterly or annual) dividend payments, according to the firm's dividend payout policy. Total net dividends also include cash flows to common equity shareholders through stock buybacks. Further, cash flows from the shareholders to the firm when the firm issues shares are *negative* dividends. Thus, to measure total value-relevant net dividends that encompass all of the cash flows from the firm to common equity shareholders each period, you should include the following three components:

+ Quarterly or annual ordinary dividend payments to common equity shareholders
+ Net cash flows to shareholders from common equity share repurchases
− Net cash flows from shareholders through common equity issues

= Total dividends to common equity shareholders

An alternative and equivalent way of computing total net dividends relies on how shareholders' equity is accounted for under the assumption of *clean surplus accounting*. Under clean surplus accounting, income must include *all* revenues, expenses, gains, and losses generated by the firm for common equity shareholders. Under U.S. GAAP and IFRS, clean surplus income is measured by comprehensive income (that is, net income plus all of the unrealized gains and losses included in other comprehensive income). Under clean surplus accounting, book value of equity also increases or decreases as a result of direct capital transactions between the firm and the common equity shareholders, such as periodic dividend payments, share issues, and share repurchases.[11]

The general principles of clean surplus accounting represent common equity as follows:

$$BV_t = BV_{t-1} + CI_t - D_t$$

where: BV_t denotes the book value of equity at the end of year t

   CI denotes comprehensive income for year t

   D denotes net direct capital transactions between the firm and common shareholders (dividend payments, stock issues, and stock repurchases) during year t.

To isolate all of the net cash flows between the firm and the shareholders during year t, simply rearrange the equation as follows:

$$D_t = CI_t + BV_{t-1} - BV_t$$

Therefore, total dividends used in valuation should equal comprehensive income each year, adjusted for the change in the book value of common equity as a result of direct capital transactions.

Measuring Dividends for PepsiCo

This section illustrates the dividends-based valuation approach using **PepsiCo**. We derive our dividends expectations from our projected financial statements for PepsiCo in Chapter 10. We projected that (amounts in millions, allow for rounding):

- PepsiCo would pay Year +1 common equity dividends equal to 55% of net income available to common shareholders, amounting to $3,387 million [0.55 × ($6,168.0 net income − $10.5 income attributable to noncontrolling interests)].
- PepsiCo's common stock and additional paid-in capital would remain roughly 5.6% of total assets. Our projections expect common stock and additional paid-in capital will grow from $4,204 million to $4,249 million by the end of Year +1, implying new stock issues of $45 million (in effect, negative dividends of −$45 million).
- PepsiCo would engage in net repurchases of common shares totaling $3,150 million ($3,000 + $150) in Year +1, as follows:
  - PepsiCo would pay $3,000 million to repurchase common shares, net of any shares reissued for stock options exercises.
  - PepsiCo would use treasury share repurchases as the flexible financial account to balance the balance sheet, so an additional $150 million in capital would be distributed to common equity shareholders through additional share repurchases.

---

[11]Also assume that direct capital transactions between the firm and common equity shareholders are arms-length exchanges of fair value. That is, the firm does not generate gains or losses from trading in its own shares because the shares are issued or repurchased for fair value.

Bringing these components together, we project that total value-relevant dividends to common equity shareholders in Year +1 will be as follows (in millions; allow for rounding):

Periodic dividend payments	$3,387
Common stock issues	(45)
Net purchases of treasury stock	3,150
Total dividends to common equity shareholders	$6,491

This computation can be reconciled with the clean surplus accounting approach as follows: The Year +1 forecast of comprehensive income is $6,158 million. Total book value of common shareholders' equity (before noncontrolling interests) is $22,417 million at the beginning of Year +1 and $22,020 million at the end of Year +1. Using the clean surplus accounting approach, total dividends in Year +1 are as follows (in millions; allow for rounding):

$$D_t = CI_t + BV_{t-1} - BV_t = \$6,158 + \$22,417 - \$22,020 = \$6,554$$

Recall, however, that book value of equity was reduced in Year +1 by the $63 million of the liquidating dividend to repurchase and retire the outstanding preferred stock. After deducting this amount (which pertains to preferred rather than common shareholders), the projected net amount of dividends to common shareholders using the clean surplus approach is identical to the amount computed above, as follows (in millions):

$$\$6,554 - \$63 = \$6,491$$

Exhibit 11.5 demonstrates these computations for Years +1 through +5.

Exhibit 11.5

Computation of PepsiCo's Total Dividends for the Dividends-Based Valuation Approach (amounts in millions, allow for rounding)

	Computing Total Dividends Using Components				
	Year +1	**Year +2**	**Year +3**	**Year +4**	**Year +5**
Dividends paid to common shareholders	$3,387	$3,507	$3,629	$3,835	$3,885
Less: Common stock issues	(45)	(152)	(154)	(225)	(94)
Plus: Common stock repurchases	3,150	2,624	2,792	2,852	3,217
Total dividends to common equity	$6,491	$5,979	$6,267	$6,462	$7,008

	Computing Total Dividends Using Clean Surplus Accounting				
	Year +1	**Year +2**	**Year +3**	**Year +4**	**Year +5**
Comprehensive income	$ 6,158	$ 6,377	$ 6,598	$ 6,972	$ 7,064
Less: Retirement of preferred shares	(63)	(0)	(0)	(0)	(0)
Comprehensive income available for common equity	$ 6,095	$ 6,377	$ 6,598	$ 6,972	$ 7,064
Plus: Beginning book value of common equity	22,417	22,020	22,418	22,749	23,260
Less: Ending book value of common equity	(22,020)	(22,418)	(22,749)	(23,260)	(23,316)
Total dividends to common equity	$ 6,491	$ 5,979	$ 6,267	$ 6,462	$ 7,008

Selecting a Forecast Horizon

For how many future years should you project future payoffs from an investment? The correct answer is the expected life of the investment being valued. This life is a finite number of years for an investment in a machine, a building, or any resource with limits to its physical existence or a financial instrument with a finite stated maturity (such as a bond, mortgage, or lease). In equity valuation, however, the resource to be valued is an ownership claim on the firm, which has an indefinite expected life. Therefore, in the case of an equity security, you must project future dividends that, in theory, extend indefinitely.

Of course, as a practical matter, you cannot precisely predict a firm's dividends very many years into the future. Therefore, analysts commonly develop specific forecasts of dividends over an explicit finite forecast horizon (perhaps five or ten years) depending on the industry, the maturity of the firm, and the expected growth and predictability of the firm's business activities. After the finite forecast horizon, analysts then typically use general steady-state growth assumptions to project the future dividends that will persist indefinitely. Therefore, you will find it desirable to develop specific forecasts of income statements, balance sheets, and cash flows over an explicit forecast horizon that extends until the point at which you expect a firm's growth pattern will settle into steady-state equilibrium, during which time you can expect dividends will grow at a steady, predictable rate indefinitely.

Selecting a forecast horizon involves trade-offs. You can make reasonably reliable projections over longer forecast horizons for stable and mature firms. Projections for such firms, like **PepsiCo** demonstrated in Chapter 10, capture relatively steady-state operations. On the other hand, it is more difficult to develop reliable projections over long forecast horizons for young high-growth firms, like **Tesla Motors**, because their future operating performance is more uncertain. This difficulty is exacerbated by the fact that a much higher proportion of the value of young growth firms will be achieved in distant future years, after they reach their potential steady-state profitability. Thus, you face the dilemma of depending most heavily on long-run forecasts for young growth firms for which long-run projections are most uncertain and most difficult to project. The forecasting and valuation process is particularly difficult for growth firms when you project the near-term dividends will be zero or negative, as is common for rapidly growing firms that finance growth by issuing common stock. In this case, the firm's value depends entirely on dividends to be generated in years far into the future.

Unfortunately, there is no way to avoid this dilemma. The predictive accuracy of your dividend forecasts many years into the future is likely to be limited for even the most stable and predictable firms. You must recognize that forecasts and value estimates for all firms, but especially growth firms, have a high degree of uncertainty and estimation risk. To mitigate this uncertainty and estimation risk, you should adhere to the following coaching tips:

- Diligently and comprehensively follow all six steps of the analysis framework. By thoroughly analyzing the firm's industry and strategy, the firm's accounting quality, and the firm's financial performance and risk, you will have more information to use to develop long-term forecasts that are as reliable as possible.
- To the extent possible, directly confront the problem of long-term uncertainty by developing specific projections of dividends derived from projected income statements and balance sheets that extend five or ten years into the future, at which point the firm may reasonably be projected to reach steady-state growth.
- Assess the sensitivity of the forecast projections and value estimates across the reasonable range of growth assumptions.

Projecting and Valuing Continuing Dividends

This section describes techniques to project continuing dividends using a steady-state growth rate beyond the explicit forecast horizon and to measure the present value of continuing dividends. We refer to them as *continuing dividends* because they reflect the cash flows from the firm to the common equity shareholders continuing into the long-run future.

In some circumstances, however, you may not find it necessary to forecast dividends continuing beyond the explicit forecast horizon if you can reliably predict that the share will receive a future liquidating dividend. In such circumstances, the liquidating dividend is the final cash flow to the shareholder. The liquidating dividend might arise when the firm liquidates its assets at the end of its business life and distributes the proceeds to shareholders to retire their shares. Alternatively, the liquidating dividend might arise when a firm's shares are acquired by another firm in a merger or acquisition transaction, or when the shareholder sells the share, creating a liquidating dividend from the selling price.

Projecting Continuing Dividends

If you cannot reliably predict whether or when your shares will receive a liquidating dividend, then you need to forecast dividends over an explicit forecast horizon until the point at which you expect the firm to mature into steady-state growth, and you can assume dividends will grow at a constant steady-state rate. You can project the long-run sustainable growth rate (denoted as g) in future continuing dividends to be positive, negative, or zero. Sustainable growth in dividends will be driven by long-run expectations for inflation, the industry's sales, the economy in general, and the firm's strategy. You should select a growth rate that captures realistic long-run expectations for Year $T+1$ and beyond.

Unfortunately, a shortcut some analysts sometimes use (and a common error some analysts make) in computing the continuing dividends for Year $T+1$ is to multiply the dividends for Year T by one plus the growth rate $(1 + g)$ instead of deriving the Year $T+1$ dividends from the projected Year $T+1$ income statement and balance sheet. If you want to avoid this error and compute internally consistent and identical estimates of firm value using dividends, free cash flows, and earnings, you should *not* project dividends for Year $T+1$ by simply multiplying dividends for Year T by $(1 + g)$. Doing so ignores the necessary growth in all of the elements of the balance sheet and the income statement, which can introduce inconsistent forecast assumptions for dividends, cash flows, and earnings. Even if you simply project that Year $T+1$ dividends, cash flows, and earnings will grow at an identical rate $(1 + g)$, you may obtain inconsistent value estimates if Year T dividends, cash flows, and earnings are not internally consistent with their long-run continuing amounts.

Example: Projecting Continuing Dividends Incorrectly

Suppose you develop the following forecasts for the firm in Year T–1 and Year T:

	Assets	=	Liabilities	+	Shareholders' Equity
Year T–1 balances	$100	=	$60	+	$40
Net income	+ 20				+ 20
New borrowing	+ 6		+ 6		
Dividends paid	− 10				− 10
Year T balances	$116	=	$66	+	$50

Suppose you project that the firm will grow at a steady-state rate of 10% in Year T+1 and thereafter. If you simply (and erroneously) project Year T dividends to grow by 10%, the Year T+1 projection will be only $11 ($10 Year T dividends × 1.10). Then, if you project that future earnings will grow at the same 10% steady-state rate, the projected Year T+1 earnings would be $22 ($20 Year T net income × 1.10). Even though you have used the same growth rate, you have used inconsistent assumptions. As we show in the next section, if assets, liabilities, and shareholders' equity all increase by 10%, then dividends and net income cannot simultaneously increase by 10%; the clean surplus relationship will not hold. This error will force the estimated value of the firm based on dividends to be lower than the value estimates based on earnings.

Example: Projecting Continuing Dividends Correctly

To project continuing dividends in Year T+1 correctly, you should derive the continuing dividends from the projected Year T+1 income statement and balance sheet. To do so correctly, you should use the expected long-run growth rate (g) to project all of the items of the Year T+1 income statement and balance sheet. That is, you should project each item on the Year T+1 income statement and balance sheet by multiplying each item for Year T times $(1 + g)$. You can then derive Year T+1 dividends using clean surplus accounting as follows:

$$D_{T+1} = CI_{T+1} + BV_T - BV_{T+1}$$

Comprehensive income and book value in Year T+1 are therefore, $CI_{T+1} = CI_T \times (1 + g)$ and $BV_{T+1} = BV_T \times (1 + g)$. Substitute these terms into the D_{T+1} equation, as follows:

$$D_{T+1} = [CI_T \times (1 + g)] + BV_T - [BV_T \times (1 + g)]$$

You must impose the long-run growth rate assumption $(1 + g)$ uniformly on the Year T+1 income statement and balance sheet projections to derive the dividends for Year T+1 correctly. In the long run, assuming that the firm itself will grow at a steady-state rate, all of the elements of the firm—revenues, expenses, income, assets, liabilities, shareholders' equity, cash flows, and therefore, dividends—will grow at the same rate. By applying a uniform growth rate across all of the items of the income statement and balance sheet, you will achieve internally consistent steady-state growth across all of the your projections, keeping the balance sheet in balance throughout the continuing forecast horizon, and keeping growth in dividends, cash flows, and earnings internally consistent with each other.

Returning to the example, to compute continuing dividends in Year T+1 correctly, you should project Year T+1 net income, assets, liabilities, and shareholders' equity to grow by 10% each and then compute Year T+1 continuing dividends as follows:

	Assets	=	Liabilities	+	Shareholders' Equity
Year T balances	$ 116	=	$ 66	+	$ 50
Growth	×1.10		×1.10		×1.10
Year T+1 balances	$127.6	=	$72.6	+	$ 55

The projected net income would be $22 ($20 × 1.10). The Year T+1 dividends projection would therefore be $17 ($22 net income + $50 beginning shareholders' equity — $55 ending shareholders' equity). Note that the correct projected Year T+1 dividend amount of $17 is substantially larger than the erroneous $11 dividend projection in the previous section. Also note that the $17 Year T+1 dividend is substantially larger than the $10 dividend amount for Year T. The reason the firm can begin to pay larger dividends in Year T+1 and beyond is that the firm's long-run growth rate of 10% is lower than the Year T growth rate in assets (16%) and shareholders' equity (25%) shown in the explicit financial statement forecasts in the previous section; thus, this firm will not need to reinvest as much of its earnings to fund growth and will be able to pay larger dividends in Year T+1 and beyond.

In projecting continuing dividends in Year T+1 and beyond, analysts assume that the firm will settle into a long-run sustainable growth rate. Often analysts assume that the firm's long-run sustainable growth rate will be consistent with long-run growth in the economy, on the order of 3%–5%. For firms that have been growing faster than that in the years leading up to Year T+1, the long-run sustainable growth rate implies that the firm will maintain a lower growth rate in assets and equity and thus will be able to pay out substantially larger dividends. By projecting Year T+1 net income, assets, and equity using the long-run sustainable growth rate, it is possible to solve for the long-run sustainable dividends the firm can pay. The continuing dividend amount derived for Year T+1 may be significantly larger than the amounts the firm actually paid during its higher-growth-rate years. The Year T+1 dividend amount reflects the firm's transition from a high rate of reinvestment to finance high growth in assets to lower reinvestment for lower growth.

Computing Continuing Value

One you have computed continuing dividends for Year T+1, you can compute continuing value (sometimes called terminal value) of continuing dividends in Year T+1 and beyond using the perpetuity-with-growth valuation model. At the end of Year T, assume that the continuing value of the common equity of the firm (denoted as V_T) will equal the present value of all expected future continuing dividends in Year T+1 and beyond, which can be expressed as follows:

$$V_T = \sum_{t=1}^{\infty} \frac{D_{T+t}}{(1 + R_E)^t}$$

As described in the preceding section, we project the Year T+1 dividend by assuming that each line item on the Year T income statement and balance sheet will grow at the long-run steady state growth rate $(1 + g)$ and then deriving the Year T+1 dividend. As shown above, we assume that accounting for the book value of the shareholders' equity (BV) follows the general principle of adding comprehensive income (CI) and subtracting dividends to common shareholders each period (that is, $BV_t = BV_{t-1} + CI_t - D_t$). Comprehensive income and book value in Year T+1 therefore equal $CI_{T+1} = CI_T \times (1 + g)$ and $BV_{T+1} = BV_T \times (1 + g)$. The D_{T+1} equation can then be rewritten as follows:

$$D_{T+1} = CI_{T+1} + BV_T - BV_{T+1} = [CI_T \times (1 + g)] + BV_T - [BV_T \times (1 + g)]$$

Assuming that D_{T+1} will grow in perpetuity at rate g, the firm can be valued at the end of Year T using the perpetuity-with-growth model, as follows:[12]

$$V_T = \sum_{t=1}^{\infty} \frac{D_{T+t}}{(1 + R_E)^t} = \frac{D_{T+t}}{(R_E - g)} = \frac{[CI_T \times (1 + g)] + BV_T - [BV_T \times (1 + g)]}{(R_E - g)}$$

---

[12]This formula is simply the algebraic simplification for the present value of a growing perpetuity.

Example: Valuing Continuing Dividends

Suppose you forecast that the dividends of a firm in Year +5 will be $30 million and that Year +5 earnings and cash flows also will be $30 million. For simplicity in this example, assume you expect that the firm's income statements and balance sheets will grow uniformly over the long run and, therefore, so will cash flows, earnings, and dividends. But you are uncertain about the steady-state long-run growth rate in Years +6 and beyond. You believe that the growth rate will most likely be zero but could reasonably fall in the range between +6% and −6% per year; so you derived the range of Year +6 dividends shown in the following table. Assuming a 15% cost of capital, the table shows the range of possible continuing values (in millions) for the firm in present value at the beginning of the continuing value period (that is, the beginning of Year +6) and in present value as of today; that is, the continuing value is discounted to today using a factor of $1/(1.15)^5$:

Dividends Year +5 (T)	Long-Run Growth Rate	Dividends Year +6 (T+1)	Perpetuity with Growth Factor	Present Value of Continuing Value as of: Beginning of Year +6 (T+1)	Today
$30.00	0%	$30.00	$1/(0.15 - 0.0)$ = 6.67	$200.00	$ 99.44
$30.00	+6%	$31.80	$1/(0.15 - 0.06)$ = 11.11	$353.30	$175.65
$30.00	−6%	$28.20	$1/(0.15 + 0.06)$ = 4.76	$134.23	$ 66.74

Analysts also can estimate continuing value using a multiple of dividends in the first year of the continuing value period. The following table shows the continuing value multiples using $1/(R - g)$ for various costs of equity capital and growth rates. The multiples increase with growth for a given cost of capital, and they decrease as the cost of capital increases for a given level of growth.

Continuing Value Multiples (i.e., Perpetuity with Growth Factors)						
	Long-Run Growth Rates					
Cost of Equity Capital	0%	2%	3%	4%	5%	6%
6%	16.67	25.00	33.33	50.00	100.00	N/A
8%	12.50	16.67	20.00	25.00	33.33	50.00
10%	10.00	12.50	14.29	16.67	20.00	25.00
12%	8.33	10.00	11.11	12.50	14.29	16.67
15%	6.67	7.69	8.33	9.09	10.00	11.11
18%	5.56	6.25	6.67	7.14	7.69	8.33
20%	5.00	5.56	5.88	6.25	6.67	7.14

The continuing value computation using the perpetuity-with-growth valuation model does not work when the growth rate equals or exceeds the discount rate (that is, when $g \geq R$) because the denominator in the computation is zero or negative and the resulting continuing value estimate is meaningless. In this case, you cannot use the perpetuity computation illustrated here. Instead, you must forecast dividend amounts for each year beyond the forecast horizon using the terminal period growth rate and then discount each year's dividends to present value using the discount rate. You also should reconsider whether it is realistic to expect the firm's dividend growth rate to exceed the discount rate (the expected rate of return) in perpetuity. This scenario can exist for some years, but is not likely to be sustainable indefinitely. Competition, technological change, new entrants into an industry, and similar dynamic factors eventually reduce growth rates.

An alternative approach for estimating the continuing value is to use the dividend multiples for comparable firms that currently trade in the market. You can identify comparable companies by studying characteristics such as industry, firm size and age, past growth rates in dividends, profitability, risk, and similar factors. Chapter 14 discusses valuation multiples in more depth.

Because of the uncertainty inherent in long-run growth rate forecasts and because continuing value amounts are commonly large proportions of value estimates, analysts should conduct sensitivity analysis to assess how sensitive the firm value estimate is to variations in the long-run growth assumption. For example, suppose you are valuing a young high-growth company and can reliably forecast dividends five years into the future. After that horizon, you expect the firm to grow at 6% per year, although this is highly uncertain, and long-run growth could range from −3% per year to as much as 9% per year. You should conduct sensitivity analysis on the projections and valuation, varying long-run growth across the range from −3% to 9% per year.

LO 11-6

The Dividends-Based Valuation Model

Bring all of the elements together to formulate the dividends-based valuation model.

This section presents the dividends-based valuation model that determines the value of common shareholders' equity in the firm. The sections following demonstrate how to implement the model using **PepsiCo**.

The dividends-based valuation model determines the value of common shareholders' equity in the firm (denoted as V_0) as the sum of the present value of all future dividends to shareholders over the life of the firm, which is indefinite. The dividends-based valuation model includes all-inclusive dividends (denoted as D) that encompass all of the net cash flows from the firm to shareholders through periodic dividend payments and stock buybacks and subtracts cash flows from the shareholders to the firm when the firm issues shares. We discount the stream of future dividends to present value using the required return on common equity capital in the firm (denoted as R_E). The following general model expresses the dividends valuation approach:

$$V_0 = \sum_{t=1}^{\infty} \frac{D_t}{(1 + R_E)^t} = \frac{D_1}{(1 + R_E)^1} + \frac{D_2}{(1 + R_E)^2} + \frac{D_3}{(1 + R_E)^3} + \dots$$

Suppose we can reliably forecast dividend amounts through Year T. At the end of Year T, we assume that the continuing value of the common equity of the firm (denoted as V_T) will equal the present value of all expected future continuing dividends in Year T+1 and beyond (a perpetuity of D_{T+1} in every year), which can be expressed as follows:

$$V_T = \sum_{t=1}^{\infty} \frac{D_{T+t}}{(1 + R_E)^t}$$

Thus, the value of the firm today can be expressed using periodic dividends over a finite horizon to Year T plus continuing value based on dividends in Year T+1 and beyond as follows:

$$V_0 = \sum_{t=1}^{\infty} \frac{D_t}{(1 + R_E)^t} = \frac{D_1}{(1 + R_E)^1} + \frac{D_2}{(1 + R_E)^2} + \frac{D_3}{(1 + R_E)^3} + \cdots \frac{D_T}{(1 + R_E)^T} + \frac{V_T}{(1 + R_E)^T}$$

This equation reveals that the estimate of value today (V_0) depends on the estimate of value in the future (V_T).

As described in the preceding section, we assume that accounting for book value of shareholders' equity (BV) follows the general principle of adding comprehensive income (CI) and subtracting dividends to common shareholders each period (that is, $BV_t = BV_{t-1} + CI_t - D_t$). We therefore project the Year T+1 dividend by assuming that each line item on the Year T income statement and balance sheet will grow at the expected long-run steady-state growth rate of the firm and then deriving the Year T+1 dividend as follows:

$$D_{T+1} = CI_{T+1} + BV_T - BV_{T+1} = [CI_T \times (1 + g)] + BV_T - [BV_T \times (1 + g)]$$

Assuming that D_{T+1} will grow in perpetuity at rate g, the firm can be valued at the end of Year T using the perpetuity-with-growth model as follows:

$$V_T = \sum_{t=1}^{\infty} \frac{D_{T+t}}{(1 + R_E)^t} = \frac{D_{T+1}}{(R_E - g)} = \frac{[CI_T \times (1 + g)] + BV_T - [BV_T \times (1 + g)]}{(R_E - g)}$$

Therefore, the dividends-based valuation model estimates the present value of common equity as follows:

$$V_0 = \sum_{t=1}^{\infty} \frac{D_t}{(1 + R_E)^t}$$

$$= \frac{D_1}{(1 + R_E)^1} + \frac{D_2}{(1 + R_E)^2} + \frac{D_3}{(1 + R_E)^3} + \cdots + \frac{D_T}{(1 + R_E)^T} + \frac{V_T}{(1 + R_E)^T}$$

$$= \frac{D_1}{(1 + R_E)^1} + \frac{D_2}{(1 + R_E)^2} + \frac{D_3}{(1 + R_E)^3} + \cdots + \frac{D_T}{(1 + R_E)^T} + \frac{[CI_T \times (1 + g)] + BV_T - [BV_T \times (1 + g)]}{(R_E - g) \times (1 + R_E)^T}$$

Applying the Dividends-Based Valuation Model to Value PepsiCo

LO 11-7

Apply the dividends valuation techniques to estimate firm value.

Applying the dividends-based valuation model to determine the value of the common shareholders' equity in a firm involves measuring the following three elements:

1. The discount rate (denoted as R_E in the valuation model) used to compute the present value of the future dividends.
2. The expected future dividends over the forecast horizon (denoted as D_t in periods $t=1$ through T in the valuation model).
3. The expected dividend at the final period of the forecast horizon, which we refer to as the *continuing dividend* (denoted as D_{T+1} in the valuation model) and a forecast of the long-run growth rate (denoted as g in the model) in the continuing dividend beyond the forecast horizon.

Prior sections of this chapter have discussed each of these elements. We now bring them all together to estimate the value for **PepsiCo** shares at the end of 2012.

Using the Dividends-Based Valuation Model to Value PepsiCo

At the end of 2012, trading in PepsiCo shares on the New York Stock Exchange closed at a *price* of $68.43 per share. But what is our best estimate of the *value* of a PepsiCo share? The valuation of PepsiCo shares uses the techniques described in this chapter and the forecasts developed in Chapter 10. The forecasts and valuation estimates are applied using the Forecasts and Valuation spreadsheets in FSAP (Appendix B).

PepsiCo's Dividends in Year +1 through Year +5

We estimate the present value of a share of common equity in PepsiCo at the end of 2012 (equivalently, the start of Year +1) using the risk-adjusted rate of return on Pepsi-Co's equity capital as the appropriate discount rate. A prior section of this chapter computed the PepsiCo cost of equity capital using the CAPM to be 7.5%. Exhibit 11.5 summarizes the computations of PepsiCo's projected dividends in Years +1 to +5. Discounting these future dividends using a discount rate of 7.5% yields a present value estimate of $25,977.2 million. The top portion of Exhibit 11.6 illustrates these computations.

PepsiCo's Continuing Dividends beyond Year +5

To compute the present value of PepsiCo's dividends continuing in Year +6 and beyond, we project that continuing dividends will grow at a 3% rate in perpetuity, consistent with long-run average growth in the economy. We forecast Year +6 dividends as follows:

$$
\begin{aligned}
D_6 &= [CI_5 \times (1 + g)] + BV_5 - [BV_5 \times (1 + g)] \\
&= [\$7,064 \text{ million} \times 1.03] + \$23,316 \text{ million} - [\$23,316 \text{ million} \times 1.03] \\
&= \$7,276 \text{ million} + \$23,316 \text{ million} - \$24,015 \text{ million} \\
&= \$6,576.6 \text{ million}
\end{aligned}
$$

We use the perpetuity-with-growth model to discount dividends in the continuing value period to present value as of the beginning of Year +6 (the beginning of the continuing value period) using PepsiCo's 7.5% cost of equity capital, as follows (allowing for rounding):

$$
\begin{aligned}
\text{Continuing Value}_0 &= D_6 \times [1/(R_E - g)] \\
&= \$6,576.6 \text{ million} \times [1/(0.075 - 0.030)] \\
&= \$6,576.6 \text{ million} \times 22.222 \\
&= \$146,147.6 \text{ million}
\end{aligned}
$$

We then discount the continuing value as of the beginning of Year +6 to present value, as follows (allow for rounding):

$$
\begin{aligned}
\text{Present Value of Continuing Value}_0 &= \$146,147.6 \text{ million} \times [1/(1 + R_E)^5] \\
&= \$146,147.6 \text{ million} \times [1/(1 + 0.075)^5] \\
&= \$146,147.6 \text{ million} \times 0.697 \\
&= \$101,800.3 \text{ million}
\end{aligned}
$$

Exhibit 11.6

Valuation of PepsiCo
Present Value of Dividends to Common Equity
Year +1 through Year +5 and Beyond
(allow for rounding)

	Valuation of Dividends in Year +1 through Year +5				
	Year +1	Year +2	Year +3	Year +4	Year +5
Total dividends to common equity (from Exhibit 11.5)	$ 6,491	$ 5,979	$ 6,267	$ 6,462	$ 7,008
Present value factors ($R_E = 7.50\%$)	0.930	0.865	0.805	0.749	0.697
Present value of dividends	$ 6,038.5	$5,173.9	$5,044.5	$4,828.8	$4,881.5
Sum of present value dividends, Years +1 through +5	$25,977.2				

Continuing Value Based on Dividends in Year +6 and Beyond

Project Year +6 Dividends (allow for rounding):

$$D_6 = [CI_5 \times (1+g)] + BV_5 - [BV_5 \times (1+g)]$$
$$= [\$7,064 \text{ million} \times 1.03] + \$23,316 \text{ million} - [\$23,316 \text{ million} \times 1.03]$$
$$= \$7,276.1 \text{ million} + \$23,316 \text{ million} - \$24,015 \text{ million}$$
$$= \$6,576.6 \text{ million}$$

$$\text{Continuing Value}_0 = [D_6 \times (1/\{R_E - g\})]$$
$$= \$6,576.6 \text{ million} \times [1/(0.075 - 0.030)]$$
$$= \$6,576.6 \text{ million} \times 22.222$$
$$= \$146,147.6 \text{ million}$$

$$\text{Present Value of Continuing Value}_0 = \$146,147.6 \text{ million} \times [1/(1 + R_E)^5]$$
$$= \$146,147.6 \text{ million} \times [1/(1 + 0.075)^5]$$
$$= \$146,147.6 \text{ million} \times 0.697$$
$$= \$101,800.3 \text{ million}$$

Total Value of PepsiCo's Dividends

Present value of dividends through Year +5	$ 25,977.2	million
Present value of continuing value	+ 101,800.3	million
Present value of common equity	= $127,777.5	million
Adjust for midyear discounting (multiply by $1 + [R_E/2]$)	× 1.0375	
Total present value of common equity	= $132,569.1	million
Divide by number of shares outstanding	÷ 1,544.0	million
Value per share of PepsiCo common equity	= $ 85.86	

PepsiCo's Total Dividends

The total present value of **PepsiCo**'s dividends to common equity shareholders is the sum of these two parts:

Present value of dividends through Year +5	$ 25,977.2 million
Present value of continuing value	101,800.3 million
Present value of common equity	$127,777.5 million

Midyear Discounting

Present value calculations like those used here discount amounts for full periods. Thus, the valuation computations discount Year +1 dividends for a full year, Year +2 dividends for two full years, and so on, which is appropriate if the dividends being discounted occur at the end of each year. Dividends often occur throughout the period. If this is the case, present value computations with full-year discounting will over-discount these flows. To avoid "over-discounting," you can compute the present value discount factors as of the midpoint of each year, thereby effectively discounting the dividends as if they occur, on average, in the middle of each year. Suppose you use a discount rate of 10% ($R = 0.10$). You would discount the Year +1 dividends from the middle of Year +1 using a factor of $1/(1 + R)^{0.5} = 1/(1.10)^{0.5} = 0.9535$; the Year +2 dividends from the middle of Year +2 using a factor of $1/(1 + R)^{1.5} = 1/(1.10)^{1.5} = 0.8668$; and so on.

You also can use a shortcut approach to this correction by adjusting the total present value to a midyear approximation by adding back one-half year of discounting. To make this midyear adjustment, multiply the total present value of the discounted dividends by a factor of $1 + (R/2)$. For example, if $R = 0.10$, the midyear adjustment is 1.05 [$1 + (0.10/2)$]. The Valuation spreadsheet computations in FSAP use this shortcut adjustment.[13]

Applying the midyear discounting adjustment to the computation of the present value of **PepsiCo** dividends results in the following:

Present value of common equity	$127,777.5 million
Midyear adjustment factor [$1 + (0.075/2)$]	× 1.0375
Total present value of common equity	$132,569.1 million

Computing Common Equity Value per Share

Dividing the total present value of common equity of $132,569.1 million by 1,544 million shares outstanding indicates that **PepsiCo**'s common equity shares have a value of $85.86 per share. This value estimate is roughly 25% higher than the market price of $68.43 at the end of 2012 (but very close to the price range at which PepsiCo shares

---

[13]The valuation models described in this chapter estimate the present value of the firm as of the first day of the first year of the forecast horizon; for example, January 1 of Year +1 for a firm with an accounting period that matches the calendar year. However, analysts estimate valuations every day of the year. Suppose the analyst values a firm as of June 17 and compares the value estimate to that day's market price. A present value calculation that determines the value of the firm as of January 1 will ignore the value accumulation between January 1 and June 17 of that year. To refine the calculation, the analyst can adjust the present value as of January 1 to a present value as of June 17 by multiplying V_0 by a future value factor that reflects value accumulation for the appropriate number of days (in this case, 168 days). For example, if the valuation date is June 17 and if $R = 0.10$, the analyst can update the January 1 value estimate by multiplying V_0 by $(1 + R)^{(168/365)} = (1 + 0.10)^{(168/365)} = 1.0448$.

were trading during mid 2013). We will obtain identical value estimates for PepsiCo when we apply the free-cash-flows-based valuation model in Chapter 12 and the earnings-based valuation model in Chapter 13. Exhibit 11.7 presents the dividend s-based valuation model from FSAP (Appendix B, which can be found online at the book's companion website at www.cengagebrain.com).

Exhibit 11.7						
Valuation of PepsiCo in FSAP: **Present Value of Dividends to Common Equity Year +1 through Year +5 and Beyond** **Using the Dividends-Based Valuation Model**						

FSAP OUTPUT: VALUATION MODELS
Analyst Name: Wahlen, Baginski & Bradshaw
Company Name: PepsiCo

	1	2	3	4	5	Continuing Value
Dividends-Based Valuation	**Year +1**	**Year +2**	**Year +3**	**Year +4**	**Year +5**	**Year +6**
Dividends Paid to Common Shareholders	3,387	507	3,629	3,835	3,885	
Less: Common Stock Issues	−45	−152	−154	−225	−94	
Plus: Common Stock Repurchases	3,150	2,624	2,792	2,852	3,217	
Dividends to Common Equity	6,491	5,979	6,267	6,462	7,008	6,577
Present Value Factors	0.930	0.865	0.805	0.749	0.697	
Present Value Net Dividends	6,038.5	5,173.9	5,044.5	4,838.8	4,881.5	
Sum of Present Value Net Dividends	25,977.2					
Present Value of Continuing Value	101,800.3					
Total	127,777.5					
Adjust to midyear discounting	1.0375					
Total Present Value Dividends	132,569.1					
Shares Outstanding	1,544.0					
Estimated Value per Share	**$85.86**					
Current share price	$68.43					
Percent difference	25%					

Sensitivity Analysis and Investment Decision Making

LO 11-8

Assess the sensitivity of firm value estimates to key valuation parameters, such as discount rates and expected long-term growth rates, and make investment decisions.

You should not place too much confidence in the *precision* of firm value estimates using these (or any) forecasts over the remaining life of any firm, even a mature firm such as **PepsiCo**. Although we have constructed these forecasts and value estimates with care, the forecasting and valuation process has an inherently high degree of uncertainty and estimation error. Therefore, you should not rely too heavily on any one point estimate of the value of a firm's shares and instead should describe a reasonable range of share values.

Two critical forecasting and valuation parameters in most valuations are the long-run growth rate assumption and the cost of equity capital assumption. You should conduct sensitivity analyses to test the effects of these and other key valuation parameters and forecast assumptions on the share value estimate. Sensitivity analyses should allow you to vary valuation parameters individually and jointly for additional insights into the correlation between share values, growth rates, and discount rate assumptions.

For PepsiCo, the base case assumptions indicate PepsiCo's share value to be roughly $85.86. The base case valuation assumes a long-run growth rate of 3.0% and a cost of equity capital of 7.5%. The sensitivity of the estimates of PepsiCo's share value can be assessed by varying these two parameters (or any other key parameters in the valuation) across reasonable ranges. Exhibit 11.8 contains the results of sensitivity analysis varying the long-run growth rate from 0%–10% and the cost of equity capital from 5%–20%. The data in Exhibit 11.8 (from FSAP) show that as the discount rate increases, holding growth constant, share value estimates of PepsiCo fall. Likewise, value estimates fall as growth rates decrease, holding discount rates constant. Note that we omit value estimates from this analysis when the assumed growth rate equals or exceeds the assumed discount rate because the continuing value computation is meaningless.

Considering the downside possibilities first, sensitivity analyses should consider how sensitive the share value estimate for PepsiCo is to adverse changes in long-run growth and discount rates. For example, by reducing the long-run growth assumption from 3.0% to 2.0% while holding the discount rate constant at 7.5%, PepsiCo's share value falls to $74.81, still above current market price of $68.43. Similarly, while holding constant the long-run growth assumption at 3.0%, increasing the discount rate from 7.5% to 8.0% produces a share value estimate of $77.56, which is above current market price, whereas

Exhibit 11.8

Valuation of PepsiCo
Sensitivity Analysis of Value to Growth and Equity Cost of Capital

Dividends Valuation Sensitivity Analysis:

					Long-Run Growth Assumptions				
	85.86	**0%**	**2%**	**3%**	**4%**	**5%**	**6%**	**8%**	**10%**
Discount Rates:	5%	91.96	135.32	189.52	352.10				
	6%	76.74	102.04	127.33	177.92	329.69			
	7%	65.88	82.07	96.23	119.84	167.05	308.67		
	7.50%	61.54	74.81	85.86	103.23	134.50	207.46		
	8%	57.74	68.75	77.56	90.77	112.79	156.83		
	9%	51.42	59.24	65.11	73.32	85.64	106.18	270.44	
	10%	46.37	52.11	56.21	61.68	69.33	80.82	138.23	
	11%	42.23	46.56	49.53	53.35	58.44	65.58	94.10	236.75
	12%	38.80	42.12	44.33	47.10	50.65	55.40	72.00	121.80
	13%	35.89	38.48	40.17	42.23	44.80	48.11	58.70	83.42
	14%	33.40	35.45	36.76	38.33	40.24	42.63	49.82	64.18
	15%	31.25	32.89	33.92	35.13	36.59	38.36	43.45	52.60
	18%	26.23	27.12	27.65	28.26	28.96	29.78	31.91	35.10
	20%	23.74	24.34	24.70	25.10	25.56	26.08	27.38	29.20

increasing the discount rate further to 9.0% produces a value estimate of $65.11, just below market price. If we revise both assumptions at once, and reduce the long-run growth assumption to 2.0% and increase the discount rate assumption to 8.0%, PepsiCo's share value falls to $68.75, nearly equivalent to current market price of $68.43.

On the upside, reducing the discount rate to 7.0% while holding growth constant at 3.0% suggests PepsiCo shares could have a value of $96.23. Increasing the long-run growth assumption from 3.0% to 4.0% while holding the discount rate constant at 7.5%, the value estimates jump to $103.23. If we reduce the discount rate further, or increase the long-run growth rate further, the share value estimates for PepsiCo jump dramatically higher. For example, increasing the growth rate assumption to 4.0% and decreasing the discount rate assumption to 7.0% moves the share value estimate to nearly $120.

These data suggest that the value estimate is sensitive to slight variations in the baseline assumptions of 3.0% long-run growth and a 7.5% discount rate, which yield a share value estimate of roughly $86. Adverse variations in valuation parameters could reduce PepsiCo's share value estimates to $65 or lower, whereas favorable variations could increase PepsiCo's share value to over $100.

If the forecast and valuation assumptions are realistic, the baseline value estimate for PepsiCo is $85.86 per share at the end of 2012. At that time, the market price of $68.43 per share indicates that PepsiCo shares were underpriced by about 25%. Under our forecast assumptions, PepsiCo's share value could vary within a range of a low of $65 per share to a high of $120 per share with only minor perturbations in the growth rate and discount rate assumptions. Given PepsiCo's $68.43 share price, these value estimates would have supported a buy recommendation at the end of 2012 because the sensitivity analysis reveals limited downside potential but substantial upside potential for the value of PepsiCo shares.

Summary

This chapter illustrated the computation of risk-adjusted required rates of return on equity and the weighted-average cost of capital, which analysts use as discount rates in valuation models. In valuation, analysts use these discount rates to compute the present value of future dividends, cash flows, or earnings. This chapter also described the dividends-based valuation model and applied it to value **PepsiCo**'s shares at the end of 2012.

The principal *advantages* of the dividends-based valuation method include the following:

- This valuation method focuses on dividends. Economists argue that dividends provide the classical approach to valuing shares. Dividends reflect the payoffs that shareholders can consume.
- Projected amounts of dividends result from projecting expected amounts of revenues, expenses, assets, liabilities, and shareholders' equity. Therefore, they reflect the implications of the analyst's expectations for the future operating, investing, and financing decisions of a firm.

The principal *disadvantages* of the dividends-based valuation method include the following:

- The continuing value (terminal value) tends to dominate the total value in many cases. For firms that do not pay periodic dividends or repurchase shares, the continuing value can comprise the total value of the firm, which requires you to forecast the future value of the firm in order to compute the present value of the firm. Continuing value estimates are sensitive to assumptions made about growth rates after the forecast horizon and discount rates.

- The projection of dividends can be time-consuming, making it costly when you follow many companies and must regularly identify under- and over-valued firms.

As with the preparation of projected financial statements in Chapter 10, the reasonableness of the valuations depends on the reliability of the forecast assumptions and the valuation parameters. You should assess the sensitivity of the valuation to alternative long-run growth and discount rate parameters and to other key drivers of value. To validate value estimates using the dividends-based valuation approach, you also should compute the value of the firm using other approaches, such as the free-cash-flows-based approaches discussed in Chapter 12, the earnings-based approaches discussed in Chapter 13, and the valuation-multiples approaches described in Chapter 14.

Questions, Exercises, Problems, and Cases

Questions and Exercises

LO 11-1

11.1 The Dividends-Based Valuation Approach. Explain the theory behind the dividends-based valuation approach. Why are dividends value-relevant to common equity shareholders?

LO 11-2

11.2 Valuation Approach Equivalence. Conceptually, why should an analyst expect the dividends-based valuation approach to yield equivalent value estimates to the valuation approach that is based on free cash flows available to be distributed to common equity shareholders?

LO 11-3

11.3 The Risk-Return Trade-Off. Explain why analysts and investors use risk-adjusted expected rates of return as discount rates in valuation. Why do investors expect rates of return to *increase* with risk?

LO 11-3

11.4 The Components of the CAPM. The CAPM computes expected rates of return using the following model (described in the chapter):

$$E[R_{Ej}] = E[R_F] + \beta_j \times \{E[R_M] - E[R_F]\}$$

Explain the role of each of the three components of this model.

LO 11-3

11.5 Nondiversifiable and Diversifiable Risk Factors. Identify the types of firm-specific factors that increase a firm's nondiversifiable risk (systematic risk). Identify the types of firm-specific factors that increase a firm's diversifiable risk (nonsystematic risk). Why do models of risk-adjusted expected returns include no expected return premia for diversifiable risk?

LO 11-3

11.6 Debt and the Weighted-Average Cost of Capital. Why do investors typically accept a lower risk-adjusted rate of return on debt capital than equity capital? Suppose a stable, financially healthy, profitable, tax-paying firm that has been financed with all equity now decides to add a reasonable amount of debt to its capital structure. What effect will the change in capital structure likely have on the firm's weighted-average cost of capital?

LO 11-4

11.7 Firms That Do Not Pay Periodic Dividends. Why is the dividends-based valuation approach applicable to firms that do not pay periodic (quarterly or annual) dividends?

11.8 Dividend Policy Irrelevance. The chapter asserts that dividends are value-relevant even though the firm's dividend policy is irrelevant. How can that be true? What is the key assumption in the theory of dividend policy irrelevance?

LO 11-4

11.9 Measuring Value-Relevant Dividends. The chapter describes how the dividends-based valuation approach measures value-relevant dividends to encompass various transactions between the firm and the common shareholders. What transactions should you include in value-relevant dividends for the purposes of implementing the dividends-based valuation model? Why?

LO 11-5

Problems and Cases

11.10 Calculating Required Rates of Return on Equity Capital across Different Industries. The data in Exhibit 11.3 on industry median betas suggest that firms in the following three sets of related industries have different degrees of systematic risk.

LO 11-3

	Median Beta during 2003–2012
Utilities versus Petroleum and Natural Gas	0.77 versus 1.31
Food Products (Grocery Stores) versus Apparel (Retailers)	0.68 versus 1.09
Banking (Depository Institutions) versus Financial Trading (Security and Commodity Brokers)	0.76 versus 1.09

REQUIRED

a. For each matched pair of industries, describe factors that characterize a typical firm's business model in each industry. Describe how such factors would contribute to differences in systematic risk.

b. For each matched pair of industries, use the CAPM to compute the required rate of return on equity capital for the median firm in each industry. Assume that the risk-free rate of return is 4.0% and the market risk premium is 5.0%.

c. For each matched pair of industries, compute the present value of a stream of $1 dividends for the median firm in each industry. Use the perpetuity-with-growth model and assume 3.0% long-run growth for each industry. What effect does the difference in systematic risk across industries have on the per-dollar dividend valuation of the median firm in each industry?

11.11 Calculating the Cost of Capital. Whirlpool manufactures and sells home appliances under various brand names. **IBM** develops and manufactures computer hardware and offers related technology services. **Target** operates a chain of general merchandise discount retail stores. The data in the following table apply to these companies (dollar amounts in millions). For each firm, assume that the market value of the debt equals its book value.

LO 11-3

	Whirlpool	IBM	Target Stores
Total assets	$13,532	$109,524	$44,106
Interest-bearing debt	$ 2,597	$ 33,925	$18,752
Average pretax borrowing cost	6.1%	4.3%	4.9%
Common equity:			
Book value	$ 3,006	$ 13,465	$13,712
Market value	$ 2,959	$110,984	$22,521
Income tax rate	35.0%	35.0%	35.0%
Market equity beta	2.27	0.78	1.20

REQUIRED

a. Assume that the intermediate-term yields on U.S. government Treasury securities are 3.5%. Assume that the market risk premium is 5.0%. Compute the cost of equity capital for each of the three companies.

b. Compute the weighted-average cost of capital for each of the three companies.

c. Compute the unlevered market (asset) beta for each of the three companies.

d. Assume that each company is a candidate for a potential leveraged buyout. The buyers intend to implement a capital structure that has 75% debt (with a pretax borrowing cost of 8.0%) and 25% common equity. Project the weighted-average cost of capital for each company based on the new capital structure. To what extent do these revised weighted-average costs of capital differ from those computed in Requirement b?

LOs 11-3–11-8

11.12 Calculation of Dividends-Based Value. Royal Dutch Shell is a petroleum and petrochemicals company. It engages primarily in the exploration, production, and sale of crude oil and natural gas and the manufacture, transportation, and sale of petroleum and petrochemical products. The company operates in approximately 200 countries in North America, Europe, Asia-Pacific, Africa, South America, and the Middle East. Assume that during the past three years (Year −2, −1, and 0), Royal Dutch Shell generated the following total dividends to common equity shareholders (in USD millions):

	Year −2	Year −1	Year 0
Common dividend payments	$ 8,142	$ 9,001	$ 9,516
Stock repurchases	8,047	4,387	3,573
Total dividends	$16,189	$13,388	$13,089

Analysts project 5% growth in earnings over the next five years. Assuming concurrent 5% growth in dividends, the following table provides the amounts that analysts project for Royal Dutch Shell's total dividends for each of the next five years. In Year +6, total dividends are projected for Royal Dutch Shell assuming that its income statement and balance sheet will grow at a long-term growth rate of 3%.

	Year +1	Year +2	Year +3	Year +4	Year +5	Year +6
Projected growth	5%	5%	5%	5%	5%	3%
Projected total dividends to common equity	$13,743	$14,431	$15,152	$15,910	$16,705	$17,206

At the end of Year 0, Royal Dutch Shell had a market beta of 0.71. At that time, yields on intermediate-term U.S. Treasuries were 3.5%. Assume that the market required a 5.0% risk premium. Suppose Royal Dutch Shell had 6,241 million shares outstanding at the beginning of Year +1 that traded at a share price of $24.87.

REQUIRED

a. Calculate the required rate of return on equity for Royal Dutch Shell as of the beginning of Year +1.

b. Calculate the sum of the present value of total dividends for Years +1 through +5.

c. Calculate the continuing value of Royal Dutch Shell at the start of Year +6 using the perpetuity-with-growth model with Year +6 total dividends. Also compute the present value of continuing value as of the beginning of Year +1.

d. Compute the total present value of dividends for Royal Dutch Shell as of the beginning of Year +1. Remember to adjust the present value for midyear discounting.

e. Compute the value per share of Royal Dutch Shell as of the beginning of Year +1.

f. Given the share price at the start of Year +1, do Royal Dutch Shell shares appear underpriced, overpriced, or correctly priced?

11.13 Valuing the Equity of a Privately Held Firm. Refer to the financial statement forecasts for Massachusetts Stove Company (MSC) prepared for Case 10.2. The management of MSC wants to know the equity valuation implications of adding gas stoves under the best, most likely, and worst-case scenarios. Under the three scenarios from Case 10.2, the actual amounts of net income and common shareholders' equity for Year 7 and the projected amounts for Years 8 through 12 are as follows:

LOs 11-5–11-8

	Actual	Projected				
	Year 7	**Year 8**	**Year 9**	**Year 10**	**Year 11**	**Year 12**
Best-case scenario:						
Net income	$154,601	$148,422	$123,226	$173,336	$ 271,725	$ 390,639
Common equity	$552,080	$700,502	$823,728	$997,064	$1,268,789	$1,659,429
Most likely scenario:						
Net income	$154,601	$135,343	$ 74,437	$ 72,899	$ 109,357	$ 149,977
Common equity	$552,080	$687,423	$761,860	$834,759	$ 944,116	$1,094,093
Worst-case scenario:						
Net income	$154,601	$128,263	$ 18,796	$ (39,902)	$ (58,316)	$ (77,156)
Common equity	$552,080	$680,343	$699,139	$659,238	$ 600,921	$ 523,766

MSC is not publicly traded and therefore does not have a market equity beta. Using the market equity beta of the only publicly traded woodstove and gas stove manufacturing firm and adjusting it for differences in the debt-to-equity ratio, income tax rate, and privately owned status of MSC yields a cost of equity capital for MSC of 13.55%.

REQUIRED

a. Use the clean surplus accounting approach to derive the projected total amount of MSC's dividends to common equity shareholders in Years 8 through 12.

b. Given that MSC is a privately held company, assume that ending book value of common equity at the end of Year 12 is a reasonable estimate of the value at which the common shareholders' equity could be liquidated. Calculate the value of the equity of MSC as of the end of Year 7 under each of the three scenarios. Ignore the midyear discounting adjustment.

c. How do these valuations affect your advice to the management of MSC about adding gas stoves to its woodstove line?

11.14 Dividends-Based Valuation of Common Equity. Problem 10.16 projected financial statements for **Walmart** for Years +1 through +5. The following data for Walmart include the actual amounts for 2012 and the projected amounts for Years +1 through +5 for comprehensive income and common shareholders' equity, assuming it will use implied dividends as the financial flexible account to balance the balance sheet (amounts in millions).

LOs 11-3–11-8

	Actual	**Projected**				
	2012	**Year +1**	**Year +2**	**Year +3**	**Year +4**	**Year +5**
Comprehensive income	$18,579	$17,666	$18,416	$19,195	$20,007	$20,851
Common shareholders' equity:						
Paid-in Capital	$ 3,952	$ 4,163	$ 4,282	$ 4,392	$ 4,491	$ 4,581
Retained Earnings	72,978	75,625	77,023	77,934	78,213	77,859
Accumulated Other Comprehensive Income	(587)	(587)	(587)	(587)	(587)	(587)
Total Common Equity	$76,343	$79,201	$80,719	$81,738	$82,117	$81,853

Assume that the market equity beta for Walmart at the end of 2012 was 1.00. Assume that the risk-free interest rate was 3.0% and the market risk premium was 6.0%. Also assume that Walmart had 3,314 million shares outstanding at the end of 2012, and share price was $69.09.

REQUIRED

a. Use the CAPM to compute the required rate of return on common equity capital for Walmart.

b. Compute the weighted-average cost of capital for Walmart as of the start of Year +1. At the end of 2012, Walmart had $48,222 million in outstanding interest-bearing debt on the balance sheet and no preferred stock. Assume that the balance sheet value of Walmart's debt is approximately equal to the market value of the debt. Assume that at the start of Year +1, it will incur interest expense of 4.2% on debt capital and that its average tax rate will be 32.0%. Walmart also had $5,395 million in equity capital from noncontrolling interests. Assume that this equity capital carries a 15.0% required rate of return. (For our forecasts, we assume noncontrolling interests are similar to preferred shares and receive dividends equal to the required rate of return each year.)

c. Use the clean surplus accounting approach to derive the projected dividends for common shareholders for Years +1 through +5 based on the projected comprehensive income and shareholders' equity amounts. (Throughout this problem, you can ignore dividends to noncontrolling interests.)

d. Use the clean surplus accounting approach to project the continuing dividend to common shareholders in Year +6. Assume that the steady-state long-run growth rate will be 3% in Years +6 and beyond.

e. Using the required rate of return on common equity from Requirement a as a discount rate, compute the sum of the present value of dividends to common shareholders for Walmart for Years +1 through +5.

f. Using the required rate of return on common equity from Requirement a as a discount rate and the long-run growth rate from Requirement d, compute the continuing value of Walmart as of the beginning of Year +6 based on its continuing dividends in Years +6 and beyond. After computing continuing value, bring continuing value back to present value at the start of Year +1.

g. Compute the value of a share of Walmart common stock, as follows:

(1) Compute the sum of the present value of dividends including the present value of continuing value.

(2) Adjust the sum of the present value using the midyear discounting adjustment factor.

(3) Compute the per-share value estimate.

h. Using the same set of forecast assumptions as before, recompute the value of Walmart shares under two alternative scenarios. To quantify the sensitivity of your share value estimate for Walmart to these variations in growth and discount rates, compare (in percentage terms) your value estimates under these two scenarios with your value estimate from Requirement g.

- Scenario 1: Assume that Walmart's long-run growth will be 2%, not 3% as before, and assume that its required rate of return on equity is 1 percentage point higher than the rate you computed using the CAPM in Requirement a.
- Scenario 2: Assume that Walmart's long-run growth will be 4%, not 3% as before, and assume that its required rate of return on equity is 1 percentage point lower than the rate you computed using the CAPM in Requirement a.

i. What reasonable range of share values would you expect for Walmart common stock? Where is the current price for Walmart shares relative to this range? What do you recommend?

INTEGRATIVE CASE 11.1

Starbucks

Dividends-Based Valuation of Starbucks' Common Equity

LOs 11-3–11-8

Integrative Case 10.1 projected financial statements for **Starbucks** for Years +1 through +5. This portion of the Starbucks Integrative Case applies the techniques of this chapter to compute Starbucks' required rate of return on equity and Starbucks' share value using the dividends-based valuation model. This case also compares the value estimate to Starbucks' share price at the time of the case development to provide an investment recommendation.

Assume the market equity beta for Starbucks at the end of 2012 was 0.75. Assume that the risk-free interest rate was 3.0% and the market risk premium was 6.0%. Starbucks had 749.3 million shares outstanding at the end of 2012, and the share price was $50.15.

REQUIRED

a. Use the CAPM to compute the required rate of return on equity capital for Starbucks.

b. Compute the weighted-average cost of capital for Starbucks as of the start of Year +1. At the start of Year +1, Starbucks had $550 million in outstanding interest-bearing debt on the balance sheet and no preferred stock. Assume that the balance sheet value of Starbucks' debt is approximately equal to the market value of the debt. Assume that at the start of Year +1, Starbucks will incur interest expense of 6.25% on debt capital and that Starbucks' average tax rate is 33.0%.

c. From your forecasts of Starbucks' financial statements for Years +1 through +5, derive the projected dividends using the projected amounts for the plug to dividends minus the net amounts of common stock issued each year (if any). Then compute projected dividends for Starbucks for Years +1 through +5 using the clean surplus accounting approach based on projected amounts for comprehensive income and common shareholders' equity. The projected amounts of dividends under the two approaches should be identical.

d. Use the clean surplus accounting approach to project the continuing dividend in Year +6. Assume that the steady-state long-run growth rate will be 3% in Year +6 and beyond.

e. Using the required rate of return on common equity capital from Requirement a as a discount rate, compute the sum of the present value of dividends for Starbucks for Years +1 through +5.

f. Using the required rate of return on common equity capital from Requirement a as a discount rate and a 3.0% long-run growth rate, compute the continuing value of Starbucks as of the beginning of Year +6 based on Starbucks' continuing dividends in Year +6 and beyond. After computing continuing value, discount it to present value at the start of Year +1.

g. Compute the value of a share of Starbucks' common stock, as follows:

    (1) Compute the sum of the present value of dividends including the present value of continuing value.

    (2) Adjust the sum of the present value using the midyear discounting adjustment factor.

    (3) Compute the per-share value estimate.

h. Using the same set of forecast assumptions as before, recompute the value of Starbucks' shares under two alternative scenarios. To quantify the sensitivity of your estimate of share value for Starbucks to variations in long-run growth and discount rates, compare (in percentage terms) your value estimates under these two scenarios with your value estimate from Requirement g.

- Scenario 1: Assume that Starbucks' long-run growth will be 2%, not 3% as before, and assume that Starbucks' required rate of return on equity is 1 percentage point higher than the rate you computed using the CAPM in Requirement a.
- Scenario 2: Assume that Starbucks' long-run growth will be 4%, not 3% as before, and assume that Starbucks' required rate of return on equity is 1 percentage point lower than the rate you computed using the CAPM in Requirement a.

i. What reasonable range of share values would you expect for Starbucks' common stock? Where is the current price for Starbucks' shares relative to this range? What do you recommend?

Valuation: Cash-Flow-Based Approaches

LO 12-1 Describe cash-flow-based valuation models and their conceptual and practical strengths and weaknesses.

LO 12-2 Measure free cash flows for all debt and equity stakeholders, as well as free cash flows for common equity shareholders, and explain when each measure is appropriate.

LO 12-3 Estimate firm value using the:

a. present value of future free cash flows for common equity shareholders, discounted at the required rate of return on equity capital.

b. present value of future free cash flows for all debt and equity stakeholders, discounted at the weighted-average cost of capital.

LO 12-4 Understand how to implement the free-cash-flows-based valuation approaches by applying them to estimate share value for PepsiCo.

LO 12-5 Assess the sensitivity of firm value estimates to key valuation parameters such as discount rates and expected long-term growth rates.

Chapter Overview

This chapter relies on the financial statement forecasts developed for **PepsiCo** in Chapter 10, as well as the valuation concepts and techniques introduced and applied in Chapter 11. This chapter develops *free-cash-flows-based* valuation approaches and applies them to PepsiCo. If you are not familiar with the forecasting techniques introduced in Chapter 10 and the valuation concepts and techniques introduced in Chapter 11, we strongly encourage you to read those chapters carefully before proceeding with this chapter. Many of the concepts that are explained and demonstrated in those chapters are applied in this one.

Recall that economic theory teaches that the value of an investment equals the present value of the expected future payoffs from the investment, discounted at a rate that reflects the time value of money and the risk inherent in those expected payoffs. The general model for estimating the present value of a security (denoted as V_0, present value at time $t = 0$) with an expected life of n future periods is as follows:[1]

$$V_0 = \sum_{t=1}^{n} \frac{\text{Expected Future Payoffs}_t}{(1 + \text{Discount Rate})^t}$$

[1]In this chapter, as in the previous chapter, t refers to accounting periods. The valuation process determines an estimate of firm value, denoted as V_0, in present value as of today, when $t = 0$. The period $t = 1$ refers to the first accounting period being discounted to present value. Period $t = n$ is the period of the expected final payoff.

The dividends-based valuation approach demonstrated in the previous chapter, the free-cash-flows-based approaches demonstrated in this chapter, and the earnings-based approaches demonstrated in the next two chapters are all designed to produce reliable estimates of the value of the firm's equity shares. These approaches produce value estimates that provide the basis for intelligent investment decisions because, even in relatively efficient securities markets, price does not necessarily equal value for every security at all times. Price is observable, but value is not; value must be estimated. Therefore, estimating the value of a security is a common objective of financial statement analysis. The financial statement analysis and valuation process enables investors, analysts, portfolio managers, investment bankers, and corporate managers to determine a reliable appraisal of the value of shares of common equity. Comparing value to price then yields a reliable basis to assess whether a firm's equity shares are underpriced, overpriced, or fairly priced in the capital markets.

Whether you will produce reliable estimates of share value as a result of the financial statement analysis and valuation process depends entirely on whether you carefully and thoughtfully apply each step of the six-step analysis framework that forms the structure of this book (Exhibit 1.2 in Chapter 1). Following the first three steps, you should first understand the economics of the industry, then assess the particular firm's strategy, and then carefully evaluate the quality of the firm's accounting, making adjustments if necessary. In the fourth step, you should evaluate the firm's profitability and risk. All of these analyses should provide you with useful information for the fifth step, projecting the firm's future financial statements. You can then use those financial statement forecasts to derive expectations of future earnings, cash flows, and dividends, which are the fundamental payoff measures used in valuation. In the sixth and final step, you apply valuation models to these expectations to estimate the value of the firm. Your expectations for future payoffs (the numerator in the valuation model) depend on your forecasts of future earnings, cash flows, or dividends. Assessing an appropriate risk-adjusted discount rate (the denominator in the valuation model) requires an unbiased assessment of the inherent riskiness in the set of expected future payoffs. Therefore, reliable estimates of firm value depend on unbiased expectations of future payoffs and an appropriate risk-adjusted discount rate, all of which depend on all six steps of the framework.

As explained in the previous chapter, when you derive forecasts of future earnings, cash flows, and dividends from a set of internally consistent financial statement forecasts for a firm and use the same discount rate in correctly specified models to compute present values, the earnings-, cash-flows-, and dividends-based valuation models will yield *identical* estimates of value for a firm. In Chapter 11, we applied the dividends-based valuation approach to PepsiCo and estimated that, given our forecast assumptions and valuation parameters, PepsiCo's share value should be within a fairly narrow range of around $85.86 at the time of our analysis. Chapter 11 also illustrated the theoretical equivalence of the dividends and free-cash–flows-based valuation approaches. This chapter demonstrates the practical equivalence of the dividends- and free-cash-flows-based valuation approaches with the valuation of PepsiCo. The next chapter will describe and apply the earnings-based valuation approach and demonstrate its theoretical and practical equivalence with both the dividends and free-cash-flows approaches.[2]

---

[2]For examples of research on the complementarity of these approaches, see Stephen Penman and Theodore Sougiannis, "A Comparison of Dividend, Cash Flow, and Earnings Approaches to Equity Valuation," *Contemporary Accounting Research* 15, No. 3 (Fall 1998), pp. 343–383, and Jennifer Francis, Per Olsson, and Dennis Oswald, "Comparing the Accuracy and Explainability of Dividend, Free Cash Flow, and Abnormal Earnings Equity Value Estimates," *Journal of Accounting Research* 38, no. 1 (Spring 2000), pp. 45–70.

It is important that you understand the similarities and differences in the dividends-, free-cash-flows-, and earnings-based valuation approaches and see their theoretical and practical equivalence. Our experience strongly suggests that applying several different valuation approaches yields better insights about the value of a firm than relying on only one approach in all cases. In addition, it is our experience that you will be better equipped to work successfully with clients, managers, colleagues, and subordinates in the financial statement analysis and valuation process if you thoroughly understand all three valuation approaches.

All four valuation chapters—Chapters 11–14—emphasize that the objective of the valuation process is not necessarily a single point estimate of value. Instead, the objective is to determine the distribution of value estimates across the relevant ranges of critical forecast assumptions and valuation parameters. By assessing the sensitivity of value estimates across a distribution of relevant forecast assumptions and valuation parameters, we seek to determine the most likely range of values for a share, which we then compare to the share's current price for an intelligent investment decision.

Rationale for Cash-Flow-Based Valuation

LO 12-1

Describe cash-flow-based valuation models and their conceptual and practical strengths and weaknesses.

As we demonstrated in the previous chapter, the value of a share of common equity is the present value of the expected future dividends. Dividends are fundamental expected future payoffs that you can use to value shares because they represent the distribution of wealth to you, the shareholder. You invest cash when you purchase the share, and then you receive cash through dividends as the payoffs from holding the share, including the final *liquidating dividend* when you sell the share. In dividends-based valuation, we define *dividends* broadly to encompass all cash flows from the firm to the common equity shareholders through periodic dividend payments, stock buybacks, and the liquidating dividend, as well as cash flows from the shareholders to the firm when the firm issues shares (negative dividends).

You should consider cash-flow-based valuation and dividends-based valuation to be two sides of the same coin: you can value the firm based on the cash flows *into* the firm that will be used to pay dividends or, equivalently, value the firm based on the cash flows *out of* the firm in dividends to common shareholders. We apply the same fundamental valuation concepts and techniques to value expected future dividends in Chapter 11 and free cash flows here in Chapter 12. These fundamental concepts are listed in Exhibit 12.1. Instead of focusing on wealth distribution through dividends, the free-cash-flow-based approach focuses on cash flows generated by the firm that create dividend-paying capacity. In any given period, the amount of cash flow into the firm and the amount of dividends paid out of the firm will likely differ; the equivalence of these two valuation approaches arises because over the lifetime of the firm, the cash flows into and out of the firm will be equivalent.

The cash-flow-based valuation approach measures and values the cash flows that are "free" to be distributed to shareholders. That is, *free cash flows* are the cash flows each period that are available for distribution to shareholders, unencumbered by necessary reinvestments in operating assets or required payments to debtholders, preferred stockholders, or other claimants. Free cash flows can be used instead of dividends as the value-relevant measures of expected future payoffs to the investor in the numerator of the general value model set forth at the outset of this chapter. Both approaches, if implemented with consistent assumptions, lead to identical estimates of value.

Exhibit 12.1

Fundamental Valuation Concepts

Important Note to Readers: The following key concepts apply to all the valuation models demonstrated in this text. All of these concepts are explained and demonstrated in Chapter 11 (pages 864 to 891). So to minimize redundancy, we do not repeat them in this chapter. If you have not yet read Chapter 11, or want a thorough discussion and explanation of these topics, we strongly encourage you to read Chapter 11 carefully.

- Risk, expected rates of return, and the weighted-average cost of capital
- Cash flows to the investor versus cash flows to the firm
- Nominal versus real cash flows
- The forecast horizon
- Computing continuing value

The principal advantages of using the free-cash-flows-based valuation methods include the following:

- Cash is the medium of exchange, and therefore a fundamental source of value. When individuals and firms invest cash in an economic resource, they delay current consumption in favor of future consumption. A resource has value because of its ability to provide future cash flows that will enable investors to consume goods and services in the future. The free-cash-flows approach measures value based on the projected cash flows that the firm will generate that will be distributed to investors.
- Cash is a measurable common denominator for comparing the future benefits of alternative investment opportunities. One might compare very different investment opportunities involving a bond, a stock, or real estate, but comparing these alternatives requires a common measuring unit of their future benefits. The future cash flows serve that function.
- Projected amounts of free cash flows result from projected amounts of revenues, expenses, assets, liabilities, and shareholders' equity, which result from projected future operating, investing, and financing decisions of a firm.
- Free cash flows valuation focuses directly on net cash inflows to the entity that are available to distribute to capital providers, as opposed to focusing on dividends to common equity shareholders. This cash flow perspective is especially pertinent to acquisition decisions.
- Free cash flows valuation approaches are widely used in practice.

The principal disadvantages of using the free-cash-flows-based valuation methods include the following:

- The projection of free cash flows can be time-consuming, making it costly when you follow many companies and must regularly identify under- and overvalued firms.
- The continuing value (terminal value) tends to dominate the total value in many cases. This continuing value is sensitive to assumptions made about growth rates after the forecast horizon and discount rates.

■ You must be very careful that free cash flow computations are internally consistent with long-run assumptions regarding growth and payout. Failure to do so can result in unnecessary estimation errors that produce poor valuations that are inconsistent with those derived from expected future dividends and earnings.

Measuring Free Cash Flows

LO 12-2

Measure free cash flows for all debt and equity stakeholders, as well as free cash flows for common equity shareholders, and explain when each measure is appropriate.

This section first presents a conceptual framework for measuring free cash flows. Then it describes specific practical steps to measure free cash flows from two different perspectives—free cash flows to all debt and equity stakeholders and free cash flows to common equity shareholders—and when to use each.

A Conceptual Framework for Free Cash Flows

A conceptual framework for free cash flows emanates from the familiar balance sheet equation:

$$A = L + SE$$

Recall from Chapter 5 the demonstration of an alternative ROCE decomposition into operating and financial leverage components. Using the same approach, separate all of the assets and liabilities into two categories: operating or financing:

$$OA + FA = OL + FL + SE$$

Operating assets (denoted as OA) and operating liabilities (denoted as OL) relate to the firm's day-to-day operations in the normal course of business. For most firms, operating assets include cash and short-term investment securities necessary for operating liquidity purposes; accounts receivable; inventory; property, plant, and equipment; intangible assets (for example, licenses, patents, trademarks, and goodwill); and investments in affiliated companies. Operating liabilities typically include accounts payable, accrued expenses, accrued taxes, deferred taxes, pension obligations, and other retirement benefits obligations.

Financial liabilities (denoted as FL) include interest-bearing liabilities that are part of the financial capital structure of the firm. Financial liabilities are those that trigger a cost of financing and include short-term notes payable; current maturities of long-term debt; and long-term debt in the forms of mortgages, bonds, notes, and capital lease obligations. Insofar as outstanding preferred stock contains features that make it economically similar to debt (features such as limited life, mandatory redemption, and guaranteed dividends), you should include preferred stock with financial liabilities.

In some circumstances, firms may hold financial assets (denoted as FA) such as excess cash and short- or long-term investment securities to provide the firm with liquidity to repay debt, pay dividends, and repurchase common stock. Distinguishing financial assets that the firm will use for its financial capital structure from cash and marketable securities the firm will use for liquidity for operating purposes requires that you make a judgment call. Analysts typically consider financial assets to be part of the financial structure of the firm if the firm intends to use the financial assets to retire debt or if the financial assets exceed the firm's needs for operating liquidity purposes. and therefore could be used to retire debt, pay dividends or repurchase common equity shares. For example, such financial assets may exist if a firm is accumulating cash or investment securities for the purpose of retiring debt, holding certain amounts of restricted cash under a loan covenant, or accumulating a sinking fund for bond retirement under the terms of a bond debenture. Analysts typically do not consider financial assets such as cash and cash equivalents and marketable securities to be part of the financial capital structure of a firm when these financial assets are necessary to manage the liquidity needs of the firm's operating activities across different seasons or business cycles. Analysts also typically do not consider financial assets to be part of the financial capital structure of the firm when the financial assets include investment securities that are part of the long-term strategy of the firm, such as investments in affiliated subsidiaries with related operating activities or investments in potential acquisition targets.[3] Capital held in these types of accounts for the purposes of operating liquidity or strategic investments should be considered operating assets, not financial assets.

Once you have separated the balance sheet into operating and financing components, rearrange the equation to put operating accounts on one side and financing accounts and shareholders' equity on the other, as follows:

$$OA - OL = FL - FA + SE,$$

which is equivalent to

$$NetOA = NetFL + SE$$

where $NetOA = OA - OL$ and $NetFL = FL - FA$. For most firms, operating assets are likely to exceed operating liabilities and financial liabilities are likely to exceed financial assets. (Financial borrowing usually exceeds financial assets because the firm uses the funds obtained from borrowing to purchase operating assets.)

This balance sheet arrangement provides a useful basis to conceptualize free cash flows to the firm. If we substitute for each term the present values of the expected future net cash flows associated with operating activities, financing activities, and shareholders' equity, we can express the balance sheet as follows:

Present Value of Expected Future Net Cash Flows from Operations
= *Present Value of Expected Future Net Cash Flows Available for Debt Financing*
+ *Present Value of Expected Future Net Cash Flows Available for Shareholders' Equity*

This expression indicates that the present value of the expected net cash flows from operations of the firm determines the sum of the values of the debt and equity claims on the firm. Therefore, one can value the debt and equity capital of the firm by valuing the net cash flows from operations that are "free" to service debt and equity claims. We refer to this measure of free cash flows as *the free cash flows for all debt and equity stakeholders* because they reflect the cash flows that are available to the debt and equity stakeholders in the firm.

We can rearrange the balance sheet equation slightly further:

$$NetOA - NetFL = SE$$

---

[3]The calculation of the rate of return on assets, or ROA, in Chapter 4 assumed that all assets were operating assets and that operating income is equal to net income excluding the after-tax cost of financial liabilities. Thus, Chapter 4 made no adjustment to eliminate interest income on financial assets from net income in the numerator of ROA and no adjustment to eliminate financial assets in the denominator. Most manufacturing, retailing, and service firms hold only minor amounts of financial assets, so ignoring adjustments for financial assets does not usually introduce a material amount of bias to the calculation of ROA. A more precise calculation of ROA for firms with a material amount of financial assets in the capital structure adjusts the numerator to eliminate interest income and adjusts the denominator of ROA for the portions of financial assets (cash, marketable securities, and investment securities) that are part of the financial capital structure and are not directly related to operating activities.

Using the same present value cash flow terms as before, we can express this form of the balance sheet equation as follows:

Present Value of Expected Future Net Cash Flows from Operations
  −Present Value of Expected Future Net Cash Flows Available for Debt Financing
  = Present Value of Expected Future Net Cash Flows Available for Shareholders' Equity

With this expression, we can conceptualize free cash flows specifically attributable to the equity shareholders of the firm. The present value of free cash flows produced by the operations of the firm minus the present value of cash flows necessary to service claims of the net debtholders yields *free cash flows available for common equity shareholders.* This measure captures the net free cash flows available to equity shareholders after debt claims are satisfied.

Free Cash Flows Measurement

The following sections describe how you should measure free cash flows from the two perspectives described above—*free cash flows for all debt and equity stakeholders* and *free cash flows for common equity shareholders*—and when you should use each free cash flow measure. In practice, different analysts compute free cash flows from various starting points: the statement of cash flows, net income, EBITDA (earnings before interest, tax, depreciation, and amortization), and NOPAT (net operating profit adjusted for tax). For completeness, we describe how to measure free cash flows from each starting point.

Measuring Free Cash Flows: The Statement of Cash Flows as the Starting Point

Under U.S. GAAP and IFRS, firms report the statement of cash flows by decomposing the net change in cash into operating, investing, and financing activity components. These three categories do not exactly match the operating and financing classifications we need for computing free cash flows. Thus, you need to reclassify some of the components of the statement of cash flows to compute free cash flows for valuation purposes. Exhibit 12.2 describes the computations.

Cash flow from operations from the projected statement of cash flows is the most direct starting point for computing both measures of free cash flows because it requires the fewest adjustments. Recall from Chapter 3 that the statement of cash flows measures cash flow from operations by beginning with net income, adding back any non-cash expenses or losses (such as depreciation and amortization expenses), subtracting any non-cash income or gains (such as income from equity-method affiliates), and then adjusting for changes in receivables, inventory, accounts payable, and accrued expenses.

Free Cash Flows for All Debt and Equity Capital Stakeholders

Free cash flows for all debt and equity capital stakeholders are the cash flows available to make interest and principal payments to debtholders, redeem preferred shares or pay dividends to preferred shareholders, retire or pay dividends to noncontrolling interests, and pay dividends and buy back shares from common equity shareholders. To measure these free cash flows, we begin with cash flows from operations from the projected statement of cash flows, as shown in the left side of Exhibit 12.2. To measure cash flows from operations before the effects of the firm's financial capital structure, you must add back the interest expense on financial liabilities, net of any income tax savings from interest expense. If you make the judgment call that some or all of the firm's financial

Exhibit 12.2

Measurement of Free Cash Flows

Free Cash Flows for All Debt and Equity Stakeholders:	Free Cash Flows for Common Equity Shareholders:
Operating Activities:	**Operating Activities:**
Cash Flow from Operations	**Cash Flow from Operations**
Begin with cash flow from operations on the projected statement of cash flows.	Begin with cash flow from operations on the projected statement of cash flows.
$+/-$ **Net Interest after Tax**	
Add back interest expense (net of tax) Also subtract interest income (net of tax) from financial assets if you deem them to be part of the financial capital structure of the firm and not part of the operating activities of the firm.	
$+/-$ **Changes in Cash Required for Liquidity**	$+/-$ **Changes in Cash Required for Liquidity**
Subtract an increase or add a decrease in cash required for purposes of liquidity for operations.	Subtract an increase or add a decrease in cash required for purposes of liquidity for operations.
$=$ *Free Cash Flows from Operations for All Debt and Equity*	$=$ *Free Cash Flows from Operations for Equity*
Investing Activities:	**Investing Activities:**
$+/-$ **Net Capital Expenditures**	$+/-$ **Net Capital Expenditures**
Subtract cash outflows for capital expenditures and add cash inflows from sales of assets that comprise the productive capacity of the operations of the firm (including property, plant, and equipment; affiliated companies; and intangible assets).	Subtract cash outflows for capital expenditures and add cash inflows from sales of assets that comprise the productive capacity of the operations of the firm (including property, plant, and equipment; affiliated companies; and intangible assets).
$=$ *Free Cash Flows for All Debt and Equity Stakeholders*	
	Financing Activities:
	$+/-$ **Debt Cash Flows**
	Add cash inflows from new borrowings or subtract cash outflows for repayments of short- and long-term interest-bearing debt.

(Continued)

Exhibit 12.2 (Continued)

+/− **Financial Asset Cash Flows**

Subtract cash outflows invested in cash, short-term, and long-term investment securities (or add cash inflows from these accounts) if you deem these financial assets to be part of the financial capital structure of the firm and not part of the operating activities of the firm.

+/− **Preferred Stock Cash Flows**

Add cash inflows from new issues of preferred stock or subtract cash outflows for preferred stock retirements and dividend payments.

+/− **Noncontrolling Interest Cash Flows**

Add cash inflows from new investments by noncontrolling interests or subtract cash outflows for noncontrolling interest retirements and dividend payments.

= *Free Cash Flows for Common Equity Stakeholders*

assets (such as excess cash holdings or marketable securities) are intended to retire debt and pay dividends and are part of the financial capital structure of the firm (rather than part of the operating liquidity management of the firm), you should subtract the interest income on those financial assets, net of the income taxes paid on that interest income. To adjust interest expense and interest income for tax effects multiply interest expense and interest income by one minus the firm's marginal tax rate.[4]

You should also add or subtract any change in the cash balance that the firm will require for operating liquidity. Cash that the firm must maintain for operating liquidity purposes is not available for distribution to debt or equity stakeholders and therefore is *not* part of free cash flow. If the firm improves its cash management efficiency and reduces the amount of cash required for operating liquidity, the firm has additional free cash flow that can be distributed to debt or equity stakeholders. If the firm expands its operations into new markets or countries, it will require additional amounts of cash for operating liquidity, reducing free cash flow available for debt and equity stakeholders.[5] Procedurally, you should project the required amounts of cash for working capital

---

[4]Technically, analysts should make these adjustments using the cash amounts of interest paid and interest received rather than the accrual amounts of interest expense and interest income. However, as a practical matter, it is reasonable to assume that forecasted amounts of interest expense will equal interest paid and forecasted amounts of interest income will equal interest received.

[5]For example, suppose you are valuing a retail store chain and the chain must maintain the equivalent of seven days of sales in checking accounts and cash on hand at each store for purposes of conducting retail sales transactions. When the chain opens new stores, it is required to hold additional cash as part of operations (as it would need to hold additional inventory). These additional cash requirements are not available for debt and equity capital providers if the firm intends to maintain its operations.

purposes each period and add or subtract the change in required cash balances to determine free cash flow from operations for debt and equity stakeholders.

Next, adjust for cash flows related to capital expenditures on long-lived assets that are a part of the firm's productive capacity (for example, property, plant, and equipment; affiliated companies; intangible assets; and other investing activities). You should subtract cash outflows for capital expenditures and investments, and add cash inflows from sales of these types of assets, pulling the amounts from the investing activities section of the projected statement of cash flows.

As noted earlier, you must make a judgment call about the amounts of the firm's financial assets (for example, in cash and cash equivalents, short-term securities, or long-term investment securities) that are (1) necessary for the liquidity and operating capacity of the firm or (2) part of the financial capital structure of the firm and therefore distributable to debt or equity stakeholders. For example, if you project that the firm will retain financial assets by saving some portion of its cash flows in a securities account each period and that this cash will ultimately be used to repay debt, pay dividends, or buy back shares, then you should deem these cash flows as free cash flows for debt and equity capital. For instance, the firm may be required by a bond indenture agreement to maintain a sinking fund of cash or liquid securities that will be available to repay the bond when it matures. In this case, you should include the amount of cash added to the bond sinking fund as free cash flows for debt and equity capital.

This adjustment requires a judgment call because in some circumstances, firms retain seemingly excess amounts of cash, marketable securities, or investment securities accounts when these assets are in fact not free for potential distribution to capital stakeholders. For example, in some cases, firms with seasonal business need to maintain large balances in cash or securities accounts in order to provide needed liquidity during particular seasons. In other cases, firms build up large balances in investment securities accounts that represent investments in key affiliates. In scenarios such as these, you should not assess these cash flows as "free" for potential distribution to capital stakeholders, but instead should consider these cash flows necessary investments in the liquidity and productive capacity of the firm.

Together, these computations result in free cash flows available to service debt; pay dividends to preferred, common, and noncontrolling interest shareholders; and buy back shares. A later section describes the approach to estimate the present value of the debt and equity claims on the firm by discounting free cash flows for debt and equity stakeholders using the weighted-average cost of capital of the firm.

Free Cash Flows for Common Equity Shareholders

Free cash flows for common equity shareholders are the cash flows specifically available to the common shareholders after all debt service payments to lenders and dividends to preferred and noncontrolling interest shareholders. To measure free cash flows for common equity shareholders, you can again begin with cash flow from operations from the projected statement of cash flows, as presented in the right side of Exhibit 12.2. As in the previous section, you should subtract any increase in the cash balance required operating liquidity because this cash is not free for distribution to equity shareholders (or add any decrease in the required cash balance because it means more cash is free for equity shareholders).[6]

---

[6]Note that unlike the computation of free cash flows for all debt and equity stakeholders, we do not adjust for interest expense or interest income after tax when we compute free cash flows for equity. Our measure of free cash flow for equity already reflects net cash flows for interest payments for interest-bearing debt capital because the statement of cash flows starts with net income to compute cash flow from operations and because net income already reflects interest expense after tax.

Also, as in the previous section, you should adjust for cash flows for capital expenditures on long-lived assets that are a part of the firm's productive capacity. You should subtract cash outflows for purchases and add cash inflows from sales of assets related to the firm's long-term productive activities.

You should also include cash flows related to debt claims by adding cash inflows from new borrowing in short- and long-term debt and subtracting cash outflows for repayments of short- and long-term debt. If you make the judgment call that the firm saves financial capital beyond its immediate liquidity needs in a cash or investment securities account, these cash flows reflect financing activities. Therefore, you must (1) subtract the amount of cash outflow to purchase the securities because this cash obviously is not paid out to equity shareholders or (2) add the amount of cash inflow received from selling such securities because this cash inflow is available for distribution to equity shareholders. For example, if the firm maintains a bond sinking fund for the retirement of bonds when they mature, the cash invested in the sinking fund is not available for common equity shareholders. You also should add cash inflows from new issues of preferred stock and subtract cash outflows from preferred-stock retirements and dividend payments.[7] Finally, you should also add cash inflows from new investments of capital by noncontrolling interests, and subtract cash outflows from retirements and dividend payments to noncontrolling interests. These computations measure free cash flows available to common equity shareholders for dividends, stock buybacks, or reinvestment. As described in a later section of this chapter, we will discount free cash flows for common equity at the cost of equity capital to determine the value of the common equity of the firm.

Measuring Free Cash Flows: Alternative Starting Points

In practice, different analysts use different starting points to compute free cash flows. The approaches described above began with cash flows from operations from the projected statement of cash flows because it is the most direct starting point, requiring the fewest adjustments. However, it is more common for analysts to compute free cash flows by beginning with projected net income, EBITDA, or NOPAT, each of which is more complicated and prone to error than starting with cash flows from operations. Exhibit 12.3 describes the steps you must take to adjust each of these starting points to determine free cash flows to all debt and equity stakeholders. Exhibit 12.4 (page 917) describes the steps you must take to adjust each of these starting points to determine free cash flows to common equity shareholders.

If you start with net income and want to determine free cash flows for all debt and equity stakeholders, Exhibit 12.3 indicates that you must add back all non-cash expenses (such as depreciation and amortization expenses), subtract all non-cash income items (such as accrued income from equity method affiliates), and adjust for changes in working capital accounts (receivables, inventory, payables). These adjustments bring you to our previous starting point, cash flows from operations. You should then incorporate the remaining steps by adjusting for net interest expense after tax, changes in cash required for liquidity, and capital expenditures.

---

[7]It might seem inappropriate to include changes in debt and preferred stock financing, which appear in the financing section of the statement of cash flows, in the valuation of a firm. Economic theory suggests that the capital structure (that is, the proportion of debt versus equity) should not affect the value. Changes in debt and preferred stock, however, affect the amount of cash available to the common shareholders. You should include cash flows related to debt and preferred stock financing in free cash flows for common equity shareholders but adjust the cost of equity capital to reflect the amounts of such senior financing in the capital structure.

Exhibit 12.3

Measurement of Free Cash Flows for All Debt and Equity Stakeholders from Alternative Starting Points

Starting Point:

Net Income:	EBITDA:[a]	NOPAT:[b]
Operating Activities:	*Operating Activities:*	*Operating Activities:*
Net income	EBITDA	NOPAT
+ Add back all non-cash expenses	+ Add back all non-cash expenses other than depreciation and amortization	+ Add back all non-cash expenses
− Subtract all non-cash income items	− Subtract all non-cash income items	− Subtract all non-cash income items
+/− Working capital cash flows	+/− Working capital cash flows	+/− Working capital cash flows
+/− Net interest after tax	− Subtract cash taxes paid, net of tax savings on interest expense	
+/− Changes in cash required for liquidity	+/− Changes in cash required for liquidity	+/− Changes in cash required for liquidity
= *Free Cash Flows from Operations for All Debt and Equity Stakeholders*	= *Free Cash Flows from Operations for All Debt and Equity Stakeholders*	= *Free Cash Flows from Operations for All Debt and Equity Stakeholders*
Investing Activities:	*Investing Activities:*	*Investing Activities:*
+/− Net capital expenditures	+/− Net capital expenditures	+/− Net capital expenditures
= *Free Cash Flows for All Debt and Equity Stakeholders*	= *Free Cash Flows for All Debt and Equity Stakeholders*	= *Free Cash Flows for All Debt and Equity Stakeholders*

[a]EBITDA denotes earnings before interest, tax, depreciation, and amortization.
[b]NOPAT denotes net operating profit after tax, which equals net income adjusted for net interest expense after tax.

Exhibit 12.4

Measurement of Free Cash Flows for Common Equity Shareholders from Alternative Starting Points

Net Income:	Starting Point:
	EBITDA:[a]

EBITDA:[a]

Operating Activities:

EBITDA
+ Add back all non-cash expenses other than depreciation and amortization
− Subtract all non-cash income items
+/− Working capital cash flows
− Subtract net interest expense
− Subtract taxes
+/− Changes in cash required for liquidity

= *Free Cash Flows from Operations for Equity*

Investing Activities:
+/− Net capital expenditures

Financing Activities:
+/− **Debt cash flows**
+/− Financial asset cash flows
+/− Preferred stock cash flows
+/− Noncontrolling interest cash flows

= *Free Cash Flows for Common Equity Stakeholders*

NOPAT:[b]

Operating Activities:

NOPAT
+ Add back all non-cash expenses
− Subtract all non-cash income items
+/− Working capital cash flows
− Subtract net interest expense after tax
+/− Changes in cash required for liquidity

= *Free Cash Flows from Operations for Equity*

Investing Activities:
+/− Net capital expenditures

Financing Activities:
+/− **Debt cash flows**
+/− Financial asset cash flows
+/− Preferred stock cash flows
+/− Noncontrolling interest cash flows

= *Free Cash Flows for Common Equity Stakeholders*

Net Income:

Operating Activities:

Net income
+ Add back all non-cash expenses
− Subtract all non-cash income items
+/− Working capital cash flows
+/− Changes in cash required for liquidity

= *Free Cash Flows from Operations for Equity*

Investing Activities:
+/− Net capital expenditures

Financing Activities:
+/− **Debt cash flows**
+/− Financial asset cash flows
+/− Preferred stock cash flows
+/− Noncontrolling interest cash flows

= *Free Cash Flows for Common Equity Stakeholders*

---

[a]EBITDA denotes earnings before interest, tax, depreciation, and amortization.
[b]NOPAT denotes net operating profit after tax, which equals net income adjusted for net interest expense after tax.

Other analysts compute free cash flows for all debt and equity by starting with EBITDA, which already adds back non-cash income items for depreciation and amortization, interest expense (but usually not interest income) and *all* of the provision for income taxes. From this starting point, you must adjust further by adding back any other non-cash expenses (other than depreciation and amortization), adjust for non-cash income items, and adjust for changes in working capital accounts. In addition, because EBITDA adds back all of the provision for income taxes, you must subtract cash taxes paid, net of tax savings on interest expense. These adjustments bring you to our previous starting point, cash flows from operations. You then incorporate the remaining steps by adjusting for changes in cash required for operating liquidity and capital expenditures.

Finally, other analysts begin the computation of free cash flows for all debt and equity stakeholders using NOPAT, which is net income with net interest expense (adjusted for tax savings) added back. From this starting point, you should add back all non-cash expenses (such as depreciation and amortization expenses), subtract all non-cash income items (such as accrued income from equity method affiliates), and adjust for cash flows for changes in working capital accounts. You then incorporate the remaining steps by adjusting for changes in cash required for liquidity and capital expenditures.

In practice, some analysts also use net income, EBITDA, and NOPAT as starting points to compute free cash flows for equity shareholders. Exhibit 12.4 shows the steps necessary to adjust each of these starting point amounts to complete measures of free cash flows for common equity. Note that many, but not all, of the additional adjustments are similar to those demonstrated in Exhibit 12.3. Also note that although it occurs in practice, starting with EBITDA or NOPAT is inefficient because it is then necessary to subtract interest expense after tax.

The starting point of the computation of free cash flows is less important than the ending point. You can begin the computation with cash flow from operating activities on the statement of cash flows, net income, EBITDA, or NOPAT, so long as you properly make all of the necessary adjustments to compute a complete measure of free cash flows as described in Exhibits 12.2–12.4.

Which Free Cash Flow Measure Should Be Used?

The appropriate free cash flow measure to use—free cash flows to all debt and equity stakeholders or free cash flows to equity shareholders—depends on your objective.

- If your objective is to value net operating assets or, equivalently the sum of the debt and equity capital of a firm, you should use the free cash flow for all debt and equity stakeholders, discounted using the weighted-average cost of capital.
- If your objective is to value the common shareholders' equity of a firm, you should use the free cash flow for common equity shareholders, discounted at the cost of equity capital.

The difference between these two valuations is the value of total debt financing, preferred stock, and noncontrolling interests. To reconcile the two valuations, one could value the debt financing instruments by discounting all future debt service cash flows (including repayments of principal) at the after-tax cost of debt capital, all preferred-stock dividends at the cost of preferred equity, and all noncontrolling interest dividends at the appropriate cost of equity capital for the subsidiary firm. Subtracting these present values of debt financing, preferred stock, and noncontrolling interests from the present value of the sum of debt and equity capital yields the present value of common equity. The approach to use depends on the valuation setting.

Example 1: Valuing an Asset Acquisition. One firm wants to acquire the net operating assets of another firm. The acquiring firm will replace the financing structure of the target with a financing structure that matches its own. The relevant free cash flows for valuing the target's net operating assets are the operating cash flows the assets will generate minus the expected capital expenditures in operating assets or, equivalently, the free cash flows for all debt and equity capital. The acquiring firm will discount these projected free cash flows for all debt and equity capital at the expected future weighted-average cost of capital of the acquiring firm because it will use a similar financing structure for the target.

Example 2: Valuing Equity Shares. An investor wants to value 1,000 shares of common stock in a firm. The relevant cash flows are the free cash flows available for common equity shareholders. These free cash flows measure the cash flows generated from using the assets of the firm minus the cash required to service the debt. Thus, free cash flows for common equity shareholders should capture the cash generated by operating the assets of the firm plus any beneficial effects of financial leverage on the value of the common equity minus the cash flows required to service debt capital. The investor should discount these projected free cash flows at the required return on equity capital.

Example 3: Valuing a Leveraged Buyout. The managers of a firm intend to acquire a target firm through a leveraged buyout (LBO). The managers offer to purchase the outstanding shares of the target firm by investing their own equity (usually 20%–25% of the total) and borrowing the remainder from various lenders. The tendered shares serve as collateral for the loan (often called a *bridge loan*) during the transaction. After gaining voting control of the firm, the managers will have the firm engage in sufficient new borrowing to repay the bridge loan. Following an LBO, the firm will likely have a significantly higher debt level in the capital structure from the use of leverage to execute the takeover.

Determining the value of the common shares acquired follows the usual procedure for an equity investment (see prior example.) This value should equal the present value of free cash flows for common equity discounted at the cost of common equity capital. The valuation of the equity must reflect the new capital structure and the related increase in debt service costs. Also, the cost of equity capital will likely increase as a result of the higher level of debt in the capital structure; the common shareholders bear more risk as residual claimants on the assets of the firm. Therefore, the valuation must be based on the expected new cost of equity capital.

As an alternative approach that will produce the same value for the common equity, you can treat an LBO as a purchase of assets (similar to Example 1). That is, compute the present value of the free cash flows for all debt and equity capital stakeholders using the expected future weighted-average cost of debt and equity capital, using weights that reflect the newly leveraged capital structure of the acquired firm. This amount represents the value of net operating assets. Subtract from the present value of net operating assets the present value of debt raised to execute the LBO.[8] The result is the present value of the common equity.

---

[8]It is irrelevant whether any debt on the books of the target firm remains outstanding after the LBO or whether the firm engages in additional borrowing to repay existing debt, as long as the weighted-average cost of capital properly includes the costs of each financing arrangement.

LO 12-3

Estimate firm value using the:

a. present value of future free cash flows for common equity shareholders, discounted at the required rate of return on equity capital.

b. present value of future free cash flows for all debt and equity stakeholders, discounted at the weighted-average cost of capital.

Cash-Flow-Based Valuation Models

Thus far, this chapter has discussed all of the elements of free-cash-flow-based valuation. To bring all of the elements together, we next present the free-cash-flow-based valuation models. In each of these equations, all of the variables used to compute firm value are *expectations* of future free cash flows, future discount rates, and future growth rates.

Valuation Models for Free Cash Flows for Common Equity Shareholders

The following equation values the common equity of a firm as of time $t=0$ (denoted as V_0) using the present value of free cash flows for common equity shareholders discounted at the required rate of return on equity capital (R_E):

$$V_0 = \sum_{t=1}^{\infty} \left[\text{Free Cash Flow Equity}_t / (1 + R_E)^t \right]$$

This valuation approach expresses the value of the common equity of the firm as a function of the present value of the free cash flows the firm will generate for the common equity shareholders after the firm has met all other cash requirements for working capital, capital expenditures, principal and interest payments on debt financing, preferred stock dividends, and noncontrolling interests dividends. Given that common equity shareholders are the residual risk-bearers of the firm, this valuation approach estimates common equity value using the residual free cash flows available to them. Therefore, it is appropriate to discount these payoffs to present value using a discount rate that reflects the risk-adjusted required rate of return on common equity capital of the firm.

The following equation also computes the present value of common equity as of time $t = 0$, but in this equation, we compute the present value of the expected future free cash flows for common equity shareholders over a finite forecast horizon through Year T plus the present value of continuing value of free cash flows continuing in Year T+1 and beyond.[9] We compute continuing value based on the forecast assumption that the firm will grow indefinitely at rate g beginning in Year T+1 and continuing thereafter. We derive free cash flows for common equity shareholders in Year T+1 from the projected income statement and balance sheet for Year T+1, in which we project all of the elements of the Year T income statement and balance sheet to grow at rate g beginning in Year T+1. The equation is as follows:

$$V_0 = \sum_{t=1}^{T} \left[\text{Free Cash Flow Equity}_t / (1 + R_E)^t \right]$$
$$+ \text{Free Cash Flow Equity}_{T+1} \times \left[1/(R_E - g) \right] \times \left[1/(1 + R_E)^T \right]$$

Both of these equations represent the value of the common equity of the firm. The Valuations spreadsheet in FSAP provides a template that calculates V_0 using the present value of free cash flows for common equity shareholders, including the continuing value computation.

---

[9]Note that this valuation model is essentially identical to the dividends valuation model described in Chapter 11 (page 891). The only difference between the two models is the payoff being valued—dividends versus free cash flows for equity shareholders.

Valuation Models for Free Cash Flows for All Debt and Equity Stakeholders

The following equation determines the present value of the net operating assets of a firm as of time $t=0$ (denoted as $VNOA_0$) by computing the present value of all future free cash flows for all debt and equity capital stakeholders (denoted as *Free Cash Flow All*):

$$VNOA_0 = \sum_{t=1}^{\infty} \left[\text{Free Cash Flow All}_t / (1 + R_A)^t \right]$$

This equation differs from the models in the previous section in three important ways. First, this valuation approach does not compute the value of common shareholders' equity (V_0); instead, it computes the value of the *net operating assets* of the firm or, equivalently, the value of all of the debt, preferred, noncontrolling interests, and common equity claims on the net assets of the firm. Second, this model includes expected future free cash flows to all debt and equity stakeholders. The prior equation focused specifically on the expected future free cash flows to common equity shareholders. Third, this equation discounts the free cash flows to present value using R_A, which denotes the expected future weighted-average cost of capital (which should reflect the weighted-average required rate of return on the net operating assets of the firm). Previously, we relied on a discount rate using the required rate of return to equity (R_E).

This valuation approach expresses the value of the financial claims (debt, preferred, noncontrolling interests, and common equity) on the firm as a function of the present value of the free cash flows the firm's net operating assets will generate and that can ultimately be distributed to debtholders, preferred stockholders, noncontrolling investors, and common shareholders. Thus, the value-relevant payoff measure in this approach is the excess cash the firm's operations generate that will be available to satisfy all financing claims. Given that these free cash flows will be distributed to debt, preferred, noncontrolling, and common equity stakeholders, it is appropriate to discount these payoffs to present value using a discount rate that reflects the weighted-average cost of capital across these different capital claims.

The next equation summarizes the same computation but uses the present value of free cash flows for all debt and equity stakeholders over a finite forecast horizon through Year T (for example, T may be five or ten years in the future) plus the present value of continuing value. We compute continuing value based on the forecast assumption that the firm will grow indefinitely at rate g beginning in Year T+1 and continuing thereafter. We derive free cash flows for all debt and equity capital stakeholders in Year T+1 from the projected income statement and balance sheet for Year T+1, in which we project all elements of the Year T income statement and balance sheet to grow at rate g beginning in Year T+1. The equation is as follows:

$$V_0 = \sum_{t=1}^{T} \left[\text{Free Cash Flow All}_t / (1 + R_A)^t \right]$$
$$+ \text{Free Cash Flow All}_{T+1} \times \left[1/(R_A - g) \right] \times \left[1/(1 + R_A)^T \right]$$

Both of the prior equations estimate the value of the net operating assets of the firm, which is equivalent to the sum of the values of debt, preferred, noncontrolling, and common equity capital. To isolate the value of common equity capital, we must subtract the present value of all interest-bearing debt, preferred stock, and noncontrolling interests. The equation to compute the value of equity (denoted as V_0) is as follows:

$$V_0 = VNOA_0 - VDebt_0 - VPreferred_0 - VNCI_0$$

The Valuations spreadsheet in FSAP provides a template that calculates $VNOA_0$ and V_0 using the present value of free cash flows for all debt and equity capital stakeholders, including the continuing value computation.

In theory, the value of common equity using this valuation approach should be identical to the value of common equity using the free-cash-flows-to-equity approach, the dividends-based valuation approach discussed in the previous chapter, and the earnings-based approaches discussed in the following chapters. As a practical matter, however, it is sometimes difficult to get the equity value estimate from the free cash flows to all debt and equity stakeholders to match the other value estimates. The main reason is the added degrees of circularity in this valuation approach. For these different approaches to agree, the market-value-based weights for debt, preferred stock, noncontrolling interests, and common equity capital used in computing the weighted-average cost of capital must be consistent with the value estimates for debt, preferred stock, noncontrolling interests, and common equity. Thus, additional degrees of circularity arise because the value estimates depend on the weighted-average cost of capital, and the weighted-average cost of capital depends on the value estimates. Obtaining an internally consistent set of value estimates for each type of capital and an internally consistent weighted-average cost of capital may require a number of iterations until all of the weights and value estimates agree.

LO 12-4

Understand how to implement the free-cash-flows-based valuation approaches by applying them to estimate share value for PepsiCo.

Free Cash Flows Valuation of PepsiCo

At the end of 2012, trading in **PepsiCo** shares on the New York Stock Exchange closed at $68.43 per share. Therefore, we know the *price* at which we could buy or sell PepsiCo shares at that time. The free cash flows valuation methods enable us to estimate the *value* of these shares. This section illustrates the valuation of PepsiCo shares using the free cash flows valuation techniques described in this chapter and the forecasts developed in Chapter 10. We develop these forecasts and value estimates using the Forecast and Valuation spreadsheets in FSAP (see Appendix C).

In this section, we estimate the value of PepsiCo's shares at the end of 2012 (equivalently, the start of forecast Year +1) two ways, by estimating (a) the present value of free cash flows to *common equity* shareholders, discounted at the *equity* cost of capital; and (b) the present value of free cash flows to *all debt and equity* stakeholders, discounted using PepsiCo's *weighted-average* cost of capital; we then subtract the present value of debt claims.

To proceed with each valuation, we follow four steps:

1. Estimate the appropriate discount rates for PepsiCo.
2. Derive the free cash flows from the projected financial statements for PepsiCo described in Chapter 10 and make an assumption about free cash flows growth in the continuing periods beyond the forecast horizon.
3. Discount the free cash flows to present value, including continuing value.
4. Make the necessary adjustments to convert the present value computation to an estimate of share value for PepsiCo.

Once we have our benchmark estimate of PepsiCo's share value, we conduct sensitivity analysis to determine the reasonable range of values for PepsiCo shares. Finally, we compare this range of reasonable values to PepsiCo's share price in the market and suggest an appropriate investment decision indicated by our analysis. As we saw in the previous chapter using the dividends-based valuation approach, our value estimate was $85.86. Because of the equivalence of models, we should obtain the same value estimates here.

PepsiCo Discount Rates

To discount free cash flows to common equity shareholders, we need to compute PepsiCo's required rate of return on equity capital. To discount free cash flows to all debt and equity capital, we need to compute PepsiCo's weighted-average cost of capital. The following sections briefly describe the computations. Recall from Chapter 11 our computations of PepsiCo's required rate of return on equity capital and weighted-average cost of capital. This section will only briefly review those computations.

Computing the Required Rate of Return on Equity Capital for PepsiCo

At the end of 2012, different sources provided different estimates of market beta for PepsiCo common stock, ranging from 0.50 to 1.00. Historically, PepsiCo's market beta has varied around 0.75 over time, so we will assume that PepsiCo common stock has a market beta of 0.75 as of the end of 2012. At that time, U.S. Treasury bills with ten years to maturity traded with a yield of approximately 3.0%, which we use as the risk-free rate. Assuming a 6.0% market risk premium, the CAPM indicates that PepsiCo has a cost of common equity capital of 7.5% [7.5% = 3.0% + (0.75 × 6.0%)]. At the end of 2012, PepsiCo had 1,544 million shares outstanding and a share price of $68.43 for a total market capital of common equity of $105,656 million.

Computing the Weighted-Average Cost of Capital for PepsiCo

The following subsections demonstrate how to compute the costs of capital for the debt and other components of PepsiCo's capital structure, and then how to compute the PepsiCo's weighted-average cost of capital.

Debt Capital. PepsiCo's balance sheet (Appendix A) at the end of 2012 shows interest-bearing debt from short-term obligations of $4,815 million and long-term debt obligations of $23,544 million, totaling $28,359 million. In Note 10, "Financial Instruments" (Appendix A), PepsiCo discloses that the fair value of outstanding debt obligations at the end of 2012 is $30,500 million. Thus, PepsiCo has experienced an unrealized (and unrecognized) loss of $2,141 million ($28,359 million − $30,500 million) on its debt capital. We use the current fair value (as a proxy for market value) of PepsiCo's debt for weighting purposes. Recall that in Chapter 10, we used information disclosed in Note 9, "Debt Obligations and Commitments" (Appendix A), to assess stated interest rates on PepsiCo's interest-bearing debt. We determined that in 2012, PepsiCo's outstanding debt carries a weighted-average interest rate of approximately 3.65%. Given that many of PepsiCo's outstanding debt obligations were recently issued in 2012 and that prevailing yields to maturity are expected to be temporarily low, we forecast in Chapter 10 that PepsiCo's cost of debt capital will continue to approximate 3.65% in Year +1 and beyond. In Note 5, "Income Taxes" (Appendix A), PepsiCo discloses that the combined average federal, state, and foreign tax rate is approximately 25.2% in 2012. In Chapter 10, we forecast that PepsiCo will face average tax rates of roughly 27% in Year +1 and beyond. Therefore, our projections imply that PepsiCo faces an after-tax cost of debt capital of 2.66% [3.65 × (1 − 0.27)].

Preferred Stock and Noncontrolling Interests. PepsiCo has a net *negative* balance of $123 million in preferred stock on the 2012 balance sheet. Chapter 10 projected that PepsiCo will retire the remaining outstanding preferred stock during Year +1 and not issue any additional preferred stock capital in future years. Therefore, we include no preferred stock in the computation of PepsiCo's weighted-average cost of capital. PepsiCo's 2012 balance sheet also reports $105 million in equity capital attributable to noncontrolling interests. Chapter 10 projected that noncontrolling interests would earn a 10% rate of return, so we will use that as an estimate of the cost of capital for noncontrolling interests.

PepsiCo's Weighted-Average Cost of Capital. Bringing the costs of debt and equity capital together, we compute PepsiCo's weighted-average cost of capital to be 6.42%, as follows (allow for rounding):

Capital	Value Basis	Amounts in Millions	Weight	After-Tax Cost of Capital	Weighted-Average Component
Debt	Fair	$ 30,500	22.38%	2.66%	0.596%
Common equity	Market	105,656	77.54%	7.50%	5.816%
Noncontrolling interests	Book	105	0.08%	10.00%	0.008%
Totals		$136,261	100.00%		6.420%

Note that this is just our *initial* estimate of PepsiCo's weighted-average cost of capital. As described earlier, the weighted-average cost of capital must be computed iteratively until the weights used are consistent with the present values of debt and equity capital.

Computing Free Cash Flows for PepsiCo

This section first describes the computations for **PepsiCo**'s free cash flows for all debt and equity stakeholders, then describes the computations for PepsiCo's free cash flows for common equity shareholders. Recall that Exhibits 12.2–12.4 presented the steps to compute free cash flows, beginning with the statement of cash flows. Chapter 10 described detailed projections of PepsiCo's future statements of cash flows by making specific assumptions regarding each item on the income statement and balance sheet and then deriving the related cash flow effects over a five-year forecast horizon. We use these projections of PepsiCo's statements of cash flows (see Exhibit 10.6) to compute projected free cash flows. We report the projections of free cash flows for all debt and equity stakeholders, as well as the present value computations, in Exhibit 12.5. We report the projections and present value computations of free cash flows for common equity shareholders in Exhibit 12.6 (page 926).

PepsiCo's Free Cash Flows to All Debt and Equity Capital Stakeholders

In Exhibit 12.5, we begin our computation of free cash flows with cash flows from operations from the projected statements of cash flows developed in Chapter 10 for **PepsiCo** for Year +1 through Year +5.[10] In Year +1, for example, we project that PepsiCo's cash

---

[10]Please note that in Chapter 10, we present forecast amounts without decimals for ease of exposition. In this chapter, we present those same amounts rounded to one decimal place, for greater precision in estimating share value. Also, please allow for rounding in all of the computations in this chapter.

Exhibit 12.5

Projected Free Cash Flows to All Debt and Equity Stakeholders for PepsiCo Year +1 through Year +6 (dollar amounts in millions; allow for rounding)

Free Cash Flows for All Debt and Equity	Year +1	Year +2	Year +3	Year +4	Year +5	Year +6
Net cash flow from operations	$ 9,104.3	$ 9,850.3	$10,344.0	$11,221.7	$11,113.7	$ 8,764.4
Add back: Interest expense after tax	765.7	793.4	829.4	872.8	911.3	938.6
Subtract: Interest income after tax	(0.0)	(0.0)	(0.0)	(0.0)	(0.0)	(0.0)
Decrease (Increase) in cash required for operations	1,065.3	(218.3)	(229.6)	(355.5)	(140.5)	(185.3)
Free cash flow from operations for all debt and equity stakeholders	$10,935.3	$10,425.4	$10,943.8	$11,739.0	$11,884.5	$ 9,517.7
Net cash flows for investing activities	(4,480.6)	(4,974.8)	(5,207.4)	(6,280.2)	(4,955.4)	(3,035.9)
Add back: Net cash flows into financial assets	0.0	0.0	0.0	0.0	0.0	0.0
Free cash flows—all debt and equity stakeholders	$ 6,454.7	$ 5,450.6	$ 5,736.4	$ 5,458.8	$ 6,929.1	$ 6,481.9
Present value factors ($R_A = 6.42\%$)	0.940	0.883	0.830	0.780	0.733	
Present value free cash flows	$ 6,065.3	$ 4,812.8	$ 4,759.7	$ 4,256.1	$ 5,076.6	
Sum of present value of free cash flows for all debt and equity stakeholders, Year +1 through Year +5	$24,970.5					

flows from operations will be $9,104.3 million. We then adjust for net interest, adding back interest expense after tax. Specifically, in Year +1, we add back $765.7 million in interest expense after tax [$1,049.0 million × (1 – 0.27)]. We do not subtract interest income after tax because we assume that all of PepsiCo's interest income relates to financial assets (cash and short-term investments) that are used for liquidity in operating activities and strategic investments and are not part of the capital structure. We also adjust cash flow from operations for required investments in operating cash. In Chapter 10, we projected that PepsiCo would maintain roughly 28 days of sales in cash for liquidity purposes; therefore, Pepsi-Co's required cash balance varies with sales. For example, at the end of Year +1, we project that PepsiCo's cash balance will be $5,231.7 million, equivalent to 28 days of sales. Given that this balance is lower than PepsiCo's 2012 year-end cash balance of $6,297.0 million, it implies that PepsiCo will reduce its cash balance by $1,065.3 million. This increment of cash is available in Year +1 to satisfy debt and equity claims, so we add it to free cash flows. In Year +2, we project that the cash balance will grow by $218.3 million to $5,450.0 million. This additional increment of cash is required for liquidity in Year +2 and therefore is not a free cash flow, so we subtract it. As a result of these adjustments, we project that PepsiCo's free cash flows from operations for all debt and equity stakeholders will be $10,935.3 million in Year +1 and $10,425.4 million in Year +2, and so on.

Exhibit 12.6

Projected Free Cash Flows to Common Equity Shareholders for PepsiCo Year +1 through Year +6 (dollar amounts in millions; allow for rounding)

Free Cash Flows for Common Equity Shareholders	Year +1	Year +2	Year +3	Year +4	Year +5	Year +6
Net cash flow from operations	$ 9,104.3	$ 9,850.3	$10,344.0	$11,221.7	$11,113.7	$ 8,764.4
Decrease (increase) in cash required for operations	1,065.3	(218.3)	(229.6)	(355.5)	(140.5)	(185.3)
Free cash flow from operations for common equity shareholders	$10,169.6	$ 9,632.0	$10,114.4	$10,866.2	$10,973.2	$ 8,579.1
Net cash flows for investing activities	(4,480.6)	(4,974.8)	(5,207.4)	(6,280.2)	(4,955.4)	(3,035.9)
Net cash flows from debt financing	752.9	1,332.4	1,370.2	1,886.6	1,000.6	1,041.1
Net cash flows into financial assets	0.0	0.0	0.0	0.0	0.0	0.0
Net cash flows—preferred stock and noncontrolling interests	49.5	(10.5)	(10.5)	(10.5)	(10.5)	(7.7)
Free cash flow for common equity shareholders	$ 6,491.4	$ 5,979.0	$ 6,266.7	$ 6,462.1	$ 7,008.0	$ 6,576.6
Present value factors ($R_E = 7.50\%$)	0.930	0.865	0.805	0.749	0.697	
Present value of free cash flows	$ 6,038.5	$ 5,173.9	$ 5,044.5	$ 4,838.8	$ 4,881.5	
Sum of present value free cash flows for common equity shareholders, Year +1 through Year +5	$25,977.2					

Next, we subtract cash flows for capital expenditures using the amount of net cash flow for investing from PepsiCo's projected statements of cash flows. For example, in Year +1, we projected that net cash flows for investing activities will be $4,480.6 million. These investing cash flows include cash outflows for purchases of property, plant, and equipment; acquisitions of goodwill and other intangible assets; and purchases of marketable securities and investment securities. We consider purchases of marketable securities and investment securities to be investing activities (rather than financing activities) because these securities are for the purposes of operating liquidity, so we make no adjustment for cash flows into financial assets. Therefore, we subtract the full amount of net cash flow for investing activities from the free cash flow from operations. We forecast that PepsiCo's free cash flows for all debt and equity capital stakeholders will be $6,454.7 million ($10,935.3 million − $4,480.6 million) in Year +1. We repeat these steps each year through Year +5.

We estimate the present value of these free cash flows in Year +1 through Year +5 by discounting them using PepsiCo's weighted-average cost of capital, which we estimated to be 6.42%. Exhibit 12.5 shows that PepsiCo's free cash flows for all debt and equity through Year +5 have a present value of $24,970.5 million.

To project PepsiCo's free cash flows continuing in Year +6 and beyond, we forecast that PepsiCo will sustain a long-run growth rate of 3.0%, consistent with expected long-term growth in the economy. To compute continuing free cash flows in Year +6, we project each line item on PepsiCo's Year +5 income statement and balance sheet to grow at 3.0% per year in Year +6. We use these Year +6 projected income statement and balance sheet amounts to derive the Year +6 free cash flows for all debt and equity, which we project will be $6,481.9 million. We assume that this free cash flow amount is the beginning of a perpetuity of continuing free cash flows that PepsiCo will generate beginning in Year +6, growing at 3% each year thereafter. The computations are shown in detail in the Forecast and Valuation spreadsheets in FSAP (Appendix C), which permit specific forecast assumptions to extend as far as Year +5 into the future, with continuing value assumptions thereafter.

PepsiCo's Free Cash Flows to Common Equity

Exhibit 12.6 presents estimates of **PepsiCo**'s free cash flows for common equity share-holders through Year +6. The computations begin with the Year +1 projection of $9,104.3 million of cash flows from operations, as described earlier. As in the previous section, we adjust cash flow from operations in Year +1 by adding the increment of $1,065.3 million of cash no longer required for liquidity. Also as in the previous section, we subtract $4,480.6 million of projected cash outflows for capital expenditures and other investing activities in Year +1. Note that, unlike the previous section, we make no adjustment for net interest expense after tax because we need to measure the free cash flows available to equity shareholders net of all debt-related cash flows. Because our starting point, cash flows from operations, is derived from net income (after interest expense), our cash flows amount is net of interest expense.

To further refine these cash flows to free cash flows available to common equity, we need to adjust them for cash flows related to debt, preferred stock, and noncontrolling interest financing. We first add any cash inflows from new borrowing and subtract any cash outflows for debt repayments. For example, in Year +1, we add $752.9 million in cash flows for our projections of PepsiCo's additional short-term and long-term bor-rowing. We also subtract any cash outflows and add any cash inflows related to financial asset accounts that are part of PepsiCo's capital structure (which we have deemed to be zero). Next, we add inflows and subtract outflows related to transactions with pre-ferred stock and noncontrolling interest shareholders (if any). In Year +1, we add $49.5 million to free cash flows for preferred stock and noncontrolling interests. To obtain this amount, we include the $123.0 million adjustment to zero out the negative pre-ferred stock account, and subtract the projected $63.0 million payment in Year +1 to retire the remaining preferred shares. In addition, we subtract the projected dividends of $10.5 million in Year +1 to noncontrolling interests (which we projected to be equal to 100% payout of earnings attributable to noncontrolling interests). The net of all of these adjustments is a $49.5 million increase in free cash flows for equity in Year +1 ($123.0 million − $63.0 million − $10.5 million). (In Year +2 to Year +5, we simply subtract the projected $10.5 million in dividends to noncontrolling shareholders.) The computations project $6,491.4 million in free cash flows for PepsiCo's common equity shareholders in Year +1. We repeat these steps each year through Year +5.

We estimate the present value of these free cash flows in Year +1 through Year +5 by discounting them using PepsiCo's 7.50% risk-adjusted required rate of return on equity capital. Exhibit 12.6 shows that PepsiCo's free cash flows for common equity through Year + 5 have a present value of $25,977.2 million.

To project PepsiCo's free cash flows for common equity continuing in Year +6 and beyond, we again forecast that PepsiCo will sustain long-run growth of 3.0%. We

project the Year +5 income statement and balance sheet amounts to grow at a rate of 3.0% in Year +6 and derive free cash flows to common equity from the projected Year +6 statements. Our computations indicate that free cash flows to common equity in Year +6 will be $6,576.6 million (shown in detail in the Forecast and Valuation spreadsheets in FSAP in Appendix C). We assume that these free cash flows will continue to grow at 3.0% per year thereafter.

Valuation of PepsiCo Using Free Cash Flows to Common Equity Shareholders

We estimate the value of a share of common equity in **PepsiCo** at the end of 2012 (equivalently, the start of Year +1) by discounting to present value the free cash flows to equity using PepsiCo's 7.50% risk-adjusted required rate of return on equity capital as the appropriate discount rate. As shown in Exhibit 12.6, PepsiCo's free cash flows for common equity through Year +5 have a present value of $25,977.2 million.

We compute the present value of PepsiCo's continuing value as the present value of a growing perpetuity of free cash flows beginning in Year +6, which we project will be $6,576.6. We project these free cash flows to grow at 3.0% and discount them to present value using the 7.50% discount rate. The present value of these cash flows is $101,800.3 million. As shown in Exhibit 12.7, the present value of PepsiCo's free cash flows to common equity shareholders is the sum of these two parts:

Present value free cash flows through Year +5	$ 25,977.2 million
Present value of continuing value in Year +6 and beyond	101,800.3 million
Present value of common equity	$127,777.5 million

As described in the previous chapter, we need to correct our present value calculations for over-discounting. To make the correction, we multiply the present value sum by the midyear adjustment factor of 1.0375 $[1 + (R_E /2) = 1 + (0.0750/2)]$. The total present value of free cash flows to common equity shareholders should be $132,569.1 million ($127,777.5 million $\times$ 1.0375). Dividing the total value of common equity of PepsiCo by 1,544 million shares outstanding indicates that PepsiCo's common equity shares have a value of $85.86 per share. This share value estimate is identical to the share value estimate we computed using dividends in the previous chapter. Exhibit 12.8 presents these computations from the Valuations spreadsheet in FSAP.

Valuation of PepsiCo Using Free Cash Flows to All Debt and Equity Stakeholders

We also estimate the present value of a share of common equity in **PepsiCo** at the end of 2012 by discounting the free cash flows to all debt and equity stakeholders using PepsiCo's 6.42% weighted-average cost of capital as the appropriate discount rate. Exhibit 12.5 shows that PepsiCo's free cash flows for all debt and equity stakeholders through Year +5 have a present value of $24,970.5 million. To compute the present value of PepsiCo's continuing value, we compute the continuing value in Year +6 and beyond using the perpetuity-with-growth model. First, as described earlier and shown in Exhibit 12.5, we project that PepsiCo will generate free cash flows of $6,481.9 million in Year +6, and that these free cash flows will grow at a rate of 3.0% indefinitely.

Exhibit 12.7

Valuation of PepsiCo Using Free Cash Flows to Common Equity Shareholders (allow for rounding)

Present Value of Free Cash Flows to Common Equity Shareholders in Year +1 through Year +5:

From Exhibit 12.6:	$ 25,977.2 million

Present Value of Continuing Value of Free Cash Flows to Common Equity in Year +6 and Beyond:

Projected Year +6 Free Cash Flows to Common Equity (Exhibit 12.6): $6,576.6 million

Continuing Value in Present Value (R_E = 7.50% and g = 3.0%):

Continuing Value $= \text{Free Cash Flow}_{\text{Year}+6} \times [1/(R_E - g)]$
$= \$6,576.6 \text{ million} \times [1/(0.0750 - 0.0300)]$
$= \$6,576.6 \text{ million} \times 22.2222$
$= \$146,147.5 \text{ million}$

Present Value of Continuing Value $= \text{Continuing Value} \times [1/(1 + R_E)^5]$
$= \$146,147.5 \text{ million} \times [1/(1 + 0.0750)^5]$
$= \$146,147.5 \text{ million} \times 0.697$ | $=\$101,800.3$ million

Total Value of PepsiCo's Free Cash Flows to Common Equity Shareholders:

Present value of free cash flows through Year +5	$ 25,977.2 million
Present value of continuing value	+ 101,800.3 million
Present value of common equity	$127,777.5 million
Adjust for midyear discounting (multiply by 1 + [R /2])	× 1.0375
Total present value of common equity	$132,569.1 million
Divide by number of shares outstanding	÷ 1,544 million
Value per share of PepsiCo common equity	$ 85.86

Exhibit 12.9 (page 931) demonstrates that in present value, PepsiCo's continuing value has a present value of $138,874.5 million.[11] The present value of PepsiCo's free cash flows to all debt and equity capital stakeholders is the sum of these two parts:

Present value free cash flows through Year +5	$ 24,970.5 million
Present value of continuing value Year +6 and beyond	138,874.5 million
Present value of free cash flows for all debt and equity	$163,845.0 million

Necessary Adjustments to Compute Common Equity Share Value

To narrow this computation to the present value of common equity, we need to subtract the market value of interest-bearing debt, preferred stock, and noncontrolling interests,

---

[11]Because of the effects of rounding, it appears the present value of continuing value computation may be slightly in error. But when computed with greater precision and less rounding the computation is correct, as follows: *Continuing Value = Free Cash Flow*$_{\text{Year}+6} \times [1/(R_A - g)] \times [1/(1 + R_A)^5]$ = $6,481.888 million × [1/(0.0641957 − 0.0300)] × [1/(1 + 0.0641957)^5]$ = $6,481.888 million × 29.243443 × 0.732643 = $138,874.457 million.

Exhibit 12.8

FSAP Valuation of PepsiCo Using Free Cash Flows to Common Equity Shareholders through Year +5 and Beyond (in millions, except per-share amounts; allow for rounding)

Free Cash Flows for Common Equity Shareholders	Year +1	Year +2	Year +3	Year +4	Year +5	Continuing Value Year +6
Net cash flow from operations	$ 9,104.3	$ 9,850.3	$10,344.0	$11,221.7	$11,113.7	$ 8,764.4
Decrease (Increase) in cash required for operations	1,065.3	(218.3)	(229.6)	(355.5)	(140.5)	(185.3)
Net cash flows for investing activities	(4,480.6)	(4,974.8)	(5,207.4)	(6,280.2)	(4,955.4)	(3,035.9)
Net cash flows from debt financing	752.9	1,332.4	1,370.2	1,886.6	1,000.6	1,041.1
Net cash flows into financial assets	0.0	0.0	0.0	0.0	0.0	0.0
Net cash flows—preferred stock and noncontrolling interests	49.5	(10.5)	(10.5)	(10.5)	(10.5)	(7.7)
Free cash flow for common equity shareholders	$ 6,491.4	$ 5,979.0	$ 6,266.7	$ 6,462.1	$ 7,008.0	$ 6,576.6
Present value factors ($R_E = 7.50\%$)	0.930	0.865	0.805	0.749	0.697	
Present value of free cash flows	$ 6,038.5	$ 5,173.9	$ 5,044.5	$ 4,838.8	$ 4,881.5	
Sum of present value free cash flows for common equity shareholders, Year +1 through Year +5	$ 25,977.2					
Present value of continuing value	101,800.3					
Total	$127,777.5					
Adjust to midyear discounting	1.0375					
Total present value of free cash flows to equity	$132,569.1					
Shares outstanding	1,544.0					
Estimated value per share	$ 85.86					
Current share price	$ 68.43					
Percent difference	25%					

Exhibit 12.9

Valuation of PepsiCo Using Free Cash Flows to All Debt and Equity Stakeholders (allow for rounding)

Present Value of Free Cash Flows to All Debt and Equity Stakeholders in Year +1 through Year +5:

From Exhibit 12.5:	**$ 24,970.5 million**

Present Value of Continuing Value of Free Cash Flows to All Debt and Equity Stakeholders in Year +6 and Beyond:

Projected Year +6 Free Cash Flows to All Debt and Equity Stakeholders
(Exhibit 12.5): $6,481.9 million

Continuing Value in Present Value ($R_A = 6.42\%$ and $g = 3.0\%$):

Continuing Value	$= \text{Free Cash Flow} \times [1/(R - g)]$
	$= \$6,481.9 \text{ million} \times [1/(0.0642 - 0.030)]$
	$= \$6,481.9 \text{ million} \times 29.240$
	$= \$189,552.7 \text{ million}$

Present Value of Continuing Value	$= \text{Continuing Value} \times [1/(1 + R)^5]$	
	$= \$189,552.7 \text{ million} \times [1/(1 + 0.0642)^5]$	
	$= \$189,552.7 \text{ million} \times 0.733$	$=\$138,874.5$ million

Total Value of PepsiCo's Free Cash Flows to All Debt and Equity Stakeholders:

Present value of free cash flows through Year +5	$ 24,970.5	million
+ Present value of continuing value	+ 138,874.5	million
Present value of all debt and equity	$163,845.0	million
Subtract fair value of debt	− 30,500.0	million
Subtract fair value to retire preferred stock	− 63.0	million
Subtract book value of noncontrolling interests	− 105.0	million
Add fair value of financial assets in the capital structure	+ 0.0	million
Present value of common equity	$133,177.0	million
Adjust for midyear discounting [multiply by $1 + (R_A/2) = 1 + (0.0642/2)$]	× 1.0321	
Total present value of common equity	$137,451.7	million
Divide by number of shares outstanding	÷ 1,544	million
Value per share of PepsiCo common equity	$ 89.02	

and add the present value of interest-earning financial assets that are part of the firm's financial capital structure. Exhibit 12.9 summarizes all of these computations, and Exhibit 12.10 (page 932) presents the computations to arrive at PepsiCo's common equity share value using the free cash flows to all debt and equity stakeholders approach in the Valuations spreadsheet in FSAP.

Relying on PepsiCo's book values of debt, we subtract $30,500 million for the fair value of outstanding debt. We also assumed that PepsiCo would retire the outstanding preferred stock during Year +1, so we subtract the $63 million cash outflow that will be required to retire that preferred stock. We also subtract the $105 million book value (as a proxy for fair value) of equity capital attributable to noncontrolling interests.

Exhibit 12.10

FSAP Valuation of PepsiCo Using Free Cash Flows to All Debt and Equity Stakeholders through Year +5 and Beyond (in millions, except per-share amounts; allow for rounding)

Free Cash Flows for All Debt and Equity Stakeholders	Year +1	Year +2	Year +3	Year +4	Year +5	Continuing Value Year +6
Net cash flow from operations	$ 9,104.3	$ 9,850.3	$10,344.0	$11,221.7	$11,113.7	$ 8,764.4
Add back: Interest expense after tax	765.7	793.4	872.8	872.8	911.3	938.6
Subtract: Interest income after tax	0.0	0.0	0.0	0.0	0.0	0.0
Decrease (Increase) in cash required for operations	1,065.3	(218.3)	(229.6)	(355.5)	(140.5)	(185.3)
Free cash flow from operations	$ 10,935.3	$10,425.4	$10,943.8	$11,739.0	$11,884.5	$ 9,517.7
Net cash flow from investing activities	(4,480.6)	(4,974.8)	(5,207.4)	(6,280.2)	(4,955.4)	(3,035.9)
Add back: Net cash flows into financial assets	0.0	0.0	0.0	0.0	0.0	0.0
Free cash flow for all debt and equity stakeholders	$ 6,454.7	$ 5,450.6	$ 5,736.4	$ 5,458.8	$ 6,929.1	$ 6,481.9
Present value factors ($R_E = 6.42\%$)	0.940	0.883	0.830	0.780	0.733	
Present value of free cash flows	$ 6,065.3	$ 4,812.8	$ 4,759.7	$ 4,256.1	$ 5,076.6	
Sum of present value free cash flows for all debt and equity stakeholders, Year +1 through Year +5	$ 24,970.5					
Present value of continuing value	138,874.5					
Total present value of free cash flows to equity and debt	$163,845.0					
Less: Value of outstanding debt	(30,500.0)					
Value of preferred stock	(63.0)					
Noncontrolling interests	(105.0)					
Plus: Value of financial assets	0.0					
Present value of equity	$133,177.0					
Adjust to midyear discounting	1.0321					
Total present value of free cash flows to equity	$137,451.7					
Shares outstanding	1,544.0					
Estimated value per share	$ 89.02					
Current share price	$ 68.43					
Percent difference	30%					

We assume that PepsiCo's financial assets are not part of the financial capital structure, so we do not adjust for them. After these adjustments, the present value of PepsiCo's common equity capital is $133,177.0 million ($163,845.0 million − $30,500.0 million − $63.0 million − $105.0 million).

As described earlier, our present value calculations have over-discounted these cash flows because we have discounted each year's cash flows for a full period when, in fact, PepsiCo generates cash flows throughout each period and we should discount them from the midpoint of each year to the present. Therefore, to make the correction, we multiply the present value sum by the midyear adjustment factor of 1.0321 $[1 + (R_A/2) = 1 + (0.0642/2)]$. Therefore, the total present value of free cash flows to common equity shareholders is $137,451.7 million ($133,177.0 million × 1.0321). Dividing by 1,544 million shares outstanding indicates that PepsiCo's common equity shares have a value of $89.02 per share.

Note that our calculation of an $89.02 value for PepsiCo's common equity shares is slightly different from the value of $85.86 per share obtained from the free-cash-flows-to-common-equity approach described previously and the dividends-based approach in the previous chapter. This is because we used the current market price per share of PepsiCo common stock ($68.43) in the initial weighted-average cost of capital computation, rather than our previous value estimate ($85.86). As a consequence, we did not place enough weight on the market value of equity in the initial cost of capital computation. To iterate the valuation approach, we can use the share value estimate of $85.86 to determine that the total value of PepsiCo common equity in the weighted-average cost of capital computation. To further iterate the valuation approach, we can recompute the weighted-average cost of equity capital each forecast year because our projections indicate that PepsiCo's common equity in the capital structure will gradually fall in proportion to the debt financing in the capital structure in future years. After a number of iterations, the valuation computations and the weights we use to compute the weighted-average cost of capital converge (which highlights the circularity of this approach, namely that we require an estimate of share value to compute share value). The equity value estimate of $132,569.1 million, or $85.86 per share, is the internally consistent value.

Sensitivity Analysis and Investment Decision Making

LO 12-5

Assess the sensitivity of firm value estimates to key valuation parameters such as discount rates and expected long-term growth rates.

As we emphasized in the previous chapter, forecasts of cash flows over the remaining life of any firm, even a mature firm such as **PepsiCo**, contain a high degree of uncertainty; so we should not place too much confidence in the *precision* of value estimates using these forecasts. Although we have constructed these forecasts and value estimates with care, the forecasting and valuation process has an inherently high degree of uncertainty and estimation error. Therefore, do not rely too heavily on any one point estimate of the value of a firm's shares; instead, you should describe a reasonable range of values for a firm's shares.

Two critical forecasting and valuation parameters in most valuations are the long-run growth rate assumption and the cost of equity capital assumption. You should conduct sensitivity analyses to test the effects of these and other key forecast assumptions and valuation parameters on the share value estimate. Sensitivity analysis tests should allow you to vary these assumptions and parameters individually and jointly for additional insights into the correlation between share value, growth rates, and discount rate assumptions.

For PepsiCo, our base case assumptions indicate PepsiCo's share value to be roughly $85.86. Our base case valuation assumptions include a long-run growth rate of 3% and a cost of equity capital of 7.50%. We can assess the sensitivity of our estimates of PepsiCo's share value by varying these two parameters (or any other key parameters in the valuation) across reasonable ranges. Exhibit 12.11 contains the results of sensitivity analysis varying the long-run growth rate from 0–10% and the cost of equity capital from 5–20%. The data in Exhibit 12.11 show that as the discount rate increases, holding growth constant, share value estimates of PepsiCo fall. Likewise, value estimates fall as growth rates decrease, holding discount rates constant.

Considering the downside possibilities first, if we reduce the long-run growth assumption to 2.0% while holding the discount rate constant at 7.50%, PepsiCo's share value falls to $74.81, still above current market price. Similarly, if we increase the discount rate to 8.0 or 10.0% while holding the long-run growth assumption constant at 3.0%, PepsiCo shares have a value of roughly $77.56. If we revise both assumptions at once and reduce the long-run growth assumption to 2% and increase the discount rate assumption to 8.0%, PepsiCo's share value falls to roughly $68.75, which is slightly above the market price of $68.43.

On the upside, if we reduce the discount rate to 7.0% while holding long-run growth constant at 3.0% or if we increase the long-run growth assumption from 3.0% to 4.0% while holding the discount rate constant at 7.50%, the value estimates jump to roughly $96 per share or $103 per share, respectively. If we reduce the discount rate assumption further or increase the long-run growth rate further, our share value estimates for PepsiCo jump dramatically higher.

These data suggest that our value estimate is sensitive to slight variations of our baseline assumptions of 3.0% long-run growth and a 7.50% discount rate, which yield a

Exhibit 12.11

Valuation of PepsiCo:
Sensitivity Analysis of Value to Growth and Equity Cost of Capital

Free Cash Flows to Equity Valuation Sensitivity Analysis:

	Long-Run Growth Assumptions								
85.86	**0%**	**2%**	**3%**	**4%**	**5%**	**6%**	**8%**	**10%**
Discount Rates:								
5%	91.96	135.32	189.52	352.10				
6%	76.74	102.04	127.33	177.92	329.69			
7%	65.88	82.07	96.23	119.84	167.05	308.67		
7.50%	61.54	74.81	85.86	103.23	134.50	207.46		
8%	57.74	68.75	77.56	90.77	112.79	156.83		
9%	51.42	59.24	65.11	73.32	85.64	106.18	270.44	
10%	46.37	52.11	56.21	61.68	69.33	80.82	138.23	
11%	42.23	46.56	49.53	53.35	58.44	65.58	94.10	236.75
12%	38.80	42.12	44.33	47.10	50.65	55.40	72.00	121.80
13%	35.89	38.48	40.17	42.23	44.80	48.11	58.70	83.42
14%	33.40	35.45	36.76	38.33	40.24	42.63	49.82	64.18
15%	31.25	32.89	33.92	35.13	36.59	38.36	43.45	52.60
18%	26.23	27.12	27.65	28.26	28.96	29.78	31.91	35.10
20%	23.74	24.34	24.70	25.10	25.56	26.08	27.38	29.20

share value estimate of $85.86. Adverse variations in valuation parameters could reduce PepsiCo's share value estimates to $68 or lower, whereas favorable variations could increase PepsiCo's share value up to or above $100.

If our forecast and valuation assumptions are realistic, our baseline value estimate for PepsiCo is approximately $85.86 per share at the end of 2012. At that time, the market price of $68.43 per share indicates that PepsiCo shares were underpriced by about 25%. Under our forecast assumptions, PepsiCo's share value could vary within a range of a low of $68 per share to a high of $103 per share with only minor perturbations in our growth rate and discount rate assumptions. Given PepsiCo's $68.43 share price, these value estimates would have supported a buy recommendation at the end of 2012 because the valuation sensitivity analysis reveals limited downside potential but substantial upside potential for the value of PepsiCo shares.

Summary

This chapter illustrates valuation using the present value of future free cash flows. As with the preparation of financial statement forecasts in Chapter 10, the reasonableness of the valuations depends on the reasonableness of the assumptions. You should assess the sensitivity of the valuation to alternative assumptions regarding growth and discount rates. To validate value estimates using a free-cash-flows-based approach, you also should compute the value of the common equity of the firm using other approaches, such as the dividends-based approach described in Chapter 11, the earnings-based approach described in Chapter 13, and the market-based approaches described in Chapter 14.

Questions, Exercises, Problems, and Cases

Questions and Exercises

12.1 Free Cash Flows. Explain "free" cash flows. Describe which types of cash flows are *free* and which are not. How do free cash flows available for debt and equity stakeholders differ from free cash flows available for common equity shareholders?   `LO 12-1`

12.2 Free-Cash-Flows-Based Valuation Approaches. Explain the theory behind the free cash flows valuation approaches. Why are free cash flows value-relevant to common equity shareholders when they are not cash flows to those shareholders but rather are cash flows into the firm?   `LO 12-1`

12.3 Valuation Approach Equivalence. Conceptually, why should you expect valuation based on dividends and valuation based on the free cash flows for common equity shareholders to yield identical value estimates?   `LO 12-1`

12.4 Measuring Value-Relevant Free Cash Flows. The chapter describes free cash flows for common equity shareholders. If the firm borrows cash by issuing debt, how does that transaction affect free cash flows for common equity shareholders in that period? If the firm uses cash to repay debt, how does that transaction affect free cash flows for common equity shareholders in that period?   `LO 12-2`

12.5 Measuring Value-Relevant Free Cash Flows. The chapter describes free cash flows for common equity shareholders. Suppose a firm has no debt and uses marketable securities to manage operating liquidity. If the firm uses cash to purchase marketable securities, how does that transaction affect free cash flows for common equity shareholders in that period? If the firm sells marketable securities for cash, how does that transaction affect free cash flows for common equity shareholders in that period?

LO 12-3

12.6 Valuation When Free Cash Flows Are Negative. Suppose you are valuing a healthy, growing, profitable firm and you project that the firm will generate negative free cash flows for equity shareholders in each of the next five years. Can you use a free-cash-flows-based valuation approach when cash flows are negative? If so, explain how a free-cash-flows approach can produce positive valuations of firms when they are expected to generate negative free cash flows over the next five years.

LO 12-2, LO 12-3, LO 12-4

12.7 Using Different Free-Cash-Flows-Based Approaches. The chapter describes valuation using free cash flows for all debt and equity stakeholders as well as free cash flows for equity shareholders. For each approach, give one example of valuation settings in which that approach is appropriate.

LO 12-2, LO 12-3, LO 12-4

12.8 Appropriate Discount Rates. Describe valuation settings in which the appropriate discount rate to use is the required rate of return on equity capital versus settings in which it is appropriate to use a weighted-average cost of capital.

LO 12-2, LO 12-3, LO 12-4

12.9 Free Cash Flows and Discount Rates. Describe circumstances and give an example of when free cash flows to equity shareholders and free cash flows to all debt and equity stakeholders will be identical. Under those circumstances, will the required rate of return on equity and the weighted-average cost of capital be identical too? Explain.

Problems and Cases

LO 12-2

12.10 Calculating Free Cash Flows. The **3M Company** is a global diversified technology company active in the following product markets: consumer and office; display and graphics; electronics and communications; health care; industrial; safety, security, and protection services; and transportation. At the consumer level, 3M is probably most widely known for products such as Scotch® Brand transparent tape and Post-it® notes. Exhibit 12.12 presents information from the statement of cash flows and income statement for the 3M Company for 2006–2008. From 2006 through 2008, 3M increased cash and cash equivalents. Assume that 3M considers these increases in cash and cash equivalents to be necessary to sustain operating liquidity. The interest income reported by 3M pertains to interest earned on cash and marketable securities. 3M holds only small amounts of investments in marketable securities. 3M's income tax rate is 35%.

REQUIRED

    a. Beginning with cash flows from operating activities, calculate the amount of free cash flows to all debt and equity capital stakeholders for 3M for 2006, 2007, and 2008.

    b. Beginning with cash flows from operating activities, calculate the amount of free cash flows 3M generated for common equity shareholders in 2006, 2007, and 2008.

    c. Reconcile the amounts of free cash flows 3M generated for common equity shareholders in 2006, 2007, and 2008 from Requirement b with 3M's uses of cash flows for equity shareholders, including share repurchases and dividend payments.

LO 12-2

12.11 Calculating Free Cash Flows. **Dick's Sporting Goods** is a chain of full-line sporting goods retail stores offering a broad assortment of brand name sporting goods equipment, apparel, and footwear. Dick's Sporting Goods had its initial public offering of

Exhibit 12.12

3M Company
Selected Information from the Statement of Cash Flows
(amounts in millions)
(Problem 12.10)

	2008	2007	2006
Operating Activities:			
Cash Flow from Operating Activities	$ 4,118	$ 4,363	$ 3,896
Investing Activities:			
Fixed assets acquired, net	(1,384)	(1,319)	(1,119)
(Acquisition) Sale of businesses, net	(1,306)	358	321
(Purchase) Sale of investments	291	(406)	(662)
Cash Flow from Investing Activities	$(2,399)	$(1,367)	$(1,460)
Financing Activities:			
Increase (Decrease) in short-term borrowing	361	(1,222)	882
Increase (Decrease) in long-term debt	676	2,444	253
Increase (Decrease) in common stock	(1,405)	(2,389)	(1,820)
Dividends paid	(1,398)	(1,380)	(1,376)
Cash Flow from Financing Activities	$(1,766)	$(2,547)	$(2,061)
Net increase (decrease) in cash & equivalents	$ (47)	$ 449	$ 375
Cash at beginning of year	$ 1,896	$ 1,447	$ 1,072
Cash at end of year	$ 1,849	$ 1,896	$ 1,447
Interest income	$ 105	$ 132	$ 51
Interest expense	$ 215	$ 210	$ 122

Source: 3M Company, Form 10-K for Fiscal Year Ended December 31, 2008.

shares in fiscal 2003. Since then, Dick's Sporting Goods has grown its chain of retail stores rapidly and has acquired several other chains of retail sporting goods stores, including Golf Galaxy and Chick's Sporting Goods in the fiscal year ending in 2008. As of the end of the fiscal year ending in 2009, Dick's Sporting Goods operated 409 stores in 40 states of the United States. Exhibit 12.13 presents information from the statement of cash flows and income statement for Dick's Sporting Goods for the fiscal years ending in 2007 through 2009. Dick's Sporting Goods requires all of its cash and cash equivalents for operating liquidity and reports no interest income on the income statement. The average income tax rate for Dick's Sporting Goods during 2007 through 2009 is 40%.

REQUIRED

a. Beginning with cash flows from operating activities, calculate free cash flows to all debt and equity capital stakeholders for Dick's Sporting Goods for fiscal years ending in 2007, 2008, and 2009.

b. Beginning with cash flows from operating activities, calculate free cash flows for common equity shareholders for Dick's Sporting Goods for fiscal years ending in 2007, 2008, and 2009.

Exhibit 12.13

Dick's Sporting Goods
Selected Information from the Statement of Cash Flows
(amounts in thousands)
(Problem 12.11)

	Fiscal year ended		
	January 31, 2009	February 2, 2008	February 3, 2007
CASH FLOWS FROM OPERATING ACTIVITIES:			
Net (loss) income	$ (35,094)	$ 155,036	$ 112,611
Adjustments to reconcile net (loss) income to net cash provided by operating activities:			
Depreciation and amortization	90,732	75,052	54,929
Impairment of store assets, goodwill and other intangible assets	193,350	—	—
Deferred income taxes	(45,906)	(32,696)	(1,110)
Various addbacks to net income	24,709	2,462	(7,371)
Changes in assets and liabilities, net of acquired assets and liabilities:			
Accounts receivable	3,090	(10,982)	(2,142)
Inventories	29,581	(127,027)	(105,766)
Prepaid expenses and other assets	(10,554)	(4,267)	(29,039)
Accounts payable	(56,709)	12,337	24,444
Accrued expenses	(7,575)	26,222	42,479
Income taxes payable/receivable	(63,089)	114,706	4,750
Deferred construction allowances	19,452	22,256	19,264
Deferred revenue and other liabilities	17,689	29,869	26,560
Net cash provided by operating activities	**$ 159,676**	**$ 262,968**	**$ 139,609**
CASH FLOWS USED IN INVESTING ACTIVITIES:			
Capital expenditures	(191,423)	(172,366)	(162,995)
Purchase of corporate aircraft	(25,107)	—	—
Proceeds from sale of corporate aircraft	27,463	—	—
Proceeds from sale-leaseback transactions	44,873	28,440	32,509
Payment for the purchase of Golf Galaxy, net of $4,859 cash acquired	—	(222,170)	—
Payment for the purchase of Chick's Sporting Goods	—	(69,200)	—
Net cash used in investing activities	**$(144,194)**	**$(435,296)**	**$(130,486)**
CASH FLOWS FROM FINANCING ACTIVITIES:			
Increase (Decrease) Short-term borrowing	(9,927)	4,785	8,829
Long-term borrowing—Construction allowance receipts	11,874	13,282	17,902

(Continued)

Exhibit 12.13 (Continued)			
Payments on long-term debt and capital leases	(6,793)	(1,058)	(184)
Proceeds from sale of common stock	13,894	69,684	63,708
Net cash provided by financing activities	$ 9,048	$ 86,693	$ 90,255
NET INCREASE (DECREASE) IN CASH	$ 24,530	$ (85,635)	$ 99,378
CASH, BEGINNING OF PERIOD	50,307	135,942	36,564
CASH, END OF PERIOD	$ 74,837	$ 50,307	$ 135,942
Cash paid during the year for interest	$ 8,021	$ 12,314	$ 9,286

Source: Dick's Sporting Goods, Form 10-K for the Fiscal Year Ended January 31, 2009.

c. Reconcile the amounts of free cash flows for common equity shareholders for Dick's Sporting Goods for fiscal years ending in 2007, 2008, and 2009 with Dick's Sporting Goods' sources of cash flows from equity shareholders.

d. Why do the free cash flows to all debt and equity capital stakeholders for Dick's Sporting Goods change so much from year to year? In each of these three years, why do the free cash flows to all debt and equity capital stakeholders differ so much from the free cash flows to common equity shareholders?

e. In each of these three years, Dick's Sporting Goods produces negative free cash flows for common shareholders. Does that imply that Dick's Sporting Goods is destroying the value of common equity? Explain.

12.12 Valuing a Leveraged Buyout Candidate. May Department Stores

LO 12-4

Company (May) operates retail department store chains throughout the United States. Assume that at the end of Year 2, May's balance sheet reports debt of $4,658 million and common shareholders' equity at book value of $3,923 million. The market value of its common stock is $6,705, and its market equity beta is 0.88.

Suppose an equity buyout group is considering an LBO of May as of the beginning of Year 3. The group intends to finance the buyout with 25% common equity and 75% debt carrying an interest rate of 10%. Assume the group projects that the free cash flows to all debt and equity capital stakeholders of May will be as follows: Year 3, $798 million; Year 4, $861 million; Year 5, $904 million; Year 6, $850 million; Year 7, $834 million; Year 8, $884 million; Year 9, $919 million; Year 10, $947 million; Year 11, $985 million; and Year 12, $1,034 million. The group projects free cash flows to grow 3% annually after Year 12.

This problem sets forth the steps you might follow in deciding whether to acquire May and the value to place on the firm.

REQUIRED

a. Compute the unlevered market equity (asset) beta of May before consideration of the LBO. Assume that the book value of the debt equals its market value. The income tax rate is 35%. (See Chapter 11.)

b. Compute the cost of equity capital with the new capital structure that results from the LBO. Assume a risk-free rate of 4.2% and a market risk premium of 5.0%.

c. Compute the weighted-average cost of capital of the new capital structure.

d. Compute the present value of the projected free cash flows to all debt and equity capital stakeholders at the weighted-average cost of capital. Ignore the midyear adjustment related to the assumption that cash flows occur, on average, over the year. In computing the continuing value, apply the projected growth rate in free cash flows after Year 12 of 3% directly to the free cash flows of Year 12.

e. Assume that the buyout group acquires May for the value determined in Requirement d. Assuming that the realized free cash flows coincide with projections, will May generate sufficient cash flow each year to service the interest on the debt? Explain.

12.13 Valuing a Leveraged Buyout Candidate. At the end of Year 5, Experian Information Solutions, Inc. (Experian) has total assets of $555,443, long-term debt of $1,839, and common equity at book value of $402,759 (amounts in thousands). Suppose an equity buyout group is planning to acquire Experian in an LBO as of the beginning of Year 6. The group plans to finance the buyout with 60% debt that has an interest cost of 10% per year and 40% common equity. Analysts for the buyout group project free cash flows to all debt and equity capital stakeholders as follows (in thousands): Year 6, $52,300; Year 7, $54,915; Year 8, $57,112; Year 9, $59,396; and Year 10, $62,366. Because Experian is not a publicly traded firm, it does not have a market equity beta. The company most comparable to Experian is Equifax. Equifax has an equity beta of 0.86. The market value of Equifax's debt is $366.5 thousand, and its common equity is $4,436.8 thousand. Assume an income tax rate of 35% throughout this problem.

This problem sets forth the steps you might follow in valuing an LBO candidate.

REQUIRED

a. Compute the unlevered market equity (asset) beta of Equifax. (See Chapter 11.)

b. Assuming that the unlevered market equity beta of Equifax is appropriate for Experian, compute the equity beta of Experian after the buyout with its new capital structure.

c. Compute the weighted-average cost of capital of Experian after the buyout. Assume a risk-free interest rate of 4.2% and a market risk premium of 5.0%.

d. The analysts at the buyout firm project that free cash flows for all debt and equity capital stakeholders of Experian will increase 5.0% each year after Year 10. Compute the present value of the free cash flows at the weighted-average cost of capital. Ignore the midyear adjustment related to the assumption that cash flows occur, on average, over the year. In computing the continuing value, apply the 5.0% projected growth rate directly to the free cash flows of Year 10.

e. Assume that the buyout group acquires Experian for the value determined in Requirement d. Assuming that actual free cash flows to all debt and equity capital stakeholders coincide with projections, will Experian generate sufficient cash flow each year to service the debt? Explain.

12.14 Applying Various Present Value Approaches to Valuation. An equity buyout group intends to acquire Wedgewood as of the beginning of Year 8. The buyout group intends to finance 40% of the acquisition price with debt bearing a 10% interest rate and 60% with common equity. The income tax rate is 40%. The cost of equity capital is 14%. Analysts at the buyout firm project the following free cash flows for all debt and equity capital stakeholders for Wedgewood (in millions): Year 8, $2,100; Year 9, $2,268; Year 10, $2,449; Year 11, $2,645; and Year 12, $2,857. The analysts project that free cash flows for all debt and equity capital stakeholders will increase 8% each year after Year 12.

REQUIRED

a. Compute the weighted-average cost of capital for Wedgewood based on the proposed capital structure.

b. Compute the total purchase price of Wedgewood (debt plus common equity). To do this, discount the free cash flows for all debt and equity capital stakeholders at the weighted-average cost of capital. Ignore the midyear adjustment related to the assumption that cash flows occur, on average, over the year. In computing the continuing value, apply the 8% projected growth rate in free cash flows after Year 12 directly to the free cash flows of Year 12.

c. Given the purchase price determined in Requirement b, compute the total amount of debt, the annual interest cost, and the free cash flows to common equity shareholders for Year 8 to Year 12.

d. The present value of the free cash flows for common equity shareholders when dis-counted at the 14% cost of equity capital should equal the common equity portion of the total purchase price computed in Requirement b. Determine the growth rate in free cash flows for common equity shareholders after Year 12 that will result in a present value of free cash flows for common equity shareholders equal to 60% of the purchase price computed in Requirement b.

e. Why does the implied growth rate in free cash flows to common equity shareholders determined in Requirement d differ from the 8% assumed growth rate in free cash flows for all debt and equity capital stakeholders?

f. The adjusted present value valuation approach separates the total value of the firm into the value of an all-equity firm and the value of the tax savings from interest deductions. Assume that the cost of unlevered equity is 11.33%. Compute the present value of the free cash flows to all debt and equity capital stakeholders at this unlevered equity cost. Compute the present value of the tax savings from interest expense deductions using the pretax cost of debt as the discount rate. Compare the total of these two present values to the purchase price determined in Requirement b.

12.15 Valuing the Equity of a Privately Held Firm. Refer to the projected [LO 12-3]

financial statements for Massachusetts Stove Company (MSC) prepared for Case 10.2. The man-agement of MSC wants to know the equity valuation implications of not adding gas stoves ver-sus adding gas stoves under the best, most likely, and worst scenarios. Under the three scenarios from Case 10.2 and a fourth scenario involving not adding gas stoves, the projected free cash flows to common equity shareholders for Year 8 to Year 12, and assumed growth rates thereafter, are as follows:

Year	Best	Most Likely	Worst	No Gas
8	$ 73,967	$ 47,034	$ 3,027	$162,455
9	$ 52,143	$ (3,120)	$(84,800)	$132,708
10	$213,895	$135,939	$ 48,353	$106,021
11	$315,633	$178,510	$ 36,605	$ 81,840
12	$432,232	$220,010	$ 10,232	$ 60,007
13–17	20% Growth	10% Growth	Zero Growth	Zero Growth
After Year 17	10% Growth	5% Growth	Zero Growth	Zero Growth

MSC is not publicly traded and therefore does not have a market equity beta. Using the market equity beta of the only publicly traded woodstove and gas stove manufacturing firm and adjusting it for differences in the debt-to-equity ratio, income tax rate, and privately owned status of MSC yields a cost of equity capital for MSC of 13.55%.

REQUIRED

a. Calculate the value of the equity of MSC as of the beginning of Year 8 under each of the four scenarios. Ignore the midyear adjustment related to the assumption that cash flows occur, on average, over the year. Apply the growth rates in free cash flows to common equity shareholders after Year 12 directly to the free cash flow of the preceding year. (That is, Year 13 free cash flow equals the Year 12 free cash flow times the given growth rate; Year 18 free cash flow equals the Year 17 free cash flow times the given growth rate.)

b. How do these valuations affect your advice to the management of MSC regarding the addition of gas stoves to its woodstove line?

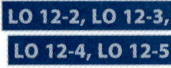

12.16 Free-Cash-Flows-Based Valuation. The **Coca-Cola Company** is a
global soft drink beverage company (ticker symbol = KO) that is a primary and direct competitor with **PepsiCo**. The data in Exhibits 12.14–12.16 (pages 943–946) include the actual amounts for 2010, 2011, and 2012 and projected amounts for Year +1 to Year +6 for the income statements, balance sheets, and statements of cash flows for Coca-Cola (in millions). The market equity beta for Coca-Cola at the end of 2012 is 0.75. Assume that the risk-free interest rate is 3.0% and the market risk premium is 6.0%. Coca-Cola has 4,469 million shares outstanding at the end of 2012, when Coca-Cola's share price was $35.48.

REQUIRED

Part I—Computing Coca-Cola's Share Value Using Free Cash Flows to Common Equity Shareholders

a. Use the CAPM to compute the required rate of return on common equity capital for Coca-Cola.

b. Derive the projected free cash flows for common equity shareholders for Coca-Cola for Years +1 through +6 based on the projected financial statements. Assume that Coca-Cola's changes in cash each year are necessary for operating liquidity purposes. The financial statement forecasts for Year +6 assume that Coca-Cola will experience a steady-state long-run growth rate of 3% in Year +6 and beyond.

c. Using the required rate of return on common equity from Requirement a as a discount rate, compute the sum of the present value of free cash flows for common equity share holders for Coca-Cola for Years +1 through +5.

d. Using the required rate of return on common equity from Requirement a as a discount rate and the long-run growth rate from Requirement b, compute the continuing value of Coca-Cola as of the start of Year +6 based on Coca-Cola's continuing free cash flows for common equity shareholders in Year +6 and beyond. After computing continuing value as of the start of Year +6, discount it to present value at the start of Year +1.

e. Compute the value of a share of Coca-Cola common stock.
   (1) Compute the total sum of the present value of all future free cash flows for equity shareholders (from Requirements c and d).
   (2) Adjust the total sum of the present value using the midyear discounting adjustment factor.
   (3) Compute the per-share value estimate.

Part II—Computing Coca-Cola's Share Value Using Free Cash Flows to All Debt and Equity Stakeholders

f. At the end of 2012, Coca-Cola had $32,610 million in outstanding interest-bearing short-term and long-term debt on the balance sheet and no preferred stock. Assume that the balance sheet value of Coca-Cola's debt is approximately equal to the market value of the debt. The forecasts assume that Coca-Cola will face

Exhibit 12.14

The Coca-Cola Company
Income Statements for 2010 through 2012 (Actual) and Year +1 through Year +6 (Projected)
(amounts in millions; allow for rounding)
(Problem 12.16)

	Actuals			Forecasts					
	2010	2011	2012	Year +1	Year +2	Year +3	Year +4	Year +5	Year +6
Revenues	$35,119	$46,542	$48,017	$50,418	$52,939	$55,586	$58,365	$61,283	$63,122
Cost of goods sold	(12,693)	(18,215)	(19,053)	(20,167)	(21,175)	(22,234)	(23,346)	(24,513)	(25,249)
Gross Profit	$22,426	$28,327	$28,964	$30,251	$31,763	$33,351	$35,019	$36,770	$37,873
Selling, general, and admin. expenses	(13,194)	(17,422)	(17,738)	(18,655)	(19,587)	(20,567)	(21,595)	(22,675)	(23,355)
Other operating expenses	(819)	(732)	(447)	(504)	(529)	(556)	(584)	(613)	(631)
Operating Profit	$ 8,413	$10,173	$10,779	$11,092	$11,647	$12,229	$12,840	$13,482	$13,887
Interest income	317	483	471	360	396	412	430	448	461
Interest expense	(733)	(417)	(397)	(978)	(1,006)	(1,065)	(1,125)	(1,188)	(1,223)
Income from equity affiliates	1,025	690	819	857	900	945	992	1,041	1,073
Other income	5,185	529	137	0	0	0	0	0	0
Income before Tax	$14,207	$11,458	$11,809	$11,330	$11,936	$12,521	$13,137	$13,784	$14,197
Income tax expense	(2,370)	(2,812)	(2,723)	(2,606)	(2,745)	(2,880)	(3,021)	(3,170)	(3,265)
Net Income	$11,837	$ 8,646	$ 9,086	$ 8,724	$ 9,191	$ 9,641	$10,115	$10,613	$10,932
Net income attributable to noncontrolling interests	(50)	(62)	(67)	(57)	(57)	(57)	(57)	(57)	(58)
Net Income Attributable to Common Shareholders	$11,787	$ 8,584	$ 9,019	$ 8,668	$ 9,134	$ 9,585	$10,058	$10,557	$10,873
Other comprehensive income items	(771)	(1,265)	(611)	0	0	0	0	0	0
Comprehensive Income	$11,116	$ 7,319	$ 8,408	$ 8,668	$ 9,134	$ 9,585	$10,058	$10,557	$10,873

Source for Actuals: The Coca-Cola Company, Form 10-K for the Fiscal Year Ended December 31, 2012.

Exhibit 12.15

The Coca-Cola Company
Balance Sheets for 2010 through 2012 (Actual) and Year +1 through Year +6 (Projected)
(amounts in millions; allow for rounding)
(Problem 12.16)

	Actuals			Forecasts					
	2010	2011	2012	Year +1	Year +2	Year +3	Year +4	Year +5	Year +6
ASSETS									
Cash and cash equivalents	$ 8,517	$ 12,803	$ 8,442	$ 11,050	$ 11,603	$ 12,183	$ 12,792	$ 13,432	$ 13,835
Marketable securities	2,820	1,232	8,109	8,352	8,603	8,861	9,127	9,401	9,683
Accounts receivable (net)	4,430	4,920	4,759	5,111	5,366	5,635	5,916	6,212	6,399
Inventories	2,650	3,092	3,264	3,370	3,539	3,716	3,902	4,097	4,220
Prepaid expenses and other current assets	3,162	3,450	2,781	2,920	3,066	3,219	3,380	3,549	3,656
Assets held for sale	0	0	2,973	0	0	0	0	0	0
Current Assets	$ 21,579	$ 25,497	$ 30,328	$ 30,804	$ 32,177	$ 33,614	$ 35,118	$ 36,691	$ 37,792
Long-term investments in affiliates	7,585	8,374	10,448	10,970	11,519	12,095	12,700	13,335	13,735
Property, plant & equipment (at cost)	21,706	23,151	23,486	26,486	29,636	32,944	36,416	40,063	41,265
Accumulated depreciation	(6,979)	(8,212)	(9,010)	(10,945)	(13,111)	(15,518)	(18,180)	(21,107)	(21,740)
Amortizable intangible assets (net)	1,377	1,250	1,150	1,050	950	850	750	650	670
Goodwill	11,665	12,219	12,255	12,868	13,511	14,187	14,896	15,641	16,110
Other nonamortizable intangibles	13,867	14,200	13,932	14,629	15,360	16,128	16,934	17,781	18,315
Other noncurrent assets	2,121	3,495	3,585	3,764	3,952	4,150	4,358	4,575	4,713
Total Assets	$72,921	$79,974	$86,174	$89,626	$93,995	$98,449	$102,992	$107,629	$110,857

(Continued)

	Actuals			Forecasts					
	2010	2011	2012	Year +1	Year +2	Year +3	Year +4	Year +5	Year +6
LIABILITIES									
Accounts payable—trade	$ 1,887	$ 2,172	$ 1,969	$ 2,222	$ 2,339	$ 2,456	$ 2,579	$ 2,708	$ 2,789
Current accrued liabilities	6,972	6,837	6,711	7,047	7,399	7,769	8,157	8,565	8,822
Notes payable and short-term debt	8,100	12,871	16,297	17,113	18,118	19,158	20,233	21,347	21,987
Current maturities of long-term debt	1,276	2,041	1,577	1,656	1,753	1,854	1,958	2,066	2,128
Income taxes payable	273	362	471	448	470	492	515	538	554
Liabilities of segments held for sale	0	0	796	0	0	0	0	0	0
Current Liabilities	$ 18,508	$ 24,283	$ 27,821	$ 28,485	$ 30,079	$ 31,729	$ 33,442	$ 35,223	$ 36,280
Long-term debt	14,041	13,656	14,736	15,474	16,383	17,323	18,295	19,302	19,881
Deferred tax liabilities—noncurrent	4,261	4,694	4,981	5,181	5,433	5,690	5,953	6,221	6,408
Other noncurrent liabilities	4,794	5,420	5,468	5,741	6,028	6,330	6,646	6,979	7,188
Total Liabilities	$ 41,604	$ 48,053	$ 53,006	$ 54,881	$ 57,923	$ 61,072	$ 64,337	$ 67,725	$ 69,757
SHAREHOLDERS' EQUITY									
Common stock + paid-in capital	$ 10,937	$ 12,092	$ 13,139	$ 13,665	$ 14,331	$ 15,011	$ 15,703	$ 16,410	$ 16,902
Retained earnings	49,278	53,621	58,045	62,369	66,917	71,688	76,695	81,950	84,409
Accum. other comprehensive income (loss)	(1,450)	(2,774)	(3,385)	(3,385)	(3,385)	(3,385)	(3,385)	(3,385)	(3,385)
Treasury stock	(27,762)	(31,304)	(35,009)	(38,283)	(42,170)	(46,315)	(50,737)	(55,450)	(57,215)
Common Shareholders' Equity	$ 31,003	$ 31,635	$ 32,790	$ 34,367	$ 35,693	$ 36,999	$ 38,277	$ 39,525	$ 40,711
Noncontrolling interests	314	286	378	378	378	378	378	378	389
Total Equity	$ 31,317	$ 31,921	$ 33,168	$ 34,745	$ 36,071	$ 37,377	$ 38,655	$ 39,903	$ 41,100
Total Liabilities and Equities	$ 72,921	$ 79,974	$ 86,174	$ 89,626	$ 93,995	$ 98,449	$102,992	$107,629	$110,857

Source for Actuals: The Coca-Cola Company, Form 10-K for the Fiscal Year Ended December 31, 2012.

Exhibit 12.16

The Coca-Cola Company
Projected Implied Statements of Cash Flows for Year +1 through Year +6
(amounts in millions; allow for rounding)
(Problem 12.16)

			Forecasts			
	Year +1	Year +2	Year +3	Year +4	Year +5	Year +6
IMPLIED STATEMENT OF CASH FLOWS						
Net Income	$ 8,705	$ 9,151	$ 9,600	$10,071	$10,567	$10,884
Add back depreciation expense (net)	1,935	2,166	2,407	2,661	2,928	633
(Increase) Decrease in receivables (net)	(352)	(256)	(268)	(282)	(296)	(186)
(Increase) Decrease in inventories	(106)	(169)	(177)	(186)	(195)	(123)
(Increase) Decrease in prepaid expenses	(139)	(146)	(153)	(161)	(169)	(106)
Increase (Decrease) in accounts payable—trade	253	117	117	123	129	81
Increase (Decrease) in current accrued liabilities	336	352	370	388	408	257
Increase (Decrease) in income taxes payable	(23)	22	22	23	23	16
Net change in deferred tax assets and liabilities	200	253	257	263	268	187
Increase (Decrease) in other noncurrent liabilities	273	287	301	316	332	209
Cash flows from assets/liabilities of segment sold	2,177	0	0	0	0	0
Net Cash Flows from Operations	$13,259	$11,778	$12,476	$13,217	$13,995	$11,852
(Increase) Decrease in prop., plant, & equip., at cost	(3,000)	(3,150)	(3,308)	(3,473)	(3,647)	(1,202)
(Increase) Decrease in marketable securities	(243)	(251)	(258)	(266)	(274)	(282)
(Increase) Decrease in investment securities	(522)	(549)	(576)	(605)	(635)	(400)
(Increase) Decrease in amortizable intangible assets (net)	100	100	100	100	100	(20)
(Increase) Decrease in goodwill and nonamort. intang.	(1,309)	(1,375)	(1,444)	(1,516)	(1,592)	(1,003)
(Increase) Decrease in other non-current assets	(179)	(188)	(198)	(208)	(218)	(137)
Net Cash Flows from Investing	$ (5,154)	$ (5,412)	$ (5,683)	$ (5,967)	$ (6,265)	$ (3,043)
Increase (Decrease) in short-term debt	895	1,103	1,140	1,180	1,221	702
Increase (Decrease) in long-term debt	738	909	940	973	1,007	579
Increase (Decrease) in common stock + paid-in capital	526	666	679	693	707	492
Increase (Decrease) in accum. OCI and other equity adjs.	0	0	0	0	0	0
Increase (Decrease) in treasury stock	(3,274)	(3,887)	(4,145)	(4,422)	(4,713)	(1,765)
Dividends	(4,324)	(4,547)	(4,771)	(5,007)	(5,255)	(8,367)
Dividends to noncontrolling interests	(57)	(57)	(57)	(57)	(57)	(47)
Net Cash Flows from Financing	$ (5,496)	$ (5,813)	$ (6,214)	$ (6,641)	$ (7,091)	$ (8,405)
Net Change in Cash	$ 2,608	$ 553	$ 580	$ 609	$ 640	$ 403

an interest rate of 3.0% on debt capital and that Coca-Cola's average tax rate will be 23% (based on the past five-year average effective tax rate). Coca-Cola also had non-controlling interests of $378 million at that time. The forecasts assume a 15.0% cost of capital for noncontrolling interests. (For our forecasts, we assume noncontrolling interests receive dividends equal to the required rate of return each year.) Compute the weighted-average cost of capital for Coca-Cola as of the start of Year +1.

g. Beginning with projected net cash flows from operations, derive the projected free cash flows for all debt and equity stakeholders for Coca-Cola for Years +1 through +6 based on the projected financial statements. Assume that the change in cash each year is related to operating liquidity needs.

h. Using the weighted-average cost of capital from Requirement f as a discount rate, compute the sum of the present value of free cash flows for all debt and equity stakeholders for Coca-Cola for Years +1 through +5.

i. Using the weighted-average cost of capital from Requirement f as a discount rate and the long-run growth rate from Requirement b, compute the continuing value of Coca-Cola as of the start of Year +6 based on Coca-Cola's continuing free cash flows for all debt and equity stakeholders in Year +6 and beyond. After computing continuing value as of the start of Year +6, discount it to present value as of the start of Year +1.

j. Compute the value of a share of Coca-Cola common stock.
   (1) Compute the total value of Coca-Cola's net operating assets using the total sum of the present value of free cash flows for all debt and equity stakeholders (from Requirements h and i).
   (2) Subtract the value of outstanding debt to obtain the value of equity.
   (3) Adjust the present value of equity using the midyear discounting adjustment factor.
   (4) Compute the per-share value estimate of Coca-Cola's common equity shares.

Note: Do not be alarmed if your share value estimate from Requirement e is slightly different from your share value estimate from Requirement j. The weighted-average cost of capital computation in Requirement f used the weight of equity based on the market price of Coca-Cola's stock at the end of 2012. The share value estimates from Requirements e and j likely differ from the market price, so the weights used to compute the weighted-average cost of capital are not internally consistent with the estimated share values.

Part III—Sensitivity Analysis and Recommendation

k. Using the free cash flows to common equity shareholders, recompute the value of Coca-Cola shares under two alternative scenarios.
   Scenario 1: Assume that Coca-Cola's long-run growth will be 2%, not 3% as before, and assume that Coca-Cola's required rate of return on equity is 1% higher than the rate you computed for Requirement a.
   Scenario 2: Assume that Coca-Cola's long-run growth will be 4%, not 3% as before, and assume that Coca-Cola's required rate of return on equity is 1% lower than the rate you computed in Requirement a. To quantify the sensitivity of your share value estimate for Coca-Cola to these variations in growth and discount rates, compare (in percentage terms) your value estimates under these two scenarios with your value estimate from Requirement e.

l. Using these data at the end of 2012, what reasonable range of share values would you have expected for Coca-Cola common stock? At that time, what was the market price for Coca-Cola shares relative to this range? What investment strategy (buy, hold, or sell) would you have recommended?

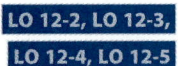

12.17 Free-Cash-Flows-Based Valuation. In Problem 10.16, we projected financial statements for **Walmart Stores, Inc.** (Walmart) for Years +1 through +5. The data in Exhibits 12.17–12.19 (pages 948–950) include the actual amounts for 2012 and the projected amounts for Year +1 to Year +5 for the income statements, balance sheets, and statements of cash flows for Walmart (in millions). These forecast amounts assume Walmart will use implied dividends as the financial flexible account to balance the balance sheet.

The market equity beta for Walmart at the end of 2012 was 1.00. Assume that the risk-free interest rate was 3.0% and the market risk premium was 6.0%. Walmart had 3,314 million shares outstanding at the end of 2012, and a share price of $69.09.

REQUIRED

Part I—Computing Walmart's Share Value Using Free Cash Flows to Common Equity Shareholders

a. Use the CAPM to compute the required rate of return on common equity capital for Walmart.

b. Beginning with projected net cash flows from operations, derive the projected free cash flows for common equity shareholders for Walmart for Years +1 through +5 based on the projected financial statements. Assume that Walmart uses cash for operating liquidity purposes.

c. Project the continuing free cash flow for common equity shareholders in Year +6. Assume that the steady-state, long-run growth rate will be 3% in Year +6 and beyond. Project that the Year +5 income statement and balance sheet amounts will

---

Exhibit 12.17

Walmart Stores, Inc.
Income Statements for 2012 (Actual) and Year +1 through Year +5 (Projected)
(amounts in millions; allow for rounding)
(Problem 12.17)

	Actual	Projected				
	2012	Year +1	Year +2	Year +3	Year +4	Year +5
Revenues	$ 469,162	$ 487,928	$ 507,446	$ 527,743	$ 548,853	$ 570,807
Cost of goods sold	(352,488)	(365,946)	(380,584)	(395,808)	(411,640)	(428,105)
Gross Profit	$ 116,674	$ 121,982	$ 126,861	$ 131,936	$ 137,213	$ 142,702
Selling, general, and administrative expenses	(88,873)	(92,706)	(96,415)	(100,271)	(104,282)	(108,453)
Interest income	187	202	202	202	202	202
Interest expense	(2,251)	(2,308)	(2,377)	(2,448)	(2,522)	(2,597)
Income before tax	$ 25,737	$ 27,170	$ 28,272	$ 29,419	$ 30,612	$ 31,853
Income tax expense	(7,981)	(8,694)	(9,047)	(9,414)	(9,796)	(10,193)
Income attributable to noncontrolling interests	(757)	(809)	(809)	(809)	(809)	(809)
Net Income Attributable to Common Shareholders	$ 16,999	$ 17,666	$ 18,416	$ 19,195	$ 20,007	$ 20,851

Source for Actual 2012: Walmart Stores, Inc., Form 10-K for the Fiscal Year Ended January 31, 2013.

Exhibit 12.18

Walmart Stores, Inc.
Balance Sheets for 2012 (Actual) and Year +1 through Year +5 (Projected)
(amounts in millions; allow for rounding)
(Problem 12.17)

	Actual	Projected				
	2012	Year +1	Year +2	Year +3	Year +4	Year +5
ASSETS						
Cash and cash equivalents	$ 7,781	$ 7,781	$ 7,781	$ 7,781	$ 7,781	$ 7,781
Accounts receivable—net	6,768	7,106	7,462	7,835	8,227	8,638
Inventories	43,803	44,114	45,879	47,714	49,622	51,607
Prepaid expenses and other current assets	1,588	1,652	1,718	1,786	1,858	1,932
Current Assets	$ 59,940	$ 60,653	$ 62,839	$ 65,116	$ 67,488	$ 69,958
Property, plant & equipment—at cost	171,724	184,224	196,724	209,224	221,724	234,224
Accumulated depreciation	(55,043)	(64,254)	(74,090)	(84,552)	(95,638)	(107,349)
Goodwill and other assets	26,484	27,543	28,645	29,791	30,983	32,222
Total Assets	$203,105	$208,166	$214,118	$219,579	$224,556	$ 229,055
LIABILITIES						
Accounts payable—trade	$ 38,080	$ 38,131	$ 39,806	$ 41,398	$ 43,054	$ 44,777
Current accrued expenses	18,808	19,560	20,343	21,156	22,003	22,883
Notes payable and short-term debt	6,805	7,009	7,219	7,436	7,659	7,889
Current maturities of long-term debt	5,914	6,091	6,274	6,462	6,656	6,856
Income taxes payable	2,211	2,277	2,346	2,416	2,488	2,563
Current Liabilities	$ 71,818	$ 73,069	$ 75,988	$ 78,869	$ 81,861	$ 84,967
Long-term debt	41,417	42,660	43,939	45,257	46,615	48,014
Deferred tax liabilities—noncurrent	7,613	7,841	8,077	8,319	8,568	8,826
Redeemable noncontrolling interest	519	0	0	0	0	0
Total Liabilities	$121,367	$123,570	$128,004	$132,446	$137,045	$ 141,807
SHAREHOLDERS' EQUITY						
Common stock + paid-in capital	3,952	4,163	4,282	4,392	4,491	4,581
Retained earnings	72,978	75,625	77,023	77,934	78,213	77,859
Accum. other comprehensive income (loss)	(587)	(587)	(587)	(587)	(587)	(587)
Common Shareholders' Equity	$ 76,343	$ 79,201	$ 80,719	$ 81,738	$ 82,117	$ 81,853
Noncontrolling interests	5,395	5,395	5,395	5,395	5,395	5,395
Total Equity	81,738	84,596	86,114	87,133	87,512	87,248
Total Liabilities and Equities	$203,105	$208,166	$214,118	$219,579	$224,556	$ 229,055

Source for Actual 2012: Walmart Stores, Inc., Form 10-K for the Fiscal Year Ended January 31, 2013.

Exhibit 12.19

Walmart Stores, Inc.
Projected Implied Statements of Cash Flows for Year +1 through Year +5
(amounts in millions; allow for rounding)
(Problem 12.17)

	Projected				
	Year +1	Year +2	Year +3	Year +4	Year +5
IMPLIED STATEMENTS OF CASH FLOWS					
Net income	$ 18,476	$ 19,225	$ 20,005	$ 20,816	$ 21,660
Add back depreciation expense (net)	9,211	9,836	10,461	11,086	11,711
(Increase) Decrease in receivables—net	(338)	(355)	(373)	(392)	(411)
(Increase) Decrease in inventories	(311)	(1,765)	(1,835)	(1,909)	(1,985)
(Increase) Decrease in prepaid expenses	(64)	(66)	(69)	(71)	(74)
Increase (Decrease) in accounts payable—trade	51	1,675	1,592	1,656	1,722
Increase (Decrease) in current accrued liabilities	752	782	814	846	880
Increase (Decrease) in income taxes payable	66	68	70	72	75
Net change in deferred tax assets and liabilities	228	235	242	250	257
Net Cash Flows from Operations	$ 28,072	$ 29,636	$ 30,908	$ 32,355	$ 33,835
(Increase) Decrease in prop., plant, & equip., at cost	(12,500)	(12,500)	(12,500)	(12,500)	(12,500)
(Increase) Decrease in goodwill and nonamort. intang.	(820)	(853)	(887)	(922)	(959)
(Increase) Decrease in other noncurrent assets	(239)	(249)	(259)	(269)	(280)
Net Cash Flows from Investing Activities	$(13,559)	$(13,602)	$(13,646)	$(13,692)	$(13,739)
Increase (Decrease) in short-term debt	382	393	405	417	429
Increase (Decrease) in long-term debt	1,243	1,280	1,318	1,358	1,398
Increase (Decrease) in redeemable noncontrolling interest	(519)	0	0	0	0
Increase (Decrease) in common stock + paid-in capital	211	119	109	100	90
Increase (Decrease) in accumulated OCI	0	0	0	0	0
Dividends	(15,020)	(17,017)	(18,285)	(19,728)	(21,204)
Increase (Decrease) in noncontrolling interests	(809)	(809)	(809)	(809)	(809)
Net Cash Flows from Financing Activities	$(14,513)	$(16,035)	$(17,262)	$(18,663)	$(20,096)
Net Change in Cash	$ 0	$ 0	$ 0	$ 0	$ 0

grow by 3% in Year +6; then derive the projected statement of cash flows for Year +6. Derive the projected free cash flow for common equity shareholders in Year +6 from the projected statement of cash flows for Year +6.

d. Using the required rate of return on common equity from Requirement a as the discount rate, compute the sum of the present value of free cash flows for common equity shareholders for Walmart for Years +1 through +5.

e. Using the required rate of return on common equity from Requirement a as a discount rate and the long-run growth rate from Requirement c, compute the continuing value of Walmart as of the start of Year +6 based on Walmart's continuing free cash flows for common equity shareholders in Year +6 and beyond. After computing continuing value as of the start of Year +6, discount it to present value at the start of Year +1.

f. Compute the value of a share of Walmart common stock.

(1) Compute the total sum of the present value of all future free cash flows for equity shareholders (from Requirements d and e).

(2) Adjust the total sum of the present value using the midyear discounting adjustment factor.

(3) Compute the per-share value estimate.

Note: If you worked Problem 11.14 in Chapter 11 and computed Walmart's share value using the dividends valuation approach, compare your value estimate from that problem with the value estimate you obtain here. They should be the same.

Part II—Computing Walmart's Share Value Using Free Cash Flows to All Debt and Equity Stakeholders

g. At the end of 2012, Walmart had $48,222 million in outstanding interest-bearing short-term and long-term debt on the balance sheet and no preferred stock. Assume that the balance sheet value of Walmart's debt is approximately equal to the market value of the debt. During 2012, Walmart's income statement included interest expense of $2,251 million, implying an average interest expense of roughly 4.2%. Assume that at the start of Year +1, Walmart will continue to incur interest expense of 4.2% on debt capital and that Walmart's average tax rate will be 32.0%. In addition, at the end of 2012, Walmart had noncontrolling interests of $5,395 million, with an expected return of 15%. (For our forecasts, we assume noncontrolling interests receive dividends equal to the required rate of return each year.) Compute the weighted-average cost of capital for Walmart as of the start of Year +1.

h. Beginning with projected net cash flows from operations, derive the projected free cash flows for all debt and equity stakeholders for Walmart for Years +1 through +5 based on the projected financial statements.

i. Project the continuing free cash flows for all debt and equity stakeholders in Year +6. Use the projected financial statements for Year +6 from Requirement c to derive the projected free cash flow for all debt and equity stakeholders in Year +6.

j. Using the weighted-average cost of capital from Requirement g as a discount rate, compute the sum of the present value of free cash flows for all debt and equity stakeholders for Walmart for Years +1 through +5.

k. Using the weighted-average cost of capital from Requirement g as a discount rate and the long-run growth rate from Requirement c, compute the continuing value of Walmart as of the start of Year +6 based on Walmart's continuing free cash flows for all debt and equity stakeholders in Year +6 and beyond. After computing continuing value as of the start of Year +6, discount it to present value as of the start of Year +1.

l. Compute the value of a share of Walmart common stock.

    (1) Compute the total value of Walmart's net operating assets using the total sum of the present value of free cash flows for all debt and equity stake holders (from Requirements j and k).

    (2) Subtract the value of outstanding debt to obtain the value of equity.

    (3) Adjust the present value of equity using the midyear discounting adjustment factor.

    (4) Compute the per-share value estimate of Walmart's common equity shares.

Note: Do not be alarmed if your share value estimate from Requirement f is slightly different from your share value estimate from Requirement l. The weighted-average cost of capital computation in Requirement g used the weight of equity based on the market price of Walmart's stock at the end of 2012. The share value estimates from Requirements f and l likely differ from the market price, so the weights used to compute the weighted-average cost of capital are not internally consistent with the estimated share values.

Part III—Sensitivity Analysis and Recommendation

m. Using the free cash flows to common equity shareholders, recompute the value of Walmart shares under two alternative scenarios.

    Scenario 1: Assume that Walmart's long-run growth will be 2%, not 3% as before, and assume that Walmart's required rate of return on equity is 1 percentage point higher than the rate you computed using the CAPM in Requirement a.

    Scenario 2: Assume that Walmart's long-run growth will be 4%, not 3% as before, and assume that Walmart's required rate of return on equity is 1 percentage point lower than the rate you computed using the CAPM in Requirement a. To quantify the sensitivity of your share value estimate for Walmart to these variations in growth and discount rates, compare (in percentage terms) your value estimates under these two scenarios with your value estimate from Requirement f.

n. Using these data at the end of 2012, what reasonable range of share values would you have expected for Walmart common stock? At that time, what was the market price for Walmart shares relative to this range? What would you have recommended?

INTEGRATIVE CASE 12.1

Starbucks

Free Cash Flows Valuation of Starbucks' Common Equity

In Case 10.1, we projected financial statements for Starbucks for Years +1 through +5. In this portion of the Starbucks Integrative Case, we use the projected financial statements from Case 10.1 and apply the techniques learned in this chapter to compute Starbucks' required rate of return on equity and share value based on the free cash flows valuation models. We also compare our value estimate to Starbucks' share price at the time of the case development to provide an investment recommendation.

The market equity beta for Starbucks at the end of 2012 is 0.75. Assume that the risk-free interest rate is 3.0% and the market risk premium is 6.0%. Starbucks has 749.3 million shares outstanding at the end of 2012. At the start of Year +1, Starbucks' share price was $50.15.

REQUIRED

Part I—Computing Starbucks' Share Value Using Free Cash Flows to Common Equity Shareholders

a. Use the CAPM to compute the required rate of return on common equity capital for Starbucks.

b. Using your projected financial statements from Case 10.1 for Starbucks, begin with projected net cash flows from operations and derive the projected free cash flows for common equity shareholders for Starbucks for Years +1 through +5. You must determine whether your projected changes in cash are necessary for operating liquidity purposes.

c. Project the continuing free cash flow for common equity shareholders in Year +6. Assume that the steady-state, long-run growth rate will be 3% in Year +6 and beyond. Project that the Year +5 income statement and balance sheet amounts will grow by 3% in Year +6; then derive the projected statement of cash flows for Year +6. Derive the projected free cash flow for common equity shareholders in Year +6 from the projected statement of cash flows for Year +6.

d. Using the required rate of return on common equity from Requirement a as a discount rate, compute the sum of the present value of free cash flows for common equity share holders for Starbucks for Years +1 through +5.

e. Using the required rate of return on common equity from Requirement a as a discount rate and the long-run growth rate from Requirement c, compute the continuing value of Starbucks as of the start of Year +6 based on Starbucks' continuing free cash flows for common equity shareholders in Year +6 and beyond. After computing continuing value as of the start of Year +6, discount it to present value at the start of Year +1.

f. Compute the value of a share of Starbucks common stock.

   (1) Compute the total sum of the present value of free cash flows for equity shareholders (from Requirements d and e).

   (2) Adjust the total sum of the present value using the midyear discounting adjustment factor.

   (3) Compute the per-share value estimate.

Note: If you worked Integrative Case 11.1 from Chapter 11 and computed Starbucks' share value using the dividends valuation approach, compare your value estimate from that case with the value estimate you obtain here. They should be the same.

Part II—Computing Starbucks' Share Value Using Free Cash Flows to All Debt and Equity Stakeholders

g. At the end of 2012, Starbucks had $1,263 million in outstanding interest-bearing short-term and long-term debt on the balance sheet and no preferred stock. Assume that the balance sheet value of Starbucks' debt equals the market value of the debt. Starbucks faces an interest rate of roughly 6.25% on its outstanding debt. Assume that Starbucks will continue to face the same interest rate on this outstanding debt capital over the remaining life of the debt. Assume that Starbucks will continue to face a 33% income tax rate over the forecast horizon. Compute the weighted-average cost of capital for Starbucks as of the start of Year +1. Compare your computation of Starbucks' weighted-average cost of capital with your estimate of Starbucks' required return on equity from Requirement a. Why do the two amounts differ?

h. Based on your projections of Starbucks' financial statements, begin with projected net cash flows from operations and derive the projected free cash flows for all debt and equity stakeholders for Years +1 through +5. Compare your forecasts of Starbucks' free cash flows for all debt and equity stakeholders Years +1 through +5 with your forecast of Starbucks' free cash flows for equity shareholders in Requirement b. Why are the amounts not identical—what causes the difference each year?

i. Project the continuing free cash flows for all debt and equity stakeholders in Year +6. Use the projected financial statements for Year +6 from Requirement c to derive the projected free cash flows for all debt and equity stakeholders in Year +6.

j. Using the weighted-average cost of capital from Requirement g as a discount rate, compute the sum of the present value of free cash flows for all debt and equity stakeholders for Starbucks for Years +1 through +5.

k. Using the weighted-average cost of capital from Requirement g as a discount rate and the long-run growth rate from Requirement c, compute the continuing value of Starbucks as of the start of Year +6 based on Starbucks' continuing free cash flows for all debt and equity stakeholders in Year +6 and beyond. After computing continuing value as of the start of Year +6, discount it to present value at the start of Year +1.

l. Compute the value of a share of Starbucks common stock.

    (1) Compute the value of Starbucks' net operating assets using the total sum of the present value of free cash flows for all debt and equity stakeholders (from Requirements j and k).

    (2) Subtract the value of outstanding debt to obtain the value of equity.

    (3) Adjust the present value of equity using the midyear discounting adjustment factor.

    (4) Compute the per-share value estimate.

m. Compare your share value estimate from Requirement f with your share value estimate from Requirement l. These values should be similar.

Part III—Sensitivity Analysis and Recommendation

n. Using the free cash flows to common equity shareholders, recompute the value of Starbucks shares under two alternative scenarios.

    Scenario 1: Assume that Starbucks' long-run growth will be 2%, not 3% as before, and assume that Starbucks' required rate of return on equity is 1 percentage point higher than the rate you computed using the CAPM in Requirement a.

    Scenario 2: Assume that Starbucks' long-run growth will be 4%, not 3% as before, and assume that Starbucks' required rate of return on equity is 1 percentage point lower than the rate you computed using the CAPM in Requirement a. To quantify the sensitivity of your share value estimate for Starbucks to these variations in growth and discount rates, compare (in percentage terms) your value estimates under these two scenarios with your value estimate from Requirement f.

o. At the end of 2012, what reasonable range of share values would you have expected for Starbucks common stock? At that time, where was the market price for Starbucks shares relative to this range? What would you have recommended?

p. If you computed Starbucks' common equity share value using the dividends-based valuation approach in Case 11.1, compare the value estimate you obtained in that case with the estimate you obtained in this case. They should be identical.

CASE 12.2

Holmes Corporation

LBO Valuation

Holmes Corporation is a leading designer and manufacturer of material handling and process equipment for heavy industry in the United States and abroad. Its sales have more than doubled, and its earnings have increased more than sixfold in the past five years. In material handling, Holmes is a major producer of electric overhead and gantry cranes, ranging from 5 tons in capacity to 600-ton giants, the latter used primarily in nuclear and conventional power-generating plants. It also builds underhung cranes and monorail systems for general industrial use carrying loads up to 40 tons, railcar movers, railroad and mass transit shop maintenance equipment, and a broad line of advanced package conveyors. Holmes is a world leader in evaporation and crystallization systems and furnishes dryers, heat exchangers, and filters to complete its line of chemical processing equipment sold internationally to the chemical, fertilizer, food, drug, and paper industries. For the metallurgical industry, it designs and manufactures electric arc and induction furnaces, cupolas, ladles, and hot metal distribution equipment.

The information below and on the following pages appears in the Year 15 annual report of Holmes Corporation.

Highlights

	Year 15	Year 14
Net sales	$102,698,836	$109,372,718
Net earnings	6,601,908	6,583,360
Net earnings per share	3.62*	3.61*
Cash dividends paid	2,241,892	1,426,502
Cash dividends per share	1.22*	0.78*
Shareholders' equity	29,333,803	24,659,214
Shareholders' equity per share	16.07*	13.51*
Working capital	23,100,863	19,029,626
Orders received	95,436,103	80,707,576
Unfilled orders at end of period	77,455,900	84,718,633
Average number of common shares outstanding during period	1,824,853*	1,824,754*

*All per-share amounts throughout the case have already been adjusted for June, Year 15, and June, Year 14, 5-for-4 stock distributions.

Net Sales, Net Earnings, and Net Earnings per Share by Quarter

	Year 15			Year 14		
	Net Sales	Net Earnings	Per Share	Net Sales	Net Earnings	Per Share
First quarter	$ 25,931,457	$1,602,837	$0.88	$ 21,768,077	$1,126,470	$0.62
Second quarter	24,390,079	1,727,112	0.95	28,514,298	1,716,910	0.94
Third quarter	25,327,226	1,505,118	0.82	28,798,564	1,510,958	0.82
Fourth quarter	27,050,074	1,766,841	0.97	30,291,779	2,229,022	1.23
	$102,698,836	$6,601,908	$3.62	$109,372,718	$6,583,360	$3.61

Common Stock Prices and Cash Dividends Paid per Common Share by Quarter

| | Year 15 | | | Year 14 | | |
| | Stock Prices | | Cash Dividends per Share | Stock Prices | | Cash Dividends per Share |
	High	Low		High	Low	
First quarter	$22½	$18½	$0.26	$11¼	$ 9½	$0.16
Second quarter	25¼	19½	0.26	12⅜	8⅞	0.16
Third quarter	26¼	19¾	0.325	15⅞	11⅝	0.20
Fourth quarter	28⅛	23¼	0.375	20⅞	15⅞	0.26
			$1.22			$0.78

Management's Report to Shareholders

Year 15 was a pleasant surprise for all of us at Holmes Corporation. When the year started, it looked as though Year 15 would be a good year but not up to the record performance of Year 14. However, due to the excellent performance of our employees and the benefit of a favorable acquisition, Year 15 produced both record earnings and the largest cash dividend outlay in the company's 93-year history.

There is no doubt that some of the attractive orders received in late Year 12 and early Year 13 contributed to Year 15 profit. But of major significance was our organization's favorable response to several new management policies instituted to emphasize higher corporate profitability. Year 15 showed a net profit on net sales of 6.4%, which not only exceeded the 6.0% of last year but represents the highest net margin in several decades.

Net sales for the year were $102,698,836, down 6% from the $109,372,718 of a year ago but still the second largest volume in our history. Net earnings, however, set a new record at $6,601,908, or $3.62 per common share, which slightly exceeded the $6,583,360, or $3.61 per common share earned last year.

Cash dividends of $2,241,892 paid in Year 15 were 57% above the $1,426,502 paid a year ago. The record total resulted from your Board's approval of two increases during the year. When we implemented the 5-for-4 stock distribution in June, Year 15, we maintained the quarterly dividend rate of $0.325 on the increased number of shares for the January payment. Then, in December, Year 15, we increased the quarterly rate to $0.375 per share.

Year 15 certainly was not the most exuberant year in the capital equipment markets. Fortunately, our heavy involvement in ecology improvement, power generation, and international markets continued to serve us well, with the result that new orders of $95,436,103 were 18% over the $80,707,576 of Year 14.

Economists have predicted a substantial capital spending upturn for well over a year, but, so far, our customers have displayed stubborn reluctance to place new orders amid the uncertainty concerning the economy. Confidence is the answer. As soon as potential buyers can see clearly the future direction of the economy, we expect the unleashing of a large latent demand for capital goods, producing a much-expanded market for Holmes' products.

Fortunately, the accelerating pace of international markets continues to yield new business. Year 15 was an excellent year on the international front as our foreign customers continue to recognize our technological leadership in several product lines. Net sales of Holmes products shipped overseas and fees from foreign licensees amounted to $30,495,041, which represents a 31% increase over the $23,351,980 of a year ago.

Management fully recognizes and intends to take maximum advantage of our technological leadership in foreign lands. The latest manifestation of this policy was the acquisition of a controlling interest in Societé Francaise Holmes Fermont, our Swenson process equipment licensee located in Paris. Holmes and a partner started this firm 14 years ago as a sales and engineering organization to function in the Common Market. The company currently operates in the same mode. It owns no physical manufacturing assets, subcontracting all production. Its markets have expanded to include Spain and the East European countries.

Holmes Fermont is experiencing strong demand in Europe. For example, in early May, a $5.5 million order for a large potash crystallization system was received from a French engineering company representing a Russian client. Management estimates that Holmes Fermont will contribute approximately $6 to $8 million of net sales in Year 16.

Holmes' other wholly owned subsidiaries—Holmes Equipment Limited in Canada, Ermanco Incorporated in Michigan, and Holmes International, Inc., our FSC (Foreign Sales Corporation)—again contributed substantially to the success of Year 15. Holmes Equipment Limited registered its second-best year. However, capital equipment markets in Canada have virtually come to a standstill in the past two quarters. Ermanco achieved the best year in its history, while Holmes International, Inc. had a truly exceptional year because of the very high level of activity in our international markets.

The financial condition of the company showed further improvement and is now unusually strong as a result of very stringent financial controls. Working capital increased to $23,100,863 from $19,029,626, a 21% improvement. Inventories decreased 6% from $18,559,231 to $17,491,741. The company currently has no long-term or short-term debt, and has considerable cash in short-term instruments. Much of our cash position, however, results from customers' advance payments which we will absorb as we make shipments on the contracts. Shareholders' equity increased 19% to $29,393,803 from $24,690,214 a year ago.

Plant equipment expenditures for the year were $1,172,057, down 18% from $1,426,347 of Year 14. Several appropriations approved during the year did not require expenditures because of delayed deliveries beyond Year 15. The major emphasis again was on our continuing program of improving capacity and efficiency through the purchase of numerically controlled machine tools. We expanded the Ermanco plant by 50%, but since this is a leasehold arrangement, we made only minor direct investments. We also improved the Canadian operation by adding more manufacturing space and installing energy-saving insulation.

Labor relations were excellent throughout the year. The Harvey plant continues to be non-union. We negotiated a new labor contract at the Canadian plant, which extends to March 1, Year 17. The Pioneer Division in Alabama has a labor contract that does not expire until April, Year 16. While the union contract at Ermanco expired June 1, Year 15, work continues while negotiation proceeds on a new contract. We anticipate no difficulty in reaching a new agreement.

We exerted considerable effort during the year to improve Holmes' image in the investment community. Management held several informative meetings with security analyst groups to enhance the awareness of our activities and corporate performance.

The outlook for Year 16, while generally favorable, depends in part on the course of capital spending over the next several months. If the spending rate accelerates, the quickening pace of new orders, coupled with present backlogs, will provide the conditions for another fine year. On the other hand, if general industry continues the reluctant spending pattern of the last two years, Year 16 could be a year of maintaining market positions while awaiting better market conditions. Management takes an optimistic view and thus looks for a successful Year 16.

The achievement of record earnings and the highest profit margin in decades demonstrates the capability and the dedication of our employees. Management is most grateful for their efforts throughout the excellent year.

T. R. Varnum   T. L. Fuller
President   Chairman
March 15, Year 16

Review of Operations

Year 15 was a very active year although the pace was not at the hectic tempo of Year 14. It was a year that showed continued strong demand in some product areas but a dampened rate in others. The product areas that had some special economic circumstances enhancing demand fared well. For example, the continuing effort toward ecological improvement fostered excellent activity in Swenson process equipment. Likewise, the energy concern and the need for more electrical power generation capacity boded well for large overhead cranes. On the other hand, Holmes' products that relate to general industry and depend on the overall capital spending rate for new equipment experienced lesser demand, resulting in lower new orders and reduced backlogs. The affected products were small cranes, underhung cranes, railcar movers, and metallurgical equipment.

Year 15 was the first full year of operations under some major policy changes instituted to improve Holmes' profitability. The two primary revisions were the restructuring of our marketing effort along product division lines and the conversion of the product division incentive plans to a profit-based formula. The corporate organization adapted extremely well to the new policies. The improved profit margin in Year 15, in substantial part, was a result of the changes.

International activity increased markedly during the year. Surging foreign business and the expressed objective to capitalize on Holmes' technological leadership overseas resulted in the elevation of Mr. R. E. Foster to officer status as Vice President-International. The year involved heavy commitments of the product division staffs, engineering groups, and manufacturing organization to such important contracts as the $14 million Swenson order for Poland, the $8 million Swenson project for Mexico, the $2 million crane order for Venezuela, and several millions of dollars of railcar movers for all areas of the world.

The acquisition of control and commencement of operating responsibility of Societé Francaise Holmes Fermont, the Swenson licensee in Paris, was a major milestone in our international strategy. This organization has the potential of becoming a very substantial contributor in the years immediately ahead. Its long-range market opportunities in Europe and Asia are excellent.

Material Handling Products

Material handling equipment activities portrayed conflicting trends. During the year, when total backlog decreased, the crane division backlog increased. This was a result of several multimillion dollar contracts for power plant cranes. The small crane market, on the other hand, experienced depressed conditions during most of the year as general industry withheld appropriations for new plant and equipment. The underhung crane market experienced similar conditions. However, as Congressional attitudes and policies on investment unfold, we expect capital spending to show a substantial upturn.

The Transportation Equipment Division secured the second order for orbital service bridges, a new product for the containment vessels of nuclear power plants. This design is unique and allows considerable cost savings in erecting and maintaining containment shells.

The Ermanco Conveyor Division completed its best year with the growing acceptance of the unique XenoROL design. We expanded the Grand Haven plant by 50% to effect further cost reduction and new concepts of marketing.

The railcar moving line continued to produce more business from international markets. We installed the new 11TM unit in six domestic locations, a product showing signs of exceptional performance. We shipped the first foreign 11TM machine to Sweden.

Process Equipment Products

Process equipment again accounted for slightly more than half of the year's business.

Swenson activity reached an all-time high level with much of the division's effort going into international projects. The large foreign orders required considerable additional work to cover the necessary documentation, metrification when required, and general liaison.

We engaged in considerably more subcontracting during the year to accommodate one-piece shipment of the huge vessels pioneered by Swenson to effect greater equipment economies. The division continued to expand the use of computerization for design work and contract administration. We developed more capability during the year to handle the many additional tasks associated with turnkey projects. Swenson's research and development efforts accelerated in search of better technology and new products. We conducted pilot plant test work at our facilities and in the field to convert several sales prospects into new contracts.

The metallurgical business proceeded at a slower pace in Year 15. However, with construction activity showing early signs of improvement and automotive and farm machinery manufacturers increasing their operating rates, we see intensified interest in metallurgical equipment.

Financial Statements

The financial statements of Holmes Corporation and related notes appear in Exhibits 12.20–12.22 (pages 960–962). Exhibit 12.23 (page 963) presents five-year summary operating information for Holmes.

Notes to Consolidated Financial Statements Year 15 and Year 14

Note A—Summary of Significant Accounting Policies. Significant accounting policies consistently applied appear below to assist the reader in reviewing the company's consolidated financial statements contained in this report.

Consolidation—The consolidated financial statements include the accounts of the company and its subsidiaries after eliminating all intercompany transactions and balances.

Inventories—Inventories generally appear at the lower of cost or market, with cost determined principally on a first-in, first-out method.

Property, plant, and equipment—Property, plant, and equipment appear at acquisition cost minus accumulated depreciation. When the company retires or disposes of properties, it removes the related costs and accumulated depreciation from the respective accounts and credits, or charges any gain or loss to earnings. The company expenses maintenance and repairs as incurred. It capitalizes major betterments and renewals. Depreciation results from applying the straight-line method over the estimated useful lives of the assets as follows:

Buildings	30 to 45 years
Machinery and equipment	4 to 20 years
Furniture and fixtures	10 years

Exhibit 12.20

Holmes Corporation
Balance Sheet
(amounts in thousands)
(Case 12.2)

	Year 10	Year 11	Year 12	Year 13	Year 14	Year 15
Cash	$ 955	$ 962	$ 865	$ 1,247	$ 1,540	$ 3,857
Marketable securities	0	0	0	0	0	2,990
Accounts/Notes receivable	6,545	7,295	9,718	13,307	18,759	14,303
Inventories	7,298	8,685	12,797	20,426	18,559	17,492
Current Assets	$14,798	$16,942	$23,380	$34,980	$38,858	$38,642
Investments	0	0	0	0	0	422
Property, plant, and equipment	12,216	12,445	13,126	13,792	14,903	15,876
Less: Accumulated depreciation	(7,846)	(8,236)	(8,558)	(8,988)	(9,258)	(9,703)
Other assets	470	420	400	299	343	276
Total Assets	$19,638	$21,571	$28,348	$40,083	$44,846	$45,513
Accounts payable—trade	$ 2,894	$ 4,122	$ 6,496	$ 7,889	$ 6,779	$ 4,400
Notes payable—nontrade	0	0	700	3,500	0	0
Current portion long-term debt	170	170	170	170	170	0
Other current liabilities	550	1,022	3,888	8,624	12,879	11,142
Current Liabilities	$ 3,614	$ 5,314	$11,254	$20,183	$19,828	$15,542
Long-term debt	680	510	340	170	0	0
Deferred tax	0	0	0	216	328	577
Other noncurrent liabilities	0	0	0	0	0	0
Total Liabilities	$ 4,294	$ 5,824	$11,594	$20,569	$20,156	$16,119
Common stock	$ 2,927	$ 2,927	$ 2,927	$ 5,855	$ 7,303	$ 9,214
Additional paid-in capital	5,075	5,075	5,075	5,075	5,061	5,286
Retained earnings	7,342	7,772	8,774	8,599	12,297	14,834
Accumulated other comprehensive income	0	0	5	12	29	60
Treasury stock	0	(27)	(27)	(27)	0	0
Total Shareholders' Equity	$15,344	$15,747	$16,754	$19,514	$24,690	$29,394
Total Liabilities and Shareholders' Equity	$19,638	$21,571	$28,348	$40,083	$44,846	$45,513

Intangible assets—The company has amortized the unallocated excess of cost of a subsidiary over net assets acquired (that is, goodwill) over a 17-year period. Beginning in Year 16, U.S. GAAP no longer requires amortization of goodwill.

Research and development costs—The company charges research and development costs to operations as incurred ($479,410 in Year 15, and $467,733 in Year 14).

Pension plans—The company and its subsidiaries have noncontributory pension plans covering substantially all of their employees. The company's policy is to fund accrued pension costs as determined by independent actuaries. Pension costs amounted to $471,826 in Year 15 and $366,802 in Year 14.

Exhibit 12.21

Holmes Corporation
Income Statement
(amounts in thousands)
(Case 12.2)

	Year 11	Year 12	Year 13	Year 14	Year 15
Sales	$ 41,428	$ 53,541	$ 76,328	$109,373	$102,699
Other revenues and gains	0	41	0	0	211
Cost of goods sold	(33,269)	(43,142)	(60,000)	(85,364)	(80,260)
Selling and administrative expense	(6,175)	(7,215)	(9,325)	(13,416)	(12,090)
Other expenses and losses	(2)	0	(11)	(31)	(1)
Operating Income	$ 1,982	$ 3,225	$ 6,992	$ 10,562	$ 10,559
Interest expense	(43)	(21)	(284)	(276)	(13)
Income tax expense	(894)	(1,471)	(2,992)	(3,703)	(3,944)
Net Income	$ 1,045	$ 1,733	$ 3,716	$ 6,583	$ 6,602

Revenue recognition—The company generally recognizes income on a percentage-of-completion basis. It records advance payments as received and reports them as a deduction from billings when earned. The company recognizes royalties, included in net sales, as income when received. Royalties totaled $656,043 in Year 15 and $723,930 in Year 14.

Income taxes—The company provides no income taxes on unremitted earnings of foreign subsidiaries since it anticipates no significant tax liabilities should foreign units remit such earnings. The company makes provision for deferred income taxes applicable to timing differences between financial statement and income tax accounting, principally on the earnings of a foreign sales subsidiary which existing statutes defer in part from current taxation.

Note B—Foreign Operations. The consolidated financial statements in Year 15 include net assets of $2,120,648 ($1,847,534 in Year 14), undistributed earnings of $2,061,441 ($1,808,752 in Year 14), sales of $7,287,566 ($8,603,225 in Year 14), and net income of $454,999 ($641,454 in Year 14) applicable to the Canadian subsidiary. The company translates balance sheet accounts of the Canadian subsidiary into U.S. dollars at the exchange rates at the end of the year and translates operating results at the average of exchange rates for the year.

Note C—Inventories. Inventories used in determining cost of sales appear below.

	Year 15	Year 14	Year 13
Raw materials and supplies	$ 8,889,147	$ 9,720,581	$ 8,900,911
Work in process	8,602,594	8,838,650	11,524,805
Total inventories	$17,491,741	$18,559,231	$20,425,716

Note D—Short-Term Borrowing. The company has short-term credit agreements which principally provide for loans of 90-day periods at varying interest rates. There were no borrowings in

Exhibit 12.22

Holmes Corporation
Statement of Cash Flows
(amounts in thousands)
(Case 12.2)

	Year 11	Year 12	Year 13	Year 14	Year 15
OPERATIONS					
Net income	$ 1,045	$ 1,733	$ 3,716	$ 6,583	$ 6,602
Depreciation and amortization	491	490	513	586	643
Other addbacks	20	25	243	151	299
Other subtractions	0	0	0	0	(97)
(Increase) Decrease in receivables	(750)	(2,424)	(3,589)	(5,452)	4,456
(Increase) Decrease in inventories	(1,387)	(4,111)	(7,629)	1,867	1,068
Increase (Decrease) accounts payable—trade	1,228	2,374	1,393	1,496	(2,608)
Increase (Decrease) in other current liabilities	473	2,865	4,737	1,649	(1,509)
Cash Flow from Operations	$ 1,120	$ 952	$ (616)	$ 6,880	$ 8,854
INVESTING					
Fixed assets acquired, net	$ (347)	$ (849)	$ (749)	$(1,426)	$(1,172)
Investments acquired	0	0	0	0	(3,306)
Other investing transactions	45	0	81	(64)	39
Cash Flow from Investing	$ (302)	$ (849)	$ (668)	$(1,490)	$(4,439)
FINANCING					
Increase in short-term borrowing	$ 0	$ 700	$ 2,800	$ 0	$ 0
Decrease in short-term borrowing	0	0	0	(3,500)	0
Increase in long-term borrowing	0	0	0	0	0
Decrease in long-term borrowing	(170)	(170)	(170)	(170)	(170)
Issue of capital stock	0	0	0	0	315
Acquisition of capital stock	(27)	0	0	0	0
Dividends	(614)	(730)	(964)	(1,427)	(2,243)
Other financing transactions	0	0	0	0	0
Cash Flow from Financing	$ (811)	$ (200)	$ 1,666	$(5,097)	$(2,098)
Net Change in Cash	$ 7	$ (97)	$ 382	$ 293	$ 2,317
Cash, beginning of year	955	962	865	1,247	1,540
Cash, End of Year	$ 962	$ 865	$ 1,247	$ 1,540	$ 3,857

Year 15. In Year 14, the maximum borrowing at the end of any calendar month was $4,500,000 and the approximate average loan balance and weighted-average interest rate, computed by using the days outstanding method, was $3,435,000 and 7.6%. There were no restrictions upon the company during the period of the loans and no compensating bank balance arrangements required by the lending institutions.

Exhibit 12.23

Holmes Corporation
Five-Year Summary of Operations
(Case 12.2)

	Year 11	Year 12	Year 13	Year 14	Year 15
Orders received	$55,454,188	$89,466,793	$121,445,731	$ 80,707,576	$ 95,436,103
Net sales	41,427,702	53,540,699	76,327,664	109,372,718	102,698,836
Backlog of unfilled orders	32,339,614	68,265,708	113,383,775	84,718,633	77,455,900
Earnings before taxes on income	$ 1,939,414	$ 3,203,835	$ 6,708,072	$ 10,285,943	$ 10,546,213
Taxes on income	894,257	1,470,489	2,991,947	3,702,583	3,944,305
Net earnings	1,045,157	1,733,346	3,716,125	6,583,360	6,601,908
Net property, plant, and equipment	$ 4,209,396	$ 4,568,372	$ 4,803,978	$ 5,644,590	$ 6,173,416
Net additions to property	346,549	848,685	748,791	1,426,347	1,172,057
Depreciation and amortization	491,217	490,133	513,402	585,735	643,231
Cash dividends paid	$ 614,378	$ 730,254	$ 963,935	$ 1,426,502	$ 2,242,892
Working capital	11,627,875	12,126,491	14,796,931	19,029,626	23,100,463
Shareholders' equity	15,747,116	15,754,166	19,514,358	24,690,214	29,393,803
Earnings per common share (1)	$ 0.57	$ 0.96	$ 2.03	$ 3.61	$ 3.62
Dividends per common share (1)	0.34	0.40	0.53	0.78	1.22
Book value per common share (1)	8.62	9.18	10.68	13.51	16.07
Number of shareholders, December 31	1,787	1,792	1,834	2,024	2,157
Number of employees, December 31	1,303	1,425	1,551	1,550	1,549
Shares of common outstanding, December 31(1)	1,827,515	1,824,941	1,824,754	1,824,754	1,824,853
Percent of net sales by product line:					
Material Handling Equipment	63.0%	54.4%	51.3%	43.6%	46.1%
Processing Equipment	37.0%	45.6%	48.7%	56.4%	53.9%

Note E—Income Taxes. Provision for income taxes consists of:

	Year 15	Year 14
Current		
Federal	$2,931,152	$2,633,663
State	466,113	483,240
Canadian	260,306	472,450
Total current provision	$3,657,571	$3,589,353
Deferred		
Federal	$ 263,797	$ 91,524
Canadian	22,937	21,706
Total deferred	$ 286,734	$ 113,230
Total provision for income taxes	$3,944,305	$3,702,583

Reconciliation of the total provision for income taxes to the current federal statutory rate of 35% is as follows:

	Year 15		Year 14	
	Amount	**%**	**Amount**	**%**
Tax at statutory rate	$3,691,000	35.0%	$3,600,100	35.0%
State taxes, net of U.S. tax credit	302,973	2.9	314,106	3.1
All other items	(49,668)	(0.5)	(211,623)	(2.1)
Total provision for income taxes	$3,944,305	37.4%	$3,702,583	36.0%

Note F—Pensions. The components of pension expense appear below.

	Year 15	Year 14
Service cost	$ 476,490	$ 429,700
Interest cost	567,159	446,605
Expected return on pension investments	(558,373)	(494,083)
Amortization of actuarial gains and losses	(13,450)	(15,420)
Pension expense	$ 471,826	$ 366,802

The funded status of the pension plan appears below.

	December 31:	
	Year 15	**Year 14**
Accumulated benefit obligation	$5,763,450	$5,325,291
Effect of salary increases	1,031,970	976,480
Projected benefit obligation	$6,795,420	$6,301,771
Pension fund assets	6,247,940	5,583,730
Excess pension obligation	$ 547,480	$ 718,041

Assumptions used in accounting for pensions appear below.

	Year 15	Year 14
Expected return on pension assets	10%	10%
Discount rate for projected benefit obligation	9%	8%
Salary increases	5%	5%

Note G—Common Stock. As of March 20, Year 15, the company increased the authorized number of shares of common stock from 1,800,000 shares to 5,000,000 shares. On December 29, Year 15, the company increased its equity interest (from 45% to 85%) in Societé Francaise Holmes Fermont, a French affiliate, in exchange for 18,040 of its common shares in a transaction accounted for as a purchase. The company credited the excess of the fair value ($224,373) of the company's shares issued over their par value ($90,200) to additional contributed capital. The excess of the purchase cost over the underlying value of the assets acquired was insignificant.

The company made a 25% common stock distribution on June 15, Year 14, and on June 19, Year 15, resulting in increases of 291,915 shares in Year 14 and 364,433 shares in Year 15, respectively. We capitalized the par value of these additional shares by a transfer of $1,457,575 in Year 14 and $1,822,165 in Year 15 from retained earnings to the common stock account. In Year 14 and Year 15, we paid cash of $2,611 and $15,340, respectively, in lieu of fractional share interests.

In addition, the company retired 2,570 shares of treasury stock in June, Year 14. The earnings and dividends per share for Year 14 and Year 15 in the accompanying consolidated financial statements reflect the 25% stock distributions.

Note H—Contingent Liabilities. The company has certain contingent liabilities with respect to litigation and claims arising in the ordinary course of business. The company cannot determine the ultimate disposition of these contingent liabilities but, in the opinion of management, they will not result in any material effect upon the company's consolidated financial position or results of operations.

Note I—Quarterly Data (unaudited). Quarterly sales, gross profit, net earnings, and earnings per share for Year 15 appear below (first quarter results restated for 25% stock distribution):

	Net Sales	Gross Profit	Net Earnings	Earnings per Share
First	$ 25,931,457	$ 5,606,013	$1,602,837	$0.88
Second	24,390,079	6,148,725	1,727,112	0.95
Third	25,327,226	5,706,407	1,505,118	0.82
Fourth	27,050,074	4,977,774	1,766,841	0.97
Year	$102,698,836	$22,438,919	$6,601,908	$3.62

Auditors' Report

Board of Directors and Stockholders

Holmes Corporation

We have examined the consolidated balance sheets of Holmes Corporation and Subsidiaries as of December 31, Year 15 and Year 14, and the related consolidated statements of earnings and cash flows for the years then ended. Our examination was made in accordance with generally accepted auditing standards and accordingly included such tests of the accounting records and such other auditing procedures as we considered necessary in the circumstances. In our opinion, the financial statements referred to above present fairly the consolidated financial position of

Holmes Corporation and Subsidiaries at December 31, Year 15 and Year 14, and the consolidated results of their operations and changes in cash flows for the years then ended, in conformity with generally accepted accounting principles applied on a consistent basis.

SBW, LLP
Chicago, Illinois
March 15, Year 16

REQUIRED

A group of Holmes' top management is interested in acquiring Holmes in an LBO.

- **a.** Briefly describe the factors that make Holmes an attractive and, conversely, an unattractive LBO candidate.
- **b.** (This question requires coverage of Chapter 10.) Prepare projected financial statements for Holmes Corporation for Year 16 through Year 20 excluding all financing. That is, project the amount of operating income after taxes, assets, and cash flows from operating and investing activities. State the underlying assumptions made.
- **c.** Ascertain the value of Holmes' common shareholders' equity using the present value of its future cash flows valuation approach. Assume a risk-free interest rate of 4.2% and a market premium of 5.0%. Note that information in Requirement e may be helpful in this valuation. Assume the following financing structure for the LBO:

Type	Proportion	Interest Rate	Term
Term debt	50%	8%	7-year amortization[a]
Subordinated debt	25	12%	10-year amortization[a]
Shareholders' equity	25		
	100%		

[a]Holmes must repay principal and interest in equal annual payments.

- **d.** (This question requires coverage of Chapter 13.) Ascertain the value of Holmes' common shareholders' equity using the residual income approach.
- **e.** (This question requires coverage of Chapter 14.) Ascertain the value of Holmes' common shareholders' equity using the residual ROCE model and the price-to-earnings ratio and the market value to book value of comparable companies' approaches. Selected data for similar companies for Year 15 appear in the following table (amounts in millions):

Industry:	Agee Robotics Conveyor Systems	GI Handling Systems Conveyor Systems	LJG Industries Cranes	Gelas Corp. Industrial Furnaces
Sales	$4,214	$28,998	$123,034	$75,830
Net income	$ 309	$ 2,020	$ 9,872	$ 5,117
Assets	$2,634	$15,197	$ 72,518	$41,665
Long-term debt	$ 736	$ 5,098	$ 23,745	$ 8,869
Common shareholders' equity	$1,551	$ 7,473	$ 38,939	$26,884
Market value of common equity	$6,915	$20,000	$102,667	$41,962
Market beta	1.12	0.88	0.99	0.93

- **f.** Would you attempt to acquire Holmes Corporation after completing the analyses in Requirements a–e? If not, how would you change the analyses to make this an attractive LBO?

Valuation: Earnings-Based Approach

LEARNING OBJECTIVES

LO 13-1 Describe earnings-based valuation and explain the different valuation implications of earnings, dividends, and free cash flows.

LO 13-2 Describe the conceptual and practical strengths and weaknesses of earnings-based valuation.

LO 13-3 Demonstrate a conceptual understanding of and apply practical techniques for residual income valuation by:
   a. Utilizing book value of common shareholders' equity, comprehensive income, dividends, and clean surplus accounting in valuation.
   b. Measuring required (or "normal") income by multiplying beginning-of-period book value of equity by the risk-adjusted required rate of return on equity capital.
   c. Measuring residual (or "abnormal") income by subtracting required income from expected future income.
   d. Determining the value of common equity as the sum of book value of common shareholders' equity plus the present value of expected future residual income.

LO 13-4 Apply the residual income valuation method to value common shares and assess the sensitivity of value estimates to key valuation parameters, such as discount rates and expected long-term growth rates.

LO 13-5 Describe four important implementation issues for the residual income valuation approach.

LO 13-6 Identify potential causes of errors if the residual income, free cash flows, and dividend valuations do not produce identical value estimates.

Chapter Overview

Reported earnings numbers are the single most widely followed measures of firm performance. Accounting standard setters (most notably the FASB and IASB), along with the accounting profession and the community of financial statement users, have designed the accrual accounting process to measure earnings as the bottom line of the firm's profitability each period. As a result, firms' reported earnings numbers play a central role as the primary value-relevant measures of performance used in the capital markets for share pricing and capital allocation.

Because of the demand in the capital markets for earnings information, firms usually release quarterly and annual earnings to the public as soon as accountants have prepared and verified the numbers, often weeks *before* the firms actually release their detailed quarterly and annual income statements, balance sheets, statements of cash flows, and notes. Firms commonly announce earnings during conference calls and press conferences attended by investors, analysts, managers, board members, and the financial press. Analysts often spend enormous amounts of time and effort building (and when new information arrives, revising) forecasts of firms' upcoming quarterly and annual earnings. Sell-side analysts disseminate their earnings forecasts to interested investors, brokers, and fund managers. Commercial firms such as **I/B/E/S** and **First Call** have built businesses on compiling and distributing daily data on analysts' earnings forecasts. The financial media (broadcast, print, and online) provide daily coverage of firms' earnings announcements. For example, *The Wall Street Journal* provides daily reports of firms' earnings announcements as well as daily data on each firm's stock price and price-earnings ratio. In fact, because of the demand for and attention devoted to earnings among capital markets participants, U.S. GAAP and IFRS require firms to report earnings scaled on a per-share basis in their financial statements. (See the related discussion in Chapter 4.)[1]

Firms' share prices usually react quickly to earnings announcements, and the direction and magnitude of the market's reaction depends on the direction and magnitude of the earnings news relative to what investors expected. Firms that announce earnings beating the market's expectations ("good news") often experience significant jumps in share price during the day of and the days immediately following the announcement. Likewise, firms that announce earnings falling short of the market's expectations ("bad news") may experience immediate sharp declines in share price. As noted in several prior chapters, the seminal Ball and Brown (1968) study and many other research studies, including the Nichols and Wahlen (2004) study[2] described in Chapter 1, have shown that firms' stock returns are highly positively correlated with changes in firms' earnings.

Because earnings provide such important information to investors and other external stakeholders, earnings also play key roles in decisions that firms make with regard to internal capital allocation. New project proposals within firms are often evaluated based on the effects they will have on reported earnings. In addition, corporate governance processes commonly reward or punish managers with compensation and bonus plans based on whether firm performance meets (or fails to meet) certain earnings targets. The following observations establish the important roles of earnings:

- Earnings is the primary measure of firm performance produced by the accrual accounting system.
- Earnings has a direct impact on the capital markets and the pricing of shares.
- Corporate managers and boards of directors use earnings for internal capital allocation and for aligning the incentives of managers with shareholders.
- Because of the tremendous demand for earnings information among stakeholders, the financial press and the analyst community devote tremendous time and attention to reporting, analyzing, and forecasting earnings.

Therefore, it is logical that accounting earnings would also provide a basis for valuation. This chapter describes the conceptual and practical strengths and weaknesses of the earnings-based valuation model known as the *residual income valuation model*. This valuation model bases valuation on expected future earnings and the book value of common shareholders' equity.

---

[1] *FASB Codification Topic 260;* International Accounting Standards Board, *International Accounting Standard 33,* "Earnings per Share" (revised 2003).

[2] Ray Ball and Philip Brown, "An Evaluation of Accounting Income Numbers," *Journal of Accounting Research* (Autumn 1968), pp. 159–178. D. Craig Nichols and James Wahlen, "How Do Earnings Numbers Relate to Stock Returns? A Review of Classic Accounting Research with Updated Evidence," *Accounting Horizons* (December 2004), pp. 263–286.

Exhibit 13.1

Steps to Understanding Residual Income Valuation

1. *Rationale*
   - What is the rationale for using earnings as a basis for valuation?
   - What are the practical advantages and concerns associated with using earnings to determine common shareholders' equity value?

2. *Theoretical and Conceptual Foundations for Residual Income Valuation*
   - What theories and concepts support residual income valuation?
   - How do we measure residual income? What economic construct does it represent?

3. *Practical Applications*
   - How do we estimate share value using residual income valuation methods?
   - What implementation issues do we need to understand in order to use the residual income model?
   - What value estimate do we get from this approach for the common shareholders' equity of PepsiCo?

4. *Linking Residual Income Valuation to Dividends Valuation and Free Cash Flow Valuation*
   - Conceptually, why is the residual income valuation approach equivalent to the valuation approaches that rely on dividends and free cash flows?
   - Practically, does the value estimate we obtain for PepsiCo using the residual income valuation approach agree with the estimates from Chapters 11 and 12 using dividends and free cash flows to common equity?
   - What if the value estimates do not agree across these three models? How do we find and correct possible valuation errors?

This chapter takes four important steps. Exhibit 13.1 illustrates these steps and some of the key questions we address in this chapter. First, we describe the rationale behind earnings-based valuation. Second, we explain the theoretical and conceptual foundation for residual income valuation, with a number of illustrations and examples. Third, we demonstrate the residual income model by applying it to value the common shareholders' equity of **PepsiCo**. As we apply the model, we describe the key measurement and implementation issues. Finally, we demonstrate the internal consistency among dividends-based, free-cash-flows-based, and earnings-based valuation models and how to identify and correct errors when the three models seem to disagree.

The residual income valuation model in this chapter provides a powerful approach that is a complementary equivalent to the classical dividends-based valuation approach presented in Chapter 11 and to the free-cash-flows-based valuation approach presented in Chapter 12. The residual income valuation model in this chapter forms the basis for the market-based valuation multiples described in Chapter 14, including the market-to-book ratio and the price-earnings ratio.

Rationale for Earnings-Based Valuation

LO 13-1

Describe earnings-based valuation and explain the different valuation implications of earnings, dividends, and free cash flows.

Exhibit 13.1 shows that the first step toward understanding residual income valuation is to establish the theoretical and conceptual rationale for using an earnings-based valuation approach. Economic theory teaches that the value of any resource equals the present value of the expected future payoffs from the resource discounted at a rate that reflects the risk inherent in those expected future payoffs. Like Chapters 11 and 12, we start with the same general model for the present value of a security (denoted as V_0, with present value denoted as of time $t=0$) with an expected life of n future periods, as follows:[3]

$$V_0 = \sum_{t=1}^{n} \frac{\text{Expected Future Payoffs}_t}{(1 + \text{Discount Rate})^t}$$

Chapter 11 demonstrates that the value of a share of common equity should equal the present value of the *expected future dividends* the shareholder will receive. Dividends are the fundamental value-relevant payoffs because they represent the distribution of wealth from the firm to the shareholders. The equity shareholder receives dividends as the payoffs from holding a share, including the final "liquidating" dividend when the firm liquidates the share or the shareholder sells the share. Thus, to value a firm's shares using dividends, you discount to present value the expected future dividends over the life of the firm (or the expected length of time the share will be held), including the final liquidating dividend. This is a *wealth distribution* (or liquidation) approach to valuation.

Chapter 12 demonstrates that the value of a share of common equity also should equal the present value of the *expected future free cash flows* that the firm will create and ultimately distribute in *dividends* to the common equity shareholders. The free-cash-flows-based valuation approach focuses on the amounts and timing of the cash flows the firm will generate that will eventually be distributed to shareholders in future dividends. Thus, to value a firm's shares using free cash flows, you discount to present value the expected future free cash flows for common equity shareholders over the life of the firm (or the expected length of time the share will be held), including the final liquidating cash flows. This is a *distributable wealth* approach to valuation.

The residual income valuation approach presented in this chapter parallels the dividends-based and the free-cash-flows-based valuation approaches, except that it uses a different measure of payoffs. The residual income valuation approach uses book value of common shareholders' equity and expected future earnings to determine the value-relevant expected future payoffs to the investor (the numerator of the general valuation model above) in place of future dividends or future free cash flows. The rationale for the role of book value of shareholders' equity is straightforward: it is the starting point for valuation because it is the balance sheet measure of the common equity shareholders' claim on the net assets of the firm. The rationale for using expected future earnings as a basis for valuation is also straightforward: future earnings measure the net profits or losses the firm will generate for the shareholders. Over the remaining life of the firm, earnings measure the total wealth to be created by the firm for the shareholders. Instead of focusing on wealth distribution through dividends payments and instead of focusing on distributable wealth through free cash flow realizations, residual income valuation focuses on *earnings as a periodic measure of shareholder wealth creation*. Therefore, residual income is a *wealth-creation* approach to valuation. In Chapter 11, Exhibit 11.2 showed the differences in valuation approach perspectives between dividends as measures of *wealth distribution*, free cash flows as measures of *distributable wealth*, and earnings as value-relevant measures of *wealth creation*.

To measure wealth creation, the accrual accounting process measures income for the equity shareholders based on the net amount of economic resources generated and consumed by the firm each period. Accrual accounting also produces periodic

---

[3]This chapter uses the same notation as in prior chapters, where t refers to accounting periods. The valuation process determines an estimate of firm value, denoted as V_0, in present value as of today, when $t=0$. The period $t=1$ refers to the first accounting period being discounted to present value. Period $t=n$ is the period of the expected final, or liquidating, payoff.

statements of financial position—balance sheets measuring assets, liabilities, and share-holders' equity—that report the economic resources (assets) that the firm controls and uses to produce expected future economic benefits and the claims on those resources by creditors and investors (liabilities and equities). To produce informative measures of financial performance and position that are relevant and reliable, the accounting profession develops and implements accounting standards through which the accrual accounting process measures income, assets, liabilities, and shareholders' equity using estimates of economic resources earned and consumed each period, rather than just relying on cash inflows and cash outflows, which often do not reflect economic value generated or consumed each period. To measure a firm's economic performance and position in a given period, it makes sense to measure the following:

- *Revenues earned* from operating performance during that period, not just the amounts of cash collected from customers that period
- Expenses for *resources consumed* in that period, not just the amounts of cash paid out of the firm that period
- A portion of the *long-lived resources consumed* during that period, such as periodic depreciation of a building each year of its useful life (rather than recognize the full cost of the building in the year the firm pays for it and ignore the consumption of the building in all other years the firm uses it)
- *Commitments made* this period to pay in future periods for obligations incurred in the course of doing business this period, such as pension and other retirement benefits, warranties, taxes, and others (rather than ignore those commitments and measure their effects only when the firm pays cash)

Earnings under accrual accounting are far from perfect performance measures. However, recall the discussion in Chapter 2 that described how accounting standards are intended to optimize the relevance and reliability of accrual accounting information (asset and liability valuation and income recognition) for investors and other stakeholders. By virtue of accounting standards, accounting earnings will more closely match the firm's underlying economic performance—the wealth created or destroyed for equity shareholders—in a given period than will the net cash inflows or outflows of that period.

Over the life of a firm, the cash flows invested in the firm by the shareholders plus the wealth created by the firm for the shareholders will determine the cash flows that will be distributable to shareholders. Thus, valuation of shareholders' equity in a firm using the capital invested in the firm plus earnings over the life of the firm (residual income valuation) is equivalent to valuation using free cash flows over the life of the firm. And both are equivalent to valuation using dividends over the life of the firm.[4]

Earnings-Based Valuation: Practical Advantages and Concerns

LO 13-2

Describe the conceptual and practical strengths and weaknesses of earnings-based valuation.

Although earnings, cash flows, and dividends are equally valid bases for valuation, several practical advantages and concerns arise with earnings-based valuation. The first

---

[4]Over sufficiently long time periods, net income equals free cash flows to common equity. The effect of year-end accruals to convert cash flows to net income lessens as the measurement period lengthens. The correlation between firms' earnings and stock returns increases as the earnings measurement interval increases. The values of R^2 for various intervals are one year, 5%; two years, 15%; five years, 33%; and 10 years, 63%. See Peter D. Easton, Trevor S. Harris, and James A. Ohlson, "Aggregate Accounting Earnings Can Explain Most of Security Returns," *Journal of Accounting and Economics* (1992), pp. 119–142.

advantage is that the emphasis placed on earnings by firms and the capital markets makes earnings a logical starting point for valuation. Analysts, investors, the capital markets, managers, boards, and the financial press focus on earnings forecasts and earnings reports rather than free cash flow forecasts and free cash flow amounts. It is rare to find a firm holding press conferences to announce free cash flows. Analysts publish earnings forecasts far more frequently than they publish free cash flow forecasts. Boards of directors and compensation committees typically do not establish managers' bonus plans based on achieving free cash flow targets (most often relying on earnings-based measures of performance). The reason for the tendency to rely on earnings is that they align more closely than dividends or free cash flows with the focus of the capital markets and corporate managers and boards of directors on periodic performance measurement.

Another practical advantage arises because it is more direct and efficient for you to go straight from earnings to valuation rather than take a detour to free cash flows.[5] As Exhibit 13.2 depicts, estimating firm value using free cash flows adds an intermediary

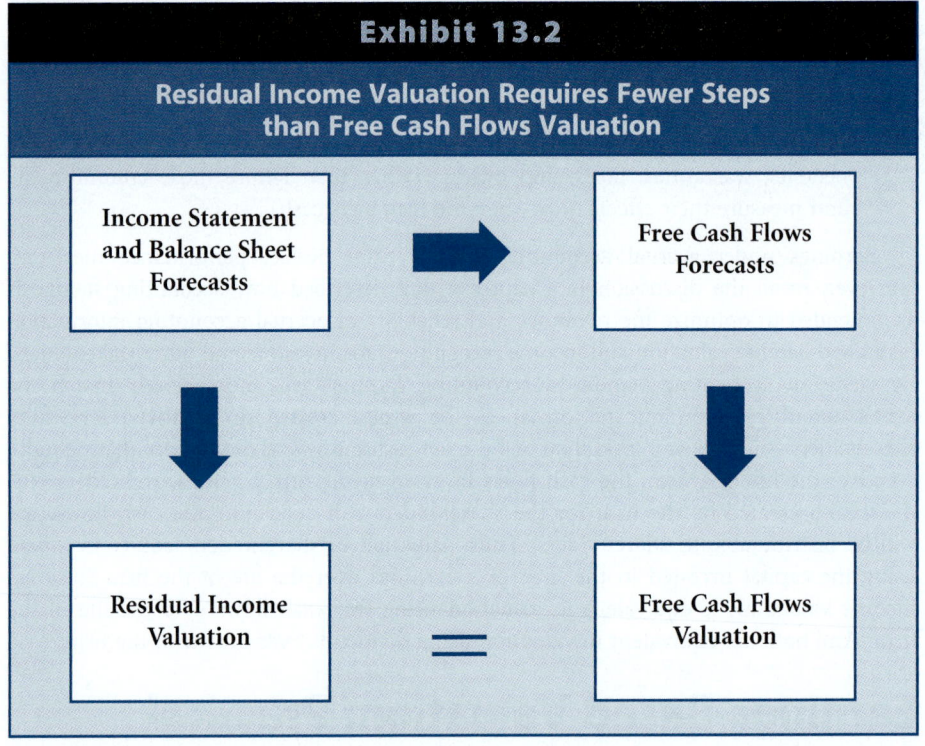

Exhibit 13.2

Residual Income Valuation Requires Fewer Steps than Free Cash Flows Valuation

Income Statement and Balance Sheet Forecasts → Free Cash Flows Forecasts

Income Statement and Balance Sheet Forecasts ↓ Residual Income Valuation

Free Cash Flows Forecasts ↓ Free Cash Flows Valuation

Residual Income Valuation = Free Cash Flows Valuation

---

[5]Researchers have directed considerable attention to the question of whether cash flows or earnings associate more closely with stock returns. This research indicates that earnings and cash flows cumulated over long periods of time are highly positively correlated with stock returns over long periods (for example, five-year periods), but that for shorter periods, earnings show a stronger association with stock returns than cash flows. See Patricia M. Dechow, "Accounting Earnings and Cash Flows as Measures of Firm Performance: The Role of Accounting Accruals," *Journal of Accounting and Economics* (1994), pp. 3–42; C. S. Cheng, Chao-Shin Liu, and Thomas F. Schaefer, "Earnings Permanence and the Incremental Information Content of Cash Flow from Operations," *Journal of Accounting Research* (Spring 1996), pp. 173–181; Richard G. Sloan, "Do Stock Prices Fully Reflect Information in Accruals and Cash Flows about Future Earnings," *The Accounting Review* (July 1996), pp. 289–315.

step to the valuation process. As demonstrated in Chapter 12, free cash flows valuation requires that we initially forecast future income statements and balance sheets. Then we derive the implied forecasts of cash flows from those income statements and balance sheets by making adjustments for the accruals in earnings, for the cash flows invested in working capital, and for capital expenditures. We use these cash flows to determine free cash flows, which we then use to compute value. Under the residual income approach, we begin valuation immediately after we forecast future income statements and balance sheets. The two valuations should ultimately be the same, but the free-cash-flows-based approach requires more computations, which requires more time and effort, and increases the potential for error.

Economists sometimes express concern that earnings are not useful for valuation because earnings are not as reliable or as meaningful as cash or dividends for valuing investments. When considering earnings, economists sometimes point out that firms pay dividends in cash, not earnings; investors can spend cash but cannot spend earnings for future consumption. This concern is alleviated in valuation, however, by the fact that the differences between earnings, cash flows, and dividends are merely timing differences: earnings measure when the firm creates wealth, whereas free cash flows measure when the firm realizes wealth in cash, and dividends measure when the firm distributes wealth to shareholders. Over the life of the firm, the present values of future earnings, cash flows, and dividends will be equal.

Some economists worry that accrual accounting earnings reflect accounting methods that no longer capture changes in underlying economic values (for example, depreciation or amortization expenses based on outdated acquisition costs of assets, expenses for research and development that have turned out to be successful, or advertising expenses that have created economically valuable brand equity). Value measurement based on expected earnings over the remaining life of the firm alleviates this concern. Over time, the accrual accounting process will ultimately self-correct measurement errors in accounting numbers. For example, if fixed asset book values are "too high" or "too low" for a company, over time (and it usually does not take long), accrual accounting will naturally correct these measurement errors because the subsequent depreciation expenses will be "too high" or "too low" accordingly. If the current balance sheet does not recognize intellectual capital value created by successful research and development or brand value created by successful marketing, accrual accounting will correct itself over time as the firm generates higher earnings from this intangible capital.[6]

Some economists voice concerns that earnings can be subject to purposeful management or manipulation by a firm. To be sure, analysts should always be alert to the possibility that earnings management (or worse, fraudulent reporting) may occur in some periods by some firms. But this is more of a concern about whether past and current earnings are useful measures to assess profitability and risk, and therefore lead to reliable forecasts of any of the payoffs, whether they be earnings, dividends, or free cash flows. As long as you perform accounting analysis carefully to ensure that your forecasts of these future payoffs are not naively based on a projection that past managed earnings will persist in future years, residual earnings valuation will be unaffected. The same can be said for dividends-based and free-cash-flows-based valuations. Earlier chapters

---

[6]Indeed, when an analyst asserts that a firm's current balance sheet accounting numbers do not reflect underlying economic values, how does the analyst know that? When an analyst asserts that a firm's balance sheet omits a valuable intangible asset in the form of intellectual property or brand equity, how has the analyst assessed the amount of the omission? Usually, analysts base assertions like these on their assessments that the firm will generate future profits from operations that utilize these economic assets. Earnings-based valuation captures *exactly* the same idea. Firm value depends on expected future earnings over the remaining life of the firm.

devoted considerable attention to helping you understand how to assess firms' accounting quality and how to build reliable forecasts.

Ironically, firms can easily manage cash flows in a given period, but economists rarely voice this concern. Free cash flows each period depend on cash inflows and outflows, which the firm can easily manipulate by accelerating or delaying certain cash payments or cash collections in that particular period. Over the remaining life of the firm, which is the focus of your forecasting and valuation, the firm's earnings and cash flows will be determined ultimately by the success of the firm's operating, investing, and financing activities, not by the manipulation of past earnings or cash flows.

LO 13-3

Demonstrate a conceptual understanding of and apply practical techniques for residual income valuation by:

a. Utilizing book value of common shareholders' equity, comprehensive income, dividends, and clean surplus accounting in valuation.

b. Measuring required (or "normal") income by multiplying beginning-of-period book value of equity by the risk-adjusted required rate of return on equity capital.

c. Measuring residual (or "abnormal") income by subtracting required income from expected future income.

d. Determining the value of common equity as the sum of book value of common shareholders' equity plus the present value of expected future residual income.

Theoretical and Conceptual Foundations for Residual Income Valuation[7]

Exhibit 13.1 indicates that the second step toward understanding residual income valuation is to establish its theoretical and conceptual foundation. The foundation for residual income valuation is the classical dividends-based valuation model from Chapter 11, in which the value of common shareholders' equity is the present value of all future dividends to shareholders over the remaining life of the firm. As described in Chapter 11, we define *dividends* to be all-inclusive measures of the cash flows between the firm and the common equity shareholders, encompassing cash flows from the firm to shareholders through periodic dividend payments, stock buybacks, and the firm's liquidating dividend, as well as cash flows from the shareholders to the firm when the firm issues shares (negative dividends).

Chapter 11 demonstrates how to estimate an appropriate discount rate (using the CAPM or some other risk-based expected returns model) based on the rate of return (denoted as R_E) that the capital markets expect for the risk associated with common equity capital in a firm. That chapter also demonstrates the dividends-based valuation approach, which measures the value of common shareholders' equity (denoted as V_0) as the present value of all expected future dividends (denoted as D) with the following general model:

$$V_0 = \sum_{t=1}^{\infty} \frac{D_t}{(1 + R_E)^t} = \frac{D_1}{(1 + R_E)^1} + \frac{D_2}{(1 + R_E)^2} + \frac{D_3}{(1 + R_E)^3} + \cdots$$

Analysts and investors commonly find it desirable to identify and forecast economic variables that determine the firm's future dividends and can therefore substitute for dividends to yield an equivalent valuation. Accounting numbers provide a solution. Accounting for the book value of common shareholders' equity (denoted as BV) in a firm can be expressed as follows:

$$BV_t = BV_{t-1} + CI_t - D_t$$

---

[7]Credit for the rigorous development of the residual income valuation model goes to James A. Ohlson, "A Synthesis of Security Valuation Theory and the Role of Dividends, Cash Flows, and Earnings," *Contemporary Accounting Research* (Spring 1990), pp. 648–676; James A. Ohlson, "Earnings, Book Values, and Dividends in Equity Valuation," *Contemporary Accounting Research* (Spring 1995), pp. 661–687; Gerald A. Feltham and James A. Ohlson, "Valuation and Clean Surplus Accounting for Operating and Financial Activities," *Contemporary Accounting Research* (Spring 1995), pp. 216–230. The ideas underlying the earnings-based valuation approach trace to early work by G.A.D. Preinreich, "Annual Survey of Economic Theory: The Theory of Depreciation," *Econometrica* (1938), pp. 219–241, and Edgar O. Edwards and Philip W. Bell, *The Theory and Measurement of Business Income* (Berkeley, CA: University of California Press), 1961.

In this expression, book value of common shareholders' equity at the end of Year t (BV_t) is equal to book value at the end of Year $t-1$ (BV_{t-1}) plus comprehensive income for Year t (CI_t) minus the all-inclusive dividends during Year t (D_t). As in the dividends valuation approach described in Chapter 11, we assume that accounting for net income and book value of shareholders' equity follows *clean surplus accounting.* Clean surplus accounting simply means that comprehensive income includes all of the recognized elements of income of the firm for common equity shareholders (that is, all of the amounts in the income statement plus all of the other comprehensive income items) and dividends include all direct capital transactions between the firm and the common equity shareholders (that is, periodic dividend payments, share repurchases, and share issues).

We can rearrange the accounting equation for the book value of common equity to isolate dividends as follows:

$$D_t = CI_t + BV_{t-1} - BV_t$$

In this expression, dividends equal comprehensive income plus the change in book value from direct capital transactions with common shareholders.

Example: Clean Surplus

Suppose a firm had shareholders' equity on the balance sheet at a book value of $5,000 at the end of Year $t-1$. Suppose during Year t, the firm earns comprehensive income of $600, pays dividends to shareholders of $360, issues new stock to raise $250 of capital, and uses $50 to repurchase common shares. The book value of shareholders' equity at the end of Year t is as follows:

$$\begin{aligned}
BV_t &= BV_{t-1} + CI_t - D_t \\
&= \$5{,}000 + \$600 - (\$360 - \$250 + \$50) \\
&= \$5{,}000 + \$600 - \$160 \\
&= \$5{,}440
\end{aligned}$$

In this example, all-inclusive dividends (D_t) in Year t amount to $160. Using the expression for dividends shows that

$$D_t = CI_t + BV_{t-1} - BV_t = \$600 + \$5{,}000 - \$5{,}440 = \$160$$

Because dividends equal comprehensive income plus the change in book value of common shareholders' equity, we can substitute comprehensive income plus the change in the book value of common shareholders' equity into the classical dividends valuation model, as follows:

$$\begin{aligned}
V_0 &= \sum_{t=1}^{\infty} \frac{D_t}{(1+R_E)^t} = \sum_{t=1}^{\infty} \frac{CI_t + BV_{t-1} - BV_t}{(1-R_E)^t} \\
&= \frac{CI_1 + BV_0 - BV_1}{(1+R_E)^1} + \frac{CI_2 + BV_1 - BV_2}{(1+R_E)^2} + \frac{CI_3 + BV_2 - BV_3}{(1+R_E)^3} + \cdots
\end{aligned}$$

Algebraically, the present value of BV_{t-1} can be rewritten as follows:

$$\frac{BV_{t-1}}{(1+R_E)^t} = \frac{BV_{t-1}}{(1+R_E)^{t-1}} - \frac{R_E \times BV_{t-1}}{(1+R_E)^t}$$

We substitute the right side expression for the present value of BV_{t-1} into the equation for V_0, rearrange terms, and simplify to obtain the following expression for the *residual income valuation model:*

$$V_0 = BV_0 + \sum_{t=1}^{\infty} \frac{CI_t - (R_E \times BV_{t-1})}{(1 + R_E)^t}$$

$$= BV_0 + \frac{CI_1 - (R_E \times BV_0)}{(1 + R_E)^1} + \frac{CI_2 - (R_E \times BV_1)}{(1 + R_E)^2} + \frac{CI_3 - (R_E \times BV_2)}{(1 + R_E)^3} + \cdots$$

The *residual income valuation model* above is therefore a valuation model for common shareholders' equity that is algebraically equivalent to dividends-based valuation, yet relies on earnings and book values.[8]

Intuition for Residual Income Measurement and Valuation

The intuition for the residual income valuation model is straightforward. The value of common shareholders' equity is equal to the book value of common equity plus the present value of all expected future *residual income,* which is the amount by which expected future earnings exceed the required earnings, for the remaining life of the firm. The *required earnings* (also known as *normal earnings*) of the firm equals the product of the required rate of return on common equity capital times the book value of common equity capital at the beginning of each period. We compute required earnings for period t as $R_E \times BV_{t-1}$. Required earnings reflect the earnings the firm must earn in period t simply to provide a return to common equity that is equal to the cost of common equity capital. Required earnings are analogous to a charge for the cost of equity capital, similar to interest expense as a charge for the cost of debt capital.

We measure *residual income* (also called *abnormal earnings*) as follows:

$$Residual\ Income_t = CI_t - (R_E \times BV_{t-1})$$

Residual income is the difference between the comprehensive income you expect the firm to generate and the required earnings of the firm. Residual income in period t measures the amount of wealth creation (if it is a positive amount; or wealth destruction if it is negative) the firm will generate in period t for common equity shareholders above (or below) the earnings required to cover the cost of equity capital. If you expect the firm to generate comprehensive income each period in the future that is exactly equal to required earnings [that is, $CI_t - (R_E \times BV_{t-1}) = 0$ residual income for all future periods], you also expect the firm to exactly cover the cost of equity capital, no more, no less. In that case, the value of the firm is exactly equal to the book value of common shareholders' equity. On the other hand, if you expect the firm to create wealth for the shareholders by earning positive amounts of residual income, the value of the firm is equal to book value of common shareholders' equity plus the present value of all expected future residual income.[9]

---

[8]Chapter 14 demonstrates a version of this residual income approach that determines the intrinsic-value-to-book-value ratio for the firm using the return on common equity (ROCE, described in Chapter 4) and expected growth in the book value of common equity.

[9]The concept of residual income in the economics literature and the accounting literature predates the commercialization of "Economic Value Added" by decades. Applications of the concept of residual income in valuation and corporate governance practices can be found in G. Bennett Stewart, *The Quest for Value* (New York: Harper Collins), 1991, and in the expanding literature on EVA®.

Illustrations of Residual Income Measurement and Valuation

The following examples illustrate residual income measurement and the residual income valuation model under various assumptions.

Example 1: Zero Residual Income, 100% Dividend Payout

Suppose investors have invested $10,000 in common equity in a company. Given the risk of the company, the investors expect to earn a 12% return, and they expect the company to pay out 100% of income in dividends each year. The required earnings of the company each period are as follows:

$$R_E \times BV_{t-1} = 0.12 \times \$10,000 = \$1,200$$

Suppose the investors forecast that the company will generate exactly $1,200 in comprehensive income each year. The investors should compute the residual income of the firm as follows:

$$CI_t - (R_E \times BV_{t-1}) = \$1,200 - (0.12 \times \$10,000) = \$0$$

Using the residual income approach, investors would value this firm based on book value plus expected future residual income as follows:

$$V_0 = BV_0 + \sum_{t=1}^{\infty} \frac{CI_t - (R_E \times BV_{t-1})}{(1 + R_E)^t}$$

$$= \$10,000 + \sum_{t=1}^{\infty} \frac{\$1,200_t - (0.12 \times \$10,000_{t-1})}{(1 + 0.12)^t}$$

$$= \$10,000 + \sum_{t=1}^{\infty} \frac{\$0}{(1 + 0.12)^t} = \$10,000$$

In this case, the firm's expected future income exactly equals the required earnings necessary to cover the cost of equity capital. So residual income is zero and the value of the firm is equal to the book value of common equity invested in the firm. The value of the firm under the residual income model is identical to the value determined using the dividends valuation model, which would value the company as a stream of dividends in perpetuity with no growth as follows:

$$V_0 = \frac{\$1,200}{0.12} = \$10,000$$

Example 2: Zero Residual Income, Zero Dividend Payout

Now assume the same facts as in Example 1, but suppose investors expect the company to pay out no dividends each year and all the earnings will be reinvested in projects that will generate the investors' required 12% rate of return.[10] The required earnings of the firm in Year +1 will be

$$R_E \times BV_0 = 0.12 \times \$10,000 = \$1,200$$

---

[10]Although this is simply an illustration, note that this is an important assumption because it presumes that the firm can scale up operations without diminishing future returns.

After retained earnings of \$1,200 are added to book value of equity at the end of Year +1, the required earnings of the company in Year +2 will be

$$R_E \times BV_1 = 0.12 \times [\$10,000 + \$1,200] = \$1,344$$

After retained earnings of \$1,344 are added to book value of equity at the end of Year +2, the required earnings of the company in Year +3 will be

$$R_E \times BV_2 = 0.12 \times [\$11,200 + \$1,344] = \$1,505$$

These computations show that the required earnings of the firm will grow as the firm retains and reinvests earnings, on which the investors expect the firm to earn the required rate of return.

Suppose the investors expect the firm to generate future earnings each year that will exactly match required earnings each year. Assuming the firm will continue to reinvest all of its earnings and generate the required 12% return each year over its remaining life (that is, continuing in Year +4 and beyond), we can determine the value of equity capital in the firm using the residual income model as follows:

$$V_0 = BV_0 + \sum_{t=1}^{\infty} \frac{CI_t - (R_E \times BV_{t-1})}{(1 + R_E)^t}$$

$$= \$10,000 + \frac{\$1,200 - (0.12 \times \$10,000)}{(1.12)^1} + \frac{\$1,344 - (0.12 \times \$11,200)}{(1.12)^2}$$

$$+ \frac{\$1,505 - (0.12 \times \$12,544)}{(1.12)^3} + \sum_{t=4}^{\infty} \frac{CI_t - (0.12 \times BV_{t-1})}{(1 + 0.12)^t}$$

$$= \$10,000 + \frac{\$0}{(1.12)^1} + \frac{\$0}{(1.12)^2} + \frac{\$0}{(1.12)^3} + \sum_{t=4}^{\infty} \frac{\$0}{(1 + 0.12)^t}$$

$$= \$10,000$$

Example 3: Declining Residual Income, Zero Dividend Payout

Now assume the same facts as in Example 2, but suppose investors expect the firm simply to reinvest the earnings in cash or other types of assets that will earn no additional return for each of the next three periods. The investors expect the firm to continue to earn \$1,200 each year on the original investment of \$10,000, but they expect the reinvestment of earnings in the first three years to produce no incremental return. Also assume for simplicity that in Year +4 and beyond, the firm will invest in projects that will earn a total of 12% return for equity shareholders.

The required earnings of the firm in Year +1 will be

$$R_E \times BV_0 = 0.12 \times \$10,000 = \$1,200$$

After retained earnings of \$1,200 are added to book value of equity at the end of Year +1, the required earnings of the company in Year +2 will be

$$R_E \times BV_1 = 0.12 \times (\$10,000 + \$1,200) = \$1,344$$

After retained earnings of \$1,200 are added to book value of equity at the end of Year +2, the required earnings of the company in Year +3 will be

$$R_E \times BV_2 = 0.12 \times (\$11,200 + \$1,200) = \$1,488$$

We can determine the value of equity capital in the firm using the residual income model as follows:

$$V_0 = BV_0 + \sum_{t=1}^{\infty} \frac{CI_t - (R_E \times BV_{t-1})}{(1 + R_E)^t}$$

$$= \$10,000 + \frac{\$1,200 - (0.12 \times \$10,000)}{(1.12)^1} + \frac{\$1,200 - (0.12 \times \$11,200)}{(1.12)^2}$$

$$+ \frac{\$1,200 - (0.12 \times \$12,400)}{(1.12)^3} + \sum_{t=4}^{\infty} \frac{CI_t - (0.12 \times BV_{t-1})}{(1 + 0.12)^t}$$

$$= \$10,000 + \frac{\$0}{(1.12)^1} + \frac{\$1,200 - \$1,344}{(1.12)^2} + \frac{\$1,200 - \$1,488}{(1.12)^3} + \sum_{t=4}^{\infty} \frac{\$0}{(1+0.12)^t}$$

$$= \$10,000 + \$0 - \$115 - \$205 + \$0$$

$$= \$9,680$$

This example shows that by reinvesting earnings to earn zero incremental return rather than the required 12% return, the firm's reinvested earnings will be $144 less than required earnings in Year +2 and $288 less than required earnings in Year +3. In present value terms, the firm will destroy $115 of shareholder value in Year +2 and $205 of shareholder value in Year +3. Therefore, investors would value the firm at only $9,680 in this example, as compared to $10,000 in the preceding two examples.

Example 4: Positive Residual Income

Now assume investors have invested $10,000 in common equity in a firm, they expect to earn a 12% return, and they expect the company to pay out 100% of income in dividends each year. Now suppose these investors expect the firm to earn net income of $1,000 in Year +1, $2,000 in Year +2, $1,500 in Year +3, and $1,200 each year thereafter. Investors should compute the residual income valuation as follows:

$$V_0 = BV_0 + \sum_{t=1}^{\infty} \frac{CI_t - (R_E \times BV_{t-1})}{(1 + R_E)^t}$$

$$= \$10,000 + \frac{\$1,000 - (0.12 \times \$10,000)}{(1.12)^1} + \frac{\$2,000 - (0.12 \times \$10,000)}{(1.12)^2}$$

$$+ \frac{\$1,500 - (0.12 \times \$10,000)}{(1.12)^3} + \sum_{t=4}^{\infty} \frac{\$1,200_t - (0.12 \times \$10,000)}{(1 + 0.12)^t}$$

$$= \$10,000 + \frac{-\$200}{(1.12)^1} + \frac{\$800}{(1.12)^2} + \frac{\$300}{(1.12)^3} + \sum_{t=4}^{\infty} \frac{\$0_t}{(1 + 0.12)^t}$$

$$= \$10,000 - \$179 + \$638 + \$214 + \$0$$

$$= \$10,673$$

In this example, the firm will generate residual income amounts of –$200 in Year +1, $800 in Year +2, $300 in Year +3, and $0 each year thereafter. The firm destroys shareholder wealth in Year +1 by failing to earn sufficient income to cover the cost of equity capital, but the firm generates increasing shareholder wealth in Years +2 and +3 and exactly covers the cost of equity capital each year thereafter. Given these assumptions, the present value of the firm under the residual income model is $10,673.

Example 5: Residual Income Valuation under Different Accounting Treatments

As mentioned earlier, like accrual accounting, the residual income valuation model will naturally correct for differences in accounting methods over the life of a firm. To illustrate, suppose we are valuing a very simple firm under the following assumptions. The firm has only one asset (cash) of $200 and a beginning book value of common equity equal to $200. Investors expect to earn a 10% rate of return. In Year 1, the firm invests $100 cash in an R&D project. In Year 1, the firm realizes no revenues, but in Year 2 realizes $200 in revenues from the R&D project. These are the only activities of this (admittedly simple) firm.

Suppose the firm immediately expenses the entire R&D in Year 1. Earnings for the firm would equal −$100 in Year 1 ($0 revenues − $100 R&D expense) and +$200 in Year 2 ($200 in revenues − $0 expenses). Using the residual income valuation model, we would value the firm as follows:

$$V_0 = BV_0 + \sum_{t=1}^{\infty} \frac{CI_t - (R_E \times BV_{t-1})}{(1 + R_E)^t}$$

$$= \$200 + \frac{-\$100 - (0.10 \times \$200)}{(1.10)^1} + \frac{\$200 - (0.10 \times \$100)}{(1.10)^2}$$

$$= \$200 + \frac{-\$120}{(1.10)^1} + \frac{\$190}{(1.10)^2}$$

$$= \$200 - \$109 + \$157 = \$248$$

Now suppose the firm capitalizes the entire R&D expenditure as an asset in Year 1, and expenses the R&D in Year 2, the period in which the R&D generates revenues. Earnings for the firm would equal $0 in Year 1 ($0 revenues − $0 R&D expense) and +$100 in Year 2 ($200 in revenues − $100 R&D expense). Using the residual income valuation model, we would value the firm as follows:

$$V_0 = BV_0 + \sum_{t=1}^{\infty} \frac{CI_t - (R_E \times BV_{t-1})}{(1 + R_E)^t}$$

$$= \$200 + \frac{\$0 - (0.10 \times \$200)}{(1.10)^1} + \frac{\$100 - (0.10 \times \$200)}{(1.1)^2}$$

$$= \$200 + \frac{-\$20}{(1.10)^1} + \frac{\$80}{(1.10)^2}$$

$$= \$200 - \$18 + \$66 = \$248$$

Notice that we arrive at exactly the same value, whether the firm capitalizes or expenses R&D in Year 1.

Now imagine that we value the firm using free-cash-flows-based or dividends-based valuation. At the end of Year 2, the firm has $300 in free cash flows, so it can pay a $300 liquidating dividend, based on the initial $200 cash investment minus $100 in cash spent on R&D in Year 1 plus $200 in cash collected in revenues in Year 2. The present value of a $300 dividend at the end of Year 2, discounted at 10%, is $248, exactly the same value as we determined by the residual income model.

Residual Income Valuation Model with Finite Horizon Earnings Forecasts and Continuing Value Computation

LO 13-4

Apply the residual income valuation method to value common shares and assess the sensitivity of value estimates to key valuation parameters, such as discount rates and expected long-term growth rates.

Analysts cannot precisely forecast firms' income statements and balance sheets for many years into the future. Therefore, analysts commonly forecast income statements and balance sheets over a foreseeable finite horizon and then make simplifying growth rate assumptions for the years continuing after the forecast horizon. We can modify the residual income valuation model to include explicit forecasts of net income and book value of common equity through Year T (where T is a finite horizon, often five or ten years in the future) and then apply a constant growth rate assumption (denoted as g) to project residual income for Year T+1 and all years thereafter. We used similar approaches to forecast dividends in Chapter 11 and free cash flows in Chapter 12.

To deal with the uncertainty in long-run forecasts, you must forecast net income, book value of shareholders' equity, and residual income over an explicit forecast horizon until the point at which you expect the firm's growth pattern to settle into steady-state growth, during which time earnings, dividends, and cash flows will grow (on average) at a steady, predictable rate. We refer to residual income in this long-run, steady-state growth period as *continuing residual income* because it reflects residual income earned by the firm continuing into the long-run future. The long-run, steady-state growth rate in future continuing residual income may be positive, negative, or zero. Steady-state growth in residual income may be driven by long-run expectations for inflation, the industry's sales, the economy in general, or the population. In some industries, competitive dynamics eventually drive long-run projections of the future returns earned by the firm (for example, the future ROCE) to an equilibrium level equal to the long-run expected cost of equity capital in the firm. Once a firm reaches that point, the firm can be expected to earn zero residual income in the future. You should select a continuing growth rate in residual income that captures realistic long-run expectations for the firm.

To compute residual income in Year T+1, you should project Year T+1 comprehensive income by multiplying Year T comprehensive income by the growth factor $(1+g)$. Year T+1 residual income (denoted as RI_{T+1}) can then be computed as follows:

$$RI_{T+1} = [CI_T \times (1 + g)] - [R_E \times BV_T]$$

By estimating RI_{T+1} this way, you also will be able to apply the same uniform long-run growth factor $(1 + g)$ to estimate Year T+1 income statement and balance sheet amounts and to compute internally consistent projections for Year T+1 free cash flows and dividends, which you can then use in free-cash-flows-based and dividends-based valuation models to determine internally consistent value estimates. Chapters 11 and 12 demonstrate these approaches.

Next, you can treat RI_{T+1} as a growing perpetuity of residual income beginning in Year T+1. You can discount the perpetuity of residual income to present value using the perpetuity-with-growth value model described in Chapters 11 and 12. We include the continuing value computation into the finite horizon residual income model as follows:

$$V_0 = BV_0 + \sum_{t=1}^{\infty} \frac{CI_t - (R_E \times BV_{t-1})}{(1 + R_E)^t}$$

$$= BV_0 + \underbrace{\sum_{t=1}^{T} \frac{CI_t - (R_E \times BV_{t-1})}{(1 + R_E)^t}}_{}$$

$$\underset{(1)}{} \qquad \underset{(2)}{}$$

$$+ \underbrace{\left(\{[CI_T \times (1 + g)] - (R_E \times BV_T)\} \times \frac{1}{(R_E - g)} \times \frac{1}{(1 + R_E)^T} \right)}_{(3)}$$

This model computes the value of common equity based on three parts, identified as (1), (2), and (3) in the preceding equation:

1. Book value of shareholders' equity at time $t=0$ (the BV_0 term)
2. Present value of residual income over the explicit forecast horizon through Year T (the summation term)
3. Present value of continuing value based on residual income as a perpetuity with growth beginning in Year T+1 (the term in brackets)

To compute continuing value, we compute residual income in Year T+1 {the term $[CI_T \times (1 + g)] - (R_E \times BV_T)$}. We assume that residual income in Year T+1 will grow at constant rate g in perpetuity beginning in Year T+1, so we compute continuing value as of the start of Year T+1 using the perpetuity-with-growth valuation factor [the term $1/(R_E - g)$]. Finally, we discount continuing value to present value at time $t = 0$ using the present value factor [the term $1/(1 + R_E)^T$].

Coaching Tip: Avoid This Common Mistake

The preceding section describes how to compute residual income in Year T+1, as follows:

$$RI_{T+1} = [CI_T \times (1 + g)] - (R_E \times BV_T)$$

By estimating RI_{T+1} this way, you will effectively apply a uniform long-run growth factor $(1 + g)$ to comprehensive income to compute residual income. Recall that Chapters 11 and 12 also demonstrated how to correctly compute free cash flows and dividends in Year T+1 by applying the same long-run growth factor $(1 + g)$ to project all of the Year T+1 income statement and balance sheet amounts and then deriving internally consistent projections for Year T+1 free cash flows and dividends. With this simple but important step, you can determine internally consistent value estimates across all three valuation models (and therefore avoid the all-too-common mistake of deriving *different* values for the *same* firm using *different* valuation models).

The common mistake analysts make (and you can avoid with the tip indicated above) is forecasting RI_{T+1} by simply projecting $RI_{T+1} = RI_T \times (1 + g)$. This (likely erroneous) shortcut projection implicitly assumes that $RI_T \times (1 + g) = [CI_T - (R_E \times BV_{T-1})] \times (1 + g) = CI_T \times (1 + g) - [R_E \times BV_{T-1} \times (1 + g)]$. This assumption requires BV_T to equal $BV_{T-1} \times (1 + g)$, which is not necessarily true. Residual income in Year T+1 depends on book value at the end of Year T. We assume constant growth at rate $(1 + g)$ in residual income beginning in Year T+1. Thus, the only way residual income in Year T+1 will equal residual income in Year T times $(1 + g)$ is if book value in Year T happened to grow (by coincidence) at the same rate $(1 + g)$. Such a coincidence is rare. You can easily avoid this forecasting and valuation error for RI_{T+1} by correctly computing $RI_{T+1} = [CI_T \times (1 + g)] - (R_E \times BV_T)$.

Valuation of PepsiCo Using the Residual Income Model

Step three toward understanding residual income valuation, as Exhibit 13.1 illustrates, is the practical applications step in which we apply the residual income valuation approach to value the common shareholders' equity in **PepsiCo**. As Chapters 11 and 12 describe, PepsiCo shares closed trading at $68.43 on the New York Stock Exchange at the end of 2012. In Chapter 11, we determined our central estimate of the value of PepsiCo shares at the end of 2012 to be roughly $85.86 using the projected financial statement forecasts developed in Chapter 10 and applying the dividends-based valuation approach. We obtained the same $85.86 value estimate for PepsiCo shares in Chapter 12 using the free-cash-flows-based valuation approaches. Next, we illustrate the valuation of PepsiCo shares using the residual income valuation model techniques described in this chapter and the forecasts developed in Chapter 10. The Forecasts and Valuation spreadsheets of FSAP (Appendix C) also demonstrate the forecasts and valuation estimates.

We value PepsiCo with the residual income approach following these seven steps:

1. Estimate the appropriate discount rate using the risk-adjusted required rate of return on equity capital.
2. Determine the book value of common shareholders' equity on PepsiCo's 2012 balance sheet.
3. Project expected future residual income from the financial statement forecasts for PepsiCo described in Chapter 10.
4. Project long-run growth in residual income in the continuing periods beyond the forecast horizon.
5. Discount the expected future residual income to present value, including continuing value.
6. Add the book value of equity and the present value of expected future residual income to determine the total value of common shareholders' equity, correct for midyear discounting, and divide by the number of shares outstanding to convert this total to an estimate of share value for PepsiCo.
7. Analyze the sensitivity of the estimate of PepsiCo's share value to determine the reasonable range of values for PepsiCo shares.

After illustrating this seven-step valuation process, we will compare the range of reasonable values to PepsiCo's share price in the market and suggest an appropriate investment decision indicated by the analysis.

Discount Rates for Residual Income

To compute the appropriate discount rate for residual income, we again use the CAPM to estimate the market's required rate of return on **PepsiCo**'s common stock, as demonstrated in Chapters 11 and 12. At the end of 2012, PepsiCo's common stock had a market beta of roughly 0.75. At the same time, U.S. Treasury bills with ten years to maturity traded with a yield of approximately 3.0%, which we use as the risk-free rate. Assuming a 6% market risk premium, the CAPM indicates that PepsiCo had a cost of common equity capital of 7.5% [$R_E = 7.5\% = 3.0\% + (0.75 \times 6.0\%)$] at the end of 2012, the beginning of the valuation period. We used this same cost of common equity capital to value PepsiCo shares in Chapter 11 using the present value of future dividends and in Chapter 12 using the present value of free cash flows to common equity shareholders'.

Using the residual income valuation model, we do not need to compute the weighted-average cost of capital. This does not mean that we ignore debt capital or the costs related to debt capital. Instead, we rely on accounting to capture the effects of debt. We project book value of shareholders' equity after subtracting debt from total assets, and we project net income after subtracting interest expense net of tax savings.

PepsiCo's Book Value of Equity and the Projection of Residual Income

According to **PepsiCo**'s balance sheet (Appendix A), book value of common shareholders' equity is $22,417.0 million at the end of 2012. This amount is the starting point for the residual income valuation model, the term denoted BV_0 in the valuation equations.

We project residual income each period in the finite forecast horizon using the following four steps:

1. Forecast expected future comprehensive income for each period.
2. Forecast expected future book value of common shareholders' equity at the beginning of each period.
3. Compute expected future required income, which is the product of the cost of equity capital times the book value of common shareholders' equity at the beginning of each period ($R_E \times BV_{t-1}$).
4. Determine expected future residual income by subtracting expected future required income from expected future comprehensive income [$CI_t - (R_E \times BV_{t-1})$].

We completed the first and second steps in Chapter 10. Chapter 10 developed our projections of PepsiCo's future comprehensive income by making specific assumptions regarding each line item on the income statement. Chapter 10 also developed specific forecasts of common shareholders' equity on the balance sheet by making specific assumptions about PepsiCo's assets, liabilities, and common equity, including specific forecasts of dividends, stock issues, and stock buybacks. For projections of comprehensive income and book value of shareholders' equity beyond Year +5, we assume that PepsiCo will grow in steady state at a rate of 3.0% per year in Year +6 and beyond. Exhibit 13.3 presents projections of PepsiCo's comprehensive income, book value of shareholders' equity, required income, and residual income through Year +5 using the forecasts discussed in Chapter 10 and a 7.5% cost of equity capital.

In Chapter 10, for example, we projected PepsiCo's net income attributable to PepsiCo common shareholders will be $6,157.7 million in Year +1. We forecasted other comprehensive income items will be zero, so projected comprehensive income and net income will be equal. (Recall from the earlier discussion that the residual income model requires that we measure income for common equity shareholders comprehensively by using clean surplus accounting.) We projected that preferred stock outstanding

Exhibit 13.3

Valuation of PepsiCo:
Present Value of Residual Income Year +1 through Year +5
(dollar amounts in millions; allow for rounding)

	Year +1	Year +2	Year +3	Year +4	Year +5
Common shareholders' equity (at beginning of year; denoted BV_{t-1})	$ 22,417.0	$22,020.3	$22,417.9	$22,749.5	$23,259.5
Comprehensive income available for common shareholders (denoted CI_t)	$ 6,094.7	$ 6,376.6	$ 6,598.3	$ 6,972.2	$ 7,064.2
Required income ($R_E \times BV_{t-1}$; $R_E = 7.5\%$)	(1,681.3)	(1,651.5)	(1,681.3)	(1,706.2)	(1,744.5)
Residual income [$CI_t - (R_E \times BV_{t-1})$]	$ 4,413.5	$ 4,725.1	$ 4,917.0	$ 5,266.0	$ 5,319.7
Present value factors ($R_E = 7.5\%$)	0.930	0.865	0.805	0.749	0.697
Present value of residual income	$ 4,105.6	$ 4,088.8	$ 3,958.0	$ 3,943.2	$ 3,705.5
Sum of present value residual income Year +1 through Year +5	$19,801.0				

would be liquidated, requiring liquidating dividends of $63.0 million (the fair value of the preferred stock) in Year +1; so comprehensive income available to common shareholders will be $6,094.7 million. Given that PepsiCo's book value of common shareholders' equity at the beginning of Year +1 is $22,417.0 million and PepsiCo's cost of equity capital is 7.5%, we project Year +1 required earnings to be $1,681.3 million (0.075 × $22,417.0 million). Therefore, we project Year +1 residual income will be $4,413.5 million ($6,094.7 million – $1,681.3 million).

To project PepsiCo's residual income continuing in Year +6 and beyond, we forecast that PepsiCo can sustain long-run growth of 3.0% per year, consistent with long-run average growth in the economy. It is the same assumption we made in forecasting long-run growth in Year +6 and beyond for dividends in Chapter 11 and for free cash flows in Chapter 12. We project Year +6 residual income will be $5,527.4 million, computed by projecting Year +5 comprehensive income to grow by 3.0% and subtracting required earnings, measured as the equity cost of capital times book value at the end of Year +5, as follows:

$$RI_6 = [CI_5 \times (1 + g)] - [R_E \times BV_5]$$
$$= (\$7,064.2 \text{ million} \times 1.03) - (0.075 \times \$23,315.8 \text{ million})$$
$$= \$7,276.1 \text{ million} - \$1,748.7 \text{ million} = \$5,527.4 \text{ million}$$

Discounting PepsiCo's Residual Income to Present Value

We discount residual income to present value using **PepsiCo**'s 7.5% cost of equity capital. Exhibit 13.3 shows that the sum of the present value of PepsiCo's residual income from Year +1 through Year +5 is $19,801.0 million.

We compute the present value of PepsiCo's continuing value of residual income as a perpetuity beginning in Year +6 with growth at a 3.0% rate. To compute the continuing value estimate, we use the perpetuity-with-growth valuation model, which determines the present value of the growing perpetuity at the start of the perpetuity period. We then discount that value back to present value at time $t=0$. We compute the present value of the continuing value of PepsiCo's residual income as follows (allowing for rounding):

$$Present\ Value\ of\ Continuing\ Value_0$$
$$= \{[CI_5 \times (1+g)] - (R_E \times BV_5)\} \times [1/(R_E - g)] \times [1/(1 + R_E)^5]$$
$$= (\$7,064.2\ million \times 1.03) - (0.075 \times \$23,315.8\ million)$$
$$\times [1/(0.075 - 0.03)] \times [1/(1 + 0.075)^5]$$
$$= (\$7,276.1\ million - \$1,748.7\ million) \times 22.2222 \times 0.697$$
$$= \$5,527.4\ million \times 22.2222 \times 0.697$$
$$= \$85,559.5\ million$$

The total present value of PepsiCo's residual income is the sum of these two parts:

Present value of residual income Year +1 through Year +5 (Exhibit 13.3)	$ 19,801.0 million
Present value of continuing value in Year +6 and beyond	85,559.5 million
Present value of residual income	$105,360.5 million

Computing PepsiCo's Common Equity Share Value

To compute the total value of common equity, we add **PepsiCo**'s book value of common equity to the present value of residual income. The total value of common equity of PepsiCo as of the beginning of Year +1 is the sum of these two amounts:

Present value of residual income	$105,360.5 million
Book value of common shareholders' equity	22,417.0 million
Present value of common shareholders' equity before midyear discounting	$127,777.5 million

As Chapters 11 and 12 describe, our present value calculations over-discount because they discount each year's residual income for full periods when, in fact, residual income is generated throughout each period and should be discounted from the midpoint of each year to the present. Therefore, to make the correction, we multiply the total by the midyear adjustment factor of 1.0375 $[1 + (R_E/2) = 1 + (0.075/2)]$. Therefore, the total present value of common shareholders' equity should be computed as follows:

Present value of common shareholders' equity before midyear discounting	$127,777.5 million
Midyear discounting adjustment factor	$\times$ 1.0375
Total present value of common shareholders' equity	$132,569.1 million

Dividing the total present value of common shareholders' equity of $132,569.1 million by 1,544 million shares outstanding indicates that PepsiCo's common equity shares have a value of $85.86 per share. This value estimate is identical to the value estimate based on dividends in Chapter 11 and free cash flows to common equity shareholders in Chapter 12. Exhibit 13.4 summarizes the computations to arrive at PepsiCo's common equity share value. Exhibit 13.5 presents the residual income model application for PepsiCo from FSAP.

Sensitivity Analysis and Investment Decision Making

We cautioned in Chapters 11 and 12 and we reiterate here that you should not place too much confidence in the precision of a single point estimate of firm value using these (or any) forecasts for residual income over the remaining life of any firm, even a mature firm such as **PepsiCo**. Although we have constructed these forecasts and value estimates with care, the forecasting and valuation process has an inherently high degree of uncertainty and estimation error. Therefore, rather than relying too heavily on any one point estimate of the value of a firm's shares, you should describe a reasonable range of values for a firm's shares.

Two critical forecasting and valuation parameters are the long-run growth assumption, which we forecast to be 3.0%, and the cost of equity capital, which we forecast to be 7.5%. With these assumptions, our base case estimate is that PepsiCo common shares should be valued at roughly $85.86 per share. As in Chapters 11 and 12, we assess the sensitivity of our estimate of PepsiCo's share value by varying these two parameters across reasonable ranges. Exhibit 13.6 contains the results of sensitivity analysis in FSAP varying the long-run growth assumption from 0–10% and the cost of equity capital

Exhibit 13.4

Valuation of PepsiCo Using the Residual Income Valuation Model
(dollar amounts in millions except per-share amounts)

Valuation Steps	Computations	Amounts
Sum of present value of residual income, Year +1 through Year +5	See Exhibit 13.3.	$ 19,801.0
Add present value of continuing value	Year +6 residual income assumed to grow at 3.0%; discounted at 7.5%	+ 85,559.5
Total present value of residual income		$105,360.5
Add: Beginning book value of equity	Beginning book value of equity from 2012 balance sheet	+ 22,417.0
Total		$127,777.5
Adjust to midyear discounting	Multiply by $1 + (R_E/2)$	× 1.0375
Total present value of common equity		$132,569.1
Divide by shares outstanding	1,544 million shares outstanding	÷ 1,544.0
Estimated value per share		$ 85.86
Current price per share		$ 68.43
Percent difference	Positive number indicates underpricing	25%

Exhibit 13.5

Valuation of PepsiCo:
Residual Income Valuation Approach in FSAP
(dollar amounts in millions, except per-share amounts)

RESIDUAL INCOME VALUATION	1 Year +1	2 Year +2	3 Year +3	4 Year +4	5 Year +5	Continuing Value Year +6
Comprehensive income available for common shareholders	$ 6,094.7	$ 6,376.6	$ 6,598.3	$ 6,972.2	$ 7,064.2	$ 7,276.1
Lagged book value of common shareholders' equity (at $t-1$)	$ 22,417.0	$22,020.3	$22,417.9	$22,749.5	$23,259.5	$23,315.8
Required earnings	$ 1,681.3	$ 1,651.5	$ 1,681.3	$ 1,706.2	$ 1,744.5	$ 1,748.7
Residual Income	$ 4,413.5	$ 4,725.1	$ 4,917.0	$ 5,266.0	$ 5,319.7	$ 5,527.4
Present value factors	0.930	0.865	0.805	0.749	0.697	
Present value residual income	$ 4,105.6	$ 4,088.8	$ 3,958.0	$ 3,943.2	$ 3,705.5	
Sum of present value residual income	$ 19,801.0					
Present value of continuing value	85,559.5					
Total	$105,360.5					
Add: Beginning book value of equity	22,417.0					
Present value of equity	$127,777.5					
Adjust to midyear discounting	1.0375					
Total present value of equity	$132,569.1					
Shares outstanding	1,544.0					
Estimated value per share	$ 85.86					
Current share price	$ 68.43					
Percent difference	25%					

Exhibit 13.6

Valuation of PepsiCo:
Sensitivity Analysis of Share Value Estimates to Growth and Equity Cost of Capital

RESIDUAL INCOME VALUATION SENSITIVITY ANALYSIS

Long-Run Growth Assumptions

	85.86	0%	2%	3%	4%	5%	6%	8%	10%
Discount Rates:	5%	91.96	135.32	189.52	352.10				
	6%	76.74	102.04	127.33	177.92	329.69			
	6.5%	70.89	90.94	109.56	143.08	221.27	612.25		
	7.5%	61.54	74.81	85.86	103.23	134.50	207.46		
	8.5%	54.40	63.63	70.77	81.08	97.28	126.45	534.73	
	10%	46.37	52.11	56.21	61.68	69.33	80.82	138.23	
	11%	42.23	46.56	49.53	53.35	58.44	65.58	94.10	236.75
	12%	38.80	42.12	44.33	47.10	50.65	55.40	72.00	121.80
	13%	35.89	38.48	40.17	42.23	44.80	48.11	58.70	83.42
	14%	33.40	35.45	36.76	38.33	40.24	42.63	49.82	64.18
	15%	31.25	32.89	33.92	35.13	36.59	38.36	43.45	52.60
	16%	29.36	30.69	31.51	32.46	33.59	34.94	38.66	44.85
	18%	26.23	27.12	27.65	28.26	28.96	29.78	31.91	35.10
	20%	23.74	24.34	24.70	25.10	25.56	26.08	27.38	29.20

from 5–20%. The data in Exhibit 13.6 show that value estimates of PepsiCo are inversely related to discount rates, holding growth constant. In contrast, share value estimates are positively related to growth rates, holding discount rates constant. We omit value estimates from this analysis when the growth rate equals or exceeds the discount rate, because the continuing value computation is meaningless.

As we observed in our sensitivity analyses in Chapters 11 and 12, these data suggest that our value estimate is sensitive to slight variations of our baseline assumptions of 3.0% long-run growth and a 7.5% discount rate. Slight adverse variations in valuation parameters (such as 2.0% long-run growth and an 8.5% discount rate) reduce PepsiCo's share value to roughly $63, whereas slightly more favorable variations (such as 4.0% long-run growth and a 6.5% discount rate) increase PepsiCo's share value to $143. If our forecast and valuation assumptions are realistic, our baseline value estimate for PepsiCo is $85.86 per share at the end of 2012. At that time, the market price of $68.43 per share indicates that PepsiCo shares were underpriced by about 25%. Under our forecast assumptions, PepsiCo's share value could vary within a range of a low of $63 per share to a high of $143 per share with only minor perturbations in our growth rate and discount rate assumptions. Given PepsiCo's $68.43 share price, these value estimates would have supported a buy recommendation at the end of 2012.

LO 13-5

Describe four important implementation issues for the residual income valuation approach.

Residual Income Model Implementation Issues

The residual income valuation model is a rigorous and straightforward valuation approach, but you should be aware of four important implementation issues

1. "Dirty surplus" accounting items
2. Common stock transactions
3. Portions of net income attributable to equity claimants other than common shareholders
4. Negative book value of equity

The next four sections describe these issues and how to deal with them.

Dirty Surplus Accounting

The first implementation issue arises because the residual income model requires that you follow clean surplus accounting in developing expectations for future comprehensive income, dividends, and book values. This means that the expected future income amounts should include all of the income recognized by the firm for the common equity shareholders and that all-inclusive dividends should include all capital transactions with common equity shareholders. Currently, U.S. GAAP and IFRS do *not* measure net income using clean surplus accounting. U.S. GAAP admits four *dirty surplus* items. These items are the other comprehensive income amounts that firms recognize directly in shareholders' equity. The four dirty surplus items are

1. unrealized fair value gains and losses on available-for-sale investment securities.
2. foreign currency translation gains and losses.
3. changes in assets and liabilities related to pensions and postemployment benefits that arise from plan amendments and actuarial experience.
4. the fair value gains and losses from cash flow hedges.

U.S. GAAP requires that firms recognize these items within *comprehensive income* but does not allow firms to recognize them in net income until they are realized (for example, when the firm realizes gains or losses by selling an available-for-sale investment security). Under U.S. GAAP and IFRS, firms usually report comprehensive income in a separate statement of performance to accompany the income statement. In residual income valuation, be sure to use projected comprehensive income (rather than net income) to be consistent with clean surplus accounting.

For example, **PepsiCo** reported in its 2012 consolidated statement of comprehensive income (Appendix A) that other comprehensive income items totaled +$706 million. As a result of these items, PepsiCo's comprehensive income was $6,920 million (net income of $6,214 million plus other comprehensive income items totaling $737 million minus comprehensive income attributable to noncontrolling interests of $31 million). By the end of 2012, total accumulated other comprehensive loss (which measures total accumulated other comprehensive income adjustments over the life of PepsiCo and is included as a component of shareholders' equity) was –$5,487 million. As Chapters 8 and 10 describe, the main two culprits driving other comprehensive income for PepsiCo have been foreign currency translation adjustments, amounting to +$737 million in 2012 with a cumulative total of –$1,946 million, and pension and retiree benefits adjustments, amounting to –$73 million in 2012 with a cumulative total of –$3,491 million.

The four dirty surplus items in U.S. GAAP typically arise because of unrealized gains and losses attributable to changes in market prices, such as changes in investment security fair values, foreign currency exchange rates, or interest rates. Thus, in expectation, you may determine that such gains and losses are certain to occur but that it is impossible to predict with precision either the direction or amount of the future unrealized gains and losses. In that case, you would likely forecast the expected future other comprehensive income items to be zero, on average, and therefore forecast net income and comprehensive income to be equal. We used this assumption in building forecasts for PepsiCo in Chapter 10.

On the other hand, if you can reliably project the amounts and timing of any of these items, you should incorporate them in your comprehensive income forecasts. To allow for either possibility (expectations of zero or nonzero comprehensive income items in the future), the residual income model in the Valuation spreadsheet in FSAP begins with forecasts of future comprehensive income.

Common Stock Transactions

Common stock transactions that change the intrinsic value of existing common shareholders' equity also can cause violations of the clean surplus accounting relation and hinder the ability of the residual income model to measure firm value correctly. To illustrate, consider the firm that sells common shares or repurchases common shares at transaction prices that exactly reflect the intrinsic value of the shares (that is, share sales or repurchases that are zero net present value projects for existing shareholders). Such transactions leave the existing shareholders' value unchanged, and clean surplus accounting holds for these transactions. On the other hand, suppose the firm issues common shares at a price that is lower than their intrinsic value. This transaction has a dilutive effect on (that is, reduces the value of) all of the existing common shares. Comprehensive income and the all-inclusive dividend do not reflect this loss in value to existing shareholders, so it violates clean surplus accounting.

It is reasonable to expect that clean surplus accounting holds for most common stock transactions, because most issues and repurchases of common shares are accounted for at market value. As such, they will likely have zero net present value effects on existing shareholders and will conform to clean surplus accounting. The most prominent exception, however, is the issuance of common equity shares for employee stock options exercises. As Chapter 7 discusses, the exercise of stock options by employees at strike prices below the prevailing market price dilutes the existing shareholders' equity value. If the firm estimates the fair value of the employee stock options at the time it grants them and recognizes the estimated value of the grants as an expense in measuring net income, it mitigates the violation of clean surplus accounting. In this case, you should forecast the fair value of expected future options grants and subtract these estimated expenses when forecasting expected future net income. We follow this approach in Chapter 10 in building our forecasts of net income for **PepsiCo**, because PepsiCo expenses the fair value of stock options at the date of grant. Under Statement No. 123 (Revised 2004) and IAS 2, firms are required to expense the fair value of stock options by amortizing them over the vesting period, beginning at the date of grant.[11]

---

[11]The FASB *Statement No. 123* (*Revised 2004*) "Accounting for Share-Based Payment," and the IASB *International Financial Reporting Standard 2* "Share-Based Payment" were issued in 2004.

It is not uncommon for firms to repurchase common equity shares in the open market and then use these shares to fulfill stock option exercises. In that case, the accounting for the stock repurchase at market value and the issue of the treasury shares at the option strike price captures the dilutive effect of the option exercise on shareholders' equity. For example, if the firm repurchases a share in the market for $60 and issues it to an employee exercising an option with a strike price of $40, the net effect of the accounting will capture the $20 decrease in shareholders' equity. On the other hand, if the firm fulfills stock option exercises by issuing new shares (or treasury shares repurchased in prior periods at prices that do not reflect the current period market value), the accounting will reflect the issue of the shares at the option's strike price and the dilutive effect on existing shareholders will violate clean surplus accounting.

For example, PepsiCo reports in its 2012 consolidated statement of common shareholders' equity (Appendix A) that it repurchased a total of 47 million shares for $3,219 million, implying an average cost of $68.49 per share. PepsiCo also discloses in that statement that it reissued 24 million shares for options exercises, thereby increasing equity capital by $1,057 million ($1,488 million in the Repurchased Common Stock account minus $431 million in the Capital in Excess of Par Value account), for an average book value of $44.04 per share issued. The difference between the average cost of $68.49 per share and the average book value of $44.04 per share indicates an average dilution of $24.45 per share issued. Given that PepsiCo issued 24 million shares, the total dilution is $586.8 million. With 1,544 million shares outstanding, that amounts to $0.38 dilution per outstanding share, which is roughly 0.6% of the year-end share price of $68.43.

You should devote particular time and attention to stock-based compensation when valuing a firm with substantial amounts of options outstanding and/or that will likely grant large numbers of options in the future, if you expect that these options will likely be exercised (options that you expect will ultimately expire or be forfeited pose no problems for valuation). In these cases, you should explicitly forecast future stock-based compensation expenses that include the fair values of future options grants. In addition, you should forecast the future dilutive effects of options exercises on the book value of common equity. You should capture both effects in your valuation.[12]

Portions of Net Income Attributable to Equity Claimants Other Than Common Shareholders

Residual income valuation should be based on the comprehensive income available for common equity shareholders. In some circumstances, a portion of comprehensive income is attributable to equity claimants other than common shareholders. For example, preferred stockholders may be entitled to preference in dividends over common shareholders. Also, noncontrolling interest shareholders have a claim on the portion of comprehensive income that is attributable to their share of the equity in the subsidiary they own. For purposes of residual income measurement and valuation, these portions of comprehensive income are not available to the common equity shareholders and should be excluded from residual income (just as we excluded the noncontrolling interest on the balance sheet from our beginning book value of equity in the residual income valuation model). For **PepsiCo** in Year +1, for example, we forecast that PepsiCo will

---

[12]For an illustration of stock options and valuation, see Leonard Soffer, "SFAS No. 123 Disclosures and Discounted Cash Flow Valuation," *Accounting Horizons* Vol. 14, No. 2 (June 2000), pp. 169–189.

pay a $63 million liquidating dividend to retire outstanding preferred stock, so we measure residual income after subtracting this dividend to determine comprehensive income available to common equity shareholders. Also note that for PepsiCo, our income statement projections subtract from net income $10.5 million for net income that is attributable to noncontrolling interests each year. Thus, our residual income valuation is based correctly on comprehensive income available to common shareholders.

Negative Book Value of Common Shareholders' Equity

Some firms report negative amounts for total common shareholders' equity (liabilities exceed assets). This is not common, but it can arise among firms that are in the start-up phase of the life cycle, when the firm's operations may be generating significant losses. Negative book value of common equity also can arise following a significant releveraging, during which time the firm may use debt capital to repurchase shares or pay dividends, driving total shareholders' equity below zero. Negative book value of equity can also arise for firms that are in severe distress and at high risk of bankruptcy (essentially, liabilities exceed total assets).

In these uncommon cases, you should not use the residual income valuation approach because the computation of required earnings ($R_E \times BV_{t-1}$) will be negative. The computation of residual income [$CI_t - (R_E \times BV_{t-1})$] will then effectively result in *adding* (subtracting a negative amount) required earnings to net income, which is not correct. In this situation, you should use only the dividends-based and free-cash-flows-based valuation approaches.[13]

Consistency in Residual Income, Dividends, and Free Cash Flows Valuation Estimates

LO 13-6

Identify potential causes of errors if the residual income, free cash flows, and dividend valuations do not produce identical value estimates.

As Exhibit 13.1 illustrates, the fourth and final step toward understanding residual income valuation—and valuation in general—is to follow the internal consistency among the dividends-based, free-cash-flows-based, and earnings-based valuation approaches. Throughout Chapters 11–13, we have anchored the discussions of each of the valuation approaches on the general valuation model (presented in the introduction to each of these chapters) and have conceptually and theoretically linked each valuation approach to that general model. Along the way, we have demonstrated the internal consistency of these approaches through our analysis and valuation of **PepsiCo** and have demonstrated the equivalence of value estimates based on residual income, free cash flows, and dividends.

The former baseball player and coach Yogi Berra is reported to have said, "In theory, practice and theory are the same. In practice, they're not." In theory, all three valuation models, *when correctly implemented with internally consistent assumptions,*

---

[13]Note that this implementation issue arises only when total book value of common shareholders' equity is negative. This implementation issue does not arise when retained earnings is a negative amount (in such circumstances, it is termed *retained deficit*), but when total book value of common shareholders' equity is positive. This situation is not uncommon among firms that have generated significant operating losses, particularly during the start-up phase.

will produce the same estimates of value. In practice, you may discover that the three models yield different value estimates. If so, check your analysis for one or more of the following three common errors:[14]

1. *Incomplete or inconsistent earnings and cash flow forecasts.* You should make sure that projected earnings, cash flows, and dividends are complete and based on assumptions that are consistent with one another. As Chapter 10 emphasized, you can reduce the chance of incomplete or inconsistent forecasts by forecasting complete financial statements in which the balance sheets balance, the income statements measure comprehensive income for common shareholders, and the statements of cash flows articulate with the income statements and the changes in the balance sheets. You also should ensure that projected shareholders' equity reflects clean surplus accounting. As suggested in Chapter 10, relying on the additivity and articulation of financial statements will help you avoid inconsistent forecasts and valuations.

2. *Inconsistent estimates of weighted-average costs of capital.* Suppose you compute the present value of free cash flows to all debt and equity capital using the weighted-average cost of capital as a discount rate and then subtract the present value of debt and preferred stock to determine the present value of common equity (as shown in Chapter 12). The only way the value estimates from this approach will be identical with value estimates from the residual income approach or the dividends approach is if the weighted-average cost of capital uses weights that are perfectly internally consistent with the present values of debt, preferred stock, and common equity. Thus, you may have to iterate the computation of the weighted-average cost of capital a number of times until all of the weights and present values are internally consistent.

3. *Incorrect continuing value computations.* Chapters 11–13 emphasize that you must carefully estimate continuing value, particularly the Year T+1 amount for residual income, free cash flows, and dividends. If you use inconsistent assumptions to project the beginning amounts to compute continuing value, your resulting value estimates will not agree. To avoid this problem, you should first project the Year T+1 income statement and balance sheet amounts assuming a uniform rate of growth $(1 + g)$ and then use these projections to derive the Year T+1 amounts for residual income, free cash flows, and dividends. The derived amounts for Year T+1 can then be used as the starting values of the perpetuity to calculate continuing value. A common error that analysts make is simply to assume that all residual income, free cash flows, and dividends in Year T will grow at the same rate g. This shortcut will *not* ensure consistent assumptions and valuation.

Summary

Chapters 11–13 have described and applied three different but equivalent approaches to valuation using the present value of projected dividends, the present value of projected free cash flows, and the present value of projected residual income. Together, these approaches are theoretically sound and practical techniques for estimating a firm's value.

---

[14]For a more complete description of diagnosing errors that can cause differences in the three valuation model estimates, see Russell Lundholm and Terry O'Keefe, "Reconciling Value Estimates from the Discounted Cash Flow Model and the Residual Income Model," *Contemporary Accounting Research* (Summer 2001), pp. 1–26.

Our experience with valuation suggests that using several valuation approaches yields more useful insights than using just one approach in all circumstances. Chapter 14 demonstrates a variety of additional valuation techniques, including the use of market-based valuation multiples, such as market-to-book ratios and price-earnings ratios.

Questions, Exercises, Problems, and Cases

Questions and Exercises

13.1 Valuation Approach Equivalence. Conceptually, why should an analyst expect a valuation based on dividends, a valuation based on the free cash flows for common equity shareholders, and a valuation based on residual income to yield equivalent value estimates for a given firm?

LO 13-1, LO 13-2

13.2 Required Income. Explain required income. What does required income represent? How is required income conceptually analogous to interest expense?

LO 13-3

13.3 Residual Income. Explain residual income. What does residual income represent? What does residual income measure?

LO 13-3

13.4 Residual Income Valuation Theory. Explain the theory behind the residual income valuation approach. Why is residual income value-relevant to common equity shareholders?

LO 13-3

13.5 Residual Income Valuation Approach. Explain the two roles of book value of common shareholders' equity in the residual income valuation approach.

LO 13-3

13.6 Interpreting Residual Income. If a firm's residual income for a particular year is positive, does that mean the firm was profitable? Explain. If a firm's residual income for a particular year is negative, does that mean the firm necessarily reported a loss on the income statement? Explain. What does it mean when a firm's residual income is zero?

LO 13-3

13.7 Effects of Investments on Residual Income. Assume that the firm's cost of equity capital is 10% and that the firm's existing assets and operations generate a 10% return on common equity. If the firm raises additional equity capital and invests in assets that will generate a return less than 10%, what effect will that investment have on the firm's residual income? If the firm raises additional equity capital and invests in assets that will generate a return that exceeds 10%, what effect will that investment have on the firm's residual income?

LO 13-3

13.8 Effects of Borrowing on Residual Income. If the firm borrows capital from a bank and invests it in assets that earn a return greater than the interest rate charged by the bank, what effect will that have on residual income for the firm? How does that effect compare with the effects of capital structure leverage described in Chapters 4 and 5?

LO 13-3

13.9 Effects of Competition on Residual Income. If the firm is in a very competitive, mature industry, what effect will the competitive conditions have on residual income for the firm and others in the industry? Now suppose the firm holds a competitive advantage in its industry, but the advantage is not likely to be sustainable for more than a few years. As the firm's competitive advantage diminishes, what effect will that have on that firm's residual income?

LO 13-3

LO 13-2 **13.10 Effects of Conservative Accounting on Residual Income Valuation.** Suppose you are applying the residual income valuation model to value a firm with extremely conservative accounting. Suppose, for example, the firm is following U.S. GAAP or IFRS, but the firm does not recognize a substantial intangible asset on the balance sheet. (Perhaps the firm has expensed substantial amounts of R&D expenditures that have led to valuable intellectual property or substantial amounts of advertising that have created a valuable brand name). As a consequence of this conservative accounting, the firm reports assets and equity at book values that are much lower than their respective economic values. Explain why the residual income value estimates will not be distorted by conservative accounting. How does the residual income valuation model correct for the effects of conservative accounting and understated book values of equity?

LO 13-2 **13.11 Effects of Aggressive Accounting on Residual Income Valuation.** Suppose you are applying the residual income valuation model to value a firm with extremely aggressive accounting. Suppose, for example, the firm has a substantially overvalued asset on the balance sheet. (Perhaps the firm has a large amount of goodwill on the balance sheet from a prior acquisition and has delayed recording a necessary impairment charge that would write off the value of the goodwill.) As a consequence of this aggressive accounting, the firm reports assets and equity at book values that are much higher than their respective economic values. Explain why the residual income value estimates will not be distorted by aggressive accounting. How does the residual income valuation model correct for the effects of aggressive accounting and overstated book values of equity?

LO 13-4 **13.12 Appropriate Discount Rates.** Why is it appropriate to use the required rate of return on equity capital (rather than the weighted-average cost of capital) as the discount rate when using the residual income valuation approach?

Problems and Cases

LO 13-3 **13.13 Computing Residual Income.** Suppose the following hypothetical data represent total assets, book value, and market value of common shareholders' equity (dollar amounts in millions) for Abbott Labs, IBM, and Target Stores. Abbott Labs manufactures and sells health care products. IBM develops and manufactures computer hardware and offers related technology services. Target Stores operates a chain of general merchandise discount retail stores. In addition, these data include hypothetical market betas for the three firms and analysts' consensus forecasts of net income for Year +1. Assume that for each firm, analysts expect other comprehensive income items for Year +1 to be zero, so Year +1 net income and comprehensive income will be identical. Assume that the risk-free rate of return in the economy is 4.0% and the market risk premium is 5.0%.

(amounts in millions)	Abbott Labs	IBM	Target Stores
Total assets	$42,419	$109,524	$44,106
Common equity:			
Book value	$17,480	$ 13,466	$13,712
Market value	$83,050	$166,420	$34,600
Market equity beta	0.27	0.73	1.09
Analysts' consensus forecasts			
of net income for Year +1	$ 5,750	$ 12,956	$ 2,384

REQUIRED

a. Using the CAPM, compute the required rate of return on equity capital for each firm.
b. Project required income for Year +1 for each firm.
c. Project residual income for Year +1 for each firm.
d. What do the different amounts of residual income imply about each firm? Do the projected residual income amounts help explain the differences in market value of equity across these three firms? Explain.

13.14 Computing Residual Income. Suppose the following hypothetical data represent total assets, book value, and market value of common shareholders' equity (dollar amounts in millions) for Microsoft, Intel, and Dell, three firms involved in different aspects of the computer technology industry. Microsoft engages primarily in the development, manufacture, license, and support of software products. Intel develops and manufactures semiconductor chips and microprocessors for the computing and communications industries. Dell designs and manufactures a range of computer hardware systems, such as laptops, desktops, and servers. These data also include hypothetical market betas for these three firms and analysts' consensus forecasts of net income for Year +1. For each firm, analysts expect other comprehensive income items for Year +1 to be zero, so Year +1 net income and comprehensive income will be identical. Assume that the risk-free rate of return in the economy is 4.0% and the market risk premium is 5.0%.

LO 13-3

(amounts in millions)	Microsoft	Intel	Dell
Total assets	$ 77,888	$ 50,715	$26,500
Common equity:			
Book value	$ 39,558	$ 39,088	$ 4,271
Market value	$264,510	$112,480	$26,000
Market equity beta	0.96	1.12	1.28
Analysts' consensus forecasts			
of net income for Year +1	$ 16,250	$ 8,060	$ 1,882

REQUIRED

a. Using the CAPM, compute the required rate of return on equity capital for each firm.
b. Project required income for Year +1 for each firm.
c. Project residual income for Year +1 for each firm.
d. Rank the three firms using expected residual income for Year +1 relative to book value of common equity.
e. What do the different amounts of residual income imply about each firm? Do the projected residual income amounts help explain the differences in market value of equity across these three firms? Explain.

13.15 Computing Residual Income. Suppose the following hypothetical data represent total assets, book value, and market value of common shareholders' equity (dollar amounts in millions) for three firms. Each of these firms, Southwest Airlines, Kroger, and Yum! Brands, operates in a different industry, but all of them operate in very competitive industries. Southwest Airlines is a U.S. domestic airline that provides low-cost point-to-point air transportation services. Kroger operates retail supermarkets across the United States. Yum! Brands operates and franchises quick-service restaurants, including KFC, Pizza Hut, Taco Bell,

LO 13-3

Long John Silver's, and A&W All American Food restaurants. These data also include hypothetical market betas for the three firms and analysts' consensus forecasts of net income for Year +1. For each firm, analysts expect other comprehensive income items for Year +1 to be zero; so Year +1 net income and comprehensive income will be identical. Assume that the risk-free rate of return in the economy is 4.0% and the market risk premium is 5.0%.

(amounts in millions)	Southwest Airlines	Kroger	Yum! Brands
Total assets	$14,308	$23,211	$ 7,242
Common equity:			
Book value	$ 4,953	$ 5,176	$ 1,139
Market value	$ 7,490	$14,870	$15,950
Market equity beta	1.10	0.35	1.04
Analysts' consensus forecasts			
of net income for Year +1	$ 252	$ 1,263	$ 1,010

REQUIRED

   a. Using the CAPM, compute the required rate of return on equity capital for each firm.
   b. Project required income for Year +1 for each firm.
   c. Project residual income for Year +1 for each firm.
   d. Rank the three firms using expected residual income for Year +1 relative to book value of common equity.
   e. What do the different amounts of residual income imply about each firm? Do the projected residual income amounts help explain the differences in market value of equity across these three firms? Explain.

13.16 Equity Valuation Using the Residual Income Model. Morrissey

Tool Company manufactures machine tools for other manufacturing firms. The firm is wholly owned by Kelsey Morrissey. The firm's accountant developed the following long-term forecasts of comprehensive income:

Year +1:	$213,948
Year +2:	$192,008
Year +3:	$187,444
Year +4:	$196,442
Year +5:	$206,667

The accountant expects comprehensive income to grow 5% annually after Year +5. Kelsey withdraws 30% of comprehensive income each year as a dividend. Total common shareholders' equity on January 1, Year +1, is $1,111,141. Kelsey expects to earn a rate of return on her invested equity capital of 12% each year.

REQUIRED

   a. Using the residual income valuation model, compute the value of Morrissey Tool Company as of January 1, Year +1.
   b. What advice would you give Kelsey regarding her ownership of the firm?

13.17 Equity Valuation Using the Residual Income and Dividend Discount Models.

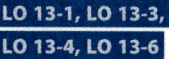

Priority Contractors provides maintenance and cleaning services to various corporate clients in New York City. The firm has provided the following forecasts of comprehensive income for Year +1 to Year +5:

Year +1:	$478,246
Year +2:	$491,882
Year +3:	$485,568
Year +4:	$515,533
Year +5:	$554,198

Total common shareholders' equity was $2,224,401 on January 1, Year +1. The firm does not expect to pay a dividend during the period of Year +1 to Year +5. The cost of equity capital is 12%.

REQUIRED

a. Compute the value of Priority Contractors on January 1, Year +1, using the residual income valuation model. The firm expects comprehensive income to grow 5% annually after Year +5.

b. Compute the value of Priority Contractors on January 1, Year +1, using the dividend discount model. The firm will pay its first dividend in Year +6. (Hint: Solve for the dividend amount using clean surplus accounting and 5% growth in comprehensive income and shareholders' equity in Year +6.)

13.18 Equity Valuation Using the Residual Income, Free Cash Flow, and Dividend Discount Models.

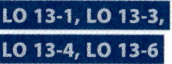

Exhibit 13.7 presents selected hypothetical data from projected financial statements for Steak 'n Shake for Year +1 to Year +11. The amounts for Year +11 reflect a long-term growth assumption of 3%. The cost of equity capital is 9.34%. Assume net income and comprehensive income will be identical.

REQUIRED

a. Compute the value of Steak 'n Shake as of January 1, Year +1, using the residual income model.

b. Repeat Requirement a using the present value of expected free cash flows to the common equity shareholders.

c. Repeat Requirement a using the dividend discount model.

d. Identify the reasons for any differences in the valuations in Requirements a–c.

e. Suppose the market value of Steak 'n Shake on January 1, Year +1, is $309.98 million. Based on your valuations in Requirements a–c, what is your assessment of the market value of this firm?

13.19 Residual Income Valuation.

The **Coca-Cola Company** is a global soft drink beverage company (ticker: KO) that is a primary and direct competitor with **PepsiCo**. The data in Chapter 12's Exhibits 12.14, 12.15, and 12.16 (pages 943–946) include the actual amounts for 2010, 2011, and 2012 and projected amounts for Year +1 to Year +6 for the income statements, balance sheets, and statements of cash flows, respectively, for Coca-Cola. The market equity beta for Coca-Cola at the end of 2012 is 0.75. Assume that the risk-free interest rate is 3.0% and the market risk premium is 6.0%. Coca-Cola had 4,469 million shares outstanding at the end of 2012, when Coca-Cola's share price was $35.48.

Exhibit 13.7

Steak 'n Shake
Selected Financial Information
(amounts in millions; allow for rounding)
(Problem 13.18)

	Year +1	Year +2	Year +3	Year +4	Year +5	Year +6	Year +7	Year +8	Year +9	Year +10	Year +11[a]
Common equity, beginning of year	$165.8	$177.6	$192.0	$206.0	$216.6	$227.7	$234.2	$238.1	$239.4	$255.8	$269.5
Net income	24.5	25.8	27.6	29.6	31.8	34.2	36.8	39.5	53.9	57.0	58.7
Dividends	(12.7)	(11.4)	(13.6)	(19.0)	(20.8)	(27.7)	(32.9)	(38.2)	(37.4)	(43.3)	(50.6)
Common equity, end of year[b]	$177.6	$192.0	$206.0	$216.6	$227.7	$234.2	$238.1	$239.4	$255.8	$269.5	$277.6
Cash flow from operations	$ 45.4	$ 51.2	$ 56.3	$ 61.5	$ 67.1	$ 72.9	$ 78.9	$ 85.2	$ 85.6	$ 92.4	$ 73.2
Cash flow for investing	(35.2)	(41.1)	(41.9)	(42.7)	(43.5)	(44.4)	(45.2)	(46.0)	(47.3)	(48.1)	(22.1)
Cash flow for long-term debt	(0.5)	2.0	—	1.0	(2.0)	—	—	—	—	—	—
Cash flow for dividends	(12.7)	(11.4)	(13.6)	(19.0)	(20.8)	(27.7)	(32.9)	(38.2)	(37.4)	(43.3)	(50.6)
Net change in cash	$ (3.0)	$ 0.7	$ 0.8	$ 0.8	$ 0.8	$ 0.8	$ 0.8	$ 1.0	$ 0.9	$ 1.0	$ 0.5

[a]The amounts for Year +11 result from increasing each income statement and balance sheet amount by the expected long-term growth rate of 3% and then deriving the amounts for the statement of cash flows.
[b]Amounts on this line may reflect the effects of rounding of intermediate computations.

REQUIRED

Part I—Computing Coca-Cola's Share Value Using the Residual Income Valuation Approach

a. Use the CAPM to compute the required rate of return on common equity capital for Coca-Cola.

b. Derive the projected residual income for Coca-Cola for Years +1 through +6 based on the projected financial statements. The financial statement forecasts for Year +6 assume that Coca-Cola will experience a steady-state, long-run growth rate of 3% in Year +6 and beyond.

c. Using the required rate of return on common equity from Requirement a as a discount rate, compute the sum of the present value of residual income for Coca-Cola for Years +1 through +5.

d. Using the required rate of return on common equity from Requirement a as a discount rate and the long-run growth rate from Requirement b, compute the continuing value of Coca-Cola as of the start of Year +6 based on Coca-Cola's continuing residual income in Year +6 and beyond. After computing continuing value as of the start of Year +6, discount it to present value at the start of Year +1.

e. Compute the value of a share of Coca-Cola common stock.

   (1) Compute the total sum of the present value of all residual income (from Requirements c and d).

   (2) Add the book value of equity as of the beginning of the valuation (that is, as of the end of 2012, or the start of Year+1).

   (3) Adjust the total sum of the present value of residual income plus book value of common equity using the midyear discounting adjustment factor.

   (4) Compute the per-share value estimate.

Part II—Sensitivity Analysis and Recommendation

f. Using the residual income valuation approach, recompute the value of Coca-Cola shares under two alternative scenarios.

   Scenario 1: Assume that Coca-Cola's long-run growth will be 2%, not 3% as above, and that Coca-Cola's required rate of return on equity is 1% higher than that calculated in Requirement a.

   Scenario 2: Assume that Coca-Cola's long-run growth will be 4%, not 3% as above, and that Coca-Cola's required rate of return on equity is 1% lower than that calculated in Requirement a.

   To quantify the sensitivity of your share value estimate for Coca-Cola to these variations in growth and discount rates, compare (in percentage terms) your value estimates under these two scenarios with your value estimate from Requirement e.

g. Using these data at the end of 2012, what reasonable range of share values would you have expected for Coca-Cola common stock? At that time, what was the market price for Coca-Cola shares relative to this range? What would you have recommended?

h. If you completed Problem 12.16 in Chapter 12, compare the value estimate you obtained in Requirement e of that problem (using the free cash flows to common equity shareholders valuation approach) with the value estimate you obtain here using the residual income valuation approach. The value estimates should be the same. If you have not completed Problem 12.16, you would benefit from doing so now.

13.20 Residual Income Valuation. In Problem 10.16, we projected financial statements for **Walmart Stores, Inc.** (Walmart) for Years +1 through +5. The data in Chapter 12's Exhibits 12.17, 12.18, and 12.19 (pages 948–950) include the actual amounts for 2012 and the projected amounts for Year +1 to Year +5 for the income statements, balance sheets, and statements of cash flows, respectively, for Walmart. The market equity beta for Walmart at the end of 2012 was 1.00. Assume that the risk-free interest rate was 3.0% and the market risk premium was 6.0%. Walmart had 3,314 million shares outstanding at the end of 2012 and a share price of $69.09.

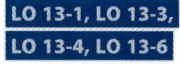

LO 13-1, LO 13-3,
LO 13-4, LO 13-6

REQUIRED

Part I—Computing Walmart's Share Value Using the Residual Income Valuation Approach

a. Use the CAPM to compute the required rate of return on common equity capital for Walmart.

b. Derive the projected residual income for Walmart for Years +1 through +5 based on the projected financial statements.

c. Project the continuing residual income in Year +6. Assume that the steady-state, long-run growth rate will be 3% in Year +6 and beyond. Project that the Year +5 income statement and balance sheet amounts will grow by 3% in Year +6; then derive the projected amount of residual income for Year +6.

d. Using the required rate of return on common equity from Requirement a as a discount rate, compute the sum of the present value of residual income for Walmart for Years +1 through +5.

e. Using the required rate of return on common equity from Requirement a as a discount rate and the long-run growth rate from Requirement c, compute the continuing value of Walmart as of the start of Year +6 based on Walmart's continuing residual income in Year +6 and beyond. After computing continuing value as of the start of Year +6, discount it to present value at the start of Year +1.

f. Compute the value of a share of Walmart common stock.

    (1) Compute the total sum of the present value of all future residual income (from Requirements d and e).

    (2) Add the book value of equity as of the beginning of the valuation (that is, as of the end of 2012, or the start of Year +1).

    (3) Adjust the total sum of the present value of residual income plus book value of common equity using the midyear discounting adjustment factor.

    (4) Compute the per-share value estimate.

Part II—Sensitivity Analysis and Recommendation

g. Using the residual income valuation method, recompute the value of Walmart shares under two alternative scenarios.

    Scenario 1: Assume that Walmart's long-run growth will be 2%, not 3% as above, and that Walmart's required rate of return on equity is 1 percentage point higher than the rate you computed using the CAPM in Requirement a.

    Scenario 2: Assume that Walmart's long-run growth will be 4%, not 3% as above, and that Walmart's required rate of return on equity is 1 percentage point lower than the rate you computed using the CAPM in Requirement a.

To quantify the sensitivity of your share value estimate for Walmart to these variations in growth and discount rates, compare (in percentage terms) your value estimates under these two scenarios with your value estimate from Requirement f.

h. Using these data at the end of 2012, what reasonable range of share values would you have expected for Walmart common stock? At that time, what was the market price for Walmart shares relative to this range? What would you have recommended?

i. If you worked Problem 11.14 from Chapter 11 and computed Walmart's share value using the dividends valuation approach, compare your value estimate from Requirement g of that problem with the value estimate you obtained here. Similarly, if you worked Problem 12.17 from Chapter 12 and computed Walmart's share value using the free cash flows to common equity shareholders, compare your value estimate from Requirement f of that problem with the value estimate you obtained here. You should obtain the same value estimates for Walmart shares under all three approaches. If you have not worked both of those problems, you would benefit from doing so now.

INTEGRATIVE CASE 13.1

Starbucks

Residual Income Valuation of Starbucks' Common Equity

LO 13-1, LO 13-3, LO 13-4, LO 13-6

In Integrative Case 10.1, we projected financial statements for **Starbucks** for Years +1 through +5. In this portion of the Starbucks Integrative Case, we use the projected financial statements from Integrative Case 10.1 and apply the techniques in Chapter 13 to compute Starbucks' required rate of return on equity and share value based on the residual income valuation model. We also compare our value estimate to Starbucks' share price at the time of the case to provide an investment recommendation. The market equity beta for Starbucks at the end of 2012 is 0.75. Assume that the risk-free interest rate is 3.0% and the market risk premium is 6.0%. Starbucks has 749.3 million shares outstanding at the end of 2012. At the start of Year +1, Starbucks' share price was $50.15.

REQUIRED

Part I—Computing Starbucks' Share Value Using the Residual Income Valuation Approach

a. Use the CAPM to compute the required rate of return on common equity capital for Starbucks.

b. Using your projected financial statements from Integrative Case 10.1 for Starbucks, derive the projected residual income for Starbucks for Years +1 through +5.

c. Project the continuing residual income in Year +6. Assume that the steady-state, long-run growth rate will be 3% in Year +6 and beyond. Project that the Year +5 income statement and balance sheet amounts will grow by 3% in Year +6; then derive the projected residual income for Year +6.

d. Using the required rate of return on common equity from Requirement a as a discount rate, compute the sum of the present value of residual income for Starbucks for Years +1 through +5.

e. Using the required rate of return on common equity from Requirement a as a discount rate and the long-run growth rate from Requirement c, compute the continuing value of Starbucks as of the start of Year +6 based on Starbucks' continuing residual income in Year +6 and beyond. After computing continuing value as of the start of Year +6, discount it to present value at the start of Year +1.

f. Compute the value of a share of Starbucks common stock.

   (1) Compute the total sum of the present value of all future residual income (from Requirements d and e).

   (2) Add the book value of equity as of the beginning of the valuation (that is, as of the end of 2012, or the start of Year +1).

   (3) Adjust the total sum of the present value of residual income plus book value of common equity using the midyear discounting adjustment factor.

   (4) Compute the per-share value estimate.

Part II—Sensitivity Analysis and Recommendation

g. Using the residual income valuation approach, recompute the value of Starbucks shares under two alternative scenarios.

   Scenario 1: Assume that Starbucks' long-run growth will be 2%, not 3% as above, and that Starbucks' required rate of return on equity is 1 percentage point higher than the rate you computed using the CAPM in Requirement a.

Scenario 2: Assume that Starbucks' long-run growth will be 4%, not 3% as above, and that Starbucks' required rate of return on equity is 1 percentage point lower than the rate you computed using the CAPM in Requirement a. To quantify the sensitivity of your share value estimate for Starbucks to these variations in growth and discount rates, compare (in percentage terms) your value estimates under these two scenarios with your value estimate from Requirement f.

h. At the end of 2012, what reasonable range of share values would you have expected for Starbucks common stock? At that time, where was the market price for Starbucks shares relative to this range? What would you have recommended?

i. If you computed Starbucks' common equity share value using the dividends valuation approach in Integrative Case 11.1 in Chapter 11, compare the value estimate you obtained in that case with the estimate you obtained in this case. Similarly, if you computed Starbucks' common equity share value using the free cash flows to common equity shareholders valuation approach in Integrative Case 12.1 in Chapter 12, compare the value estimate you obtained in that case with the estimate you obtained in this case. You should obtain the same value estimates under all three approaches. If you have not worked both of those cases, you would benefit from doing so now.

Valuation: Market-Based Approaches

LO 14-1 Explain the use of market-based valuation multiples such as market-to-book (MB) and price-earnings (PE) ratios to assess the capital market's relative valuation of a particular stock, along with the practical advantages and disadvantages of using market-based valuation multiples.

LO 14-2 For market-to-book ratios:

    a. Apply a version of the residual income valuation model to compute the value-to-book (VB) ratio.

    b. Make investment decisions by comparing the VB ratio to the MB ratio.

    c. Explain why VB and MB ratios differ across firms and the impact of the following factors on VB and MB ratios: (1) risk and the cost of equity capital, (2) growth, (3) differences between current and expected future earnings, and (4) alternative accounting methods and principles.

LO 14-3 For price-earnings ratios:

    a. Compute and use the firm's value-earnings (VE) ratio.

    b. Incorporate growth into the VE ratio to compute the value-earnings-growth (VEG) ratio.

    c. Use VE and VEG ratios to analyze firm value over time and across firms, and to make investment decisions.

    d. Explain why VE and PE ratios differ across firms and the impact of the following factors on VE and PE ratios: (1) risk and the cost of equity capital, (2) growth, (3) differences between current and expected future earnings, and (4) alternative accounting methods and principles.

LO 14-4 Estimate the price differential, which is the difference between market price and "risk-neutral value."

LO 14-5 Reverse engineer a firm's stock price to determine the implied expected return or the implied expected long-run growth rate.

LO 14-6 Explain the notion of capital market efficiency in valuation and the academic evidence on the degree to which the capital markets efficiently impound earnings information into share prices.

Chapter Overview

Chapters 1-13 focus on using the information in accounting numbers, financial statements, and related notes to analyze firms' fundamental characteristics of profitability, risk, growth, and value. These chapters establish a disciplined and effective six-step framework to attack a very difficult but fascinating problem—how to analyze and value a firm. To use this framework, we must first understand the firm's industry and business strategy and then use that understanding to assess the quality of the firm's accounting, making adjustments as necessary. We then evaluate the firm's profitability, risk, growth, efficiency, liquidity, and leverage, using a set of financial ratios. Using these steps as a foundation, we forecast the firm's future business activities, measuring the expected outcomes of these activities with projected future balance sheets, income statements, and statements of cash flows. We derive from our financial statement forecasts the firm's expected future dividends, free cash flows, and residual income, which we then use to value the firm. We also use the value models to assess the sensitivity of firm value estimates to key valuation parameters such as the cost of capital, the expected long-run growth rate, and other parameters. To culminate this process, we compute a realistic range of firm value estimates and compare this range to the firm's share price in the market in order to make an intelligent investment decision.

Exhibit 14.1 provides a summary representation of this fundamentals-driven valuation process. The top of the exhibit depicts the firm's value drivers, such as expected future earnings, cash flows, dividends, growth, and risk, which comprise the economic foundations of valuation. We capture these determinants of value in forecasts of future financial statements, and then convert these forecasts into estimates of firm value using the residual income model, the free cash flows model, and the dividends model.

In this chapter, we continue our focus on fundamental characteristics of profitability, risk, growth, and value, but we augment that analytical approach with techniques that allow us to exploit the information in *share price*. We describe and apply a variety of techniques that compare the firm's share price to the firm's fundamentals. The techniques described in this chapter include commonly used market multiples—market-to-book (MB) ratios, price-earnings (PE) ratios, and price-earnings-growth (PEG) ratios—which provide efficient shortcuts in the valuation process. As Exhibit 14.2 depicts, market multiples require an understanding of the same set of value drivers as discussed in

Exhibit 14.1

Fundamentals of Valuation

**Fundamental Value Drivers over the Remaining Life of the Firm:
Expected Future Earnings, Cash Flows, Dividends Growth, Risk**

Financial Statement Forecasts

**Compute:
Book Value of Common Equity + Present Value of Expected Future Residual Income
= Present Value of Expected Future Free Cash Flows to Common Equity Shareholders
= Present Value of Expected Future Dividends**

Firm Value

Exhibit 14.2

Market Multiples

**Fundamental Value Drivers over the Remaining Life of the Firm:
Expected Future Earnings, Cash Flows, Dividends Growth, Risk**

**Summary Accounting Numbers:
Book Value of Common Equity per Share,
Earnings per Share, Long-Run Earnings Growth**

**Market Multiples:
Market-to-Book Ratios, Price-Earnings Ratios,
Price-Earnings-Growth Ratios**

Firm Value

Chapters 11–13—expected earnings, cash flows, dividends, growth, and risk—but market multiples collapse the valuation process in two important ways:

1. Instead of developing financial statement forecasts, market multiples use just one or two summary accounting numbers (such as earnings per share or book value of common equity per share) to summarize the value drivers.
2. Instead of using extensive present value computations, market multiples utilize simple ratios of share price relative to summary accounting numbers.

In this chapter, we also demonstrate two additional techniques to infer and exploit the information in share prices. First, we introduce a measure of the impact of risk on share price, which we call the *price differential*. Second, we demonstrate *reverse engineering* share prices, a technique which enables you to infer the assumptions the capital market appears to be making in pricing a particular share. In the last section of the chapter, we summarize a few key insights from the last 40 years of accounting and finance research suggesting that the capital markets are highly but not perfectly efficient in using accounting earnings information to price stocks. These research findings are encouraging for those interested in using earnings and accounting information for fundamental analysis and valuation of stocks and for developing trading strategies to exploit accounting information.

Market Multiples of Accounting Numbers

Throughout this text, we have described how to analyze accounting numbers to exploit the wide array of information available in financial statements: earnings, balance sheet amounts, cash flows, footnote data, supplemental management disclosures, financial

LO 14-1

Explain the use of market-based valuation multiples such as market-to-book (MB) and price-earnings (PE) ratios to assess the capital market's relative valuation of a particular stock, along with the practical advantages and disadvantages of using market-based valuation multiples.

ratios, growth rates, and many others. However, we have not analyzed and exploited the information in one very important number: *share price*. The market price for a share of common equity is a special and informative number: it aggregates the expectations of all of the market participants (investors, potential investors, analysts, and others) following that particular stock. The market price is the result of the market's trading activity in that stock. It summarizes the information the market participants have about the firm and their aggregate expectations for the firm's future profitability, growth, risk, and value.

The market price of a share does not mean that all market participants agree that the price is the correct value for the share. In fact, the prices at which potential buyers or sellers may be willing to trade may differ widely across market participants and over time. Indeed, the market price simply indicates that the momentary point of equilibrium in which the forces of supply (market participants potentially willing to sell the stock—the "ask" side of trading) and the forces of demand (market participants potentially willing to buy the stock—the "bid" side of trading) are in balance. Stock prices are dynamic, constantly changing with the arrival of new information that changes investors' expectations about share value and triggers trading in the firm's shares. We can analyze share price to obtain a wealth of information.

Market participants commonly calibrate firm valuation using market value or share price expressed as a multiple of a fundamental summary accounting number, such as the market-to-book ratio or the price-earnings ratio. These market multiples play two important roles for analysts: as analytical tools and as valuation tools. As analytical tools, market multiples capture *relative* valuation per dollar of book value or per dollar of earnings. In this way, market multiples measure share price relative to a key accounting number as a common denominator, thereby enabling you to draw inferences about a particular firm's relative market capitalization, to assess changes in a firm's relative valuation over time, to compare values across firms, and to project comparable firms' values. For example, PE ratios allow you to quickly gauge and compare the multiples at which the market is capitalizing different firms' annual earnings. As analytical tools, market multiples enable you to conduct time-series and cross-sectional analyses to summarize and compare how the capital markets are valuing stocks (in the same way you would compare other ratios such as ROA and ROCE across firms and over time).

Market multiples also can serve as useful and efficient fundamental valuation tools, but you must apply and interpret them carefully, after considering the firm's expected future profitability, growth, and risk. Multiples such as MB and PE ratios are *relative* value metrics, in which market value is denominated relative to a summary accounting measure of equity or performance; therefore, they are not meaningful as standalone valuation measures. For example, you cannot determine whether a particular firm's PE ratio should be 10, 20, 50, or some other number unless you know the firm's fundamental characteristics—expected future profitability, growth, and risk. Similarly, you cannot determine whether a particular firm's PE ratio should be higher or lower than some other firm's PE ratio or the industry average PE ratio unless you know how the firm's expected future profitability, growth, and risk characteristics compare to those characteristics of the other firm or the industry as a whole. For example, a firm may have a very high PE ratio at a particular point in time for very different reasons: perhaps the share price is too high, perhaps the market expects and prices very high future earnings growth, or perhaps the firm experienced temporarily low earnings last period (because of a restructuring charge, for example). If you use market multiples to draw naive inferences about the firm's market price without carefully researching the firm's fundamentals, you risk badly misinterpreting market multiples.

Market multiples can be very useful shortcut valuation tools. Unfortunately, analysts sometimes apply market multiples as valuation tools to estimate value in ad hoc and simplistic ways, and this "quick-and-dirty" approach, may be misleading. A naive analyst might be tempted to value a firm simply by using its historical average or the industry average market multiple. The firm's historical average MB ratio, for example, may be an appropriate fit for the valuation of the firm today, but only if the firm's current fundamental characteristics match those of the past. In the same vein, an industry average PE multiple may be an appropriate yardstick for valuing a particular firm, but only if that firm's fundamental characteristics match the industry averages. If the firm's fundamentals are now different or do not match the industry averages, then you must adjust market multiples to reflect the firm's fundamental characteristics.

This chapter continues to emphasize the distinction between *value* and *price*. The chapter focuses on how you should compute *value*-based multiples that properly reflect the firm's fundamentals and that can be reliably compared to market *price*-based multiples. This focus also directs your attention to the factors that drive multiples so that you can adjust historical or industry average multiples correctly to reflect the firm's expected future profitability, growth, and risk appropriately.

Market-to-Book and Value-to-Book Ratios

The MB ratio can be computed easily by dividing the firm's market value of common equity at a point in time by the book value of common equity from the firm's most recent balance sheet. For example, on December 31, 2012, **PepsiCo**'s market value was $105,656 million ($68.43 per share × 1,544 million shares) and PepsiCo's 2012 book value of common shareholders' equity was $22,417 million (Appendix A). Thus, PepsiCo was trading at an MB ratio equal to 4.7 ($105,656 million/$22,417 million). The MB ratio measures market value as a multiple of accounting book value at a point in time. The MB ratio reflects what the market value *is*, but it does not tell us what the ratio *should be* given our estimate of intrinsic value.

A Theoretical Model of the Value-to-Book Ratio[1]

We can compute the ratio of the firm's intrinsic value of common shareholders' equity divided by the book value of common shareholders' equity—the value-to-book (VB) ratio—using a version of the residual income model developed in Chapter 13. In fact, the VB ratio model is simply the residual income model scaled by book value of common shareholders' equity. The numerator of the VB ratio is the estimated intrinsic value of

LO 14-2

For market-to-book ratios:
a. Apply a version of the residual income valuation model to compute the value-to-book (VB) ratio.
b. Make investment decisions by comparing the VB ratio to the MB ratio.
c. Explain why VB and MB ratios differ across firms and the impact of the following factors on VB and MB ratios: (1) risk and the cost of equity capital, (2) growth, (3) differences between current and expected future earnings, and (4) alternative accounting methods and principles.

---

[1]As noted in Chapter 13, credit for the rigorous development of the residual income model and its extension to the value-to-book ratio model goes to James A. Ohlson, "A Synthesis of Security Valuation Theory and the Role of Dividends, Cash Flows, and Earnings," *Contemporary Accounting Research* (Spring 1990), pp. 648–676; James A. Ohlson, "Earnings, Book Values, and Dividends in Equity Valuation," *Contemporary Accounting Research* (Spring 1995), pp. 661–687; Gerald A. Feltham and James A. Ohlson, "Valuation and Clean Surplus Accounting for Operating and Financial Activities," *Contemporary Accounting Research* (Spring 1995), pp. 216–230. The ideas underlying the value-to-book ratio also trace to early work by G.A.D. Preinreich, "Annual Survey of Economic Theory: The Theory of Depreciation," *Econometrica* (1938), pp. 219–241 and Edgar O. Edwards and Philip W. Bell, *The Theory and Measurement of Business Income* (Berkeley, CA: University of California Press), 1961.

common equity, which takes into account the book value of common shareholders' equity, expected future profitability, growth, risk, and the time value of money. The denominator of the VB ratio (denoted BV_0) is the total book value of common shareholders' equity (excluding equity of noncontrolling interests). You can compare the VB ratio to the MB ratio to evaluate share price and make an investment decision the same way previous chapters compared intrinsic value to share price. You also can use the VB ratio of one firm to estimate the value of a comparable firm provided you make the appropriate and necessary adjustments to the VB ratio so that it reflects the comparable firm's fundamental profitability, risk, and growth characteristics. This section demonstrates the theoretical and empirical relation among intrinsic value, book value, and market value.

Using the same notation from prior chapters, we compute the VB ratio using the following model:

$$\frac{V_0}{BV_0} = 1 + \sum_{t=1}^{\infty} \frac{(ROCE_t - R_E) \times \dfrac{BV_{t-1}}{BV_0}}{(1 + R_E)^t}$$

In short, the VB ratio should be equal to 1 plus the present value of expected future residual return on common equity [the $(ROCE - R)$ term above] times cumulative growth in book value (the BV_{t-1}/BV_0 term above). The growth in book value indicates the increase in net assets on which firms can earn residual income. The growth in book value depends on ROCE, dividend payout, and changes in common stock outstanding from share issues or repurchases. As the model shows, if a firm generates greater positive residual ROCE ($ROCE_t - R_E$) and generates greater growth in book value (through reinvested earnings and/or stock issues) on which the firm will earn positive residual ROCE, the firm will create greater value for shareholders (the numerator on the right side will increase, so the value-to-book ratio will increase).

To derive this model, recall from Chapter 13 the residual income valuation model:

$$V_0 = BV_0 + \sum_{t=1}^{\infty} \frac{CI_t - (R_E \times BV_{t-1})}{(1 + R_E)^t}$$

This model estimates the value of common shareholders' equity as equal to the book value of common equity plus the present value of all expected future residual income, which is the amount by which expected future comprehensive income exceeds required earnings for the remaining life of the firm.[2] We compute the required earnings (or "normal" earnings) of the firm in Year t as the product of the required rate of return on common equity capital times the book value of common equity at the beginning of Year t ($R_E \times BV_{t-1}$). Required earnings captures the amount of income the firm must generate to provide a return to common equity capital that is equal to the cost of common equity capital. We measure *residual income* (or "abnormal" earnings) by the subtraction term: $CI_t - (R_E \times BV_{t-1})$. Residual income is the difference between expected comprehensive income in Year t and required earnings of the firm in Year t. Residual income measures the amount of wealth you expect the firm to create (or destroy) in Year t for common equity shareholders above (or below) the required return to equity capital.

---

[2]Chapter 13 described that the residual income valuation model depends on clean surplus accounting for book value of common shareholders' equity, which requires expected future earnings forecasts to be comprehensive measures of income for the firm's common equity shareholders and expected future dividends to reflect all capital transactions between the firm and common equity shareholders. Throughout this chapter, when we refer to expected future "earnings" or "net income" in the context of residual income valuation, we mean expected future comprehensive income available for common shareholders under clean surplus accounting.

To convert the residual income model into a model for the VB ratio, we scale both sides of the equation by BV_0, which produces the following equation:

$$\frac{V_0}{BV_0} = \frac{BV_0}{BV_0} + \sum_{t=1}^{\infty} \frac{\dfrac{CI_t}{BV_0} - \left(R_E \times \dfrac{BV_{t-1}}{BV_0}\right)}{(1+R_E)^t}$$

The term BV_0 divided by BV_0 is, of course, equal to 1. We rewrite the CI_t/BV_0 term as follows:

$$\frac{CI_t}{BV_0} = \frac{CI_t}{BV_{t-1}} \times \frac{BV_{t-1}}{BV_0} = ROCE_t \times \frac{BV_{t-1}}{BV_0}$$

To rewrite CI_t/BV_0 this way, we state $ROCE_t = CI_t/BV_{t-1}$. Note that this computation of $ROCE_t$ divides comprehensive income in period t by book value of common equity at the *beginning* of period t.[3] Also note that BV_{t-1}/BV_0 is the cumulative growth factor in book value of common equity between year 0 (the date of the valuation) and period $t-1$. As indicated previously, growth in book value is a function of the earnings generated each period plus additional capital contributions by shareholders, minus equity capital paid out to shareholders through dividends and stock buybacks. The growth in book value indicates growth in net assets, on which a firm can earn residual income.[4]

By decomposing the term CI_t/BV_0 into these two parts, we can restate CI_t/BV_0 as the product of profitability times growth: *ROCE* in Year t times the cumulative growth in book value from Year 0 to the start of Year t. Return on common equity is a function of profitability relative to beginning-of-year common equity; beginning-of-year common equity is a function of cumulative growth. We then substitute these two components of CI_t/BV_0 into the VB equation as follows:

$$\frac{V_0}{BV_0} = 1 + \sum_{t=1}^{\infty} \frac{\left(ROCE_t \times \dfrac{BV_{t-1}}{BV_0}\right) - \left(R_E \times \dfrac{BV_{t-1}}{BV_0}\right)}{(1+R_E)^t}$$

Now both terms in the numerator of the summation term are multiplied by the same cumulative book value growth factor. We rearrange that equation as follows:

$$\frac{V_0}{BV_0} = 1 + \sum_{t=1}^{\infty} \frac{(ROCE_t - R_E) \times \dfrac{BV_{t-1}}{BV_0}}{(1+R_E)^t}$$

We now have a useful model for the VB ratio. Let's consider each term.

First, as a starting point, the VB ratio will equal 1, to reflect the book value of common equity invested in the firm. Second, the summation term indicates how the VB ratio should differ from 1 as a function of the firm's expected future abnormal profitability (the $ROCE_t - R_E$ term) times the firm's cumulative growth in book value (the BV_{t-1}/BV_0 term), all of which is discounted to present value, reflecting the firm's cost of equity capital (R_E) and the time value of money. Thus, the residual income model specifies the firm's VB ratio as a function

---

[3]Theoretical and empirical research on the VB ratio defines ROCE as net income to common shareholders for a year divided by common shareholders' equity at the *beginning* of the year. In contrast, in prior chapters (particularly Chapter 4) we used *average* common shareholders' equity in the denominator of ROCE. The theoretical development and application of the VB model in this section uses comprehensive income rather than net income and shareholders' equity at the beginning of the year. These changes are theoretically correct, and as a practical matter they should not be particularly significant for most firms.

[4]Indeed, as we will discuss in more detail later, if a firm increases common shareholders' equity through retained earnings or common equity issues and it does not generate future earnings increases, the firm will experience a decline in the value-to-book ratio.

of the firm's value drivers: capital in place, profitability, growth, cost of equity capital, risk, and the time value of money. The VB model provides a valuation approach in which all of the inputs to valuation can be expressed as forecasts of rates—expected future ROCE, R_E, and growth. The only dollar amount you need in order to use the VB ratio to compute the dollar value of common shareholders' equity is the book value of common shareholders' equity, which is observable from the shareholders' equity section of the balance sheet.

Example

Suppose you want to value a firm with $1,000 of book value of common equity and a cost of equity capital equal to 10%. Assume that you forecast the firm will earn ROCE of 15% from Year +1 through Year +3, but that after Year +3, the firm will earn ROCE equal to 10%. You also expect the firm will reinvest all income (that is, pay zero dividends) and not issue or repurchase stock. Using the VB ratio approach, you should assign the firm a VB ratio equal to 1 plus the present value of future residual ROCE times growth. The present value of future residual ROCE times growth is determined as follows:

Year	Expected ROCE	Residual ROCE $(ROCE - R_E)$	Cumulative Book Value Growth Factor to Year $t - 1$	Residual ROCE $\times$ Cumulative Growth	PV Factor	PV of Residual ROCE $\times$ Cumulative Growth
+1	0.15	0.05	$1.00 = (1.15)^0$	0.05000	0.9091	0.04546
+2	0.15	0.05	$1.15 = (1.15)^1$	0.05750	0.8264	0.04752
+3	0.15	0.05	$1.3225 = (1.15)^2$	0.06613	0.7513	0.04968
+4	0.10	0.00	$1.5209 = (1.15)^3$	0.00000	0.6830	0.00000
					Total	0.14266

The sum of the present values of residual ROCE times cumulative growth through Year +3 equals 0.14266, and the sum in all years after Year +3 is zero. Adding this present value amount to 1 (to reflect the book value of equity already in place), the VB ratio of this firm is 1.14266. Note that we have determined this VB ratio with all of the inputs expressed in rates. We can multiply the VB ratio by book value of equity to determine that firm value is $1,142.66 (1.14266 VB ratio × $1,000 book value of equity). We can confirm this value using dollar amounts and the residual income approach from Chapter 13 as follows:

Year	Expected ROCE	Expected Earnings	Cumulative Book Value at the end of Year $t-1$ (BV_{t-1})	Required Income $(BV_{t-1} \times R_E)$	Residual Income	PV Factor	PV of Residual Income
+1	0.15	$150.00 $= 0.15 \times \$1,000$	$1,000	$100 $= \$1,000 \times 0.10$	$50.00 $= \$150 - \$100$	0.9091	$ 45.46
+2	0.15	$172.50 $= 0.15 \times \$1,150$	$1,150 $= \$1,000 + \$150$	$115 $= \$1,150 \times 0.10$	$57.50 $= \$172.50 - \$115$	0.8264	47.52
+3	0.15	$198.38 $= 0.15 \times \$1,322.5$	$1,322.5 $= \$1,150 + \$172.5$	$132.25 $= \$1,322.5 \times 0.10$	$66.13 $= \$198.38 - \$132.25$	0.7513	49.68
+4	0.10	$152.09 $= 0.10 \times \$1,520.9$	$1,520.9 $= \$1,322.5 + \$198.4$	$152.09 $= \$1,520.9 \times 0.10$	$0.00 $= \$152.09 - \$152.09$	0.6830	0.00
						Total	$142.66

The sum of the present values of residual income through Year +3 equals $142.66, the sum in all years after Year +3 is zero, and book value of equity is $1,000; so the residual income model confirms that firm value is $1,142.66.

The Value-to-Book Model with Finite Horizon Earnings Forecasts and Continuing Value Computation

As we discussed in Chapters 11–13, analysts commonly forecast income statements, balance sheets, and cash flows over a foreseeable, finite horizon and then make simplifying growth rate assumptions for the years continuing after the forecast horizon. We can modify the VB model to include specific forecasts of comprehensive income, book value of common equity, and ROCE through Year T (where T is a finite horizon, for example, five or ten years in the future) and then apply a constant growth rate assumption (denoted as g) to project ROCE for Year T+1 and all years thereafter. We used similar approaches to forecast and value dividends in Chapter 11, free cash flows in Chapter 12, and residual income in Chapter 13.

To develop the VB model with finite horizon earnings forecasts and continuing value computations, we follow the same approach used in Chapter 13, with only slight modifications. Recall from Chapter 13 that we used specific forecasts of financial statements for a finite horizon through Year T and then projected Year T+1 comprehensive income by multiplying Year T comprehensive income by the long-run growth factor $(1 + g)$. We then computed Year T+1 residual income (denoted as RI_{T+1}) as follows:

$$RI_{T+1} = [CI_T \times (1 + g)] - (R_E \times BV_T)$$

By estimating RI_{T+1} this way, we apply the same uniform long-run growth factor $(1 + g)$ to estimate Year T+1 income statement and balance sheet amounts and compute internally consistent projections for Year T+1 free cash flows, dividends, and residual income.

As we discussed in Chapter 13, after computing RI_{T+1}, you can treat RI_{T+1} as a growing perpetuity of residual income beginning in Year T+1. You can compute the present value of the perpetuity of residual income using the perpetuity-with-growth value model as follows:

Present Value of
Continuing Value$_0$ $= [CI_T \times (1 + g)] - (R_E \times BV_T) \times [1/(R_E - g)] \times [1/(1 + R_E)^T]$

We can modify this computation to adapt it to the value-to-book model with two steps:

1. Divide the term $[CI_T \times (1 + g)]$ by BV_T to convert it to an ROCE measure for Year T+1.
2. Divide the BV_T term by BV_0 to measure the cumulative growth in book value.

The result of these two steps is a continuing value computation based on projected future residual ROCE and book value growth as follows:

Present Value of Continuing Value$_0$

$$= \{[CI_T \times (1 + g)/BV_T] - R_E\} \times (BV_T/BV_0) \times [1/(R_E - g)] \times [1/(1 + R_E)^T]$$
$$= [ROCE_{T+1} - R_E] \times [BV_T/BV_0] \times [1/(R_E - g)] \times [1/(1 + R_E)^T]$$
$$\quad\quad (1) \quad\quad\quad\quad (2) \qu\quad\quad\quad (3) \qu\quad\quad\quad (4)$$

The first term in the computation is projected residual ROCE in Year T+1. The second term is the cumulative growth in book value from present (BV_0) to the beginning of the continuing value period (BV_T). The third term is the familiar perpetuity-with-growth factor, computing the present value of the perpetuity as of the start of the continuing value period. The fourth term is the present value factor that discounts continuing value to present value today.

We include the continuing value computation into the finite horizon value-to-book model as follows:

$$\frac{V_0}{BV_0} = 1 + \sum_{t=1}^{T} \frac{(ROCE_t - R_E) \times \dfrac{BV_{t-1}}{BV_0}}{(1 + R_E)^t} + (ROCE_{T+1} - R_E) \times (BV_T/BV_0) \times [1/(R_E - g)] \times [1/(1 + R_E)^T]$$

$$\text{(1)} \qquad\qquad \text{(2)} \qquad\qquad\qquad \text{(3)}$$

This model computes the value-to-book ratio of common equity based on three parts: (1) book value scaled by book value (BV_0/BV_0, which is of course equal to 1), (2) the present value of residual ROCE over the explicit forecast horizon through Year T (the summation term), and (3) the present value of continuing value based on residual ROCE as a perpetuity with growth beginning in Year T+1.

Reasons Why VB Ratios and MB Ratios May Differ From 1

But the expression for the VB ratio provides some deeper insights into valuation. First, let's focus on a number of *economic* reasons why VB and MB ratios may differ from 1:

Economics teaches that in long-run equilibrium firms should expect to earn a return equal to the cost of capital (that is, ROCE = R_E). The VB model indicates that a firm in steady-state equilibrium earning ROCE = R_E will maintain (not create or destroy) shareholder wealth and will be valued at book value. That is, for firms in equilibrium, we would expect VB = 1.

- The firm may have competitive advantages that enable it to earn an ROCE that is greater than R_E. To the extent that the firm can sustain these competitive advantages, the firm will increase the magnitude and persistence over time of the degree to which ROCE exceeds R_E, thereby increasing the VB and MB ratios. A firm's value should be greater than its book value of common equity if the firm is expected to generate wealth for common equity shareholders by earning a return (ROCE) that exceeds the cost of capital (R_E). That is, VB > 1 if ROCE > R_E. By contrast, firms that are expected to earn a return that is less than the cost of equity capital (that is, ROCE < R_E) will destroy shareholder wealth and will be valued below book value (that is, VB < 1).
- By itself, growth does not add value. Growth adds value to shareholders only if the growth creates additional residual income for common equity shareholders. If expected ROCE equals R_E on new projects (that is, zero NPV projects), these new projects will not create or destroy common shareholders' equity value. New projects will create new wealth for equity shareholders (that is, will be positive NPV projects) only when expected ROCE exceeds R_E.
- The risk of the firm increases the equity cost of capital, R_E. Increasing the equity cost of capital reduces firm value in two ways: (1) by increasing the required ROCE the firm must earn to cover the increased R_E (that is, the "hurdle rate" goes up in the numerator) and (2) by increasing the discount rate used to compute the present value of residual income (which increases the denominator).

- If a firm's VB ratio differs from the industry average VB ratio, it should be because the firm's expected future ROCE, R_E, and/or book value growth differ from the industry averages.
- If a firm's VB ratio changes over time, current expectations for the firm's future ROCE, R_E, and/or book value growth should differ from past expectations for the firm's future ROCE, R_E, and/or book value growth, respectively.

A firm's VB and MB ratio may differ from 1 for *accounting* reasons in addition to economic reasons.[5] The firm may have investments in projects for which accounting methods and principles cause ROCE to differ from R_E. For example, firms may make substantial investments in successful R&D projects, brand equity, human capital, or other intangible resources. If these investments are internally generated through R&D activities, marketing and advertising activities, or human capital recruiting and training activities, firms are typically required to expense them according to conservative accounting principles (as is common under U.S. GAAP and IFRS).[6] If these investments subsequently develop into profitable resources, the firm will have substantial off-balance-sheet assets and off-balance-sheet common shareholders' equity. These off-balance-sheet assets generate net income, but by being off-balance-sheet, they cause common shareholders' equity to be understated, so ROCE is relatively high. These effects can be observed among certain firms in many industries, such as pharmaceuticals, biotechnology, software, and consumer goods.

PepsiCo and **Coca-Cola** have created substantial off-balance-sheet brand equity over many years of successful product development, advertising, and brand-building activities. Following U.S. GAAP, these firms have expensed their investments in these activities. Thus, for these firms, the book value of common shareholders' equity does not recognize the off-balance-sheet value of brand equity. Relative to R_E, ROCE for PepsiCo and Coca-Cola is very high and likely will continue to be very high for many years in the future.

Over a sufficiently long period of time, however, the impact of accounting principles on the VB and MB ratio will diminish because economics teaches us to expect that competitive equilibrium forces will drive ROCE to R_E in the long run. Also, the self-correcting nature of accounting will eventually eliminate conservative biases in ROCE and book value of equity. For example, consider a biotechnology company that for several years invests in R&D to develop a particular drug. During the initial years of research, the firm incurs research costs that the firm is required to expense under U.S. GAAP. Its ROCE and book value of equity will be "low" during these years. After successfully developing and marketing the drug, ROCE will be "high" because the firm generates revenues without matching expenses for research costs. The "high" ROCE will increase retained earnings, and over time, the initial conservative biases in ROCE and book value will be corrected.

---

[5]Stephen Ryan (1995) found that book value changes lag market value changes in part because U.S. GAAP uses historical cost valuations for assets. The lag varies in part based on the degree of capital intensity of firms. See Stephen Ryan, "A Model of Accrual Measurement and Implications for the Evolution of the Book-to-Market Ratio," *Journal of Accounting Research* (Spring 1995), pp. 95–112.

[6]U.S. GAAP and IFRS typically require expensing (rather than capitalizing) expenditures on internally generated intangible resources such as R&D (except IFRS does permit capitalization of development costs), advertising, and human capital because the highly uncertain future cash flows associated with them are inherently difficult to measure reliably.

Application of the Value-to-Book Model to PepsiCo

In Chapter 13, we determined that **PepsiCo**'s share value at the end of 2012 should be within a reasonable range centered on $85.86. We determined this amount using the financial statement forecasts developed in Chapter 10 and the residual income valuation model. Given that we already have an estimate of share value, we can simply divide by book value of equity per share to determine the VB ratio. PepsiCo's book value per share at the end of 2012 was $14.5188 ($22,417.0 million/1,544 million shares). Thus, PepsiCo's VB ratio at the end of 2012 should be 5.914 ($85.86 value per share/$14.5188 book value equity per share).

We illustrate the valuation of PepsiCo shares using the VB model to illustrate the rigor of the VB model and its consistency with the residual income valuation approach in Chapter 13. To apply to VB model to PepsiCo, we rely on the same financial statement forecasts developed in Chapter 10, the same equity cost of capital (7.5%), the same expected long-run growth rate (3.0%), and the same residual income computations and valuation steps developed in Chapter 13. We summarize the computations to arrive at PepsiCo's common equity share value using the VB approach in Exhibit 14.3, where we present the VB model for PepsiCo from FSAP. We present all of the forecasts and valuation models in the FSAP Forecasts and Valuation spreadsheets in Appendix C.

In applying the VB model to PepsiCo, note that the first two rows of information in Exhibit 14.3 are identical to the amounts used in Exhibit 13.5 on page 988 to apply the residual income valuation model: the projected amounts of comprehensive income available to common shareholders and projected book values of common shareholders equity. Using these amounts, the Year +1 projected ROCE is 27.2%, ($6,094.7 million/ $22,417.0 million). The residual ROCE is 19.7% after subtracting 7.5% for the cost of equity capital. The cumulative growth factor in book value (BV_{t-1}/BV_0) in Year +1 is 1.0 because Year +1 is the first year of the valuation horizon.[7] Therefore, the product of Year +1 residual ROCE times the cumulative growth factor is 19.7%, which we discount to present value using the 7.5% cost of equity capital. Exhibit 14.3 presents these computations for PepsiCo for Year +1 through Year +5. The sum of the present value of residual ROCE times growth in Year +1 through Year +5 is 0.88.[8]

For purposes of computing continuing value, as described in the previous chapter, we project comprehensive income in Year +6 to grow by the 3.0% long-run growth rate. Using projected book value as of the start of Year +6 (the end of Year +5), we compute implied residual ROCE and multiply by the cumulative growth factor in book value up to the beginning of Year +6. The projected ROCE in Year +6 is 31.2% $\{[CI_5 \times (1+g)]/BV_5 = ($7,064.2$ million $\times$ 1.03)/$23,315.8 million $=$ $7,276.1 million/$23,315.8 million$\}$. After subtracting the 7.5% cost of equity capital, the projected residual ROCE in Year +6 is 23.7%. Cumulative growth in book value from Year 0 to the beginning of Year +6 (the end of Year +5) is 1.04 $(BV_5/BV_0 = $23,315.8$ million/$22,417.0 million). Therefore, we project that in Year +6, the

---

[7]We project that PepsiCo's book value of common equity will decrease slightly to $22,020.3 million by the end of Year +1. Therefore, the cumulative growth factor in book value of common equity as of the start of Year +2 will be 0.982 ($22,020.3 million/$22,417.0 million).

[8]This amount should be interpreted as a component of the VB ratio because all of the computations in the model are scaled by BV_0. Thus, the amount 0.88 should be interpreted as an estimate of the amount of residual income PepsiCo will create in Years +1 through +5 that, in present value, is equal to 0.88 times the book value of common equity. To reconcile this computation with the residual income model computations in Chapter 13, recognize that 0.88 times book value of $22,417.0 million equals $19,801.0 (allow for rounding), which is the sum of the present value of residual income in Year +1 through Year +5 computed in Exhibit 13.2.

Exhibit 14.3

Valuation of PepsiCo
Value-to-Book Approach
(dollar amounts in millions, except per-share amounts; allow for rounding)

RESIDUAL INCOME VALUATION						Continuing Value
	1	2	3	4	5	
Value-to-Book Approach	Year +1	Year +2	Year +3	Year +4	Year +5	Year +6
Comprehensive income available for common shareholders	$ 6,094.7	$ 6,376.6	$ 6,598.3	$ 6,972.2	$ 7,064.2	$ 7,276.1
Book value of common shareholders' equity (at $t-1$)	$ 22,417.0	$22,020.3	$22,417.9	$22,749.5	$23,259.5	$23,315.8
Implied ROCE	27.2%	29.0%	29.4%	30.6%	30.4%	31.2%
Residual ROCE	19.7%	21.5%	21.9%	23.1%	22.9%	23.7%
Cumulative growth factor in common equity as of $t-1$	100.0%	98.2%	100.0%	101.5%	103.8%	104.0%
Residual ROCE times cumulative growth	19.7%	21.1%	21.9%	23.5%	23.7%	24.7%
Present value factors	0.930	0.865	0.805	0.749	0.697	
Present value residual ROCE times growth	0.183	0.182	0.177	0.176	0.165	
Sum of present value residual ROCE times growth	0.88					
Present value of continuing value	+ 3.82					
Total present value residual ROCE	4.70					
Add one for book value of equity at $t-1$	+ 1.00					
Sum	5.70					
Adjust to mid-year discounting	×$ 1.0375					
Implied value-to-book ratio	5.9138					
Times beginning book value of equity	22,417.0					
Total present value of equity	132,569.1					
Shares outstanding	÷ 1,544.0					
Estimated value per share	$ 85.86					
Current share price	$ 68.43					
Percent difference	25%					

Sensitivity analysis for the value-to-book approach should be identical to that of the residual income approach.

product of residual ROCE times cumulative growth is 24.7% (23.7% $\times$ 1.04). The present value of continuing value is computed as follows (allow for rounding):

Present Value of Continuing Value$_0$

$$= [(\{[CI_5 \times (1 + g)]/BV_5\} - R_E) \times (BV_5/BV_0)] \times [1/(R_E - g)] \times [1/(1 + R_E)^5]$$
$$= (\{[(\$7{,}064.2 \times 1.03)/\$23{,}315.8] - 0.075\} \times (\$23{,}315.8/\$22{,}417.0))$$
$$\times [1/(0.075 - 0.030)] \times [1/(1 + 0.075)^5]$$
$$= 0.237 \times 1.040 \times 22.222 \times 0.697$$
$$= 3.82$$

To compute the VB ratio, we need to add the present value of future residual income and PepsiCo's beginning book value of common equity expressed as a ratio of beginning book value of equity, which is, of course, equal to 1. Also, as described in prior chapters, our present value calculations over-discount because they discount each year's residual ROCE for full periods. Therefore, we multiply the present value sum by the midyear discounting adjustment factor of 1.0375 [1 + (R_E/2) = 1 + (0.075/2)]. The implied VB ratio is computed as follows:

Present value of residual ROCE in Year +1 through Year +5	0.88
Present value of continuing value of residual ROCE in Year +6 and beyond	3.82
Present value of all future residual ROCE	4.70
Add: Beginning book value	+ 1.00
Total	5.70
Multiply by the midyear discounting factor	×1.0375
Implied VB ratio	5.9138

These computations confirm that PepsiCo common equity should be valued at 5.9138 times the book value of equity at the end of 2012. At that time, PepsiCo's market value was $105,656 million ($68.43 per share $\times$ 1,544 million shares) and PepsiCo's book value of common shareholders' equity was $22,417.0 million. Thus, PepsiCo was trading at an MB ratio equal to 4.7 ($105,656.0 million/$22,417.0 million). The VB ratio of 5.9138 is 25% greater than the MB ratio of 4.7, implying that PepsiCo shares were underpriced by 25% at that time.

Equivalently, we can convert the VB ratio into a share value estimate for purposes of comparing to market price per share. If we multiply book value equity by the VB ratio, we obtain the value estimate of PepsiCo common equity of $132,569.1 million ($22,417.0 million $\times$ 5.9138 VB ratio). Dividing by 1,544 million shares outstanding indicates that PepsiCo's common equity shares have a value of $85.86 per share, which is identical to the value estimates we obtained from the residual income model in Chapter 13, the free cash flows to common equity shareholders model in Chapter 12, and the dividend models in Chapter 11. Comparing the share value estimate of $85.86 to market price per share of $68.43 also indicates that PepsiCo's shares were underpriced by 25% at the end of 2012.

We can conduct a sensitivity analysis for the estimate of PepsiCo's VB ratio to assess a reasonable range of VB ratios for PepsiCo. We will find that the sensitivity of the VB ratio estimate is identical to the sensitivity of the residual income model value estimates demonstrated in Chapter 13. This is to be expected because both models use the same forecasts and valuation assumptions and the VB model is a scaled version of the residual income model.

Empirical Data on MB Ratios

Exhibit 14.4 presents descriptive statistics for MB ratios across 47 industries during the decade from 2003–2012 (the same industries and years for which Exhibit 11.3 in Chapter 11 provided data on market betas).[9] The median MB ratio for the 48,184 firm-years in this sample is 1.86. These data reveal substantial variation in MB ratios across industries and within industries during this period. The descriptive statistics on MB and other ratios across industries and years in Appendix D (which can be found online at the book's companion website at www.cengagebrain.com) also reveal substantial variation in MB ratios.

The differences across industries in median MB ratios in Exhibit 14.4 likely relate, in part, to differences in competitive conditions driving differences in growth and ROCE relative to R_E as well as differences in applicable accounting principles across firms and time. Economically, in a mature and competitive industry, the median firm will likely generate ROCE that is close to R_E and will not likely generate unusually high rates of growth. Such firms tend to have median MB ratios closer to 1. For example, firms in mature competitive industries such as insurance, textiles, banking, fabrication, construction, agriculture, transportation, real estate, securities trading, and utilities, tend to have MB ratios that are lower than the sample average.

The assets of firms in some of these industries—particularly banks and insurers—are primarily investments in financial assets, some of which appear on the balance sheet at fair value; thus, MB ratios are closer to 1. In contrast, some of the industries

Exhibit 14.4

Descriptive Statistics on Market-to-Book Ratios, 2003–2012
Forty-Seven Industries Sorted by Median Market-to-Book Ratios

Industry	25th Percentile	Median	75th Percentile
Full Sample (*n* = 48,184 firm-years)*	**1.18**	**1.86**	**3.12**
Insurance	0.87	1.21	1.70
Textiles	0.84	1.22	2.01
Banking	0.85	1.33	1.94
Fabricated Products	0.98	1.38	1.95
Construction	1.05	1.54	2.24
Agriculture	0.95	1.60	3.07
Transportation	1.03	1.60	2.62
Real Estate	0.92	1.60	2.80
Trading	1.07	1.61	2.73
Utilities	1.30	1.64	2.15
Consumer Goods	1.01	1.64	2.88
Business Supplies	1.13	1.65	2.35
Wholesale	1.08	1.66	2.59
Automobiles and Trucks	1.12	1.67	2.93

(Continued)

---

[9]Our sincere thanks to Professor Matt Wieland for providing these data and the data in Exhibits 11.3 and 14.7.

Exhibit 14.4 (Continued)

Industry	25th Percentile	Median	75th Percentile
Recreation	1.08	1.68	2.68
Steel Works	1.10	1.69	2.34
Construction Materials	1.09	1.72	2.47
Apparel	1.13	1.78	2.87
Rubber and Plastic Products	1.22	1.79	2.79
Electronic Equipment	1.17	1.82	3.02
Retail	1.18	1.89	3.16
Communication	1.26	1.92	3.37
Electrical Equipment	1.30	1.93	3.08
Food Products	1.28	1.94	3.36
Entertainment	1.19	1.96	3.45
Petroleum and Natural Gas	1.35	2.05	3.04
Shipbuilding, Railroad Equipment	1.29	2.05	3.06
Printing and Publishing	1.30	2.06	3.62
Machinery	1.35	2.08	3.20
Measuring and Control Equipment	1.38	2.09	3.32
Aircraft	1.32	2.13	3.36
Restaurants, Hotels, Motels	1.23	2.14	3.66
Personal Services	1.29	2.17	3.94
Chemicals	1.51	2.20	3.59
Healthcare	1.31	2.21	3.51
Computers	1.53	2.33	3.74
Business Services	1.45	2.42	4.13
Shipping Containers	1.79	2.43	3.59
Precious Metals	1.70	2.60	4.17
Candy & Soda	1.72	2.68	4.06
Beer & Liquor	1.34	2.69	5.01
Non-Metallic and Industrial Metal Mining	1.70	2.73	4.48
Medical Equipment	1.67	2.80	4.71
Defense	1.73	2.82	4.65
Coal	1.76	3.24	5.46
Pharmaceutical Products	2.12	3.59	6.03
Tobacco Products	3.82	5.47	11.64

*To compute these descriptive statistics on market-to-book value ratios, we deleted firm-years with negative book value of equity. We also deleted firm-year observations in the top 1% of the distribution to reduce the influence of potential outliers.

with relatively high MB ratios are more likely to have off-balance-sheet assets and shareholders' equity. For example, the tobacco industry contains firms with significant off-balance-sheet brand equity and the pharmaceutical industry includes firms with substantial value in off-balance-sheet R&D assets. The balance sheet understates the economic value of key resources in these industries. These industries have MB ratios considerably in excess of 1.

Empirical Research Results on the Predictive Power of MB Ratios

Several empirical studies have found that MB ratios are fairly stable, mean reverting slowly over time, and that MB ratios are reliable predictors of future growth in book value and expected future ROCE (implying that ROCE also mean reverts slowly).[10] For example, Victor Bernard grouped roughly 1,900 firms into ten portfolios each year between 1972 and 1981 based on their MB ratios. He then computed the mean ROCE for each portfolio in the formation year and for each of the ten subsequent years. Exhibit 14.5 summarizes a portion of Bernard's results, grouping firms in the lowest three MB portfolios, middle four MB portfolios, and highest three MB portfolios.[11]

The data in Exhibit 14.5 indicate that firms with the highest MB ratios tend to have the highest ROCEs through Year +10 and firms with the lowest MB ratios tend to have the lowest ROCEs through Year +10. The results from the Bernard study also indicate that firms with the highest MB ratios have the highest growth rates in book value of equity through Year +10 and firms with the lowest MB ratios have the lowest growth rates through

Exhibit 14.5

The Relations among MB Ratios, Future ROCE, and Future Book Value Growth

MB Portfolio	Mean MB Ratio	Median ROCE for Year:			
		0	+1	+5	+10
Low	0.67	0.11	0.09	0.12	0.12
Medium	1.15	0.11	0.13	0.14	0.14
High	2.65	0.10	0.17	0.16	0.20

MB Portfolio	Mean MB Ratio	Cumulative Percentage Increase in Book Value through Year:			
		0	+1	+5	+10
Low	0.67	0%	15%	54%	190%
Medium	1.15	0%	15%	69%	204%
High	2.65	0%	21%	139%	394%

[10]Victor L. Bernard, "Accounting-Based Valuation Methods, Determinants of Market-to-Book Ratios and Implications for Financial Statement Analysis," *Working Paper*, University of Michigan (1993); Jane A. Ou and Stephen H. Penman, "Financial Statement Analysis and the Evaluation of Market-to-Book Ratios," *Working Paper*, Columbia University (1995); Stephen H. Penman, "The Articulation of Price-Earnings Ratios and Market-to-Book Ratios and the Evaluation of Growth," *Journal of Accounting Research*, Vol. 34, No. 2 (Autumn 1996), pp. 235–259; William H. Beaver and Stephen G. Ryan, "Biases and Lags in Book Value and Their Effects on the Ability of the Book-to-Market Ratio to Predict Book Return on Equity," *Journal of Accounting Research*, Vol. 38, No. 1 (Spring 2000), pp. 127–149.

[11]To reduce the effects of survivorship bias, Bernard included firms that did not survive the entire ten-year future horizon and included any gain or loss on the cessation of the firm (from bankruptcy, takeover, or liquidation) in the final year ROCE.

Year +10. In addition, the results in the Bernard study indicate (although it is not apparent from the summary of results in Exhibit 14.5) that the predictive power of MB ratios for future ROCEs tends to diminish as the horizon lengthens. In Year +10, for example, there is relatively little difference in ROCEs across firms in the third through ninth MB portfolios, as these firms experience ROCEs that tended to converge to 14% during Bernard's sample period. These results are consistent with the mean reversion in ROCEs over time, consistent with movement toward competitive equilibrium.

LO 14-3

For price-earnings ratios:
a. Compute and use the firm's value-earnings (VE) ratio.
b. Incorporate growth into the VE ratio to compute the value-earnings-growth (VEG) ratio.
c. Use VE and VEG ratios analyze firm value over time and across firms, and to make investment decisions.
d. Explain why VE and PE ratios differ across firms and the impact of the following factors on VE and PE ratios: (1) risk and the cost of equity capital, (2) growth, (3) differences between current and expected future earnings, and (4) alternative accounting methods and principles.

Price-Earnings and Value-Earnings Ratios

As noted in Chapter 13, the capital markets devote enormous amounts of time and energy to forecasting and analyzing firms' earnings. Therefore, it is no surprise that the market multiple that receives most frequent use and attention is the PE ratio. Analysts' reports and the financial press frequently refer to PE ratios. *The Wall Street Journal* reports PE ratios as part of the daily coverage of stock prices and trading activity. The capital markets increasingly evaluate ratios that integrate the PE ratio with expected future earnings growth to capture explicitly the links between price, profitability, and growth.

This section begins by computing the value-earnings (VE) ratio for **PepsiCo** and describing a theoretical model for computing VE ratios. The section then describes computing and using PE ratios from a practical perspective. It discusses the strict assumptions implied by PE ratios, the conditions in which PE ratios may not capture appropriately the theoretical relation between value and earnings for most firms, and the difficulties encountered in reconciling actual PE ratios with those indicated by the theoretical value-earnings model. This section also incorporates earnings growth and examines PEG ratios. The section concludes by describing empirical data on PE ratios, the predictive power of PE ratios, and the empirical evidence on the articulation between PE ratios and MB ratios.

A Model for the Value-Earnings Ratio with Application to PepsiCo

Beginning from the most conceptually sound and theoretically correct standpoint, the VE ratio should be computed as the value of common shareholders' equity divided by earnings for a single period. The previous chapter described how to determine common equity value as a function of present value of expected *future* earnings using the residual income model. In the residual income model, we use clean surplus accounting and measure future earnings as expected future comprehensive income available to common shareholders. Thus, in theory, you should measure the VE ratio as the value of common equity divided by the next period's expected comprehensive income. This way, the VE ratio achieves consistent alignment of *perspective* (numerator and denominator both forward-looking) and *measurement* (numerator and denominator both based on comprehensive income).

If one has already computed firm value using the forecasting and valuation models developed in the last four chapters, computing the theoretically correct VE ratio is a simple matter of division. For example, in the preceding section and in prior chapters, we estimated **PepsiCo**'s common shareholders' equity value to be $132,569.1 million at the end of 2012. We also projected that Year $+1$ comprehensive income will equal net income available for common shareholders, which will equal $6,094.7 million. Thus, we can compute the VE ratio for PepsiCo at the end of 2012 as follows:

$$V_0/E_1 = \$132,569.1 \text{ million}/\$6,094.7 \text{ million} = 21.75$$

Or equivalently, the VE ratio can be computed on a per-share basis, as follows:

$$Vps_0/Eps_1 = (\$132,569.1 \text{ million}/1,544 \text{ million shares})/(\$6,094.7 \text{ million}/1,544 \text{ million shares})$$
$$= \$85.86/\$3.95$$
$$= 21.75$$

We also can derive the VE ratio from the VB ratio determined using the residual income model in the previous section. For this derivation, we employ a simple algebraic step, as follows:

$$V_0/E_1 = V_0/BV_0 \times BV_0/E_1 = V_0/BV_0 \times (1/ROCE_1)$$

This formula shows that the same factors that drive the VB ratio (V_0/BV_0) also drive the VE ratio. In fact, the model shows that the VE ratio should be a multiple of the VB ratio, where the multiple is the inverse of ROCE. However, the VE ratio also makes an additional simplifying and restrictive assumption: that value can be summarized by one-period-ahead ROCE. A consequence of this assumption is that VE ratios vary *inversely* with expected future ROCE. Holding the VB ratio constant, a firm with a temporarily high level of expected ROCE next period will have a temporarily low VE ratio, and vice versa.

Using this approach, we can derive PepsiCo's VE ratio from the VB ratio we computed in the previous section, as follows:

$$V_0/E_1 = V_0/BV_0 \times BV_0/E_1 = V_0/BV_0 \times (1/ROCE_1)$$
$$= (\$132,569.1 \text{ million}/\$22,417.0 \text{ million}) \times (\$22,417.0 \text{ million}/\$6,094.7 \text{ million})$$
$$= 5.9138 \times 3.678$$
$$= 5.9138 \times (1/0.272)$$
$$= 21.75$$

Thus, PepsiCo's VE ratio should equal 21.75. We convert PepsiCo's VB ratio of 5.9138 into the VE ratio by multiplying by $1/ROCE_1$, which we project will be the inverse of 27.2%.

Notice that we derived the VE ratio simply from the computation that PepsiCo's value is equal to $132,569.1 million, which is based on specific forecasts of PepsiCo's future earnings. Obviously, using value to compute a VE ratio will not provide any new information about PepsiCo's value. So what is the point of computing a VE ratio?

The VE ratio provides you with a theoretically correct benchmark to evaluate the firm's PE ratio. We can compare PepsiCo's VE ratio of 21.75 to PepsiCo's PE ratio to assess the market value of PepsiCo shares. This comparison is equivalent to comparing V to P (that is, value to price). We compute the PE ratio for PepsiCo as of the end of 2012 using our forecast that Year $+1$ earnings (comprehensive income available to common shareholders) will be $6,094.7 million as follows:

$$P_0/E_{+1} = Price\ per\ Share_0/Earnings\ per\ Share_{+1}$$
$$= \$68.43/(\$6,094.7 \text{ million}/1,544 \text{ million shares})$$
$$= \$68.43/\$3.95$$
$$= 17.32$$

Thus, at the end of 2012, PepsiCo shares traded at a multiple of 17.32 times the Year +1 earnings forecast. PepsiCo's VE ratio of 21.75 is 25% greater than PepsiCo's PE ratio of 17.32 at the end of 2012, consistent with our prior estimates of PepsiCo's value.

With the theoretically correct VE ratio, we also can project VE ratios for other firms after we have made any necessary adjustments to capture the other firms' fundamental characteristics of profitability, growth, and risk. In addition, with the theoretically correct VE ratio, we have a benchmark to gauge other firms' PE ratios to assess whether the market is under- or overpricing their shares.

In the next section, we illustrate the process by which PE ratios can be used as a shortcut valuation metric, highlighting the necessary assumptions in the process and evaluating their theoretical soundness. We also discuss the practical advantages and disadvantages in using PE ratios as shortcut valuation metrics.

PE Ratios from a Theoretical Perspective: Projecting Firm Value from Permanent Earnings

PE ratios are practical tools used by analysts interested in valuation shortcuts. In some circumstances, you may need to react with timely ballpark value estimates, and PE ratios can provide a quick and efficient way to estimate firm value as a multiple of earnings. You can also assess benchmark PE ratios that you might expect a firm to have based on past PE ratios for that firm, on industry-average PE ratios, or on comparable firms' PE ratios. You use benchmarks such as these to project a firm's PE ratio quickly, using one-period earnings as a common denominator for relative valuations rather than engaging in the extensive computations necessary to determine the correct VE ratio to assess whether the market has priced the firm's shares appropriately. But what should a firm's PE ratio be? If you have not computed firm value to determine the VE ratio and need to use a shortcut PE ratio instead, what is the correct PE ratio to use?

In projecting firm value using a simple PE ratio (that is, one that uses only one period of earnings and ignores earnings growth), you impose a *very strong assumption* on the earnings for a single period: you treat these earnings (whether trailing earnings or a one-period-ahead earnings forecast) as the beginning amount of a *permanent* stream of earnings, valued as a perpetuity. In essence, the PE assumes that one year of earnings is sufficient information to value a firm and to determine share price. Conceptually, suppose the firm's common shareholders' equity value equals its market value, the firm's earnings will be constant in the future, and the firm's investors expect a constant rate of return R_E. Under these restrictive conditions, we can value the firm's common equity using one-year-ahead earnings (denoted as E_1) as a perpetuity, as follows:

$$V_0 = P_0 = E_1/R_E$$

Rearranged slightly, under these assumptions, the firm's VE and PE ratios are:

$$V_0/E_1 = P_0/E_1 = 1/R_E$$

Thus, strictly speaking, the PE multiple assumes that firm value is the present value of a constant stream of expected future earnings, which is discounted at a constant expected future discount rate. Under these conditions, you can value the firm using simply a multiple of one-period-ahead earnings and the PE ratio of the firm is simply the inverse of the discount rate.

To illustrate this model, assume that the market expects the firm to generate earnings of $700 next period and requires a 14% return on equity capital. The market value of the firm at the beginning of the next period should be \$5,000 (\$700/0.14). Note that the inverse of the 14% discount rate translates into a PE ratio of 7.14 (1/0.14). Thus, \$700 times 7.14 equals \$5,000.

The simple PE ratio assumes that future earnings will be permanent, which is not realistic for most firms. Most firms' earnings are not expected to remain constant; most firms' earnings are expected to grow. We have already seen that such strict assumptions do not fit **PepsiCo**. Under the assumptions that PepsiCo's earnings will be constant in the future and that PepsiCo's constant future ROCE will equal the 7.5% cost of equity capital, PepsiCo's PE ratio should be 13.33 (1/0.075). This PE ratio is far below the theoretically derived VE ratio of 21.75 for PepsiCo.

Price-Earnings Ratios from a Practical Perspective

As a practical matter, analysts, the financial press, and financial databases commonly measure PE ratios as current period share price divided by reported (historical) earnings per share for the most recent prior fiscal year or the most recent four quarters (sometimes referred to as the *lagged* or *trailing-twelve-months earnings per share*).[12] *The Wall Street Journal* and financial data websites such as Yahoo! Finance commonly compute PE ratios this way. With this approach, the PE ratio for **PepsiCo** as of the end of 2012 is equal to price per share$_{2012}$/basic earnings per share$_{2012}$ = \$68.43/\$3.96 = 17.28. Thus, at the end of 2012, PepsiCo shares traded at a PE multiple of 17.28 times 2012 basic earnings per share.[13]

The common approach to compute the PE ratio by dividing market price per share by basic earnings per share for the most recent year is practical because you can readily observe price and earnings per share for most firms. This approach is efficient because it does not require you to produce a computation of value or a forecast of earnings. However, this common approach creates a logical misalignment for valuation purposes because it divides *historical* earnings into share price, which reflects the present value of *future* earnings. If historical earnings contain unusual or nonrecurring gains or losses that are not expected to persist in future earnings, you should normalize the reported historical earnings by removing these effects to compute a PE ratio that reflects earnings that are likely to persist in the future. Chapters 3 and 6 describe techniques to identify elements of income that are unusual and nonrecurring, adjust reported earnings to eliminate their effects, and thereby measure recurring, persistent earnings.

As an alternative approach to create a more logical alignment of price and earnings, you can compute the "*forward PE ratio*" by dividing share price by a forecast of future

---

[12]In theory, to be consistent with clean surplus accounting and residual income valuation, the denominator should be based on comprehensive income per share. However, analysts, the financial press, and financial databases rarely compute PE ratios based on comprehensive income per share, in part because (1) U.S. GAAP does not yet require reporting comprehensive income on a per-share basis and (2) the other comprehensive income items are usually unrealized gains and losses that are not likely to be a permanent component of income each period. We follow traditional practice in this chapter and compute PE ratios using reported earnings figures.

[13]The common approach to computing PE ratios also can be slightly distorted by differences in the number of shares outstanding at year-end that the market uses to compute share price versus the weighted-average number of shares outstanding used to compute earnings per share under U.S. GAAP. If we compute PepsiCo's PE ratio using amounts in millions rather than per-share amounts, we obtain a PE ratio of 17.10 [\$105,656.0 million/(net income attributable to PepsiCo shareholders of \$6,178 million − \$1 million preferred dividends)]. This PE ratio is slightly lower than the PE ratio of 17.28 based on per-share amounts, because PepsiCo reports earnings per share based on the weighted-average number of common shares outstanding during the year (as required by U.S. GAAP) rather than the number of shares outstanding at year-end.

earnings per share (for example, analysts' consensus forecast of expected earnings per share one year ahead). A PE ratio based on expected future earnings, however, requires you to forecast future earnings (or have access to an analyst's forecast). Thus, the reliability of a forward PE ratio depends on the reliability of the earnings forecast. Earnings forecast errors will distort forward PE ratios. In addition, as discussed previously for VE ratios, PE ratios will vary inversely with transitory earnings components. If you use trailing or forward earnings that are temporarily increased by transitory gains or temporarily decreased by transitory losses, the PE ratio will be temporarily biased down or up, respectively.

Recall that in the preceding subsection, we computed the forward PE ratio for PepsiCo as of the end of 2012 using our forecast that Year $+1$ earnings (comprehensive income available to common shareholders) as follows: price per share$_0$/earnings per share$_{+1}$ = \$68.43 per share/(\$6,094.7 million/1,544 million shares) = \$68.43/\$3.95 = 17.28. Thus, at the end of 2012, PepsiCo shares traded at a forward PE multiple of 17.28 times the Year $+1$ earnings forecast. PepsiCo's VE ratio of 21.75 is 25% greater than PepsiCo's forward PE ratio of 17.28 at the end of 2012, consistent with our prior estimates of PepsiCo's value.[14]

Notice that we derived the PE ratios in this section simply by dividing PepsiCo's market share price by earnings per share of the past year or by our forecasts of PepsiCo's future earnings per share. Obviously, using price to compute a PE ratio will not provide any new information about PepsiCo's share *value*.

PE Ratio Measurement Issues

Thus far, we have discussed a variety of different measurement issues for PE ratios. Forward-looking PE ratios divide share price by one-year-ahead earnings forecasts, which is theoretically more correct. However, at least two problems arise in using forward PE ratios. First, one-year-ahead earnings forecasts are not readily available for all firms. Second, the accuracy of the forecasts depends on your forecast assumptions, which can differ widely. Therefore, as noted earlier, in practice PE ratios are most commonly measured as share price divided by earnings per share for the most recent prior fiscal year or for the most recent four quarters. This is a sensible approach because historical earnings are observable and unique; however, computation of PE ratios using historic earnings introduces the potential for bias. To recap, you should be aware of (at least) the following types of potential measurement errors in PE ratios:

1. *Growth.* Simple PE ratios do not explicitly consider firm-specific differences in long-term earnings growth. The price-earnings-growth ratio described in a later section provides a mechanism that addresses this potential bias by incorporating growth into price-earnings multiples.

2. *Transitory earnings.* Past earnings are historical and may not be indicative of expected future "permanent" earnings levels. Insofar as historic earnings contain transitory gains or losses (or other elements that are not expected to recur), temporarily high or low earnings can cause the PE ratio to vary considerably. You should normalize the earnings figure by removing the effects of nonrecurring or unusual gains or losses.

3. *Dividends.* A potential bias in PE ratios can arise because of differences in firms' dividend payouts. Dividends displace future earnings. A dividend paid in Year *t* reduces market price by the amount of the dividend, but the dividend is not subtracted from earnings. The dividend paid will cause future earnings to decline, all

---

[14]In this case, our forecasts of net income and comprehensive income for PepsiCo in Year $+1$ are the same, so the PE ratio using earnings per share is equal to that using comprehensive income per share.

else equal, because the firm has paid out a portion of its resources to shareholders. Therefore, price should decline by the present value of the firm's forgone amount of expected future return on assets distributed as dividends. Thus, for dividend-paying firms, dividends cause a mismatch between current period price and lagged earnings. To eliminate this mismatch, you can compute a PE ratio with growth for a dividend-paying firm as follows: $(P_t + D_t)/E_t = 1/(R_E - g)$.[15]

Benchmarking Relative Valuation: Using Market Multiples of Comparable Firms

In addition to using PE ratios as shortcut valuation metrics, you can also use PE ratios as potentially informative benchmarks to compare valuations across companies or to project the valuations of other companies. For example, you could compare **PepsiCo**'s PE ratio to the PE ratios of **Coca-Cola**, **Cadbury Schweppes**, or other beverage companies. You also might use PepsiCo's PE ratio to project valuations for these beverage companies. You also can value privately held firms (whose common shares are not publicly traded) or divisions of companies by using PE ratios (and MB) ratios of comparable firms that are publicly traded. Investment bankers use comparable companies' PE ratios, for example, to benchmark reasonable ranges of share prices for IPOs (initial public offerings) and merger and acquisition transactions.

PE ratios have the advantage of speed and efficiency, but they are not necessarily precise valuation estimates. Therefore, when using PE ratios, you must be careful to adjust them to match the fundamental characteristics of different companies. For example, PepsiCo's PE ratio should differ from Coca-Cola's insofar as the fundamental characteristics of profitability, growth, and risk differ across the two firms. Such differences might arise, for example, because PepsiCo derives a major portion of earnings from the snack food business and Coca-Cola does not. Coca-Cola derives more of its earnings from international beverage sales than does PepsiCo. These and other factors cause the profitability, growth, and risk of PepsiCo and Coca-Cola to differ and therefore cause their PE ratios to differ. In later sections, we describe PE ratio differences in more detail and provide descriptive data.

Selecting appropriate firms to use as comparable or peer firms in relative valuation analysis using PE ratios (or BM ratios) can be a challenging task. The theoretical models assist in this task by identifying the variables you should use in selecting comparable firms. Bhojraj and Lee (2002) demonstrate a technique for selecting comparable firms in multiples-based valuation by computing "warranted multiples" based on factors that drive cross-sectional differences in multiples, such as expected profitability, growth, and cost of capital.[16] Alford (1992) examined the accuracy of the PE valuation models using industry, risk, ROCE, and earnings growth as the bases for selecting comparable firms.[17] The results indicate that industry membership, particularly at a three-digit SIC code level, provides a useful basis for comparisons if firms in the same industry experience similar profitability, face similar risks, and grow at similar rates. Thus, in some circumstances, industry membership serves as an effective proxy for the variables in the PE

---

[15]While this adjustment to PE ratios for differences in dividend policies is technically correct, it is not commonly implemented in practice.

[16]Sanjeev Bhojraj and Charles M.C. Lee, "Who Is My Peer? A Valuation-Based Approach to the Selection of Comparable Firms," *Journal of Accounting Research*, Vol. 40, No. 2 (May 2002), pp. 407–439.

[17]Andrew W. Alford, "The Effect of the Set of Comparable Firms on the Accuracy of the Price-Earnings Valuation Method," *Journal of Accounting Research* (Spring 1992), pp. 94–108.

valuation model. However, as the data in Exhibit 14.4 reveal for MB ratios, and as the data described in the next section reveal for PE ratios, substantial differences commonly exist across firms in the same industry. The warranted-multiples approach of Bhojraj and Lee provides a mechanism to determine comparable companies within similar industries and across different industries.

Descriptive Data on PE Ratios

Exhibit 14.6 includes descriptive statistics on forward PE ratios (share price divided by one-year-ahead earnings before extraordinary items: P_t/E_{t+1}) for the same 47 industries described in Exhibit 14.4 (MB ratios) and Exhibit 11.3 (market betas) during 2003–2012. These data represent a broad cross-sectional sample of 28,732 firm-years drawn from the Compustat database, excluding all firm-years with negative earnings.[18] Exhibit 14.6 lists the industries in ascending order of the median PE ratios. Descriptive statistics on PE and other ratios across industries and years also appear in Appendix D.

Exhibit 14.6

Descriptive Statistics on Forward Price-Earnings Ratios (P_t/E_{t+1}), 2003–2012
Forty-Seven Industries Sorted by Median Forward PE Ratio

Industry	25th Percentile	Median	75th Percentile
Full Sample (N = 28,732 firm-years)*	**11.40**	**16.37**	**25.40**
Insurance	7.94	10.92	16.35
Steel Works	6.42	11.54	19.10
Petroleum and Natural Gas	8.57	12.45	20.73
Automobiles and Trucks	9.87	13.16	20.98
Tobacco Products	11.62	13.23	15.17
Coal	8.18	13.30	20.20
Defense	9.07	13.40	22.44
Fabricated Products	8.53	14.08	22.85
Shipping Containers	11.40	14.29	19.03
Non-Metallic and Industrial Metal Mining	8.96	14.38	25.97
Transportation	9.52	14.41	21.71
Apparel	10.96	14.53	21.46
Construction	8.24	14.59	23.21
Chemicals	10.07	14.60	20.92
Wholesale	9.92	14.69	19.76
Business Supplies	9.92	14.79	21.85
Candy & Soda	11.89	14.84	19.91
Utilities	12.46	14.95	19.27
Electrical Equipment	11.38	15.11	20.35
Aircraft	12.48	15.28	19.49

(Continued)

---

[18]It does not make sense to compute PE ratios on the basis of negative earnings. PE ratios assume that earnings are permanent; negative earnings cannot be permanent.

Exhibit 14.6 (Continued)			
Industry	**25th Percentile**	**Median**	**75th Percentile**
Banking	12.01	15.45	21.33
Retail	10.98	15.49	22.24
Rubber and Plastic Products	11.69	15.68	21.84
Shipbuilding, Railroad Equipment	12.85	15.82	26.87
Communication	11.00	15.88	25.24
Machinery	11.73	15.97	22.50
Healthcare	12.19	16.02	22.50
Construction Materials	11.62	16.37	24.19
Recreation	10.57	16.50	25.26
Consumer Goods	11.99	16.74	22.69
Textiles	9.16	17.01	24.13
Beer & Liquor	13.24	17.33	19.78
Food Products	12.31	17.34	25.80
Real Estate	9.51	17.64	41.76
Printing and Publishing	12.37	17.81	23.75
Restaurants, Hotels, Motels	13.35	18.04	27.80
Pharmaceutical Products	12.97	18.99	30.45
Agriculture	11.17	19.35	28.05
Measuring and Control Equipment	13.75	19.38	30.24
Trading	12.43	19.51	33.10
Electronic Equipment	12.32	19.57	32.24
Personal Services	13.68	20.11	30.55
Business Services	13.74	20.84	33.81
Computers	14.48	21.79	36.96
Entertainment	15.02	22.42	33.88
Medical Equipment	15.74	22.79	34.98
Precious Metals	14.15	25.53	48.10

*To compute these descriptive statistics on price-earnings ratios, we divided firm value (computed as year-end closing price times number of shares outstanding) by one-year-ahead net income before extraordinary items. We deleted firm-years with negative one-year-ahead net income.

These descriptive data indicate substantial differences in median PE ratios across industries during 2003–2012. The firms in the insurance, steel, petroleum and natural gas, and auto and truck industries experienced the lowest median PE ratios during the period, whereas firms in the precious metals, medical equipment, entertainment, computers, and business services industries experienced the highest median PE ratios. These data also depict wide variation in PE ratios across firms in each industry. For example, most of these 47 industries experienced wide differences between the 25th percentile and the 75th percentile PE ratio during 2003–2012. With only a few exceptions, the 75th percentile PE ratio in most industries was more than double the 25th percentile PE ratio.[19]

---

[19]You must be careful with PE ratios because they are sensitive to earnings that are near zero. Firms with earnings that are positive but temporarily very low will experience PE ratios that are temporarily very high.

What Factors Cause PE Ratios to Differ across Firms?

The same set of economic factors that can cause firms' MB ratios to differ also can cause firms' PE ratios to differ. The primary drivers of variation in PE ratios across firms are the fundamental drivers of value: risk, profitability, and growth. In addition to economic factors, differences across firms in accounting methods and accounting principles and differences in earnings across time also can drive differences in PE ratios. We describe the effects of each of these determinants of PE ratios in the following sections, saving growth for last because we will expand on the role of growth in determining PE ratios.

Risk and the Cost of Capital. As the previous discussion points out, firms with equivalent amounts of earnings but different levels of risk and therefore different costs of equity capital will experience different PE ratios (and different VE ratios). All else equal, a riskier firm will experience a lower market value and PE ratio.

Profitability. A firm with competitive advantages will be able to earn ROCE that exceeds R_E. To the extent that the firm can sustain these competitive advantages, the persistence over time of the degree to which ROCE exceeds R_E will increase, thereby increasing the PE ratio relative to similar firms that do not have sustainable competitive advantages. Thus, both the magnitude and persistence of the amount by which ROCE exceeds R_E will increase PE ratios across firms.

Accounting Differences. In addition to economic factors, firms' PE ratios may differ for a variety of accounting reasons, including the periodic nature of earnings measurement and differences in accounting methods and principles. Some firms select accounting methods that are conservative with respect to income recognition and asset measurement (for example, LIFO for inventories during periods of rising input prices and accelerated depreciation of fixed assets). Some firms invest in projects for which accounting principles are conservative. For example, firms may make substantial expenditures on intangible activities that must be expensed under conservative accounting principles, leading to economic assets that are off-balance-sheet, such as successful R&D, brand equity, or human capital. The effects of accounting methods and principles on reported earnings and PE ratios will likely change over the life of the firm. All else equal, conservative accounting will reduce reported earnings early in the life of the firm (for example, when accelerated depreciation charges are high or R&D is being expensed), thereby increasing the PE ratio. Ironically, later in the life of the firm, after the investments have been completely expensed, reported earnings will be higher and PE ratios will be lower.

Accounting Measures Earnings in Annual Periods. Firms' PE ratios will be significantly different when one-period earnings are unusually high or low and therefore not representative of persistent earnings. For example, if earnings include an unusual loss that will not persist, the firm's PE ratio will be unusually high. The transitory nature of a single period of accounting earnings can cause PE ratios to be more volatile than the long-run expectations of earnings warrant. In particular, if you use PE ratios based on trailing-twelve-months earnings that include gains or losses that are not expected to persist, the PE ratios will be artificially volatile. The impact of unusual and nonrecurring items on net income will have an inverse impact on PE ratios. That is, nonrecurring gains will temporarily drive net income up and PE ratios down, whereas nonrecurring losses will temporarily drive net income down but PE ratios up.

Continuing the simple example introduced earlier, assume that you expect the firm to generate earnings of $600 next period instead of $700 because the firm will recognize a nonrecurring $100 restructuring charge. Because this charge is nonrecurring (not a permanent change in earnings), the market price should fall to roughly $4,900 ($5,000 − $100) in the no-growth scenario and the PE ratio for that period will be 8.17 ($4,900/$600) instead of 7.14 ($5,000/$700). Conversely, if the current period's earnings exceed their expected permanent level, the PE ratio will be lower than normal.

You must assess whether the lower or higher level of earnings for the period (and therefore higher or lower PE ratio) represents a transitory event or a change to a new level of permanent earnings. If you expect that the decrease in earnings from $700 to $600 will be permanent, the market price (assuming no change in risk or growth) should decrease to $4,286 ($600/0.14). Thus, the PE ratio remains the same at 7.14 (1/0.14).

To illustrate the effects of accounting differences on PE ratios across firms, consider the historical data in the following table, which includes PE ratios (computed as year-end share price over trailing earnings per share) for **PepsiCo** and **Coca-Cola** for 2000 and 2001.

		PE Ratio	Price per Share	Earnings per Share
2000:	PepsiCo	31.9	$46.25	$1.45
	Coca-Cola	69.3	$60.94	$0.88
2001:	PepsiCo	34.2	$46.18	$1.35
	Coca-Cola	29.5	$47.15	$1.60

Considered at face value, the PE ratios for PepsiCo and Coca-Cola in 2000 indicate that the market valued Coca-Cola's earnings at a multiple of 69.3, more than twice PepsiCo's earnings multiple of 31.9, implying that Coca-Cola had lower cost of capital, higher growth, and/or greater profitability than PepsiCo. To the contrary, however, Coca-Cola recognized a large restructuring charge in income in 2000, driving EPS down to only $0.88, thereby temporarily inflating Coca-Cola's PE ratio. Thus, the big jump in Coca-Cola's PE ratio occurred largely because earnings temporarily declined that year and did not reflect the market's expectations for Coca-Cola's long-term earnings. In 2001, both firms reported earnings closer to normal levels and their PE ratios were quite similar.

Growth. All else equal, market values and PE ratios will be greater for firms that the market expects will generate greater earnings growth with future investments in abnormally profitable projects. In the next section, we discuss techniques that analysts use to incorporate earnings growth into PE ratios.

Incorporating Earnings Growth into PE Ratios

Analysts commonly modify the PE ratio to incorporate earnings growth. In this section, we describe and apply two related approaches to include expected future earnings growth in the computation of the PE ratio: (1) the perpetuity-with-growth approach and (2) the price-earnings-growth approach.

The Perpetuity-with-Growth Approach

The perpetuity-with-growth approach assumes that the firm's current period earnings will grow at a constant rate g. Therefore, the firm can be valued as the present value of a permanent stream of future earnings that will grow at constant rate g. In this case, we can express forward VE and forward PE ratios as perpetuity-with-growth models as follows:

$$V_0 = P_0 = \frac{E_0 \times (1+g)}{(R_E - g)} = \frac{E_1}{(R_E - g)}, \text{ so } \frac{V_0}{E_1} = \frac{P_0}{E_1} = \frac{1}{(R_E - g)}$$

To continue the illustration, assume that the firm generated \$666.67 in earnings in the current period. The market expects the firms' earnings to grow 5% next year and each year thereafter, so that Year +1 earnings will be \$700. The model suggests that the forward PE ratio incorporating growth should be 11.11 [1.0/(0.14 − 0.05)] and market value should be \$7,778 (\$700 × 11.11). The present value of the expected future growth in earnings adds \$2,778 (\$7,778 − \$5,000) to the value of the firm.

Note that the above expression describes forward VE and forward PE ratios because they use E_1 (one-year-ahead earnings). As mentioned earlier, PE ratios are commonly measured in practice using historical earnings. If current period (historical) earnings are expected to grow at the constant rate g and if the VE and PE ratios are expressed as multiples of current period (historical) earnings (E_0):

$$V_0 = P_0 = \frac{E_1}{(R_E - g)} = \frac{E_0 \times (1+g)}{(R_E - g)}, \text{ so } \frac{V_0}{E_0} = \frac{P_0}{E_0} = \frac{(1+g)}{(R_E - g)}$$

Continuing with the illustration, the VE and PE ratios based on current period earnings would then be 11.667 [(1 + g)/(R_E − g) = 1.05/(0.14 − 0.05)]. Note that using this VE and PE ratio will lead to market value for the firm of \$7,778 (\$666.67 × 11.667). This is the same market value as we determined using the forward VE and PE ratios.

PE ratios are particularly sensitive to the growth rate. If the growth rate in our illustration becomes 6% instead of 5%, the forward PE ratio becomes 12.50 [1.0/(0.14 − 0.06)] and the market value becomes \$8,750 (\$700 × 12.50). The sensitivity occurs because the model assumes that the firm will grow at the specified growth rate in perpetuity. Competition, new discoveries or technologies, or other factors eventually erode rapid growth rates in an industry. In using the constant growth version of the PE ratio, you should select a long-run equilibrium growth rate in earnings.

This expression for the VE and PE ratio underscores the joint importance of risk and growth in valuation. Given the relation between expected return (R_E) and risk, the VE and PE ratios should be inversely related to risk. Holding earnings and growth constant, higher risk levels should translate into lower PE and VE ratios, and vice versa. Risk-averse investors will not pay as much for a higher-risk security as for a lower-risk security with identical expected earnings and growth. In contrast, VE and PE should relate positively to growth. Holding earnings and R_E constant, firms with higher expected long-run growth rates in earnings should experience higher VE and PE ratios.

With respect to our valuation of **PepsiCo** at the end of 2012, we assumed that PepsiCo would experience a long-run growth rate of 3.0% beginning in Year +6 and beyond. If we were instead to assume that PepsiCo will experience a 3.0% constant growth rate in earnings beginning in Year +1, using the perpetuity-with-growth approach, we calculate the forward PE ratio for PepsiCo as follows:

$$\frac{P_0}{E_1} = \frac{1}{(R_E - g)} = \frac{1}{(0.075 - 0.030)} = 22.222$$

Clearly, incorporating growth makes a big difference in PepsiCo's forward PE ratio [as compared to the PE ratio of 13.33 (1/0.075) that ignores growth]. Assuming that

PepsiCo's earnings will grow at 3.0% per year beginning in Year +1, this forward PE-with-growth ratio would value PepsiCo shares at a multiple of 22.222 times the Year +1 earnings forecast. This PE ratio is only slightly greater than the theoretically correct VE ratio of 21.7.

The Price-Earnings-Growth Approach

An alternative ad hoc approach to incorporate growth into PE ratios has emerged from practice in recent years. Using this approach, we divide the PE ratio by the expected medium-term earnings growth rate (expressed as a percent). Some analysts use the expected earnings growth rate over a three- to five-year horizon. This approach produces the so-called PEG ratio seen with increasing frequency in practice. You can compute the PEG ratio as follows:

$$PEG = (Price\ per\ Share_0/Expected\ Earnings\ per\ Share_1)/(g \times 100)$$

Analysts and the financial press use the PEG ratio as a rule of thumb to assess share price relative to earnings and expected future earnings growth. Although there is little theoretical foundation for this rule of thumb (which tends to vary among analysts), proponents of PEG ratios generally assert that firms should have PEG ratios roughly equal to 1.0, indicating that market price fairly reflects expected earnings and growth.

This rule of thumb implies the following value model for a VEG ratio under the following set of assumptions:

- The firm's earnings behave as a perpetuity with growth.
- The firm's earnings generate an ROCE equivalent to R_E.
- All of the firm's growth arises from reinvesting all of its earnings.
- All of the reinvested earnings generate an ROCE equivalent to R_E, so the firm's earnings growth rate is equivalent to R_E.

Under this set of restrictive assumptions, the VEG ratio follows. [For notation, assume that $(g \times 100) = G = R_E$.]

$$
\begin{aligned}
VEG_0 &= (Value\ per\ Share_0/Expected\ Earnings\ per\ Share_1)/(g \times 100) \\
&= V_0/E_1/G \\
&= 1/R_E/R_E \\
&= 1
\end{aligned}
$$

Alternatively, note that the VEG ratio is mathematically equivalent to a simple valuation model that estimates share value as next year's earnings per share multiplied by the growth rate times 100 (that is, $V_0 = E_1 \times G$).

Using the rule of thumb that VEG ratios should equal 1, proponents assert that market prices for firms with PEG ratios below 1 are underpriced given earnings and expected earnings growth and that market prices for firms with PEG ratios above 1 are overpriced relative to earnings and expected earnings growth. Proponents of PEG ratios argue that this heuristic provides a convenient means to rank stocks, taking into account one-year-ahead earnings and expected earnings growth.[20]

In Chapter 10, we assumed that **PepsiCo** would experience earnings growth of roughly 2.7% per year through Year +5. Using this growth rate assumption and our

---

[20]Mark Bradshaw (2002) demonstrates that sell-side analysts' target price estimates are highly correlated with valuation estimates based on the PEG model in "The Use of Target Prices to Justify Sell-Side Analysts' Stock Recommendations," *Accounting Horizons*, Vol. 16, No. 1 (March 2002), pp. 27–41.

projected earnings per share of $3.95 for Year +1, we compute PepsiCo's PEG ratio at the end of 2012 as follows:

$$PEG_{2012} = (Price\ per\ Share_{2012}/Expected\ Earnings\ per\ Share_{+1})/(g \times 100)$$
$$= (\$68.43/\$3.95)/(0.027 \times 100)$$
$$= 17.32/2.7$$
$$= 6.42$$

Thus, PepsiCo shares traded at the end of 2012 at a PEG ratio of 6.42. Based on the PEG heuristic, PepsiCo's PEG ratio suggests that the market price for PepsiCo shares reflect substantial *overpricing* of PepsiCo's earnings and expected earnings growth. However, the PEG ratio heuristic does not take into account differences in risk and costs of equity capital across firms. For example, PepsiCo's PEG ratio seems high because it does not account for the fact that PepsiCo's expected future ROCE is significantly greater than PepsiCo's R_E because of PepsiCo's substantial off-balance-sheet brand equity. In addition, this heuristic does not take into account the fact that PepsiCo is likely to achieve this future earnings growth with relatively low risk. (PepsiCo's beta is 0.75.) The PEG ratio deserves considerable attention from researchers and practitioners so that its uses and limitations can be tested and understood.

Empirical Properties of PE Ratios

The theoretical models indicate that the PE ratio is related to R_E, the cost of equity capital, and g, the growth rate in future earnings. Several empirical studies have examined the relations among PE ratios, risk (measured using market beta), and growth (measured using realized prior growth rates or analysts' forecasts of future growth). These studies have found that approximately 50–70% of the variability in PE ratios across firms relates to risk and growth.[21]

PE Ratios as Predictors of Future Earnings Growth

Stephen Penman, a leading scholar in the relations among earnings, book values, and market values, studied the relation between PE ratios and changes in earnings per share. Penman collected data from the CRSP and Compustat databases on roughly 2,574 firms during 1968–1985.[22] For each year, Penman grouped firms into 20 portfolios based on the level of their PE ratios, computed using lagged earnings per share. He then computed the percentage change in earnings per share for the formation year and for each of the nine subsequent years. Penman then aggregated the results across years. The table below presents a subset of the aggregate results.

PE Portfolio	Median Percentage Change in Earnings per Share in:				
	Year 0	**Year +1**	**Year +2**	**Year +3**	**Year +4**
High	3.9%	52.2%	17.5%	17.8%	15.0%
Medium	14.0%	11.8%	11.6%	13.7%	15.8%
Low	18.4%	4.8%	10.2%	12.3%	13.1%

[21]See William Beaver and Dale Morse, "What Determines Price-Earnings Ratios?," *Financial Analysts Journal* (July–August 1978), pp. 65–76; Paul Zarowin, "What Determines Earnings-Price Ratios: Revisited," *Journal of Accounting, Auditing and Finance* (Summer 1990), pp. 439–454.

[22]Stephen H. Penman, "The Articulation of Price-Earnings Ratios and Market-to-Book Ratios and the Evaluation of Growth," *Journal of Accounting Research*, Vol. 34, No. 2 (Autumn 1996), pp. 235–259.

The results for the portfolio formation year are consistent with transitory components in earnings in Year 0. Firms with high PE ratios experienced, on average, low percentage changes in earnings (and many experienced earnings declines) during Year 0 relative to the preceding year. Firms with low PE ratios experienced high percentage changes in earnings during Year 0. The results for Year +1 suggest a counterbalancing effect of the earnings change in the prior year. A low percentage increase (or decrease) in earnings is followed by a high percentage earnings increase for the high PE portfolios, and vice versa for the low PE portfolios.

The results for subsequent years reflect the tendency toward mean reversion in percentage earnings changes to a level in the mid-teens. This result is consistent with the data presented in Exhibit 14.5 for ROCE, where Victor Bernard observed a mean reversion in ROCE toward the mid-teens during his sample period. The mean reversion suggests systematic directional changes in earnings growth over time (that is, serial autocorrelation), but the reversion takes several years to occur.

Articulation of MB and PE Ratios. In the same research study, Penman also ranked and grouped the firms into three MB ratio portfolios, classifying MB ratios below 0.90 as low, MB ratios above 1.10 as high, and MB ratios between 0.90 and 1.10 as normal. He then utilized the residual income valuation model and empirical data to examine the articulation between firms' PE and MB ratios.[23] Exhibit 14.7 presents a matrix summarizing a portion of the results from Penman's study. The matrix presents residual

Exhibit 14.7

The Articulation of Market-to-Book (MB) and Price-Earnings (PE) Ratios

PE Ratio Portfolios	MB Ratio Portfolios		
	High	**Normal**	**Low**
High (Portfolios 15–20)	CRI < FRI > 0 CRI: −0.50 to 0.07 FRI_1: −0.07 to 0.08 FRI_6: 0.01 to 0.11	CRI < FRI = 0 CRI: −0.36 to −0.04 FRI_1: −0.13 to −0.03 FRI_6: −0.06 to 0.07	CRI < FRI < 0 CRI: −0.24 to −0.06 FRI_1: −0.13 to −0.06 FRI_6: −0.01 to 0.02
Normal (Portfolios 7–14)	CRI = FRI > 0 CRI: 0.07 to 0.10 FRI_1: 0.08 to 0.10 FRI_6: 0.11 to 0.14	CRI = FRI = 0 CRI: −0.02 to 0.04 FRI_1: −0.02 to 0.04 FRI_6: 0.01 to 0.06	CRI = FRI < 0 CRI: −0.05 to 0.00 FRI_1: −0.04 to 0.00 FRI_6: −0.02 to 0.03
Low (Portfolios 1–6)	CRI > FRI > 0 CRI: 0.12 to 0.41 FRI_1: 0.12 to 0.25 FRI_6: 0.11 to 0.24	CRI > FRI = 0 CRI: 0.05 to 0.22 FRI_1: 0.05 to 0.15 FRI_6: 0.07 to 0.12	CRI > FRI < 0 CRI: 0.00 to 0.06 FRI_1: −0.01 to 0.04 FRI_6: 0.03 to 0.05

Note: CRI denotes current period residual income and FRI denotes future residual income. Source: We obtained these data from Table 4 in Stephen H. Penman, "The Articulation of Price-Earnings Ratios and Market-to-Book Ratios and the Evaluation of Growth," *Journal of Accounting Research,* Vol. 34, No. 2 (Autumn 1996), pp. 235–259.

---

[23]Stephen H. Penman, *op. cit.*

income scaled by book value of equity (essentially residual ROCE) figures after assuming a 10.0% cost of capital for all firm-years. We denote current period residual income as CRI and future residual income one year ahead and six years ahead as FRI_1 and FRI_6, respectively.

Penman's research results generally support his predictions and shed light on the residual income conditions that cause MB ratios and PE ratios to covary. His results show that future residual income is substantially *higher* for *high* MB firms than for *low* MB firms. Examining future residual income across columns of the matrix, Penman's results show that MB ratios are positive predictors of future residual income, consistent with the results from Bernard in Exhibit 14.5. Examining the results across rows, high PE ratio firms tend to have current period residual income that is much *lower than* future residual income, suggesting that PE ratios for these firms are temporarily high because residual income is temporarily low. In contrast, firms with low PE ratios tend to have current residual income amounts that are *greater than* the future residual income amounts, suggesting that these firms are experiencing low PE ratios because residual income is temporarily high. Penman's results provide intuition about when MB ratios should be high, low, or normal and, concurrently, when PE ratios should be high, low, or normal.

- Summarizing, the VE and PE ratios are determined by:
  - risk.
  - growth.
  - differences between current and expected future earnings.
  - alternative accounting methods and principles.
- You must assess each of these elements when estimating VE ratios, particularly when comparing VE ratios to PE ratios to determine whether shares appear to be under- or overpriced and when projecting VE ratios to value other firms.
- You should be aware of the following considerations when using VE and PE ratios:
  - The VE ratio is particularly sensitive to the cost of equity capital and to the earnings growth rate because it assumes that a firm can grow earnings at that rate indefinitely. You should select a sustainable long-term growth rate when computing the VE model.
  - The VE model does not work when the growth rate in earnings exceeds the cost of equity capital. Firms are not likely to grow earnings forever at rates exceeding the cost of equity capital. Competition will eventually force growth rates to diminish.
  - The VE model should not be used when the cost of equity capital and the growth rate in earnings are similar in amount. The denominator of the VE model ($R_E - g$) approaches zero, and the VE ratio becomes exceedingly large.
  - The VE and PE models should not be used when earnings are negative because the VE and PE models assume that earnings are permanent, and negative earnings cannot persist in perpetuity.
  - When you compare a VE ratio to a PE ratio for a particular firm, be sure that the earnings numbers in the denominators are internally consistent with each other.
  - When comparing PE ratios across firms, you should consider the impact of the firms' use of different accounting methods and principles, and be sure that the earnings numbers in the denominators are internally consistent across firms.

Price Differentials

LO 14-4

Estimate the price differential, which is the difference between market price and "risk-neutral value."

In light of the critical role of risk and expected returns in valuation and in light of the uncertainty surrounding how to measure risk and expected returns, you need a variety of tools to assess the impact of risk on share prices and firm values. One such tool involves computing *price differentials*.[24] Price differentials can be used to address questions such as: What is the impact of risk on share price? Is the share price impact too large or too small relative to risk? We rely on an adaptation of the residual income model to address these questions by computing the price differential—the amount the market has discounted share price for risk.

As described in detail in the previous chapter, the residual income model determines the present value of common shareholders' equity as follows:

$$V_0 = BV_0 + \sum_{t=1}^{\infty} \frac{CI_t - (R_E \times BV_{t-1})}{(1 + R_E)^t}$$

To implement this model, you must estimate the cost of equity capital (R_E) and then use it to compute residual income $[CI_t - (R_E \times BV_{t-1})]$ and discount residual income to present value at $1/(1 + R_E)^t$. But state-of-the-art in financial economics does not provide a clear understanding of how R_E should be determined. Substantial controversy surrounds expected returns models such as the CAPM. What is the appropriate measure for market beta? In addition to market betas, what other risk factors belong in the expected returns model, such as firm size, MB ratios, or some other set of risk factors? Assuming that one can identify the appropriate risk factors that are priced in the market, what are the appropriate risk premia to use to determine expected returns for each of these factors? At an even more fundamental level, questions arise about whether risk and expected returns should be measured based on covariation between a firm's returns and a market index of returns. These questions arise in part because market-based models such as the CAPM are essentially circular—should stock returns be used to estimate risk to determine expected returns to evaluate stock prices? Or should risk and expected returns be based on covariation between a firm's returns and its fundamental risk characteristics (such as volatility in earnings)? Or should risk and expected returns derive from the covariation between a firm's stock returns and an economy-wide measure of consumption, on the theory that investors' risk aversion is driven by the need to diversify volatility in expected future consumption?

The procedure for computing the price differential offers an alternative approach for evaluating the market's pricing of risk. To begin, substitute the prevailing risk-free rate of interest (denoted R_F; for example, the yield on ten-year U.S. Treasury securities) for the cost of equity capital (R_E) and use the residual income model to estimate risk-neutral value (denoted as RNV_0), which is an estimate of the hypothetical value of the firm in a risk-neutral market:

$$RNV_0 = BV_0 + \sum_{t=1}^{\infty} \frac{CI_t - (R_F \times BV_{t-1})}{(1 + R_F)^t}$$

Risk-neutral value represents the value of the firm, based on book value of equity and forecasts of expected future comprehensive income, in the absence of discounting for risk. Dividing risk-neutral value by the number of shares outstanding gives risk-neutral value per share, which represents the hypothetical value at which shares would trade in

---

[24]This section relies heavily on Stephen Baginski and James Wahlen, "Residual Income Risk, Intrinsic Values, and Share Prices," *The Accounting Review,* Vol. 78, No. 1 (January 2003), pp. 327–351.

a risk-neutral market. Market price per share of common equity reflects the risk-discounted value in the real world, which is risk-averse. Therefore, market price per share can be subtracted from risk-neutral value per share to determine the total amount by which share price has been discounted for risk. We refer to this difference as the *price differential* (denoted as PDIFF), computed as follows:

$$PDIFF_0 = RNV \text{ per Share}_0 - \text{Price per Share}_0$$

You can also divide $PDIFF_0$ by RNV_0 to determine the *PDIFF percentage*, as follows:

$$PDIFF\%_0 = (RNV \text{ per Share}_0 - \text{Price per Share}_0)/RNV \text{ per Share}_0$$

You can evaluate the PDIFF% to assess whether the market discount for risk is sufficient to compensate the investor to hold the firm's shares and bear risk. You can also compare PDIFF% across time for a given firm or across firms to evaluate the extent to which the market is discounting share prices for risk. If you assesses that *PDIFF%* is large relative to the risk of the firm, the firm's shares may be overdiscounted for risk (underpriced). On the other hand, if you assesses that *PDIFF%* is small relative to firm risk, perhaps the firm's shares are underdiscounted for risk (over-priced). In the next section, we illustrate how to compute the PDIFF% for PepsiCo. In the following section that discusses reverse engineering, we describe and apply more formal methods to gauge the relative magnitude of PDIFF%.

Computing PDIFF for PepsiCo

To compute the price differential of **PepsiCo** as of the end of 2012, we rely on the forecast assumptions developed in Chapter 10 and the residual income model developed in the previous chapter. However, instead of using a 7.5% cost of equity capital for PepsiCo for purposes of computing residual income and discounting it to present value, we use the risk-free interest rate at the time of the valuation. At the end of 2012, U.S. Treasury bills with ten years to maturity yielded roughly 3.0%. Exhibit 14.8 reports the present

Exhibit 14.8

Price Differential of PepsiCo: Present Value of Residual Income in Year +1 through Year +5 after Discounting at the Risk-Free Rate of Interest (3.0%) (dollar amounts in millions; allow for rounding)

	Year +1	Year +2	Year +3	Year +4	Year +5
Lagged book value of common shareholders' equity (at $t-1$)	$ 22,417.0	$ 22,020.3	$ 22,417.9	$ 22,749.5	$ 23,259.5
Comprehensive income available for common shareholders	$ 6,094.7	$ 6,376.6	$ 6,598.3	$ 6,972.2	$ 7,064.2
Less: Required earnings	− 672.5	− 660.6	− 672.5	− 682.5	− 697.8
Residual income	$ 5,422.2	$ 5,716.0	$ 5,925.8	$ 6,289.7	$ 6,366.4
Present value factors	× 0.9709	× 0.9426	× 0.9151	× 0.8885	× 0.8626
Present value of residual income	$ 5,264.3	$ 5,387.9	$ 5,422.9	$ 5,588.3	$ 5,491.7
Sum of present value of residual income, Year +1 through Year +5	$ 27,155.1				

value of PepsiCo's expected future residual income in Year +1 through Year +5 amounts to $27,155.1 million, computed using the 3.0% risk-free discount rate.

To compute continuing value, we use the now-familiar perpetuity-with-growth model $[1/(R_F - g)]$ assuming that long-term growth for PepsiCo will be 1.0% and that the risk-free discount rate is 3.0%. [Note: Simply for purposes of demonstrating PDIFF computations, we assume long-run growth will be only 1%. In prior chapters, we assumed PepsiCo's long-run growth would be 3%. However, when the long-run growth rate is equal to (or greater than) the discount rate (in this case $R_F = 3\%$), then $(R_F - g)$ is zero or negative, and the perpetuity with growth computation produces nonsensical results.]

The present value of continuing value under this approach is $277,559.7 million. After adding book value of common equity at the end of 2012, adjusting for midyear discounting, and dividing by the number of shares outstanding, we estimate that PepsiCo shares have a risk-neutral value of $215.05. Subtracting the market price on December 31, 2012 of $68.43 per share, we estimate the PDIFF to be $146.62 per share. These computations suggest that PepsiCo shares have been discounted by a risk-averse market by roughly $146.62 per share below the value at which they would trade in a hypothetical risk-neutral market, conditional on the forecast assumptions made in Chapter 10. The PDIFF% is 68.2% [computed as PDIFF / RNV = $146.62/$215.05]. These computations indicate that, at a price of $68.43, PepsiCo's shares have been discounted 68.2% relative to the risk-neutral value. Equivalently, at $68.43 at the end of 2012, PepsiCo's shares traded at a price equal to roughly 32% of risk-neutral value ($68.43/$215.05). Exhibit 14.9 presents these computations.

Exhibit 14.9

Price Differential of PepsiCo
(dollar amounts in millions, except per-share amounts; allow for rounding)

Valuation Steps	Computations	Amounts
Sum of present value residual income in Year +1 through Year +5	Discounted at the risk-free rate of interest of 3.0%. (See Exhibit 14.8.)	$ 27,155.1
Add continuing value in present value	Year +6 residual income assumed to grow at 1.0% in perpetuity; discounted at 3.0%. (Computations not shown.)	+ 277,559.7
Total present value residual income		$304,714.9
Add: Beginning book value of equity	From 2012 balance sheet	+ 22,417.0
		$327,131.9
Adjust to midyear discounting	Multiply by $1 + (R_F/2)$	× 1.015
Present value of common equity		$332,038.8
Shares outstanding		÷ 1,544.0
Estimated risk-neutral value per share		$ 215.05
Current price per share		− 68.43
Price differential		$ 146.62
Price differential as a percent of risk-neutral value		68.2%

In Chapters 11–13, we estimated that PepsiCo shares may have been underpriced at the end of 2012 by roughly 25%, conditional on our forecast assumptions and valuation models. The price differential computation indicates that the market imposed a substantial discount to PepsiCo's expected future residual income relative to the risk of PepsiCo. To more formally evaluate the relative magnitude of the price differential, we turn to the method of reverse engineering market values.

LO 14-5

Reverse engineer a firm's stock price to determine the implied expected return or the implied expected long-run growth rate.

Reverse Engineering

Reverse engineering is an analytical approach through which you can deduce and evaluate the assumptions implicit in a stock price. Throughout this text, we have emphasized the process of using a firm's fundamental characteristics to estimate firm value independent of the prevailing market value. The valuation process can be characterized essentially as a puzzle with four pieces, or as an equation with four variables, as follows:

1. Expected future profitability
2. Expected long-run future growth
3. Expected risk-adjusted discount rates
4. Firm value

Thus far, we have developed forecasts and expectations about three of the variables—expected future profitability, long-run growth, and risk-adjusted discount rates—and have used them to solve for the fourth variable: firm value. In fact, we can make assumptions about any three of the four variables and then solve for the fourth variable.

For example, we can treat the market value of common equity as one of the "known" variables by assuming that V_0 equals market price. (That is, we can assume that the market is correct; hence, price equals value.) We can then develop forecast assumptions for any two other variables and solve for the missing fourth variable. We refer to this process as *reverse engineering* stock prices because it takes the valuation process and reverses it. It is a process in which you assume that the market is efficient and share value equals market price, and then solve for the assumptions the market appears to be making to price the firm's shares. For example, if we assume that a firm's share value equals the market's share price and use the consensus analysts' forecasts for future earnings and growth as reasonable proxies for the market's expectations, we can solve for the implied expected risk-adjusted rate of return on common equity that is consistent with the observed market price. This is essentially equivalent to solving for the internal rate of return on the stock.

As another example, suppose we assume that share value equals market price, that the market's risk-adjusted expected return on a stock can be determined by an expected returns model such as the CAPM, and that analysts' consensus earnings forecasts through Year +5 are reasonable proxies for the market's earnings expectations. We can then solve for the long-run growth rate implicit in the firm's stock price, conditional on the other assumptions.

The process of reverse engineering stock prices allows you to infer a set of assumptions that the market appears to have impounded into a share price. You can then assess whether the assumptions the market appears to be making are realistic, optimistic, or pessimistic. If you determine that the market's assumptions seem optimistic, it suggests that the market has overpriced the stock (or perhaps you will question whether you are more pessimistic than the market). Alternatively, if you determine that the market's assumptions seem pessimistic, it suggests that the market has underpriced the stock (or you may be less pessimistic than the market).

Reverse Engineering PepsiCo's Stock Price

To illustrate the process of reverse engineering, we apply the approach to **PepsiCo** using the December 31, 2012 market price of $68.43 per share. To reverse engineer PepsiCo's share price, we again rely on the residual income model in the previous chapter and the forecasts developed in Chapter 10.

Assume that we want to solve for the expected rate of return (that is, the risk-adjusted discount rate) implied by PepsiCo's 2012 share price of $68.43. Also assume that our forecasts of earnings and book value of common equity for PepsiCo through Year +5 and our forecast of 3.0% long-run growth are realistic proxies for the market's expectations. Armed with share price, earnings and growth forecasts through Year +5, and a constant long-run growth assumption beyond Year +5, we can use the residual income value model to solve for the discount rate that reduces future earnings and book value to a present value equal to the $68.43 market price per share.

Procedurally, one way to solve for the implied expected return on PepsiCo stock, conditional on the price, earnings, and growth assumptions, is to estimate the value of common equity using the risk-free discount rate, as in the price differential illustration above. The risk-neutral value will likely far exceed the market price because the future residual income has not been discounted for risk. In applying the price differential model to PepsiCo in the previous section, we determined that PepsiCo's risk-neutral value was $215.05 per share. To reverse engineer the share price, steadily increase the discount rate as necessary until the residual income model value exactly agrees with the market price of $68.43 per share. Following this approach, the implied expected rate of return on PepsiCo stock is 8.696%. At this discount rate, conditional on our residual income and growth assumptions, the present value of PepsiCo shares is $68.43 per share, exactly equal to market price. Recall that we assumed that PepsiCo common equity had a required rate of return of 7.5% based on the CAPM. However, this reverse engineering approach indicates that if we buy a share of PepsiCo stock at the market price of $68.43, *it will yield an 8.696% rate of return*, conditional on our other assumptions. The Valuation spreadsheet in FSAP allows you to make these iterative computations easily by varying the discount rate for equity capital.

To demonstrate another example, we can reverse engineer PepsiCo's 2012 year-end stock price to solve for the implicit long-run growth assumption. To illustrate, we again take the market price of $68.43 per share as given and our earnings and book value forecasts through Year +5 as reasonable proxies for the market's expectations. We return to our original assumption that the CAPM the risk-adjusted discount rate for PepsiCo stock is 7.5%. With this, we have established three assumptions—value, earnings through Year +5, and the risk-adjusted discount rate—and can solve for the missing piece of the puzzle: long-run implied growth. We begin with the long-run growth assumption set at zero. We compute our first estimate of firm value using a zero growth assumption and compare that estimate to market price. The first estimate is normally substantially lower than market price because market price probably includes the present value of the market's expectations for long-run growth. This turns out to be the case for PepsiCo, as the initial value estimate assuming zero growth is only $61.54 per share—well below current share price. To determine the implied long-run growth rate impounded in price, we steadily increase the long-run growth parameter assumption as necessary until the present value from the residual income model equals market price.[25] In the case of PepsiCo at the end of 2012, market price of $68.43 reflects *long-run growth* of 1.192%, which is significantly lower than our expectation of 3.0% long-run growth. That is, conditional on our assumptions for residual income through Year +5, on PepsiCo's cost of equity capital at 7.5%, and on the market's expectations for long-run growth at 1.192% per year, the present value of PepsiCo shares exactly agrees with the market price of $68.43. Given that PepsiCo will not likely experience such low long-run growth, it further confirms our assessment that PepsiCo shares are underpriced at the end of 2012. Again, note that the Valuation spreadsheet in FSAP is a useful tool that allows you to establish assumptions for earnings and cost of capital and then vary the long-run growth assumption for reverse engineering.

LO 14-6

Explain the notion of capital market efficiency in valuation and the academic evidence on the degree to which the capital markets efficiently impound earnings information into share prices.

The Relevance of Academic Research for the Work of the Security Analyst

Throughout this text, we have referred to relevant examples of empirical accounting research, including the classic study by Ball and Brown (1968) that helped set the stage for future research by being the first to show that changes in earnings correlate with unexpected changes in stock prices.[26] As demonstrated in Exhibit 1.21 in Chapter 1, the Nichols and Wahlen (2004) replication of the Ball and Brown results indicate that during their sample period 1988–2002, merely the difference in the sign of the change in annual earnings (whether positive or negative) was associated with nearly a 35% difference in annual market-adjusted stock returns. The average sample firm that reported an earnings increase in a given year experienced stock returns that, on average, "beat" the market average returns by 19%, while the average sample firm that reported an earnings decrease in a given year experienced stock returns that, on average, fell 16% short of the market average returns. The results suggest earnings numbers are very informative for the capital markets.

The results of academic research in accounting have provided many insights into multifaceted dimensions of the relations between accounting numbers and a variety of capital market variables such as stock prices, stock price reactions around earnings announcements, stock returns cumulated over long periods of time, trading volume, analysts' and managements' earnings forecasts, equity costs of capital, implied market risk premia, market betas and other risk factors, bankruptcy, earnings management, and fraud. This concluding section summarizes the role of market efficiency and describes some striking empirical evidence on the relative degree of market efficiency with respect to earnings. In addition, this section describes an empirical study that used the residual income valuation models demonstrated in this chapter and in Chapter 13 to pick stocks and form portfolios. We consider the results to date to be very encouraging for analysts and investors.

What Does "Capital Market Efficiency" Really Mean?

Academics generally perceive market efficiency from the perspective of the big picture, with a view of large samples and market movements in general. In contrast, analysts and investors view their task as the constant pursuit of market inefficiencies—temporarily mispriced

---

[25]Note that you must vary the long-run growth parameter assumption in two places: (1) projecting the terminal year financial statement amounts and (2) calculating the valuation equations.

[26]Ray Ball and Philip Brown, "An Empirical Evaluation of Accounting Income Numbers," *Journal of Accounting Research* (Autumn 1968), pp. 159–178.

securities. Investors see market efficiency from the front lines, experiencing daily swings in market prices that are sometimes hard to explain in the context of an efficient market. Thus, it is not surprising that the perspective on the degree of market efficiency (or the lack thereof) differs substantially between academics and professional investors. This section seeks to reach a common understanding, and the next section provides some striking evidence on the degree of market efficiency with respect to earnings and accounting information.

Capital markets may be described as "efficient" with regard to accounting information based on the degree to which market prices react *completely* and *quickly* to available accounting information. Notice that efficiency should be described as a matter of *degree*, not as an absolute. The issue is not whether the capital markets are or are not efficient. Rather, the issue is the degree to which the capital markets impound in prices all the available value-relevant information.

The term *completely* in this description implies the degree to which share prices reflect the value-relevant implications of all available accounting information without systematic bias. A capital market that is relatively efficient will impound in stock prices the economic implications of all value-relevant financial statement information, even including accounting items that may be disclosed in the notes.

The term *quickly* in this description suggests that market participants cannot consistently earn abnormal returns using accounting information for a long period of time after the information has been made public. If capital markets exhibit a high degree of efficiency, market prices should react quickly (within a matter of days) to capture any value-relevant signals in the accounting information or other sources of information about the firm.

The degree of efficiency, or the completeness and speed of price reactions, in an information-efficient capital market depends on analysts and financial statement analysis. Analysts and investors study accounting information to assess appropriate values for stocks and to take positions in under- or overpriced securities, thereby driving stock market prices to efficient levels. Share prices move to new efficient levels based on the speed with which they can forecast and anticipate accounting information before it is released and on the speed with which they can analyze and react quickly to surprises in accounting information when it is released.

Also consider what a high degree of market efficiency *does not imply*. A capital market with a high degree of information efficiency does not necessarily price all stocks correctly every day. As a practical matter, relatively efficient markets experience valuation errors at the level of the individual firm, but these random inefficiencies cancel out at an aggregated market level and do not persist for long periods of time.[27] Analysts and investors are driving forces involved in identifying and correcting security mispricings. A capital market with a high degree of information efficiency does not necessarily have perfect foresight—surprises happen. Firms frequently surprise the market by announcing earnings that are higher or lower than the market's expectations. Again, analysts and investors drive market prices to react quickly and completely to new information.

Striking Evidence on the Degree of Market Efficiency and Inefficiency with Respect to Earnings

Two studies by Victor Bernard and Jacob Thomas (1989 and 1990) provide the most striking evidence to date on the degree of market efficiency and inefficiency with respect

---

[27]For a discussion of these issues, see Ray Ball, "The Earnings-Price Anomaly," *Journal of Accounting and Economics* (1992), pp. 319–345.

to accounting earnings.[28] The Bernard and Thomas results during the post-earnings-announcement period suggest that the market's reaction to quarterly earnings news is highly, but not completely, efficient. Nichols and Wahlen (2004) used data from 1988–2002 to replicate the seminal results in Bernard and Thomas (which were based on data from 1974–1986). Nichols and Wahlen collected a sample of 90,470 quarterly earnings announcements for firms on the CRSP and Compustat databases. They ranked all sample firms each quarter into ten portfolios on the basis of each firm's unexpected earnings. (Unexpected earnings (denoted as UE) equals actual earnings per share minus analysts' consensus forecast of earnings per share, scaled by price per share as of 60 trading days prior to the earnings announcement for cross-sectional comparability.) They studied the average abnormal (market-adjusted) stock returns to each portfolio over the 60 trading days leading up to the quarterly earnings announcement and over the 60 trading days following the announcement. Exhibit 14.10 depicts a portion of the Nichols and Wahlen results, which mirror the Bernard and Thomas results.

The results in Exhibit 14.10 during the pre-announcement period indicate that the market is highly efficient in anticipating and reacting to quarterly earnings surprises. Firms with quarterly earnings surprises in the "good news" portfolios—UE portfolios 6 through 10—experience positive cumulative abnormal returns during the 60 days prior to and including the release of earnings. Firms with quarterly earnings surprises in the "bad news" portfolios—UE portfolios 1 through 4—experience negative cumulative abnormal returns during the 60 days prior to and including the release of earnings. The average difference in cumulative abnormal returns between UE portfolio 10 (roughly +6.7%) and UE portfolio 1 (roughly −6.8%) was 13.5% *per quarter*. These results suggest that the market anticipates and reacts quickly to quarterly earnings information.

The results in Exhibit 14.10 during the post-announcement period suggest that the market's reaction to quarterly earnings news is highly, but not completely, efficient. In the post-announcement period, Nichols and Wahlen measured the cumulative abnormal returns to the exact same portfolios over the 60 trading days *after* the earnings announcements. If the market's reactions to quarterly earnings were, on average, quick and complete, these portfolios should exhibit no systematic abnormal returns in the post-announcement period. Upon the announcement of earnings, market prices should adjust efficiently within a few days of the announcement. Post-announcement abnormal returns should arise only from new information that arrives during those 60 days, and the post-announcement abnormal returns should not be associated with the prior quarter's earnings news.

The results for the post-announcement period clearly indicate significant cumulative abnormal returns for the firms in UE portfolio 10 (best news) and UE portfolio 1 (worst news). Mean cumulative abnormal returns amount to roughly +3.0% and −2.2% for the best and worst unexpected earnings news portfolios, respectively. In a follow-up study, Bernard and Thomas (1990) show that, in part, the market seems to underreact to the persistence in current period earnings for future period earnings, failing to fully anticipate the momentum in quarterly earnings changes.

Taken together, the Bernard and Thomas studies reveal that the market is highly, but not completely, efficient with respect to quarterly earnings. The results from the Nichols and Wahlen study using current data suggest that the Bernard and Thomas

---

[28]Victor Bernard and Jacob Thomas, "Post-Earnings Announcement Drift: Delayed Price Response or Risk Premium?" *Journal of Accounting Research* Vol. 27, (Supplement, 1989), pp. 1–36; and "Evidence that Stock Prices Do Not Fully Reflect the Implications of Current Earnings for Future Earnings," *Journal of Accounting and Economics* Vol. 13, No. 4 (1990), pp. 305–340.

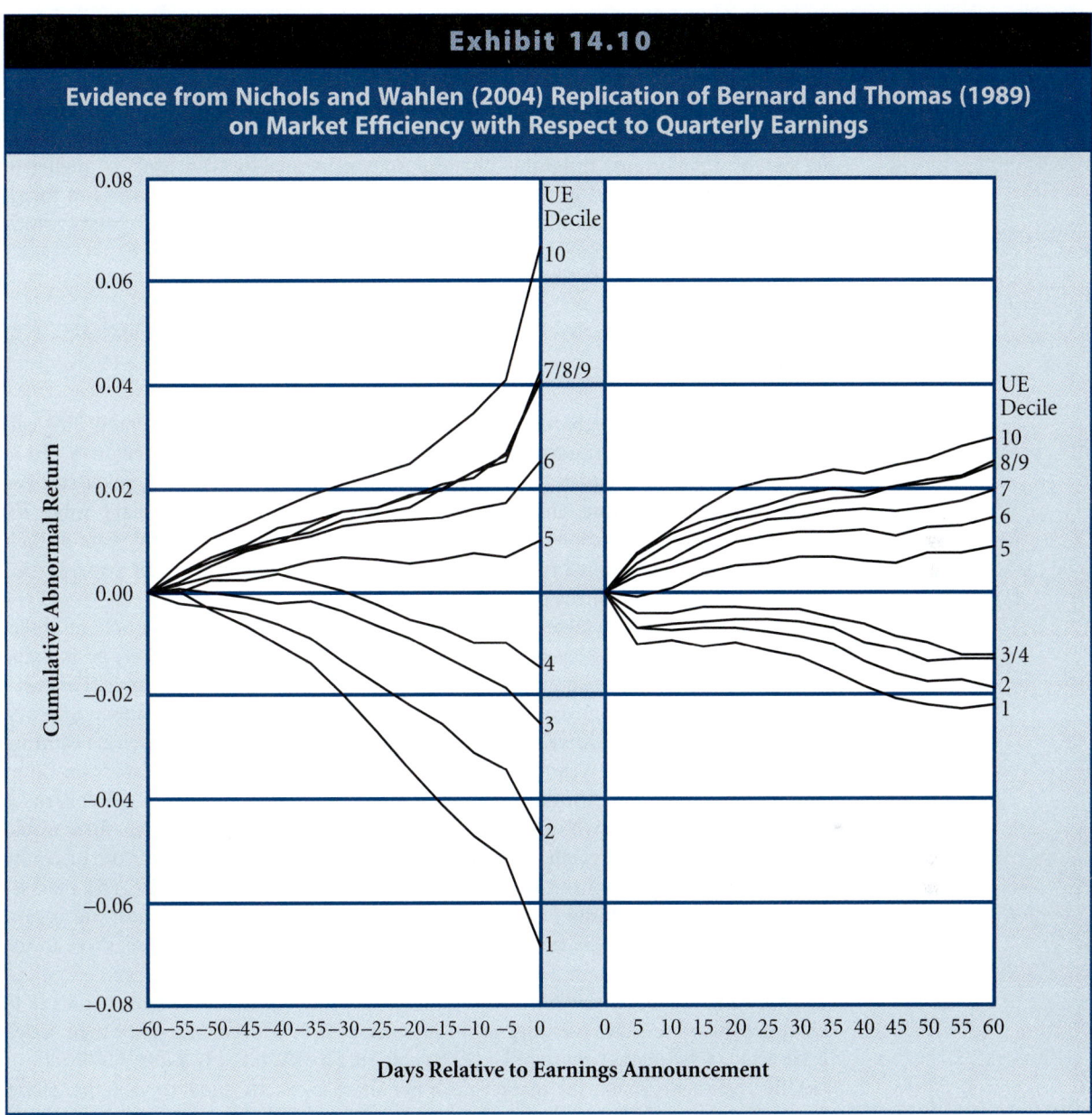

Exhibit 14.10

Evidence from Nichols and Wahlen (2004) Replication of Bernard and Thomas (1989) on Market Efficiency with Respect to Quarterly Earnings

findings still hold. We consider these results to be very encouraging for analysts. We interpret the results to suggest that analysts who can sharpen their ability to forecast future earnings and take long positions in (buy) shares of firms experiencing earnings increases and short positions in (sell) shares of firms experiencing earnings decreases during the 60-day pre-announcement period have the potential to earn some portion of the pre-announcement abnormal returns. Similarly, analysts who can sharpen their ability to react appropriately once earnings are announced have some potential to earn a portion of the post-announcement abnormal returns. These findings suggest that there are returns to be earned by being good at forecasting and reacting to earnings.

We believe that the state of the art of market efficiency is exactly where analysts would like it to be. The market is very efficient with respect to accounting information, but not perfectly efficient. Some stocks are temporarily mispriced, but the market tends to correct mispricings in a relatively short time. Financial statement analysis, particularly focusing on earnings, can help you identify stocks whose prices may be temporarily out of equilibrium. Insightful financial statement analysis can lead to intelligent investment decisions and better-than-average returns. Moreover, the analysis of financial statements leads to additional information being impounded in stock prices, which contributes to market efficiency.

Striking Evidence on the Use of Valuation Models to Form Portfolios

An empirical study by Richard Frankel and Charles Lee (1998) provides compelling evidence on the use of the residual income valuation models (which were demonstrated in this chapter and in Chapter 13) to pick stocks and form portfolios.[29] Frankel and Lee implemented the residual income model to compute fundamental share value for 18,162 firm-year observations from 1976 through 1993. During the early years of their study, the sample contained roughly 500 firms per year, while in the later years, it contained more than 1,300 firms per year.

To implement the residual income valuation model across a large sample of observations, Frankel and Lee needed data on earnings forecasts, book values, book value forecasts, and the cost of equity capital (R_E) for each firm-year in the sample. For earnings forecasts, Frankel and Lee collected from I/B/E/S the consensus analysts' forecasts of one-year-ahead and two-years-ahead earnings per share as well as consensus earnings growth rate forecasts for Year +3. They collected book-value-per-share data from Compustat and projected that future book value per share would grow with the consensus earnings-per-share forecast minus future dividends, assuming that each firm would maintain the current dividend payout policy. Finally, to determine the cost of equity capital, Frankel and Lee used an industry-average, three-factor (beta, size, and market-to-book) expected returns model. They also assumed a constant cost of capital (11%, 12%, or 13%) across time and firms. Their results were not very sensitive to the R_E estimate.

Applying the three-year-horizon residual income model enabled Frankel and Lee to compute value per share (denoted as V) for each sample observation. They then scaled each firm's V by market share price (P) to compute a V/P ratio. If a firm's V/P ratio is exactly 1, it suggests that the market price per share is exactly equal to value per share. If a V/P ratio is greater than 1, it suggests that the share price is underpriced, whereas a V/P ratio of less than 1 suggests that the share is overpriced. During each year of the study, Frankel and Lee ranked all of the sample firms from highest to lowest V/P. They then formed five portfolios, from the quintile of firms with the highest V/P ratios that year (the top 20%) down to the quintile of firms with the lowest V/P ratios that year (the bottom 20%). They presumed a 36-month holding period for these portfolios and cumulated the average returns.

Exhibit 14.11 presents the Frankel and Lee results averaged across all of the years of their study. Judging by the bars in the graph and the axis on the left side of the exhibit,

---

[29]Richard Frankel and Charles M.C. Lee, "Accounting Valuation, Market Expectation, and Cross-Sectional Stock Returns," *Journal of Accounting and Economics,* Vol. 25 (1998), pp. 283–319.

the bottom quintile portfolio had an average V/P ratio of roughly 0.40, implying that these firms tended to be significantly overpriced. The top quintile portfolio had an average V/P ratio of roughly 1.5, indicating that these firms tended to be underpriced. The square dots and the right axis of the graph indicate the average buy-and-hold returns cumulated by each portfolio over the 36 months after portfolio formation. Notice that the lowest quintile V/P firms generated, on average, cumulative three-year returns of only 35%, whereas the highest quintile V/P firms generated average cumulative three-year returns of nearly 65%. Frankel and Lee's study also included various sensitivity analyses and control tests indicating that their results were robust. The V/P ratio seemingly distinguished under- and overpriced stocks.

These results suggest that the valuation models we have discussed and demonstrated are useful in estimating share values and in evaluating which stocks are more likely to be under- or overpriced. Although these results are very encouraging for analysts, the results do not imply that the valuation process is easy or error-proof. Indeed, we strongly encourage you to carefully apply all six steps of the analysis framework demonstrated throughout this book to conduct thorough financial statement analysis, develop accurate forecasts, and determine reliable estimates of value to increase the likelihood of making good investment decisions.

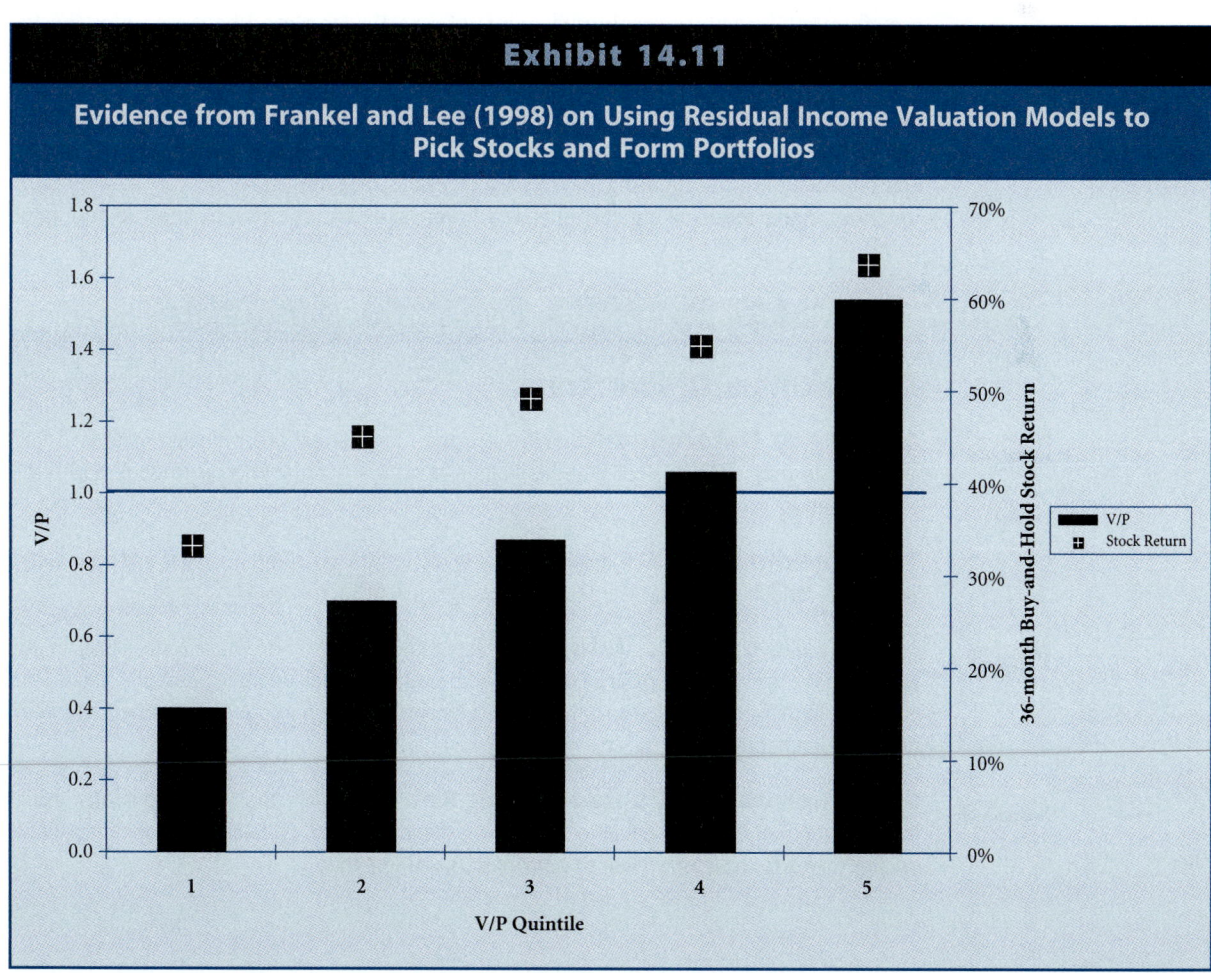

Exhibit 14.11

Evidence from Frankel and Lee (1998) on Using Residual Income Valuation Models to Pick Stocks and Form Portfolios

Summary

This chapter examines the use of market multiples in valuation by relying on the residual income model to develop the theoretical rationale relating market prices to economic drivers of value and to accounting fundamentals. This chapter describes the conceptual bases and practical applications of market multiples such as the market-to-book value ratio, the price-earnings ratio, and the price-earnings-growth ratio. The chapter focuses on four factors that affect these market multiples:

1. Risk and the cost of equity capital
2. Expected future growth in earnings
3. The presence of permanent and transitory components in the earnings of a particular year
4. The effects of accounting methods and principles on reported earnings and the book value of common shareholders' equity

For decades, analysts have relied heavily on price-earnings ratios to relate market prices to earnings. However, in recent years, analysts and academics alike increasingly recognize that transitory elements in earnings and earnings growth can cloud the interpretation of the price-earnings ratio as an indicator of value. Analysts and academics are shifting emphasis to the market-to-book ratio and to the price-earnings-growth ratio. Transitory earnings elements of a particular period have less effect on the market-to-book ratio. This chapter also demonstrates techniques to exploit the information in market value by calculating price differentials and by reverse engineering stock prices to infer the assumptions the market appears to be making. The chapter concludes by describing the relevance of academic research for the professional analyst, including highlighting key research results that appear to be very encouraging for those interested in using earnings and financial statement data to analyze and value firms.

Questions, Exercises, Problems, and Cases

Questions and Exercises

LO 14-1

14.1 Value Determinants. What are the fundamental determinants of share value, and how do they affect market-based valuation multiples, such as market-to-book and price-earnings ratios?

LO 14-2

14.2 Residual ROCE. Explain *residual* ROCE (return on common shareholders' equity). What does residual ROCE represent? What does residual ROCE measure?

LO 14-2

14.3 Value-to-Book Valuation Approach. In conceptual terms, explain the value-to-book valuation approach. Explain how the value-to-book approach described and demonstrated in this chapter relates to the residual income valuation approach described and demonstrated in Chapter 13.

LO 14-2

14.4 Interpreting Value-to-Book Ratios. Explain the implications of a value-to-book ratio that is exactly equal to 1. Compare the implications of a value-to-book ratio that is greater than 1 to those of a value-to-book ratio that is less than 1.

14.5 Interpreting Value-to-Book Ratios. Explain the implications of a value-to-book ratio that is greater than the market-to-book ratio. Explain the implications of a value-to-book ratio that is less than the market-to-book ratio.

LO 14-2

14.6 Value-to-Book Ratio Drivers. Identify three economic factors that will drive a firm's value-to-book ratio to be higher than that of other firms in the same industry. Identify three accounting factors that will drive a firm's value-to-book ratio to be higher than that of other firms in the same industry.

LO 14-2

14.7 Value-to-Book Ratio Drivers. Identify three economic factors that will drive a firm's value-to-book ratio to decrease over time. Identify three accounting factors that will drive a firm's value-to-book ratio to decrease over time.

LO 14-2

14.8 The Value-Earnings Ratio. In conceptual terms, explain the value-earnings ratio. Explain the difference between the value-earnings ratio and the price-earnings ratio. What is the critical assumption about future earnings in both the value-earnings and price-earnings ratio?

LO 14-3

14.9 The Price-Earnings Ratio. In practice, it is common to observe price-earnings ratios measured as current period price divided by trailing-twelve-months (or most recent annual) earnings per share. Identify and explain three potential flaws inherent in this measurement of the price-earnings ratio as a valuation multiple.

LO 14-3

14.10 Price-Earnings Ratio Drivers. Identify three economic factors that will drive a firm's price-earnings ratio to be higher than that of other firms in the same industry. Identify three accounting factors that will drive a firm's price-earnings ratio in a given period to be higher than that of other firms in the same industry.

LO 14-3

14.11 Price-Earnings Ratio Drivers. Identify three economic factors that will drive a firm's price-earnings ratio to decrease over time. Identify three accounting factors that will drive a firm's price-earnings ratio down in a given period.

LO 14-3

14.12 Market-to-Book versus Price-Earnings Ratios. Explain why market-to-book valuation multiples demonstrate less variance over time and across firms than do price-earnings valuation multiples.

LO 14-2, LO 14-3

14.13 Price Differentials. Explain Price Differentials in Conceptual Terms. What does a price differential measure? How does a price differential relate to risk?

LO 14-4

14.14 Reverse Engineering Share Prices. Explain reverse engineering of share prices in conceptual terms. How does reverse engineering of share prices enable an analyst to infer (or deduce) the assumptions that the capital markets appear to impound in share price?

LO 14-5

14.15 Market Efficiency. What does market efficiency mean? What does market efficiency not mean? Explain how market efficiency relates to the *amount* of information that affects share prices and the *speed* with which information affects share prices.

LO 14-6

14.16 Analysts' Role in Market Efficiency. Explain the role of analysts in increasing capital market efficiency.

LO 14-6

14.17 Market Efficiency with Respect to Quarterly Earnings Surprises. Using the evidence presented in Exhibit 14.10, describe the extent to which the market is efficient with respect to quarterly earnings surprises during the 60 trading days *prior to* quarterly earnings announcements. Using the evidence presented in Exhibit 14.10, describe the extent to which the market is efficient with respect to quarterly earnings surprises during the 60 trading days *following* quarterly earnings announcements.

Problems and Cases

14.18 Using Market Multiples to Assess Values and Market Prices. Problem 13.18 and Exhibit 13.7 in Chapter 13 present selected hypothetical data from projected financial statements for Steak 'n Shake for Year +1 to Year +11. The amounts for Year +11 reflect a long-term growth assumption of 3%. The cost of equity capital is 9.34%. The market value of common shareholders' equity in Steak 'n Shake on January 1, Year +1, is $309.98 million.

REQUIRED

a. Compute the value-to-book ratio as of January 1, Year +1, using the residual ROCE valuation method.

b. Using the analyses developed in Requirement a, prepare an exhibit summarizing the following ratios for Steak 'n Shake as of January 1, Year +1:

(1) Value-to-book ratio (using the amounts from Requirement a)

(2) Market-to-book ratio

(3) Value-earnings ratio, using reported earnings for Year 0 of $21.8 million

(4) Price-earnings ratio, using reported earnings for Year 0 of $21.8 million

(5) Value-earnings ratio, using projected earnings for Year +1 of $24.5 million

(6) Price-earnings ratio, using projected earnings for Year +1 of $24.5 million

c. Compute the risk-neutral value of Steak 'n Shake as of January 1, Year +1, using a risk-free rate of 4.2%. Use the projected earnings for Year +1 to Year +10 and the projected earnings for Year +11 given in Exhibit 13.7. Maintain the continuing value growth assumption of 3%. Compute the price differential for Steak 'n Shake as of January 1, Year +1. Compute the ratio of market value to risk-neutral value for Steak 'n Shake as of January 1, Year +1.

d. Use reverse engineering to solve for the long-run growth rate in continuing residual income in Year +11 and beyond that is implicitly impounded in the market value of Steak 'n Shake on January 1, Year +1. Use the 9.34% cost of equity capital and the projected earnings amounts for Year +1 to Year +10 in Exhibit 13.7 before solving for the long-run growth rate in continuing residual income.

e. Using the analyses in Requirements a–d, evaluate the extent of the market's mispricing (if any) of Steak 'n Shake.

14.19 Interpreting Market-to-Book Ratios. Exhibit 14.12 presents data on market-to-book ratios, ROCE, the cost of equity capital, and price-earnings ratios for seven pharmaceutical companies. (Note that price-earnings ratios for these firms typically fall in the 30–35 range.) Exhibit 14.12 also provides historical data on the five-year average rate of growth in earnings and dividend payout ratios for each firm. The data on excess earnings years represent the number of years that each firm would need to earn a rate of return on common shareholders' equity (ROCE) equal to that in Exhibit 14.12 in order to produce value-to-book ratios that equal the market-to-book ratios shown. For example, **Bristol-Myers Squibb** would need to earn an ROCE of 48.9% for 58.3 years in order for the present value of the excess earnings over the cost of equity capital to produce a value-to-book ratio that matches the market-to-book ratio of 13.9.

Exhibit 14.12

Selected Data for Pharmaceutical Companies
(Problem 14.19)

Company	MB	ROCE	Cost of Equity Capital	Dividend Payout Ratio	PE	Growth in Earnings	Excess Earnings Years
Bristol-Myers Squibb	13.9	0.489	0.134	0.77	32.4	0.068	58.3
Warner-Lambert	13.0	0.350	0.133	0.48	42.7	0.051	32.2
Eli Lilly	12.4	0.281	0.155	0.42	49.3	0.110	89.8
Pfizer	11.2	0.350	0.143	0.43	40.4	0.152	27.8
Abbott Laboratories	10.4	0.428	0.113	0.39	26.9	0.116	13.5
Merck	10.3	0.331	0.154	0.46	31.8	0.130	41.9
Wyeth	6.9	0.340	0.138	0.51	25.0	0.065	24.6

REQUIRED

Assume that market share prices for each firm are reasonably efficient. That is, do not simply assume that the market has over- or undervalued these firms. Considering the theoretical determinants of the market-to-book ratio, discuss the likely reasons for the relative ordering of these seven companies on their market-to-book ratios.

14.20 Sensitivity of Value-Earnings and Value-to-Book to Changes in Assumptions.

LO 14-2, LO 14-3

This problem explores the sensitivity of the value-earnings and value-to-book models to changes in underlying assumptions. We recommend that you design a computer spreadsheet to perform the calculations, particularly for the value-to-book ratio.

REQUIRED

a. Assume that current period earnings per share were $1.00 for each of the following nine scenarios (A through I). Compute the value-earnings ratio based on projected one-year-ahead earnings under each of the following sets of assumptions:

Scenario	Cost of Equity Capital	Growth Rate in Earnings
A	0.15	0.06
B	0.15	0.08
C	0.15	0.10
D	0.13	0.06
E	0.13	0.08
F	0.13	0.10
G	0.11	0.06
H	0.11	0.08
I	0.11	0.10

b. Assess the sensitivity of the value-earnings ratio to changes in the cost of equity capital and changes in the growth rate.

c. Compute the value-to-book ratio under each of the following nine sets of assumptions (A through I). Assume zero abnormal ROCE in the periods following the number of years of excess earnings.

Scenario	ROCE	Cost of Equity Capital	Dividend Payout Percentage	Years of Excess Earnings
A	0.20	0.13	0.30	10
B	0.18	0.13	0.30	10
C	0.14	0.13	0.30	10
D	0.18	0.15	0.30	10
E	0.18	0.11	0.30	10
F	0.18	0.13	0.40	10
G	0.18	0.13	0.20	10
H	0.18	0.13	0.30	15
I	0.18	0.13	0.30	20

d. Assess the sensitivity of the value-to-book ratio to changes in the assumptions made about the various underlying variables.

LO 14-5

14.21 Market Multiples and Reverse Engineering Share Prices. In 2000, **Enron** enjoyed remarkable success in the capital markets. During that year, Enron's shares increased in value by 89%, while the S&P 500 index fell by 9%. At the end of 2000, Enron's shares were trading at roughly $83 per share and all of the sell-side analysts following Enron recommended the shares as a "buy" or a "strong buy." With 752.2 million shares outstanding, Enron had a market capitalization of $62,530 million and was one of the largest firms (in terms of market capital) in the United States. At year-end 2000, Enron's book value of common shareholders' equity was $11,470 million.

At year-end 2000, Enron posted earnings per share of $1.19. Among sell-side analysts following Enron, the consensus forecast for earnings per share was $1.31 per share for 2001 and $1.44 per share for 2002, with 10% earnings growth expected from 2003–2005. At the time, Enron was paying dividends equivalent to roughly 40% of earnings and was expected to maintain that payout policy.

At year-end 2000, Enron had a market beta of 1.7. The risk-free rate of return was 4.3%, and the market risk premium was 5.0%. (Note: The data provided in this problem, and the inferences you draw from them, do not depend on foresight of Enron's declaring bankruptcy by the end of 2001.)

REQUIRED

a. Use the CAPM to compute the required rate of return on common equity capital for Enron.
b. Use year-end 2000 data to compute the following ratios for Enron:
  (1) Market-to-book
  (2) Price-earnings (using 2000 earnings per share)
  (3) Forward price-earnings (using consensus forecast earnings per share for 2001)
c. Reverse engineer Enron's $83 share price to solve for the implied expected return on Enron shares at year-end 2000. Do the reverse engineering under the following assumptions:
  (1) Enron's market price equals value.
  (2) The consensus analysts' earnings-per-share forecasts through 2005 are reliable proxies for market expectations.
  (3) Enron will maintain a 40% dividend payout rate.
  (4) Beyond 2005, Enron's long-run earnings growth rate will be 3.0%.
d. What do these analyses suggest about investing in Enron's shares at a price of $83?

14.22 Valuation of Coca-Cola Using Market Multiples. The Coca-Cola

LO 14-2, LO 14-3,
LO 14-4, LO 14-5,
LO 14-6

Company is a global soft-drink beverage company that is a primary and direct competitor with **PepsiCo**. The data in Chapter 12 Exhibits 12.14–12.16 include the actual amounts for 2012 and projected amounts for Year +1 to Year +6 for the income statements, balance sheets, and statements of cash flows for Coca-Cola.

The market equity beta for Coca-Cola at the end of 2012 is 0.75. Assume that the risk-free interest rate is 3.0% and the market risk premium is 6.0%. Coca-Cola has 4,469 million shares outstanding at the end of 2012, when Coca-Cola's share price was $35.48.

REQUIRED

Part I—Computing Coca-Cola's Value-to-Book Ratio Using the Value-to-Book Valuation Approach

a. Use the CAPM to compute the required rate of return on common equity capital for Coca-Cola.

b. Using the projected financial statements in Exhibits 12.14–12.16, derive the projected residual ROCE (return on common shareholders' equity) for Coca-Cola for Years +1 through +5.

c. The projected income statements and balance sheets for Year +6 assume Coca-Cola will grow at a steady state growth rate of 3.0%. Derive the projected residual ROCE for Year +6 for Coca-Cola.

d. Using the required rate of return on common equity from Requirement a as a discount rate, compute the sum of the present value of residual ROCE for Coca-Cola for Years +1 through +5.

e. Using the required rate of return on common equity from Requirement a as a discount rate and the long-run growth rate from Requirement c, compute the continuing value of Coca- Cola as of the start of Year +6 based on Coca-Cola's continuing residual ROCE in Year +6 and beyond. After computing continuing value as of the start of Year +6, discount it to present value at the start of Year +1.

f. Compute Coca-Cola's value-to-book ratio as of the end of 2012 with the following three steps:

(1) Compute the total sum of the present value of all future residual ROCE (from Requirements d and e).

(2) To the total from Requirement f (1), add 1 (representing the book value of equity as of the beginning of the valuation as of the end of 2012).

(3) Adjust the total sum from Requirement f (2) using the midyear discounting adjustment factor.

g. Compute Coca-Cola's market-to-book ratio as of the end of 2012. Compare the value-to-book ratio to the market-to-book ratio. What investment decision does the comparison suggest? What does the comparison suggest regarding the pricing of Coca-Cola shares in the market: underpriced, overpriced, or fairly priced?

h. Use the value-to-book ratio to project the value of a share of common equity in Coca-Cola.

i. If you computed Coca-Cola's common equity share value using the free cash flows to common equity valuation approach in Problem 12.16 in Chapter 12 and/or the residual income valuation approach in Problem 13.19 in Chapter 13, compare the value estimate you obtained in those problems with the estimate you obtained in this case. You should obtain the same value estimates under all three approaches. If you have not yet worked those problems, you would benefit from doing so now.

Part II—Analyzing Coca-Cola's Share Price Using the Value-Earnings Ratio, Price-Earnings Ratio, Price Differentials, and Reverse Engineering

j. Use the forecast data for Year +1 to project Year +1 earnings per share. To do so, divide the projection of Coca-Cola's comprehensive income available for common shareholders in Year +1 by the number of common shares outstanding at the end of 2012. Using this Year +1 earnings-per-share forecast and the share value computed in Requirement h, compute Coca-Cola's value-earnings ratio.

k. Using the Year +1 earnings-per-share forecast from Requirement j and using the share price at the end of 2012, compute Coca-Cola's price-earnings ratio. Compare Coca-Cola's value-earnings ratio with its price-earnings ratio. What investment decision does the comparison suggest? What does the comparison suggest regarding the pricing of Coca-Cola shares in the market: underpriced, overpriced, or fairly priced? Does this comparison lead to the same conclusions you reached when comparing value-to-book ratios with market-to-book ratios in Requirement g?

l. Note: For this part only, assume Coca-Cola's long-run growth beginning in Year +6 will be 1% rather than 3%. With a 1% growth rate, Year +6 comprehensive income will be $10,615 million. Compute Coca-Cola's price differential at the end of 2012. Compute Coca-Cola's price differential as a percentage of Coca-Cola's risk-neutral value. What dollar amount and what percentage amount has the market discounted Coca-Cola shares for risk?

m. Reverse engineer Coca-Cola's share price at the end of 2012 to solve for the implied expected rate of return. First, assume that value equals price and that the earnings and 3% long-run growth forecasts through Year +6 and beyond are reliable proxies for the market's expectations for Coca-Cola. Then solve for the implied expected rate of return (the discount rate) the market has impounded in Coca-Cola's share price. (Hint: Begin with the forecast and valuation spreadsheet you developed to value Coca-Cola shares. Vary the discount rate until you solve for the discount rate that makes your value estimate exactly equal the end of 2012 market price of $35.48 per share.)

n. Reverse engineer Coca-Cola's share price at the end of 2012 to solve for the implied expected long-run growth. First, assume that value equals price and that the earnings forecasts through Year +5 are reliable proxies for the market's expectations for Coca-Cola. Also assume that the discount rate implied by the CAPM (computed in Requirement a) is a reliable proxy for the market's expected rate of return. Then solve for the implied expected long-run growth rate the market has impounded in Coca-Cola's share price. (Hint: Begin with the forecast and valuation spreadsheet you developed to value Coca-Cola shares and use the CAPM discount rate. Set the long-run growth parameter initially to zero. Increase the long-run growth rate until you solve for the growth rate that makes your value estimate exactly equal the end of 2012 market price of $35.48 per share.)

14.23 Analysis of Comparable Companies Using Market Multiples.
In this chapter, we evaluated shares of common equity in **PepsiCo** using the value-to-book approach, market multiples, price differentials, and reverse engineering. **The Coca-Cola Company** competes directly with PepsiCo. The data in Chapter 12 Exhibits 12.14–12.16 include the actual amounts for 2012 and projected amounts for Year +1 to Year +6 for the income statements, balance sheets, and statements of cash flows for Coca-Cola. In Problem 14.22, you evaluated shares of common equity in Coca-Cola using the value-to-book approach, market multiples, price differentials, and reverse engineering.

REQUIRED

a. Prepare an exhibit using the data and analyses for PepsiCo from this chapter and the data and analyses for Coca-Cola from the previous problem that will allow you to compare these two competitors on the following dimensions:
  (1) Cost of equity capital (R_E)
  (2) ROCE for 2012

(3) Projected ROCE for Year +1

(4) Book value of common shareholders' equity

(5) Market value of common shareholders' equity

(6) Intrinsic value of common shareholders' equity

(7) Value-to-book ratio

(8) Market-to-book ratio

(9) Value-earnings ratio (using Year +1 projected comprehensive income)

(10) Price-earnings ratio (using Year +1 projected comprehensive income)

(11) Value-earnings ratio (using 2012 reported earnings per share)

(12) Price-earnings ratio (using 2012 reported earnings per share)

(13) Price differential (on a per-share basis; assume 1% long-run growth for both firms for this part of the problem)

(14) Price differential as a percentage of risk-neutral value (assume 1% long-run growth for both firms for this part of the problem)

(15) Reverse engineer share price to solve for implied expected rate of return (assuming 3% long-run growth)

(16) Reverse engineer share price to solve for implied long-run growth (assuming the cost of equity capital as the discount rate)

b. What inferences can you draw from these comparisons about the valuation of PepsiCo versus Coca-Cola? In the chapter, we concluded that PepsiCo shares were underpriced by roughly 25% in the market at the end of 2012. In the previous problem, you determined whether Coca-Cola was under- or overpriced. Are the comparisons here consistent with your previous conclusions regarding both PepsiCo and Coca-Cola shares at the end of 2012? Explain.

14.24 Valuation of Walmart Using Market Multiples. In Problem 10.16, we projected financial statements for Walmart Stores for Years +1 through +5. The data in Chapter 12 Exhibits 12.17–12.19 include the actual amounts for 2012 and the projected amounts for Year +1 to Year +5 for the income statements, balance sheets, and statements of cash flows for Walmart (in millions).

LO 14-2, LO 14-3, LO 14-4, LO 14-5, LO 14-6

The market equity beta for Walmart at the end of 2012 was 1.00. Assume that the risk-free interest rate was 3.0% and the market risk premium was 6.0%. Walmart had 3,314 million shares outstanding at the end of 2012, and the share price was $69.09.

REQUIRED

Part I—Computing Walmart's Value-to-Book Ratio Using the Value-to-Book Valuation Approach

a. Use the CAPM to compute the required rate of return on common equity capital for Walmart.

b. Using the projected financial statements in Chapter 12 Exhibits 12.17–12.19, derive the projected residual ROCE (return on common shareholders' equity) for Walmart for Years +1 through +5.

c. Assume that the steady-state, long-run growth rate will be 3% in Year +6 and beyond. Project that the Year +5 income statement and balance sheet amounts will grow by 3% in Year +6; then derive the projected residual ROCE for Year +6 for Walmart.

d. Using the required rate of return on common equity from Requirement a as a discount rate, compute the sum of the present value of residual ROCE for Walmart for Years +1 through +5.

e. Using the required rate of return on common equity from Requirement a as a discount rate and the long-run growth rate from Requirement c, compute the continuing value of Walmart as of the start of Year +6 based on Walmart's continuing residual ROCE in Year

+6 and beyond. After computing continuing value as of the start of Year +6, discount it to present value at the start of Year +1.

f. Compute Walmart's value-to-book ratio as of the end of 2012 with the following three steps:

   (1) Compute the total sum of the present value of all future residual ROCE (from Requirements d and e).

   (2) To the total from Requirement f (1), add 1 (representing the book value of equity as of the beginning of the valuation as of the end of 2012).

   (3) Adjust the total sum from Requirement f (2) using the midyear discounting adjustment factor.

g. Compute Walmart's market-to-book ratio as of the end of 2012. Compare the value-to-book ratio to the market-to-book ratio. What investment decision does the comparison suggest? What does the comparison suggest regarding the pricing of Walmart shares in the market: underpriced, overpriced, or fairly priced?

h. Use the value-to-book ratio to project Walmart's share value.

i. If you computed Walmart's common equity share value using the dividends valuation approach in Problem 11.14 in Chapter 11, and/or the free cash flows to common equity valuation approach in Problem 12.17 in Chapter 12, and/or the residual income valuation approach in Problem 13.20 in Chapter 13, compare the value estimate you obtained in those problems with the estimate you obtained in this case. You should obtain the same value estimates under all four approaches. If you have not yet worked those problems, you would benefit from doing so now.

Part II—Analyzing Walmart's Share Price Using the Value-Earnings Ratio, Price-Earnings Ratio, Price Differentials, and Reverse Engineering

j. Use the forecast data for Year +1 to project Year +1 earnings per share. To do so, divide Walmart's projected comprehensive income available for common shareholders in Year +1 by the number of common shares outstanding at the end of 2012. Using this Year +1 earnings-per-share forecast and the share value computed in Requirement h, compute Walmart's value-earnings ratio.

k. Using the Year +1 earnings-per-share forecast from Requirement j and using the share price of $69.09 at the end of 2012, compute Walmart's price-earnings ratio. Compare Walmart's value-earnings ratio with its price-earnings ratio. What does the comparison suggest regarding the pricing of Walmart shares in the market: underpriced, overpriced, or fairly priced? What investment decision does the comparison suggest? Does this comparison lead to the same conclusions you reached when comparing value-to-book ratios with market-to-book ratios in Requirement g?

l. Note: For this part only, assume Walmart's long-run growth beginning in Year +6 will be 1% rather than 3%. With a 1% growth rate, Year +6 comprehensive income will be $21,059 million. Compute Walmart's price differential at the end of 2012. Compute Walmart's price differential as a percentage of Walmart's risk-neutral value. What dollar amount and what percentage amount has the market discounted Walmart shares for risk?

m. Reverse engineer Walmart's share price at the end of 2012 to solve for the implied expected rate of return. First, assume that value equals price and that the earnings and 3% long-run growth forecasts in Year +6 and beyond are reliable proxies for the market's expectations for Walmart. Then solve for the implied expected rate of return (the discount rate) the market has impounded in Walmart's share price. (Hint: Begin with the forecast and valuation spreadsheet you developed to value Walmart shares.

Vary the discount rate until you solve for the discount rate that makes your value estimate exactly equal the end-of-2012 market price of $69.09 per share.)

n. Reverse engineer Walmart's share price at the end of 2012 to solve for the implied expected long-run growth. First, assume that value equals price and that the earnings forecasts through Year +5 are reliable proxies for the market's expectations for Walmart. Also assume that the discount rate implied by the CAPM (computed in Requirement a) is a reliable proxy for the market's expected rate of return. Then solve for the implied expected long-run growth rate the market has impounded in Walmart's share price. (Hint: Begin with the forecast and valuation spreadsheet you developed to value Walmart shares and use the CAPM discount rate. Set the long-run growth parameter initially to zero. Increase the long-run growth rate until you solve for the growth rate that makes your value estimate exactly equal the end-of-2012 market price of $69.09 per share.)

INTEGRATIVE CASE 14.1

Starbucks

Valuation of Starbucks' Common Equity Using Market Multiples

In Integrative Case 10.1, we projected financial statements for **Starbucks** for Years +1 through +5. In this portion of the Starbucks Integrative Case, we use the projected financial statements from Integrative Case 10.1 and apply the techniques in Chapter 14 to compute Starbucks' required rate of return on equity and share value based on the value-to-book valuation model. We also compare our value-to-book ratio estimate to Starbucks' market-to-book ratio at the time of the case to determine an investment recommendation. In addition, we compute the value-earnings and price-earnings ratios and the price differential, and we reverse engineer Starbucks' share price as of the end of 2012.

The market equity beta for Starbucks at the end of 2012 is 0.75. Assume that the risk-free interest rate is 3.0% and the market risk premium is 6.0%. Starbucks has 749.3 million shares outstanding at the end of 2012, and the share price was $50.15.

REQUIRED

Part I—Computing Starbucks' Value-to-Book Ratio Using the Value-to-Book Valuation Approach

a. Use the CAPM to compute the required rate of return on common equity capital for Starbucks.

b. Using your projected financial statements from Integrative Case 10.1 for Starbucks, derive the projected residual ROCE (return on common equity) for Starbucks for Years +1 through +5.

c. Assume that the steady-state, long-run growth rate will be 3% in Year +6 and beyond. Project that the Year +5 income statement and balance sheet amounts will grow by 3% in Year +6; then derive the projected residual ROCE for Year +6.

d. Using the required rate of return on common equity from Requirement a as a discount rate, compute the sum of the present value of residual ROCE for Starbucks for Years +1 through +5.

e. Using the required rate of return on common equity from Requirement a as a discount rate and the long-run growth rate from Requirement c, compute the continuing value of Starbucks as of the start of Year +6 based on Starbucks' continuing residual ROCE in Year +6 and beyond. After computing continuing value as of the start of Year +6, discount it to present value at the start of Year +1.

f. Compute Starbucks' value-to-book ratio as of the end of 2012 with the following three steps:

   (1) Compute the total sum of the present value of all future residual ROCE (from Requirements d and e).

   (2) To the total from Requirement f (1), add 1 (representing the book value of equity as of the beginning of the valuation as of the end of 2012).

   (3) Adjust the total sum from Requirement f (2) using the midyear discounting adjustment factor.

g. Compute Starbucks' market-to-book ratio as of the end of 2012. Compare the value-to-book ratio to the market-to-book ratio. What does the comparison suggest regarding the pricing of Starbucks' shares in the market: underpriced, overpriced, or fairly priced? What investment decision does the comparison suggest?

h. Use the value-to-book ratio to project Starbucks' share value.

i. If you computed Starbucks' common equity share value using the dividends valuation approach in Integrative Case 11.1 in Chapter 11, and/or the free cash flows to common equity valuation approach in Integrative Case 12.1 in Chapter 12, and/or the residual income valuation approach in Integrative Case 13.1 in Chapter 13, compare the value estimate you obtained in those cases with the estimate you obtained in this case. You should obtain the same value estimates under all four approaches. If you have not yet worked those prior cases, you would benefit from doing so now.

Part II—Analyzing Starbucks' Share Price Using the Value-Earnings Ratio, the Price-Earnings Ratio, Price Differentials, and Reverse Engineering

j. Use your forecast data for Year +1 to project Year +1 earnings per share. To do so, divide your projection of Starbucks' comprehensive income available for common shareholders in Year +1 by the number of common shares outstanding at the end of 2012. Using this Year +1 earnings-per-share forecast and using the share value computed in Requirement h, compute Starbucks' value-earnings ratio.

k. Using the Year +1 earnings-per-share forecast from Requirement j and using the share price at the end of 2012, compute Starbucks' price-earnings ratio. Compare Starbucks' value-earnings ratio with its price-earnings ratio. What investment decision does the comparison suggest? What does the comparison suggest regarding the pricing of Starbucks' shares in the market: underpriced, overpriced, or fairly priced? Does this comparison lead to the same conclusions you reached when comparing value-to-book ratios with market-to-book ratios in Requirement g?

l. Note: For this part only, assume Starbucks's long-run growth beginning in Year +6 will be 1% rather than 3%. With a 1% growth rate, Year +6 comprehensive income will be $2,900 million. Compute Starbucks' price differential at the end of 2012. Compute Starbucks's price differential as a percentage of risk-neutral value. What dollar amount and what percentage amount has the market discounted Starbucks' shares for risk?

m. Reverse engineer Starbucks' share price at the end of 2012 to solve for the implied expected rate of return. First, assume that value equals price and that your earnings and 3% long-run growth forecasts through Year +6 and beyond are reliable proxies for the market's expectations for Starbucks. Then solve for the implied expected rate of return (the discount rate) the market has impounded in Starbucks' share price. (Hint: Begin with the forecast and valuation spreadsheet you developed to value Starbucks' shares. Vary the discount rate until you solve for the discount rate that makes your value estimate exactly equal the end-of-2012 market price of $50.15 per share.)

n. Reverse engineer Starbucks' share price at the end of 2012 to solve for the implied expected long-run growth. First, assume that value equals price and that your earnings forecasts through Year +5 are reliable proxies for the market's expectations for Starbucks. Also assume that the discount rate implied by the CAPM (computed in Requirement a) is a reliable proxy for the market's expected rate of return. Then solve for the implied expected long-run growth rate the market has impounded in Starbucks' share price. (Hint: Begin with the forecast and valuation spreadsheet you developed to value Starbucks' shares and use the CAPM discount rate. Set the long-run growth parameter initially to zero. Increase the long-run growth rate until you solve for the growth rate that makes your value estimate exactly equal the market price of $50.15 per share.)

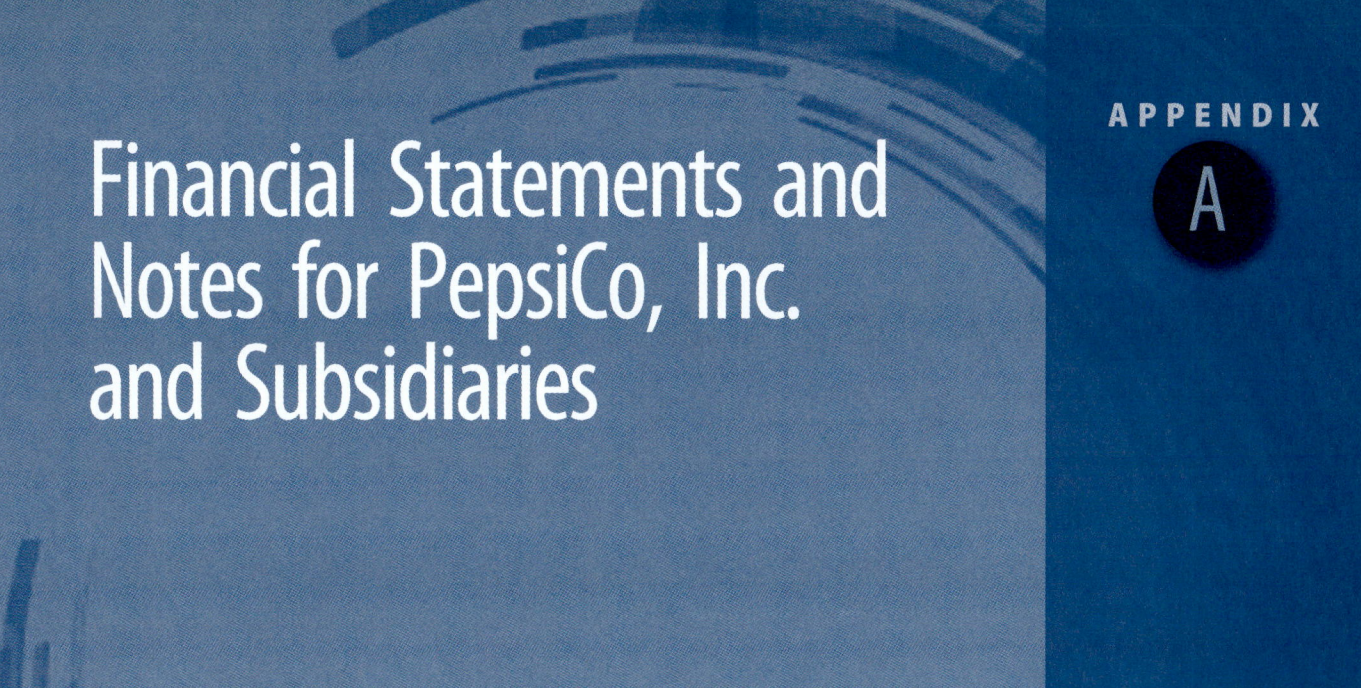

Financial Statements and Notes for PepsiCo, Inc. and Subsidiaries

Consolidated Statement of Income
PepsiCo, Inc. and Subsidiaries
Fiscal years ended December 29, 2012, December 31, 2011 and December 25, 2010
(in millions except per share amounts)

	2012	2011	2010
Net Revenue	$ 65,492	$ 66,504	$ 57,838
Cost of sales	31,291	31,593	26,575
Selling, general and administrative expenses	24,970	25,145	22,814
Amortization of intangible assets	119	133	117
Operating Profit	9,112	9,633	8,332
Bottling equity income	—	—	735
Interest expense	(899)	(856)	(903)
Interest income and other	91	57	68
Income before income taxes	8,304	8,834	8,232
Provision for income taxes	2,090	2,372	1,894
Net income	6,214	6,462	6,338
Less: Net income attributable to noncontrolling interests	36	19	18
Net Income Attributable to PepsiCo	$ 6,178	$ 6,443	$ 6,320
Net Income Attributable to PepsiCo per Common Share			
Basic	$ 3.96	$ 4.08	$ 3.97
Diluted	$ 3.92	$ 4.03	$ 3.91
Weighted-average common shares outstanding			
Basic	1,557	1,576	1,590
Diluted	1,575	1,597	1,614
Cash dividends declared per common share	$ 2.1275	$ 2.025	$ 1.89

See accompanying notes to consolidated financial statements.

Consolidated Statement of Comprehensive Income
PepsiCo, Inc. and Subsidiaries
Fiscal years ended December 29, 2012, December 31, 2011 and December 25, 2010
(in millions)

	2012		
	Pre-tax amounts	Tax benefit/(expense)	After-tax amounts
Net income			$ 6,214
Other Comprehensive Income			
Currency translation adjustment	$ 737	$ —	737
Cash flow hedges:			
Net derivative losses	(50)	10	(40)
Reclassification of net losses to net income	90	(32)	58
Pension and retiree medical:			
Net prior service cost	(32)	12	(20)
Net losses	(41)	(11)	(52)
Unrealized gains on securities	18	—	18
Other	—	36	36
Total Other Comprehensive Income	$ 722	$ 15	737
Comprehensive income			6,951
Comprehensive income attributable to noncontrolling interests			(31)
Comprehensive Income Attributable to PepsiCo			$ 6,920

	2011		
	Pre-tax amounts	Tax benefit/(expense)	After-tax amounts
Net income			$ 6,462
Other Comprehensive Loss			
Currency translation adjustment	$ (1,464)	$ —	(1,464)
Cash flow hedges:			
Net derivative losses	(126)	43	(83)
Reclassification of net losses to net income	5	4	9
Pension and retiree medical:			
Net prior service cost	(18)	8	(10)
Net losses	(1,468)	501	(967)
Unrealized losses on securities	(27)	19	(8)
Other	(16)	5	(11)
Total Other Comprehensive Loss	$ (3,114)	$ 580	(2,534)
Comprehensive income			3,928
Comprehensive income attributable to noncontrolling interests			(84)
Comprehensive Income Attributable to PepsiCo			$ 3,844

	2010		
	Pre-tax amounts	Tax benefit/(expense)	After-tax amounts
Net income			$ 6,338
Other Comprehensive Income			
Currency translation adjustment	$ 299	$ —	299
Cash flow hedges:			
Net derivative losses	(69)	23	(46)

Reclassification of net losses to net income		75		(25)	50
Pension and retiree medical:					
Net prior service credit		35		(13)	22
Net losses		(260)		124	(136)
Unrealized gains on securities		24		(1)	23
Other		(25)		(36)	(61)
Total Other Comprehensive Income	$	79	$	72	151
Comprehensive income					6,489
Comprehensive income attributable to noncontrolling interests					(5)
Comprehensive Income Attributable to PepsiCo				$	6,484

See accompanying notes to consolidated financial statements.

66

Consolidated Statement of Cash Flows
PepsiCo, Inc. and Subsidiaries
Fiscal years ended December 29, 2012, December 31, 2011 and December 25, 2010
(in millions)

		2012		2011		2010
Operating Activities						
Net income	$	6,214	$	6,462	$	6,338
preciation and amortization		2,689		2,737		2,327
Stock-based compensation expense		278		326		299
Merger and integration costs		16		329		808
Cash payments for merger and integration costs		(83)		(377)		(385)
Restructuring and impairment charges		279		383		—
Cash payments for restructuring charges		(343)		(31)		(31)
Restructuring and other charges related to the transaction with Tingyi		176		—		—
Cash payments for restructuring and other charges related to the transaction with Tingyi		(109)		—		—
Gain on previously held equity interests in PBG and PAS		—		—		(958)
Asset write-off		—		—		145
Non-cash foreign exchange loss related to Venezuela devaluation		—		—		120
Excess tax benefits from share-based payment arrangements		(124)		(70)		(107)
Pension and retiree medical plan contributions		(1,865)		(349)		(1,734)
Pension and retiree medical plan expenses		796		571		453
Bottling equity income, net of dividends		—		—		42
Deferred income taxes and other tax charges and credits		321		495		500
Change in accounts and notes receivable		(250)		(666)		(268)
Change in inventories		144		(331)		276
Change in prepaid expenses and other current assets		89		(27)		144
Change in accounts payable and other current liabilities		548		520		488
Change in income taxes payable		(97)		(340)		123
Other, net		(200)		(688)		(132)
Net Cash Provided by Operating Activities		8,479		8,944		8,448

(Continued on following page)

Consolidated Statement of Cash Flows (continued)
PepsiCo, Inc. and Subsidiaries
Fiscal years ended December 29, 2012, December 31, 2011 and December 25, 2010
(in millions)

Investing Activities			
Capital spending	(2,714)	(3,339)	(3,253)
Sales of property, plant and equipment	95	84	81
Acquisitions of PBG and PAS, net of cash and cash equivalents acquired	—	—	(2,833)
Acquisition of manufacturing and distribution rights from DPSG	—	—	(900)
Acquisition of WBD, net of cash and cash equivalents acquired	—	(2,428)	—
Investment in WBD	—	(164)	(463)
Cash payments related to the transaction with Tingyi	(306)	—	—
Other acquisitions and investments in noncontrolled affiliates	(121)	(601)	(83)
Divestitures	(32)	780	12
Short-term investments, by original maturity			
More than three months – purchases	—	—	(12)
More than three months – maturities	—	21	29
Three months or less, net	61	45	(229)
Other investing, net	12	(16)	(17)
Net Cash Used for Investing Activities	(3,005)	(5,618)	(7,668)

67

	2012	2011	2010
Financing Activities			
Proceeds from issuances of long-term debt	$ 5,999	$ 3,000	$ 6,451
Payments of long-term debt	(2,449)	(1,596)	(59)
Debt repurchase	—	(771)	(500)
Short-term borrowings, by original maturity			
More than three months – proceeds	549	523	227
More than three months – payments	(248)	(559)	(96)
Three months or less, net	(1,762)	339	2,351
Cash dividends paid	(3,305)	(3,157)	(2,978)
Share repurchases – common	(3,219)	(2,489)	(4,978)
Share repurchases – preferred	(7)	(7)	(5)
Proceeds from exercises of stock options	1,122	945	1,038
Excess tax benefits from share-based payment arrangements	124	70	107
Acquisition of noncontrolling interests	(68)	(1,406)	(159)
Other financing	(42)	(27)	(13)
Net Cash (Used for)/Provided by Financing Activities	(3,306)	(5,135)	1,386
Effect of exchange rate changes on cash and cash equivalents	62	(67)	(166)
Net Increase/(Decrease) in Cash and Cash Equivalents	2,230	(1,876)	2,000
Cash and Cash Equivalents, Beginning of Year	4,067	5,943	3,943
Cash and Cash Equivalents, End of Year	$ 6,297	$ 4,067	$ 5,943
Non-cash activity:			
Issuance of common stock and equity awards in connection with our acquisitions of PBG and PAS, as reflected in investing and financing activities			$ 4,451

See accompanying notes to consolidated financial statements.

Consolidated Balance Sheet
PepsiCo, Inc. and Subsidiaries
December 29, 2012 and December 31, 2011
(in millions except per share amounts)

	2012	2011
ASSETS		
Current Assets		
Cash and cash equivalents	$ 6,297	$ 4,067
Short-term investments	322	358
Accounts and notes receivable, net	7,041	6,912
Inventories	3,581	3,827
Prepaid expenses and other current assets	1,479	2,277
Total Current Assets	18,720	17,441
Property, Plant and Equipment, net	19,136	19,698
Amortizable Intangible Assets, net	1,781	1,888
Goodwill	16,971	16,800
Other nonamortizable intangible assets	14,744	14,557
Nonamortizable Intangible Assets	31,715	31,357
Investments in Noncontrolled Affiliates	1,633	1,477
Other Assets	1,653	1,021
Total Assets	$ 74,638	$ 72,882
LIABILITIES AND EQUITY		
Current Liabilities		
Short-term obligations	$ 4,815	$ 6,205
Accounts payable and other current liabilities	11,903	11,757
Income taxes payable	371	192
Total Current Liabilities	17,089	18,154
Long-Term Debt Obligations	23,544	20,568
Other Liabilities	6,543	8,266
Deferred Income Taxes	5,063	4,995
Total Liabilities	52,239	51,983
Commitments and Contingencies		
Preferred Stock, no par value	41	41
Repurchased Preferred Stock	(164)	(157)
PepsiCo Common Shareholders' Equity		
Common stock, par value $1^2/_3$¢ per share (authorized 3,600 shares, issued, net of repurchased common stock at par value: 1,544 and 1,565 shares, respectively)	26	26
Capital in excess of par value	4,178	4,461
Retained earnings	43,158	40,316
Accumulated other comprehensive loss	(5,487)	(6,229)
Repurchased common stock, in excess of par value (322 and 301 shares, respectively)	(19,458)	(17,870)
Total PepsiCo Common Shareholders' Equity	22,417	20,704
Noncontrolling interests	105	311
Total Equity	22,399	20,899
Total Liabilities and Equity	$ 74,638	$ 72,882

See accompanying notes to consolidated financial statements.

Consolidated Statement of Equity
PepsiCo, Inc. and Subsidiaries
Fiscal years ended December 29, 2012, December 31, 2011 and December 25, 2010
(in millions)

	2012		2011		2010	
	Shares	Amount	Shares	Amount	Shares	Amount
Preferred Stock	0.8	$ 41	0.8	$ 41	0.8	$ 41
Repurchased Preferred Stock						
Balance, beginning of year	(0.6)	(157)	(0.6)	(150)	(0.6)	(145)
Redemptions	—	(7)	—	(7)	—	(5)
Balance, end of year	(0.6)	(164)	(0.6)	(157)	(0.6)	(150)
Common Stock						
Balance, beginning of year	1,565	26	1,582	26	1,566	26
Repurchased common stock	(21)	—	(17)	—	(67)	(1)
Shares issued in connection with our acquisitions of PBG and PAS	—	—	—	—	83	1
Balance, end of year	1,544	26	1,565	26	1,582	26
Capital in Excess of Par Value						
Balance, beginning of year		4,461		4,527		250
Stock-based compensation expense		278		326		299
Stock option exercises/RSUs converted [a]		(431)		(361)		(500)
Withholding tax on RSUs converted		(70)		(56)		(68)
Equity issued in connection with our acquisitions of PBG and PAS		—		—		4,451
Other		(60)		25		95
Balance, end of year		4,178		4,461		4,527
Retained Earnings						
Balance, beginning of year		40,316		37,090		33,805
Net income attributable to PepsiCo		6,178		6,443		6,320
Cash dividends declared – common		(3,312)		(3,192)		(3,028)
Cash dividends declared – preferred		(1)		(1)		(1)
Cash dividends declared – RSUs		(23)		(24)		(12)
Other		—		—		6
Balance, end of year		43,158		40,316		37,090
Accumulated Other Comprehensive Loss						
Balance, beginning of year		(6,229)		(3,630)		(3,794)
Currency translation adjustment		742		(1,529)		312
Cash flow hedges, net of tax:						
Net derivative losses		(40)		(83)		(46)
Reclassification of net losses to net income		58		9		50
Pension and retiree medical, net of tax:						
Net pension and retiree medical losses		(493)		(1,110)		(280)
Reclassification of net losses to net income		421		133		166
Unrealized gains/(losses) on securities, net of tax		18		(8)		23
Other		36		(11)		(61)
Balance, end of year		(5,487)		(6,229)		(3,630)

Repurchased Common Stock						
Balance, beginning of year	**(301)**	**(17,870)**	(284)	(16,740)	(217)	(13,379)
Share repurchases	**(47)**	**(3,219)**	(39)	(2,489)	(76)	(4,977)
Stock option exercises	**24**	**1,488**	20	1,251	24	1,487
Other	**2**	**143**	2	108	(15)	129
Balance, end of year	**(322)**	**(19,458)**	(301)	(17,870)	(284)	(16,740)
Total PepsiCo Common Shareholders' Equity		**22,417**		20,704		21,273
Noncontrolling Interests						
Balance, beginning of year		**311**		312		638
Net income attributable to noncontrolling interests		**36**		19		18
Distributions to noncontrolling interests, net		**(37)**		(24)		(6)
Currency translation adjustment		**(5)**		65		(13)
Acquisitions and divestitures		**(200)**		(57)		(326)
Other, net		**—**		(4)		1
Balance, end of year		**105**		311		312
Total Equity	$	**22,399**	$	20,899	$	21,476

(a) Includes total tax benefits of $84 million in 2012, $43 million in 2011 and $75 million in 2010.

See accompanying notes to consolidated financial statements.

Notes to Consolidated Financial Statements

Note 1 — Basis of Presentation and Our Divisions

Basis of Presentation

Our financial statements include the consolidated accounts of PepsiCo, Inc. and the affiliates that we control. In addition, we include our share of the results of certain other affiliates using the equity method based on our economic ownership interest, our ability to exercise significant influence over the operating or financial decisions of these affiliates or our ability to direct their economic resources. We do not control these other affiliates, as our ownership in these other affiliates is generally less than 50%. Intercompany balances and transactions are eliminated. Our fiscal year ends on the last Saturday of each December, resulting in an additional week of results every five or six years. In 2011, we had an additional week of results (53rd week).

On February 26, 2010, we completed our acquisitions of PBG and PAS. The results of the acquired companies in the U.S. and Canada were reflected in our consolidated results as of the acquisition date, and the international results of the acquired companies have been reported as of the beginning of the second quarter of 2010, consistent with our monthly international reporting calendar. The results of the acquired companies in the U.S., Canada and Mexico are reported within our PAB segment, and the results of the acquired companies in Europe, including Russia, are reported within our Europe segment. Prior to our acquisitions of PBG and PAS, we recorded our share of equity income or loss from the acquired companies in bottling equity income in our income statement. Our share of income or loss from other noncontrolled affiliates is reflected as a component of selling, general and administrative expenses. Additionally, in the first quarter of 2010, in connection with our acquisitions of PBG and PAS, we recorded a gain on our previously held equity interests of $958 million, comprising $735 million which was non-taxable and recorded in bottling equity income and $223 million related to the reversal of deferred tax liabilities associated with these previously held equity interests. See Notes 8 and 15 to our consolidated financial statements, and for additional unaudited information on items affecting the comparability of our consolidated results see "Items Affecting Comparability" in Management's Discussion and Analysis of Financial Condition and Results of Operations.

As of the beginning of our 2010 fiscal year, the results of our Venezuelan businesses are reported under hyperinflationary accounting. See "Our Business Risks" and "Items Affecting Comparability" in Management's Discussion and Analysis of Financial Condition and Results of Operations.

In the first quarter of 2011, QFNA changed its method of accounting for certain U.S. inventories from the last-in, first-out (LIFO) method to the average cost method as we believe that the average cost method of accounting improves our financial reporting by better matching revenues and expenses and better reflecting the current value of inventory. The impact of this change on consolidated net income in the first quarter of 2011 was approximately $9 million (or less than a penny per share). Prior periods were not restated as the impact of the change on previously issued financial statements was not considered material.

Raw materials, direct labor and plant overhead, as well as purchasing and receiving costs, costs directly related to production planning, inspection costs and raw material handling facilities, are included in cost of sales. The costs of moving, storing and delivering finished product are included in selling, general and administrative expenses.

The preparation of our consolidated financial statements in conformity with generally accepted accounting principles requires us to make estimates and assumptions that affect reported amounts of assets, liabilities, revenues, expenses and disclosure of contingent assets and liabilities. Estimates are used in determining, among other items, sales incentives accruals, tax reserves, stock-based compensation, pension and retiree medical accruals, amounts and useful lives for intangible assets, and future cash flows associated with impairment testing for perpetual brands, goodwill and other long-lived assets. We evaluate our estimates on

71

an ongoing basis using our historical experience, as well as other factors we believe appropriate under the circumstances, such as current economic conditions, and adjust or revise our estimates as circumstances change. As future events and their effect cannot be determined with precision, actual results could differ significantly from these estimates.

While our North America results are reported on a weekly calendar basis, most of our international operations report on a monthly calendar basis. In 2011, we had an additional week of results (53rd week). The following chart details our quarterly reporting schedule for all other reporting periods presented:

Quarter	U.S. and Canada	International
First Quarter	12 weeks	January, February
Second Quarter	12 weeks	March, April and May
Third Quarter	12 weeks	June, July and August
Fourth Quarter	16 weeks	September, October, November and December

See "Our Divisions" below, and for additional unaudited information on items affecting the comparability of our consolidated results, see "Items Affecting Comparability" in Management's Discussion and Analysis of Financial Condition and Results of Operations.

Tabular dollars are in millions, except per share amounts. All per share amounts reflect common per share amounts, assume dilution unless noted, and are based on unrounded amounts. Certain reclassifications were made to prior years' amounts to conform to the 2012 presentation.

Our Divisions

We manufacture or use contract manufacturers, market and sell a variety of salty, convenient, sweet and grain-based snacks, carbonated and non-carbonated beverages, dairy products and other foods in over 200 countries and territories with our largest operations in North America (United States and Canada), Russia, Mexico, the United Kingdom and Brazil. Division results are based on how our Chief Executive Officer assesses the performance of and allocates resources to our divisions. For additional unaudited information on our divisions, see "Our Operations" in Management's Discussion and Analysis of Financial Condition and Results of Operations. The accounting policies for the divisions are the same as those described in Note 2, except for the following allocation methodologies:

•stock-based compensation expense;
•pension and retiree medical expense; and
•derivatives.

Stock-Based Compensation Expense

Our divisions are held accountable for stock-based compensation expense and, therefore, this expense is allocated to our divisions as an incremental employee compensation cost. The allocation of stock-based compensation expense in 2012 was approximately 16% to FLNA, 2% to QFNA, 5% to LAF, 25% to PAB, 14% to Europe, 12% to AMEA and 26% to corporate unallocated expenses. We had similar allocations of stock-based compensation expense to our divisions in 2011 and 2010. The expense allocated to our divisions excludes any impact of changes in our assumptions during the year which reflect market conditions over which division management has no control. Therefore, any variances between allocated expense and our actual expense are recognized in corporate unallocated expenses.

72

Pension and Retiree Medical Expense

Pension and retiree medical service costs measured at a fixed discount rate, as well as amortization of costs related to certain pension plan amendments and gains and losses due to demographics, including salary experience, are reflected in division results for North American employees. Division results also include interest costs, measured at a fixed discount rate, for retiree medical plans. Interest costs for the pension plans, pension asset returns and the impact of pension funding, and gains and losses other than those due to demographics, are all reflected in corporate unallocated expenses. In addition, corporate unallocated expenses include the difference between the service costs measured at a fixed discount rate (included in division results as noted above) and the total service costs determined using the plans' discount rates as disclosed in Note 7 to our consolidated financial statements.

Derivatives

We centrally manage commodity derivatives on behalf of our divisions. These commodity derivatives include agricultural products, metals and energy. Certain of these commodity derivatives do not qualify for hedge accounting treatment and are marked to market with the resulting gains and losses recognized in corporate unallocated expenses. These gains and losses are subsequently reflected in division results when the divisions take delivery of the underlying commodity. Therefore, the divisions realize the economic effects of the derivative without experiencing any resulting mark-to-market volatility, which remains in corporate unallocated expenses. These derivatives hedge underlying commodity price risk and were not entered into for speculative purposes.

73

	Net Revenue			Operating Profit [a]		
	2012	2011	2010	2012	2011	2010
FLNA	$ 13,574	$ 13,322	$ 12,573	$ 3,646	$ 3,621	$ 3,376
QFNA	2,636	2,656	2,656	695	797	741
LAF	7,780	7,156	6,315	1,059	1,078	1,004
PAB	21,408	22,418	20,401	2,937	3,273	2,776
Europe [b]	13,441	13,560	9,602	1,330	1,210	1,054
AMEA	6,653	7,392	6,291	747	887	708
Total division	65,492	66,504	57,838	10,414	10,866	9,659
Corporate Unallocated						
Mark-to-market net impact gains/(losses)				65	(102)	91
Merger and integration charges				—	(78)	(191)
Restructuring and impairment charges				(10)	(74)	—
Pension lump sum settlement charge				(195)	—	—
53rd week				—	(18)	—
Venezuela currency devaluation				—	—	(129)
Asset write-off				—	—	(145)
Foundation contribution				—	—	(100)
Other				(1,162)	(961)	(853)
	$ 65,492	$ 66,504	$ 57,838	$ 9,112	$ 9,633	$ 8,332

(a) For information on the impact of restructuring, impairment and integration charges on our divisions, see Note 3 to our consolidated financial statements.
(b) Change in net revenue in 2011 relates primarily to our acquisition of WBD.

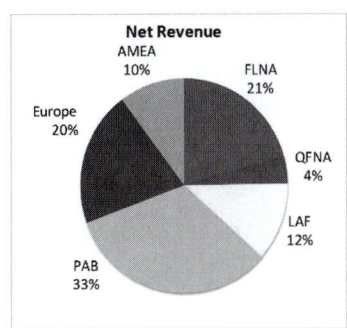

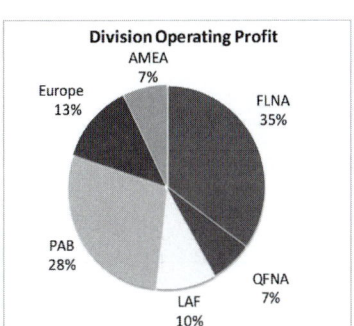

Corporate

Corporate includes costs of our corporate headquarters, centrally managed initiatives such as our ongoing global business transformation initiative and research and development projects, unallocated insurance and benefit programs, foreign exchange transaction gains and losses, certain commodity derivative gains and losses and certain other items.

Other Division Information

	Total Assets			Capital Spending		
	2012	2011	2010	**2012**	2011	2010
FLNA	$ **5,332**	$ 5,384	$ 5,276	$ **365**	$ 439	$ 515
QFNA	**966**	1,024	1,062	**37**	43	48
LAF	**4,993**	4,721	4,041	**436**	413	370
PAB	**30,899**	31,142	31,571	**702**	1,006	973
Europe [a]	**19,218**	18,461	13,018	**575**	588	517
AMEA	**5,738**	6,038	5,557	**510**	693	610
Total division	**67,146**	66,770	60,525	**2,625**	3,182	3,033
Corporate [b]	**7,492**	6,112	7,389	**89**	157	220
Investments in bottling affiliates	—	—	239	—	—	—
	$ **74,638**	$ 72,882	$ 68,153	$ **2,714**	$ 3,339	$ 3,253

(a) Changes in total assets in 2011 relate primarily to our acquisition of WBD.

(b) Corporate assets consist principally of cash and cash equivalents, short-term investments, derivative instruments and property, plant and equipment.

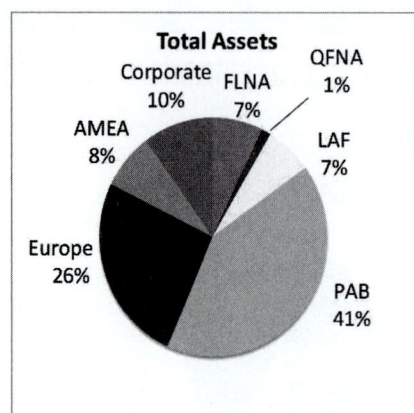

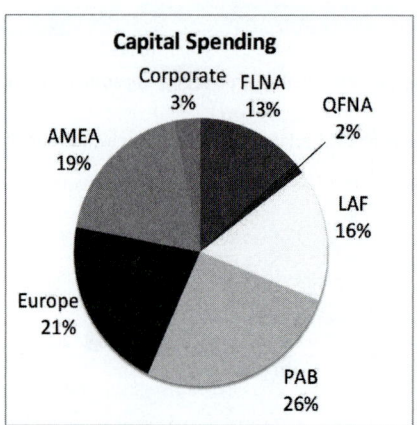

	Amortization of Intangible Assets			Depreciation and Other Amortization		
	2012	2011	2010	**2012**	2011	2010
FLNA	$ **7**	$ 7	$ 7	$ **445**	$ 458	$ 448
QFNA	—	—	—	**53**	54	52
LAF	**10**	10	6	**248**	238	213
PAB	**59**	65	56	**855**	865	749
Europe	**36**	39	35	**522**	522	355
AMEA	**7**	12	13	**305**	350	294
Total division	**119**	133	117	**2,428**	2,487	2,111
Corporate	—	—	—	**142**	117	99
	$ **119**	$ 133	$ 117	$ **2,570**	$ 2,604	$ 2,210

75

	Net Revenue			Long-Lived Assets[a]		
	2012	2011	2010	**2012**	2011	2010
U.S.	**$ 33,348**	$ 33,053	$ 30,618	**$ 28,344**	$ 28,999	$ 28,631
Russia [b]	**4,861**	4,749	1,890	**8,603**	8,121	2,744
Mexico	**3,955**	4,782	4,531	**1,237**	1,027	1,671
Canada	**3,290**	3,364	3,081	**3,294**	3,097	3,133
United Kingdom	**2,102**	2,075	1,888	**1,053**	1,011	1,019
Brazil	**1,866**	1,838	1,582	**1,134**	1,124	677
All other countries	**16,070**	16,643	14,248	**10,600**	11,041	11,020
	$ 65,492	$ 66,504	$ 57,838	**$ 54,265**	$ 54,420	$ 48,895

(a) Long-lived assets represent property, plant and equipment, nonamortizable intangible assets, amortizable intangible assets and investments in noncontrolled affiliates. These assets are reported in the country where they are primarily used.

(b) Change in 2011 relates primarily to our acquisition of WBD.

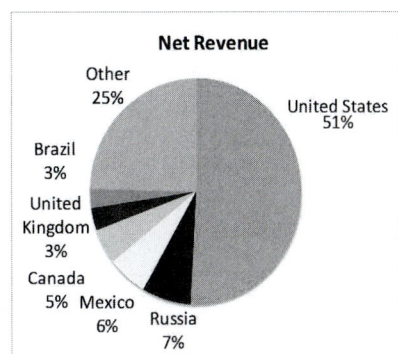

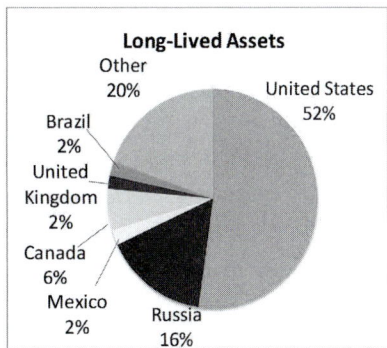

Note 2 — Our Significant Accounting Policies

Revenue Recognition

We recognize revenue upon shipment or delivery to our customers based on written sales terms that do not allow for a right of return. However, our policy for DSD and certain chilled products is to remove and replace damaged and out-of-date products from store shelves to ensure that consumers receive the product quality and freshness they expect. Similarly, our policy for certain warehouse-distributed products is to replace damaged and out-of-date products. Based on our experience with this practice, we have reserved for anticipated damaged and out-of-date products. For additional unaudited information on our revenue recognition and related policies, including our policy on bad debts, see "Our Critical Accounting Policies" in Management's Discussion and Analysis of Financial Condition and Results of Operations. We are exposed to concentration of credit risk by our customers, including Wal-Mart. In 2012, Wal-Mart (including Sam's) represented approximately 11% of our total net revenue, including concentrate sales to our independent bottlers which are used in finished goods sold by them to Wal-Mart. We have not experienced credit issues with these customers.

Total Marketplace Spending

We offer sales incentives and discounts through various programs to customers and consumers. Total marketplace spending includes sales incentives, discounts, advertising and other marketing activities. Sales incentives and discounts are primarily accounted for as a reduction of revenue and totaled $34.7 billion in 2012, $34.6 billion in 2011 and $29.1 billion in 2010. Sales incentives and discounts include payments to customers for performing merchandising activities on our behalf, such as payments for in-store displays, payments to gain distribution of new products, payments for shelf space and discounts to promote lower

76

retail prices. It also includes support provided to our independent bottlers through funding of advertising and other marketing activities. While most of these incentive arrangements have terms of no more than one year, certain arrangements, such as fountain pouring rights, may extend beyond one year. Costs incurred to obtain these arrangements are recognized over the shorter of the economic or contractual life, as a reduction of revenue, and the remaining balances of $335 million as of December 29, 2012 and $313 million as of December 31, 2011, are included in current assets and other assets on our balance sheet. For additional unaudited information on our sales incentives, see "Our Critical Accounting Policies" in Management's Discussion and Analysis of Financial Condition and Results of Operations.

Advertising and other marketing activities, reported as selling, general and administrative expenses, totaled $3.7 billion in 2012, $3.5 billion in 2011 and $3.4 billion in 2010, including advertising expenses of $2.2 billion in 2012 and $1.9 billion in both 2011 and 2010. Deferred advertising costs are not expensed until the year first used and consist of:

*   media and personal service prepayments;
*   promotional materials in inventory; and
*   production costs of future media advertising.

Deferred advertising costs of $88 million and $163 million at year-end 2012 and 2011, respectively, are classified as prepaid expenses on our balance sheet.

Distribution Costs

Distribution costs, including the costs of shipping and handling activities, are reported as selling, general and administrative expenses. Shipping and handling expenses were $9.1 billion in 2012, $9.2 billion in 2011 and $7.7 billion in 2010.

Cash Equivalents

Cash equivalents are highly liquid investments with original maturities of three months or less.

Software Costs

We capitalize certain computer software and software development costs incurred in connection with developing or obtaining computer software for internal use when both the preliminary project stage is completed and it is probable that the software will be used as intended. Capitalized software costs include only (i) external direct costs of materials and services utilized in developing or obtaining computer software, (ii) compensation and related benefits for employees who are directly associated with the software project and (iii) interest costs incurred while developing internal-use computer software. Capitalized software costs are included in property, plant and equipment on our balance sheet and amortized on a straight-line basis when placed into service over the estimated useful lives of the software, which approximate 5 to 10 years. Software amortization totaled $196 million in 2012, $156 million in 2011 and $137 million in 2010. Net capitalized software and development costs were $1.1 billion as of December 29, 2012 and $1.3 billion as of December 31, 2011.

Commitments and Contingencies

We are subject to various claims and contingencies related to lawsuits, certain taxes and environmental matters, as well as commitments under contractual and other commercial obligations. We recognize liabilities for contingencies and commitments when a loss is probable and estimable. For additional information on our commitments, see Note 9 to our consolidated financial statements.

Research and Development

We engage in a variety of research and development activities and continue to invest to accelerate growth in these activities and to drive innovation globally. These activities principally involve the development of

77

new products, improvement in the quality of existing products, improvement and modernization of production processes, and the development and implementation of new technologies to enhance the quality and value of both current and proposed product lines. Consumer research is excluded from research and development costs and included in other marketing costs. Research and development costs were $552 million in 2012, $525 million in 2011 and $488 million in 2010 and are reported within selling, general and administrative expenses.

Other Significant Accounting Policies

Our other significant accounting policies are disclosed as follows:

*   *Property, Plant and Equipment and Intangible Assets* – Note 4, and for additional unaudited information on goodwill and other intangible assets see "Our Critical Accounting Policies" in Management's Discussion and Analysis of Financial Condition and Results of Operations.
*   *Income Taxes* – Note 5, and for additional unaudited information see "Our Critical Accounting Policies" in Management's Discussion and Analysis of Financial Condition and Results of Operations.
*   *Stock-Based Compensation* – Note 6.
*   *Pension, Retiree Medical and Savings Plans* – Note 7, and for additional unaudited information see "Our Critical Accounting Policies" in Management's Discussion and Analysis of Financial Condition and Results of Operations.
*   *Financial Instruments* – Note 10, and for additional unaudited information, see "Our Business Risks" in Management's Discussion and Analysis of Financial Condition and Results of Operations.
*   *Inventories* – Note 14. Inventories are valued at the lower of cost or market. Cost is determined using the average; first-in, first-out (FIFO) or last-in, first-out (LIFO) methods.
*   *Translation of Financial Statements of Foreign Subsidiaries* – Financial statements of foreign subsidiaries are translated into U.S. dollars using period-end exchange rates for assets and liabilities and weighted-average exchange rates for revenues and expenses. Adjustments resulting from translating net assets are reported as a separate component of accumulated other comprehensive loss within common shareholders' equity as currency translation adjustment.

Recent Accounting Pronouncements

In July 2012, the Financial Accounting Standards Board (FASB) issued new accounting guidance that permits an entity to first assess qualitative factors to determine whether it is more likely than not that an indefinite-lived intangible asset is impaired as a basis for determining whether it is necessary to perform a quantitative impairment test. An entity would continue to calculate the fair value of an indefinite-lived intangible asset if the asset fails the qualitative assessment, while no further analysis would be required if it passes. The provisions of the new guidance are effective as of the beginning of our 2013 fiscal year. We do not expect the new guidance to have an impact on the 2013 impairment test results.

In September 2011, the FASB issued new accounting guidance that permits an entity to first assess qualitative factors of whether it is more likely than not that a reporting unit's fair value is less than its carrying amount before applying the two-step goodwill impairment test. An entity would continue to perform the historical first step of the impairment test if it fails the qualitative assessment, while no further analysis would be required if it passes. The provisions of the new guidance were effective for, and had no impact on, our 2012 annual goodwill impairment test results.

In December 2011, the FASB issued new disclosure requirements that are intended to enhance current disclosures on offsetting financial assets and liabilities. The new disclosures require an entity to disclose both gross and net information about derivative instruments accounted for in accordance with the guidance on derivatives and hedging that are eligible for offset on the balance sheet and instruments and transactions

78

subject to an agreement similar to a master netting arrangement. The provisions of the new disclosure requirements are effective as of the beginning of our 2014 fiscal year. We are currently evaluating the impact of the new guidance on our financial statements.

In September 2011, the FASB amended its guidance regarding the disclosure requirements for employers participating in multiemployer pension and other postretirement benefit plans (multiemployer plans) to improve transparency and increase awareness of the commitments and risks involved with participation in multiemployer plans. The new accounting guidance requires employers participating in multiemployer plans to provide additional quantitative and qualitative disclosures to provide users with more detailed information regarding an employer's involvement in multiemployer plans. The provisions of this new guidance were effective as of the beginning of our 2011 fiscal year and did not have a material impact on our financial statements.

In June 2011, the FASB amended its accounting guidance on the presentation of comprehensive income in financial statements to improve the comparability, consistency and transparency of financial reporting and to increase the prominence of items that are recorded in other comprehensive income. The new accounting guidance requires entities to report components of comprehensive income in either (1) a continuous statement of comprehensive income or (2) two separate but consecutive statements. The provisions of the guidance were effective as of the beginning of our 2012 fiscal year. Accordingly, we have presented the components of net income and other comprehensive income for the fiscal years ended December 29, 2012, December 31, 2011 and December 25, 2010 as separate but consecutive statements. In February 2013, the FASB issued guidance that would require an entity to provide enhanced footnote disclosures to explain the effect of reclassification adjustments on other comprehensive income by component and provide tabular disclosure in the footnotes showing the effect of items reclassified from accumulated other comprehensive income on the line items of net income. The provisions of this new guidance are effective as of the beginning of our 2013 fiscal year. We do not expect the adoption of this new guidance to have a material impact on our financial statements.

In the second quarter of 2010, the Patient Protection and Affordable Care Act (PPACA) was signed into law. The PPACA changes the tax treatment related to an existing retiree drug subsidy (RDS) available to sponsors of retiree health benefit plans that provide a benefit that is at least actuarially equivalent to the benefits under Medicare Part D. As a result of the PPACA, RDS payments will effectively become taxable in tax years beginning in 2013, by requiring the amount of the subsidy received to be offset against our deduction for health care expenses. The provisions of the PPACA required us to record the effect of this tax law change beginning in our second quarter of 2010, and consequently we recorded a one-time related tax charge of $41 million in the second quarter of 2010. In the first quarter of 2012, we began pre-paying funds within our 401(h) voluntary employee beneficiary associations (VEBA) trust to fully cover prescription drug benefit liabilities for Medicare eligible retirees. As a result, the receipt of future Medicare subsidy payments for prescription drugs will not be taxable and consequently we recorded a $55 million tax benefit reflecting this change in the first quarter of 2012.

Note 3 — Restructuring, Impairment and Integration Charges

In 2012, we incurred restructuring charges of $279 million ($215 million after-tax or $0.14 per share) in conjunction with our Productivity Plan. In 2011, we incurred restructuring charges of $383 million ($286 million after-tax or $0.18 per share) in conjunction with our Productivity Plan. All of these charges were recorded in selling, general and administrative expenses and primarily relate to severance and other employee related costs, asset impairments, and consulting and contract termination costs. The Productivity Plan includes actions in every aspect of our business that we believe will strengthen our complementary food, snack and beverage businesses by leveraging new technologies and processes across PepsiCo's operations; go-to-market and information systems; heightening the focus on best practice sharing across the globe; consolidating manufacturing, warehouse and sales facilities; and implementing simplified organization structures, with wider spans of control and fewer layers of management. The Productivity Plan is expected to enhance PepsiCo's cost-competitiveness, provide a source of funding for future brand-building and innovation initiatives, and serve as a financial cushion for potential macroeconomic uncertainty.

A summary of our Productivity Plan charges in 2012 was as follows:

	Severance and Other Employee Costs		Asset Impairments		Other Costs		Total
FLNA	$	14	$	8	$	16	$	38
QFNA		—		—		9		9
LAF		15		8		27		50
PAB		34		43		25		102
Europe		14		16		12		42
AMEA		18		—		10		28
Corporate		(6)		—		16		10
	$	89	$	75	$	115	$	279

A summary of our Productivity Plan charges in 2011 was as follows:

	Severance and Other Employee Costs		Other Costs		Total
FLNA	$	74	$	2	$	76
QFNA		18		—		18
LAF		46		2		48
PAB		75		6		81
Europe		65		12		77
AMEA		9		—		9
Corporate		40		34		74
	$	327	$	56	$	383

A summary of our Productivity Plan activity in 2011 and 2012 was as follows:

	Severance and Other Employee Costs		Asset Impairments		Other Costs		Total
2011 restructuring charges	$	327	$	—	$	56	$	383
Cash payments		(1)		—		(29)		(30)
Non-cash charges		(77)		—		—		(77)
Liability as of December 31, 2011		249		—		27		276
2012 restructuring charges		89		75		115		279
Cash payments		(239)		—		(104)		(343)
Non-cash charges		(8)		(75)		(2)		(85)
Liability as of December 29, 2012	$	91	$	—	$	36	$	127

In 2012, we incurred merger and integration charges of $16 million ($12 million after-tax or $0.01 per share) related to our acquisition of WBD, including $11 million recorded in the Europe segment and $5 million recorded in interest expense. All of these net charges, other than the interest expense portion, were recorded in selling, general and administrative expenses. The majority of cash payments related to these charges were paid by the end of 2012.

In 2011, we incurred merger and integration charges of $329 million ($271 million after-tax or $0.17 per share) related to our acquisitions of PBG, PAS and WBD, including $112 million recorded in the PAB segment, $123 million recorded in the Europe segment, $78 million recorded in corporate unallocated expenses and $16 million recorded in interest expense. All of these net charges, other than the interest expense portion, were recorded in selling, general and administrative expenses. These charges also include closing costs and advisory fees related to our acquisition of WBD. Substantially all cash payments related to the above charges were made by the end of 2011.

In 2010, we incurred merger and integration charges of $799 million related to our acquisitions of PBG and PAS, as well as advisory fees in connection with our acquisition of WBD. $467 million of these charges were recorded in the PAB segment, $111 million recorded in the Europe segment, $191 million recorded in corporate unallocated expenses and $30 million recorded in interest expense. All of these charges, other than the interest expense portion, were recorded in selling, general and administrative expenses. The merger and integration charges related to our acquisitions of PBG and PAS were incurred to help create a more fully integrated supply chain and go-to-market business model, to improve the effectiveness and efficiency of the distribution of our brands and to enhance our revenue growth. These charges also include closing costs, one-time financing costs and advisory fees related to our acquisitions of PBG and PAS. In addition, we recorded $9 million of merger-related charges, representing our share of the respective merger costs of PBG and PAS, in bottling equity income. Substantially all cash payments related to the above charges were made by the end of 2011. In total, these charges had an after-tax impact of $648 million or $0.40 per share.

A summary of our merger and integration activity was as follows:

	Severance and Other Employee Costs		Asset Impairments		Other Costs		Total	
2010 merger and integration charges	$	396	$	132	$	280	$	808
Cash payments		(114)		—		(271)		(385)
Non-cash charges		(103)		(132)		16		(219)
Liability as of December 25, 2010		179		—		25		204
2011 merger and integration charges		146		34		149		329
Cash payments		(191)		—		(186)		(377)
Non-cash charges		(36)		(34)		19		(51)
Liability as of December 31, 2011		98		—		7		105
2012 merger and integration charges		(3)		1		18		16
Cash payments		(65)		—		(18)		(83)
Non-cash charges		(12)		(1)		(1)		(14)
Liability as of December 29, 2012	$	18	$	—	$	6	$	24

Note 4 — Property, Plant and Equipment and Intangible Assets

	Average Useful Life (Years)		**2012**		2011		2010
Property, plant and equipment, net							
Land and improvements	10 – 34	$	**1,890**	$	1,951		
Buildings and improvements	15 – 44		**7,792**		7,565		
Machinery and equipment, including fleet and software	5 – 15		**24,743**		23,798		
Construction in progress			**1,737**		1,826		
			36,162		35,140		
Accumulated depreciation			**(17,026)**		(15,442)		
		$	**19,136**	$	19,698		
Depreciation expense		$	**2,489**	$	2,476	$	2,124

Property, plant and equipment is recorded at historical cost. Depreciation and amortization are recognized on a straight-line basis over an asset's estimated useful life. Land is not depreciated and construction in progress is not depreciated until ready for service.

Amortizable intangible assets, net	Average Useful Life (Years)	2012				2011			2010
		Gross	Accumulated Amortization		Net	Gross	Accumulated Amortization	Net	
Acquired franchise rights	56 – 60	$ 931	$	(67)	$ 864	$ 916	$	(42) $ 874	
Reacquired franchise rights	1 – 14	110		(68)	42	110		(47) 63	
Brands	5 – 40	1,422		(980)	442	1,417		(945) 472	
Other identifiable intangibles	10 – 24	736		(303)	433	777		(298) 479	
		$ 3,199	$	(1,418)	$ 1,781	$ 3,220	$	(1,332) $ 1,888	
Amortization expense					$ 119			$ 133	$ 117

Amortization of intangible assets for each of the next five years, based on existing intangible assets as of December 29, 2012 and using average 2012 foreign exchange rates, is expected to be as follows:

	2013	2014	2015	2016	2017
Five-year projected amortization	$ 110	$ 95	$ 86	$ 78	$ 72

Depreciable and amortizable assets are only evaluated for impairment upon a significant change in the operating or macroeconomic environment. In these circumstances, if an evaluation of the undiscounted cash flows indicates impairment, the asset is written down to its estimated fair value, which is based on discounted future cash flows. Useful lives are periodically evaluated to determine whether events or circumstances have occurred which indicate the need for revision. For additional unaudited information on our policies for amortizable brands, see "Our Critical Accounting Policies" in Management's Discussion and Analysis of Financial Condition and Results of Operations.

Nonamortizable Intangible Assets

Perpetual brands and goodwill are assessed for impairment at least annually. If the carrying amount of a perpetual brand exceeds its fair value, as determined by its discounted cash flows, an impairment loss is recognized in an amount equal to that excess. We did not recognize any impairment charges for goodwill in the years presented. We recorded impairment charges on certain brands in Europe of $23 million and $14 million in 2012 and 2011, respectively. The change in the book value of nonamortizable intangible assets is as follows:

	Balance, Beginning 2011	Acquisitions/(Divestitures)	Translation and Other	Balance, End of 2011	Acquisitions/ (Divestitures)	Translation and Other	Balance, End of 2012
FLNA							
Goodwill	$ 313	$ —	$ (2)	$ 311	$ —	$ 5	$ 316
Brands	31	—	(1)	30	—	1	31
	344	—	(3)	341	—	6	347
QFNA							
Goodwill	175	—	—	175	—	—	175
LAF							
Goodwill	497	331	(35)	793	(61)	(16)	716
Brands	143	20	(6)	157	75	(9)	223
	640	351	(41)	950	14	(25)	939
PAB							
Goodwill	9,946	(27)	13	9,932	23	33	9,988
Reacquired franchise rights	7,283	77	(18)	7,342	(33)	28	7,337
Acquired franchise rights	1,565	(1)	(2)	1,562	9	2	1,573
Brands	182	(20)	6	168	—	(15)	153
Other	10	(9)	(1)	—	—	—	—
	18,986	20	(2)	19,004	(1)	48	19,051
Europe [(a)]							
Goodwill	3,040	2,131	(271)	4,900	78	236	5,214
Reacquired franchise rights	793	—	(61)	732	—	40	772
Acquired franchise rights	227	—	(9)	218	—	5	223
Brands	1,380	3,114	(316)	4,178	(96)	202	4,284
	5,440	5,245	(657)	10,028	(18)	483	10,493
AMEA							
Goodwill	690	—	(1)	689	(142)	15	562
Brands	169	—	1	170	(24)	2	148
	859	—	—	859	(166)	17	710
Total goodwill	14,661	2,435	(296)	16,800	(102)	273	16,971
Total reacquired franchise rights	8,076	77	(79)	8,074	(33)	68	8,109
Total acquired franchise rights	1,792	(1)	(11)	1,780	9	7	1,796
Total brands	1,905	3,114	(316)	4,703	(45)	181	4,839
Total other	10	(9)	(1)	—	—	—	—
	$ 26,444	$ 5,616	$ (703)	$31,357	$ (171)	$ 529	$ 31,715

(a)Net increase in 2011 relates primarily to our acquisition of WBD.

Note 5 — Income Taxes

	2012	2011	2010
Income before income taxes			
U.S.	$ 3,234	$ 3,964	$ 4,008
Foreign	5,070	4,870	4,224
	$ 8,304	$ 8,834	$ 8,232
Provision for income taxes			
Current: U.S. Federal	$ 911	$ 611	$ 932
Foreign	940	882	728
State	153	124	137
	2,004	1,617	1,797
Deferred: U.S. Federal	154	789	78
Foreign	(95)	(88)	18
State	27	54	1
	86	755	97
	$ 2,090	$ 2,372	$ 1,894
Tax rate reconciliation			
U.S. Federal statutory tax rate	35.0 %	35.0 %	35.0 %
State income tax, net of U.S. Federal tax benefit	1.4	1.3	1.1
Lower taxes on foreign results	(6.9)	(8.7)	(9.4)
Tax benefit related to tax court decision	(2.6)	—	—
Acquisitions of PBG and PAS	—	—	(3.1)
Other, net	(1.7)	(0.8)	(0.6)
Annual tax rate	25.2 %	26.8 %	23.0 %
Deferred tax liabilities			
Investments in noncontrolled affiliates	$ 48	$ 41	
Debt guarantee of wholly owned subsidiary	828	828	
Property, plant and equipment	2,424	2,466	
Intangible assets other than nondeductible goodwill	4,388	4,297	
Other	260	184	
Gross deferred tax liabilities	7,948	7,816	
Deferred tax assets			
Net carryforwards	1,378	1,373	
Stock-based compensation	378	429	
Retiree medical benefits	411	504	
Other employee-related benefits	672	695	
Pension benefits	647	545	
Deductible state tax and interest benefits	345	339	
Long-term debt obligations acquired	164	223	
Other	863	822	
Gross deferred tax assets	4,858	4,930	
Valuation allowances	(1,233)	(1,264)	
Deferred tax assets, net	3,625	3,666	
Net deferred tax liabilities	$ 4,323	$ 4,150	

		2012		2011		2010
Deferred taxes included within:						
Assets:						
Prepaid expenses and other current assets	$	740	$	845		
Liabilities:						
Deferred income taxes	$	5,063	$	4,995		
Analysis of valuation allowances						
Balance, beginning of year	$	1,264	$	875	$	586
Provision		68		464		75
Other (deductions)/additions		(99)		(75)		214
Balance, end of year	$	1,233	$	1,264	$	875

For additional unaudited information on our income tax policies, including our reserves for income taxes, see "Our Critical Accounting Policies" in Management's Discussion and Analysis of Financial Condition and Results of Operations.

Reserves

A number of years may elapse before a particular matter, for which we have established a reserve, is audited and finally resolved. The number of years with open tax audits varies depending on the tax jurisdiction. Our major taxing jurisdictions and the related open tax audits are as follows:

- U.S. – during 2012, we received a favorable tax court decision related to the classification of financial instruments. We continue to dispute three matters related to the 2003-2007 audit cycle with the IRS Appeals Division. We are currently under audit for tax years 2008-2009;

- Mexico – audits have been completed for all taxable years through 2005. We are currently under audit for 2006-2008;

- United Kingdom – audits have been completed for all taxable years through 2009;

- Canada – domestic audits have been substantially completed for all taxable years through 2008. International audits have been completed for all taxable years through 2005; and

- Russia – audits have been substantially completed for all taxable years through 2008. We are currently under audit for 2009-2011.

While it is often difficult to predict the final outcome or the timing of resolution of any particular tax matter, we believe that our reserves reflect the probable outcome of known tax contingencies. We adjust these reserves, as well as the related interest, in light of changing facts and circumstances. Settlement of any particular issue would usually require the use of cash. Favorable resolution would be recognized as a reduction to our annual tax rate in the year of resolution. For further unaudited information on the impact of the resolution of open tax issues, see "Other Consolidated Results" in Management's Discussion and Analysis of Financial Condition and Results of Operations.

We believe that it is reasonably possible that our reserves for uncertain tax positions could decrease by approximately $1.5 billion within the next twelve months as a result of the completion of audits in various jurisdictions, including the potential settlement with the IRS for the taxable years 2003-2009.

As of December 29, 2012, the total gross amount of reserves for income taxes, reported in income taxes payable and other liabilities, was $2,425 million. Any prospective adjustments to these reserves will be recorded as an increase or decrease to our provision for income taxes and would impact our effective tax rate. In addition, we accrue interest related to reserves for income taxes in our provision for income taxes and any associated penalties are recorded in selling, general and administrative expenses. The gross amount of interest accrued, reported in other liabilities, was $670 million as of December 29, 2012, of which $10 million was recognized in 2012. The gross amount of interest accrued, reported in other liabilities, was $660 million as of December 31, 2011, of which $90 million was recognized in 2011.

A rollforward of our reserves for all federal, state and foreign tax jurisdictions, is as follows:

	2012	2011
Balance, beginning of year	$ 2,167	$ 2,022
Additions for tax positions related to the current year	275	233
Additions for tax positions from prior years	161	147
Reductions for tax positions from prior years	(172)	(46)
Settlement payments	(17)	(156)
Statute of limitations expiration	(3)	(15)
Translation and other	14	(18)
Balance, end of year	$ 2,425	$ 2,167

Carryforwards and Allowances

Operating loss carryforwards totaling $10.4 billion at year-end 2012 are being carried forward in a number of foreign and state jurisdictions where we are permitted to use tax operating losses from prior periods to reduce future taxable income. These operating losses will expire as follows: $0.2 billion in 2013, $8.2 billion between 2014 and 2032 and $2.0 billion may be carried forward indefinitely. We establish valuation allowances for our deferred tax assets if, based on the available evidence, it is more likely than not that some portion or all of the deferred tax assets will not be realized.

Undistributed International Earnings

As of December 29, 2012, we had approximately $32.2 billion of undistributed international earnings. We intend to continue to reinvest earnings outside the U.S. for the foreseeable future and, therefore, have not recognized any U.S. tax expense on these earnings.

Note 6 — Stock-Based Compensation

Our stock-based compensation program is designed to attract and retain employees while also aligning employees' interests with the interests of our shareholders. Stock options and restricted stock units (RSU) are granted to employees under the shareholder-approved 2007 Long-Term Incentive Plan (LTIP).

In 2012, certain executive officers were granted PepsiCo equity performance units (PEPUnits). These PEPUnits are earned based on achievement of a cumulative net income performance target and provide an opportunity to earn shares of PepsiCo common stock with a value that adjusts based upon absolute changes in PepsiCo's stock price as well as PepsiCo's Total Shareholder Return relative to the S&P 500 over a three-year performance period.

The Company may use either authorized and unissued shares or repurchased common stock to meet share requirements resulting from the exercise of stock options and the vesting of restricted stock awards.

At year-end 2012, 124 million shares were available for future stock-based compensation grants.

The following table summarizes our total stock-based compensation expense:

	2012	2011	2010
Stock-based compensation expense	$ 278	$ 326	$ 299
Merger and integration charges	2	13	53
Restructuring and impairment (benefits) / charges	(7)	4	—
Total [(a)]	$ 273	$ 343	$ 352
Income tax benefits recognized in earnings related to stock-based compensation	$ 73	$ 101	$ 89

(a) $86 million recorded in 2010 was related to the unvested PBG/PAS acquisition-related grants.

In connection with our acquisition of PBG in 2010, we issued 13.4 million stock options and 2.7 million RSUs at weighted-average grant prices of $42.89 and $62.30, respectively, to replace previously held PBG equity awards. In connection with our acquisition of PAS in 2010, we issued 0.4 million stock options at a weighted-average grant price of $31.72 to replace previously held PAS equity awards. Our equity issuances included 8.3 million stock options and 0.6 million RSUs which were vested at the acquisition date and were included in the purchase price. The remaining 5.5 million stock options and 2.1 million RSUs issued were unvested at the issuance date and are being amortized over their remaining vesting period, up to three years from the issuance date.

As a result of our annual benefits review in 2010, the Company approved certain changes to our benefits programs to remain market competitive relative to other leading global companies. These changes included ending the Company's broad-based SharePower stock option program. Consequently, beginning in 2011, no new awards were granted under the SharePower program. Outstanding SharePower awards from 2010 and earlier continue to vest and are exercisable according to the terms and conditions of the program. See Note 7 for additional information regarding other related changes.

Method of Accounting and Our Assumptions
We account for our employee stock options under the fair value method of accounting using a Black-Scholes valuation model to measure stock option expense at the date of grant. In addition, we use the Monte-Carlo simulation option-pricing model to determine the fair value of market-based awards. The Monte-Carlo simulation option-pricing model uses the same input assumptions as the Black-Scholes model, however, it also further incorporates into the fair-value determination the possibility that the market condition may not be satisfied. Compensation costs related to awards with a market-based condition are recognized regardless of whether the market condition is satisfied, provided that the requisite service has been provided.

All stock option grants have an exercise price equal to the fair market value of our common stock on the date of grant and generally have a 10-year term. We do not backdate, reprice or grant stock-based compensation awards retroactively. Repricing of awards would require shareholder approval under the LTIP.

87

The fair value of stock option grants is amortized to expense over the vesting period, generally three years. Awards to employees eligible for retirement prior to the award becoming fully vested are amortized to expense over the period through the date that the employee first becomes eligible to retire and is no longer required to provide service to earn the award. Executives who are awarded long-term incentives based on their performance are generally offered the choice of stock options or RSUs. Executives who elect RSUs receive one RSU for every four stock options that would have otherwise been granted. Senior officers do not have a choice and, through 2012, are granted 50% stock options and 50% performance-based RSUs. Our weighted-average Black-Scholes fair value assumptions are as follows:

	2012	2011	2010
Expected life	6 years	6 years	5 years
Risk-free interest rate	1.3%	2.5%	2.3%
Expected volatility	17%	16%	17%
Expected dividend yield	3.0%	2.9%	2.8%

The expected life is the period over which our employee groups are expected to hold their options. It is based on our historical experience with similar grants. The risk-free interest rate is based on the expected U.S. Treasury rate over the expected life. Volatility reflects movements in our stock price over the most recent historical period equivalent to the expected life. Dividend yield is estimated over the expected life based on our stated dividend policy and forecasts of net income, share repurchases and stock price.

A summary of our stock-based compensation activity for the year ended December 29, 2012 is presented below:

Our Stock Option Activity

	Options[a]	Average Price[b]	Average Life (years)[c]	Aggregate Intrinsic Value[d]
Outstanding at December 31, 2011	91,075	$ 55.92		
Granted	3,696	$ 67.13		
Exercised	(23,585)	$ 47.33		
Forfeited/expired	(3,041)	$ 63.81		
Outstanding at December 29, 2012	68,145	$ 59.15	5.04	$ 614,322
Exercisable at December 29, 2012	48,366	$ 56.44	4.45	$ 567,761
Expected to vest as of December 29, 2012	19,432	$ 65.79	7.85	$ 45,374

(a) Options are in thousands and include options previously granted under PBG, PAS and Quaker legacy plans. No additional options or shares may be granted under the PBG, PAS and Quaker plans.
(b) Weighted-average exercise price.
(c) Weighted-average contractual life remaining.
(d) In thousands.

Our RSU Activity

	RSUs[a]	Average Intrinsic Value[b]	Average Life (years)[c]	Aggregate Intrinsic Value[d]
Outstanding at December 31, 2011	12,340	$ 62.96		
Granted	4,404	$ 66.64		
Converted	(3,436)	$ 57.76		
Forfeited	(1,326)	$ 64.80		
Outstanding at December 29, 2012	11,982	$ 65.60	1.49	$ 815,051
Expected to vest as of December 29, 2012	11,616	$ 65.58	1.34	$ 790,128

(a) RSUs are in thousands and include RSUs previously granted under a PBG plan. No additional RSUs or shares may be granted under the PBG plan.
(b) Weighted-average intrinsic value at grant date.
(c) Weighted-average contractual life remaining.
(d) In thousands.

Our PEPUnit Activity

	PEPUnits[a]	Average Intrinsic Value[b]	Average Life (years)[c]	Aggregate Intrinsic Value[d]
Outstanding at December 31, 2011	—	$ —		
Granted	410	$ 64.85		
Converted	—	$ —		
Forfeited	(42)	$ 64.51		
Outstanding at December 29, 2012	368	$ 64.89	2.26	$ 25,031
Expected to vest as of December 29, 2012	334	$ 64.85	2.26	$ 22,721

(a) PEPUnits are in thousands.
(b) Weighted-average intrinsic value at grant date.
(c) Weighted-average contractual life remaining.
(d) In thousands.

Other Stock-Based Compensation Data

	2012	2011	2010
Stock Options			
Weighted-average fair value of options granted	$ 6.86	$ 7.79	$ 13.93
Total intrinsic value of options exercised[a]	$ 512,636	$ 385,678	$ 502,354
RSUs			
Total number of RSUs granted[a]	4,404	5,333	8,326
Weighted-average intrinsic value of RSUs granted	$ 66.64	$ 63.87	$ 65.01
Total intrinsic value of RSUs converted[a]	$ 236,575	$ 173,433	$ 202,717
PEPUnits			
Total number of PEPUnits granted[a]	410	—	
Weighted-average intrinsic value of PEPUnits granted	$ 64.85	$ —	
Total intrinsic value of PEPUnits converted[a]	—		

(a) In thousands.

As of December 31, 2012, there was $389 million of total unrecognized compensation cost related to nonvested share-based compensation grants. This unrecognized compensation is expected to be recognized over a weighted-average period of two years.

Note 7 — Pension, Retiree Medical and Savings Plans

Our pension plans cover certain full-time employees in the U.S. and certain international employees. Benefits are determined based on either years of service or a combination of years of service and earnings. Certain U.S. and Canada retirees are also eligible for medical and life insurance benefits (retiree medical) if they meet age and service requirements. Generally, our share of retiree medical costs is capped at specified dollar amounts, which vary based upon years of service, with retirees contributing the remainder of the costs.

Gains and losses resulting from actual experience differing from our assumptions, including the difference between the actual return on plan assets and the expected return on plan assets, and from changes in our assumptions are determined at each measurement date. If this net accumulated gain or loss exceeds 10% of the greater of the market-related value of plan assets or plan liabilities, a portion of the net gain or loss is included in expense for the following year based upon the average remaining service period of active plan participants, which is approximately 11 years for pension expense and approximately 8 years for retiree medical expense. The cost or benefit of plan changes that increase or decrease benefits for prior employee service (prior service cost/(credit)) is included in earnings on a straight-line basis over the average remaining service period of active plan participants.

In connection with our acquisitions of PBG and PAS, we assumed sponsorship of pension and retiree medical plans that provide benefits to certain U.S. and international employees. Subsequently, during 2010, we merged the pension plan assets of the legacy PBG and PAS U.S. pension plans with those of PepsiCo into one master trust.

During 2010, the Compensation Committee of PepsiCo's Board of Directors approved certain changes to the U.S. pension and retiree medical plans, effective January 1, 2011. Pension plan design changes included implementing a new employer contribution to the 401(k) savings plan for all future salaried new hires of the Company, as salaried new hires are no longer eligible to participate in the defined benefit pension plan, as well as implementing a new defined benefit pension formula for certain hourly new hires of the Company. Pension plan design changes also included implementing a new employer contribution to the 401(k) savings plan for certain legacy PBG and PAS salaried employees (as such employees are also not eligible to participate in the defined benefit pension plan), as well as implementing a new defined benefit pension formula for certain legacy PBG and PAS hourly employees. The retiree medical plan design change included phasing out Company subsidies of retiree medical benefits. As a result of these changes, we remeasured our pension and retiree medical expenses and liabilities in 2010, which resulted in a one-time pre-tax curtailment gain of $62 million included in retiree medical expenses.

In the fourth quarter of 2012, the Company offered certain former employees who have vested benefits in our defined benefit pension plans the option of receiving a one-time lump sum payment equal to the present value of the participant's pension benefit (payable in cash or rolled over into a qualified retirement plan or IRA). In December 2012, we made a discretionary contribution of $405 million to fund substantially all of these payments. The Company recorded a pre-tax non-cash settlement charge of $195 million ($131 million after-tax or $0.08 per share) as a result of this transaction. See "Items Affecting Comparability" in Management's Discussion and Analysis of Financial Condition and Results of Operations.

The provisions of both the PPACA and the Health Care and Education Reconciliation Act are reflected in our retiree medical expenses and liabilities and were not material to our financial statements.

Selected financial information for our pension and retiree medical plans is as follows:

| | Pension | | | | Retiree Medical | |
| | U.S. | | International | | | |
	2012	2011	2012	2011	2012	2011
Change in projected benefit liability						
Liability at beginning of year	$ **11,901**	$ 9,851	$ **2,381**	$ 2,142	$ **1,563**	$ 1,770
Acquisitions/(divestitures)	**—**	11	**—**	(63)	**—**	—
Service cost	**407**	350	**100**	95	**50**	51
Interest cost	**534**	547	**115**	117	**65**	88
Plan amendments	**15**	21	**—**	(16)	**—**	3
Participant contributions	**—**	—	**3**	3	**—**	—
Experience loss/(gain)	**932**	1,484	**200**	224	**(63)**	(239)
Benefit payments	**(278)**	(414)	**(76)**	(69)	**(111)**	(110)
Settlement/curtailment	**(633)**	(20)	**(40)**	(15)	**—**	—
Special termination benefits	**8**	71	**1**	1	**5**	1
Foreign currency adjustment	**—**	—	**102**	(41)	**2**	(1)
Other	**—**	—	**2**	3	**—**	—
Liability at end of year	$ **12,886**	$ 11,901	$ **2,788**	$ 2,381	$ **1,511**	$ 1,563
Change in fair value of plan assets						
Fair value at beginning of year	$ **9,072**	$ 8,870	$ **2,031**	$ 1,896	$ **190**	$ 190
Acquisitions/(divestitures)	**—**	11	**—**	(1)	**—**	—
Actual return on plan assets	**1,282**	542	**206**	79	**35**	—
Employer contributions/funding	**1,368**	63	**246**	176	**251**	110
Participant contributions	**—**	—	**3**	3	**—**	—
Benefit payments	**(278)**	(414)	**(76)**	(69)	**(111)**	(110)
Settlement	**(627)**	—	**(33)**	(30)	**—**	—
Foreign currency adjustment	**—**	—	**86**	(23)	**—**	—
Fair value at end of year	$ **10,817**	$ 9,072	$ **2,463**	$ 2,031	$ **365**	$ 190
Funded status	$ **(2,069)**	$ (2,829)	$ **(325)**	$ (350)	$ **(1,146)**	$ (1,373)

	Pension				Retiree Medical	
	U.S.		International			
	2012	2011	**2012**	2011	**2012**	2011
Amounts recognized						
Other assets	$ —	$ —	$ **51**	$ 55	$ —	$ —
Other current liabilities	**(51)**	(91)	**(2)**	(1)	**(71)**	(124)
Other liabilities	**(2,018)**	(2,738)	**(374)**	(404)	**(1,075)**	(1,249)
Net amount recognized	$ **(2,069)**	$ (2,829)	$ **(325)**	$ (350)	$ **(1,146)**	$ (1,373)
Amounts included in accumulated other comprehensive loss (pre-tax)						
Net loss/(gain)	$ **4,212**	$ 4,217	$ **1,096**	$ 977	$ **(44)**	$ 32
Prior service cost/(credit)	**121**	122	**(3)**	(2)	**(92)**	(118)
Total	$ **4,333**	$ 4,339	$ **1,093**	$ 975	$ **(136)**	$ (86)
Components of the (decrease)/increase in net loss/(gain) included in accumulated other comprehensive loss						
Change in discount rate	$ **776**	$ 1,710	$ **188**	$ 302	$ **84**	$ 115
Employee-related assumption changes	**135**	(140)	**(2)**	(51)	**(67)**	(125)
Liability-related experience different from assumptions	**66**	(85)	**14**	(27)	**(80)**	(210)
Actual asset return different from expected return	**(486)**	162	**(60)**	57	**(13)**	14
Amortization and settlement of losses	**(451)**	(147)	**(64)**	(55)	**—**	(12)
Other, including foreign currency adjustments	**(45)**	(9)	**43**	(16)	**—**	(20)
Total	$ **(5)**	$ 1,491	$ **119**	$ 210	$ **(76)**	$ (238)
Liability at end of year for service to date	$ **11,643**	$ 11,205	$ **2,323**	$ 1,921		

The components of benefit expense are as follows:

	Pension						Retiree Medical		
	U.S.			International					
	2012	2011	2010	**2012**	2011	2010	**2012**	2011	2010
Components of benefit expense									
Service cost	$ **407**	$ 350	$ 299	$ **100**	$ 95	$ 81	$ **50**	$ 51	$ 54
Interest cost	**534**	547	506	**115**	117	106	**65**	88	93
Expected return on plan assets	**(796)**	(704)	(643)	**(146)**	(136)	(123)	**(22)**	(14)	(1)
Amortization of prior service cost/(credit)	**17**	14	12	**1**	2	2	**(26)**	(28)	(22)
Amortization of net loss	**259**	145	119	**53**	40	24	**—**	12	9
	421	352	293	**123**	118	90	**67**	109	133
Settlement/curtailment loss/(gain) [(a)]	**185**	(8)	(2)	**4**	30	1	**—**	—	(62)
Special termination benefits	**8**	71	45	**1**	1	3	**5**	1	3
Total	$ **614**	$ 415	$ 336	$ **128**	$ 149	$ 94	$ **72**	$ 110	$ 74

(a)Includes pension lump sum settlement charge of $195 million in 2012. This charge is reflected in items affecting comparability (see "Items Affecting Comparability" in Management's Discussion and Analysis of Financial Condition and Results of Operations).

The estimated amounts to be amortized from accumulated other comprehensive loss into expense in 2013 for our pension and retiree medical plans are as follows:

	Pension		Retiree Medical
	U.S.	International	
Net loss	$ 289	$ 68	$ 1
Prior service cost/(credit)	18	1	(22)
Total	$ 307	$ 69	$ (21)

The following table provides the weighted-average assumptions used to determine projected benefit liability and benefit expense for our pension and retiree medical plans:

	Pension						Retiree Medical		
	U.S.			International					
	2012	2011	2010	2012	2011	2010	2012	2011	2010
Weighted-average assumptions									
Liability discount rate	4.2%	4.6%	5.7%	4.4%	4.8%	5.5%	3.7%	4.4%	5.2%
Expense discount rate	4.6%	5.7%	6.0%	4.8%	5.5%	6.0%	4.4%	5.2%	5.8%
Expected return on plan assets	7.8%	7.8%	7.8%	6.7%	6.7%	7.1%	7.8%	7.8%	7.8%
Liability rate of salary increases	3.7%	3.7%	4.1%	3.9%	4.1%	4.1%			
Expense rate of salary increases	3.7%	4.1%	4.4%	4.1%	4.1%	4.1%			

The following table provides selected information about plans with liability for service to date and total benefit liability in excess of plan assets:

	Pension				Retiree Medical	
	U.S.		International			
	2012	2011	2012	2011	2012	2011
Selected information for plans with liability for service to date in excess of plan assets						
Liability for service to date	$ (11,643)	$ (11,205)	$ (711)	$ (471)		
Fair value of plan assets	$ 10,817	$ 9,072	$ 552	$ 344		
Selected information for plans with projected benefit liability in excess of plan assets						
Benefit liability	$ (12,886)	$ (11,901)	$ (2,542)	$ (2,191)	$ (1,511)	$ (1,563)
Fair value of plan assets	$ 10,817	$ 9,072	$ 2,166	$ 1,786	$ 365	$ 190

Of the total projected pension benefit liability at year-end 2012, $761 million relates to plans that we do not fund because the funding of such plans does not receive favorable tax treatment.

Future Benefit Payments and Funding

Our estimated future benefit payments are as follows:

	2013	2014	2015	2016	2017	2018-22
Pension	$ 560	$ 570	$ 600	$ 650	$ 705	$ 4,465
Retiree medical[a]	$ 120	$ 125	$ 125	$ 130	$ 130	$ 655

(a)Expected future benefit payments for our retiree medical plans do not reflect any estimated subsidies expected to be received under the 2003 Medicare Act. Subsidies are expected to be approximately $13 million for each of the years from 2013 through 2017 and approximately $90 million in total for 2018 through 2022.

These future benefits to beneficiaries include payments from both funded and unfunded plans.

In 2013, we expect to make pension and retiree medical contributions of approximately $240 million, with up to approximately $17 million expected to be discretionary. Our contributions for retiree medical are estimated to be approximately $70 million in 2013.

Plan Assets

Pension

Our pension plan investment strategy includes the use of actively managed securities and is reviewed periodically in conjunction with plan liabilities, an evaluation of market conditions, tolerance for risk and cash requirements for benefit payments. Our investment objective is to ensure that funds are available to meet the plans' benefit obligations when they become due. Our overall investment strategy is to prudently invest plan assets in a well-diversified portfolio of equity and high-quality debt securities to achieve our long-term return expectations. Our investment policy also permits the use of derivative instruments which are primarily used to reduce risk. Our expected long-term rate of return on U.S. plan assets is 7.8%. Our target investment allocations are as follows:

	2013	2012
Fixed income	40%	40%
U.S. equity	33%	33%
International equity	22%	22%
Real estate	5%	5%

Actual investment allocations may vary from our target investment allocations due to prevailing market conditions. We regularly review our actual investment allocations and periodically rebalance our investments to our target allocations.

The expected return on pension plan assets is based on our pension plan investment strategy and our expectations for long-term rates of return by asset class, taking into account volatility and correlation among asset classes and our historical experience. We also review current levels of interest rates and inflation to assess the reasonableness of the long-term rates. We evaluate our expected return assumptions annually to ensure that they are reasonable. To calculate the expected return on pension plan assets, our market-related value of assets for fixed income is the actual fair value. For all other asset categories, we use a method that recognizes investment gains or losses (the difference between the expected and actual return based on the market-related value of assets) over a five-year period. This has the effect of reducing year-to-year volatility.

Our pension contributions for 2012 were $1,614 million, of which $1,375 million was discretionary. Discretionary contributions included $405 million pertaining to pension lump sum payments.

Retiree Medical

In 2012 and 2011, we made non-discretionary contributions of $111 million and $110 million, respectively, to fund the payment of retiree medical claims. In 2012, we made a discretionary contribution of $140 million to fund future U.S. retiree medical plan benefits. This contribution was invested consistently with the allocation of existing assets in the U.S. pension plan.

Fair Value

The guidance on fair value measurements defines fair value, establishes a framework for measuring fair value and expands disclosures about fair value measurements. The fair value framework requires the categorization of assets and liabilities into three levels based upon the assumptions (inputs) used to price the assets. Level 1 provides the most reliable measure of fair value, whereas Level 3 generally requires significant management judgment.

Plan assets measured at fair value as of fiscal year-end 2012 and 2011 are categorized consistently by level in both years, and are as follows:

	2012				2011
	Total	Level 1	Level 2	Level 3	Total
U.S. plan assets*					
Equity securities:					
U.S. common stock[a]	$ 626	$ 626	$ —	$ —	$ 514
U.S. commingled funds[b]	3,106	—	3,106	—	3,003
International common stock[a]	1,597	1,597	—	—	1,089
International commingled fund[c]	948	—	948	—	776
Preferred stock[d]	20	—	20	—	19
Fixed income securities:					
Government securities[d]	1,287	—	1,287	—	1,032
Corporate bonds[d][e]	2,962	—	2,962	—	2,653
Mortgage-backed securities[d]	110	—	110	—	24
Other:					
Contracts with insurance companies[f]	27	—	—	27	24
Real estate commingled funds[g]	331	—	—	331	—
Cash and cash equivalents	117	117	—	—	78
Sub-total U.S. plan assets	11,131	$ 2,340	$ 8,433	$ 358	9,212
Dividends and interest receivable	51				50
Total U.S. plan assets	$ 11,182				$ 9,262
International plan assets					
Equity securities:					
U.S. commingled funds[b]	$ 278	$ —	$ 278	$ —	$ 246
International commingled funds[c]	863	—	863	—	729
Fixed income securities:					
Government securities[d]	202	—	202	—	171
Corporate bonds[d]	230	—	230	—	196
Fixed income commingled funds[h]	600	—	600	—	530
Other:					
Contracts with insurance companies[f]	35	—	—	35	30
Currency commingled funds[i]	64	—	64	—	52
Real estate commingled fund[g]	60	—	—	60	56
Cash and cash equivalents	125	125	—	—	16
Sub-total international plan assets	2,457	$ 125	$ 2,237	$ 95	2,026
Dividends and interest receivable	6				5
Total international plan assets	$ 2,463				$ 2,031

(a) Based on quoted market prices in active markets.

(b) Based on the fair value of the investments owned by these funds that track various U.S. large, mid-cap and small company indices. Includes one large-cap fund that represents 25% and 30%, respectively, of total U.S. plan assets for 2012 and 2011.

(c) Based on the fair value of the investments owned by these funds that track various non-U.S. equity indices.

(d) Based on quoted bid prices for comparable securities in the marketplace and broker/dealer quotes that are not observable.

(e) Corporate bonds of U.S.-based companies represent 22% and 24%, respectively, of total U.S. plan assets for 2012 and 2011.

(f) Based on the fair value of the contracts as determined by the insurance companies using inputs that are not observable.

(g) Based on the appraised value of the investments owned by these funds as determined by independent third parties using inputs that are not observable.

(h) Based on the fair value of the investments owned by these funds that track various government and corporate bond indices.

(i) Based on the fair value of the investments owned by these funds. Includes managed hedge funds that invest primarily in derivatives to reduce currency exposure.

* 2012 and 2011 amounts include $365 million and $190 million, respectively, of retiree medical plan assets that are restricted for purposes of providing health benefits for U.S. retirees and their beneficiaries.

The change in Level 3 plan assets for 2012 is as follows:

	Balance, End of 2011	Return on Assets Held at Year End	Return on Assets Sold	Purchases and Sales, Net	Balance, End of 2012
Real estate commingled funds	$ 56	$ 15	$ 1	$ 319	$ 391
Contracts with insurance companies	54	9	—	(1)	62
Total	$ 110	$ 24	$ 1	$ 318	$ 453

Retiree Medical Cost Trend Rates

An average increase of 7% in the cost of covered retiree medical benefits is assumed for 2013. This average increase is then projected to decline gradually to 5% in 2020 and thereafter. These assumed health care cost trend rates have an impact on the retiree medical plan expense and liability. However, the cap on our share of retiree medical costs limits the impact. In addition, as of January 1, 2011, the Company started phasing out Company subsidies of retiree medical benefits. A 1-percentage-point change in the assumed health care trend rate would have the following effects:

	1% Increase	1% Decrease
2012 Service and interest cost components	$ 4	$ (4)
2012 Benefit liability	$ 40	$ (38)

Savings Plan

Certain U.S. employees are eligible to participate in 401(k) savings plans, which are voluntary defined contribution plans. The plans are designed to help employees accumulate additional savings for retirement, and we make Company matching contributions on a portion of eligible pay based on years of service.

In 2010, in connection with our acquisitions of PBG and PAS, we also made Company retirement contributions for certain employees on a portion of eligible pay based on years of service.

As of January 1, 2011, a new employer contribution to the 401(k) savings plan became effective for certain eligible legacy PBG and PAS salaried employees as well as all eligible salaried new hires of PepsiCo who were not eligible to participate in the defined benefit pension plan as a result of plan design changes approved during 2010. In 2012 and 2011, our total Company contributions were $109 million and $144 million, respectively.

As of February 2012, certain U.S. employees earning a benefit under one of our defined benefit pension plans were no longer eligible for the Company matching contributions on their 401(k) contributions.

For additional unaudited information on our pension and retiree medical plans and related accounting policies and assumptions, see "Our Critical Accounting Policies" in Management's Discussion and Analysis of Financial Condition and Results of Operations.

Note 8 — Related Party Transactions

On February 26, 2010, we completed our acquisitions of PBG and PAS, at which time we gained control over their operations and began to consolidate their results. See Notes 1 and 15 to our consolidated financial statements. Prior to these acquisitions, our significant related party transactions were with PBG and PAS as they represented our most significant noncontrolled bottling affiliates. In 2010, prior to the date of acquisition of PBG and PAS, we reflected the following related party transactions in our consolidated financial statements: net revenue of $993 million, cost of sales of $116 million and selling, general and administrative expenses of $6 million. As a result of these acquisitions, our related party transactions in 2011 and 2012 were not material.

We also coordinate, on an aggregate basis, the contract negotiations of sweeteners and other raw material requirements, including aluminum cans and plastic bottles and closures for certain of our independent bottlers. Once we have negotiated the contracts, the bottlers order and take delivery directly from the supplier and pay the suppliers directly. Consequently, these transactions are not reflected in our consolidated financial statements. As the contracting party, we could be liable to these suppliers in the event of any nonpayment by our bottlers, but we consider this exposure to be remote.

In addition, our joint ventures with Unilever (under the Lipton brand name) and Starbucks sell finished goods (ready-to-drink teas and coffees) to our noncontrolled bottling affiliates. Consistent with accounting for equity method investments, our joint venture revenue is not included in our consolidated net revenue.

In 2010, we repurchased $357 million (5.5 million shares) of PepsiCo stock from the master trust which holds assets of PepsiCo's U.S. qualified pension plans at market value.

Note 9 — Debt Obligations and Commitments

	2012	2011
Short-term debt obligations		
Current maturities of long-term debt	$ 2,901	$ 2,549
Commercial paper (0.1% and 0.1%)	1,101	2,973
Other borrowings (7.4% and 7.6%)	813	683
	$ 4,815	$ 6,205
Long-term debt obligations		
Notes due 2012 (3.0%)	$ —	$ 2,353
Notes due 2013 (2.3%)	2,891	2,841
Notes due 2014 (4.4% and 4.6%)	3,237	3,335
Notes due 2015 (1.5% and 2.3%)	3,300	1,632
Notes due 2016 (3.9%)	1,878	1,876
Notes due 2017 (2.0% and 5.0%)	1,250	258
Notes due 2018-2042 (4.4% and 4.8%)	13,781	10,548
Other, due 2013-2020 (9.3% and 9.9%)	108	274
	26,445	23,117
Less: current maturities of long-term debt obligations	(2,901)	(2,549)
Total	$ 23,544	$ 20,568

The interest rates in the above table reflect weighted-average rates at year-end.

In 2012, we issued:

- $750 million of 0.750% senior notes maturing in March 2015;
- $900 million of 0.700% senior notes maturing in August 2015;
- $1 billion of 1.250% senior notes maturing in August 2017;
- $1.250 billion of 2.750% senior notes maturing in March 2022;
- £500 million of 2.500% senior notes maturing in November 2022;
- $750 million of 4.000% senior notes maturing in March 2042; and
- $600 million of 3.600% senior notes maturing in August 2042.

The net proceeds from the issuances of all the above notes were used for general corporate purposes, including the repayment of commercial paper.

In the second quarter of 2012, we extended the termination date of our four-year unsecured revolving credit agreement (Four-Year Credit Agreement) from June 14, 2015 to June 14, 2016 and the termination date of our 364-day unsecured revolving credit agreement (364-Day Credit Agreement) from June 12, 2012 to June 11, 2013. Funds borrowed under the Four-Year Credit Agreement and the 364-Day Credit Agreement may be used for general corporate purposes of PepsiCo and its subsidiaries, including, but not limited to, working capital, capital investments and acquisitions.

In addition, as of December 29, 2012, our international debt of $857 million related to borrowings from external parties including various lines of credit. These lines of credit are subject to normal banking terms and conditions and are fully committed at least to the extent of our borrowings.

Long-Term Contractual Commitments [a]

			Payments Due by Period		
	Total	2013	2014 – 2015	2016 – 2017	2018 and beyond
Long-term debt obligations[b]	$ 22,858	$ —	$ 6,450	$ 3,105	$ 13,303
Interest on debt obligations[c]	8,772	915	1,477	1,252	5,128
Operating leases	2,061	445	634	362	620
Purchasing commitments[d]	1,738	741	808	135	54
Marketing commitments[d]	2,332	298	605	490	939
	$ 37,761	$ 2,399	$ 9,974	$ 5,344	$ 20,044

(a) Based on year-end foreign exchange rates.
(b) Excludes $2,901 million related to current maturities of long-term debt, $349 million related to the fair value step-up of debt acquired in connection with our acquisitions of PBG and PAS and $337 million related to the increase in carrying value of long-term debt representing the gains on our fair value interest rate swaps.
(c) Interest payments on floating-rate debt are estimated using interest rates effective as of December 29, 2012.
(d) Primarily reflects non-cancelable commitments as of December 29, 2012.

Most long-term contractual commitments, except for our long-term debt obligations, are not recorded on our balance sheet. Operating leases primarily represent building leases. Non-cancelable purchasing commitments are primarily for packaging materials, oranges and orange juice, and sugar and other sweeteners. Non-cancelable marketing commitments are primarily for sports marketing. Bottler funding to independent bottlers is not reflected in our long-term contractual commitments as it is negotiated on an annual basis. Accrued liabilities for pension and retiree medical plans are not reflected in our long-term contractual commitments because they do not represent expected future cash outflows. See Note 7 to our consolidated financial statements for additional information regarding our pension and retiree medical obligations.

Off-Balance-Sheet Arrangements

It is not our business practice to enter into off-balance-sheet arrangements, other than in the normal course of business. See Note 8 to our consolidated financial statements regarding contracts related to certain of our bottlers.

See "Our Liquidity and Capital Resources" in Management's Discussion and Analysis of Financial Condition and Results of Operations for further unaudited information on our borrowings.

Note 10 — Financial Instruments

We are exposed to market risks arising from adverse changes in:

* commodity prices, affecting the cost of our raw materials and energy;

* foreign exchange risks and currency restrictions; and

* interest rates.

In the normal course of business, we manage these risks through a variety of strategies, including the use of derivatives. Certain derivatives are designated as either cash flow or fair value hedges and qualify for hedge accounting treatment, while others do not qualify and are marked to market through earnings. Cash flows from derivatives used to manage commodity, foreign exchange or interest risks are classified as operating activities. We classify both the earnings and cash flow impact from these derivatives consistent with the underlying hedged item. See "Our Business Risks" in Management's Discussion and Analysis of Financial Condition and Results of Operations for further unaudited information on our business risks.

For cash flow hedges, changes in fair value are deferred in accumulated other comprehensive loss within common shareholders' equity until the underlying hedged item is recognized in net income. For fair value hedges, changes in fair value are recognized immediately in earnings, consistent with the underlying hedged item. Hedging transactions are limited to an underlying exposure. As a result, any change in the value of our derivative instruments would be substantially offset by an opposite change in the value of the underlying hedged items. Hedging ineffectiveness and a net earnings impact occur when the change in the value of the hedge does not offset the change in the value of the underlying hedged item. If the derivative instrument is terminated, we continue to defer the related gain or loss and then include it as a component of the cost of the underlying hedged item. Upon determination that the underlying hedged item will not be part of an actual transaction, we recognize the related gain or loss on the hedge in net income immediately.

We also use derivatives that do not qualify for hedge accounting treatment. We account for such derivatives at market value with the resulting gains and losses reflected in our income statement. We do not use derivative instruments for trading or speculative purposes. We perform assessments of our counterparty credit risk regularly, including a review of credit ratings, credit default swap rates and potential nonperformance of the counterparty. Based on our most recent assessment of our counterparty credit risk, we consider this risk to be low. In addition, we enter into derivative contracts with a variety of financial institutions that we believe are creditworthy in order to reduce our concentration of credit risk.

Commodity Prices

We are subject to commodity price risk because our ability to recover increased costs through higher pricing may be limited in the competitive environment in which we operate. This risk is managed through the use of fixed-price purchase orders, pricing agreements and derivatives. In addition, risk to our supply of certain raw materials is mitigated through purchases from multiple geographies and suppliers. We use derivatives, with terms of no more than three years, to economically hedge price fluctuations related to a portion of our anticipated commodity purchases, primarily for agricultural products, metals and energy. For those derivatives that qualify for hedge accounting, any ineffectiveness is recorded immediately in corporate unallocated expenses. Ineffectiveness was not material for all periods presented. During the next 12 months, we expect to reclassify net losses of $12 million related to these hedges from accumulated other comprehensive loss into net income. Derivatives used to hedge commodity price risk that do not qualify for hedge accounting are marked to market each period and reflected in our income statement.

Our open commodity derivative contracts that qualify for hedge accounting had a face value of $507 million as of December 29, 2012 and $598 million as of December 31, 2011.

Our open commodity derivative contracts that do not qualify for hedge accounting had a face value of $853 million as of December 29, 2012 and $630 million as of December 31, 2011.

Foreign Exchange

Our operations outside of the U.S. generate 49% of our net revenue, with Russia, Mexico, Canada, the United Kingdom and Brazil comprising approximately 25% of our net revenue. As a result, we are exposed to foreign currency risks.

Additionally, we are also exposed to foreign currency risk from foreign currency purchases and foreign currency assets and liabilities created in the normal course of business. We manage this risk through sourcing purchases from local suppliers, negotiating contracts in local currencies with foreign suppliers and through the use of derivatives, primarily forward contracts with terms of no more than two years. Exchange rate gains or losses related to foreign currency transactions are recognized as transaction gains or losses in our income statement as incurred.

Our foreign currency derivatives had a total face value of $2.8 billion as of December 29, 2012 and $2.3 billion as of December 31, 2011. During the next 12 months, we expect to reclassify net losses of $14 million related to foreign currency contracts that qualify for hedge accounting from accumulated other comprehensive loss into net income. Additionally, ineffectiveness for our foreign currency hedges was not material for all periods presented. For foreign currency derivatives that do not qualify for hedge accounting treatment, all losses and gains were offset by changes in the underlying hedged items, resulting in no net material impact on earnings.

Interest Rates

We centrally manage our debt and investment portfolios considering investment opportunities and risks, tax consequences and overall financing strategies. We use various interest rate derivative instruments including, but not limited to, interest rate swaps, cross-currency interest rate swaps, Treasury locks and swap locks to manage our overall interest expense and foreign exchange risk. These instruments effectively change the interest rate and currency of specific debt issuances. Certain of our fixed rate indebtedness has been swapped to floating rates. The notional amount, interest payment and maturity date of the interest rate and cross-currency swaps match the principal, interest payment and maturity date of the related debt. Our Treasury locks and swap locks are entered into to protect against unfavorable interest rate changes relating to forecasted debt transactions.

The notional amounts of the interest rate derivative instruments outstanding as of December 29, 2012 and December 31, 2011 were $8.1 billion and $8.3 billion, respectively. For those interest rate derivative instruments that qualify for cash flow hedge accounting, any ineffectiveness is recorded immediately. Ineffectiveness was not material for all periods presented. During the next 12 months, we expect to reclassify net losses of $23 million related to these hedges from accumulated other comprehensive loss into net income.

As of December 29, 2012, approximately 27% of total debt, after the impact of the related interest rate derivative instruments, was exposed to variable rates, compared to 38% as of December 31, 2011.

Fair Value Measurements

The fair values of our financial assets and liabilities as of December 29, 2012 and December 31, 2011 are categorized as follows:

	2012		2011	
	Assets[a]	Liabilities[a]	Assets[a]	Liabilities[a]
Available-for-sale securities[b]	$ 79	$ —	$ 59	$ —
Short-term investments – index funds[c]	$ 161	$ —	$ 157	$ —
Prepaid forward contracts[d]	$ 33	$ —	$ 40	$ —
Deferred compensation[e]	$ —	$ 492	$ —	$ 519
Derivatives designated as fair value hedging instruments:				
Interest rate derivatives[f]	$ 276	$ —	$ 300	$ —
Derivatives designated as cash flow hedging instruments:				
Foreign exchange contracts[g]	$ 5	$ 19	$ 25	$ 5
Interest rate derivatives[f]	6	—	—	69
Commodity contracts[h]	8	24	3	78
	$ 19	$ 43	$ 28	$ 152
Derivatives not designated as hedging instruments:				
Foreign exchange contracts[g]	$ 8	$ 6	$ 17	$ 20
Interest rate derivatives[f]	123	153	107	141
Commodity contracts[h]	40	45	10	62
	$ 171	$ 204	$ 134	$ 223
Total derivatives at fair value	$ 466	$ 247	$ 462	$ 375
Total	$ 739	$ 739	$ 718	$ 894

(a) Financial assets are classified on our balance sheet within prepaid expenses and other current assets and other assets, with the exception of available-for-sale securities and short-term investments, which are classified as short-term investments. Financial liabilities are classified on our balance sheet within accounts payable and other current liabilities and other liabilities. Unless specifically indicated, all financial assets and liabilities are categorized as Level 2 assets or liabilities.

(b) Based on the price of common stock. Categorized as a Level 1 asset.

(c) Based on price changes in index funds used to manage a portion of market risk arising from our deferred compensation liability. Categorized as a Level 1 asset.

(d) Based primarily on the price of our common stock.

(e) Based on the fair value of investments corresponding to employees' investment elections. As of December 29, 2012 and December 31, 2011, $10 million and $44 million, respectively, are categorized as Level 1 liabilities. The remaining balances are categorized as Level 2 liabilities.

(f) Based on LIBOR forward rates and recently reported market transactions of spot and forward rates.

(g) Based on recently reported market transactions of spot and forward rates.

(h) Based on recently reported transactions in the marketplace, primarily swap arrangements.

The effective portion of the pre-tax (gains)/losses on our derivative instruments are categorized in the table below.

| | Fair Value/Non-designated Hedges | | Cash Flow Hedges | | | |
| | (Gains)/Losses Recognized in Income Statement[a] | | Losses/(Gains) Recognized in Accumulated Other Comprehensive Loss | | Losses/(Gains) Reclassified from Accumulated Other Comprehensive Loss into Income Statement[b] | |
	2012	2011	2012	2011	2012	2011
Foreign exchange contracts	$ (23)	$ 14	$ 41	$ (9)	$ 8	$ 26
Interest rate derivatives	17	(113)	(2)	84	19	15
Commodity contracts	(23)	25	11	51	63	(36)
Total	$ (29)	$ (74)	$ 50	$ 126	$ 90	$ 5

(a) Interest rate derivative losses are primarily from fair value hedges and are included in interest expense. These losses are substantially offset by decreases in the value of the underlying debt, which is also included in interest expense. All other gains/losses are from non-designated hedges and are included in corporate unallocated expenses.

(b) Interest rate derivative losses are included in interest expense. All other gains/losses are primarily included in cost of sales.

The carrying amounts of our cash and cash equivalents and short-term investments approximate fair value due to the short-term maturity. Short-term investments consist principally of short-term time deposits and index funds used to manage a portion of market risk arising from our deferred compensation liability. The fair value of our debt obligations as of December 29, 2012 and December 31, 2011 was $30.5 billion and $29.8 billion, respectively, based upon prices of similar instruments in the marketplace.

Note 11 — Net Income Attributable to PepsiCo per Common Share
Basic net income attributable to PepsiCo per common share is net income available for PepsiCo common shareholders divided by the weighted average of common shares outstanding during the period. Diluted net income attributable to PepsiCo per common share is calculated using the weighted average of common shares outstanding adjusted to include the effect that would occur if in-the-money employee stock options were exercised and RSUs and preferred shares were converted into common shares. Options to purchase 9.6 million shares in 2012, 25.9 million shares in 2011 and 24.4 million shares in 2010 were not included in the calculation of diluted earnings per common share because these options were out-of-the-money. Out-of-the-money options had average exercise prices of $67.64 in 2012, $66.99 in 2011 and $67.26 in 2010.

The computations of basic and diluted net income attributable to PepsiCo per common share are as follows:

	2012		2011		2010	
	Income	Shares[a]	Income	Shares[a]	Income	Shares[a]
Net income attributable to PepsiCo	$ 6,178		$ 6,443		$ 6,320	
Preferred shares:						
Dividends	(1)		(1)		(1)	
Redemption premium	(6)		(6)		(5)	
Net income available for PepsiCo common shareholders	$ 6,171	1,557	$ 6,436	1,576	$ 6,314	1,590
Basic net income attributable to PepsiCo per common share	$ 3.96		$ 4.08		$ 3.97	
Net income available for PepsiCo common shareholders	$ 6,171	1,557	$ 6,436	1,576	$ 6,314	1,590
Dilutive securities:						
Stock options and RSUs	—	17	—	20	—	23
ESOP convertible preferred stock	7	1	7	1	6	1
Diluted	$ 6,178	1,575	$ 6,443	1,597	$ 6,320	1,614
Diluted net income attributable to PepsiCo per common share	$ 3.92		$ 4.03		$ 3.91	

(a)Weighted-average common shares outstanding (in millions).

Note 12 — Preferred Stock

As of December 29, 2012 and December 31, 2011, there were 3 million shares of convertible preferred stock authorized. The preferred stock was issued for an ESOP established by Quaker and these shares are redeemable for common stock by the ESOP participants. The preferred stock accrues dividends at an annual rate of $5.46 per share. At year-end 2012 and 2011, there were 803,953 preferred shares issued and 186,553 and 206,653 shares outstanding, respectively. The outstanding preferred shares had a fair value of $63 million as of December 29, 2012 and $68 million as of December 31, 2011. Each share is convertible at the option of the holder into 4.9625 shares of common stock. The preferred shares may be called by us upon written notice at $78 per share plus accrued and unpaid dividends. Quaker made the final award to its ESOP plan in June 2001.

	2012		2011		2010	
	Shares[a]	Amount	Shares[a]	Amount	Shares[a]	Amount
Preferred stock	0.8	$ 41	0.8	$ 41	0.8	$ 41
Repurchased preferred stock						
Balance, beginning of year	0.6	$ 157	0.6	$ 150	0.6	$ 145
Redemptions	—	7	—	7	—	5
Balance, end of year	0.6	$ 164	0.6	$ 157	0.6	$ 150

(a)In millions.

Note 13 — Accumulated Other Comprehensive Loss Attributable to PepsiCo

Comprehensive income is a measure of income which includes both net income and other comprehensive income or loss. Other comprehensive income or loss results from items deferred from recognition into our income statement. Accumulated other comprehensive income or loss is separately presented on our balance sheet as part of common shareholders' equity. Other comprehensive income/(loss) attributable to PepsiCo was $742 million in 2012, $(2,599) million in 2011 and $164 million in 2010. The accumulated balances for each component of other comprehensive loss attributable to PepsiCo were as follows:

		2012		2011		2010
Currency translation adjustment	$	**(1,946)**	$	(2,688)	$	(1,159)
Cash flow hedges, net of tax		**(94)**		(112)		(38)
Unamortized pension and retiree medical, net of tax [a]		**(3,491)**		(3,419)		(2,442)
Unrealized gain on securities, net of tax		**80**		62		70
Other		**(36)**		(72)		(61)
Accumulated other comprehensive loss attributable to PepsiCo	$	**(5,487)**	$	(6,229)	$	(3,630)

(a) Net of taxes of $1,832 million in 2012, $1,831 million in 2011 and $1,322 million in 2010.

Note 14 — Supplemental Financial Information

		2012		2011		2010
Accounts receivable						
Trade receivables	$	**6,215**	$	6,036		
Other receivables		**983**		1,033		
		7,198		7,069		
Allowance, beginning of year		**157**		144	$	90
Net amounts charged to expense		**28**		30		12
Deductions [a]		**(27)**		(41)		(37)
Other [b]		**(1)**		24		79
Allowance, end of year		**157**		157	$	144
Net receivables	$	**7,041**	$	6,912		
Inventories [c]						
Raw materials	$	**1,875**	$	1,883		
Work-in-process		**173**		207		
Finished goods		**1,533**		1,737		
	$	**3,581**	$	3,827		

(a) Includes accounts written off.

(b) Includes adjustments related to acquisitions, currency translation and other adjustments.

(c) Approximately 3%, in both 2012 and 2011, of the inventory cost was computed using the LIFO method. The differences between LIFO and FIFO methods of valuing these inventories were not material.

	2012	2011
Other assets		
Noncurrent notes and accounts receivable	$ **136**	$ 159
Deferred marketplace spending	**195**	186
Pension plans	**62**	65
Other investments (a)	**718**	89
Other	**542**	522
	$ **1,653**	$ 1,021
Accounts payable and other current liabilities		
Accounts payable	$ **4,451**	$ 4,083
Accrued marketplace spending	**2,187**	2,105
Accrued compensation and benefits	**1,705**	1,771
Dividends payable	**838**	813
Other current liabilities	**2,722**	2,985
	$ **11,903**	$ 11,757

(a)Net increase in 2012 primarily relates to our 5% indirect equity interest in Tingyi-Asahi Beverages Holding Co. Ltd. (TAB).

	2012	2011	2010
Other supplemental information			
Rent expense	$ **581**	$ 589	$ 526
Interest paid	$ **1,074**	$ 1,039	$ 1,043
Income taxes paid, net of refunds	$ **1,840**	$ 2,218	$ 1,495

Note 15 — Acquisitions and Divestitures

PBG and PAS

On February 26, 2010, we acquired PBG and PAS to create a more fully integrated supply chain and go-to-market business model, improving the effectiveness and efficiency of the distribution of our brands and enhancing our revenue growth. The total purchase price was approximately $12.6 billion, which included $8.3 billion of cash and equity and the fair value of our previously held equity interests in PBG and PAS of $4.3 billion. The acquisitions were accounted for as business combinations, and, accordingly, the identifiable assets acquired and liabilities assumed were recorded at their estimated fair values at the date of acquisition. Our fair market valuations of the identifiable assets acquired and liabilities assumed were completed in the first quarter of 2011.

WBD

On February 3, 2011, we acquired the ordinary shares, including shares underlying ADSs and Global Depositary Shares (GDS), of WBD, a company incorporated in the Russian Federation, which represented in the aggregate approximately 66% of WBD's outstanding ordinary shares, pursuant to the purchase agreement dated December 1, 2010 between PepsiCo and certain selling shareholders of WBD for approximately $3.8 billion in cash (or $2.4 billion, net of cash and cash equivalents acquired). The acquisition of those shares increased our total ownership to approximately 77%, giving us a controlling interest in WBD. Under the guidance on accounting for business combinations, once a controlling interest is obtained, we were required to recognize and measure 100% of the identifiable assets acquired, liabilities assumed and noncontrolling interests at their full fair values. Our fair market valuations of the identifiable assets acquired and liabilities assumed were completed in the first quarter of 2012 and the final valuations did not materially differ from those fair values reported as of December 31, 2011.

On March 10, 2011, we commenced tender offers in Russia and the U.S. for all remaining outstanding ordinary shares and ADSs of WBD for 3,883.70 Russian rubles per ordinary share and 970.925 Russian rubles per ADS, respectively. The Russian offer was made to all holders of ordinary shares and the U.S. offer was made to all holders of ADSs. We completed the Russian offer on May 19, 2011 and the U.S. offer on May 16, 2011. After completion of the offers, we paid approximately $1.3 billion for WBD's ordinary shares (including shares underlying ADSs) and increased our total ownership of WBD to approximately 98.6%.

On June 30, 2011, we elected to exercise our squeeze-out rights under Russian law with respect to all remaining WBD ordinary shares not already owned by us. Therefore, under Russian law, all remaining WBD shareholders were required to sell their ordinary shares (including those underlying ADSs) to us at the same price that was offered to WBD shareholders in the Russian tender offer. Accordingly, all registered holders of ordinary shares on August 15, 2011 (including the ADSs depositary) received 3,883.70 Russian rubles per ordinary share. After completion of the squeeze-out in September 2011, we paid approximately $79 million for WBD's ordinary shares (including shares underlying ADSs) and increased our total ownership to 100% of WBD.

Tingyi-Asahi Beverages Holding Co. Ltd.

On March 31, 2012, we completed a transaction with Tingyi. Under the terms of the agreement, we contributed our company-owned and joint venture bottling operations in China to Tingyi's beverage subsidiary, TAB, and received as consideration a 5% indirect equity interest in TAB. As a result of this transaction, TAB is now our franchise bottler in China. We also have a call option to increase our indirect holding in TAB to 20% by 2015. We recorded restructuring and other charges of $150 million ($176 million after-tax or $0.11 per share), primarily consisting of employee-related charges, in our 2012 results. This charge is reflected in items affecting comparability. See "Items Affecting Comparability" in Management's Discussion and Analysis of Financial Condition and Results of Operations.

106

Management's Responsibility for Financial Reporting

To Our Shareholders:

At PepsiCo, our actions – the actions of all our associates – are governed by our Global Code of Conduct. This Code is clearly aligned with our stated values – a commitment to sustained growth, through empowered people, operating with responsibility and building trust. Both the Code and our core values enable us to operate with integrity – both within the letter and the spirit of the law. Our Code of Conduct is reinforced consistently at all levels and in all countries. We have maintained strong governance policies and practices for many years.

The management of PepsiCo is responsible for the objectivity and integrity of our consolidated financial statements. The Audit Committee of the Board of Directors has engaged independent registered public accounting firm, KPMG LLP, to audit our consolidated financial statements, and they have expressed an unqualified opinion.

We are committed to providing timely, accurate and understandable information to investors. Our commitment encompasses the following:

Maintaining strong controls over financial reporting. Our system of internal control is based on the control criteria framework of the Committee of Sponsoring Organizations of the Treadway Commission published in their report titled *Internal Control – Integrated Framework*. The system is designed to provide reasonable assurance that transactions are executed as authorized and accurately recorded; that assets are safeguarded; and that accounting records are sufficiently reliable to permit the preparation of financial statements that conform in all material respects with accounting principles generally accepted in the U.S. We maintain disclosure controls and procedures designed to ensure that information required to be disclosed in reports under the Securities Exchange Act of 1934 is recorded, processed, summarized and reported within the specified time periods. We monitor these internal controls through self-assessments and an ongoing program of internal audits. Our internal controls are reinforced through our Global Code of Conduct, which sets forth our commitment to conduct business with integrity, and within both the letter and the spirit of the law.

Exerting rigorous oversight of the business. We continuously review our business results and strategies. This encompasses financial discipline in our strategic and daily business decisions. Our Executive Committee is actively involved – from understanding strategies and alternatives to reviewing key initiatives and financial performance. The intent is to ensure we remain objective in our assessments, constructively challenge our approach to potential business opportunities and issues, and monitor results and controls.

Engaging strong and effective Corporate Governance from our Board of Directors. We have an active, capable and diligent Board that meets the required standards for independence, and we welcome the Board's oversight as a representative of our shareholders. Our Audit Committee is comprised of independent directors with the financial literacy, knowledge and experience to provide appropriate oversight. We review our critical accounting policies, financial reporting and internal control matters with them and encourage their direct communication with KPMG LLP, with our General Auditor, and with our General Counsel. We also have a Compliance & Ethics Department, led by our Chief Compliance & Ethics Officer, to coordinate our compliance policies and practices.

Providing investors with financial results that are complete, transparent and understandable. The consolidated financial statements and financial information included in this report are the responsibility of management. This includes preparing the financial statements in accordance with accounting principles generally accepted in the U.S., which require estimates based on management's best judgment.

PepsiCo has a strong history of doing what's right. We realize that great companies are built on trust, strong ethical standards and principles. Our financial results are delivered from that culture of accountability, and we take responsibility for the quality and accuracy of our financial reporting.

February 21, 2013

/s/ MARIE T. GALLAGHER
_____

Marie T. Gallagher
Senior Vice President and Controller

/s/ HUGH F. JOHNSTON
_____

Hugh F. Johnston
Chief Financial Officer

/s/ INDRA K. NOOYI
_____

Indra K. Nooyi
Chairman of the Board of Directors and
Chief Executive Officer

108

Report of Independent Registered Public Accounting Firm

The Board of Directors and Shareholders
PepsiCo, Inc.:

We have audited the accompanying Consolidated Balance Sheets of PepsiCo, Inc. and Subsidiaries ("PepsiCo, Inc." or "the Company") as of December 29, 2012 and December 31, 2011, and the related Consolidated Statements of Income, Comprehensive Income, Cash Flows and Equity for each of the fiscal years in the three-year period ended December 29, 2012. We also have audited PepsiCo, Inc.'s internal control over financial reporting as of December 29, 2012, based on criteria established in Internal Control - Integrated Framework issued by the Committee of Sponsoring Organizations of the Treadway Commission (COSO). PepsiCo, Inc.'s management is responsible for these consolidated financial statements, for maintaining effective internal control over financial reporting, and for its assessment of the effectiveness of internal control over financial reporting, included in the accompanying Management's Report on Internal Control over Financial Reporting under Item 9A. Our responsibility is to express an opinion on these consolidated financial statements and an opinion on the Company's internal control over financial reporting based on our audits.

We conducted our audits in accordance with the standards of the Public Company Accounting Oversight Board (United States). Those standards require that we plan and perform the audits to obtain reasonable assurance about whether the financial statements are free of material misstatement and whether effective internal control over financial reporting was maintained in all material respects. Our audits of the consolidated financial statements included examining, on a test basis, evidence supporting the amounts and disclosures in the financial statements, assessing the accounting principles used and significant estimates made by management, and evaluating the overall financial statement presentation. Our audit of internal control over financial reporting included obtaining an understanding of internal control over financial reporting, assessing the risk that a material weakness exists, and testing and evaluating the design and operating effectiveness of internal control based on the assessed risk. Our audits also included performing such other procedures as we considered necessary in the circumstances. We believe that our audits provide a reasonable basis for our opinions.

A company's internal control over financial reporting is a process designed to provide reasonable assurance regarding the reliability of financial reporting and the preparation of financial statements for external purposes in accordance with generally accepted accounting principles. A company's internal control over financial reporting includes those policies and procedures that (1) pertain to the maintenance of records that, in reasonable detail, accurately and fairly reflect the transactions and dispositions of the assets of the company; (2) provide reasonable assurance that transactions are recorded as necessary to permit preparation of financial statements in accordance with generally accepted accounting principles, and that receipts and expenditures of the company are being made only in accordance with authorizations of management and directors of the company; and (3) provide reasonable assurance regarding prevention or timely detection of unauthorized acquisition, use, or disposition of the company's assets that could have a material effect on the financial statements.

Because of its inherent limitations, internal control over financial reporting may not prevent or detect misstatements. Also, projections of any evaluation of effectiveness to future periods are subject to the risk that controls may become inadequate because of changes in conditions, or that the degree of compliance with the policies or procedures may deteriorate.

In our opinion, the consolidated financial statements referred to above present fairly, in all material respects, the financial position of PepsiCo, Inc. as of December 29, 2012 and December 31, 2011, and the results of its operations and its cash flows for each of the fiscal years in the three-year period ended December 29, 2012, in conformity with U.S. generally accepted accounting principles. Also in our opinion, PepsiCo, Inc. maintained, in all material respects, effective internal control over financial reporting as of December 29, 2012, based on criteria established in Internal Control − Integrated Framework issued by COSO.

/s/ KPMG LLP
New York, New York
February 21, 2013

110

Management's Discussion and Analysis for PepsiCo, Inc. and Subsidiaries

Appendix B can be found online at the book's companion website at www.cengagebrain.com

Financial Statement Analysis Package (FSAP)

OUTPUT FROM FSAP FOR PEPSICO INC. AND SUBSIDIARIES

The Financial Statement Analysis Package (**FSAP**) that accompanies this text is a user-friendly, adaptable series of Excel®-based spreadsheet templates. FSAP enables the user to manually input financial statement data for a firm and then perform financial statement analysis, forecasting, and valuation. FSAP contains five spreadsheets: Data, Analysis, Forecasts, Forecast Development, and Valuation.

Appendix C presents the output of these spreadsheets using the data for PepsiCo. The output includes the financial statement data for the years 2003–2008, the profitability and risk ratios for the years 2007–2012, financial statement forecasts, and a variety of valuation models applied to the forecasted data for PepsiCo.

FSAP contains a series of User Guides that provide line-by-line instructions on how to use FSAP. You can download a blank FSAP template as well as the FSAP output for PepsiCo from this book's companion website, which you'll find by going to www.cengagebrain.com and searching for this book by its author or title. FSAP data files also are available for various problems and cases in the book. The FSAP icon has been used throughout the book to denote potential applications for FSAP.

Data Spreadsheet

Analyst Name:	Wahlen, Baginski & Bradshaw					
Company Name:	PepsiCo					

Year (Most recent in far right column.)	2007	2008	2009	2010	2011	2012
BALANCE SHEET DATA						
Assets:						
Cash and cash equivalents	910	2,064	3,943	5,943	4,067	6,297
Marketable securities	1,571	213	192	426	358	322
Accounts and notes receivable—net	4,389	4,683	4,624	6,323	6,912	7,041
Inventories	2,290	2,522	2,618	3,372	3,827	3,581
Prepaid expenses and other current assets	991	1,324	1,194	1,505	2,277	1,479
Deferred tax assets—current						
Other current assets (1)						
Other current assets (2)						
Current Assets	**10,151**	**10,806**	**12,571**	**17,569**	**17,441**	**18,720**
Investments in noncontrolled affiliates	4,354	3,883	4,484	1,368	1,477	1,633
Property, plant, and equipment—at cost	21,896	22,552	24,912	33,041	35,140	36,162
<Accumulated depreciation>	−10,668	−10,889	−12,241	−13,983	−15,442	−17,026
Amortizable intangible assets (net)	796	732	841	2,025	1,888	1,781
Goodwill	5,169	5,124	6,534	14,661	16,800	16,971
Other nonamortizable intangible assets	1,248	1,128	1,782	11,783	14,557	14,744
Deferred tax assets—non current						
Other assets	1,682	2,658	965	1,689	1,021	1,653
Total Assets	**34,628**	**35,994**	**39,848**	**68,153**	**72,882**	**74,638**
Liabilities and Equities:						
Accounts payable	2,562	2,846	2,881	3,865	4,083	4,451
Current accrued expenses	5,040	5,427	5,246	7,058	7,674	7,452
Notes payable and short-term debt	0	369	464	4,898	6,205	4,815
Current maturities of long-term debt						
Deferred tax liabilities—current						
Income taxes payable	151	145	165	71	192	371
Other current liabilities (2)						
Other current liabilities (1)						
Current Liabilities	**7,753**	**8,787**	**8,756**	**15,892**	**18,154**	**17,089**
Long-term debt obligations	4,203	7,858	7,400	19,999	20,568	23,544
Long-term accrued liabilities	4,730	6,541	5,591	6,729	8,266	6,543
Deferred tax liabilities—noncurrent	646	226	659	4,057	4,995	5,063
Other noncurrent liabilities (1)						
Other noncurrent liabilities (2)						
Total Liabilities	**17,332**	**23,412**	**22,406**	**46,677**	**51,983**	**52,239**

Data Spreadsheet (Continued)

Year (Most recent in far right column.)	2007	2008	2009	2010	2011	2012
Preferred stock	−91	−97	−104	−109	−116	−123
Common stock + Additional paid in capital	480	381	280	4,558	4,487	4,204
Retained earnings <deficit>	28,184	30,638	33,805	37,090	40,316	43,158
Accum. other comprehensive income <loss>	−952	−4,694	−3,794	−3,630	−6,229	−5,487
<Treasury stock> and other equity adjustments	−10,387	−14,122	−13,383	−16,745	−17,870	−19,458
Total Common Shareholders' Equity	**17,325**	**12,203**	**16,908**	**21,273**	**20,704**	**22,417**
Noncontrolling interests	62	476	638	312	311	105
Total Equity	**17,296**	**12,582**	**17,442**	**21,476**	**20,899**	**22,399**
Total Liabilities and Equities	**34,628**	**35,994**	**39,848**	**68,153**	**72,882**	**74,638**

INCOME STATEMENT DATA	2007	2008	2009	2010	2011	2012
Revenues	39,474	43,251	43,232	57,838	66,504	65,492
<Cost of goods sold>	−18,038	−20,351	−20,099	−26,575	−31,593	−31,291
Gross Profit	**21,436**	**22,900**	**23,133**	**31,263**	**34,911**	**34,201**
<Selling, general and administrative expenses>	−14,196	−15,877	−15,026	−22,814	−25,145	−24,970
<Research and development expenses>						
<Amortization of intangible assets>	−58	−64	−63	−117	−133	−119
<Other operating expenses (1)>						
<Other operating expenses (2)>						
Other operating income (1)						
Other operating income (2)						
Non-recurring operating gains <losses>						
Operating Profit	**7,182**	**6,959**	**8,044**	**8,332**	**9,633**	**9,112**
Interest income	125	41	67	68	57	91
<Interest expense>	−224	−329	−397	−903	−856	−899
Income <Loss> from equity affiliates	560	374	365	735	0	0
Other income or gains <Other expenses or losses>						
Income before Tax	**7,643**	**7,045**	**8,079**	**8,232**	**8,834**	**8,304**
<Income tax expense>	−1,973	−1,879	−2,100	−1,894	−2,372	−2,090
Income <Loss> from discontinued operations						
Extraordinary gains <losses>						
Changes in accounting principles						
Net Income	**5,670**	**5,166**	**5,979**	**6,338**	**6,462**	**6,214**
Net income attributable to noncontrolling interests	−12	−24	−33	−18	−19	−36
Net Income attributable to common shareholders	5,658	5,142	5,946	6,320	6,443	6,178
Net Income (enter reported amount as a check)	5,658	5,142	5,946	6,320	6,443	6,178
Other comprehensive income items	1,282	−3,817	867	146	−2,618	706
Comprehensive Income	**6,952**	**1,349**	**6,846**	**6,484**	**3,844**	**6,920**

(Continued)

Data Spreadsheet (Continued)

Year (Most recent in far right column.)	2007	2008	2009	2010	2011	2012
STATEMENT OF CASH FLOWS DATA						
Net Income	5,670	5,166	5,979	6,338	6,462	6,214
Add back depreciation and amortization expenses	1,426	1,543	1,635	2,327	2,737	2,689
Add back stock-based compensation expense	260	238	227	299	326	278
Deferred income taxes	118	573	284	500	495	321
<Income from equity affiliates, net of dividends>	−441	−202	−235	42	0	0
<Increase> Decrease in accounts receivable	−405	−549	188	−268	−666	−250
<Increase> Decrease in inventories	−204	−345	17	276	−331	144
<Increase> Decrease in prepaid expenses	−16	−68	−127	144	−27	89
<Increase> Decrease in other current assets						
<Increase> Decrease in other noncurrent assets						
Increase <Decrease> in accounts payable	522	718	−133	488	520	548
Increase <Decrease> in income taxes payable	128	−180	319	123	−340	−97
Increase <Decrease> in other current liabilities						
Increase <Decrease> in other noncurrent liabilities						
Other addbacks to <subtractions from> net income	97	496	−1,077	−1,689	456	−1,257
Other operating cash flows	−221	−391	−281	−132	−688	−200
Net CF from Operating Activities	**6,934**	**6,999**	**6,796**	**8,448**	**8,944**	**8,479**
Proceeds from sales of property, plant, and equipment	47	98	58	81	84	95
<Property, plant, and equipment acquired>	−2,430	−2,446	−2,128	−3,253	−3,339	−2,714
<Increase> Decrease in marketable securities	−383	1,282	55	−212	66	61
Investments sold	27	364	99	12	780	−32
<Investments acquired>	−1,320	−1,925	−500	−4,279	−3,193	−427
Payments for acquisitions of intangible assets	315	−40				
Other investment transactions			15	−17	−16	12
Net CF from Investing Activities	**−3,744**	**−2,667**	**−2,401**	**−7,668**	**−5,618**	**−3,005**
Increase <Decrease> in short-term borrowing	−395	445	−1,018	2,482	303	−1,461
Increase <Decrease> in long-term borrowing	1,589	3,070	831	5,892	633	3,550
Issue of capital stock	0	0	0	0	0	0
Proceeds from stock option exercises	1,108	620	455	1,145	1,015	1,246
<Share repurchases—treasury stock>	−4,312	−4,726	−7	−4,983	−2,496	−3,226
<Dividend payments>	−2,204	−2,541	−2,732	−2,978	−3,157	−3,305
Other financing transactions (1)	208	107	0	−159	−1,406	−68
Other financing transactions (2)			−26	−13	−27	−42
Net CF from Financing Activities	**−4,006**	**−3,025**	**−2,497**	**1,386**	**−5,135**	**−3,306**
Effects of exchange rate changes on cash	75	−153	−19	−166	−67	62
Net Change in Cash	**−741**	**1,154**	**1,879**	**2,000**	**−1,876**	**2,230**
Cash and cash equivalents, beginning of year	1,651	910	2,064	3,943	5,943	4,067
Cash and cash equivalents, end of year	910	2,064	3,943	5,943	4,067	6,297

Data Spreadsheet (Continued)

Year (Most recent in far right column.)	2007	2008	2009	2010	2011	2012
SUPPLEMENTAL DATA						
Statutory tax rate	35.0%	35.0%	35.0%	35.0%	35.0%	35.0%
Average tax rate implied from income statement data	25.8%	26.7%	26.0%	23.0%	26.9%	25.2%
After-tax effects of nonrecurring and unusual items on net income	71	−745	100	−355	−592	−276
Depreciation expense	1,304	1,422	1,500	2,124	2,476	2,489
Preferred stock dividends (total, if any)	2	1	2	1	1	1
Common shares outstanding	1,605	1,553	1,566	1,582	1,565	1,544
Earnings per share (basic)	3.48	3.26	3.81	3.97	4.08	3.96
Common dividends per share	1.37	1.64	1.74	1.88	2.02	2.14
Share price at fiscal year end	65.86	48.14	56.22	61.95	64.86	68.43

FINANCIAL DATA CHECKS						
Assets − Liabilities − Equities	0	0	0	0	0	0
Net Income (computed) − Net Income (reported)	0	0	0	0	0	0
Cash Changes	0	0	0	0	0	0

Analysis Spreadsheet

Analyst Name:	Wahlen, Baginski & Bradshaw
Company Name:	PepsiCo

DATA CHECKS

Assets – Liabilities – Equities	0	0	0	0	0
Net Income (computed) – Net Income (reported)	0	0	0	0	0
Cash Changes	0	0	0	0	0

PROFITABILITY FACTORS:

Year	2008	2009	2010	2011	2012
RETURN ON ASSETS (based on reported amounts):					
Profit Margin for ROA	12.4%	14.4%	12.0%	10.6%	10.4%
× Asset Turnover	1.2	1.1	1.1	0.9	0.9
= Return on Assets	15.2%	16.4%	12.8%	10.0%	9.2%
RETURN ON ASSETS (excluding the effects of nonrecurring items):					
Profit Margin for ROA	14.2%	14.2%	12.6%	11.4%	10.8%
× Asset Turnover	1.2	1.1	1.1	0.9	0.9
= Return on Assets	17.3%	16.2%	13.5%	10.8%	9.6%
RETURN ON COMMON EQUITY (based on reported amounts):					
Profit Margin for ROCE	11.9%	13.7%	10.9%	9.7%	9.4%
× Asset Turnover	1.2	1.1	1.1	0.9	0.9
× Capital Structure Leverage	2.4	2.6	2.8	3.4	3.4
= Return on Common Equity	34.8%	40.8%	33.1%	30.7%	28.6%
RETURN ON COMMON EQUITY (excluding the effects of nonrecurring items):					
Profit Margin for ROCE	13.6%	13.5%	11.5%	10.6%	9.9%
× Asset Turnover	1.2	1.1	1.1	0.9	0.9
× Capital Structure Leverage	2.4	2.6	2.8	3.4	3.4
= Return on Common Equity	39.9%	40.1%	35.0%	33.5%	29.9%
OPERATING PERFORMANCE:					
Gross Profit/Revenues	52.9%	53.5%	54.1%	52.5%	52.2%
Operating Profit/Revenues	16.1%	18.6%	14.4%	14.5%	13.9%
Net Income/Revenues	11.9%	13.8%	10.9%	9.7%	9.4%
Comprehensive Income/Revenues	3.1%	15.8%	11.2%	5.8%	10.6%
PERSISTENT OPERATING PERFORMANCE (excluding the effects of nonrecurring items):					
Persistent Operating Profit/Revenues	16.1%	18.6%	14.4%	14.5%	13.9%
Persistent Net Income/Revenues	13.6%	13.5%	11.5%	10.6%	9.9%
GROWTH:					
Revenue Growth	9.6%	0.0%	33.8%	15.0%	−1.5%
Net Income Growth	−9.1%	15.6%	6.3%	1.9%	−4.1%
Persistent Net Income Growth	5.4%	−0.7%	14.2%	5.4%	−8.3%

Analysis Spreadsheet (Continued)

PROFITABILITY FACTORS:

Year	2008	2009	2010	2011	2012
OPERATING CONTROL:					
Gross Profit Control Index	97.5%	101.1%	101.0%	97.1%	99.5%
Operating Profit Contol Index	88.4%	115.6%	77.4%	100.5%	96.1%
Profit Margin Decomposition:					
Gross Profit Margin	52.9%	53.5%	54.1%	52.5%	52.2%
Operating Profit Index	30.4%	34.8%	26.7%	27.6%	26.6%
Leverage Index	101.2%	100.4%	98.8%	91.7%	91.1%
Tax Index	73.3%	74.0%	77.0%	73.1%	74.8%
Net Profit Margin	11.9%	13.8%	11.0%	9.7%	9.5%
Comprehensive Income Performance:					
Comprehensive Income Index	26.1%	114.5%	102.3%	59.5%	111.4%
Comprehensive Income Margin	3.1%	15.8%	11.2%	5.8%	10.6%

RISK FACTORS:

Year	2008	2009	2010	2011	2012
LIQUIDITY:					
Current Ratio	1.23	1.44	1.11	0.96	1.10
Quick Ratio	0.79	1.00	0.80	0.62	0.80
Operating Cash Flow to Current Liabilities	84.6%	77.5%	68.5%	52.5%	48.1%
ASSET TURNOVER:					
Accounts Receivable Turnover	9.5	9.3	10.6	10.0	9.4
Days Receivables Held	38	39	35	36	39
Inventory Turnover	8.5	7.8	8.9	8.8	8.4
Days Inventory Held	43	47	41	42	43
Accounts Payable Turnover	7.6	7.1	8.1	8.1	7.3
Days Payables Held	48	52	45	45	50
Net Working Capital Days	33	34	31	33	32
Revenues/Average Net Fixed Assets	3.8	3.5	3.6	3.4	3.4
Cash Turnover	29.1	14.4	11.7	13.3	12.6
Days Sales Held in Cash	12.5	25.4	31.2	27.5	28.9
SOLVENCY:					
Total Liabilities/Total Assets	65.0%	56.2%	68.5%	71.3%	70.0%
Total Liabilities/Total Equity	186.1%	128.5%	217.3%	248.7%	233.2%
LT Debt/LT Capital	38.4%	29.8%	48.2%	49.6%	51.2%
LT Debt/Total Equity	62.5%	42.4%	93.1%	98.4%	105.1%
Operating Cash Flow to Total Liabilities	34.4%	29.7%	24.5%	18.1%	16.3%
Interest Coverage Ratio (reported amounts)	22.4	21.4	10.1	11.3	10.2
Interest Coverage ratio (recurring amounts)	22.4	21.4	10.1	11.3	10.2

(Continued)

Analysis Spreadsheet (Continued)

RISK FACTORS:

Year	2008	2009	2010	2011	2012
Bankruptcy Predictors:					
Altman Z Score	5.05	5.45	3.34	3.29	3.33
Bankruptcy Probability	0.00%	0.00%	0.96%	1.11%	0.98%
Earnings Manipulation Predictors:					
Beneish Earnings Manipulation Score	−2.73	−2.59	−2.31	−2.54	−2.61
Earnings Manipulation Probability	0.31%	0.48%	1.05%	0.55%	0.46%
DIVIDEND and STOCK MARKET-BASED RATIOS:					
Stock Returns	−24.4%	20.4%	13.5%	8.0%	8.8%
Price-Earnings Ratio (reported amounts)	14.8	14.8	15.6	15.9	17.3
Price-Earnings Ratio (recurring amounts)	12.9	15.0	14.8	14.5	16.5
Market Value to Book Value Ratio	6.1	5.2	4.6	4.9	4.7
Common Dividends per Share	$1.64	$1.74	$1.88	$2.02	$2.14
Common Dividend Payout (% of Net Income)	−49.4%	−45.9%	−47.1%	−49.0%	−53.5%
Common Dividend Yield (% of Share Price)	3.4%	3.1%	3.0%	3.1%	3.1%

INCOME STATEMENT ITEMS AS A PERCENT OF REVENUES:

Year	2008	2009	2010	2011	2012
Revenues	**100.0%**	**100.0%**	**100.0%**	**100.0%**	**100.0%**
<Cost of goods sold>	−47.1%	−46.5%	−45.9%	−47.5%	−47.8%
Gross Profit	**52.9%**	**53.5%**	**54.1%**	**52.5%**	**52.2%**
<Selling, general and administrative expenses>	−36.7%	−34.8%	−39.4%	−37.8%	−38.1%
<Research and development expenses>					
<Amortization of intangible assets>	−0.1%	−0.1%	−0.2%	−0.2%	−0.2%
<Other operating expenses (1)>					
<Other operating expenses (2)>					
Other operating income (1)					
Other operating income (2)					
Non-recurring operating gains <losses>					
Operating Profit	**16.1%**	**18.6%**	**14.4%**	**14.5%**	**13.9%**
Interest income	0.1%	0.2%	0.1%	0.1%	0.1%
<Interest expense>	−0.8%	−0.9%	−1.6%	−1.3%	−1.4%
Income <Loss> from equity affiliates	0.9%	0.8%	1.3%		
Other income or gains <Other expenses or losses>					
Income before Tax	**16.3%**	**18.7%**	**14.2%**	**13.3%**	**12.7%**
<Income tax expense>	−4.3%	−4.9%	−3.3%	−3.6%	−3.2%
Income <Loss> from discontinued operations					
Extraordinary gains <losses>					
Changes in accounting principles					
Net Income	**11.9%**	**13.8%**	**11.0%**	**9.7%**	**9.5%**
Net income attributable to noncontrolling interests	−0.1%	−0.1%	0.0%	0.0%	−0.1%
Net Income attributable to common shareholders	**11.9%**	**13.8%**	**10.9%**	**9.7%**	**9.4%**
Other comprehensive income items	−8.8%	2.0%	0.3%	−3.9%	1.1%
Comprehensive Income	**3.1%**	**15.8%**	**11.2%**	**5.8%**	**10.6%**

Analysis Spreadsheet (Continued)

INCOME STATEMENT ITEMS: GROWTH RATES

Year	2008	2009	2010	2011	2012	COMPOUND GROWTH RATE
		YEAR TO YEAR GROWTH RATES				
Revenues	9.6%	0.0%	33.8%	15.0%	−1.5%	10.7%
<Cost of goods sold>	12.8%	−1.2%	32.2%	18.9%	−1.0%	11.6%
Gross Profit	**6.8%**	**1.0%**	**35.1%**	**11.7%**	**−2.0%**	**9.8%**
<Selling, general and administrative expenses>	11.8%	−5.4%	51.8%	10.2%	−0.7%	12.0%
<Research and development expenses>						
<Amortization of intangible assets>	10.3%	−1.6%	85.7%	13.7%	−10.5%	15.5%
<Other operating expenses (1)>						
<Other operating expenses (2)>						
Other operating income (1)						
Other operating income (2)						
Non-recurring operating gains <losses>						
Operating Profit	**−3.1%**	**15.6%**	**3.6%**	**15.6%**	**−5.4%**	**4.9%**
Interest income	−67.2%	63.4%	1.5%	−16.2%	59.6%	−6.2%
<Interest expense>	46.9%	20.7%	127.5%	−5.2%	5.0%	32.0%
Income <Loss> from equity affiliates	−33.2%	−2.4%	101.4%	−100.0%		−100.0%
Other income or gains <Other expenses or losses>						
Income before Tax	**−7.8%**	**14.7%**	**1.9%**	**7.3%**	**−6.0%**	**1.7%**
<Income tax expense>	−4.8%	11.8%	−9.8%	25.2%	−11.9%	1.2%
Income <Loss> from discontinued operations						
Extraordinary gains <losses>						
Changes in accounting principles						
Net Income	**−8.9%**	**15.7%**	**6.0%**	**2.0%**	**−3.8%**	**1.8%**
Net income attributable to noncontrolling interests	100.0%	37.5%	−45.5%	5.6%	89.5%	24.6%
Net Income attributable to common shareholders	**−9.1%**	**15.6%**	**6.3%**	**1.9%**	**−4.1%**	**1.8%**
Other comprehensive income items	−397.7%	−122.7%	−83.2%	−1893.2%	−127.0%	−11.2%
Comprehensive Income	**−80.6%**	**407.5%**	**−5.3%**	**−40.7%**	**80.0%**	**−0.1%**

(Continued)

Analysis Spreadsheet (Continued)

COMMON SIZE BALANCE SHEET—AS A PERCENT OF TOTAL ASSETS

Year	2008	2009	2010	2011	2012
Assets:					
Cash and cash equivalents	5.7%	9.9%	8.7%	5.6%	8.4%
Marketable securities	0.6%	0.5%	0.6%	0.5%	0.4%
Accounts and notes receivable—net	13.0%	11.6%	9.3%	9.5%	9.4%
Inventories	7.0%	6.6%	4.9%	5.3%	4.8%
Prepaid expenses and other current assets	3.7%	3.0%	2.2%	3.1%	2.0%
Deferred tax assets—current					
Current Assets	**30.0%**	**31.5%**	**25.8%**	**23.9%**	**25.1%**
Investments in noncontrolled affiliates	10.8%	11.3%	2.0%	2.0%	2.2%
Property, plant, and equipment—at cost	62.7%	62.5%	48.5%	48.2%	48.4%
<Accumulated depreciation>	−30.3%	−30.7%	−20.5%	−21.2%	−22.8%
Amortizable intangible assets (net)	2.0%	2.1%	3.0%	2.6%	2.4%
Goodwill	14.2%	16.4%	21.5%	23.1%	22.7%
Other nonamortizable intangible assets	3.1%	4.5%	17.3%	20.0%	19.8%
Deferred tax assets—non current					
Other assets	7.4%	2.4%	2.5%	1.4%	2.2%
Total Assets	**100.0%**	**100.0%**	**100.0%**	**100.0%**	**100.0%**
Liabilities and Equities:					
Accounts payable	7.9%	7.2%	5.7%	5.6%	6.0%
Current accrued expenses	15.1%	13.2%	10.4%	10.5%	10.0%
Notes payable and short-term debt	1.0%	1.2%	7.2%	8.5%	6.5%
Current maturities of long-term debt					
Deferred tax liabilities—current					
Income taxes payable	0.4%	0.4%	0.1%	0.3%	0.5%
Current Liabilities	**24.4%**	**22.0%**	**23.3%**	**24.9%**	**22.9%**
Long-term debt obligations	21.8%	18.6%	29.3%	28.2%	31.5%
Long-term accrued liabilities	18.2%	14.0%	9.9%	11.3%	8.8%
Deferred tax liabilities—noncurrent	0.6%	1.7%	6.0%	6.9%	6.8%
Total Liabilities	**65.0%**	**56.2%**	**68.5%**	**71.3%**	**70.0%**
Preferred stock	−0.3%	−0.3%	−0.2%	−0.2%	−0.2%
Common stock + Additional paid in capital	1.1%	0.7%	6.7%	6.2%	5.6%
Retained earnings <deficit>	85.1%	84.8%	54.4%	55.3%	57.8%
Accum. other comprehensive income <loss>	−13.0%	−9.5%	−5.3%	−8.5%	−7.4%
<Treasury stock> and other equity adjustments	−39.2%	−33.6%	−24.6%	−24.5%	−26.1%
Total Common Shareholders' Equity	**33.9%**	**42.4%**	**31.2%**	**28.4%**	**30.0%**
Noncontrolling interests	1.3%	1.6%	0.5%	0.4%	0.1%
Total Equity	**35.0%**	**43.8%**	**31.5%**	**28.7%**	**30.0%**
Total Liabilities and Equities	**100.0%**	**100.0%**	**100.0%**	**100.0%**	**100.0%**

Analysis Spreadsheet (Continued)

BALANCE SHEET ITEMS: GROWTH RATES

Year	2008	2009	2010	2011	2012	
	YEAR TO YEAR GROWTH RATES					COMPOUND GROWTH RATE
Assets:						
Cash and cash equivalents	126.8%	91.0%	50.7%	−31.6%	54.8%	47.2%
Marketable securities	−86.4%	−9.9%	121.9%	−16.0%	−10.1%	−27.2%
Accounts and notes receivable—net	6.7%	−1.3%	36.7%	9.3%	1.9%	9.9%
Inventories	10.1%	3.8%	28.8%	13.5%	−6.4%	9.4%
Prepaid expenses and other current assets	33.6%	−9.8%	26.0%	51.3%	−35.0%	8.3%
Deferred tax assets—current						
Current Assets	**6.5%**	**16.3%**	**39.8%**	**−0.7%**	**7.3%**	**13.0%**
Investments in noncontrolled affiliates	−10.8%	15.5%	−69.5%	8.0%	10.6%	−17.8%
Property, plant, and equipment—at cost	3.0%	10.5%	32.6%	6.4%	2.9%	10.6%
<Accumulated depreciation>	2.1%	12.4%	14.2%	10.4%	10.3%	9.8%
Amortizable intangible assets (net)	−8.0%	14.9%	140.8%	−6.8%	−5.7%	17.5%
Goodwill	−0.9%	27.5%	124.4%	14.6%	1.0%	26.8%
Other nonamortizable intangible assets	−9.6%	58.0%	561.2%	23.5%	1.3%	63.9%
Deferred tax assets—non current						
Other assets	58.0%	−63.7%	75.0%	−39.6%	61.9%	−0.3%
Total Assets	**3.9%**	**10.7%**	**71.0%**	**6.9%**	**2.4%**	**16.6%**
Liabilities and Equities:						
Accounts payable	11.1%	1.2%	34.2%	5.6%	9.0%	11.7%
Current accrued expenses	7.7%	−3.3%	34.5%	8.7%	−2.9%	8.1%
Notes payable and short-term debt		25.7%	955.6%	26.7%	−22.4%	
Current maturities of long-term debt						
Deferred tax liabilities—current						
Income taxes payable	−4.0%	13.8%	−57.0%	170.4%	93.2%	19.7%
Current Liabilities	**13.3%**	**−0.4%**	**81.5%**	**14.2%**	**−5.9%**	**17.1%**
Long-term debt obligations	87.0%	−5.8%	170.3%	2.8%	14.5%	41.1%
Long-term accrued liabilities	38.3%	−14.5%	20.4%	22.8%	−20.8%	6.7%
Deferred tax liabilities—noncurrent	−65.0%	191.6%	515.6%	23.1%	1.4%	51.0%
Total Liabilities	**35.1%**	**−4.3%**	**108.3%**	**11.4%**	**0.5%**	**24.7%**
Preferred stock	6.6%	7.2%	4.8%	6.4%	6.0%	6.2%
Common stock + Additional paid in capital	−20.6%	−26.5%	1527.9%	−1.6%	−6.3%	54.3%
Retained earnings <deficit>	8.7%	10.3%	9.7%	8.7%	7.0%	8.9%
Accum. other comprehensive income <loss>	393.1%	−19.2%	−4.3%	71.6%	−11.9%	42.0%
<Treasury stock> and other equity adjustments	36.0%	−5.2%	25.1%	6.7%	8.9%	13.4%
Total Common Shareholders' Equity	**−29.6%**	**38.6%**	**25.8%**	**−2.7%**	**8.3%**	**5.3%**

(Continued)

Analysis Spreadsheet (Continued)

BALANCE SHEET ITEMS: GROWTH RATES

Year	2008	2009	2010	2011	2012	
	YEAR TO YEAR GROWTH RATES					**COMPOUND GROWTH RATE**
Noncontrolling interests	667.7%	34.0%	−51.1%	−0.3%	−66.2%	11.1%
Total Equity	−27.3%	38.6%	23.1%	−2.7%	7.2%	5.3%
Total Liabilities and Equities	3.9%	10.7%	71.0%	6.9%	2.4%	16.6%

RETURN ON ASSETS ANALYSIS (excluding the effects of non-recurring items)

Level 1	RETURN ON ASSETS		
	2010	2011	2012
	13.5%	10.8%	9.6%

Level 2	PROFIT MARGIN FOR ROA			ASSET TURNOVER		
	2010	2011	2012	2010	2011	2012
	12.6%	11.4%	10.8%	1.1	0.9	0.9

Level 3	2010	2011	2012	2010	2011	2012	Turnovers:
Revenues	100.0%	100.0%	100.0%	10.6	10.0	9.4	Receivables
<Cost of goods sold>	−45.9%	−47.5%	−47.8%	8.9	8.8	8.4	Inventory Fixed
Gross Profit	54.1%	52.5%	52.2%	3.6	3.4	3.4	Assets
<Selling, general and administrative expenses>	−39.4%	−37.8%	−38.1%				
Operating Profit	14.4%	14.5%	13.9%				
Income before Tax	14.2%	13.3%	12.7%				
<Income tax expense>	−3.3%	−3.6%	−3.2%				
Profit Margin for ROA*	12.6%	11.4%	10.8%				

*Amounts do not sum.

RETURN ON COMMON SHAREHOLDERS' EQUITY ANALYSIS
(excluding the effects of non-recurring items)

	2010	2011	2012
Return on Common Shareholders' Equity	35.0%	33.5%	29.9%
Profit Margin for ROCE	11.5%	10.6%	9.9%
Asset Turnover	1.1	0.9	0.9
Capital Structure Leverage	2.8	3.4	3.4

Analysis Spreadsheet (Continued)

RETURN ON COMMON SHAREHOLDERS' EQUITY ANALYSIS: Alternative Approach to Disaggregation

	RETURN ON COMMON SHAREHOLDERS' EQUITY		
	2010	2011	2012
ROCE	35.0%	33.5%	29.9%
INPUT VARIABLES			
Total Revenues	57,838	66,504	65,492
Net Operating Profit After Tax (NOPAT)	7,387	7,679	7,162
Net Financing Expense After Tax	714	646	710
Average Net Operating Assets	35,840	47,023	49,215
Average Financing Obligations	16,749	26,034	27,655
Average Common Equity	19,091	20,989	21,561
Profit margin for operating ROA	0.128	0.115	0.109
Net operating asset turnover	1.614	1.414	1.331
Operating ROA (NOPAT/Average NOA)	0.206	0.163	0.146
Net Borrowing Rate	0.043	0.025	0.026
Spread	0.163	0.138	0.120
Leverage	0.877	1.240	1.283
Leverage*Spread	0.143	0.172	0.154
ROCE = Operating ROA + Leverage*Spread	0.350	0.335	0.299

(Continued)

Analysis Spreadsheet (Continued)

STATEMENT OF CASH FLOWS: SUMMARY

Year	2008	2009	2010	2011	2012
Operating Activities:					
Net Income	5,166	5,979	6,338	6,462	6,214
Add back depreciation and amortization expenses	1,543	1,635	2,327	2,737	2,689
Net cash flows for working capital	−424	264	763	−844	434
Other net addbacks/subtractions	714	−1,082	−980	589	−858
Net CF from Operating Activities	**6,999**	**6,796**	**8,448**	**8,944**	**8,479**
Investing Activities:					
Capital expenditures (net)	−2,348	−2,070	−3,172	−3,255	−2,619
Investments	−279	−346	−4,479	−2,347	−398
Other investing transactions	−40	15	−17	−16	12
Net CF from Investing Activities	**−2,667**	**−2,401**	**−7,668**	**−5,618**	**−3,005**
Financing Activities:					
Net proceeds from short-term borrowing	445	−1,018	2,482	303	−1,461
Net proceeds from long-term borrowing	3,070	831	5,892	633	3,550
Net proceeds from share issues and repurchases	−4,106	448	−3,838	−1,481	−1,980
Dividends	−2,541	−2,732	−2,978	−3,157	−3,305
Other financing transactions	107	−26	−172	−1,433	−110
Net CF from Financing Activities	**−3,025**	**−2,497**	**1,386**	**−5,135**	**−3,306**
Effects of exchange rate changes on cash	−153	−19	−166	−67	62
Net Change in Cash	**1,154**	**1,879**	**2,000**	**−1,876**	**2,230**

Forecasts Spreadsheet

FSAP OUTPUT: FINANCIAL STATEMENT FORECASTS

Analyst Name: Wahlen, Baginski & Bradshaw
Company Name: PepsiCo

Year +6 and beyond:

| Long-Run Growth Rate: | 3.0% |
| Long-Run Growth Factor: | 103.0% |

Row Format:
Actual Amounts
Common Size Percentage
Rate of Change Percentage

Row Format:
Forecast Amounts
Forecast assumption
Forecast assumption explanation

Year	Actuals			Forecasts					
	2010	2011	2012	Year +1	Year +2	Year +3	Year +4	Year +5	Year +6
INCOME STATEMENT									
Revenues	57,838	66,504	65,492	68,198	71,044	74,038	78,672	80,504	82,919
common size	100.0%	100.0%	100.0%	4.1%	4.2%	4.2%	6.3%	2.3%	
rate of change		15.0%	−1.5%	See Forecast Development worksheet for details of revenues forecasts.					
<**Cost of goods sold**>	−26,575	−31,593	−31,291	−32,667	−34,101	−35,612	−37,920	−38,883	−40,050
common size	−45.9%	−47.5%	−47.8%	−47.9%	−48.0%	−48.1%	−48.2%	−48.3%	
rate of change		18.9%	−1.0%	Assume slowly increasing cost of goods sold as a percent of sales.					
Gross Profit	31,263	34,911	34,201	35,531	36,943	38,426	40,752	41,621	42,869
common size	54.1%	52.5%	52.2%	52.1%	52.0%	51.9%	51.8%	51.7%	51.7%
rate of change		11.7%	−2.0%	3.9%	4.0%	4.0%	6.1%	2.1%	
<**Selling, general and administrative expenses**>	−22,814	−25,145	−24,970	−25,984	−27,068	−28,208	−29,974	−30,672	−31,592
common size	−39.4%	−37.8%	−38.1%	−38.1%	−38.1%	−38.1%	−38.1%	−38.1%	
rate of change		10.2%	−0.7%	Assume steady SG&A expense as a percent of sales.					
<**Research and development expenses**>	0	0	0	0	0	0	0	0	0
common size	0.0%	0.0%	0.0%	0.0%	0.0%	0.0%	0.0%	0.0%	0.0%
rate of change				Explain assumptions.					
<**Amortization of intangible assets**>	−117	−133	−119	−110	−95	−86	−78	−72	−74
common size	−0.2%	−0.2%	−0.2%						
rate of change		13.7%	−10.5%	Amounts based on PepsiCo disclosures in Note 4.					

(Continued)

Forecasts Spreadsheet (Continued)

	Actuals			Forecasts					
Year	2010	2011	2012	Year +1	Year +2	Year +3	Year +4	Year +5	Year +6
<Other operating expenses (1)>	0	0	0	0	0	0	0	0	0
common size	0.0%	0.0%	0.0%	0.0%	0.0%	0.0%	0.0%	0.0%	0.0%
rate of change				Explain assumptions.					
<Other operating expenses (2)>	0	0	0	0	0	0	0	0	0
common size	0.0%	0.0%	0.0%	0.0%	0.0%	0.0%	0.0%	0.0%	0.0%
rate of change				Explain assumptions.					
Other operating income (1)	0	0	0	0	0	0	0	0	0
common size	0.0%	0.0%	0.0%	0.0%	0.0%	0.0%	0.0%	0.0%	0.0%
rate of change				Explain assumptions.					
Other operating income (2)	0	0	0	0	0	0	0	0	0
common size	0.0%	0.0%	0.0%	0.0%	0.0%	0.0%	0.0%	0.0%	0.0%
rate of change				Explain assumptions.					
Non-recurring operating gains <losses>	0	0	0	0	0	0	0	0	0
common size	0.0%	0.0%	0.0%	0.0%	0.0%	0.0%	0.0%	0.0%	0.0%
rate of change				Explain assumptions					
Operating Profit	**8,332**	**9,633**	**9,112**	**9,438**	**9,780**	**10,131**	**10,700**	**10,877**	**11,203**
common size	14.4%	14.5%	13.9%	13.8%	13.8%	13.7%	13.6%	13.5%	13.5%
rate of change		15.6%	−5.4%	3.6%	3.6%	3.6%	5.6%	1.6%	
Interest income	**68**	**57**	**91**	**61**	**56**	**58**	**61**	**63**	**65**
common size	0.1%	0.1%	0.1%	1.0%	1.0%	1.0%	1.0%	1.0%	1.0%
rate of change		−16.2%	59.6%	Assume 1.0% interest earned on avg. balance in cash and marketable securities.					
<Interest expense>	**−903**	**−856**	**−899**	**−1,049**	**−1,087**	**−1,136**	**−1,196**	**−1,248**	**−1,286**
common size	−1.6%	−1.3%	−1.4%	−3.65%	−3.65%	−3.65%	−3.65%	−3.65%	−3.65%
rate of change		−5.2%	5.0%	Weighted average interest rate on financial liabilities.					

Income <Loss> from equity affiliates	735	0	0	0	0	0	0	0	0
common size	1.3%	0.0%	0.0%	0.0%	0.0%	0.0%	0.0%	0.0%	0.0%
rate of change		−100.0%	0.0%	0.0%	Explain assumptions	0.0%	0.0%	0.0%	0.0%
Other income or gains <Other expenses or losses>	0	0	0	0	0	0	0	0	0
common size	0.0%	0.0%	0.0%	0.0%	0.0%	0.0%	0.0%	0.0%	0.0%
rate of change	0.0%	0.0%	0.0%	0.0%	Explain assumptions	0.0%	0.0%	0.0%	0.0%
Income before Tax	8,232	8,834	8,304	8,450	8,749	9,053	9,565	9,691	9,982
common size	14.2%	13.3%	12.7%	12.4%	12.3%	12.2%	12.2%	12.0%	12.0%
rate of change		7.3%	−6.0%	1.8%	3.5%	3.5%	5.7%	1.3%	3.0%
<Income tax expense>	−1,894	−2,372	−2,090	−2,281	−2,362	−2,444	−2,583	−2,617	−2,695
common size	−3.3%	−3.6%	−3.2%	−27.0%	−27.0%	−27.0%	−27.0%	−27.0%	−27.0%
rate of change		25.2%	−11.9%	−27.0%	Assume effective income tax rate equal to that of past two years.	−27.0%	−27.0%	−27.0%	−27.0%
Income <Loss> from discontinued operations	0	0	0	0	0	0	0	0	0
common size	0.0%	0.0%	0.0%	0.0%	0.0%	0.0%	0.0%	0.0%	0.0%
rate of change	0.0%	0.0%	0.0%	0.0%	Explain assumptions	0.0%	0.0%	0.0%	0.0%
Extraordinary gains <losses>	0	0	0	0	0	0	0	0	0
common size	0.0%	0.0%	0.0%	0.0%	0.0%	0.0%	0.0%	0.0%	0.0%
rate of change	0.0%	0.0%	0.0%	0.0%	Explain assumptions	0.0%	0.0%	0.0%	0.0%
Changes in accounting principles	0	0	0	0	0	0	0	0	0
common size	0.0%	0.0%	0.0%	0.0%	0.0%	0.0%	0.0%	0.0%	0.0%
rate of change	0.0%	0.0%	0.0%	0.0%	Explain assumptions	0.0%	0.0%	0.0%	0.0%
Net Income	6,338	6,462	6,214	6,168	6,387	6,609	6,983	7,075	7,287
common size	11.0%	9.7%	9.5%	9.0%	9.0%	8.9%	8.9%	8.8%	8.8%
rate of change		2.0%	−3.8%	−0.7%	3.5%	3.5%	5.7%	1.3%	3.0%

(Continued)

Forecasts Spreadsheet (Continued)

| | Actuals | | | Forecasts | | | | | |
Year	2010	2011	2012	Year +1	Year +2	Year +3	Year +4	Year +5	Year +6
Net income attributable to noncontrolling interests	−18	−19	−36	−10.5	−10.5	−10.5	−10.5	−10.5	−10.8
common size	0.0%	0.0%	−0.1%	10%	10%	10%	10%	10%	10%
rate of change		5.6%	89.5%	Assume noncontrolling interests earn a 10% rate of return.					
Net Income attributable to common shareholders	6,320	6,443	6,178	6,158	6,377	6,598	6,972	7,064	7,276
common size	10.9%	9.7%	9.4%	9.0%	9.0%	8.9%	8.9%	8.8%	8.8%
rate of change		1.9%	−4.1%	−0.3%	3.6%	3.5%	5.7%	1.3%	3.0%
Other comprehensive income items	146	−2,618	706	0	0	0	0	0	0
common size	0.3%	−3.9%	1.1%	0.0	0.0	0.0	0.0	0.0	0
rate of change		−1893.2%	−127.0%	Assume random walk with mean zero.					
Comprehensive Income	6,484	3,844	6,920	6,158	6,377	6,598	6,972	7,064	7,276
common size	11.2%	5.8%	10.6%	9.0%	9.0%	8.9%	8.9%	8.8%	8.8%
rate of change		−40.7%	80.0%	−11.0%	3.6%	3.5%	5.7%	1.3%	3.0%

Forecasts Spreadsheet (Continued)

FSAP OUTPUT: FINANCIAL STATEMENT FORECASTS

Analyst Name: Wahlen, Baginski & Bradshaw
Company Name: PepsiCo

Row Format:
Actual Amounts
Common Size Percent
Rate of Change Percent

Row Format:
Forecast Amounts
Forecast assumption
Forecast assumption explanation

Year +6 and beyond:
Long-Run Growth Rate: 3.0%
Long-Run Growth Factor: 103.0%

	Actuals		Forecasts					
Year	**2010**	**2011**	**2012**	**Year +1**	**Year +2**	**Year +3**	**Year +4**	**Year +5**	**Year +6**
BALANCE SHEET									
ASSETS:									
Cash and cash equivalents	5,943	4,067	6,297	5,232	5,450	5,680	6,035	6,176	6,361
common size	8.7%	5.6%	8.4%	28.0	28.0	28.0	28.0	28.0	
rate of change		−31.6%	54.8%	Assume ending cash balances equal to 28 days sales.					
Marketable securities	426	358	322	293	267	243	221	201	207
common size	0.6%	0.5%	0.4%	−9%	−9%	−9%	−9%	−9%	
rate of change		−16.0%	−10.1%	Assume 9 percent decline, consistent with trend since 2010.					
Accounts and notes									
receivable—net	6,323	6,912	7,041	7,287	7,591	7,911	8,406	8,602	8,860
common size	9.3%	9.5%	9.4%	39.0	39.0	39.0	39.0	39.0	
rate of change		9.3%	1.9%	Assume ending accounts receivable equals 39 days sales.					
Inventories	3,372	3,827	3,581	3,938	4,158	4,391	4,727	4,900	5,047
common size	4.9%	5.3%	4.8%	44.0	44.5	45.0	45.5	46.0	
rate of change		13.5%	−6.4%	Assume continued increase in ending inventory, consistent with recent trend.					
Prepaid expenses and other									
current assets	1,505	2,277	1,479	1,540	1,604	1,672	1,777	1,818	1,873
common size	2.2%	3.1%	2.0%	4.1%	4.2%	4.2%	6.3%	2.3%	
rate of change		51.3%	−35.0%	Assume growth with SG&A expenses, which grow with sales.					
Deferred tax assets—current	0	0	0	0	0	0	0	0	0
common size	0.0%	0.0%	0.0%	0%	0%	0%	0%	0%	
rate of change		0.0%	0.0%	Explain assumptions					

(Continued)

Forecasts Spreadsheet (Continued)

Year	Actuals			Forecasts					
	2010	2011	2012	Year +1	Year +2	Year +3	Year +4	Year +5	Year +6
Other current assets (1)	0	0	0	0	0	0	0	0	0
common size	0.0%	0.0%	0.0%	0%	0%	0%	0%	0%	0%
rate of change				Explain assumptions					
Other current assets (2)	0	0	0	0	0	0	0	0	0
common size	0.0%	0.0%	0.0%	0%	0%	0%	0%	0%	0%
rate of change				Explain assumptions					
Current Assets	**17,569**	**17,441**	**18,720**	**18,290**	**19,070**	**19,896**	**21,166**	**21,697**	**22,348**
common size	25.8%	23.9%	25.1%	24.1%	24.3%	24.5%	24.8%	24.9%	24.9%
rate of change		−0.7%	7.3%	−2.3%	4.3%	4.3%	6.4%	2.5%	3.0%
Investments in noncontrolled affiliates	**1,368**	**1,477**	**1,633**	**1,764**	**1,905**	**2,057**	**2,222**	**2,399**	**2,471**
common size	2.0%	2.0%	2.2%	8%	8%	8%	8%	8%	8%
rate of change		8.0%	10.6%	Assume 8% growth, consistent with past two years.					
Property, plant, and equipment—at cost	**33,041**	**35,140**	**36,162**	**39,162**	**42,572**	**46,126**	**49,902**	**53,766**	**55,379**
common size	48.5%	48.2%	48.4%						
rate of change		6.4%	2.9%	PP&E assumptions—see schedule in forecast development					
<Accumulated depreciation>	**−13,983**	**−15,442**	**−17,026**	**−19,760**	**−22,732**	**−25,953**	**−29,437**	**−33,190**	**−34,186**
common size	−20.5%	−21.2%	−22.8%						
rate of change		10.4%	10.3%	See depreciation schedule in forecast development worksheet.					
Amortizable intangible assets (net)	**2,025**	**1,888**	**1,781**	**1,671**	**1,576**	**1,490**	**1,412**	**1,340**	**1,380**
common size	3.0%	2.6%	2.4%	−110	−95	−86	−78	−72	
rate of change		−6.8%	−5.7%	Assume amortization per PepsiCo disclosures in Note 4.					
Goodwill	**14,661**	**16,800**	**16,971**	**17,672**	**18,410**	**19,185**	**20,386**	**20,861**	**21,487**
common size	21.5%	23.1%	22.7%	4.1%	4.2%	4.2%	6.3%	2.3%	3.0%
rate of change		14.6%	1.0%	Assume growth with sales.					
Other nonamortizable intangible assets	**11,783**	**14,557**	**14,744**	**15,353**	**15,994**	**16,668**	**17,711**	**18,124**	**18,667**
common size	17.3%	20.0%	19.8%	4.1%	4.2%	4.2%	6.3%	2.3%	3.0%
rate of change		23.5%	1.3%	Assume growth with sales.					

Account / metric									
Deferred tax assets—non current	0	0	0	0	0	0	0	0	0
common size	0.0%	0.0%	0.0%	0.0%	0.0%	0.0%	0.0%	0.0%	0.0%
rate of change		0.0%	0.0%	*Explain assumptions*	0.0%	0.0%	0.0%	0.0%	0.0%
Other assets	1,689	1,021	1,653	1,721	1,793	1,869	1,986	2,032	2,093
common size	2.5%	1.4%	2.2%	2.3%	2.3%	2.3%	2.3%	2.3%	2.3%
rate of change		−39.6%	61.9%	4.1%	4.2%	4.2%	6.3%	2.3%	3.0%
				Assume growth with sales.					
Total Assets	68,153	72,882	74,638	75,873	78,587	81,338	85,348	87,029	89,640
common size	100.0%	100.0%	100.0%	100.0%	100.0%	100.0%	100.0%	100.0%	100.0%
rate of change		6.9%	2.4%	1.7%	3.6%	3.5%	4.9%	2.0%	3.0%
LIABILITIES:									
Accounts payable	3,865	4,083	4,451	4,524	4,701	4,910	5,241	5,350	5,511
common size	5.7%	5.6%	6.0%	50.0	50.0	50.0	50.0	50.0	50.0
rate of change		5.6%	9.0%	*Assume a 50 day payment period consistent with prior year.*					
Current accrued expenses	7,058	7,674	7,452	7,760	8,084	8,424	8,952	9,160	9,435
common size	10.4%	10.5%	10.0%	10.2%	10.3%	10.4%	10.5%	10.5%	10.5%
rate of change		8.7%	−2.9%	4.1%	4.2%	4.2%	6.3%	2.3%	3.0%
				Assume growth with SG&A expenses, which grow with sales.					
Notes payable and short-term debt	4,898	6,205	4,815	4,943	5,169	5,402	5,722	5,892	6,069
common size	7.2%	8.5%	6.5%	6.5%	6.6%	6.6%	6.7%	6.8%	6.8%
rate of change		26.7%	−22.4%	2.7%	4.6%	4.5%	5.9%	3.0%	3.0%
				Assume growth that is one perrcent faster than total assets growth.					
Current maturities of long-term debt	0	0	0	0	0	0	0	0	0
common size	0.0%	0.0%	0.0%	0.0%	0.0%	0.0%	0.0%	0.0%	0.0%
rate of change		0.0%	0.0%	*Explain assumptions*	0.0%	0.0%	0.0%	0.0%	0.0%
Deferred tax liabilities—current	0	0	0	0	0	0	0	0	0
common size	0.0%	0.0%	0.0%	0.0%	0.0%	0.0%	0.0%	0.0%	0.0%
rate of change		0.0%	0.0%	*Explain assumptions*	0.0%	0.0%	0.0%	0.0%	0.0%
Income taxes payable	71	192	371	379	393	407	427	435	448
common size	0.1%	0.3%	0.5%	0.5%	0.5%	0.5%	0.5%	0.5%	0.5%
rate of change		170.4%	93.2%	*Assume a constant 0.5% of total assets.*					

(Continued)

Forecasts Spreadsheet (Continued)

Year	Actuals			Forecasts					
	2010	2011	2012	Year +1	Year +2	Year +3	Year +4	Year +5	Year +6
Other current liabilities (2)	0	0	0	0	0	0	0	0	0
common size	0.0%	0.0%	0.0%	0.0%	0.0%	0.0%	0.0%	0.0%	
rate of change				Explain assumptions					
Other current liabilities (1)	0	0	0	0	0	0	0	0	0
common size	0.0%	0.0%	0.0%	0.0%	0.0%	0.0%	0.0%	0.0%	
rate of change				Explain assumptions					
Current Liabilities	15,892	18,154	17,089	17,606	18,347	19,143	20,341	20,837	21,463
common size	23.3%	24.9%	22.9%	23.2%	23.3%	23.5%	23.8%	23.9%	23.9%
rate of change		14.2%	−5.9%	3.0%	4.2%	4.3%	6.3%	2.4%	
Long-term debt obligations	19,999	20,568	23,544	24,169	25,275	26,413	27,979	28,810	29,674
common size	29.3%	28.2%	31.5%	2.7%	4.6%	4.5%	5.9%	3.0%	
rate of change		2.8%	14.5%	Assume growth that is one percent faster than total assets growth.					
Long-term accrued liabilities	6,729	8,266	6,543	6,813	7,098	7,397	7,860	8,043	8,284
common size	9.9%	11.3%	8.8%	4.1%	4.2%	4.2%	6.3%	2.3%	
rate of change		22.8%	−20.8%	Assume growth with SG&A expenses, which grow with sales.					
Deferred tax liabilities— noncurrent	4,057	4,995	5,063	5,159	5,344	5,531	5,804	5,918	6,095
common size	6.0%	6.9%	6.8%	6.8%	6.8%	6.8%	6.8%	6.8%	
rate of change		23.1%	1.4%	Assume a constant 6.8% of total assets.					
Other noncurrent liabilities (1)	0	0	0	0	0	0	0	0	0
common size	0.0%	0.0%	0.0%	0.0%	0.0%	0.0%	0.0%	0.0%	
rate of change				Explain assumptions					
Other noncurrent liabilities (2)	0	0	0	0	0	0	0	0	0
common size	0.0%	0.0%	0.0%	0.0%	0.0%	0.0%	0.0%	0.0%	
rate of change				Explain assumptions					
Total Liabilities	46,677	51,983	52,239	53,748	56,064	58,484	61,984	63,608	65,516
common size	68.5%	71.3%	70.0%	70.8%	71.3%	71.9%	72.6%	73.1%	73.1%
rate of change		11.4%	0.5%	2.9%	4.3%	4.3%	6.0%	2.6%	3.0%

SHAREHOLDERS' EQUITY:									
Preferred stock	−109	−116	−123	0	0	0	0	0	0
common size	−0.2%	−0.2%	−0.2%	0.0	0.0	0.0	0.0	0.0	0.0
rate of change		6.4%	6.0%	Assume preferred stock retired.					
Common stock + Additional paid in capital	4,558	4,487	4,204	4,249	4,401	4,555	4,779	4,874	5,020
common size	6.7%	6.2%	5.6%	5.6%	5.6%	5.6%	5.6%	5.6%	5.6%
rate of change		−1.6%	−6.3%	Assume steady percent of total assets.					
Retained earnings <deficit>	37,090	40,316	43,158	45,866	48,735	51,705	54,842	58,021	59,762
common size	54.4%	55.3%	57.8%						
rate of change		8.7%	7.0%	Add net income and subtract dividends; see dividends forecast box below.					
Accum. other comprehensive income <loss>	−3,630	−6,229	−5,487	−5,487	−5,487	−5,487	−5,487	−5,487	−5,487
common size	−5.3%	−8.5%	−7.4%						
rate of change		71.6%	−11.9%	0.0	0.0	0.0	0.0	0.0	0.0
				Add other comprehensive income items from income statement					
<Treasury stock> and other equity adjustments	−16,745	−17,870	−19,458	−22,608	−25,231	−28,023	−30,875	−34,092	−35,279
common size	−24.6%	−24.5%	−26.1%						
rate of change		6.7%	8.9%	−3,150	−2,624	−2,792	−2,852	−3,217	
				Treasury stock repurchases, net of treasury stock reissues.					
Total Common Shareholders' Equity	21,273	20,704	22,417	22,020	22,418	22,749	23,260	23,316	24,015
common size	31.2%	28.4%	30.0%	29.0%	28.5%	28.0%	27.3%	26.8%	26.8%
rate of change		−2.7%	8.3%	−1.8%	1.8%	1.5%	2.2%	0.2%	3.0%
Noncontrolling interests	312	311	105	105	105	105	105	105	105
common size	0.5%	0.4%	0.1%	0.0	0.0	0.0	0.0	0.0	0.0
rate of change		−0.3%	−66.2%	0.0	0.0	0.0	0.0	0.0	108.2
				Assume noncontrolling interests remain constant; all earnings distributed.					
Total Equity	21,585	21,015	22,522	22,125	22,523	22,854	23,365	23,421	24,123
common size	31.7%	28.8%	30.2%	29.2%	28.7%	28.1%	27.4%	26.9%	26.9%
rate of change		−2.6%	7.2%	−1.8%	1.8%	1.5%	2.2%	0.2%	3.0%

(Continued)

Forecasts Spreadsheet (Continued)

	Actuals			Forecasts					
Year	**2010**	**2011**	**2012**	**Year +1**	**Year +2**	**Year +3**	**Year +4**	**Year +5**	**Year +6**
Total Liabilities and Equities	**68,153**	**72,882**	**74,638**	**75,873**	**78,587**	**81,338**	**85,348**	**87,029**	**89,640**
common size	100.0%	100.0%	100.0%	100.0%	100.0%	100.0%	100.0%	100.0%	100.0%
rate of change		6.9%	2.4%	1.7%	3.6%	3.5%	4.9%	2.0%	3.0%
Check figures: Balance Sheet									
A = L + OE?	0	0	0	0	0	0	0	0	0
			Initial adjustment needed to balance the balance sheet:						
				−150	376	208	148	−217	−1,187

Dividends forecasts:

Common dividends:				3,387	3,507	3,629	3,835	3,885	5,535
				55.0%	55.0%	55.0%	55.0%	55.0%	
			Assume 55% payout of net income available to common shareholders.						
Preferred dividends:				63	0	0	0	0	0
				63.0	0.0	0.0	0.0	0.0	
			Assume $63 million paid to retire preferred shares.						
Total dividends:				**3,450**	**3,507**	**3,629**	**3,835**	**3,885**	**5,535**
			Total dividend forecast amounts.						

Treasury Stock Purchases:

Flexible Financial Account:									
Original Forecast Amounts:									
Treasury Stock Purchases:				−3,000	−3,000	−3,000	−3,000	−3,000	
				−3,000	−3,000	−3,000	−3,000	−3,000	
			Treasury stock repurchases, net of reissues, per PepsiCo disclosures.						
Implied adjustments:				−150	376	208	148	−217	−1,187
			Adjustment needed to balance the balance sheet, from above.						
Total:				**−3,150**	**−2,624**	**−2,792**	**−2,852**	**−3,217**	**−1,187**
			Total Treasury Stock Purchase Amounts						

Forecasts Spreadsheet (Continued)

FSAP OUTPUT: FINANCIAL STATEMENT FORECASTS

Analyst Name: Wahlen, Baginski & Bradshaw
Company Name: PepsiCo

	Actuals		Forecasts					
IMPLIED STATEMENT OF CASH FLOWS	2011	2012	Year +1	Year +2	Year +3	Year +4	Year +5	Year +6
Net Income	**6,462**	**6,214**	**6,168**	**6,387**	**6,609**	**6,983**	**7,075**	**7,287**
Add back depreciation expense (net)	1,459	1,584	2,734	2,972	3,220	3,484	3,754	996
Add back amortization expense (net)	133	119	110	95	86	78	72	74
<Increase> Decrease in receivables—net	−589	−129	−246	−304	−320	−495	−196	−258
<Increase> Decrease in inventories	−455	246	−357	−220	−233	−336	−173	−147
<Increase> Decrease in prepaid expenses	−772	798	−61	−64	−68	−105	−41	−55
<Increase> Decrease in other current assets (1)	0	0	0	0	0	0	0	0
<Increase> Decrease in other current assets (2)	0	0	0	0	0	0	0	0
Increase <Decrease> in accounts payable—trade	218	368	73	178	209	330	110	161
Increase <Decrease> in current accrued liabilities	616	−222	308	324	341	527	208	275
Increase <Decrease> in income taxes payable	121	179	8	14	14	20	8	13
Increase <Decrease> in other current liabilities (1)	0	0	0	0	0	0	0	0
Increase <Decrease> in other current liabilities (2)	0	0	0	0	0	0	0	0
Net change in deferred tax assets and liabilities	938	68	96	185	187	273	114	178
Increase <Decrease> in long-term accrued liabilities	1,537	−1,723	270	284	299	463	183	241
Increase <Decrease> in other noncurrent liabilities (1)	0	0	0	0	0	0	0	0
Increase <Decrease> in other noncurrent liabilities (2)	0	0	0	0	0	0	0	0
Net Cash Flows from Operations	**9,668**	**7,502**	**9,104**	**9,850**	**10,344**	**11,222**	**11,114**	**8,764**
<Increase> Decrease in property, plant, & equip. at cost	−2,099	−1,022	−3,000	−3,410	−3,554	−3,776	−3,864	−1,613
<Increase> Decrease in marketable securities	68	36	29	26	24	22	20	−6
<Increase> Decrease in investment securities	−109	−156	−131	−141	−152	−165	−178	−72
<Increase> Decrease in amortizable intangible assets (net)	4	−12	0	0	0	0	0	−114
<Increase> Decrease in goodwill and nonamort. intangibles	−4,913	−358	−1,311	−1,378	−1,450	−2,244	−887	−1,170

(Continued)

Forecasts Spreadsheet (Continued)

IMPLIED STATEMENT OF CASH FLOWS	Actuals		Forecasts					
	2011	2012	Year +1	Year +2	Year +3	Year +4	Year +5	Year +6
<Increase> Decrease in other noncurrent assets (1)	0	0	0	0	0	0	0	0
<Increase> Decrease in other noncurrent assets (2)	668	−632	−68	−72	−76	−117	−46	−61
Net Cash Flows from Investing Activities	**−6,381**	**−2,144**	**−4,481**	**−4,975**	**−5,207**	**−6,280**	**−4,955**	**−3,036**
Increase <Decrease> in short-term debt	1,307	−1,390	128	226	233	320	170	177
Increase <Decrease> in long-term debt	569	2,976	625	1,106	1,138	1,566	831	864
Increase <Decrease> in preferred stock	−7	−7	123	0	0	0	0	0
Increase <Decrease> in common stock + paid in capital	−71	−283	45	152	154	225	94	146
Increase <Decrease> in accum. OCI	−2,599	742	0	0	0	0	0	0
Increase <Decrease> in treasury stock and other equity adjs.	−1,125	−1,588	−3,150	−2,624	−2,792	−2,852	−3,217	−1,187
Dividends	−3,217	−3,336	−3,450	−3,507	−3,629	−3,835	−3,885	−5,535
Increase <Decrease> in noncontrolling interests	−20	−242	−11	−11	−11	−11	−11	−8
Net Cash Flows from Financing Activities	**−5,163**	**−3,128**	**−5,689**	**−4,657**	**−4,907**	**−4,586**	**−6,018**	**−5,543**
Net Change in Cash	**−1,876**	**2,230**	**−1,065**	**218**	**230**	**356**	**141**	**185**
Check Figure:								
Net change in cash − Change in cash balance	0	0	0	0	0	0	0	0

Forecasts Spreadsheet (Continued)

FSAP OUTPUT: FINANCIAL STATEMENT FORECASTS

Analyst Name: Wahlen, Baginski & Bradshaw
Company Name: PepsiCo

	Actuals			Forecasts					
	2010	2011	2012	Year +1	Year +2	Year +3	Year +4	Year +5	Year +6
FORECAST VALIDITY CHECK DATA:									
GROWTH:									
Revenue Growth Rates:	33.8%	15.0%	−1.5%	4.1%	4.2%	4.2%	6.3%	2.3%	3.0%
Net Income Growth Rates:	6.3%	1.9%	−4.1%	−0.7%	3.5%	3.5%	5.7%	1.3%	3.0%
Total Asset Growth Rates	71.0%	6.9%	2.4%	1.7%	3.6%	3.5%	4.9%	2.0%	3.0%
RETURN ON ASSETS (based on reported amounts):									
Profit Margin for ROA	12.0%	10.6%	10.4%	10.2%	10.1%	10.0%	10.0%	9.9%	9.9%
× Asset Turnover	1.1	0.9	0.9	0.9	0.9	0.9	0.9	0.9	0.9
= Return on Assets	12.8%	10.0%	9.2%	9.2%	9.3%	9.3%	9.4%	9.3%	9.3%
RETURN ON ASSETS (excluding the effects of nonrecurring items):									
Profit Margin for ROA	12.6%	11.4%	10.8%	10.2%	10.1%	10.0%	10.0%	9.9%	9.9%
× Asset Turnover	1.1	0.9	0.9	0.9	0.9	0.9	0.9	0.9	0.9
= Return on Assets	13.5%	10.8%	9.6%	9.2%	9.3%	9.3%	9.4%	9.3%	9.3%
RETURN ON COMMON EQUITY (based on reported amounts):									
Profit Margin for ROCE	10.9%	9.7%	9.4%	9.0%	9.0%	8.9%	8.9%	8.8%	8.8%
× Asset Turnover	1.1	0.9	0.9	0.9	0.9	0.9	0.9	0.9	0.9
× Capital Structure Leverage	2.8	3.4	3.4	3.4	3.5	3.5	3.6	3.7	3.7
= Return on Common Equity	33.1%	30.7%	28.6%	27.5%	28.7%	29.3%	30.4%	30.4%	30.8%
RETURN ON COMMON EQUITY (excluding the effects of nonrecurring items):									
Profit Margin for ROCE	11.5%	10.6%	9.9%	9.0%	9.0%	8.9%	8.9%	8.8%	8.8%
× Asset Turnover	1.1	0.9	0.9	0.9	0.9	0.9	0.9	0.9	0.9
× Capital Structure Leverage	2.8	3.4	3.4	3.4	3.5	3.5	3.6	3.7	3.7
= Return on Common Equity	35.0%	33.5%	29.9%	27.5%	28.7%	29.3%	30.4%	30.4%	30.8%

(Continued)

Forecasts Spreadsheet (Continued)

FSAP OUTPUT: **FINANCIAL STATEMENT FORECASTS**

Analyst Name: Wahlen, Baginski & Bradshaw
Company Name: PepsiCo

	Actuals				Forecasts				
	2010	2011	2012	Year +1	Year +2	Year +3	Year +4	Year +5	Year +6
OPERATING PERFORMANCE:									
Gross Profit/Revenues	54.1%	52.5%	52.2%	52.1%	52.0%	51.9%	51.8%	51.7%	51.7%
Operating Profit Before Taxes/Revenues	14.4%	14.5%	13.9%	13.8%	13.8%	13.7%	13.6%	13.5%	13.5%
ASSET TURNOVER:									
Revenues/Avg. Accounts Receivable	10.6	10.0	9.4	9.5	9.6	9.6	9.6	9.5	9.5
COGS/Average Inventory	8.9	8.8	8.4	8.7	8.4	8.3	8.3	8.1	8.1
Revenues/Average Fixed Assets	3.6	3.4	3.4	3.5	3.6	3.7	3.9	3.9	4.0
LIQUIDITY:									
Current Ratio	1.1	1.0	1.1	1.0	1.0	1.0	1.0	1.0	1.0
Quick Ratio	0.8	0.6	0.8	0.7	0.7	0.7	0.7	0.7	0.7
SOLVENCY:									
Total Liabilities/Total Assets	68.5%	71.3%	70.0%	70.8%	71.3%	71.9%	72.6%	73.1%	73.1%
Total Liabilities/Total Equity	217.3%	248.7%	233.2%	244.1%	250.1%	257.1%	266.5%	272.8%	272.8%
Interest Coverage Ratio	10.1	11.3	10.2	9.1	9.0	9.0	9.0	8.8	8.8

Forecast Development Spreadsheet

Analyst Name: Wahlen, Baginski & Bradshaw
Company Name: PepsiCo

Sales Revenue Forecast Development

	Actuals				Forecasts			
Year	2010	2011	2012	Year +1	Year +2	Year +3	Year +4	Year +5
Revenues	57,838	66,504	65,492	68,198	71,044	74,038	78,672	80,504
rate of change		15.0%	−1.5%	4.1%	4.2%	4.2%	6.3%	2.3%
				Sales growth rate assumptions.				
Sales Forecasts Combined by Divisions:								
Frito-Lay North America	12,573	13,322	13,574	13,984	14,406	14,841	15,584	15,751
Quaker Foods North America	2,656	2,656	2,636	2,636	2,636	2,636	2,686	2,635
Latin America Foods	6,315	7,156	7,780	8,415	9,101	9,844	10,852	11,516
PepsiCo Americas Beverages	20,401	22,418	21,408	22,055	22,721	23,407	24,577	24,842
Europe	9,602	13,560	13,441	13,984	14,549	15,137	16,051	16,385
Asia, Middle East & Africa	**6,291**	**7,392**	**6,653**	**7,125**	**7,631**	**8,173**	**8,922**	**9,375**
PepsiCo Total Net Revenues	**57,838**	**66,504**	**65,492**	**68,198**	**71,044**	**74,038**	**78,672**	**80,504**
growth rates		15.0%	−1.5%	4.1%	4.2%	4.2%	6.3%	2.3%
Sales Forecasts for PepsiCo by Division:								
Frito-Lay North America	12,573	13,322	13,574	13,984	14,406	14,841	15,584	15,751
overall growth rates		6.0%	1.9%	3.0%	3.0%	3.0%	5.0%	1.1%
growth in volume		2.0%	−1.0%	1.0%	1.0%	1.0%	1.0%	1.0%
growth from price changes		2.0%	4.8%	2.0%	2.0%	2.0%	2.0%	2.0%
impact of foreign currency translation		0.0%	0.0%	0.0%	0.0%	0.0%	0.0%	0.0%
53rd week effect		1.9%	−1.9%	0.0%	0.0%	0.0%	1.9%	−1.9%
Quaker Foods North America	2,656	2,656	2,636	2,636	2,636	2,636	2,686	2,635
overall growth rates		0.0%	−0.8%	0.0%	0.0%	0.0%	1.9%	−1.9%
growth in volume		−5.0%	−1.0%	−1.0%	−1.0%	−1.0%	−1.0%	−1.0%
growth from price changes		2.1%	2.1%	1.0%	1.0%	1.0%	1.0%	1.0%
impact of foreign currency translation		1.0%	0.0%	0.0%	0.0%	0.0%	0.0%	0.0%
53rd week effect		1.9%	−1.9%	0.0%	0.0%	0.0%	1.9%	−1.9%

(Continued)

Forecast Development Spreadsheet (Continued)

Sales Forecasts for PepsiCo by Division:

Year	2010	2011	2012	Year +1	Year +2	Year +3	Year +4	Year +5
Latin America Foods	6,315	7,156	7,780	8,415	9,101	9,844	10,852	11,516
overall growth rates		13.3%	8.7%	8.2%	8.2%	8.2%	10.2%	6.1%
growth in volume and acquisitions		3.5%	6.0%	4.0%	4.0%	4.0%	4.0%	4.0%
growth from price changes		5.9%	11.6%	4.0%	4.0%	4.0%	4.0%	4.0%
impact of foreign currency translation		2.0%	-7.0%	0.0%	0.0%	0.0%	0.0%	0.0%
53rd week effect		1.9%	-1.9%	0.0%	0.0%	0.0%	1.9%	-1.9%
PepsiCo Americas Beverages	20,401	22,418	21,408	22,055	22,721	23,407	24,577	24,842
overall growth rates		9.9%	-4.5%	3.0%	3.0%	3.0%	5.0%	1.1%
growth in volume and acquisitions		6.0%	-7.5%	1.0%	1.0%	1.0%	1.0%	1.0%
growth from price changes		1.0%	4.9%	2.0%	2.0%	2.0%	2.0%	2.0%
impact of foreign currency translation		1.0%	0.0%	0.0%	0.0%	0.0%	0.0%	0.0%
53rd week effect		1.9%	-1.9%	0.0%	0.0%	0.0%	1.9%	-1.9%
Europe	9,602	13,560	13,441	13,984	14,549	15,137	16,051	16,385
overall growth rates		41.2%	-0.9%	4.0%	4.0%	4.0%	6.0%	2.1%
growth in volume and acquisitions		36.0%	2.0%	2.0%	2.0%	2.0%	2.0%	2.0%
growth from price changes		0.3%	6.0%	2.0%	2.0%	2.0%	2.0%	2.0%
impact of foreign currency translation		3.0%	-7.0%	0.0%	0.0%	0.0%	0.0%	0.0%
53rd week effect		1.9%	-1.9%	0.0%	0.0%	0.0%	1.9%	-1.9%
Asia, Middle East & Africa	6,291	7,392	6,653	7,125	7,631	8,173	8,922	9,375
overall growth rates		17.5%	-10.0%	7.1%	7.1%	7.1%	9.2%	5.1%
growth in volume and acquisitions		10.0%	-9.0%	5.0%	5.0%	5.0%	5.0%	5.0%
growth from price changes		3.6%	3.9%	2.0%	2.0%	2.0%	2.0%	2.0%
impact of foreign currency translation		2.0%	-3.0%	0.0%	0.0%	0.0%	0.0%	0.0%
53rd week effect		1.9%	-1.9%	0.0%	0.0%	0.0%	1.9%	-1.9%

Forecast Development Spreadsheet (Continued)

Forecast Development: Capital Expenditures, Property, Plant and Equipment, and Depreciation

Capital Expenditures:

	2010	2011	2012	CAPEX Forecasts:				
				Year +1	Year +2	Year +3	Year +4	Year +5
CAPEX:								
PP&E Acquired	3,253	3,339	2,714					
PP&E Sold	−81	−84	−95					
Net CAPEX	**3,172**	**3,255**	**2,619**	**3,000**	**3,410**	**3,554**	**3,776**	**3,864**
Net CAPEX as a percent of:								
Gross PP&E	12.7%	9.9%	7.5%	8.3%	8.7%	8.3%	8.2%	7.7%
Revenues	5.5%	4.9%	4.0%	4.4%	4.8%	4.8%	4.8%	4.8%
			4.8%					

Property, Plant and Equipment and Depreciation

Property, Plant and Equipment and Depreciation Forecasts:

	2010	2011	2012	Year +1	Year +2	Year +3	Year +4	Year +5
PP&E at cost:								
Beg. balance at cost:				36,162	39,162	42,572	46,126	49,902
Add: CAPEX forecasts from above:				3,000	3,410	3,554	3,776	3,864
End balance at cost:	**33,041**	**35,140**	**36,162**	**39,162**	**42,572**	**46,126**	**49,902**	**53,766**
Accumulated Depreciation:								
Beg. Balance:				−17,026	−19,760	−22,732	−25,953	−29,437
Subtract: Depreciation expense forecasts from below:				−2,734	−2,972	−3,220	−3,484	−3,754
End Balance:	**−13,983**	**−15,442**	**−17,026**	**−19,760**	**−22,732**	**−25,953**	**−29,437**	**−33,190**
PP&E—net	**19,058**	**19,698**	**19,136**	**19,402**	**19,840**	**20,173**	**20,466**	**20,576**

(Continued)

Forecast Development Spreadsheet (Continued)

	Year +1	Year +2	Year +3	Year +4	Year +5	Year +6
Depreciation Expense Forecast Development:						
		Depreciation expense forecast on existing PP&E:				
Existing PP&E at cost:	36,162	2,525	2,525	2,525	2,525	2,525
Remaining balance to be depreciated.	19,136	16,611	14,087	11,562	9,037	6,513
PP&E Purchases:		Depreciation expense forecasts on new PP&E:				
Capex Year +1	3,000	209	209	209	209	209
Capex Year +2	3,410		238	238	238	238
Capex Year +3	3,554			248	248	248
Capex Year +4	3,776				264	264
Capex Year +5	3,864					270
Total Depreciation Expense		2,734	2,972	3,220	3,484	3,754

Depreciation methods:	2010	2011	2012
PPE at Cost	33,041	35,140	36,162
Avg Depreciable PPE		34,091	35,651
Depreciation Expense	2,124	2,476	2,489
Implied Avg. Useful Life in Years		13.8	14.32
Useful Life Forecast Assumption:			14.32
			(in years)

Valuation Spreadsheet

DATA CHECKS—Estimated Value per Share

Dividend Based Valuation	$85.86
Free Cash Flow Valuation	$85.86
Residual Income Valuation	$85.86
Residual Income Market-to-Book Valuation	$85.86
Free Cash Flow for All Debt and Equity Valuation	$89.02

Check: All Estimated Value per Share amounts should be the same, with the possible exception of the share value from the Free Cash Flow for All Debt and Equity model.

FSAP OUTPUT: VALUATION MODELS

Analyst Name:	**Wahlen, Baginski & Bradshaw**
Company Name:	**PepsiCo**

VALUATION PARAMETER ASSUMPTIONS

Current share price	$ 68.43			
Number of shares outstanding	1,544.0	**COST OF PREFERRED STOCK**		
Current market value	**$105,656**	Preferred stock capital	$	—
GROWTH		Preferred dividends	$	—
Long-run growth assumption used in forecasts	3.0%	**Implied yield**		**0.00%**
Long-run growth assumption used in valuation. (Both long-run growth assumptions should be the same.)	3.0%	**COST OF NONCONTROLLING INTERESTS' CAPITAL**		
		Noncontrolling interests capital	$	105
COST OF EQUITY CAPITAL		Earnings attributable to noncontrolling		
Equity risk factor (market beta)	0.75	interests	$	10.5
Risk free rate	3.0%	**Implied yield**		**10.00%**
Market risk premium	6.0%	**WEIGHTED AVERAGE COST OF CAPITAL**		
Required rate of return on common equity:	**7.50%**	Weight of equity in capital structure		0.7754
		Weight of debt in capital structure		0.2238
COST OF DEBT CAPITAL		Weight of preferred in capital structure		0.0000
Debt capital	$ 30,500	Weight of noncontrolling interests in		
Cost of debt capital, before tax	3.65%	capital structure		0.0008
Effective tax rate	−27.0%	**Weighted average cost of capital**		**6.42%**
After-tax cost of debt capital	**2.66%**			

(Continued)

Valuation Spreadsheet (Continued)

FSAP OUTPUT: **VALUATION MODELS**

Analyst Name: Wahlen, Baginski & Bradshaw
Company Name: PepsiCo

	1	2	3	4	5	Continuing Value
DIVIDENDS-BASED VALUATION	Year +1	Year +2	Year +3	Year +4	Year +5	Year +6
Dividends Paid to Common Shareholders	3,386.8	3,507	3,629	3,835	3,885	
Less: Common Stock Issues	−44.9	−152	−154	−225	−94	
Plus: Common Stock Repurchases	3,149.5	2,624	2,792	2,852	3,217	
Dividends to Common Equity	**6,491.4**	**5,979**	**6,267**	**6,462**	**7,008**	**6,576.6**
Present Value Factors	0.930	0.865	0.805	0.749	0.697	
Present Value Net Dividends	6,038.5	5,173.9	5,044.5	4,838.8	4,881.5	
Sum of Present Value Net Dividends	25,977.2					
Present Value of Continuing Value	101,800.3					
Total	127,777.5					
Adjust to midyear discounting	1.0375					
Total Present Value Dividends	132,569.1					
Shares Outstanding	1,544.0					
Estimated Value per Share	**$85.86**					
Current share price	$68.43					
Percent difference	25%					

Valuation Spreadsheet (Continued)

FSAP OUTPUT: **VALUATION MODELS**

Analyst Name:	Wahlen, Baginski & Bradshaw
Company Name:	PepsiCo

	1	2	3	4	5	Continuing Value
FREE CASH FLOWS FOR COMMON EQUITY	Year +1	Year +2	Year +3	Year +4	Year +5	Year +6
Net Cash Flow from Operations	9,104.3	9,850.3	10,344.0	11,221.7	11,113.7	8,764.4
Decrease (Increase) in Cash Required for Operations	1,065.3	−218.3	−229.6	−355.5	−140.5	−185.3
Net Cash Flow from Investing	−4,480.6	−4,974.8	−5,207.4	−6,280.2	−4,955.4	−3,035.9
Net Cash Flow from Debt Financing	752.9	1,332.4	1,370.2	1,886.6	1,000.6	1,041.1
Net Cash Flow into Financial Assets	0.0	0.0	0.0	0.0	0.0	0.0
Net Cash Flow—Pref. Stock and Noncontrolling Interests	49.5	−10.5	−10.5	−10.5	−10.5	−7.7
Free Cash Flow for Common Equity	**6,491.4**	**5,979.0**	**6,266.7**	**6,462.1**	**7,008.0**	**6,576.6**
Present Value Factors	0.930	0.865	0.805	0.749	0.697	
Present Value Free Cash Flows	6,038.5	5,173.9	5,044.5	4,838.8	4,881.5	
Sum of Present Value Free Cash Flows	25,977.2					
Present Value of Continuing Value	101,800.3					
Total	127,777.5					
Adjust to midyear discounting	1.0375					
Total Present Value Free Cash Flows to Equity	132,569.1					
Shares Outstanding	1,544.0					
Estimated Value per Share	**$85.86**					
Current share price	$68.43					
Percent difference	25%					

(Continued)

Valuation Spreadsheet (Continued)

FSAP OUTPUT: **VALUATION MODELS**

Analyst Name:	**Wahlen, Baginski & Bradshaw**
Company Name:	**PepsiCo**

DIVIDENDS VALUATION SENSITIVITY ANALYSIS:

		Long-Run Growth Assumptions							
	85.86	**0%**	**2%**	**3%**	**4%**	**5%**	**6%**	**8%**	**10%**
Discount	5%	91.96	135.32	189.52	352.10				
Rates:	6%	76.74	102.04	127.33	177.92	329.69			
	7%	65.88	82.07	96.23	119.84	167.05	308.67		
	7.50%	61.54	74.81	**85.86**	103.23	134.50	207.46		
	8%	57.74	68.75	77.56	90.77	112.79	156.83		
	9%	51.42	59.24	65.11	73.32	85.64	106.18	270.44	
	10%	46.37	52.11	56.21	61.68	69.33	80.82	138.23	
	11%	42.23	46.56	49.53	53.35	58.44	65.58	94.10	236.75
	12%	38.80	42.12	44.33	47.10	50.65	55.40	72.00	121.80
	13%	35.89	38.48	40.17	42.23	44.80	48.11	58.70	83.42
	14%	33.40	35.45	36.76	38.33	40.24	42.63	49.82	64.18
	15%	31.25	32.89	33.92	35.13	36.59	38.36	43.45	52.60
	18%	26.23	27.12	27.65	28.26	28.96	29.78	31.91	35.10
	20%	23.74	24.34	24.70	25.10	25.56	26.08	27.38	29.20

Valuation Spreadsheet (Continued)

FSAP OUTPUT: **VALUATION MODELS**

Analyst Name: **Wahlen, Baginski & Bradshaw**
Company Name: **PepsiCo**

	1	2	3	4	5	Continuing Value
RESIDUAL INCOME VALUATION	Year +1	Year +2	Year +3	Year +4	Year +5	Year +6
Comprehensive Income Available for Common Shareholders	6,094.7	6,376.6	6,598.3	6,972.2	7,064.2	7,276.1
Lagged Book Value of Common Shareholders' Equity (at t-1)	22,417.0	22,020.3	22,417.9	22,749.5	23,259.5	23,315.8
Required Earnings	1,681.3	1,651.5	1,681.3	1,706.2	1,744.5	1,748.7
Residual Income	**4,413.5**	**4,725.1**	**4,917.0**	**5,266.0**	**5,319.7**	**5,527.4**
Present Value Factors	0.930	0.865	0.805	0.749	0.697	
Present Value Residual Income	4,105.6	4,088.8	3,958.0	3,943.2	3,705.5	
Sum of Present Value Residual Income	19,801.0					
Present Value of Continuing Value	85,559.5					
Total	105,360.5					
Add: Beginning Book Value of Equity	22,417.0					
Present Value of Equity	127,777.5					
Adjust to midyear discounting	1.0375					
Total Present Value of Equity	132,569.1					
Shares Outstanding	1,544.0					
Estimated Value per Share	**$85.86**					
Current share price	$68.43					
Percent difference	25%					

(Continued)

Valuation Spreadsheet (Continued)

FSAP OUTPUT: **VALUATION MODELS**

Analyst Name:	Wahlen, Baginski & Bradshaw
Company Name:	PepsiCo

RESIDUAL INCOME VALUATION SENSITIVITY ANALYSIS:

		Long-Run Growth Assumptions							
	85.86	**0%**	**2%**	**3%**	**4%**	**5%**	**6%**	**8%**	**10%**
Discount	5%	91.96	135.32	189.52	352.10				
Rates:	6%	76.74	102.04	127.33	177.92	329.69			
	7%	65.88	82.07	96.23	119.84	167.05	308.67		
	7.50%	61.54	74.81	**85.86**	103.23	134.50	207.46		
	8%	57.74	68.75	77.56	90.77	112.79	156.83		
	9%	51.42	59.24	65.11	73.32	85.64	106.18	270.44	
	10%	46.37	52.11	56.21	61.68	69.33	80.82	138.23	
	11%	42.23	46.56	49.53	53.35	58.44	65.58	94.10	236.75
	12%	38.80	42.12	44.33	47.10	50.65	55.40	72.00	121.80
	13%	35.89	38.48	40.17	42.23	44.80	48.11	58.70	83.42
	14%	33.40	35.45	36.76	38.33	40.24	42.63	49.82	64.18
	15%	31.25	32.89	33.92	35.13	36.59	38.36	43.45	52.60
	18%	26.23	27.12	27.65	28.26	28.96	29.78	31.91	35.10
	20%	23.74	24.34	24.70	25.10	25.56	26.08	27.38	29.20

Valuation Spreadsheet (Continued)

FSAP OUTPUT:	VALUATION MODELS
Analyst Name:	Wahlen, Baginski & Bradshaw
Company Name:	PepsiCo

RESIDUAL INCOME VALUATION	1	2	3	4	5	Continuing Value
Market-to-Book Approach	Year +1	Year +2	Year +3	Year +4	Year +5	Year +6
Comprehensive Income Available for Common Shareholders	6,094.7	6,376.6	6,598.3	6,972.2	7,064.2	7,276.1
Book Value of Common Shareholders' Equity (at t-1)	22,417.0	22,020.3	22,417.9	22,749.5	23,259.5	23,315.8
Implied ROCE	27.2%	29.0%	29.4%	30.6%	30.4%	31.2%
Residual ROCE	19.7%	21.5%	21.9%	23.1%	22.9%	23.7%
Cumulative growth factor in common equity as of t-1	100.0%	98.2%	100.0%	101.5%	103.8%	104.0%
Residual ROCE times cumulative growth	**19.7%**	**21.1%**	**21.9%**	**23.5%**	**23.7%**	**24.7%**
Present Value Factors	0.930	0.865	0.805	0.749	0.697	
Present Value Residual ROCE times growth	0.183	0.182	0.177	0.176	0.165	
Sum of Present Value Residual ROCE times growth	0.88					
Present Value of Continuing Value	3.82					
Total Present Value Residual ROCE	4.70					
Add one for book value of equity at t-1	1.0					
Sum	5.70					
Adjust to mid-year discounting	1.0375					
Implied Market-to-Book Ratio	5.914					
Times Beginning Book Value of Equity	22,417.0					
Total Present Value of Equity	132,569.1					
Shares Outstanding	1,544.0					
Estimated Value per Share	**$85.86**					
Current share price	$68.43					
Percent difference	25%					

Sensitivity analysis for the market-to-book approach should be identical to that of the residual income approach.

(Continued)

Valuation Spreadsheet (Continued)

FSAP OUTPUT: **VALUATION MODELS**

Analyst Name:	Wahlen, Baginski & Bradshaw
Company Name:	PepsiCo

Free Cash Flows for All Debt and Equity	1 Year +1	2 Year +2	3 Year +3	4 Year +4	5 Year +5	Continuing Value Year +6
Net Cash Flow from Operations	9,104.3	9,850.3	10,344.0	11,221.7	11,113.7	8,764.4
Add back: Interest Expense after tax	765.7	793.4	829.4	872.8	911.3	938.6
Subtract: Interest Income after tax	0.0	0.0	0.0	0.0	0.0	0.0
Decrease (Increase) in Cash Required for Operations	1,065.3	−218.3	−229.6	−355.5	−140.5	−185.3
Free Cash Flow from Operations	10,935.3	10,425.4	10,943.8	11,739.0	11,884.5	9,517.7
Net Cash Flow from Investing	−4,480.6	−4,974.8	−5,207.4	−6,280.2	−4,955.4	−3,035.9
Add back: Net CFs into Financial Assets	0.0	0.0	0.0	0.0	0.0	0.0
Free Cash Flows—All Debt and Equity	**6,454.7**	**5,450.6**	**5,736.4**	**5,458.8**	**6,929.1**	**6,481.9**
Present Value Factors	0.940	0.883	0.830	0.780	0.733	
Present Value Free Cash Flows	6,065.3	4,812.8	4,759.7	4,256.1	5,076.6	
Sum of Present Value Free Cash Flows	24,970.5					
Present Value of Continuing Value	138,874.5					
Total Present Value Free Cash Flows to Equity and Debt	163,845.0					
Less: Value of Outstanding Debt	−30,500.0					
Less: Value of Preferred Stock	−63.0					
Less: Noncontrolling Interests	−105.0					
Plus: Value of Financial Assets	0.0					
Present Value of Equity	133,177.0					
Adjust to midyear discounting	1.0321					
Total Present Value of Equity	137,451.7					
Shares Outstanding	1,544.0					
Estimated Value per Share	**$89.02**					
Current share price	$68.43					
Percent difference	30%					

Financial Statement Ratios: Descriptive Statistics by Industry and by Year

Appendix D can be found online at the book's companion website at www.cengagebrain.com

Preparing a Term Project

Appendix 1.1 can be found online at the book's companion website at www.cengagebrain.com